History of the 89th Division

MAJOR GENERAL
LEONARD WOOD
MAJOR GENERAL
WILLIAM M. WRIGHT
MAJOR GENERAL
FRANK L. WINN

HISTORY

OF THE

89TH DIVISION, U. S. A.

From its Organization in 1917, through its Operations in the World War, the Occupation of Germany and Until Demobilization in 1919

With Maps, Photographs, Official Reports, Honor and Casualty Lists, Etc.

By

GEORGE H. ENGLISH, Jr.

Official Historian, War Society of the 89th Division,
Formerly Lieutenant Colonel, Infantry, 353d Infantry and, later,
Adjutant 177th Infantry Brigade, 89th Division

Published by
The War Society of the 89th Division
1920

PRESS OF
SMITH-BROOKS PRINTING COMPANY
DENVER, COLORADO

PREFACE

The author is conscious that for thousands of men, including himself, life reached its climax in the acts related in this history; that for thousands of others, whose hearts were with loved ones in the fighting line while their bodies must perforce remain at home, these events, dimly perceived at the time through the veil of the censorship and even as yet only partially known, evoked emotions which will never die away. He is aware that even among the actual participants, including himself, a very limited knowledge of the great whole was ever possible to any one man.

His attempt has been to present a connected view of the division, not only of its parts in relation to each other, but in the division's relation to the great war, to the entire body of the American Expeditionary Forces and to the enemy. He has endeavored to tell his story simply, avoiding fulsome praise and the attempt to be eloquent, yet not shrinking from the narration of disagreeable incidents nor from making criticism which he deemed just. He has, to the utmost of his ability, reconciled conflicting reports of the same operation or event, has weighed the available evidence and stated the result as it appeared to his impartial judgment. He has striven for accuracy above all things else. He is conscious of many shortcomings in execution, but of none in desire to do justice to his subject.

Necessarily his viewpoint is that of the division as a whole. Exploits of individuals and accomplishments of the separate organizations within the division have been used as typical incidents illustrating the general narrative. But for anything like a complete account of such details, reference must of necessity be made to the histories of the various organizations, some of which have already been published. In dealing with such subjects the historian was limited by availability of information. He could tell only what he knew from his own experience or from data which came into his hands in the form of military reports or personal anecdotes. The lack of such information was especially felt in respect to the Artillery Brigade, the Trains and special units.

It is too much to hope no errors have been committed. Certainly no intentional injustice has been done, but there is inevitable in a work of this kind the injustice of failing to describe events well deserving description. Furthermore, there are probably cases where errors exist in reports, which errors have been carried over into the narrative. The historian will be very grateful to be corrected where he has erred, even in respect to mere inaccuracies of spelling, initials, dates and the like, and to receive accounts of incidents and events which should be included in a second edition, if one is demanded.

The author has enjoyed the benefits of most cordial assistance from many members of the division. He is particularly under obligations to General Wright and General Winn for information and advice; to Colonel John C. H. Lee for invaluable services in the supervision of the maps; to Major Joseph E. Brown for the preparation of rosters and statistics; to Major C. J. Masseck for valuable data acquired in the preparation of the Brief History of the division; and above all, to Lieutenant Colonel Burton A. Smead for procuring official photographs, assisting in every part of the narrative, and indefatigable services in respect to the printing, proofreading and assembling of the appendices. It is mere justice to say that without the aid of Colonel Smead, the author feels that he would have failed in his undertaking. The Smith-Brooks Printing Company, of Denver, Colorado, gave aid and encouragement without stint. Rinkle & Whitehead, of Kirwin, Kansas, generously contributed a number of photographs taken by them as official photographers for the 353rd Infantry; Captain Merle Walker, 341st Field Artillery, and Major Walter C. Cole, 314th Motor Supply Train, furnished photographs; and many doubtful points were cleared up by correspondence with other officers and men of the division, whose kind co-operation and assistance the historian would gladly acknowledge in each individual case if space permitted.

Whatever may be the deficiencies of the present volume, the true history of the 89th Division, written in the hearts of the men and graved on the soil of France, is one that no soldier can ever contemplate without pride.

GEORGE H. ENGLISH, JR.

Kansas City, Mo.
11 November, 1920.

TABLE OF CONTENTS

APPENDIX

TABLE OF CONTENTS—Concluded

ILLUSTRATIONS

MAPS

Large Insert Maps

Small Maps

COMPARATIVE DIAGRAMS

CARTOONS

PHOTOGRAPHS

ILLUSTRATIONS—Continued

ILLUSTRATIONS—Concluded

CHAPTER I.

ORGANIZATION AND TRAINING

The 89th Division can with justice claim to typify the best results of the mighty effort made by the United States to put into the field an efficient fighting force in the minimum of time. Drawn from the great Middle West, its composition was largely that of the native born, agricultural class, which is the most truly representative of American traditions and ideals. Organized in September and October, 1917, under officers the majority of whom received their first military training beginning in May of that year, it entered the battle line in August, 1918, a well-trained military unit; and within fourteen months from the day the first raw recruit reported for duty, the Division had participated in two of the major engagements of the great war, had been flung against the choicest troops of the German Army on a front vital to the enemy and had conquered them in open fight. The energy, the resource, the intelligence and the martial vigor of America have never been better exemplified than in the National Army Divisions in this war, and our division has proof that it is regarded as one of the best of these.

Napoleon is reported to have said: "I have no such things as good and bad regiments; I merely have good and bad colonels." But the dictum of this great soldier, ascribing success or failure solely to the character and ability of the leader, cannot be accepted. Without good leadership, the success of even the best of troops is, of course, impossible. But with good leadership, the failure of such troops as ours would have been equally impossible. The 89th Division has been singularly fortunate in the character of its commanding officers. For its organization and its early formative period it had Major General Leonard Wood, universally recognized as one of the greatest military organizers, who had for years devoted all the force of tremendous native ability and wide military experience to stimulating our country to more adequate military preparation, and was the founder of the system of training camps which furnished the great majority of his junior officers. For part of its training in America and all of its training in France, and for its service in trench warfare in front of Toul, the Division had Major General Frank L. Winn, a master of every detail of the military art, and an exponent of thoroughness in all things. In battle it had Major General William M. Wright, bold, aggressive and valiant. Each of its leaders possessed precisely the qualities needed at the time of his leadership. But back of all features of leadership lay the quality of the rank and file of the Division. The mention of the composite characteristics of the men of this division is merely a catalogue of soldierly virtues—bravery, docility, intelligence, loyalty, initiative and physical soundness and vigor. They were the flower of the youth of the best section of the United States. They excited the admiration of every observer, both of our own country and of our allies—and even of our enemies. They deserve the largest measure of the credit for the success of the Division. Their achievements form the subject matter of this history.

OFFICERS' TRAINING CAMP

The history of the 89th Division may properly be said to begin with the first Officers' Training Camp at Fort Riley. This was one of the fourteen such camps established under the plan adopted for training and educating the prospective officers necessary for the huge army to be raised under the provisions of the Selective Service Law of 1917. The camp at Fort Riley was the location of the 14th Provisional Training Regiment. It was opened about one month after the entry of the United States into the war, receiving its first increment of civilian aspirants on May 8th, 1917. These camps were an extension of the so-called Plattsburg idea, which in its initiation and development was almost entirely the work of Major General Leonard Wood. The first training camp for civilians was inaugurated in 1913 at Gettysburg, Pennsylvania, with a relatively small attendance of eastern college students. The next year the camp was held at Fort Oglethorpe, Georgia, and the next two summers saw the first Plattsburg camps. By this time the idea had taken hold and to the Plattsburg camps and to a similar camp at Fort Douglas, near Salt Lake City, there came several thousand young men, mostly college graduates and students who wished to devote themselves to qualifying as officers in case of the contingency of war. By the time that war became an actuality, the system of instruction in these camps had become fairly well settled and the great expansion in number of the aspirants for commissions could be trained under a uniform and demonstrably successful method.

These camps were each organized as a provisional regiment with companies of a convenient size, approximately 160 men to each. Each camp, as well as each of the companies, was commanded by an officer of the regular army. The subjects of instruction for each period of the camp were prescribed by orders, and included intensive training from the elements of military science in the School of the Soldier, up to many of the most essential of the higher branches of that science. In the field there was drill, practice marching and camping, target practice, trench digging and field exercises in small problems. In the class room, study and recitations on the service manuals, field service regulations, minor tactics, topography, map making and army regulations. Trench warfare and bayonet drill were made features. Intense competition prevailed at all times, as but relatively few of the aspirants were to be chosen, and the elimination of the unfit or unprepared was merciless and continuous.

Fort Riley is a long-established military post. It is situated in the central part of Kansas, at the confluence of the Republican and Smoky Hill Rivers, which form the Kaw or Kansas River. The Fort is the seat of a cavalry post, an artillery post and of the Mounted Service School. The Military Reservation of the Fort comprises about 25,000 acres, shaped somewhat like a fan, and lying on the north side of the Republican and Kaw Rivers. The buildings of the post are of substantial stone construction. Most of the students were quartered in these barracks, which were empty of troops of the Regular Army because of the service at the time on the Mexican Border. Others were quartered in temporary wooden barracks.

The course of instruction was arduous. Hard work in the field by day under the scorching sun of a Kansas summer, was followed by intense mental work in the evening in the study room or in the class room. There was little time for recreation and the minimum for rest. The survivors of this course had proved themselves physically and mentally fit for commissions in the service of the United States and they were commissioned on August 15th, 1917. Hard as was the work of the training camp, however, they found it but play compared with what followed.

BUILDING CAMP FUNSTON

During the period of the training camp, the construction of the vast establishment necessary to house the men and material for the coming army was begun. A site was selected on the Fort Riley Military Reservation near its eastern border and two or three miles from the Post. The place was in a large river flat in a bend of the Kaw River containing several hundred acres. It was named Camp Funston, in honor of General Frederick Funston, a native of Kansas, celebrated for his intrepid service in Cuba and the Philippines, and no less for his prompt mastery of conditions in a time of great civil catastrophe —the earthquake and fire of San Francisco.

The story of the almost magical construction of these great cantonments has been often told. During the months of June, July and August a vast wooden city was being built, capable of housing over 50,000 men. It was supplied with a system of waterworks and sewers, electric lights and steam heat. Not all the conveniences nor even all the buildings were complete when the troops of the first increment began to arrive in early September, but all received shelter as needed. The mere construction of this and the similar cantonments all over the country is a marvel of the creative energy of the Nation.

While the construction of the Army cantonments on the scale and in the time was, as a whole, a wonderful feat, it would not be consistent with the facts to leave the impression that the accomplishment was free from shortcomings and that it could not be improved upon in another emergency of the same kind.

The plans for all the Army cantonments, down to even very minute details of location of buildings, were determined on in Washington and the purchase of all the material entering into them was through agencies of the War Department at the National Capital. No doubt this system resulted on the whole in large economies and in the prevention of local profiteering. But in many instances it resulted in delays in delivery of materials and loss of opportunity to purchase economically local supplies. The government purchased or paid for all labor and materials and the contractors received ten per cent on all expenditures for the use of their organization and for their supervision of the work. This arrangement was unquestionably best for both parties under the circumstances, because in the fluctuating state of the market under war conditions and in view of the enormous demands, the ordinary system of competitive bidding would have been a mere gamble on the part of the contractor, bringing him sometimes undue profits and sometimes ruin, entailing delays in the initial bids and often failures to perform the contracts, for which no monetary penalty could compensate. But to be entirely successful and just to both parties, this system required constant, thorough, intelligent and authoritative inspection and supervision by the government, a service which the government was not always able to perform adequately. Consequently some abuses arose and delays occurred.

At Camp Funston, delay in sending forward the recruits had to be asked because of the incomplete state of the cantonment. The first increment was only five per cent of the total draft, and was followed by small increments, some of which had to be postponed. The heating system was not in operation, even in part, until well along in the fall, and a premature cold spell in October caused real suffering. Thievery of material was discovered, and dishonest and unpatriotic working men scamped their work or loafed on their highly-paid jobs. But in spite of all difficulties and delays, the work was accomplished as a whole in a wonderful way and the Division was housed and sheltered, equipped and fed.

ORGANIZING THE DIVISION

Late in August General Wood came to the camp, having been assigned to the command of the 89th Division, now to be organized, and assumed command of the camp in consequence of his seniority in rank. The camp was to contain not only the 89th Division, but also the 164th Depot Brigade (originally a part of the Division), portions of the 92nd Division (colored troops), a remount station and other elements. The Commanding General brought with him, or soon assembled, an efficient staff, some of whom, despite all vicissitudes, were destined to serve throughout the entire career of the Division. For his Chief of Staff he brought Lieutenant Colonel (later Brigadier General) Charles E. Kilbourne, already decorated with the coveted Medal of Honor, and fated to win the D. S. C. on the field of St. Mihiel. As assistant Chief of Staff there came an officer of Engineers, Captain (later Colonel) John C. H. Lee, afterwards to become the energetic and aggressive Chief of Staff of the Division during its hardest fighting. Also the indefatigable Major (later Lieutenant Colonel) Frank Wilbur Smith, originally brought into the military service by General Wood for the purpose of setting up a system of military post offices, but never employed on that duty, and who after serving in a number of capacities, settled down in a place for which he proved eminently qualified, the head of the Intelligence Department, A. C. of S., G-2. Also General Wood found at Fort Riley, acting as Post Quartermaster, Colonel Warren W. Whitside, who was made the first Division Quartermaster and ultimately became the "wheel horse" of the Division Staff as the Commander of Trains and Military Police.

General Wood also brought with him a number of young men, undergraduates of Harvard University, who had had special training in trench warfare under the personal instruction of Lieutenant Colonel Paul Azan, of the French Army, the author of the best text book on the War of Positions. These young men devoted themselves to giving lectures and instructions on the methods of this new warfare to the new officers when they reported.

Then came a number of officers from the Regular Army for assignment to the new Division as higher commanders, Brigadier General Frank L. Winn to the 177th Infantry Brigade, Brigadier General Thomas G. Hanson to the 178th Infantry Brigade, Colonel James H. Reeves to the 353rd Infantry, Colonel Americus Mitchell to the 354th Infantry, Colonel Wm. G. Sills to the 355th Infantry, Colonel (later Brigadier General) Louis M. Nuttman to the 356th Infantry and Major (later Lieutenant Colonel) R. E. Smyser to the 340th Machine Gun Battalion, with many others who for one reason or another did not remain with the Division throughout its life.

Early in September there came the newly commissioned officers from the training camp. Those from one of the provisional training companies were ordinarily assigned to form the line officers of a single regiment. Those from companies which did not form the officers of a regiment were assigned to the Machine Gun Battalions, the trains and separate units of the Division, the remainder to the 164th Depot Brigade.

There reported also some non-commissioned officers of the Regular Army of sufficient number to assign two to each company of infantry and battery of artillery. Many of these men were of inestimable value in drilling the new recruits and in the preparation of the vast amount of paper work which was required of the new organization, in which work most of the officers and men were entirely inexperienced. Many of these army non-commissioned officers had been recently promoted as a result of the great expansion of the Regular Army whereby commissions had been issued to a large number of the best qualified men, leaving only the less qualified men available for non-commissioned officers. As a class these non-commissioned officers did not accommodate themselves well to the new conditions, and were not so valuable as the better educated and more highly skilled men from civil life, of which there were a number in every company or battery.

Then, on the memorable day of September 5th, 1917, there began to arrive the first increment of five per cent of the National soldiers who had been called to the colors under the Selective Service Act. The Draft Boards had been asked to send, in this five per cent, men who had had previous military experience or who had had experience in cooking. And thus the skeleton of an effective military organization, with prospective non-commissioned officers and cooks, was formed before the great body of men reported.

Soon after the other increments began to report as ordered and as quarters became available. With their arrival the Division began to take form and shape. For their coming all that had gone before had been mere preparation. The real fighting men were now at hand and an Army was being born.

In the assignment of men to different organizations, one of the first things thought of was to attempt to place the men of special qualifications in the special service best adapted to their experience. Thus, to the 314th Engineers were assigned increments from the river counties of Missouri, on the assumption that there would be among them men skilled in boating who would be useful as pontooneers; and increments from the mining counties of southeast Missouri, among whom would be found prospective sappers; and increments from the Ozark counties, among whom were bound to be woodsmen and men skilled in the use of the ax; and increments from the cities of Missouri, from whom many excellent mechanics could be taken. In this manner, the Engineer Regiment was largely filled from the diversified population of Missouri.

As far as possible, the recruits from a certain section were all assigned to the same organization and thus their state identity was preserved, and with it local pride and friendly and familiar associations in the new surroundings were fostered.

The states from which the Division was drawn were Missouri, Kansas, Colorado, Nebraska, South Dakota, Arizona and New Mexico. The men from Kansas were for the most part assigned to the 353rd Infantry, which became and is still known as the All-Kansas Regiment, since every county in the state has, at one time or another, been represented in its ranks. Missouri, which furnished by far the largest number of men of all the states represented in the Division, because of her greater population, filled the 354th Infantry with men from the southeastern and eastern parts of the state, with a large number over for the 314th Engineers, filled the 356th Infantry with men from northwest Missouri and the 342nd Field Artillery from southeast Missouri. Nebraska furnished the men for the 355th Infantry and the 314th Ammunition Train. Personnel of the other trains was drawn from the several states. Some of the companies of the 314th Sanitary Train had been organized originally as Red Cross units, others came from the training camp at Fort Riley. South Dakota sent men to the 340th Machine Gun Battalion. The city of Omaha furnished all the men for the 341st Machine Gun Battalion. The 342nd Machine Gun Battalion received men from South Dakota, New Mexico and Arizona. Arizona and Colorado supplied the 340th and 341st Regiments of Field Artillery, respectively. Surplus men from all the states served to fill the 164th Depot Brigade.

The 314th Field Signal Battalion, when called into service Oct. 5th, 1917, was composed entirely of men of the Signal Enlisted Reserve Corps. It was recruited largely in Chicago, but contained representatives of almost every state.

Company "A," the Radio company, was recruited from employees of the Western Electric Co., most of them specialists in some branch of radio work.

Company "B," the Wire company, consisted of telephone, telegraph and railroad employees, all being either telephone or telegraph men.

Company "C," the Outpost company, was largely composed of telegraphers and telephone men, with a sprinkling of specialists such as cable splicers, telephone installers, etc.

During the training period at Camp Funston the Signal Battalion was drawn on heavily for specialists of all sorts. Some were called away for duty elsewhere in the United States, and many were sent overseas for duty requiring their especial skill long before the Division went. Before the Division moved the battalion was filled up to strength with recruits, some skilled, and those lacking technical knowledge were largely of a quality to readily absorb the necessary training.

The history of the early organization of the Division, as of the whole National Army, is a history of minor discomforts and small but perplexing difficulties borne and overcome with typical American good humor and ingenuity. The barracks were new and clean. It was determined to spare no effort to keep them so. Therefore, no incoming recruit was allowed to set foot in them until he had been bathed, had discarded his civilian clothing (part of which was collected and sent to destitute Belgium), and had been outfitted with new clothing and had been examined for the presence of obvious contagious disease. The responsibility for these preliminary measures rested upon the company commander, who was also required, by existing orders, to personally supervise the fitting of the shoes upon his men. The trains bearing the incoming recruits ordinarily arrived in the night, usually between midnight and 2 o'clock in the morning, the train schedule being thus arranged to interfere as little as possible with the regular railroad service, already strained to the limit with the transportation of material and an enhanced passenger traffic. The contingents of recruits were met at the station by officers detailed for the purpose, assigned to the organizations to be recruited from their section and provided with guides to conduct them thither. On arrival at their new homes, noses were counted to see that all were present, then, a few at a time, they were admitted to the detached lavatories of the barracks, required to strip and take a shower bath and a good scrub. The water heating system had not yet been installed; and this icy bath in the small hours of the cool nights of early fall was a splendid test of the qualities of the embryo soldiers. It was borne with the same nonchalance, good humor and uncomplaining loyalty with which the same men, a year later, in the blackness of a November night, plunged into the icy waters of the Meuse to swim across and reconnoiter the enemy's positions on the further shore.

But a different sort of reconnaissance followed this first contact with the water. Armed with an electric torch, the company commander scrutinized the superficies of the shrinking recruit for signs of disease that might contaminate others. If such signs were found, the recruit was bundled off to the hospital. If not, he dressed himself in new government underclothing and overalls and entered the barrack building. There hot coffee and sandwiches were usually awaiting him; then with his blankets he lay down on a straw filled bedsack on a steel spring cot to snatch an hour or so of his first army sleep.

PREVENTING AND FIGHTING DISEASE

He arose next morning to begin a routine of days so full of duties that one recruit expressed his feelings by saying plaintively that Sunday in the Army was just like Monday on the farm! Elementary military instruction began immediately, and an early hour of his first morning in camp usually found the recruit lined up with others learning to fall in in double ranks, to stand at attention and to execute squads right and left. Very soon his company marched away to the hospital to receive the first "shot in the arm" and to be vaccinated. The shot was a hypodermic injection of a prophylactic against typhoid fever. It was repeated at intervals of not over ten days until three had been taken. The results obtained from this measure alone form one of the most striking triumphs of modern preventive medicine. Typhoid fever has been one of the scourges of every army in the past. During our Spanish-American War, typhoid fever alone caused 85 per cent of the total number of deaths and slew more than four times as many soldiers as were slain by the enemy; in the present war, as a result of this compulsory vaccination against typhoid, combined with better medical service, better sanitation and better hospitals, typhoid fever has been practically eliminated and the total deaths from this disease have been only one-half of one per cent of all the deaths.

While intestinal diseases, of which typhoid is a type, which have their origin in filth and foul water, had been practically eliminated, other diseases, especially those propagated through the air, remained to be combatted. The Division fortunately was spared the experience of the frightful pandemic of influenza which swept over this country in the fall of 1918. But during the fall and winter of 1917, the medical department was engaged in combat with the respiratory diseases. Pneumonia proved to be the worst of the scourges and was the cause of most of the deaths by disease in the Division, as in the entire Army of the United States; next in deadliness, though far behind as a cause in the total number of deaths, was spinal meningitis. To combat the spread of these and other contagious diseases, many devices were adopted under the supervision of Colonel John L. Shepard, the Division surgeon. Some of Colonel Shepard's methods were novel and were afterwards adopted with success throughout the army.

Of course, the underlying principle of the fight against air-borne disease is simply to furnish the men with pure, fresh air and to keep them from breathing air which has been exhaled by any infected person. But to accomplish this is not simple among large bodies of men living of necessity in barracks. First of all, attention was paid to the ventilation of the sleeping quarters. Orders were issued requiring that there should be no overcrowding of the barracks; the capacity of all rooms was calculated and the number of men allowed to sleep in each room was plainly marked on the walls of the rooms. Orders required that the ventilators in the ceilings of the sleeping rooms and also windows should be kept open during the night and these orders were enforced by constant and rigid inspections. For many men, not sufficiently educated in the matters of hygiene, seemed perversely bent on closing the windows on cold nights. The company commander, the officer of the day and a medical officer were each required independently to inspect every sleeping room of the organization each night to see that the ventilation was proper.

Shelter tent halves were stretched so as to partition off each bunk slightly from its neighbor, thus minimizing the effect of coughing, as a disseminator of disease.

When a case of contagious disease, such as meningitis, measles or scarlet fever, appeared, all the men of the company were quarantined, were required to drill separately and were not permitted to join any assembly with other men. Daily inspections of those quarantined was made. Cultures from the nose and throat of all the men were taken frequently and where the germs of meningitis were found, though the man was not sick, he was quarantined in a separate camp as a carrier. Organizations in which the disease appeared were required to have a daily disinfecting spray of nose and throat.

The floors of all buildings were washed daily with disinfectants. Every utensil used at the table was sterilized after each meal with scalding water.

It was evident that the dust of the camp was responsible for the spread of disease as well as for irritations of the throat and nose which would increase susceptibility, and successful efforts were made to reduce the amount of dust. By General Wood's order, Colonel Whitside, the Division Quartermaster, not without great difficulty, obtained crude oil in sufficient quantities to oil the roads bearing the heavy traffic, and finally enough to oil all the roads and the especially dusty portions of the bare ground. Over $400,000 worth of crude oil was used for this purpose, and it was well worth it. Every effort was made to preserve the grass by changing drill grounds frequently. In many places alfalfa was planted which alleviated conditions the following spring.

BONDS AND INSURANCE

The recruit found himself involved in a maze of intricate business transactions which seemed to him to resolve themselves into attacks upon his pay. He had not thought very much about his pay. He perhaps realized that his pay of $30 per month was enormous in comparison to what the other nations were paying their soldiers, but it didn't seem very much to him, and now everybody seemed to be trying to take even that away. He and his fellows were assembled and required to listen to long explanations from his officers as to how he must make an allotment of half of it to his wife, to which the government would add as much again (or more, if he was well blessed with children); and how he might allot part of it to anyone he chose, if he had no dependents; he was urged to take out government insurance on his life, and shown how he could insure himself up to $10,000 at low rates, thus relieving himself of anxiety about the future of his loved ones; and above all, he was importuned to subscribe and pay by allotment from his pay for the Liberty Loan.

With characteristic good sense and good humor, the men as a whole accepted the opportunities thus presented to them. The government insurance was almost universally taken advantage of to the limit, over 99 per cent of the Division becoming insured, a record equalled by only one other camp and excelled by none. The 340th Field Artillery regiment had a record of insurance which could not be excelled, since every officer and man was reported insured to the full amount,—100 per cent of full insurance. The response to the appeal to subscribe to the Liberty Loan more than met the expectations of the Commanding General, and deserves space for a few words of comment. The campaign for subscriptions for the Liberty Loan in the Army had significance in more than one respect. The amount subscribed was no inconsiderable proportion of the whole, and contributed in the way of mere brute dollars and cents to raising the gigantic sums necessary to carry on the war. But beyond this, it had a tremendous moral and political significance. It was an unmistakable index of the spirit and feeling of the men of our new-born National Army. It shattered the delusion of our enemy that the heart of America was not in the war; it refuted the sneers of some, even of our own mistaken politicians, who, oblivious to the true democracy of universal military service, voiced the sentiment that an army of conscripts was somehow analogous to an army of convicts; it demonstrated to the world that the common people of America represented by these young men drawn with inexorable impartiality from every class, condition, race and occupation, had entered the war against the foes of democracy and humanity with willing and eager hearts, determined to conquer at whatever expense of money, or blood, or life itself.

CHOW

The important feature of proper preparation of food for the new army was given careful attention. A number of suitable officers had been detailed from the Training Camp for special instruction as mess officers, and had received a brief but thorough course of training in these duties. A large army school for cooks and bakers was already in operation at Fort Riley. Through Colonel W. W. Whitside, the organization of this school was made available for the instruction of the cooks and bakers of the new army; thus the very best training in this most important subject was obtained. Civilian cooks were also employed, to serve the new organizations until they could develop cooks of their own from the schools or from men of that occupation. Under the supervision of the mess officers, the messes were opened, supplies and utensils installed and cooks were ready to function in each company before the arrival of the first recruits.

This feature of the organization of the Division was a remarkable success. The new recruit, almost without exception, found himself provided from the day of his arrival with an abundance of wholesome and well prepared food.

The training of the cooks continued, and men who showed an aptitude for the work or who had previous experience of the kind were given instruction in the school throughout the entire training period. Excellent cooks were thus developed, whose services in the trying days overseas were an element of the utmost importance in maintaining the health and morale of the command. Nor did the cooks fail in other soldierly qualities when occasion arose in the field. Men must be fed when they fight and when they hold the line. So in the hard days in the battle lines, kitchens were always brought as near to the front as possible. A kitchen is a hard thing to conceal, and it was always a favorite target for the enemy's artillery and air men. So the cooks and their kitchens came in for a great deal of shelling and were the object of many an air raider's sudden swoop. But never did the cooks, as a class, fail because of danger, to perform their homely and necessary tasks. On one occasion, in the trenches of the Toul Sector, just before the St. Mihiel battle, a daring German trench raiding party penetrated to a point near a well advanced kitchen of the 353rd Infantry, driving back the outposts. A determined and resourceful sergeant nearby organized the cooks and kitchen police into a little combat group, and advancing on the enemy, covered the retreat and reorganization of the outpost, assisted it in repelling the raid and in inflicting losses on the raiders.

So also on one occasion in those days of stress following the Battle of the St. Mihiel salient, Private Elmer P. Richards, Company "D," 354th Infantry, while acting as cook for his company, was wounded by a piece of flying shrapnel and given the anti-tetanic treatment. Later in the day he found that owing to the intense shelling he could not prepare food for the front line troops some two miles away and to the north of Xammes. So, on his own initiative, and wounded as he was, he procured a quantity of chocolate and carried it himself to the front line through shell fire and personally saw that each man received a portion.

CLOTHING

Uniforms were not forthcoming. "Very well," said General Wood to his supply officers, "Go out and buy blue denim overalls for them." These would all look alike and would cover the body, which, essentially, is all that any uniform can do. There were no rifles. "Very well," said General Wood, "Let them whittle rifles out of wood." These would do for them to learn the manual of arms, and to get the knack of coming to a halt with a "one, two" and a "one, two, three."

And so presently comical blue denim columns began to wind over the hills; many an officer, used to better things, had to make violent efforts to suppress a titter when a ludicrous sentry in campaign hat and with overalls turned up a mile at the bottom, came solemnly to a present with a wooden gun. Comical, ludicrous, you say? Well, only at first sight. When that officer came in actual contact with these men and began to command them, there came an appreciation of what lay under the uncouth exterior. These men, taken, as some thought, against their own will from peaceful pursuits, were found to be responding to the national will. Sober, undemonstrative, cool, sound in body, wholesome in mind, they were willingly and cheerfully and uncomplainingly making the best of things in order to fit themselves for a great task, and were deliberately making themselves into the finest individual soldiers in the world. The thrill that followed the realization of the true character of the American soldier has never departed from many an officer, and recurs whenever he sees a body of troops on the march or thinks of what they have endured and what they have accomplished.

IMPROVISING TRAINING MATERIAL

It was in the Artillery Brigade that the lack of material for training was most keenly felt, and where the greatest ingenuity was displayed in supplying the deficiencies. Through the early training period the Brigade was under the command of Colonel (later Brigadier General) George A. Nugent, who also commanded the 342nd Field Artillery. With rare insight into the problems of the transition of a great mass of untrained men from civilian life into the complex and highly specialized organization of the artillery, Colonel Nugent inspired his command with the determination to get the utmost of training with the means at hand. His subsequent transfer was felt to be a great loss to the Division. Foot drill was followed by "mounted drill" on foot. Gun positions were marked upon the ground, and the men trained to take their positions at imaginary guns. On the running gear of condemned escort wagons, logs were mounted. Some of the old muzzle-loading guns captured from the enemy in the Spanish War, preserved at Fort Riley as relics, were hauled down and served to reduce the amount of imagination necessary for the preliminary drill of the gun squads. Later, with much mechanical skill, some really wonderful wooden models of guns were made, complete even to the breech mechanism, and better drill was had. Barrels were mounted on wooden legs, saddled and served to teach the soldier the proper position of a mounted man. Even instruments were improvised to serve as B. A. instruments and panoramic sights; the computation of firing data and the measurements of angles obtained by squinting along a stick were not without value when the proper instruments were finally obtained.

During the fall a miniature terrain was constructed, on the scale of 1:1000. On this tiny landscape white woolen balls would be dropped to simulate "bursts," and from these, observers equipped with field glasses would report the locations and the firing data would be computed. During the winter a similar terrain was constructed indoors and this invaluable practice was continued, the balls representing hits being dropped from a simple mechanism in the ceiling.

There were no drill manuals available adapted to the guns which would later be actually used. So the French Artillery Drill Regulations, supplied by Captain Monroe, were translated and mimeographed. A Brigade School of Artillery Fire was established under the direction of Lieutenant Colonel Stephen A. Mould with the invaluable assistance of Captain Francois Monroe of the French mission. Beginning in November, two officers a month from each regiment departed for a three-months course in the School of Fire at Fort Sill, Oklahoma. On their return these officers became instructors in the Division Schools.

In November some animals were received, and in December the full complement of animals for the two regiments of light artillery. The 342nd Field Artillery, the heavies, did not receive their authorized motor equipment until the war was over, while they were in Germany. They fought throughout with animal-drawn guns. But in preparation for their duties, thirty men a week were sent during the fall and winter to the Kansas State Agricultural College for a short course in motors and tractors, and the regiment received four trucks for practice work.

In December, a battery of three-inch guns was issued for the use of the two regiments of light artillery and a battery of 4.7 howitzers to the heavies. With these guns, target practice began in April on the artillery range at Fort Riley, culminating in May in a barrage laid down with gratifying accuracy in front of the trenches on Carpenter Hill.

Thus the artillery training, so much more specialized and complicated than the training of the infantry, especially for the officers, was accomplished under great handicaps. But that the training was thorough and sound, nevertheless, conclusively appeared by the splendid progress and fine record made by the artillery brigade overseas.

The training of the auxiliary services and organizations presents the same features of intense endeavor, of difficulties overcome and successful outcome, as those which characterized the combat troops. The 314th Motor Supply Train, originally under the command of Lieutenant Colonel G. M. Grimes, was for the most part trained under the supervision of Captain (afterward Major) Walter C. Cole, who later became its commanding officer. On reporting in November, 1917, Captain Cole found 500 men, most of them with little or no mechanical experience. In an incredibly brief space of time, these were converted into a well-organized Motor Supply Train, with efficient truckmasters, mechanics and chauffeurs. A few trucks were borrowed for instruction purposes from Truck Company 59 and a condemned motor was procured for evening class-room instruction. From it Sergeants Wait and Pinckney very ingeniously made a skeleton motor to demonstrate its operation. Soon all the trucks of Truck Company 59 were being operated by the men of the Supply Train and the repair shop for the Motor Transportation of the Fuller Construction Company had many mechanics from the Supply Train rendering good service while at the same time perfecting themselves in the arts soon to be so useful to the Division. A detail from the Supply Train which was sent to the Velie Plant at Moline, Illinois, to convoy Liberty trucks to Funston, found on its arrival that the convoy was not ready. The men were at once put to work in the Velie Plant assembling Liberty Trucks and when the convoy was ready to move, every man had become familiar with the construction and operation of the Liberty truck and the methods of its assembly and manufacture.

The 314th Ammunition Train was first classed as an infantry organization and its first few months training was largely in infantry drill, with detachments on special supply work and instruction. Shortly after the first of the year the four motor companies received twenty-two F. W. D. and Nash Quad ammunition trucks; the two caisson companies were issued sixteen caissons each and their full quota of horses, while the wagon company drew thirty-three combat wagons and limbers and one hundred fifty mules.

CONSCIENTIOUS OBJECTORS

The conscientious objector became a feature of the army at an early stage, and must not be passed without mention. Experience developed the fact that there were three types of conscientious objectors; first, men whose religious beliefs or ethical convictions made them genuinely and conscientiously opposed to the resistance of evil by force; second, German sympathizers; and third, cowards. Of the first class, there were a few. Any general condemnation of the conscientious objector would do a grave injustice to these few men, real heroes of conscience, however mistaken in the present state of society. A number of these men expressed their willingness to serve their country in any capacity, no matter how dangerous nor how menial, provided the service did not violate their scruples; some of them were sent to and willingly served among the sanitary troops; others, without complaint, performed the necessary but distasteful tasks of scavengers and like occupations; and not a few, on more mature reflection and with wider knowledge of the inhuman character of the warfare waged by the German, abandoned their previous convictions and took their places with the rest of the troops. They were of the same stuff as Sergeant York, of another division, and displayed the same bravery and conscientiousness in the application of force as they had in refusing to apply it. Their number was small; but under cover of the fact that there were such men, a goodly number of the other two classes sought to evade the call of duty.

A small incident which occurred early in the organization showed what was coming. A little delegation of men dressed in clerical garb appeared in the office of the Chief of Staff and requested an interview with the Commanding General. The acting chief of staff, as usual, made inquiry of their mission and was told that they wished to protest to the General against the compulsion to military duty of young men of their faith, who would soon be selected for service. The Chief of Staff asked them upon what they based their faith that resistance to evil by force was wrong; and they said that they based it upon the teachings of Jesus Christ. Major Lee then advanced the argument that the Saviour had not disdained to use force against evil on occasion, and pointed to the scourging of the money-changers from the Temple as supporting his view. This brought on a theological discussion, in the course of which need rose for the actual text of the passage; and not having at hand a copy of the Holy Writ, Major Lee asked if any of the ministers had a pocket copy with him. With a little reluctance, a Testament was produced; but it failed to solve the point at issue, because it was printed in the German tongue.

Of course, it does not follow that because of his German parentage or his adherence to a sect the members of which have so low an ideal of the duties of citizenship as to refuse the use of the language of the country of their adoption, a man cannot have conscientious scruples against war. But a suspiciously large number of the conscientious objectors came from that class.

As to the cowards, many of them had become converts to the teachings of non-resistance after the passage of the Selective Service Act. About that time they began to think seriously concerning a number of things that they had never thought of before. Some of them became the founders of entirely new sects and denominations with very limited membership,—only one member, in a great many instances. Their conscience played queer tricks with them, too. For example, their conscience did not revolt against their eating Government food or sleeping under Government blankets in cold weather; but these same singular consciences would not permit them to wash the dishes from which they had eaten their food, or to make up the beds on which they had slept. When they found that the War Department, desiring to err, if at all, on the side of mercy and humanity, would permit them to be imprisoned, but would permit no other coercion or punishment of them, insolence and shameless effrontery were manifested. Jeers and derision greeted the guards, who were compelled to perform the most menial functions to keep the quarters of the recalcitrants fit for human habitation. With impish and malicious tricks and with unconcealed delight they celebrated the strategem whereby honest and dutiful men were compelled to perform the offices of common decency for them; and whereby, in their stead, hosts of brave young soldiers were meeting the shock of battle and laying down their lives in far-off France.

It was a trying situation and was handled as well as circumstances and existing orders would permit. Men professing conscientious objection to the military service were put to the performance of tasks of a necessary but non-military nature, collecting garbage, removing manure, working on the roads, serving as kitchen police and the like. When, as frequently, they refused to perform any duty whatever, they were, after due trial, imprisoned. They were of course left behind on the departure of the Division for France, and the later development of the situation concerning them forms no part of this history.

TRENCH WARFARE AND TRAINING FOR IT

Of course, the main pursuit of the Division was military training, to which everything else was necessarily subordinate. It was realized that the Great War had introduced new methods with which no one in America was familiar except by report. On the Western Front of Europe the Warfare of Position had superseded the open warfare to which our Army had been trained.

The war of position or trench warfare developed as a result of the improvement in fire power through the use of rapid-fire weapons, particularly the machine gun. This result had been foreseen and predicted by a few far-sighted military critics before the war. But the actual evolution of this form of warfare seems not to have been anticipated generally by any of the belligerents, at least not to the extent to which it had developed at the time of the entry of America into the war.

When men fought hand to hand with sword and lance the fighting was necessarily in the open field. With the introduction of firearms, the use of shelter became more general, and from the time of our Civil War on, the importance of cover and earthworks increased with the increase of the accuracy and range of the small arm. And yet, up to the time of the Great War, it had always been an accepted military principle that a numerically superior force, if well led, could take any position held by a numerically inferior force, equal in weapons, skill and morale. This was necessarily so, because while an equal number of assailants could engage the defenders in a fire fight in which the volume of fire would be practically equal on both sides, other elements of the attacking force could, without exposure to fire of sufficient volume to stop them, encircle the position or penetrate it at some point of weakness. This method was universally regarded as the solution of all problems of the attack of fortified places and it was believed to be a sufficient solution. The experience of the Boer War and of the Russo-Japanese War confirmed the opinion. No position, however skillfully fortified or heroically held, had ever resisted the attack of sufficiently determined and numerous assailants.

With the advent of the period of stabilization which followed the earlier onslaughts of the Germans in the first year of the war, it was found that a revision of these principles was necessary. The enormous number of men engaged enabled the position to be made continuous along the entire Western Front between two impassable barriers,—neutral Switzerland and the Sea. Indeed this enormous extension of the lines had been occasioned by the successive efforts of each adversary to outflank the other. But more important than this in producing the condition of trench warfare, was the introduction on a large scale of the machine gun. This weapon, firing small arms ammunition, had more than fifty times the fire power of the rifle. A handful of machine guns, distributed over a given front and manned by very few men, was capable of delivering as great a volume of fire as a whole regiment of infantry armed with the rifle; and furthermore, the gun being mounted on a fixed base, this fire could be kept low and thus be made more effective against masses of troops. Obviously, the method of engaging a substantially equal number of attackers and defenders in a fire fight on a given front could no longer be employed; if practicable to engage machine gun with machine gun, which it is not, the front would become too greatly extended for a single operation, for the defenders could always hold a relatively wide front with relatively few men and retain their main forces in the rear to concentrate against any encirclement or penetration of the line. When the tremendous advantage which the machine gun gave the defense was supplemented by the construction of the barbed wire entanglements to hold the attacking forces within the field of fire (first used, by the way, in our Civil War) and by trenches which afforded the defenders almost complete protection against rifle and artillery fire until the very moment that their fire became necessary, and by the construction of position after position of the same sort far to the rear, it became manifest through bitter experience that neither side could expect to advance against the other without such appalling losses as to render victory fruitless. Thus the war settled down into a sort of deadlock, while both sides awaited the happening of some event, or the introduction of some new method or appliance which would force the adversary into the open field and enable a decisive result to be attained. The only possible solution, aside from the mere process of attrition, seemed to be the increase of the power and volume of the artillery so that it might perform all the functions of the offense by destroying the wire entanglements, demolishing the trenches and covering with a curtain of fire called a barrage, the advance of the infantry. Thus protected, the infantry could enter a position without much loss and if given time to organize it by the construction of new entanglements on the side towards the enemy and by repairing the trenches, could then hold the position thus gained against anything except a similar methodical attack. But advance by these methods was so slow and expensive that it seemed that the war would be simply a test of endurance unless some startling change of conditions intervened.

This form of warfare had developed practices and methods peculiar to itself, which the 89th Division, in common with the rest of the Army, was endeavoring by every means to master. But side by side with the instruction and training in the new methods of trench warfare went instruction in the methods and principles of warfare in the open. For it seems to have been at all times the faith and belief of our Army that some time and somehow this stalemate would come to an end; that finally the enemy would be forced into the open and would have to come to conflict face to face and breast to breast; that the general principles of warfare are immutable and are unchanged from age to age by the introduction of new appliances and new details; that our own methods were sound and in accordance with those principles. This faith and belief were justified by events. The sturdy adherence to it, the refusal to accept the condition of deadlock as anything more than a phase of the conflict, the tenacious conviction that ultimately the winning of the war would be accomplished by the well-trained infantry soldier armed with the rifle, was no small part of America's military contribution to the final victory.

It is felt that the importance of this feature has not always been appreciated, and that any contribution to the literature of the war from American sources should not fail to give it due emphasis. In the final report of Sir Douglas Haig, the justly-honored commander of our British allies, it is stated, in substance, that the war was simply one immense battle and, like all battles, it had three stages; first, maneuvering for advantages; second (if the forces are about equal), the great wearing-down process—attrition—the price of victory; and third, the final effort by the stronger remaining side, which wins. Sir Douglas gives it as his opinion that the war was won in the second stage and he alludes most scantily to the American participation. Without making the braggart's boast that America won the war nor minimizing the glorious staunchness of our Allies in the preceding phases of the conflict, the candid student of the war will be compelled to admit that the conclusion of the phase of attrition found Germany with her Eastern front free of danger; with men and supplies adequate to assume the most formidable offensive of the war; and with the will and power to end the war of position and seek a conclusion in the open field. In this time of peril, an element of victory far more important than their mere numbers, was the advent of the American troops, consistently trained in open warfare and masters of the use of the rifle. The effectiveness of the American rifle fire delivered by our 6th Engineers in Cary's heroic British stop-gap Army, followed by that of our 2nd, 3rd and 4th Divisions along the Marne, unquestionably induced an attitude on the part of our Allies which might be expressed as follows: "Our old, seasoned, trench warfare troops must break the line and your dashing fellows carry through in the open."

Frank recognition of the deficiencies of the Allies in open warfare followed, which reached all parts of the allied armies. For example, at a conference of his corps commanders on the 26th of June, 1918, General de Boissoudy, commanding the 7th French Army, commented on the criticism of General Ludendorff on the recent German offensive along the Marne and stated that the French had been led astray by the tactics of trench warfare and when the Germans broke through they did not know what to do; he gave urgent directions for immediate training in open warfare and pointed out that the American troops under his command were ahead of the French in that respect.

Thus did future events vindicate the judgment of the American Army. That judgment had been voiced and effectuated by the great soldier who commanded the American Expeditionary Forces, for the instructions for training our Division received from the War Department in the fall of 1917 quoted a letter of General Pershing, which insisted upon the necessity of training in open warfare and musketry.

FOREIGN OFFICERS

But it was imperative that the methods of the War of Position should also be mastered, and there were no American officers who had first-hand knowledge of this mode of fighting. To aid in our training in these modern methods of warfare, there reported early in November a number of French and British officers, sent to this country by their governments for that purpose, Major Hall, Captain Few and Lieutenant Baumber, of the British Army, gave special attention to the training, respectively, in machine gunnery, gas warfare and bayonet fighting. Captain Francois Monroe, Captain Henri

Bloch, Lieutenant Hoffmann, Lieutenant Reich and Lieutenant Boucher, of the French Army, supervised respectively, the training in artillery, field maneuvers, automatic rifles, bombs and liaison. Captain Macdonald, of the Canadian Forces, came later and instructed the Stokes Mortar platoons in the use of this weapon. These officers were welcome guests. Their opinions on the subjects of their specialties were taken as final. They were members of the mess of the Commanding General and were assigned quarters in a building originally erected for the Red Cross and furnished tastefully by the Chapter of the Daughters of the American Revolution of Kansas City, Missouri.

CARPENTER HILL, THE GAS HOUSE AND SMOKY HILL FLATS

Assisted by these officers, an elaborate system of trenches was laid out and constructed by the troops on Carpenter Hill. The system covered an area about a thousand yards square and comprised three lines of trenches with communicating trenches, dugouts, wire entanglements and machine gun emplacements. In its construction the men got their first taste of the digging which was to become such a feature of their life in the coming days after St. Mihiel. Constant training in the features of trench warfare was held here throughout the following winter and spring,—reliefs by night of each element by another were practiced, trench orders were issued for the attack and defense of the place, plans of defense were drawn up providing for the conduct of the troops under every possible condition of enemy attack and penetration of the position, then these conditions were simulated and the plans were put into effect.

A gas house was built, in which the men, after having been drilled in the use of their gas masks, were all required to endure a long period of contact with deadly gases, to demonstrate the absolute protection afforded by the mask and give them confidence in it.

In the late winter and early spring, instruction in all the varied forms of modern warfare went on in Smoky Hill Flats, some five miles from Camp Funston. This instruction was conducted by the Division School of Arms under the command of Major E. A. Keyes and the foreign officers. Here a more elaborate system of trenches was constructed or indicated and larger problems of trench warfare were worked out. Hand and rifle grenades were furnished and the men trained in their use. Target practice with the one-pound cannon was had. Continual instruction in bayonet fighting was conducted.

An enormous target range with three hundred targets was constructed on Republican Flats. Ranges of 100, 200 and 300 yards were available there, while on the smaller range on the reservation, ranges of 500 and 600 yards could be used. Here, throughout the winter and spring the rattle of rifle fire was continually heard. Individual coaches were provided for each man while he was firing, and no one was permitted to fire on the range until he had had preliminary instruction in sighting, aiming, nomenclature and loading of his piece. Fairly good scores were made with the Enfield rifle, with which the troops were equipped. Although not regarded as so good a weapon on the range as the old Springfield, it proved in action to be a reliable service weapon.

CHRISTMAS CELEBRATION

It had been hoped that at Christmas time liberal passes would be issued to the men so that a large number would be enabled to pass the holidays at home, and preliminary orders looking to this end were issued. At the last moment, however, orders from the War Department came which limited severely the number of passes which could be granted. The occasion for this limitation was the state of the nation's transportation system, which bade fair to break down under the stress of war needs. The addition of several hundred thousand soldiers on furlough as passengers at the time was not considered advisable. In Funston, the Division Commander cast about for some means of entertaining his men and allaying the disappointment occasioned by the curtailment of holiday passes. It was determined to have a "Rodeo" and Captain Chauncey M. Dewey, of the 164th Depot Brigade, was detailed to organize the event.

Cow ponies and steers were imported from all over the West; a huge corral was built in which an exhibition of riding, roping and Wild West sports generally was held in the morning. In the afternoon, an attack of Indians and bandits upon a wagon train was staged, the soldier spectators acting the part of the bandits and robbing the wagon train of the freight of Christmas candies and delicacies.

The construction of the zone, with its stores, restaurants and theaters, the Kansas and Nebraska buildings, with their conveniences and entertainment of the men without leaving camp, together with the K. C. and regimental "Y" huts and other special features contributing to the welfare of the soldiers, all deserve description, for which space cannot be given.

FIRE PROTECTION

The possibility of a disastrous fire in this vast cantonment of wooden buildings induced constant vigilance and preparation. Fire drills in the various units were frequently held, in which the men were assembled outside their barracks and special details manned the fire apparatus at designated points. Fire drill on a larger scale was the feature of several winter nights, for the contingency of the total destruction of the entire camp was provided against as far as possible. Such a catastrophe would have turned fifty thousand men out into a bleak and sparsely settled country without food or shelter. The orders for the drill therefore provided for the assembly of all organizations at designated points on the borders of the camp, carrying with them their clothing, arms, blankets and two days' rations, preservation of the essential records of the organizations, assembly and protection of the animals, together with the detail of suitable elements to fight the fire. In the midst of several bitter winter nights, the general fire alarm was sounded, all the lights were cut off from the central lighting plant, as was assumed would be the case in the event of such a disaster, and the prearranged, orderly assembly of the great camp took place. Fortunately, a real occasion for such a maneuver never arose. Much credit for averting serious damage by fire is due the camp fire department, which was frequently called out to extinguish incipient fires. The stress laid by camp orders upon the instruction of sentinels of the ordinary military guard for fire protection, with the constant inspection, drill and training of them in such duties, was one of the efficient causes of our immunity from this ever present danger.

GENERAL WOOD GOES TO FRANCE

On November 26th, 1917, Major General Wood was detailed for observation duty in France, and took abroad with him Colonel Kilbourne, his Chief of Staff. In the short period of three months he had organized the Division into a living, functioning unit and had impressed it with characteristics of energy, resource and ambition which never left it.

The departure of General Wood was made the occasion for the first assembly of the Division as a unit. The men had just been equipped with overcoats and rifles. Without the knowledge of General Wood, orders were issued that the Division be assembled and the troops formed in line on both sides of the road through which he would pass on his way to the station. The kindly secret had been well kept, and the formation was an agreeable and affecting surprise to the General. It was more than that. The appearance and bearing of these soldiers of less than three months training was such as to astonish and delight even those who had been daily in observation of them. One of the British officers, in generous enthusiasm, remarked that the entire British Army could not turn out such a body of men.

While in Europe, General Wood and Colonel Kilbourne were both severely wounded by the explosion of a trench mortar, and their return to the Division was delayed until April 12, 1918. During the absence of General Wood, the Division was under the command of Brigadier General Frank L. Winn, who thus, for a large part of the time from its organization to its departure overseas, conducted the training and equipment.

During this period the Division was constantly being made and re-made. Large contingents of men equipped and partially trained in Camp Funston, were sent to fill deficiencies in other divisions which were supposed to be destined for earlier service overseas than we were. Thus contingents were sent to Camp Kearney, others to Camp Doniphan for the 35th Division, and finally, in the late winter and early spring large quotas of men were sent directly overseas to serve as replacements for divisions already engaged or about to be engaged with the enemy. Many of these men were assigned to the 3rd and 4th Divisions, and participated in the fighting of the spring and summer of 1918 at Chateau-Thierry and along the Vesle.

As a result of these transfers the Division was much depleted on the return of General Wood on April 12th, 1918. Replacements soon began to flow in. Some of them were partially trained men from Camp Grant. Early in May a large contingent of newly drafted men reported in numbers sufficient to fill all vacancies. These men were received within two weeks of the departure of the Division for overseas, and those weeks were crowded weeks for them. They were equipped, trained in the elements of marching and of the manual of arms, given their typhoid prophylaxis and vaccination, all at breakneck speed. But nearly all their time they spent upon the rifle range. General Wood was determined that no soldier of his Division should go overseas until he knew how to shoot. So these raw recruits were hurried to the targets and carefully instructed in the use of their weapons. The good scores made by them were surprising. The success of this hurried training gave striking testimony to the willing eagerness of these recruits to perfect themselves in the duties of a fighting man, and demonstrated how fortunate it was that these Western men, unlike some of those recruited from crowded Eastern centers, were already familiar with the use of firearms. In a short space of time these newcomers had been assimilated in the Division, and by the time of their arrival overseas it would have been impossible for an observer to divine that the Division contained so large a proportion of men only a few weeks separated from the farm and factory.

PREPARATION FOR OVERSEAS

During early May it became known that the Division would depart for overseas during the month. It was high time. The great German offensive of early spring had disclosed the imperative need of our Allies for the military aid of America. It was the dramatic moment of the war, when Germany sought to make good her insolent boast that she would end the war in victory before America could prepare and throw into the conflict an effective force. It was a challenge to all the force and energy of this country, and the events of the next six months disclosed how it was met. But it was nearly true. Our previous inactivity had made our condition such that only by colossal exertions were our forces enabled to arrive in the nick of time. The German had not deemed us capable of making this exertion, and thus invited his own ruin. And in retrospect, with fuller knowledge of what was done, we stand amazed at our country's accomplishments.

Preparations for the departure were hastened, all deficiencies in equipment were made up by hard work in the supply departments, inspections of troops and equipment were personally made by General Wood, and the hour of departure found all ready.

On May 21st the first units of the Division drew out of Camp Funston, bound for "an American port" which later proved to be New York. By the 27th all the Division except the artillery and trains had departed and was assembled at Camp Mills, on Long Island. The Artillery Brigade soon followed overseas, but not as a part of the Division. It went directly to the Artillery Training Camp near Bordeaux, and did not join the Division until the last day of the battle of St. Mihiel.

From the departure of the Division from Camp Funston until its arrival at the training area in France, its passage was marked by spontaneous cheering from the inhabitants of every country and community. It seemed one continuous and inspiring ovation.

GENERAL WOOD RELIEVED

After the concentration of the Division in Camp Mills and on the very eve of its embarkation, an order was received relieving General Wood of the command of the Division and assigning him for duty in the United States. Assembling his officers, he bade them farewell and wished them "the best o' luck" in a brief and soldierly, but touching address, which none of his auditors will ever forget. No reason has ever been assigned by the War Department for the sudden relief of General Wood. It is known, however, that it was not due to physical condition which denied active service to so many of our older officers, for General Wood had recently and successfully passed a thorough physical examination by the official Board of Examiners.

Brigadier General Winn again assumed command of the Division. the troops were transported by train to the docks, and on June 3rd embarked upon the vessels that were to take them overseas. On the very day of the embarkation the story of German submarine activities along the coast of the United States was made known. In the few days preceding, some twenty or thirty small craft had been sunk by submarine raiders, some within forty miles of the harbor of New York. This was a piece of German terrorism, intended to delay and hinder the transportation of troops, as is now manifest from the fact that the cowardly pirates of the sea confined their attacks to small and defenseless vessels. But their presence in our waters did not delay our departure a single instant.

OFF FOR FRANCE

On June 4th, in the blazing light of a midday of June, the vessels forming the convoy swung out from their various docks, steamed down the harbor of New York and took up their voyage to those lands towards which the Goddess of Liberty from her pedestal seemed to turn a wistful gaze. Nine great vessels, striped with the bizarre patterns of their camouflage, crowded with those fighting men who formed part of the hope of civilization, swept down the channel and, without pause, into the open sea. They were all British ships, some of them P. and O., Cunard and White Star liners, some converted cargo boats, some from the Australian trade lines. A British cruiser accompanied them all the way. A number of American torpedo boat destroyers escorted the convoy for the first day and then left it. Two naval aeroplanes circled before and on the flanks of the convoy for the first few miles of the voyage and an observation balloon searched the seas for lurking submarines. When the open sea was reached, the convoy took up a definite formation in three columns with distances of about five hundred yards between the vessels and maintained the formation with the utmost precision for the entire voyage.

There was a shortage of crew in some of the vessels and volunteers from among the troops were called for to serve as stokers. The response was instant. More men applied than were needed. Although their commanding officers explained to them that the service would be entirely voluntary and pointed out the danger attending their position in case of submarine attack,

Caronia, camouflaged, in 1918, when she carried overseas the Headquarters 89th Division (Division Staff, Headquarters Troop and Detachment), 356th Infantry, 342nd Machine Gun Battalion and part of the 353rd Infantry. S. C. 154273.

they gladly served throughout the voyage, receiving the compensation from the ship captain ordinarily paid for such service.

The course taken was far to the north of the usual lines of ocean travel. On approaching the danger zone off the coast of Ireland, a number of British torpedo boats appeared to escort the convoy and the habitual course of the ships became a series of sharp zigzags. No submarine attack occurred and the convoy reached Liverpool safely on the 16th of June, twelve days out of New York. The headquarters of the 177th Infantry Brigade, the 354th Infantry and the 341st Machine Gun Battalion did not cross on this convoy, but went by rail from New York, through Montreal to Halifax and sailed thence to London, joining the Division at its point of concentration, a rest camp near the quaint old cathedral city of Winchester. Some elements of the Division, however, were held at Knotty Ash rest camp near Liverpool, proceeding thence directly to Southampton.

Less than a week was spent in this rest camp, a misnomer by the way, for little rest was experienced there. The troops were sent out to drill on the morning after their arrival and engaged in training every day of their stay.

Here the first glimpse was caught of German prisoners of war, many of whom were kept at work about the camp, great, hairy fellows who stared curiously at the stalwart Americans and perhaps began for the first time to doubt the veracity of their Kaiser when he assured his people that they might ignore the rights and lives of Americans, for they would never take any military part in the war.

ENGLAND IN WAR TIME

England, as it displayed itself, seemed short of food and low of spirit. Some British soldiers, in talking to our men, expressed the sentiment that they were sorry that we had come; that the Allies were whipped and we could not change the result; and that our coming would only prolong the war, which otherwise would have been terminated already. Such pessimistic talk did not in the least daunt our men. It was thought to be in part inspired by German propaganda, and partly the result of the depressing surroundings, as most of the British soldiers about were wounded men from large hospitals in the vicinity. The events of the next few weeks showed that there was no lack of the traditional British pluck among the soldiers at the front, nor in the people at home in England.

Further experience in England gave testimony of the way the whole country was in the war. Scarcely any able-bodied men were to be seen. As the troop trains passed factories, women workers in overalls waved their greetings and resumed their work. Major Meade and Captain Withington, calling on some connections of the latter, found that their host, a wealthy broker, spent four hours a day in overalls, handling pig iron; his beautiful daughter was forewoman in a munitions plant.

There was a noticeable shortage of food. Sugar was not to be had in private life and public restaurants. Small saccharine tablets formed a sorry substitute. Our men, while in England, were furnished the rations issued to the British troops. These consisted largely of cheese, black bread, tea and jam. While we were assured that this ration contained a food value comparable to the American ration and amply sufficient to maintain health and vigor, still it did not seem to fill the American stomach and there was much grumbling about the "chow." Our appreciation of the pluck of the British Army was enhanced when we obtained this first-hand knowledge of the sort of food it fought upon, and reached its climax, later, after the armistice, when we tried out the kind of shoes it fought in. After a few days of refitting and drill at Winchester, the Division was transported by rail to Southampton for embarkation across the Channel to France. The transports were mostly channel packets, fast flying, frail boats driven at high speed by turbine engines.

No separate escort was provided for them and they relied for protection against the submarines on their speed and the general anti-submarine defenses of the Channel. The boats were packed with troops to the utmost of their capacity. There were, of course, no bunks, and scarcely room for the men to stretch out on the decks and floors of the compartments. The voyage was one of the most uncomfortable that our men were ever called upon to endure. It lasted but a few hours, however, and the early morning found us safe off the harbor of Le Havre, which we entered soon after daylight. The Division was soon debarked and the troops were formed to march to their rest camp a few miles from the town. The 89th had at last reached France.

CHAPTER II.

TRAINING BEHIND THE LINES

When the units of the Division landed, mostly at Le Havre, a few at Cherbourg, between June 20th and June 29th, 1918, they were marched forthwith to one of the so-called "rest camps" which were a feature of every port. The trip through the streets of Le Havre consequently afforded most of the

"Hommes 40—Chevaux 8." The standard type of railroad transportation for troops by "side-door Pullmans" in France. S. C. 7029.

men their first glimpse of the country they had come to fight for, and it was with mingled feelings of admiration, sympathy, curiosity and wonder that they looked on this strange people, these narrow streets, odd buildings and signs of unknown meaning. Here the men again caught sight of the enemy, as they went past small groups of German and Austrian prisoners of war, working under guard of a "poilu" or two. Here, too, were seen the oriental laborers used everywhere to release Frenchmen for the front.

There came now a few days at the rest camp, when all had an opportunity to write home from "somewhere in France," and a chance to become acquainted with French money, which they found not complicated in itself, but of elusive value. To the end of their stay in France most of the men were unable to estimate values in terms of francs.

Only a brief period of confinement and inactivity at the rest camp was needed to make orders to proceed inland more than welcome. By night the troops were marched to a dark railroad yard, and stopped beside an unlighted train, the caution being out of deference to the not infrequent German air raids. The men were now introduced to the "Hommes 40—Chevaux 8" box-cars which were to serve them for Pullmans in all their continental travels, while the officers squeezed into the tiny compartments of third-class French coaches. In the middle of the night the journey to an unknown destination began. But if the night was cold and the floor hard the morning brought forgetfulness, for the troops awoke to see the beautiful countryside of Normandy flitting by. And Normandy in June, with its green valleys dotted with little white towns, its fair fields strewn with the reddest of poppies, its leafy woods hiding here and there an old chateau, constitutes for ordinary mortals nothing less than fairyland.

When the train stopped at one and another of the small villages along the way the French children came running to greet "les Americains," and to clamor for "Biskee, Biskee," as they termed the army hardtack. Near Paris many freight trains full of French troops were passed, some going toward the front and some the other way. There were other trains, long and quiet, that carried the wounded, and still others with prisoners of war, who expressed themselves, to those who understood German, as glad to be out of the fight.

THE REYNEL TRAINING AREA

The trip which should have taken only twelve or fifteen hours lasted about two days. But at last the train came to a stop between Chaumont and Neufchateau, and the troops detrained in an area in the Haute-Marne that became officially known as the "Fourth Training Area," and commonly called the "Reynel Training Area." Though not in the most picturesque or the most prosperous part of France, the Division was now hardly more than sixty kilometers from the front, and therefore available for use against the rumored fourth German drive. It was also most conveniently located with reference to higher headquarters, for at that time the headquarters of the Fourth Army Corps, to which the Division was to be assigned, were at Neufchateau, while Chaumont was the seat of General Pershing's headquarters ("G. H. Q."), throughout almost the entire history of the American Expeditionary Forces.

The beautiful seventeenth-century chateau of Reynel had already been chosen by the advance party for Division headquarters. Upon arrival the troops of the Division were scattered over the area, some being lodged in the portable "Adrian barracks," and the rest being billeted upon the population. The 177th Brigade Headquarters were placed in the town of Rimaucourt, the 178th Brigade Headquarters at Prez-sous-Lafauche. Headquarters of the 353rd Infantry were established at Manois, with troops also at Rimaucourt and St. Blin. The 354th Infantry Headquarters were located at Trampot, and in addition the regiment occupied Busson, Leurville, Chambroncourt, and Morionvilliers. The towns of Grand, Brechainville and Aillianville were taken by the 355th Infantry, Grand being used for regimental headquarters. The 356th Infantry was sent to Liffol le Grand and the nearby town of Villouxel. The 340th Machine Gun Battalion was located in St. Blin. The 341st Machine Gun Battalion was stationed at Chalvraines, and the 342nd Machine Gun Battalion at Vesaignes. The 314th Engineers occupied Orquevaux and Humberville, and the 314th Field Signal Battalion shared St. Blin with the battalion of infantry and the machine gun battalion already mentioned as being there. Other units of the Division were distributed as follows: The 314th Sanitary Train at Prez-sous-Lafauche and Liffol le Petit; the Headquarters Troop and Detachment at Reynel, and the 314th Military Police at Rimaucourt. The 314th Supply Train came overseas with the 164th Field Artillery Brigade, and did not reach the divisional training area until August 2, 1918, just in time to assist in the movement of the Division to the front. The Supply Train was stationed at Rimaucourt and was here issued its trucks, not one of which was ever salvaged except those directly hit by enemy artillery.

The Fourth (Reynel) Training Area, Haute Marne, France, where the 89th Division trained.

The surroundings in which the men of the Division now found themselves proved novel in the extreme, though, as they later discovered, they were merely living in typical French communities. The red-roofed houses looked as if they might have been built a thousand years before. The town laundry and the town pump were strange institutions, as were the stores, which unfortunately were found to contain none of the accustomed American delicacies. Chocolate sweetened with saccharine turned out to be the best available substitute for candy. Ice cream was replaced by the French national beverages—vin blanc and vin rouge. Along with these other novelties there must also be mentioned, the greatest novelty of all—the cool French summer. That it was a welcome surprise after the scorching heat of Kansas goes without saying. And in view of the intensive training that had to be done in the next few weeks it was as fortunate as it was welcome.

Due to the presence of quantities of manure and other filth in the streets these towns were extremely unsanitary. All the water was contaminated, and had to be chlorinated before being used for drinking purposes. Primitive is a mild word to describe the living conditions of the men. A few fortunate ones had bunks; others slept in hay lofts or barns. They were under the same roof with horses, cows, pigs and chickens,—indeed it was nothing unusual for a soldier to come home and find his billet overrun with chickens, or a calf on his doorstep.

Lessons in French were begun immediately, and the men were soon able to "parley" with the "mademoiselles." Relations with the peasants were very friendly. The French liked the Americans because they had come to fight alongside their poilus, and the Americans liked the French because of their natural, instinctive friendliness for anyone they meet.

The story of the training area would be incomplete without a special tribute to the conduct of the men in their relations to French among whom they lived. So excellent it was that to visitors in the area since, and most of all such members of the Division as returned, the praise of our men is most striking.

The vision of the fight he was soon to enter lay now at the heart of each man. Upon coming across the sea the Division had found the hopes and spirits of the Allies at a very low ebb. Everywhere there seemed to be sense of coming disaster. Though the last advance had been turned back at Chateau-Thierry, many feared that another drive would bring the invaders to Paris. There was, however, none of this gloomy foreboding in the minds of the men of the Division. When on still nights they heard the guns at the front they were only the more impressed with the seriousness of their undertaking.

INTENSIVE TRAINING AGAIN

Training began in grim earnestness. Again the fundamentals of infantry training were rehearsed with new formations for attack against machine guns. Target ranges were promptly constructed, though with some difficulties about material and locations. After playing with dummies at Camp Funston the men were now given real grenades that exploded when they were thrown. Practice with live rifle grenades was held, too, though several accidents, occasioned by using an improper tromblon with the Enfield rifle, marred the exercises. All the infantry troops had a turn at occupying a network of practice trenches near Goncourt, where they learned to construct and repair entanglements, to snipe at sawdust enemies, to make camouflage, to execute trench raids, and to "stand to" for an enemy attack. The keynote of all training was, of course, attention to discipline. The rigid attention, upright bearing and willing obedience now required of every soldier served to create in him that spirit of discipline and intensity of purpose necessary to success in battle. In this and other training areas there was now being laid the foundation that made it possible for the American Expeditionary Forces to set a new standard of discipline for an American Army.

The infantry soldier was taught that the rifle and the bayonet are his principal weapons, and he was made to feel himself expert as a marksman and invincible as a bayonet fighter. The rifle practice held at this time is worthy of special comment. It can be no exaggeration to say that only an American division would have felt the compulsion of this practice so keenly that, without a sign of a target or a place to use one, it would undertake the job of building its own ranges. For in building these ranges it was necessary, first, to search the area carefully for suitable range sites, then to obtain permission from the French authorities to cut wood, to go to the forests and cut it, and finally to construct pits and frames and improvise targets. Notwithstanding a multitude of difficulties most of the men were firing on the range in the second or third week of their stay in the training area, and before the Division went to the front every man had fired all ranges up to and including 600 yards.

More important even than target practice was the training given in the new method of platoon attack. This instruction showed the platoon leader how to scatter out his platoon in two lines twenty or thirty yards apart, with the men six or seven yards from each other in each line. Troops were taught that the machine gun which held up their advance must be taken by flanking, and not by a frontal attack. The proper formations for artillery fire were rehearsed, and general instructions given in the offensive conduct of small units. The tremendous value of this training may be seen from the experience of the First and Second Divisions, which entered the line without it. In their early engagements at Chateau-Thierry and Soissons, clinging to the old extended order formation of the Infantry Drill Regulations, and advancing with only a yard between men, they were mowed down by the German machine gun fire, suffering terrible losses before they learned to spread out. It was costly knowledge. To the acquisition of it in the training area may be partly attributed the relatively small losses suffered by the 89th Division in its two major operations. Use of casualties as a measure of combat accomplishment is frequently a false standard, for lack of thorough training often caused great and unnecessary losses. These the 89th avoided.

The machine gun organizations spent their time in learning the intricacies of the new Vickers guns, which they had received just before leaving Camp Funston. The Engineers spent day after day at their specialties, bridge construction, the surveying and digging of trenches, the construction of barbed wire entanglements, and the building of roads. The Sanitary Train was likewise being prepared for the role it was to play at the front, while the Signal Troops were finding both experience and hard work in maintaining telephones, buzzers, projectors, wireless and other means of communication for the maneuvers and terrain exercises that were held almost daily. Many officers and men were sent away at this time to various schools, rejoining the Division later with a fund of specialized knowledge.

Imaginary battles were staged daily—long, furious battles that could only be decided by the umpire. Constant maneuver work over varied terrain gave all officers experience in handling troops under war conditions. The topography of the Reynel area bears a strong resemblance to that of the Argonne, where the Division was destined to see its greatest conflict and win its greatest fame. Thus, whether by accident or design, the steep hills and dense woods of the area served an important purpose in preparing the Division for future operations. To the end of coördinating the service of communication and developing the tactical knowledge of commanding officers, numerous terrain exercises were held under plans of the Division and the Corps. These gave to staff and line invaluable experience in working together, and developed the confidence of all. A familiar figure in these exercises was Lieutenant Colonel Stuart Heintzelman (later Brigadier General), Chief of Staff of the Fourth Army Corps, who brought to the critiques held at the close of each exercise a store of sound military principles coupled with no little knowledge of actual conditions at the front. In all the maneuvers and terrain exercises Colonel Heintzelman and other officers from higher headquarters placed the greatest emphasis upon the principles of open warfare. Orders from General Pershing required that all instruction must contemplate the assumption of a vigorous offensive. This was in accordance with his belief that the American Army had been sent overseas, not to help hold the trenches, but to gain as speedy a victory as possible. Hence our troops were now being trained for the great drive that would sweep past the defenses of position warfare, and, forcing the enemy ever backward, cut his line of communication and compel his surrender.

July Fourth came and went. Rumors reached the Division of a stirring parade in Paris on that day. In the training area, however, the holiday was celebrated with speeches and baseball games. A beautiful and touching ceremony took place at Division Headquarters. The Mayor, Council, teacher and school children of Reynel came to the chateau and in well-chosen words expressed to General Winn their gratitude for America's aid in the war. Similar ceremonies took place in other towns in the area. As the French had in courtesy to America observed the Fourth as a holiday, so the American Expeditionary Forces paid tribute to France on July Fourteenth by celebrating the fall of the Bastille. Our Division was honored by being selected to furnish the troops for that occasion and the 1st Battalion of the 353rd Infantry, under command of Lieutenant Colonel (then Major) George H. English, Jr., marched to Chaumont and paraded before the Commander-in-Chief. Their easy discipline, splendid vigor, and indomitable air made of these men a visible embodiment of the spirit of America for all who were there present and elicited warm commendation from General Pershing.

TRAINING THE ARTILLERY AT DE SOUGE

During all this period the 164th Artillery Brigade was separated from the remainder of the Division. It landed in France between July 2nd and July 13th, and was at once sent to a billeting area near Bordeaux, there to wait its chance to enter Camp de Souge, the American artillery training center in France. The 314th Ammunition Train was likewise billeted near Bordeaux and trained at Camp de Souge. Moving into Camp de Souge early in August, the artillery units entered upon a period of six weeks specialized and intensified training, conducted along the accepted traditions of French artillery practice. The wooden guns and caissons, the imaginary teams and other training devices of Camp Funston were now forgotten with the issue of real guns, animals and combat equipment. The 340th and 341st regiments received French 75 mm. guns, model 1897, while the 342nd Field Artillery was equipped with 155 mm. howitzers, model 1915, known as Schneiders. Though, under the tables of organization, the 342nd was to be a motorized outfit, and though it had been given considerable mechanical training with this in view, tractors and motor equipment now failed to materialize, and the regiment had perforce to acquaint itself with the duties and problems of horse-drawn artillery. Actual firing on the range, which had been very difficult at Camp Funston, was now the daily routine. Thorough training was given in the use of the telephone, radio and various other means of communication. Much time was devoted to the computation of firing data and the study of firing methods, as well as to the construction of gun emplacements and the erection of camouflage. Nor was the necessity for constant training in liaison with the infantry overlooked. There were technical schools of almost infinite variety, and tactical problems and artillery fire demonstrations in numbers that could not be counted. Day after day this rigorous course of training continued, each man being trained and trained and trained again for his particular work at the front, until finally, during the St. Mihiel offensive, the brigade rejoined the Division at the front.

Meanwhile in the Reynel area the Division was being equipped for the fight. The time-honored campaign hat had already been discarded for the overseas cap. Russet shoes were exchanged for field shoes, a wrap leggin replaced the one of canvas. Infantry companies were equipped with the French Chauchat automatic rifle. And at last there were given out those two articles, that, producing the most hateful of first impressions, eventually became the inseparable friends of every soldier—the steel helmet and the gas mask. With the issue of these and other articles of combat came, of course, instruction in their use. Helmets were worn until they no longer produced stiff necks. Gas training was given daily, until presently the donning of the mask became a matter of instant habit. After the ups and downs of a year's preparation, the 89th was now almost ready.

DIVISION INSIGNIA

It was during this period that the Division insignia was adopted. The device consists of the letter W enclosed in a circle. The official explanation of its meaning made at the time is that it designates the "Middle West" Division, as the central letter can in one aspect be read as an M and in another as a W. The official explanation also adds that in another aspect the letter can be read as a Greek Sigma, the symbol of summation; and that the circle implies the ability to exert force in any direction and to rest in any position. In other words, if the observer be rotated about his center, as in turning what the small boys call a cart wheel, he will, at successive periods of his revolution be enabled to read M for Middle, W for West and, if he is a Greek scholar, Sigma for summation. Probably, however, the part about coming to rest in any position would not apply in the case supposed.

Notwithstanding the official explanation, there is ground for the suspicion that the symbol has another and esoteric meaning. The W in the circle might serve to recall to memory an old general pining in inaction in the states and be read as "Wood's Own;" while at the same time it could with equal propriety suggest the personality of the assiduous and conscientious leader who was then shaping the Division for its great task, and be read as "Winn's Own." By a happy turn of circumstance, the general destined later to lead the Division into battle bore the same initial, rounding out its combat history as "Wright's Own." Thus the Division's insignia will ever serve to call to remembrance the trinity of commanding officers, so different in type, yet each so uniquely qualified for the work of the moment, and all held equal in respect and regard by the Division. The happy combination of names also served sometimes as a sort of slogan, "Wright, Wood, Winn,"—"Right would win."

The adoption of insignia by the different divisions became, about this time, universal in the A. E. F. Aside from the satisfaction of the instinctive desire of all human organizations to adopt some device other than a mere numerical designation, these symbols served a distinct military purpose by facilitating the identification of our own troops and making the work of the enemy's spies more difficult. It was realized, of course, that all these symbols would soon become known to the Intelligence Department of the German High Command. But the ordinary spy, the small village shopkeeper or workman, would not in the nature of things have this information. In reporting the presence or movement of a body of troops to his superiors he would often be compelled to resort to a description of the symbol; such description was often inaccurate and always difficult to put into a code or brief message.

CHANGES AND MORE TRAINING

During all this time the Division remained under the command of Brigadier General Frank L. Winn. It was the general opinion that, having commanded the Division so long, he would now be permitted to take it into action and would ultimately receive his promotion to the grade of Major General. Just at the close of the training period, Colonel James H. Reeves relinquished command of the 353rd Infantry, which had been under him since its formation, and took the brigade into action. Colonel William G. Sills, who had commanded the 355th Infantry since September, 1917, was now detached from the Division and sent to General Headquarters, much to the regret of his regiment and the entire Division. In his stead Lieutenant Colonel James D. Taylor of the same regiment, who had just been made a full colonel, was assigned as regimental commander. There were other changes of officers, too, the most important of which were those occurring when, on the eve of the departure of the Division for the front, a number of officers were selected to return to the United States and help to train the new divisions then being formed. It was a cruel disappointment to these that the armistice prevented them from returning to Europe and assisting in the downfall of Germany.

It was on July 15th, it will be remembered, that the Germans launched their dreaded fourth offensive, attacking both east and southwest of Rheims with the plan of effecting a junction of the attacking forces, thus broadening the Marne salient preparatory to the final drive on Paris. It was just three days later that Marshal Foch inaugurated his marvelous counter-attack that cut the German communication on the tip of the salient, and in a few days eliminated the "Marne pocket" entirely. While these momentous pages of history were being written the 89th waited and trained behind the lines, ready and eager to take its place beside those other American divisions already in the fight. So if the Division trained well and thoroughly, much of its earnestness of purpose and zest for work can be ascribed to the noise of the distant battle.

Through all the days, and not a few of the nights, of July, the training continued. The fine appearance, soldierly bearing, and excellent work of the Division had won it the approval of G. H. Q., the lethargy induced by the trip overseas had been thrown off, and the severe training had prepared each man for the hardships that were to come. Frequent inspections by higher officers, with as frequent criticisms, had rounded off the rough places, and the Division was now fit for battle. Feeling their own readiness, the men began to circulate rumors of a move to the front. In these, speculation was divided between the St. Mihiel salient, north of Toul, and the part of the Vosges bordering Alsace. A partial basis for the rumors was laid on the 30th of July, when representatives from the Division staff and from each organization were sent to the trenches for a tour of observation. They went to the Toul sector, which had been for months a quiet section of the front, and had already served as a training ground for several American divisions. These officers and men came back fired with confidence and enthusiasm. But scarcely had they begun to relate their experiences, when the entire Division, ready and anxious for the real test, received its orders to go forward to that same Toul sector, where it was presently to receive its baptism of fire, hold its first trenches, and capture its first Germans. Finally, it was on this front that the Division was to engage in its first offensive—was to advance with the best American divisions, and prove itself second to none.

The main street in Seicheprey on September 17th, 1918. Prior to the St. Mihiel Offensive, five days earlier, this was in our front line, in the subsector of the 355th Infantry. Then no mules ambled through the uncleared streets and soldiers moved around but little by daylight. Telephone lines on roadside at right. City Hall at right. "Dry wall" of stone in center of picture protected from shellfire the dugout behind and below it. S. C. 25256.

CHAPTER III.

IN THE TRENCHES

On August 3 and 4, 1918, the 89th Division loaded itself into trucks and started for a front line sector north of Toul. Moving northeast the columns of trucks passed through busy Neufchateau and came to Toul. Now Toul is not an attractive place. It is an ungainly railroad junction and canal town, whose chief claim to general interest lies in its great natural defenses and in the fact that strong fortifications had made it one of the four bulwarks of France along the German frontier. To men, however, who had just come from a two months' stay in the small unsightly villages of the Reynel Area, the town assumed large proportions and woudrous beauty, and it was with the keenest regret that they traveled through it to billets in towns farther north.

EMBUSSING TO THE FRONT

The movement by bus from the Reynel Training Area to the front line is noteworthy in several respects. It was the first movement of American troops by this method of transportation conducted entirely by the American organization and in American trucks. All previous movements of the kind had been conducted by the experienced transportation service of our allies. Furthermore, it afforded the Division an opportunity once more to display its ability to overcome unforeseen and unexpected difficulties.

The orderly movement of large bodies of men is difficult and requires careful forethought and intelligent plans. The preparation of these plans is a function of the staff. The members of the Division staff had received theoretical instruction in such matters at the Staff College. They had been taught that in such movements the truck train would be assembled under an officer of the Transportation Department in charge of a thoroughly organized Bus Park; that this officer would command the train and run it on schedule like a railway train, prescribing the places for halting and having under him an organization of officers and men to arrange all details of the route; that such officers would report to the Division headquarters several days in advance of the move and, in conference with the Division staff officers, arrange the times and places for the troops to meet the trucks; that it was the function of the Division staff to have the troops at those places at those times; and that it was the function of the Bus Park commander to control the movement of the train from that point on to the destination. So when the orders came that the Division was to move by bus to its new station in the line, the Division staff made the preliminary plans for the assembling of the troops and awaited the reporting of the Bus Park commander. But no Bus Park commander reported. When the time for the move was getting perilously near, an officer was sent to Corps Headquarters at Neufchateau to ascertain the cause for the delay and perhaps to hold the conference there. He was informed that no Bus Park had been formed, no officer designated to command

"Embussing" for a troop movement by truck. S. C. 18341.

the movement of the trucks; that the trucks had been ordered from all over the A. E. F. to report to the Division on a certain day and that it was up to the Division to organize the train and conduct the movement. This meant quick work in organizing a force for an entirely novel proceeding; but the success of the movement showed how well it was performed. Major (afterward Lieutenant Colonel) John Franklin, Division Signal officer, who had had truck service in Mexico, was designated to command the train, and made all the preliminary preparations. The actual movement, however, was placed under the charge of Captain (later Major) Walter C. Cole, of the 314th Motor Supply Train. Officers having some experience in the management of trucks and transportation were sought from all organizations of the Division and detailed for duties with the separate parts. A careful schedule of the movement of each organization was made out, provision made for the transportation of the advance parties and billeting details and for the route of the animal-drawn transportation. So when the trucks began reporting from every direction they were met by a well organized body of officers and men and assigned to their places without undue confusion. When the trucks were all assembled it was found that one essential of a truck movement was lacking,—gasoline. On the night of August 2, the Division had but 500 gallons of gasoline; 60,000 were required. Captain Cole hastily organized a convoy, which made the trip to Is-sur-Tille and returned with the needed fuel by starting time, August 3. The difficulties of the movement were enhanced by the fact that it had to be made through the area of the 4th Corps, which was just in the process of organization and was as yet uncontrolled by American military police. The 89th Division Military Police (then called the 314th Military Police), under command of Major James Smallwood, therefore assumed and magnificently performed the task of posting and instructing military police at all cross roads, thus controlling not only the movement of the trucks and animal-drawn transportation of the 89th Division, but all the front, rear and lateral traffic as well.

The movement of the animal-drawn transportation of the Division was under the direction of Captain (afterward Major) Robert K. Schutt, and the difficult task of bringing this unwieldly, slow-moving mass to its proper place at the proper time was well done. The whole movement under the impromptu organization proceeded without hitch, accident or delay; it deserved and received the commendation of higher commanders who knew the difficulties and appreciated the manner in which they had been overcome. The incident was important in constituting one of a chain of events which demonstrated the dependability of the 89th. The Division gained the reputation of accomplishing its missions, no matter what the difficulties. Doubtless each accomplishment enhanced its reputation and occasioned its selection for the next most arduous task. The truck movement and its service in the trenches perhaps induced corps and army commanders to assign to the 89th the sector of Mort Mare, the strongest German position on the front of the St. Mihiel operation. Our success against Mort Mare perhaps earned us the honor of assaulting the Heights of Barricourt, the strongest and most vital position of the enemy in the last phase of the Meuse-Argonne battle, and our actions there earned us our place in the Army of Occupation.

RELIEVING THE 82ND

The Division was to relieve the 82nd American Division in the occupation of a sector of the front line lying north of Toul and between the towns of Remenauville and Bouconville, forming part of the southern face of the St. Mihiel salient. This sector had previously been occupied and had served as a training ground in trench warfare by the 1st and 26th Divisions. It had been regarded as a quiet sector to which green troops could be sent for their first contact with the enemy, and to which exhausted divisions of both combatants could be sent to perform perfunctory service in holding the line. The sector seemed bound to remain always a quiet one and never likely to become the scene of large operations on either side. For any considerable advance by our forces on this front would have brought us to the supposedly impregnable fortified area of Metz. A corresponding advance by the German would have brought him to the equally impregnable fortified area of Toul. But, as will be related, the serenity of the sector became greatly disturbed after the arrival of the 89th Division, and the activity increased steadily until its culmination in the great battle of the St. Mihiel salient.

A certain distinction marked the relief of the 82nd by the 89th Division. It is said that our division was the first American division ever permitted to enter the line as a unit and without having been previously brigaded with French or British troops. The first American troops sent into the line were sent in by battalions as parts of a regiment (or, among the British, of a brigade), the regiment or brigade being under the command of the foreign officer, no American officer of higher rank than a major being in immediate command of troops. When the 82nd went in, its regiments went in as units, but with a French regiment between each two American regiments and the French colonel in command of the adjacent regiment, commanding both his own and the American regiment. After a little seasoning, the American colonels assumed direct command of their regiments, but the brigade, composed of American and French regiments, remained under the command of the French brigade commander. Still later, the American brigade and division commanders assumed their proper commands, commanding both the American and French troops in their sector until, finally, all the French troops would be withdrawn.

IN THE FRENCH ARMY

The process of gradual assimilation was not followed when the 89th entered the line. Our division went in as a division, though as a part of the French Army, under a French Corps commander and with French Artillery support. We became a part of the 32nd French Army Corps, under command of General Passaga, a highly regarded French officer whose commanding presence and high military attainments entitled him to the phrase "every inch a soldier," and under whom it was a pleasure and a privilege to serve. The 32nd French Corps was in turn part of the Eighth French Army, at that time under the command of General Gerard.

An incident which occurred very soon after the entry of the Division into the sector served to promote the good relations between our division and the French. The left flank of our division joined the right flank of the 39th French Division, and formed the junction point, not only of the divisions but of Corps and Armies, for there the sector of the 8th French Army terminated and that of the 2nd French Army began. It was therefore a critical point in the line. The plans for the defense of this point had been prepared and adopted by the French. These plans involved the maintenance of an infantry battalion and machine gun company from our division of the 8th Army to be stationed at Cornieville. Its mission was to garrison the position Cote de Reugnon, Jouy-sous-les-Cotes, Jouy and Gironville forts so as to cover the left flank of the Lucey sector in the event that the Heights of Gironville were attacked; in such event it was to be under the command of the colonel commanding the Gironville sector in the zone of the 2nd (French) Army.

When our division took over the sector, a study of the ground convinced General Winn that the disposition was faulty in that this battalion's position afforded such field of fire that it did not in reality guard our left flank, but guarded only the right flank of the French 2nd Army; while the guarding of our left flank was dependent upon the troops of the right division of the 2nd Army on the tactical line of Drominchamp-Le Petit Bois. And that the disposition could be much improved by extending our boundaries so as to include all of Lake Vargevaux, Le Bois Brule and the eastern half of Le Petit Bois. Accordingly General Winn made the suggestion to the French commanders that their plans should be changed in these respects. His suggestions were adopted by the commanders of the two armies and the sectors and dispositions of troops were changed in conformity.

It is thought that the incident served to induce the French commanders to repose increasing confidence in the military attainments of the American forces; and, on our part, to convince us that the French officers were free from pride of opinion and were deferential to our views.

The countersign and parole gave some trouble at first, because they were French names. Weird sounds were usually produced when a sentry challenged and called for the countersign. The countersign and parole were published by the Army for the use of all troops in its zone. They were changed at noon and in force for a period of twenty-four hours.

On August 20th the higher command of the sector passed from the French to the American Army. The 1st and 4th Corps of the United States Army had previously been organized and they took over the defensive zone of Toul, which had up to that time been under the 32nd French Army Corps. Our division was a part of the 4th Corps, under the command of Major General Dickman with headquarters at Toul. Command passed on August 20th, at 3 P. M. The 1st Corps took over the sector to our right, command passing August 22nd.

It was with genuine feeling of regard on both sides that the Division parted with its French Corps commander. General Passaga, on relinquishing command, expressed through a general order his high appreciation of the Division. And even after the severance of command was complete, he continued in the most friendly and considerate manner to furnish valuable advice and suggestions. An instance of this illustrates not only the kindly impulse and sound common sense of the French commanders, but also how slight was the anticipation, even in the high command, of the swiftness of the current of events that was leading to the collapse of the German military power. General Gerard, the French Army commander, and General Passaga suggested to General Winn that battery emplacements and barracks located in the woods be covered by wire netting, suspended from the trees, so that when the forest leaves began to fall, they would be caught by the netting and the locations thus camouflaged by Nature herself throughout the winter. But within a few days of the giving of this sagacious counsel, the German had been driven far beyond the possibility of harming these emplacements and barracks; and before all the leaves had fallen, his armies were in full retreat along the entire front and he was suing for peace!

HOLDING THE LINE

The first relief in this sector had already been made before the major part of the 89th Division reached the front; Field Hospital 355 of the 314th Sanitary Train had taken over a Field Hospital of the 82nd Division near Minorville on August 2, 1918. Other units moved up and released elements of the 82nd Division as fast as orders allowed. The first combat element of the 89th Division to enter the line was the 1st Battalion of the 355th Infantry, which relieved a battalion of the 327th Infantry, 82nd Division, near Beaumont on the night of August 4-5. Battalions of the 353rd, 354th and 356th regiments quickly followed, and by the morning of August 10th the Division was holding the entire line.

The mission of the Division in this sector was, of course, principally to hold it secure against the enemy and at the same time to prepare itself for future aggressive action. The main activities during the period were therefore holding and occupying the advance post positions, continuous patrolling and raiding, both for our own security and to obtain information of the enemy, work on the position of resistance and training in the rear.

The division sector was divided into four regimental sectors. Running from west to east these sectors were designated respectively as Centers U, V, W and X, and were occupied respectively by the 356th, 355th, 354th and 353rd Infantry Regiments. The regimental headquarters, in the same order, were at Raulecourt, Ansauville, Noviant and Manonville. While officially located in these towns the 356th actually maintained headquarters in the woods two and a half kilometers south of Raulecourt, and one echelon of the 353rd P. C. was in the woods north of Manonville. The Brigade Headquarters were, for the left brigade, the 178th, in the Foret de la Reine about two and a half kilometers south of Ansauville; and for the right brigade, the 177th, at Minorville. Division Headquarters were at Lucey. There was a rail head at Boucq and later another at Menil-la-Tour where the trains were principally located. The enemy opposed this front with parts of two divisions. Opposite the X center was the 419th Regiment of the 77th Reserve Division, and opposite the W center was the 257th Regiment of the same division, which extended about one-fourth over into the V center. The remainder of the V center was opposed by the 477th Regiment and the U center was opposed by the 417th Regiment and a part of the 441st. These last three regiments were part of the 227th German Division.

The sector to the right of our division was at the time of the relief being taken over by the 1st American Division, with headquarters at Saiserais. The sector to our left was held by the 34th French Division, with headquarters at Commercy.

OUR SECTOR

Roughly paralleling the Metz-St. Dizier road, the Division's sector extended from a point opposite the eastern edge of the town of Remenauville to the middle of the Vargevaux Pond (Etang de Vargevaux)—a total distance of more than sixteen kilometers. Like all sectors of the old front line, it consisted of a number of trenches fenced by wire and parallel to a shell-pitted strip of ground, beyond which lay some thicker wire and the parapet of the foremost

Shell-wrecked church in Limey, in the line held by 89th Division prior to the St. Mihiel offensive. S. C. 25278.

enemy trench. All advantages of position and observation were on the side of the enemy. He had taken up his position in natural strongholds and had made them stronger and stronger. From his lookout posts he commanded a view of our trenches and rear areas for many miles, while our only view was of No Man's Land and the nearest of the strongholds.

At the extreme right of the sector were a number of spurs jutting out from the east, each covered with a dark clump of woodland. Well behind our line one of these clumps, the Bois des Hayes, formed one of the strongest points in our line of resistance, where the final stand against an enemy attack in force would be made. Just inside the enemy position, and only two hundred yards from our observation groups, was the town of Remenauville, a mass of ruins, honeycombed with galleries and dugouts. Swerving to the south our line came in front of Limey, torn and smashed, but still recognizable as an erstwhile pretty town. The battered church remained standing, though it had formed a target for hundreds of German shells. The Germans used to fire at the tower of this church every Sunday morning in an effort, as it seemed to the soldiers, to ring the bell for services. But the tower stood in spite of the boche and many men were cheered and comforted thereby. In the cemetery of Limey there was to be seen a sample of German workmanship. During the early part of the war the German lines were several hundred yards farther south, and included Limey. While here the enemy had constructed a machine gun emplacement in one of the monuments of the cemetery, and had no doubt used this skillfully concealed position with deadly effect against the French. Later in the war the Germans had voluntarily withdrawn from most of the low ground in this sector, leaving the French no course but to move up and take worse positions than they already had. In front of most of this part of our line the ground rises sharply toward the enemy trenches, so that our soldiers could see little in front of them but the slope.

In front of Limey No Man's Land was green and wide, and sprinkled thick with poppies. Through it ran a number of old German trenches, now abandoned and blocked at our end, so that no enemy patrol could steal inside our lines without our knowledge. A few of these trenches were left open, however, for our own patrols, and here a tense sentinel stood guard day and night, never knowing when a German bayonet might stare him in the face. Opposite Limey were the old Ansoncourt and Robert Menil Farms. The two names no longer designated peaceful farmhouses, but sets of ruins in which the enemy had built himself deep machine gun emplacements, powerfully revetted trenches, and dugouts of wood and iron capable of withstanding the heaviest shells. When the attack of September 12th passed by, the bodies of many of our officers and men were found in front of these strongholds, riddled with machine gun bullets. It is well to add that the garrisons were found dead at their posts only a few yards away.

The line passing westward now comes in front of shattered Flirey, whose outward aspect was one of whiteness and desolation. In some of the ruins, however, the cellars had been strengthened with beams and girders, and several groups of men were always sheltered here. Across from Flirey was that tower of defense in the German line—the Mort Mare Wood. All that could be seen of it from our lines was a confusion of wire and gnarled trees. But the enemy had dug and cut and tunneled and wired and builded until he had made the wood a more impregnable fortress than the strongest castle of old. In its strong dugouts large numbers could be held ready to repel an attack, meanwhile living in comparative safety and moderate comfort. Its concrete pill boxes were carefully made, and its wire was high and wide. So strong was this position deemed by the Division commander that in his preparations for the St. Mihiel drive he planned no frontal attack against it, choosing instead to send troops around each flank and mop it up from the rear.

Behind Flirey lay the two woods known as the Bois de la Voisogne and the Bois de la Hazelle, and to the west was the Bois de Jury. Running westward, our lines now sloped into an open, marshy country, a projection of the plain of the Woevre. Within our lines about four kilometres west of Flirey, was situated the ruins of the village of Seicheprey, the scene of the first serious conflict of the American troops with the boche. Here, on April 20th, 1918, a strong raiding party of Germans attacked vigorously Americans of the 26th

In front of Rambucourt. Our wire and telephone line in immediate foreground, trenches in middle distance, Xivray beyond, and to the left Montsec, which had been in possession of the Germans since the first year of the war. Village of Montsec on its right slope. The lines were practically stationary here for four years and until the American St. Mihiel offensive, Sept. 12th, 1918. Photographed Sept. 17, 1918. S. C. 25255.

Division, and met with a reception which gave them a taste of the fighting spirit of their new adversaries. The initial conflict between American and German troops had taken place here also, a minor clash of outposts some three months previously, when the 1st Division held the sector.

North of Seicheprey about two kilometers and in the enemy lines was the village of Lahayville, now converted into an enemy strong point. About four kilometers to the northwest of Seicheprey the German lines ran through the village of Richecourt, also strongly fortified. Passing on westward through Xivray, our lines terminated in the pond or lake of Vargevaux, to the north and a little east of which was the camel's hump called Mont Sec. While Mont Sec itself was a capital point of observation of our lines, the strength of the German positions about St. Mihiel lay in the possession of high ground further west. These heights bordered the river Meuse and separated it from the plain of the Woevre, which is a rather high but marshy plateau lying between the heights which border the valleys of the Moselle and the Meuse.

NEW TACTICS IN POSITION WARFARE

The front line trenches on both sides were elaborately constructed, with wide belts of wire, deep dugouts and a maze of communicating trenches. One of the first impressions of the observer was that of the tremendous amount of human labor expended in the construction of this vast system extending from Switzerland to the ocean, and the thought of what benefit to humanity would have been conferred if this mighty effort on both sides had been applied to the arts of peace instead of being made part of a process of destruction.

Yet at the time the Division took over the trenches a new development of the tactics of defensive warfare had already rendered the greater part of this great trench system useless, left it largely unused and in many places dilapidated and caving away to disintegration.

In the early days of the warfare of position both sides held the front line trenches with strong forces and endeavored to repel from them all attacks of the enemy. With the increase of the power, volume and accuracy of the artillery, however, it was found that this method of defense presented serious disadvantages. A sufficiently heavy artillery preparation could and did demolish the front line defenses and cause frightful losses to the defenders, who were unable to retaliate with their own weapons. When, after such preparation, the enemy flung his infantry at the position he was almost always able to occupy it with little loss. The result was, where the front line position was held by strong forces and the main fight was made there, that the defense was greatly handicapped, was often compelled to withdraw its forces under fire and lost the battle when losing the position.

Though this method of advance was certain, it had limitations. In the first place it was necessarily very slow. Only one position could be taken at a time. If the defenders withdrew to a similar position constructed in the rear, the whole process had to be repeated for the next position, and so on ad infinitum. The artillery must be brought forward to the range of the new position, the vast accumulation of ammunition for the next advance must be made, firing data computed anew and prolonged study of the enemy's positions made before the detailed plans for the reduction of the next position could be formed. The greatest difficulty was, of course, the accumulation of sufficient artillery and especially the ammunition for it to assure the demolition of the front line defenses. It was calculated, in the first few years of the war, that three months were required to accumulate the ammunition necessary to maintain six hours drum fire, as the most intense possible fire of massed artillery was sometimes called. Artillery concentration for such methodical attacks was also limited by the fact that such concentration could not be so close to the front as to be within range of weapons which could be fired from the trenches themselves, such as trench mortars and minnenwerfers, nor within the zones of possible raids from the trenches, and also by the difficulty of finding sufficient gun positions for so large a mass of artillery. Consequently, the defenders' second position could be located far enough to the rear so that adequate artillery preparation upon it could not be made without moving forward the artillery after the first position was reduced, and yet sufficiently close to the original front line to cover the withdrawal of the troops there and to launch a counter attack upon the original front line before the attacking infantry could have time to organize it for defense.

When this situation became fully developed, and it was obvious that the offense could, by sufficient preparation, though at great expense of time and ammunition, always take the enemy front line position, the tacticians on both sides, considering the status from the viewpoint of the defense, asked themselves why it was necessary to hold the front line strongly and stake the battle on conflict there; why not give battle in positions not exposed to destruction by artillery, and hold the front line with only enough men to prevent an infantry advance unaccompanied by intense artillery preparation.

The great advantage which the introduction of the rapid firing small arm gave to the defense has already been pointed out and this made feasible a new method of defensive warfare. Both armies adopted the new method, and in the winter of 1917-1918 began adapting their trench systems to it. This change was still in progress when the 89th Division entered the line in the Toul sector and a very large part of its activities was devoted to perfecting it.

In brief, the new plan of defense consisted in holding the front line, or more accurately, the advance position (for it is a zone rather than a line), with small and scattered groups of men, plentifully supplied with machine guns and automatic rifles. These groups were not arranged in the form of a continuous line, but were scattered about in checkerboard fashion. In strength they were ordinarily a platoon, of from 25 to 50 men. They were so placed that each group could cover with its fire the front or flanks of some other group and the gaps between. Their orders were to hold their positions to the last, even if cut off or surrounded, unless authorized to retire by special authority of the general commanding the army. Further to the rear were larger groups, ordinarily a company in size, so located as to support the combat groups by fire and close enough to advance to the support of the combat groups and fight by their side in case of partial penetration of the position or the cutting off of a combat group. From these supports, small detachments as patrols, observers and sentinels were thrown forward in advance of the line of combat groups. Their functions were to give the alarm in case of attack and to offer preliminary resistance. They were to retire fighting, passing between the combat groups and to rejoin the supports. This whole system of advance elements, combat groups and supports made up what was known as the Advance Post Position, and took the place of what had formerly been practically a continuous line or lines in the front trenches. In the regimental sector the Advance Post Position was commonly held by one battalion. Its elements, instead of being arranged side by side in one or two lines, were scattered over an area usually about three of four kilometers in width by from two to three kilometers in depth.

The only contingency which permitted the troops of the Advance Post Position to retire to positions further back, was the direct command of the Army Commander. As a practical matter, such orders would not probably be given in battle. They would be appropriate only as part of a large strategy, as when a general attack was foreseen in advance, and for some reason the Advance Post Position would be evacuated before the attack.

Back of the Advance Post Position and running roughly parallel with it at a distance of four to eight kilometers from the extreme front line positions, was located the Position of Resistance. This was the position upon which, under the new system of defense, the main battle would be fought in the event of an attack upon a large and serious scale. This position was fortified with all the art of military science. Its defensive strength lay in a number of strong points, or centers of resistance, each containing one or more concrete pill boxes or machine gun nests so located as to afford a field of fire parallel to our front, but it was also to consist of a continuous line to resist infiltration. It is an axiom of machine gun tactics that flanking fire is essential to get the full power of this weapon. Direct fire to the front is of little more value with a machine gun than with a rifle, because of the wide intervals between men taken by attacking forces; but if a line of advancing men can be taken in the flank by fire, only a slight horizontal movement of the piece (called "traverse") is necessary to bring the entire line under fire, and fearful execution is the result. In consequence of this characteristic of the machine gun, which of course applies to rifle fire also to a certain extent, all field fortifications are laid out in the form of zigzags; the angles pointing to the enemy are called salients, and those pointing to the rear are called re-entrants. By locating the machine gun near a re-entrant, it is enabled to fire parallel to the side of the adjacent salient and thus sweep from the flank the wire entanglements and the ground in front of them.

The position of resistance in the Toul sector was being constructed in conformity with these principles when the 89th Division entered the sector. Some of the concrete pill boxes had already been constructed and the barbed wire entanglements around them and connecting them with one another had been put in place. But the trenches which would lie behind (but not always parallel with), the wire, had not been dug, nor were there shelters or dugouts for the garrisons. In this work the 89th was vigorously engaged during its occupation of the sector, the new position of resistance having been occupied on August 19th.

Ordinarily, in the regimental sector, one battalion would be stationed on the position of resistance as the garrison of this position. As a routine occupation, this battalion worked on the trenches through the night and slept either in the trenches or in shelter nearby during the day.

In rear of the position of resistance the remaining battalion of the regiment would be held as a reserve. This battalion was ordinarily billeted in some town within a few minutes' march of the position of resistance and would ordinarily engage in training during the day under such conditions as to preclude, as far as possible, enemy observation.

It will be seen from the foregoing description of the new system of defense, that in case of a serious attack, the enemy would meet with increasing resistance from our forces, and the further he progressed from his supporting artillery the stronger the resistance became. The system has been well likened to the compression of a spring, the resistance becoming stronger as the pressure increases until a point is reached where no further progress can be made. The system seems heartless at first thought, in its requirements that the troops of the Advance Post Positions must die in their positions rather than yield, sacrificing themselves to break up the advance so that it can be shattered on the Position of Resistance. But on further reflection it is perceived that the total of casualties in the action will be far less than if strong forces were kept in the front lines to be subjected to the frightful shower of artillery projectiles there and compelled to fight the enemy infantry under such tremendous disadvantages. Another function of the combat groups of the Advance Post Position makes it imperative that they hold their posts to the last. Even if the enemy overwhelms and passes the Advance Post Position, it seldom happens that all the defenders are destroyed. And if the enemy's attack on the Position of Resistance fails, the survivors in the islands of resistance of the Advance Post Position can inflict severe losses on his retreating troops and increase their confusion.

ARTILLERY SUPPORT

The supporting artillery was mostly French, though one battalion of 75's of the 15th Field Artillery of the 2nd U. S. Division was in the sector when the relief of the 82nd Division took place. The artillery was so disposed that the bulk of it was in rear of the position of resistance and these guns were permitted to fire only upon order of the Division Commander or of the Division Artillery Commander, except in cases of an important attack, if the telephone wires were cut. Artillery positions in front of the line of resistance were occupied by pieces detached from these in the combat positions. The proportion of these forward guns to the total effective strength was from one-quarter to one-half of the 75's and one-quarter to one-third of the 155 short. The 75 millimeter gun is of approximately 3-inch caliber, the 155th millimeter approximately 6-inch, the latter being of two classes, the "short" or howitzer firing at a high angle, like a mortar, and being divisional artillery, and the long (G. P. F.'s) firing at a flatter angle, of greater range, and used only as a corps or army artillery. The advance position guns executed the daily fires, certain barrage fires and local counter-preparations. A certain amount of ammunition was alloted to them for daily harrassing fire and reprisal fire requested by the infantry commanders.

A wall or curtain of fire laid down by the shells of the artillery or the bullets of the machine guns is called a barrage. Of course such projectiles cannot fall precisely in a line and in effect what is obtained is a zone of at least 50 meters depth within which the fire falls. Three such barrage lines were provided and the guns were prepared at all times to lay their fire on these lines if called for. Rocket signals from the infantry as well as the ordinary artillery liaison service were used to call for these barrages as needed. At the time of the relief of the 82nd Division the signals were a large green star rocket for the barrage before the advance observation posts of the infantry, executed exclusively by the pieces in the advanced positions; a large red star rocket for a barrage before the line of combat groups, executed at first only by the pieces in the advanced positions, but if necessary participated in, under the orders of the division commander, by pieces from the rear of the position of resistance; and a large white star rocket for the barrage before the position of resistance, participated in by all batteries. The barrage lines were laid as near to the front of the elements protected as safety would permit, and one gun was assigned to cover not over 50 meters of front. A caterpillar rocket sent up simultaneously with the barrage rocket called for counter-preparation fire; a caterpillar rocket alone indicated that the artillery was firing short or that it was desirable to increase the range for other reasons; an attack by tanks was indicated by a yellow smoke bomb and a gas attack by a green parachute. These signals were subsequently changed, but the same system of barrages remained.

PLANS OF DEFENSE

A feature of position warfare in general is the preparation of elaborate plans of defense. In view of the changes in progress in the method of holding the sector, this became an important part of the duties of the officers of all grades, each in his own sphere.

The standing orders of the French Higher Command prescribed the defense of the sector in conformity with the principles above described. In addition, a host of eventualities was provided for. A certain number of battalions of the troops in the reserve positions were required to be designated as army reserves. In the event of an attack on the division sector, the withdrawal of these troops from the control of the division commander was not contemplated. But they were required to be constantly equipped, prepared and available for transportation to other points of the army's sector if an attack fell elsewhere. The proper commanders were required to designate positions in the Position of Resistance to be occupied by each of these reserve battalions in the event of attack; and troop leaders, even down to non-commissioned officers of these battalions, were required to reconnoiter these positions and the routes to them. On the Position of Resistance itself a certain percentage (one-sixteenth) of the troops were required to be kept at all times, day and night, under arms and on the watch, while the other troops on the position were at work or in repose.

Positions far to the rear of the area occupied by our division were also fortified, and the French plans of defense detailed the methods of retirement to them and the garrisons for the various forts. These positions in our rear were part of a system known as the Toul Barrage, and during the period of our occupation were entirely garrisoned by the French.

Subordinate to these general plans, detailed plans were prepared down to even the smallest subdivisions, each in conformity to the plans of the next higher unit. The division headquarters drew plans covering every eventuality of enemy attack upon or penetration of the division sector, prescribing the general duties of the reserves and of the line troops in each case. Upon these plans the brigade commanders based their own plans of defense, prescribing the duties of the regiments; they in turn prescribed the duties of the companies; and they, of the platoons. The plans for the conduct of each unit were required to be kept at the headquarters of that unit, and there were frequent inspections by each higher authority to assure himself that his subordinates had and understood these plans. When a unit was relieved in the occupation of a sector, the relief was not deemed complete until these plans, as well as maps of the sector and trench stores, had been turned over to the relieving commander and receipted for by him.

CODES

The use of codes and code names for communication by telephone, telegraph and radio was a necessary but vexatious feature of the constant reports which conditions imposed upon us. It was well known that the enemy had tapped in on our system of telephone wires, no difficult matter in that sector where four years of occupation had covered the country with a network of telephone wires strung through miles of trenches, many of them merely laid upon the open ground. A vast amount of this wire was no longer in use. Much of it was in positions in the old trenches of the front lines which were little frequented except by patrols of both armies. Spies and patrols doubtless connected up this wire with wires in use, or by other means got connection with our wire.

There was no doubt about the fact that the Germans were on our lines of wire. One day, soon after the occupation of the sector, a voice called up two different ambulance stations, and, giving the proper code names for the regimental headquarters, requested that two ambulances be sent at once to the headquarters of the 353rd and 354th Infantry. The ambulances were at once sent, but on arrival found that no request had been made for them from the regiments. The trip of the ambulances had, however, been watched without doubt by the German observers from their balloons, and the location of the headquarters of the two regiments was thus made known to the enemy. A little later brisk shelling of these points became a feature of the enemy's harassing artillery fire. It was necessary, therefore, to assume in all telephone conversations. that Fritz was listening in, and codes were used in an attempt to thwart him.

The code names in use by the 82nd Division were taken over by us on the relief. These consisted in assigning to locations and the troops there stationed arbitrary names. These were all names of birds, Redbird, Jaybird, Crow and the like designating the units stationed in the Bois de Voisogne, Manonville, Lironville, and so forth. The bodies of all messages were coded under a code issued by the Army and frequently changed. These codes were simple, a combination of letters or figures being assigned to represent each letter of the alphabet and words and phrases in common use. In the use of letter codes over the telephone it was found that the succession of disconnected letters was hard to understand because of the similarity of sound of so many of the letters like b, c, d, t and others pronounced with the recurrence of the "ee" sound. Also some letters like "f" and "s" are absolutely indistinguishable from one another over the telephone. In consequence of this difficulty, the system was adopted of further describing each letter by some word in which it occurred, as "a for able," "p for pup" and so on. Even this system had to be used with intelligence, many words like "fox" and "socks" sounding exactly alike over the telephone, as the reader can demonstrate if he chooses.

It will be imagined how trying upon the nerves it was to send or receive an important message over the phone under these conditions, a long succession of "a for able's" and "p for pup's" being requisite for a very short communication, and requiring coding and decoding at both ends. It formed, however, a valuable schooling in the splendid habit of brevity.

About the time of the St. Mihiel operation a system of numbers to indicate officers and staff sections, uniform throughout the Army, went into effect. This system continued without change until the dissolution of the Division. The code names of the organizations of each division all commenced with the same letter. In our division, these names all began with the letter "I;" in the 42nd Division with the letter "C;" in the 78th, the letter "F;" in the 90th, the letter "T" and so on.

The numbers indicating the officers and staff sections were the following:

No.	Army	Army Art.	Corps	Division	Brigade	Regiment	Smaller Units	No.
1	C. G.	C. G.	C. G.	C. G.	C. G.	Col.	C. O.	1
2	A. D. C.	A. D. C.	A. D. C.	A. D. C.	A. D. C.	Lt. Col..	....	2
3	C. of S.	C. of S.	C. of S.	C. of S.	....	....	....	3
4	Sec. G. S.	....	Sec. G. S.	....	....	....	....	4
5	G-1	....	G-1	G-1	....	....	....	5
6	G-2	Inf.	G-2	G-2	Intl. O.	Intl. O.	Intl. and Op. O.	6
7	G-3	Opr.	G-3	G-3	Opr. O.	Opr. O.	....	7
8	G-4	....	....	....	....	....	....	8
9	G-5	....	....	....	....	....	....	9
10	Signals	Art. Sig.	Signals	Signals	Signals	Signals	Signals	10
11	A. G.	Adj.	A. G.	A. G.	Adj.	Adj.	Adj.	11
12	I. G.	....	I. G.	I. G.	....	....	....	12
13	J. A.	....	J. A.	J. A.	....	....	....	13
14	C. Q. M.	....	C. Q. M.	C. Q. M.	....	Sup. Off.	Sup. Off.	14
15	C. Surg.	Surg.	C. Surg.	C. Surg.	Surg.	Surg.	Surg.	15
16	C. E. O.	Eng.	C. E. O.	....	....	....	....	16
17	M. T. S.	....	....	M. T. S.	....	....	....	17
18	C. O. O.	Ord.	C. O. O.	C. O. O.	....	....	....	18
19	C. A. S.	....	C. A. S.	....	....	....	....	19
20	C. C. W. S	....	C. C. W. S	C. C. W. S.	....	Gas Off.	Gas Off.	20
21	P. M. G.	....	P. M. G.	P. M.	....	....	....	21
22	C. T. C.	....	C. T. C.	....	....	....	....	22
23	C. G. Art.	....	C. G. Art.	....	....	....	....	23
24	Hdq.Com.	....	Hdq.Com.	Hdq. Tr.	Hdq. Det.	Hdq. Co.	Hdq.Det.	24
25	Fr. Miss.	....	Fr. Miss.	Fr. Miss.	....	....	....	25
26	....	....	....	M. G. O.	....	....	....	26
27	....	....	....	Stat. O.	....	....	....	27

The code names for the principal combat units, which the reader examining the field messages and dispatches of the Division will constantly encounter, are the following which is copied literally from the official order. This order was based upon the composition of the staff of higher headquarters and naturally contains some officials who served on such staff but for whom there was no corresponding official in the Division, the code number being preserved for the sake of uniformity of corresponding officials on all staffs. These were the Secretary of the General Staff, G-4, G-5, and some others. Furthermore, the abbreviations used are those, in many instances, appropriate only to the staff of a higher unit than a division, the principal variations and corresponding officer in a division being the following: A. G., Division Adjutant; I. G., Division Inspector; C. Q. M., Division Quartermaster; C. Surg., Division Surgeon; C. E. O., Division Engineer; C. O. O., Division Ordnance Officer; C. A. S., Air Service Liaison Officer; C. C. W. S., literally, Chief of Chemical Warfare Service, actually the same as the Division Gas Officer; P. M. G., Commander of the Military Police.

The list:

NAME	CODE NAME
Commanding General	Immortal No. 1
A. D. C.	Immortal No. 2
Chief of Staff	Immortal No. 3
Sec. G. S.	Immortal No. 4
G-1	Immortal No. 5
G-2	Immortal No. 6
G-3	Immortal No. 7
G-4	Immortal No. 8
G-5	Immortal No. 9
Signal Officer	Immortal No. 10
A. G.	Immortal No. 11
I. G.	Immortal No. 12
J. A.	Immortal No. 13
C. Q. M.	Immortal No. 14
C. Surgeon	Immortal No. 15
C. E. O.	Immortal No. 16
M. T. S.	Immortal No. 17
C. O. O.	Immortal No. 18
C. A. S.	Immortal No. 19
C. C. W. S.	Immortal No. 20
P. M. G.	Immortal No. 21
C. T. C.	Immortal No. 22
C. G. Art.	Immortal No. 23
Hdq. Com.	Immortal No. 24
Fr. Mission	Immortal No. 25
M. G. O.	Immortal No. 26
Stat. O.	Immortal No. 27
C. O. Sig. Bn.	Immortal No. 28
Radio Station	Immortal No. 29
Supply Train	Immortal No. 30
Amm. Tr. Hdq.	Immortal No. 31
San. Tr. Hdq.	Immortal No. 32
Hdq. Amb. Sec.	Immortal No. 33
Hdq. Tr.	Immortal No. 35
Corps Vetr.	Immortal No. 36
Message Center	Immortal No. 37
Air Service	Immortal No. 38
Gas Officer	Immortal No. 39
Munitions Officer	Immortal No. 40

NAME	CODE NAME
354th Ambulance Co.	Imploro
355th Ambulance Co.	Illustrate
356th Ambulance Co.	Impose
353rd Ambulance Co. Dressing Stat.	Imploy
354th Ambulance Co. Dressing Stat.	Improvise
Commanding Officer, Field Hospitals and Ambulance Sections	Import
Dental Corps	Impulse
177th Brigade Hdq.	Illustrious
Hdq. 353rd Infantry	Ideal
1st Battalion	Identical
2nd Battalion	Idiom
3rd Battalion	Idol
Hdq. 354th Infantry	Ignatius
1st Battalion	Igloo
2nd Battalion	Ignite
3rd Battalion	Ignore
178th Brigade Hdq.	Immanity
Hdq. 355th Infantry	Immense
1st Battalion	Immediate
2nd Battalion	Immeasurable
3rd Battalion	Immaculate
Hdq. 356th Infantry	Illimitable
1st Battalion	Illative
2nd Battalion	Illegible
3rd Battalion	Illogical
340th Machine Gun Bn.	Imbricate
342nd Machine Gun Bn.	Imbrute
340th Field Artillery	Immature
341st Field Artillery	Immemorial
342nd Field Artillery	Improve
Div. Artillery Officer	Implant
Div. Camouflage Officer	Important
Division Engineer	Implicit
314th Supply Train	Impeach

NAME	CODE NAME
Mobile Ord. Repair Shop	Immortal No. 52
Hdq. Motor Bn. Am. Tr.	Immortal No. 53
21st Engineers	Rod
314th Engineers	Imp
1st Battalion	Impact
2nd Battalion	Impart
314th Engineers Train	
Engineer Dump	Ignorant
314th Field Signal Bn.	Imperial
353rd Field Hospital	Ignoble
354th Field Hospital	Illumine
355th Field Hospital	Imagine
356th Field Hospital	Immobile
353rd Ambulance Co.	Impetuous

NAME	CODE NAME
164th Artillery Brigade Headquarters	Immaterial
44th Artillery, 2nd Bn.	Nonsense
42nd Division	Optimus
78th Division	Faraday
69th Balloon Company	
Division Balloon	
Hdq. Tr. and M. P.	Ignition
Remount Officer	Immane
Mobile Veterinary Sec.	Impassion
Sales Commissary	Implicate
Ammunition Dumps, Small Arms	Implicate
Supply Dump	Impetus
314th Ammunition Tn.	Immit

Thus, the writer, acting both as Brigade Adjutant and Operations Officer of the 177th Brigade, answered to the call of the name "Illustrious" and either of the magic figures 7 or 11.

THE FIRST GAS ATTACK

Soon after the front line battalions of the 82nd Division had been relieved and just before the final completion of the relief, the Division received its

Gas Hollow, back of Flirey. Until the St. Mihiel offensive of Sept. 12th, 1918, these dugouts were in the third line and had been occupied for about four years, the last six weeks by troops of the 89th Division. It was the battalion P. C. of the 1st Battalion, 354th Infantry in the center of the German gas of Aug. 7-8, 1918. S. C. 25261.

first taste of the realities of war, and that in one of its most hideous forms. On the night of the 7th-8th of August, the front line battalions in Bois de Jury, Bois de la Hazelle and to the south and west of Flirey were subjected to a most severe bombardment of gas shells. The first attack started at 10:30 in the evening and continued until midnight. The shelling then ceased until about 1 o'clock and was then resumed for nearly two hours more. Between 9,000 and 10,000 shells were fired during the bombardment. About 95 per

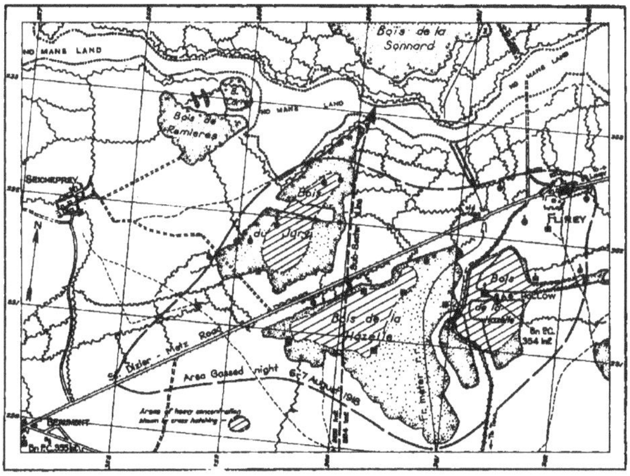

Scene of the gas attack August 7-8, 1918, on positions of the 354th Infantry and 355th Infantry, between Beaumont and Flirey. Kilometer grid. From map accompanying the official report and Mort Mare map.

cent of the shells were of mustard gas and phosgene, interspersed with many high explosives. The chief concentration of the shelling was in the vicinity of the headquarters of the 1st Battalion of the 354th Infantry in a ravine in Bois de la Hazelle, about a kilometer southwest of Flirey, which from that night on was known as "Gas Hollow." Other areas of heavy concentration were in Bois de Jury and the western portion of Bois de la Hazelle, falling chiefly on the 1st Battalion of the 355th Infantry.

The casualties of our Division reported up to August 21st as a result of this attack were 556, most of them light, though up to that date forty-two officers and men had suffered the horrible death of gas poisoning. The casualties of the 82nd Division were some 150 in addition.

This gas attack was undoubtedly in retaliation for a gas attack which had been launched by a special gas detachment of army troops while the 82nd Division was in occupation of the sector some weeks previously. While it served to display most notably the spirit of devotion to duty in the Division, and to afford the occasion for the exhibition of many individual cases of heroism, it brought out quite as emphatically an omission in the orders for the occupation of the sector.

Proper gas discipline requires that alternative positions for the combat groups be designated, so that in case of a gas attack the troops can be moved to an area which is not so exposed to the poison fumes. It is obvious that any positions which the enemy has gassed can be deemed for the time being safe from enemy attack, for the gas is just as deadly to the enemy as it is to us. There had been no similar gassing during the occupancy of the sector by the 82nd Division and no such alternative positions had been selected, nor was their necessity explained to our troops. On the contrary, the plan of defense which was in force in the 82nd Division and probably had been in force in the sector since the period of the French occupation and which the 89th at the time was bound by and required to conform to, expressly provided that the troops were to hold their positions to the last and under all conditions unless withdrawn by order of the Army Commander.

Gas patients brought to Field Hospital north of Royaumeix (St. Mihiel Sector) Aug. 8th, 1918, after the severe gas attack which greeted the 89th Division when it first entered the line. Most of them were from the 354th Inf. and 355th Inf., on whom the attack centered. They were brought in so rapidly by ambulances and trucks that capacity of the hospital was exceeded and many received preliminary treatment out in the open, after which they were hurried back to hospitals in and near Toul. The white cloths over the faces of the patients are soaked with a neutralizing solution. Note the mittens on hands of nurse and attendant. S. C. 22012.

In consequence the troops stayed doggedly and heroically in their positions, though many of them, with no experience in mustard gas and without that complete discipline which can come only through experience, removed their masks when the shelling was over, and others next morning went to their kitchens in the low ground, in ignorance of that property of the gas which causes it to vaporize again at the rising of the sun.

Many of the officers, including the medical officers, realized the danger of the premature removal of the masks and the vaporization by daylight, and undoubtedly saved many lives by passing among the troops, maintaining discipline and caring for the casualties.

Conspicuous among these was the case of Major Nathan C. Shiverick, who had just been assigned to the 354th Infantry as second in command and had assumed command of the first line troops during the progress of the attack. Utterly disregarding his own safety, he went among his men giving instructions and caring for the casualties. He received severe burns all over the body, but would not permit himself to be evacuated until all known casualties had been cared for. His injuries were so severe that after lingering long in the hospital, he was returned to the United States, against his urgent protests, where he did duty in the Inspector General's Department, and was eventually discharged from the service. Thus the Division lost an officer whose valuable services during the training period gave promise of great worth in action.

A like case also was that of Major John E. Morrison, who was just being relieved of command of the front line battalion of the 354th Infantry by Major Shiverick that very evening. Although he received severe infection from the gas and might have regarded himself as relieved of responsibility by the presence of Major Shiverick, he remained at his post, encouraging and instructing his men with great coolness, and was not evacuated until the following morning when the situation was well in hand.

Major (then Captain) Paul Withington, Medical Corps, displayed in this emergency those qualities which had made him famous as a Harvard athlete and were to accompany his career on the trying fields of the later battles. He was at the time attached to the 1st Battalion, 354th Infantry, as Medical Officer, and as such assumed charge of the medical work in the gassed area. He worked all night in the gassed area, not only as attending surgeon but even as litter bearer when necessary. His superb physical strength and great determination carried him through the trying period, although he received burns as severe as those for which he evacuated many of the soldiers. He administered treatment to himself during intervals in his treatment of others and escaped with painful but not permanent injuries to his eyes.

Similar devotion was shown by Major (then Captain) Harvey E. McCarthy, on duty as regimental surgeon in the 355th Infantry, who passed about in the gassed area and personally removed many men from gassed dugouts. He worked continuously, dressing the wounded and assisting in their evacuation until all had been evacuated or cared for.

Major Thomas F. Wirth, who commanded the front line battalion of the 355th Infantry, also personally aided in getting the gas victims out of the dugouts and by his good judgment and qualities of command kept the situation in control without confusion or disorder.

Corporal John A. Johnson, Company "A," and Private Louis H. Schumaker, Company "D," both of the 355th Infantry, were conspicuous in the difficult and dangerous tasks of carrying messages between the Battalion

Loading gas patients at Field Hospital north of Royaumeix (St. Mihiel Sector) Aug. 8th, 1918, after gas attack on the 89th Division, for removal to hospitals in Toul. Stretcher bearers wear special mittens to protect hands from gas-infected clothing of victims. S. C. 22013.

Headquarters and the companies in the gassed area. To perform this duty in the darkness of the night, wearing a gas mask and passing through the continuous rain of gas and high explosive shells, required qualities of the highest order.

Considering the serious character of the attack, the fact that it occurred at the trying time of a relief and when the command of the sector had not passed, the imcomplete state of the orders respecting a gas attack, and above all the fact that it was the first time that the Division had been in contact with the enemy, the casualties were lighter than might have been expected, and the stamina and courage displayed by the men gave promise of a glorious future for the Division as an intrepid combat unit.

The two lessons learned by the gas attack were that the 89th Division was absolutely dependable, that the control of officers and discipline of the men were all that could be desired, and that we must determine and issue our own orders in English and not merely translate and publish the French orders. The French order to hold the front line at all costs should have been interpreted to provide alternative positions in case of gas attack.

That the lessons of the defense against gas were well learned soon appeared. On August 21st and again on the 31st, more limited but highly concentrated gas shell attacks were made on platoons of the 353rd Infantry, in the position of resistance and in the front line. The men evacuated the districts in good order and sustained no casualties.

It is noteworthy as an example of the value of bitter experience as a teacher, that the regiments which suffered most severely from these attacks developed the highest state of gas discipline. Early in October the entire line was again subjected to a series of local but violent attacks with gas. Few and light casualties resulted in the 353rd, 354th and 355th Infantry regiments. But the 356th, which had escaped the gassing in August, suffered severely in comparison with the others.

The deficiency in the standing orders for the troops of the Advance Post Position was at once supplied by orders designating three alternative positions for each combat group in case of gas attack, the selection to be governed by the direction of the wind at the time. "Gas Hollow" and the areas of heavy concentration were surrounded by wire and sentries posted to prevent any entrance until the gas had cleared. It was several weeks after the attack before these positions could be safely re-occupied, so persistent is the effect of the mustard gas.

ROUTINE TRENCH LIFE

There is a certain charm attached to life in the trenches and position warfare in general which, it is believed, accounts in part for the fortitude displayed by the French and British forces during the discouraging four years of the war and which induced a frame of mind on the part of our Allies which might be described as a sort of cheerful pessimism. The impression left by contact with the French Army was that while there was no thought of ever giving up the conflict, there was no way to be seen by which the existing situation could ever be terminated. And trench life seemed to be anticipated as a normal condition of existence indefinitely. Trench life wasn't such a bad life, after all. It had sufficient excitement and variety and danger to give zest; and yet it permitted an orderly routine, a fair amount of comfort and reasonably regular periods for relaxation and recreation. It afforded an agreeable alternative to the deadly grind of the training period on the one hand and the fearful tension of battle on the other. Many a man will look back upon the days in the trenches of the Lucey sector for his most satisfactory reminiscences of the war.

Each regiment normally kept one battalion in the Advance Post Position, one on the Position of Resistance and one in reserve. The troops in the

Advance Post Position worked at improving their positions and engaged nightly in patrolling and raiding; troops on the position of resistance worked, in conjunction with the Engineers, in digging trenches and dugouts, stringing wire and improving the position; while those in reserve were engaged in resting, refitting and training. The companies of the brigade machine gun battalions and the regimental machine gun companies were divided among the infantry elements in each of the three positions and engaged in like occupations as the infantry.

The troops in each position were relieved approximately every ten days. Carefully prepared schedules for the relief of troops were issued, so devised that the machine guns would not be relieved at the same time as the infantry in the sector, nor would adjacent infantry regiments be making reliefs on the same night.

Early in August Companies B and C, 314th Ammunition Train, reached Andelot, and, after brief further training there, proceeded to Leonval, near Boucq, when the Division entered the line. On August 9th their first trucks were received and two days (or rather nights) later both companies made their first haul of ammunition to the front, small arms ammunition, hand grenades and detonators. Days and nights of unremitting toil followed. The novelty of driving ammunition-laden trucks over shell-pitted roads at night, without lights and sometimes under fire, soon wore off, but cheerfully the miles were ground out with little thought for the lack of sleep, cold rations, rain and mud.

PATROLS AND RAIDS

The service of patrolling and raiding was one upon which both the French higher command and our own division commander laid great stress, the standing orders from the French Grand General Headquarters requiring each infantry division to identify the enemy in front of it twice a week. This service was prosecuted with such marked intelligence, vigor and courage as to win commendation from the French and American higher commands and, as was ascertained later from captured documents, from our enemies also.

From the very beginning of the occupation, penetrating patrols were sent out against enemy positions in a systematic manner. A schedule for these patrols was prepared far in advance. Each regiment was required to send out a patrol each night. The sector of each regiment was considered as consisting of three parts, the left, center and right, and the Division schedule for the patrols was so arranged that no regiment would have a patrol out in front of the right or left of its sector at the same time that an adjacent regiment had one out on the left or right, as the case might be. By the use of this schedule confusion or conflict between the patrols was avoided, each infantry organization and the supporting artillery were constantly advised of the locality of the patrol and time was afforded for the patrol leaders to be selected, and for them to organize their patrols and reconnoiter as far as possible during the daylight the ground to be traversed at night; most important of all, it assured the examination of all points on the front, and frustrated enemy ambuscades through the irregularity of the hours and itineraries of the patrols. General Passaga was so impressed with the value of the schedule that he published it as a service note for the information of all the divisions under his command in the sector.

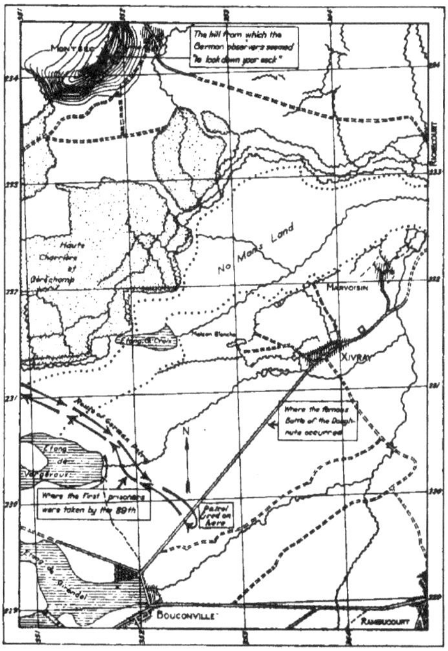

Bouconville-Xivray area, where the first prisoners of the 89th Division were captured on the night of August 13-14, 1918, and the Battle of the Doughnuts occurred September 2, 1918. Both of these exploits were by members of the 356th Infantry. Kilometer grid. From Mort Mare map.

Our predecessors in the sector had been unfortunate in the matter of capturing prisoners for identifications, though they had not been remiss in their efforts in this direction. On the night of the 5th of August and during the progress of the relief, the 82nd Division had made an elaborately-prepared raid upon the German positions with strong artillery support in the way of a heavy box barrage and violent general shelling. But either through some disclosure of the plans or mere mishap, the raiders found the German positions unoccupied, and returned, not only without prisoners but with severe casualties of their own from the German counter-barrage. On the night of the 7th-8th another raid on the right of the sector was in progress by troops of the 82nd Division, when the great gas attack on the center of our line took place. The low grounds through which the raiders were to pass were found to be filled with the gas, and the raid was abandoned. Observers from our division attended both these operations, as far to the front as existing orders of the 82nd Division permitted.

The vigor with which the 89th Division took up the task of obtaining prisoners, coupled with, perhaps, better luck than attended the 82nd, brought results almost at once. On the night of August 13th-14th, only four days after the Division had completely taken over the sector, a patrol from the 2nd Battalion, 356th Infantry, consisting of twenty-six men under the command of 1st Lieutenant Francis N. Jordan, Company "H," encountered two German patrols endeavoring to penetrate our lines before Bouconville. They engaged the enemy and, at the cost of only one slight casualty, captured four prisoners who gave valuable information. For this exploit, to which Sergeants Charles P. Smith ond B. J. Wicker, Company H, 356th Infantry, contributed skill and initiative, the Division was warmly commended by

First German prisoners captured by the 89th Division. They were taken by a patrol of the 356th Inf. which met and defeated a German patrol Aug. 13th, 1918. The corporal, at the left, is 24 years old and has been in the German army four years. The other three, whom he calls "recruits," are 19 and have been in service since September, 1917. In background (left to right) are Capt. T. R. Gowenlock, assistant G-2, 89th Division, Major James Smallwood, 314th Military Police, 89th Division, and the guard of the prisoners. S. C. 22811.

General Passaga, our French Corps Commander, both formally and informally. A day or two later the 355th Infantry captured its first prisoners.

Deserters also began to come into our lines, principally Alsatians from the 77th German Reserve Division. The first of these were very much downcast to find themselves in the hands of Americans. They had wanted to desert to the French and moreover had been told that the Americans were savages who took no prisoners, but murdered every one of the enemy they captured. When, however, they found themselves well treated, the news seemed somehow to leak over into the German lines and an increasing number of them began to come over, much to the disgust of the German commander, as captured documents afterwards showed.

Early in the morning of August 19th, 1918, the enemy attempted an elaborate and fruitless raid against our lines in one of his desperate attempts to secure identifications from us. At 4:10 a heavy bombardment of high explosives and shrapnel along the entire front was started, which included a well defined box barrage around an area of a little less than a kilometer square before Flirey. During the bombardment, a single white rocket was sent up from within this area, which was repeated from the high ground to the north. At this, the barrage moved southward directly upon the town of Flirey, where it was held until 4:55. In this sector we had maintained an advance post until the night previous, when it had been withdrawn. In consequence, not a single soldier of our forces was within the area surrounded by the box barrage. When the bombardment ceased, our patrols went at once into the area and found a number of German wire cutters, automatic pistols, many grenades and signs of blood; also, at the point where our Decauville trench crossed the railroad, a wooden box with handles and wire attached, full of explosives, was discovered.

We suffered no losses and no casualties, except one man killed by the covering bombardment and outside of the sector of the raid. The raid wholly failed in its object, and the raiders apparently suffered some casualties from the vigorous fire which our supporting French artillery placed on the raided area.

A patrol led by 2nd Lieutenant Vernon C. Swihart, Co. I, 355th Infantry, on the night of August 27-28, was the occasion of a special letter of commendation to that officer from the Division Commander, which was published to the entire Division in General Orders.

On the night of the 30th-31st August, 1918, at about 3:45 A. M., the Germans attempted a typical trench raid on a rather elaborate scale, as a part of their increasing efforts to obtain identifications from our sector. The attack was cunningly planned, being directed at what is always a weak point in a line, the junction of two organizations. The point selected was the junction of the 353rd and 354th Infantry regiments, about midway between Flirey and Limey, near a small cemetery. As at all points of contact of organizations, there was stationed here an outpost composed of members of both units, the whole under the command of the senior officer present, no matter which organization he belonged to. The raid was preceded and accompanied by a box barrage—that is by a line of fire from the artillery on both sides and to the rear of the position to be raided—and also by a general shelling of the entire sector. After penetrating our line at the Metz road, the raiders proceeded due east along the south side of the road, following the trench which parallels the road, until they reached the position of the outpost platoon of Company "L," 353rd Infantry. The members of the mixed outpost

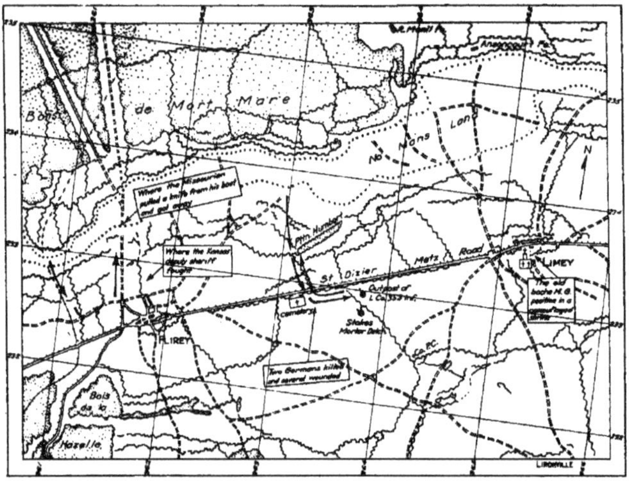

Raids on 353rd Infantry and 354th Infantry on the night of August 30-31, 1918, between Flirey and Limey. Other raids also occurred in the same area. Kilometer grid. From Mort Mare map.

commanded by Corporal Frank R. Rice retired before the raiders, firing and giving the alarm, Corporal Rice himself killing one of the enemy.

As soon as the barrage lifted off the outpost, the outpost commander, Sergeant Harry G. Hyndman, deployed his men facing west in front of the enemy, his right resting on the Metz road. The Germans advanced, calling out in English, "Don't fire, we are the 354th; don't shoot your own men!" and other remarks. Our men withheld their fire until the enemy was only seventy-five yards distant, when they opened fire and drove the raiding party off. As the raiders retreated along the way they had come, the Stokes mortar detachment stationed at the outpost, under command of Lieutenant Harold Leedy, 353rd Infantry, fired eight shots upon them while they were in the little cemetery about three hundred yards from the outpost. The raiders left two of their dead there and must have carried away some wounded; for six German

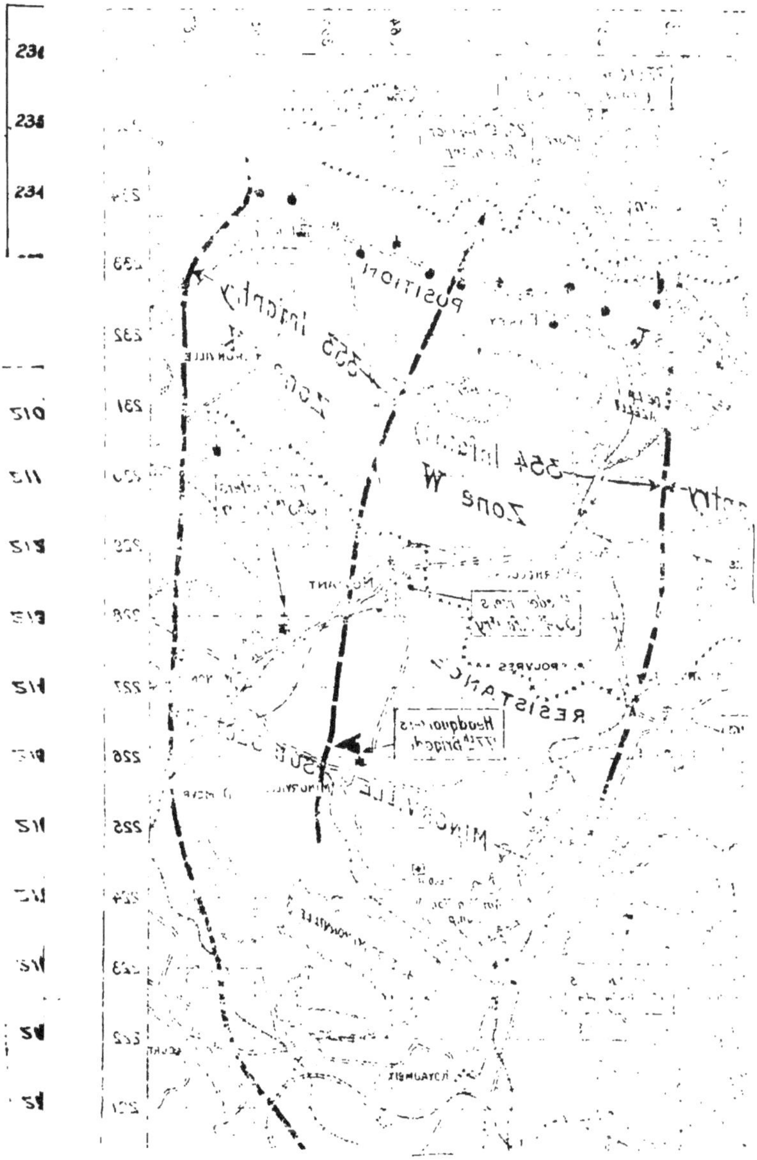
354 Infantry
Zone W
Headquarters 177th Brigade
POSITION
RESISTANCE
MINORVILLE

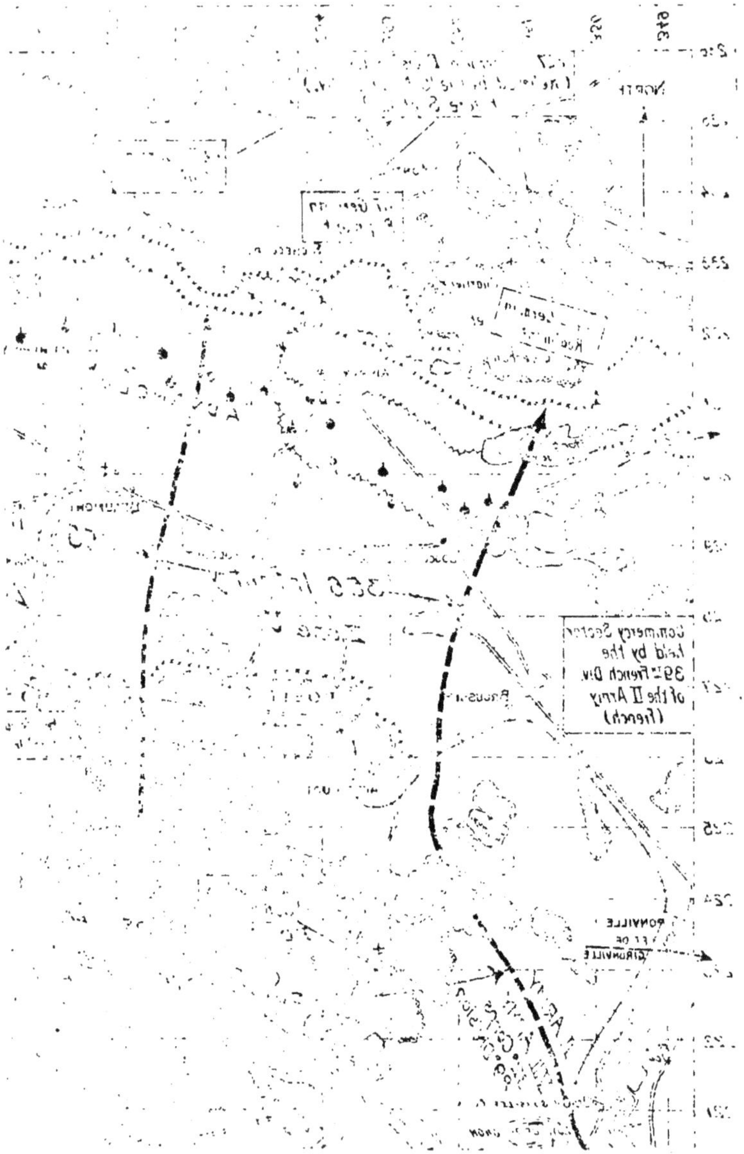

NORTH
Commercy Sector held by the 39th French Div. of the II Army (French)

helmets and a number of rifles, machine gun ammunition and wire cutters were found there.

A letter found on one of the dead Germans disclosed that the raid had been carefully planned and was carried out by shock troops of the 77th Reserve Division. It was a complete failure, as our troops suffered no losses and the raiders, though numerically stronger than those of our troops engaged, were driven off after suffering casualties.

In late August and early September, the activity of our patrols was increased by orders to penetrate the German lines more and more deeply in order to ascertain the depth, width and character of the trenches and the condition of the wire entanglements. This was, of course, part of the preparation for the forthcoming attack on the St. Mihiel salient. Many brisk encounters and striking incidents occurred as a part of the day's work in these minor but important operations.

An incident which occurred late in August served to increase the impression of the low state of morale of the enemy troops and to confirm the reports of the callous indifference of German officers towards their men. A German patrol of one officer and twenty men from the 398th Regiment, 10th German Division, encountered one of our patrols from the 356th Infantry in No Man's Land south of Richecourt. A sharp engagement followed in which three Germans were captured and a number hit by our fire. Our patrol leader, having gained his identifications, checked the number of his men, and, finding them all present, returned with his full patrol and prisoners. On the follow-

Communication trench passing under the Metz-St. Dizier Road between Flirey and Limey at the point of the German raid on the night of August 30-31, 1918.

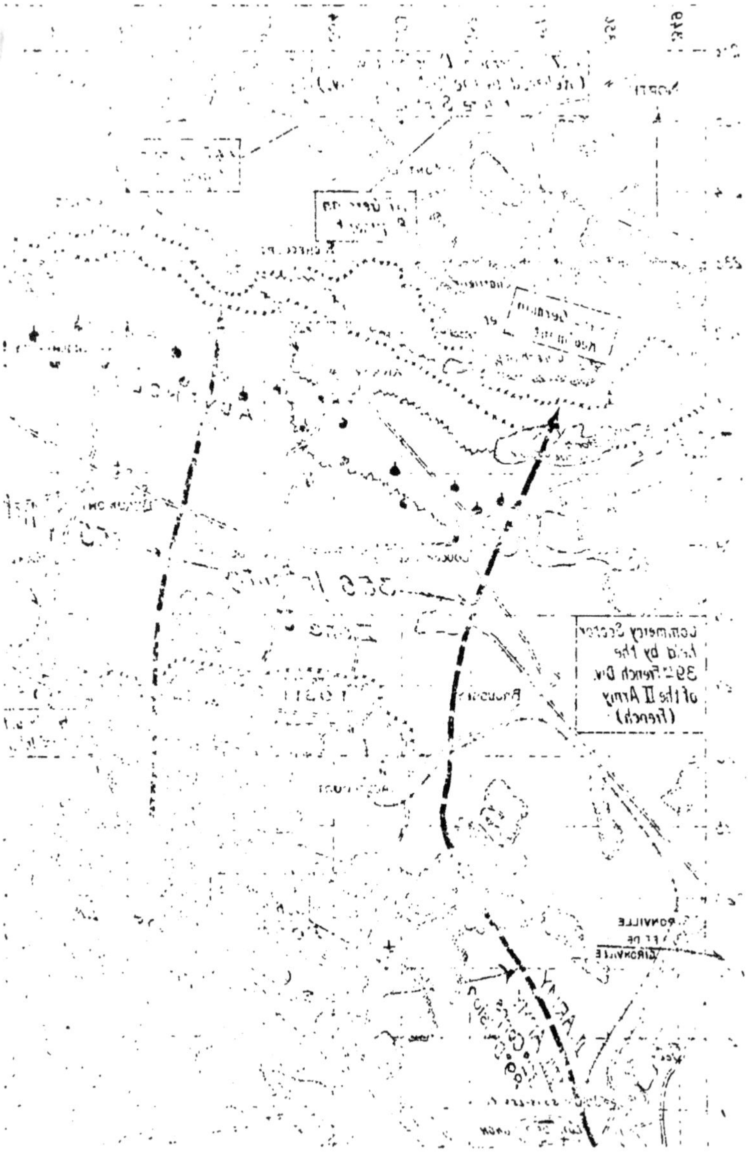

ing day, another of our patrols found German dead and wounded on the scene of the encounter, lying in such position in No Man's Land that it was necessary to cross much open ground to reach them. As soon as possible, under cover of darkness, the wounded were brought in by our men, cared for and evacuated to an American hospital.

This conduct of the German officer and his patrol in leaving his wounded to perish in No Man's Land and his dead to go unburied, called forth a

Scene of the German raid on the night of August 30-31, 1918. The road in the foreground is the Metz-St. Dizier road. The trenches are old French trenches which parallel the road for several kilometers. At this point the sectors of the 353rd and 354th Infantry regiments joined. The raiders came from the direction of the right of the picture and crossed the trench, following it in the direction of the foreground, the mixed outpost retiring before them in that direction, falling back, firing, to the position of the support platoon of Co. "L," 353rd Infantry. Here the raid was repulsed by the outpost with casualties which were increased by fire from the Stokes mortar detachment nearby. Wire can be seen to the right of the road.

memorandum from our Division Commander in which the conduct of the Germans was called wretched and dastardly and was contrasted with the conduct of our own troops, in that our own officers and men willingly accepted the danger the Germans refused and rescued wounded enemies where German troops failed to rescue comrades.

BATTLE OF THE DOUGHNUTS

An operation, which came to be known as the "Battle of the Doughnuts" was fought on the night of September 2nd. The troops engaged on the American side were commanded by Corporal (later Sergeant) Walter Rudy, Company "M," 356th Infantry, and consisted of Private (later Corporal) Peter Sweet of the same company. The enemy forces comprised a patrol of seven men. The American detachment was acting as convoy to supplies intended for an outpost of their company stationed in Xivray. The supplies consisted of a can of doughnuts, worth about a million dollars each to hungry soldiers in an outpost. The disposition of the American forces was as follows: Corporal Rudy acted as point, advance party and advance guard, Private Sweet, forming the main body and personally transporting the supplies, following the advance guard at a distance of about two paces. While in this formation, the enemy debouched from the bushes on the flank of the advance guard. The entire American detachment at once opened fire with their pistols with such effect that one German fell, mortally wounded, another was taken prisoner by Corporal Rudy and the rest fled. The report of the engagement, by Private Sweet, was as follows: "Never lost a doughnut."

On the night of 6-7 September, a violent effort was made by the enemy to penetrate our lines and obtain identifications. Following a heavy barrage two raiding parties were sent against different parts of our line. One of about 60 was repulsed by the 354th Infantry and a similar party of about 100 was driven back by the 353rd Infantry. Both parties of the enemy suffered considerable loss. Six German prisoners were taken and three German dead left in our hands, but not an American was captured.

It was at this time that a Missourian, Corporal Hayden McDowell, Company E, 354th Infantry, fought the German patrol with his bayonet until overpowered and stunned, when the boche, as they supposed, completely disarmed him. As they started back across No Man's Land carrying their unconscious prisoner the barrage fell and all scattered to shell holes, the three carrying the Missourian sticking with him. While in the shell hole the Ozark mountaineer regained consciousness and realized his condition. His hand slid down his "laig" to his puttee, wherein lay hidden his trusty trench knife. In the scrimmage which followed two Germans were killed and the third reached the German wire exhausted and breathing hard, sans the prisoner, who made his way back to the American lines in spite of a wound in his shoulder. The record of the 89th of not losing a man by capture remained unbroken.

Another corporal, whose name and organization, unfortunately, are not now available, heard a commotion where his squad was on post. Running down the trench to the rescue he was confronted by several Germans in the trench and one above on each side. The corporal jammed his bayonet into boche No. 1 in the trench, disengaged and, from the hip, shot the man above to the right just before the one to the left jumped down on him. The corporal took the shock standing and hurled the jumping man into the face of the next German in the trench. They beat a retreat, followed by the fire of the corporal. When it was over his left arm felt "funny" and at the first aid station the surgeon found a broken collar-bone, patched it and asked: "Were'nt you scared?" "Hell, no," says the corporal, "that's nothin'; I'm a deputy sheriff from Kansas!"

THE 314TH MOTOR SUPPLY TRAIN

During the period of trench occupation and as the preparations for the coming battle developed, the work of the Motor Supply Train became of increasing importance and difficulty. The Sanitary Train was practically without transportation; the Engineer Train entirely so; and only Companies "B" and "C" of the Motor Battalion of the 314th Ammunition Train had come to the Division. All these deficiencies of transportation were met by extra exertion of the Motor Supply Train. Every night found these splendid troops of the train driving their unwieldy trucks, without lights, hauling food for the soldiers, or soldiers themselves when relieved, barbed wire for entanglements, rock for the engineers to use in road repair, ammunition for infantry and artillery. Under the heavy stress, the trucks began to wear out and spare parts for their repair were almost unobtainable. General Winn ordered Captain (later Major) Cole to establish a Division Machine Shop for repairs. Practically creating the equipment out of nothing but spare tools and such equipment as could be "salvaged" in the vicinity, Captain Cole had the shop operating under Lieutenant G. W. Bottorf within five days, and making invaluable repairs for all the divisional transportation.

On September 6th, the 314th Mobile Ordnance Repair Shop reported to the Division and was assigned a station in the Artillery Park at Royaumeix. This unit had come overseas with the Artillery Brigade, but had been detached for instruction at Is-sur-Tille since July 19th. It now began work on the repair of the artillery attached to the Division.

MORE TRAINING

The training of the troops in the reserve positions was continued most vigorously. This had to be conducted with precautions against enemy observation and air raids. These precautions consisted of training the men in small groups in places protected from observation from the enemy lines by slopes of the hills; by requiring all men and vehicles on the move to stop still, and, if possible, to lie down on the approach of an enemy plane; by giving frequent and valuable practice in marching by compass in thick woods and at night.

Improved formations for the reduction of machine gun nests were suggested and put into practice by Colonel Conrad S. Babcock, who was assigned to the Division during this time and was attached as commanding officer to the 353rd Infantry while Colonel Reeves of that regiment was in command of the 177th Infantry Brigade. At a later period, when General Winn took command of the brigade and Colonel Reeves of his regiment, Colonel Babcock was assigned to the 354th Infantry, vice Colonel Americus Mitchell relieved, and commanded it thereafter until the Division left Germany for the United States, when on his own application, he remained as Town Commander at Trier. He later commanded the composite regiment which marched in the great victory celebration in London and Paris during the summer of 1919, and in Washington upon the final return of the 1st Division. Colonel Babcock had been in command of a regiment of the 1st Division during some of the earlier fighting and his experience in the field had taught him the value of using extremely small groups in the advance of infantry against machine gun positions. He instructed both regiments of the 177th Brigade in the formation of a combat group into a diamond formation of smaller groups of three or four men each, the foremost of which engaged the gun while the two flank groups encircled it. This formation, which was also prescribed in the manuals, was successfully used in the subsequent fighting throughout the Division, and, it is believed, the proficiency of the troops in taking this formation enabled them to overcome the resistance of machine guns with surprisingly small casualties.

Another feature of the training during this period was that of the problems of liaison, participated in by the intelligence and liaison personnel of the organizations. Troops were assumed to be in the occupation of certain positions, and orders for and reports of their movements were transmitted by all the means of communication available,—visual signalling by flags and projectors, buzzers, telephones, radio and runners. These exercises were also carried out under actual trench conditions, and test messages were sent to and from the front line troops under various assumed conditions, such as that the wire connections were cut, runners killed or captured, etc. There was also practice in liaison through air planes. Troops would be assumed to be in positions not known to the air men. The plane would fly over, disclosing its character as the divisional plane by the display of the prescribed rocket signal. It would then give the signal, "Mark your positions," and panel details would spread the muslin panels on the ground, marking by appropriate symbols the supposed location of the front lines and the battalion, regimental and brigade headquarters. The panels were maintained until the plane signalled "Understood." From the division or brigade headquarters would be displayed a panel meaning, "What is the position of my left (or other) regiment?" And the observer in the plane would mark the positions on a map and drop it at the supposed headquarters. Such exercises were conducted sometimes near the positions of the reserve battalions, only eight or ten kilometers from the front lines, and sometimes in the vicinity of the Air Squadron Park near Toul.

FIREWORKS

Among the supplies left by the French in the trenches were vast quantities of pyrotechnics, rockets, flares, light bombs and the like. Most of these were quite useless to us, as our rocket signals were few and simple, calls for a barrage in case of an attack or raid, and a signal that our own artillery was firing short. The presence of these surplus supplies imported a bit of danger that in the excitement of an attack the wrong signal might be set off. And as our troops had had no practice in the use of pyrotechnics, the means seemed at hand for getting a little useful training and at the same time disposing usefully of this accumulation.

Accordingly, Colonel James H. Reeves, commanding the 177th Brigade, having obtained the necessary permission and having notified all adjacent units to pay no attention to rocket signals from his sector during a certain time, gave orders that every man in the trenches was to fire off three pieces of fireworks within a specified fifteen minutes.

This maneuver was a brilliant success. No such display had ever been seen by any of us on any Fourth of July. Rockets of every color burst in splendour, white star bombs lit up No Man's Land like day. All enjoyed a lovely spectacle, except poor Fritz, who displayed signs of nervousness. Rocket signals on his side of the line broke out, his artillery began to drop a useless

American ammunition dump north of Royaumeix and Menil la Tour (St. Mihiel Sector) blown up Aug. 30th, 1918, by German long-distance artillery or aeroplane bombs. What part of the dump looked like when the fireworks were over. S. C. 22165.

barrage in front of his lines and in No Man's Land, showing us where his barrage line ran, and doubtless many a comfortable German nap was broken and double-jointed German swear words were hurled across the lines at the crazy Americans.

MINES AND COUNTERMINES

In rear of the headquarters of the 177th Infantry Brigade was a large dugout, said to be capable of holding 800 men. It had been constructed as the headquarters of a division of the French Army while the French held the sector. In it was established the switchboard for the brigade telephone system. One night the telephone operators reported that they heard the sound of digging near the dugout. Colonel Reeves, commanding the brigade, and all his staff listened and could hear the sounds of a pick digging regularly.

Commandant Donnio, the French major commanding the supporting artillery, could hear it and agreed that it was someone digging a mine. Sergeant McKibben, of the 353rd, an old and experienced miner, was sent for the next night. The sounds were still audible and seemed to be getting nearer. The sergeant was sure that someone was digging a drift towards the dugout. Col. Johnson, the Division Engineer, was sent for and though expressing doubts about its being a countermine, thought it might be that. The entrance could not be far away, so a search of all the cellars of Minorville was made in the middle of the night, with no results other than accurate information of the prevailing styles of night garments in the village. A countermine was started in the part of the dugout nearest the sound. But about the time that the digging of the countermine began to be irksome, it came to be believed that the sound came from the trampling of horses on the cobblestones of the stables of the village, and that the noise was transmitted to the dugout by some peculiarity of the soil. At all events, though the sound continued at intervals thereafter, the mine, if there was one, was never exploded, and the German spy, if there was one, had his labor for his pains.

AIR BATTLES

Air activity was intense on both sides during this time. Nearly every clear afternoon fighting was going on in the air over our lines between German raiders and our own planes. From high in the air would come the faint popping of the machine guns; the tiny fighting planes could scarcely be discerned, until a glint of sunlight from their shining wings would disclose their position. At almost any hour of the day, the buzz of a German observing plane might be heard, soon to be accompanied by the booming of the anti-aircraft batteries stationed all about, and if the plane was not too high, by the insistent tap-tap-tap of our machine guns from the ground. Daring raids were made on our observation balloons, and too often were successful. The huge sausage would be floating serenely in the air, when suddenly from behind some fleecy cloud would dart a swift plane, sweeping toward the balloon, pouring forth a stream of bright tracer bullets. If one of these penetrated the huge bag of inflammable gas, there would be a great burst of fire and smoke and the remnants of the balloon and its car would sink flaming to the earth. The occupant of the balloon seldom waited for this to happen. On the first approach of the plane, the balloon would be frantically pulled down; and if it went too slowly, a little speck would be seen to detach itself from the great mass and float slowly to earth. This would be the observer, going home in his parachute. One afternoon a German plane, darting swiftly from one balloon to another, shot down three of our balloons in as many minutes and flew safely back. Our own planes made similar attacks on the German balloons, and when we left the sector the score was slightly in our favor.

On every clear night, German raiders would be heard going overhead to drop bombs on Toul and the railroad stations in the rear. Soon the giant searchlights would sweep the sky from half a dozen different points. If one of them picked out the raider, all would soon be concentrated upon him, and then the booming of the "Archies" (anti-aircraft guns) would begin and the bright explosions of their shells high in the air, the great beams of the search lights, the procession of long, caterpillar rockets sent up from the German lines to show the night wanderers the way home, all made up a picture of terrible beauty which its observers will never forget.

Our men soon learned to distinguish, or to think that they could, the pulsating roar of the German planes from the steady roar of our own. But it is undeniable that some of the German planes roared steadily, while some of ours throbbed, so the identification was not always complete.

Difficulty was also experienced in distinguishing the airplanes by their markings, and the air service complained that our own planes were sometimes fired on from our front lines. The markings were on the lower surface of the wings. Allied planes were all marked with a series of three concentric circles,—American, red, blue and white, from the circumference toward the center; French, red, white and blue in the same order; and British, blue, white and red. The German planes were marked with either a Maltese or a Greek cross. But with the evident object of so disguising the marking as to deceive us and yet remain within the laws of war, they took to making the cross very small on a white field and surrounding it with a red circle.

PROPAGANDA

A rather amusing feature of this period was the German propaganda. Nearly every night when the wind was blowing towards us, paper balloons would float over to us from the German lines. Attached to these were newspapers and pamphlets, badly printed in comical English and containing the crudest possible appeals to the American soldiers to quit fighting and go home or to come over and surrender. Many of them were evidently intended to excite animosity towards the British; the means adopted to attain this end was to recite the history of the Revolutionary War, though with the omission of the part played by the Hessians therein. So far as is known, the only emotion ever excited by these efforts was that of derision. There was never a deserter in the 89th Division. And it was not until the Germans were soundly trounced that the soldiers of the Division quit fighting and went home.

CHAPTER IV.

THE ST. MIHIEL OFFENSIVE

As is well known, there are but two practicable routes for an invading army from the north to descend upon central France. One is along the coast through Belgium; the other through the region of Verdun. One or the other of these routes has always been followed by the barbarous German invaders since the dawn of European history.

In the beginning of the present war, the German attempted to advance by both routes. In the Verdun opening he was able to push forward a portion of his lines across the Meuse at the village of St. Mihiel and to form a projection in the front which came to be known as the St. Mihiel salient. The lines ran approximately north and south from before Verdun to St. Mihiel and then turned sharply and directly to the east. They had occupied substantially this position since the first few weeks of the war. This salient was a menace, a dagger pointed at the heart of France. Its maintenance was made possible by the high, rugged country on the right bank of the river and by the existence within the nose of the salient of an eminence called Mont Sec from which perfect observation of the allied lines on both sides of the angle, and far across the Meuse, was possible. The French in 1915 had made a determined effort to reduce this salient, but had been repulsed. Its reduction had long been planned by General Pershing as the first American offensive on a large scale. The general plans for the battle had been prepared by the General Staff of the A. E. F. in the fall of 1917, a year before the battle, which took place September 12-16, 1918. The signal success of this operation was, in the terse language of the Commander-in-Chief: "Of prime importance. The Allies found they had a formidable army to aid them, and the enemy learned finally that he had one to reckon with." To bear a part and an honorable one in this great operation was now the lot of the 89th Division.

In preparation for the attack, the First American Army was formed on August 10th, and our division, which had entered the line as a part of the 8th French Army, became a part of the American 1st Army. The sector occupied by the 1st Army began at Port-sur-Seille, east of the Moselle, and extended to the west to the position before St. Mihiel, thence north to a point opposite Verdun.

PERSHING'S SUMMARY OF THE OPERATION

The general conduct of the operation is described as follows in the official report of the Commander-in-Chief:

"From Les Eparges around the nose of the salient of St. Mihiel to the Moselle River the line was roughly forty miles long and situated on commanding ground, greatly strengthened by artificial defenses. Our First Corps (82nd, 90th, 5th and 2nd Divisions), under command of Major General Hunter Liggett, resting its right on Pont-a-Mousson, with its left joining our Fourth Corps (the 89th, 42nd and 1st Divisions), under Major General Joseph T. Dickman, in line to Xivray, were to swing in toward Vigneulles, on the pivot of the Moselle River, for the initial assault. From Xivray to Mouilly the Second French Colonial Corps was in line in the center, and our Fifth Corps, under command of Major General George H. Cameron, with the 26th and 4th Divisions and the 15th French Colonial Division at the western base of the salient, were to attack three difficult hills, Les Eparges, Combres and Amaranthe. Our First Corps had in reserve the 78th Division, our Fourth Corps the 3rd Division, and our First Army the 35th and 91st Divisions, with the 80th and 33rd Divisions available. It should be understood that our corps organizations are very elastic, and that we have at no time had permanent assignments of divisions to corps.

"After four hours' artillery preparation the seven American divisions in the front line advanced at 5 A. M. on September 12th, assisted by a limited number of tanks, manned partly by Americans and partly by the French. These divisions, accompanied by groups of wire cutters and others armed with bangalore torpedoes, went through the successive bands of barbed wire that protected the enemy's front line and support trenches in irresistible waves on schedule time, breaking down all defense of an enemy demoralized by the great volume of our artillery fire and our sudden appearance out of the fog.

"Our First Corps took Thiaucourt, while our Fourth Corps curved back to the southwest through Nonsard. The Second French Colonial Corps made the slight advance required of it on very difficult ground, and the Fifth Corps took its three ridges and repulsed a counter-attack. A rapid march brought reserve regiments of a division of the Fifth Corps into Vigneulles in the early morning, where it linked up with patrols of our Fourth Corps, closing the salient and forming a new line west of Thiaucourt to Vigneulles and beyond Fresnes-en-Woevre. At the cost of only 7,000 casualties, mostly light, we had taken 13,751 prisoners and 443 guns, a great quantity of material, released the inhabitants of many villages from enemy domination and established our lines in a position to threaten Metz."

The plans for this attack required our division to go into the fight from our own trenches, which we had been holding for considerably over a month. All the other divisions participating came up from the rear, where they had had some refitting and rest. Our former front was shortened by divisions coming in on our right and left and we jumped off on a front of about four kilometers. Previously we had occupied a front of about sixteen kilometers, extending generally parallel to the St. Dizier-Metz road from a point opposite Remenauville on the east to one south and a little east of Mont Sec. Our new front ran from before the western edge of Limey to about a kilometer west and north of Flirey. We found ourselves in excellent company for our first fight. On our right was the 2nd Division, whose infantry consisted of the celebrated Marine Brigade of two regiments and the no less valiant 3rd Brigade, made up of the 9th and 23rd Infantry. On our left was the Rainbow Division, the 42nd, and beyond them the 1st Division. Our neighbors were thus veteran divisions, tried and tested in many of the previous engagements of the American forces, gallant fighting men, every one of them.

THE TERRAIN

The task assigned to the 89th was not an easy one. Directly across our front lay the forest of Mort Mare, described in the Army estimate of the situation, as the key to the German positions between St. Mihiel and Pont-a-Mousson. It, with part of the adjacent Bois de la Sonnard (which was continuous with and generally considered part of Mort Mare), covered our entire front, except a few hundred meters to the east. This open ground to the east consisted of a high bare ridge, known as the Promenade des Moines, and the long slope leading up to it. The ridge and the slope were all covered with German trenches and wire, and two strong points, miniature fortresses, had been constructed there in the ruins of French farmsteads—the Robert Menil Farm and the Ansoncourt Farm. The First German lines or position con-

German trenches in the defense system north of Flirey from which they were driven in the St. Mihiel offensive Sept. 12th, 1918. At this point trenches were old, caved in and held but lightly at intervals or visited by patrols. Note coils of wire in the trench and concrete dugout to left, above which can be seen a dense mass of wire and beyond a little American cemetery. The background to right is a maze of trenches, shell holes and wire. Photographed Sept. 24th, 1918. S. C. 25232.

sisted of three well defined trenches and numerous connecting and switch trenches, the whole interspersed with carefully made dugouts and strong points, the result of four years work by the Germans to make the position impregnable. Into the very heart of Mort Mare forest they had conducted a narrow-gauge railroad, protected from observation and fire by the forest and the high ridge which ran through the forest ond out into the open on the east. Northeast of Mort Mare and practically continuous with it, were two more dense woods, Bois d'Euvezin and Bois de Beau Vallon. It is obvious that the enemy in these last named woods could fire both to the south on our troops advancing through the open over the Promenade des Moines and also to the west on our lines as they emerged from the northern edge of Mort Mare. In consequence the enemy had located his second line of defense on rising ground, extending to the west, which passed south of Euvezin. This position, like the first, consisted of several lines of trenches protected by bands of barbed wire, with the usual dugouts and strong points. But it was not so elaborate as the first line.

North of the heights of Euvezin the ground dropped once more into a valley down which flowed the little stream called the Rupt de Mad, on the banks of which stood the villages of Bouillonville and Thiaucourt. After rising sharply from this valley the ground stretched away to the north and east in a high, bare plateau on which were situated the villages of Xammes and Beney, with dense forests on the east and west. On this height, between Beney and Xammes, lay the enemy's third line of defense, only partially completed, with wire strung but trenches merely indicated. From it, however, troops on the open heights of Euvezin and in the valley of the Rupt de Mad could be brought under rifle and machine gun fire.

The ground over which the attack was to be made can be roughly conceived of as three swelling billows of the sea, respectively corresponding to the Promenade des Moines, the heights of Euvezin and the heights beyond Bouillonville. Running diagonally across these hills and valleys a continuous belt of dense forest—the woods of Sonnard, Mort Mare, Euvezin and Beau Vallon. Picture the commanding positions and the thick forests, an intricacy of barbed wire and trenches and you have the terrain over which our division was to make its first attack.

While, as above stated, the general project of the reduction of the St. Mihiel salient by the American forces had been in contemplation by the Commander-in-Chief from practically the time of the arrival of the first of the American troops, and the general outline of the attack had been prepared as early as September 5th, 1917, still the actual execution of the operation was determined on and carried out with considerable haste. This was due to the temporary abandonment of the plans and their subsequent resumption, occasioned by the events on the other fronts. The Russian collapse released many German divisions from the eastern front and enabled the enemy to inaugurate his terrific offensive in the spring of 1918 against the Channel Ports and Paris. The desperate situation called for every available man at the threatened points and impelled the Allies to agree upon the plan for a unification of command of the Allied forces under Marshal Foch. While there was much newspaper talk of "Foch's Strategical Reserve," this was entirely newspaper imagination, and the bitter fact was that Foch had no reserve forces whatever. So even before the unity of command was adopted, all the plans of General Pershing and his staff for an American offensive against the salient in the summer of 1918 were given up. The American troops were placed entirely at the disposal of Marshal Foch and were used by him in stemming the tide at Chateau-Thierry and Cantigny.

When, however, through the gallantry of the Allied forces in the field, the German drive had been stopped and when through the titanic efforts of England in transporting and America in training, equipping and furnishing that host of American troops, Marshal Foch found himself able to assume the offensive with the balance of reserve power in his hands, he allowed General Pershing to go back to his original plans of holding the St. Mihiel sector and conducting a major operation there. So, finally, in the late summer, orders were received at G. H. Q. to carry out the St. Mihiel attack as soon after September 5th as possible.

PREPARATION

Much had to be done to put the plans into action. The First Army was organized, corps were organized, scattered troops assembled, vast supplies of ammunition and equipment brought up, all in an incredibly short space of time. The concentration for this operation, which was to be a surprise, involved the movement, mostly at night, of 600,000 troops. The general plans for the operation were slightly changed in the midst of the preparations, so that instead of a deep penetration to the outer fortifications of Metz, as originally contemplated, only an advance to a limited objective, wiping out the salient, was determined on. This change was made because developments on the other fronts justified the undertaking of a larger operation north of Verdun, which promised greater results in cutting the southern German line of communication at Mezieres.

In consequence of this situation, there occurred many difficulties in our division which enhanced the difficulties inseparable from the first engagement. Orders were received from higher commands with very limited time in which to execute them and to make them understood by the smaller units.

The control of the traffic incidental to bringing up the enormous quantity of supplies needed in the coming attack presented great difficulties. Of course, this great increase in movement on the roads could not be wholly concealed from the enemy. But much could be and was done by the enforcement of strict traffic regulations to mislead him. Movement of the truck trains was made at night. No lights on the cars were permitted. The military police were supplemented by guards and sentinels from the troops to enforce the orders that the roads must be cleared by the break of day and kept clear in daylight hours. The work of the truck trains was marvelous. Few serious collisions or accidents occurred, though long convoys of trucks, hundreds of single cars, trucks, motorcycles and wagons passed all night long over the slippery and shell-torn roads.

The enemy would not have been deceived if all traffic had been suspended during his hours of observation. The problem was to keep it as nearly normal as possible to that required by ordinary occupation of the trenches. This was accomplished, and a small strategem also succeeded in further deluding him. It was reasoned that the enemy would be sure to know that the greatly increased night traffic portended some attack and that the day traffic would be kept at normal; but that a small increase in day traffic with no attempt at concealment would induce the belief on his part that the attack had been abandoned or postponed. Therefore, for a few days preceding the attack, the day traffic was increased by permitting the bringing up of trench stores, ammunition and road material. This ruse was successful. For in the attack there was captured an intelligence report of one of the regiments of the 10th German Division, in which it was stated that, judging by the character and amount of the traffic circulation, the projected American attack had probably been postponed. Furthermore, the captured official report of the German Army Group on the operation discloses that the attack was not anticipated until a few days later and that it actually caught the German artillery on the move.

General Pershing leaving Headquarters 89th Division at Lucey, Sept. 9, 1918, three days before the St. Mihiel offensive. Major General W. M. Wright, commanding 89th Division, standing in the doorway. S. C. 25288.

Supplies, particularly compasses and maps, were inadequate. Movements of troops which could have been made with ease in a longer space of time, had often to be made simultaneously by several units with attendant confusion and exhaustion. These difficulties were overcome and did not mar the result.

The Corps orders for the attack were very complete. They were several times revised, and, in important features, such as the time for moving to the Corps objective of the day and the duration of the artillery preparation, were changed almost at the last moment. These orders were first brought to

Division headquarters late at night by Captain Wickersham of the Corps staff and were explained by him to the Division Commander, General Winn and his staff, in a dramatic but satisfactory manner. The theatrical atmosphere of this midnight conference was intensified by the suspicion that a spy might be listening, and the meeting was adjourned while a thorough but vain search of the building was made for spies and dictaphones.

The Division orders were carefully drawn under direction of General Winn, who was later of the opinion that they were too detailed, especially for inexperienced troops, whose need is the greater for simple and direct orders than is that of troops of more proficiency in the art of war. These orders were necessarily revised from time to time in conformity with the changes received from Army and Corps; and as these changes gave rise to some discussion and resulted in some confusion the whole subject of the plans for this battle will be gone into in considerable detail.

PLANS OF BATTLE

The mission of the Division, as fixed by the Corps order, is thus stated in the Division Field Order for the attack:

"This Division will attack in the general direction of Dampvitoux, supporting the advance of the 42nd Division on our left *by exerting the main effort on our left* to include the Rupt de Mad, thence assist the advance of the 2nd Division, 1st Corps, by turning the Bois d'Euvezin, Bois de Beau Vallon and Thiaucourt from the west. By the capture of the east edges of the Bois Mort Mare, this division will assist the initial advance of the 2nd Division, 1st Corps. If the 2nd Division is delayed, the 89th Division will capture Thiaucourt and turn it over to the 2nd Division."

With this mission, with a front entirely too extended for a penetrating attack along the entire line, and with the flanks separated by the seemingly impassable obstacle of the Bois de Mort Mare, the Division, in preparing the plans for attack, was confronted by the alternatives of either making a direct frontal attack on Mort Mare, which would be costly in lives, almost certainly delay the advance and hinder in giving the necessary support to the divisions on the right and left; or to make the Division attack on both flanks, with Mort Mare separating them, which would necessarily divide the command and run the risk of an interruption of liaison between the brigades of the Division. The Division Commander chose the latter alternative as most promising of success.

GENERAL WRIGHT ASSUMES COMMAND

The Corps order made the mission of the 42nd Division the most important of all and directed our main effort to be on the left. It was therefore determined to support the 42nd Division with General Hanson's entire brigade, the 178th, on a front approximately half as wide as that assigned to the other brigade; while from the 177th Brigade, then commanded by Colonel James H. Reeves, the junior brigade commander, was taken the Division reserve, and this brigade, thus of lesser strength than the other, was given the subordinate mission of supporting the attack of the 2nd Division. The plans and orders were determined and the plans issued to the brigade commanders, and preliminary plans for the details of their operation had been submitted by the brigade commanders, when command of the Division was assumed by Major General William M. Wright, on September 6th. General Winn thereupon assumed command of his brigade, the 177th, Colonel Reeves of his regiment, the 353rd, and Colonel Conrad S. Babcock, who had theretofore been attached to the 353rd Infantry as commanding officer, was assigned to the command of the 354th Infantry. It thus fell to General Winn to take over his own divisional plan and execute the mission of the 177th Infantry Brigade as reduced in strength in accordance with the divisional scheme.

The numerical weakness of the 177th Infantry Brigade, from which the 354th Infantry was detached to form the Division and Brigade reserves, together with the width of front assigned to it, necessitated adopting a plan which would conform to its strength and at the same time protect its exposed flank. The solution was found by making no frontal advance whatever on Mort Mare in the 177th Brigade sector, but in flanking the forest by moving forward in conjunction with the 2nd Division and mopping up the woods with detachments that would accompany the attacking troops and turn off into the woods as the successive German defensive positions were reached.

As to the 178th Brigade, it must of necessity advance directly against and through Mort Mare on its sector, for the forest extended to the western boundary of the Division. It was realized that this brigade had a difficult task; but there were two broad straight openings, each two or three hundred meters wide, extending through the woods and bordering the roads from Flirey to Essey and Euvezin respectively, also some small open spaces in the western part of the woods; and it was thought that these were approaches that might be negotiated by strong infantry columns.

On the morning of September 11th the brigade commanders were assembled at Division headquarters and the plans gone over. The final orders were handed to brigade commanders at this time. This final order omits the original plan for awaiting orders before advancing to the Corps objective of the day after securing the high ground in the vicinity of and to the south of Bouillonville. In the action, as will be later noted, there was a delay after the capture of Bouillonville, which had no effect on the result, as the line of the Corps objective was entirely controlled by our occupation of Bouillonville and the heights immediately south of the town.

The night of September 11-12 was dismal, cold and rainy. The trenches were filled with water and mud, and the roads slippery and congested with moving troops, guns and supply trains. All seemed confusion and disorder. There was no thrill for the coming conflict, no pomp and circumstance whatever as the tired troops plowed their way through the mud to their allotted positions or huddled in their trenches vainly trying to keep dry and to snatch a little rest. But suddenly at 1 o'clock in the morning the roar of the unprecedented artillery preparation burst forth and continued with unbroken violence for four hours. Such a concentration of artillery had not been previously known in the war, which had now reached the stage where the artillery had become the weapon of offense, blasting out the enemy from the desired position, which the infantry was to advance to and hold against counter attack.

ARTILLERY PREPARATION

In support of the 89th Division was the 55th Field Artillery Brigade, under the command of Brigadier General J. A. Shipton, and consisting of two regiments of light guns, 75s, and one regiment of howitzers, 155s; also two regiments and two battalions of French Field Artillery, the 250th, 212th and 160th, respectively; also three Trench Mortar Batteries, the 105th, and 108th United States and the 176th French. In addition, Army and Corps artillery of large calibre was pounding away from positions in our rear upon targets in our sector. Altogether the Allied artillery fired a million rounds in these four hours of preparation, the most intense concentration of artillery fire known in history.

The enemy's response to our artillery was comparatively feeble. It afterwards developed that by a lucky chance a large amount of the German artillery was on the move and our attack came as a surprise. The Germans were expecting it, but not so soon.

No account of the artillery branch of the battle would be complete without an expression of appreciation of the service rendered by Colonel de Chaunac Lanzac, 250th Regiment of French Field Artillery. His regiment had been in support of the Division during the period of occupation of the sector and had deserved and gained the esteem of all. When the command of the Divisional Artillery was taken by General Shipton, Colonel de Chaunac Lanzac was requested to assume the duties of his chief of staff. His detailed knowledge of the terrain and conditions in the sector as well as his high military attainments enabled him to perform this function in a particularly satisfactory manner; and the assistance rendered by him in the preparation of the artillery program contributed in no small degree to the unquestioned success of this feature of the battle.

The action proceeded as planned. The 178th Brigade forced its way through the forest, mopping up as it went; the 177th Brigade, skirting the eastern edge of Mort Mare, mopped up the portion of the forest in its sector by means of detachments. After the lines had passed the forest, the two brigades obtained contact with one another. The Division then advanced to the position originally designated as the limit of its independent action—the heights north of Euvezin. Here the line halted and the troops were reorganized. This halt was a little longer than was contemplated in the orders for the battle, partly because our division had advanced more rapidly than the divisions on our right and left and partly because of a slight misconception of orders occasioned by the change of the objective of the day to the heights north of Bouillonville in the orders as finally issued. During this pause, the troops in the line received the orders that the objective for the day would be still further advanced to the line Xammes—the center of Forest of Dampvitoux.

Accordingly, in the late afternoon, the advance was resumed and continued into the night until the designated objective was reached. When the morning of the 13th came, the Division was on this Army objective, originally planned to be the exploitation line for the second day's fighting, and found itself confronting the Hindenburg Line and under fire from guns of the fortified area of Metz.

Let us now narrate in detail the actions of the brigades and their subordinate units, in this their first battle.

OPERATIONS OF THE 177TH INFANTRY BRIGADE

The 177th Infantry Brigade, Brigadier General Frank L. Winn commanding, consisted in the action of the following troops: 353rd Infantry, Colonel James H. Reeves commanding; 341st Machine Gun Battalion, Major Ernest E. Watson commanding, and the 1st Battalion, 354th Infantry, Captain Alonzo W. Harlow commanding, this battalion acting as Brigade Reserve. A battery of artillery had also been assigned to the Brigade to accompany the advance of the infantry, but it did not come up in time to participate in the fight. The 354th Infantry, excepting the battalion named, was held in Division Reserve.

The honor of leading the attack on the 177th Brigade sector fell to the 2nd Battalion of the 353rd Infantry, under the command of Captain (later Lieutenant Colonel) James L. Peatross. During the night the battalion had been assembled in the front line trenches, and at 4:40 A. M. the men as silently as possible scrambled up the muddy walls of their trenches, their own Colonel James H. Reeves among them, and moved forward into the valley at the edge of our wire 150 yards in front of the enemy front line. "E" and "F" Companies comprised the first wave, and "G" and "H" Companies the second. On the moment, at 5 o'clock, our barrage fell upon the enemy front line and the troops followed it as it advanced. But the enemy's machine guns had not been silenced by the barrage. East of Ansoncourt farm and in its ruins a nest of these guns played with deadly effect on the advancing troops and "F" Company attacked them with little groups of three and four men widely separated in a diamond formation. The nest was soon encircled and the gunners killed or captured, but at the cost of the life of gallant young Lieutenant James Nixon, who fell with a mortal wound. From the edge of Mort Mare and the Promenade des Moines, other guns enfiladed the line. These fell to the lot of "E" Company. Every officer of the company was either killed or wounded in the first fifteen minutes of the fight, but Captain (later Major) Milton E. Portmann, of "E," though painfully wounded, continued to lead his men against these guns and put them out of action. First Lieutenant Charles A. Shaw, Company "E," encountering a machine gun position, surrounded by unbroken wire, leaped into the wire at the head of his men, putting the gun out of action by their impetuous charge, only to lose his life by machine gun fire a few moments later. So the attack swept irresistibly on. Old Captain Moses D. Atkins, of Company "H," a veteran of the Spanish War and of many a fight in the Philippines, was wounded in the leg. He found, however, that he could hobble along fairly well on the level ground and that when he came to a trench he could send his runners down into it to boost him over. So he continued to fight until evening, when another wound forced him out. Second Lieutenant J. Hunter Wickersham, of the same company, was advancing with his platoon when he was severely wounded in four places by the bursting of a high explosive shell. Before receiving any aid for himself, he dressed the wounds of his orderly, who was wounded at the same time. He then ordered and accompanied the advance of his platoon, although weakened by loss of blood. His right hand and arm being disabled by wounds, he continued to fire his revolver with his left hand, until exhausted by loss of blood he fell and died from his wounds before aid could be administered. When he became unconscious he was endeavoring to tie his pistol halyard around his right arm as a ligature to stop the bleeding. Posthumous award of the Medal of Honor was made to this gallant young officer.

When the assault battalion had passed the open ground east of Mort Mare it entered the Woods of Euvezin. Contact with the other brigade of the Division was acquired by connecting with troops of the 355th Infantry. Contact had been maintained at all times during the advance with the 9th Infantry of the 2nd Division, which was on the right. So the important feature of presenting an unbroken line to the enemy was not lacking, in spite of the temporary gap caused by Mort Mare.

The Bois d'Euvezin, however, was not to be gone around. The troops advanced through the woods, dense as they were, keeping with surprising accuracy their formation. A large number of prisoners was taken by them in these woods, including a major.

After passing through the woods, the troops were halted at the northern edge to reform before entering the Bois de Beau Vallon. Along the southern edge of Beau Vallon, it will be remembered, ran the German second position, ugly trenches and barbed wire. But our troops were not to be denied and pressed forward into the woods, taking fifteen machine guns and 200 prisoners, then halting on the northern edge to reform and let the third battalion pass the lines and take up the burden of the advance.

The 1st Battalion of the 353rd under Captain Clay Crump, had been assigned the two tasks of mopping up Mort Mare and of maintaining contact with the troops of the 2nd Division. For this latter mission, Company "A" under Captain Allen Barnett was selected. The company proceeded along the right boundary of the zone of the Division's advance, keeping near a similar body of the 9th Infantry, and meeting little opposition from the enemy. The other companies of the battalion advanced immediately behind the assault battalion. When the trench system along the southern edge of Mort Mare was reached, Company "B," under Captain Hazlett, turned off to the left and proceeded down the trenches. At the trenches running through the center of the woods, Company "D" under Lieutenant (later Captain) Hugh Kellogg, turned off; and Company "C," under Captain Ward Ellis entered and mopped up the upper portion of Mort Mare and the western part of Bois d'Euvezin. Each of these companies encountered surprised and desperate bodies of the enemy, who were looking for an attack from the front and not from the flank and rear. Some hand-to-hand fighting was done and a large number of prisoners and machine guns taken. German snipers had taken positions in the trees. One of them, in the eastern edge of the woods, was firing upon the lines advancing in the open, and very bravely ignoring the presence of the moppers up in the forest beneath him. His nest, well concealed in the tree

One of the entrances to the large dugout in Bouillonville where Sergt. Harry Adams, 353rd Infantry, captured 300 Germans single handed and with an empty pistol.

tops, was finally located and one of our riflemen, long trained in squirrel shooting in our western woods, brought him tumbling headlong from his lofty perch.

When the mopping up was done, the battalion was assembled at the northern edge of Bois d'Euvezin and followed the advance as support to the 3rd Battalion, which had passed the lines of the 2nd Battalion and had become the assault battalion for the remainder of the action.

During the process of mopping up, remarkable daring and initiative were shown by Private Joseph A. Szczepanik of Company "M," 353rd Infantry. Scouting about alone, he sought the hiding places into which enemy soldiers had been driven by our barrage. Through his efforts about 150 Germans were captured before they had a chance to come out from cover and man their machine guns. He was later wounded while attempting to enter barracks in which several of the enemy had taken refuge.

The Brigade Headquarters of the 177th Brigade for the jump-off had been established in a dugout located on the St. Dizier-Metz road about midway between Limey and Flirey. When the troops had taken the first objective Brigade Headquarters moved forward to the Ansoncourt Farm and then almost immediately to the Robert Menil Trench about four hundred meters northwest of the Ansoncourt Farm, at which point the P. C., which was established before 8 o'clock in the morning, remained until the assault battalion had passed through the woods of Euvezin and Beau Vallon. General Winn, however, remained at the P. C. only a short time and then personally moved forward and joined the supports of the assault battalion and finished the first phase of the day's fighting with these troops.

The Brigade continued the advance and halted on the heights south of Bouillonville. Patrols were pushed forward vigorously to the front. Lieutenant Colonel Boschen, 353rd Infantry, with a few men entered Bouillonville and returned with several hundred prisoners, mostly sanitary troops of the 10th German Division, who had been cut off by our artillery fire and were waiting to surrender to some one. Sergeant Harry Adams, Company "K," 353rd Infantry, saw a German soldier in Bouillonville run into a house. He followed in time to see his prey disappear into an opening in the hillside behind the house, which led, as afterwards developed, into a large dugout. Adams had two shots only left in his pistol. He fired these into the door and called on the occupants to surrender. Soon they began to pour out, more and more and more, until the astonished sergeant found himself the sole custodian of approximately three hundred prisoners, including seven officers, one of whom was a Lieutenant Colonel. Coolly assembling them under the menace of his empty

Flashlight of interior of the dugout in Bouillonville where Sergt. Harry J. Adams, 353rd Infantry, captured 300 Germans.

pistol, he convoyed them safely to the rear, startling his platoon commander, Lieutenant Chase, as the column approached, into the conviction that it was a German counter attack which threatened.

The enemy artillery was not idle. Admirably directed by low-flying aeroplanes, the light artillery directed a galling fire upon our men; wherever

A concentration of rolling kitchens of the 89th Division (which was broken up as soon as the Division commander saw it!) under partial protection of the hill at Bouillonville, Sept. 16th, 1918, during the St. Mihiel offensive. Good commanders crowded the rolling kitchens forward, even though thereby many were hit by German shells, for hot food added greatly to comfort of the men. S. C. 25262.

a few men were collected together the shells would soon begin to fall. But as the formation adopted consisted of wide separation of the men, relatively light casualties resulted.

OPERATIONS OF THE 178TH INFANTRY BRIGADE

We turn now to the action of the 178th Brigade from the jump-off until junction was effected with the 177th Brigade. The general axis of the advance of this brigade took it directly through the Mort Mare forest. The only opening in the dense forest was that made by the roads from Flirey to Essey and such lines and openings in the German wire and in the forest as had been blasted by our artillery fire. The troops advanced promptly at 5 o'clock. There had been great effort and some confusion occasioned by the fact that many of the troops had been on the move both the night preceding the assault and the night previous to that. The contraction of the front had occasioned the relief of elements of both of these regiments by troops of the 1st and 42nd Divisions, which took over the entire sector formerly occupied by the Brigade, and relief by this Brigade of troops of the 177th Brigade which were occupying the departure trenches. These reliefs were effected at night over roads slippery with mud and congested almost to the point of impassibility by traffic—supply trains, artillery and other troops on the move. As a result all the men went into the departure trenches and started out on the attack tired, muddy and uncomfortable, but there was no grumbling and no reluctance. When the hour came all moved out promptly and eagerly to the first fight. The attack was made by the brigade with two infantry regiments in line abreast of one another; the 355th Infantry on the right and the 356th on the left. This brigade was compelled to pass over a rather wide strip of open ground in No Man's Land between the jump-off line and the German position in the edge of Mort Mare woods. The difficulty of the initial attack was enhanced by the fact that the departure trench lay at a 45-degree angle to the direction of the assault and the first objective, consisting of the German trenches in the edge of Mort Mare, lay at the same angle to the axis of the advance. These difficulties, however, were soon overcome. The 355th Infantry, under the command of Colonel James D. Taylor, was charged with the duty not only of advancing through the woods but also with capturing by a flank attack the main German communication trench called Boyau de Faunes, protecting the right flank of the brigade and the divisional line of communication, mopping up Mort Mare from its western side and reëstablishing liaison with the 177th Brigade when the woods of Mort Mare should be passed. This difficult mission of mopping up was entrusted to the 2nd Battalion, 355th Infantry, which also was to act as Brigade Reserve.

The assault battalion was the 3rd Battalion, commanded by Captain (afterwards Major) J. F. Symes.

The 1st Battalion, under command of Major Thomas F. Wirth, advanced as support to the assault battalion and later passed the lines of the assault battalion and continued as assault battalion in the operations of the latter part of the day.

The 356th Infantry was formed with the 3rd Battalion as the assault battalion under the command of Major Henry W. Hobson, and the 1st Battalion in support commanded by Major William Bland. The 2nd Battalion of this regiment was Brigade Reserve. No passage of lines was made by this regiment, as the commander of the assault battalion had his troops so well in hand that none was necessary.

The assault battalion of the 355th Infantry had sustained some losses during the night and upon departure from its trenches suffered from machine gun fire and a few enemy shells. Soon after the jump-off Lieutenant John H. Ale of Company "M" was badly wounded, losing his right hand and receiving wounds in both legs and in his chest. Notwithstanding these wounds he returned to his platoon and addressed his men, telling them that he was unable to go with them but that he had confidence in their ability to go ahead without him. Inspired by his grit, his platoon went ahead and ably performed its duty.

Sergeant Martin J. Janssen, Company A, 355th Infantry, coming up in the rear of two platoons of the battalion ahead, which were held up by machine gun fire from front and flank, fearlessly exposed himself running from end to end of the line encouraging the men, and by his inspiring leadership, carried the line forward. Corporal (then Bugler) Chauncey W. Porter, Company B, 355th Infantry, charged a machine gun alone, killed one man with his automatic pistol, and drove the rest of the enemy back along the trench, thereby enabling the advance of his platoon. Private Marcelino Serna, of the same company, single-handed, charged and captured twenty-four Germans. Private Edwin Wiese, Company C, 355th Infantry, crept forward alone under machine gun fire and captured two machine guns which had delayed the advance of his organization.

89th Division P. C. (post of command or headquarters) under wrecked railroad bridge at Flirey, Sept. 14th, 1918, during the St. Mihiel offensive, showing Col. C. E. Kilbourne, Chief of Staff, examining a map. Until Sept. 12th this was part of the second line trench system. S. C 25260.

The battalion took its first and second objective on time, but before reaching the third objective (the Trench de l'Eperon) it encountered a number of machine guns which had to be outflanked and taken by the infantry at the cost of losses, especially among officers. One-half company having strayed off the regimental sector to the left, the battalion was coolly halted and reformed for the attack upon the third objective, which was taken in spite of machine gun fire from the right. By the taking of the third objective the line had emerged from Mort Mare and by extending to the right came in contact with troops of the 353rd Infantry, thus reëstablishing the line and justifying the plan of the Division Commander in attacking Mort Mare from the flanks even at the expense of advancing his line with so wide a gap.

Sergeant John Brinda, Co. B, 355th Infantry, without awaiting orders, alone charged a concealed machine gun which was holding up his platoon, killed the gunner and captured four others, thereby enabling the platoon to advance.

The 3rd Battalion of the 356th Infantry, under Major Henry W. Hobson, led the assault of the left sector of the brigade. Very little reconnaisance of the departure trench and of the ground over which the attack had to be made had been possible, but the assaulting battalion passed over No Man's Land without much loss until just before reaching Mort Mare woods, where strong machine gun resistance was encountered. Major Hobson was twice wounded within ten minutes after the beginning of the advance, once in the shoulder by a machine gun bullet and once by shrapnel in the leg. His adjutant, Lieutenant Earl W. Moore, was killed, and several of his runners wounded by the same shell which wounded the Major. Notwithstanding his wounds, Major Hobson continued to accompany and direct his command throughout the day, even though at halts he had to be assisted to lie down and get up. When the fighting of the day was over he then, and not until then, permitted himself to be evacuated to the hospital and Captain A. Y. Wear of Company "L" took command of the battalion. The first decoration received by a member of the 89th Division was the D. S. C. awarded to Major Hobson.

Captain Wear's company started out with but three officers and came out with none, Captain Wear commanding the battalion, his other two officers wounded.

Sergeant Gable of Company "L," 356th Infantry, was a private at this time, but when his platoon leader had been wounded he took command of his platoon and lead it on to the final objective, where he was seriously gassed.

When Major Hobson was wounded Lieutenant (later Captain) Arthur S. Champeny, who had been acting as Intelligence Officer, maintained the liaison personnel and made many a journey himself through the heavy shelling to keep up connections. Later, when Major Hobson had finally been evacuated, and before Captain Ware could be notified to take command, this young lieutenant assumed command of the battalion and moved it to its proper position on the final objective of the day.

Private Ora L. Dutcher, 355th Infantry, on duty as an observer at battalion headquarters, twice volunteered to carry important messages to the company commanders, passing through heavy barrages on these missions.

Second Lieutenant Oscar P. May attacked and captured a machine gun without assistance.

Lieutenant Leon P. Shinn, 356th Infantry, wounded in the leg during the first twenty minutes of the engagement, continued to lead his platoon until the third objective was reached.

The support battalion had few difficulties. It was compelled to pass through the enemy's counter barrage at the jump-off and captured about 100 prisoners lurking in dugouts which had not been mopped up by the preceding troops. It suffered a great loss, however, when its commander, Major William Bland, was killed by a shell fragment soon after emerging from Mort Mare. Captain John W. Harris then assumed command of the battalion and led it through the remainder of the engagement.

THE FIRST OBJECTIVE ATTAINED

The front of the Division having now become united, all troops pressed on to the objective of the first phase of the battle, the heights south of Bouillonville and of the Rupt de Mad and north of Euvezin. The right brigade, the 177th, had been able to advance exactly on schedule and arrived at this line at 11 A. M., having only a slight advance to make to rectify its alignment. The

Doughboys of the 178th Infantry Brigade, 89th Division, resting in trench near Beney during the St. Mihiel offensive. Wire in middle distance and village in background. S. C. 25287.

178th Brigade on the left, coming directly through Mort Mare, could not advance so rapidly, the 356th Infantry arriving on the objective at noon and the 355th by 3 P. M. The front line from right to left then consisted of 3rd Battalion 353rd Infantry, Ist Battalion 355th Infantry and 3rd Battalion 356th Infantry.

At this juncture there developed one of those incidents which often affect the result of battles and the fate of empires. The original Field Order under which the attack was made had provided that the advance would halt at the attainment of the objective of the first phase and await orders before advancing to the objective of the day. As before stated this order had been modified so as to require the advance to continue from this objective to that of the 2nd phase —the objective of the first day, namely a line extending approximately from about two kilometers south of Beney to about a kilometer north of Thiaucourt, and passing about half a kilometer north of Bouillonville. But both brigades halted on the lines mentioned as the objectives of the 1st phase of the first day, sending only patrols to the front.

In the meantime, while the action was in progress, the Division Commander had received orders that the attack was not to halt even on the first day's objective, but was to be pushed on to the Army objective which had been previously decided on as the limit of the second day's fighting and of the operation itself. This line, so far as our Division was concerned, extended from the center of the Bois de Dampvitoux, at a point some four kilometers north of Beney, to Xammes. It will be noted that this line is almost at right angles to the line of the first day's objective. The latter ran in a direction almost southwest to northeast. The new objective ran in a direction almost northwest to southeast. The extreme left of the line would have to swing round, the line turning on a pivot near Xammes.

THE SECOND DAY'S OBJECTIVE ATTAINED

In order, therefore, to correct the misconception of the lower commanders as to the day's objective and to give the new orders for the further advance to the Army objective, General Wright sent forward officers of his staff to see in person that the orders were transmitted and understood. On Colonel C. E. Kilbourne, Chief of Staff, this duty principally devolved. Riding far beyond the foremost positions he satisfied himself personally of conditions to the front, visited each battalion, regimental and brigade commander and saw to it that all was understood and in process of performance before returning to his post at Division Headquarters.

When the 177th Brigade had attained the heights south of Bouillonville and its patrols had entered the town and had sent back numerous prisoners, Colonel Reeves informed General Winn that his troops were abreast of, if not in advance of, the 2nd Division. The 178th Brigade had not come up and was not in sight. General Winn gave directions to Colonel Reeves to keep close liaison with the 2nd Division and to prepare to move forward in conjunction with it. He then went to the left of his brigade and then to the front as far as Bouillonville for the purpose of getting in touch with General Hanson or his troops. On returning to the temporary P. C. of the Brigade, near the P. C. of the 353rd Infantry, he found Colonel Kilbourne there. Colonel Kilbourne had already noted the delay incident to moving forward to the Corps objective, and had directed the battalion commanders on the ground to move forward at once, which was done. He also brought the orders to move to the Army or 2nd day objective, for which orders to the troops were immediately issued.

In the meanwhile Colonel Kilbourne had given orders to the troops of the 355th and 356th Infantry, and these were already on the move to the front.

The 355th Infantry had been first notified and in consequence moved forward first. It resulted that the advance of the Division was in crescent shape, the center leading and the two flanks retired. The center arrived on the

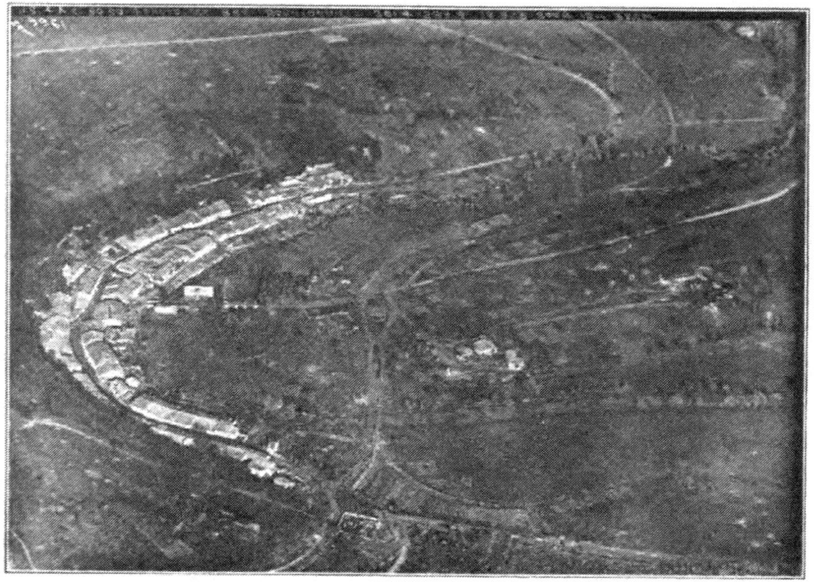

Bouillonville (familiarly known as "Soup-town"), captured by the 89th Division in the St. Mihiel offensive, as it appeared from an altitude of 300 meters (a little less than 1,000 feet), on Sept. 13, 1918. The shell holes shown were from the American artillery fire, which was terrific at this point. A German wagon train and escort was caught in this fire while retreating along the road to Thiaucourt, which leaves the town in the upper part of the picture. This road and the sloping hillside about it were thickly strewn with bodies of men and animals killed in this fire. The steep, curved hill under which the town was built was between us and the enemy and afforded much appreciated protection for the numerous P. Cs. and hospital detachments located there. A. S. 9961.

day's new objective at 6 P. M., September 12th, the left at about 8 o'clock that evening and on the right the 353rd Infantry reached the day's objective near Xammes about midnight, the 354th Infantry, coming up from its position in reserve during the night, took its place in the line in the early morning, and all troops of the 177th Brigade were reported on the line of the objective at about 10 o'clock A. M., September 13th. This further advance was without much organized opposition except from the artillery.

THE NIGHT AFTER THE BATTLE

The advance through the gathering dusk and the deep night, though devoid of excitement, was stirring to the emotions of every participant. The weather had cleared and brilliant stars were looking down upon the field of battle. The continuous roar of the artillery and the rattle of small arms had ceased. At long intervals, the boom of a distant gun was heard. After toiling upward from the dark valleys, a scene of rare and terrible beauty greeted the soldier on the heights. For, far to the southwest, in the angle of the old St. Mihiel salient, now no more a salient, blazed hundreds of fires. They were from military stores and supplies, barracks and even villages which the defeated enemy had sought to destroy to prevent their falling into the hands of the victors.

In the towns some few civilians, men and women, who had clung to their homes, emerged from their hiding places, still half stunned from the fearful pounding of the artillery, scarce able yet to realize that the hated invader had at last been driven out, and timidly greeted the passing troops, with feelings almost too deep for expression.

In Bouillonville and Xammes, fires were still burning in the stoves of the military kitchens and huge kettles of food were found, still hot, for which, no doubt, many empty German stomachs were clamoring, over there in the dark behind the wire of the Hindenburg Line.

The fearful execution done by our artillery fire was everywhere in evidence. The road from Bouillonville to Thiaucourt presented a gruesome sight. A wagon train moving out supplies had evidently been caught there in our fire. The bodies of many German soldiers lay in the road itself, and the hillside above, over which they had attempted to flee, was thickly strewn with corpses. In the road were many loaded wagons, the horses lying dead in the harness, twisted into grotesque shapes by the fearful explosions. Passing over this road in the faint light of the stars and winding in and out to avoid treading on these ghastly obstacles, was an experience to which none of the horrors of the battle field in the open day could compare.

Not until late at night, when his command had intrenched under fire and was settled at least until morning, did Captain Fred F. Moore, 355th Infantry, take time to allow his wounded shoulder to be dressed and two pieces of shrapnel removed therefrom, although he had been wounded in the morning and continued all day to lead his company gallantly and efficiently.

Promptly after passage of the infantry, the Engineers had started that morning construction of a road north from Flirey across No Man's land and over the trenches in spite of shortage of road-making material. By noon the motor transport of the 340th Machine Gun Battalion picked its way across and claims the honor of taking the first motor vehicles into the re-conquered territory. Artillery was pushed forward as quickly as possible, and thereafter

Digging fox holes at a battalion P. C. of the 355th Infantry, 89th Division, on the outskirts of Beney, Sept. 16th, 1918, St. Mihiel offensive. S. C. 25314.

the herculean efforts of the engineers were continued, building and improving the road while still allowing traffic to pass over it.

General Winn, with the headquarters of the 177th Brigade, followed the advancing troops through Bouillonville and to the western edge of Thiaucourt, arriving about midnight. A brief rest in a deserted mill there was interrupted by a message from Division Headquarters that several thousand Germans were massing at Mon Plaisir Farm for a counter attack in the direction of Thiaucourt. It appears from the captured German reports of the battle, that this counter attack was in fact ordered; but it never took place. Brigade Headquarters, however, moved to the more central location of Bouillonville at about 3 A. M., and established its Command Post there and by daylight had reports of the locations of all of its elements and control of its scattered troops. General Hanson had established the headquarters of the 178th Brigade at Euvezin for the night. On the following day headquarters moved to Beney, then and at all times a favorite target for enemy shell fire, but well located for control of the sector of the brigade.

Too much cannot be said in praise of the advance of these raw troops in the night following their first battle. Maps were scarce, the platoon commanders and many company commanders not being supplied; the ground was unknown; the enemy could be expected to make a stand at any moment and to launch a counter attack. The men were approaching the limit of physical exhaustion. Nearly all of them had marched all night before and some the night before that under trying conditions of weather and traffic. Troops of the division on the right and left had strayed over into our sector and added to the confusion and difficulty. To crown all, the line had to swing to a 45-degree change of direction. It would have been a difficult maneuver for a peace time field problem. Yet these midwest farmer boys, many of whom had been on their farms five months before, led by officers who for the most part had, of technical military training, only three months of training camp, advanced to their objective, marching by compass bearing, and placed themselves on the line which, in the original plans, it had not been expected they could attain until twenty-four hours later. Well indeed had they justified their country's pride and confidence. Gone forever was the German delusion that America would be able to do little in a military way in the war.

During the night of September 12-13, the 354th Infantry, which had been, except one battalion, held in the rear as Division Reserve, advanced to Bouillonville. In the early morning it pushed forward and took its place in the line between the 353rd and the 355th, the regiments thus occupying the line

Troops of the 178th Infantry Brigade, 89th Division, dug in, open style, in shallow trenches on the new line north of Beney, Sept. 24th, 1918, after the St. Mihiel offensive. Machine gun in center of picture. S. C. 23943.

in numerical order from right to left. This movement was not accomplished without losses. Practically the entire front of the Division was in the open, only the extreme left of the line having the advantage of shelter in the Bois de Dampvitoux. The whole of the plateau was under complete observation by the enemy from many points, particularly a height east of Charey known as Mon Plaisir Farm. With perfect observation the enemy artillery could and did inflict severe losses upon the troops taking position in the open. Fortunately the weather, which seemed to have been ordered to suit the American forces, again changed, so clouds and gusts of rain hindered somewhat the enemy's observation and concealed the movements. As it was, it seemed to the observer that the open ground between Xammes and the Bois de Dampvitoux was crammed with troops, our own coming into the line and rectifying their positions and strays from the 42nd Division and from the Marines. Soon, however, the men had reached their approximate positions and had begun to dig in.

On the afternoon of Sept. 14th occurred one of those incidents characteristic of American soldiers. Private Frank Curtis, 23rd Infantry, 2nd Division, was lying in No Man's land, wounded and abandoned by the enemy. On learning of the fact, Ambulance Driver Charles L. Grout, accompanied by Wagoner Victor W. Allen acting as ambulance orderly, fearlessly drove him ambulance in broad daylight into No Man's Land north of Xammes, under observation of the Germans and in imminent danger of both fire and capture, rescued the wounded soldier. Both men were members of Ambulance Co. 355, 314th Sanitary Train.

ACCOMPLISHMENT BEYOND EXPECTATION

There are several circumstances which induce the conjecture that in the Battle of the St. Mihiel Salient the 89th Division accomplished a great deal more than was expected of it in advance by the commanders of the Corps and Army. It alone, of all the divisions called upon to make an extended advance, went into the action without opportunity for refitting and rest after prolonged contact with the enemy. Strict orders from higher authority prohibited the relief of any of its front line elements for several days before "D" day, until the very night preceding the attack. The contraction of the front, delayed thus until the night before the battle, necessitated exhausting marches under trying road conditions by troops already wearied with prolonged service in the front line trenches, and would probably not have been imposed deliberately upon troops from whom severe fighting and an extended advance on the following day were to be expected. Of course, it is entirely obvious that the order against relief of the front line elements until the last moment was a part of the arrangements to insure the secrecy of the operation. If, in the few days preceding the attack, the enemy had been successful in his repeated attempts to capture prisoners in our sector, the information which he would have obtained from them would have been of little value. They would have been troops that had been long in the sector and would

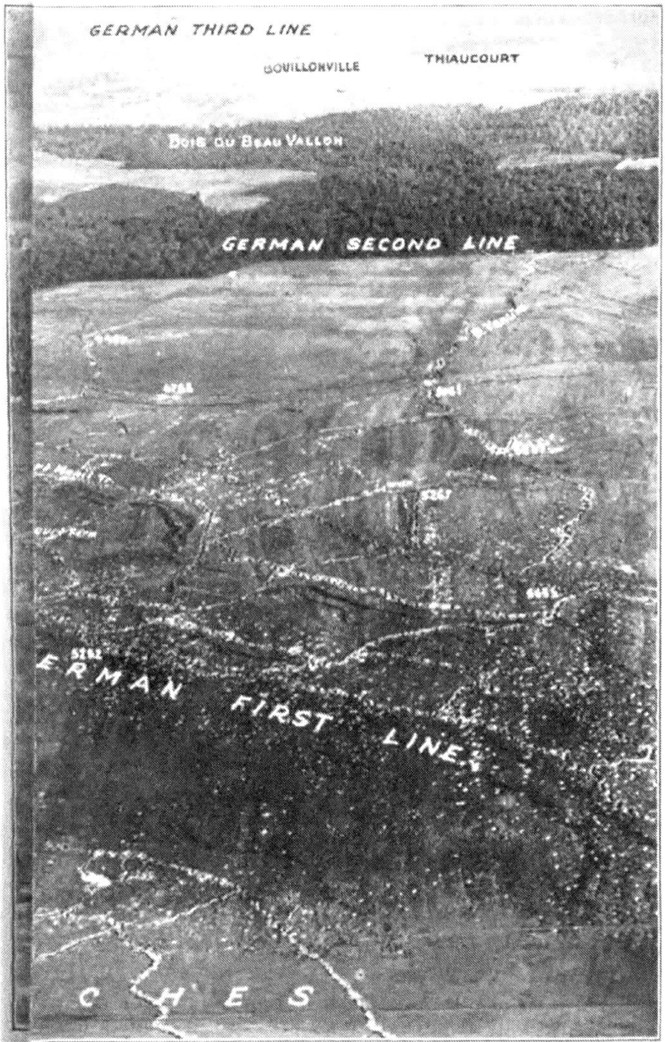

he country and dense forests. The 177th Infantry Brigade attacked over
at the extreme left, part of the ground over which it fought in the early
made prior to the attack, so there is necessarily some distortion in per-

have had no observation of the extensive preparations which were going on in the rear areas. So, while the reason for the extra hardship imposed upon our troops is plain enough and proper enough from a military standpoint, the inference is that it would not have been exacted of troops expected to play a decisive part in the battle. Ostensibly the mission assigned to the 89th Division was the most difficult of accomplishment on the entire front. The Forest of Mort Mare, which lay wholly within the sector of its advance, was the most formidable position of defense on the entire southern side of the salient, and in the Army estimate of the enemy's defensive system was stated unequivocally to be the key to the enemy's positions between Pont-a-Mousson and St. Mihiel. If it had been the Army Commander's intention to reduce this position by a direct frontal assault, he would undoubtedly have thrown against it his most experienced and freshest troops. Instead, he assigned to this sector our division, which, though it had evidently shown good quality in the trenches, was as yet untested in actual battle. Furthermore, it was not even a rested division, since it had already been nearly six weeks in the trenches, and was called on for extra exertions on the night before battle. The conclusion is irresistible, therefore, that the real mission of our division, in the mind of the higher commander, was that of what is called a holding mission; that our attack on Mort Mare was expected merely

Captured German trench mortars, heavy and light, brought back to Flirey after the St. Mihiel offensive. Painted on the side of the large one is the word "Wotan." S. C. 29877.

to engage the enemy's attention, while the real attack would be made around the flanks of the woods, by the rested and veteran 42nd and 2nd Divisions on our left and right; and that in accordance with universal military policy, this holding attack was not so designated in the orders.

This conjecture is confirmed by the language used in assigning the mission of the Division, which, after stating the direction of the advance, added the

Captured Boche narrow-gauge engine and cars manned by the 314th Engineers, 89th Division, at Bouillonville, St. Mihiel offensive, Sept. 16th, 1918. S. C. 25320.

words, "supporting the advance of the 42nd Division on our left by exerting the main effort on the left, * * * assist the advance of the 2nd Division * * *. If the 2nd Division is delayed, the 89th Division will capture Thiaucourt." Such expressions are typical of those invariably used to order a holding attack and are inconsistent with the idea that the plan of the commander contemplated that the main burden of reducing Mort Mare would rest upon the 89th Division.

We have seen, however, that the 89th did reduce Mort Mare, and without assistance from its neighbors; that it kept up with the advance of the whole line and finished the day on its objectives and ahead of the splendid divisions on its right and left. Its success must have been as gratifying as it was unexpected to the higher commanders. The Division had been given a task that was believed to be beyond its powers and had accomplished it. It felt that it was entitled to more credit than if it had merely done what was expected of it.

DEFECTS IN BATTLE

Though the Division performed most creditably in its first engagement and succeeded beyond all expectation, it would not be consistent with the facts to leave the impression that our performance was unmarred by serious defects in execution.

The most striking of these was the failure of liaison. Throughout the day there was great difficulty in communicating with the fighting elements. The Division was in fairly good telephone communication with the 178th Brigade, but the brigade was not in communication with the troops; in the other brigade, the reverse was the case, for General Winn was at all times in good communication with the troops, but out of touch with the Division. From the standpoint of the Division Commander the result was the same in both cases. The Field Signal Battalion had not been remiss in its preparations for maintaining telephone liaison and detachments from the battalion went over the top with the troops of the assault battalions; but the difficulty of getting up the wire carts over No Man's Land, made their efforts futile and

Railroad bridge at Flirey, blown up by the French to impede the German advance in 1914. P. C. of the 89th Division during the St. Mihiel offensive was in dugouts under the right end of the wrecked bridge. This photograph, made Sept. 13th, 1918, the second day of the drive, shows the two lines of trucks (one disappearing in background behind the bridge) interspersed with other transportation and artillery, which moved in solid column (or stood still, blocked) for 80 hours during the advance. S. C. 25253.

it was not until the second day that good telephone connections were available.

Liaison by airplane was also a failure. This was due in part to the failure of the troops to make use of this means of communication; and, also in part to the destruction of the divisional plane early in the day. The pilot of the divisional plane, over zealous in the performance of his duties, or

Flirey on Sept. 14th, 1918, during the St. Mihiel offensive, with trucks loaded with Q. M. supplies entering the town. A large stone in church tower may be seen hanging in the air, suspended by an almost invisible iron tie rod. S. C. 25258.

perhaps taking the risks inseparable from their performance, flew so low as to come into the zone of our artillery barrage. His plane came down in flames, a terrible and moving sight.

A fearful jam of traffic occurred following the operation. The road from Flirey north was the sole practicable artery of supply for the 42nd and 89th Divisions. Through some failure of the promulgation or enforcement or coördination of traffic regulations, together with inadequate provision for road construction and repair across No Man's Land and beyond, a terrific congestion of vehicles of all kinds occurred at Flirey which lasted for more than two days and caused serious difficulties in the supply of troops with food and ammunition, the evacuation of the wounded, and worst of all, the movement of the artillery. Responsibility for road conditions, from which followed so many other difficulties, was on the corps at least in part, but the Division was not blameless.

A grave defect in the operation was the failure to get to the troops an adequate supply of maps. The platoon and company commanders of the assault troops were practically all without maps of the terrain over which they were to operate, and their effectiveness was thereby much impaired. The sad part of the situation was that the maps were actually available, but through the fault of someone, as yet unknown, or by some circumstance as yet unexplained, they did not get to the troops.

There were numerous defects, characteristic of green troops—"waiting for orders" by small groups of men, which almost amounted to straggling; eating up reserve rations without orders; throwing away of raincoats and other equipment sadly needed later, and general confusion and disorder on a small scale.

By the time the Division was again in an offensive all these defects were reduced to a minimum.

THE GERMAN VERSION

It will be of interest now to consider the operation from the enemy's viewpoint. This we are enabled to do from documents captured and the statements of prisoners.

The captured German documents relating to this battle consist of two reports of Lieutenant General Fuchs, commanding Army Detachment "C," which was the designation of the entire body of troops occupying the St. Mihiel salient; these reports are both dated 19 September; the first of them relates the events up to the evening of September 11th, the second, the events of September 12th. There is also the report of the Corps Commander, General Leuthold, commanding the 12th Reserve Corps, not dated but obviously made very soon after the action and covering the events of the 12th of September in great detail. There were also a number of letters of German soldiers, mostly dated September 11th, which had been dropped for mailing into an outgoing mail box and were captured on our advance.

Of these, the report of General Fuchs is the most interesting, because of its subject matter, the evidence it gives of the complete success of our strategy in deluding the enemy not only as to our immediate plans but to our wider designs, and finally of the picture it presents to the imagination of the surly, defeated commander, striving to extract some comfort out of the situation and to cast the blame upon someone else.

From these documents and the reports of our intelligence service the following information of the German dispositions before the battle is known. The St. Mihiel salient was held by troops under the command of Lieutenant General Fuchs. The command was described as Army Detachment "C." The sector assigned to this detachment commenced on the western face of the salient at a point almost due east and a little south of Verdun, near the small village of Eix. Thence it extended around the nose of the salient and along the southern face to a point about two kilometers east of Regnieville. The German forces holding this line were divided into three so-called groups; of which the Combres Group held the western face to a point about eight kilometers north of St. Mihiel; the Mihiel Group held the nose of the salient and the southern face to a point about midway between Loupmont and Xivray, while the Gorz Group held the balance of the southern face. East of the limits of the sector of Army Detachment "C" was the 19th German Army, under General von Bothmer. This army was astride the Moselle; the sector lying west of the Moselle up to the boundary of Detachment "C" was held by one Division, the 255th, and was about five kilometers in length.

German "pill box" or machine gun emplacement in Bois de Mort Mare.

The Combres Group was organized as the Fifth Corps, the Mihiel Group as the 12th Reserve Corps; while the Gorz Group, against which the 89th Division attacked, was not, so far as is known, organized as a corps.

In examining these reports, it must be kept in mind that the German clock time was an hour faster than our own, so that six o'clock in the morning in German reports means five o'clock in ours.

The German forces opposite our immediate front were, from east to west, the 77th Reserve Division commanded by Lieutenant General Adams, and composed of the 332nd, 419th and 257th Regiments of Infantry, in the order named. Its sector extended from the vicinity of Remeneauville on the east to a point just west of Flirey on the west. Then came the 10th Division, holding the line in the vicinity of Loupmont on the west, commanded by Major General Gresster and consisting of the 6th Grenadier and 398th Regiments of Infantry. Thus the adversaries of our 353rd and 355th Infantry were troops of the German 77th Division and the adversaries of our 356th Infantry were troops of the German 10th Division.

By the French Intelligence Service, the 77th German Reserve Division was rated a third-class division, on a scale of excellence of five grades. On the other hand, the 10th Division was rated by the French as a first-class division.

The 10th Division had seen hard service in some of the most important engagements of the war. It had been originally formed in Polish Silesia, but had received a large injection of Prussians. It had been engaged at Verdun, on the Aisne and Chemin des Dames. It had been severely defeated by the French in the Douaumont sector at Verdun in October, 1916, and had had severe fighting during the campaigns of 1917. It had participated in the spring offensives of the German Army in 1918, going into the line on March 23rd and for a second time in the Aisne offensive where it reached Chateau-Thierry. It also entered the line again in July on the Marne and participated in the retreat over the Vesle until the beginning of August. It entered the line opposite to us on August 20th, relieving the 227th German Division.

It will thus be seen that the enemy troops were no novices, but seasoned, veteran divisions, formidable opponents. The reports do not recite how many divisions were in Detachment "C," but state that the front of 84 kilometers was held with an average sector of 12 kilometers to the division, thus indicating seven divisions in the line, which number was confirmed by our own

Searching German prisoners before admitting them to the 4th Corps prisoners' enclosure, Menil la Tour, Sept. 15, 1918. Nearly all prisoners taken by the 89th Division in the St. Mihiel offensive were cleared through this enclosure, part of which may be seen in background. S. C. 25169.

intelligence reports; it further states that there was at first only one division as a reserve behind the army and that three more were hurriedly brought up later. It therefore appears that at least eleven German divisions were engaged, with the possibility of more. As a comparison to these facts, it will be remembered that the 89th Division, before the attack, was holding a sector the front of which was sixteen kilometers, and that the whole battle on the American side was fought by nine American and one French divisions, not counting the French Corps which held the nose of the angle and did not advance, nor reserves which did not participate in the action. It must not be forgotten, however, that the American divisions, both nominally and actually, are much stronger numerically than the German divisions and that in the all important matter of morale of the troops there was little likeness between our high-spirited men and the discouraged and disillusioned German soldiers. These advantages, however, might have been expected to have been offset somewhat by the greater experience of the German forces, particularly in the higher commands and the staffs; and also by the fact that they were defending carefully prepared positions, with every advantage of terrain and the practically impregnable defenses of Metz behind them.

THE REPORT OF GENERAL FUCHS

The report of General Fuchs starts off with something of an excuse and a slur upon the troops of the command. The writer mentions that he had among his troops the 3rd Landwehr Division, the 1st Austro-Hungarian Division, "the completely used up 192nd Division" and the 77th Reserve Division, "considered unreliable." He states that the difficulty of holding this dangerous salient with only a slight force had always been clearly realized, that only a defensive battle called "Michel" was worked out and that to prevent deep penetration of the salient before evacuation was completed he had requested four assault divisions, two field artillery regiments, ten battalions of heavy artillery and a reinforcement of the air forces. In as much as he had twelve divisions under his command (counting the 255th), tremendous advantages of position and was intending to fight only a rear-guard action, it would seem that General Fuchs was not one to take a chance if he could help it. He then quotes in full the letter he had previously written to his superiors requesting the relief of the 77th Reserve Division because of the number of desertions from the Alsace-Lorrainers in that organization and mentions the requests he had made for another division or two to put in between the 10th and 77th Reserve Divisions "in order to re-inforce the obviously too-weakly held front at that point." It will be remembered that the point of junction of these two divisions was the supposedly impregnable Bois de Mort Mare. The writer also goes on to remark that on August 27th and September 2nd he had made representations relative to assigning to his command the sector of the 255th Division, "shown to be especially urgent in view of the tense situation;" and that this request was not granted until 5:45 A. M. on the day of the battle. This sector was that lying between the left of the 77th Reserve Division and the River Moselle. Thus having cleared his decks for action by taking a fling at his own troops and his next higher commander, the General is ready to tell what happened. It is all very human. What defeated commander ever failed to blame his troops for his defeat; and what military person is there anywhere, from the lowest private to the highest general in any army, who fails to harbor a more or less vivid sense of irritation towards his next higher commander?

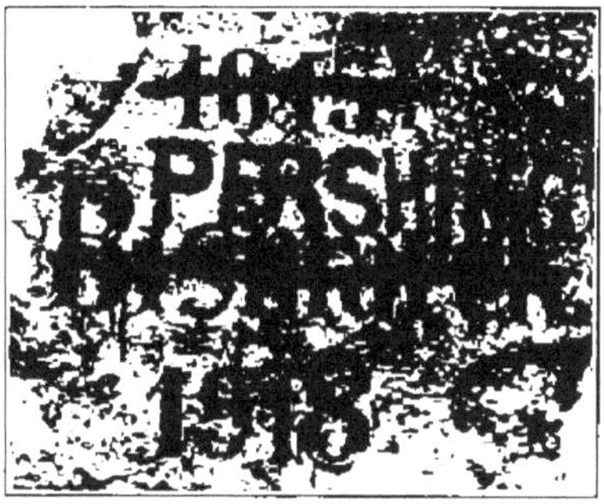

American revision of a German sign at Bouillonville after the St. Mihiel offensive, Sept. 22, 1918. S. C. 25333.

The importance attached to the sector over which the 89th Division advanced is shown by the mention that special orders were issued in anticipation of the battle providing for the assembling of the reserve divisions behind the army at Dampvitoux, St. Julian and Onville, "and for conducting them into the sectors of the 77th Reserve and the 10th Division."

The report then details the frantic efforts to fortify the positions upon which the battle was to be fought. The main line of resistance was to be the "line of artillery protection," and this is identified in other parts of the report as the line, on our front, of the heights above Bouillonville running from Thiaucourt to Beney. Beginning August 25th all working forces, minnenwerfer companies, pioneer companies, gas projector companies and even resting Austrian regiments were set to work to complete this line. Thus it appears that nearly three weeks of intensive work had been put in to fortify a line which our troops penetrated on the first day of the attack. To this line also, the report states, the Army sent its entire artillery reserve, nine squadrons and three light batteries on September 5th, "to support that flank, which was considered to be especially endangered."

On September 7th it was decided, and on September 9th the plans were all worked out, for an attack on the southern front (ours), the object of which was "to shatter the enemy's offensive preparations." But this plan was abandoned. Why, oh why, General Fuchs? You say in your report, "because a highly important change in the situation had occurred in the meantime—the probability of a simultaneous hostile attack against the western front of Army Detachment 'C' had increased materially." But had you not been feeling out this same southern front for days and weeks? Had you not sent against it first your patrols, and then your specially selected shock troops and finally had you not launched elaborate raids with heavy artillery preparations? Had you not issued peremptory orders to your divisions and regiments that our positions must be penetrated at all costs, and spurred the flagging spirits of your men by the offer of reward for the capture of American prisoners?—All, all in vain.

LETTERS OF GERMAN SOLDIERS

The sturdy Americans frustrated every attempt. It is all very well for you and your division commanders, "in conference at Montmedy" to make plans

German prisoners marching through the streets of Bouillonville. They were mostly from the 10th German Division with some from the 77th Reserve Division. The picture shows them to be in fine physical condition and of proper military age. They were cut off in Bouillonville by our heavy artillery fire and the rapid advance of the infantry. Note the French civilian woman, one of many who remained in their homes through the entire battle.

and to put into your reports pompous phrases about shattering the enemy; but what about your men who are to do the shattering? How about the spirit of your old veterans of your famous 10th Division,—your "decima legio,"—like Grenadier Langner of the 6th Grenadiers who was writing about this time to some "Dear Joseph" complaining that "every evening strong patrols are sent out to bring in prisoners but they are always driven off by the Americans." Or Grenadier Erich Becker, one of the Scout Detachment of the same regiment who was writing that on the very day, September 9th, when you were shattering the enemy's offensive preparations on paper at Montmedy, he and his comrades "ran on to the Americans with from 40 to 50 men. There was a damned mix-up. We had one severely and one slightly wounded. It was right by the enemy's lines. So you see that we can't sleep at night and have to tend to that by day. And then we are all full of mud and wet through."

Or Heinrich Kirschke, of the 47th Infantry Regiment, writing from Pannes, whose regiment seems to have been a little more lucky than the rest and captured a couple of American prisoners (not from the 89th Division, be it said). These prisoners had the bad manners, so Heinrich reports, to say that the Americans would be in Germany in eight days. Which induced Heinrich to add, plaintively, "We few fellows cannot hold up this superior might and must all go helplessly into captivity and of course most of the prisoners are murdered."

Oh no, General Fuchs, your bold words are merely words. The Americans are on your front. You have tested their temper and you know it is true and ardent. The lies which you and your kind have circulated have come home to you; and poor, stupid Heinrich Kirschke whom, with his comrades, you thought to frighten into holding fast by fostering the belief that the Americans murdered their prisoners, has been, by that very lie, thrown into a panic. It is not time to shatter the enemy's preparations, though you have the men and the material. Better get back to safer places. And so you do. "It was decided to obtain an order from the Higher Command for the immediate starting of the Michel movement (withdrawal to the Michel positions)."

WORK OF REMOVAL AND DESTRUCTION

The report goes on to state that on September 10th, before the desired order was received the work of removal and destruction was ordered to commence, and telegraphic request for reinforcements was made. "Army Head-

German gun wrecked by our artillery fire. Perhaps one of those referred to as "burst in bore" in the German official reports of the St. Mihiel engagement.

quarters gave its approval and stipulated that the movement which had been in preparation for weeks should be completed by 4 A. M., September 12th. Thus, on the morning of September 12th, the work of removal and destruction was in full progress. Some of the unmounted batteries had already been withdrawn (Mihiel Group) and the others were to be withdrawn that night. The Gorz Group was engaged in moving back its main line of resistance. The available counter-attack divisions were so placed that they could be used either on the western or southern front. This was the situation when the enemy's attack struck the Army Detachment by surprise on the night of September 11-12."

Poor Fuchs, what a time you had! After your enemy's intention to attack was so obvious as to be common knowledge of even the soldiers in the ranks, after you had spent nearly three weeks in preparation of a new line of resistance, after you had brought up and placed your counter-attack troops, after all this, to be surprised!

In the few lines of this report, General Fuchs catalogues every excuse that a defeated general ever gave for his defeat,—poor troops, a higher command at times dilatory and again unreasonably impatient, superior forces of the enemy and, finally, surprise.

THE ATTACK BEGINS

The next document is another report of General Fuchs detailing the events of September 12th. It is dated, like the first, on September 19th. In it he relates the commencement of our artillery preparation, which convinced him "that the expected large scale attack had begun." Accordingly he alerted three divisions which he had in reserve, the 31st, 123rd and 88th, and sent them forward, the 31st to Xammes and the 123rd to La Grange en Hays Farm before the infantry attack began.

The report proceeds: "The enemy's infantry attacked at 6 A. M. At 4:20 A. M. it was reported to the Army Group, in reply to an inquiry, that the evacuation would not be begun as there were no compelling reasons for such action at that time."

Naturally enough. There were no compelling reasons, for the infantry had not attacked. If, however, it had been the intention to evacuate the salient, the time to do so would have been before the infantry attacked.

The report proceeds "The events which took place after the attack had begun, showed, however, that the lightly held southern front was not capable of sustaining the attack of greatly superior forces."

By 11:15 (German time) it was reported that the enemy had broken through the 77th Division. This would be our 89th and 2nd Divisions. Telephone communication with the Gorz Group had been broken, and the commander of that group on his own responsibility had, at 10:45 and 11 ordered the 31st and 123rd Divisions to make a simultaneous attack against the flank of the advancing enemy, the former through Thiaucourt, the latter in the direction of Vieville. At 11:50 the Gorz Group reported:

"The enemy is southeast of Thiaucourt and at Tautecourt Farm. The 77th Reserve Division appears to be annihilated. No information yet concerning the counter-attack of the 31st and 123rd Divisions."

General Fuchs then proceeds: "At the time of this report, the enemy had, therefore, already advanced to within one kilometer of the main line of resistance of the 'Michel' position. Furthermore, the left wing of the 10th Division had undoubtedly been outflanked and driven back by the 6-kilometer penetration near Thiaucourt. There was not only the danger of a break through at the vital point of the 'Michel' position, but also a serious threat at the line of retreat of the Mihiel Group which was still in the salient."

This comment makes clear the fact that the main line of resistance of the Michel position was not the Hindenburg line, to which the Germans were finally driven, but was the line of entrenchments on the heights above Thiaucourt and Bouillonville; for Thiaucourt is nearly six kilometers from the Hindenburg line running through Dampvitoux, Charey and Rembercourt. It shows further that the main line of resistance upon which all available labor had been spent since the first intimation of the coming attack, August 25th, and upon which General Fuchs intended to fight the coming battle, was threatened within five hours of the jump-off. It was entirely in our hands by early afternoon. There can be no pretense that the Battle of the St. Mihiel Salient was merely "a long-premediated withdrawal to previously prepared positions." General Fuchs kept his main forces in their lines on the faces of the salient, after he was convinced that the large scale attack was about to begin. He intended to hold these lines if he could, but at all events to fight

German minnenwerfer emplacement in Bois de Euvezin. This was a portion of the German second position on the south face of the St. Mihiel salient. Note the tree branches fastened to the front of emplacement and scattered on the ground below. These were used as camouflage.

Thiaucourt being shelled by the Germans and burning after its capture by the 2nd Division, supported by the 89th in the St. Mihiel offensive. S. C. 25273.

the battle to a decision on the Michel position on the heights above Thiaucourt and Bouillonville. His troops were expelled by force from the front lines of the old salient and were driven back in such disorder by our impetuous advance, that he was unable to make a stand at the chosen position. He was defeated at every point and in every phase of the battle on the testimony of his own report. There remained to him nothing but to try to save from capture as many men as possible.

At noon (German time, 11 o'clock by ours) he issued the following order to the Mihiel Group: "The withdrawal will begin at once." Accordingly the retreat of this 12th Reserve Corps began. As appears from the report of its commander, its headquarters were in the chateau at St. Benoit. Keen anxiety was manifested at Corps Headquarters lest the attacks to the east of this point (which were being made by our Division and the 42nd) should penetrate to St. Benoit and cut off the retreat and especially Corps Headquarters itself. Some reserves were hurried up to prevent this—some companies which had been sent back to work on the entrenchment of the Michel position and the 65th Landwehr Infantry from the 5th Landwehr Division. In the meanwhile, the main body of the Group consisting of the 5th Landwehr Division and 192nd Division were hurrying to the rear. They had not been heavily engaged through the morning, for no attack on their positions was contemplated. The activity on their front was merely a diversion, made by the French Colonials around the nose of the salient. Yet it is characteristic of the German fondness for big words and sounding phrases to have described these sorties in the following manner in the report of the 12th Reserve Corps: "The 192nd Division reported at 2:15 P. M. that the enemy had attacked the division. In front of Sector E. I. North the enemy had been annihilated in the wire entanglements."

THE RETREAT FROM THE SALIENT

The retreat of the 12th Reserve Corps was parallel to the line of our advance. It began shortly after noon under verbal orders of General Leuthold, which were confirmed in a written order issued at 1:10 (German time). This order provided for the commencement of what was called in the quaint German fashion the "Loki" movement and directs the transfer of the defense to the "Schroeter Zone," a line running from one kilometer east of Deuxnouds to Champrez Pond. But by 1:52, the 5th Landwehr Division reported that Pannes and Nonsard had been surrounded and captured, which, to General Leuthold "signified that the situation had grown decidedly worse" and that "the order issued by Army Headquarters at noon to hold the Schroeter Zone had become obsolete."

The 5th Landwehr Division reported that on its own responsibility it had sent two resting battalions which were already in the Schroeter Zone as a garrison, to counter attack in the region north of Heudicourt, and "drive back the enemy beyond the line Pannes-Beney in the direction of Bouillonville."

And General Leuthold agreed to this arrangement, stating in his report, in a tone of despair, "There were no other forces in sight for the protection of the flanks."

It will be remembered that at this time, shortly after noon by our time, our division was in the occupation of the heights north of Euvezin and confronting the high ground along the line Thiaucourt-Beney. The 42nd Division,

French refugees from behind the German lines arriving at Flirey Sept. 14th, 1918, during the St. Mihiel offensive. They were fed by the 89th Division and transported to the rear by trucks. S. C. 25305.

on our left, had taken Pannes and Nonsard. These German reports show that two counter attacks on these positions had been ordered, one by the troops of the 5th Landwehr Division from the direction of Heudicourt, which would have taken us directly from the left flank; and one by the entire 31st German Division, which was assembled at Xammes with orders to attack through Thiaucourt, which would have struck the point of junction of our right flank with the left of the 2nd Division. The German counter-attack troops were all fresh, none of them having been engaged; our men, on the contrary, were naturally somewhat disorganized and exhausted by hard fighting and the rapid advance through the muddy field. It is quite likely that had these counter-attacks been made simultaneously and pressed with courage and determination they would have given us considerable discomfort, but they were not pressed. It is doubtful if they were ever even launched. It is certain that they did not delay our advance an instant. The only possible explanation of the collapse of the German defense is that the morale of the enemy, already low, had completely evaporated under our artillery preparation and spirited infantry advance.

MORE LETTERS

Who would have expected H. Walter, of the 6th Grenadiers, to do much effective counter attacking in the frame of mind which he exhibited the day previously, writing to his "Dear Aunt and Uncle," to whom he said: "For here it rains day in and day out. We are lying outdoors here under the open heavens. We never get dry and the things we have on our bodies will certainly rot. You have no idea how bad we feel. We get such bad food, worse than a dog, and the men have no more courage."

T. Tiedthe, of the 47th Infantry, was on the same day, writing to his "Dear Meta": "We are expecting every day an American attack and when the bombardment starts we will get it from three sides. * * * What have we done that the whole world has designs on our lives? If the Americans attack we will be in Metz in two days."

Front of chateau of St. Benoit, St. Mihiel Sector. The building was the headquarters of the 12th German Reserve Corps, and from the roof General Leuthold and his staff watched the retreat of their troops from the salient. The chateau was unharmed during the battle and was used immediately after as headquarters for a brigade of the 42nd Division. Realizing that the place was too conspicuous for this purpose, the brigade moved to other quarters. The following day the German artillery opened upon it, setting it afire and reducing it to the ruin shown in the picture. When the 89th Division took over the sector of the 42nd, headquarters of the 353rd Infantry were established in the cellar of the ruins and occupied until the Division was relieved.

Fritz Pieper, a non-commissioned officer of the 47th Infantry, wrote: "The men are so embittered that they have no interest in anything and they only want the war to end, no matter how. We are certainly only the slaves of our government." And M. W. Herman, of the same regiment wrote: "I am so nervous that at the sound of every shell I fall to my knees and trembling overcomes me. I never used to have that."

Compare the state of mind of the writers of such letters with that of our own gallant men, who had also been lying out under the open heavens and on whom just as much rain had fallen, and it will be very plain why the ordered counter attacks failed, why the retreat of the German army from the St. Mihiel salient became a rout, and the opportunity for obtaining a measure of success on that stricken field passed.

The rest of the story is soon told. At 2:30 (German time) the headquarters of the 12th Corps was transferred to La Chausee from St. Benoit. The main body of the corps retreated through St. Benoit and by roads to the west, their right flank protected by the 10th German Division which was being forced back to the vicinity of Beney, but which was maintaining its front. Assault troops were being brought up by rail from Briey. The 88th Division was en route from Conflans by automobile to relieve the 5th Landwehr. This news was communicated to the troops. Orders were issued to retire to the Michel I Zone, which seems to have indicated what we call the Hindenburg line, and is to be distinguished from the Michel Zone, the line parallel to the old southern face of the salient, and practically a bretelle or switch line connecting the old positions with the new.

Some works of destruction were accomplished during the retreat. Water towers at Heudicourt and at several railroad stations were destroyed, and, as General Leuthold states in his report, "The Roman Fort was systematically blown up, the majority of villages and camps were set on fire." These were the fires which presented so terrible and beautiful a sight to the observer passing over the heights to Bouillonville in the early evening, and which excited mingled feelings of exultation at the visible token of the enemy's defeat and withdrawal and at the same time regret and resentment for the destructive processes of war.

BACK TO THE HINDENBURG LINE

During the night, the 12th Corps reached the Hindenburg Line, and reinforced, took up positions for defense. It had lost 1,100 men and three guns, but this was a matter for congratulation to its commander and to the Detachment Commander. It had been able to outrun our advancing columns and to take a position which our orders did not permit us to assault. This fact affords the only consolation for the German commanders. Hear them:

General Leuthold: "The very great danger which had been continually threatening during the afternoon and evening of September 12, namely, that the enemy would advance from Dampvitoux Woods into the Michel I Zone and break through at that point before forces were available for its defense, was obviated. The enemy had not followed."

General Fuchs: "It is due only to the energetic stand of the Combres Group, to the splendid leadership and conduct of the Mihiel Group, and to the timely decision made by the Army Command upon its own responsibility, that the Mihiel Group was able to make the 30 kilometer flank march with heavy rear guard fighting and the loss of only 1,100 men and three guns (with burst in bore) and was able to reach the Michel position next morning after having been joined by the Assault Regiment and the 88th Division. Two flank detachments of the 5th Ldw. Division and the failure of the Americans to recognize their tactically favorable position prevented the latter from bringing catastrophe to Army Detachment 'C.' At the same time the attacks of the 31st and 123rd Infantry Divisions, even though they gained but little ground, prevented the penetration of the Michel position northeast of Thiaucourt."

This comment of General Fuchs seems hardly to do justice to his 10th Division, which though driven back with fearful losses did not lose its organization and was always between our forces and the 12th Reserve Corps. He does not omit a tribute to his own sagacity in ordering the retreat of the 12th Corps, which, however, would probably have retreated about this time without orders. The comment of both generals shows how lucky they thought themselves to have escaped greater disaster. And it is but justice to the 12th Reserve Corps to admit that they ran well.

But the interesting feature to us is the complete obliviousness to the greater peril to their cause from the American operations then taking shape elsewhere. Both generals criticise us for not following up our advantage and penetrating the Hindenburg line. But that was no part of the plans of our Commander-in-chief. Even while you are penning your reports, Generals Fuchs and Leuthold, the American artillery is on the move to the scene of another and greater battle. The Hindenburg line will be penetrated, never fear; but not where you expect it to be. Your great fortress of Metz will be cut off, but not on your front. Take what comfort you can from the situation, there is little enough. The despised Americans, whom you and your ilk have assured your deluded troops and countrymen were too fond of the dollar to risk their skins in the field, have met you breast to breast and man to man. Our inexperienced staff has planned a major operation and executed it precisely as planned; while the vaunted foresight and skill of your high commanders and your experienced staffs have failed to accomplish a single one of the results they set for themselves even in an anticipated and purely defensive battle.

GENERAL LUDENDORFF'S ACCOUNT

The impression prevails in some quarters that the St. Mihiel operation was practically the mere pursuit of an enemy already in the act of withdrawal. That this is not the fact appears from the account of the operation by General Ludendorff in his recently published Memoirs. He states that at the end of August, an American offensive between St. Mihiel and the Moselle had seemed probable and that General Headquarters had pushed up reserves. That he (Ludendorff) had discussed the evacuation of the salient with the Chief of

German machine gun in place, abandoned in second line trench when American troops swept over the German lines in the St. Mihiel offensive Sept. 12, 1918. Empty shells under the machine gun and filled belt to left, behind which is short ladder used to climb in and out of trench. Empty belt to right of machine gun. Above it and to right gas alarm signal horn. Dugout shelter for machine gunner is underneath. S. C. 23439.

Staff of the army group and of Army Detachment "C," but that local commanders were confident in spite of his demurs, that General Headquarters was reluctant to evacuate the salient, on account of the industrial centers lying behind, and unfortunately did not order this step until September 8. His account of the operation is as follows:

"The work of evacuation had not been carried very far when, on September 12, the attack developed between the Rupt and the Moselle, accompanied by a secondary offensive movement against the northern end of the salient on the Combres heights. The enemy penetrated our line in both places. On the southern sector he broke through a Prussian division, and the reserves were not sufficiently close enough up to restore the position immediately. On the Combres heights there was an Austro-Hungarian division, which might have fought better. As early as noon the local army headquarters ordered the evacuation of the salient. I was dissatisfied with myself, but also with the local command. The earlier reports indicated that the evacuation was proceeding satisfactorily, this being facilitated by the enemy not following up. I founded my official communique, which turned out later to be too favorable, on these reports."

The phrases "penetrated our line" and "broke through a Prussian division" are incompatible with any other idea than that of a successful assault of positions determinedly held. It is gratifying to the 89th Division also to note that the direction of the atttack on the south face of the salient,

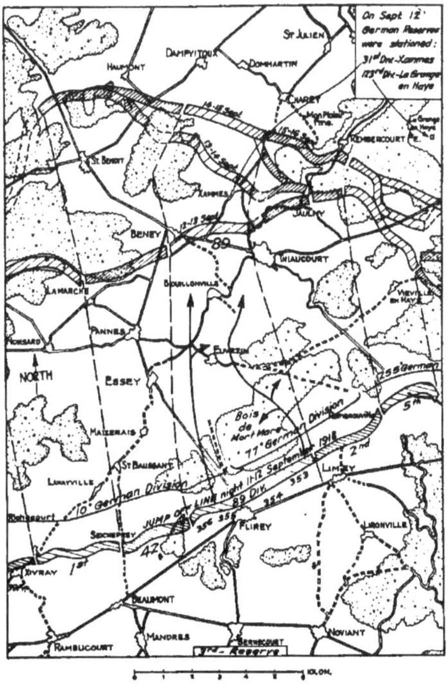

St. Mihiel offensive, September 12-15, 1918. Sectors and lines of advance of the 89th and adjacent Divisions, showing their approximate position each midnight. From Metz-Commercy map.

as shown on the map of the operation in Ludendorff's Memoir, is substantially our sector and that of the 2nd Division, namely from a point slightly east of Flirey to one slightly east of Regnieville.

CONSOLIDATING THE POSITIONS

During the next few days, the 13th to the 15th, the troops were engaged in consolidating the position, digging first shallow pits usually called fox-holes, then connecting these up so as to form a trench, stringing wire in front and generally preparing the ground for their own comfort and security against harassing fire and attack.

This was a most trying period. In the first place, all the men were tired after the long stay in the trenches and the rapid advance in the battle. Supplies of all kinds were slow in getting up and there was many an empty stomach. The labor was arduous and had to be done at night and all night, while in the day time little genuine rest could be had by men lying in cramped positions in their little fox-holes, subjected all day long to galling and well regulated artillery fire.

But the most disheartening feature was the apparently useless changes of position, so that it seemed to the tired man that the work he did on one night would be sure to be abandoned on the next night and recommenced only a few yards further forward or back. The man swinging the pick could not and did not know of or understand the reasons for these, to him, purposeless and vexatious changes. He did not realize that our front was only a little part of the whole army front and that all the parts of the whole had to be adjusted to one another; that we were confronting the Hindenburg line which had been prepared by the German engineers in entire deliberation and after prolonged study both of the ground to be occupied by them and the ground to be occupied by us; that every slight accident of the ground, every fold of the earth, had its military advantage or disadvantage, all of which had been cunningly taken into account by the enemy and which required corresponding skill and care on our part if we were to have an equal chance with him; the soldier did not know of the larger plans involving the attack then in preparation in the Argonne and that in consequence it was required that our line be made so strong that it could be held by few or exhausted troops while the new fight was going on elsewhere. The man with the pick and shovel didn't know or realize these things. He didn't like to dig, anyway; he would rather fight. He hoped we would push on up to Metz and get into the German trenches, which were at least deep enough even if the dugouts did face the wrong way. And so he grumbled and growled but, nevertheless, went on and did his duty as he was told in a very competent way.

It was during this period that Private Charles W. Earl, Headquarters Troop, 89th Division, was wounded while making a special trip with General Wright. In spite of his injury he refused to be evacuated when advised and remained at his post as courier, courageously fulfilling all his duties and assisting in maintaining liaison between Division Headquarters and the advanced elements.

Most of the wiring was done by the Engineers, who also supervised and did much of the work on the trench system and shelters throughout the area, in addition to road work.

CHANGES OF POSITION

Summarizing and anticipating the narrative of events up to the time of our departure from this sector, it will give some idea of our ceaseless activity to say that in addition to countless minor shifts of position and reliefs within organizations, the following movements took place between September 13th and October 8th, when the Division left the sector. On the night of September 15-16 the outpost line on the right was advanced nearly a kilometer; on the nights of the 16th-17th and 17th-18th our own divisional artillery joined us, relieving French artillery; the night of the 19th-20th and the following night the 354th Infantry took over from the 353rd Infantry the right sub-sector, the latter regiment going into brigade and division reserve; the night of September 21-22 the 177th Infantry Brigade took over the entire Division front, the other brigade going to the rear as division reserve and for training; as a part of this movement the 353rd Infantry relieved the 356th Infantry on this and the following nights; the night of the 22nd-23rd was further enlivened by a raid on the German positions made by troops of the 356th Infantry.

On September 26th a raid with artillery preparation was made at dawn by the 354th Infantry near Charey, netting prisoners; on the nights of September 29-30 and September 30-October 1 the 178th Infantry Brigade relieved the 177th Infantry Brigade in the occupation of the front lines (or Trench Zone), the latter supposing it was going to the rear as division reserve and for training, and that for the first time since August 6th all parts of this brigade would be out of immediate contact with the enemy; but on the night of September 30-October 1 our division took over the sector occupied by the 42nd Division on our left, the 177th Brigade occupying the position with the 353rd Infantry in the line and the 354th in reserve; on the night of October 4-5, our front was extended to the right so as to hold half of the sector till then held by the 78th Division, which had previously relieved the 2nd Division in this sector. The 356th Infantry took over this sub-sector; and thus we touched elbows again with the 90th Division on our right, renewing old acquaintances of trench days and forming new ties which were to be strengthened a little later in the Meuse-Argonne fighting. Finally, on the night of October 7th-8th and 8th-9th, the Division was relieved in the entire sector by the 37th Division and was assembled on the 8th and 9th in the vicinity of Commercy. It had been in the line or in battle continuously for two months and a day, perhaps the longest period of uninterrupted conflict which any American division was called upon to endure.

THE NEW SECTOR

Our sector, as finally occupied, was known as the Limey-Flirey-Pannes Sector. It extended from the Lake of La Chausee, inclusive, on the west, to

Hill 321.4, about half a kilometer southeast of Rembercourt, on the east. It was between ten and eleven kilometers of front. It was divided into four substantially equal sub-sectors called, respectively, from west to east, the Benoit, Bois, Xammes and Jaulny sub-sectors. These were held, in the order named, by the 353rd, 354th, 355th and 356th Infantry Regiments. On our right was the 90th Division and on our left the 39th French Division. Head-

Pannes (St. Mihiel Sector) being shelled by the Germans Sept. 27, 1918. Dust from shell breaks at left. American observation balloon over church in distance. The town was captured by the 42nd Division and later occupied by the 89th Division when the latter took over sector of the former after the advance. S. C. 25291.

quarters of the Division were Euvezin; of the 177th Infantry Brigade at Pannes; of the 178th Infantry Brigade, in the woods just west of the Essey-Bouillonville Road, about a kilometer north of the Euvezin cross road. The headquarters of the 353rd Infantry were in the chateau of St. Benoit, from the tower of which the officers of the 12th German Corps had watched the retreat of their troops, but which now was in ruins as a result of the continual fire of the German batteries. The headquarters of the 354th Infantry were in huts in the woods in the southwest part of Bois de Dampvitoux; of the 355th Infantry, at Beney, and of the 356th Infantry, in a ravine near the railroad station east of Thiaucourt.

THE 164TH ARTILLERY BRIGADE

Our own splendid artillery brigade furnished our supporting artillery, the 341st Field Artillery supporting the 177th Infantry Brigade and the 340th supporting the 178th Infantry Brigade. The howitzers of the 342nd Field Artillery were divided between the sectors. Companies "A" and "D" of the Motor Battalion of the Ammunition Train left Camp de Souge, Sept. 13th, traveling overland in 70 trucks to join the rest of the battalion with the Division. The Horse Battalion joined on September 22nd. The train was stationed at St. Baussant, where Company "F" was placed in charge of an ammunition dump and remained, much to its disappointment, till the close of the war.

The first shot fired by the 340th Field Artillery against the foe, perhaps the first from the brigade, was from Battery F, Captain Donald S. Lamm commanding, located near Thiaucourt, at 10 P. M., September 16th. Sergeant Warren O. Engelbrecht was chief of the section, and the gunner corporal, appropriately named, was Corporal Vincent L. Shotwell.

The high state of discipline and training of our artillery brigade, the fine dash and enthusiasm of its officers, the excellent liaison established with the infantry, all contributed to make this period of trench warfare highly satisfactory, so far as the coöperation of the two arms of the service was concerned. It was with deep regret that we parted with the artillery brigade when the division was relieved, and many an effort was made thereafter by General Wright to secure its return to us for use in the great coming battle.

The disposition of the troops in the sector was in conformity with that which had prevailed before the advance. We had now become experienced in the routine of this mode of warfare, reliefs moved off without friction, liaison groups were established as a matter of course, trench stores and plans of defense were properly preserved and turned over, and generally all the modes of trench life were again resumed.

Elaborate plans of defense of the Division, brigade and regiments were made, and on relief, duly turned over to the 37th Division.

THE ENEMY'S DISPOSITIONS

Through observation of the ground, airplane photographs, reports of patrols, captured German maps and the examination of prisoners, we soon came to know quite a great deal about the positions in the enemy's lines and his troops and their dispositions.

The general line which the Germans occupied was called by both armies the Hindenburg line. The name for it in this sector, given by the Germans, was the Michel I Zone for the advanced positions and the Michel II Zone for those more retired. It was organized by them on the same general plan as our own positions, with lightly held advance positions garrisoned by scattered combat groups, and with a main line of resistance further to the rear. Work upon the position had been commenced two years before in conformity with the general principles governing the entire Hindenburg line—selection of defensive positions on the reverse slopes, tremendous use of concrete in the construction of dugouts and emplacements and great use of wire and accessory defenses. The dugouts and wire were complete, but the trench system was unfinished, large sections of the trenches being little more than traces on the ground. The rear positions were not organized in the open, but the woods had been at least partially prepared for defense. The flanks of the sector were well protected by natural obstacles, the wooded heights east of Rembercourt on the enemy's left and the impassable pond of La Chausee on his right. The intervening country was in the main open and rolling. His line passed through Rembercourt, Mon Plaisir Farm, Charey, Dommartin and

Men of 314th Sanitary Train, 89th Division, caring for wounded at Bouillonville, St. Mihiel Sector, Sept. 20th, 1918. S. C. 25322.

Dampvitoux, each of which had been converted into a strong center of resistance, surrounded both front and rear with bands of wire. The dominating feature of the front was an eminence upon which was situated Mon Plaisir Farm. The high ground which terminated in this eminence extended northeasterly for several kilometers. From it, observation of nearly our entire line was possible. Dampvitoux was also high, affording from its buildings good views of our lines.

Four German divisions were in the line opposite us—the 123rd on the east up to the railroad running southwest from Rembercourt; the 31st from this point on to Mon Plaisir Farm; the 88th to the vicinity of Haumont; and the 5th Landwehr to the western limits of the sector. By this time they could all be considered poor troops. The German regiments had all been reorganized with three companies to the battalion instead of four as formerly. All three of the companies of the front line battalions were in line, each with a platoon on outpost in front of the line and equipped with two machine guns. The second platoon of each company was in the front trenches, the third in the support trenches. The use of two machine guns in each outpost platoon indicated the great reliance the enemy placed on this weapon for fire effect.

A GERMAN PLANE COMES DOWN

On September 24th, shortly before noon, a fine new German L. V. C. two-seated biplane, with its aero camera intact, was brought down, landing in the open ground near Xammes. The pilot and the observer were captured uninjured. The anti-aircraft machine gun detachment had alone fired at the circling plane and is believed to have brought it down. The observer, however, bitterly accused the pilot of treachery. The pilot claimed that his plane was not hit, but was forced to descend because of broken steering gear. The pilot had lived in the United States and spoke English well. As the two prisoners were being taken in an automobile to the rear, the German artillery opened up its usual noon-day harassing fire on Bouillonville and the roads nearby, searching for our kitchens and the artillery ammunition dump

The result of a direct hit by a German shell on an American truck at the Div. Q. M. dump at Bouillonville Sept. 24, 1918. Two men were killed and two wounded, in rescuing whom Corporal Billie Belt, 314th Supply Train, won the D. S. C. Two German aviators, who had been brought down within our lines, were being taken to the rear when this truck was hit nearby. Both jumped from the automobile and, without seeking to escape, sought safety in flight. S. C. 30020.

in the vicinity. One of the shells broke near the car carrying the two prisoners and set fire to an American truck in the Quartermaster dump at Bouillonville. With one accord, the two prisoners leapt from the car and fled wildly across the country, seeking not liberty but safety. They were soon rounded up and resumed their journey.

These Germans could have witnessed, at this time, one of those act of heroism of which all the American soldiers seemed capable in emergencies. The truck which was hit was loaded with gasoline, which took fire and began to explode. Two of the men on the truck were killed and two were severely wounded by the shell, and were in deadly peril. Corporal Billie Belt, of Company "B," 314th Supply Train, who was rear lookout on a truck that had just passed, rushed to the burning truck, in spite of the danger from exploding bidons of gasoline, and rescued one of the men. After carrying him to safety he returned and attempted to disentangle the second man from the burning wreckage, but found it impossible.

RAIDS ON DOMMARTIN WOOD AND CHAREY

On the night of September 22-23, 1918, the 1st Battalion of the 356th Infantry, then commanded by Major Mark Hanna, made a raid from the shelter of Bois de Dampvitoux and Bois de Charey upon the enemy's positions in Bois de Dommartin. The raiders were compelled to advance from the shelter of the woods and cross nearly a kilometer of open country before gaining the enemy's positions. Supported by heavy artillery fire, and identified to one another by white bands around the arm, two companies of the battalion, with the other two in support, dashed across No Man's Land through heavy artillery and machine gun fire, encountered and engaged the enemy, inflicting severe losses and returned with four prisoners.

Private John J. Dorgan, Co. C, 356th Infantry, although wounded four times at the start of the engagement, continued with the advance and was of great assistance to his platoon sergeant in maintaining control under heavy fire. Lieutenant Eilert Heiken, 356th Infantry, wounded in the shoulder at the beginning of the attack on Bois de Dommartin, likewise continued until his mission was successfully accomplished.

Rather severe casualties were suffered by the raiders. Their efforts were all the more gallant and praiseworthy, because, on the previous night this battalion had been relieved in the occupation of this sector and had marched, after the relief, nearly nine kilometers back to the vicinity of Essey and had repeated the fatiguing march over the muddy trails through the woods on the night of the raid in order to get into position by "H" hour.

On the night of 25-26 September, 1918, or rather in the early morning of the 26th, a picked party of 100 men of the 354th Infantry, under the command of Captain (then 2nd Lieutenant) Marshall P. Wilder, executed a raid on the plateau Grande Fontaine about a kilometer southwest of Charey. The raid was a part of the demonstration made that night along the entire front of the American Army in order to support the attack then being begun in the Argonne and delude the enemy as to the location of the real attack. The men who executed this raid had been specially selected and trained for such activities out of the entire regiment. To promote the efficiency of his regiment in this important function, Colonel Babcock, the commanding officer, had conceived the idea of forming a sort of corps d'elite of raiders, men who showed special aptitude for the work and who should be characterized by courage, dash and initiative. They were authorized to wear a special device on their uniforms. The honor of belonging to this body was eagerly sought. They were placed under the command of Captain Wilder, whose qualities of leadership, cool intrepidity and powerful physique peculiarly qualified him for the position. Many raids and patrols had been conducted by this organization. Subsequently another such unit of 100 was organized under Captain Herman McNulty, which alternated with the first in these operations.

For the occasion in question, careful preparations were made and a rehearsal of the part each man was to play was conducted in the rear areas; the ground was reconnoitered in advance, both by daylight observation and by night patrols; the artillery preparation was carefully coördinated with the infantry movements. As a result the raid was entirely successful. Two prisoners were captured who furnished valuable information, many of the enemy were killed and our own casualties were light. The raiders penetrated as far as Charey itself.

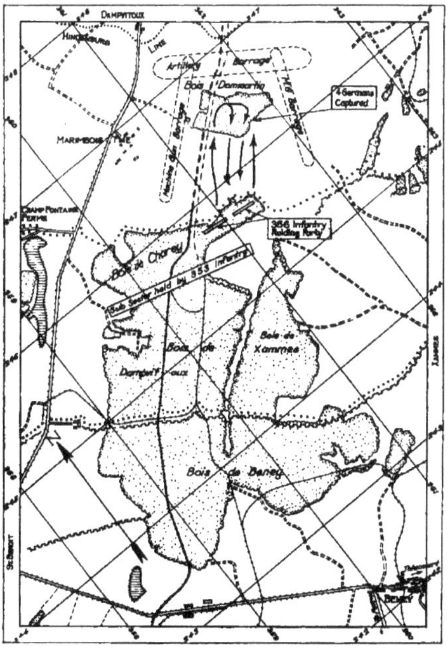

Bois de Dampvitoux and vicinity. Scene of raid by the 356th Infantry on the Bois de Dommartin, Sept. 22-23, 1918.

One feature of the raid in question showed the value of careful forethought and preparation. It frequently happens, in operations of the kind, that most of the casualties occur on the return from the raid. The raiding party, having the advantage of surprise and the protection of our artillery fire, usually can penetrate to the desired position without much loss. But on the return trip they are exposed to the enemy's retaliatory and barrage fire and ordinarily suffer most of their losses then. A striking example was the raid made by the 82nd Division during the period of the relief of that division

A street in Thiaucourt Sept. 21st, 1918, during the shelling and burning of the town by the Germans after its occupancy by American troops during the St. Mihiel offensive. S. C. 25329.

by our own; the raiders suffered no casualties until nearly back to their own lines, when the enemy's artillery caused them severe losses.

To avoid this danger, advantage was taken of the terrain. The objective of the raid was a German position situated on a high plateau running from southwest to northeast; this plateau fell away sharply on the side towards our lines in a steep slope covered with clumps of trees and underbrush. Instead of retiring directly to our lines, the raiding party, as planned, halted after the raid in the shelter of this slope in No Man's Land, and the inevitable hostile barrage fell harmlessly between them and our trenches. The position was kept until the barrage ceased; then, in broad daylight, the entire party trickled back in small groups to the shelter of our trenches, taking advantage of the cover afforded by vegetation and the folds of the ground. Thus all the party returned safely to our lines, and with but a few casualties.

The raiding party was formed into 5 groups, 3 of them of about 20 men each, comprising the fighting line, and 2 groups of 26 and 9, respectively, in support. The party was also accompanied by 15 engineers and a medical detachment of 14 men, under Major (then Captain) Paul Withington. In addition a support detail with machine guns and automatic rifles, under command of Lieutenant Holcombe, guarded the flanks of the raiders with their fire. The raiding party was assembled in our front line position north of Xammes at 11 P. M. on the night of September 25th. The artillery demonstration commenced at 11:30 in a wonderful roar of guns extending from the Argonne around the positions before Verdun, across the base of the old St. Mihiel salient and down through the Vosges to the extreme limit of the American sector.

Under cover of this fire the raiding party passed the wire, crossed No Man's Land and assembled under the bluffs which form a bold barrier facing southwest at the extremity of Plateau of Grande Fontaine. Here places were assigned to each man and small outpost parties were pushed forward part way up the hill. The movement had attracted no attention from the enemy and drew no fire. In the shelter of this high bluff, within a stone's throw of the German position the raiders lay through the entire night prepared to make the assault at dawn. Promptly at 5:30 the barrage which had been playing upon the German positions upon the Plateau and back at Charey, lifted and commenced creeping along the Plateau. A whistle signal of three sharp blasts was given and the advance started. The left com-

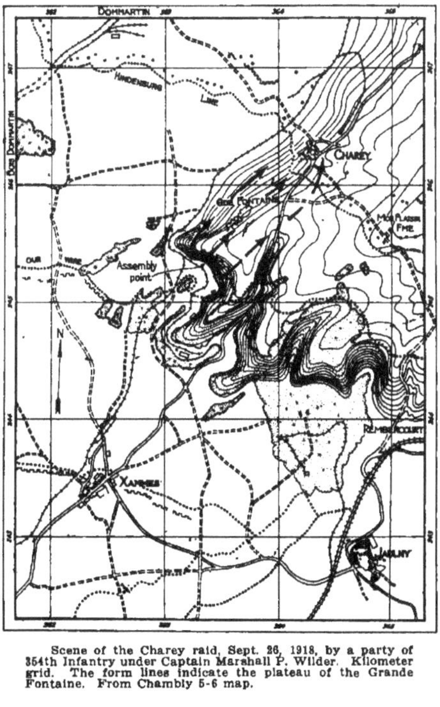

Scene of the Charey raid, Sept. 26, 1918, by a party of 354th Infantry under Captain Marshall P. Wilder. Kilometer grid. The form lines indicate the plateau of the Grande Fontaine. From Chambly 5-6 map.

bat group, under command of Sergeant Bargfrede, Company "H," 354th Infantry, met with little resistance as it surmounted the crest of the hill. It met and overcame resistance offered by four light machine guns and a body of about twenty riflemen. The route of this group lay along the slope of the hill, its left resting upon the railroad track which runs to the northeast. The center group met severe resistance at the very crest of the hill from at least three machine guns of the light type. The right flank group, under command of Sergeant Anthony, Company "B," 354th Infantry, was confronted by three machine guns of the heavy type which were abandoned by their gunners on the advance of the raiders. The guns were too heavy to be moved and were left behind by the raiders as they returned after they had disabled them as far as possible by firing rifle shots into the mechanism. This party encountered three dugouts which were blown up—in one seven dead Germans were found. To overcome the resistance in the center and on the right, the supports were brought up by Lieutenant Wilder and with their aid the enemy was overcome, but this early resistance had cost about ten precious minutes, during which the barrage had crept forward. Upon clearing the crest of the hill the raiders were compelled to run to catch up with the barrage, firing as they ran upon the retreating Germans.

The advance continued following the barrage until the designated objective was gained, Lieutenant Wilder commanding the entire advance from a position with the center group. The German wire was found to be in rather poor shape and the engineers had little to do to enable the infantry to penetrate it. By 6 o'clock the raiding party had penetrated the German wire on its objective, the right group having partially encircled Charey and penetrated to its outskirts from the southeast. Thereupon Lieutenant Wilder sent up rockets which had been agreed upon as the signal for retiring. The party came back, blowing up two dugouts on the way and carrying their dead and wounded. At least twenty Germans were known to be killed—the number of wounded was, of course, unknown. The woods and trees were searched for possible live Germans. The two prisoners captured were sent to the rear carrying our wounded in a litter.

The raid demonstrated that the enemy had no actual position of resistance between our lines and Charey and that the hill was merely an outpost position strongly held by riflemen and machine guns. The opinion of Lieutenant Wilder was that Charey could be taken at any time in 30 minutes.

The raiding party reassembled at the foot of the bluff from which the raid had begun. All men were then accounted for and the raid was over by 6:30 A. M. During the day the party in small groups returned without accident to our lines. Our own losses were one dead and seven severely and four slightly wounded.

Sergeant Bargfrede, who performed excellent service in this raid, was afterwards distinguished by being commissioned 2nd Lieutenant for gallantry in action, the only enlisted man in the Division and one of very few in the A. E. F. commissioned without passing through the schools.

352 353

On the night
lieved the 42
249 had held the
The 42nd no
Battle.
This practica
248 sector, exten
Chaussee an
Benoit and
held by an en
247 front.
This new sect
177th Inf. Brig
the 340th F.A.
246 by the 178th Inf. B

An excellent bit of patrolling was done about this time by 2nd Lieutenant Harry W. Pine, battalion scout officer of the 3rd Battalion, 353rd Infantry, who had previously won distinction immediately after the St. Mihiel drive by alone reconnoitering in advance of our lines, crossing a wide No Man's Land, walking along the wire of the Hindenburg line and actually penetrating gaps in it, being the first man of this Division to accomplish this feat. On October 4th, 1918, Lieutenant Pine, with a patrol of eight men, moved out of the lines of his regiment north of St. Benoit with the mission of reconnoitering in the vicinity of Haumont and gaining identifications of the enemy from the town, which was an outpost in the Hindenburg line, and had been most bitterly held. He worked his way with his patrol through the enemy outposts, circled the town to the west and came to a road leading into it from the north. Here he heard an enemy patrol coming down the road. Waiting until he could actually see them in the dark, he opened fire with an automatic shot gun, killing one and seriously wounding another. He kept his patrol well together. and after a short wait boldly entered the town from the north, down the same road that the enemy's patrol had come, and proceeded through the entire length of the town. There he encountered two German soldiers, whom he made prisoners and brought in, as valuable identifications, to our lines.

On the night of October 5-6 a shell burst directly above an ambulance on a narrow road near Jaulnay, killing the driver. Wagoner Roscoe C. McTeer, 354th Ambulance Company, 314th Sanitary Train, who was acting as

Haumont, where Lieutenant Pine's patrol, after encircling the town and driving off a relief detail, entered the town from the rear and engaged the garrison, making some of them prisoners.

ambulance orderly with him, grasped the wheel with great presence of mind, brought the machine to the side of the road so a following ambulance could pass. In spite of the constant shelling of the road ambulance service was maintained, McTeer taking the place of the fallen man for the remainder of the day.

THE 37TH RELIEVES US

The 164th Artillery Brigade was not included in the relief of the Division, but remained in support of the 37th Division, which came to the sector without artillery. The incoming division had been utterly worn out in the grueling conflict of the Argonne and the relief was not completed until the night of Oct. 8-9. Units of the 89th Division upon being relieved slung packs and marched back some twenty or thirty kilometers to the vicinity of Commercy. Here, billeted in towns beyond the range of any German gun save Fat Bertha herself, and able for the first time in two months to hang gas mask and "tin derby" on a nail, all hoped for a few days' rest. Nor was this hope entirely abandoned when on October 9th, the Division again started on the move, this time in French trucks, with a rear area in the Argonne as the ultimate destination. But when on arrival the Division was made part of the reserve of the First American Army, and when maps and descriptions of the Argonne territory began to be distributed, it was clearly brought home to all that the hoped for rest was but a change of sectors, and that the only rest would be that incidental to the shift. Yet weary as they were, the prospect of entering the new battle accorded with the spirit of the men of the Division. We had seen successively the 1st, 2nd, 42nd and finally the 78th taken from our sector and sent into the Argonne fight. We did not want to be left out. We wanted a little rest and then to get at the enemy again.

EN ROUTE TO THE ARGONNE

The route of the Division to its new area lay through the towns of Gironville and Boncourt and thence to Erize St. Dizier, just beyond which it fell for a distance of fifteen kilometers along the famous "Verdun Road," the "Sacred Way." It is related concerning this road that in the fall of 1914, General Petain, who was commanding the French forces about Verdun, anticipated that the Germans would in time direct a strong attack against Verdun, and that such an attack would undoubtedly cut the railroad lines supplying the city and the surrounding territory. He therefore ordered the road connecting Verdun with Souilly and Bar-le-Duc remade and widened. Consequently when the German attack in the summer of 1916 did cut the railroad lines, as he had so remarkably prophesied, a line of communication from Verdun to the rear was still open, and the Crown Prince, watching the bloody battle from the heights of Montfaucon, was at last forced to turn way in disappointment. Forsaking this road at Erize la Petite the column proceeded along the valley of the River Aire through Fleury, Rarecourt and Auzeville to the vicinity of Recicourt. The 314th Supply Train and other motor transportation of the Division, however, did not follow this route, but proceeded through the recently captured St. Mihiel, down the valley of the

Meuse almost to Verdun itself, and thence by way of Blercourt and Dombasle to its destination. In order to avoid congestion of the roads the field trains of the Division were routed to the new area in still another way.

In this move the Division experienced for the first time an acute shortage of transportation. With some difficulty and a succession of hauls all baggage and supplies had been moved from the front, but now the organizations were forced to leave behind great stores of property, including many trophies of the St. Mihiel fight, which they could only hope to send for later.

The French trucks that accomplished the move were driven by swarthy orientals from the French colonies of Annam and Tonkin. Because of scarcity of man power the French Army used these men in all troop movements by truck transportation, saving its own drivers and mechanics for use at the front. The trip to Recicourt and vicinity was made by the French trucks in a single night, the night hours being chosen for traveling so that the movement might not be perceived by the enemy. All equipment and troops other than foot troops were moved by the 314th Supply Train.

The district in which the Division now found itself lay immediately east of the central part of the great Argonne Forest, and south of the road from Verdun to Ste. Menehould. Since being overrun by the Germans in 1914, it had been in a continual state of poverty and desolation—a state that had not been improved by its long use as a rest area for troops entering or leaving the line. It was just in rear of the ruins of Avocourt, which had formed a central starting point for the terrific American attack on Sept. 26th, and close enough to the present German lines to be the scene of nightly bombing attacks. Since the small dilapidated towns in the area could only accommodate a few men, most of the troops were obliged to camp in the woods.

INTENSIVE TRAINING AGAIN

Here the Division at once set about the cleaning up, refitting and training so long anticipated and so sorely needed. Five hours of intensive training were given daily. The regimen consisted of such disciplinary training as was thought necessary to bring the command up to its standard, and instruction in combat exercises for the remainder of the time, special emphasis being laid on the nature of the resistance to be expected in the Argonne sector and the means of overcoming it. At this time new men were received from the 86th Division, which had been broken up and used for replacement purposes immediately on arriving overseas. These replacements were fine stalwart men from Michigan and Wisconsin, eager to participate in the training, and well qualified to take a place among the veterans of the 89th.

WE JOIN THE FIFTH CORPS

On leaving the Commercy Area the Division had been assigned to the Third Army Corps, still remaining in the First Army, commanded by Lieutenant General Hunter Liggett. On Oct. 12th, however, it was transferred from the Third Corps to the Fifth Corps, which at this time comprised the 32nd and 42nd Divisions, both occupying front line positions. The 89th was ordered to move to the vicinity of Eclisfontaine and Epinonville in support of these divisions. The Fifth Army Corps, of which the 89th now became part, had, under the command of Major General George H. Cameron, played a decisive part in the St. Mihiel operation by descending from the hills on the western face of the salient, known as the Cotes de Meuse, into the Woevre Plain, and there effecting a junction with the troops that had attacked on the south. Coming to the theater of operations between the Meuse and the Argonne Forest it had on Sept. 26th in conjunction with the Third and First Corps, carried the primary defensive positions of the enemy, including the dominating height of Montfaucon. When the 89th came up in its rear Major General Charles P. Summerall had just been placed in command, and the Corps was in the act of capturing the formidable Kriemhilde Stellung.

On October 13th the Division left the Recicourt Area, and, winding in succession past the stones that had once been Avocourt, the shell torn No Man's Land to the north, and the endless lines of wire and trenches that had been concealed by the blasted stumps of Cheppy Wood, spent the night under the shadow of Montfaucon. Next morning the troops again took up the march, and about noon came to bivouac in the mud around Epinonville and Eclisfontaine. Division headquarters was established at the former town, the 177th Infantry Brigade at the latter, and the 178th Infantry Brigade on a hillside midway between the two. Due to traffic jams on the roads most of the rolling kitchens did not catch up with the organizations until late on October 14th, but the men endured both hunger and exhaustion without a murmur.

UNDER FIRE AGAIN

Thus, on October 14th, only five days after its last elements had been withdrawn from the front line in the sector of Thiaucourt-Xammes-Beney-St. Benoit-Pannes, the 89th found itself once more under shell fire, acting as reserve of the 5th Corps in rear of the 32nd Division and awaiting orders to relieve that division in the line of battle. The next five days were spent in making thorough reconnoissance of the routes to the positions held by the 32nd Division, in training and refitting as well as circumstances and the necessity of concealment from the enemy would permit.

Finally the orders came to relieve the 32nd on the night of October 19th-20th. So well had the previous reconnaissance been performed and so thorough was the discipline now established in the 89th, that the relief of the 32nd was accomplished practically without the use of guides from that division. This was most gratifying to the 32nd, worn out by the hard fighting it had just gone through, and furnished the occasion for a much appreciated letter of commendation from Major General W. G. Haan, the Commanding General of the 32nd Division.

And now, after only ten days respite, half of which had been spent on the move, and the other half within the zone of artillery fire, our division once more was in immediate contact with the enemy and engaged in the great Meuse-Argonne battle, which had been begun, as an American operation, on the 26th of September and was destined to continue until the victorious termination of the war.

CHAPTER V.

THE MEUSE-ARGONNE OFFENSIVE

The war sped to its denouement in the campaign of the summer and fall of 1918, with a celerity that amazed the world and astounded even the belligerents themselves. The German began the campaign in the spring with the avowed intention of terminating the war before America could throw her military power into the conflict. The devotion and gallantry of the French and British prevented the attainment of anything more than local successes and denied the enemy that decision in the field which he coveted, and his victories brought him nothing but exhaustion. He had won the battles and lost the war.

The stupendous effort of America in organizing, training and equipping her vast forces and of Britain in assuming the chief burden of transporting them turned the scale of war in midsummer, and within four months crushing defeat in the field forced the German to forever abandon the high hopes which had been his in the spring, and to acknowledge himself vanquished.

PERSHING'S DECISION TO COMMENCE THE OFFENSIVE

It has been noted how the sudden fluctuation of the fortunes of the Allies had first caused the abandonment of the plans for the operation at St. Mihiel and their sudden resumption. The continued success of the British and French on the other fronts had afforded the prospect of even greater results from more extended operations. So that even before the St. Mihiel operation was commenced, plans were revised and a greater and more promising offensive was determined upon by General Pershing. Accordingly instead of pushing the St. Mihiel advance to the fortified area of Metz and maintaining through the winter the menace of the fortress, as had been originally planned, the advance was limited to the location of the Hindenburg line and preparations were begun for a great offensive north of Verdun in the Argonne district. A successful advance here would cut the vital railway communications between the German armies on the eastern and western portions of the line. Such an offensive had been in contemplation for the campaign of 1919. But since the Germans were reeling under the succession of blows delivered all along the front, General Pershing with boldness and audacity determined to take the chance of delivering a fatal thrust with what forces he had and in the state of preparation they then were. He sought and obtained permission of the Supreme Commander for the attempt. With a staff and army working at top speed the plans were perfected, the enormous concentration of men and material was effected without premature disclosure to the enemy, and the attack was launched on September 26th, just two weeks after the beginning of the St. Mihiel operation. The grim purpose of the Commander-in-chief is expressed in the following words in his report:

"We expected to draw the best German divisions to our front and consume them, while the enemy was held under grave apprehension lest our attack should break his line, which it was our firm purpose to do."

THE TERRAIN

The terrain over which this great battle was fought was what is known as the Argonne region, from the Forest of Argonne which lies in it. It is a rough and hilly country lying between the marshy plains of the Woevre on the east and the level, chalky Champagne district on the west. The Meuse River flows through it in the general direction of southeast to northwest. There are many forests besides the Argonne, most of the woods and forests lying on high ground. The valleys are cultivated as far as possible, but there are many steep hills and deep ravines.

Both sides of the Meuse valley are bordered with high, wooded hills. Protected by the range of hills beyond the Meuse ran the important railway from Metz, through Mezieres and Sedan to the districts of Belgium and northern France. In the southern border of the Forest of Argonne and across the Meuse to the north of Verdun had run the enemy's lines for four years. Strongly organized for defense, both by the nature of the country and by every device of military art, this line had held, though strong attacks had been made upon it by the French earlier in the war.

GENERAL DESCRIPTION OF THE BATTLE

Only a few divisions that had been tried in battle were available for the initial attack. The veteran divisions were either engaged in the St. Mihiel operations or refitting after their efforts there. Of the nine divisions in the line of battle, only two had previously participated in serious fighting. But with the dash and courage which had characterized all the American troops the initial attack swept irresistibly forward, mastering on the first day all the first-line defenses. The advance continued on the 27th and 28th against increasing resistance as the enemy flung into the conflict division after division of his reserve troops. By the night of the 28th a period of relative stability had arrived. But the advance had penetrated from three to seven miles; our troops had taken more than 10,000 prisoners, had gained commanding positions at Montfaucon, Exermont, Ivoiry, Epinonville and elsewhere, and more than all had gained our point of forcing the battle into the open. From this time to the end of the war there was no more trench warfare on this part of the American front; strongly organized positions there were—machine guns cunningly sited, entanglements and trenches to overcome—but no settling down into a position to hold it. Every halt in the attack meant merely the bringing up of reinforcements, artillery and supplies to resume the advance.

A strong reaction by the enemy after the initial advance was to be expected, for the German High Command was keenly alive to the catastrophe which would follow success on this front, and good roads and ample railroad facilities were available for bringing up artillery and reserves. General Pershing's desire and expectation to draw the best German divisions to this front and consume them, were fully met. Division after division, the pick of the German Army, advanced in vain counter attacks or clung with desperate courage to every point of vantage. But with steady, persistent pressure, with determination to advance that could not be resisted, the American divisions were sent forward to fight to the point of exhaustion, then yield place to fresh divisions who took up the advance. Slow and plodding was the progress for the next few days through the impenetrable thickets of the Argonne Forest, and the woods and fields east of it, for which so many gallant Frenchmen had given their lives in vain in the earlier stages of the war. Fierce counter attacks in strong force on every part of the line were repelled, though strongly supported by artillery with the continual use of gas shells. Every advantage of the ground was with the enemy, for notwithstanding his reinforcements it was we who were doing the driving, and the broken character of the country favored the defense and subserved the methods which he employed, the prodigal use of machine guns manned by highly trained veterans and artillery firing at short ranges. But step by step and inch by inch the enemy was forced back.

This slow progress was terminated, and what is regarded as the second phase of the battle was begun on October 4th, when a concerted attack commenced all along the front. Continual and brilliant fighting went on, until by the 10th of October the Argonne Forest had been cleared of the enemy and positions were within reach from which a final assault on the heights of the Meuse could be launched. The attaining of these positions by a series of local thrusts marked the conclusion of the second phase of the battle. During this period the 89th Division was brought into the line, and its operation in clearing the Bois de Bantheville was one of the last of the operations which placed in our hands the positions from which the final, great attack of the war was to depart. This second phase of the battle terminated on the 23rd of October. From this time until the 1st of November no attempt was made to advance, but every effort was concentrated on the preparation for the great coming attack.

THE SECOND ARMY FORMED

In consequence of the enormous number of men engaged and the great extension of the front, it had become necessary to constitute a Second Army before the final offensive. General Pershing, who had personally commanded the First Army in addition to performing the functions of Commander-in-chief, now turned over the command of the First Army to Lieutenant General

Hunter Liggett. The divisions which were in the sector of the Woevre, east of Verdun, were organized as the Second Army under the command of Lieutenant General Robert L. Bullard. Major General Dickman was assigned to the command of the 1st Corps, Major General Charles P. Summerall to the 5th Corps and Major General Hines to the 3rd Corps. These changes occurred on the 10th of October, while the 89th Division was en route to the

Road near Forges in the Meuse-Argonne camouflaged to prevent observation of traffic from any direction. Oct., 1918. S. C. 26103.

Meuse-Argonne battle. It thus became a part of the Second Army on the 10th and 11th of October, but on the 12th was transferred to the First Army and ultimately assigned to the 5th Corps, which then consisted of the 1st, 2nd, 32nd and 42nd Divisions in addition to our own.

PERSHING'S REPORT

The following extracts from the final report of General Pershing covering the last phase of the Meuse-Argonne offensive will serve to show the relative importance of the operations of the 89th Division.

"On the 21st my instructions were issued to the First Army to prepare thoroughly for a general attack on October 28th, that would be decisive, if possible. In order that the attack of the First Army and that of the Fourth French Army on its left should be simultaneous, our attack was delayed until

November 1. The immediate purpose of the First Army was to take Buzancy and the Heights of Barricourt, to turn the forest north of Grandpre, and to establish contact with the Fourth French Army near Boult-aux-Bois. The Army was directed to carry the heights of Barricourt by nightfall of the first day and then to exploit this success by advancing its left to Boult-aux-Bois in preparation for the drive towards Sedan. * * *

On the morning of November 1st, three army corps were in line * * *; the Fifth Corps occupied the center of the line with the 89th and 2nd Divisions, and was to be the wedge of the attack on the first day.

By nightfall, the Fifth Corps, in the center, had realized an advance of almost 9 kilometers, to the Bois de la Folie, and had completed the capture of the heights of Barricourt. * * * By the evening of the 4th, our troops had reached Laneuville, opposite Stenay, and had swept through the great Foret de Dieulet, reaching the outskirts of Beaumont. * * *

On the night of the 10th-11th and the morning of the 11th, the Fifth Corps, in the First Army, forced a crossing of the Meuse east of Beaumont and gained the commanding heights within the rëentrant of the river, thus completing our control of the Meuse River line. At 6 A. M. on the 11th notification was received from Marshal Foch's headquarters that the armistice had been signed and that hostilities would cease at 11 A. M. Preparatory measures had already been taken to insure the prompt transmission to the troops of the announcement of an armistice. However, the advance east of Beaumont on the morning of the 11th had been so rapid and communication across the river was so difficult that there was some fighting on isolated portions of that front after 11 A. M."

RELIEVING THE 32ND

When the 89th Division relieved the 32nd Division on the night of the 19th-20th October, it had been planned and was anticipated that the general attack would be launched immediately. In consequence, the relieving troops entered the line in order of battle. Their formation was in conformity to the orders of the Corps Commander, whose experience was that the highest efficiency of the Division was best obtained by the formation of the brigades side by side and the regiments of the brigades side by side, each regiment formed in column of battalions, with one battalion in the fighting line and one in support; this formation thus left four additional battalions, of which one was to serve as brigade reserve for each brigade, and two for division reserve.

The 32nd Division was considerably disorganized by the violent fighting it had had. Just previously it had taken by storm strongly fortified positions forming part of the German line known as the Kriemhilde Stellung. All four of its infantry regiments were in the line, but their elements, through the exigencies of battle, had become considerably intermingled, so much so that a regular relief by brigades was impossible. The organizations were much depleted, the exact location of the lines in the Forest of Bantheville, which covered a large part of the front, was uncertain, and the disorganization which followed their severe fighting was so great that the troops had been unable to bury their own and the enemy dead for several days.

CAPTURE OF COL. BROWN

An interesting and unfortunate event at this time was the capture of Lieutenant Colonel Levi G. Brown, the highest ranking American officer captured by the enemy during the campaign. Colonel Brown was acting as G-3 of our division. On October 18th the Division was bivouaced around Epinonville, acting as reserve for the 5th Corps and expecting to relieve the 32nd

Mud Camp of the 314th Field Signal Battalion and other troops of the 89th Division at Epinonville in the Meuse-Argonne, Oct. 16th, 1918. No matter whether you dug a fox hole to sleep in, which filled with water before morning, or merely lay down in the mud without digging hole, you wished you'd done the other thing. S. C. 30014.

Division in the line at once. In preparation for the relief, Colonel Brown started out on the morning of the 18th to reconnoiter the front of the sector held by the 32nd as reported by that division the night of the 17th. On his way to the front, Colonel Brown was informed by four different members of that division that the line was five kilometers north of a line through Romagne, his last informant locating our front lines about a kilometer and a half north of La Dhuy Farm. In point of fact, La Dhuy Farm itself and all the northern part of the Bois de Bantheville were still held by the enemy. Colonel Brown and his orderly, Private Charles Garrison, Headquarters Troop, 89th Division, rode forward to a point about 75 meters from the road running through Landres-et-St. Georges and La Dhuy Farm and about two kilometers east of Landres-et-St. Georges. They there dismounted and were at once fired on by machine guns from Bois des Hazois. Colonel Brown's horse was killed and the orderly's horse ran toward the German lines. Colonel Brown and Private Garrison took cover in shell holes nearby and then, running from shell hole to shell hole under continuous fire, succeeded in getting nearly three hundred yards back towards our lines. At this point Colonel Brown lost contact with his orderly. He feared that Garrison had been hit and was unwilling to leave him wounded and alone in No Man's Land. So he remained for thirty minutes, calling at times for Garrison. It transpired that Garrison had been wounded, but that he had, before this, succeeded in gaining cover in the Bois de Bantheville and was seeking troops to come to the rescue of Colonel Brown. In the meantime the Germans sent a patrol from the direction of La Dhuy Farm. Colonel Brown was surrounded by them and taken to the German lines. The orderly reported the events as far as he knew them, and in spite of his wounds, accompanied patrols which were at once sent out from our lines. The ground was reconnoitered as far as possible in the day time and thoroughly by night by a patrol led by 1st Lieutenant R. G. Hudson, but of course without avail.

Colonel Brown was conducted to the headquarters of the 41st German Division at Le Champy Haut. His route lay through Bois des Hazois, Remonville, Barricourt and Nouart, places which fell into our hands some weeks later. The German corps headquarters were at Stenay and an officer from the Corps conducted the prisoner thither and then questioned him. Colonel Brown refused to answer questions and the officer thereupon recounted to him correctly every move the 89th Division had made from the time it entered the Lucey sector, stating when and where we had received replacements, and giving our move by truck from Commercy to Recicourt. He said we had relieved the 32nd Division the night of October 17th, thus displaying powers of prophecy as well as of divination, since the relief did not actually take place until the night of the 19th-20th. It was an excellent demonstration of the efficiency of the German Intelligence Service. This officer spoke freely of the prospects of peace and was fearful that the Allies, elated by their successes, would not abide by President Wilson's fourteen points. He indicated a line on a map running through Namur-Mezieres-Sedan-Stenay-Metz, which he claimed would be difficult for the Allies to break that winter, stating that by spring they would probably give Germany better terms of peace than at that time. He doubted the ability of the Americans to conduct a winter campaign. He treated Colonel Brown very courteously and rationed him at his own mess while Colonel Brown remained in Stenay. Colonel Brown was finally taken to a prison camp for American officers at Villinen. He was well treated, except for food, but after October 25th received abundant food, clothing and other necessities through the American Red Cross. While in prison he was paid at the rate of 100 marks per month and required to pay board at the rate of 54 marks per month.

After the signing of the Armistice, of which the prisoners were informed with its terms, on the 11th of November, they were still kept under guard and restrictions, though promised release from day to day. Finally, the party of 245 officers and men, without formal discharge but without restraint, set out from the prison camp and made their way to Switzerland. Colonel Brown was able to join the Division again just before Christmas in Germany. He had little to complain of as to his personal treatment, but reported that there appeared much hatred on the part of the civilian population in the vicinity of the prison camp towards the Americans, and that from other prisoners of war he learned that the German treatment of them had improved rapidly from July, 1918, as the Allied successes increased.

MOPPING UP BOIS DE BANTHEVILLE

The operation of clearing the Bois de Bantheville had an importance of which the active participants at the time were unaware. As now appears from General Pershing's final report, the entire First Army was at this time awaiting the result of four important local operations which were essential to adjust the positions preparatory to a renewed general assault. One of these was the clearing of the Bois de Bantheville; the others were the advance through Grandpre by the First Corps; the occupation of Cunel Heights by the Third Corps and the occupation of the main ridge south of La Grande Montagne by the 17th French Corps.

The importance of the secure possession of Bois de Bantheville before the final advance on this sector of the front, grew out of the enemy's tenure of the strong position of Landres-et-St. Georges, just west of the forest. The 42nd Division, on our left, had repeatedly assaulted Landres-et-St. Georges and had been unable to take it; as is mentioned elsewhere, the ridge running from Bois d' Andevanne southwest enabled the enemy to supply and reinforce the garrison at Landres-et-St. Georges. The Bois de Bantheville flanked this position and a relatively short advance from the forest would cut this line of communication. But if the Bois de Bantheville as well as Landres-et-St. Georges remained in the enemy's hands at the time of a general assault, a delay might be caused which would imperil the success of the entire operation; for the chief objective on this sector was the Heights of Barricourt which could not be attained except through the Bois de Bantheville and Landres-et-St. Georges. Thus the operation in Bois de Bantheville was the subject of keen solicitude up to the Commanding General of the Army, manifesting itself in continual pressure from the corps upon the Division and from the Division upon the brigades to report the successful conclusion of the operation.

This pressure increased a tenseness within the Division caused by the unexpected difficulties of accomplishing the missions assigned to the two infantry brigades, by changes in the dispositions of the troops after the operation was ordered and by the not unusual little slips in the transmission and execution of orders.

Summarizing for the sake of clearness the details stated elsewhere, the 89th Division took over the sector on October 19th with the two brigades abreast, the 178th Brigade having the sector which included the Bois de Bantheville. The expectation was for an immediate attack in this formation. The clearing of the Bois de Bantheville was assigned as a mission to the 178th Brigade, and from the information received from the 32nd Division this was not expected to be a very severe task. Before the operation could be commenced, the corps order for the coming general attack was changed so as to require it to be conducted with one brigade only as the assault brigade, the other to be in reserve. The 177th Brigade having been chosen for the assault brigade, it was ordered to relieve the 178th in Bois de Bantheville when that brigade should have cleared the woods. The operation proved far more difficult than anticipated and instead of requiring only two platoons as at first planned, three battalions of infantry were at one time and another engaged. Friction developed between the brigades, the battalion commanders of the 178th contending that their mission was accomplished when their troops had reached the northern edges of the forest; and the battalion commander of the troops of the 177th contending that he was not authorized to relieve the 178th until all the enemy had been driven out. All difficulties, both from within and without, were ultimately and gloriously overcome.

The assault battalions of the 178th Infantry Brigade in the relief of the elements of the 32nd Division in the Bois de Bantheville were the 2nd Battalion, 355th Infantry, commanded by Captain Neville C. Fisher and the 1st Battalion, 356th Infantry, commanded by Captain (later Major) John W. Harris. At about 10 A. M., October 20th, these battalion commanders were ordered to co-operate with each other in mopping up the woods. Relying upon the information received from the 32nd Division that the woods were practically clear of the enemy, they decided that a platoon from each battalion would be adequate for the task and agreed to commence the operation on that basis at 2 P. M. About noon, orders came to Captain Fisher that the 3rd Battalion of his regiment would be substituted for his in the operation. This order was later rescinded, but it had the effect of delaying the commencement of the mopping up until late in the afternoon. In the meantime, Captain Fisher had sent a reconnoitering patrol into the woods which reported at about 4:30 P. M. that the woods were strongly held by the enemy and that it would require a considerable force to dislodge them. Revising their plans as a a result of this information, the two battalion commanders decided to use one company from each battalion for the task and selected "F" Company of the 355th and "D" Company of the 356th. The hour set for the assault was 8 P. M. The companies were to form in front of the position then held by "E" Company, 355th, on the hill at 06.15-87.20 and to proceed from there to the north edge of the woods, the 355th taking the west half of the woods and the 356th the east half. At the hour set, Captain Fisher's battalion was at the appointed place, but the company of the 356th had not joined. Two hours were spent by Captain Fisher in an effort to obtain contact with the company of the 356th. It developed later that Captain Harris' battalion had advanced along the eastern portion of the forest independently.

Giving up the attempt to connect with the 356th, Captain Fisher determined to advance unaided and at 10 P. M., sent forward Company "F"

First Aid Station of 353rd Infantry on Romagne-Sommerance Road just south of Bois de Bantheville. Here the wounded in the bloody fighting in Bois de Bantheville were given first aid. This is a concrete dugout forming part of the Kriemhilde Stellung. A direct hit by a German shell in one of the entrances wounded Captain Fox of the 353rd Infantry Medical Detachment and several wounded men.

under the command of Lieutenant Charles K. Bowser, with "E" and "G" Companies in support and reserve respectively. There were but three companies in the battalion, "H" Company having been detached. The delay had given the enemy opportunity to divine our intentions and heavy artillery fire developed along the line of advance. Severe machine gun fire was also encountered from the hill at 06.0-87.8, the southern slopes of which were gained by 3:30 A. M., October 21st. "F" Company was so reduced by losses as to form scarcely the strength of a platoon. At this point, Captain Fisher halted the advance to reform and to obtain, if possible, artillery assistance and contact with Captain Harris.

The 1st Battalion, 353rd Infantry, was at this time in rear of Captain Fisher's battalion. Captain (later Major) Milton Portmann, who had been in command, was severely wounded by a shell fragment in the night and had been succeeded by Captain Allen Barnett.

While Captain Fisher was waiting at his P. C. for a response from the brigade to his request for artillery support, Captain Harris and Captain Barnett came up. Captain Harris reported that his troops had gained the northeastern portion of the forest and, regarding his part of the mopping up as completed, demanded of Captain Barnett that his battalion be relieved at once. Captain Barnett, whose orders were to make the relief when the mopping up of the forest was complete and aware of the strong resistance which Captain Fisher's advance was meeting, did not regard the mission of the 178th Infantry Brigade as accomplished and declined to make the relief.

Brigade Headquarters refused to call for artillery fire on the northern tip of the forest without the assurance from Captain Fisher that there were no friendly troops in front of his position. This assurance he was unable to give. In consequence, he returned to his task unaided and resumed the advance the morning of the 21st with "G" Company as the assault company, "E" Company in support and the scant remnant of "F" Company in reserve. For more than two hours the advance met with sharp opposition from machine guns, but happily without artillery fire from the enemy.

By 1:30 P. M. of the 21st, the enemy was driven from the position on the hill which had stopped the advance, having lost five or six prisoners and ten or more machine guns. From this point the advance proceeded with little opposition; at about 4:30 P. M. the objective in the northwest corner of the woods was reached on a line of approximately 05.60-88.45 to 05.90-88.65.

Captain Fisher then returned to his P. C. to arrange for the relief of his battalion, leaving the battalion under the immediate command of 1st Lieutenant Mack V. Traynor. Lieutenant Traynor selected a good defensive position and had his men dig in. In the night, he received word from Captain Fisher that he was to be relieved by the 353rd. He thereupon sent runners to the 353rd to tell them that he was ready to be relieved, and at 3 A. M., on October 22nd, being, in effect, relieved on the position attained by the assumption of responsibility for the sector by the 177th Brigade, led his men back through the woods that they had conquered without meeting any resistance on the return.

The advance of the 1st Battalion, 356th, commenced at 8 P. M., October 20th, from a position along the edge of the woods north of the road running west out of Bantheville. In order to gain this position, the battalion had had to do some fighting to drive out detachments of the enemy located near the jump-off position and in the edges of the woods. Company "C," commanded by 1st Lieutenant (later Captain) Frank B. Welsh, formed the assault element, with Company "B," under the command of Captain W. H. Schwinn starting in support; but before the action was over, portions of all the companies had been engaged. Organized machine gun resistance was encountered just south of Hill 270, at about 06.3-88.2, and the advance was made under continuous shell fire. The assault elements of the battalion reached the northern tip of the woods at about 5 o'clock A. M., October 21st.

A German artillery officer was captured during the advance. An outpost line was established within the northern edge of the woods, and the front was patrolled along the Remonville-Bantheville road. The main body of the battalion remained in position south of Hill 270 at about point 06.4-87.6. The assault elements in the tip of the forest consisted of "C" Company and a portion of Company "A," commanded by 1st Lieutenant (later Captain) Matthew Winters. After organizing their position, these troops found themselves practically isolated from the main body of the battalion. The enemy was found to be on the front and both flanks. A few runners succeeded in getting through to the battalion commander, but until the final relief by the troops of the 353rd Infantry on the afternoon of October 22nd, no supplies could be sent them and communication was at all times uncertain.

A portion of the "Kriemhilde Stellung," the strong German trench system in the Bois de Bantheville, taken in the Meuse-Argonne offensive by the 89th Division during the latter part of October, 1918. S. C. 31488.

It was during the fighting in the Bois de Bantheville that Private Alex J. Barbier, Headquarters Company, 356th Infantry, although painfully wounded in the head, refused to go to the rear, remained on duty with his platoon and took an active part in the action for twenty-four hours after he was hit.

The situation on the evening of the 21st of October was that the assault battalions of the 355th and 356th regiments had penetrated to the northwest and northeast edges of the forest respectively; their commanders and the commander of their brigade regarded their mission as accomplished and were insisting on being relieved by the troops of the 177th Infantry Brigade. Yet as developed from the reconnaissances made by the 353rd, the enemy was undoubtedly occupying the central northern portion of the woods, was holding on tenaciously, and the 177th Brigade troops were dubious of their right and duty to participate in the necessary mopping up. A delay occurred, the more exasperating to the Division Commander, because of the pressure being applied by the corps on the Division for the completion of the operation.

In view of the demands of General Hanson for the relief of his troops in the forest, demands made with increasing acerbity, both upon the Division and upon the 177th Infantry Brigade, General Winn expressed his willingness to assume the responsibility for the sector; and at 8:05 P. M., on October 21st, General Hanson reported that fact to the Division and in his report stated: "Battalions concerned have instructions to withdraw as prescribed in the instructions from your office." The fact that notwithstanding these instructions, the troops of Captain Harris' battalion in the tip of the forest were not withdrawn until the evening of the 22nd when the troops of the other brigade fought their way through to them, indicates what a misconception there was as to the enemy's forces in the forest and how different was the mission of the 177th Brigade from the mere relief of troops who had been reported as in the secure possession of the position, after mopping it up.

On assuming responsibility for the sector in the early evening of the 21st, General Winn gave orders to the 353rd Infantry to relieve the elements of the 178th Brigade in the forest; but it had now become apparent that the relief could only be effected if the 353rd itself mopped up the forest, a task of appalling difficulty in the night with little preliminary reconnaissance, and the troops as yet not concentrated for an assault. It was not until the following morning that the detailed orders for the advance as a mopping up operation, rather than a relief, were actually issued to the immediate commanders of the troops. The company commanders of Captain Barnett's battalion were summoned to the battalion P. C. in the forest. Colonel Reeves in person supervised the preliminary preparations and General Winn came to the position to see that all was well. Extremely heavy shelling with high explosives and gas shells was in progress, communication with the companies was very greatly hampered, and the battalion P. C. rendered entirely untenable. Considerable delay in starting the operation resulted from this heavy fire, but finally, at 1 P. M. the attack began.

The formation adopted was with the four companies of the battalion abreast, in the order from east to west, "B" Company, commanded by Captain Francis Leigh; "C" Company, commanded by 1st Lieutenant (afterwards Captain) Vernon D. Hunter; "D" Company, commanded by Captain Frank M. Wood and "A" Company, commanded, at the beginning of the operation by 1st Lieutenant William Dolan, and, upon his becoming incapacitated, by 2nd Lieutenant (later 1st Lieutenant) Ruby M. Hulen. The battalion was under the command of Captain Allen Barnett. The objective of companies "A" and "D" was the Remonville-Bantheville road which curved around the northern tip of the woods, Company "A" to clear the northwestern edges of the woods; while the objective of companies "C" and "B" on the right was the northeastern edges of the woods, Company "B" to clear the eastern edges. All four companies encountered stubborn resistance and suffered severe casualties. The fighting was the most desperate that any element of the Division had encountered up to this time. It developed from the examination of prisoners later that substantially an entire regiment of the 13th German division was holding the woods.

Company "B," on the right flank not only encountered severe fire from machine guns on its left in the sector of Company "C," but also found the enemy in a strong position in the eastern edge of the forest. One of the machine gun nests in this position was reduced single-handed by Private John I. Dugan after his teeth and lips had been shot away. In the sector of Company "C" severe machine gun fire was encountered in the center of the woods; after overcoming these guns, the company advanced to the position held by the two companies of the 356th Infantry. They were found dug in at approximately 6.6 x 8.4 and reported Germans to the front and on both flanks in the woods. These companies were relieved and went to the rear. Patrols were thrown out forward and the enemy was encountered across the clearing at 6.6 x 8.5, but withdrew without serious resistance. Company "D" encountered numerous machine guns along a slight ridge at 5.8 x 8.5. So stubborn was the resistance offered by these guns that Captain Wood called for the aid of the Stokes Mortar detachment which accompanied the battalion. Sergeant Harry E. Bayly, of this detachment, brought up his gun and directing its fire by holding it with hands and knees assisted the attack and the enemy was driven out. Sergeant Walter S. Witt, though severely wounded in the face, refused first aid and led his platoon until the final objective was attained. Company "A" encountered the enemy in the western edges of the forest at a point southeast of La Dhuy Farm. After a hard fight the enemy was driven out, suffering severely as they ran across the open. Sergeant Lee B. McDaniels, of this company, though severely wounded, continued to lead his men against the machine guns until they had been taken, and not till then permitted himself to receive medical attention.

At several points in this engagement, the enemy exhibited that treachery of which we had heard, but had never before encountered. After surrendering, a hidden machine gun would be opened on our men as they went up to take the prisoners. Some individuals, incensed beyond control by this treachery, refused to take prisoners during the balance of the engagement.

The entire engagement consumed four hours of bloody fighting. By 5 o'clock P. M., October 22nd, the entire edge of the forest was in our hands, all the elements of the battalion being in contact with each other, and thereafter no Germans entered the Bois de Bantheville except as prisoners.

The spirit of the men is well illustrated by that of Private Earl A. Hoffman, Company C, 341st Machine Gun Battalion, who was severely wounded while dressing the wounds of his comrades, but continued his work until he fainted from pain and was evacuated.

Of the same sort was Private Edward Sittler of the same organization, who gave aid to other wounded men and helped carry them back to the first aid station. Although severely wounded himself he refused to have his own wounds attended to until the others had received attention.

It was during these trying days also that Private 1-cl. Martin L. Larson, Company B, 355th Infantry, and Corporal James L. Melton, Company D, 356th Infantry, distinguished themselves by effective service as runners under heavy shell fire.

The 1st Battalion, 353rd Infantry, remained in the position under severe conditions until the 31st of October, when it was relieved by the 3rd Battalion for the assault of November 1st. Major James L. Peatross was placed in command of the 1st Battalion on October 23rd and commanded it throughout this period.

WAITING FOR THE ORDER TO ATTACK

The 177th Infantry Brigade, having taken over the entire Divisional front, in anticipation of leading off the attack, was subjected to some of its most trying experiences during the period of waiting. The day of the attack was from time to time postponed, awaiting developments on other sectors of the front; and the troops remained in their positions, organizing them, patrolling the front and preparing for the attack from October 21st until November 1st. The 353rd Infantry occupied the right half of the Division's sector, holding the tip and sides of the Bois de Bantheville. On October 28th, the 90th Division took over the northeastern borders of the Bois de Bantheville, the dividing point for the jump-off being the extreme northern tip of the forest. The 354th Infantry held the left half of the sector, the line extending in a southwesterly direction so as to connect with the 42nd Division, whose lines were less advanced than our own because of the German occupation of the strong point at Landres-et-St. Georges.

As soon as our possession of the whole forest was secure, the enemy inaugurated a campaign of harassment that made the holding of the position one of severe hardship. Continuous shelling of the position was coupled with airplane raids upon the troops in the edge of the woods. Worst of all was the establishment of a gassed area extending across the central portion of the forest, which was maintained by an almost uninterrupted bombardment for days with the gas shells. Communication and supply of troops in the tip of the forest must be through this gassed area. The heroism and devotion to duty of the carrying parties, the runners, the litter bearers carrying wounded, and the telephone linemen, whose duties took them constantly through this dangerous area, are alone worthy of a chapter.

CONTINUOUS GASSING

The gassing became exceptionally severe in the last few days before the attack. On October 26th and again on October 27th, beginning about 2:30 o'clock in the morning and continuing until nearly 6:00 o'clock, several thousand gas and high explosive shells were thrown into the southern portions of the Bois de Bantheville and the northern part of Bois de Romagne. The area of concentration was between the front line battalion of the 353rd Infantry in the tip of Bois de Bantheville, and its support battalion in the southern part of the woods. Consequently no troops were in positions of high concentration. In the 354th Infantry, whose outposts were in the open beyond the woods, the area of high concentration was upon positions occupied by the support companies of the front line battalion, the 2nd battalion. Company "F" of this regiment suffered most severely in the bombardment of the night of October 26th, and many casualties resulted from direct hits splashing the gas on the men. The intensity of the bombardment and the darkness of the night prevented the men from being moved until towards

Effect of a direct hit by a German 220 on one of the German concrete dugouts in the Kriemhilde Stellung. This dugout had been occupied by Major Geo. W. Blackinton, 353rd Infantry, as a battalion P. C. until a few hours before it was hit Meuse-Argonne Offensive.

morning, when the troops in the area of high concentration were withdrawn further to the rear, strong outposts and machine guns, however, being left to hold the front lines. The troops in the outposts were supplied with rations during the nights, these being carried up on a horse which was led along the narrow-gauge track southwest of the woods and thence through the open to the troops in the northwestern part of the forest.

Although these gas bombardments produced many casualties, and called for the display of the highest qualities of courage and determination in the men, especially on the part of runners, food details and signal corps men repairing wires in the dark, yet it was demonstrated that the measures of gas defense were effective. Troops who were well disciplined and instructed in gas defense, who used their masks intelligently, kept their clothes carefully buttoned up, did not sit down or linger in low places and reported for treatment at the first sign of injury from the effects of the gas, escaped with slight losses and light cases, even of those affected.

It was also noticeable that the quality of the German gas had deteriorated. It was not nearly so virulent as the gas which had been thrown upon us in the Lucey sector.

A typical, though somewhat gruesome, illustration of the way the men met the conditions is the case of Private 1-cl. Wendell W. Jacobs, Company C, 341st Machine Gun Battalion. When six men of his section were wounded and his own hand was partly severed by a shell fragment, he had another soldier cut it off with a pocket knife and bandage the stump, after which Jacobs assisted the other wounded men before he proceeded to the first aid station, whence he was evacuated to the hospital.

AIR RAIDS ON OUR INFANTRY

It was during this period that the doughboy formed his unchangeable opinion of the air service,--all air and no service. The German planes were exceedingly active over the front lines. Flying low over the outposts and up and down the lines, they machine-gunned the troops cowering in their little fox holes. With no apparent retaliation from our own air forces, they

P. C. Reeves,—Headquarters of 353rd Infantry, on Romagne-Sommerance Road just south of Bois de Bantheville. A typical German dugout in the Kriemhilde Stellung. The tops of these dugouts are flush with the ground and are about five feet thick, of solid concrete. A concrete partition two feet thick runs parallel with the front and entrance to the inner portion is through a door placed opposite the space between the two outer doors, thus protecting the garrison from the effect of even a direct hit in one of the outer doors. The inner partition is pierced with loopholes to enable the defenders to fight even when the attackers penetrate the outer chamber of the dugout. The garrison with its machine guns remains inside during the artillery preparation, but on the approach of the infantry, places the machine guns on top of the dugout and operates them from the fire steps shown on both sides and between the doors.

raided our front lines at will, firing until their ammunition was all expended and then returning to their own lines for more and coming back to repeat the performance. They were gorgeously painted planes, the remnants of the celebrated German squadron known as the "Richthofen Circus."

In point of fact, the official reports show that our air forces were engaged in the performance of excellent service both of observation and fighting back of the German lines. But to our infantry it seemed that the enemy was the undisputed master of the air, on our front at least.

Bois de Bantheville, showing operations Oct. 21st-Nov. 1st, 1918. Kilometer grid. From Dun sur Meuse map.

PRELIMINARY PREPARATIONS

On November 1, 1918, began the great attack which was destined to continue for eleven days of continuous fighting for our Division, to take us forward across the Meuse, twenty-five kilometers away, and to result in the final severance of the German communication with Metz and the collapse of the enemy's resistance.

The contrast with the conditions of the St. Mihiel battle which we had fought six weeks before, was striking. Though for ten days our men had engaged in stubborn fighting in the Bantheville woods, and had borne a succession of daily gas and aerial attacks and constant artillery fire, their spirit was at its height. The Division was thoroughly well equipped, thoroughly well prepared and straining at the leash. The replacements who had joined us about two weeks previously had proved to be of splendid mettle and fine training. They had been by now completely assimilated and were of one bone and spirit with us. Time had been afforded for careful preparation and transmittal of orders. Maps and compasses in sufficient quantities had been obtained. Every man knew the part he was to perform and was eager to be about it.

ENHANCING MORALE

One of the most important of the preliminary preparations for the coming conflict was that which was addressed to the spiritual side of the troops, if it may be so put, the enhancement of the morale, and the perfection of such discipline as would result in perfect control. General Pershing personally visited the Division P. C. at Epinonville and cautioned General Wright particularly as to the necessity for control and taking advantage of American experience in recent operations. And General Wright, by speaking personally to the officers, formally or informally, by addressing the non-commissioned officers of the various organizations, and by talking with the men of every grade, explained the outline, principles and reasons involved in his orders and appealed to their loyalty for control. It was brought home to every individual man that perhaps upon him and upon him alone the success of the entire operation might depend, as, indeed, in the previous fighting, it had been found that the attainment of some critical point by even a single determined man or a single squad, sufficed to gain the position for all.

The Corps Commander, Major General Charles P. Summerall, made daily visits to the Division, often assembling officers and men and speaking directly to them.

The talk of General Summerall to the assembled officers was in tone grim, blunt and somber,—the talk of a fighting man to fighting men. In substance, he spoke as follows:

Entrance of corduroy road to Bois de Bantheville. All supplies to the troops of the 1st Battalion, 353rd Infantry and all the wounded were carried by hand over the corduroy road shown at the right of the picture from the 22nd of October to the 1st of November. This portion of the wood was continually gassed by the enemy and the carrying details and litter bearers had to make their way through the mud at night, without lights and wearing their gas masks.

"When a division enters the line in an attack, it is given an objective to take. That objective must be reached. There is no excuse for failure. Either you take your objective or you do not take it. Casualties among officers will be heavy, as well as among men, although probably eighty per cent of the wounded will come back. Officers must keep well to the front, and when anything goes wrong, it is the duty of the next commander to go up and see what is the matter. The toll of casualties of the senior officers will of necessity be increased by this practice, but the results are more than commensurate with the costs. Control is vital. Divisions have been frittered away by straggling or the pernicious practice of sending details to the rear. In this corps, it is the order that no riflemen are to be taken from a company for any purpose. The best way to safeguard the wounded is to push ahead and defeat the enemy. Pitiful examples have occurred in the present offensive wherein units have allowed their strength to be weakened by details for carrying wounded, and in the face of a counter attack have been driven back, leaving their wounded to die. To halt plays the enemy's game, since he is fighting a defensive action with machine guns and artillery. To halt means losses. But if you push on the losses will not be much greater and you will have gained something. No officer should ever say that he is tired, or allow his men to say it. No man is ever so tired that he cannot take one step forward.

Don't ask for relief. Those in higher command are constantly considering the matter of relief. It is expected that the full measure of the organization's strength will be demanded of it before it is pulled out. It must be so if we win. When you have reached the stage that the gains you are making do not justify the losses you are sustaining, you will be taken out. Don't worry about your flanks. Distribution in depth protects them. Troops must hold their ground. To fall back allows the enemy to play his guns on you, causing losses, and these losses, with the ones you have sustained in the advance, will be in vain. But even a squad, or a platoon, if it holds its ground, will enable the whole line to advance. In the last few days, a patrol of twenty men, by fighting and holding its ground on a hill enabled a whole division to advance. The best way to take machine guns is to go and take 'em! Press forward. The finest tribute that can be paid to a division is: It takes its objective!"

General Summerall concluded his talk with the characteristic remark that he would get down to see us as often as he could. That he would try to see us if things went well. If things did not go well, we would certainly see him soon.

Another example of this sort of preparation is General Wright's "Battle Memorandum", as follows:

"HEADQUARTERS
EIGHTY-NINTH DIVISION
FRANCE.

Secret.
Read and Destroy. October 26, 1918.

BATTLE MEMORANDUM FOR COMMANDERS:

You can expect heavy counter-attack before you reach the woods. It may come just after you enter the woods but it will probably come and come hard. It may come while we are halted on an objective. It may come while we are in motion. In any case, we must hold our ground. First line battalion must immediately develop its full fire action in place, mow down the enemy and capture any of them who penetrate among us. Warn your men about this. The Boche will try to surprise us. Be constantly on the alert for it. There is no question but that we can whip him. The more of them we get in the counter-attack, the fewer we will have to fight later on. When he counter-attacks he plays our game, but we must be ready.

Assault battalions will move at distances and intervals of not less than ten meters between men. The staggered formation of advance keeping closely behind the barrage is believed to be the best. In all cases, great depth is essential for your flank protection.

Don't worry about fire on your flanks. When that comes, it is a sign we are succeeding, that we are pulling the other people forward, that we are getting inside the Boche lines, that we are hurting him, and if we drive resolutely forward, we are going to defeat him badly.

Explain thoroughly and train your men while passing through woods to depend ONLY on compass bearings. Take your time about it. Sight along the compass, stationary, steady, and pick the next point to march on. Then march on it. Again sight along your compass, pick your points. Never guess at it in the woods. Never rely on a trail. When you know you are off slightly from your original line, don't try to go back on the point you started from. Drive straight ahead along your compass bearing. Always move forward on your compass bearing. Your slight deflections to the right and left will compensate. They make no difference. Always start out again on your compass bearing.

As you reach the edge of the woods, get your men in hand. Don't let them break out of the woods in disorder. Form them up in their combat groups well inside the woods. Then send forward your scouts. Then put your staggered groups out *TOGETHER*. If they go out singly the enemy can concentrate on them. If they go out together it will take the heart out of him.

In going through woods, it is best to avoid paths, roads and railroad tracks if the Boche is shelling. He has these spotted and it may cause you heavy losses.

We can expect bitter fighting—many machine guns. To overcome this we must have full development of fire action, great development in depth and resolute determination to go forward at all costs. The more we hesitate the greater will be our losses. The halts on our objectives are taken according to the best previous experience in order for the infantry to be coördinated with the barrage. All other halts should be avoided. Troops must drive on and leave strong points to be mopped up by the support detachments. This mopping up must not be neglected, however; special detachments are detailed for it, but the assault elements should pass on and gain the main objective.

Don't forget your communications. Send back reports of how you are getting along. Then we can help you. Then we can keep the attack going. If your phone doesn't work, try the buzzer. Remember you will have pigeons and runners.

Infantry must never be advanced in the open without a tremendous fire of machine guns or artillery. You must organize for this. Move your supporting machine guns when your infantry is halted. Then move the infantry forward under their fire. Machine gun officers must study the terrain and study the maps of the forward areas in great detail, deciding where they can best site their guns to accomplish this mission. Remember that the German often puts his organized shell holes 50 to 100 meters in advance of the woods.

Read carefully confidential publication No. 1376-G-5, Notes on Recent Operations, No. 3.

We are going to supply you maps down to your platoon commanders. If you don't get them, we want you to say so and keep talking until you do get them. There were some hitches in this during the St. Mihiel drive, although the maps were available. They are no good unless they are in the hands of the men who need them.

This Division accomplished its big share in the St. Mihiel drive in company with the veteran divisions of the American Expeditionary Forces. Now, at a time when the Allies have this great opportunity to win, we have again been selected for a big task and in company best guaranteed to succeed. We must take our objectives. The Corps Commander, the Commander-in-chief, the Allied Governments, count on us. This can well be the climax of the Division's service. That's what we have all been living for. Burn this into your minds. Tell it to your men. Hold them together. Set your teeth. Put it across.

WRIGHT, Commanding."

Such appeals as these had a marked effect upon the conduct of the Division in the battle. It would be hard to conceive of better fighting spirit than was shown by all ranks. The lesson of control was well learned; the total of straggling for the entire division was only a fraction of one per cent.

THE ENGINEERS BUILD A ROAD

The lesson of the St. Mihiel attack respecting the importance of omitting nothing that would facilitate bringing up supplies from the rear, was applied in this offensive. Every available route was reconnoitered and the work was pressed night and day. The taking of the town of Bantheville by the 90th Division opened the possibility of the use of the Bantheville-Remonville road, once the enemy was driven from the Bois d'Andevanne. But reliance was not placed on this route, and the Division Commander determined to have a road leading to the front that would be wholly within the Division's sector, and that would enable him to be assured of ability to bring up supplies and ammunition from the rear as the attack progressed. Accordingly a road known as the Engineer Road was constructed by the troops of the Division, principally by the Engineer regiment. This road ran from the road fork on the Romagne-Sommerance Road about two kilometers west of Romagne, following, northwesterly, the general line of the clearing and the valley to the St. Georges-La Dhuy Farm road. This road was worked as far north as enemy observation and fire would permit. At night, this meant working up to a point about 50 meters west of the most western tip of the Bois de Bantheville, within 1500 yards of the enemy's line. The engineers also did work on the roads through Bantheville and due north through the Bois de Bantheville. The result was that, due to the energy of the engineers and fortunate fair weather, the Engineer Road was completed and served for horse-drawn transportation and light motor vehicles by 10 o'clock on the morning of the attack. Moreover, animal-drawn transportation, mainly ambulances, came back through the Northern road.

A rigid system of priority was enforced, guaranteeing that only animal-drawn transportation would be permitted over the roads concerning which there was any question of maintenance. Restrictions were placed even on staff cars and motor ambulances. Definite limits were given to all trucks beyond which they could not pass until the Corps Engineer was satisfied that the roads would stand the traffic.

The Division Engineers also opened an old German 60 centimeter railroad from Cierges north to Romagne, and prepared to advance it to the Bois des Hazois. The engineers likewise perfected their plans for men and material to be used on road work close behind the infantry as the advance progressed.

The result of this preparation was that there was no such jam of traffic as marred the St. Mihiel operation and that the great difficulty of getting up supplies was to a large extent obviated.

The 314th Supply Train not only performed its normal functions, but also organized a provisional company to drive light trucks distributed among the infantry regiments, sent one half-company with the 340th Machine Gun Battalion, a company with the 314th Sanitary Train to handle wounded, and furnished a large detail which served with the 341st Machine Gun Battalion until the armistice.

EQUIPMENT

Another feature of the preparation which made for the success of the attack was the unremitting attention given to equipping the men. In addition to his regular equipment, each infantry soldier was required to carry two bandoleers of small arms ammunition, one automatic rifle clip or the equivalent number of cartridges, two hand grenades and two rifle grenades and one white panel. The packs of the assaulting troops were left under guard and each man went forward with only a slicker for protection. Maps were issued down to and including platoon commanders showing the Divisional boundaries, and the corrected magnetic lines of the advance. At the last practicable moment the latest information in regard to enemy dispositions, machine guns and artillery was sent out on maps to platoon commanders. Each platoon commander was also supplied with a time table for each objective with space for him to fill in the exact time as soon as H hour was known, and also the local description of his part of each objective. He was also given the principal liaison signals of panels and rockets on card form, and a brief admonition about reports, to report often the date, place, time, coördinates of his front line, and the regimental numbers of the prisoners he had taken.

Special effort was made to secure extra compasses for the infantry, and every available supply at Corps and Army dumps was exhausted, including the salvage dumps in the vicinity. All troops had been carefully instructed in marching by compass. There was no report in the operation of loss of direction.

The machine gun battalions sent details into Bois de Bantheville to prepare in advance machine gun emplacements which would be occupied just before the drive and to establish ammunition dumps nearby.

LIAISON, WHAT IT IS, AND WHAT WE DID

In preparation for the coming battle, a new and complete plan of liaison was issued from the Division Headquarters, which embodied the results of previous successes and failures in this important feature of active operations.

In as much as the liaison in the battle was successfully maintained and the Division reached its nearest point to perfection in this service during the operation, a description of the plan and its operation is essential to a complete understanding of the events which followed.

The term "liaison" is used to designate the whole system of communication and connection between the complex elements of a modern army. The importance of such communication and connection has greatly increased under the conditions of modern warfare, primarily because of the increase in the dependence of each element upon every other unit for success of the whole. Moreover, the vast areas over which modern battles are fought, and the enormous number of men engaged, have made the task of direction of a great force impossible without more effective means of communication both of information and orders than was ever needed in the past. At the battle of Waterloo, Napoleon and Wellington could both take positions from which the whole of the conflict would be visible. They needed little more than mounted messengers to carry reports and orders. In a modern battle there is no point from which even a regimental commander can observe more than a small fraction of his command in an engagement. A single battalion in attack formation will have a front of more than a quarter of a mile and a depth of nearly three-quarters of a mile; and its ability to advance upon a given occasion will often depend upon the ability of its commander to inform the artillery of enemy machine guns or defenses on its front, or inform the higher commanders of conditions on the flanks which can be met by the action of other units. Multiply these infantry battalions by twelve, for the divisional infantry, add the artillery and auxiliary troops, and then multiply the total by the great number of divisions engaged and in reserve, and the reader will have some conception of the difficulty of the problem involved in directing the great machine to its destination in the enemy's lines.

Fortunately modern invention has supplied many instruments for quick and accurate communication which Napoleon and Wellington did not have or need. The messenger is still the most reliable means of all, but he is now equipped with a motorcycle or automobile. The modern army also employs the telephone, telegraph, radio, buzzer phone, earth telegraph (T. P. S.) pyrotechnics, projectors, wig-wag flags, airplanes, pigeons, dogs, and balloons.

The Division plan of liaison provided for an officer from its staff to represent it as liaison officer with each of the infantry brigades and also one with each adjacent division. Lieutenant J. K. B. Hockaday continued to perform this function with the 177th Brigade, having well performed these duties since the time the Division first entered the line. Lieutenant James E. Freeman was detailed to the 178th Infantry Brigade; Lieutenant H. H. Tenney to the division on the right and Lieutenant (later Captain) James C. Crockett to the division on the left. These officers remained habitually with the element to which they were designated. They visited the Division Headquarters at least once daily for instructions at the evening conference. The brigade liaison officers carried and explained the orders of the division commander to the brigades and served the brigades by stating and explaining the needs of the brigades to the division commander and his staff.

In the brigades, an officer from each regiment performed similar duties between regiment and brigade. And in the assault brigade, officers were detailed to and received from the adjacent brigades of the neighboring divisions. In like manner, the regimental commanders had agents of liaison operating between their headquarters and their battalions, and adjacent regiments; the battalion commanders, such agents between them and their companies; and the company commanders, between them and their platoons.

An artillery officer was attached to the headquarters of each infantry brigade, each regiment and each battalion in the front line as liaison agent for the supporting artillery. And these officers had under their control systems of telephones and couriers independent of the similar systems of the infantry, so as to promote and assure direct and immediate connection with the artillery.

At Division Headquarters a message center was organized before leaving Reynel and maintained under direction of the Assistant Chief of Staff G-3. During the Meuse-Argonne offensive it was in charge of Captain Gregory Vigeant, 354th Infantry. This office received and despatched all messages and communications to and from Division Headquarters. A daily courier service was maintained from this center with the Army Corps, brigades, independent units of the Division, rear echelons of the Division and the divisions on the right and left. The couriers made three trips daily and special couriers were available in emergencies.

An advance message center was organized for the coming battle, and in charge of it, at his own request, was placed Lieutenant Colonel (then Major) Burton A. Smead, the Division Adjutant. This message center was placed as close to the P. C. of the leading brigade as practicable and was to be maintained at the wire-head, usually abreast of the advance brigade P. C. In the action it was often ahead of this point, and in the later phases, was at one time actually in advance of the advance battalion and with the outpost platoon in the town of Laneuville.

The construction and maintenance of these telephone systems was, of course, the work of the 314th Field Signal Battalion, at this time under the command of Major Harry F. Strider. The telephone liaison throughout the fighting was marvelously good, made so by the devotion of the Signal Battalion men, who were always close up to the infantry, often laying their wire by hand through gassed or heavily shelled areas. On November 1st, the Advance

Message Center Signal Corps detachment carried the Brigade wire the last two kilometers to Remonville about noon, the reel carts bringing up the Division circuits a couple of hours later. In the hard fighting from November 4 to 11, the Signal Battalion detachment, under 1st Lieutenant N. B. Forrest, laid and maintained the lines between Tailly and Laneuville under such trying conditions of constant shell fire that the Distinguished Service Cross was awarded to four of its members—Sergeants Charles A. Lemasters, Harold B. Mansfield, Elgin J. Moore and Roy M. Sauers. For their work during the advance, Lieutenant Forrest and Sergeant Charles M. Huber, Company B, 314th Field Signal Battalion, were cited in Division Orders.

The great majority of messages were sent and received by telephone, though naturally this service was continually interrupted through the destruction of the telephone lines by shell fire. For the coming battle, a telephone axis of liaison was prescribed, beginning at Gesnes and to run west of the Bois de Bantheville through La Dhuy Farm, La Bergerie Farm and Remonville. This line was to be laid as rapidly as the advance of the Division would permit. It was to consist of five metallic circuits from Division Headquarters forward, one of which was at the disposition of the artillery. Normally, one brigade P. C. and one regimental P. C. were to be located on the axis.

The brigades were, of course, connected with their regiments by telephone, and the regiments with their front line battalions.

Each regiment and brigade had a radio set, and the call letters for each unit and the wave lengths to be used were all prescribed in the plan of liaison. Sending "in clear" was prohibited over the radio and all messages had to be coded.

The earth telegraph (T. P. S.), although issued down to battalions, was not carried into the assault, but was to be brought forward with the combat train and installed when the objectives of the Division were reached. Its weight made it difficult to transport, and furthermore, this appliance had not worked satisfactorily in the Lucey sector, where its use from the front-line trenches was often attempted. Since the Division never became stablized in the battle but was advancing until the cessation of hostilities, these instruments were never used. The projector also was not used.

A divisional observation post was established on an eminence called Hill 288 and placed in charge of Captain W. P. Montgomery, who had performed excellent service in a similar capacity in the St. Mihiel battle. Low visibility during the operations, however, impaired the service from this point and the others to which the observation post was advanced, until the attack passed the heights north of Tailly. From thence to the river, the observation post performed excellent service.

For communication between airplanes and the infantry careful preparation was made. Each soldier was required to carry white strips of cloth to lay upon the ground to mark out the position of the front line when called upon to do so by the signal of the divisional plane. Bengal flares were also carried into action by the troops for use for this purpose during periods of low visibility. Panels were also provided and taken into action by battalion, regimental and brigade headquarters and a code of communications by means of these panels was prescribed in the plan of liaison. The 104th U. S. Air Squadron (less one flight) and the 7th Balloon company were attached to the Division for the operation.

However, as the divisional airplane never appeared in the battle, the panels proved useless. Throughout the operation the enemy dominated the air. For this reason, as well as low visibility, the airplane liaison failed. And the enemy shot down our balloons almost as fast as we could raise them, so observation from them also failed.

A new code of pyrotechnic signals was prescribed in the plan of liaison and the troops were provided with the rockets and Very pistols for exhibiting these signals. The other means of liaison, however, served sufficiently well and these signals were not used.

Pigeons were supplied to the brigades and regiments and messages were sent by their means. Their cotes were too far in the rear, however, and their value was slight.

However, the most dependable means of liaison, here as everywhere else, was the gallant and devoted runner. In rcognition of the courage and accomplishments of the runners, General Wright's last orders before leaving the Division, just after the armistice, directed that the runners should receive first consideration in granting furloughs to the leave areas in southern France.

SHELL FIRE INCIDENTS

The headquarters of the 177th Brigade were in a concrete dugout built in the Kriemhilde Stellung near the road from Romagne to Sommerance and in the southern part of the Bois de Romagne. It was an eligible situation except for the northern exposure. Southern exposures for dwelling places in those conditions were decidedly preferable, so long as the enemy artillery remained north of us. However, no hit was obtained by the enemy's conscientious efforts in the entrance, though one shell exploded harmlessly on the very top of the dugout. There was room for but six or seven persons in the little place, so that some of the headquarters detachment must needs find shelter in fox holes and folds of the ground near by. A shell broke in one of these little shelters in the small hours of one night and wounded every man of a detachment of eight of the 314th Engineers, who were attached to brigade headquarters for duty on the advance. The casualty was reported to the commanding officer of the Engineers with the request that another detail be supplied. As this relief detail of nine men was marching through Romagne to take its post, a shell exploded among them, killing or wounding every man of the detachment. A third detachment was sent, which arrived without mishap and served throughout the advance without undue casualties.

"Official Photo from Mid-Week Pictorial, by permission"

Romagne, Meuse-Argonne Offensive, as it appeared from the air when the fighting had moved on. Shell holes, stripped trees, battered houses and the ruined church are plainly visible. The road running from the church to the top of the picture is the Romagne-Sommerance road, which passes south of Bois de Bantheville about 1,000 yards west of Romagne. This road, particularly at the point where it leaves the town, was under constant artillery fire, and as all the supplies for the brigade in the line had to be transported over it many casualties occurred. At the right of the road, near the top of the picture is seen the French cemetery. Just beyond this is now the great American cemetery, where are buried our soldiers who fell in the Argonne battle.

The headquarters of the 341st Machine Gun Battalion were in a large dugout in Romagne. One day a gas shell was dropped into the very entrance of the dugout, knocking down by the concussion Major Ernest E. Watson, the commanding officer, and filling the place with the deadly fumes. Crawling on his hands and knees, Major Watson assembled his men and led them out of another entrance to the place. He was taken to a dressing station and bathed with the neutralizing solution; but persuaded the medical officer not to evacuate him to the rear, and returned to duty the following day in time to participate in the great advance of November 1st.

Early on the morning of October 28th, Captain (then 1st Lieutenant) John L. Crofut, of the 89th Military Police Company, originally called the 314th Military Police, was out inspecting traffic control posts in the vicinity of Romagne. He was accompanied by his driver, Private David A. Reavis, of the same company. Romagne was under heavy shell fire, as usual. In the southern part of the town was a large ammunition dump, consisting of a quantity of boxed "Seventy-fives" placed on top of a considerable number of "One Hundred Fifty-fives." A shell exploded near the dump and set fire to a number of the boxes containing the 75's. Taking Reavis with him,

An ammunition shed hit by an Austrian 88 near Headquarters 89th Division, Gesnes, during the Meuse-Argonne offensive, Nov. 1st, 1918. S. C. 31483.

Lieutenant Crofut went at once to the blazing dump and the two carried the burning boxes of ammunition to a place of safety, putting out the fire with their bare hands. During this time, another shell burst about fifty yards away, blowing one soldier to pieces and seriously wounding Lieutenant Sargent, of the 16th Field Artillery. After putting out the fire, Lieutenant Crofut went immediately to the help of the wounded officer and assisted in getting him to the dressing station in Romagne.

Gesnes, which was Division Headquarters, was a favorite target for German shelling at intervals.

On October 31st, 1918, the day before the great advance, unusual efforts were made to obtain final information of the enemy's dispositions, and daylight patrols were sent out to develop the enemy positions and, if possible, obtain identifications. The enemy was found to be holding his positions in force and with determination, and two of these patrols, sent from the lines of the 354th Infantry, were caught under the enemy's rifle and machine gun fire and were unable either to advance or to withdraw to our lines. One man finally succeeded in crawling from the position into our lines and brought back word that two of the officers were lying wounded in No Man's Land. Two stretcher bearers of Company "L", 354th Infantry, 1st Class Privates Charles D. Barger and Jesse N. Funk, on hearing the news, and without any special order to do so, ran out with their stretcher through a very hail of machine-gun fire and brought in 2nd Lieutenant John Millis, who, fearfully wounded in both legs, had ordered the men of his patrol to return without him. After bearing him to a place of safety, they returned again to the inferno of fire and brought in the other officer, Lieutenant Rowell. For these acts of conspicuous gallantry, over and beyond the call of their duties, they were both most justly awarded later the highest reward for gallantry in action, the Medal of Honor.

THE TERRAIN OF OUR ADVANCE

The line from which the attack was to be launched began at the northern tip of the Bois de Bantheville and extended almost due southwest. It was about two kilometers in length. It lay almost at right angles to the axis of the advance, which was to the northeast. This formation was occasioned by the fact that the Bois de Bantheville, which we had conquered and held, constituted a salient into the enemy's line, the Germans still holding the village of Landres-et-St. Georges in the sector to our left, which village was nearly a kilometer and a half less advanced than the point we had attained. From our front the ground sloped gently to a valley in which lay La Dhuy Farm, consisting of a number of stone buildings and constituting a strong point in the German line, well defended with machine guns.

Beyond this valley the ground rose steeply to a ridge, on which, south and west of our sector, lay the strongly held Bois des Hazois; small, scattered patches of timber lay in the open ground on these heights, and further on, to the right, our advance passed through a portion of the Bois d'Andevanne, still on high ground. These little tracts of timber each concealed a machine gun nest skillfully placed, and the Bois d'Andevanne had been organized with machine gun emplacements and wire. This ridge, running from Bois d'Andevanne to Hill 263, northeast of Landres-et-St. Georges, formed a natural switch line which, by covering communications, had enabled the enemy to hold Landres-et-St. Georges and a little fragment of the Kriemhilde Stellung after the greater part of that position had been taken. From these heights the ground sloped down to the valley in which lay, in the left of our sector, the village of Remonville. It then rose to high ground on which, extending across our entire front, was the formidable, dense Forest of Barricourt. The objective of the first day's attack was the northern edge of this forest on the right, and high open ground beyond it on the left. This forest constituted an extremely strong natural fortress. An advance on it was dominated and flanked by natural bastions such as the Bois d'Andevanne and the town of Remonville. The long slope immediately in front of it was, in effect, a glacis, affording a beautiful field of fire, while the outpost position, including the Bois des Hazois, the scattered woods and hills in the vicinity of La Dhuy Farm, afforded excellent machine gun positions and fields of fire from reverse slopes.

But the position was one that must needs be taken by us if we were to advance; and it must needs be held by the German if calamity to him was to be averted. For these heights of Barricourt dominated everything as far as the River Meuse. Small wonder that when it was reported to Marshal Foch that the Heights of Barricourt had been taken, he sprang to his feet, overturning his table in his emotion, and exclaimed, "Then the war is over." And we of the 89th may well be proud that to us fell the honor of storming and taking this formidable position.

The plan of attack was not complicated. The 177th Infantry Brigade was to make the initial assault, capture the Heights of Barricourt at all costs and push on to the Exploitation Line. The 178th Infantry Brigade was to act as support during the first day's advance, when it was to pass the lines of the other brigade and continue the advance as the assault brigade.

ARTILLERY SUPPORT

The artillery was to furnish an intense preparation fire for two hours preceding the attack, and then to lay down a creeping barrage in front of the advancing troops. This barrage was to be very heavy, consisting of a high explosive rolling barrage of almost twice the usual density, together with a rolling barrage of shrapnel 75's and a jumping barrage on successive targets by 75's, 105's, 155's and 8-inch howitzers. To this was to be added a rolling barrage of machine gun fire, sweeping the enemy's terrain 500 meters in advance of the infantry as far as the first objective, which was the crest of the ridge between the valleys of Remonville and of Landres-et-St. Georges. The infantry Stokes Mortars of the reserve brigade and the detachment of gas and flame troops were placed under the orders of the Artillery

Brigade Commander, in conjunction with his trench mortar batteries, during the preliminary bombardment. The smoke barrage laid down by the gas and flame troops and these mortars contributed quite a little to the success of the initial jump-off. Two machine gun companies of the leading brigade, assigned to join later the reserve infantry battalions thereof, also the machine gun companies of the division reserve and the one-pounder platoons of the brigade, were placed under the orders of the Division machine gun officer, Lieutenant Colonel Rudolph E. Smyser, for use during the preliminary bombardment and for covering the advance of the infantry as far as the first objective.

The supporting artillery left little to be desired on the first day except the wish that it was our own. It consisted of the 57th Field Artillery Brigade, the 203rd (French) Regiment of 75mm., the 58th Field Artillery Brigade. Brigadier General Irwin, commanding the 57th Field Artillery Brigade, commanded all the Divisional artillery during the preliminary bombardment and during the first day of the attack. It was provided in the orders that his brigade should be relieved at the end of the first day, it having been long in action and being much depleted both in personnel and in animals, and that the command of the Divisional artillery should then pass to Brigadier General H. D. Todd, Jr., commanding the 58th Field Artillery Brigade, which brigade, with the French regiment and attached elements would alone support the further advance. Unfortunately, during the forenoon of October 30th, General Todd was wounded by shell splinters while reconnoitering roads to be used during the advance. Brigadier General E. A. Millar, 6th F. A. Brigade, without the opportunity for personal preliminary reconnaissance, commanded the brigade until November 6th, when General Todd returned.

The success of the artillery preparation and support of the first day's advance was in part due to the accomplishment by the Corps Air Service of the difficult mission of photographing the enemy positions under trying conditions both of visibility and of enemy opposition. Photographs of practically the entire front to a depth of five kilometers were obtained on October 27th and 29th. The results of these photographs were embodied by the Corps in a combined Infantry Assault and Artillery Objective map; and the benefits were confirmed by the statements of many prisoners taken on the 1st of November that the reason that they were taken was that the artillery concentrations were so effective that they were confined to their shelters and isolated in small groups. Artillery prisoners said they were unable to leave their shelters to serve their guns. Officers were in some cases entirely cut off from communication with their troops.

The preliminary bombardment and the support of the infantry advance of November 1st are, so far as this Division is concerned, to be deemed near to perfect performance of the function of the artillery. During the night of October 31st-November 1st, some 60,000 shells were expended by the light artillery alone. At about 10:00 P. M. October 31st, 2,000 gas shells were placed by Corps order on what is known technically as "sensitive points", — that is, positions where enemy activities are known or suspected, battery positions, machine gun nests, important cross roads, command posts, headquarters, ammunition and supply depots, kitchens and the like. The heavy artillery delivered a covering fire on the enemy back areas. Behind the Divisional artillery, Corps and Army delivered a like fire and continued it all the following day. The success of this heavy artillery fire was very great and was plainly noted when the infantry passed over the shelled area.

At the jump-off at 5:30 A. M., November 1st, seventeen batteries, distributed over the Divisional front, placed the high explosive barrage combined with non-persistent gas. Nine other batteries placed, four hundred meters ahead of the first mentioned barrage, a fire of shrapnel mixed with smoke, which had the effect of forcing the machine gunners to their dugouts. Six other batteries were placing still further ahead a highly concentrated fire on certain selected sensitive points. In short, thirty-two batteries, 128 guns, were used for the barrage under which our infantry advanced.

It is little to be wondered at that when, on the following day, only twenty-two guns were available for the barrage, the infantry, accustomed to the magnificent support of the preceding day by 128 guns on a front only half as extended, could not recognize the feeble popping as a barrage at all.

The relative failure of the artillery support on the second day is to be noted, but not by way of undue censure of the artillery. The necessity for the relief of the entire 57th Field Artillery Brigade was doubtless great. The change of command during the course of the engagement was bad. And the inability of two regiments of the 58th Field Artillery Brigade to get forward and participate in the barrage is to be ascribed in part to difficulties on the roads. It is true, however, that the Artillery Commander attempted to displace an entire regiment of artillery instead of moving forward by battalions as ordered. And it is further true that one whole regiment of light artillery failed to get into the action as a direct consequence of failure of its commander to follow the road which he was directed to take to his position. The road from Remonville to Andevanne was known to be in bad condition and all the artillery was directed to take the road from Remonville due north into the Bois de Barricourt and to take positions in the woods on both sides of this road, so that the single movement would attain positions from which the advance could be covered to well beyond the line of Nouart and Tailly. Nevertheless, one regimental commander attempted to proceed by way of Andevanne and thence northward by the road which skirts the eastern edge of the Bois de Barricourt, passing through Les Tuilleries. The entire regiment was mired and did not get into the action until late in the day.

Communications with the artillery were also in poor condition during the second day's operations. From their shell hole in advance of the lines of the 354th Infantry, luckily, General Winn and Colonel Babcock were able, through the artillery liaison officer attached to the 354th Infantry, to obtain the fire of light artillery upon German positions plainly visible in their front. Later in the day, from the northern edge of the Bois de Barricourt, General Winn obtained direct telephone connection with Colonel J. C. H. Lee, the Chief of Staff of the Division, who in turn gave direct orders to the "heavies" of the Artillery Brigade and thus succeeded in getting fire upon the German positions above Barricourt.

ENEMY TROOPS AND MORALE

The enemy troops on our front were the 88th German Division. Previous to the attack the 13th German Division had been holding the sector, but it was soon ascertained from prisoners that the 13th had been relieved by the 88th on the night of October 29th-30th. The 13th, however, was not withdrawn, but merely placed in support, part of it in the Bois d'Andevanne and part in the Bois de Barricourt. Both the 13th and 88th, as well as other German troops, were in action against the 177th Brigade on the first day.

While there is no question but that at the time of this drive the morale of the German troops as a whole had fallen, still these two divisions were rated highly in the German Army. There were among them replacements of older men who had been doing garrison and frontier guard duty and also young men from the class of 1919. Yet the greater portion of the German troops opposite this Division were young, vigorous, aggressive soldiers,—the best that the German Army had to furnish to hold the most critical point of its entire line at the time.

The 88th Division was comparatively fresh, having come into the line from the Woevre front after resting eight days at Fosse. It consisted of the 352nd, 353rd and 426th Regiments of German Infantry.

It was an old acquaintance of ours, having been, as before noted, in reserve in the St. Mihiel battle, during which it went into the line on the left of the 5th Landwehr Division. During the period of stabilization following the battle it had held the sector on our front in the vicinity of Charey, where its troops were in contact with nearly all of our infantry at different times.

OUR NEIGHBORING DIVISIONS

The attack was to commence with two divisions on the front of our Corps, the 5th. The 2nd was the left division and ours the right. The 42nd Division was in the line on our left up to the moment of the attack, confronting the strongly held village of Landres-et-St. Georges. Its lines were passed by the 2nd Division, at the jump-off, which was to continue the advance to the end. The left division of the 3rd Corps, which held the sector to our right, was the 90th. So that our good neighbors in the coming fray were the veteran 2nd and the less experienced 90th, destined to prove itself in this fight as good as the best.

OBJECTIVES

Because of our advanced position relatively to the troops on our left and to adjust our advance with that of the troops on our right, an intermediate objective was established upon which our left assault battalion could wait for the 2nd Division to come up and enter the Bois des Hazois. This intermediate objective began at the southern edge of the clearing in Bois d'Andevanne and ran thence in the form of an arc, bowed to the northwest, to a point midway between La Dhuy Farm and Bois des Hazois. It was to be reached at H hour plus 48 minutes, and to be departed from at H hour plus one hour and eight minutes. The first objective was a line beginning at the northern extremity of Bois d'Andevanne at Hill 300 and running southeast along the northern edge of a line of small, scattered woods and La Bergerie Farm. It was to be reached at H plus 2 hours and 30 minutes and departed from at H plus three hours. It represented an advance from the jump-off of about 2 km. The second objective was along the ridge in the midst of Bois de Barricourt. It was to be reached at H plus 5 hours and 25 minutes and departed from at H plus 6 hours and 50 minutes. It was about four and a half kilometers from the jump-off line. The third objective, the limit of the day's advance, ran from Les Tuilleries Farm, along the northern edge of Bois de Barricourt to an eminence called La Follard, about a kilometer south of and overlooking the village of Barricourt. This line represented an average advance of about six kilometers from the jump-off. No time was set for its attainment. It was to be reached at all costs and to be held against all counter attacks. From it, vigorous exploitation towards the front, to the line of Tailly and Nouart, was directed.

When H hour was, on the night before the attack, announced as 5:30 A. M., the platoon leaders and higher commanders knew that they would depart from each of these objectives on the following schedule:

Jump-off Line	5:30 A. M
Intermediate Objective	6:38
First Objective	8:30
Second Objective	12:20 P. M.
Third Objective	?

The non-military reader will find it difficult to appreciate the degree of preliminary preparation and coördination in action requisite to make an attack of the kind that now confronted us. With the enemy holding every advantage of position, at least equal in number to us, equipped with every death-dealing weapon that modern inventiveness has conceived of, success was possible only by team work of the highest order. The only condition under which the infantry could advance against the enemy's defense, unless at frightful loss, was by following closely the artillery barrage, which kept the enemy machine gunners and riflemen under cover until our own infantry was upon them. And this barrage can only be regulated by means of the strictest time table whereby the guns, far to the rear, and out of sight of the advancing lines, can be permitted to fire by watch and map according to careful prearrangement. As has been said, the first day's advance in this attack was practically a perfect example of such an advance. The infantry was able to advance by keeping close behind the artillery barrage. And the barrage was there on schedule at all critical times.

THE JUMP-OFF

All being ready, the troops took their places on the jump-off line during the night of October 31st-November 1st. General Winn, with his aids, liaison officer and a little group of runners and telephone men, occupied a shallow shelter in the front line in the edge of Bois de Bantheville. Colonel Reeves and Colonel Babcock were in similar holes near the leading troops of their regiments.

The 353rd Infantry attacked over the right half of the sector, the 354th Infantry over the left. The regiments were each formed in column of battalions and were well distributed in depth, that is, there was maintained a distance of 1,000 meters between the rear elements of each battalion and the leading element of the battalion in its rear. The battalions themselves were also formed in depth, with two companies on the fighting line and two in support, the companies also being formed with platoons to the front and rear. When fully distributed in this manner an attacking battalion covered a distance from front to rear of about 500 meters. The result of this arrangement was that the advance presented the appearance of many lines of men, widely separated from one another or advancing in small groups of three or four. Thus the effect of the enemy's artillery fire was largely minimized and the possibility of a flank attack could be ignored.

In the 353rd Infantry the 3rd battalion, under Lieutenant Colonel (then Major) George W. Blackinton, led the attack. The 2nd battalion, under Lieutenant Colonel (then Major) James L. Peatross, was in support; while the 1st battalion, under Captain (then 1st Lieutenant) Vernon D. Hunter was in reserve. In the 354th Infantry the 1st battalion, under Major (then Captain) Morton T. Jones, led off, with the 3rd battalion, under Captain (later Major) Hugh M. Pinkerton in support, and the 2nd battalion, under Captain Frank P. Root, in reserve. One company from the 341st Machine Gun Battalion was assigned to each infantry regiment, thus giving, with the regimental machine gun companies, a machine gun company to each battalion in the fighting line and in the support. The remainder of the machine gun battalion, under Major Ernest E. Watson, participated in the preliminary bombardment and then joined the reserve battalions, thus giving each of them a company of machine guns.

Company "D," 353rd Infantry, under Captain Frank M. Wood, with a platoon of machine guns, had orders to unite with a similar detachment from the 90th Division, and advance along the boundary between the divisions, protecting the flanks and maintaining contact between the divisions. Company "F," of the 354th Infantry, under Captain Marshall P. Wilder, was given a similar mission on the left, with orders to effect the junction with the 2nd Division at the first objective.

At 3:30 A. M. the artillery preparation began, a truly intensive preparation. It will be remembered that there were assigned to the Division two whole brigades and a regiment of field artillery, with additional detachments from Army and Corps. The roar of this array of guns, intermingled with the booming of the mortars and the insistent tap-tap-tapping of the machine guns made a soul-shaking din.

The enemy artillery responded vigorously. The Germans evidently assumed that the jump-off would be made from the edge of the Bois de Bantheville, and heavily shelled this line. Our jump-off line, however, had been established in the open in front of the woods for the most part, and in consequence the enemy's fire had little effect on the troops, but made it extremely uncomfortable for the General, Colonels and assault battalion commanders who all had established P. C's. in the edge of the timber.

At 5:30 A. M. it was barely light at this late season of the year. With the usual luck in the matter of weather which had attended all of our attacks, a heavy fog hung over the field at dawn. Moreover, the last three minutes of the artillery preparation had consisted mostly of smoke shells on the German positions. So the troops moved forward veiled in smoke and mist and must have seemed to the cowering enemy outposts to be vengeful specters taking form from clouds.

Following closely the barrage, battering down resistance wherever it was manifested, exterminating machine gun nests wherever they were encountered, the attack swept on down the slope, through the valley and attained the intermediate objective on the heights beyond by 6:15. The machine gun nest and strong point in La Dhuy Farm had been overcome with little difficulty, though the German dead scattered about, mingled with our own, showed that it had not been given up without a struggle.

THE FIRST AND SECOND OBJECTIVES TAKEN

Promptly on schedule time the artillery barrage began advancing, and with the troops following it closely, it rolled on to the first and second objectives, the enemy resistance decreasing as the advance continued, and the objectives being reached precisely on time.

Almost immediately after the jump-off the assault companies of the 3rd Battalion, 353rd Infantry, were met by withering machine gun fire from the woods just north of Bois de Bantheville, which delayed the advance and caused severe casualties. First Lieutenant Harold A. Furlong, arming himself with a rifle, went ahead of his line, crossing an open space several hundred yards wide and attained a position on the flank and to the rear of the enemy's machine guns. From this point he closed in on them, and one by one silenced their fire, killing a number of the machine gunners himself by his fire and driving twenty of them as prisoners into our lines. For this deed, he was awarded the Medal of Honor.

But for the magnificent barrage, however, the 354th Infantry would have found serious trouble in taking the town of Remonville. The approaches of this town had been strongly fortified, each clump of trees forming the shelter of a nest of machine guns. Hasty barricades had been constructed in the streets,

One of the guns of a battery of 9.2 of German heavy howitzers captured by the 353rd Infantry at Les Tuilleries at the eastern edge of Bois de Barricourt, November 1, 1918.

while the small stream south of the town, and the wood known as La Grande Fontaine had, with organization, been converted into serious obstacles. But here, as everywhere, the unhesitating advance swept all before it, the resistance affording opportunity, however, for some of the most heroic feats recorded in the history of the Division. When a battery of German 77's only a few hundred yards distant fired on his company, point blank, 2nd Lieutenant Henry Henderson, 354th Infantry, without orders, led his platoon at a run around the flank of the battery, across the stream south of Remonville and up its farther bank, and charged the battery with the bayonet, driving the enemy gunners from their posts, and capturing the entire battery. Just southeast of Remonville the platoon of 2nd Lieutenant William E Maloney, 354th Infantry, encountered a machine gun nest of six guns. Lieutenant Maloney at once brought his men forward and rushed the guns, during which he was rendered unconscious by the explosion of a shell. On regaining consciousness, he hurried after his platoon, which had gone forward, and resumed command. Sergeant Roy L. Keller, Company "B", 354th Infantry, who had been acting as mess sergeant, at his own request was given command of a combat group in this action. Being fired on by two machine guns, Sergeant Keller led his men in a charge around the flank of the position, personally killing one gunner and making possible the capture of the remaining enemy. And many were the similar deeds performed at this time, as one or another combat group encountered a machine gun, and heroically rushed to its capture. It was near Remonville, too, that Sergeant Arthur J. Forrest, Company "D", 354th Infantry, performed the act of conspicuous gallantry and intrepidity for which he has been awarded the Congressional Medal of Honor. When the advance of his company was stopped by the fire of a nest of six machine guns, he charged this nest single-handed and drove out the enemy in disorder, thereby enabling his company to resume its advance. Second only to this was the feat of Private Patrick Garrity, Company "C", 354th Infantry, who, with an empty rifle, charged a machine gun single-handed, and at the point of his bayonet captured the gun and its operators.

When Private John W. Childers, Company "B", 354th Infantry, saw that his platoon commander and his platoon sergeant were both wounded and out of action, he called on some of the remaining corporals to take command of the platoon. They did not do so, and, disregarding all rank and asserting the prerogative of the natural leader, Childers took command of the platoon himself, reorganized the groups and courageously led them forward against fierce resistance, attaining all objectives on schedule time. He was made a sergeant for this deed.

Captured German field piece in position in south edge of Bois de Barricourt.

After such fighting as this, it is small wonder that a prisoner taken on November 11 from the 352nd Regiment, 88th (German) Division, stated that the entire second battalion of his regiment had been captured on November 1st at Remonville.

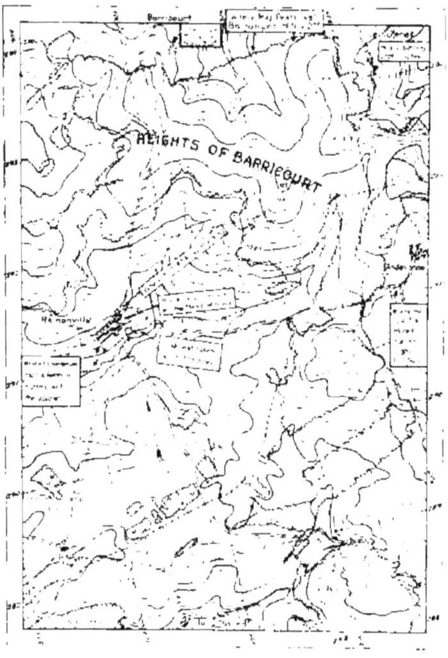

The wooded heights of Barricourt, taken in assault by the 89th Division Nov. 1st, 1918. Actual contours shown, contour interval 5 meters. Kilometer grid. From Dun sur Meuse map.

THE HEIGHTS OF BARRICOURT

At the second objective, the 2nd battalion, 353rd Infantry, and the 3rd battalion, 354th Infantry, passed the lines of the leading battalions and continued the advance on the third objective, the hills north of the Bois de Barricourt. The enemy was found in force in the Bois de Barricourt and on the heights north of it, and stubborn resistance was encountered. The natural strength of this position has already been referred to. It is a dense forest and in it trenches and dugouts were found. Snipers fought from the tree tops. Field guns, left as a forlorn hope of staying the advance, continued to fire until actually surrounded. But foot by foot the way was won through the forest and by 4 o'clock in the afternoon the troops were on their third objective.

The Heights of Barricourt had been won.

A dense fog came up at this time and the short day was coming to its end. Further pursuit of the enemy by advancing the line was impracticable. Patrols were sent out to the front, hasty entrenchments were dug, machine guns sited so as to prepare for a counter attack, and the tired men slept on their arms, waiting for daylight to advance again.

The night of November 1 and 2 was spent by the troops in reorganizing, bringing up artillery and supplies, evacuating the wounded and generally in preparation for resuming the attack on the following day. Orders received in the night provided in substance that the attack would be resumed at 5:30, November 2nd, not preceded by artillery preparation but accompanied by a rolling barrage which would advance at the same rate as the barrage of the previous day. The Exploitation Line of the previous day's attack, namely, the line running from Tailly to Nouart, was designated as the objective for the day. The 177th Infantry Brigade was not to be relieved by the 178th Infantry, as previously ordered, but was to continue as the assault brigade.

THE SECOND DAY

It was found impossible to bring up a sufficient amount of artillery during the night. The 57th Brigade of Field Artillery had been relieved on attaining the first day's objective and in consequence of the failure to bring up all the artillery, as above related, the barrage at 5:30 on the morning of November 2nd proved to be wholly ineffective. This served as the occasion for one of the most heroic achievements in the history of

P. C. Reeves in Bois de Barricourt, night of November 1-2, 1918. This tree and the muddy shell hole at the right formed the only shelter available for the headquarters of the 353rd Infantry for the second day's fighting of the last phase of the Argonne battle. The woods still contained many enemy snipers. Sheltered from observation by a blanket over the shell hole, the orders for the next day's fighting were read and the regimental orders prepared with no light except a pocket electric flash light.

the Division—the successful advance of the troops against bitter resistance of the enemy in strong and well-prepared positions across the open and with the use of practically nothing but the infantry's own weapons.

WEAK ARTILLERY SUPPORT

At the hour set for the advance, brisk shelling of our lines was in progress. The barrage which had been ordered consisted, for reasons heretofore given, of only twenty-two light guns on the entire Division sector, a front of approximately four kilometers. Neither regiment was able to distinguish this light fire as a barrage and so none advanced. When it was reported to the brigade commander that the infantry had not advanced, immediate arrangements were made with the artillery through the artillery liaison officer at Brigade Headquarters to recall and start the barrage again at the hour of 10 o'clock. The guns still had not come up and this second barrage also proved too feeble to afford the infantry protection or even to be recognized as a barrage. An intense fire of machine guns was being directed upon the lines of the 353rd Infantry in the edges of the Bois de Barricourt from the woods about 500 meters to the north and upon the 354th Infantry from the trenches and machine gun positions on the slopes of the hills northwest and southeast of Barricourt. In addition, heavy shelling of the lines was going on from German artillery in the rear. Our own barrage was indistinguishable from the enemy's fire and was not comparable to it in intensity. And so the infantry still did not advance.

General Winn had in the meanwhile gone forward to the sector occupied by the 354th Infantry, and from a shell hole in front of the front line was observing the progress of the action. He gave orders to the 354th Infantry to keep pressing forward irrespective of the lack of artillery support. The 353rd Infantry, with which telephone communication had for a time been interrupted, called up Brigade Headquarters for instructions. The Brigade Adjutant, correctly surmising what would be the will of the Commanding General in the circumstances, gave directions in his name that the infantry should advance on the enemy, using what means they had to overcome resistance.

On the left, on the front of the 354th Infantry, after an all-day fight with rifle and machine gun, Stokes mortar and one-pounder, only a very slight advance of the line was possible. It would have been practicable to flank the German position from the left. But this movement would have taken the troops into the sector of the 2nd Division which, it was at the time supposed, would shortly be advancing over this ground. The 2nd Division, however, did not advance during the day, but failure of liaison with that Division had prevented word of its plans from reaching the Brigade. When night fell the lines of the 354th Infantry had been advanced to the crests of the hills which dominated Barricourt on the southeast and southwest, so that during the night the enemy evacuated the place and the 178th Brigade entered it without opposition the following morning.

While this part of the line had been unable to advance as a whole, still patrols had been pushed out which encircled the town of Barricourt, and one patrol of this regiment, commanded by Lieutenant William E. Maloney, who had fought so gallantly the previous day, and accompanied by Captain Paul Withington, of the Medical Corps, entered the town of Nouart, on the day's objective, occupied it on the night of November 2 and 3, and was in possession when troops of the 178th Brigade entered it on the following day.

There was no passage of lines in the night of November 1 and 2, and the fighting line all next day consisted of the troops which had gained the objective of the day before, Captain Hugh Pinkerton's battalion, the 3rd, with two companies from the 2nd battalion doing the day's fighting for the 354th Infantry.

THE INFANTRY ADVANCES WITHOUT ARTILLERY SUPPORT

In the 353rd Infantry the burden of continuing the advance also fell on the troops which had gained the previous day's final objective, Major Peatross' battalion, the 2nd. Major Peatross had been wounded in the fighting of the previous day, but had refused to be evacuated. He was unable to talk above a whisper and was in a thoroughly weakened condition, physically. But, establishing his P. C. in the edge of the woods, he

German prisoners carrying a wounded man past one of the barricades in the streets of Remonville during the Meuse-Argonne offensive, Nov. 2nd, 1918. The town was taken the day before by the 354th Inf., 89th Division. S. C. 31477.

personally directed the attack. When the order was received to advance, a direct frontal attack on the enemy's positions was attempted. Every man who emerged from the line of the woods was shot in his tracks. It was decided then to encircle the position. Using the one-pounders and Stokes mortars and especially rifle grenades to engage the enemy's attention from the front, Major Peatross, after widely extending his line, ad-

Street scene in Remonville, Nov. 2nd, 1918, during the Meuse-Argonne offensive Boxes of 75 mm. ammunition brought thus far by the Ammunition Train, are opened and transferred to the caissons from the batteries and hurried forward to the guns north of the town, to support the further advance of the 89th Division. The town was taken by the 354th Inf., 89th Division, the day before. S. C. 160039.

vanced on both flanks. This maneuver proved successful, and when the flanking troops had pressed beyond the enemy's position and began to close in, the resistance was broken.

The rifle grenade proved to be one of the most effective weapons for the work of reducing machine gun nests, when operated by determined and courageous grenadiers. On this occasion, when the infantry was thrown upon its own resources, it proved its worth. For example, a rifle grenadier, Private, First Class, Cecil E. Reed, of Company "E", 353rd Infantry, advanced out of the forest into the open ground to obtain a range for his grenades, though the place was under withering machine gun fire and his comrades were seeking what cover they could find. Kneeling in the open he fired his entire supply of ammunition, then dashed back and obtained more from the other men. He returned to his firing position and when all his grenades were again fired, returned for the second time to get more. This time he moved forward to a still more advanced position, from which he succeeded in placing shots so close to the enemy machine gunners that he drove them from their shelters and they were killed by the other men of the company.

Such a feat of arms as this advance from the woods of Barricourt could not have been accomplished without acts of individual heroism and sad losses. For example, Privates Leo. L. Sandman and Quincy R. Seymour of Company "F", 353rd Infantry, made the supreme sacrifice in this action. They went forward as scouts to locate the position of the enemy machine guns and drew their attention while the rest of their company should attack them from the flanks. They located the guns and Sandman succeeded in signaling their location to his comrades before both were killed. They had advanced more than 200 yards through murderous fire before they fell.

The enemy was thus driven from his positions by the courage and determination of this matchless infantry. And on this right sector of the front he fell back in the early afternoon. The troops pressed on, meeting

Bringing ammunition through Remonville Nov. 2nd, 1918. Barricades in the street were thrown up by the Germans for defense of the town, which was captured by the 354th Inf., 89th Division, Nov. 1st. Ambulances and first-aid station in background. S. C. 31484.

and overcoming some resistance from the positions on their left, where the enemy was still making a stand before the village of Barricourt and holding up the advance of the 354th Infantry in the left sector. But the advance continued until early evening, when the day's objective was reached and Tailly was occupied. Major Peatross went to bed in the shattered village of Tailly and obtained much-deserved and needed repose in the con-

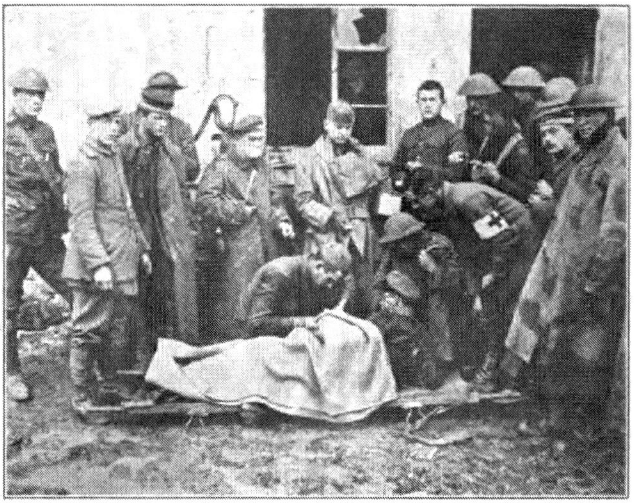

Chaplain C. S. Darley, 356th Infantry, 89th Division, ministering to a wounded German officer brought in by captured German hospital corps men, at dressing station of 354th Ambulance Co., 314th Sanitary Train, 89th Division, in Remonville, Nov. 2, 1918, during the Meuse-Argonne offensive. S. C. 31485.

sciousness that his men had accomplished their task beyond all expectation.

The 3rd battalion, under Major Blackinton, advancing in support, swung to the left, maintaining contact with the 354th Infantry through the night.

LUCKY LIAISON WITH THE 90TH

Although communication between the assault brigade and the 2nd Division on our left was interrupted during this day, it was fortunately preserved with the 90th Division on our right. During the advance of the 353rd Infantry from the Bois de Barricourt, Colonel Reeves reported by telephone to Brigade Headquarters that the barrage of the 90th Division was extending over half of his regimental sector; that it had passed over the lines of the support battalion, the 3rd, and was creeping towards the assault battalion, the 2nd, which was then heavily engaged. Through the quick and skillful efforts of Sergeant Knowles, the signal corps telephone operator at Brigade Headquarters, the Brigade Adjutant obtained almost immediately connection with the Chief of Staff of the 90th Division, informed him of the situation and requested that the barrage be recalled. The barrage was stopped before reaching the advance battalion. This was a fortunate occurrence, as the telephone wires both to the regiments and to the rear were frequently broken during the day by shell fire and it rarely happened that through communication of the kind could be counted on.

THE ENEMY BEGINS RETREAT ACROSS THE MEUSE

As had been anticipated, upon the taking of the Heights of Barricourt, the enemy began to withdraw his forces across the Meuse, leaving only rear guards to delay our advance. As all the troops of the 177th Infantry Brigade had been engaged on November 1 and 2, the Division Commander ordered the 178th Brigade to pass the lines in the night of the 2-3 and to continue the advance as the assault brigade.

Scene of the bitter fight of the 354th Inf., 89th Division, Nov. 2, 1918. The village of Barricourt lies in the valley ahead and to left of picture. The slopes on both sides of the road were covered with trenches and held strongly by the enemy. This picture was taken two days later, Nov. 4th, and shows the condition to which the road was reduced by the passage of artillery and trucks hauling supplies, yet it was the only road available. Caterpillar tractors were used to pull trucks and wagons down the hill. S. C. 35347.

From the passage of the lines on the position Nouart-Tailly, November 3, until a period of comparative stabilization had been reached along the banks of the Meuse November 7, the history is one of exhausting marches through mud and forest, with some bitter but not continuous fighting, and the ever-present harassing fire of the enemy artillery from across the river.

The boundaries of the Division's sector had been designated originally as running, on the right, between Halles and Beauclair to the western edge of Stenay; and on the left from Le Champy Haut to Inor. This gave an axis of advance nearly northeast and a gradually widening sector so that the front along the Meuse would be a little over six kilometers. During the advance the sector of the Division was extended to the left by running its boundary from Le Champy Haut to Letanne, with a jog to the eastern edge of Beaumont. This change added a V-shaped segment which included the Forest of Jaulnay, making the extreme width of the sector, in an air line from Beaumont to Stenay, about twelve kilometers, but in reality, following the bend of the River Meuse, much longer.

TERRAIN ALONG THE RIVER

The Meuse flows nearly north from Stenay to Inor then a short distance below Inor it doubles back around a large bend to flow southwest by Pouilly, and then in another bend, resumes its general northerly and westerly direction. In its course this section of the river may be likened to a great fish hook, with Stenay at the eye, Inor just above the bend, and Pouilly just above the point. Within this bend lies the Forest of Jaulnay, its length running northeast and southwest. At its southern extremity this forest joins the Forest of Dieulet, the length of which runs from northwest to southeast and which lay entirely across the sector of our division. The two forests form, roughly, an inverted "T", Dieulet the cross bar and Jaulnay the shank. And around the shank ran the river.

THE 178TH BRIGADE ASSAULTS

The mission assigned to the 178th Brigade for the 3rd of November was to attack and carry the heights overlooking Le Champy Haut and Beauclair and to push strong reconnaissance toward Stenay. The Division's sector was divided into two subsectors by the line of the road from Tailly to Beauclair to Beaufort, thence in a straight line to Laneuville. The right subsector was given to the 355th Infantry under command of Lieutenant Colonel T. P. Bernard, the left subsector to the 356th Infantry under command of Colonel Robert H. Allen. The objective for the day was taken without opposition, and at 9:30 A. M. it was evident that the enemy had withdrawn from the heights which overlook Le Champy Haut, Beauclair and Beaufort, but that fire could be expected from these places and the southern borders of the Foret de Dieulet and Bois la Dame. General Hanson was therefore ordered to press forward at once with his reconnaissances towards Stenay and to the north.

Because of the widening of the Division's sector, the advance was resumed with three battalions abreast. The right battalion, which advanced on Beauclair and Laneuville, was the 1st battalion, 355th Infantry, commanded by Major Thomas F. Wirth. The center which attacked Beaufort, was the 3rd battalion, 355th Infantry, under Captain (later Major) John F. Symes. The left, advancing on Le Champy Bas and Bois la Dame, was the first battalion, 356th Infantry, under Captain Frank Smith. Severe fighting on the right and left marked the advance of this day.

BEAUCLAIR TAKEN

By about noon. Major Wirth's battalion was in the woods north and east of Tailly, Captain Symes' battalion which had preceded it in the morning advance, having drawn off to the left to occupy the center sector. There was some delay in taking up the advance owing to lack of artillery coördination and the time required to communicate the orders for the new advance. Major Smead rode forward on a motorcycle from the advance message center, then being opened at Tailly, to locate the positions of the troops. Finding that the definite orders for the advance had not been received by Major Wirth, he rode back, procured from the Chief of Staff orders for Major Wirth to resume the advance and again rode forward with the orders, crossing the open ground under heavy fire several times on this mission. The advance on Beauclair began in the early afternoon. Intense fire developed from Beauclair and from artillery in the woods to the north. Company "B," 355th Infantry, under Captain Edmund Rogers, soon gained the edge of the Bois de Halles and there

Street scene in Tailly showing German sign on house, "Gott Strafe die Engländer."

gained contact with a detachment from the 90th Division, who gave the information that the enemy was still in these woods, and a detachment from Company "B" was sent to occupy a high knoll in the northern extremity of the woods. Company "C," coming up on the left, the advance continued on Beauclair under heavy fire from the town and the road leading from it to the west. Lieutenant Frank Fisher's platoon, inspired by his bravery and resolu-

The first American trucks (314th Supply Train, 89th Division) entering Beauclair with supplies during the Meuse-Argonne offensive while Fritz was shelling the town, which was captured on the evening of November 3rd, 1918, by the 355th Infantry, 89th Division. S. C. 31481.

tion, encircled the town and by about 3 o'clock had occupied an old German trench lying east of the Beauclair-Laneuville road, between Beauclair and the Foret de Dieulet.

In the meanwhile, our artillery was not functioning with the precision that was essential. Two accompanying guns for each assault battalion had been ordered, but these had not reported to the battalion commanders. A stray battery, which had been designated to accompany the infantry, was found by Colonel Lee, Chief of Staff, on the road south of Tailly. Perceiving the enemy resistance offered from Beauclair, Colonel Lee directed this battery to fire on the southern edges of the town, personally adjusting the fire from a position in a tree nearby. The enemy fire from Beauclair decreased, though the effect of our own artillery fire compelled Lieutenant

Fisher to withdraw his platoon to the Beauclair-Halles road. Early in the night the troops advanced on the town and meeting no further resistance, passed through it and took up a position along the Beauclair-Laneuville road, 500 yards northeast of Beauclair.

In the fighting around Beauclair, 2nd Lieutenant Frank J. Fisher displayed such conspicuous gallantry that he is personally credited with having advanced our front line two kilometers. Going out in advance, he captured two German machine guns and killed their crews. Later, when the line was halted by heavy fire, he exposed himself fearlessly in passing among his men to steady them and direct the consolidation of the position they held. While so doing, he was mortally wounded.

The center battalion, under Captain Symes, passed through Tailly on the morning of the 3rd of November and entered and cleared the woods to the east of the town during the day.

LE CHAMPY BAS TAKEN

On the left the 356th Infantry was meeting with opposition in the vicinity of Le Champy Bas. The 1st battalion had passed the lines of the 2nd battalion and had taken up the advance as assault battalion, being under the command of Captain Frank Smith. Shortly after the advance began, Captain Smith was wounded and Captain Marcellus H. Chiles took command of the battalion. The battalion was under severe fire from the woods in front and from the village of Le Champy Haut on the left flank, and could not advance. Accross the front ran a small stream. Picking up the rifle of a dead soldier, Captain Chiles called on his men to follow and led the advance across this little stream, which proved to be waist deep. On reaching the opposite bank, he fell, mortally wounded in the abdomen, the victim of a sniper's fire. Corporal William B. Whitaker, Company "A", 356th Infantry, who was following closely, disregarding his personal safety, sought and killed the sniper, and then assisted in evacuating Captain Chiles, who, though so wounded that he died in the hospital in a few days, refused to be sent to the rear until he had made complete arrangements for turning over the command to the next senior officer, 1st Lieutenant Matthew Winters. Posthumous award of the Medal of Honor was made to Captain Chiles.

The hard work and danger and gallant deeds were by no means confined to the infantry. The engineers were performing marvels in keeping the roads in repair and in reconnoitering roads and bridges to the front. 2nd Lieutenant Frank J. Hoeynck and Private 1-cl Edward A. Dietz of Companv "F", 314th Engineers, reconnoitered the bridges at Barricourt and Nouart and, while the enemy still held part of the village of Nouart, removed a mine from one of the bridges and saved it from destruction.

Under the inspiration of these examples the troops pressed on and, overcoming the resistance, passed through the small Bois la Dame and by night had attained the southeastern edges of the Bois de Belval.

Reconnoitering detachments were sent out in the night. That from the 356th Infantry proceeded in the direction of Beaumont with the mission of obtaining contact with the 2nd Division. This failed, for the 2nd Division had not yet come up. The detachment from the 355th Infantry penetrated to the outskirts of Beaufort.

WE ASK NOT TO BE RELIEVED

During the evening of this day, orders were received at Division Headquarters from the 5th Corps that the 1st Division, which was in reserve in our rear, would send a column through our lines and that we were to be assembled in its rear. General Wright immediately called the Corps by telephone and asked permission to remain in the line and to continue the advance. He stated that his troops were in fine condition, were in touch with the situation and could certainly make further progress the next day. He desired to gain possession of the Forest of Dieulet, which would afford artillery positions for long guns to break the German railroad beyond Stenay, and also to endeavor to get the bridgehead at Laneuville. The Corps Commander granted the request.

Accordingly orders were issued to General Hanson to advance and seize Laneuville, the northern edge of the Foret de Dieulet and to push reconnaissances forward to the Meuse and reconnoiter for river crossings.

The advance under these orders on November 4th was slow and on the whole unsatisfactory to General Wright, though the Division ultimately gained its objective. The troops of the line cannot be charged with the delay.

Major Wirth's battalion on the right encountered severe machine gun fire from the edges of the Foret de Dieulet where the Beauclair-Laneuville road enters it, and to the east of this point. They were unable to advance without artillery assistance which was not forthcoming, and remained most of the day engaged in a fire fight with the machine guns in these positions and from the trench which Lieutenant Fisher's platoon had occupied the previous day. Severe casualties were suffered in this position.

BEAUFORT FALLS AND THE RIVER IS REACHED

In the center, Captain Symes' battalion, moving from its position near Tailly at midnight, attacked Beaufort early in the morning and after some resistance and quite a number of casualties, especially among officers, it captured the town about 7:30 and took position near by, awaiting the barrage which was scheduled to commence on the edge of the forest at 8:30. General Hanson had expected to overcome the resistance by a standing barrage of the artillery for thirty minutes, beginning at 8:30 and laid along the edge of the woods, and had ordered the infantry to advance after this artillery preparation. But the artillery was not able to lay this barrage for the reason that sufficient ammunition had not come up, and the Division Commander countermanded the order. Thus much time was lost, during which Captain Symes and his troops were chafing at the delay in receiving orders to advance, and repeatedly requested permission to attack without artillery support. A rolling barrage against the enemy's position was then arranged, but was of little avail. Captain Symes determined to advance on his own responsibility and had given orders at 3 o'clock to do so, when he and Major Wirth finally received orders to advance without artillery support. Both battalions pressed forward, Major Wirth's troops, being closest, first penetrating the woods, and the two columns gained the northern edge of the Foret de Dieulet by midnight. Officers' patrols penetrated Laneuville, Luzy and Cesse, which made reconnaissance of the destroyed bridges and railroad in the vicinity. The left had met with little serious resistance and advanced during the day through the Foret de Dieulet, with some conflicts with isolated groups, reporting itself on its objective about an hour after dark.

The enemy had, however, succeeded in delaying our advance sufficiently to save himself from severe losses. Large numbers of the enemy and many vehicles had been observed crossing the river back of Laneuville during the day, but the reconnaissance in the night disclosed that the Germans had completely and with excellent engineering skill destroyed a series of stone culverts under the causeway from Laneuville to Stenay and had closed sufficient culverts to cause a large overflow of the upper valley to the south of the bridge. They also found opportunity to place many troublesome mines in the river villages, as will be mentioned later. On the whole, General Wright felt that the attack had not been pushed with sufficient vigor, and it is believed that if the commanders of the assault battalions had been permitted to press forward without waiting for the artillery, they would have captured a large number of the heavy guns which got across the river early that morning, and might have prevented the destruction of the bridges.

WE AGAIN DECLINE RELIEF

The Division was now in position overlooking the Meuse river. It had had four days of continuous, bitter fighting and had advanced against the enemy more than twenty-one kilometers. Evidently the Corps Commander thought we had done our share. For during the evening orders were received that the Division would assemble in the vicinity of Beaufort and Laneuville and await further orders. But still General Wright felt that the undaunted spirit of his men made them capable of rendering further service, and so for the second time he asked the Corps Commander for permission to stay in line and clear the enemy from the west side of the river. The permission was accorded and in addition authority to include in the operation the Foret de Jaulnay. Accordingly, orders were issued stating the mission to continue the advance and drive the enemy across the Meuse and seize and hold the bridges in the front. The 178th Brigade was given the mission of the Division and the 177th Brigade was directed to move forward all of its elements in support except two

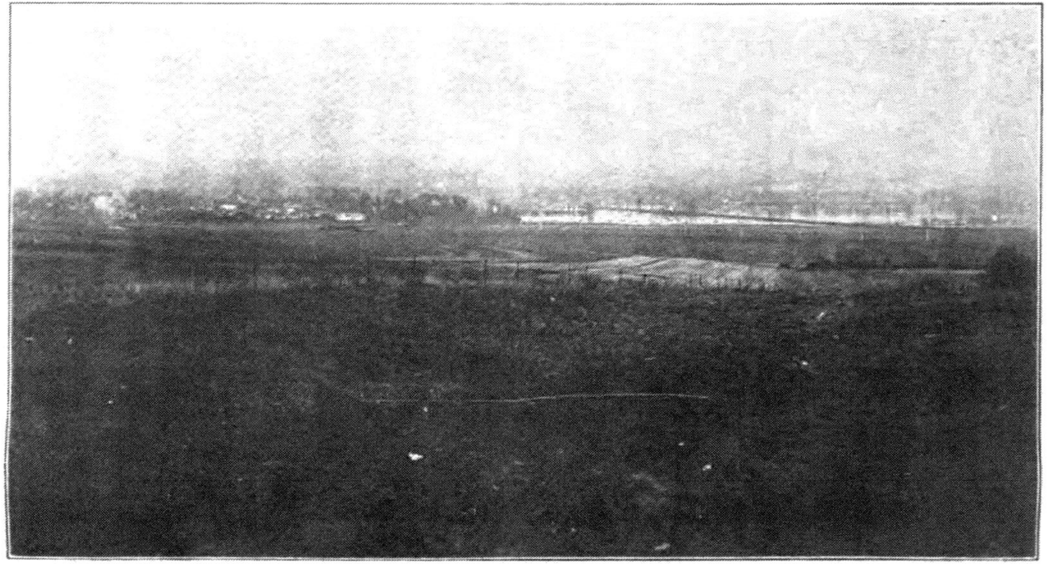

Laneuville (at left), the flooded Meuse and Stenay (at right) as they appeared from the edge of the Foret de Dieulet, Nov. 10th, 1918. A shell burst is seen at the left. Laneuville was seized by the 356th Inf., 89th Division, on the night of Nov. 4th, 1918. S. C. 34980.

battalions which were to remain on the heights and continue the organization of the positions there.

On the following day, November 5th, before noon, the Corps Commander issued instructions that the 89th Division would hold the heights east of the Meuse in its present front. This, of course, meant obtaining a river crossing. It meant that what had before been efforts for the common good in advancing to the river and seizing bridge heads, perhaps to be used by some other division in the further advance, had now become the definite and individual mission of the 89th Division, for the accomplishment of which no effort must be spared. The history from this time until the cessation of hostilities is a history of the preparation for and the final glorious accomplishment of this mission. It will be understood, of course, that there was, as yet, no order for the actual crossing of the river in force. That order was not issued until November 10th, and was carried out the night of the 10th and 11th.

Engineer reconnaissances early on the 5th disclosed that the enemy had destroyed all the bridges across the Meuse from Stenay to Inor. The bridge at Pouilly had been badly damaged, but it could still be crossed by men singly.

O. P. (observation post) of Capt. William P. Montgomery on the edge of the Foret de Dieulet, overlooking Laneuville, the Meuse and Stenay. It is a tower made of sections of German narrow-gauge railway, camouflaged with brush, and the observer is looking through a "scissors glass" projecting above the top, reporting to the men below, who repeat over the field telephone to headquarters in the rear, the effect of artillery fire, movements of the enemy, etc. Meuse-Argonne offensive, Nov. 10th, 1918. S. C. 34931.

The bridge at Inor had not been destroyed during the day of the 5th, but later it was blown up. It had been hoped that one of these bridges could be secured and held from destruction, but the enemy was able to thwart our efforts. He had succeeded in getting the bulk of his army across the river, though at the expense of heavy losses of men, and had been compelled to abandon vast quantities of stores, particularly artillery ammunition.

RECONNAISSANCES OF POUILLY

The orders extending the Division's sector so as to include the forest of Jaulnay were communicated through the brigade to the 356th Infantry at 5:30 A. M., November 5th, and that regiment was ordered to advance through the forest, clearing it of the enemy as far as the point extending beyond Pouilly in the direction of Inor. Owing to the length of time required to bring up the 3rd Battalion from its position in support of the battalion of the 355th in the center of the line, the jump-off could not be made till 8 o'clock. At this hour the advance began, with the 1st Battalion, under Captain (later Major) John W. Harris, as the assault battalion, and the 3rd Battalion, under Captain Arthur Y. Wear, in support. The advance continued throughout the day and the 1st Battalion reached a point overlooking the town of Inor at 4:30 P. M., November 5th. In the course of the operation, orders were received from the regiment to detach the 3rd Battalion from the support of the 1st, and to send it to the bridgehead at Pouilly to reconnoiter the bridgehead, and if the bridge was still intact, to hold the bridgehead and prevent any destructive operations. The order contained specific instructions, however, not to attempt to force a crossing at Pouilly, even if the bridge was found intact. Major Mark Hanna, whose battalion was to be in support of Captain Wears battalion, was designated to command both battalions in the operation. During the morning orders were received by the Division from the Corps by telephone for the 89th to hold the heights east of the river, which required a crossing. The 178th Brigade was then ordered to seize and hold the Pouilly bridge, but this order, probably because of difficulties in communication, apparently did not reach the battalion.

Captain Wear directed a preliminary reconnaissance and as a result reported in the afternoon of the 5th that the bridge was still intact. This report was evidently erroneous; the error may have been due to an error in the available maps, which showed only two branches of the river before Pouilly. In point of fact there were three; and the principal destruction was in the portion of the bridge which crossed the branch of the river nearest the town. Colonel Lee, the Chief of Staff, accompanied by Lieutenant Colonel Brehon B. Somervell, who was at the time serving with the Division as a volunteer, was sent forward by General Wright in the afternoon to get in touch with the situation on the ground. He found, after making a personal reconnaissance along the causeway, across the damaged lockgates of the canal (the bridge having been destroyed) and to the vicinity of the next bridge, that there was no outpost at the bridgehead and that the bridge had been badly damaged. He was accompanied by Lieutenant Hook and a ser-

precarious way across the sluice gates of the dam in the canal, he slipped unperceived into the town and remained there two hours. He saw many enemy soldiers who seemed to come unconcernedly into the town for their meals and could hear the women who were cooking for them talking in German; he made valuable observations of the locations of machine guns. Major Hanna returned over the bridge in broad daylight and was not fired on until after passing the railroad several hundred yards. While in the town he was on the main street within speaking distance of German soldiers who were so unconcerned that they did not notice that he was an enemy. The very audacity of this exploit seemed to have rendered him immune.

On the morning of the 6th of November, Captain Harris was returning along his runner chain from his position above Inor to Regimental Headquarters. On his way, he met a platoon of Marines from the 2nd Division on our left, and asked the commander where he was going. He replied that his orders were to drive the boche out of the northern edge of the Forest of Jaulnay. Captain Harris told him that would be a useless mission, as his battalion was in the northern edge of the woods at the time. Further back Captain Harris encountered another platoon of Marines and inquired of the commander how he happened to be in the 89th Division sector; the lieutenant responded that he had been sent over to take a patrol into Pouilly. The patrol passed on, and coming to the bridgehead was met by a patrol from 3rd Battalion, 356th Infantry, returning from the island before Pouilly across the wreckage of the destroyed bridge. It is related that when the commander of the platoon of Marines saw the situation and the condition of the bridge he exclaimed, "Good God! No wonder they talk about the 89th."

In some accounts of the operations along the Meuse, the gallant Marine Brigade has been given credit for the mopping up of the Forest of Jaulnay. Doubtless this error grew out of the fact that the orders of the 2nd Division for the mopping up were issued before the forest was placed in the sector of the 89th Division. It is an incontestable fact, however, that the forest was completely in the possession of the 356th Infantry before the mopping up parties of the 2nd Division came up.

INOR BRIDGE

The progress of the 178th Infantry Brigade on the 4th, 5th and 6th of November was not as rapid as the Division Commander thought essential. After the Heights of Barricourt fell, it was obvious that the enemy would withdraw across the Meuse, fighting only a rear-guard action. Vigorous pursuit was demanded by the situation, especially since the orders contemplated most aggressive exploitation.

The bridge at Inor had been reported as being intact on the afternoon of the 5th, by an engineer reconnaissance party which had observed it from the northeastern tip of the Forest of Jaulnay. On the 7th, the 356th Infantry reported that the bridge had been demolished, that Inor itself was occupied by the enemy who seemed to be living there, and that the road from Inor to Martincourt was being worked upon by large parties of the enemy in plain sight from our positions. This report passed through the headquarters of the 178th Brigade, without comment from the Commanding General. On its receipt at the Division, General Wright sent an inquiry to General Hanson, asking why he permitted this condition to exist on his front, in view of his mission to hold the river front and protect the bridge crossings. General Hanson responded, denying that he had permitted the conditions or had failed to use any of the instrumentalities at his disposal to prevent them. But the fact remained that the bridge had been blown up, probably on the afternoon of the 7th, and that the enemy's activities continued. General Wright, on the 8th of November, issued orders relieving General Hanson of command of his brigade, and General Herman Hall, then attached to the Division, was assigned to the command.

GALLANT EXPLOITS DURING THE ADVANCE

In recording the rush of events during the first week of November but little room has been given to exploits of individual gallantry. So numerous were they that scores, perhaps hundreds, received no recognition save in the minds of those who saw them done and in the proud consciousness of the performers that they were tried by fire and not found wanting. Those honored by decorations or citations are listed elsewhere in this book, but it was not humanly possible for all worthy cases to be reported, nor is it practicable, in the space available, to do more in this history than to touch upon a few incidents, typical rather than exceptional, of the conduct of these middle western boys on the field in France.

Encounters with machine guns, in which the individual courage and enterprise of one or two men put them out of action and permitted the continuance of the advance without undue casualties, were frequent. Among them may be mentioned Sergeant Clayton Malone, Company "I," Corporal John W. McKay, Company "M," Sergeant Elmer F. Guthrie, Company "E." all in the 353rd Infantry, on November 1st. That such enterprises require a price in blood was illustrated the same day by the experiences of Sergeant John A. Hartung, Corporal Alexander Folz and Private John J. Farrell, all of Company "B," 354th Infantry, all of whom successfully accomplished such missions, but paid with their lives for their valorous deeds. Similar were the exploits of 2nd Lieutenant Frank J. Fisher (who also made the supreme sacrifice), 355th Infantry, and Sergeant (then Corporal) George G. Hollis, Company "E," 356th Infantry, during the next two days. 2nd Lieutenant Irving LeN. Ragsdale, 356th Infantry, performed repeated acts of gallantry, advancing over open ground under intense fire to clean up machine gun nests.

On November 2nd, near Barricourt, 2nd Lieutenant Howard A. Bair, 354th Infantry, calling on his platoon to follow, pushed forward to the attack of machine gun nests. Here occurred one of the cases of suspected treachery, although the evidence is not conclusive. After killing two of the enemy, Lieutenant Bair was killed by a hand grenade while accepting the surrender of another German.

Machine gunners, placing their guns in the open, often ahead of the infantry and under heavy fire, distinguished themselves and proved the mobility and effectiveness of their weapons under adverse conditions. A striking instance of this is the case, on November 1st, of Sergeant (then Corporal) George Colville, Jr., Corporal Thomas Stirling and Private Fred S. Smith, all of the Machine Gun Company, 354th Infantry, who fired at close range in the open field until their gun was disabled, when they charged with their pistols, capturing men and machine guns and turning the latter on the foe. The following day Private Smith was killed when he went out from cover to warn comrades they were in the line of fire. Corporal Joseph C. Hahn and Private 1-cl. Clifford C. Kidd, of the same company, drew fire and honor manning a machine gun in the open ahead of the infantry on November 1st, as did Corporal Frantz Koeppe, Company "C," 341st Machine Gun Battalion, on the same day by a similar act which silenced by direct frontal fire the German machine gun nest which was delaying the advance of the infantry company to which he was attached. Similar effective service was rendered by Private 1-cl. Archie Comstock, Machine Gun Company, 356th Infantry, on November 4th, and by Roy E. McComb, of the same company, who led his section with great skill and gallantry, exposing himself fearlessly to get the greatest fire effect, until he was fatally wounded.

In the rescue of the wounded and administering to their needs, often in the open and under intense fire, those characteristics were displayed which call for no less courage than does any form of strictly combat service. Thus Private David Kline, Medical Detachment, 341st Machine Gun Battalion, disregarded his own safety in succoring the wounded in full view of the enemy and in an area swept by the fire of all arms, on November 1st, and Private 1-cl. (then Private) Almon E. Sprague, Medical Detachment, 355th Infantry, on November 4th, exposed himself at the front and made trips toward the rear and back to get first aid supplies and attend to the wounded, all under heavy fire. Sergeant (then Private) Gus Bordkas, Medical Detachment, 354th Infantry, not only displayed great bravery in the care of the wounded on November 1st, but while accompanying the front echelon, rescued and dragged into a shell hole a wounded comrade, under withering machine gun fire. On the afternoon of November 1st, northeast of Remonville, Private William E. Williams, Company "A," 314th Engineers, crawled out in advance of his company to aid a wounded comrade. On the morning of November 6th, near Luzy, Private Sigurd Lundstedt, Company "B," 342nd Machine Gun Battalion, under intense machine gun fire from German aeroplanes, rescued a wounded American aviator from under the wrecked plane which they had just brought down. About the same time Supply Sergeant Court E. Krumvieda, Company "A," 340th Machine Gun Battalion, voluntarily made an extended reconnaissance for food and ammunition much needed by his organization, capturing a German and rescuing a wounded American soldier while engaged in the enterprise. During the last week before the armistice, after all the medical officers with the battalion had been wounded, 1st Lieutenant Robert O. Smith, Dental Surgeon, 2nd Battalion, 356th Infantry, performed their duties for six days, moving the first aid station forward and maintaining it under heavy fire.

To "carry on" after being wounded, continuing in the performance of duty when every instinct points the other way and a valid reason exists to throw the torch to other hands, calls for possibly the highest type of human courage, yet such instances were so frequent during the drive that many were not reported. A few cases must suffice for this narrative: Sergeant Harry E. Flannery, of Company "D," 341st Machine Gun Battalion, though painfully wounded November 1st, maintained excellent control over his men and refused first aid until others had been cared for. Private John R. Manning, of the same company, disregarding painful injuries, continued on duty through the action and until relieved and ordered to the first aid station. Second Lieutenant Albert E. Birch, 342nd Machine Gun Battalion, wounded on November 1st, refused to go to the rear during the critical period and served with his company until killed on November 11th. Sergeant John R. Slay, Company "G," 354th Infantry, continued with the attack on November 2nd after being severely wounded until ordered to the rear. Likewise Sergeant Rudolph A. Zimmerman, of the Machine Gun Company, 354th Infantry, was wounded but continued to lead his section until relieved. Near Beauclair, on November 3rd, Private 1-cl. Charles J. Gude, Company "D," 342nd Machine Gun Battalion, after being twice wounded and unconscious, revived and took command successively of his squad and section as others were wounded, refusing first aid until relieved. Early in the action near Beaufort, on November 4th, 1st Lieutenant Verne A. Morgan, 355th Infantry, was wounded, but returned to his company immediately after receiving first aid and led it throughout the day. Private Roy A. Bess, of Company "L," 355th Infantry, wounded near Beaufort about the same time, fought on with his company for two days without treatment. 1st Lieutenant Harold W. Kenaston, 356th Infantry, although severely gassed on the 4th, continued on duty, going the next day for reserve rations for his regiment and working continuously day and night under constant fire, distinguishing himself again in the last twenty-four hours before the armistice by valuable and dangerous service.

The combat arms were not alone in danger nor in the courageous performance of duty. Corporal John H. Koontz, Company "C," 314th Ammunition Train, was with a convoy of trucks loaded with hand grenades and trench mortar ammunition near Beaufort on November 7th, when one of the trucks was hit by a high explosive shell. After removing the other trucks from the immediate vicinity he proceeded to extinguish the flames of the burning truck with a fire extinguisher, regardless of risk from exploding ammunition.

Danger was great and casualties were heavy among the runners, who formed the most reliable means of communication during active operations, when the maintenance of liaison was one of the most difficult of the many problems, and lack of it at times not only made for uncertainty but cost casualties. Barrages might fall and machine guns sputter, but the runner went through, by day or night. Bugler Frank F. Tomanek, Company I, 353rd Infantry, volunteered to maintain liaison with the assault battalion, November 1st, during a heavy counter barrage, and within two hours successfully carried out four such missions. On November 2nd Corporal Lloyd Farber, Headquarters Company, and Private Don Greene, Company H, both in the 353rd Infantry, carried important messages through heavy fire, and the same day Private John Kelly, Company "A," 341st Machine Gun Battalion, performed similar service from an advanced position, exposing himself fearlessly by a trip in the open to save his machine gun section from friendly fire and returning to it when he had informed the troops of its location. During the advance of the 356th Infantry on November 4th, Private Clarence Loken, Company "M," unhesitatingly made his trips back and forth through the bombarded area between the front line and the support battalion. The following day Private 1-cl. (then Private) John P. Donovan, Company "L," 356th Infantry, crossed on the ruined Pouilly bridge, saved his patrol leader, and brought back valuable information.

And so might the list be extended indefinitely, every name on the list of honors standing for some such exploit as those so briefly sketched here and elsewhere through the narrative.

PAUSE AT THE RIVER

The armies now confronted one another across the valley of the Meuse. The Germans were engaged in organizing the heights beyond the river for defense. Their artillery and machine gun fire swept the entire river and dominated every possible crossing. On our side the infantry rested upon their arms, guarding the crossings, patrolling and reconnoitering the banks of the stream and preparing for the coming fight. During this interim the infantry was stationed during most of the time as follows: The 1st battalion, 356th Infantry, in the Bois de la Vache at the extreme left of the sector; the 2nd battalion south of the Laneuville-Beaumont road at the junction of the Forest of Jaulnay with the Forest of Dieulet; the 3rd battalion in the Forest of Jaulnay on the heights overlooking Pouilly during the day, and at night along the railroad track and the head of the bridge leading into the town. The 355th Infantry held the southeastern edge of the Forest of Jaulnay and the northeastern edge of the Forest of Dieulet, forming an angle and overlooking the valley of the Meuse from Stenay to Inor, with two platoons in each of the towns of Luzy, Cesse and Laneuville, and constant patrols along the banks of the river. The Brigade P. C. was at Beauclair. The 177th Brigade was in the southern edges of the Foret de Dieulet and in the vicinity of Beauclair, Beaufort and Le Champy Haut. Its headquarters were first at Nouart, but from November 7th to the end, at Beaufort.

The artillery had been pushed well up to the front and was stationed for the most part along the road at the point of union of the Forests of Jaulnay and Dieulet. The 122nd F. A. was in support of the 356th Infantry in the left sub-sector and the 124th F. A. supported the 355th Infantry in the right sub-sector. The 11th F. A., 155 mm. howitzers, had two battalions along the Laneuville-Beaumont road, three kilometers northwest of Laneuville, one battery a kilometer southwest of Laneuville and another near Beaufort.

The plucky little 314th Mobile Ordnance Repair Shop, which always believed in keeping close to the front, where damage to ordnance was greatest,

Trucks loaded with Y. M. C. A. supplies going through shellfire in the streets of Laneuville in November, 1918. The town was captured by the 355th Infantry, 89th Division. S. C. 31482.

had established its small arms section in Remonville on November 4th. The artillery section soon came up and the entire shop, after opening at Beaufort and having been driven out by severe shelling and lack of shelter, was transferred to Beauclair where it worked through the stormy days up to the armistice.

DECISION TO FORCE CROSSING AT POUILLY

When, on November 5th, the Division had come actually to the banks of the river, General Wright had tentatively decided that the situation at Pouilly afforded the best opportunities for forcing the crossing of the river. Further reflection and the reports of reconnaissances confirmed this opinion, and it was definitely determined to make the crossing there. Preparations were immediately begun to carry out the decision.

The considerations which induced the selection of Pouilly were the following: The demolished condition of the causeway approaches and of the main bridge over the Meuse proper at Stenay made it manifestly impracticable to attempt the main crossing there. The flat, open character of the country around Cesse and Luzy facing the commanding bluffs on the enemy side and the character of the existing bridges eliminated these locations from consideration. There remained Inor and Pouilly. Good bridges had existed at both these places and the demolitions had been only partially complete. The enemy's position was parallel to the main course of the Meuse, which, to a point just below Inor, ran almost from south to north. Inor and the approaches thereto were therefore exposed to direct observation and fire from all portions of the enemy's line on our front. Just below Inor the river bent sharply to the southwest. Within the bend lay the Forest of Jaulnay, covering a rather high ridge. Along this reach the river ran fairly close to this ridge and the edges of the forest, and at about the center of it lay Pouilly. Pouilly, therefore was protected from observation and direct fire from all that part of the enemy's line lying to the south of the positions opposite Inor. Thus a concentration of artillery and machine gun fire which was possible at Inor was denied the enemy at Pouilly. On the other hand, since Inor was opposite the tip of the Forest of Jaulnay while Pouilly was opposite the center of its longest extent, it was plain that the protecting fire of our own artillery and machine guns scattered throughout the forest could be concentrated over Pouilly; while at Inor the narrow width of the forest denied us such concentration.

Again, our reconnaissances had been more successfully pushed at Pouilly, giving us better knowledge of the terrain and indicating that the place was not so strongly held as Inor. There were strongly held, wooded heights back of Inor, which dominated the crossing; at Pouilly the country on the opposite bank was more open and flat. And, finally, the engineer officer operating with the bridge train recommended the Pouilly crossing from a technical standpoint.

The plan adopted therefore was to force a crossing near Pouilly, drive eastward to the heights back of Inor and then exploit to the south, this to be done with one brigade. In the meanwhile the other brigade would maintain contact with the 90th Division, advancing on our right, and as soon as the 90th Division should have taken Stenay, which was in their sector, it would advance north along the east bank of the Meuse, clearing the enemy as far as the heights and connecting up with the troops which would cross at Pouilly. The orders for the crossing, issued November 10th, embody this plan and assign the mission of crossing at Pouilly to the 178th Brigade and of crossing at Stenay in liaison with the 90th Division to the 177th Brigade.

PREPARATIONS FOR CROSSING

When, on November 5th, General Wright was advised that in addition to holding its front the Division would reorganize in preparation for its advance to the north, special inspections and conferences were had to determine the exact status of the Division. And on November 6th he reported that the 178th Brigade needed a day or two of recuperation before energetic work could be expected of them; that the 177th Brigade, which had been in reserve for several days, was fit and approximately sixty per cent strength, but that the Division needed replacements of 306 officers and 6,153 men. That the artillery was able to make one shift of position, but before being pushed across the river over temporary structures and poor roads to engage in open warfare should have 500 good animals. That the bridge at Pouilly could, in a week's time, be put into condition for heavy vehicles, while infantry and light trains could probably be put over in four days. That the roads to the bridges between Stenay and Pouilly were reported bad, except the one to Inor.

The four days' cessation of actual advance gave the infantry opportunity for some recuperation, though changes of position occurred which involved exhausting marches through the forest over muddy roads, especially for the machine guns. There was constant artillery and machine gun fire upon our positions, however, causing many casualties. And the record of the patrols and reconnaissances made during this period is one of glorious achievement.

ENGINEER RECONNAISSANCES

Some of the most valuable of these reconnaissances were made by the engineers to gain information regarding bridges and possible crossings. On one of these, 2nd Lieutenant Frank J. Hoeynck, Company "F," 314th Engineers, was instantly killed on the island just south of Pouilly, by a machine gun sniper, receiving two bullets in the head. Private 1st Cl. Edward W. A. Dietz, of the same company, who accompanied him, was wounded in the hand. Private Dietz lay motionless beside the body of the dead officer during the entire day, discovering the position of the machine gun which killed Lieutenant Hoeynck, and made his escape after darkness had fallen. He returned at 2 P. M. on the 8th of November, bringing back the information which the officer and he had been ordered to secure, having been out since 3 o'clock P. M., November 6.

On the three days of Nov. 5th, 6th and 7th, Ist Lieutenant (then 2nd Lieutenant) Percy G. Forman, 314th Engineers, accompanied by Private Brewer, Company F, 314th Engineers, made valuable reconnaissances, exposed to the fire of friend and foe alike, through the shell swept Foret de Jaulnay, ascertaining the condition of the bridge at Inor and reporting on roads near there and Luzy.

SWIMMING THE MEUSE

On the afternoon of the 8th of November, Colonel Allen of the 356th Infantry received orders to send patrols across the Meuse at all hazards to reconnoiter the further bank for landing places, ascertain the enemy's dispositions and take prisoners for identification. The use of rafts for crossing was suggested. The battalion commanders of the 1st and 3rd battalions were sent for and the orders communicated to them. The 1st battalion was holding the left of the sector along the river on the regimental front and the 3rd battalion the right, the 2nd being in reserve.

No tools for the construction of rafts were at hand. A small quantity of wire was found and the attempt was made to bind together logs from the woods with this, but without success. Bags of charcoal were found and rafts out of this material were constructed, but would not hold up a man. So that ultimately to carry out the mission, many of the members of the patrols made the attempt to cross by swimming. All were volunteers who essayed this perilous feat. The river was 150 to 200 feet in width, with a swift current. The water was ice cold, the season being substantially that of winter. The men who so bravely dared this crossing had been ten days in active battle; they had only the clothes upon their backs, not even blankets to wrap in when they came out of the water. A determined enemy held the opposite shore and they knew that if they survived the perils of the crossing they would probably have to fight upon the further shore, wet and exhausted as they would be. The prospect might well have daunted the stoutest heart; but when volunteers were called for, more men responded than were needed.

On the sector of the 1st battalion, Captain Schwinn, who was in command, decided to send three patrols of two men each, at different points of his sector, each patrol to be covered by a small detachment of riflemen on the hither shore. Of the six men who made this attempt, two succeeded and two were drowned. On the left of the sector, at a point about 500 meters south of Letanne, Sergeant Waldo M. Hatler, Company "B", and Corporal John W. McAfee, Company "D", entered the stream and commenced the swim across. Before reaching the opposite bank, Corporal McAfee, chilled and exhausted, sank to rise no more. Notwithstanding, Sergeant Hatler pressed on, gained the opposite bank, ascertained its character, located an enemy outpost and reëntering the stream swam back to the point of his departure. He was drawn from the water, suffering severely from exhaustion and exposure, and taken to the regimental aid station, though not until he had given the substance of his report.

In the center of the sector, Lieutenants St. George S. Creaghe of Company "A", and Lieutenant Hayes, of Company "D", made the attempt. After they had entered the water at the mouth of the little creek Wame, a boat bearing a German patrol came directly at them. Remaining still and quiet in the icy stream, they were compelled to watch the enemy patrol land and the boat be returned by a soldier to the other shore. Leaving the stream at that point, they went further down stream to try again, but found that they were confronted by a German sentinel on the further shore, whose voice they heard in time to save themselves a rencontre. Morning was coming, and worn out by their efforts, they were compelled to abandon their attempt.

On the right of the sector, nearer Pouilly and near the mouth of the Wame, which they had followed in error, thinking it another stream which empties higher up the Meuse, Sergeant (then Private 1st Class) Harold I. Johnston, Company "A", and Private David B. Barkeley, of the same company, both succeeded in swimming the stream. On the other bank, Johnston crawled over 150 yards back from the stream without being detected by the enemy outpost in the vicinity and fully ascertained the character of the banks and found them suitable for the landing of the troops. On the return, Barkeley succumbed to the cold and effort and was drowned, but Johnston succeeded, though exhausted, in reaching shore with his information.

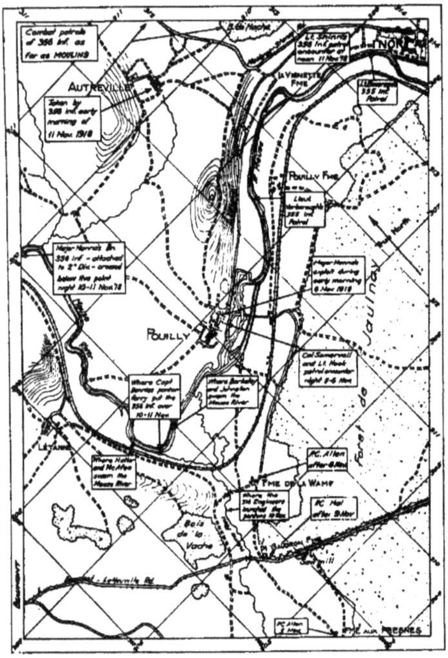

Scene of operations by the 355th Infantry and 356th Infantry in the vicinity of Pouilly and Letanne, Nov. 5-11, 1918. Kilometer grid. From Stenay map.

For these exploits Sergeant Hatler, Private 1-cl. Johnston and Private Barkeley were awarded the Medal of Honor, the award to the last named being posthumous.

On the sector of the 3rd battalion four patrols were sent out, but two of them were driven back by machine gun fire from Pouilly, and one, which attempted to cross on rafts abandoned the attempt, while the fourth, which attempted to swim, could not get across.

On the night of the 9th-10th, some captured German pontoons had come up to the 356th Infantry. One of them was floated down the Wame and used to transport a patrol of twenty-four men under Lieutenant Heiken, which made a complete and successful reconnaissance in the vicinity of Pouilly. They located an enemy outpost in the bend of the river below

Pouilly, and captured three of them, who furnished valuable information. Later, in the outskirts of Pouilly, a part of the patrol encountered an enemy patrol; one of the enemy threw a hand grenade, which exploded without causing damage; our men returned the fire with their rifles, killing two and wounding one of the enemy. They returned without casualties.

On the night of the 9th-10th, the 355th Infantry also took up the task of throwing patrols over the river on its front. A patrol of two officers and four men of the 2nd battalion, all having volunteered for the danger ous mission, attempted to cross the river by part of them swimming in the vicinity of Pouilly Farm, about a kilometer and a half up river from Pouilly. The foremost swimmers were met while in the water by the fire of machine guns and grenades from the enemy shore. Lieutenant Walter S. Yarbrough, commanding the patrol, and six men were either killed by the fire, drowned or captured, as their bodies were never found. The missing were Sergeant Mack Christian, Company "F"; Corporal Earnest C. Sexton, Company "H"; Sergeant Victor C. Lee, Company "H"; Private Ole Alendale, Company "H", and Corporal Carl Heath, Company "H". Private James V. Ponder, Company "G", was captured, and, after the Armistice, returned to his company. He knew nothing of the fate of his missing comrades. The other members of the patrol, consisting of 2nd Lieutenant John H. Davidson, Sergeant Edward R. Winebar, Private Alfred Moen, all of Company "G"; Sergeant Walter L. Lewis, Privates Onezie Suire, George Desseles, Robert C. McGill, Theodore Campbell and Henry H. Becher, all of Company "H", being slightly in the rear of the leading swimmers, were driven back.

Just west of Inor a patrol from the 3rd battalion under Lieutenant Columbus C. Beverage attempted to cross by swimming, carrying a rope on which they hoped to bring the rest of the patrol across. The current and the cold of the water proved too much for them and the attempt failed. The officer and Corporal Roscoe W. Grisham, Company "K", Privates Joseph Gross, H. F. Goettsch, Roma Brannan and James R. Cook, Company "L", were all taken from the water in an exhausted and semi-conscious condition.

A third patrol from the regiment reconnoitered the bridges near Stenay.

REMOVING MINES

During the period of preparation for the forcing of the passage of the Meuse, the engineers, among other activities, were engaged in the search for and removal of mines left by the treacherous and retreating enemy. A detail of two sergeants and fourteen men of Company "E", 314th Engineers. made a two days' examination of the buildings, bridges and roads in the vicinity of Cesse and Laneuville. They found none in the bridges which had already been demolished as completely as the enemy could do so. But they found and removed sixty-five mines in the buildings of Laneuville and eight in buildings in Cesse.

There is something particularly diabolical in the leaving of a mine to be exploded by someone coming later in ignorance of the danger. The practice is not forbidden by the laws of war and was indulged in by belligerents on both sides. But it has an unsportsmanlike cast which seemed to appeal to the German mind, and the Germans were especially good at it. Whenever they could do so, they left cunningly concealed engines of de-

314th Engineers removing mines left by the Germans in houses in Laneuville during the Meuse-Argonne offensive. The town was captured by the 355th Infantry. S. C. 31480.

struction to be exploded by the advancing troops of their adversaries. A nation whose idea of the sport of hunting is to have beaters drive the game up to the concealed hunter for slaughter, could be expected to adopt the method of killing off their adversaries with the minimum of personal danger. The feature which makes the use of concealed mines repulsive is that it does not give the victim a chance to engage with the individual who slays him—a chance which he has in fair, stand-up fighting in the open; and furthermore, it seems to healthy-minded men such an impersonal way of killing, since he who leaves the mine has no conception of who his victim will be. The mine may be exploded by a civilian, a chaplain, a Red Cross nurse—by anyone from whose slaughter all genuine soldiers would shrink. But such considerations do not appeal to the German. To him, war consists in killing as many of his adversaries as possible with the least danger and effort to himself; and concealed mines seem to him admirably adapted to that end.

So far as is known, no American troops ever left a concealed mine in this war; but it must be confessed also that they never had an opportunity to do so, for they were never compelled to evacuate a position.

Of the mines found in Laneuville and Cesse, practically all were in cellars, or on the first floor over the cellar or against the ceiling of cellars, evidently being intended to destroy the cellar. These mines were provided with a fuse from nine to ten inches in length. They ordinarily consisted of 77mm. shell cases filled with explosives, each case provided with a detonator. From five to nineteen of such cases would be placed together, with one fuse lighter and one fuse.

About half of those found in Laneuville were under a board or stone directly in front of a stove; the fuse lighter left in the grate. Thus anyone buiding a fire would light the fuse and explode the mine. A number of mines in basements or cellars were held against the ceiling by a board, and were connected with a wire running across the doorway in such a position as to be tripped by anyone entering the cellar. In such cases the fuse was only nine to twelve inches long and the charges heavy.

FORCING THE CROSSING

The crossing of the Meuse near Pouilly was effected in rafts made of pontoons captured from the enemy on another front. The transportation of the troops was assigned to Captain F. E. Dennie and his company, "C", of the 314th Engineers. The pontoons had been brought up on the afternoon of November 8th by a detachment of the 603rd Engineers under command of Captain McGeachin, and were parked that night on the Laneuville-Beaumont road in the northern edge of the Foret de Dieulet and carefully camouflaged. On consultation with Colonel Allen, 356th Infantry, Captain Dennie decided not to attempt the building of a pontoon bridge for the first crossing because his men were not familiar with the German pontoons. It was decided to build rafts of several pontoons and ferry the men across by means of cables on both ends.

One pontoon was used on the night of the 9th to take a patrol of the infantry across. The boat was poled across the river and returned with five prisoners.

The final order for the crossing was issued on the 10th. The hour set for the crossing in the orders was 6 P. M., at which time, at that season, it would be pitch dark. Teams were hitched to the pontoon wagons and they started from their park shortly before 6 o'clock. They were drawn on the wagons along the road through the forest, thence down the river road, passing Bois de la Vache, to a point near where a little stream called Ruisseau la Wame empties into the Meuse. The boats were then carried by hand and launched in this little stream three or four hundred yards above its mouth and floated down to the river. The mouth of the Wame is about one and one-half kilometers below Pouilly, and at this point the crossing was made. A raft was then made of three pontoons by placing them side by side and lashing three balks across them. The pontoons being made of metal, boards were placed in the bottoms so that the hobnails on the men's shoes would not make too loud a noise as the men stepped into the pontoons. Ropes were attached to both ends of each of the side boats, making two ropes on each end of the raft. The first one was

Ferme de la Wame in foreground. Behind it are the railroad and the Meuse. Pouilly (to the right, beyond the Meuse) had been penetrated by patrols previously, and was seized on the morning of Nov. 11th, 1918, by the 356th Infantry, 89th Division, operating from Ferme de la Wame and crossing the river in boats, manned by the 314th Engineers. The pontoon rafts used in crossing were constructed on the stream which passes this farm and floated down to the Meuse just before the crossing. About the same time one battalion of the 356th Infantry also crossed the Meuse below Letanne (which is seen in the far distance at the left) in a joint operation with troops of the 2nd Division, and suffered heavy casualties, including the death of the battalion commander, Major Mark Hanna. S. C. 34979.

completed by 7.45 P. M., and sixteen engineers and a covering detachment of twenty-two infantrymen were rowed across, and when the boats were unloaded they were pulled back by the ropes. Captain Dennie crossed with this first boat and accompanied the infantry detachment to their covering position. The infantry commander expressed doubt about being able to hold the position, but Captain Dennie encouraged him with the remark, "If you come back here you'll find me with a gun looking for you." The engineers, with Lieutenant Fournet in charge, remained on the further bank to pull the raft across. The infantry began arriving at 8:30 and were ferried across in this raft continuously until 10. Twenty-five men were placed in each boat, making seventy-five in all for each raft load. Thus the 1st battalion of the 356th Infantry and a part of the 3rd battalion were taken across within an hour and a half. While the first raft was operating, a second one of the same sort was launched a little further up the Wame and was ready to haul infantry across by 9:30 o'clock. Lieutenant Welles was in charge of the engineer detail on the north side of the river at this raft. By 2 o'clock in the morning of November 11th, these rafts had transported the rest of the 3rd battalion of the 356th and the 3rd battalion of the 355th, hauling back wounded on the return trips. Detachments of the Field Signal Battalion crossed with the infantry and found means to get their wire across on old German telephone poles.

Thus the dreaded crossing of the Meuse was effected, and without a casualty. The enemy had been wholly deceived by the careful concealment of the pontoons before their use, and by a ruse which induced him to think that the crossing was being attempted at Pouilly itself. For while the crossing below Pouilly was going on, the engineers under the cover of a brisk artillery fire on the river towns proceeded with the construction of two foot-bridges over the ruins of the old bridge into Pouilly. The enemy outposts discovered this work and called down on it machine gun and artillery fire of sufficient severity to stop it temporarily. The actual crossing was not known to the German garrison in Pouilly until the town had been encircled and our position well secured on the heights beyond. The town was then entered from the rear and more than a hundred prisoners taken.

The enemy was further deceived in the operation by the conduct of the artillery. Before the 9th of November our artillery did not fire on the towns east of the river, as they were known to be occupied by French women and children. It was realized, however, that these towns were affording shelter to the enemy and must be subjected to fire if our troops were to take them. So General Wright arranged through the air service to warn the inhabitants that the towns would be shelled, commencing the 9th of November. That evening, therefore, the towns east of the river opposite the Division front were briskly shelled. On the evening of the 10th, while the crossing was under way, the shelling of the river towns was repeated. The German garrison of Pouilly apparently took to the cellars, believing that the shelling was a mere repetition of that of the night before, and in consequence failed to discover the actual crossing.

OPERATIONS ACROSS THE MEUSE

We come now to the operations of the 178th Infantry Brigade across the Meuse. The brigade was under the command of Brigadier General Herman Hall, who had succeeded Brigadier General Hanson in command on the 9th. The headquarters were at a former German prison camp located at the Point Gaudron Farm on the Laneuville-Beaumont road near its crossing over the Wame. Though the hour designated in the Corps order for beginning the operation was 4 P. M., General Hall was advised by the Marine Brigade of the 2nd Division on our left that they would not begin the advance from the river until 9.30 P. M., and he adjusted his plans accordingly. The artillery destructive fire began on the town of Pouilly up to and including the left Divisional sector at 9:30. This fire was followed by a rolling barrage. Under its cover, the 1st battalion, 356th Infantry, under Captain Ray K. Puffer, advanced from the river bank promptly at 9:30. This battalion was followed by the 3rd battalion, 356th Infantry, under Captain Dale D. Ernsberger, and the 3rd battalion, 355th Infantry, under Major (then Captain) John F. Symes. Each battalion was accompanied by a machine gun company. While the direction of the crossing of the river had been to the northwest, the advance was to the northeast, to gain the heights above Pouilly and Inor. Marching by the compass, but meeting with no resistance in the night, Captain Puffer's battalion had by midnight reached the high hill to the northeast of Pouilly and had formed a line extending from the river to the Division boundary. This boundary ran from Letanne (excluded) to Autreville (included), thus running parallel to the southwest reach of the Meuse, at a distance of a little less than two kilometers. By 6 o'clock in the morning of November 11th this battalion had advanced to the Bois de Hache with reconnoitering parties towards the Bois de Soiry, well up towards the high ground north of the Meuse. At 8 o'clock a company, which had been detached from the 3rd battalion, 356th Infantry, occupied Autreville and the high hill to the west of that town. The morning was foggy and dismal. The troops had gained their objective and were engaged in mopping up the country in their vicinity and rear and in reconnoitering to the front. At 8:55 word was received at Brigade Headquarters that an Armistice had been agreed to and that hostilities would cease at 11 o'clock. The order was sent to the troops at

A white flag put up by the Germans, or perhaps by French civilians, in Pouilly, when the town was taken by the 356th Infantry, 89th Division, on the morning of Nov. 11th, 1918, just before the armistice went into effect. S. C. 34946.

once, but the outlying reconnoitering parties could not be all reached before the hour of eleven, and some of them were still fighting as late as noon.

While advancing up the river from Pouilly in the direction of Bois de Hache the 3rd battalion, 356th Infantry, encountered rather stiff resistance. A machine gun nest from the right flank was causing losses and threatening complete annihilation of the battalion. A little group of five from Company "I" was sent out to flank the nest. They were commanded by Lieutenant John H. Murphy and consisted of Corporal Augustine Martinez and Privates Benjamin T. Tubbs, Clarence E. Lauber, and Andrew W. Dilbeck. Moving to the flank of the nest under heavy fire, they worked to within thirty yards of the nest before opening fire. One of the enemy machine guns was turned upon them from this distance and the five, without an instant's hesitation, rushed directly upon it. When within a few feet, the gun ceased firing and six Germans charged them with the bayonet. Corporal Martinez fired twice from a distance of only a few feet, killing the non-commissioned officer and one of the men. The others fled. Corporal Martinez pursued them until they were lost in the fog, and returned to the position to find Lieutenant Murphy wounded and the other three men dead within ten feet of the enemy's weapon. All the Germans had fled, leaving three hot machine guns. This gallant little attack undoubtedly saved the battalion extremely heavy losses.

While the main body of the 178th Infantry Brigade met with comparatively little loss, the fortune of war brought tragedy and glory to one of its elements. The 2nd battalion of the 356th Infantry, under Major Mark Hanna, had been designated as a liaison group to cross the Meuse with the Marine Brigade of the 2nd Division on our left and after the crossing to obtain and maintain contact between the right of the 2nd Division and the left of ours.

The orders were late in coming and the battalion was put on the march about 6 P. M., November 10th. Its orders were to report to the commanding general of the Marine Brigade at La Sartelle Farm, a distance from its station in the Bois de Dieulet of about seven kilometers. The battalion arrived, after a hard march, just before the advance began. The 2nd Division was crossing over a pontoon bridge in front of Bois de l'Hospice. The crossing was made in the face of most deadly machine gun and artillery fire. The bridge head on the enemy side had been most accurately located by the enemy and the battalion, which had suffered already severe losses in the German counter barrage on the approach to the bridge, was here met by a withering fire of machine guns and artillery. Passing through this inferno again and again to bring his men up to their positions, Major Hanna was killed on his third trip through the barrage. Captain Carlson took command of the battalion, placed it in formation for the attack, and advanced. The losses were terrific. Company "G", which was to have been one of the assault companies, was found to be reduced to nineteen men and two non-commissioned officers, all its officers having been killed or wounded.

This little remnant attached itself to Company "F" and went bravely forward. After the crossing, little further resistance was encountered, and the battalion moved up on the boundary of the divisions, performing its mission and effected junction with the rest of the regiment next morning.

During these operations, as so many times before, there were striking cases of personal courage and individual military efficiency.

Sergeant (later 1st Sergeant) Clyde H. Dewalt, Company "K," 356th Infantry, volunteered and led a patrol against a machine gun nest which was flanking his company, capturing men and guns. Repeated trips were made through heavy shell fire by 2d Lieutenant Charles R. Hanger, 356th Infantry, and Private Earl V. Wright, Company "K," locating and guiding troops during the fog. Valuable runner service was performed by Sergeant (then Private) Carl R. Olson, of Company "E," and by Corporal George W. Blankenship, Private 1-cl. Edward J. Huchins and Private Archie D. Dunaway, all of Company "F," 356th Infantry. In the laying and maintaining of telephone wires, to, across and beyond the Meuse, much of the work being done under fire, and the repairing of breaks being particularly hazardous, 2nd Lieutenant Edmund Field, 356th Infantry, Sergeant Wesley E. Wendt, Corporal Edgar D. Egelston and Private 1-cl. Casper G. Wolfskill, all of the Headquarters Company, 356th Infantry, earned especial praise.

THE 177TH BRIGADE ENTERS THE LINE

The 177th Infantry Brigade was brought into the line for the attack. During the period of preparation for the crossing of the river, it had remained in the rear of the Foret de Dieulet, refitting, training and generally preparing for new services. Its headquarters were at Beaufort, which place, being also the location of a ration dump, had become an attractive target for the enemy artillery. On the evening of the 9th a direct hit was obtained on the ration dump in this town, about 100 yards from the Brigade P. C., and fourteen men were killed and fourteen wounded. A splendid example of chivalrous consideration was given on this occasion by Lieutenant E. M. Young of the Division Quartermaster's office, who, though mortally wounded, refused to be taken out of the dangerous locality until all his wounded men had been removed.

For the operation, the brigade was directed to relieve the two battalions of the 355th Infantry along the river front between the points opposite Inor and Stenay, to gain combat liaison with the 90th Division and push northward from the far side of the river, clearing the heights and gaining contact with the 178th Brigade north of Inor.

The 354th Infantry relieved the battalions along the river front with two of its battalions, and sent one battalion, the 1st, under Major Morton T. Jones, to relieve Major Hanna's ill-fated battalion of the 356th in the Forest of Jaulnay and act as escort to the Divisional Artillery. When the movement of the troops of the 178th Brigade across the river had been completed, the rafts were brought upstream to the vicinity of Pouilly, and this battalion of the 354th, on the morning of the 11th, crossed the river at Pouilly and under the vigorous artillery fire which continued during the morning, advanced along the right bank of the river and occupied the heights above Pouilly before the hostilities ceased. The 2nd battalion, under Captain Marshall P. Wilder, was brought up to relieve the 1st battalion as escort for the artillery and suffered severe casualties from the German fire shortly before the hour at which the armistice went into effect. A single shell breaking in the midst of "H" company killed three men outright and wounded Lieutenant John H. Collins and twenty-four men, of whom the officer and four men later died of their wounds.

The 353rd Infantry, under Colonel James H. Reeves, less one battalion, proceeded up the river in the night of the 10th-11th and crossed in the vicinity of Villefranche, in the sector of the 90th Division. Its mission was to pass through Stenay, when the 90th should have taken the place, and to push northeastward toward Olizy until contact should be gained with the 178th Brigade. The 1st battalion, under Captain Frank M. Wood, remained in the vicinity of Laneuville with directions also to cross when Stenay should be taken and push forward from there with the regiment. The original orders had provided that the regiment should cross at Stenay

Bridge over the Meuse at Stenay as it was crossed by Co. "A," 353rd Infantry, on the morning of the armistice. This picture was taken Nov. 13th, 1918, when 314th Engineers, 89th Division, began reconstruction. Picture was taken looking west, toward the Foret de Dieulet and Laneuville. Buildings at the right are in the foundry enclosure occupied by 89th Division troops for some days before the armistice. The Stenay railroad station is behind these buildings. S. C. 48462.

from Laneuville and one battalion only should be sent to Villefranche as a liaison detachment to maintain contact with the 90th Division and cover the crossing of the rest of the regiment. This order was based on the report that a foot-bridge crossing existed in the vicinity of Stenay. A personal reconnaissance by Captain Case, Company "A", 314th Engineers, disclosed that the report was erroneous and there was no way of crossing at Stenay except upon the ruins of the demolished bridge, which would involve considerable wading. Thereupon General Winn determined to send the main body of the regiment around by the crossing at Villefranche, thus expecting to get a larger force to the north of Stenay more quickly than seemed possible by the precarious crossing between Laneuville and Stenay, since the reports from the 90th Division indicated that Stenay had been penetrated and its capture was imminent. During the night, Company "A," 314th Engineers, commenced work on a rought foot-bridge across the ruins, but only the first of the broken arches of the causeway approach to the bridge proper had been spanned when the troops began the crossing.

Co. A, 353rd Infantry, 89th Division, passing German defensive barricade in front of the church in Stenay, Meuse-Argonne offensive, at 10:58 a. m. Nov. 11th, 1918, with two minutes more to fight. The clock in the church tower was not running, but the photographer vouches for the time. S. C. 34981.

STENAY ENTERED

At 9:30 on the morning of the 11th a patrol of nine men from the third platoon of Company "A", 353rd Infantry, conducted by 2nd Lieutenant Edward M. Connors, began picking its way across the ruins of the causeway and bridge, passing through brisk shell fire on the causeway, wading part of the time and throwing pieces of the destroyed structures across the channels of the river and the spillways of the canal. At 9:45 they were followed by the balance of their platoon, under 2nd Lieutenant Clifford Chalmer and accompanied by Lieutenant Benning, commander of the regimental Signal Platoon. The patrol entered the town at 10:00 and was joined in fifteen minutes by the rest of the platoon. No German or American troops were seen. The inhabitants surrounded these troops with such expressions of joy that Lieutenant Benning jokingly sent back word that he had been elected Mayor of Stenay. The patrol was divided and moved about the town, taking three German prisoners and establishing an outpost at the north end of the town. At 10:40 a patrol from the 90th Division came up. Precisely at 11 o'clock the platoon which had been mopping the town was assembled in the square north of the church and indulged in hearty cheering for the end of the war. In a few minutes the rest of Company "A", under Lieutenant Hulen, came up, outposts were placed extending from the hill north of Stenay to the southern edge of Cervisy, and locations of headquarters for the regiment and brigade were made.

WHO TOOK STENAY?

Since there has been some spirited, though fortunately not acrimonious discussion between the 89th and 90th Divisions on the subject, "Who took Stenay?" the facts as derived from the reports of the actual participants of both divisions in the operations about the place will be stated in some detail.

Celebration of the armistice on steps of church at Stenay shortly after 11 a. m., Nov. 11th, 1918, by Co. A, 353rd Infantry, 89th Division. Lieut. R. M. Hulen, in command, at left. French civilians in center. A couch standing on end, which was part of the German street barricade, at extreme right. S. C. 38553.

Stenay was a city of some 8,000 civilian inhabitants in pre-war times. It was also a French garrison town, being the station of some 9,000 troops. Its chief industry was the manufacture of steel or steel products. There were two large steel foundries or factories in the outskirts of the place. One, which was the scene of the fighting of the 90th Division, was situated about half a kilometer south of the town proper, on the east bank of the Meuse river. The other was on the west bank of the Meuse river, directly across the river from the town, and extending from the river almost to the railway station. This latter was the larger of the two establishments. Both were in large enclosures surrounded by high walls, containing a number of buildings.

The transportation features of the town consisted of a railway and a canal. The railway followed the valley of the Meuse, running on the west side of the river. The railway station was about midway between Stenay and the village of Laneuville, and rather closer to Laneuville. It was about a kilometer from the center of the town of Stenay. The canal ran along the eastern side of the valley of the Meuse, merging with the river in front of the town proper.

The French garrison had been quartered principally in extensive barracks at a place called Le Blanc Fontaine, about a kilometer southeast of the city on the road to Mouzay. In the southern part of the town proper were other extensive barracks, where artillery was quartered.

The town had been in the occupation of the Germans since the first few months of the war. During their occupation the Germans operated both the steel foundries above described and quartered a large number of troops in the barracks. The town was the headquarters of the German Crown Prince for two years and a half, during which the battle of Verdun was fought.

The road from Laneuville to Stenay, after passing the railroad station, runs upon a long causeway which rests upon eight arches of masonry. These span low lands along the river which are subject to inundation, and the causeway constitutes the approach to the bridge over the river. After passing over the river bridge, the road passes over another bridge across the canal and then enters the town at the southwest side, the river front of the town running somewhat northwest to southeast.

THE 90TH ATTACKS STENAY

The 3rd Corps, having the 90th and 5th Divisions in the fighting line, had crossed the Meuse at the vicinity of Dun sur Meuse on November 5th. Changing front to the north, these troops were pressing down the river astride of it, thus advancing on Stenay from the south. By November 9th they had attained the line Mouzay-Louppy. At 6 o'clock on the morning of the 10th they moved out of Mouzay for the attack on Stenay, which was about four kilometers distant. The troops were those of the 179th Infantry Brigade, commanded by Brigadier General J. P. O'Neil. The assault regi ment was the 358th Infantry, commanded by Colonel E. M. Leary. It was formed with the 2nd battalion under Major Souther in the fighting line and the 1st battalion under Major Canenhauer in support.

Advancing under heavy fire of machine guns and artillery, these troops reached the barracks at Blanc Fontaine by 7 o'clock. The morning was foggy and the location of the machine guns was difficult to determine. Swinging to the left, the assault battalion stormed and occupied the steel foundry between 8 and 9 o'clock. Thirteen prisoners were captured in the enclosure. Strong combat patrols were sent forward but were driven back by the severity of the enemy fire. The battalion was so depleted, both by losses here and previously, that it could muster only 130 effective men. It was subjected to an intense fire of high explosives from the German artillery. Machine guns from the island in the river on the left flank poured in a destructive fire. The buildings of the foundry were in the southern part of the enclosure, which was reported as four hundred yards square, though shown on the map as not so large. The enclosure was surrounded by a stone wall about ten feet high. Beyond this, towards Stenay, were woods held by the enemy from which sniping continued and any attempt to pass was met with machine gun fire.

Colonel Leary came up in person, bringing some more men. He conferred on the spot with the commander of the Corps Artillery and arranged with him for counter battery work against the German artillery. Believing that the counter battery work had silenced the enemy's fire, he directed Major Souther to push on. But it was impossible to advance with so few men against such intense fire, and the position was organized for defense. And here this battalion, exposed to galling fire of artillery and machine guns, clung to the position it had gained throughout the day of the 10th and the night of the 10th-11th. Its casualties were 12 killed, 48 wounded and 3 missing. But of the enemy, 52 were buried after the engagement and 17 prisoners were taken.

In the meanwhile the support battalion had also endeavored to advance from Le Blanc Fontaine barracks, but could gain only the crest of the hill overlooking the town, because of fire from the artillery barracks in the town and also from the flank. In its attempt, it lost 12 killed and 35 wounded during the engagement.

All this happened on the 10th. The 90th Division did no fighting here on the 11th.

It is an inspiring record, one worthy of the best traditions of the American Army. No one can read without a thrill the story of the little group of 130 men who pushed on in the face of destructive fire falling on them out of the mysterious fog, occupied their position and held it against a torrent of high explosive shells and machine gun fire from the front and flank, of the personal presence of the regimental commander urging his men onward, and finally of the mute record of the enemy dead and captured, exceeding in number the total of their own casualties in killed, wounded and missing. Gallantly and effectively they fought for Stenay.

There has never been anything but admiration for this achievement in the attitude of the 89th Division. Nothing has been said, or will be said, or could be said that would disparage the just pride of the 90th Division in this exploit.

THE 90TH CLAIMS SOLE CREDIT

But the documents and reports of the officers of the 90th Division from which these facts were adduced were furnished by the Commanding General of the 90th Division in support of an official request that that division alone be credited with the capture of Stenay. The request was embodied in a formal letter, dated 28th of April, 1919, from Major General C. H. Martin, then commanding the 90th Division, to the A. C. of S., G-3, G. H. Q. American Expeditionary Forces, entitled, as subject. "Capture of Stenay by the 90th Division, 10-11 of November." And the claim of the 90th Division is therein couched in the following language:

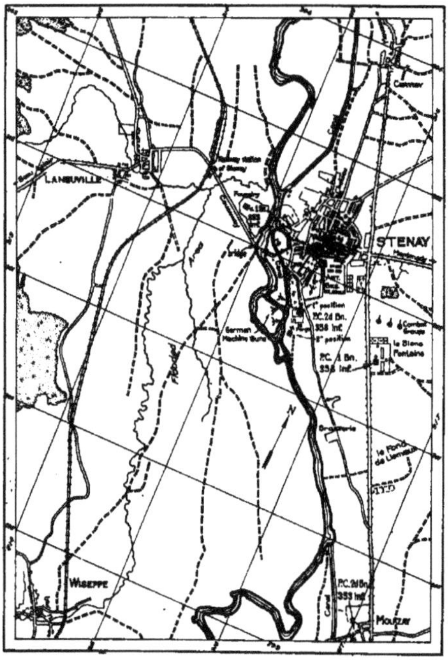

Stenay and environs, showing position of elements of the 89th and 90th Divisions, Nov. 10-11, 1918.

"4. The determination of exact lines during battle is extremely difficult, and in order to reconcile differences after the cessation of hostilities, divisions, in cases of conflict, must adopt a liberal attitude and be willing to meet each other half way. In the present case, however, I feel that we must insist that it be definitely decided that this division alone be credited with the capture of Stenay. Any other decision will be manifestly unfair to the troops of this division who went through severe fighting in driving the enemy out of the town. Twenty-four men of the 358th Infantry of this division are buried near the building in Stenay which they captured twenty-four hours before patrols of the 89th Division arrived. Those patrols did not enter the town until after the enemy, as a result of our fighting, had evacuated."

It is felt that the facts do not warrant so wide a claim; that at least some of credit is due to the 89th Division; nor is it thought that the evacuation of Stenay by the enemy is to be ascribed solely to the fighting of the 90th Division, glorious as that fighting was.

A copy of General Martin's letter to G. H. Q., together with copies of the enclosures which accompanied it, consisting of the reports of the officers of the 358th Infantry and field messages of the commanding officers of that regiment and of the 1st and 2nd battalions sent during the action, was transmitted by General Martin to the Commanding General of the 89th Division. From these the quotations herein were made.

Two aeroplane photographs joined to show Stenay, Laneuville and environs. The pictures were taken a few days before the armistice, while Stenay was held by the Germans, and are not retouched. Stenay is in the center of the picture and Laneuville in the upper left corner. The factory inclosures and woods referred to in the narrative, the river roads and various details may all be seen clearly. By reference to it and the map on opposite page the operations in this vicinity may be followed closely.

SUMMARY OF OPERATIONS OF 90TH

From them it appears conclusively that the nearest approach to Stenay gained by fighting was the crest of the hill overlooking the town, gained by the 1st battalion, and the enclosure south of the town in which were located the factory buildings gained by the 2nd battalion. That between the factory enclosure and the town of Stenay proper there were woods and other fortified positions held by the enemy from which he was never expelled by force. That the earliest penetration of the troops of the 90th Division into Stenay proper was on the morning of the 11th of November, when troops of the 89th Division were found to be already in the occupation of the town. And that during the day of November 10th and the following night the 2nd battalion organized its position for defense, its information of the enemy being that the town of Stenay proper was held by one regiment of Germans, that a battalion of German infantry was in position along the line of the canal and the river and that both units were strongly supported by machine guns.

A few quotations from the reports will serve to elucidate these points and are the more necessary because of the use of expressions, unintentionally, no doubt, which would convey the impression that the town proper had been in part at least conquered.

For example, in the letter of General Martin to G. H. Q., it is stated:

"The 2nd battalion of the 358th Infantry shortly after 9 o'clock on November 10, had forced its way into Stenay and occupied a large factory building in the southern portion of the town."

In the report of Colonel Leary, entitled "Capture of Stenay," it is stated:

"It will be seen that this battalion (the 2nd) established its P. C. in the southwest corner of Stenay at 9:15, November 10th, 1918; at dusk (4:30), the 2nd battalion had pushed its advance about 400 meters into Stenay."

The field message of the commanding officer of the 2nd battalion at 9:15, November 10th, states:

"Have established a P. C. in southwest corner of Stenay in factory building. Have 13 prisoners and am now mopping up town."

In the report of the commanding officer of the 2nd battalion, dated November 20, entitled "Capture of Stenay," it is stated:

"By 9.00 o'clock this battalion occupied and controlled the southwestern part of Stenay."

These expressions are accurate enough if it be borne in mind that they are limited to the enclosure above described in the outskirts of the city, with a determined enemy resistance in the city and in the woods lying between it and the city. In the absence of such qualifying circumstances they seem to bear a wider import.

FIELD MESSAGES AND REPORTS

Let us examine the report of Colonel Leary that at 4:30 the 2nd battalion had pushed its advance 400 meters into Stenay, in the light of the field messages and reports made at the time, in order to determine in what sense this expression was used. It occurs in a formal report made by Colonel Leary under date of November 20, 1918, to the Commanding General, 90th Division, which is entitled "Capture of Stenay."

The field messages pertinent to the matter follow.

"E-6-1" was the code name for Major Souther, the commanding officer of the 2nd battalion. "Tell. 1" was the code name for Colonel Leary, the commanding officer of the 358th Infantry. "Tyson 1" was the code name for General O'Neil. "X-1-1" was the code name for the commanding officer of the first battalion, Major Canenhauer.

"From E-6-1, at 315.5-301.7 10 Nov. 18, 9h. 15, by runner to Tell 1. Have established a P. C. in S. W. corner of Stenay in factory building. Have 13 prisoners and am now mopping up town. P. C. 315.5-301.7."

"From E-6-1 at 315.5-301-7, 10 Nov. 18, 10 h. 20, by runner to Tell 1. We hold an area about 400 yards square enclosed in high brick wall in S. W. corner of Stenay. The enemy is defending this wall with M. G. fire. Have requested 1st Bn. to come to our assistance by MOUZAY-STENAY road. Have had rather severe losses. Several enemy machine guns are on island just west of present location."

"From E-6-1 at 315.5-301.7, 10 Nov. 18, 11 h. 20, by runner to Tyson 1. We hold an area about 400 meters square in S. W. corner of STENAY. The Germans have M.G.'s on west bank of Meuse. This enclosure we hold is surrounded by a stone wall about 10 ft. high. The Germans are in woods on other side of wall. Any attempt to pass is met with machine gun fire. Have asked our 1st Bn. to come to town on MOUZAY-STENAY road, but have had no answer to two requests. If the 1st Bn. is not in town request some artillery assistance."

"From E-6-1, at 315.5-301.7, 10 Nov. 18, 12 h. 20, by runner to Tell 1. Have been heavily shelled by artillery for past hour. Now preparing to mop up town with aid of 1st Bn."

"From E-6-1, at 315.5-301.7, 10 Nov. 18, 12 h. 50, by runner to Tell 1. We can only get together 80 infantrymen and the scouts and runners, making a total of about 130 men. M. G. across canal on our left flank gives us trouble. Impossible to give exact location of gun, but its approximate location is 314.8-302.3. Without some artillery preparation consider it a hard task for such a small amount of men. Will hold ground taken until further orders. With such a small amount of men and machine guns on flanks I consider it dangerous to advance. Am not certain 1st Bn. has entered STENAY. With 130 men it would be impossible to thoroughly mop up a town the size of STENAY."

"From Tell 1, to Tell P. C. 17.5-98.8, 10 Nov. 18, 14 h. 25, by telephone, General O'Neil taking the message.

"I came to E-6-1 and found he had established P. C. as reported and was holding some part of the town west of the branch road from MOUZAY at large factory building of some kind, also stone building to the north of that. At the time I was there, however, H. E. shells were falling one right after the other and it required mine and Major Souther's personal influence to hold the men at times. I had brought up there some 150 men myself. In addition to the H. E. every line of exit was covered by M. G.'s and snipers. When the artillery was placed on the Boche artillery, after the return of Colonel Lanza who was out there at the same time I was the H. E. stopped and I had the Major immediately take the men he had before and the men I brought him and push right on mopping up the town. Lieutenant Boylan, the adjutant, just reported here. From his report I gathered they did not get very far, about 400 meters. I followed the telephone line until I found X-1-1 in the Barracks. He was in the same state as E-6 was, except for H. E.—there was none of those so far. That is the situation now. He is attemping to filter a few men at a time but the casualties as he reported are quite stiff. M. G.'s and snipers are very active on all sides except the south. In my opinion at least one other battalion is indicated for an attack on the country to the east of the town and the high road. I don't believe that the throwing of shells would make any appreciable difference on account of the fact that the M. G. emplacements are so located that it would be very hard to hit them."

"From E-6-1, 315.5-301.5, 10 Nov. 18, 15. h. By runner to Tell 7. M. G. at 315.5-301.9 giving us trouble. (Approximate.) Also ask for artillery preparation north of 315.5-302.0 on woods. There are snipers and machine guns in these woods. Ask for a raking fire over these woods. Also machine gun at 315.0-302.7."

"From E-6-1 at P. C. 10 Nov. 18, 15 h. by runner to Tell 7. Have chow brought up in ration carts on river road to point west of Blanc Fontaine. One car can haul it as chow for about 150 men is all that is needed. Have so many men carrying wounded it hardly leaves anyone. Did Boylan call you on 'phone. He left here about 12 h. 40 and has not returned."

The formal report of the commanding officer of the 2nd battalion, entitled "Capture of Stenay," and dated 20 Nov., 1918, states:

"By 9:00 hour this battalion occupied and controlled the southwestern part of Stenay, the battalion being organized in the quadrangle formed by bakery building in southwestern part of Stenay on banks of Meuse. We held this position throughout November 10th and the night of November 10th-11th."

The report of the commanding officer of Company "E", dated 19 November, 1918, is as follows:

"Advance from Mouzay started at dawn of the 10th of Nov. Time of entry into factory on southern edge of Stenay, 9 A. M., 10 November. No men of this company spent night outside of residence near bakery except out guards."

The report of the commanding officer of Company "F", dated 19 November 1918, is as follows:

"This company advanced steadily as part of the assaulting battalion from Mouzay, under artillery and heavy machine gun fire, until reaching large bakery in the southeastern portion of Stenay about 8 hour. Intense machine gun fire from front and flanks forced us to take cover in large building north of bakery. Strong combat patrols were sent forward about 50 to 100 yards, but encountered by such severe machine gun and artillery fire that they were forced to withdraw. At this point the battalion organized for defense."

The report of Captain H. P. Jordan, company not stated but presumed to be Company "G", and dated 19 November, '18, is as follows:

"I entered Stenay with 12 men at 7 h. 15, 10 November, 1918, men continued to join me constantly thereafter. This company took 12 prisoners in the quadrangle in southern edge of Stenay."

The report of 2nd Lieutenant Thomas F. Quinn, company not stated, under date of 19 November, 1918, is as follows:

"On 10 November, 1918, at 6 h. the 2nd Bn. of this regiment advanced on Stenay from Mouzay. Heavy enemy and machine gun fire was encountered and overcome, and all companies of this Bn. entered S. E. portion of Stenay at 8 h. We occupied the bakery and the buildings 75 yards N. of the bakery and kept up an active fire from those places against enemy machine guns and snipers on our front and flanks. Strong combat patrols were pushed forward to the N. and to the E. for 100 or 150 yards, causing a considerable enemy withdrawal, but our patrols were obliged to withdraw at about 11 h. to the vicinity of the bakery. Prisoners taken reiterated information that one German regiment occupied Stenay proper, that one Bn. of German Inf. were in position along line Canal-Meuse River, and that both units were strongly supported by machine guns.

This battalion organized the occupied portions for defense.

At 17 hr. outposts were thrown out and each hour thereafter a patrol advanced into Stenay from our position, for about 100 yards.

During the night no enemy resistance was encountered."

Colonel Leary's formal report, so far as relates to the operations on the 10th, is as follows:

Headquarters 358 Infantry,
Blanc Fontaine Barracks, France,
20 November, 1918.

From: Commanding Officer,
To: Commanding General, 90th Division, A.E.F., (Thru Commanding General, 179th Brigade.)

Subject: Capture of Stenay.

1. I submit herewith copies of messages sent from and received at the P. C. of this regiment on November 10th and 11th, 1918, relative to the attack on Stenay, which was our objective. Also statements of the officers of the 2nd battalion of this regiment relative to the same.

2. It will be seen that this battalion established its P. C. in the southwest corner of Stenay at 9 h. 15, November 10th, 1918; that it was subjected to high explosive shells and shrapnel, machine gun and sniper fire there but was supported by the advance of the 1st Battalion, 358th Infantry, from the barracks of Le Blanc Fontaine; that about 14 h. I brought up about 150 men consisting of one company of machine gunners and a platoon of riflemen from the vicinity of Stand to reinforce the 2nd Battalion; that I gave Colonel Conrad Lanza, Corps Artillery, near the corner of the wall at south edge of town, verbal information of targets for artillery, and that as soon as the enemy artillery fire, then very heavy, slackened, as I supposed due to Colonel Lanza's action, I ordered Major Souther to push on his battalion and mop up the town and proceeded to Major Canenhauer's battalion then at Blanc Fontaine barracks to see that he supported his advance.

3. Both battalions pushed forward, the 2nd battalion advancing about 400 meters according to Lieut. Boylan, adjutant of the 2nd battalion. The advance of the 1st battalion was delayed by cross fire of machine guns and snipers from the cemetery and the artillery barracks in Stenay and enfilade fire from the slopes of Aviation hill. At dusk, 4:30, the 2nd battalion had pushed its advance about 400 meters into Stenay. The 1st battalion held the crest of the hill overlooking Stenay between Blanc Fontaine barracks and the artillery barracks, and both battalions had received orders to dig in and hold the ground already gained and mop up the rest of the town in the morning, and during the night to intensively patrol Stenay to keep the Germans worried. All of this was done."

COMMENT ON MESSAGES AND REPORTS

Now, except in the telephone report of Colonel Leary to General O'Neil at 2:25 P. M. and in his formal report on the capture of Stenay, there is, neither in the reports above quoted nor in any other reports furnished by the 90th Division, any mention of an advance by the 2nd battalion after the occupation of the factory enclosure, which was reported at 9:15 A. M., November 10th. On the contrary, the formal reports of the company and battalion commanders negative the idea that any such advance occurred by definite assertions that by 9 o'clock the battalion was organized in the quadrangle and held this position throughout the 10th, as the battalion commander states; and that after reaching the bakery building at 8 A. M., strong combat patrols were thrown forward 50 to 100 yards, but were driven back by intense fire, and that at that point the battalion organized for defense, as is stated by Captain Mack, of Company "F".

The field messages of Major Souther, sent during the day, establish conclusively that no advance of the battalion occurred after its occupation of the quadrangle in the early morning. His message at 9.15 is sanguine in tone and states that he is mopping up the town. Doubtless the basis of this was the sending out of the combat patrols. By 10:20 the enemy's resistance had developed and he reports that the enemy was defending the walls of the enclosure with machine guns. At 11:20 the situation was unchanged, for he reported to General O'Neil that the Germans were in the woods on the other side of the wall and that any attempt to pass was met with machine gun fire. Both these last named messages state that he was requesting the 1st battalion to aid his operation by pushing into the town along the Mouzay road. At 12:20 he reports that he is preparing to mop up the town with the aid of the 1st battalion. But as the events showed, that battalion was never able to render the aid requested. And at 12:50, reporting that he could get together only 130 men and could not ascertain whether the 1st battalion was in Stenay, he states that he considered it dangerous to advance and would hold his ground until further orders. Plainly no advance had occurred at this time, ten minutes before 1 P. M. Nor had Colonel Leary visited the battalion, for he brought with him 150 men to add to Major Souther's force, and ordered the advance to take place with their aid. His visit was about 2 P. M.

At 2:25 P. M., Colonel Leary reports to General O'Neil that he had visited the battalion, had there conferred with the chief of the corps artillery and arranged with him for counter battery work which apparently had the effect of stopping the enemy artillery fire and had then ordered Major Souther to proceed with mopping up. He then left the position and proceeded to the headquarters of the 1st battalion. And he stated on the authority of Lieutenant Boylan, the battalion adjutant, who had just come up, that the mopping up had advanced 400 meters.

Aside from the reports of the battalion and company commanders above commented on, it is certain from Major Souther's next field message that this advance did not take place. This message was sent to Colonel Leary's operations officer at 3:00 P. M. It is dated from coördinates 315.5-301.5. It states the approximate location of an enemy machine gun at 315.5-301.9. It asks for artillery preparation and raking fire north of 315.5-302.0 on woods and states that there are snipers and machine guns in these woods. [See note on Map Reading, page 503.]

It will be noted that the previous field messages since the factory buildings were occupied had all been dated from coördinates 315.5-301.7. And that four localities are mentioned, all of which lie on X coördinate 315.5, namely, the point from which this message was sent; the point from which the previous field messages since 9:15 A. M. had been sent; the approximate location of an enemy machine gun; and, finally, the point in the woods from which raking artillery fire to the north was requested. It is a curious coincidence that the church in the center of Stenay is approximately on the same X coördinate—the figures which are written before the dash. The increase of each whole unit in the Y coördinate (the figures written after the dash) indicates a distance, going northward, of one kilometer; and, of course, the increase of each unit in that part of the coördinate next after the decimal point means a distance northward of one-tenth of a kilometer or 100 meters. It is, therefore, possible, even without a map, to locate the distance of all these points from Major Souther's position. And it thus appears that between 12:50 P. M. and 3:00 P. M., Major Souther moved his P. C. straight south 200 meters; that an enemy machine gun was at the time located at approximately 400 meters due north of the P. C. he was occupying at 3:00 o'clock, which was only 200 meters due north of the P. C. which he occupied at 12:50; and that at 3:00 P. M. he was requesting artillery fire on a point in the woods 500 meters due north of his then P. C., which point was only 300 meters to the north of the P. C. he occupied at 12:50; and that he reported the presence of snipers and machine guns in woods still to the north of this spot and asked for a raking fire on them.

With these enemy obstacles in the line of his advance and only 200 or 300 meters from the position from which the advance would have started, it is perfectly obvious that a misapprehension of the situation induced Colonel Leary's report to General O'Neil, which was carried over into his formal report; and that the advance never took place.

The documents enable us to make a conjecture as to how the misapprehension arose. Both in his telephone report to General O'Neil and in his formal report on the capture of Stenay, Colonel Leary states that his authority for reporting the advance is the report of Lieutenant Boylan, the adjutant of the 2nd battalion. And in his report to General O'Neil, Colonel Leary stated that Lieutenant Boylan had just reported. That was at 2:25 P. M., November 10th. At 3:00 P. M., Major Souther's message to the operations officer of the 358th Infantry contains the following. "Did Boylan call you on 'phone? He left here about 12 h. 40 and has not returned."

Evidently, therefore, Lieutenant Boylan could only report on events which occurred before 12:40, when he left his battalion, and he may have had in mind the morning advance which took the troops into the quadrangle, which was estimated as 400 meters square. On the other hand, Colonel Leary had in mind, of course, the advance which he had just ordered Major Souther to make, and may have inferred that Lieutenant Boylan was reporting a further advance.

But however the misconception arose, it is certain from all the other reports that the statement that by dusk of the 10th the 2nd battalion had pushed forward 400 meters into Stenay is an error. And all such expressions in the reports as "entering Stenay," "occupying and controlling the southwest portion of Stenay," and "pushing forward into Stenay" and the like must be taken in the sense that the factory enclosure alone is to be understood as the part of Stenay entered, occupied or pushed forward into.

With equal propriety might the troops of the 89th Division have been described as entering Stenay when they occupied the railway station of the town, lying between Laneuville and Stenay, several days previously. Or when they entered the enclosure of the steel foundry lying between the railway station and the town proper, an establishment of precisely similar character to that of the one occupied by the troops of the 90th Division and lying, on its river front, even closer to the town proper. But it is thought hardly accurate to apply such expressions to any of these localities, so long as the town proper was held by a determined and unconquered enemy.

THE SITUATION AS IT AFFECTED THE 89TH

We turn now to the situation as it affected and was affected by the 89th Division. It was the mission of the 90th Division to capture Stenay under the Army orders for the advance across the Meuse. Reconnaissances showed that it was physically possible for troops to cross the demolished bridge leading to the town when once the enemy had been driven out and that this crossing was the only practicable one on the right sector of our front. During all of the 10th of November our Division was anxiously awaiting the results of the operations of the 90th, since it seriously affected our operations planned for the night of the 10th-11th. The capture of Stenay would enable the troops of our right brigade to cross on the bridge and, passing through the town, connect up with the other brigade which was to force the crossing at Pouilly. The reports from the 90th Division on the 10th induced the belief that the town had been penetrated from the south and that its mopping up was under way and thus that its complete capture was imminent. On this assumption, the battalion of the 353rd Infantry which had been sent across the river at Villefranche as a liaison group with the 90th Division, was, during the night of the 10th-11th, augmented by the rest of the 353rd Infantry, except one battalion left in the vicinity of Laneuville. When on the morning of the 11th, the word was received that the Armistice would take effect at 11 o'clock, the desire that that hour should find Stenay in American rather than in German hands was increased by the reflection that it would form the best place in the vicinity for our troops to rest and clean themselves during the period of waiting that would follow the termination of hostilities. With winter approaching, with nothing but shell-wrecked villages behind us, the importance of obtaining shelter for our battle-wearied troops can hardly be appreciated by those who have not endured the hardships to which the troops had been exposed. It seemed that a little effort on our part would confer on us these benefits and deny them to our enemies.

Lieutenant Colonel (then Major) James L. Peatross was in command of the battalion (the 2nd) of the 353rd Infantry which was sent as liaison group between the divisions. He reports, under date of 3rd May when an investigation was ordered following receipt of copy of General Martin's letter to G. H. Q., that his battalion crossed the Meuse about 9:30 P. M., November 10th, south of Mouzay. His orders were to follow the 90th division into Stenay, and from that position cover the crossing of the 353rd Infantry. He went to General O'Neil's headquarters in Mouzay about 1 A. M., November 11th, and stated his mission to the adjutant, who informed him that the 90th had been unable to enter Stenay and was holding a line south of the town.

In the meantime, Lieutenant Robert L. Melvin, whom Major Peatross had sent to the P. C. of the 358th Infantry, returned and reported that Stenay had not been captured; that two regiments of Germans were reported in the town; and that Colonel Leary asked that Major Peatross' battalion take position on his left and attack with him at 6 A. M. Major Peatross remained at the headquarters of the 179th Brigade. While he was there orders came to the brigade to change front to the right and attack, leaving Stenay to the left and making no attack on it. Major Peatross discussed this situation with the brigade adjutant, pointing out that his mission of covering the crossing of the remainder of the 353rd could not be carried out if the 90th passed Stenay without attacking it. So Major Peatross moved his battalion into Mouzay at 3 A. M., and prepared to attack Stenay himself when the 90th attacked to the north. Later the orders to pass by Stenay were cancelled and the Brigade of the 90th was ordered to dig in and to make no advance beyond the line held at the time. Rumors were current that an Armistice had been signed and that no further advance would be made. At about 8 A. M. of the 11th, Major Peatross sent a radio message to the Commanding General of the 89th Division asking for instructions, since his orders from the Division were to follow the 90th into Stenay and the 90th had no information at that

314th Engineers, 89th Division, completing longest span of bridge across the Meuse at Stenay, Nov. 16th, 1918, replacing bridge blown up by the retreating Germans. S. C. 38549.

time of its troops being in Stenay and evinced no intention of making an attack on the town. At about this time Colonel Reeves came into Mouzay, accompanying the 3rd battalion of his regiment. He found himself unable to perform the mission assigned him, since the lines of the 90th reached to the river south of Stenay and no advance was taking place. He was informed, though of course, not by an official order, that because of the Armistice there would be no advance.

At this time, troops of the 89th Division were practically as close to the center of Stenay as those of the 90th Division. Company "A" of the 353rd Infantry was stationed about 50 to 75 yards east of the railway station which lay between Laneuville and Stenay and served both towns. This point was about 1075 meters distant from the church in the public square of the town as against about 900 meters distant from the same point to the P. C. and station of the 2nd battalion, 358th Infantry, in the southern part of the steel works. Our patrols and reconnaissance parties had during the night reconnoitered the causeway and the bridge at the very entrance of the town and reported it possible to cross.

In view of the situation and the importance of the occupation of the town not only to the 89th Division but to all the American forces, General Wright decided to push on across the river and take the town. Orders were sent accordingly to the 177th Brigade and the movement was begun by the advance parties of Company "A", 353rd Infantry, and completed as has been related.

There was a dense fog that morning and it was impossible to see the town or be seen from it until the troops were well on their way across the causeway. Then the fog lifted. It seems that it was not until this time that the final rear guards of the Germans withdrew from the town. For on the following day, a German Lieutenant in charge of a detachment then in the town of Cervisy came to our outposts and requested permission to enter our lines in order to bury his dead and care for his wounded. He stated to Lieutenant Robert L. Melvin, of the 2nd battalion, 353rd Infantry, that he had been holding the southern portion of Stenay, but had to withdraw suddenly as the American troops were coming into Stenay from Laneuville and would have made it impossible to retreat.

CONCLUSIONS

From all the foregoing, it is believed that the facts justify the following summary of the whole matter, made by Colonel John C. H. Lee, the Chief of Staff of the 89th Division, after an investigation following the receipt of the formal claim of the 90th Division to be alone credited with the capture of the town.

"It was the mission of the 90th Division to capture Stenay. Prior to November 11th they had attacked the outskirts and threatened the town. They had probably entered the southern part of the town but had not succeeded in dislodging the Germans nor assuring the occupancy of Stenay. Colonel Reeves had the mission of the 177th Brigade, that of passing through Stenay as soon as it should have been captured by the 90th Division and of cleaning the river bank and heights to the east, connecting up with the 178th Brigade, which was attacking near Pouilly.

All reports indicate that the 90th Division did not, on the morning of November 11th, intend to force the issue at Stenay. The town had not been reported as captured and several officers informed officers of this division that the town was not to be further attacked and cleared out because of the Armistice scheduled for 11 o'clock.

I believe that the movement of our patrol and first company from Laneuville actually forced the Boche to evacuate his final rear guards from Stenay. Moreover, I believe that the 89th Division operations at Pouilly had shaken the morale of the Boche quite as much as the former and possibly less successful attempts of the 90th Division to force an entrance from the southern part of Stenay. I, moreover, believe that if the patrol from Laneuville had made no attempt to get into the town the Germans would have remained there and claimed occupancy during the first period of the Armistice.

There is no question in my mind but that the 89th Division at least shared in the taking of Stenay, and this fact was apparently recognized at the time by the Corps and Army drawing the boundary in the town, giving the northern and larger part of the town to the 89th Division.

There is no attempt on the part of this division to steal glory from the 90th Division. Our troops took a chance and entered the town to clinch it, while the 90th Division apparently sat still and waited for the cessation of hostilities."

CONDITIONS IN STENAY

On entering Stenay only about two hundred civilian inhabitants were found. Soon after the final American advance of November 1st began, the German commander in Stenay had, on two hours' notice, forced the civil population to evacuate the place, enforcing the order at the point of the bayonet. One young man who refused to depart was put against a wall and threatened with shooting if he did not yield. Only a few remained—mostly old people and the parish priest.

From the inhabitants many stories of the German occupation, which seems to have been typical of this part of the line, were obtained. The town was occupied during the first invasion of the war, about the end of August, 1914. It never came within the zone of active operations until the period of the American advance in the fall of 1918. For more than two years it was the headquarters and residence of the German Crown Prince, who was domiciled in the chateau. French domestic servants of the owner of the chateau who remained at their posts throughout reported that he had been quiet and well behaved and had strictly protected the chateau and its occupants and contents from molestation by his troops. They said that he seemed little of the soldier and devoted much time to amusing himself with his dogs, of which he maintained fifteen in a kennel in the park of the chateau. The Kaiser visited him occasionally and once was accompanied by the Kaiserin. When the Crown Prince took his departure, German soldiers occupied the place and displayed less consideration. Indeed, evidence of their boorishness was manifest on our entry in the stopped up plumbing, prints of muddy boots on the beds and filth generally in the quarters occupied by them.

A visit to the Blanc Fontaine Barracks between Stenay and Mouzay which had been occupied by the German troops left unfavorable impressions of the discipline and soldierly qualities of the Germans. They were in an indescribably vile and filthy condition, not merely the disorder and dirt left by the sudden evacuation, but dirt of several years' standing was in evidence. The towns of Stenay and Laneuville were also dirty and unkempt. This condition found in the garrison of the headquarters of the Army group of the Verdun sector was mute evidence of the deterioration of the morale of the German Army, and an indication also that that great Army which had been pictured as the greatest fighting machine which the world had ever seen, was defective in one of the important military virtues, cleanliness, which is a token of self respect.

The civilian inhabitants of the town reported that during the first year of the occupation sternly repressive measures were taken against them, and some misconduct on the part of the troops was not restrained. Soldiers entered their homes with pistol in hand making searches and seizures. Nearly every month the houses were searched for rubber, white metal and copper; a woman named May Router who had succeeded in hiding the smashed instruments of the French military band, was, when her secret was betrayed by a French deserter, punished by beating until she bled. Once, for some offense, the parish priest, Pere Hazard, was tied to a horse; an act, which, to the simple and devout people of the place, was blasphemous.

The people, men, women and children over thirteen were required to work in the fields or in the factories, the usual pay being one mark (paper money) a day.

No such incidents of ruthless terrorism as occurred in Belgium were reported, however.

"Calamity Jane," a 155-mm. howitzer belonging to Battery E, 11th Field Artillery (attached to 89th Division) in the Bois de la Haie, near Laneuville-Beauclair road, Nov. 11th, 1918. It is said this howitzer fired the last shot of the war on the American front; official time, 10:59.59, but somebody's watch was slow, and, according to the photographer, actual time was 11:05!

The 342nd Field Artillery, 89th Division, was armed with weapons like this. S. C. 34958.

THE ARMISTICE

The hour of the cessation of hostilities thus found our division in complete contact with the enemy. Seven of the twelve battalions of infantry of the Division had crossed the Meuse and portions of two other battalions were also across; a pontoon bridge was in process of construction at Pouilly; a foot bridge was being constructed at Inor; the artillery was in position to support the defense of the heights east of Inor, and, in the opinion of the Division Commander, the chances of success for the entire operation were well in our favor. Moreover, the position attained by our infantry at this time enabled us to completely control the important railway communications of the German armies running through Mezieres and Sedan. This railway was essential to lateral communication of the German armies; it had been the real objective of the entire operation which began September 26th; the consequences of cutting it were realized by the German High Command as involving almost certain disaster, and this realization accounted for the stubborn resistance opposed by the very flower of the German Army to the American advance. Certain it is that only the Armistice saved the Germans from the most crushing military catastrophe that any nation has ever experienced.

And so, at this hour, the fighting ceased and the war was won. It might be supposed that wild scenes of jubilation occurred along the front, such as took place throughout the countries of the Allies. But the contrary was true. Except for a little cheering by our troops in Stenay, no demonstrations were manifest. The silence of the guns seemed to invite sober tranquility and quiet joy. There was audible the sound of celebration among the Germans, detachments of whom were still in Cervisy and Inor. But among our own troops silence reigned.

FIGHTING AFTER THE ARMISTICE

The delay in the receipt of the orders in reference to the taking effect of the armistice occasioned a regrettable incident. Inor was in the sector of the 356th Infantry and the mission of capturing it, after the crossing of the Meuse, had been assigned by Colonel Allen to his 3rd battalion, which was in support. Intense machine gun fire from the town had been directed on the flanks of the assault battalion as it passed. The operation for the capture of Inor was under way when the hour of the taking effect of the armistice arrived, but Colonel Allen did not receive the orders until 11:40; and the Commander of the 3rd battalion did not receive them until 12:15. In this state of affairs, the German commander of the troops in the vicinity, assuming that the town lay between the hostile positions, sent a detachment of an officer and two men into Inor for the purpose of finding out whether the town was required by us for the quartering of troops. The party consisted of Lieutenant Thoma, Sergeant Benz and Corporal Shweiker, all of the 19th Uhlan Regiment. When about to enter Inor from the north, at about noon, the party encountered a detachment of Company "L," 356th

Infantry, under the command of 1st Lieutenant Leon P. Shinn. The Americans, unaware of the armistice, opened fire upon them, wounding the officer. The wounded officer drew his pistol and ended his life by shooting himself through the head. The sergeant escaped, but the corporal was made prisoner and sent to the rear in accordance with the usual routine in the case of prisoners.

According to a communication from the German Armistice Commission in April, 1919, requesting the release of the prisoner, later in the day of November 11th, the American Battalion Commander (presumably Captain Dale D. Ernsberger) met a German officer of the 123rd Grenadier Regiment and expressed regret at the incident, which occurred solely because the American advance had been too rapid for all units and patrols to be informed of the armistice promptly, and failure of the Germans concerned to make it clear that they were not belligerents.

Meuse-Argonne offensive, Nov. 1-11, 1918. Sectors and lines of advance of the 89th and adjacent Divisions, showing their approximate daily advance. From Buzancy Special Map.

Word was not received from the Corps that the Armistice would go into effect at 11 o'clock, until 8:30 on the morning of the 11th. When the word came to Division Headquarters, orders were sent out immediately by all available means of liaison, including officer couriers, to the front line battalions. But the advance of the preceding night had carried the troops far forward. The word was received at the 178th Brigade, the troops of which were furthest advanced and which was therefore notified first, at 8:55. But the troops were still advancing and all the outlying elements, the scouts and patrols, were not and could not be notified in time.

Furthermore, the letter of instructions giving warning as to the approaching Armistice and the directions for the conduct of the troops under its terms, was not received at Division Headquarters until about 10:30. Since General Wright was therefore not thoroughly familiar with the terms of the Armistice, he had, on receipt of the first word, directed that the troops push forward until the enemy was actually encountered, but that the enemy would not be fired on unless he attacked; that hostilities must cease, but that any terrain that might be of military value to us and which had been abandoned by the enemy would be taken and would be occupied. He intended to complete the operation by occupying the heights east of the river between Stenay and Moulins. The enemy, however, was found to be in Cervisy and Inor. Later, orders were received not to advance beyond the line held at 11 o'clock. These orders were enforced and outposts which had been established after that hour in unoccupied territory were withdrawn to the lines actually held at 11 o'clock.

The German High Command made an official complaint immediately after the armistice that the American troops on the sector held by this division had not ceased attacking at all but continued to advance. The facts are as has been stated, and when the orders were fully understood they were loyally obeyed. But there was no regret on the part of the Division Commander nor of any one that the Division had, up to the last hour, continued to carry out its offensive instructions to the fullest possible extent.

THE 164TH ARTILLERY BRIGADE

The foregoing story of the operations of the Division is not complete without an account of the activities of the 164th Field Artillery Brigade from October 9th to the Armistice. It will be remembered that on October 8-9, the 89th Division was relieved in the Euvezin sector, and that the artillery brigade, consisting of the 164th Field Artillery Brigade Headquarters, the 340th, 341st, and 342nd Field Artillery regiments, the 314th Ammunition Train (less the small arms section, Compaines C. and G which accompanied the main body of the Division to the Argonne) and the 314th Trench Mortar Battery, was left behind under Brigadier General Edward T. Donnelly to support the 37th Division. Nine days later the 37th Division was relieved by the 28th Division, and since the 28th also was without artillery the 164th Brigade, much to its disappointment, was forced to remain in the sector. And here it stayed until the cessation of hostilities, covering with its fire the German lines and back areas from La Chaussee to Rembercourt, and winning commendation from both the 37th and 28th for its splendid work.

Though the Woevre front was settled during this period the troops that held it were not. The old policy of live and let live had yielded place to one of giving more than was received. It was the purpose of the high command to keep the Boche guessing where the next attack would strike, and with this end in view the artillery was frequently called upon to fire preliminary bombardments for attacks that never took place, and accompanying barrages for simulated offensives that were only large raids. Thus the Germans were induced to retain in the vicinity of Metz several reserve divisions that might have been used to stop the real attacks elsewhere. The spectacular barrage fired in this sector at the opening of the Meuse-Argonne offensive has already been described. As each successive phase of that offensive developed, orders came for the artillery from the Meuse to the Moselle to stir things up. This duty, light enough when compared with the bitter struggle farther west, was only too gladly performed.

The artillery brigade gradually settled down to a schedule of harassing fire by day and all kinds of fire by night. The men always preferred to fire in the daylight hours, but in the course of time it became a matter of routine for them to wake in the dead of night, calculate the necessary data, and send off shell after shell until the desired number was completed. The church steeples of Charey, Dommartin, Dampvitoux and the other towns in the Hindenburg line came in for a good share of this shelling, because of their convenience as registering points for adjusting fire on the organized strong points of the enemy in the towns and in Marimbois and Monplaisir Farms. On October 19th Battery "F" of the 342nd Field Artillery fired 119 rounds on some camouflage noted by an observer near Monplaisir Farm. That night a patrol from the infantry lines found a wrecked concrete mixer at the place, with the bodies of fifteen Germans, lying in a partially constructed concrete dugout, mute evidences of the accuracy of Battery "F." Similarly Battery "C" of the same regiment adjusted on a regimental P. C. near Dampvitoux with damaging effect to the enemy.

Before the 89th Division left the sector, Corporal Lawrence C. McKee, Battery B, 341st Field Artillery, had earned special commendation (Sept. 20-22) for repairing telephone lines and operating an exchange under heavy fire and subject to other adverse conditions. The spirit and discipline of the Artillery Brigade are well shown by the following occurrence:

On the morning of October 28, 1918, during a barrage fired to cover an infantry raid on the German positions, No. 3 gun of Battery "D," 340th Field Artillery, burst, killing Private Arthur A. Wright.

For slightly more than an hour prior to the accident the battery had been firing a barrage, which had started with a difficult accompanying fire. When the gun burst and No. 1 fell, a man in the pit calmly called out "man hurt." The crew secured a stretcher and placed their comrade on it. Gunner Corporal Arthur A. Benedict, although suffering from powder burns, secured a first aid dressing and aided his Chief of Section in dressing the wound, after which the members of the crew quietly carried the man to a dressing station, some little distance away. Meanwhile, although every man in the gun pits knew that a gun had burst, the barrage was continued, No. 2 gun taking over the No. 3 gun sector and increasing its rate of fire to cover. Not a round was missed, nor a fraction of a second lost.

RAIDS

With the entry of the 28th Division into the sector a period of especial interest and activity for the artillery began. Preparations were being made for a powerful drive that would encircle Metz and force the enemy back on his own soil, and almost every night raiding parties were sent out from the infantry regiments to secure information concerning the Hindenburg line and its defenders. For these parties the artillery had to furnish support in the shape of barrages and other annoyances to the enemy. The raids were usually quite complicated, and afforded many intricate firing problems for the artillery to work out. The uniform success of the artillery on these occasions is witnessed by an unbroken series of raids that penetrated the enemy lines and brought back prisoners. Fair examples are the raids against the Bois Bonseil on November 1st and 2nd, which were supported by neutralizing fire and a box barrage. The first netted eight prisoners, and the second forty-four. A noteworthy feature of the raid of November 2nd is the heroic exploit of Captain Francis Trives, of the French field artillery, attached to the 164th Field Artillery Brigade, and 1st Lieutenant Paul M. Coleman, of 164th Field Artillery Brigade Headquarters. These two officers volunteered to accompany the raiding party in order to assist in the destruction of any artillery material that might be found. On reaching the German wire the party became confused and disorganized. Realizing that the party would soon be caught in the enemy barrage Captain Trives took command, and walking up and down in the heavy shell fire in front of the line, by his splendid example inspired the men to go forward. He continued to lead them until he was severely wounded, whereupon Lieutenant Coleman, who had captured eight Germans, made his prisoners carry Captain Trives back more than five kilometers to St. Benoit, being under artillery fire most of the way.

After two raids in succession against the Bois Bonseil, a simulated raid was planned for the following night. A barrage like that of the night before was sent over, and this was followed by an intensive gas shelling, which, according to the reports of prisoners captured in later raids, surprised the enemy and inflicted many casualties. Again on November 7th the infantry was supported in a raid that combed the Bois des Cerfs, and resulted in fourteen prisoners. And so in one after another of these minor attacks the artillery brigade was firing thousands of rounds with an accuracy and effectiveness only fully realized when the brigade crossed the German line after the Armistice. Major General William H. Hay, commanding the 28th Division, recognized and commended this good work in a memorandum of November 8th. Lieutenant General Robert L. Bullard, commanding the Second Army, had written to General Hay expressing gratification at the vigorous patrols and raids of the 28th Division, which, according to General Bullard, had "resulted in making No Man's Land our land, and in lowering the morale of the hostile units * * * * *, as well as in inflicting losses on them, and capturing a considerable number of prisoners." This letter was transmitted by General Hay to the 164th Field Artillery Brigade, with the following comment: "The 164th Field Artillery Brigade, now attached as Divisional Artillery, has done much toward the success of these operations."

CHANGES OF POSITION

Although the brigade had remained in the same sector for all this time there had been numerous changes of regiments, battalions, and batteries, some necessitated by changes of boundaries and some for reasons of safety. The exception to this was Battery "D", 340th Field Artillery. The first position located by this organization was so well concealed that it was never located by the Boche artillery, and tactical urgencies never forced a change until the last few days of the war. The position was pointed out by inspectors as a model and officers visiting the front were sent up to study it.

The plain hard labor incident to this protracted stay at the front is little realized. The bringing up of rations and supplies, the care of guns and animals, the maintenance of various means of communication—all these and other tasks were the daily lot of the artillery. There was danger connected with the labor, too. It was while laying telephone lines near Marimbois Farm that 1st Lieutenant Thorndike Deland and Private Richard

Ruined church at Dommartin, St. Mihiel Sector, as it appeared after the armistice, showing the results of artillery fire by the 164th Field Artillery Brigade, 89th Division.

B. King, Headquarters Company, 340th Field Artillery, came upon positions occupied by the enemy. Armed with hand grenades they advanced on a dugout and routed out seventeen of the enemy. These they brought back to our lines in the midst of severe shell and machine gun fire.

Meanwhile the 314th Ammunition Train was hauling shells and accessories to the front by night, and cleaning and repairing its trucks and carts by day at a dump near St. Baussant. These trucks, going well to the front, came frequently under shell-fire, and found the Boche surprisingly accurate at hitting the roads. On October 5th Company "E" was caught in a little ravine under a heavy shelling of both high explosives and gas, and before it gained the safety of a nearby ridge it had lost five men wounded, four officers and forty-five men gassed, and twenty-one animals killed.

The following week a French tank was discovered, half buried, in a trench. Members of E Company dug it out, their machinists put it in running order, and a few days later this company was operating the only "tank service" in the artillery brigade.

A PUSH STOPPED BY THE ARMISTICE

On November 10th orders were received by the 28th Division for the attack that was to have been launched against Metz on November 11th. On the afternoon of the 10th the artillery brigade covered the advance of the infantry to the wire of the Hindenburg line. In the evening orders were issued providing for an attack in three phases, to be begun at 5:45 o'clock on the morning of the 11th. The first and second phases were the occupation of the outer defenses of the Hindenburg line, of La Chaussee and Dampvitoux, respectively, while an advance on Hageville and Mars La Tour constituted the third. The attack was begun as planned, and met with success in the initial stages, but the news of the armistice prevented its further progress. At about 9:30 the artillery regiments received official word of the cessation of hostilities, and with it the order that firing was to continue until 10:55. Then after resting for four minutes each battery was to fire at maximum speed for forty-five seconds, that is, until 10:59:45. Fifteen seconds was allowed for the last projectile to make its flight into enemy territory. Promptly at 10:59, therefore, each gun opened up and fired as it had never fired before. Then silence. It is recorded that in the forty-five seconds each gun of Battery "E", 340th Field Artillery, fired twenty-four rounds. During these final operations 1st Lieutenant William T. Milligan, 341st Field Artillery, established communication between the 2nd Battalion switch board and the town of Haumont, remaining at his observation post under intense shell fire to maintain liaison between Brigade Headquarters and the advance elements.

By way of recapitulation it is to be noted that the brigade had seen fifty-six days of continuous service in support of three different divisions. It had fired about 200,000 rounds of ammunition. Though it had been frequently shelled, good luck and good management kept the casualties down, as may be seen from the following table:

	Killed		Wounded and Gassed		Missing		Total
	Offs.	Men	Offs.	Men	Offs.	Men	
164th F. A. Brigade Headquarters	0	0	0	2	0	0	2
340th F. A.	2	8	3	75	0	0	88
341st F. A.	0	3	0	32	0	0	35
342nd F. A.	0	6	1	43	0	0	50
314th Ammunition Train	0	6	0	33	0	0	39
Total	2	23	4	185	0	0	214

The discrepancy between the casualties of infantry and artillery is due not only to the normally heavier casualties in the infantry, but also to the fact that the infantry of the Division participated in two major engagements while the artillery participated in only a portion of one.

JOINING THE DIVISION IN GERMANY

After the Armistice and its attending celebrations the batteries remained for a few days in their positions and then moved to slightly more comfortable quarters in the ruined towns. Word came that the 89th Division had been selected to form part of the Army of Occupation, and it was hoped that the artillery brigade would join the Division in Germany. Consequently, the next two weeks were spent in getting men and animals into condition, and refitting the organization preparatory to the expected move.

The animals formed the greatest problem. Originally none too good, they had been fairly worn out by the long trip to the front and two months of active service. More than this, many had been killed or wounded, and

Building in Dampvitoux, St. Mihiel Sector. This was inside the German lines until after the armistice, and destruction shown was the result of shelling by the 164th Field Artillery Brigade, 89th Division.

many more had been evacuated with mange. The brigade was therefore partly immobilized for lack of animals, but extra horses were drawn soon after the Armistice, and in a brigade horse show held on November 23rd the improved conditions of all animals was a subject of the highest praise on the part of General Hay.

On November 28th, Thanksgiving Day, orders came for the artillery brigade to rejoin the Division, then on its way to Germany. Next morning all units were on the road. The first day's march led across the mud and water of No Man's Land on a makeshift road, where guns and men alike sank deep. But in a couple of days the war zone was cleared, and the night stops became enjoyable. Traveling north through the towns of Conflans, Etain, Epincourt, and Longwy the brigade after seven days of marching caught up with the Division in Luxembourg, and crossed with it into Germany on December 7th.

CHAPTER VI.

THE OCCUPATION OF GERMANY

Soon after the Armistice, it became known that the 89th Division had earned the honor of being selected as part of the Army of Occupation. The flower of the American forces was of course chosen for this duty, which was to be the visible token of the great victory won by the Allies. Since the conclusion of the fighting had found the 89th Division in the very front of the battle and on the line of advance into the enemy's territory, it was first planned that it should advance on the heels of the retreating foe. This distinction was, however, later awarded to the divisions of longer but no more honorable records in combat, and the 89th Division was made part of the second wave or support troops in the general advance.

THE THIRD ARMY FORMED

Before the Armistice there had been but two American Armies in actual existence. Our division had been at different times part of each of them—of the First Army in the St. Mihiel battle and of the Second Army just before the Meuse-Argonne fighting, and again the First Army during that struggle. There was now formed the Third Army and to it our division passed. Evidently in prevision of the end, the order for the formation of the Third Army was issued on November 7th, 1918, and Major General J. T. Dickman, of notable achievements as a Division and Corps Commander, was assigned as its commanding general. The order was not put into effect, however, until several days later; but with a speed and effectiveness worthy of the high reputation of its commander, the staff was organized and began to function by the 15th of November, and by 5:30 A. M., November 17th, 1918, when, under the terms of the Armistice, the forward movement into Germany began, all the orders and arrangements for the forward movements of over 200,000 troops had been completed.

The Third Army, the Army of Occupation, consisted in its final form of eight divisions—four Regular Army divisions, the 1st, 2nd, 3rd and 4th; two National Guard divisions, the 32nd and 42nd; and two National Army divisions, the 89th and the 90th. These were formed into three Corps, the 3rd Corps, consisting of the 2nd, 32nd and 42nd divisions; the 4th Corps, consisting of the 1st, 2nd and 4th divisions; and the 7th Corps, consisting of the 89th and 90th divisions.

The 5th Division was originally part of the Army and assigned to the 7th Corps. But on December 12, 1918, it was relieved and transferred to the Second Army. On the same day, December 12th, the 33rd Division was assigned to the 7th Corps, 3rd Army; but almost at once, on December 17th, it was also relieved and assigned to the 2nd Army. These two divisions covered the line of communications of the advance, remaining along the route through Belgium and Luxembourg, but not crossing into Germany.

It is worthy of remark that while divisions are spoken of as Regular Army, National Guard or National Army Divisions, the terms had by this time become indicative only of the origin of the divisions; and except for their traditions and their varying degrees of excellence or effectiveness, there was nothing of difference between them. By transfers of officers and replacements from all classes, and above all, by the fiery test of battle, the American Army had become practically homogeneous, and the President's order, promulgated in the previous summer and declaring that there was but one Army of the United States had become an actuality.

Between the conclusion of the Armistice and the commencement of the march into Germany, there came a much needed breathing space. The Division had been under fire, except for eight days, since August 4th and had participated in two great battles in that time. Much rest, refitting and replacements both of men and material were needed. And more than ever were the conveniences of Stenay appreciated for that purpose.

GENERAL WINN TAKES COMMAND

On November 12th, General Wright was relieved and transferred to command the 1st Corps and Major General Frank L. Winn assumed command of the Division and retained it until the end. General Winn had received notice of his promotion during October while quartered in a dismal, muddy, leaky and shell torn cottage at Eclisfontaine while the Division was in reserve of the 32nd Division, just before relieving the latter in the battle line. There he took his oath of office before his adjutant—an informal and bizarre oath, made up of his adjutant's recollection of what such an oath should be, in the absence of the proper form. It seemed to "take," however, and was placed in due form later when the proper papers came. General Winn remained in command of his brigade throughout the ensuing fighting instead of seeking a command commensurate with his new rank. He was now to take command of the Division which he, more than any other, had trained. Brigadier General Herman Hall was transferred to the command of the 177th Infantry Brigade, and Brigadier General George C. Barnhardt, having been assigned to the Division, assumed command of the 178th Infantry Brigade.

The headquarters of the Division and of the 177th Infantry Brigade and of the 353rd Infantry were in Stenay. The headquarters of the 178th Infantry Brigade were in Nouart. The intervening villages served as billets.

In Stenay were found bathing facilities and long needed and much appreciated baths were had by the men. Delousing facilities, however, were not all that could be desired and the thorough performance of this important operation was not possible until later, though bathing and the issue of new clothing did much to alleviate the conditions.

TRANSPORTATION DIFFICULTIES

A thousand administrative matters which could not be attended to during active operations, now presented themselves. Transportation was the great difficulty, as always. Many trucks from our scanty supply, and the best animals, were taken from us to be turned over to the divisions that began the march sooner than we. Many animals were needed. Many had been killed in the fighting and many more worn out. There is a vast amount of animal-drawn transportation in a division absolutely essential on the march, rolling kitchens, water carts, medical carts, machine gun carts and supply and combat wagons. So every effort was made to bring forward fresh animals to supply the deficiencies. By hook and crook they were obtained. Shaggy, wild-eyed, tired horses, some of them straight from the farms back home and that understood English, began to come in. Animals also came in that did not speak or understand English—captured German horses, and horses that the Germans had captured from the Russians and that we, in turn, had captured from the Germans, and Spanish mules and French horses. One lot of little mules, larger than jack rabbits, but not much, incited the efforts of every organization commander to shift them off on some other organization. But finally enough good animals were obtained. Then the harness was to be cleaned and repaired and the wagons, battered and stained with hard usage in the field, were to be cleaned, repaired and painted.

On the movement into Germany, although the transportation strength of the 314th Supply train was below 100 trucks, equipment was moved and the handling of forage and rations accomplished, much of the time, by running the trucks twenty-four hours a day. At one time, with train headquarters in Arlon, Belgium, it was necessary to dispatch trucks as far back as Bar-le-Duc and Commercy for the Division's supply of gasoline and oil.

SHOES AND CLOTHING

Clothing, underclothing and shoes, worn out in the hard fighting, were to be replaced. The question of shoes presented especial difficulties. They were of prime importance for the hard marching ahead of us. But there was a great shortage which was supplied by the issue of a certain proportion of British shoes, those issued to the British soldiers. And never had the American soldier appreciated the courage, pluck and grit of his British cousins until he found himself literally in the British shoes. The nation whose troops had fought for four years in shoes like those could endure anything in the way of terrors and horrors that the war could offer. There was also a difficulty in obtaining large enough sizes in shoes, a feature which throws an interesting sidelight on the physical characteristics of the American soldier. Of course, in placing the enormous contracts for supplies of articles which come in different sizes, such as shoes, clothing, hats and the like, the specifications as to the proportion of different sizes had to be made up from the statistics available to the war department; and these figures were derived from the experience of the regular army. But the war developed the fact that the average soldier of the American Expeditionary Forces had larger feet than the average of the soldiers of the regular army, or of any other of the Allied armies, for that matter. These men were the physical pick of our great, virile country; they had discarded the silly, cramping styles of shoes, which the manufacturers of America, under the pretense of catering to popular taste, had foisted upon them as civilians; and they had been doing man's work in the open. They needed larger shoes than anyone had thought they would need; and they had trouble in getting them. One stalwart engineer who could do with nothing less than size 15½ EE, did not succeed in getting suitable shoes until long after he got into Germany; and many a sizable man had to have his old ones soled and resoled, patched and repatched by the regimental cobblers long after their days of usefulness had passed.

Thus, with these and hundreds of other problems of supply and transportation before him, the life of our G-1, Lieutenant Colonel W. J. Scott, which had been merely a bad dream when it was a question of getting up food and ammunition for the fighting men, now became a nightmare, when everything had to be renewed.

MILITARY COURTESY AND TRAINING THEREIN

Another most important feature of the preparation for the occupation was the training in military discipline and courtesy. And a word to the general reader on this subject may not be out of place here.

The object of all military activities is, of course, the ultimate application to the enemy of the maximum of physical force, the use against him of the utmost possible regulated violence. Success in war, therefore, depends upon the ability to use all available means to one end, that of crushing the enemy; and this end can only be attained if every part of the whole military force is consciously, harmoniously and intelligently applied to its attainment. In unity there is strength, and when, as in war, strength is the sole aim, there can be no strength without unity. No clearer demonstration of the truth of the axiom was ever given than in the present war when we contrast the wavering fortunes of the Allies under their different commanders, no matter how able or even how successful on their immediate front, with the uniform success which attended their flags when marshalled under one supreme command.

Now all this seems trite and obvious enough when applied to armies; but it is sometimes forgotten that it is equally true of every military unit down to the squad. And it is also sometimes forgotten that this desirable unity of action does not come of itself. Like every other human accomplishment it needs training to bring it into being, and more especially it requires that the subordination of all to the common purpose ordained by the one must, by training and by constant practice, become habitual. If it is not an habitual mode of conduct and of thought, it cannot be relied upon to manifest itself in time of stress when it is most needed. Hence the greater part of sound military training has for its object the institution of the habit of willing and instantaneous acquiescence in the execution of the common purpose as declared by the individual whose duty it is to make such declaration. As it is manifestly impossible for any one individual to prescribe all the details of even the simplest operation, it follows that a division of responsibility is necessary, whereby the general results to be attained are conceived and directed by one, and the execution of the design is delegated to others, each of whom in his own sphere prescribes the general execution of his part of the whole and entrusts details to still others, and so on in descending scale until each finds his particular duty to perform. This is military system; and the various grades of functionaries from those performing the multifarious, particular duties of the common design up through those charged with the duty of prescribing more and more general activities constitute the various grades of military rank.

Such a system may or may not be best in ordinary life where success against an adversary is not the whole object of existence. But in military life, where victory over the enemy is the only thing to be attained, even at the expense of life itself, the system is essential. The experience of mankind, which has been that of almost continuous warfare since the dawn of history, has never, from first to last, devised any other successful system of military conduct. The effectiveness of armies is, and has ever been, in exact proportion to their conformity with the system. This conformity is known as discipline.

Now military courtesy is nothing more or less than the recognition of the military system and an outward token of willing acquiescence in it. Thus it serves a dual purpose; it smoothes life of some of its asperities, as courtesy does in ordinary existence; but more than this, its practice is a constant exercise of discipline, the daily practice of an act which, by constant repetition, becomes a fixed habit of recognition of the military system, so that in times of stress each and every individual can be depended upon to act in conformity with that system. The effect is psychological, and on the subconscious as much as on the conscious mind.

The reaction of the average American youth to training in military courtesy is generally one of resentment. It is only in retrospect or after long experience that its benefits are appreciated. With many a man the realization has been slow in coming that the accomplishments of the Division of which he is now so proud became possible only because of the strict discipline which irked him at the time.

Returning now from this digression (which, perhaps, should have been included in the appendix, so that the wearied reader could skip it if he chose) we find the 89th Division a fine division of a fine army and desirous of retaining its reputation and adding thereto. In consequence, training in military discipline and courtesy, which had always been prominent, was entered upon with renewed zeal.

POLICING UP

Unremitting preparations were made, with the determination that n thing should be left unprovided for that would tend to the comfort and security of the troops or that would promote their appearance of uniformity, neatness and discipline. Uniform methods of making up the pack, the distances each unit should maintain from the other units on the march, the location in the column of the various wagons and carts and what should be carried upon them were all determined on and prescribed in orders. Preliminary inspections were held to ascertain that these orders were understood and obeyed; and when the march actually began, inspectors from the Division Staff visited and accompanied the various columns, noting and reporting even the most trifling deviations from the orders and requiring their correction. Straggling, that bane of all armies on the march, was sternly repressed. Commanding officers were required to make daily reports of the hour of arrival at their destination for the day and of the number of men who failed to complete the march with the organization and the reasons why. Policing up was also a matter on which great stress was laid. The debris of meals eaten at the noon day halts was required to be neatly collected or buried; organization commanders were required to inspect the billets just before departure; and after the departure an inspector from the Division Staff would visit all the billets occupied. Woe betide the officer whose men were found to have left dirty billets behind them. It was no excuse that the dirt had been left by some organization which preceded us on the march through that place. It was regarded as the business of the 89th to leave any place it occupied clean.

To the harried organization commander, and more to the individual soldier marching along under his heavy pack, it sometimes seemed that the unflagging attention to the observance of such details was taking all the joy out of life, and there was many a sigh for the good old days in the battle lines, where everything was dirty, messy and comfortable, except for the minor annoyances of shells, casualties, tin willy and everlasting digging.

But soon the effect of this vigilant supervision of details manifested itself in the establishment of an admirable march discipline which won the encomiums of all observers. Pride in the maintenance of soldierly discipline and neatness pervaded all ranks, and the resulting individual self respect and good conduct proved the value and wisdom of action taken. The nickname of the "Policin', Salutin' 89th" which was applied to us in some quarters, was accepted as a justly deserved compliment.

RELATIONS WITH ENEMY TROOPS

Under the terms of the Armistice, the lines which had been held at 11 o'clock November 11th were the limits of our advance and were held by us with outposts. Strict orders forbade intercourse with the German troops; and though a detachment of Germans who had retreated from Stenay on our advance, were at the village of Cervisy only 400 meters distant from the outskirts of Stenay and in plain sight from the windows of the chateau where the headquarters of the 177th Infantry Brigade were located, no communication with them was permitted. Even an officer who sought permission to enter our lines to bury his dead and care for those wounded during the fighting about Stenay was denied access at the outposts. A French medical officer, whose home was at Cervisy and who had obtained a short leave of absence to visit it, requested permission to pass the lines. The Brigade Adjutant was compelled, most regretfully, to refuse. Nothing daunted the Frenchman donned civilian clothes and slipped past the outposts and found his home practically undisturbed. All would have been well for him if his joy and delight had not impelled him to return to the Brigade Adjutant and relate his exploit; and the Brigade Adjutant was therefore forced, still more regretfully, to put him in arrest, with the result that he overstayed his leave and obtained a reprimand for the violation of orders from his own commander.

There was a German prison camp and artillery dump at Margut, some 12 or 13 kilometers north of Stenay. 1,800 prisoners of war were in confinement there. When the German garrison withdrew, these prisoners were told to march off to Stenay; and the German commander, General Maur, notified us of the fact in curious English and sent a "bill with the names of the prisoners." These soon turned up and were sent back to their organizations through the proper agencies. A large number of pieces of artillery which, under the terms of the Armistice were to be turned over to the Allies, were collected by the Germans at Villers-devant-Orval, in the celebrated Ruins of the Abbey of Orval, just over the Belgian border. The 3rd Battalion, 353rd Infantry, under Major Geo. W. Blackinton was sent forward to take over the prison camp and this artillery. These were the first of our troops to penetrate into Belgium. The modest Major Blackinton at once became the target for all manner of expressions of good will on the part of the liberated French and Belgians; delegations visited him, bringing large bouquets and expressions of gratitude carefully engrossed on enormous sheets of paper; long speeches were made to him by prominent citizens of the vicinity, leading, long coated and silk hatted, processions of their fellow citizens; and whether he escaped kissing or not, history is silent.

THE MARCH BEGINS

On November 24th promptly at 7 A. M. the march into Germany began. The troops of the first wave had passed our lines on the 17th and were reported moving forward always one day's march behind the retiring Germans.

The first movement of our Division was to be abreast of the advance of the 90th Division on our right. Of course, all available roads were used by the troops, the advance consisting of many columns moving in the same direction on different roads. Careful preparation of the orders relating to the march provided schedules of the exact time of arrival and departure of all

Welcome arch erected in Mersch, Luxembourg, temporary headquarters of the 89th Division, by the civil population for the American Army of Occupation marching through into Germany. Col. W. W. Whitside, Capt. J. E. Hausmann and Capt. L. W. Hazard at right. Dec. 3rd, 1918. S. C. 40649.

the different units and practically no confusion or waiting by one element for the passage of another took place.

The first stage of the advance was a two days' march from the line of the Meuse river to the vicinity of Virton in Belgium. This first move was a concentration of the 7th Corps with a view to following the 3rd and 4th Corps after they should cross the German-Luxembourg frontier about the first of December, one of the divisions of our Corps to be in the rear of each of the other Corps of the 3rd Army, the 90th following the 4th Corps and the 89th following the 3rd Corps.

Reconnoitering parties of engineers preceded the Division by a day's march to examine the roads, bridges and means of communication. Billeting parties preceded the troops on the day of each march, proceeding direct to the day's destination and making arrangements for the shelter of their commands.

The conclusion of this phase of the advance found the Division Headquarters at Dampicourt, the 177th Infantry Brigade Headquarters at Bellefontaine and the 178th Infantry Brigade Headquarters at Meix-devant-Virton. The troops of the brigades were billeted in the towns and villages surrounding their headquarters.

A pause of several days occurred here while the advance troops of the Army were waiting to cross into Germany. Thanksgiving day on the 28th of November was observed as a holiday. The President's eloquent Thanksgiving Day proclamation was translated into French and excited much admiration among some of the devout people and even the clergy, who, assuming that since America was not Catholic it could not be Christian, were much impressed by the character of this distinctively American holiday and the sentiments of the proclamation which established it.

The other days of this halt were occupied in training and the continuance of preparation for the further advance.

INSTRUCTIONS FOR CONDUCT IN LUXEMBOURG

Before the entry into Luxembourg, a letter of instructions from General Headquarters, governing the conduct of the Army in that country, was published for the guidance of the troops. In this letter it was pointed out that although by international law we were entitled to regard Luxembourg as hostile territory, yet, as the inhabitants were generally friendly, they would not be considered enemies. That our presence in the country was not for the purpose of hostile occupation, but merely for the passage and commu-

This is not the actual size of the packs carried by the doughboy but shows what it felt like by the end of a day's march en route to Germany.

First troops of the 89th Division crossing the Sauer River from Echternach, Luxembourg, into Germany. Unfortunately, the photographer did not identify the unit. Dec. 5th, 1918. S. C. 40650.

nications which its geographical situation made necessary. Public and unoccupied buildings were to be used for military purposes as far as possible and the general billeting regulations prevailing in our Army in France were to be followed. Supplies were to be purchased at a fixed and fair valuation; but if withheld, and the local authorities on request failed to requisition them, they were to be taken and payment made as in other cases. No Luxembourg official was to be allowed to exercise any authority over any member of the Army, but to avoid just grounds for complaint, strict discipline was to be maintained and intermingling of the troops with the local population was to be prevented. The Army, however, was cautioned that safe and uninterrupted passage and communications in Luxembourg were to be insured at all costs, and offenses against the Army would be dealt with by the military authorities regardless of the nationality of the offenders. Suspected persons were to be arrested. In case of violence or resistance, the offender might be shot on the spot.

On the 30th of November the march was resumed and continued by the Division as a whole on December 1st, the Corps objective being the line Thiaumont-Clemency-Sanem. On the 2nd, 3rd and 4th, the movement continued by subdivisions, some being on the march while others were at rest. The objective of these marches was to concentrate the Division in the vicinity of Echternach in Luxembourg, on the line of the Sauer river, which is the boundary between Luxembourg and Germany, by the night of the 4th-5th of December.

The appearance and discipline of the troops on the march had showed constant improvement.

WE ENTER GERMANY

On the morning of December 5th the Division began crossing the bridge at Echternach and entering the territory of Germany. Striking changes of environment at once were noted. The sign posts, which in Belgium were in French and in Luxembourg were both in French and German, now became all German. Many sign posts indicating roads had been taken down or destroyed, evidently in a spirit of petty malice by the retreating German Army. The roads became worse and were speedily ruined by the passage of our heavy trucks. German roads are not so well constructed as French roads, having lighter foundations and a narrower roadway. The stately, spire-like poplars which line the French roads and give a characteristic tone to the landscape, were now supplanted by smaller, wide branching trees, whose gnarled and twisted limbs gave, in the winter season, a melancholy impression of suffering.

Should we mention our feelings on seeing green fields well kept—roofs and chimneys whole on the houses—fat cattle and well fed people in unharmed Germany—all after devastated France? Other emotions were sometimes excited. It is related that a disgusted K. P., engaged in digging a kitchen sink, was overheard to make the following complaint, "This is a h—l of a country; not even a shell hole to throw things in!"

The inhabitants displayed no resentment or dislike. The common people on the roads and in the streets of villages and towns gazed curiously at the passing troops but manifested no emotions whatsoever and maintained, as our troops did under orders, an attitude of reserve. The local officials, with whom dealings took place for billeting of troops in the houses of the inhabitants and for the requisition of fuel, were uniformly efficient and generally obeyed orders with alacrity and without demur. Most of them displayed an over anxiety to placate and please the invaders and in some instances showed rather disagreeable servility. Rarely was truculence manifested. The conduct of our own troops was exemplary; no disorders of any kind nor any looting or imposition on the civilian inhabitants were reported.

The high tide of march discipline was reached when our troops marched through Bitburg, the first important town in Germany. At this time, Bitburg was the headquarters of the Third Army. Army inspectors were detailed to observe and report upon the character of the discipline manifested by the troops as they marched through the place. The highest compliments were paid us by these inspectors. The ranks were solid, the men at attention, helmets, rifles, packs all in order; the wagons, rolling kitchens and machine gun carts all were clean and orderly with no straggling men accompanying them. Officers of the Division Staff who observed the march at this time were gratified beyond measure at the worthy showing made by the Division and by the encomiums it earned; they were afterwards of the opinion that the Division then presented the finest appearance in its history—not even excepting that of the final review just before its departure for home.

By December 10th all the Division had reached the area alloted to it. Some changes and readjustments of the boundaries took place, but within a few days the Division was settled down in the area it was to occupy during the entire period of the occupation.

THE AREA WE OCCUPIED

This district, in a general way, surrounded the important city of Treves, or, in German, Trier. It was about fifty miles long, from north to south and about thirty miles broad, though quite irregular in outline. For convenience in administration it was made to follow the lines of German administrative districts and thus embrace the four kreisen, or what we might call counties, of Prüm, Bitburg, Trier (Land) and Saarburg. The city of Trier itself was excluded from the jurisdiction of the 89th Division, being reserved as the advance headquarters of the General Headquarters of the American Expeditionary Forces. The district contained a civil population of over 200,000. It is largely an agricultural community, with countless little villages of 1,000 inhabitants or thereabouts, scattered closely together, from which the inhabitants go forth to work in their fields. There are no isolated farm houses, as with us.

Nearly everyone lives in a village or town. There are few industries save farming, some quarrying and manufacture of grindstones on a small scale, large railroad yards at Ehrang and a few small factories of different sorts scattered throughout and in the outskirts of Trier.

Most of the country is hilly and broken and in the northwestern part of the district is a wild, desolate region known as the Schnee Eifel. The

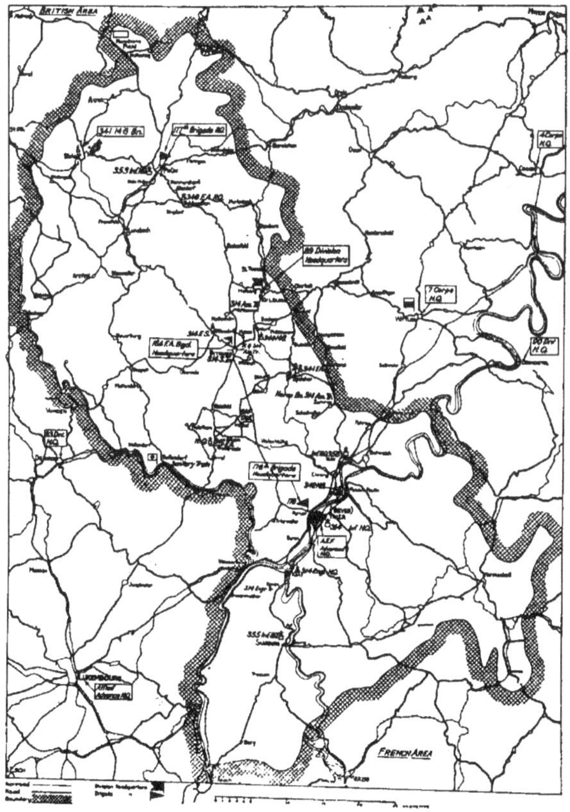

The Area in Germany occupied by the 89th Division.

whole general region bears the name Eifel, a name of great antiquity and unknown signification.

The region bears marks of volcanic origin. In the northern part are deep, circular lakes, the craters of long extinct volcanoes. The prevailing rocks are a curious, hard, red sandstone from which grindstones are made, and which, when used as everywhere for the construction of buildings, seems to defy time and the elements. For example, the church at Kylburg, part of which was built of this material in 1276, shows scarcely a trace of weathering. This sandstone is of very ancient geological origin and contains no fossils. It was formed before animal life appeared on the globe.

The principal river is the Moselle, flowing generally in the direction southeast to northwest, to empty into the Rhine at Coblenz. Its steep, bordering hills and bold headlands are devoted to growing grapes from which celebrated wines are made, and the terraced hillsides made scenes of picturesque beauty which linger long in memory. On the southwestern border of the district flows the Sauer river, dividing Germany from Luxembourg, and emptying into the Moselle at Wasserbillig. Further up the Moselle is the mouth of the Saar river, giving its name to the town and kreis of Saarburg. The upper reaches of this river, beyond our district, are the locations of the coal fields, the use of which for fifteen years was awarded to France in the Treaty of Peace as partial compensation for the malicious destruction of the French coal fields in the war zone. The little river Kyll flows from north to south through the part of the district west of the Moselle, emptying into the Moselle near Ehrang, not far from Trier.

The whole country is beautifully diversified with pine and beech forests, forming a landscape of wonderful charm. It has been a favorite resort for pleasure seekers; and hot springs and mineral water near Prüm and Gerolstein and elsewhere are supposed to have medicinal virtues.

The district was divided among the troops. The 177th Infantry Brigade, with headquarters at Prüm, occupied the Kreis of Prüm; the 164th Artillery Brigade, with headquarters at Bitburg, occupied the Kreis of Bitburg. The 178th Infantry Brigade, less the 355th Infantry, with headquarters at Pallien on the heights overlooking Trier from the west bank of the Moselle, occupied the Kreis of Trier (Land). And the 355th Infantry, with headquarters at Saarburg, occupied Kreis of Saarburg.

The headquarters of the Division were located at the village of Kyllburg, which, located near the center of the district and provided with a number of excellent summer resort hotels, furnished facilities for the accommodation of the headquarters and staff, which necessarily became much augmented by the increase of administrative work.

GENERAL CONDITIONS OF THE OCCUPATION

The Division now settled down to a sedentary life. For the combat troops training in military arts and such amusements as were possible became the order of the day. The main functions of the Division were administrative, and our narrative now enters upon rather a dry account of these activities, necessary indeed, if the reader is to gain a true picture of what our division did, but dull in comparison to the stirring scenes and events of active operations. After the first novelty of the occupation wore off, the hope and desire of all ranks was to get back home. That the Division maintained its morale, kept itself fit for any further military duty that it might be called upon to perform and displayed the same qualities of thoroughness and efficiency in garrison life as in the field will be apparent from the account which follows.

CIVIL ADMINISTRATION COMMENCED

One of the first matters demanding the attention of the Division commander was the establishment of a system of civil administration in conformity with the policy decided upon by the Allies for the government of the occupied territory. The general policy had been enunciated in the provisions of the Armistice agreement in the following language:

"5. Countries on the left bank of the Rhine will be administered by the local authorities under the control of troops of the occupation of the Allies and of the United States."

This sensible provision for utilizing the services of the civil officials under the control of the military authorities made the problem of administration much more simple and the accomplishment far more successful than previous occupations of hostile territory by United States forces had been. In the occupation of the Philippines and of Mexico a complete system of civil administration had to be first set up because the existing system was too weak to function. Vexing questions continually arose as to what features were subordinate to, concurrent with or superior to the military administration. Moreover, the necessary unfamiliarity of the civil officials of the occupying forces with local conditions impaired their efficiency, no matter how able and conscientious they were. These difficulties were avoided in Germany. The administration of civil affairs was completely under the control of the military commanders, the officers charged with the regulation of civil affairs being detailed on the staff of the various military commanders and conducting the business in the name of and as the representatives of the military authorities alone; hence there was no division of responsibility and no friction. On the other hand, by entrusting the details of administration to the local officials and supervising their performance of the duties, a high degree of efficiency was obtained. The local officials were uniformly efficient, they were naturally predisposed to the maintenance of order and the resumption of normal civil activities and were familiar with the machinery of administration. No serious case of treachery or insubordination on the part of any official occurred in the sector of the 89th Division, nor, as far as is known, in any part of the zone of American occupation. It is believed that the administration of civil affairs in the occupied territory was conspicuously successful.

General Pershing decided that an officer in charge of civil affairs in the occupied territory should be appointed, who would function directly under the Commander-in-Chief, with station in Trier. Brigadier General Harry A. Smith was so appointed. On December 13th an order of G. H. Q. was promulgated, defining the scope and organization of the Office of Civil Affairs. It provided also for the appointment of Officers in Charge of Civil Affairs for the Third Army and for each Army Corps and Division thereof, who should be on the staffs of their respective commanding generals.

Pursuant to this order Lieutenant Colonel (then Major) George H. English, Jr., then Adjutant of the 177th Infantry Brigade, was detailed as such officer for the 89th Division. He continued in the performance of the duties of this office during the entire period of the occupation, except for about six weeks during March and April, 1919, when he was detailed as Division Educational Officer. During this period Capt. S. B. McPheeters of the 340th Field Artillery was detailed for the office of civil affairs under the supervision of the A. C. of S., G-2.

The divisional area was organized with a local officer in charge of Civil Affairs for each Kreis, who kept supervision over the Landrat, the German chief administrative officer of the Kreis, and through him over the various burgomasters, who were the heads of the smaller administrative subdivisions, comprising one or several villages with their adjacent territory. Through these officials various regulations for the conduct of the civil population were promulgated and enforced. The officers in charge of Civil Affairs for the several Kreisen were as follows: Kreis Prüm, Capt. Manton Davis, 354th Infantry; Kreis Bitburg, Capt. (then Lieutenant) A. R. Baldwin, Headquarters 164th Field Artillery Brigade; Kreis Trier (Land), Capt. Edmund Rogers, 355th Infantry; and Kreis Saarburg, Lieutenant Colonel Levi G. Brown, 355th Infantry, and, for much of the time, Captain Neville C. Fisher.

Punishment of offenses by the civil population against the military regulations was under the jurisdiction of Provost Courts. An officer to serve as Inferior Provost Court was appointed in every town in which troops were stationed. These courts had limited jurisdiction, being authorized to impose punishments up to three months' imprisonment and 3,000 marks fine. Their procedure was quite simple, being analogous to that of summary courts provided for in the Manual of Courts Martial for the Army. They made weekly reports of their proceedings through the officer in charge of Civil Affairs. Fines collected were remitted directly to Advance G. H. Q. in Trier. For more serious offenses, trial was had before a Superior Provost Court, Colonel Warren W. Whitside, Commander of Trains, being appointed to serve as this court. The Superior Court had jurisdiction up to six months' imprisonment and 10,000 marks fine. Its procedure was the same as that of the inferior courts. The organization and procedure of these courts were prescribed in the orders of G. H. Q.

REGULATIONS FOR CIVILIANS

The regulations governing the conduct of the civil population were simple and moderate and in striking contrast to the harsh rules imposed by the German military authorities upon the inhabitants of Belgium and France during their occupation. Every person above the age of twelve was required to provide himself with a card of identity, containing a photograph of the individual and a certificate of his identity by his burgomaster. This, however, was already a feature of existing civil regulations of Germany, required principally, however, of travelers. Circulation of individuals outside of the American zone was prohibited without permission of the Division Commander. Such permission was not granted without a certificate from the burgomaster that the proposed journey was of pressing importance. The granting of these permits was at first under the Civil Affairs Office, but was later made a function of the Intelligence Section, G-2. It served the purpose not only of keeping the people well in hand, but also to reduce to the minimum the use of means of transportation, which were being strained to the utmost to supply the needs of the army as well as of the civilian population. Strict regulations forbade the passage of Germans into Luxembourg, and as the 89th Division held the border, the enforcement of these regulations was entrusted to our troops. The granting of such passes as were imperative was arranged by the Civil Affairs officer with the commander of the French forces occupying Luxembourg. Our regulations also required that all dramshops be closed except during a few hours of the afternoon and early evening. The sale of any intoxicant except beer and light wines was prohibited. All weapons of every sort were required to be turned over to the military authorities who collected them in depots and guarded them. Assembling of the people was forbidden without permission, which however, was always granted on request for a meeting for any lawful purpose, especially for political meetings of all parties during the period before the election of delegates to the National Assembly and the Prussian Diet. Returning German soldiers were required to remove their uniform within four days of their return. All persons in uniform were required to salute American officers and all persons were required to uncover and stand at attention when Army bands played the National anthem. Any interference with the troops or having in possession American Army stores or property was, of course, the occasion for sharp punishment. Sanitary measures were enforced, such as the isolation of contagious diseases, the marking of polluted water sources, and compulsory treatment by our own veterinarians of all horses and mules owned by civilians within the area in order to eradicate the mange, which was prevalent. Manure piles, those obtrusive features of every village in Continental Europe, were required to be neatly kept and covered with pine boughs. General cleanliness and the abatement of nuisances were required. All reported prostitutes were examined and women found with venereal diseases were arrested and sent to Trier for treatment in German hospitals.

ATHLETICS IN GERMANY.

Soon after the arrival of the Division in Germany, organized athletics became the subject of great attention by General Winn. Football, basketball, indoor baseball and soccer teams were at once formed in all organizations. In the spring a baseball league of regimental teams was formed. Athletic equipment was furnished by the Y. M. C. A., and intense and increasing interest was manifested by all ranks in wholesome outdoor sports.

Naturally, the focus of interest from the viewpoint of the Division as a whole is the Division Football Team,—our ever-victorious team which won the championship of the A. E. F.

Captain (later Major) Withington began the organization of the team in January, 1919. A small field was selected in the vicinity of Malburg, a little village only a few hundred yards from Kyllburg. Men of known ability were called on to report for practice, and the Division was combed for men who had shown skill at the game in the organization teams. Although equipment had not arrived, the men began practice in their O. D. trousers and hob-nailed shoes by the 25th of January, in the snow and slush.

The first game was played February 14th, 1919, against the team of the 90th Division at Wittlich. The final score was 89th Division, 6; 90th Division, 0. At no stage of the game was the outcome in doubt, except during the last few minutes of play when the 90th's team, within twelve yards of a touchdown, spoiled a chance to score by making an illegal substitution for which they were penalized half the length of the field. On the other hand, our team was in striking distance of the goal again and again, but the tightening of the defense and the slippery field saved the losers from a larger score. The only score came in the third quarter on a straight play by Wilder. "Potsy" Clark, who afterwards starred so brilliantly, sustained a dislocated shoulder in the first play of the game and was forced to withdraw.

The second game of the season was played at Coblenz, February 20th, against the Headquarters' Third Army. It proved to be an easy win for our team, the score being 30 to 0.

The third game, played against the 4th Division Team at Coblenz, on February 27th, determined the championship of the Third Army and our 14 to 0 victory earned us the honor of representing the Army of Occupation in the A. E. F. championship games at Paris. This game was thrilling throughout, both as regards the playing and the "accessories" and was one of the best played games. It was Harvard against Harvard, the captains of the teams being two of the greatest players who ever wore the Crimson,—Paul Withington for us and Hamilton Fish for the 4th.

The first quarter passed without a score and with little apparent advantage to either team. The break came in the second quarter with only 20 seconds left to the half. One of Lindsey's high, twisting punts was caught dangerously near the 4th's goal and the catcher downed in his tracks by our fleet ends. A kick out of danger was the only play; but "Poge" Lewis, our center, went through Sibert and knocked down the ball as it left Roderick's toe and it rolled back of the goal line; "Scrubby" Laslett had just the necessary fraction of a second more speed than the three 4th Division men who darted after it and when the legs were untangled it was seen that he was hugging the ball behind the 4th's goal line for our first touchdown. Pandemonium. The bugle corps of two hundred massed trumpeters which the 89th had organized and brought along for the occasion blew "Pay Day." A great banner bearing the Circle W broke out to the breeze. Lindsey kicked goal. Seven to zero.

The second score came as the result of smashing, straight, superior football. Clark, Lindsey and Padfield made steady gains. "Potsy," his dislocated shoulder all right by now, uncorked one of his spectacular runs through a broken field for 35 yards, being down and up three times. The ball was advanced to the three-yard line; the 4th concentrated its forces for a mass play; Quarterback Gerhardt, observing the enemy's dispositions, determined on a flank movement and sent Clark around the left end for the second touchdown. Fourteen to nothing. There was no more scoring. The fighting was furious but clean throughout. The whole game was a high example of true American sportsmanship.

There was an O. D. crowd of 7,500 to 10,000, accuracy in figures being impossible because no tickets were taken. Before the game, Eddie Rickenbacker's Aeroplane Circus gave us an exhibition of tail spins, nose spins, dives and every sort of air thriller; an observation balloon with a great American flag floated above the field; the 4th's squad of clowns lent an amusing touch. It was a great day.

The team returned home to prepare for the final struggles. Our former adversaries, generous in defeat, sent us the best of their coaches to help prepare the team for a Third Army victory. Lieutenant Trimble of the 90th Division, formerly of Harvard, and Major Pritchard of the Seventh Corps Staff, formerly of West Point, had already been assisting Captain Withington. There now came also Captain Sonsa, formerly of Harvard, Captain Denny of Brown, and Captain Moriarity, tackle of the 4th Division team. Later, after the defeat of the St. Nazaire team, Lieutenant Eddie Mahan joined the coaching staff. Throughout the team had the benefit of the services of Major F. W. O'Donnell, of our own medical corps, whose careful supervision of the team brought them into every contest in superb physical condition.

Early in March the team with its coaches went to Paris to engage in the final games for the championship. Seven teams had been the survivors of the competitions in the different armies and sections of the S. O. S. Three rounds must therefore be played before the final victor could be determined.

Our first adversary was the powerful St. Nazaire team, one of the two representatives of the S. O. S. in the finals. The game was played March 14th at the Velodrome, the great race track in Paris. The St. Nazaire team was coached by Eddie Hart, Princeton, and had in its line-up Eddie Mahan, one of Harvard's greatest kickers. The score was: 89th Division, 13; St. Nazaire, 0. Our first score came in the second quarter as a result of steady short gains beginning at our forty-yard line and sweeping down the field for a touchdown. St. Nazaire came back strongly for the second half and forced the ball to our one-yard line. Here the die-in-the-trench spirit of the 89th manifested itself and the line held for four downs. Eissler twice, Mahan, and finally Barrett were hurled desperately against the line, but those few inches could not be passed, and the ball went to us on downs. From this point the outcome was never in doubt and after consistent, short gains to striking distance of the goal, "Potsy" Clark wriggled over the line for the final touchdown. Lindsey's punts had equalled or exceeded Mahan's.

The next game, played March 22nd at the Auteuil Velodrome, was against the team representing the Intermediate Section S. O. S. The game was a typical 89th Division victory, finishing with a victorious punch after coming from behind. The final score was 17 to 3. The S. O. S. scored first, a goal from placement in the second quarter. In the second half, one of Lindsey's punts rolled past the S. O. S. safety man, who followed the ball too closely, in the hope that it would roll out of bounds for a touchback. The ball, with a freakish bound, grazed his leg and Laslett, put on side by the touch, pounced on it like a flash, giving us first down on the S. O. S. five-yard line. Three line bucks left the ball still a yard and a half away. A fake kick proved to be a short forward pass, Gerhardt to Clark, who crossed the line for a touchdown at the corner of the field. Lindsey kicked the difficult goal. A field goal by Lindsey and a touchdown by Clark with only 35 seconds to play made a thrilling finish in the last quarter.

The final game, against the 36th Division team, representing the First Army, provided a contest well worthy of a place in the classics of gridiron history. It was played March 29th at the Velodrome, Parc des Princes, Paris, before at least 15,000 spectators. General Pershing, General Liggett, and a host of officers of the highest rank attended. The commanding generals of the two divisions, each with his staff, occupied prominent places. General Edwin R. Smith was the commanding officer of the 36th. General Winn, who had not missed a game played by the team of his division, nor failed to visit and encourage the men between halves, was accompanied by 1,200 officers and soldiers of the 89th who had come from far-off Germany on special trains, with their bugle corps and bands, to root for the team.

The field was muddy, but the football played was of the highest order. The final score was 14 to 6, the 89th, as usual, coming from behind and emerging with the victory after it had seemed that the game was lost.

In the first quarter the 89th worked the ball to the one-yard line and on the fourth down tried for a field goal, but the slippery ball went wide. After neither side had gained much advantage in close play in the middle of the field, Mahseet delivered a terrific punt that carried more than fifty yards and passed the safety man of the 89th, who let it roll over the line for a touchback. On the first play, the ball was passed badly to Lindsey, who fumbled and the ball rolled over the line. McCuller fell on it for the first touchdown of the game. Mahseet missed goal. The quarter ended without further scoring.

Neither side scored in the second quarter, the play rather favoring the 36th Division, for after Mahseet had again punted over the line for a touchback and the ball had been put in play on the 89th twenty-yard line, three bucks on the 36th line actually lost ground. The half ended with the score 6 to 0 in favor of the 36th. With victory apparently in sight, the 36th Division swarmed on the field for a snake dance.

Between halves, in addition to the usual scorching talks from the coaches, General Winn spoke to the team. Many of the players afterward said that his appeal to their pride in the Division, his encouragement of their efforts, was one of the most effective of such appeals that they had ever listened to. Certain it is that something was instilled into the team between halves that called forth reserve powers that had not been displayed before.

Beginning the third quarter, Lindsey returned the Indian's kick-off forty-one yards by one of the most brilliant runs of the game. In three plays on the line the 89th gained first down. The 36th then stiffened and a punting duel followed, in which a blocked punt gave the 89th the ball on the seven-yard line, but a fumble by Clark lost the chance to score. Finally a pretty forward pass to Clark and a run netting twenty-two yards put the ball within striking distance. Lindsey and Gerhardt dropped back as if to try for a field goal. Gerhardt received the ball, shot it back to Lindsey, who passed it far down the field to Clark. Clark received it almost on the goal line and stepped across for the first touchdown. Clark kicked a difficult goal, and the 89th, amid a bedlam of cheering, went into the lead, not to be headed again.

The game came to a fitting climax with the last score. The 89th obtained the ball on its own thirty-five-yard line. On the first play, the linemen opened a hole for "Potsy" Clark. Eluding the first defense men, the fleet half-back was off down the muddy field with only the safety man between him and a touchdown. Clark proved to be the best mudder and passed the safety man like a streak, ending the most sensational play of the game, a sixty-five-yard run, with a touchdown. Clark kicked goal, thus being accredited individually with all his team's points.

Before the close of the game, General Pershing came upon the field, personally greeted the players and congratulated them on their splendid game and fine spirit. Paris was not dull that night.

Line-up and score:

89th Division.	Position.	36th Division.
Pvt. Laslett	Left End	Pvt. McCuller
Corp. Thompson	Left Tackle	Sgt. Tolbert
Capt. Withington	Left Guard	Pvt. Brown
Lieut. Lewis	Center	Sgt. Frye
Lieut. Garside	Right Guard	Pvt. Mahseet
Lieut. Schweiger	Right Tackle	Sgt. Gray
Lieut. W. K. Clark	Right End	Musician Bellieu
Capt. Gerhardt	Quarter-back	Capt. Whitney
Lieut. G. Clark	Left Half-back	Lieut. S. Clarke
Lieut. Lindsey	Right Half-back	Pvt. Lockabaugh
Sgt. Nelson	Full-back	Sgt. Cranfill

Substitutions—89th Division: Flannigan for Garside, Higgins for W. Clark, Fletcher for Higgins, Higgins for Fletcher, Padfield for Nelson. 36th Division: Gray for Tolbert, Leiter for Gray, Kendricks for Bellieu, Fetterolf for S. Clarke, Watson for Fetterolf, S. Clarke for Watson. Touchdowns—Lieut. G. Clark 2, Pvt. McCuller. Goals following touchdown—Lieut. G. Clark 2. Goals missed following touchdown—Mahseet. Referee, Lieut.-Col. W. Withington (Michigan), 7th Division; Umpire, Capt. J. J. O'Hare (West Point), Advance Section S.O.S.; Field Judge, Lieut. John W. Leonard, 5th Division; Head Linesman, Col. Carl L. Ristine (Missouri), 35th Division; Assistant Linesmen, Major George Woodruff and Major David H. Nelson. Time of periods—15 minutes each. Score by quarters:

89th Division	0	0	7	7—14
36th Division	6	0	0	0— 6

The victorious team was given a well-earned leave of absence in the rest area of Nice, and finally, on the 15th of April returned to the Division's area in Germany. The return was made a triumphal entry. They were entertained at dinner at Trier by General Winn and his staff. Coming into Kyllburg, they passed under a series of arches erected over the road from Malburg on. Fireworks of every description were set off in the square at Kyllburg, and amid applause they were escorted to the great ball room of the Eifelerhof, where a reception, dance and presentation of small silver footballs as trophies followed. General Winn made the presentation of the decorations, and was surprised and gratified when Captain Withington, in behalf of the team, presented him with one in return, with the comment that the General's speeches at each game had been largely instrumental in its success.

The division had given promise of success in football during its training period at Funston, the team there developed, and which contained many of those who made up our champion team, having been the only one to conquer the strong team of the Great Lakes Training Camp.

TRACK AND FIELD

The 89th Division track and field meet held at Goeben Kaserne, an old German military barracks, in Trier, was won by the team from the 355th Infantry, which registered 66 points. The 356th Infantry was second with 39 points and the 341st Field Artillery third with 29½. Summaries:

100 YARDS DASH—11 2-5s., Corp. Imlay, 355th Inf., won; Sgt. Blackburn, 355th Inf., second; Pvt. Meets, 355 Inf., third. 220 YARDS DASH—30s., Sgt. Blackburn, 355th Inf., won; Pvt. Williams, 340th M. G. Bat., second; Sgt. Armen, 356th Inf., third. 440 YARDS RUN—1m. 4s., Lieut. Kenaston, 356th Inf., won; Pvt. Halleman, 356th Inf., second; Sgt. Heinicke, 314th Engrs., third. 880 YARDS RUN—2m. 20s., Lieut. MacKenzie, 340th M. G. Bn., won; Corp. Clapp, 355th Inf., second; Sgt. Potter, 355th Inf., third. 1 MILE RUN—Corp. Duncan, 356th Inf., won; Lieut. Foster, 356th Inf., second; Pvt. Andrews, 356th Inf., third. ROAD RACE (four miles)—24m. 33s., Sgt. Claiborne, 340th F. A., won; Lieut. Foster, 356th Inf., second; Pvt. Smith, 355th Inf., third. 120 YARDS HIGH HURDLES—22 3-5s., Sgt. Brooks, 341st F. A., won; Corp. Weder, 314th Signal Bn., second; Capt. Crawford, 164th F. A. Brig. Hqs., third. 120 YARDS LOW HURDLES—17 3-5s., Corp. Hilterbrand, 314th Engrs., won; Capt. Crawford, 164th F. A.

Brig. Hdqs., second; Sgt. Dorland, 355th Inf., third. 1 MILE RELAY (eighth, quarter, half-mile laps)—356th Inf., won; 355th Inf., second; 340th Mach. Gun Bn., third.

RUNNING HIGH JUMP—5ft. 6in., Pvt. Woodruff, 355th Inf., won; Corp. Hilterbrand, 314th Engrs., second; Capt. Crawford, 164th F. A. Brig. Hdqs., and Sgt. Henry, 341st F. A., tied for third. RUNNING BROAD JUMP—Pvt. Wood, 340th M. G. Bn., won. STANDING BROAD JUMP—Pvt. Metheny, 314th Signal Bn., third. HOP, STEP AND JUMP—38ft. 2in., Corp. Hilterbraud, 314th Engrs., won; Pvt. Bayley, 341st F. A., second; Pvt. Carpenter, 355th Inf., third. POLE VAULT—9ft., Pvt. Woodruff, 355th Inf., won; Sgt. Henry, 341st F. A., second; Pvt. Phillips, 356th Inf., third. SHOT PUT—41ft. 5in., Sgt. Henry, 341st F. A., second; Pvt. Phillips, 356th Inf., third. SHOT PUT—41ft. 5in., Sgt. Carpenter, 355th Inf., won; Sgt. Sanders, 356th Inf., second; Corp. Goodrich, 341st F. A., third. JAVELIN THROW—121ft. 8in., Pvt. Walt, 314th San. Train, won; Sgt. Sanders, 356th Inf., second; Sgt. Brooke, 341st F. A., third. DISCUS THROW—106ft. 5in., Pvt. Woodruff, 355th Inf., won; Lieut. Modisette, 341st F. A., second; Sgt. Landers, 356th Inf., third. TUG-OF-WAR—355th Inf., won; 340th M. G. Bn., second.

The Third Army track and field meet was held at Coblenz on April 24th as a part of the Third Army Carnival. The 3rd Division won the meet with a total of 78 points. The 89th was second with a total of 67, while the next nearest competitor, the Third Army Headquarters Troop had only 33, and the others trailed. We won the tug of war, and Nelson won first place for us in the 100-yard dash, and Davis another first in the running high jump. The most spectacular win, however, was that of the Cochem-Coblenz relay, a relay race of 52 kilometers, which our team won in the excellent time of 3 hours, 27 minutes, 30 seconds, and by the decisive margin of a lead of over four hundred yards at the finish.

The Third Army Carnival was held at Coblenz April 23rd to 27th. It consisted of a Horse Show, a Motor Show and a Field and Track Meet. All the divisions and the Corps and Army Troops participated. In points won in the three branches of the Carnival, the 89th Division was third with a total of 119 points, being surpassed only by the Third Army Troops with a total of 132 and the 3rd Division with a total of 120.

In track and field athletics, the Division sent a worthy representative to the A E. F. finals in the person of Captain M. P. Wilder, 354th Infantry, who had previously won distinction by gallantry in action. The finals were held at the Colombes Stadium near Paris on May 30th and 31st, and June 1st, 1919. Wilder, who was left behind to participate in the games on the departure of the Division, won the penthalon event with a total of 3,201.32 points, a margin of 154.10 points over his nearest competitor. His records in the event were as follows: 200-meter Dash—24 4-5s., 736; Running Broad Jump—20ft. 1in., 682.50; 16-lb. Shot put—36ft. 4¾in., 577; Discus Throw—110ft. 3½in., 479.02; 1,500-meter Run—4m. 34 1-5s., 776.80.

BASEBALL

The Division's departure in May prevented its participation to any great extent in the baseball contests outside of the Division. Great expectations for success in baseball had been entertained because of the fine showing in inter-regimental games within the Division. The 342nd Field Artillery, especially, had developed a strong baseball team with a wealth of fine players. A number of well-known players were on this team, among them Grover C. Alexander, the celebrated pitcher of the Chicago Cubs, who had served throughout as a sergeant in that regiment. The team had met all comers while at the Artillery Camp near Bordeaux and had won every series.

WE EDUCATE OURSELVES

In late February orders came in a rush providing for the putting into effect of the Army's educational programme. Through the Y. M. C. A., some of the foremost educators of the United States had been working upon an elaborate scheme for affording educational advantages to the American Expeditionary Forces. They were men of vision and experience who saw in this vast assemblage of the very flower of American youth an unexampled opportunity for doing good, for providing means for increasing the technical skill of a vast body of prospective industrial workers, for instilling and cultivating a taste for higher education among those fitted for it, and finally and most important of all, for taking a great step towards eliminating a humiliating percentage of illiteracy, which, when brought to universal attention by the statistics obtained from the enforcement of the Selective Service Act, has proved startling to all lovers of democracy in our great Republic.

The question of illiteracy was first attacked. Orders from G. H. Q. required imperatively that every illiterate should receive instruction in reading, writing and elementary arithmetic. Post schools were accordingly established in the Division, conducted for the most part by the regimental chaplains or under their direction. The entire system was under the general supervision of the Division Chaplain, S. E. Griffiths, and, later, Otis E. Gray. A survey was had to ascertain the number of illiterates in the Division. A man was regarded as illiterate who could not read intelligently ordinary printed matter, such as the daily newspapers, and who could not write an intelligible letter. The percentage of such illiterates found corresponded closely to the percentage of illiteracy of the population of the states from which the Division was largely drawn, namely about 3%. This proved to be a much smaller percentage than that of many other divisions. The Post Schools promptly set to work to remove this condition. The men were required to attend them and were relieved from military duties which would interfere with their attendance. Their feelings were respected as far as possible and the schools were held without unnecessary publicity and as privately as possible. These schools were continued in operation as long as practicable, some of them up to the very moment of the dissolution of the Division. Their benefits are apparent when it is stated that over 80 per cent of these men were discharged from the Post Schools as having satisfactorily completed the course; that is to say, they left the service of the United States with the ability to read understandingly the ordinary means of communicating intelligence and the ability to express intelligibly their thoughts in writing.

One lad's sister had been a school teacher. He said: "No use, my sister's tried all her life to teach me to write—it can't be done." He wrote his sister several letters before he left Germany.

The A. E. F. educational programme included also the offering of opportunities for higher education. Arrangements were made with leading universities of England and France for the attendance of American students from our military forces and approximately 150 members of the 89th Division obtained the benefit of these courses. A great university was organized out of the very body of the American forces and opened at Beaune, France, using the extensive buildings which had been erected at that place for a hospital, and which, through the unexpectedly early termination of the war, were felicitously empty of their intended occupants. The history of this A. E. F. University, brief as it is, would be well worthy of a volume and constitutes an inspiring record of American energy applied to high intellectual and spiritual ends. Suffice it to say, that in an incredibly brief time, the University was in full operation, offering courses of bewildering variety in fine and applied arts, languages, mathematics, agriculture and a host of other subjects under a faculty that would bear comparison with that of any institution of higher learning in our country. The instructors embraced many men of eminence in the profession of teaching, who had been enlisted in the work through the efforts of the educational branch of the Y. M. C. A. But the numerically greater number of them were taken from the military forces, a striking testimony of the universal character of the participation of all classes and grades of America in the military service. In April the Y. M. C. A. educational system was taken over by the Army, and the instructors, who were not military persons, became the direct employes of the government on the same or more favorable terms as under their contracts with the Y. M. C. A.

The A. E. F. University had an attendance of over 6,000 students of whom upwards of 250 students and instructors came from the 89th Division.

The orders relating to education also provided for the establishment in each division of an educational center and indicated the character of instruction that it was thought practicable to offer in such centers. Pursuant to these orders the Division Commander detailed Lieutenant Colonel (then Major) George H. English, Jr., as Divisional Educational Officer for the organization of this center and general supervision over educational matters. The Educational Officer was given cordial and unlimited support in the performance of his duties by the detail of the best and most fully qualified officers for the heads of the different schools and the selection of instructors from the Division. Much preliminary work had been done in making a survey of the Division for instructors and students and locations for the schools by Division Chaplain Captain Otis E. Gray and Captain W. E. Crockett.

On March 17th three schools were opened and continued in operation until the preparations for the return of the Division in early May compelled their closing.

The largest of these, a Technical School, was opened in the large German munitions plant at Kehr, near Halschlag in the extreme northern part of the area. It was under the command of Lieutenant Colonel O. M. Leland, 314th Engineers, who, in civil life was of the faculty of Cornell University, and of Lieutenant Colonel John H. Hinemon, Jr., Division Signal Officer, who, as an officer of the Regular Army had devoted much attention to the study and instruction of communications by radio, telegraph and telephone. This school had an attendance of about 250 students. The most popular course offered was that of automobile repair. Theoretical and practical instruction was given, using some of our own autos and trucks and some of the captured German machines. Some 50 students, not so well qualified as the others for theoretical instruction, received practical training with the repair units of the Division Trains. Courses in telegraphy, telephony, radio, wood-working, surveying, mechanical drawing, English and mathematics were also offered. The barracks at which the German workmen in the plant had been lodged, were, after cleaning, made use of for the accommodation of the students; and such tools and appliances as could be used for our purposes in the plant were made use of for instruction.

A general school, offering courses analogous to those of the Freshman and Sophomore years of college, was opened in the German Convent at Prüm. This school was under the command of Major Ernest E. Watson, 341st Machine Gun Battalion, who, a lawyer in civil life, had nevertheless remained in close touch with educational matters. The convent was the foundation of a Sisterhood of Nuns, and in ordinary times was used as a gymnasium, or High School for German boys. Excellent dormitories and class rooms were found here. The good Sisters were undisturbed in their ordinary activities. Courses in English Literature, French, Spanish, Algebra, Geometry and Trigonometry, Economics and other subjects, were pursued by about 125 students.

A School of Agriculture was opened at Hermeskail in the extreme southeastern part of the area, under the command of Lieutenant Colonel Alva S. Perkins, 342nd Field Artillery. There had been at this place a small German Agricultural Institute, such as exist in many places throughout Germany, where courses in agriculture are offered during the winter months to the farmers of the vicinity. Some small amount of material in the way of anatomical models of animals and specimens of plants was available, as well as limited class room space. The school offered instruction to about 150 students in Animal Husbandry, Agronomy and English. The unexampled opportunity for the study of European methods of agriculture and comparison with our own methods was appreciated, and it was determined to utilize these to the utmost possible extent. Accordingly, after obtaining the permission of the Division commander, the Educational Officer went to Bonn on the Rhine and there arranged for a course of four lectures to be given this school by instructors from the great German University there. Three of these were to be given by instructors from the Agricultural Institute on the subjects of Forestry, Road Construction and Plant Breeding. The fourth by a professor of the University of a more elaborate character on a comparison of American and European methods of agriculture as affected by the varying conditions of climate and labor in the two countries. The funds for the payment of these lecturers had been arranged for with the Y. M. C. A. Educational Officer of the 3rd Army. The early closing of the school prevented the completion of this course of lectures—one only having been given. But several lectures were also given by the Director of the Local Institute at Hermskail on various agricultural topics.

The method of giving these lectures was to have the lecturer furnish in advance a synopsis of his lecture; this was translated into English and mimeographed or placed on the blackboard for the students. The lecturer then gave his lecture orally in German, a translator standing by his side and translating as he proceeded. Questions were then asked, translated and answered.

Stock judging of local animals and of condemned Army animals was also a feature of the school, and arrangements were made for the students to attend some of the Horse Shows that were held by the divisions and corps, for the purpose of judging the animals exhibited.

The schools of the 89th Division won commendation from the higher authorities, and it is thought conferred considerable benefit on those who attended them. An element of their success was the cordial and effective support and aid given them by the 3rd Army Y. M. C. A. Educational Supervisor, Dr. Guy Potter Benton, in private life the President of the University of Vermont, and by the 3rd Army Educational Officer, Major Frederick Hackett. With funds made available by the Y. M. C. A., text books, drawing instruments and seeds for the experimental gardens were purchased in the open market and the German lecturers paid for their services.

Many difficulties, of course, had to be overcome by improvisation of facilities. Text books on many subjects were lacking through transportation and other difficulties from the rear. French lessons for a time were given from the French page of the European edition of the New York Herald. Tables of logarithms for the trigonometry classes were mimeographed from Engineers Field Manuals. Copies of the Tauchnitz Edition of English Classics were purchased in Trier, Coblenz and Cologne, a few at a place, until enough were obtained for the literature classes. Mechanical drawing instruments were acquired in the same way.

CHANGES IN ORGANIZATION

During the period of the occupation, some slight changes in the organization of the Division occurred. The military police were reorganized as the 89th Division Military Police Company, in conformity to changes in the regulations governing the organization of the Army. Under the quartermaster were placed the following attached organizations: Salvage Squad No. 1; Laundry Unit No. 354; Bakery Company No. 349; Clothing and Bath Unit No. 326; Sales Commissary Unit No. 5.

In the medical department, the Divisional Medical Supply Unit was established; and the 314th Mobile Veterinary Section was attached.

The American Post Office No. 761 had long been the Divisional post office.

Service Park Units Numbers 390 and 397 were also attached to the Division.

COLLECTION OF ABANDONED WAR MATERIAL

Large quantities of German war material remained in the area, having been abandoned by the German Army on its retreat. This consisted principally of artillery ammunition, trucks and horses. The location of this material was ascertained by the Kreis commanders and it was collected by the ammunition train under the supervision of G-1, placed at convenient points along the railroad and guarded by the troops. No disposition of this material was ordered by the Third Army and it was finally left in the sector, being turned over to the railroad guards of the 6th Division, which relieved us as railroad guards on our departure.

It developed that a shabby trick had been played by the German government upon its own subjects in respect to much of this property. The terms of the Armistice expressly provided that war material which was not removed from the territory to be occupied would be treated as captured property. Notwithstanding this provision, it was found that a great deal of this material, especially horses, trucks and supplies that could be used by the civilian population and that could not be removed by the Germany Army on its retreat, had been sold, under orders from Berlin, to the civilians. This was a clear evasion of the terms of the Armistice and amounted to a conversion of property which, under the laws of war, belonged to the United States. This property was seized, wherever found, and the proceeds of the sales, when these funds were found in the hands of the local authorities, were impounded.

There was located at Kehr, near Halschlag, in the extreme northern part of the district, in a desolate and sparsely settled portion of the country, a large munitions plant. At the time of the occupation, a vast amount of high explosives and a large quantity of filled and empty shell cases were found there. Guards were placed over this dangerous material, and at a later period the plant was made use of as the location for the Technical School.

The proprietors of this establishment were typical of the modern commercial class of Germany. Their conduct was in striking contrast with that of the local and chiefly agricultural population and was marked by a spirit of greed, deceit and clumsy improbity. The plant was the property of a private corporation and was used in the manufacture of high explosives. Its course of business was to fill with explosives shells furnished by the German Imperial Government. A large quantity of filled and empty shell cases was on hand at the time of the occupation and the proprietors of the plant claimed them as private property and failed to report them as public war materials, which was required by the terms of the Armistice and the regulations. The claim of these shell cases, which were of considerable value, was based upon an alleged sale of them to the plant, claimed to have been made in June, 1918, by the German government. Aside from the utter improbability that the German government would, at a time when it was engaged in its most tremendous military effort of the war, make sale of any of its war material, the documents produced as evidence of the sale were suspiciously informal and appeared to have been subsequently prepared. Later, when the plant was occupied as a school, preposterous claims for damages and rental were made. While, under the terms of the Armistice, these claims, though paid at the time by the United States, would ultimately be repaid by the German government as expenses of the occupation, they were so palpably outrageous in amount that a board of officers was appointed by the Division commander to examine and report upon them; this board made an allowance of 10,000 marks, upon claims of over 600,000 marks, and felt that it had made a liberal allowance at that.

GUARDS

A frontier guard was established along the Luxembourg border in accordance with orders of the higher authority which prohibited intercourse between the occupied territory and Luxembourg. This guard was established on the 26th of December. The arrangements for it had been made in the city of Luxembourg, on Christmas day, at a conference between the French Commandant de Armes of Luxembourg, General Latour, on the one part, and Colonel Fitch, operations officer of the Seventh Corps and the 89th Division officer in charge of civil affairs. All the responsibility for maintaining this guard between the American occupied zone and Luxembourg was placed upon the 89th Division since it occupied the entire border. The establishment of this guard was shortly followed by a change of civil government in the duchy of Luxembourg.

Guards were maintained at all bridge crossings and ferries under the orders of the Kreis commanders, inspected by them and also occasionally by the Division Staff. The orders of these guards were to deny circulation across the border, particularly by Germans, into Luxembourg. Some slight inconvenience was at first occasioned by the sudden establishment of this guard. Many German farmers on the border had farms in Luxembourg; school children from Echternachbrücke attended school in Echternach; towns along the border in Luxembourg received coal and other supplies only through the German railroads across the border. As circulation was not permitted except upon approval, both of the American military authorities in Germany and the French Commandant de Armes in Luxembourg, there were at first some slight hardships imposed upon the civil population of both districts because of the inability of these authorities promptly to pass upon reasonable applications for civilian circulation. These difficulties were soon eliminated and the guard was maintained continuously until taken over by troops of the 5th Division on the departure of the 89th Division in May.

Not all the troubles of the 314th Engineers mounted patrols were caused by the German civil population. Sometimes there was lack of coördination between the plans for advance of the Engineer and the views of the steed from the Ozarks on which he was mounted.

An extensive railroad guard was organized as soon as the Division arrived in the area. This guard covered the important points along the main lines and branches of all railroads in the district, guarding particularly the tunnels, bridges, culverts, water points, switches and railroad stations. Later, only such points on the main lines were guarded. The guard was maintained and inspected by the Kreis commanders. At first, considerable difficulty in the way of transportation for the purpose of inspection and the supply of the guards was encountered. These difficulties were finally obviated by the use of gasoline driven "speeders" and by the use of Ford trucks for supply.

Weekly patrols were made to all towns of over 200 inhabitants. These patrols were carried on by each Kreis commander. Their duties were to visit officially the burgomaster and interrogate him as to general conditions. Also to inspect and report upon the condition of the town as to sanitation, regulations regarding discharged German soldiers, the observance of liquor regulations and the like.

The Engineers used mounted patrols, but their "mounts" were mules from the Ozarks. The difficulties of the conquerors on such patrols were not entirely those created by the German population.

ROAD REPAIR

One of the most important duties assumed by our troops was the repair and maintenance of the German roads. This work was placed under the immediate control of the Division Engineer, supervised by the Assistant Chief of Staff, G-1. In the occupation of the area the roads were found to be in poor condition, having been passed over by the retreating German army and by the entire Third American Army. There had been no road repairing or maintenance since the passage of these armies and little road work during the war in comparison to that done in normal times. German roads are far inferior to French roads for durability under heavy conditions. In consequence the unusual traffic over these roads had reduced them to far worse condition than similar and greater traffic had in France. It was felt that the German population should be required to repair and maintain their roads under the supervision of the Americans, both because such road repairing would constitute a permanent improvement of the country and because it was desired to avoid a situation where American soldiers would be working on a road traveled over by enemy inhabitants. The use of labor by our soldiers on the road could not always be avoided because of the extreme importance of keeping them in shape for our own service of supply, but for the most part the work was done by the requisition of German civilian labor.

The work was commenced under the supervision of the Division Engineer, then Lieutenant Colonel O. M. Leland. The many details of opening up quarries from which stone for road repair was to be procured, getting into operation the existing plants and machinery and calling out the German road officials, were gradually mastered. The maintenance of these roads had become of great importance because of the damage done to them by the moving of the heavy artillery to the foremost elements of the Army of Occupation and especially because through the inadequacy of the railroads to handle the traffic, a vast amount of transportation of supplies from the SOS was brought overland by trucks to the Rhine. This heavy traffic, coming in the winter season during periods of rain, freezing and thaw soon produced a critical situation upon the roads. In January Colonel D. D. Pullen became Division Engineer and with intense vigor soon improved the road conditions in the divisional area. Each Kreis commander took steps to see that all the available German laborers were put on the roads and within a short space of time over 2,000 German civilians were engaged in this work. Several quarries were opened up and sufficient repair machinery was put into operation so that the use of soldier labor on the roads which had become necessary as late as March was obviated and by April the roads of the entire divisional area were in very good condition.

In order to save road travel and economize on motor transportation, practically all supply was arranged by rail or by light truck. Troops were stationed as far as possible on railroad lines or close thereto, to facilitate the supplying of them by rail.

As part of the road work, the Engineers also prosecuted a vigorous program of posting the roads and repairing the existing German signs, many of which had been, through neglect or malice, taken down or damaged. By the middle of April the entire area was so well posted that travel even without a map was quite easy.

A work of preparation which fortunately never had to be used was the organization to keep the roads open in case of heavy snowfall during the winter. In this mountainous region heavy snowfalls were to be expected. The Engineers provided a sufficient number of snowplows which were turned over to the Kreis commanders and necessary instructions from division headquarters were issued to guarantee that they would be put in operation as soon as a heavy snowfall started. Fortunately the winter was mild and only moderate falls of snow occurred, which did not obstruct the traffic unduly.

Several excellent supplies of rock for road material were found in the district, the principal one being at the town of Birresborn. Under the supervision of the Division Engineer these quarries were so operated as not only to furnish the material necessary for road repair in our own district but also to ship similar material to other areas of the Army of Occupation. Furthermore, the quarry at Birreseborn was made use of as a disciplinary prison for German civilians who were convicted of violations of our regulations. Able bodied Germans with sentences of less than one month were sent there to work in the quarries.

The whole subject of road maintenance and repair was handled upon the same lines as the general civil administration, that is, by making use of the local administrative machinery. The German road supervisors in their graded capacities were held responsible for the performance of their functions under the supervision of the Division Engineer so far as this was possible. Communication with these officials was at first through the Civil Affairs Office, but later was maintained directly by the Division Engineer.

POLICING UP AND BUILDING

Directly connected with the general supervision and repair of the roads was the policing of the roadside. A great deal of litter had been left by the two armies, German and American, which passed through the district. Furthermore, the German inhabitants were not governed by as high a standard of neatness and cleanliness, apparently, as those maintained by our division. The Division Engineer gave this matter especial attention, as did also the local commanders.

The German inhabitants were required to bury the dead animals, many of which had died on the march of the armies through the area, and to remove all litter and trash. It is certain that the Division left this area, as it did all other areas ever occupied by it, far cleaner than it found it.

Among other activities of the Engineers, there was met the demand for a considerable amount of new construction which was ordered by the Division Commander, to improve the general living conditions of the troops. Delousing plants, kitchens, store-rooms, mess-halls, stables, barracks, latrines and rough articles of furniture were constructed by the engineers. Priority on these constructions was determined by the Division Commander in the following order: First, kitchens. Second, mess-halls. Third, stables. A large quantity of lumber was required for this construction, which was purchased by the Division Engineer in the open market with funds made available from the German government as part of the expense of the Army of Occupation. As an example of the American way of doing things on a large scale, Colonel Pullen's purchase of this lumber may be cited. As soon as he became aware of the amount of construction that his department would be called upon to furnish, he went immediately to Trier, visited the local lumber dealers and purchased the entire stock of lumber on hand in this large town. He also opened and operated a sawmill in the vicinity of Mürlenbach and by these energetic measures was able to supply the demand of construction very efficiently.

When the Division left the area, all the buildings erected by the Engineers and all the furniture were listed by the zone major and the local burgomasters were given to understand that in each case they were responsible for the turning over of this construction to the incoming troops in good condition.

REGULATING PUBLIC UTILITIES

Another activity of the Engineers was the supervision of all public utilities within the area, especially the water, light and sewer systems. In every town occupied by American troops, where such utilities were available, officers or reliable non-commissioned officers were stationed who made an examination of these utilities and took special care to see that they were not overloaded by the demands of the troops in addition to those of the normal civil population. Extensive surveys of such towns were made and accurate data obtained as to the normal use and the capacity of the existing plants. Then restrictions were placed upon the use of water and electricity, both by troops and the civil population, so that the essential needs could be met without a breakdown. Co-operating with the sanitary personnel, special investigations as to the purity of the water supply were made and steps were taken to improve the quality of the water.

The Engineers also maintained an efficient lithographic plant which turned out large numbers of road maps and printed matter generally, for the use of the Division. Most excellent work was done in this plant and some of the calendars and programs for the horse shows and other divisional activities were works of art which would bear comparison with the very best of civilian products.

The Engineers also constructed three dipping vats, used in dipping animals to eradicate the mange. One of these, at Bitburg, was made of concrete and proved of more satisfactory construction than the other two, which were wooden lined, and located, one at Trier, and one at Niederprüm.

They also constructed delousing plants for the use of the troops. These plants consisted of a small underground room built near a bathhouse, which construction proved to be the most satisfactory type. Delousing plants in which the sterilization was accomplished by steam were procured from the quartermaster and some were captured from the German army. These, however, were not so satisfactory as the underground dry heat plants.

During the last part of the period, the entire engineer regiment was assembled at Conz in order to refit it and get the men in hand. This was the more necessary since the regiment had been scattered throughout the divisional area engaged in its multitudinous tasks ever since the occupation began. During this period of concentration, however, the engineers were called upon to furnish two companies for construction of remount corral and stations at Wengenohr under the supervision of the corps engineer and also to stake out the reviewing field at Trier. smooth off the rougher portions of the grounds and build reviewing stands, all for the final grand review of the Division made by the Commander in Chief shortly before its departure.

On the whole, the activities of the 314th Engineers during the period of the occupation were very great, very important, and the results of their work were such as to reflect great credit upon the regiment of engineers and upon the Division as a whole.

BILLETING

One of the essential activities of an occupying army is the arrangement for the billeting of the troops in the houses of the civil population. Existing orders governed generally the subject of billeting. Some slight interpretations of the rights of the occupying forces, however, not covered by the regulations, were made with a view to the comfort of our men. It was found that the disposition of the German inhabitants, naturally enough, was, if possible, to furnish the troops billeted upon them with surplus or spare quarters so as to be disturbed as little as possible in their normal domestic arrangements. This sometimes was found to be unsatisfactory and the guiding principle was adopted in our Division, that whatever accommodations were available, the best or the equivalent of the best, was to be allotted to the American military personnel. Accordingly, each billeting officer would ascertain by a personal investigation, being accompanied by the burgomaster, just what living space was necessary for the German inhabitants of a particular dwelling, in order that the German women and decrepit males might be assured of proper quarters and each family of the necessary living space. All other space was considered to be available as billets for the American army. It was considered incompatible with the prestige of the occupying troops that any German should have more favorable living conditions than those of Americans in the same dwelling. A curious characteristic of the American troops was continually noted by the inspectors. Far from assuming the attitude of conquerors or displaying arrogance or insolence under the circumstances of the occupation, the average soldier was prone to display even too great consideration for the local inhabitants. Time after time in the inspection of the billets, commanding officers would find the troops sleeping on the floor or in second-class rooms when under the regulations far better quarters were available, and on inquiring why they permitted themselves to be so slighted, the answer in hundreds of cases was that they did not wish to discommode the people and were entirely satisfied with things as they were. It is a striking example of the old adage that "the bravest are the tenderest," for these men, who had met the choicest troops of the German army in continuous open fighting, had never retreated, but had displayed the highest qualities of dash and courage, permitted themselves to be discommoded and refused even to assert their unquestioned rights, rather than annoy or discommode the civilian inhabitants of the enemy country.

All billeting arrangements and payment therefor were made under the supervision of Division Headquarters through the office of the zone major, at first Captain C. W. Cook and later Major E. B. Hopkins, and locally through the town major in each case. The Division's claims officer, Major E. B. Hopkins, covered all claims presented against the United States, made the investigations necessary and submitted recommendations as required. When the Division left the area Major Hopkins, with the necessary assistants, including a bonded disbursing officer, was left in the area in order to wind up the affairs of that office.

Kylburg, Germany. Headquarters of the 89th Division in the Army of Occupation. In the background are the terraced hillsides which became so familiar a sight to the American troops in Germany. The Kyll River makes a horseshoe around the town. It may be seen behind the trees at the extreme right, and also at the extreme left, under the road leading to Malburg. S. C. 44350.

CHAPTER VII.

ADMINISTRATION

The narrative of the career of the Division up to this time has been largely that of the combat troops. But no true picture of the Division would be complete without a narrative of its composition and some brief description of its place and function as a typical combat division in the American Expeditionary Forces; nor without a detailed description of those administrative duties performed by the staff without which success in battle would have been wholly impossible.

ORGANIZATION OF THE A. E. F.

A division was only a small part of the A. E. F., and its operations were inextricably tied up in the operations and efficiency of other divisions, of larger units and troops in the rear, and the commanders and staffs directing them. The A. E. F. was divided roughly into two zones:

(1) The combat zone, an area parallel to the front and perhaps 40 kilometers deep, containing combat troops and the auxiliaries directly serving them, and

(2) The zone of the Services of Supply (the S. O. S.) including the rest of France clear back to the base ports. The S. O. S. had but one mission. It received, cared for, and delivered to the armies in the field, men and material needed in combat, and received back and cared for the salvage of broken men and material. All American troops in France were known as the American Expeditionary Forces and were commanded from General Headquarters (commonly known as G. H. Q.) at Chaumont.

ARMIES

The largest combat organization was an Army, consisting of two or more Corps, together with other troops (operating directly under Army Headquarters) commonly known as "Army Troops." These consisted of heavier artillery than that assigned to Divisions or Corps, extra engineer, signal, air service, motor transport and other special service troops. In general, the Army troops occupied a zone in the rear of that held by its Corps, received and distributed supplies, repaired roads and railroads, wire communications, controlled air service operations, and delivered long distance heavy artillery fire. Strategic operations were conducted by the Army. Three American

Armies were formed, the First for the St. Mihiel Offensive, the Second at the time of the Meuse-Argonne Offensive, for the purpose of taking over that part of the American line east of Verdun (the St. Mihiel area), and the Third for the Army of Occupation.

CORPS

A Corps consisted of two or more Divisions, together with other troops (operating directly under Corps Headquarters) commonly known as "Corps Troops." They consisted of heavier artillery than that assigned to Divisions, extra engineer, signal, air service, motor transport and other special service troops. In general the Corps troops occupied and were responsible for an area intermediate between the Army area and the sectors in the line held by Divisions. Its work was like that of the Army, on a smaller scale.

In the A. E. F. there was no permanent assignment of Divisions to Corps nor Corps to Armies. A Corps occupied a broad section of the front, a Division was assigned to it, went into the line, became depleted and tired, was then relieved by another Division and withdrawn. In theory the Division was rested, refitted and filled up to strength again with replacements and probably transferred to another sector and Corps, before rëentering the line. During the strenuous days in the fall of 1918, the "resting" was conspicuous by its absence. Thus Corps and Army were flexible in composition and the unit which actually did most of the fighting, the largest unit possessing a permanent organization and successfully developing esprit, was the Division.

DIVISIONS

An Infantry Division at full strength consists of about 28,000 men and officers. It is the smallest complete battle unit, with balanced forces of infantry, artillery, engineers, signal and sanitary troops, trains (motor and horse drawn transportation), staffs and auxiliary services necessary for a mobile force to play the game of war "on its own."

BRIGADES AND REGIMENTS

The combat troops of the division are divided into brigades, and these into regiments, and these into battalions and the battalions into companies of infantry or batteries of artillery.

The administrative units are the regiment and company or battery. In principle the brigade (like the battalion and platoon) is a tactical, not an administrative unit.

In questions of supply, the division ordinarily deals directly with the regiment, the regiment with its companies and the company with the individual soldier. So also rosters, casualty and change reports and other administrative details are handled. Brigade, battalion, platoon and squad are arbitrary subdivisions, primarily for expediency in maneuver and combat, but each is an incomplete part of the larger administrative unit, not an administrative unit itself.

There was a tendency in the A. E. F. to develop and model the organization of brigade headquarters along the line of division headquarters under the brigade adjutant as Chief of Brigade Staff, with administrative, operations and intelligence officers detailed as assistants, and many enlisted men to perform clerical and other special duties, although there was no provision for this in tables of organization. The wisdom of the policy is doubtful, chiefly because it inserts one more intermediate channel to complicate action and slow up the game, and thus to impair the efficiency of these organizations as purely fighting units.

A regiment is frankly and properly organized in imitation of the division. A regimental commander has his adjutant, operations, intelligence and supply officers as a staff to do the work. Their functions correspond closely to similar officers at Division Headquarters and are obvious. Miniature staffs are found within the battalion and company, where the battalion commander has his adjutant and scout officer, the company its supply sergeant, mess sergeant, and company clerk, a personnel familiar to all. None will dispute that the "top" is the Company Commander's efficient Chief of Staff!

COMPOSITION OF THE 89TH DIVISION

The organization of the 89th Division during the greater part of 1918-1919, with devolution of authority, is shown on the following table:

Note:—Figures in brackets show maximum authorized strength in officers and men according to Tables of Organization of Dec. 1st, 1918. Seldom, if ever, did organizations reach full strength. Usually they were somewhere from 65% to 85% of authorized strength.

Discrepancies in totals are due to omission, within units, of minor headquarters detachments and small attached elements.

89TH DIVISION, A. E. F. (28105)

Division Headquarters (304)
- (a) Division Commander and Staff (51)
- (b) Headquarters Detachment (128)
- (c) Headquarters Troop (125)

1. 177th Infantry Brigade (8475)
   - 1 Brigade Headquarters (25)
     with veterinary field unit attached
   - (a) 353rd Infantry (3834)
     - 12 Rifle Companies, A to M, inclusive, in 3 battalions (each Co. 256)
     - 1 Headquarters Company (343)
       with medical detachment
     - 1 Machine Gun Company (178)
     - 1 Supply Company (170)
       with ordnance detachment
   - (b) 354th Infantry (3834)
     (Organized same as 353rd Infantry)
   - (c) 341st Machine Gun Battalion (778)
     - 1 Headquarters (47)
       with medical and ordnance detachments
     - 4 Machine Gun Companies, A to D, inclusive (each 178)
2. 178th Infantry Brigade (8475)
   - 1 Brigade Headquarters (25)
     with veterinary field unit attached
   - (a) 355th Infantry (3834)
     (Organized same as 353rd Infantry)

(b) 356th Infantry (3834)
(Organized same as 353rd Infantry)

(c) 342nd Machine Gun Battalion (778)
(Organized same as 341st Machine Gun Battalion)

3. 164th Field Artillery Brigade (5069)
1 Brigade Headquarters (79)

(a) 340th Field Artillery (1565)
6 Batteries, A to F, inclusive, in two Battalions (each Battery 199)
(armed with 75 m.m. French gun)
1 Headquarters Company (201)
with medical detachment and and two veterinary field units
1 Supply Company (125)
with ordnance detachment

(b) 341st Field Artillery (1565)
(Organized same as the 340th F. A.)

(c) 342nd Field Artillery (motorized in Germany) (1678)
6 Batteries, A to F, inclusive, in three Battalions (each battery 210)
(armed with 155 m.m. French howitzer)
1 Headquarters Company (251)
with medical detachment
1 Supply Company (117)
with ordnance detachment

(d) 314th Trench Mortar Battery (177)
(armed with 6" Stokes Trench Mortars)

4. 340th Machine Gun Battalion, Motorized (395)
(Controlled by G-3, usually through Division M. G. officer)
1 Headquarters (30)
with medical and ordnance detachments
2 Machine Gun Companies, A and B (each 178)

5. 314th Engineers (1749)
(Controlled by G-1 through Division Engineer)
1 Headquarters (172)
with medical and ordnance detachments
6 Companies, A to F, inclusive, in two Battalions (each Co. 256)

6. 314th Field Signal Battalion (488)
(Controlled by G-3 through Division Signal Officer)
Companies A to C, inclusive
1 Headquarters (15)
with medical detachment and supply section
1 Radio Company (A) (78)
1 Wire Company (B) (78)
1 Outpost Company (C) (285)

7. 314th Train Headquarters (68)
(Controlled by G-1 through C. O. Trains and M. P.)
Operations of Military Police, the Supply Train and (to a greater or less degree according to the tactical situation) directs or coördinates actions of other trains.
With medical and ordnance detachments, 3 veterinary field units and mobile veterinary section.

8. 89th Military Police Company (205)
(Controlled by G-1 through C. O. Trains and M. P.)
(Previously called 314th Military Police and consisting of two troops, "A" and "B".)

9. 314th Motor Supply Train (501)
(Controlled by G-1, usually through C. O. Trains and M. P.)
1 Headquarters (16)
with medical detachment
6 Truck Companies, A to F, inclusive (each 79)

10. 314th Engineer Train (84)
(Controlled by G-1, usually through Division Engineer)
One Company.

11. 314th Ammunition Train (1341)
    (Controlled by G-1, different sections usually under the Artillery Commander, Munitions Officer, C. O. Trains, M. O. R. S. under Division Ordnance Officer, etc., according to the tactical situation).
    1 Headquarters (32)
        with medical and ordnance detachments
    1 Motor Battalion (629)
        1 Battalion Headquarters (33)
        4 Truck Companies, A to D, inclusive (each 149)
    1 Horse Battalion (568)
        1 Battalion Headquarters (24)
            Companies E to G, inclusive
        2 Caisson Companies (each 194)
        1 Wagon Company (156)
    314th Mobile Ordnance Repair Shop (attached) (56)

12. 314th Sanitary Train (951)
    (Controlled by G-1, through Division Surgeon)
    1 Headquarters (18)
    1 Ambulance Section (546)
        1 Section Headquarters (7)
        3 Ambulance Companies, motorized, Nos. 353 to 355, inclusive (each 127)
        1 Ambulance Company, No. 356, animal drawn (158)
    1 Field Hospital Section (362)
        1 Section Headquarters (7)
        3 Field Hospital Companies, Nos. 353 to 355, inclusive, motorized (each 89)
        1 Field Hospital Company, No. 356, animal drawn (88)
    8 Camp Infirmaries (16)
    1 Division Medical Supply Unit (9)

THE STAFF

The staff has been called the brains and nervous system of the army. In their possession of large and well trained staffs lay the greatest assumed superiority of European over American armies, and it was on his efficient staff that the German relied largely for victory.

It was apparent that America could recruit large forces, but that it could improvise a competent staff to train, equip and handle large armies in the field was questioned even by our friends. The preference of the French and English for our troops to be used as replacements in their own units rather than for the formation of an American Army was no doubt due in large part to distrust of our ability to develop quickly enough an able American staff and higher commanders to direct our own immense new forces.

That General Pershing did create an adequate staff system and develop an able staff, one which met and overcame tremendous difficulties, is regarded by many competent judges as the crowning achievement of American participation in the war. The staffs of the entire A. E. F., including those of divisions and lesser units, were in a constant state of development from the arrival of the first troops in Europe to the departure of the last. With the period of the occupation, however, the operations of the staff had reached the point of greatest efficiency, and since the activities of divisions in the Army of Occupation were so largely administrative, a detailed account of the work of the staff departments at that time is essential.

During active operations duties of the staff were more important and difficult, but they were also then more simple and obvious. They are shown on the organization table below, but the detailed discription following refers largely to the period of occupation when activities were multifarious.

THE "G" SYSTEM

The Division Commander is, of course, the supreme executive power, concerning himself with the larger questions of tactics and policy. Working out the details, preparing the orders and supervising their execution devolve upon the Divisional General Staff, headed by the Chief of Staff, through whom the Division Commander acts and under whose direction three Assistant Chiefs of Staff sketch in the form within broad outlines indicated by the Division Commander.

The three Assistant Chiefs of Staff represent three sections of the General Staff, each with its distinct field of duty to be handled separately, but requiring constant coördination with the others to avoid conflict or inconsistent action. They are known as G1, G2, and G3, and from this designation the whole staff system created in the A. E. F. is known as the "G" system. Broadly, the field of the G's is divided into transportation and supply under G1; information and intelligence under G2, and operations under G3. Larger units than the division had two more G's, known as G4 and G5, who performed, respectively, some of the functions assigned to G3 and G1 in the division. While all executive functions are exercised by these three, and ordinarily most of the divisional staff report to them, the exigencies of the service require considerable latitude in practice, and there are three division staff officers, the Adjutant, Inspector and Judge Advocate, whose duties are of such character that the original form of organization of the A. E. F. provided for them to report direct to the Chief of Staff. Although subsequently modified in some organizations, the 89th Division adhered substantially to the original conception. The G System was promulgated by General Order 31, G. H. Q., A. E. F., February 16, 1918.

Properly the duties of G1, G2 and G3 are executive and coördinative, the actual tactical and administrative duties being the function of commanding officers of organizations within the division and of the technical and administrative services concerned.

ORGANIZATION OF THE 89TH DIVISION STAFF

The organization of the Division staff, under the Chief of Staff, with classification of duties, during the greater part of 1918-1919, is shown on the following table, which requires no explanation beyond, perhaps, the statement that a staff officer issues orders only to carry out policies established by the commander, and in his name. Temporary changes in responsibility and channels are not shown.

CHIEF OF STAFF

The directing and coördinating head of all staff activities.
Executive officer for the Division Commander.

1. Assistant Chief of Staff, G-1 (Administration)
   Supervision and control of supply and salvage, traffic and transportation. Sanitary service, evacuations and burials. Assignment of replacement. Police, prisoners and captured material. Technical troops on construction work, roads, communications, billets. Welfare organizations. Postal service. (See Table A.)

2. Assistant Chief of Staff, G-2 (Intelligence)
   Information of the enemy, examination of prisoners and captured documents. Preparation of maps and data as to terrain. Translations, codes and ciphers. Censorship and control of passes (in Germany only). Photographs and visitors. Secret service and counter espionage. Civil affairs (in Germany only).
   (a) Intelligence Officers with organizations.
   (b) Civil Affairs Officer (in Germany only).
   Relations with civil authorities and population in occupied territory in Germany.
   (c) Circulation Bureau for civilians (in Germany only).
   (d) German Press Censorship Bureau (in Germany only).

3. Assistant Chief of Staff, G-3 (Operations).
   Operation and combat plans. Operation orders and reports. Supervision and control of operations. Receipt and delivery of messages and orders. Training and athletics. (See Table B.)

4. Division Adjutant.
   Routine administration. Administrative orders. Commissioned and enlisted personnel. Correspondence and records. Strength and statistical rosters, records and returns. Casualty reports. Identification cards. Office supplies and blank forms. Recruiting (in Germany only).
   (a) Division Personnel Adjutant.
   Strength and statistical reperts and returns, casualty reports. Rosters and individual card records of all members of Division.
   (b) Recruiting Officer (in Germany only).
   Re-enlistment of men desiring further service in Europe.

5. Division Inspector.
   Investigations of all classes and establishments, including efficiency, organization, camps, misconduct, etc. Inspections of property. Verification of money accounts. (Under G-1 from Sept. 6 to Nov. 12, 1918.)

6. Division Judge Advocate.
   General supervision of Courts-Martial. Examination and tentative review of court-martial cases requiring action of the Division Commander. Court-Martial orders. Supervision and administration of military law. Submission of legal opinions on request. Rentals, requisitions and claims (during part of the time only).
   (Under G-1 from Sept. 6 to Nov. 12, 1918.)

TABLE A.

G-1 Section, Administrative Staff.

1. Division Quartermaster.
   Quartermaster supplies, including clothing, subsistence, fuel, forage, etc., sales commissary, laundries, bakeries, baths, salvage service.
   (a) Finance officer, payment of troops, etc.
2. Division Ordnance Officer.
   Ordnance material, artillery, machine guns, automatic rifles, small arms, pistols, grenades, etc. Ordnance equipment and supplies. Ordnance repairs. Supervision of the 314th Mobile Ordnance Repair shop.
3. Division Engineer. (C. O. 314th Engineers.)
   Field fortifications, roads, bridges, constructions of all kinds. Engineer supplies. Camouflage. Supervision of municipal electric light and water plants (in Germany only). Supervision of 314th Engineer train.
4. C. O. Trains and Military Police.
   Supervision of Division Field Trains. Inspection of trains and transportation within the Division. Supervision of
   (a) 314th Supply Train.

(b) 314th Ammunition Train (when not under Artillery Commander).
(c) Division Motor Transport Officer.
Technical supervision of motor transport, repairs, spare parts, etc.
(d) 314th (later 89th) Military Police.
Control of road traffic. Apprehension of stragglers. Maintenance of order. Custody of prisoners of war.
(e) Division Veterinarian.
Care of horses. Meat inspections.
Technical supervision of veterinarians with organizations.
(f) Division Remount Officer.
Replacements of horses and mules.

5. Division Surgeon.
Health of the command. Collection, care and evacuation of sick and wounded. Medical supplies. Sanitary inspections. Technical supervision of surgeons with organizations. Supervision of
(a) 314th Sanitary Train.
(Field Hospitals and Ambulance Companies.)
(b) Division Dental Surgeon.
(c) Sanitary Inspector.
(d) Medical Supply Depot.

6. Rental Requisitions and Claims Officer.
Accounts with civil population for billets, supplies, damage claims, etc.

7. Division Postal Officer.
A. P. O. No. 761—Receipt and distribution of Postoffice mail (not official mail, which is handled by Motor Dispatch Service).

8. Senior Chaplain.
Supervision of chaplains and religious activities. Burials. Post Schools.

9. Welfare Officer (in Germany only).
Supervision of welfare work in the Division and operations of the Y. M. C. A., K. C. and R. C. Distribution of luxuries, establishment of clubs and canteens, etc.

10. Entertainment Officer (in Germany only).
Supervision and routing of shows and entertainments in the divisional area, both soldier and professional.

TABLE B.

G-3 Section, Administrative Staff.

1. Division Signal Officer.
Installation and operation of telephone, telegraph and radio communication service. Signal Corps material. Technical supervision of signal officers with organizations. Division Message Center (in Germany only).
Supervision 314th F. S. Bn.

2. Division Machine Gun Officer.
Technical adviser as to training and use in combat of machine gun units. Supervision of 340th M. G. Bn. (the divisional M. G. unit).

3. Division Gas Officer.
Gas defense, measures and supplies.

4. C. O. Headquarters Troop and Detachment.
Administration of Division Headquarters (supervision of billets, mess supplies, enlisted personnel). Courier service and headquarters transportation (during active operations only).

5. Officer in charge of Division Message Center.
(During active operations directly under G-3. Later supervised by Division Signal Officer.)
Receipt and dispatch of operations orders and reports, official mail and messages. Courier service within the Division.

6. French Mission.
French liaison officers attached to the Division.

7. Educational Officer. (In Germany only.)
Supervision of special schools established in Germany.

8. Athletic Officer. (In Germany only.)
Supervision of athletics.

CONFLICT BETWEEN LINE AND STAFF

The irrepressible conflict in point of view between line and staff, which always has existed and no doubt always will exist, took on certain phases in the A. E. F. worthy of brief comment.

Throughout the A. E. F. there was a tendency, on the part of General Staff Officers, in an over-anxiety to direct things properly, to grasp and manage administrative functions which could be more efficiently handled by the services or technicians directly concerned, and to prescribe in minute detail matters better left to the discretion of the commanding officers of troops who would have to act. There was also a tendency on the part of staffs and higher commanders, in the zest of the game, and through a commendable desire for results, to overlook, in issuing orders, their relative importance and certain factors entering into their execution whose importance was absolute: the surrounding circumstances and mental processes of their subordinates; the human element or psychology of the thing, and above all, the amount of time required to transmit orders to the troops and to execute them. It was very easy to issue an order, without fully visualizing its effect, when clear visualization might have altered and sometimes even prevented the order. Service in the line, in close contact with troops, is necessary to realize clearly the capabilities and limitations of the several arms of the service as they must be known to get best results with a minimum of friction or lost motion.

Conversely there was limited vision on the part of many organization commanders, a failure to appreciate clearly their respective parts in the vast operations being carried on, an inclination towards the conviction that each should be free to fight his own little war. A wider perspective would have shown that he had only a small part to play which must always be in harmony with, and sometimes subordinated or even sacrificed for, the teamwork of the whole. A battalion commander would perhaps bitterly resent, as a matter of petty, inopportune inquisitiveness, the inquiry "just where is your front line?" although without that information the artillery support he was loudly demanding could not be given. Regimental commanders frequently saw only through the eyes of the regiment, when staff experience and broader vision would have simplified their problems and eased their minds.

These faults, though characteristic of all armies at all times, were in our case also partly the result of the earnestness with which each one was playing the game. It was one new to all, and with the weight of his own work heavy on his shoulders, each man found it hard to see large enough the responsibility and burdens carried by others and to realize that factors beyond his ken entered into the orders he received; that there was a reason, even though it was not obvious. With the growth of experience the faults and difficulties lessened, and men whose judgment and discretion did not meet the requirements were given other assignments.

The foregoing applies to the entire A. E. F., and the 89th Division had no more than its share of such trouble. Indeed, it functioned (to use a word dear to the heart of the army) more efficiently and with less friction than most divisions of comparable experience.

THE CHIEF OF STAFF

The staff organization of the Division was handled entirely by the Chief of Staff, originally Colonel C. E. Kilbourne, and after his promotion to the rank of Brigadier General, Colonel John C. H. Lee. During active operations no matters, except in emergency, were presented to the Division Commander from the staff, except through the Chief of Staff, who also signed all papers of routine administration for the Division Commander. With the change of Division commanders following the Armistice and with the decrease in purely military activities and the large increase in purely administrative work, a wide expansion and some change of policy in the staff occurred. General Winn desired to see his staff officers and the heads of departments regularly in person. Accordingly, he established the routine of daily interviews with the Division adjutant, handled court-martial cases directly with the Division judge advocate, and expressed his desire to see any staff officers as often as desired. The policy of the staff was ever that of service to the Line. Division staff conferences were resumed and continued throughout the period of the occupation. These conferences met three times a week and were attended by all the heads of the departments and sub-departments of the Division staff as well as by brigade and separate organization commanders.

The Chief of Staff met the three assistant chiefs of staff in informal conference three times daily, thus promoting perfect liaison and coördination. During the period of occupation the personnel of the Division staff was greatly augmented by the addition of several new officers, including civil affairs, education, welfare, athletics, entertainment, zone major and circulation officers, though the personnel was kept at a minimum so far as the wide ramifications of the Division's activities made it practicable. The personnel of the Division staff as it stood at the time the Division left the occupied area exemplified the survival of the fittest. By a continuous process of elimination and occasional selection there had been built up a staff organization fit and trained to cope with any divisional situation, either tactical or administrative.

THE G-1 OFFICE

The G-1 office, originally under Colonel Charles B. Clark, was, during the greater part of the period of active operations, and on the 11th of November, in charge of Lieutenant Colonel W. J. Scott, General Staff, who served in that capacity until the latter part of January, when he was relieved for assignment as Provost Marshal, First Army. During the short intervening period the office was in charge of Captain (afterwards Major) C. E. Boesch, until taken over by Lieutenant Colonel Brehon B. Somervell, who was relieved from duty as G-3 in order to reorganize the G-1 office, and acted as G-1 until the Division left Germany. Work of the Division Engineer has been covered in the previous chapter.

G-1 OFFICE. THE QUARTERMASTER

The duties of the quartermaster were performed by Lieutenant Colonel James L. Costella. The finance department, under the direction of Major C. W. Bartlett, showed particular efficiency, starting with the handicap that a majority of the organizations in the Division had not been paid for some time because the continuous service of the Division on the line of battle had prevented preparation of payrolls. This condition was soon remedied and during the last few months of occupation every regimental and separate supply officer received the full pay for his organization on or before the first of each month. The finance office also undertook the handling of the company fund accounts, which formed a difficult task because of the absence of civilian financial institutions with whom such business could be transacted. The sales commissary of the quartermaster's office maintained branches at Bitburg and Prüm. Uniforms for the officers were in great demand, for the hard fighting and absence of baggage rendered the situation quite difficult and it was much desired that the command present a good appearance. The sales commissary undertook to meet this deficiency, a quartermaster of tailoring experience was placed on duty in Trier and satisfactory arrangements were made with a local German tailor to supply uniforms at a nominal cost under the supervision of the American officer.

Rations and forage were handled by the quartermaster through three rail heads at Bitburg, Prüm and Trier.

G-1 OFFICE. THE ORDNANCE OFFICER

The ordnance officer was Lieutenant Colonel Wilson Potter, whose office was operated so smoothly and efficiently that little need be said about it except that the ordnance needs of the Division were always met.

The 314th Mobile Ordnance Repair Shop, under 1st Lt. George R. Conover, was opened in Bitburg. The Artillery Section repaired a number of the heavy guns, and the Small Arms Section unpacked, tested and equipped the entire Division with Browning Machine Guns and Browning Automatic Rifles.

G-1 OFFICE. THE TRAINS

The Commanding Officer of Trains was Colonel W. W. Whitside, under whose orders were the ammunition train (except when, in whole or in part, it was under the artillery commander), the supply train and the military police. During the march into Germany the Commanding Officer of Trains labored under the greatest difficulty of shortage in transportation. It was necessary to move up immediately the equipment of the Division, keep the Division supplied with forage and rations and also bring up the heavier equipment by degrees. That the Division was never seriously short of rations was due to the splendid work of Colonel Whitside. One of his duties during the occupation was the inspection service of both animal-drawn and motor transportation. The animal transportation of the Division had been greatly reduced just after the Armistice, to supply the needs of the divisions which were to move sooner than our own. The animals which were left were culls of inferior quality and condition. Consequently the Division received large assignments of new animals, many of which were infected with mange. At first there was a severe shortage of veterinary medicines and disinfectants and it was also true that during the period of active operations, the animals could not be cared for with such thoroughness as might have prevented, to some extent, the spread of this disease. Over 2,000 cases of mange on animals developed in the Division. The situation was met under the general supervision of the Commander of Trains with vigorous and drastic measures. Colonel Rudolph Smyser, the divisional machine gun officer, of long service in the cavalry of the regular army, was relieved of other duties and directed to devote his entire time to the eradication of this disease. In consultation with the division veterinarian, Major Palmer, the engineers constructed three dipping vats which were filled with disinfecting solution and every animal in the Division was ordered clipped, diseased animals were treated both before and after clipping and all stables were thoroughly disinfected. Every animal was dipped three or four times and the solution was well rubbed in after dipping. By the middle of April the Division had been entirely cleared of all active cases of the mange.

The subject of motor transportation was given constant attention, both as to appearance and maintenance. The Division Commander ordered that each truck and car be cleaned daily and that proper provisions for washing vehicles be provided in each of the towns where transportation was centered. The driver of a truck or car was held to the same responsibility that the driver of a horse or mule was; that is, in finishing the day's work, he was required to groom his charge and see to it that his vehicle was washed, oiled and supplied with gasoline before he was authorized to look out for his own comfort. The result was a great improvement in the appearance and value of the transportation.

G-1 OFFICE. THE M. P.'S

Under the supervision of the commander of trains and the regulation of the military police, thorough instructions regarding road discipline were promulgated and enforced. One valuable regulation was the rule that each truck should maintain a lookout in the rear in order to give warning of the approach of faster moving vehicles. The German population, moreover, were held to strict account for the observance of road regulations and were required to keep to the proper side of the road on the approach of motor vehicles, to keep children out of the streets of villages through which direct roads ran, and generally to observe all traffic regulations.

The military police, under the supervision of the commander of trains, were used on the march to facilitate the location of troops at the close of each day's march and were finally posted in the occupied area to enforce circulation and traffic rules. As soon as this duty could be turned over to the Kreis commanders, the military police company, under 1st Lieutenant (later Captain) John L. Crofut, was assembled at division headquarters for re-equipping and training.

In January, the Division Commander established a disciplinary detachment at Malburg under the supervision of the military police. Soldiers sentenced for violation of the articles of war were sent to this detachment and were required to perform strenuous military drill in the morning and hard labor in the afternoons. They were required to live in an exemplary manner as to cleanliness and policing and practically all of the hours of the day were filled with prescribed duties. A high degree of military esprit developed in this detachment, which was under the command of Captain Henry Crofut. The general policy of the detachment followed that of the disciplinary barracks of the United States Army at Leavenworth. Rewards were instituted for good conduct and the results were highly satisfactory.

Another activity under the general control of Colonel Whitside was the horse shows instituted within the Division. A show was first held in each brigade and subsequently a division show at Trier. The result of these horse shows was a great increase in the interest and efficiency of the organizations of the Division having animals under their control and an extraordinarily

The broken railroad bridge at Bouillonville, St. Mihiel Sector. This is a reproduction of a German post card photograph seized in the occupied area in Germany during the period the 89th Division was in the Army of Occupation. When the 89th Division reached Bouillonville, September 12th, 1918, artillery fire had thoroughly demolished this bridge and most of it was on the ground.

fine showing was made considering the quality of the animals furnished the Division. Subsequently a motor show was held to select vehicles for the corps and army shows. The Division made entries for both the corps and army horse shows which were very creditable to the Division.

G-1 OFFICE. MOTOR TRANSPORT

The motor transport officer of the Division was the commanding officer of the supply train, Major Walter C. Cole, who made the most of the machines assigned to the Division by careful maintenance and repair. There was always a shortage in transportation, both at Division headquarters and throughout the Division. The headquarters motor transportation was pooled, with the exception of the car assigned to the Division Commander, one to the Chief of Staff and those assigned to brigade and regimental commanders. Large economies were effected by this system, though at the expense at times of complete efficiency of the staff in the matter of transportation.

G-1 OFFICE. RELIGION, WELFARE AND ENTERTAINMENT

Acting under the assistant chief of staff G-1, was the Division chaplain, who at the time of the Armistice was Chaplain Griffiths and later Chaplain Otis E. Gray. The religious needs of the organization were not overlooked and the Division chaplain saw to it that proper religious services were held throughout the entire division and in addition participated in the work of education as already mentioned.

Under G-1 also was the welfare office, organized under the supervision of Major J. W. Sutphen, in order to coördinate the work of the various welfare societies throughout the area. The office proved to be very necessary and worked out for a large increase in efficiency. Practical supervision was undertaken over the sales of supplies by the Y. M. C. A. and other welfare organizations and these were made of record, coördinated, and very largely increased. Distribution of gratuitous articles was supervised, guaranteeing more equitable procedure than had prevailed in this matter where, very often, troops who were inconvenient of access and who for that reason all the more needed cigarettes and candy and all the little knick-knacks of life, were not getting these articles because they were distributed to troops more easily reached. The supply of reading matter and magazines was greatly increased and placed in the hands of the men more promptly. Sales points were established in forty-two of the fifty-five towns occupied by the Division. Canteen workers were also controlled by this office.

The entertainment office was also under G-1. This office was organized under the supervision of Captain G. A. Davis, later promoted to the rank of Major in recognition of his excellent work in the line before coming to the 89th and later in the department here described. This office had charge of all entertainment in the Division, not only soldier shows but professional entertainments provided by the Y. M. C. A. All lectures and moving picture shows were scheduled and routed by this office. After the entertainment office was fully organized, the various organizations of the Division averaged two or three entertainments a week. Motor transportation was used to get men in from outlying towns to the larger centers where theatrical accommodations were to be had. Working in conjunction with this office, Miss Anna Purnell, formerly a theatrical critic, and employee of the Y. M. C. A., worked especially at developing soldier shows and ascertaining latent talent in the Division itself.

G-1 OFFICE. THE SURGEON

Under G-1 also was the Division surgeon, who was held responsible for the entire sanitary personnel of the Division, for sanitary inspections and the eradication of vermin as well as the work of the dental officers. While in each organization the organization surgeon was under the immediate orders of the organization commander, the Division surgeon was required to maintain an inspection service to guarantee that each organization commander was satisfied with the efficiency of his medical personnel, in addition to exercising direct command of the medical personnel in purely medical matters. At the time of the Armistice Major F. W. O'Donnell was the Division surgeon, having served in that capacity during the recent fighting, but during November, Colonel L. P. Williamson of the Regular Army was assigned to the Division and acted as Division surgeon during the period of occupation and until just before the departure of the Division from Germany. At this time Colonel Williamson was relieved and Lieutenant Colonel F. W. O'Donnell, who had been in the meantime promoted in recognition of his efficient service and who had been in command of the sanitary train, assumed again the office of Division surgeon. One of the first and most important duties of the Division surgeon was to insure the eradication of vermin which inevitably collects upon the men during the period of active operations in Europe. Strenuous efforts were made by the erection of delousing plants by the engineers and frequent supervision to insure that the dangerous pests were entirely eliminated, and ultimately this was accomplished, though not without difficulties.

Under the Division surgeon and sanitary inspector, Lieutenant Colonel Frank L. Morse, active sanitary measures were required from the civil population. Sources of water pollution were investigated and abated and a careful examination of all the troops for contagious and venereal diseases was constantly kept up and the Division's record in respect to the health of the men was remarkable. Two field hospitals were kept in constant operation at Bitburg. One was placed in temporary operation in Saarburg and another in partial operation at Bollendorf, the headquarters of the train. The ambulance cars were used throughout the area in the evacuation of the sick and in transporting to entertainments.

During the period of the occupation the entire command was again required to take a typhoid vaccination and the sore arms of the new recruit days were again in evidence.

Work of the 314th Sanitary Train, under the Division Surgeon, was always unobtrusive, but effective. Its ambulances transported and its field hospitals cared for the sick and wounded from organizations of the Division, returning to duty the slightly wounded and those sick for brief periods; and sending back to evacuation and base hospitals in the rear those whose condition was more serious. In addition to information elsewhere, the following information regarding these necessary organizations will be of interest:

Ambulance Company 353 was organized originally as Red Cross Ambulance Co. No. 16, largely through the efforts of Dr. (later Major) Edgar C. Duncan and Dr. (later Captain) Walter P. Guy. It was recruited mostly in Fredonia, Wilson County, Kansas, in May, 1917. Later the men were taken into the Enlisted Medical Reserve Corps and absorbed into the National Army and 89th Division in October, 1917. During the St. Mihiel offensive 600 patients were evacuated through its dressing stations, and in the Meuse-Argonne offensive over 1,000 passed through during the first five days of November.

Ambulance Company 354 was originally Company No. 16 at the Fort Riley training camp. Almost 500 of the gas casualties of the gas attack of August 7-8 were handled by this company, a strenuous introduction to its duties in the field. Again it handled 200 gas casualties on October 6th. This company enjoyed a novel experience the next day when it found itself actually holding the front line, with no infantry ahead, due to some slip-up in the relief and the non-arrival of troops of the relieving division.

Ambulance Company 355 was originally Red Cross Ambulance Co. No. 24, of Kansas City, organized by Captain Ernest W. Cavaness. This company established the gas hospital at Boullionville, and while in that sector operated its ambulances, not only from the regimental dressing stations, but even directly from the front line trenches on occasions.

Ambulance Company 356 was also originally a part of Company No. 16 at Fort Riley. It was the only horse drawn unit in the Ambulance Section of the 314th Sanitary Train. As such it was called on for less service in the field, as a unit, than the motorized companies, and was held in reserve much of the time. Its personnel, however, saw its full share of strenuous service. While in reserve at Andilly, these men served in the field and evacuation hospitals at Royaumeix and Toul. Work was especially arduous in the gas wards at Toul, where shifts were without relief, during periods of stress, of two and three days. Later many of its men were on detached service with the infantry and machine gun organizations.

That it was (theoretically) non-combatant service did not prevent their suffering their share of casualties. Especially during the Meuse-Argonne offensive the ambulance companies did most excellent work evacuating the wounded under fire. Many an ambulance bore the marks of breaking shells and some casualties occurred in this service.

In the Lucey Sector the stations of the Ambulance Companies, before the St. Mihiel Drive, were:

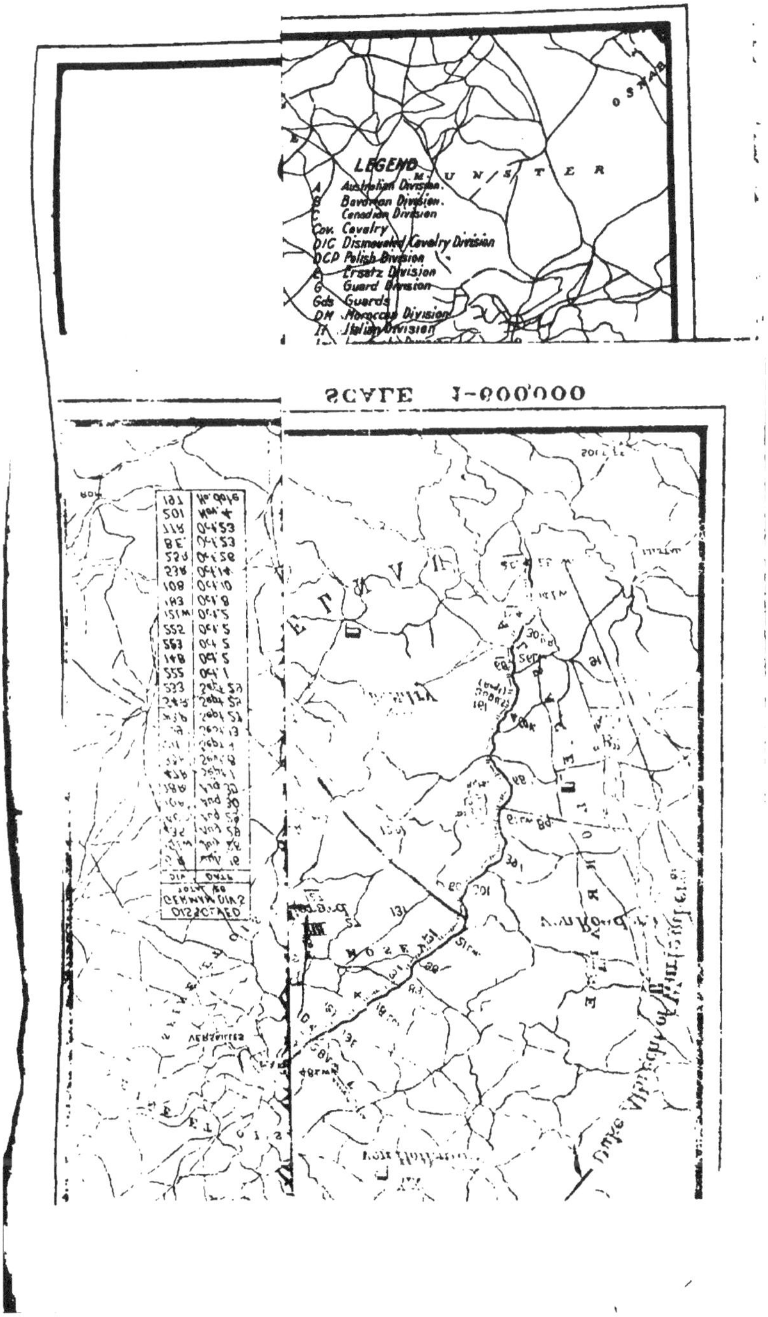

M U N S T E R
LEGEND
A Australian Division.
B Bavarian Division.
C Canadian Division
Cav. Cavalry
DIC Dismounted Cavalry Division
DCP Polish Division
E Ersatz Division
G Guard Division
Gds Guards
DM Moroccan Division
It Italian Division

ORDER OF BATTLE ON 1

11 A.M. NOV 11.

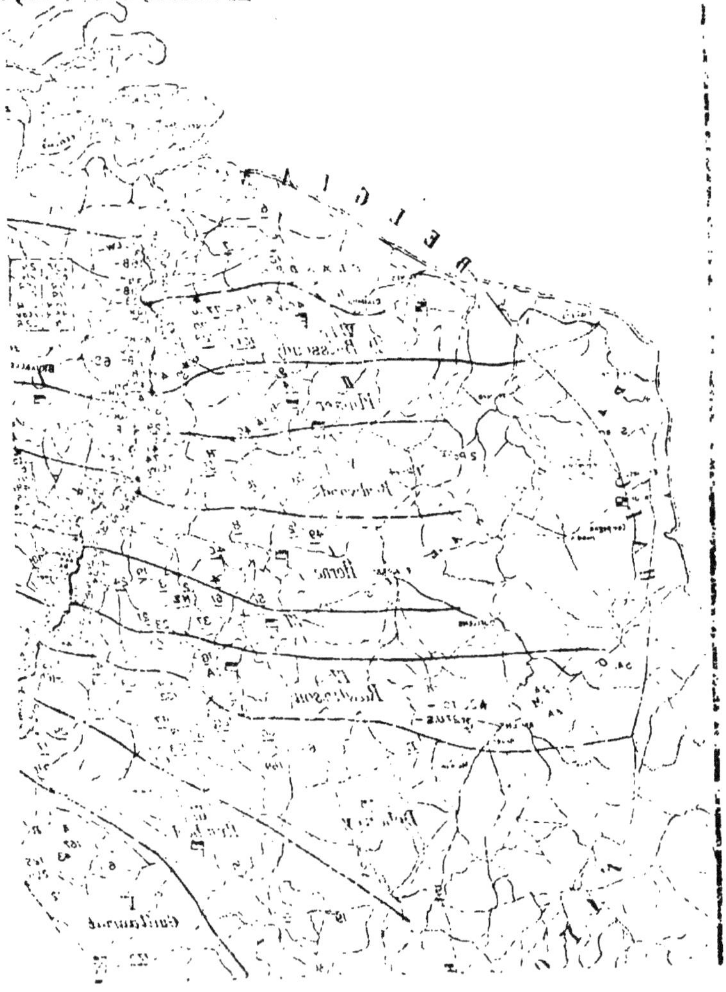

Ambulance Company 353, Minorville, with advance dressing station at Noviant.

Ambulance Company 354, Menil la Tour, with advance dressing station in Rehenne Woods.

Ambulance Company 355, Rongeval, with advance dressing station some distance north.

Ambulance Company 356, in reserve at Andilly.

Headquarters were at Boullionville later, and in the Meuse-Argonne several stations were held. Just before the drive, November 1st, headquarters were on the main road between Charpentry and Eclisfontaine, where brisk shelling by the Germans (probably intended for an ammunition dump not far away) suggested the wisdom of moving further back. During the balance of the period of active operations to November 11th the work was done in the field ahead, but headquarters was immobilized for lack of transportation.

The arrangements devised and put in effect for classification and separate care of those wounded in different degrees, gassed and casualties of other kinds, drew strong commendations from the G. H. Q. inspectors.

On the night of September 22nd, while the Sanitary Train was at Bouillonville, Wagoners Paul S. Phelps and Howard G. Rounds, Medical Supply Depot No. 2, rendered help under heavy shell fire which saved the lives of several wounded men.

Field Hospital Company 353, commanded by Captain (later Major) Fred E. Harvey, took over part of the Justice group of barracks in Toul August 9, 1918, where almost 1,200 patients were admitted in 18 days. Later stations were the French Evacuation Hospital Barracks near Royaumiex, in the woods between Essey and Flirey, and Bernecourt.

In the Meuse-Argonne it was at Montfaucon, and then on the Eclisfontaine road near Charpentry. Here it was shelled by the Germans, with casualties in killed and wounded. It was acting as the Division Triage at that time, and while the surgical unit continued work during the shelling, evacuations were quickly made and that night the hospital was moved back of Charpentry.

In the Army of Occupation this hospital was located first at Manderscheid, and later at Bitburg. To January 31, 1919, it had handled almost 4,000 patients.

The other field hospitals also rendered excellent service.

THE G-2 OFFICE

The position of Assistant Chief of Staff, G-2, was held during almost the entire period of active operations by Major (later Lieutenant Colonel) J. W. Goodman, and later during the entire period of the occupation by Lieutenant Colonel Frank Wilbur Smith, General Staff, who was promoted from Major in recognition of his excellent service. During the period of reorganization and during the march into Germany, the intelligence organization of the Division was kept in both positive and negative operation. German prisoners, deserters, discharged German soldiers were all interviewed and information turned in to higher authority. During the march the G-2 office showed great energy in locating German maps, getting them out to the troops and in providing a large number of road maps for organization commanders and supply officers.

Drawn By G. [illegible], Hdqs. 89th. Div.

Summary Sam cartoon, from Summary of Intelligence, published by G-2, 89th Division in the Army of Occupation.

In the occupied area the G-2 office expanded into a wide range of activities. The office of civil affairs, which was originally started out directly under the Chief of Staff, was placed under G-2 The circulation of individuals, originally under the civil affairs office, was ultimately regulated and controlled by the G-2 office, which established a sub-office at Division headquarters, to which civilians desiring to leave the area were required to apply for passes. At least seventy-five such applications, on an average, were examined daily. Only urgent personal reasons, authenticated by the certificate of the local burgomaster, were regarded as cause for granting such permission.

Under G-2 also was the censorship of all publications within the area. Local newspapers, of which there were four in the divisional area, were required to send copies to the G-2 office where official notices which local authorities were required to issue, were translated and checked and general supervision over publication was exercised. Special investigations were also made by the personnel of the G-2 office. There were some cases of thefts of United States property. Violations of American regulations, cases of suspected prostitution, complaint and criticism of welfare organizations, thefts of supplies on the route from the SOS, irregular sales of liquor and constant and thorough investigation regarding the living conditions, welfare and food, industrial conditions and opinions of the German population came also under this office.

An important function was the registration of returned German discharged soldiers. Every returned German soldier was, under our regulations, required to be reported by the local authorities on his return. He was then interviewed by an agent of the G-2 office as to his military career, place of his discharge, conditions of the army at that point and other matters. The record of these returned soldiers was also used to form the basis of labor requisitions and was of great value to the Division Engineer. Over 20,000 discharged soldiers returned to the divisional area during the period of occupation and were examined in this manner. The G-2 office published daily a summary of intelligence in accordance with instructions from higher authority. This was a mimeographic publication, frequently containing eight or ten pages. It included intelligence information, together with radio news of general interest, and in the later stages of the occupation contained a page of cartoons, the hero of which was known as "Summary Sam." These cartoons were prepared by Private G. Rohlfing of the statistical section of the adjutant's office, and were frequently pointedly humorous and always interesting. The Summary of Intelligence established a reputation for the Division throughout the Army of Ocupation, at American G. H. Q. and at adjacent divisions of our allied armies.

THE G-3 OFFICE

The position of Assistant Chief of Staff, G-3, was held at the time of the Armistice by Lieutenant Colonel B. B. Somervell, Corps of Engineers, who was shortly afterwards appointed on the General Staff, American Expeditionary Forces. During the march into Germany Lieutenant Colonel Somervell also performed the duties of Division Engineer. In late January, when he was relieved as G-3, in order to reorganize the G-1 office, Major (later Lieutenant Colonel) F. A. Doniat reported for duty in the Division and was assigned as G-3. He held this position until the middle of May when (upon return of the Division to the United States) he was relieved for further service overseas. During the period of reorganization and march into Germany the work in the G-3 office was important and satisfactory. March orders and march tables were worked out with satisfactory detail and distributed in ample time to permit the brigade and separate organization commanders to have the necessary information for the movement. An adequate inspection service was maintained throughout the march, which included not only road discipline but also assisted in clearing up difficulties regarding routes and billeting areas.

In occupied territory the work of training was promptly taken up in accordance with orders received from higher authority. A new series of training bulletins was commenced at the first of the year and embodied from the start all instructions received from higher authority so that the successive commanders had no need to refer to past files or files of other headquarters. Throughout the training the G-3 office furnished an inspection service so as to keep the Division commander informed as to the progress of training and

Battery E, 340th Field Artillery, 89th Division, firing a 21-gun salute as part of the commemorative exercises in honor of ex-President Roosevelt, whose death had just been announced. Near Prüm, Germany, Jan. 8th, 1919. S. C. 49013.

to assist the subordinate commanders in the interpretation of division orders. The problems conducted by the Division commander were prepared in the G-3 office and the divisional preparations for the liaison problems conducted by the corps commander were also under G-3. The thoroughness with which this work was done and the orders drawn up and compiled brought exceptionally favorable comment from the corps commander. Periods of training were roughly divided into two classes:

1. Tactical training for each successive unit up to include the Division, conducted in the form of field problems, maneuvers and liaison exercises.

2. A period which gave more attention to the instruction of the individual soldier, including rifle practice.

The first period which was carried on in conformity with the orders received from G. H. Q. had for its purpose the training and development of platoon, company, battalion, regimental and brigade commanders and their staffs, taking advantage of existing opportunities of command. During the first month of training the results obtained in the smaller demonstrations for platoons and companies were not generally satisfactory, though regimental and brigade exercises were very good. The Division problem conducted by the corps commander was rated by him as very good. In the second month considerable improvement was noticed particularly in regard to the firing exercises and demonstrations with service ammunition as conducted in the smaller units. During the last period a more thorough and complete training of the individual soldier was undertaken, with a view to his preparation for his future service as an instructor in case of further emergency. In addition to the incentive of excellence in marksmanship covered by the return of the system of recognizing by award the attainment of the standard of expert riflemen, sharpshooters and marksmen and in the publication of plans for the A. E. F. match, the Division commander offered and gave a silver trophy to the best shooting infantry platoon and the best shooting infantry company in the Division. Results of this competition are given in the Appendix.

Through both periods of training the maintenance of a high standard of discipline was demanded by the Division commander. The excellence achieved in training was the principal factor in the rating of the organizations of the Division.

The comparative rating of the organizations within the Division was started early in the year for the purpose of creating additional interest on the part of the individual soldier and each successive organization commander. The ratings were based on ten general factors, covering, as far as possible, the points on which a comparison could be obtained from actual ratings and accomplishments. This rating was published at the close of each period and included the name of the organization commander in each case.

As a mark of distinction, members of winning organizations were authorized to wear white patches in one or more of the sections outside the "W" and within the circle of the Division Insignia, the number and location depending upon whether the organization was the best company, the best regiment, etc. This system is fully described in the Appendix.

G-3 OFFICE. THE SIGNAL OFFICER

From the organization of the Division and through the greater part of active operations the Division Signal Officer was Lieutenant Colonel John F. Franklin, whose transfer was regarded as a distinct loss. He was succeeded by Lieutenant Colonel John H. Hinemon, Jr. G-3 was held responsible for the efficiency and training of the 314th Field Signal Battalion, and through the Signal Officer, performed in a way the function of regimental commander in regard to these troops.

The first casualties of the Field Signal Battalion occurred in Company "C" during the initial gas attack, Aug. 7-8, 1918, and from that time the battalion paid its toll each month for the very necessary work of establishing and maintaining communication with the Division.

In the Lucey Sector the Signal men greatly improved the wire facilities and developed other means of communication, with projector stations between Division Headquarters and the front lines, telephones from all battalion headquarters back, buzzer phones from each battalion headquarters to its companies, and wireless at regimental, brigade and Division Headquarters.

Company "C" maintained the lines forward of brigade, its platoons being associated in their work with the infantry signal platoons. Constant effort was made to have available other means of communication, including pigeons, for use if wires broke down.

After the St. Mihiel Offensive they established the permanent wire net when the new line stabilized, Company "B" using to advantage captured cable. In fact, then and always thereafter, German material was used whenever possible, and proved a very present help in time of trouble, one of the greatest difficulties of the work being, at all times, shortage of material, especially wire.

The first work in the Meuse-Argonne was with the signal men of the 32nd Division, extending wires before the 89th took over the line. The 314th Field Signal Battalion assumed responsibility for communications at the same time the Division took over the line. Thereafter lines were improved and in the following ten or twelve days a good system was built up and carried ahead with the small advances, telephones even being carried forward with patrols at times to permit instant communication with the rear.

In spite of the rapid advance beginning November 1st, with bad roads, shortage of supplies and constant breaking of lines by fire, wires on the divisional axis of liaison were carried forward promptly, and lateral communication kept up, the work being done not infrequently by men in gas masks stringing hand coils where the reel carts could not travel.

On the first day roads were repaired so reel carts reached La Dhuy farm by 11:30 A. M., Remonville during the afternoon, and beyond before night.

On the 3rd, reel carts passed Tailly, on the 4th, Beauclair, again under heavy shelling which required constant repairing of breaks. On the 5th

Laneuville was reached in spite of the destroyed bridge on the edge of the Foret de Dieulet and trees felled across the road.

The laying and maintaining of these lines under constant fire then and during the days which followed, and the eventual carrying of the wire over the Meuse at Pouilly, Nov. 10th-11th, form a very bright page in the history of the battalion.

During the march into Germany the Signal Battalion maintained wire communication between Division and brigades, frequently using parts of the local lines. In the Army of Occupation the telephone net extended to all regiments and separate organizations. In addition the radio sets were available in emergencies. Except during periods of actual movement telegraph lines were in operation from the Division to higher headquarters and were used principally for transmitting brief administrative orders and reports important enough to require prompt transmission.

G-3 OFFICE. THE MESSAGE CENTER

In Germany the Division message center remained under the control of G-3 but was placed under the immediate supervision of the Division Signal Officer, Lieutenant Colonel John H. Hinemon, Jr. A very efficient organization was maintained and regular delivery of messages, orders and military correspondence throughout the Division was kept up, utilizing local means of communication as well as those peculiar to the army. The local telephone exchanges were operated under the supervision of the Division Signal Officer by the local companies and owners, but in every important exchange an American switch-board was also installed in which connections could be made with the German boards, and thus the German wires were used for the heavy telephone needs of the Division. A complete telephone system was thus established with substantially every one of the scattered organizations, and remarkable success in the operation of such a system with the means at hand, was obtained.

G-3 OFFICE. THE MACHINE GUN OFFICER

The Division Machine Gun Officer, Lieutenant Colonel Rudolph E. Smyser, served as an assistant to G-3 throughout the period. During active operations the work of the machine gun battalions was so closely involved with that of the infantry they supported or to which they were attached that little could be told as a separate story regarding them. Their service was faithful and efficient, and many an infantryman owes his life to the protection of their fire. In the early part of 1919 the Browning automatic rifle and heavy machine gun were issued to the troops in preparation for the training in these new weapons. The Division Machine Gun Officer was directed to organize a school for instruction in automatic weapons. This school was opened at Malberg, and after the completion of the course had prepared a sufficient number of men to act as a corps of instructors for the various organizations.

G-3 OFFICE. THE FRENCH MISSION

Under G-3 was the French Mission, a detachment of French officers and men, which, during the entire period of the Division's career overseas, was attached to it. The functions of this Mission were primarily to maintain liaison, both military and otherwise, with the French. During the training period in the Reynel area a number of instructors from the French Army gave invaluable assistance. They were under the immediate direction of Major Jean de Tarade, who remained with us during the period of trench warfare in the Toul Sector. His spare figure and wind-blown beard were a familiar sight in the trenches, many of which had been constructed by his own troops nearly four years before. He had seen hard service and had been wounded at Verdun. His sagacious advice and kindly personality made him a welcome addition to the Division personnel.

During the service in France the French Mission assisted in straightening and keeping straight all our relations with the civil population and performed valuable military service as well. In Germany not so many questions arose for the Mission.

For most of the time the Mission was under 1st Lieutenant Charles Dangelzer, and interpreters or other representatives of the Mission served with the brigades and lesser organizations. We were fortunate in the personality of these foreign officers, and their tact and good service left agreeable impressions of their country.

G-3 OFFICE. ATHLETICS AND OTHER ACTIVITIES

The Division athletic officer, Major Paul Withington (who was promoted during this period) served as assistant to G-3 during the entire occupation. Athletic matters were handled in the training bulletins. The splendid athletic record of the Division in winning the A. E. F. championship in football and in other lines is an evidence of the excellence of this branch of the work. Athletics, however, were by no means confined to the developing of championship teams. Programs were so planned as to require participation by all the men and a high degree of physical development was thereby fostered throughout the entire division.

The Division Gas Officer, originally Captain M. B. Chittick, and later Captain Hugh W. Rowan, represented the Chemical Warfare Service and worked under G-3.

Under G-3 also were the matters of citation and recommendations for decorations as well as the conducting of the ceremonies themselves. An aide to the Division commander, who was on duty in the G-3 office, handled these awards. The board which passed upon all such recommendations included the three brigade commanders and the aide as member recorder.

Under G-3 also were the educational centers already described.

INSPECTORS

The Division inspector at the time of the Armistice was Major Throop M. Wilder, who was later assigned to the First Division and after an interim was succeeded by Lieutenant Colonel H. M. Taggart; he in December was relieved by Lieutenant Colonel Ellery Farmer, and he in January by Lieutenant Colonel M. E. Spalding. In addition to his normal duties, the inspector handled special investigations, checking the reports of boards of survey and investigating (in addition to the Judge Advocate's investigations) the recommendations for all trials by court martial. Particular attention was paid by the inspector to the condition of the soldiers throughout the Division as to billeting, comfort and general living conditions. A special and important subject of his investigations was the company fund accounts, which ordinarily are a subject of much vexation and trouble and which were particularly so under conditions of the occupation and previous hard fighting, because of the necessity of changing this money from American into French money and then from French into German money and the absence of banks of deposit in which such funds could be kept. By hard work on the part of the inspector a high degree of order was finally obtained in these matters and others of similar character.

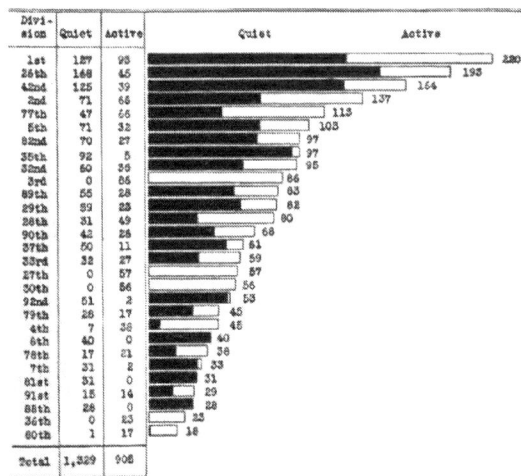

Division	Quiet	Active
1st	127	93
26th	148	45
42nd	125	39
2nd	71	66
77th	47	66
5th	71	32
82nd	70	27
35th	92	5
32nd	60	35
3rd	0	86
89th	55	28
29th	59	23
28th	31	49
90th	42	26
37th	50	11
33rd	32	27
27th	0	57
30th	0	56
92nd	51	2
79th	28	17
4th	7	38
6th	40	0
78th	17	21
7th	31	2
81st	31	0
91st	15	14
88th	28	0
36th	0	23
80th	1	17
Total	1,329	906

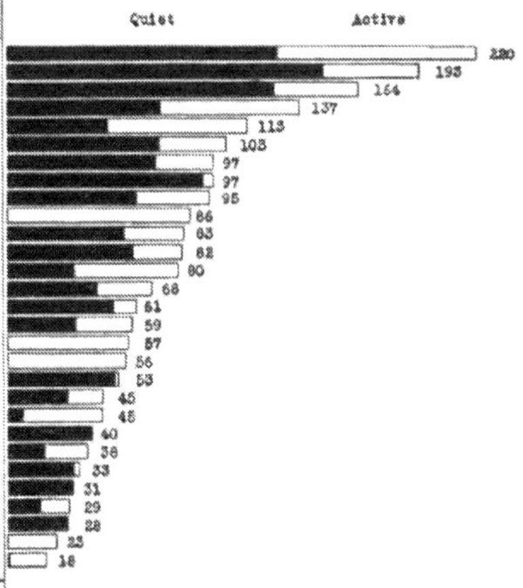

Days spent by each division in quiet and active sectors. From "The War with Germany, a Statistical Summary" (Ayres), 2nd Edition, an official compilation prepared by the Statistics Branch of the General Staff, War Department, Washington, D. C.

THE ADJUTANT'S OFFICE

The position of Division Adjutant was, during almost the entire period of active operations and until the dissolution of the Division, held by Major (later Lieutenant Colonel) Burton A. Smead. During the training period at Camp Funston, the Division Adjutant had been Major (later Colonel) Jerome G. Pillow. At that time, the G System had not been inaugurated, and the Adjutant dealt directly with members of the staff who were later under the G's. Upon his being ordered overseas in February, 1918, Lieutenant Colonel (later Colonel) Ralph McCoy acted as Adjutant until the arrival of the Division in France, and for a brief time Major Throop M. Wilder was Adjutant.

The non-military reader can have little conception of the amount of administrative and record work in a division. If he will conceive the division as an aggregation of individuals, comparable in size to the number of all the inhabitants of every age of a fair sized city; if he will then conceive that every act of every individual in that city must be authorized, either in general or specifically by a written order; and that a written record of the fact of and occasion for every movement, accomplishment, change of condition, sickness or death must be made and reported on in a number of differing phases, and that all these records, in one way and another, originate in or pass through one office, which also furnishes the administrative machinery for carrying out the orders and policies established, he will begin to have a faint conception of the duties devolving upon a division adjutant.

No account of the Division would be complete without some narration of the work done in this department, though a detailed description of the forms used, the reports made and the records kept would be impossible in a volume of this size.

Of especial importance is the work of the Statistical Section of the office, for there was kept the record of casualties, that sad but glorious roll of those for whom many a broken heart back home sought and still seeks tidings.

CLASSES OF ORDERS

Standing orders and instructions, applicable to the entire command, were published in General Orders when importance justified; those of less importance and information of temporary interest were announced in a Special Memorandum, covering a particular subject, or as paragraphs in a General Memorandum or Bulletin embracing various current subjects. In both cases copies mimeographed at Division Headquarters were distributed to the command. Orders from higher headquarters were distributed or paraphrased as occasion required. Assignments, promotions, transfers and movements of individuals not necessary to publish to the command were covered by Special Orders, a new numbered order being issued each day, with separate numbered paragraphs for each item. Copies were distributed only to the individuals and organizations concerned.

General and Special Orders, Bulletins, Memoranda, etc., are issued through the Division Adjutant as the single channel of administrative correspondence and record. The only exceptions are Training Bulletins, Field Orders and Operations Reports, issued by G3, Intelligence Reports by G2 and Administrative Annexes to Field Orders prepared by G1.

PAPER WORK AND MILITARY CORRESPONDENCE

The bête noir of all ranks was "paper work." It was one the importance and absolute necessity of which was realized only when someone fell down on the job and requisite information was unavailable or pending matters were unacted on. There was paper work a-plenty in all branches of the service, but primarily the burden of it fell upon the Adjutant General's Department at higher headquarters as the main channel of Army Administration (correspondence, orders, statistics, records, etc.), and upon the Adjutants of divisions and organizations within the division, each of whom acted for his immediate commanding officer as papers went down within the organization, and prepared them for the approval and signature of the commanding officer if to go to higher headquarters.

In the Army a letter is answered by endorsement on the original and passed up and down along the established line of command by endorsement at each headquarters. Thus does each responsible commander receive correspondence from within his command, stopping, acting on and returning that which can be handled within the limits of his authority. He forwards, with

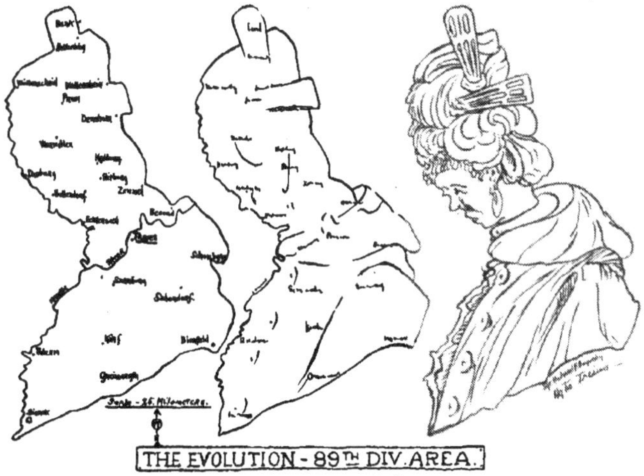

THE EVOLUTION - 89TH DIV. AREA.

FROM AREA-LINE — TO FRÄU-LEIN

One conception of the area occupied by the 89th Division in Germany.

his recommendations for or against, those requiring action by higher headquarters or reference to independent organizations. The system is laborious, but only by it can the commander know and control what is going on within his command. Any alternative permitting individual soldiers or subordinate commanders to communicate directly with higher headquarters or independent organizations would swamp all with an infinite volume of petty matters which higher authority would lack the specific knowledge to act on intelligently and concerning which independent commanders would lack also the necessary authority. Most matters, in both cases, can be more quickly and wisely disposed of by some intermediate commander. The first reaction of the temporary officer to Army channels was disapproval of the apparent lost motion. Later, with administrative experience (especially if at regimental or higher headquarters) came realization of the chaos of disorganization which would follow any alternative system.

Likewise sad experience taught higher headquarters that without a comprehensive follow-up system, and the return of even non-military papers "through channels," an irresistible impulse, seemed to lead company (yea and higher!) commanders to "lose in the field" or "inadvertantly overlook" action on papers which could be more conveniently buried than answered. The word "inadvertent" was a great asset in the Army to explain away sins.

But sound though the principle of military correspondence is, legitimate complaint can be made of its application to the handling by formal correspondence of matters which frequently could have been taken care of informally or by word of mouth, and especially of the added and unnecessary labor entailed by the habit of higher headquarters (frequently above the Division) to require formal reference of matters better left to the judgment of subordinate commanders and further to prescribe minutely by formal orders, matters of small or occasional importance. So many special and periodical detailed reports were required, many of which duplicated each other, that organizations were fairly buried under the volume. A snowstorm of orders, bulletins, memoranda and instructions issued from every headquarters, beginning with the regiment and extending up to G. H. Q. Each paragraph no doubt seemed important to the one who wrote it, but the aggregate was staggering, and from a perspective of present peace days, there is question just how much was really necessary or worth while and how much was a well meant but thoughtless blunder-bussing of orders and instructions, important (if at all) to only a small part of the target hit. With some sins of the same sort of its own to answer for, Division Headquarters became, particularly in Germany, the reluctant intermediary passing on down to the regiments, futile and changing requirements of higher authority from which before we had been happily free, and over which the veil of charity may now well be drawn.

MOBILITY OF THE OFFICE

To handle the volume of administrative work required a large force and extensive equipment, but mobility was not lost sight of and Division Headquarters could pack and move in an hour at any time, reopening for business in a few minutes. Movements were made by echelon, the new P. C. being opened before the old one closed.

Typewriters and mimeograph machines were screwed to the hinged tops of their boxes which, opened, formed the tables on which the machines were operated. The 30,000 or more statistical cards were kept in special boxes which had been ingeniously designed by Captain J. K. Strutz, Personnel Adjutant at Camp Funston, and built under his direction. Strong enough to stand rough usage, they were so constructed that, when opened, a box formed a convenient desk holding the card trays and the top an adjoining table, the whole supported at the proper height on detachable legs which were kept inside the box when it was closed. Files were kept in wooden cases with hinged doors which protected them and could be locked each night. A small canvas collapsible rack served at the Message Center for classifying papers to be distributed to organizations. - The large distributing rack, in appearance not unlike those used in post offices, in the Adjutants' office, where most of the distributing was done, was in a case, the front side of which was hinged and fell away, forming a table upon which papers were handled. It could be closed and locked in a moment, effectually sealing in a pigeon hole for each organization, those papers awaiting delivery at time movement began. Boxes of supplies were used for tables upon which field desks were mounted, other boxes serving for chairs.

KEEPING STATISTICS

Upon arrival in France a Division Statistical Section was organized by Captain (later Major) Joseph E. Brown, the Division Personnel Adjutant in compliance with G. O. 100, G. H. Q. 1918, with subsections in all units within the Division. The methods were new from the ground up, being entirely unlike the personnel and statistical work previously done in the United States. The vocational qualification cards of enlisted men were at once shipped to Central Records Office (C.R.O.) and officers' cards to G. H. Q., to be forgotten until shortly before the Division returned to the United States, when they came back again to the organizations to be placed with the individual records of the men.

Statistical work, records of personnel, strength returns, etc., acquired an importance not previously attached to them, and were kept both within organizations of the Division and at Division Headquarters under difficulties which at times seemed almost insurmountable.

In addition to records kept by the units within the Division, a complete card index record was made at Division Headquarters on 5 x 8 cards from rosters of June 30th, 1918, a card for each member of the Division. This card index was carefully kept up to date during the entire period of service in Europe, all data as to changes of status (casualties, transfers, promotions, etc.) being entered on the cards, which were filed alphabetically without regard to organization, so it was possible to tell in a moment whether or not a given individual belonged to the Division, his rank, organization, whether he became a casualty, was in the hospital, on leave, transferred or promoted; in short, a complete history of his military service with the Division.

In addition to the card index, a loose leaf roster of officers, arranged by organizations, was kept up to date at all times showing the assignment and duties of all officers within each organization.

These were invaluable records, in constant use for an infinite number of purposes, and peculiarly necessary because of the constant changes during active operations due to casualties, transfers, promotions and replacements.

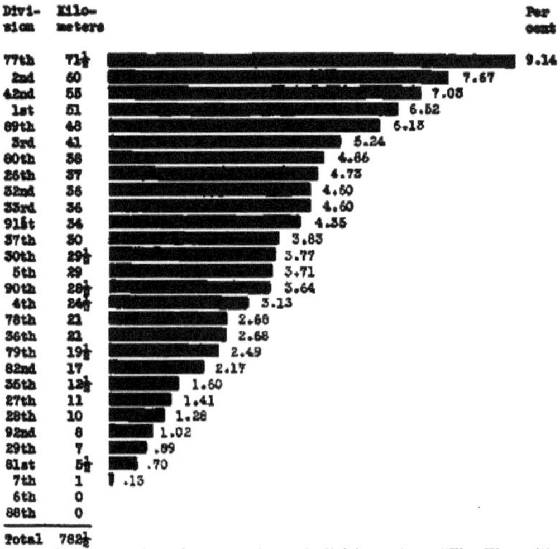

Division
Kilometers
Per cent
77th 71½ 9.14
2nd 60 7.67
42nd 55 7.03
1st 51 6.52
89th 48 6.13
3rd 41 5.24
80th 38 4.86
26th 37 4.73
32nd 36 4.60
33rd 36 4.60
91st 34 4.35
37th 30 3.83
30th 29½ 3.77
5th 29 3.71
90th 28½ 3.64
4th 24½ 3.13
78th 21 2.68
36th 21 2.68
79th 19½ 2.49
82nd 17 2.17
35th 12½ 1.60
27th 11 1.41
28th 10 1.28
92nd 8 1.02
29th 7 .89
81st 5½ .70
7th 1 .13
6th 0
88th 0
Total 782½

Kilometers advanced against the enemy by each division. From "The War with Germany, a Statistical Summary" (Ayres), 2nd Edition, an official compilation prepared by the Statistics Branch of the General Staff, War Department, Washington, D. C.

They were used to check and correct rosters and reports from organizations, which were notified when a change reported was inconsistent with the previous record. Thus errors were caught and corrections made.

In general the statistical subsections within the Division operated on similar though simpler lines, receiving reports of changes from their companies, maintaining indexes and rosters, preparing the reports of casualties and changes in proper form and furnishing other data required.

KEEPING THE RECORD OF OUR DEAD AND WOUNDED

The tragic experience with gas casualties when the Division first entered the line made it evident that a comprehensive system of reporting casualties to the Division Personal Adjutant from all possible sources of information was necessary; that at Division Headquarters these reports must be checked as to spelling and organization of the names shown, and verified when inconsistent or incomplete, to insure accuracy as to the identity of the man and degree of injury in the Division official report of each casualty.

Casualties were often evacuated through hospitals of adjoining divisions without proper report therefrom, either to the Division Personnel Adjutant or to the regiment, or perhaps moved direct in ambulances or trucks to hospitals far in the rear without record of any kind. There were emergencies when the problem was to save men and the mere record of their saving became relatively of no importance. Errors in name and organization in reports received prevented identification of casualties at times. Replacements received during actual fighting became casualties and were evacuated before they could even be picked up on the records. These are only a few of the conditions which had to be met, and in spite of which an excellent record for accuracy and completeness was established.

It is no wonder that sometimes loving, anxious mothers "back home" had their hearts wrung by tragic errors in casualty reports by the time they were repeated back to the C. R. O. and cabled to Washington for publication. But it is a great wonder that these errors were so few.

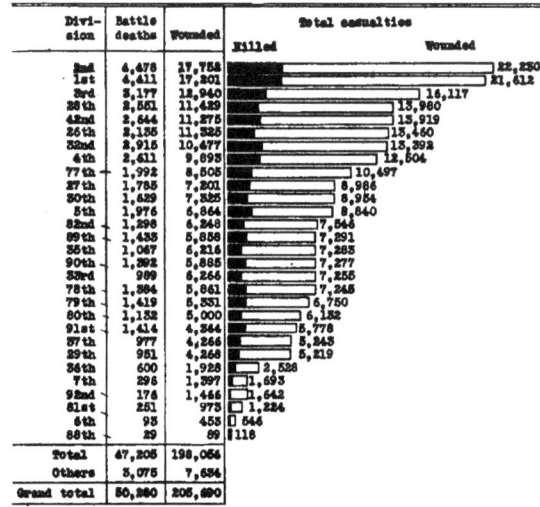

Division	Battle deaths	Wounded	Total casualties
2nd	4,478	17,752	22,230
1st	4,411	17,201	21,612
3rd	3,177	12,940	16,117
28th	2,551	11,429	13,980
42nd	2,644	11,275	13,919
26th	2,135	11,325	13,460
32nd	2,915	10,477	13,392
4th	2,611	9,893	12,504
77th	1,992	8,505	10,497
27th	1,785	7,201	8,986
30th	1,629	7,325	8,954
5th	1,976	6,864	8,840
82nd	1,298	6,248	7,546
89th	1,433	5,858	7,291
35th	1,067	6,216	7,283
90th	1,392	5,885	7,277
33rd	989	6,266	7,255
78th	1,384	5,861	7,245
79th	1,419	5,331	6,750
80th	1,132	5,000	6,132
91st	1,414	4,364	5,778
37th	977	4,266	5,243
29th	951	4,268	5,219
36th	600	1,928	2,528
7th	296	1,397	1,693
92nd	176	1,466	1,642
81st	251	973	1,224
6th	93	453	546
88th	29	89	118
Total	47,205	198,054	
Others	3,075	7,634	
Grand total	50,280	205,690	

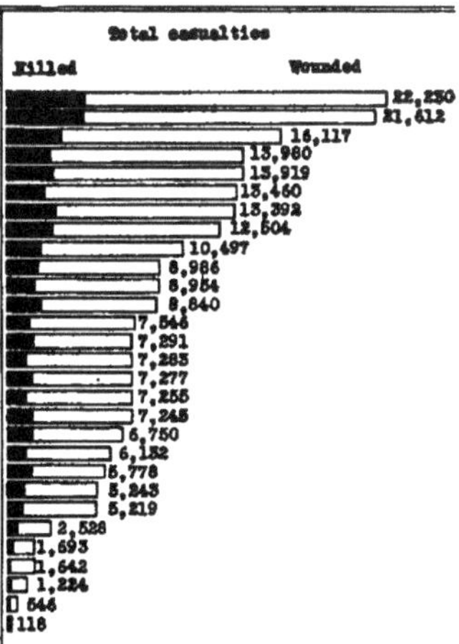

Casualties suffered by each division. From "The War with Germany, a Statistical Summary" (Ayres), 2nd Edition, an official compilation prepared by the Statistics Branch of the General Staff, War Department, Washington, D. C.

The following method of recording and reporting casualties was devised in August, and with slight modification was in effect until final demobilization. It was original in the Division and was widely complimented and copied by others. Each report of a casualty, whether shown on Casualty and Change Reports from hospitals and organizations, on Forms for Report of Casualties, Graves Location Blanks, reports of burial parties or informal memorandum, was entered on the card index previously referred to. By use of this card, before reporting a casualty to Central Records Office, mistakes in spelling or description were prevented. At the same time, if the casualty were anything more serious than slightly wounded, a separate "casualty card" was made, upon which was given all the information contained in the report, which might be included in the official report of the casualty to C. R. O. by telegram or couriergram. The casualty was then tallied on a tally sheet by which the total number of casualties, classified according to degree, was kept. No casualty was reported until verification was received, usually from more than one source. This was necessary because of frequent errors in initial reports. Casualty cards, therefore, on which no verification appeared, were returned to a suspense file when the daily report of verified casualties was made. Later reports concerning such casualties were entered on the card index and casualty card, the latter coming back to the man preparing the casualty telegram each time a new report was received on that casualty, to be entered thereon and finally to be reported to C. R. O. when he was fully convinced as to the facts.

It is characteristic of the Division's thoroughness in all things that after its dissolution and even up to the moment of present writing Major Brown has continued his activity, has checked up personally with the casualty records at Washington, all the casualties, prisoners and men reported missing, so that a final and accurate record of every man who has ever served overseas with the 89th Division is now available.

A recruiting office was opened for recruits for the Regular Army. Its history is analogous to the celebrated account of the snakes in Ireland—there were no recruits. Army life on a peace status was found to have no appeal for our men.

THE JUDGE ADVOCATE

The position of Division judge advocate, originally held by Lieutenant Colonel G. V. Packer, was held throughout the period by Major (later Lieutenant Colonel) Henry Davis, and fortunately and most creditably for the Division the records of punishments for serious offenses are quite low.

CHAPTER VIII.

THE FINALS

Before its departure for home, it was the practice of General Pershing to review each of the divisions. The review of our Division took place April 23rd in the great airplane station in Trier. It was a memorable event,—the only time that the whole Division with infantry, artillery and trains was ever assembled at one place on foreign soil. No effort was spared to make the appearance of the Division such as to be in keeping with its splendid record in the field, and the result was well worthy of the effort.

In preparation for the event, troops and trains began moving to Trier two days before the date; the engineer regiment was assembled and prepared the field by smoothing it and erecting reviewing stands; all the regimental bands were massed and, under the direction of Captain Francis Leigh, furnished a magnificent volume of music for the marching troops. The Division being formed in line of masses, was first reviewed by the Commander-in-Chief. Then followed the impressive ceremony of awarding decorations to those who had earned them by conspicuous gallantry. Most moving was the decorating of the colors of the regiments for valiant service. The infantry then passed the reviewing stand in column of battalions, each battalion in line of platoons, affording a wonderful sight as the many columns abreast marched in perfect alinement and cadence. Then followed the artillery, the 340th and 341st regiments with their horse-drawn field guns. Then followed the animal-drawn transportation of the Division, arranged in eleven columns abreast; a vast array of horses and wagons now for the first time assembled and astonishing even to the members of the Division in its quantity and in the precision of the movement of the unwieldy mass. The 342nd, now at last motorized, was parked and inspected near the Zeppelin shed. It did not pass in review, lest the heavy howitzers, now drawn by caterpillar tractors, cut the turf too greatly.

So carefully had the plans for the assembly of the Division been made, that the great body of men and vehicles, after passing in review, went at once to its appointed place and returned to its station without road jams or confusion.

After the review, all the Division, except necessary details, was assembled in the huge Zeppelin shed. There they were addressed by the Com-

Review of the 89th Division by General Pershing at Euren, near Trier (Treves), Germany, April 23, 1919. Division Wagon Trains in left foreground. Horse-drawn (340th and 341st) artillery in center, above which the infantry and machine gun organizations appear only as small dots, each dot being a whole platoon of infantry, about fifty men. To their right are aeroplanes and their hangars. At top of the picture in the center is an immense Zeppelin shed, in which Secretary of War Baker, General Pershing and Major General Summerall addressed the men of the Division after the review. In front of it and to the left is the motorized (342nd) artillery. Motor transportation of the Division was stretched out for inspection on the road to the right far beyond the picture. At the left are practice trenches, formerly used by the Germans in training. To their right a German powder magazine, surrounded by a moat. A. S. 3-A, 95 Sq., B. 269.

mander-in-Chief in a soldierly discourse which failed not to pay just tribute to the achievements of the Division in the field; Secretary of War Newton D. Baker, who had accompanied General Pershing on the occasion, also spoke to the Division, expressing the sentiments of those back home. General C. P. Summerall, our corps commander in the Argonne fighting, was also introduced, and after receiving a welcome of spontaneous and heartfelt cheering, spoke briefly and feelingly to his former troops.

RETROSPECT AND COMPARISON

After settling down in Germany, the Division began to look back over its record in the field and to compare its accomplishments with those of other combat divisions. It found its record to be one that would well bear such comparison.

Of Congressional Medals of Honor, the highest award for individual heroism in action granted by any nation, its men had won nine, a number surpassed by only one division in the A. E. F., the 30th.

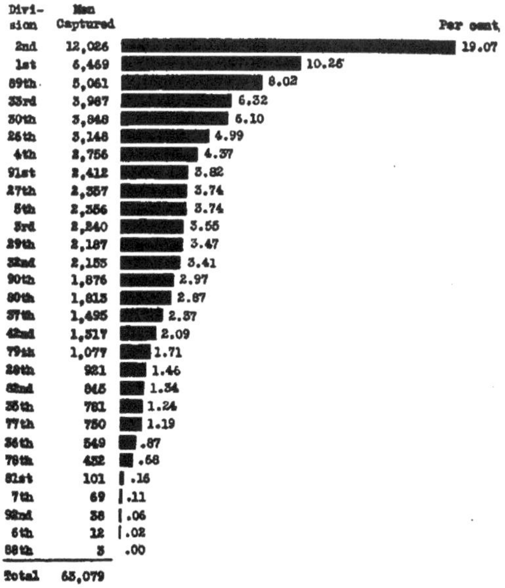
Division
Men Captured
Per cent
2nd 12,026 19.07
1st 6,469 10.26
89th 5,061 8.02
33rd 3,987 6.32
30th 3,848 6.10
26th 3,148 4.99
4th 2,756 4.37
91st 2,412 3.82
27th 2,357 3.74
5th 2,356 3.74
3rd 2,240 3.55
29th 2,187 3.47
32nd 2,153 3.41
90th 1,876 2.97
80th 1,813 2.87
37th 1,495 2.37
42nd 1,317 2.09
79th 1,077 1.71
28th 921 1.46
82nd 845 1.34
35th 781 1.24
77th 750 1.19
36th 549 .87
78th 432 .68
81st 101 .16
7th 69 .11
92nd 38 .06
6th 12 .02
88th 3 .00
Total 63,079

German prisoners captured by each division. From "The War with Germany, a Statistical Summary" (Ayres), 2nd Edition, an official compilation prepared by the Statistics Branch of the General Staff, War Department, Washington, D. C.

Four Medals of Honor were won by members of the 356th Infantry and three by members of the 354th Infantry. While official records covering the facts are not available, its is believed that only one regiment in the entire A. E. F., the 132nd Infantry, 33rd Division, with five, won more Medals of Honor than did the 356th Infantry.

Of kilometers advanced against the enemy, it had an official total of 48, constituting more than six per cent of all the advances made by all the American forces and being surpassed only by the 77th, 2nd, 42nd and 1st Divisions in this regard.

Of prisoners captured, the 89th Division is officially credited with 5,061, more than 8 per cent of all the prisoners taken by the American forces, and is surpassed in this respect only by the 2nd and 1st Divisions.

The significance of these comparisons will be the greater when it is understood that there were a total of 29 combat divisions engaged by the American forces; that all the divisions reported as having surpassed ours in any particular (except the 30th) had, by virtue of their earlier arrival in Europe, spent more time in contact with the enemy than ours, the 89th's standing among combat divisions being eleventh in this respect. Thus, though eleventh in opportunity, we were second in individual heroism, fifth in distance advanced, and third in the capture of prisoners.

In some other respects we found ourselves first: from our first entry into the line until the armistice we spent a larger percentage of time in contact with the enemy than any other division after its first contact; we were the first to move from the training area to the front by American trucks under American command; first to enter the line without previously being brigaded with French or British troops; first to be continuously in the front line for more than eight weeks, and the first National Army Division to enter Germany.

On the whole, we began to feel rather proud of ourselves and to form the opinion, which has never since been shaken, that the 89th Division was as good as the best division in the American Forces, and a long way better than most.

CASUALTY COMMENTS

A study of the casualties, by periods, shows some interesting facts not generally realized. The story of operations centers around the offensives, yet the natural conclusion that most of the casualties occurred then is not justified. Such a view ignores the fact that first digging in at the end of an advance is succeeded by the grueling task of constructing, under fire and with little protection, a system of trenches and dugouts on the new line. It forgets the wastage from day to day holding the line. It disregards the heavy losses (frequently falling on a single battalion or regiment) in minor operations, which make an impressive total. The losses of the 354th and 355th Regiments the first night the Division was in the line are an illustration at the beginning of the combat experience of the Division, and the casualties November 10-11 in Major Hanna's battalion of the 356th regiment are another at the very end of the campaign.

An itemized table of casualties, prepared after the armistice, divided into arbitrary periods corresponding closely to changes in conditions in the line, will make the situation clearer.

It should also be remembered that here, as elsewhere in this history, only the actual bona fide casualties, officially reported, are considered. Nowhere are loose approximations or round figures in excess of official figures, indulged in.

ITEMIZED TABLE OF CASUALTIES

Toul-St. Mihiel Sector	*Casualties*	
Shelling and Gas attack of night of August 7th and 8th, 1918	623	
Holding the line, August 8th to September 12th	310	
ST. MIHIEL Offensive, September 12th to 18th	1,008	
Holding the line, September 18th to October 9th	1,483	
Total St. Mihiel Sector		3,424
Meuse-Argonne Sector		
Attacking and Mopping up the BOIS de BANTHEVILLE, October 19th to 22nd	442	
Holding the line, October 22nd to November 1st, in the BOIS de BANTHEVILLE	557	
Final Phase, MEUSE-ARGONNE Offensive, November 1st to November 6th	1,646	
Holding the line along the River MEUSE, November 6th to November 10th	571	
Crossing the River MEUSE, night of November 10th and 11th	362	
Total Meuse-Argonne Sector		3,578
Grand total		7,002

To emphasize some of the surprising facts disclosed by the foregoing figures, it should be noted that:

(a) Casualties the first night in the line were six-tenths as heavy as they were during the St. Mihiel Offensive, and double those during the rest of the period in the trenches to September 12th. The total from entry into the line to the offensive was almost as great as during the offensive itself.

(b) Total casualties during the St. Mihiel Offensive were only a little over two-thirds of the losses we suffered establishing and holding the new line after that advance and to date of relief, October 9th, even though casualties during the initial digging in (Sept. 15-17) after the advance are included in those for the offensive. It cost fifty per cent more to hold than to take.

(c) Mopping up the Bois de Bantheville cost more than one-fourth, and holding it, more than a third as many casualties as were suffered during the six days advance in the final phase of the Meuse-Argonne Offensive. In other words, getting ready for that advance cost about two-thirds as many casualties as the advance itself.

(d) Holding the line on the river Meuse from Nov. 6th to 10th involved more than a third as many losses as those suffered during the advance which preceded.

(e) The last twenty hours of the war cost more than a fifth as many casualties as occurred during the Meuse-Argonne advance, most of them falling, moreover, on a single battalion.

(f) Losses in the Meuse-Argonne before and after the advance (Nov. 1-6) were materially heavier than during the advance itself.

WAR SOCIETY OF THE 89TH DIVISION

The War Society of the 89th Division was organized at Bitburg, Germany, May 4th, 1919, at a convention called by the Division Commander and composed of delegates elected by the members of all organizations in the Division.

The following sections, quoted from the constitution there adopted, give the essential facts regarding it:

SECTION II. PURPOSES AND OBJECTS:

The purposes and objects of this Society shall be: to perpetuate the memories of services in war with the 89th Division; to promote and maintain among members of the Division the comradeship and spirit engendered by active service with the 89th Division; to collect and preserve such mementos of service of the Division as members of the Society may donate or may receive from other sources; to preserve the memory of the fallen; to publish from time to time bulletins of general interest to the Society; to publish the history of the Division.

SECTION III. QUALIFICATIONS FOR MEMBERSHIP:

The following qualifications will be required for membership in this Society: Any officer, field clerk or enlisted man of the Army of the United States or of the Allied Armies, any member of an officially recognized welfare organization, and any officer, field clerk or enlisted man honorably separated from the military service of the United States or of the Allied Governments, who has served in any organization of the Division, or attached thereto, since the 25th of August, 1917, to the date of the Peace Treaty, shall be eligible to membership in this Society.

In case of the death of an individual who otherwise would be entitled to membership, his direct descendant or next of kin is eligible.

Wives, mothers, sisters and daughters of members are eligible for associate membership.

Associate membership carries full obligations, and privileges except those of voting, of holding office or of speaking from the floor of the convention.

* * * * * * * * *

SECTION IX. FEES AND FINANCES:

The initiation fees for membership in this Society shall be as follow: For commissioned officers of all grades and field clerks, ten (10) francs when paid in the A. E. F., and two (2) dollars when paid in the United States or elsewhere; for enlisted men of all grades, two (2) francs when paid in the A. E. F. and fifty cents when paid in the United States or elsewhere. The annual dues shall be such amount as may be determined by the Executive Committee, not to exceed Two ($2.00) Dollars, and shall be the same for all members. The initial fee shall cover the membership for the first year of the Society's organization. Voluntary contributions of money, in addition to the fees, may be received by the Society.

Life membership fee shall be Twenty-five ($25.00) Dollars.

Not one cent of funds so raised will be spent to support any political party.

* * * * * * * * *

The following honorary presidents were elected at the Bitburg convention: Major General Leonard Wood, Major General William M. Wright, Major General Charles P. Summerall.

The following active officers were chosen: President, Major General Frank L. Winn; Vice President, Sergeant F. R. Baker, 356th Infantry;

Secretary, Lieutenant Colonel Burton A. Smead, Headquarters 89th Division; Treasurer, Sergeant Spencer Bartlett, Finance Office, Division Quartermaster.

The Executive Committee consists of the President, Secretary and Treasurer, together with the following additional members, who were also elected at the Bitburg convention: Brigadier General Edward T. Donnelly, 164th Field Artillery Brigade; Private, 1st-class, Howard P. Laslett, Intelligence Section.

A brief history of the 89th Division (a 48-page booklet with three maps) prepared in Germany by Major C. J. Masseck, 353rd Infantry, under the super-

Awards of Medal of Honor, by Organisations.

Organizations	Number	Per cent of total
30th Division	12	15.1
89th "	9	11.3
33rd "	9	11.3
2nd "	7	8.8
77th "	6	7.5
27th "	5	6.3
91st "	4	5.0
29th "	3	3.7
1st "	2	2.5
3rd "	2	2.5
5th "	2	2.5
26th "	2	2.5
28th "	2	2.5
35th "	2	2.5
36th "	2	2.5
42nd "	2	2.5
82nd "	2	2.5
Tank Corps	2	2.5
76th Division	1	1.2
78th "	1	1.2
93rd "	1	1.2
Air Service	1	1.2
Total	79	

Awards of Medal of Honor to members of each division. Prepared from information obtained from Statistics Branch, General Staff, War Department, Washington, D. C. Data secured from the Decoration Section, Adjutant General's Office, G. H. Q., A. E. F., at Washington, in April, 1920, confirmed the foregoing figures, with the following discrepancies: 3rd Division, 3 instead of 2; 27th Division, 6 instead of 5; 28th Division, 1 instead of 2; 76th Division, 0 instead of 1. There is no discrepancy in total number awarded, and presumably the minor variations in figures noted occurred by use of different methods in crediting honors where a man was assigned to one organization but was attached to or serving with another.

vision of G-2, was published by the War Society on the return of the Division from overseas and distributed gratuitously to all members of the Division whose addresses were known.

The present complete history of the 89th Division, by the official historian of the War Society, was prepared and is published under the auspices of the War Society of the 89th Division.

THE HOME GOING

In May came the welcome news that the Division would go home. The 314th Trench Mortar Battery had already departed, having received its orders to return on January 10th. Theoretically, the Division became dissolved when it was assigned to the SOS for embarkation in May, but in point of fact a form of organization was maintained after its arrival in America.

Division Headquarters was kept intact even on board ship, at Camp Upton and subsequently at Camp Funston, for the purpose of clearing up administrative details, and thus a spark of life was kept which could represent the old Division. The movement from Germany to the port of embarkation at Brest was accompanied by a train daily from each of the three entraining points, Prüm, Erdorf and Trier. The movement was accomplished with great smoothness and dispatch. Practically without exception each organization

"For it's home, boys, home—." The Agamemnon pulling up to the dock in New York, May 24, 1919, bringing back from overseas the following 89th Division troops: 314th Ammunition Train, 314th Sanitary Train, 314th M. O. R. S., 341st Field Artillery and parts of the 340th Field Artillery and 356th Infantry. The Division insignia can be recognized on the shoulders of many of the men. S. C. 67079.

left its billets in excellent condition, arrived in ample time at the entraining point, accomplished the details of loading and of cleaning up its immediate vicinity in sufficient time for the departure of its train at the scheduled hour. Division Headquarters was the last element of the Division to leave the area of the Army of Occupation, except for the zone major and the claims officer, who were left behind to complete their work, but an advance division headquarters was established at Brest under the supervision of G-1, who sent two officers from his office and the Division personnel adjutant as an advance party several days prior to the departure of the first unit of the Division. Although the splendid organization of the SOS service at Brest made it unnecessary for the Division staff to assume any responsibility at that point other than the handling of its own immediate officers and men, the opening of this office proved satisfactory in smoothing the details. The entire Division passed through Brest without special event and started homeward with a maximum delay of only forty-eight hours in every case, with the exception of that of Division headquarters. The SOS officials at Brest complimented the manner in which the divisional units arrived, the condition of their records and their general discipline. The first element of the Division to sail from Brest embarked upon the Leviathan May 15th and comprised the 355th Infantry, the 353rd Infantry and 340th and 341st Machine Gun Battalions. On the same date also, the 354th Infantry and 177th Infantry Brigade Headquarters sailed on the Imperator. Other units were embarked on the 16th, 18th and 19th of May on the Agamemnon, the America, the Montana, and the Prinz Frederic Wilhelm. Finally, on May 19th, Division Headquarters, with the Headquarters Troop, 178th Infantry Brigade Headquarters and the 314th Supply Train, sailed on the Rotterdam, and the entire 89th Division had left foreign shores.

On arrival at New York, officers and men were sent, for the main part, to Camp Upton, where some were discharged, but most were sent out as reduced organizations or detachments to the various demobilization camps closest to their homes and there discharged. A large majority of the men were sent to Camp Funston, as well as several regimental headquarters and the Division headquarters. All general officers of the Division were relieved from duty therewith before leaving the vicinity of New York.

One by one the officers of the headquarters were discharged, or, if of the Regular Army, assigned to new duties.

General Winn was detailed to the command of Camp Custer, Michigan, where he was accompanied by his aides, Captains Lockwood and Green. For the convenient preparation of this history he requested and obtained the order of the War Department for the historian to report at Camp Custer, and thus a little remnant of the Division remained together. But soon Captain Lockwood was discharged; General Winn returned to his rank of Colonel in the regular service and was assigned to duties elsewhere; Captain Green, after remaining a short while to render valuable assistance to the historian, returned to civil life. And of all wearers of the encircled W, there remained only the historian, surrounded by his papers; who now, filled with pensive recollections of the stirring events through which he has lived again in retrospect, at last brings the Division's history to

THE END.

The American Military Cemetery at Romagne, as it appeared May 28th, 1919, when American labor troops, assisted by German prisoners, were completing the building of roads, erection of crosses and placing wreaths before Memorial Day. Members of the 89th Division killed in the Meuse-Argonne Offensive are buried here. The picture shows only about half of the cemetery. S. C. 67276.

OFFICIAL REPORTS

ST. MIHIEL OFFENSIVE

HEADQUARTERS
89TH DIVISION
AMERICAN EXPEDITIONARY FORCES.

5 December, 1918.

From: Commanding General, 89th Division.

To: Commander-in-Chief, AMERICAN EXPEDITIONARY FORCES (Operations Section, G-3, G. H. Q.)

Subject: Operation September 6th- October 7th, 1918

PART I. HOSTILE SITUATION AT THE BEGINNING OF THE OPERATION.

1. At the beginning of the operation the enemy occupied a position which he had held since shortly after the beginning of the war, about four years. It consisted of the usual wired entrenchments. Here and there were concrete dugouts. Elaborate observation posts had been constructed and a thorough system of artillery telephone communications had been extended to the rear. The wire, which was four or five bands deep in places, and the entrenchments had been maintained, improved and elaborated during the enemy's occupancy. They were in good condition. So that at the beginning of the operation the enemy occupied a carefully prepared, strongly fortified position

2. In the rear area artillery emplacements had been constructed. At one place in our advance a series of tank traps had been prepared. Concrete dugouts and other elaborate facilities for shelter existed. Furthermore, the enemy, owing to his long occupancy of the territory, was thoroughly familiar with the terrain.

3. The zone of advance of this Division was characterized by the occupancy of the BOIS de MORT MARE, almost entirely across the immediate front. These woods stood on high ground and offered a naturally strong defensive barrier to our progress.

4. The enemy held the line opposite our zone of action from east to west as follows: The 332nd Regiment, 419th Regiment and 257th Regiment of the 77th Reserve Division in the order named. Its sector extended from the vicinity of REMENAUVILLE on the east to a point just west of FLIREY on the west. The 6th Reserve Regiment, 47th Regiment, and 398th Regiment, of the 10th Division, in the order named, held the remainder of the line to the vicinity of LOUPMONT on the west. The 77th Reserve Division was a low-rated division, the 10th Division was a high-rated division. The troops of our division had forces of each of these two divisions of the enemy opposed to them. About the time that the operation was begun, enemy battalions were being reduced from four companies to three in number. Assuming that the enemy had not completed this change, as probably was the case, the method of holding the line was as follows: Two battalions occupied the line, side by side, each with two companies of each battalion in the front lines and two in support. The third battalion was in reserve. Machine gun outposts were stationed in front of the line.

PART II. INFORMATION RECEIVED OF THE ENEMY DURING THE OPERATION.

1. During the operation the enemy order of battle was confirmed by many prisoners. Some artillery and pioneer units were also identified. However, prisoners were evacuated directly to the Corps cage, where these identifications were recorded.

2. Some prisoners stated that several divisions had been held in reserve at METZ and the vicinity; that they were to take a position behind the Hindenburg Line and counter attack our forces from this line.

PART III. HOSTILE MOVEMENTS, CHANGES AND CONDUCT DURING THE OPERATION.

1. Upon our advance the enemy withdrew. There was no organized opposition to our troops during the morning of the attack and during the early afternoon. During the latter part of the afternoon our troops suffered some casualties from machine gun fire and artillery fire of small calibers. They were also sniped at by 47 mm. guns. The same sort of opposition was interposed to their progress upon the following day. At no time was there any serious opposition from the enemy infantry except as above.

2. The enemy fell back to the so-called Hindenburg Line. The 192nd Division entered the line opposite our sector. Upon approaching the Hindenburg Line our troops consolidated their gain and proceeded to organize along the line XAMMES, north of BENEY, and along the north edge of the BOIS de DAMPVITOUX. The enemy dug in along the Hindenburg Line, and when he determined that our further advance was not forthcoming, he withdrew his stronger divisions to strengthen his line at other points.

PART IV. OWN SITUATION AT THE BEGINNING OF THE OPERATION.

1. Prior to September 11, 1918, the 89th Division held the LUCEY Sector, on a front of approximately 16 kilometers to the north of the METZ Road from west of BOUCONVILLE to the east of LIMEY. A small portion of the western end of the line was taken over by the Second French Colonial Corps, on the night 8-9 September. Some units on the Position of Resistance were relieved by the 1st Division on the nights 6-7-8 September, by units of the 2nd Division on the nights 9-10-11 September, and by units of the 42nd Division on the night 10-11 September. The Advanced Post Positions were held, however, by the Division all the night 11-12, when these were taken over west of FLIREY, by units of the 1st and 42nd Divisions. The 2nd Division was scheduled to relieve the outposts east of LIMEY on the night 11-12, but did not do so.

2. The following units composed the supporting artillery: 55th F. A. Brigade, 250 R. A. P., 212 R. A. P., two battalions of 160 R. A. P. and 105th, 108th U. S. and 176 Fr. T. M. Batteries. These units were distributed in a general way south of the METZ Road within the Division Sector. A few batteries were placed north of the METZ Road and west of FLIREY. The nature of the terrain and the need of concealment made the distribution heavy on the left of the Sector, the greater number of batteries being placed in the BOIS de la HAZELLE. Corps artillery occupied the BOIS de la VOISOGNE. One battalion of 75's and one battalion of 155's were distributed in favorable positions along the LIMEY-NOVIANT Road.

3. The Zone of Action, as shown on the attached map, is described in the accompanying Field Order No. 12. The Brigade zones of operation are similarly indicated. A study of the sketch shows that the Division zone narrows from 4½ kilometers at the beginning to 2½ kilometers at its narrowest point (east and west line through BENEY) and then widens to approximately 4 kilometers along the line of the Army Objective.

4. The missions of the Division were definite, namely: The support of the advance of the 42nd Division on our left to include the capture of ESSEY by occupying the heights north of EUVEZIN; the support of the advance of the 2nd Division by capturing the eastern edge of MORT MARE Wood and by turning the woods of EUVEZIN and BEAU VALLON, and aid in the capture of THIAUCOURT.

5. With these missions and with the obstacle of the MORT MARE Forest in the immediate front of the Division, it was necessary to divide the command and run the risk of an interruption of liaison between the brigades of the Division. A frontal attack on the BOIS de MORT MARE was believed impracticable, as this would delay the advance and hinder in giving the necessary support to the divisions on the right and left. It was necessary, however, to clear the forest of the enemy in order to eliminate the danger of ambush to the troops, trains and artillery on the roads. These considerations influenced the initial arrangement for the attack.

6. The mission on the right was given to the 177th Infantry Brigade (less the 354th Regiment—plus one battalion 354th Infantry as Brigade reserve); that on the left to the 178th Infantry Brigade. Each brigade had the task of mopping the woods and other enemy locations within its zone of operation.

7. A four-hour artillery preparation, followed by a rolling barrage was directed in the Corps Order. Especial targets to be fired on during this four-hour preparation were selected by the Division Artillery Officer based on information of the enemy dispositions and routes of reinforcement or withdrawal. The plan of the barrage was based on the prescribed rate of the infantry advance, allowing for a halt after the capture of each objective. The Corps allowed six hours to reach the line 1 kilometer north of EUVEZIN—northern edge of BOIS BEAU VALLON, which marked the limit for independent action of the Division and of the first phase.

8. The time allotted for the completion of the first phase was 5 hours 45 minutes, whereas the Corps Order provided for 6 hours. The plans also allowed for a continuation of the barrage to and including the objective of the first day, without a cessation of fire. The artillery plan contemplated the advance of all batteries practicable at about H plus 3 and their siting north of BOIS de MORT MARE for continuous support of the advance. This advance did not affect the density of the barrage materially on account of the narrowing of the zone of action.

9. The following dispositions of the troops in the Division were made: The right brigade was extended in depth, with one battalion in the front line. TRENCH FERNIER ¾ kilometers north of the METZ Road; one in support, one in regimental reserve, and one battalion 354th Infantry in brigade reserve. There were attached one company of Engineers and one-half company of Pioneers, with one battery of American (4-75's) as accompanying artillery. The left brigade had two regiments in line, each with one battalion in advance, TRENCH DECAUVILLE and northwestward; one battalion in support and one battalion in brigade reserve. One company of Engineers and one-half company of Pioneers were attached to this brigade, and two batteries American Artillery (8-75's) attached as accompanying artillery. The reserve, consisting of the 354th Infantry (less one battalion) was in a ravine 1 kilometer south of FLIREY, except that three companies held the line of combat groups in the Advance Post Position, facing MORT MARE Wood between the left of the 177th Brigade and the right of the 178th Brigade. The Division Machine Gun Battalion, as part of the reserve, was disposed so as to deliver a barrage on MORT MARE Wood. Half of the machine gun companies of the brigades were likewise disposed to deliver a barrage on selected portions of the woods during the first fifteen minutes of the advance. They later joined their brigades in the advance. One battalion in each brigade was detailed to mop up the forests and prevent interference to the forward movement of troops and trains. These battalions were disposed in depth, placed on the exposed flanks of their respective brigades and instructed to take the enemy by the flank and rear. This form of attack, it was believed, would result in the surrender with less resistance than by a direct frontal attack.

10. Troops were directed to leave pack carriers in dumps, to carry the haversack and two days' reserve rations, their slickers and extra bandoleer of ammunition and ample supply of heavy wire cutters in advancing. Accompanying Engineers were equipped with Bangelor torpedoes and mobile charges.

11. The 314th Engineers (less two companies and with one company of Pioneers) were directed to clear the road over No Man's Land north of FLIREY immediately after passage of the infantry attack, and to make it passable for Artillery. The Pioneers were to be detached at nightfall, September 12th, and formed into burial squads. The further responsibility for this road was assumed by the Corps.

12. The plan of evacuation and supply was carefully prepared and functioned remarkably well, especially when the character of the road from FLIREY north and the depth of the advance of the troops are taken into consideration.

13 The Division P. C. was in the railroad cut north of NOVIANT and moved to FLIREY at 10:00 A.M., September 12th, remaining until 10:00 A.M., September 14th, when it moved to EUVEZIN, at which last point it was continued.

PART. V. OWN CHANGES, MOVEMENTS AND ACTIONS DURING THE OPERATION.

1. The artillery preparation began at 1:00 o'clock, September 12th. H hour was 5:00 o'clock and a few minutes later word was received that the infantry was advancing. The progress of the advance is shown on the map accompanying marked "A." On the right, the 177th Brigade advanced in good order and on schedule time. First Battalion, 353rd Infantry,

detailed to mop up MORT MARE Wood, turned to the flank as directed, mopped up the woods, capturing many prisoners, then reformed and by 11:00 A.M. had rejoined the regiment in position of regimental reserve. The brigade was halted on a line designated as the objective of the first phase, the limit of the independent action of the Division, at 11:00 A.M., rectifying the position by a slight advance where it remained until 4:00 P.M., due to misapprehension of the requirements of the order, the cause of which will be mentioned later. The advance of the 178th Brigade was not so favorable. The right of that brigade maintained the schedule of advance for five hours, the left being slightly retired. The left regiment overtook the right regiment and formed ahead to the line limiting the independent operation of the Division at noon. The right regiment arrived on this line at 3:00 P.M. The mopping up of MORT MARE Wood was successfully accomplished during the advance.

2. Telephonic communication failed with the 177th Brigade early in the action and was never satisfactorily restored. Communication with the 178th Brigade P. C. was maintained by telephone but information received was unsatisfactory in that there was a failure of liaison within the brigade. The Division Commander received fragmentary information from aeroplane reports dropped at the Division P. C., but by 9:00 A.M. it became evident that it would be necessary, in order to control the action, to do so by sending representatives of the Division Commander to the front line and this was done thereafter throughout the day. By this means the general misconception of the plan of action beyond the first phase was discovered and the troops were moved forward onto the day's objective. The first organization notified was the 355th Infantry forming the right regiment of the 178th Brigade. The advance of the Division to the first day's objective was made, therefore, with the center leading and the two flanks retired. The center arrived on the day's objective at 18:00 o'clock, September 12th, the left about 20:00 o'clock, September 12th, and the right at about 1:00 o'clock, September 13th.

3. The 354th Infantry in reserve advanced to BOUILLONVILLE on the night of the 12th and took its place in the line on the morning of the 13th. From the 13th to the 15th instant the troops dug in on the lines occupied. Each regiment had one battalion in the outpost position, which extended from a point about ½ km. in front of the line of resistance on the right to 1½ km. in front of the line of resistance on the left (this disposition was corrected on the night of the 15th-16th by an advance of the outpost line on the right to the new position, approximately 1,200 meters to the north of the line of resistance). P. C. of the 177th Brigade was established at BOUILLONVILLE and the 178th Brigade at BENEY.

PART VI. INFORMATION CONCERNING NEIGHBORING UNITS.

During the advance information was received by aeroplane that the divisions on our right and left were progressing with much greater speed than ours, but nothing could be done in view of our difficult ground, broad front, enforced breaking of liaison and rolling barrage time table.

PART VII. ORDERS RECEIVED DURING OPERATION.

1. Orders were received while the advance was in progress to continue on to the Army Objective originally designated to be captured on the second day.

2. On the night of the 13th and 14th orders were received to determine whether or not the Hindenburg Line was held in force by the enemy.

PART VIII. ACTION DURING THE OPERATION ON ORDERS ISSUED AND RECEIVED.

1. As the advance progressed orders were received to continue on to the Army Objective, which originally was scheduled for capture on the second day. The halt on the first day's objective, therefore, was not very long. By dawn, September 13th, the troops were occupying substantially the Army Objective. The leading elements of the 356th Infantry on the left were approximately 1½ km. North of the Army Objective; the 355th Infantry and 353rd Infantry were approximately on the objective.

2. The orders for determining the strength of the enemy on the Hindenburg Line after the objective was reached, were acted on by sending out patrols. On the night of the 13th orders were received so late that the patrol was barely able to reach the enemy wire, when they were withdrawn in order to avoid being caught under artillery fire in the open by daylight. On the night of the 14th a large patrol was misled due to mistake of a guide and became lost in the darkness, returning in the early dawn without having accomplished its mission. On both occasions machine gun fire indicated the enemy was holding a line of outposts in front of the Hindenburg Line. A request was made to continue the attempts on the night of September 15th, but as the Division on our right had succeeded in developing the Hindenburg Line on the night of the 14th, the reconnoissance was not ordered.

3. On the night of September 30-October 1, we relieved the 42nd Division on our left and on October 4-5 relieved the 78th Division to the east. Our relief by the 37th Division was ordered to be completed by 23:00 hours October 7th, but was not accomplished until 24 hours later, when the Division was assembled in the vicinity of COMMERCY.

4. From this time forward the Division consolidated its positions, constructed shelters from harassing fire and organized positions of resistance. On the 21st of September the 177th Brigade took over the subsector assigned to the 178th Brigade which went into reserve to clean up and rest. The night of September 22-23 the 356th Infantry made a regimental raid on the BOIS de DOMMARTIN. This raid was a success, the woods were cleared of the enemy and prisoners captured. A second regimental raid by the 354th Infantry was made on CHAREY the night of September 25-26. This was part of a general demonstration made all along the line to support the ARGONNE attack by the 1st Army. The raid was heavily supported by artillery and penetrated to CHAREY, although a strong machine gun fire was met.

PART IX. RESULTS OF ACTION, BOTH OWN AND ENEMY.

1. The casualties of this Division were comparatively light, especially if considered in connection with the territory recovered and other results obtained from the action.

	Killed	Wounded	Missing
Officers	14	41	6
Enlisted men	177	892	69

This Division alone captured 2,287 prisoners, practically all of whom belonged to the 10th Division and the 77th Reserve Division. The large number of prisoners captured from these divisions and their casualties rendered them incapable of further immediate service. Enemy killed is estimated as 300. Booty captured was large, including 72 cannon, 95 machine guns,

1,000 rifles and enormous quantities of artillery and small arms ammunition, grenades, clothing and blankets, engineer's stores and other equipment. Several locomotives and a number of railroad cars were taken.

2. It was learned from a document captured subsequent to the action that the enemy had planned a withdrawal. Pursuant to that plan, a large part of its artillery had been withdrawn. But the enemy had timed our advance for September 15th instead of September 12th, so that considerable artillery still remained.

3. The villages of EUVEZIN, BOUILLONVILLE, XAMMES and BENEY were captured by this Division in conjunction with neighboring divisions.

PART X. MAP ILLUSTRATING THE ABOVE.

Map of the operation attached.

PART XI. REMARKS.

1. The 55th Artillery Brigade, which supported the Division during the attack, was relieved three days later. The 250th Field Artillery (French) which accompanied the Division into the sector was relieved 16-17-18 September. Neither of these organizations have submitted report of their operations. Substantially they are as follows: The accompanying artillery of the 177th Infantry Brigade succeeded in getting over the road in time to join that brigade before its advance beyond the first phase. The accompanying artillery of the left brigade was unable to get through in time to give effective support to the brigade to which assigned. Due to the condition of roads the light artillery of the 55th Artillery Brigade did not all reach their positions until the night of the 15th. The tractor drawn French Artillery began to arrive on the 14th and was in position in time to secure the Artillery defense of the sector on the relief of the 55th Artillery Brigade, September 15, 1918.

The rolling barrage is reported by brigade commanders as being exceedingly well executed. Among other orders to the Artillery was one to avoid destruction of any bridges. The density of shell holes in sectors designated as special targets, combined with the fact that no bridge was damaged, is evidence of the accuracy of Artillery fire in this engagement.

2. The traffic congestion over the hastily patched up road leading North from FLIREY was extreme: not only the 89th Division, but a part of the artillery, and Trains of the 2nd and 42nd Divisions were endeavoring to pass over this road. Large numbers of men were at work carrying rock which sunk into the soft mud as the trucks passed over. Had the rain of the 12th continued throughout the 13th the troops would have been without food and ammunition. Fortunately the weather cleared on the 13th, enabling a limited supply to be gotten through that night. An advanced dump was established at BOUILLONVILLE. Excepting for the inadequate preparation for the rebuilding and maintenance of roads and for failures in traffic control the service of supply of the Division operated satisfactorily. The evacuation of the wounded was entirely satisfactory due to the establishment in BOUILLONVILLE of an advance hospital where the wounded could be cared for until the congestion on the roads had somewhat abated.

W. M. WRIGHT,
Major General, U. S. A

HEADQUARTERS
177TH INFANTRY BRIGADE
AMERICAN EXPEDITIONARY FORCES.

September 30, 1918.

REPORT OF OPERATION OF SEPTEMBER 12, 1918.

The 177th Infantry Brigade, as part of the 89th Division, 4th Corps, attacked on September 12th, from the position it then occupied in front of the vicinity of Limey.

The sector assigned to the brigade and its various objectives appear in the Field Orders attached. The tactical situation confronting the Brigade Commander was this:

In his immediate front was the wood of Mort Mare, which was strongly occupied and fortified, and was regarded as one of the key positions of the enemy's line. The brigade consisted of but one regiment and one battalion with some auxiliary elements, the other regiment being in divisional reserve. The objectives assigned were in rear of Mort Mare and carried the attacking forces over the open ground to the East of the same, in which was a high bare ridge, known as Promenade des Moines. Beyond this, in the line of advance, were dense woods, Bois de Euvezin and Bois de Beau Vallon. Two strong points in the open had been occupied as machine gun nests, namely Ansoncourt Farm and Robert Menil Farm. The terrain and the orders under which the attack was made rendered it wholly impracticable to maintain contact with the 178th Brigade until after passing Bois de Mort Mare. The 178th Brigade attacked from our left through the wooded ground known as Bois de Rendu and along the clearance through which ran the roads from Flirey to Essey and Euvezin.

The plan adopted to meet this situation was to flank the position of the enemy in Mort Mare and mop up his trenches from the rear. In considering this plan, it is evident that no one mopping up party could be expected to advance through the entire woods. It was therefore, determined to flank the position with the main forces at the disposal of the Brigade Commander and to mop up Mort Mare with detachments, each of which should turn off at a suitable place as the flank attack progressed.

This plan was embodied in Field Orders of which copies are attached and in the attack was carried out precisely as ordered and with excellent effect.

The attack proceeded with two battalions of the 353rd Infantry advancing over the open ground, 3 companies severally of the 353rd Infantry turning off at the various designated trenches in Bois de Mort Mare, and mopping up from the rear. Large numbers of prisoners and much material were captured, and the resistance of this highly organized position was quickly overcome and little effective fire was directed upon the flanks of the main attack. One company of the 353rd Infantry also operated on the right flank of the attack, effecting combat liaison with the 2nd Division. The objectives assigned to the brigade were each attained on time.

The final objective for the day, as originally ordered, was attained. The conclusion of the 1st phase found the brigade on the banks of the Rupt de Mad, South of Bouillonville, as ordered, and the operation concluded with the troops of this brigade in position on the Army Objective

TROOPS

353rd Infantry—Colonel Jas. H. Reeves, Commanding.
341st Machine Gun Battalion—Major Ernest E. Watson, Commanding.
1st Battalion, 354th Infantry (Brigade Reserve)—Captain Alonzo W. Harlow, Commanding

DETAILS OF ATTACK

2ND BATTALION, 353RD INFANTRY

Commanded by Captain Peatross

The 2nd Battalion of the 353rd Infantry, under Captain Peatross, was in the first wave with Companies "E" and "F" in front, and Companies "G" and "H" in support.

At 4:40 A.M. the battalion moved forward into the valley at the edge of the wire, 150 yards in front of the enemy front line and then followed the barrage. Machine guns were encountered East of Ansoncourt Farm, which were put out of action. In Bois de Mort Mare machine guns were encountered which inflicted losses, including four officers killed and three wounded. At Ansoncourt Farm several bands of wire which had escaped the artillery fire had to be cut before advancing. Advancing into Bois de Euvezin other machine guns were encountered and reduced. Company "E" encountered a number of machine guns in Promenade des Moines and put them out of action.

While advancing through the woods a fairly good formation was kept with the exception that some of the 355th Infantry advancing on our left, overlapped a little once, causing congestion. This, however, was soon adjusted. Contact was maintained at all times with the division on the right.

After cleaning out Bois de Euvezin and taking a large number of prisoners, one of whom was a major, the battalion was reorganized on the North edge of the woods before entering Bois du Beau Vallon where 15 machine guns and 200 prisoners were taken. Sixty-five of these prisoners were taken by one man.

At the North edge of the woods the battalion was again reorganized. At this point the 3rd Battalion passed the lines of the 2nd Battalion with the 2nd Battalion following in support through Bouillonville to objective. Upon arriving at the final objective, patrols were sent out to gather up stragglers.

During the advance one platoon of Company "F" moved too fast, overtaking the barrage and causing slight casualties.

Captain Portman of Company "E" and Captain Atkins of Company "H" were both wounded, but refused to stop. Captain Atkins later received another wound, forcing him out.

3RD BATTALION, 353RD INFANTRY

Commanded by Major Geo. W. Blackinton

The 3rd Battalion of the 353rd Infantry, commanded by Major Geo. W. Blackinton, was late getting into place owing to distance it had to move and the congestion of traffic. It had been in reserve at Minorville and was to move out at H hour from the trench immediately behind the METZ road extending 700 yards West of Limey. It had not come up when the preliminary bombardment started and finally arrived in position about 4:00 A.M. At 4:30 the troops left their position, cutting through the wire, followed the 2nd Battalion with Companies "M" and "L" in the first echelon, supported by Companies "I" and "K." The leading companies were preceded by a skirmish line followed by small columns in artillery formation. The rear companies followed in artillery formation. Up to the time they reached the fourth objective little opposition was encountered. On arrival at the fourth objective several machine guns were encountered and overcome. At this point the companies were reorganized and passed the lines of the 2nd Battalion. At the fifth objective about 200 prisoners were taken after putting out several machine guns. This objective was reached on time. The leading companies pushed forward patrols as far as 1,500 meters beyond objective, capturing a number of prisoners. Flank guards were posted. In Bouillonville about one thousand prisoners were taken. In Bouillonville a large supply of stores were taken, including a complete field hospital with priceless drugs and surgical implements.

At 17:00 o'clock the battalion was ordered to move North. The battalion was then formed with Companies "I" and "K" in front and Companies "L" and "M" in support. Owing to limited time, the battalion moved out without machine gun support.

At 19:00 o'clock the order was received to push to West of Xammes, covering a front of 600 yards Northwest of the town. This was done but upon arriving it was found that there were no troops on either side. These troops arrived the following day. A few prisoners were taken after daylight.

1ST BATTALION, 353RD INFANTRY

Commanded by Captain Clay Crump

The 1st Battalion of the 353rd Infantry, commanded by Captain Clay Crump, was divided. Company "A" acted as the right-flank guard of the regiment. Company "B" acted as the mopping up party for the first wave and cleaned up the South edge of Mort Mare. Company "D" was mopping up party for the second wave, and entered and mopped up the center of Mort Mare, and Company "C" for the third and mopped up the upper portion of Mort Mare and the Western part of Bois de Euvezin.

These companies advanced with their designated wave, stopping at the first, second and third trenches in order. During this cleaning up much hand to hand fighting was done in which a large number of prisoners and machine guns were taken.

The battalion assembled at the North edge of Bois de Euvezin and followed as support to the 3rd Battalion.

When the battalion assembled, the fifth objective had just been reached. Company "B" was sent forward by the Brigade Commander and joined the first wave of the regiment. Company "C" was also sent forward. The other Company "D," and a part of "C," dug in on the hill South of the fifth objective.

When the advance toward the Army Objective was made this battalion advanced in rear of the 3rd Battalion, crossed the Rupt de Mad and halted for two hours about 1½ kilometers West of Thiaucourt, and then moved to the Thiaucourt-Beney Road. The 3rd Battalion had gone ahead. Sometime after midnight the battalion received orders to go ahead in the direction of Xammes and get in touch with the 3rd Battalion. It advanced to and occupied Xammes, which had been so recently evacuated that fires were still burning. The 3rd Battalion had been missed and passed in the darkness. It came up, and the 1st Battalion dug in near Xammes, about 500 meters in rear of the 3rd Battalion.

ONE-POUND CANNON
353rd Infantry

The One-Pound Cannon Platoon of Headquarters Company, 353rd Infantry, under the command of Lieutenant Dahmke left the trenches with the assaulting battalion, proceeded around the East edge of Bois de Mort Mare to Promenade des Moines, where they went into action, firing until the Infantry reached the hill to the left of Bois du Beau Vallon. Proceeding to the hill beyond Bois du Beau Vallon, they fired on a machine gun nest located on the hill Northwest of Bois du Beau Vallon, putting it out of action. At this point they lost connection with the regiment and followed troops of the 42nd Division to the hill Northwest of Bouillonville, where they fired on a number of machine guns, causing them to withdraw, after which they rejoined their regiment West of Thiaucourt.

MACHINE GUN COMPANY
353rd Infantry

The Machine Gun Company of the 353rd Infantry, commanded by 1st Lieutenant E. A Mitchell, advanced with the leading battalion. They encountered enemy machine guns in Bois de Mort Mare, but did not go into action as no target was visible. After reaching Bouillonville several guns were used to snipe retreating Germans. The men carried their guns and ammunition by hand.

A novel method of transporting and firing the gun was devised by Sergt. C. G. Latchem, 353rd Infantry, and successfully used in this attack. The gun was strapped to the back of No. 1 man, muzzle up. When a target was presented, the man laid down, placed his helmet over the back of his head and neck to avoid injury from the flash and the gun was fired from his back. During the advance the gun was covered by a shelter half, making it almost impossible to identify the machine gun as such. Thus the guns kept up with the infantry and got into action in the minimum of time.

STOKES MORTAR PLATOON
353rd Infantry

The Stokes Mortar Platoon, under Lieutenant Leedy, went into action at Bois de Mort Mare putting three machine guns out. After this the mortar was not called on to fire.

SIGNAL PLATOON
353rd Infantry

The Signal Platoon of the Headquarters Company, 353rd Infantry, under Lieutenant Benning, advanced with Regimental Headquarters, but owing to the weight of the equipment, some of the men were compelled to drop behind. The radio set was used with success while on the move. A station was set up in Robert Menil Trench which was used by the Brigade Headquarters for communication to the rear. One carrier pigeon was released after the fifth objective was reached.

FORMATION OF THE INFANTRY

Each Infantry Battalion was distributed in depth, whether in the foremost echelon or in the support. Two companies were in the front echelon of the Battalion, and two in the rear. Each of the two companies in the front of each Battalion advanced with two platoons in front and two in support. The leading platoons were again divided into half platoons, or combat groups, and each combat group was organized into small parties of 4 men each. One party in front, either in column of files or in skirmish line with wide intervals. The 4 men on each flank were about 50 yards to the flanks and 30 yards to the rear, while the remainder of the platoon followed at about 50 yards in the rear of the leading element. The casualties in the groups of 4's were replaced from the remainder of the combat group. This combat group fought as a unit against machine guns; the leading group engaging the gun from the front while the flanking groups moved upon the flanks and attacked the gun from three sides. Each of the 4 groups was under the direct supervision of a Corporal, who remained in its rear; the entire combat group generally being commanded by a Sergeant.

The distance between the two echelons of two companies in each battalion was about 500 meters; the distance between battalions about 1,000 meters.

The advance of the regiment was made through the thick forest of Beau Vallon. This obstacle was passed in good order and the leading battalion emerged from the Northern edge of it in a fairly regular line. At the Northern line of this forest the passage of lines of the two battalions was effected with surprising good order.

The men showed natural aptitude for the work of attacking small points of resistance in small and widely separated groups. One of the most striking and gratifying features of the operation was the coolness and resolution displayed in their orderly and methodical reduction of machine gun positions.

LIAISON

The liaison was not well maintained. The original command post of the Brigade Headquarters had been prepared by the installation of telephone and buzzers and radio. During the preliminary bombardment the telephone was seldom giving good service. The buzzer afforded means of communication part of the time while the telephone was out and the wireless did not work particularly well.

When the troops had taken the first objective, Brigade Headquarters was moved forward as planned to ANSONCOURT FARM. The Signal Corps did not accompany the advance of the headquarters with the detachment and in fact no representative of the Signal Corps was with the Brigade Headquarters from the initial C. P. on. Telephone installation was found at ANSONCOURT FARM which had been set up by the Signal Corps attached to the 3rd Brigade, which was on our right. This phone was reported not to be in working order and no messages were sent over it. Brigade Headquarters then moved to a position in the ROBERT MENIL TRENCH, leaving instructions at the ANSONCOURT FARM to forward any messages to a new location in ROBERT MENIL TRENCH and to communicate the change in location through the 3rd Brigade to our Division when the telephone was established. This message did not get through. As usual, the runner was found to be the only certain means of communication. Many messages were sent and received by runner. Copies are attached.

At the location in the ROBERT MENIL TRENCH at approximately 400 meters Northwest of the ANSONCOURT FARM a wireless station was found which had been set up by the Signal Platoon of the 353rd Infantry. Through this station the message was sent to the rear to bring forward the brigade reserve which was not coming forward as rapidly as advance of the fighting line required. Messages were also sent by runners from this point to the same effect. These messages, however, were by mistake delivered to the divisional reserve.

The liaison with the aircraft was also a failure. The panels indicating the position of the brigade C. P. were in the possession of the Signal Corps and were not displayed because the Signal Corps did not bring them up. Division Aviator reports that, although he signalled repeatedly for the infantry to disclose their positions by the display of panels, he never received this information from it. This is explainable partly to the inexperience of the troops and perhaps also to the fact that the signals for the aviator to communicate with the infantry by pyrotechnics had been changed in the plan of liaison which was not promulgated in time to be communicated to the infantry. The infantry had been ordered to provide itself with panels and flares, but none of these were used; at least not so as to be observed by the aviator.

When the infantry was reorganized after attaining the first day's objective, orders for the new advance were communicated directly to the commanding officers of the troops and the only communication thereafter was by runners

ARTILLERY

The attack was preceded by preparation by artillery for four hours. This preparation was very well executed. No difficulty was experienced in gaining the first line nor in passing through the wire. The machine gun nest at ANSONCOURT FARM, to which the attention of the artillery commander had been especially called, had been so far neutralized by the artillery that it was taken with little loss. Several of the machine guns, however, remained in action and had to be taken by the infantry.

One battery of the Field Artillery assigned to the Brigade had been ordered to go forward between the first echelon and the support. This battery never came up and wholly failed to perform its mission.

The effect of our artillery fire on the enemy's rear and lines of communication was particularly good as became apparent when these positions were entered. In the road between BOUILLONVILLE and THIAUCOURT were many dead men and horses, killed by the artillery which had evidently found the range with accuracy.

The enemy artillery was chiefly 77s. These were used with skill and with excellent liaison with aeroplane. While the troops were being reorganized after attaining the first day's objective, enemy aeroplanes bearing the American insignia flew low over our lines directing artillery fire upon them which was very effective, causing us losses.

The two gas guns assigned to the brigade never reported to the Brigade Commander and if they performed any service it is not known.

BRIGADE INTELLIGENCE SERVICE

During the attack the intelligence section handled a number of messages, coding and decoding them. The majority of the messages, however, were sent in clear, the co-ordinates only being coded.

It was planned that all prisoners should come through Brigade Headquarters, there to be searched and separated into two lots. The Military Police were to take one lot to the Division G-2, the rest to the Division enclosure. During the attack there were no Military Police near Brigade Headquarters. At Robert Menil Trench and in the Bois du Beau Vallon, prisoners were questioned on their way back. South of Bouillonville two groups were carefully questioned.

In the town of Bouillonville searching parties were sent out to gather intelligence material. They collected several hundred maps and documents, a number of pamphlets and several varieties of gas masks. The maps and papers found were hurriedly examined and the most important sent to Division G-2 by special messenger.

A French inhabitant who remained in the city of Bouillonville was questioned and gave some valuable information.

Maps were furnished to a number of officers who did not have them.

In addition to those things, the Intelligence Section performed duties outside of intelligence work.

Notwithstanding the fact that the objectives were uniformly attained, and the operation and its results were entirely successful, it remains to be noted that in many particulars serious defects existed, which might have caused great damage and which should be and will be corrected in further operations. First was the general lack of certainty of knowledge of the final plans which prevailed throughout the brigade from its commander down to its last platoon leader. This was due entirely to the lack of time afforded for preparation for the attack. The Field Order from which the attack was made was not received in its final form until late in the day of September 11th, and copies for the regimental commanders were not received until some of the troops were actually on their way to take station. Important changes were made in the final order from the provisions of drafts which had previously been furnished, notably in the assignment of the Corps Objective for the day. It is also a fact that the brigade commander was not informed that he was expected to proceed to the position West of Xammes, until nearly 6:00 o'clock in the evening. The voluminous order which commanded important changes had not been received until too late for the arrangement of the many details of the evening before. The artillery plan, the plan of liaison, the plan of communications, all of them elaborate and voluminous documents, were not received in their entirety at the brigade in time even to be read by the brigade commander or his adjutant before the movement was commenced.

Not nearly sufficient numbers of maps were supplied or distributed for the use of regimental, company and platoon commanders, and practically every platoon and many company commanders went into the action without any maps at all

The Commanding Officer, 113th Field Artillery, had agreed to send forward some guns with the assaulting echelon to be used for direct fire on machine gun nests and such targets as might be presented. This battery never came up.

The Signal Corps Detachment attached to the brigade failed to maintain contact with the Brigade Commander throughout the engagement and did not join the headquarters of the brigade until the following day in Bouillonville, and no messages whatever were transmitted through the Signal Corps from the time the Brigade Commander left the jumping off place until the engagement was entirely over.

Combat liaison was maintained with the 2nd Division throughout the engagement by the company especially assigned to that duty. The duty of maintaining combat liaison between the 178th Brigade and this brigade was by the Division order assigned to the 178th Brigade. No such contact was maintained. It was not until late on the morning of September 13th that actual contact, of the lines before the enemy, between the 177th Brigade and the 178th Brigade was established.

Company B of the 341st Machine Gun Battalion, which was ordered to join the 3rd Battalion, 353rd Infantry, in the attack, never came up and did not participate in the engagement of the battalion until that battalion had attained the fifth objective and had been there some time. This failure is to be ascribed in part to the fact that too many missions were assigned to the machine gun companies. The company had been expected to join in the barrage and then to overtake the infantry. It is believed that it would have been better to assign it to the infantry alone or to the barrage alone, and that the assignment of two missions made the task of this machine gun company too great.

Two gas guns which were assigned to the brigade for use never reported and so far as known did not participate in the engagement.

Contact through the aeroplane service was practically nil and the infantry ignored the signals of the aeroplane to display panels. Brigade Headquarters panel was not displayed because of the failure of the Signal Corps Detachment to keep up and display it.

In brief, the engagement was successfully fought by the brigade as an infantry engagement with artillery support, and the enemy resistance was overcome with the infantry weapons, the rifle and machine gun. Substantially every auxiliary weapon and every auxiliary service failed.

Attached hereto are Field Orders No. 12, 89th Division, under which the attack was made, Field Order No. 1, Headquarters 177th Infantry Brigade, dated September 10, 1918, copies of the messages sent and received at Brigade Headquarters, and a map showing the positions of the various battalions at the different phases of the advance.

FRANK L. WINN,
Brigadier General, U. S. A., Commanding.

HEADQUARTERS 178TH INFANTRY BRIGADE
AMERICAN EXPEDITIONARY FORCES
REPORT ON ST. MIHIEL OFFENSIVE

18 September, 1918.

NOTE—Lettering of paragraphs is that used in Memo. of Chief of Staff, IV Corps, September 11, 1918.

A. The operation of the 178th Brigade, beginning at 5:00 A. M., September 12, 1918, consisted in a direct frontal attack on strongly entrenched positions of the enemy. Liaison with the 42nd Division on the left of our Brigade was impracticable during the first stages and all stages of the assault. No direct frontal assault was contemplated by the 177th Brigade on our right on that portion of MORT MARE Woods between the eastern Brigade boundary and the 353rd Infantry. No liaison with the 177th Brigade was possible. In order to meet this condition the 2nd Battalion 355th Infantry (in reality the Regimental support), had for its mission capture by flank attack of BOYAU de FAUNES, protection of the right flank of the Brigade and Divisional line of communication, mopping up the BOIS de MORT MARE, reëstablishment of liaison with the 177th Brigade, all to be performed during the uninterrupted advance of the attack proper. This enterprise was successful, and a large number of enemy prisoners captured by this force.

B. Terrain. Dense woods, cut up by our barrage. Much barbed wire, through which necessary lanes had been blasted by our artillery fire.

C. Initial Dispositions. Regiments side by side, each disposed in depth. On the right the 355th Infantry; one battalion in front line disposed in depth; support battalion—mission described in paragraph A above. Real support was the 1st Battalion, plus one machine gun company, 342nd Machine Gun Battalion. On the left the 356th Infantry, disposed as in the 355th Infantry. Support one battalion, plus one company, 342nd Machine Gun Battalion. Brigade reserve consisted of one battalion 356th Infantry and 342nd Machine Gun Battalion (less three companies). One regiment of Field Artillery (American) (less one battalion); one battalion Field Artillery assigned to the Brigade as advance artillery and as Infantry battery. Due to the rapid advance of the battalions, this artillery never caught up and mission was accomplished without it.

To each leading battalion was assigned one squad of engineers, plus one squad of pioneers, to each platoon of infantry in front line for wire cutting and removal of obstacles. Remaining engineers disposed for road work.

D. Stability of Formation adopted in light of subsequent events. In my opinion, the artillery barrage was so skillfully executed and the resistance so lacking in vigor, no real tests of our dispositions were obtained.

E. The attack was so conducted by each regimental commander and each battalion commander who came in contact with the enemy that changing conditions of combat and terrain were in turn met and overcome in an entirely creditable manner.

F. Various infantry weapons were handled by all commanders in an effective and skillful manner. Their handling varied in the regiments. In the 355th Infantry Stokes mortar and one-pounder appear to have been unnecessary. For varying details on these points I call attention to reports of Colonels Nuttman and Taylor.

G. Artillery Support. This appears to me to have left nothing to be desired—skillful and effective. Use of accompanying guns untested; they never took part. In my opinion all guns used in the barrage could not have ceased firing in time to join in the rapid and uncontested advance. I foresaw and predicted this result.

H. Passage of Obstacles.

I. Passage of Lines. In the 356th Infantry none took place. For reasons given by Colonel Nuttman none was necessary. In the 355th, passage of the lines was successfully and skillfully performed with the halting of the 3rd Battalion at edge of the woods and passing through of the 1st Battalion (2nd Battalion being engaged on the right flank as already described.) For details of these operations reference is made to Colonel Taylor's report.

J. Machine gun nests, etc. These appear to have been few in number, generally outflanked by automatic rifles, occupants killed or captured in considerable numbers, with small resistance. Particular reference is made to Colonel Taylor's report. My conclusion is that we could learn little from our experiences along this line, since resistance was lacking in spirit and morale.

K. Fighting in Intermediate Zone. Reference is again made to each Colonel's report. No real test of capacity of all subordinate commanders was experienced. Cohesion between our units appears to have been deficient. Individual efforts and results obtained. Our troops and their officers lack still the experience of the game by prevailing over the most stubborn resistance.

L. The Organization and Holding of Conquered Ground. Accomplished temporarily in good order. Still in operation. Strong points being organized in line of observation, disposed in depth. Small pits, accommodating two or three men, dug and occupied. These pits subsequently connected by deeper and longer trenches Particular reference is made to remarks of Colonel Taylor on this subject.

M. Liaison. During the engagement September 12 liaison practically did not exist. Telephone lines could not keep up with regiments. Brigade Headquarters reached EUVEZIN ahead of the wire. With the 356th Infantry runner service was continued, but had no effect on the outcome of the day. By the time a message was received from Regimental Headquarters and reply or order from the Brigade Commander got back to the regiment, conditions had differed and the order was not applicable. One pigeon was sent to me but failed to arrive.

GENERAL REMARKS

A summary of my views, aside from a statement of the facts, would be largely quotations from reports of my two Colonels. The most noticeable thing to avoid in the future is described in the following words of Colonel Nuttman's report; they include what I consider the greatest drawback and obstacle which was encountered in my Brigade:

"At the beginning of the operation the 89th Division held the line of the entire Corps. It was relieved by battalions at different times and these battalions moved by the flank and took their assault positions. Battalion of the 356th Infantry relieved by the 1st Division could not get away from RAMBOUCOURT until 1:00 A. M., after the barrage had started. I consider this to be an exceedingly complicated battle maneuver for experienced troops."

THOMAS G. HANSON,
Brigadier General, Commanding.

FIELD ORDERS

89th Division, France,
9 September 1918

SECRET
Field Orders
No. 12

MAPS: MORT MARE, CHAMBLEY 5-6 } 1:20,000
COMMERCY 1:80,000

I. A. (1) For the situation regarding the enemy see data from VIIIth Army already issued by G-2, and daily intelligence reports.

(2) For the estimate of the terrain see terrain study already furnished by G-2.

B. The Fourth Army Corps is to attack along the front RICHECOURT (355x233) ANSAUCOURT FARM (364.55x235.3) (1 4/5 km. N. W. of LIMEY) with the 1st, 42nd and 89th Divisions in the line from West to East, and the 3rd Division in central reserve. The 2nd Division of the 1st American Army Corps is to attack on our right.

C. The Corps objectives to be gained are:
First attack: 1st phase (first day), to pierce the enemy's outpost position, breaking through his position of resistance and seizing the line:
S. point ETANG LAMBEPINOT (355x236) (3 km. N. of RICHECOURT);
N. edge BOIS RATE (356x236) (3⅓ km. N. of RICHECOURT);
POINT (358.8x237.8) (1⅓ km. N. of ESSEY on ESSEY-PANNES Road);
R. R. CROSSING (359.9x238.5) (On PANNES-EUVEZIN Road);
Bend of River (361.7x238.9) (1¼ km. S. W. of BOUILLONVILLE);
Head of Ravine (363.5x239.5) (1⅓ km. S. of THIAUCOURT) (liaison with 2nd Division).
This attack will start on D day at H hour.

2nd phase: The general advance against the line:
E. edge ETANG LAMBEPINOT (355x236);
ROAD at edge of woods (354.9x237.3);
NONSARD (exclusive) (355x238);
1 km. N. W. of PANNES on BENEY-PANNES Road (359.1x240.05);
CROSSROADS (361.5x240.9) (½ km. N. of THIAUCOURT).
XAMMES-THIAUCOURT ROAD at (362.8x242.05) (1 km. N. of THIAUCOURT);
ROAD FORK (363.2x242.2) (1 km. N. of THIAUCOURT);
This attack will start from the objective of the first phase at H plus 6 hours. A delay of one hour may be ordered by the Corps.

(Second day). (1) On the second day it is expected that the corps axis of effort will be towards ST. BENOIT (357x244) and VIGNEULLES (351x244), the right division extending the front through BOIS DAMPVITOUX (360x245) XAMMES (362x243) to the 1st Corps, and the left division extending the front along the western edge of BOIS VIGNEULLES (3 km. S. E. of VIGNEULLES), BOIS BELLE OZEIRE (3 km. E. of HEUDICOURT) to 2nd C. A. C. (French).

(2) The Army Corps may order this advance on the first day.

(3) Thereafter the Army may direct an advance to the general line:

VIEVILLE (350x246) (inclusive);
HATTONVILLE (352x245) (inclusive);
N. edge BOIS CHAUFOUR (355x245);
Chateau ST. BENOIT (357.4x245) (200 meters N. of ST. BENOIT);
Center of BOIS DAMPVITOUX (360x245) (2.5 km. E. of ST. BENOIT);
XAMMES (362x243) (inclusive).

This line is known as the Army Objective.

D. The advance will be a frontal attack with each division pushing forward to the first objective (ETANG LAMBEPINOT-BOIS d'HEICHE) (365x240) without waiting for the adjacent divisions.

E. **Strong reconnaissance** will be pushed out by front line divisions from the objective of the second phase, first day, and from the second day's objective. Upon reaching the Army Objective strong detachments will be sent out towards the Exploitation Line.

II. A. This Division will attack in the general direction DAMPVITOUX, supporting the advance of the 42nd Division on our left by exerting the **main effort on the left** to include the RUPT de MAD, thence assist the advance of the 2nd Division, 1st Corps, by turning the BOIS d'EUVEZIN, BOIS BEAU VALLON, and THIAUCOURT from the west. By the capture of the east edges of the BOIS MORT MARE this Division will assist the initial advance of the 2nd Division, 1st Corps. If the 2nd Division is delayed, the 89th Division will capture THIAUCOURT and turn it over to the 2nd Division.

B. The zone of operations of this Division:

Eastern Boundary:

BOUVRON (inclusive).
MINORVILLE (inclusive).
NOVIANT (inclusive).
Unimproved road extending North from LIMEY to center of BOIS d'EUVEZIN (inclusive).
HILL 261 (1:80,000) or Point 362.7x238.8 (1:20,000) (exclusive).
THIAUCOURT (363x241) (exclusive).
XAMMES (362x243) (inclusive).
CHAREY (364x246) (exclusive).

Western Boundary:

LAGNEY (inclusive).
SANZEY (inclusive).
ANSAUVILLE (exclusive).
POINT 360.45x233.00—400 meters W. of R. R. at Salient RENARD.
POINT 360.45x266.85 (about 1 km. S. W. of EUVEZIN).
BENEY (360x242) (inclusive).
POINT 358.65x244.60 (N. W. tip of BOIS de DAMPVITOUX).

C. The attack will be made with two brigades in line. The Divisional Infantry Reserve will consist of one regiment of the 177th Brigade (less 1 battalion).

* * * * * * * * * * *

III. A. (1) The boundary line between brigades will be:

BERNECOURT (to the left brigade).
BERNECOURT-FLIREY Road (to the left brigade).
SALIENT 1737 (to the left brigade).
BOY des FAUNES to Point 1447 (to right brigade).
CROSSROADS 250.2 (361.5x242.3) (to the left brigade).

* * * * * * * * * * *

V. LIAISON.

A. (1) Combat flank liaison between all advancing troops is vital. Commanders will be held individually responsible for maintaining it. The only exception in this operation is the BOIS MORT MARE between the 178th and 177th Brigades. In all other cases during the operation flank liaison will be considered of importance second only to contact with the enemy.

(2) Combat liaison for our left flank is to be provided by 42nd Division.

* * * * * * * * * * *

(4) Combat liaison on our right flank will be furnished by the right brigade, and will consist of detachments advancing by bounds, each detachment to consist of at least one Infantry company, supported by one platoon of machine guns.

* * * * * * * * * * *

WRIGHT.
Commanding.

F. O. DISTRIBUTION.

SECRET
Field Orders
No. 16

89th Division, France.
12 September 1918.

MAPS: CHAMBLEY 5-6 / MORT MARE } 1:20,000

I. A. (1) The enemy has been driven beyond the first day's objective. Hostile forces of the enemy are reported in the vicinity of DAMPVITOUX and also advancing from the west to east from SPADA to VIGNEULLES and along the TRANCHES DE CAZONNE Road towards VIGNEULLES.

(2) Aviator at 6:00 P. M reports enemy on line:

BOIS CHAREY;
CROSSROADS 220.3;
MONT PLAISIR FARM;

B. The IV. Corps is to advance to the first phase, second day, but each Division is required to assure the defense of the first day's objective.

II. This Division will immediately advance to the line:

XAMMES (incl.) on the East (liaison with the 2nd Division);
BOIS DAMPVITOUX and BOIS BENEY (both incl.) on the west (liaison with 42nd Division).

III. A. Brigades will take position side by side. Division between Brigades to be adjusted by Brigade Commanders on the ground in consultation with the Chief of Staff.

B. Organization of the Ground will conform to instructions already issued in Field Orders No. 12.

C. (1) Supporting artillery will be moved forward with all speed possible, under direction of the C. O. Divisional Artillery. He will arrange supply of ammunition.

(2) Division Engineer will push forward entrenching tools as soon as they can be released from road work.

(3) Division Engineer, in co-operation with the Corps Engineer, will keep open the road FLIREY-ESSEY, as well as the Division axis road.

(4) Until further orders no trucks will be permitted over the FLIREY-ESSEY road except by specific permission in writing by the Division Commander in each case.

(5) The Division Munitions Officer will send forward combat trains (to include small arms ammunition, pyrotechnics and grenades), second in priority to the Artillery.

IV. The command must be subsisted on its present ration supply until further orders. Field and ration trains will not be sent forward until directed from these Headquarters.

V. Division P. C. and Message Center near R. R. bridge, FLIREY.
Advance Information Center, EUVEZIN.
P. C. 177th Brigade, MAUCHE ANCIEN MOULIN (364.4x239.7).
P. C. 178th Brigade, EUVEZIN.

WRIGHT,
Commanding.

OFFICIAL:
JOHN C. H. LEE,
Colonel, General Staff, G-3.
F. O. DISTRIBUTION.

THE MEUSE-ARGONNE OFFENSIVE
HEADQUARTERS
89TH DIVISION
AMERICAN EXPEDITIONARY FORCES
FRANCE

11 November, 1918.

From: Commanding General.
To: Commander in Chief, American E. F.
Subject: Report on Operations October 19, 1918, to November 11, 1918, inclusive.

PART I. SITUATION AT THE BEGINNING OF THE OPERATION.

The 89th Division, having fought through the ST. MIHIEL Operation as a first line division, organized the FLIREY Sector and took over the PANNES Sector from the 42nd Division, and the LIMEY Sector from the 78th American Division.

The 89th Division was relieved in the PANNES-FLIREY-LIMEY Sector by the 37th American Division on 9 October, 1918. The relief was accomplished without special event other than a delay of twenty-four hours caused by the fatigued condition of the relieving division. The 89th Division was thereupon assembled in the area Northeast of COMMERCY and then moved by bus to the RECICOURT area, becoming attached to the III. Corps as reserve of the First Army. This move was rapid. The French transportation was inadequate for bringing up all the necessary equipment and unsatisfactory in that the French train commanders arbitrarily parked at points other than the pre-arranged debussing places. It was several days before the Division could collect up all its rolling kitchens and other essential equipment. The animal drawn transportation arrived by long marches in good condition.

The Division went into bivouac and billets until 14 October, special care being given to completion of equipment, training preparations for active operations and open warfare, with every practical precaution for concealment. The Division Commander held conferences with his Operations Staff, Brigade and Regimental Commanders, upon tactical dispositions and control. A special effort was made to get the men bathed and in this the Division was generally successful.

On 13 October the Division marched through mud and wet weather to bivouac in the MONTFAUCON Woods and on the following day continued the march to the EPINONVILLE area in rear of the 32nd American Division.

A. Estimate of the Enemy.

When, on 19 October, 1918, the 89th Division relieved the 32nd American Division, the enemy order of battle opposite the Division from East to West was reported as follows:

123rd Division, SAXON, 3rd Class.
13th Division, WESTPHALIAN, 1st Class.
3rd Guard Division, PRUSSIA and ALSACE-LORRAINE, 1st Class.
41st Division, WEST PRUSSIAN, 2nd Class.
27th Division, WEST PRUSSIAN, 2nd Class.

The enemy's line was held by both light and heavy machine gun outposts, with Infantry filling the gaps. The ordinary line of outposts in advance of the machine guns had generally been dispensed with. The interval between the machine gun posts varied from 20 to 50 meters.

Behind this formation the enemy's Infantry and Artillery were echeloned in depth. Some light field pieces had been pushed well to the front to support the machine guns and for use against tanks.

The enemy had no rested divisions in reserve.

The 13th German Division had been holding the sector opposite by its line of outposts, strongly defended by machine guns, placed in the neighborhood of LA DHUY FERME and small woods North of the BOIS de BANTHEVILLE. The indications were that the enemy considered this front vital to his entire line and intended to hold it to the last. It developed in the attack that the 13th Division was relieved by the 88th Division on the night 29-30 October, and placed in support.

The 89th Division had been informed that the BOIS de BANTHEVILLE had been cleared of the enemy and that all that was necessary in order to completely hold these woods was to mop them up. It was found that these woods were held in force and that the mission assigned was not one of mopping up, but was virtually an advance against strong, stubborn resistance.

From 19 October, 1918, to 1 November, 1918, the enemy's situation changed from the above to the following, so that on 1 November, 1918, the enemy front line opposite the sector of this Division in general followed the BANTHEVILLE-LANDRES-ET-ST. GEORGES Road from 06-89.9 to the LA DHUY FERME at 04.4-88.4, thence it ran in a Southerly direction in front of the Southern edge of the BOIS des HAZOIS to the Western boundary of the sector of this Division at 02.8-87.8.

On 1 November, 1918, the enemy order of battle from East to West was as follows:
109th Regiment, 28th Division, BADEN, 2nd Class.
426th Regiment, 88th Division, WEST PRUSSIAN and SILESIAN, 3rd Class.
353rd Regiment, 88th Division, WEST PRUSSIAN and SILESIAN, 3rd Class.
170th Regiment, 52nd Division, BADEN, 2nd Class.

The 109th Regiment and the 426th Regiment were in contact in the BOIS de ANDEVANNE. The 426th Regiment and the 353rd Regiment were in contact East of LA DHUY FERME. The 353rd Regiment and the 170th Regiment were in contact to the West of LA DHUY FERME. As to the reserve, the 55th Regiment, 13th Division, seems to have been in reserve, to the 109th Regiment, 28th Division. It lay to the rear of the 109th Regiment in the BOIS de ANDEVANNE. The 352nd Regiment, 88th Division, was in reserve of the 426th Regiment, and the 353rd Regiment of the same division. It lay in the BOIS de BARRICOURT

The enemy's dispositions contained no entrenched or wired positions. There was an outpost line in which at intervals of about 20 to 50 meters machine guns were stationed. At certain points there was another line of guns back of this outpost line. Each machine gun location was marked by a fox hole shelter. The line of resistance of the enemy was reenforced by machine guns carefully placed to enfilade the roads and terrain, affording a good field of fire. These machine guns were usually heavy machine guns and were manned by especially trained personnel, they being in general the personnel of machine gun companies who were attached to the Army and were known as Army Troops. The infantry, as indicated by the order of battle, was well echeloned in depth.

During the period 22 October, 1918, to 1 November, 1918 (after the BOIS de BANTHEVILLE had been cleared of the enemy), the enemy defense consisted largely of stationary warfare, the Artillery being echeloned in great depth. However, some light artillery pieces were located close to our lines in order, if possible, to break up an attack of Infantry and tanks.

On 1 November, 1918, at the time of the drive, there is no question but that the morale of the German troops as a whole had fallen. However, the troops opposite this sector were rated highly in the German Army. While there were replacements of older men who had been doing garrison and frontier guard duty, and also from the 1919 class, the greater proportion of the German troops opposite this Division were young, vigorous, aggressive soldiers.

B. SITUATION OF OUR OWN TROOPS.

On 14 October the 89th Division bivouaced near EPINONVILLE under the orders of the Vth American Corps, Major-General C. P. Summerall, Commanding.

General Pershing, Commander in Chief, visited the Division P. C. at EPINONVILLE and cautioned the Division Commander particularly as to the necessity for control and for taking advantage of American experience in recent operations. The Corps Commander made daily visits to the Division, often speaking directly to the officers and men. The Division Commander, by personally speaking to the officers formally or informally, by addressing the noncommissioned officers of the various organizations, and by talking with the men, explained the outline, principles and reasons involved in his orders and appealed to their loyalty for control.

The weather during the bivouac at EPINONVILLE was generally good until just before the Division went into the line. The five days' respite gave time to complete the essential parts of the equipment, to rest the men, brush up on training and crystallize control. Thorough reconnaissances were made forward with the view of taking over the sector of the 32nd American Division.

Anticipating orders to relieve the 32nd American Division and continue the advance, the Division Commander, in compliance with the expressed opinion and wish of the Corps Commander, planned to put in his brigades side by side, with four regiments in line, each in column of battalions, giving each brigade commander one battalion as brigade reserve, and holding out two battalions as Divisional Reserve This disposition the Corps Commander had found most effective in attack. A machine gun company was to be attached to each Infantry battalion.

While in reserve in the EPINONVILLE area, the Division was disposed relatively in line to correspond to the formation outlined above.

At this time the Division had no Artillery. The 164th Field Artillery Brigade was left in the PANNES-FLIREY-LIMEY Sector attached to the 37th American Division. The Division Commander made repeated requests for the return of this Artillery Brigade with the view of establishing closer liaison between the Infantry and Artillery. Unfortunately, the Army was unable to comply with this request.

During the period at EPINONVILLE the Divisional Engineers were used on road work under the Corps Engineer. Profiting by the experience in the ST. MIHIEL offensive, the Division Commander decided to use his Engineers during the impending offensive almost entirely on communications.

Orders were received from Vth Corps (F. O. 82) during the afternoon 19 October to relieve the 32nd American Division, less its Artillery, which was to remain in support of the 89th Division. The troops in the Division had been ready for over twenty-four hours to march at an hour's notice. Reconnaissances had been made both as to routes of advance and dispositions of the 32nd American Division. Division Field Orders No. 33 divided the sector to be taken over into two sub-sectors, and directed each Infantry Brigade (less one battalion) to relieve the elements of the 32nd American Division in a sub-sector. A straight relief of brigades by organizations was impracticable because of the intermingled dispositions existing at the time in the 32nd Division. The details of the relief were arranged between the brigade commanders concerned, and command was passed by telephone with the Commanding General, 32nd American Division, when the relief of the brigades was reported on the morning 20 October.

The relief was accomplished without particular event. The 57th Field Artillery Brigade remained in position in the sector and passed under the command of the 89th Division Commander.

Major General W. G. Haan, Commanding the 32nd Division, wrote a commendatory letter on the manner in which this Division effected the relief of his troops.

The Division thus held the line extending from the vicinity of LA CAVANIERE, 3 kilometers Northwest from ROMAGNE, where liaison was had with the 42nd American Division, holding the COTE de CHATILLON; thence the line extended through the BOIS de BANTHEVILLE and included ROMAGNE, as shown on the attached map.

The 5th American Division of the III. Corps was on the right and was in liaison with our right elements near ROMAGNE.

In accordance with orders received from the Vth Corps (F. O. 83), the 89th Division issued instructions in Field Orders No. 34 to make preparations for advance, to develop the enemy's main line of resistance, and to mop up the BOIS de BANTHEVILLE during the day of 20 October. Taping and outlining of trenches of the position of resistance was ordered. Systematic Artillery bombardment was continued.

The mopping up of the BOIS de BANTHEVILLE proved to be quite an operation in itself, as the enemy defended his position with Artillery and machine guns, and put up a stubborn resistance until the afternoon of October 31st (22nd?). After this hour only a few straggling elements of the enemy, occasionally machine guns, were encountered.

The afternoon of October 20th orders were received from the Vth Army Corps (F. O. 84) for the attack of the line BOIS de HAZOIS-COTE 253. General instructions from the First Army required that the attack be made by one brigade, with the second brigade in reserve. In preparation for this, Field Orders No. 35 were issued directing the 177th Brigade to take over the entire front, placing the 178th Brigade, with the Divisional Machine Gun Battalion, in Divisional reserve. This relief was finally accomplished, after midnight October 21st-22nd. The enemy's scattered stragglers and occasional machine gunners in the BOIS de BANTHEVILLE, and his persistent gas shelling through the East central part of the woods, impeded the operation of the relief. One battalion commander, 177th Brigade, who unnecessarily delayed this operation was relieved from command and sent to the rear for reclassification.

On the 21st of October instructions were received from the Corps, by telephone, to adjust the boundary line with the 42nd American Division. This was accomplished through Field Orders No. 37, by the leading brigade of this Division taking over, on the night of October 21st-22nd, the front as far as the TUILERIE FERME from the 168th Infantry, 84th Brigade, 42nd Division.

During the 21st, 22nd, 23rd and 24th of October, the Division remained in possession of the BOIS de BANTHEVILLE, maintaining contact with the enemy and continuing preparations for advance in accordance with Field Orders No. 84, Vth Corps, and Field Orders No. 38, these Headquarters.

October 24th, new orders were received from the Corps (F. O. 90), directing a deeper attack, to include the heights of BARRICOURT and an exploitation line as far as NOUART-TAILLY. This order gave the 89th Division the mission of clearing the BOIS des HAZOIS as part of its first objective, then proceeding through REMONVILLE to take the wooded heights of BARRICOURT and exploit to the NOUART-TAILLY line. Our reconnaissances had developed the fact that the BOIS des HAZOIS was strongly held. Its position formed a serious menace to the attack, not only of this Division, but also of the Division on our left. The Division Commander, therefore, designated it as a separate mission and assigned it to a battalion of the reserve brigade, giving the leading brigade commander the mission of driving his attack through the heights of BARRICOURT, which were to be taken at all costs. It was recognized that once the enemy was driven from the heights of BARRICOURT, thus giving us the advantage of observation, he could probably be driven from beyond the MEUSE.

This plan was approved by the Corps Commander, but in the adjustment of the Corps plans a change was made, giving the BOIS des HAZOIS mission to the 2nd Division on our left. Three orders in all were issued for the attack—each in accordance with a change in plan. However, the changes were minor ones and no confusion resulted.

As shown in Field Orders No. 45, the 89th Division had finally at its disposal its entire Infantry, machine gun and Engineer strength, with 57th Field Artillery Brigade, 58th Field Artillery Brigade and certain attached French and Corps Artillery.

The plan of attack was based on a short and violent Artillery preparation of two hours, following a continuous harassing fire for several days. At "H" hour a very heavy barrage was planned, to give a high explosive rolling barrage of almost twice the usual density, together with a rolling barrage of shrapnel 75s, and a jumping barrage on successive targets by remaining 75s, 105s, 155s and 8-inch howitzers. To this barrage was added a rolling barrage of machine gun fire, sweeping the enemy's terrain 500 meters in advance of the Infantry as far as the first objective. The Infantry Stokes Mortars of the reserve brigade and the detachment of Gas and Flame Troops were placed under the orders of the Artillery Brigade Commander, in conjunction with his Trench Mortar batteries, during the preliminary bombardment. Two machine gun companies of the leading brigades assigned to join later the reserve Infantry battalions thereof, also the machine gun companies of the Divisional reserve and the one-pounder platoons of that brigade, were placed under the orders of the Division Machine Gun Officer for use during the preliminary bombardment and for covering the advance of the Infantry as far as the first objective.

Instructions to the Infantry were to follow the barrage as close as 50 meters, if practicable, and to drive straight through to their objectives.

To each assault and support battalion was assigned one machine gun company, which jumped off with it. To each assault battalion was also assigned two accompanying guns, 75s, which were to open fire upon order of the Infantry commander and to follow him.

The barrage table was adjusted and regulated by the Corps Artillery Commander. The adjustment with the III. Corps on our right necessitated an intermediate objective. Furthermore, the fact that our jump off line was well in advance of that of the 2nd Division on our left made it desirable to have an intermediate objective on which our left assault battalion could wait for the 2nd Division to come up and enter the BOIS des HAZOIS.

Accordingly, this intermediate objective, as shown on the attached map, ran from the Southern edge of the clearing in BOIS d'ANDEVANNE (800 meters North of the BOIS de BANTHEVILLE), through the small woods near Point 253 and beyond the LA DHUY FERME. The first objective included Hill 300 in the Southern point of BOIS d'ANDEVANNE, the fringe of woods to the Southwest, including the LA BERGERIE FERME and CROSS ROADS 257. The second objective included the Southern nose of the BARRICOURT heights and the Southern edge of the woods. The third objective included the BOIS de BARRICOURT from TUILERIE FERME to the Hill called LA FOLARDE, overlooking BARRICOURT. These objectives, together with the Divisional boundaries, are shown on the attached map.

The Division Commander gave the matter of battle liaison with the 90th Division special care and attention. It was realized that although the taking of the Hill 300 was absolutely essential to the advance of the 90th Division, it was also necessary for this Division's unimpeded advance. The taking of the Hill was by order of the Army, a divided mission. Detailed arrangements were made for initial liaison with the 90th Division and its maintenance throughout the action. Battle liaison with the 2nd Division was made in compliance with Corps orders, becoming secure near the Camp Aviation North of the BOIS des HAZOIS.

No developed and wire position was known to exist in our front, and the few aeroplane photographs available failed to show the development, by wiring, of the so-called STELLUNG, reported and shown on captured maps to be in the vicinity of REMONVILLE. Accordingly, the only provisions made for passing the wire were to equip the Infantry to the fullest extent possible with heavy wire cutters, believing that any enemy wire would be of hasty and light character. The Engineers were accordingly assigned only to the opening and maintenance of communication, with particular regard to the getting forward of Artillery and ammunition.

The lessons gained in the ST. MIHIEL drive were especially considered. Every available route was reconnoitered and the work pressed night and day. Use of the road through LANDRES-ST. GEORGE was closed to this Division. The taking of the town of BANTHEVILLE by the 90th Division opened the possibility of the use of the BANTHEVILLE-REMONVILLE road, once the enemy was driven from the BOIS d'ANDEVANNE. However, reliance was not placed on this route, and the Engineers proceeded with the vigorous development of the Engineer Road.

The Engineer Road ran from the Road fork on the ROMAGNE-SOMMERANGE Road near Point 05.7x84.8 Northwest, following the general line of the clearing and the valley to the ST. GEORGES-LA DHUY FERME Road. This road was worked as far North as enemy observation and fire would permit. At night this meant as far as the railroad cut in the Northern part of Square 46. Further work was done by the Engineers to open up the road through BANTHEVILLE and due North through the BOIS de BANTHEVILLE. The result was that, due to the energy of the Engineers and fortunate fair weather, the Engineer Road was completed and served for horse-drawn transportation and light motor vehicles by 10:00 hours of the morning of "D" day. Moreover, animal drawn transportation came back through the Northern road.

A rigid system of priority, as explained in the G-1 order, was laid down and approved by the Corps, guaranteeing that only animal-drawn transportation would be permitted over the roads concerning which there was any question of maintenance. Restrictions were placed even on staff cars and motor ambulances. Definite limits were given to all trucks beyond which they could not pass until the Corps Engineer was satisfied that the roads would stand the traffic.

Based on this plan and coordinated with it, was planned the advance of the Artillery of the 58th Brigade, which was to be displaced, by battalions, and moved forward so as to cover the advance of the Infantry beyond the Third Objective.

The evacuation plan contemplated the use of the Engineer Road and the road through the Northern part of the BOIS de BANTHEVILLE as a one-way and animal drawn circuit, with an advanced dressing station and transfer point for motor vehicles just West of BANTHEVILLE.

The Division Engineers opened the old German 60 centimeter railroad from CIERGES North to ROMAGNE and prepared to advance it to the BOIS des HAZOIS. All available material was collected in order to push this work forward rapidly. Salvaged German rolling stock was employed on this line before the Army Engineers connected up North of MONTFAUCON.

The Division was well equipped and supplied. In addition to his regular equipment, each infantry soldier was required to carry two bandoleers of small arms ammunition, one automatic rifle clip or the equivalent number of cartridges, two hand grenades and two rifle grenades, and one white panel. Packs of the assaulting troops were left under guard and each man went forward with only a slicker for protection. Due to extra effort on the part of the supply service and especial attention and close supervision of organization commanders, all troops in the Division were, until "D" day, getting at least one or two hot meals a day, even in the front line.

Throughout the preparatory stage of this attack, the Germans' shell-fire was constant, including considerable gas through the central portion of the BOIS de BANTHEVILLE. It was apparently the enemy's intention to infiltrate back into the Northern edge of the woods, if possible, for he threw very little gas in this part. Just prior to the attack, in retaliation, perhaps, for the gassing of BOIS des HAZOIS and other sensitive points by our Artillery, the enemy shelled with gas the edges of the BOIS de BANTHEVILLE, particularly opposite the left sub-sector. As the Jumping Off Line was well in advance of the edge of the woods, this caused no serious difficulty on the morning of the attack.

Maps were issued down to and including platoon commanders showing the Divisional boundaries, Divisional objectives and the corrected magnetic lines of advance. At the last practicable moment the latest information in regard to enemy dispositions, machine guns and Artillery was sent out on maps to platoon commanders. Each platoon commander was also supplied with a time table for each objective, with space for him to fill in the exact time as soon as "H" hour was known, and also the local description of his part of each objective. He was given also the principal liaison signals of panels and rockets on card form, and a brief admonition about reports—to report often, the date, place, time, co-ordinates of his front line, and the regimental numbers of prisoners he had taken.

Special effort was made to secure extra compasses for the Infantry, and every available supply at Corps and Army dumps was exhausted, including the salvage dumps in the vicinity. All troops had been carefully instructed in marching by compass. There was no report in the operation of loss of direction.

In accordance with the orders of the Commander in Chief, great stress was laid on control of the men. The Division Commander personally spoke to the officers and noncommissioned officers in each regiment and separate battalion. He emphasized the absolute need of holding the command together, and called on his officers and noncommissioned officers, particularly the corporals, to control the men. The Corps Commander addressed the Officers of the Division on this and similar subjects. Just prior to the operation, a straggler drive was made through the back area. For the operation a very efficient cordon of sentinels was established by the Military Police and every influence which would tend to encourage stragglers, such as Y. M. C. A. issue points and Red Cross chocolate places, were prohibited and kept well to the rear. These efforts were well repaid. The total straggling in the Division for the entire operation was only a fraction of one per cent.

Signal communications were pushed as far to the front as the enemy situation would permit. The main telephone axis of five metallic circuits was pushed up along the Engineer Road to the edge of the BOIS de BANTHEVILLE, and preparations made to carry it forward behind the Infantry. A special projector station was established on Hill 288. Wireless communications were developed through the Division, and buzzer telephones provided down to include front line battalions. Special instructions had been given to the Infantry at each available opportunity for instruction in airplane liaison. French pigeons were furnished by the Corps, but owing to the location of the cotes well to the rear of the Division P. C., runner liaison was found to be faster.

During the last week in October the weather was exceedingly fair, which fact was of particular advantage to the roads and did much to keep up the already excellent spirits of the men. One or two days of clear visibility were had and full advantage was taken by the Intelligence Department. The morning of 1 November was very hazy and offered excellent cover for the advance.

On 25 October, orders were issued to adjust the right boundary of the Division, turning over the Western edge of the BOIS de BANTHEVILLE to the 90th American Division of the III. Corps. Only the front line was relieved by the 90th American Division, but no difficulty arose, our supporting troops remaining well to the right.

The final order of attack was published by the Vth Army Corps in Field Orders No. 101, based on which was published Field Orders No. 45 of these Headquarters, involving the final changes necessitated by co-ordination between Corps and Divisions.

The Corps issued Field Orders to cover the case of enemy withdrawal, on which Field Orders No. 46, these Headquarters were based.

Between this time and 1 November there were no especial matters of interest except a continued effort to maintain the efficiency of the preparation, to complete the understanding of orders by all ranks and to guarantee a system of supply.

The Division P. C. moved to GESNES 24 October and remained there until "D" day. The Division Commander's O. P. was prepared on Hill 288, but was not occupied on "D" day on account of the poor visibility. The Advance Message Center was placed as close to the P. C. of the leading brigade as practicable. This Message Center was maintained at the wirehead, usually abreast of the Advance Brigade P. C., often ahead and, in the latter phases of the operation, was at one time actually in advance of the advance battalion in the town of LANEUVILLE. The Division Commander kept his Battle Echelon well in advance. Careful organization in this regard permitted the Division Commander's Echelon, including this General Staff, Signal Officer, his mess and personal equipment to move by automobile and light truck on half an hour's notice.

Liaison officers reported from the Corps, adjacent divisions, from the division in reserve, from the Air Service, from the Army Artillery, in addition to the regular brigade liaison officers. These officers were placed under the orders of the Corps Liaison Officer, Major Stewart, I.G.D., and were provided with all information as it came in and with copies of orders as they went out. All their messages were censored by G-3.

Special guard was placed over Division Headquarters and rigid orders enforced to keep the P. C. quiet and orderly. This condition held throughout the operation.

Just previous to the operation several observer officers from the various schools and departments of the S. O. S. reported for temporary duty with the Division. The Division Commander assigned these officers for duty with brigades and regiments where they served as second in command or actually in command of the specialties in which they were interested.

PART II. THE ATTACK:

"D" day was 1 November, 1918. "H" hour was 5:30. The preliminary bombardment commenced at 3:30.

The attack progressed in general as planned During the first day's operation each objective was reached on schedule time. The losses were relatively light, and a large number of prisoners and considerable quantity of material were captured. Detailed reports of the brigade commanders and other officers are appended hereto.

"D" DAY.

Liaison was satisfactory throughout "D" day. Telephonic communication was maintained with the advance brigade, the artillery and the divisions to the right and left.

Based on reports he had just received, the Division Commander reported to the Corps Commander at 5:15:

> "Assaulting brigade in place at 'H'—2 hours. Artillery preparation progressing satisfactorily—Reserve brigade in place. Entire morale of command excellent Weather ideal."

By 7:00 hours reports had come in of the taking of the Intermediate Objective at 6:25 and of new identifications. Reports also stated that the advance was proceeding on the 1st Objective, the advance Brigade Commander moving his P. C. forward. The Engineer Road was reported open for Artillery at 10:09, and one battalion of the 58th Field Artillery Brigade was reported going into position North of LA DHUY FERME at 11:00 hours. The advance battalion of the right regiment reported difficulty about 11:00 hours, but the advance of the left regiment indicated immediately after that it was progressing on schedule, thus permitting the right of the line to come up. About 12:30 hours word was received that troops entered the BARRICOURT woods on schedule and were taking the 3rd Objective at about 11:30 hours. At 12:30 hours the advance brigade commander moved to REMONVILLE.

At 13:50 hours, 104th Aero Squadron reported that observation was impossible on account of the weather

The Division Commander moved forward to the vicinity of the battle O. P. about 9:30 and there received reports of the taking of REMONVILLE and the Second Objective. He moved his Battle Echelon forward at 15:30 hours, joined it at the Engineer Road and proceeded to LA DHUY FERME. Here telephonic communication was opened with the advanced brigade and one Regimental Commander, as well as with the Artillery. The Artillery Commander maintained his P. C. with the Division Commander.

The Infantry succeeded in its attack by faithfully following the barrage, without hesitation, to its objectives. The German machine gunners in their fox holes cowered under the effects of the heavy barrage. Some were killed by this fire, but for the main part they were killed or captured by the Infantry before they could get the machine guns out of the holes and into action. Chaplains throughout the Division, who rapidly followed up the Infantry and buried the dead, report that the majority of the German dead had rifle bullets in their heads or upper bodies.

The enemy resistance with Artillery fire was strong at the start, but decreased later in the day as our Infantry pressed steadily forward. This fire was confined largely to the back areas, which were likely shelters for reserves. In this way the enemy inflicted rather heavy casualties on a pen of German prisoners which were first assembled near LA GAVANIERE.

By noon of 1 November elements of some ten German divisions had been reported in the front of this Division and those adjoining.

Artillery moved forward according to schedule and continued to support to and including the day's objective. Details of this movement are given in the Artillery report.

A heavy fog came up in the early afternoon, making it difficult for the advancing Infantry to be certain of its location. The position of the line was checked up by field officers, and in the left regiment by the Regimental Commander himself, and it was reported as on the Third Objective. Strong patrols were pushed out in front and developed enemy machine gun fire within a short distance.

On the night 1 November orders were received from the Vth Corps (F. O. 108), to press on the following day to the Exploitation Line. The Division Commander decided to continue the advance with the 177th Brigade which had led the attack. There had been a passage of the lines in each regiment, leaving one fresh battalion in each sub-sector. The Jump-off battalion in the left regiment was in excellent condition and none of the battalions were reported so badly disorganized. It later developed that the front line battalions at night, particularly in the right regiment, were not well in hand, due to the disorganization of attacking through the woods and difficulty of seeing in the fog.

The Reserve Brigade had moved forward, regiments side by side, each in column of battalions, open formation, with the leading battalions on the First Objective.

In order to provide adequate Artillery support, the Division Artillery Commander was directed to move up his Artillery by battalions, one regiment light Artillery to be in position as early in the morning as practicable, to be followed by the other light regiment. In the meantime, the howitzers were to be brought up by battalions.

"H" hour was set at 5:30 and a barrage ordered along the line generally 400 meters in advance of the Third Objective.

These instructions were covered by Field Orders No. 47.

2 NOVEMBER 1918.

The attack on this day was slow and uncertain, and it was not until a late hour that the Infantry was reported on its objective.

The attack of the assaulting battalions was directed to move forward when the barrage lifted and followed the barrage. This attack failed to get started because the barrage was less than one-third as dense as that of the preceding day and was not recognized as a barrage by the Infantry.

This condition was due to the fact that the Artillery support of the Division was cut in two at the close of "D" day by the relief of the 57th Field Artillery Brigade, and moreover, the Artillery Commander displaced an entire regiment of 75's instead of moving up his light guns by battalions.

Successive attacks were ordered and started during the day, but did not succeed because the Infantry was instructed to follow the barrage. It should have had orders to move forward at a definite hour regardless of the barrage.

The enemy's resistance was severe, both with Artillery and machine guns. A special detachment of Germans, Army machine gun troops, were encountered North of the BARRICOURT Woods.

Liaison was not satisfactory during this day. The Division was, for the greater part of the time, in communication with the Advance Message Center, but the Artillery Commander at the Division P. C was not in communication with his regiments. The advance Infantry Commander was intermittently in communication with the regiments of 75's. The only communication with the regiment of 155's, which were in position South of REMONVILLE, was by runner from the Advance Message Center.

It was late in the afternoon before the attack really progressed, piece by piece on the left, and on the right—under covering fire of all available Artillery. Discouraging reports were received from the right regiment, but the commander was given firm orders to proceed to his objective

About 21:00 hours the right regiment entered TAILLY and placed itself on its objective for the day, and the left regiment, although not having taken BARRICOURT—which was heavily held by machine guns, had practically encircled the town and had entered NOUART.

The Reserve Infantry Brigade moved forward, its leading elements into the BOIS de BARRICOURT, preparing to relieve the advance brigade.

The Engineers continued on road work and succeeded in maintaining communications for the Artillery, for ammunition and for evacuation. The Signal Battalion maintained a line to the Advance Message Center and, with great difficulty, between the Advance Message Center and the left regimental P. C. in the BOIS de BARRICOURT. Evacuation of wounded was slow on account of motor transportation being blocked South of REMONVILLE. Exaggerated reports were received as to the number of wounded, but all those collected were evacuated by early afternoon.

Orders from Vth Corps (F. O. 109-110), directed an extension of this Division's line to the left, based, as understood, on orders requiring exploitation to the West. This Division issued Field Orders No. 48 directing the reserve brigade to move up on this extension. However, the Corps order was rescinded by their Field Order No. 111, and the Division's Field Order No. 49 was issued accordingly, revoking No. 48.

Orders received from the Vth Corps (F. O. 112), stated that it would secure the heights overlooking BEAUCLAIR, Le CHAMPY HAUT and FORET de DIEULET; that hour of starting would be 6:00 o'clock, 3rd November. This Division was given the mission of securing the portion of the heights on its front and pushing strong reconnaissances toward STENAY.

The 177th Brigade had now been in the line as the attacking troops for two days. All of its battalions and machine gun companies had been engaged. The 178th Brigade was in reserve and had made reconnaissances necessary to pass through the lines. The Division Commander decided to make the attack on the following morning with fresh troops of the 178th Brigade.

Field Orders No. 50 were accordingly issued, stating the Division's mission to attack and carry the heights overlooking Le CHAMPY HAUT and BEAUCLAIR, and to push strong reconnaissances toward STENAY. The Division boundaries were given as indicated on the attached map. Two sub-sectors for the new attacking brigade were given. The hour of starting for them was given as 5:30, when leading elements would cross the road running Southeast from BARRICOURT. This would permit them to pass the lines of the 177th Brigade about 6:00 o'clock. Two accompanying guns (75's), were ordered for each of the two assaulting battalions, with special instructions to join their battalions before they crossed the above mentioned road, (as shown these orders were not carried out). Special instructions were given for organizing the ground taken for defense against counter-attack and from fire. The Artillery was ordered up to the Northern edge of the BOIS de BARRICOURT in support of the Infantry. Close liaison was directed, in that each Infantry Regimental Commander had approximately a regiment of 75's at his disposal. Exploiting columns, liaison, were ordered for each flank. The 177th Brigade was directed to camp in the vicinity of its existing positions, after the passage of the lines.

Division P. C. remained at LA DHUY FERME.

3 NOVEMBER 1918.

Early reports indicated that the Infantry got started satisfactorily and at 7:30 report was received that BARRICOURT had been taken, as well as the Heights East and West. At 9:30 the advance Brigade Commander reported his troops were on the objective for the day and were digging in on the heights. He was therefore ordered to press forward with his reconnaissances at once toward STENAY, and to the North. Since his accompanying guns had failed to report he was told not to wait for them, but that a battery would be sent up to join the reconnoitering battalion moving toward STENAY.

The Artillery failed to get in position with one of its regiments and failed to get up the four accompanying guns. As was the case on the day previous, it was believed this failure was due to lack of proper reconnaissances and initiative on the part of the Artillery commanders. The regiment either got lost or it attempted to use an impassable road, which, however, should have been well known by previous reconnaissances.

Reports in the latter part of the morning indicated enemy resistance developing on the right and left. At 12.05 the leading battalion of the right regiment was reported clear of the woods beyond the heights. The Division Commander moved his Battle Echelon to REMONVILLE about 9:00 hours, and immediately rode forward with the Chief of Staff to BARRICOURT. After consultation with the advance Brigade Commander and the Corps Commander there, the Division Commander proceeded to TAILLY, the Advance Message Center, where wire communication with the rear had not been secured. It was found that a battery of Artillery was standing on the road just South of TAILLY. The Division Commander returned to his new P. C. then being established at BARRICOURT and directed his Chief of Staff to get further information and make use of the Artillery Battery. Through the officer in charge of the Advance Message Center, liaison was accomplished with the advance battalion of the right regiment, which was held up before BEAUCLAIR. The Artillery battery was immediately ordered into position and had its fire adjusted on the Southern edges of BEAUCLAIR. At dusk this battery fired all its remaining ammunition in support of the Infantry attack, which moved up to the town. This was arranged in the presence of the Brigade Commander. Full possession of the town of BEAUCLAIR and patrols in HALLES was confirmed by later reports, but the Infantry did not enter BEAUFORT until morning. On the left the exploiting column had passed Le CHAMPY BAS and had entered BOIS de DAMES, as shown on the attached map. The Advance Brigade Commander was instructed that he must be in full possession of BEAUCLAIR and BEAUFORT by daylight.

During the evening orders were received from the Vth Corps that the 1st Division would send a column through our lines and this Division would be assembled in rear. The Division Commander promptly called the Corps by telephone and asked permission to remain in line and continue the advance. The Division Commander stated that his troops were in fine condition, were in touch with the situation and could certainly make further progress the next day. He desired to gain possession of the FORET de DIEULET, which would afford Artillery positions for long guns to break the German railroad beyond STENAY, and also to endeavor to get the bridgehead at LANEUVILLE. The Corps Commander granted this request.

Field Orders No. 51 were accordingly issued stating the Division's mission to advance and seize the town of LANEUVILLE, the Northern edge of the FORET de DIEULET, and to push reconnaissances forward to the MEUSE and reconnoiter for river crossings. "H" hour was left to the Commanding General of the leading brigade. He was directed to attack with a front of three battalions, each with a battalion in support, and to employ the full use of the fire power given him. The Division Commander desired that these three attacking battalions be able to exploit vigorously any advantage gained along this wider front. Instructions were given that the advance would be pushed vigorously to the final objective regardless of liaison. The reserve brigade was directed to move up to the heights.

The leading Brigade Commander set his "H" hour at 8:30, in order, as he explained, to give ample time for co-ordination and preparation.

4 NOVEMBER 1918.

Operations on this day were slow and, on the whole, unsatisfactory, although the Division gained its objective

Just before 9:00 hours word was received from the advance brigade that the Commander of the right assaulting battalion reported he was conducting a successful flanking move, and unless Artillery fire could be put down immediately, that the barrage planned for 8:30 should be called off. This was done Further reports were meager and unsatisfactory. The Division Commander and Chief of Staff accordingly went forward to the heights North of TAILLY, overlooking the operation. The inactivity of our Infantry was apparent. Beyond the river large convoys of Germans could be seen leaving STENAY. South of the FORET de DIEULET small numbers of Germans, apparently machine gunners, could be seen moving about. Our troops North of BEAUFORT were receiving fire and were not advancing Our Artillery was practically silent. The Division Commander, therefore, directed the advance Brigade Commander to drive forward his attack and take LANEUVILLE, stating that the advance so far was unsatisfactory and that if favorable reports were not received from the front, the Brigade Commander should go forward in person and conduct the operation. More favorable progress was then reported on the left, where the attacking battalion had entered the woods, although reporting steady resistance, and was followed by the support battalion. The center battalion made little progress. The battalion on the right could not advance until Artillery support was obtained.

By late afternoon it was learned that the Brigade Commander had ordered a 30 minutes standing barrage along the front edge of the woods, which was to be lifted for the Infantry to advance. The supply of ammunition would not permit this. The Corps Artillery Commander was at the Division P. C. at the time and stated the barrage should not be put down. The Division Commander countermanded the order; got in touch with the advance Battalion Commander on the right and directed him to proceed with his attack under a rolling barrage, which was immediately ordered. The attack then progressed on the right which carried up the center battalion.

The assaulting battalion on the left reported itself on its objective about an hour before dark. The Battalion Commander later reported that he could see large numbers of Germans and vehicles crossing the river behind LANEUVILLE and that he was receiving heavy fire of artillery and machine guns from his front. He made no attempt to exploit his success to the right and the opportunity was lost. His patrols did not reach the river that night. On the right, the town of LANEUVILLE was entered by an officers' patrol and reconnaissance made of the destroyed bridge and railroad in the vicinity before midnight.

Combat liaison had been maintained with the 90th Division on the right throughout the day. On our left this was not gained until about midnight. The road from BEAUCLAIR to LANEUVILLE through the Woods, was blocked by trees and a blown bridge in the Southern edge of the woods. The Germans had completely destroyed a series of stone culverts under the causeway from LANEUVILLE to STENAY, and had closed sufficient culverts to cause a large overflow of the upper valley to the South. The North side of the river, however, was at its normal width.

While the Division gained its objective, the attack was not driven with sufficient energy. Opportunity was undoubtedly lost to make large captures of men and material, and possibly hold an important river crossing.

During the evening orders were received from the Vth Corps that the 89th Division would assemble in the vicinity of BEAUFORT and LANEUVILLE and await further orders. Again the Division Commander felt that he could make further progress the following day and asked the Corps Commander by telephone for permission to stay in line and clear the enemy from the West side of the river. This permission was necessary, because continuance of the operation required the moving up of the Artillery, which could not be done under the orders received for assembling the Division. The Corps Commander granted the request and accordingly Field Orders No. 52 were issued. The Division Commander stated as his mission—to continue the advance and drive the enemy across the MEUSE; that he would include in this operation the FOREST OF JAULNAY, and seize and hold the bridges in his front. The leading brigade was given the mission of the Division and directed to prosecute vigorous patrols during the night toward the towns and bridges along the river; to hold all positions found unoccupied. He was given the entire Artillery support of the Division.

The reserve brigade was directed to move forward all of its elements in support, except two battalions, which were to remain on the heights and continue the organization of the position there. The Division Machine Gun Battalion was given to the leading Brigade Commander; he was also given a company of Engineers to assist in the bridge reconnaissances.

The Division P. C. had moved forward to TAILLY early in the morning of November 4th.

5 NOVEMBER 1918.

The Division Commander went forward with an Aide de Camp early in the day. Engineer reconnaissances soon developed the fact that the bridges from STENAY (inclusive) to INOR (exclusive) had been destroyed. Condition of the bridges at INOR and POUILLY was unknown The Division Commander, on seeing the road conditions in the forward area, determined that the POUILLY crossing afforded the best chance for getting traffic up to and away from the river. He, therefore, sent word back to the Division P. C. that he wanted the bridgehead at POUILLY seized.

About noon the Corps Commander issued instructions that the 89th Division would hold the heights East of the MEUSE in its present front. This meant obtaining a river crossing. The Chief of Staff, in the absence of the Division Commander, talked on the 'phone personally to the advance Brigade Commander and explained the situation, emphasizing the necessity of getting a crossing in compliance with the Corps and the Division Commanders' orders. It was reasoned that since the left regiment had reported resistance in the FOREST of JAULNAY that the bridge at POUILLY might still be intact, since the Germans would not destroy a crossing behind their troops. The advance Brigade Commander asked for definite orders on the subject, and he was therefore told to drive in behind the FOREST of JAULNAY, seize and hold the POUILLY bridge. He expressed satisfaction at the order and said it would be carried out.

The Division Commander returned to the P. C.—saw the orders of the Corps and sent his Chief of Staff forward to get in touch with the situation on the ground. The advance Brigade Commander was found in his P. C. in BEAUCLAIR. He stated that his Regimental Commander on the left was, by brigade order, in the FERME de MAUCOURT. Accordingly, the Chief of Staff pressed on through the FOREST of DIEULET, and on passing the P. C of the Commanding Officer, 3rd Battalion, 356th Infantry, South of the main road in Square W-13, found there the officer who had been designated to command the operation of seizing the bridge. He stated that he was preparing to go forward. It was then after 15:00 hours.

The Chief of Staff proceeded to the FOREST of JAULNAY where, about Point 110-306.5, he met the Commanding Officer of the advance troops, who stated that the POUILLY bridge was still intact and that he had an outpost on this side, and men had been within a few feet of the bridge. His troops were scattered, but he was getting them together. The Chief of Staff found, however, after ordering a further reconnaissance on the ground that the outpost was not established at the bridgehead and that the bridge had been badly damaged. Men could cross to the town singly.

The Infantry Commander was directed to put a platoon in the town and support it with the rest of his two and one-half companies and machine guns, and to assist the Engineer Officer, Acting Assistant G-3, to complete the Engineer reconnaissance. As wire communications were out, the Chief of Staff returned by way of the new P. C of the Regimental Commander. Failing to find him there or wire communications in, he returned to the Advance Message Center at

LANEUVILLE and reported the situation. The Division Commander approved of the disposition which had been made.

These facts are stated in unusual detail as the advance Battalion Commander did not carry out orders, and although the reconnaissance was well made that night, a detachment was not left in the town. The INOR bridge was found to be intact by the Engineer reconnoitering officer, but it was destroyed that night by the enemy during inactivity of our own Infantry in that vicinity.

No further instructions were received or issued that night.

6 NOVEMBER 1918.

In so much as Field Orders No. 118 of the Vth Corps required that in addition to holding its front the 89th Division would reorganize in preparation for advance to the North, special inspections and conferences were had to determine the exact status of the Division. This was reported to the Corps in Field Message No. 468:

"Division holds position to guard bridges from POUILLY to STENAY inclusive. Artillery well forward in position to support movement to cross the river. Leading brigade of Infantry needs one or two days recuperation before energetic work can be expected of them. Rear brigade is fit and is approximately sixty per cent. strength. Total replacements needed in Division 306 officers, 6,153 men, have been requested. Artillery could make one shift of position immediately, but should not be pushed across river over poor roads and temporary structures without replacement of 500 good animals. In one week's time and with 500 animals the 58th Artillery Brigade can resume active operations in open warfare. Bridges at POUILLY, INOR, LUZY, CESSE and STENAY, with intermediate crossings have been demolished by the enemy. Demolition at POUILLY was incomplete and small Infantry detachments have crossed and are holding far side supported by strong Infantry detachments and machine guns on this side. It is believed that a similar operation is possible at INOR. At POUILLY it would take a week's time to put bridge and road into condition for heavy vehicles. Infantry and light trains could probably be put over in four days. Roads leading to bridges between STENAY and POUILLY are bad, except road to INOR, which is reported as in fair condition. Road along Northwest corner FORET de JAULNAY, is practicable for first movement of Artillery and Trains, but it has not yet been determined if it can bear sustained traffic. Preparations for compliance with Field Orders No. 118 in progress. Request adjustment of boundary on left. This Division has forces in POUILLY and the FOREST of JAULNAY, which area is also covered by the 2nd Division. It is particularly necessary for this Division to hold NOUART in order to control traffic."

Shortly after noon the Corps Commander visited the Division P. C. and gave the information that the American Commander in Chief desired to have American troops to be the first to reach SEDAN, and that he was sending one division due North to be supported by the rest of the Corps, and that it might be necessary to force a crossing of the river and proceed on the far side. Later in the day orders were received from the Corps that this Division would cover the front of the MEUSE from STENAY Northward, protecting the right flank of the advance, and that strong reconnaissances would be pushed across the MEUSE and the Division be prepared to follow the advance. Accordingly, Field Orders No. 54 were issued, ordering the reserve Brigade into the line and giving general instructions as to the method of holding the outpost lightly, maintaining the main body of the troops at the principal cross-roads in rear. Reconnaissances and patrols continued along the river and were ordered to cross the MEUSE, but there was no bridge equipment available.

7 NOVEMBER 1918.

During the morning report was forwarded by the advance Brigade Commander that his left Regimental Commander had a plan for forcing a crossing at POUILLY. He was directed to proceed with it that night. He, however, asked for delays, which for one reason or another—principally being delay in bridge equipment coming up, was postponed until the final operation.

During the morning, word from the Corps was received revoking the order to extend to the Northwest. Accordingly Field Orders No. 55, revoking Field Orders No. 54 were issued, keeping the 177th Brigade in reserve.

8 NOVEMBER 1918.

Field Orders No. 122, Vth Corps, published late on November 7th, reached the Division P. C. the morning of the 8th. They directed the Division to push strong patrols across the MEUSE and maintain contact with the enemy. Accordingly Field Orders No. 56 were issued, directing the 178th Brigade to carry on aggressively the mission of the Division, and to force a crossing of the river at POUILLY that night, 8-9 November. The advance Brigade Commander asked for further delay, and on the recommendation of the Division Engineer, this was granted. However, instructions were given to push patrols across the river. Some six or seven attempts were made that night by various expeditions, including several patrols which tried to swim, regardless of the low temperature of the water. Two crossings were actually effected, but no information of value was gained other than that the enemy was holding the East bank of the river all along the front.

9 NOVEMBER 1918.

No Field Order was received from the Corps on this date.

In accordance with Field Orders No. 57, the Division maintained its position, with the 178th Brigade in the line, patrolling the river with a view to detecting enemy activity. The Reserve Brigade was kept in training in rear of the line. During these days attention was given to the care, improvement and grazing of animals throughout the Division, including the attached Artillery. Bombs and mines were removed from various towns, including LANEUVILLE and CESSE.

Word was received from the 90th Division that they were going to cross the river near SASSEY. The 2nd Division reported that they had been unable to cross the river at MOUSON.

The Commanding General of the advance Brigade (178th), was relieved this date and his Brigade turned over to Brigadier General Herman Hall.

During this period G-1 matters absorbed the main interest of the Division Commander. Roads had been difficult, transportation remained inadequate, it was difficult to get up supplies, and impracticable to do much toward the improvement of the Division. Difficulty was experienced even in getting up the packs and equipment of the troops.

During the night our patrols met with success. Using bridge equipment, detachments crossed West of POUILLY, encountered the enemy, and obtained prisoners. They also gained important data in regard to the character of the banks on that side of the river.

10 NOVEMBER 1918.

Orders received from the Corps (F. O. 124), stated that the Vth Corps would cross the MEUSE, seize the heights South of VAUX and East of INOR. The 89th Division was directed to cross the MEUSE at places already selected by the Division Commander, and seize the heights East and Northeast of INOR. The Corps order directed that the best possible use be made of machine guns and Artillery, and that the hour of beginning the operation be 16:00 hours, 10th November. Dividing lines and boundaries were given, LETANNE to the 2nd Division—AUTREVILLE to the 89th Division. On the South the boundary was STENAY (exclusive). Liaison between the Divisions of the Corps was to be maintained by combined detachment consisting of one Infantry battalion and one machine gun company from each Division under command of an officer from the 2nd Division.

The Division Commander received different recommendations as to the advisability of concentrating his forces for crossing at INOR and POUILLY, but decided on POUILLY, for the following reasons:

(a) The bend in the river made a stronger tactical solution for forcing the passage by concentration of Artillery and machine gun fire and denied such concentration to the enemy.

(b) Our reconnaissances had been more successfully pushed in the vicinity of POUILLY.

(c) The heights above INOR dominated the crossing, causing a much more serious menace than anything confronting the position at POUILLY.

(d) The Engineer officer operating with the Bridge Train recommended the POUILLY crossing from a technical standpoint.

It was recognized as impracticable to force the main crossing at STENAY, due to the demolished condition of the causeway approaches, and the main bridge over the MEUSE proper on the far side of the river. It was planned, however, to maintain careful liaison with the 90th Division, and as soon as they had taken STENAY, to force our Infantry North along the East bank of the MEUSE, clearing the enemy as far as the heights and connecting up with the troops which would cross at POUILLY.

The plan thus was to force a crossing near POUILLY, drive Eastward to the heights back of INOR, then exploit to the South and connect up with the other brigade which was to work North through STENAY in liaison with the 90th Division. This plan appeared to have the necessary elements of success.

Field Orders No. 58 were issued, based on the above plan. The 178th Brigade was given the mission of crossing at POUILLY, maintaining liaison with the 2nd Division and furnishing the combat liaison troops on that flank. The 177th Brigade was given the task of maintaining combat liaison with the 90th Division, sending troops by the foot bridge at VILLE-FRANCHE, as well as by a reported foot bridge near STENAY to push Northward on the far side of the river, clearing the heights and gaining contact with the 178th Brigade North of INOR. The Division Machine Gun Officer co-ordinated the machine gun operation near POUILLY, where the major portion of the machine gun organizations of the Division had been assigned. The Division Engineer, with the entire regiment of Engineers at his disposal, was directed to provide crossing for the troops operating near POUILLY, a battalion of the 177th Brigade which was to cross near STENAY, and later complete a pontoon bridge at the best point between INOR and STENAY. The Artillery was already in position to support the operation.

The Infantry Battalion Commander, 178th Brigade, recently holding LANEUVILLE, had reported that a light foot bridge had been discovered, affording passage into STENAY. The attacking Infantry of the 177th Brigade failed to find this foot bridge.

Up and until 9th November the Artillery of this Division did not fire on the towns to the East of the river, as they were known to be occupied by French women and children. Realising, however, that these towns were affording shelter to the enemy and must be subjected to fire if our troops were successfully to take them, the Division Commander arranged through the Air Service to warn the inhabitants that the towns would be shelled, commencing the 9th November. That evening, therefore, the towns East of the river opposite the Division front were briskly shelled.

NIGHT OF 10-11 NOVEMBER 1918.

The operation developed on the left practically as planned. The hour of starting was co-ordinated with that of the 2nd Division, and although our troops began the operation of moving boats from their camouflaged park near the main road about 16:00 hours, the crossing of the river was not under way until 21:30 hours. The Artillery repeated its program of brisk shelling of the river towns, and under the cover of this fire the Engineers proceeded with two foot bridges and the construction of a catamaran ferry. The enemy apparently took to the cellars, believing the shelling to be but a repetition of that of the night before. The enemy outposts, however, located the foot bridge work and called down on it machine gun and Artillery fire of sufficient severity to stop the work temporarily.

Under cover of this activity the Engineers constructed the catamaran ferry in the creek running from the FME. de WAME down to the river. Here they skillfully crossed a covering detachment of Engineers, and then one battalion of Infantry, without a casualty. The second battalion of Infantry followed with little difficulty. The Infantry proceeded North, circling POUILLY, and did not disturb the inhabitants or garrisons until our position was well secured on the heights beyond. The town was then mopped up, giving a large number of prisoners and material. The enemy on learning of this, shelled the town heavily. The Infantry, however, pressed on and took AUTREVILLE after daylight, and reached the heights to the East.

The combat liaison battalion and the machine gun company which was under the orders of the 2nd Division did not fare as well. Just as they were preparing to cross the river they were subjected to a very heavy concentration of enemy Artillery fire and suffered extremely heavy casualties. Their operation was delayed, but they accomplished their mission with the 2nd Division.

To the South the 177th Brigade sent one regiment, less one battalion, by way of the foot bridge at VILLE-FRANCHE, following the elements of the 90th Division. One battalion was directed to cross directly opposite STENAY as soon as opportunity afforded. The Regimental Commander with the VILLE-FRANCHE column moved up on the East side of the river just in rear of the 90th Division, and on the left flank. He was told that the town was strongly held by the Germans and that since operations were to cease later in the day, the 90th Division would not take the town.

The Engineers in LANEUVILLE again reconnoitered the crossing during the night, commenced work, which resulted in getting a platoon into STENAY about 10:00 o'clock.

11 NOVEMBER 1918.

At 8:30 hours information was received at the Division P. C. from the Corps that an armistice would go into effect at 11:00 hours, and that fire should cease at that time. Word was immediately sent out by all available means of liaison, including officer couriers, to the front line battalions. Artillery was directed to cease firing at 10:45, in order to ovoid mistakes and violations of the armistice.

The terms of the armistice, or the letter of instructions giving the warning as to the approaching armistice, was not received at the Division P. C. until about 10:30 hours.

Since the Division had been in the line a considerable period without proper bathing facilities, and since it was realized that if the enemy were permitted to remain in STENAY, our troops would be deprived of the billets and of the probable bathing facilities there, instructions were sent to the Infantry Commander at LANEUVILLE, to push forward directly and take STENAY, not waiting for any assistance or support of the 90th Division.

There has been considerable discussion over the matter of taking this town. It is well established that troops of this Division entered the town from LANEUVILLE and occupied its Northern portion about 10:00 o'clock. Those troops stated they met practically no resistance, and found no Americans in the town. The enemy, however, had patrols in the near vicinity, which were encountered near CERVISY.

Not being thoroughly familiar with the terms of the armistice, the Division Commander directed that our troops push forward until the enemy was actually encountered; that the enemy would not be fired upon, unless he attacked; that hostilities must cease, but that any terrain which might be of military value to us and which had been abandoned by the enemy, would be taken and would be occupied. It was intended to complete the operation by occupying the heights East of the river between STENAY and MOULINS. The enemy, however, was found to be in INOR and in CERVISY. Moreover, orders were later received not to advance beyond the line held at 11:00 hours, and those orders were enforced.

The German High Command made an official complaint that the American troops on the STENAY-BEAUMONT front had not ceased attacking at 11:00 hours but continued their advance.

Orders once fully understood were, however, loyally obeyed, although there was no regret that the Division had up to the last hour continued to carry out its offensive instructions to the fullest possible extent.

This operation closed with seven (7) battalions of Infantry East of the MEUSE, a ponton bridge in process of construction, Artillery in position to support the defense of the heights East of INOR and with the chances of success for the entire operation well in our favor. The line of the Division is shown on the attached map.

PART III. STATEMENT OF ENEMY UNITS ENGAGED. TIME AND PLACE.

On 24 October 1918, the 13th German Division was holding the line immediately to our front. On 1-2 November, the enemy order of battle from East to West was as follows:

109th Regiment	—28th Division.
426th Regiment 353rd Regiment	—88th Division.
170th Regiment	—52nd Division.

109th and 426th Regiments had contact in the ANDEVANNE Woods.
426th and 353rd Regiments had contact at LA DHUY FERME.
353rd and 170th Regiments had contact West of LA DHUY FERME.

On 2 November the 120th Regiment, 27th Division, was encountered Southwest of NOUART.

On 3 November the only new divisions identified were the 18th and 41st, on the ridge South of REMONVILLE.

On 4 November the 41st Division was encountered in the BOIS de BELVAL.

On 5 November prisoners from the 13th Division were taken in the FORET de DIEULET, and the 177th Division was identified in LANEUVILLE.

On 10 November the 88th Division was holding the line at POUILLY and remained there until the attack night 10-11 November.

PART IV. SUMMARY.

(a) Depth of Advance (See attached map). About 24 kilometers.

(b) PRISONERS TAKEN: FROM 19 OCTOBER, 1918:

	Officers.	Men.
To 11:00 hr. 11 November	72	1760
To 12 November	78	2013
To 16 November	78	2015
TOTAL	78	2015

(c) MATERIAL CAPTURED:

	1 9" howitzer
400 rifles.	1 anti-aircraft gun.
360 machine guns.	15 minenwerfers.
12 3" pieces.	30 caissons.
24 77 mm. guns.	7 one-pounders.
6 guns larger than 77's.	3 auto trucks
4 155 mm. guns.	1 coal oil burning truck.
5 150 mm. guns.	1 wagon train.
2 210 howitzers.	9 horses.

and large quantity of ammunition of all calibers.

(d) CASUALTIES:

	Officers.	Men.
Killed	29	771
Wounded	87	2399
Gassed	18	545
Missing	..	201

(e) EMPLOYMENT OF INFANTRY WEAPONS:

(1) Machine Guns. Throughout the operation machine guns served usefully in their mission of assisting the Infantry to advance and in maintaining positions, once taken. In the attack of November 1st, as far as the 1st Objective, a very carefully co-ordinated overhead fire was produced. Every available machine gun in the Division, with the exception of four companies attached to the two assault and two support Infantry battalions, was employed during the two hours preliminary bombardment and afforded an overhead rolling barrage 500 meters in advance of the Infantry. Special liaison and careful instructions were provided so as to guarantee that these companies, operating under the Division Machine Gun officer, should rejoin their proper brigades or battalion. Throughout the fighting, as far as the MEUSE, overhead machine gun fire was employed to prepare the way and assist the advance of the Infantry. The advance was not so rapid but that the machine guns could usually keep up, by following the Infantry after it had halted. For the operation near POUILLY a careful co-ordinated Artillery and machine gun program was worked out and fired. Full advantage was taken of the lay of the land, namely—heavy concentration of fire on the opposing enemy. In this way full tactical advantage was gained of the river bend forming a salient in the enemy's line.

Enemy machine guns were overcome, first—by our Infantry following the barrage closely and dispatching or capturing the German machine gunners in their fox holes before they could get their guns into action; second—by Infantry maneuver of small units working to the flanks and suppressing the German guns, sometimes with and sometimes without the aid of auxiliary weapons. The German machine gunners were almost without exception well provided with cover in their newly constructed holes or emplacements. They fought well until out-maneuvered, either locally or along general lines.

This subject is covered in report of Division Machine Gun Officer appended and marked "G."

(2) 37 mm. Guns. In the preliminary bombardment and initial advance of the Infantry on November 1st, these guns were employed under the Divisional Machine Gun Officer to good effect. They later joined their regiments, as did the machine gun companies. Throughout the open fighting of the operation the 37 mm. Guns served a useful purpose. They were generally up with the assault battalions of the Infantry, and the number of rounds fired (over 2,000), shows that they were frequently employed. This continued in the operation at POUILLY, where several direct hits were reported.

For further details see reports of Infantry Brigade Commanders appended and marked "C" and "D."

(3) Stokes Mortars: During the preliminary bombardment the Stokes Mortars of the Reserve Brigade were placed under orders of the Divisional Artillery Commander. They fired from the Northern edge of the BOIS de BANTHEVILLE on suitable targets, during the two hours, and then rejoined their regiments. In the 177th Brigade more use was gained in open fighting with these weapons than in the other brigade. Their use was limited, due to the fact that they could not be transported, with their ammunition, to keep up with the Infantry.

It is believed that sufficient practice and hard training has not been carried on to develop the strength and endurance needed by the Stokes Mortar men over and above that of the average Infantryman during offensive operations. The measure of success of Stokes Mortars during an advance is entirely in proportion to the strength and endurance of the men constituting the platoon. Where these Mortars were put into action they were served boldly and with good result. They were, however, too frequently left behind, because their carriers could not keep up. For further reports see reports of Infantry Brigade Commanders appended and marked "C" and "D."

(4) Rifle Grenades: Every Infantry soldier was required to carry two rifle grenades in addition to his other equipment. The 177th Brigade, leading the attack, used this weapon effectively against machine gun nests in the BOIS de BARRICOURT and just beyond. Their use thereafter was only occasional, but effective when tried. For further details see reports of Infantry Brigade Commanders appended and marked "C" and "D."

(f) EMPLOYMENT OF TANKS AND GAS TROOPS:

(1) Tanks: None were used with this Division.

(2) Gas Troops: One company of the 1st Regiment was attached to the Division and was assigned to fire during the preliminary bombardment under orders of the Divisional Artillery Commander. They were to follow the assaulting battalions of Infantry, and if these became held up to assist in the advance by overhead fire with thermite or phosphorus smoke on machine gun nests. As the Infantry advance was steady and rapid throughout the first day, the Gas Troops could not keep up and their services were not required.

In the POUILLY operation plans were laid to cover the crossing with a smoke barrage by the Gas Troops, if daylight movement was necessary, but as the crossing was made during the dark the Gas Troops did not participate.

(3) It has been the Division Commander's experience that special troops, such as these, are of very little value, due to the fact that the Infantry is not acquainted with their methods and has not, from experience, learned to have confidence in them. If these weapons are to be successfully employed, troops using them should habitually serve with the Division, train with it, be identified with it. The personnel of the Infantry and the special troops should know each other and have confidence in each other, and finally when the special troops are needed, they could probably be depended upon to be on time at the place their services could be advantageously used.

(g) ARTILLERY SUPPORT:

As stated in the body of this report, covering the plans for the operation, the Artillery support in the preliminary bombardment and accompanying barrage, as far as the 3rd Objective, was entirely satisfactory.

From D plus I day the Artillery support was not satisfactory. This was unquestionably due to two general causes. First—the Infantry Commanders were not accustomed to employing Artillery as part of their commands, and they did not therefore instantly and properly call for co-ordinated Artillery support. If Infantry Commanders are successfully to employ Artillery under their orders, they must have experience and training along these lines. Second—The Artillery lacked that high degree of efficiency necessary to operate effectively in open warfare after breaking through. The officers lacked initiative and foresight. They did not push their reconnaissances far enough forward to seek out targets and to be ready to support the Infantry, when called upon. They did not reconnoiter the roads efficiently, frequently causing counter-marches and delays. The care of their animals was poor and their march discipline far from satisfactory. Seldom, if ever, did the Artillery go promptly into position from the road and open fire. There were usually halts on the road waiting for battery positions to be selected and then further delays waiting for firing data. It is the Division Commander's belief that a much higher state of training, discipline and general efficiency should be required for operations of this character. The Artillery was accurate in its fire but lacked the power of skillful maneuver.

(h) TERRAIN:

The terrain was admirably suited for defense by the enemy. He had an extremely strong natural fortress in the wooded heights of BARRICOURT, the advance on which was dominated and flanked by natural bastions, such as the BOIS de ANDEVANNE and the town of REMONVILLE. A long glacis immediately in front of the woods afforded a beautiful field of fire. The outpost position, including the BOIS des HAZOIS, the scattered woods and hills in the vicinity of LA DHUY FERME, afforded excellent machine gun positions and fields of fire from reverse slopes.

The heights of BARRICOURT dominated everything as far as the river. The heights overlooking NOUART and BEAUCLAIR afforded a strong defensive position, which was prepared for organization by our troops. The plain between these heights and the river was broken by scattered towns, hedges, and finally the woods of DIEULET and JAULNAY. Those features afforded excellent opportunity for machine gun defense and rear guard actions. Numerous culverts, necessitated by the marshy condition of the land, and the trees alongside the road, gave opportunity for blocking them by the retreating Germans.

The MEUSE was found to be unfordable at that season. Moreover, the Germans, in their retreat, blocked the culverts of the causeway between LANEUVILLE and STENAY, thus flooding the upper region of the river.

The large bend in the MEUSE in the vicinity of POUILLY afforded a favorable opportunity to force a crossing there. As is explained in the body of the report, this position permitted our forces to dominate the operation from the start and maintain a heavy concentration of fire on the enemy.

At the close of the first day's fighting advantages of terrain came to our side.

(i) Air Service: Throughout this operation the Air Service, due to the fact that the enemy unquestionably dominated the air, was unsatisfactory. We got little or no information from airplane reconnaissances. Our balloons were driven down by the enemy almost at his pleasure. Our Infantry was continually harassed by enemy planes flying low, not only registering Artillery fire, but also using machine guns directly.

(j) The following appendices are attached:

A. File of 89th Division Field Orders.
B. File of First Army and V Corps F. O.'s concerning 89th Division.
C. 177th Infantry Brigade Commander's report.
D. 178th Infantry Brigade Commander's report.
E. 58th Field Artillery Brigade Commander's report.
F. 314th Engineer Commander's report.
G. Division Machine Gun Officer's report.
H. Division Signal Officer's report.
I. G-1's report.
J. Division Surgeon's report (1) Operations.
(2) Medical History.
K. Train Commander's report.
L. Report of Commanding Officer, Division Message Center.
M. Report of Commanding Officer, Advance Message Center.
N. Map showing sector and location of units during advance.
O. Map showing Artillery positions.
P. Roster of Commanders and Staffs.

(k) CONCLUSION:

The operation was unquestionably a success. Aside from the strategical value of reaching the objective, the MEUSE, the tactical success was most striking. The initial preparations were thorough and logical. The attack was well co-ordinated and efficiently carried out. The first day's operation is considered to have been almost without criticism. On the following days the unavoidable consequences of inexperience were apparent. The Division did not have its own Artillery—liaison with the Infantry therefore was hindered from the start. Infantry Commanders, moreover, did not realize the full benefit of the support within their power; also one Infantry Brigade Commander failed to exploit the successes to their reasonable possibilities.

In spite of the many deficiencies, which are apparent to the Division Commander, who was so closely in touch with the details, he feels that the operation was a remarkable success.

The Corps Commander, in recognition of what this Division accomplished, publishes the following letter and citation in orders:

"In addition to my telephone message, I desire to convey to you and to the officers and soldiers of the 89th Division my profound appreciation and great admiration for the splendid manner in which the Division accomplished the mission allotted to it in the advance of the Fifth Corps on November first.

"With a dash, courage, and speed that is worthy of the best traditions of our service, the 89th Division quickly overran the enemy's strong organization, followed its barrage, and planted itself on all objectives in accordance with the schedule previously arranged. It has captured many prisoners, guns, and spoils of war, showing that the enemy was afforded no opportunity to escape.

"The Division has more than justified the high confidence of the Commander in Chief when he selected it to form the advance, in the great operations that have begun.

"It is a high honor to command such troops, and beg that you will convey to your officers and soldiers the assurances of my abiding wishes for their continued success in the campaigns that lie before it."

* * * * * * * * * *

"The 1st, 2nd and 89th Divisions, V Corps, for their part in the memorable attack launched by the 1st American Army on November 1st. Throughout this operation all officers and men, by their high courage, devotion to duty, and disregard for the innumerable hardships encountered, made for themselves a place in the history of our country.

"The 89th Division, preceding the attack of November 1st, cleaned up the difficult and strongly held BOIS de BANTHEVILLE and attacked on November 1st. It broke through the enemy's lines, advanced strongly day and night, defeating the enemy and his reserves in its front, and drove him across the MEUSE. Under heavy fire and against stubborn resistance, it constructed bridges and established itself on the heights. The cessation of hostilities found this Division holding strong positions across the MEUSE and ready for a continuation of the advance."

Attention is invited to the map showing the Artillery positions of the Division, which shows the different P. C.'s of the Artillery Brigade. They are all enumerated as P. C. "Todd." General Todd's brigade was in support of the Division during the engagement, but General Todd was not in command, as he had been wounded a few days before the fight. The brigade was commanded by Brigadier General E. A. Millar.

In closing this report, I desire to express my great appreciation of the services rendered by Major General F. L. Winn, commanding the 177th Brigade; Colonel James H. Reeves, commanding the 353rd Infantry; Colonel Conrad S. Babcock, commanding the 354th Infantry; Colonel Robert H. Allen, commanding the 356th Infantry, all of whom led their troops with efficiency and gallantry. The Staff also showed a most commendable state of training and co-ordination under the control of the Chief of Staff, Colonel J. C. H. Lee. Colonel Lee was indefatigable in his work; his advice, tactically and administratively, always sound, did much to prepare for the battle and gain the objectives. He was frequently in the front line, and set an excellent example by his coolness and bravery. Lieut. Colonel W. J. Scott handled his section admirably, as did Major Frank W Smith, G-2, and Major Frederick W. O'Donnell, Division Surgeon. Colonel Roger S. Fitch, Chief of Staff of the 86th Division, voluntarily took over the duties of G-3 during the operations and rendered most efficient and gallant service.

I also desire to mention Lieut. Colonel Rudolph E. Smyser, Divisional Machine Gun Officer; Captain James H. Barney, A. D. C., Assistant G-2, and Captain Charles H. Gerhardt, A. D. C., Assistant G-3. Lieut. Colonel Brehon B. Somervell, Corps of Engineers, took part in the operations as Assistant Chief of Staff, G-3. I am glad to learn that he was awarded the Distinguished Service Cross, which he merited.

W. M. WRIGHT,
Major General, U. S. A.

APPENDIX "C"

177TH INFANTRY BRIGADE COMMANDER'S REPORT

HEADQUARTERS
177TH INFANTRY BRIGADE

12 November 1918.

REPORT OF OPERATIONS NOVEMBER 1-11, 1918.

PART I. SITUATION AT THE BEGINNING OF THE OPERATION.

On October 31, 1918, the 177th Infantry Brigade was holding the line—crossroads F6088, Northwest edge of BOIS de BANTHEVILLE, point F4570, trench F4265, point F3663. Two regiments were in line, the 353rd Infantry on the right, with the 3rd, 2nd, and 1st battalions in order from front to rear, and the 354th Infantry on the left, with its battalions in the same order. The 178th Infantry Brigade, with leading elements South on the ROMAGNE-SOMMERANCE Road constituted the Divisional Reserve. The Divisional and attached artillery were in position ready to support this brigade in the attack.

The 13th German Division was holding the sector opposite the brigade by a line of outposts, strongly defended by machine guns, in the neighborhood of LA DHUY FARM and the small woods North of the BOIS de BANTHEVILLE. The indications were that the enemy considered this front vital to his entire line and intended to hold it to the last. It developed in the attack that the 13th Division was relieved by the 88th Division on the night October 29-30th and placed in support, so that the enemy had in reality two divisions confronting this brigade.

PART II. THE ATTACK.

After two hours of intense artillery preparation the brigade moved to the attack at 5:30 A.M., November 1st. The two regiments were in line—the 353rd Infantry on the right and the 354th Infantry on the left. Each regiment was formed in column of battalions, the Third Battalion, 353rd Infantry and the First Battalion, 354th Infantry constituting the assault troops. A Machine Gun Company was assigned to each battalion. In addition, the attack of each regiment was supported by two accompanying guns of 75 mm. Company "B," 1st Gas Regiment participated in the barrage with smoke bombs discharged from 4" mortars from the Northern part of BOIS de BANTHEVILLE. The artillery preparation and the rolling barrage were well co-ordinated with the Infantry advance. A large proportion of smoke shells were fired, which materially assisted in screening the advance of the Infantry at the start. In consequence, the Intermediate Objective was taken at 6:15. The advance to the attack was made under heavy artillery and machine gun fire, but after the advance to the Intermediate Objective the resistance decreased and the First and Second Objectives were reached on scheduled time. The town of REMONVILLE was taken without serious difficulty.

At the Second Objective the Second Battalion, 353rd Infantry and the Third Battalion, 354th Infantry passed the lines of the leading battalions and continued the advance on the Third Objective, the hills North of the BOIS de BARRICOURT. The enemy was found in force on this point and on the heights North of it, and stubborn resistance was encountered. At 16:00 o'clock a heavy fog came up and the troops halted on the Third Objective—their objective for the day. Positions are shown on the map, the 353rd Infantry lines extending along the Northern edge of the BOIS de BARRICOURT and the 354th Infantry from point 06.1 x 93.9 to Hill 289 at the Western Boundary of the Division.

The night of November 1-2 was spent by the troops in reorganizing and bringing up artillery and supplies and in evacuating wounded, and generally in preparation for resuming the attack on the following day. Orders received in the night provided, in substance, that the attack would be resumed at 5:30 November 2nd, not preceded by artillery preparation but accompanied by a rolling barrage which would advance at the same rate as the barrage of the previous day. The Exploitation Line, described in the Field Order under which the attack was begun was designated as the objective for the day, 2nd November. Great difficulties were experienced in the evacuation of wounded during this night—particularly of those of the right regiment, because of the conditions of the roads. The wounded had neither blankets nor overcoats and it was found impossible to get ambulances to the Northern portion of the BOIS de BARRICOURT in the sector of the right regiment because of the condition of the roads. There were two routes only possible, one through ANDEVANNE and one to the East, along the Northern edge of the BOIS de BARRICOURT. Both of these routes were absolutely impassable to wheeled vehicles and, in consequence, the wounded were not evacuated until the following day. It was found impossible also to bring up a sufficient amount of artillery. One brigade of field artillery was relieved on obtaining the first day's objective and, in consequence of the inability to bring up heavy artillery, the artillery barrage at 5:30 on the morning of November 2nd proved to be wholly ineffective.

At the hour set for the advance to the attack brisk shelling of our front lines by the enemy was in progress. The barrage which had been ordered consisted, for the reasons above given, of only 22 guns on the entire division sector. Neither regiment was able to distinguish it as a barrage and in consequence neither regiment advanced at the hour specified. When it was reported to the brigade that the infantry had not advanced, immediate arrangements were made with the artillery to recall and start the barrage again at hour 10:00 o'clock. This second barrage also proved too feeble to afford the infantry any protection from the intense fire directed on the Northern edges of the BOIS de BARRICOURT, and still the Infantry did not advance. Orders had in the meanwhile been issued from the Brigade for the Infantry to advance without artillery support, using their own weapons. A very slight advance was made by the 354th Infantry because of intense machine gun fire from well organized positions on the slopes surrounding the town of BARRICOURT. The 353rd Infantry, however, advanced without artillery support, emerging from the woods shortly after noon. The formation adopted was to advance on both flanks of the regimental sector, supported by the fire of 1-pounders and Stokes Mortars. The attack proved successful and the enemy resistance having been broken in the immediate front of this regiment the advance was continued during the day and at 18:00 o'clock report was received that this battalion had entered TAILLY and was in occupation of the Exploitation Line—the day's objective.

In the meanwhile, also, while the lines of the left regiment had not been able to advance to the town of BARRICOURT patrols had been pushed out which encircled the town and one patrol entered the town of NOUART and occupied it on the night 2-3 November, and was in possession of the town when troops of the 178th Brigade entered the following day. On the morning of the 3rd November the lines of the 177th Brigade were passed by the 178th Brigade, which took up the assault.

After the passage of lines by the 178th Brigade the two regiments were assembled on the heights, respectively, North of TAILLY and South of NOUART. Two machine gun companies of the brigade were on the night 3-4 November sent forward to support the advance of the 178th Brigade. During the ensuing days a number of changes of position were made: the 354th Infantry occupying positions in BOIS de DIEULET and BOIS LA DAME with headquarters at FARM DE MAUCOURT, and the 353rd Infantry in the vicinity of BEAUCLAIR and BEAUFORT and the Southeastern border of BOIS de DIEULET with headquarters at TAILLY and later at BEAUCLAIR. Durigg the period of 3 November to 10 November the brigade organized these positions for defense and engaged in refitting and training. During the night 10th-11th November, when the crossing of the MEUSE was being effected, the 354th Infantry followed the 178th Brigade in the direction of POUILLY and on the morning of 11 November, when the Armistice went into effect, had crossed the MEUSE at POUILLY with two companies—the remainder of the regiment being in BOIS de DIEULET preparing to advance. During the night 10-11 November the 1st and 3rd Battalions of the 353rd Infantry had been pushed forward to LANEUVILLE while the 2nd Battalion was sent to cross the MEUSE in the vicinity of VILLEFRANCHE to act as combat liaison detachment with the 90th Division on our right. This regiment was ordered to effect a crossing of the MEUSE at STENAY, it having been reported that a foot bridge across the river had been discovered, although the road bridge had been previously demolished by the enemy. Early in the morning of November 11th, the Third Battalion, 353rd Infantry, was ordered to proceed from LANEUVILLE to VILLEFRANCHE, cross the river and join the 2nd Battalion, and both battalions were ordered to push Northward on the right bank of the MEUSE and effect an entrance to STENAY from the South. The Second and Third Battalions were unable to advance to STENAY, but the 1st Battalion which had remained in LANEUVILLE succeeded in getting troops across the river, at first by a small patrol and later with an entire company, entering and occupying the town of STENAY at 10:55 A.M. on November 11th. The town was found unoccupied and only lightly damaged by shell fire.

All hostilities ceased at 11:00 o'clock November 11th. The positions of the brigade at the time being as follows:

353rd Infantry—First Battalion, less 1 company, at LANEUVILLE. Company "A," First Battalion in STENAY. Second and Third Battalions about 2 kilometers Southeast of STENAY.

354th Infantry, less two companies, in BOIS de DIEULET. Companies "A" and "B" at POUILLY.

PART III. STATEMENT OF ENEMY UNITS ENGAGED.

Previous to the attack of November 1st, the 13th German Division had been holding the sector opposite the brigade. Within 30 minutes after H hour identification of prisoners from the 88th Division had been made. They stated that their division had relieved the 13th Division on the night of October 29-30th. The 88th Division had come into line from the WOEVRE front, after resting 8 days at FOSSE, and receiving replacements there. When these replacement troops, wearing their old insignia and shoulder straps, were captured, considerable confusion arose as to the identification of units. Prisoners of the 353rd Regiment, 88th Division, were taken near LA DHUY FARM, and from the 426th Regiment, 88th Division, North of the BOIS de BANTHEVILLE, before 7:00 o'clock. Prisoners from the 352nd Regiment of the same division were taken North of the BOIS de BANTHEVILLE before 8:00 o'clock.

By 9:00 o'clock prisoners had been captured from the 55th Regiment, 13th Division, who stated that their division on being relieved had taken up a position in support of the 88th Division. About 10:00 o'clock prisoners were taken from the 18th Division, South of REMONVILLE.

During the afternoon and during the fighting of November 2nd prisoners from the 18th and 152nd Regiments of the 41st Division came in. They were taken in the vicinity of the BOIS de BARRICOURT. During all the fighting of November 1st and 2nd large numbers of prisoners from the 88th Division continued to come in, outnumbering the prisoners from all other units.

Owing to the rapidity of the advance and the fact that most prisoners were taken by their captors direct to the Division enclosure further identifications were impossible.

PART IV.

A. THE DEPTH OF ADVANCE:

The advance of this brigade during the period it conducted the attack was 8½ kilometers. The total advance of the Division was approximately 21 kilometers.

B. PRISONERS TAKEN:

353rd Infantry—650 officers and men.
354th Infantry—653 officers and men.

C. MATERIAL CAPTURED:

In the course of the operations of November 1st and 2nd there were taken one 9" howitzer, two 210 howitzers, 5 150's, 4 105's, 24 77's, 335 machine guns, 15 minenwerfers, 1 anti-aircraft gun, 7—1-pounders, 3 auto trucks and a huge quantity of other material and ammunition.

D. CASUALTIES:

177TH INFANTRY BRIGADE HEADQUARTERS: Killed—1 man.

353RD INFANTRY:	Killed — 2 officers,	53 men.
	Wounded— 5 officers,	307 men.
	Missing — 0 officers,	66 men.
354TH INFANTRY:	Killed — 2 officers,	98 men.
	Wounded— 7 officers,	394 men.
	Missing — 0 officers,	85 men.
341ST MACHINE GUN BATTALION:	Killed — 0 officers,	13 men.
	Wounded— 6 officers,	36 men.
	Missing — 0 officers,	38 men.
TOTALS FOR BRIGADE:	Killed — 4 officers,	165 men.
	Wounded—18 officers,	737 men.
	Missing — 0 officers,	189 men.

Total casualties—22 officers, 1091 men.

E. EMPLOYMENT OF INFANTRY WEAPONS:

Two machine gun companies were used to fire a barrage before H hour, and performed their work well. During the attack the machine guns rendered excellent service, keeping pace with the combat groups at all times. Those of the support battalion contributed overhead fire during the advance. Immediately upon halting the machine guns were promptly and effectively posted for defensive work. In the 2nd day's attack the machine guns played an important and valuable part.

The 37 mm. guns were used by both regiments with good effect. The guns went forward with the assaulting battalions in each regiment and when the lines were passed by the support battalions they went on with the new assaulting battalion. In both regiments the guns kept up and scored hits on machine gun nests. In the 354th Infantry three guns were used which were separated over the front during the advance, but which assembled at previously designated assembly points at the different objectives. In the 353rd Infantry two guns were used. They kept up within 40 yards of the front wave of the assaulting battalion. 500 rounds of ammunition was fired in this regiment.

The Stokes Mortars were also used with fair effect in both regiments. They were taken forward with the assaulting battalion and advanced after the passage of lines and kept up well with the advance. In the 354th Infantry the ammunition was transported in a wagon which kept up sufficiently well so that no shortage of ammunition was experienced. In the 353rd Infantry the ammunition was transported by carriers and by the gun crew in improvised slings. Altogether 150 rounds were fired. In this regiment one enemy cannon, cal. 88, and its entire gun crew was cut out of action by a direct hit from a Stokes Mortar at a range of about 500 yards. This occurred on the ridge above REMONVILLE. The rifle grenades were also used with good effect in both regiments but their use was not extensive. In the 353rd Infantry one machine gun nest was put out of action on a trail in the BARRICOURT Woods. It was found that the moral effect of fire from Stokes Mortars and rifle grenades on machine gun nests was very great.

There seems to have been no use whatever made of the hand grenade in this operation by either regiment.

F. EMPLOYMENT OF AUXILIARY WEAPONS:

No tanks were used in the operation. One company of gas troops were assigned to the brigade and participated in the fire preparation and the beginning of the artillery barrage. These troops did not keep up with the advance and they were probably of very little use.

G. ARTILLERY, SUPPORT:

The two guns assigned to each regiment as accompanying guns participated in the barrage and afterwards went forward with the Infantry. They were not in touch with the commanding officers either of the regiment or of the assault battalion in the advance and, consequently, were not able to perform their special mission. They did, however, advance ahead of the supporting artillery and did fire on targets discovered by themselves. The value of these accompanying guns in a rapid advance such as the one in question is doubtful.

The general artillery support on the first day's advance was excellent at the start. As the advance continued, however, there was a failure of liaison because the artillery was not provided with telephones or any communication except by runner. During the second day's fighting, when the movement of the troops was much slower, liaison was effected through the telephone and effective support was had from the field artillery. In the 353rd Infantry especially good service was rendered by the artillery liaison officer who more than once located hostile guns by their flash and succeeded in getting them put out of action by the fire of our artillery.

The failure of the artillery barrage on the 2nd day has been noted above. On the morning of the 3rd a barrage laid down by the 90th Division, which was attacking on our right, lapped its sector and extended beyond into the sector occupied by troops of this brigade to 07.5 x 94.6. This barrage passed over the troops occupying the position of resistance, fortunately without causing any casualties, and before it reached the troops stationed on the advance post position at the Exploitation Line word was received at the brigade and was transmitted to the Chief of Staff of the 90th Division in time for him to stop the barrage and save the troops of the advance post position from being subjected to the fire.

H. TERRAIN:

The country through which the Brigade had to pass in the first stages of the advance was gradually rolling, with occasional patches of woods. South of LA DHUY FME and extending to the Northern edge of the BOIS de BANTHEVILLE was a considerable ridge, reached, however, by gradual slopes. The whole country was such as to afford the enemy excellent opportunity for the use of machine guns. He had prepared machine gun emplacements in great numbers, utilizing every fringe of trees and every fold of ground.

The right regiment encountered a strong position in the BOIS D'ANDEVANNE. These woods had been organized with machine gun emplacements and wire. In the neighborhood of REMONVILLE the country was open, the roads and ditches and the town itself being the only defensive positions of value.

Beyond REMONVILLE the advance was made over the wooded heights of BARRICOURT. These heights formed the strongest natural defensive position of the entire advance. From them the enemy artillery had fired with great effect during the early stages of the attack, but the advance was so rapid that the enemy had not time to reorganize here and his strongest position was gained at small cost.

The halt at dusk on the first day was made at the Northern edge of the BOIS de BARRICOURT. The country from here to the Exploitation Line was sharply rolling, consisting of a series of valleys and ridges. On the left of the brigade sector was the valley extending south-southeast from BARRICOURT, and the smaller valley extending Southwest from BARRICOURT. Each valley was dominated by machine guns on the opposite slope, with field guns very close up to control the situation. It was these features, together with the fact that the enemy had determined to make a stand here at all cost, that made the fighting of the second day the most severe that this brigade has ever seen.

I. CONCLUSIONS:

This attack was most successfully accomplished by this brigade which attained all its objectives on scheduled time. Liaison between the assaulting battalions and the artillery was relatively poor during the period of rapid advance, but quite good when the advance was slower. Liaison between the brigade and the regiments was very good. It was maintained by runners only until the evening of the first day, because of the rapid advance. During the second day telephone communication was established with good effect. The regimental wireless sets were not used during the advance, not having been brought up. This can probably be obviated by a little more energy on the part of the regimental signal platoons. The plan of having the regiments follow the brigade axis of liaison and having points where brigade and regimental headquarters shall meet, as prescribed in the Field Order, proved successful and effective. Maps illustrating the entire advance during the period the brigade was conducting the assault, and the Field Orders of the Division and of the Brigade, under which the attack was made, are hereto attached.

COMBAT LIAISON ON THE FLANKS:

The Combat Liaison Company on the right flank was unsuccessful in its mission on the first day, owing to the dense woods through which it moved, and at no time did it gain contact with the 90th Division. On the second day contact with the 90th Division was established and maintained.

The combat liaison on the left flank was only a little more successful. The afternoon of the first day the company on this flank gained liaison with this division, only to lose it again. Contact was regained the second day and again lost. Had this contact been maintained the second day, the brigade would have known that there was no advance on the left during the entire day and would have arranged its attack accordingly. This fact was not known, however, until the night of the second day.

LIAISON TO THE REAR:

All possible means of liaison to the rear were used. Telephone liaison would have been much more successful had the Divisional Axis of Liaison kept up with the brigade. The Signal Officer at brigade headquarters strung wire from the initial brigade P. C. to REMON-

VILLE, but at this point the wire gave out. During the first day and most of the second day it was the brigade wire, and not the Division wire, that maintained all telephone communication ahead of the Division P. C.

CARE OF WOUNDED:

The shortage of the medical personnel in both regiments was a serious handicap to the care of the wounded. The full table of organization strength for the Medical Department is scarcely enough for a long advance of this kind and the 353rd Infantry had less than a fourth of its proper strength. The motor ambulances did not follow the attacking battalions closely enough. During the greater part of the first day's advance it was possible for one or more motor ambulances to follow the Second Line Battalion. Later the 353rd Infantry in the BOIS de BARRICOURT was inaccessible, but it was still possible to follow the 354th Infantry more closely than they did.

BURIAL OF THE DEAD:

The band of each regiment accompanied by a Chaplain followed its regiment, covering its entire sector and burying both Americans and Germans. This plan proved very satisfactory. Special arrangements should be made for the burial of animals. It has been suggested that details of prisoners be used for this purpose.

FOOD:

Food did not come up promptly, because of blockade of the roads.

COMBAT TRAINS:

Combat trains followed at a proper distance. The combat trains of the 1-pounders and Stokes Mortars were kept well to the front.

A map illustrating the advance and copies of the Field Orders of the Brigade are attached.

FRANK L. WINN,
Major General, U. S. A.,
Commanding.

APPENDIX "D"

178TH INFANTRY BRIGADE COMMANDER'S REPORT

HEADQUARTERS
178TH INF. BRIGADE,
89TH DIVISION, FRANCE

From: Commanding General, 178th Infantry Brigade.
To: Commanding General, 89th Division.
Subject: Report of operations from night 19th-20th October, 1918, to 9th November, 1918, inclusive.

In compliance with special memorandum, 8th November, 1918, the following is submitted:

PART. I. SITUATION AT THE BEGINNING OF OPERATIONS.

On the 19th of October, 1918, the 178th Infantry Brigade was in bivouac extending from a point just north of EPINONVILLE to ECLISFONTAINE, with the 355th Infantry on the right and the 356th Infantry on the left. One company of the 342nd Machine Gun Battalion was attached to the 355th Infantry and one to the 356th Infantry and the remainder was in Brigade Reserve south of the center point between the two regiments. At this time the 32nd Division was holding the line in front of this brigade. At 3:45 P. M. the two regiments received orders to move forward and relieve the right sector of the 32nd Division, which was holding a position in front of the ROMAGNE-SOMMERANCE Road, which extended from a POINT 07.3-84.9 to 05.7-87.3. This relief was completed about 2:00 A. M., 20th of October. At this time, each regiment had a battalion in the front line, one in support and one held in the rear as Brigade Reserve. The two reserve battalions were in the woods near POINT 06.3-84.4. Brigade P. C. was just North of EPINONVILLE.

At 5:00 A. M., 20th of October, 1918, the two Regimental Commanders were given orders to mop up the BOIS de BANTHEVILLE, to be completed by midnight the 20th of October. This mission was not accomplished until about 4:30 hours 21st of October, due to the strong opposition of the enemy by means of artillery and organized machine gun fire. It will be seen from the locations of the troops that this mission was not exactly a mopping up one, but was an advance against stubborn resistance to the North edge of the woods, BOIS de BANTHEVILLE. At 3:00 hours, 22nd of October the 355th Infantry was relieved by the 353rd Infantry and at 21:30 hours 22nd of October the 356th Infantry was relieved by a battalion of the 353rd Infantry. During this period, the Machine Gun Battalion was located as above, that is, one with each regiment and two with the Brigade Reserve. Upon being relieved, the 178th Brigade withdrew and was consolidated in the BOIS de CIERGES, west of the ROMAGNE-ECLISFONTAINE Road. Brigade P. C. moved into the woods just east of the Brigade. Machine Gun Battalion was placed in the draw about 500 meters North of GESNES and the Machine Gun Companies of the regiments were united with the Machine Gun Battalions. This movement was completed the 23rd of October.

On the 20th of October, Brigade P. C. moved to the point about one kilometer South of ROMAGNE on the ROMAGNE-ECLISFONTAINE Road. On the night 26th-27th of October, the 355th Infantry moved forward and occupied a position one and one-half kilometers North-west of GESNES and the 356th Infantry occupied the square between 04-05 and 82-83. The Machine Gun Battalion remained in the draw just North of GESNES and the entire brigade remained in these positions until the night of the 31st of October. Brigade P. C. moved to a point in the N. E. outskirts of GESNES. Between the 23rd and 31st October, the Machine Gun Battalion and the Regimental Machine Gun Companies were occupied in digging emplacements in the North and Northwest edges of the BOIS de BANTHEVILLE and bringing up one and one-half million rounds of ammunition. These machine gun units had been notified that they would support the initial advance with overhead machine gun fire. During this period the Stokes Mortars and one pounder detachments were engaged in similar work.

PART II. THE ATTACK.

The 28th of October, Field Order No. 45, 89th Division, was received and in conformity with this Field Order No. 22, Headquarters 178th Infantry Brigade, dated 29th of October, was issued. On the night of the 31st of October, the Infantry Regiments of the brigade moved to a position in the BOIS de GESNES Southwest of the ridge between the grid lines 05 and 06. The Machine Gun Battalions and the Regimental Machine Gun Companies moved to the North and Northwest edge of the BOIS de BANTHEVILLE, where they had previously prepared positions. The Machine Gun Battalion and Machine Gun Companies of the regiment and the Stokes Mortars and one pounder detachments moved forward to the Northeast edge of the BOIS de BANTHEVILLE where there was prepared position. "D" day and "H" hour was 5:30 hours 1st November, 1918.

The Brigade held these positions with instructions to await orders from the Division Commander. At 3:30 hours, the artillery, machine guns, one pounders and Stokes Mortars began the preliminary bombardment which lasted until 5:30 hours. At about 13 hours, 1st November, 1918, the Infantry Regiments moved forward into the BOIS de BANTHEVILLE near POINT 05.5-86.5. They were echeloned in columns of battalions with 1000 meters distance between battalions. During this time the 177th Brigade was proceeding with the attack. After the completion of the preliminary barrage which ended at about 7:02 hours, the Machine Gun Battalion, Machine Gun Companies, Stokes Mortars and one pounders were instructed to report to the Commanding General of the Division Reserve at cross roads POINT 06.0-88.9. The Infantry Regiments were directed to move forward and take a position with the leading elements on the first objective. This they did in columns of battalions with an interval between regiments of about 500 or 600 meters, arriving at 5:00 P. M. The axis between regiments was the grid line 05. At 12 hours, the 1st of November, the Machine Gun units were directed to send to each regiment the Regimental Machine Gun Company, Stokes Mortar and one pounder units, and to send two companies of the 342nd Machine Gun Battalion as reserve to follow the rear battalion of the 355th Infantry at a distance of 1000 meters.

At midnight 1st of November, the regiments were alert and shortly afterwards moved forward and at daylight, 2nd of November, the following positions were held: Leading battalion 355th Infantry 06.7-91.9. Its right rested on the right Division sector and the two remaining battalions were each 1000 meters to the rear, with their right resting on the right Divisional sector. The 356th Infantry had one battalion just Northeast of REMONVILLE in the BOIS de BARRICOURT, one battalion about 500 meters Northwest of REMONVILLE and the remaining battalion in REMONVILLE. The two Machine Gun Companies that had been held in reserve were sent to REMONVILLE to report to the Commanding Officer 354th Infantry. At 0:30 hours, 3rd of November, 1918, Field Orders No. 50, 89th Division, was received by Regimental Commanders at Le DHUY FARME; at this time Brigade P. C. was at Le DHUY FARME. The regiments of the brigade were ordered to cross the road running Southeast of BARRICOURT in square 64 at 5:30 hours, 3rd of November. The crossing on the right was made at about 6:00 A. M. with the 355th Infantry on the right and the 356th Infantry on the left and as heretofore, in columns of battalions. The right of the 355th Infantry extended to the right Divisional line and the left of the 356th Infantry to the left Divisional line. At 11 hours, 3rd of November, 1918, the 355th Infantry had reached its objective, which was the North edge of the BOIS de TAILLY and at 10:30 hours the 356th Infantry had reached its objective, which was the heights overlooking La CHAMPY HAUT and the NOUART-BEAUCLAIR Road. At about 11 hours 3rd November, one Machine Gun Company of the 342nd Machine Gun Battalion was detached from the 356th Infantry and placed with the right battalion of the Brigade reserve. On the morning of the 3rd of November, Brigade P. C. moved to a point on the REMONVILLE-BARRICOURT Road at about 500 meters North of the BOIS de BARRICOURT. At 15 hours the 3rd of November the support battalion of the 355th Infantry passed through the first battalion on its mission of exploitation and shortly after 12 hours the support battalion 356th Infantry did the same. The Machine Gun Companies were distributed as previously mentioned.

Both of the leading battalions encountered strong resistance, from artillery and machine gun fire, after making passage of the lines, but a battalion of the 355th Infantry reached the edge of the town of BEAUCLAIR at 21:30 hours, while the leading battalion of the 356th Infantry reached its position in the Southern edge of the BOIS de BELVAL at 17 hours. During the night of the 3rd of November, an effort was made, in compliance with Divisional Orders, to send a strong exploitation column from the 355th Infantry to BEAUFORT and also one from the 356th Infantry to BEAUMONT to gain contact with the 2nd Division on the left. The column from the 355th was successfully accomplished at 6:30 hours the 4th of November, but the column from the 356th Infantry did not gain contact with the 2nd Division until the 5th of November, because the 2nd Division had not yet come up to the front line elements. At about 4 hours the 4th of November the Machine Gun Company that had been with the Brigade Reserve, joined the support battalion of the 355th Infantry just north of TAILLY. During the afternoon of the 3rd November, Brigade P. C. moved to BARRICOURT and then shortly after that, the same afternoon, on to TAILLY, and on the forenoon of the 4th of November, it had reached BEAUCLAIR. During the night of the 3rd-4th of November, Field Order No. 51 of Division was received. "H" hour was set at 8:30 hours 4th of November.

In this advance, the Divisional front was divided in three sub-sectors with three battalions in the lead and three in the support at a distance of 1000 meters. The right sub-sector and the center sub-sector under command of the Regimental Commander, 355th Infantry, were unable to advance, due to heavy machine gun and artillery fire from the enemy until 3:30 P. M. and because our own barrage had not materialized. However, they did move forward later and the FORET de DIEULET was cleared at about 17:30 hours and the Northwestern edge in their front was occupied at that time. LANEUVILLE was occupied by the right sub-sector at about 19:30 hours 4th of November. The left sub-sector moved forward at 8:30 hours and reached its objective on the Northeastern edge of the FORET de DIEULET at 14:30 hours. Liaison was maintained between the two regiments.

During the night of the 4th of November, Division Field Order No. 52 was received which extended the Western boundary to the Western edge of the FORET de JAULNAY. Brigade P. C. was still at BEAUCLAIR. During the night of the 4th-5th November, the Commanding Officer 356th Infantry received instructions to consolidate the support battalion of the center sub-sector which belonged to his regiment and the support battalion of the left sub-sector into consolidated column and cross the LANEUVILLE-BEAUMONT Road at 6 hours. Due to the late hour at which he received this order the start across the road was not made until about 8:30 hours. His instructions were to move Northeast to the FORET de JAULNAY with his left on the River MEUSE and to clear the entire salient between POUILLY and LANEUVILLE of the enemy. The Northeastern edge of the FORET de JAULNAY was reached at 16:30 hours 5th November. Brigade P. C. remained at BEAUCLAIR.

During the forenoon of the 5th of November, the Commanding Officer of the 356th Infantry received instructions from the Brigade Commander by telephone to detach a battalion and hold the bridgehead opposite POUILLY without crossing the river. This battalion had with it the Machine Gun Company belonging to the Brigade Battalion and four additional Machine Gun Companies were sent to reinforce it. The battalion was in position before dark the 5th of November. The various Machine Gun Companies except the one with the battalion joined this battalion at different hours during the night of the 5th-6th November. Two of these Machine Gun companies belonged to the Divisional Machine Gun Battalion and two were from the 177th Brigade. At 24:00 hours 5th November, the battalion opposite POUILLY had one platoon on the island across the canal East of POUILLY, one company was East of the canal and the remainder of the battalion along the railroad track and East of it. The other battalion remained at the Northeast edge of the FORET de JAULNAY. The remaining battalion of the 356th Infantry was on the Northern edge of the FORET de DIEULET and the 355th Infantry was on the right sector on the Northern edge of these woods with two platoons in each of the towns of LUZY, CESSE and LANEUVILLE with patrols along the East bank of the MEUSE. Brigade P. C. at BEAUCLAIR.

At dawn, 6th of November the battalion of the 356th Infantry which was close to the river opposite POUILLY was withdrawn to the wooded slopes in the FORET de JAULNAY. Two companies on the slope overlooking the river and two on the reverse slope with outposts along the edge of the forest overlooking the town. The machine guns, consisting of five companies, were a short distance back in the woods in emplacements. The remainder of the line was as previously stated. These positions were held by day on the 6th, the 7th and until the forenoon of the 8th of November. The 3rd Battalion, 356th Infantry, moved down to its original position close to the river at night, withdrawing at daylight. All along the line patrols were kept up along the river and two patrols were in each of the towns LUZY, CESSE and LANEUVILLE. Patrols at night were also sent across the river by swimming. Attempts were made to use rafts, but unsuccessfully, but patrols did get across at LANEUVILLE on a footbridge.

(The night of 7th-8th November, Divisional Field Order No. 55 was received). During the forenoon of the 8th of November, the Regimental Commander 356th Infantry received orders to withdraw his first battalion from the Northeast edge of the FORET de JAULNAY and place it in the BOIS de la VACHE and the second battalion from its position along the Northeastern edge of the FORET de DIEULET to a position South of the BEAUMONT-LANEUVILLE Road at about 09.3-05.3. The 3rd Battalion and Machine Guns which were Southeast of POUILLY were to remain in their present position. The movement of the 356th Infantry was completed at 15 hours, 8th November. On the same morning, 8th of November, the Reserve Battalion of the 355th Infantry moved to and occupied the square between grid lines 11 and 12, South of the ridge in the FORET de JAULNAY. Another battalion moved to and occupied the squares 26, 15 and 16, along the edge of the woods, and the remaining battalion occupied square 23 along the edge of the woods. This was accomplished before 18 hours 8th November. Outposts were put out along the river and patrols maintained between POUILLY FARME and LANEUVILLE. The dividing line between regiments extended from POUILLY FARME to the letter L in La BOUTELLE about 10.2-03.9. The left division sector was BEAUMONT exclusive, LETANNE exclusive, AUTREVILLE inclusive. The right was the river MEUSE At 24 hours 8th November, troops were located the same as at 18 hours. There was no change in the location of the troops until the evening of the 10th of November. Patrols along the river and across the river were kept up the night of the 8th-9th November and the night of the 9th-10th November. On the night of the 9th-10th November, the 356th Infantry sent patrols across in pontoon boats, capturing prisoners. The afternoon of the 9th of November, Brigade P. C. moved to Prison Camp. On 9th November, 1918, Brigadier General Hall was assigned to command the 178th Infantry Brigade.

PART III. STATEMENTS OF ENEMY ENGAGED, TIME AND PLACE.

So far as this office can learn, the enemy units engaged consisted of the 88th German Division, 13th Prussian Division, machine gun and artillery units.

PART IV. SUMMARY.

(a) DEPTH OF ADVANCE.

Depth of advance, as shown on map, was about 24 kilometers.

(b) PRISONERS TAKEN.

No effort was made here to keep an accurate record of prisoners captured. They were immediately sent to the rear to Division Headquarters.

(c) MATERIAL CAPTURED.

No record was kept by the Brigade of the amount of material captured. It included a number of field guns, machine guns, minenwerfers, ammunition and a large amount of supplies of various kinds.

(d) CASUALTIES.

	Officers.	Men
Killed	8	202
Wounded	19	668
Missing	6	209
Gassed	..	19

(e) EMPLOYMENT OF INFANTRY WEAPONS, ETC.

Machine gun and rifle fire was extensively and effectively used and also fire from the CHAUCHOT. The Stokes Mortars were used at the original jump-off November 1st, also the one-pounders. The one-pounders were also effectively used against machine gun positions on the East bank of the MEUSE. Rifle grenades could not be used in this advance as the range was too great or else the fighting was in woods or at night. Overhead Machine Gun fire was successfully used quite often, especially at Le CHAMPY HAUT, BARRICOURT and in the FORET de DIEULET. Where troops were held up by machine gun nests, they were successfully taken by strong frontal rifle and Chauchot fire and then by flank movements with fire using the same weapon.

(f) EMPLOYMENT OF ARTILLERY WEAPONS, TANKS, GAS TROOPS, ETC.

None employed. Very complete arrangements were made to use the gas troops in case the passage across the MEUSE was to be forced during the day time, but as this was done at night, the gas troops could not be used.

(g) ARTILLERY SUPPORT.

The artillery support, consisting of heavy artillery and field artillery, was very effective in the destructive fire and barrage on the 1st of November. On the 3rd and 4th of November, it did not give any support, due to the rapid advance of the Infantry; consequent difficulty in bringing up the pieces.

(h) TERRAIN.

As shown by the map, rolling at and at places timbered with thick underbrush; in consequence it was advantageous for the American method of maneuvering, but difficult in respect to supplies and evacuation on account of the lack of improved roads.

(i) CONCLUSION.

Leading battalions were aggressive and courageous. Group and platoon leaders displayed initiative and swept away enemy resistance. The successful advance shows that our methods, combined with the courage of the men, are correct.

HERMAN HALL,
Brigadier General.

HEADQUARTERS
178TH INFANTRY BRIGADE
89TH DIVISION, FRANCE.

From: Commanding General, 178th Infantry Brigade.
To: Commanding General, 89th Division.
Subject: Supplementary report of operations from night 9th-10th November, 1918, to 11th November, inclusive.

PART I. SITUATION AT THE BEGINNING OF OPERATION.

The situation was as stated at the close of the report of the operations up to the arrival of the Brigade on the West bank of the MEUSE river.

PART II. THE ATTACK.

At 3:35 P. M. 10th November, Divisional Field Order No. 58 was received and a corrected copy at 4:50 P. M. Capt. Dennie, 314th Engineers, who was to arrange the details for the crossing in pontoon boats, reported at Brigade Headquarters at 5:20 P. M. He reported that it would take three hours to make the preliminary arrangements for ferrying the troops across and such arrangements had to begin after dark to avoid detection of the enemy. Information was received from the 2nd Division that they would advance from the river at 9:30 P. M. This Brigade adjusted its plans accordingly. The Artillery destructive fire began on the town of POUILLY up to and including the left Divisional sector at 9:30 p. m., followed by a rolling barrage. The leading battalion, 356th Infantry, 1st Battalion, under Capt. Puffer, advanced from the right bank of the MEUSE at 9:30 P. M., followed by the 3rd Battalion, 356th Infantry and the 3rd Battalion, 355th Infantry, less one company; these Battalions were accompanied by a machine gun company, and the rear battalion had one extra machine gun company sent to it. The crossing was very successfully made at a point where the WAME stream enters the MEUSE.

At 4:30 hours 11th November, the town of POUILLY was mopped up, capturing over 100 prisoners. One battalion, 2nd, 356th Infantry, was sent to BEAUMONT as a liaison battalion with the 2nd Division and reported there at 19 hours 10th November. At 24 hours, 10th November, the leading battalion was beyond POUILLY on the high hill to the Northeast with the right outstanding to the river and its left to the Divisional Sector. At 6 hours 11th November, the leading battalion was in the BOIS de HACHE with reconnoitering parties towards the BOIS de SOIRY. At 8 hours 11th November, one company detached from the support battalion, 3rd, 356th Infantry, entered AUTREVILLE and occupied the high hill to the West of that town.

The morning of the 11th November was a very foggy one and between 6 hours and 11 hours, the organizations were occupied in mopping up the country in their vicinity and rear and reconnoitering to the front in order to determine their exact location. At 11 hours the Armistice became effective and hostilities ceased. At this time, 11 hours, four battalions of the 178th Infantry Brigade were on the East bank of the MEUSE. One battalion of the 355th Infantry was in the BOIS de la HACHE, transferred during the night from LANEUVILLE and square 23 to the BOIS de la HACHE having been relieved by a battalion of the 353rd Infantry. Five companies of the 355th Infantry were holding the FORET de JAULNAY and the town of LUZY. CESSE had been taken over by the 353rd Infantry. Four machine gun companies were across the river, one had gone with the liaison battalion to the left and one was in the Northeast edge of the FORET de JAULNAY.

PART III. STATEMENT OF ENEMY ENGAGED, TIME AND PLACE.

So far as this office can learn, the enemy units engaged consisted of the 88th German Division, 13th Prussian Division, machine gun and artillery units.

PART IV. SUMMARY.

(a) DEPTH OF ADVANCE.

Depth of advance, 5 kilometers.

(b) PRISONERS TAKEN.

About 174, so far as this office knows.

(c) MATERIAL CAPTURED.

No accurate record is available, but the material included field guns, machine guns, minenwerfers, warehouses, pontoon train and various supplies.

(d) CASUALTIES.

	Officers	Men
Killed	3	2
Wounded	19	249
Missing	..	2
Gassed	..	..

(e) EMPLOYMENT OF INFANTRY WEAPONS, ETC.

The same remarks will apply as given in the main report.

(f) EMPLOYMENT OF AUXILIARY WEAPONS, TANKS, GAS TROOPS, ETC.

None.

(g) ARTILLERY SUPPORT.

The destructive fire and barrage of the heavy and field guns up to and during the attack, 10th-11th November, was excellent and of great assistance. The willing co-operation of the artillery officers and the fire obtained were all to be desired.

(h) TERRAIN.

From the MEUSE to the BOIS de la HACHE, open, but hilly except to the Northeast end, where it is wooded.

(i) CONCLUSION.

This crossing of the MEUSE was very successful, due to careful plans of Colonel Allen, 356th Infantry, and assistance rendered by Captain Dennie, 314th Engineers, and arranging for ferrying the command in pontoons. The advance of the first Bn., 356th Infantry, under command of Captain Ray K. Puffer, 356th Infantry, on a dark foggy night, was highly commendable. It is believed that, in general, more time should be given regiments to prepare for the execution of orders of advance. On occasions like forcing a river passage, battalion, company and platoon commanders should be carefully instructed and when the command is scattered, this requires time.

HERMAN HALL,
Brigadier General.

APPENDIX "E"

58TH FIELD ARTILLERY BRIGADE COMMANDER'S REPORT

HEADQUARTERS
58TH FIELD ARTILLERY BRIGADE
AMERICAN EXPEDITIONARY FORCES.

18 December 1918.

REPORT OF OPERATIONS.
FROM OCTOBER 19, 1918 TO NOVEMBER 11, 1918.

SITUATION ON OCTOBER 19, 1918.

The 58th Field Artillery Brigade was in rest billets in the vicinity of VILLE SUR COUSANCE. Brigade Headquarters and the 123rd Field Artillery at VILLE SUR COUSANCE. 122nd Field Artillery at JUBECOURT, 124th Field Artillery at BROCOURT, 108th Ammunition Train at BRABANT, 108th Trench Mortar Battery at VRAINCOURT. At this time the 58th Field Artillery Brigade was attached to the 1st Army.

SUBSEQUENT EVENTS.

Per Memorandum dated Oct. 21, 1918, Hdqrs. 1st Army, the 123rd Field Artillery was ordered to entrain for DOULAINCOURT to be motorized and re-equipped. In accordance with this order the animals and part of the rolling stock of the 123rd Field Artillery were transferred to the 122nd and 124th Field Artillery.

Per Memorandum Instructions, Hdqrs. 1st Army, dated Oct. 22nd, the 58th Field Artillery Brigade, less the 123rd Field Artillery, was attached to the 5th Army Corps for duty with the 89th Division.

Special Orders No. 490, dated Oct. 25, 1918, Hdqrs. 1st Army, attached the 11th Field Artillery to this brigade to replace the 123rd Field Artillery.

Per Memorandum, Hdqrs. 5th Army Corps, dated Oct. 22nd-23rd, the brigade was directed to reconnoiter forward positions to be occupied by the batteries on the night of Oct. 24-25, 1918. In accordance with these Memoranda reconnaissances were made, and on Oct. 24th the

Brigade commenced its march via BROCOURT-RECICOURT-PAROIS-AUBREVILLE-AVOCOURT-MONTFAUCON-CIERGES-GESNES. During the night of Oct. 24th the regiments bivouacked in the BOIS DE CHEPPY and BOIS DE VERY.

On Oct. 25th the march was resumed. Brigade Headquarters was established in GESNES in the afternoon near the P. C. of the 89th Division. During the night of Oct. 25th three regiments of the brigade went into positions south and west of ROMAGNE.

Between Oct. 25th and Nov. 1st, the regiments adjusted their pieces and executed continuous harassings, interdiction and counter-battery fire. The principal targets for the harassing fire were the BOIS DE HAZOIS, BOIS L'EPASSE, BOIS D'ANDEVANNE, LA BERGERIE, LA TUILERIE and LA DHUY FERME, and REMONVILLE. Interdiction fires were executed on the principal cross roads north of BANTHEVILLE. Gas concentration fire was executed on the BOIS DE HAZOIS, BOIS D'ANDEVANNE and REMONVILLE. The 11th Field Artillery counter-battered all enemy batteries reported in action which were located.

The Artillery supporting the 89th Division was comprised of the 57th Field Artillery Brigade, the 203rd (French) Regt. 75 mm., the 58th F. A. Brigade and several units of Corps and Army Artillery. Brigadier General Irwin, Commanding General, 57th F. A. Brigade, commanded the Divisional Artillery. The plan of attack of the Division provided for one platoon from each of the 122nd and 124th F. A., to accompany each assaulting battalion of Infantry.

During the forenoon of Oct. 30th Brigadier General H. D. Todd, Jr., commanding the 58th F. A. Brigade, was wounded by shell splinters while reconnoitering roads to be used during the advance. Brigadier General E. A. Millar, 6th F. A. Brigade, was placed temporarily in command of the 58th F. A. Brigade.

5:30 A. M., November 1, 1918, was fixed as H hour for the attack. The preliminary bombardment commenced at H minus two hours and continued until H hour plus ten minutes This was followed by a rolling barrage, in which the 75 mm. regiments participated, and the covering fire by the 155 mm. Howitzers and Corps and Army Artillery.

At H plus two hours one battalion of the 122nd F. A. ceased firing and advanced to a position near LA DHUY FERME. It was followed at H plus 2:30 by the 2nd Battalion of the 122nd F. A. At H plus 5:30 and H plus 6:00 hours the battalions of the 124th F. A. advanced to positions northeast of LA DHUY FME. At H plus seven hours the 122nd F. A. was in its new position and continued the rolling barrage to and beyond the third objective. The 11th Field Artillery remained in position until the third objective was reached, and advanced to positions south of LA DHUY FME. The 57th Brigade remained in position and, according to the plan of attack, the command of the Divisional Artillery passed to the Commanding General, 58th F. A. Brigade, when the third objective was reached. At H plus 12 hours the 203rd (French) Regt. was ordered to advance, but was unable to do so because of lack of transportation. During the afternoon of D day the Brigade P. C. was established at LA DHUY FME.

Per Field Order No. 47, Hdqrs., 89th Division, dated November 1, 1918, the attack was ordered to be resumed at the same hour on November 2, 1918. By command of the Division, the 122nd F. A. was ordered to move forward at midnight November 1, 1918, to positions near REMONVILLE and be ready to fire a rolling barrage at H hour November 2, 1918. Accordingly the 122nd F. A. advanced soon after midnight, but because of road congestion and the impracticability of laying pieces in the dark, was not in position to fire until 7:00 hours November 2, 1918. The attack of the Divisional Infantry at 5:30 November 2, 1918, was supported by a rolling barrage fired by five batteries of the 124th F. A. on a four kilometer front. This barrage was necessarily thinner than the barrage of November 1, 1918, and the infantry was unable to advance under its cover. A second barrage was ordered for 10:00 hours in which the 122nd F. A. assisted, and under its cover the infantry was able to make considerable progress. The 11th Field Artillery and such of the Corps and Army Artillery as were in position, fired covering fire during the two barrages above mentioned.

During the day of November 2nd, the 122nd F. A. and 124th F. A. fired on such targets as were indicated by the Commanders of the infantry regiments which they were supporting. The heavy artillery fired on sensitive areas in advance of the Infantry and other targets which impeded the advance. The P. C. of the Divisional Artillery remained at LA DHUY FME.

Per Field Order No. 50, Hdqrs., 89th Division, the advance was to continue on Nov. 3, 1918, with the objective of securing the heights over-looking BEAUCLAIR-CHAMPY-HAUT-VAUX. The 124th F. A. was ordered to clear REMONVILLE by 2:00 hours, November 3, 1918, and proceed to a position in the northern edge of BOIS DE BARRICOURT. The 122nd F. A. was ordered to proceed to the northern edge of BOIS DE BARRICOURT as soon as the Infantry had cleared the road north of REMONVILLE. Each of these regiments was placed under the direction of the Infantry Regimental Commanders. One battery of the 124th F. A. was ordered to accompany a battalion of the 355th Infantry which was to push on as exploiting column towards STENAY.

The Divisional Artillery Commander issued orders, in accordance with the above Divisional Plan of Attack, and at 6:00 hours Nov. 3rd, 1918, the attack was resumed. Because of the uncertainty of the Infantry front line and the absence of any specified rate of advance, no rolling barrage was planned. The heavy artillery, under command of General Millar, fired on sensitive areas, lifting their fire according to the reported progress of the Infantry, and the light artillery fired under the direct orders of the Infantry Commanders. Owing to the impassability of the route indicated by the Division Commander and obstruction by the Military Police, the 124th Field Artillery was forced to make several counter-marches, and did not arrive in position in the BOIS de BARRICOURT until 7:00 hours Nov. 2, 1918. Battery C of the 124th F. A., detailed as the accompanying battery with the exploitation column, was instructed by the commander of the 355th Infantry to wait north of REMONVILLE for an Infantry escort. This escort did not arrive, and the Chief of Staff of the Division, seeing the battery inactive, ordered it, verbally, to move forward towards BARRICOURT, which it accordingly did. The progress of the Infantry was exceptionally rapid, and the two light regiments were almost continually on the march during the day, and consequently had few opportunities to fire, but as little resistance was encountered the apparent lack of artillery support was not seriously felt. During the morning of Nov. 3, 1918, General Millar moved his P. C. to REMONVILLE and during the afternoon to BARRICOURT. The 11th F. A. moved to a position near BARRICOURT during the day, and one battalion of the 301st (French) 105 mm. rifles fired effectively on LANEUVILLE and STENAY.

Per Field Orders No. 51, Headquarters 89th Division, the attack was resumed on Nov. 4, 1918. The Artillery support was similar to the support of Nov. 3, 1918; that is, the light regiments remained under the orders of the Infantry Commanders and the heavy artillery fired on sensitive areas and other points which seemed to impede the advance. During the morning the Divisional Artillery P. C. moved to TAILLY. The light regiments continued to advance during the day and fired on such targets as were assigned them by the Infantry Commanders. The 11th F. A. moved to positions one kilometer northeast of BARRICOURT.

The attack continued on Nov. 5th and the artillery maintained its supporting fire according to the needs of the Infantry as it advanced to the River MEUSE. As the Infantry advanced the artillery kept close behind. The Divisional Artillery P. C. remained in TAILLY, and on the evening of this day the 122nd Field Artillery and the 124th Field Artillery moved to positions northeast of BEAUCLAIR. The 11th Field Artillery was in position northeast of NOUART, and one battalion of the 203rd (French) 75 mm. Regt. had moved to a position one kilometer east of BEAUFORT.

Per Field Orders No. 54, Hdqrs. 89th Div., dated Nov. 6, 1918, preparations were to be made to cross the MEUSE at POUILLY and INOR, and the Divisional Artillery, in conjunction with the Corps Artillery, was directed to plan for the support of the crossing. In compliance with this order, the regiments of the 58th F. A. Brigade were ordered to advance in order to effectively cover the river, and the heights beyond. The general positions selected were near the BEAUMONT-LANEUVILLE road between three and four kilometers northwest of LANEUVILLE. The 124th Field Artillery moved to this general position during the night of Nov. 6th. The 11th Field Artillery moved to positions one kilometer southwest of BEAUFORT.

On the night of Nov. 5th Colonel Davis, 15th F. A., reported for duty to relieve General Millar. On the morning of Nov. 6th General Todd returned and again took command of the Divisional Artillery.

During the night harassing fire on the principal crossroads east and north of the River was executed by the 122nd and 203rd F. A. During the night of Nov. 6th the 122nd F. A. moved by echelon to a position north and northwest of FME. aux FRESNES, in square V84 (STENAY Map 1/20,000).

On November 7th a period of comparative stabilization had been reached pending the time when bridges crossing the river could be constructed to allow the passage of the infantry. The 122nd F. A. was assigned to the direct support of the western sub-sector of the division, and the 124th F. A. to that of the eastern sub-sector. During the night of Nov. 7th the 11th F. A. moved to new positions as follows:

1st and 2nd Battalion to positions along the BEAUMONT-LANEUVILLE road, about 3 kilometers northwest of LANEUVILLE.

Battery E to a position 1 kilometer southwest of LANEUVILLE.

Battery F, having been demobilized by the transfer of its tractors to the 2nd F. A. Brigade, remained in its position near BEAUFORT.

During the night harassing and interdiction fire was maintained on the principal crossroads north and east of the River, and Battery E, 11th F. A., executed destructive fire on the METZ-MEZIERS Railroad at LAMOUILLY.

From this time until Nov. 11th when the Armistice between the Allied Powers and Germany was signed, there was no further change in the positions of the firing units of this brigade. **Defensive Barrage and C. P. O.s:** Were planned for each night to protect the crossings of the river from counter-attacks, but it was never necessary to fire them. Nightly harassing and interdiction fire was executed on the crossroads north and east of the river, and destructive fire was executed constantly on the RAILROAD STATION at LAMOUILLY and the RAILROAD BRIDGE northeast of BROUENNE, and all enemy batteries which could be located were vigorously counter-battered. Various enemy organizations also shelled.

Casualties of the 58th F. A. Brigade in operation from Oct. 19th to Nov. 11, 1918:

Killed	1 Officer	15 Men
Wounded	15 Officers	147 Men

Ammunition expended by the firing units of the 58th F. A. Brigade during the operations Oct. 19th to Nov. 11th, 1918:

75 mm.	40,000 rounds
155 mm.	6,200 rounds

See attached map for battery positions during the operations.

(Signed) E. W. FREEMAN,
2nd Lieut., U. S. A.,
Acting Operations Officer.

APPENDIX "F"

314TH ENGINEERS COMMANDER'S REPORT

HEADQUARTERS
314TH ENGINEERS
AMERICAN E. F.

6th December 18.

REPORT OF OPERATIONS OF THE 314th ENGINEERS,
DURING OFFENSIVE ON MEUSE-ARGONNE FRONT.
NOVEMBER 1st to 11th, 19.8.

The month of November commenced with the division on the front line in the MEUSE-ARGONNE Sector with all preparations made for an attack.

The Regimental Headquarters' rear echelon remained at ECLISFONTAINE. The Division Engineer, Col. R. P. Johnston, with his adjutant, established a P. C. at GESNES with Division Headquarters and an Advanced P. C. in charge of Lt. Col. Curfman at the Engineer Dump in ROMAGNE.

The Second Battalion was assigned the work on roads in the advanced area. "C" Company was detailed to help the artillery through the BOIS de BANTHEVILLE as the roads were newly constructed and poor. "A" and "B" Companies were assigned on roads to follow up the Second Battalion. Companies "A" and "F" detailed men to Stokes Mortar Plat.

At 3:00 hours on 1st November the Artillery preparation for the advance began. At 6:00 hours the Infantry (354th Inf.) assault took place. All objectives were carried on time and the artillery moved forward without delay and transportation moved freely.

On November 2nd it began to rain and with the increased traffic over "No Man's Land" the road situation became more of a problem. By dint of hard work, the men getting very little sleep, the roads were kept passable and traffic moved forward. During this operation 2nd Lieutenant Frank J. Hoeynck, and Private Edward W. A. Dietz of Co. "F" reconnoitered the bridges at BARRICOURT and NOUART and, while the enemy still held part of the village of NOUART, removed a mine from one of the bridges and saved it from destruction.

Regimental Headquarters moved to REMONVILLE on November 3rd, to BARRICOURT and thence to TAILLY on November 4th. The regiment meanwhile kept up its work on maintenance and reconstruction of roads following the advance, building temporary bridges at all streams as the enemy had blown up all bridges in his retreat. The REMONVILLE-BARRICOURT Road was by this time in a very bad condition and being the main northern route of traffic for the division, traffic congestion was becoming imminent, when rock was rushed from the ruins of REMONVILLE and BARRICOURT and the road maintained so as to carry the steady stream of heavy traffic which crossed. Men assisted worn-out teams and stalled trucks through difficult places by means of "snatch rope". One bridge at NOUART had been blown out and was reconstructed.

The regiment continued work on the road from BARRICOURT northward, following the advance of the front line troops. Considerable difficulty was experienced on the REMONVILLE-BARRICOURT road which in a few days became almost impassable owing to the lack of a sufficient force of Engineer troops to maintain it, on account of the necessity of their presence in the advanced zone of action. The troops retained on that section of road worked hard to keep it open to traffic, but eventually all motor traffic was forced to detour through BAYONVILLE. An Engineer Dump was established at BARRICOURT, containing mostly tools and road material.

On November 5th the Fifth Corps took over all roads south of BARRICOURT and the 314th Engineers took over the maintenance of roads and bridges from BARRICOURT to the MEUSE River, across which the enemy had been driven. For several days following the regiment remained at work on roads and bridges, sending out reconnoitering parties to the MEUSE River, to gain information regarding bridges and possible crossings. These reconnaissances were made in advance of our front lines and without assistance of infantry. While making one of these reconnaissances, 2nd Lieutenant Frank J. Hoeynck was instantly killed on the island just south of POUILLY, by a machine gun sniper, receiving two bullets in the head. Private Edward W. A. Dietz, who accompanied him, was wounded in the hand. Private Dietz lay motionless beside the body of the dead officer during the entire day, discovering the position of the machine gun which killed Lieut. Hoeynck, and made his escape after darkness had fallen. He returned at 14 hours on 8th November, bringing back the information which the officer and he had been ordered to secure, having been out since 15 hours 6th November.

On the night of 8-9 November, a pontoon train was moved up to the edge of the FORET de JAULNAY. On the night 9-10 November, a detachment of 32 men from Company "C", commanded by Captain Frank E. Dennie, assisted by Lieutenants Shifrin and Avery, assisted an infantry patrol from the 355th Infantry to cross the MEUSE River on a pontoon raft. Three prisoners were captured by the patrol.

On the night 10-11 November, Company "C", lead by Captain Dennie, built two pontoon rafts, without the aid of a covering detachment, and transported the infantry across the MEUSE River, in connection with the operation of crossing the river. The operation was successfully executed, without a casualty occurring in the company. On the morning of 11 November, in connection with the same operation, Company "A", with Captain Case in command, built a foot bridge across the river at STENAY without the protection of an infantry covering detachment, and Captain Case was the first American in the town of STENAY. The infantry scheduled to cross at this point made its crossing without interruption, and was still pursuing the operation when, at 11:00 hours the armistice took effect.

BREHON SOMERVELL,
Lieut. Colonel, Engineers,
Commanding.

REPORT OF TRANSPORTING ATTACKING TROOPS ACROSS THE MEUSE RIVER BELOW POUILLY, FRANCE.

On November 8, 1918, Captain F. E. Dennie, in command of Company "C", 314th Engineers, was notified by the Commanding Officer, 314th Engineers, that his company had been detailed to arrange for transporting Infantry troops across the MEUSE River. He was informed that German pontoon equipment was being sent up by the Corps, and that it would be in BEAUCLAIR that afternoon. Captain McGeachin and about 140 men of the 603rd Engineers were accompanying the pontoon equipment. Two half sections of pontoons were already brought up into the south edge of FORET de DIEULET the preceding night.

It was decided by Company "C" officers not to attempt to throw a pontoon bridge across immediately due to not being familiar with the German Pontoons. The plan proposed, and accepted by Colonel Allen, 356th Infantry, was to build rafts of several pontoons and ferry the men across by means of cables on both ends. Two platoons of Company "C" were immediately sent out to FORET de DIEULET to practice unloading, placing together half sections of pontoon, and to become as familiar as possible with German pontoon equipment.

Captain Dennie consulted Colonel Allen, C. O. of the 356th Infantry, whose troops were to be transported across, and was informed that about 600 infantrymen were to cross. As for the exact location of point where to cross the river it was decided that, from a tactical view point, as close to POUILLY as possible was desirable, but that anywhere between POUILLY and about 1½ kilometers west of POUILLY would be satisfactory.

A reconnaissance of the river was then made by Engineer Officers, and the point 308.7-307.4 was decided upon. It was understood that the probable time of crossing would be the night of November 9th. On the return trip from the river to TAILLY the afternoon of November 8th, the trucks bringing the pontoon equipment up were met on the Route National No. 47, just north of BEAUCLAIR. Captain McGeachin and his men of the 603rd Engineers were with the train. A guide was left with the train, and instructions were given the officer in charge to haul pontoons up to the point 309.4-305.4 (STENAY Map) and park pontoon equipment off side of the LANEUVILLE-BEAUMONT road in the FORET de JAULNAY.

That night the C. O., 314th Engineers, received instructions to immediately have one pontoon sent out to the river to be used by a patrol of Col. Allen's. Lieut. Shifrin of Company "C", 314th Engineers, was sent out from TAILLY to consult with Col. Allen as to where boat was wanted, and to have pontoon brought out to river at that point. He left at about 24 hours the night of November 8th, and arrived at Col. Allen's P. C. at about 2 hours, November 9th. On the way out Lieut. Shifrin stopped off and had Captain McGeachin of the 603rd Engineers accompany him to P. C. Allen. Col. Allen was informed of the order, and due to the late hour and the time it would take to bring boat from place they were parked to river, decided that he could not use boat that night. Lieut. Shifrin then returned to TAILLY.

The next day, November 9th, no change in orders having been received, all of Company "C", 314th Engineers, left TAILLY at about 13 hours, for the FORET de JAULNEY. Captain Dennie received word at TAILLY at about 14 hours that the movement of troops across the MEUSE river would not take place that night, but that it would be necessary to have one boat in river to transport small patrol of infantrymen across. Word was immediately sent out to stop the whole company, and they were intercepted on road just north of BEAUCLAIR. Captain Dennie, Lieut. Pike and Lieut. Avery of Company "B", 314th Engineers, who had been detailed to assist, and about 32 men then went out to bring one pontoon down to river and to take patrol across and back.

A patrol of about 12 men were taken across by about eight engineers. The boat was poled across at point 308.7-307.4 (STENAY Map), and after patrol returned was pulled back by means of rope attached to boat. The patrol returned with five prisoners. The pontoon was removed from river and returned to parking point.

The next morning, November 10th, the C. O. Company "C", 314th Engineers, was informed that the crossing of troops across the MEUSE would take place that night. The entire Company left TAILLY for FORET de JAULNAY at 12 hours, November 10, 1918, and arrived at saw mill in FORET de JAULNAY about 16:30 hours. Before leaving TAILLY, arrangements were made to have enough mules and horses sent out to haul the pontoon equipage to river. Upon arrival at FORET de JAULNAY, word was immediately sent to have teams hitched up early to pull out. Lieut. Shifrin, who was in charge of Company "C" awaiting the arrival of Captain Dennie, at 17 hours received word from Major Rader, C. O. 1st Battalion, 314th Engineers, that the "H" hour was 18 hours, and that it would be necessary to cross the river as soon thereafter as possible. Captain Dennie and Lieut. Pike arrived at about 17 hours, and Captain Dennie went to P. C. Hall to consult General Hall. Meanwhile the teams were hitched up and the first pontoon wagon pulled out at about 17:45 hours. The route taken to river was along LANEUVILLE-BEAUMONT road to crossroad leading North along edge of BOIS de LAVACHE, thence North along said road to Railroad at point 308.7-307.3. From there the pontoons were unloaded from wagons and carried down to creek known as WAME RAU, from which they were floated to river. One raft of three pontoons was built as follows: Three balks were lashed across the three boats, each balk being lashed to each boat, chess were placed on the bottom of each boat so that the hob-nails would not make too loud a noise when a man stepped into the pontoon. A rope was attached to both ends of the side boats, making two ropes on each end of raft. The first raft was completed at about 19:45 hours, and 16 Engineers and the covering detachment of 22 Infantrymen, who were supposed to have been across the river several hours previous to protect troops launching rafts, were taken across. The trip across was made by rowing with oars, and when the men were unloaded the boat was pulled back. The engineers with Lieut. Fournet of Company "C" in charge remained on the north side to pull the raft across.

Infantry commenced coming at 20:30 hours, and the crossing continued until about 22 hours. Twenty-five men were placed in each boat, making seventy-five in all for a raft load. During the first hour and a half the entire 1st Battalion and a small part of the 3rd Battalion of the 356th Infantry were taken across without a mishap. A lull occurred at this time, due to the remaining part of the 3rd Battalion of the 356th Infantry being lost

While the first raft was operating, a second raft was being built under the supervision of Captain Dennie and Lieut. Pike. This raft launched a little upstream from first raft near foot bridge across creek at about point 308.75-307.35, and was ready to haul infantry across at about 21½ hours. Lieut. Welles of Company "C" was in charge of engineer detail on north side of river at this raft.

During the lull, while waiting for troops to arrive, several trips were made with the first raft hauling wounded men back. At about 23 hours troops commenced arriving again, and both rafts were working, taking troops of both the 356th and 355th Infantry across. Movement continued steadily until about 2 hours, November 11, 1918, after which time traffic became very light. The men stayed out all night operating the rafts whenever it was necessary. At about 5:30 hours, November 11th, orders were received to move both rafts upstream so that crossing would be near POUILLY. Both rafts were moved up to about point 309.5-307.6 (STENAY Map), and were operated at that point the rest of the day and the whole night. Several companies of the 354th Infantry were taken across at this point.

Orders were received the night of November 11th to move Company "C" back to TAILLY to work roads, but that the C. O. Company "C", 314th Engineers was still responsible for operation of rafts. On the morning of November 12th the entire company moved back to TAILLY, the operating of the rafts being arranged for with Captain McGeachin of the 603rd Engineers.

At about noon of November 12th, Captain Dennie was informed that it was necessary to establish means of having rolling kitchens and other ration vehicles cross the MEUSE River near POUILLY before that night. It was decided to throw a pontoon bridge across the river and Captain Dennie went out to supervise construction of bridge by the 603rd Engineers. Captain McGeachin took his men out and threw the bridge across at point 309.5-307.6, and had it completed by 18:15 hours, when traffic commenced crossing.

F. E. DENNIE,
Captain, Engineers, U. S. A

ENGINEERS REPORT ON CROSSING THE MEUSE
AT STENAY, FRANCE.

COMPANY "A",
314TH ENGINEERS,
AMERICAN E. F.

November 14th, 1918.

MEMORANDUM TO MAJOR RADER:

About 7:00 o'clock on the evening of November 10th, received verbal instructions from Major Black to send an officer and reconnaissance party of 7 men to LANEUVILLE to make reconnaissance of the river crossings in the vicinity of that place and STENAY. About 8:00 P. M. Lieut. Harris and 7 men were sent to LANEUVILLE on this work.

About 11 P. M. received communication from Lieut. Harris, stating that bridges on the LANEUVILLE-STENAY road had all been blown, and that there was no way across except by wading.

About 9:00 o'clock order was received from Major Black to have an officer and one platoon go to LANEUVILLE immediately to make repairs to foot bridge to STENAY, this platoon to go in trucks, this order stating that they were shelling on the hill in front of the town, and had gassed the town, also that the foot bridge was reported in good condition at that time and that measures were precautionary only.

About 3:30 A. M. received message from Major Black ordering that I go to LANEUVILLE, to put a punch in the work at that point, stating that nothing had been done. Left in your car, arriving at LANEUVILLE about 4:00 A. M. Made personal reconnaissance up and down the river bank, but could find no trace of foot bridge crossing the river, nor could I find any one of the infantry who knew the location of this bridge.

After coming to the conclusion that there was no foot bridge crossing the river, I made reconnaissance with runner Notari, of the openings in the main road between LANEUVILLE and STENAY. Sent report to Major Black at 7:00 o'clock. Before starting on this reconnaissance, started the company at work on rough foot bridge to assist the infantry in entering STENAY. About 9:00 or 9:30 the first infantry patrol passed, entering the town by the road of my reconnaissance. A short time later another infantry patrol passed over the same road, and a short time after that the Corps Engineers accompanied by Lieut. Harris also entered STENAY.

The dam which had been holding back the water and flooded the entire field between LANEUVILLE and STENAY was blown about 4:00 o'clock in the afternoon of the 11th, the water on the morning of the 12th having receded about 15 inches.

C. A. CASE,
Captain, Engrs., U. S.,
Cmdg. Co. "A".

FIELD ORDERS

89th Div., France,
28 Oct., 1918.

Copy No....
SECRET
Field Orders
No........45

MAPS:
REMONVILLE 1/20,000.
BUZANCY
DUN sur MEUSE 1/20,000.

1. (a) No further information of the enemy.

(b) Our Vth Corps, in conjunction with the Ist and IIIrd Corps, is to continue the attack. The 90th Division of the IIIrd Corps is to attack on our right and the 2nd Division, on our left.

(c) Field Orders No. 44, c. s., these Headquarters, are revoked.

2. (a) This Division will attack at "H" hour, on "D" day, and gain the objectives between the lines shown on the attached map.

(b) LINES AND OBJECTIVES.

RIGHT BOUNDARY:
CIERGES (excl.)—
Point 1½ KM. West of ROMAGNE—
North along Meridian 306—
Thence Northeast along the ridge between ANDEVANNE and REMONVILLE.
(See line on map)

LEFT BOUNDARY:
Hill 288 (incl.)—
LA TUILERIE FERME (incl.)—
BOIS des HAZOIS (excl.)—
Woods called CAMP D'AVIATION (incl.)—
REMONVILLE (incl.)—
ABRE D'REMONVILLE (Hill in square A-32) (excl.)—
LES BARRICOURT BOIS (Hill 290 in square A-45) (incl.)—
BARRICOURT (incl.)—
NOUART (incl.)—
(See line on map)

JUMP OFF LINE:

Road Fork, North edge BOIS de BANTHEVILLE—
North-western edge BOIS de BANTHEVILLE—
Thence South-West to Hill 242, 600 meters South of LA DHUY FERME.
(As shown on map)

INTERMEDIATE OBJECTIVE:

North edge of woods at point 06.0 x 89.7—
A line 100 meters North of Road Fork at 05.0 x 89.2—
100 meters beyond LA DHUY FERME.
(As shown on map)

FIRST OBJECTIVE:

Hill 300 (in square A-60) (incl.)—
Northern edge of line of woods and LA BERGERIE FERME (incl.)
(As shown on map)

SECOND OBJECTIVE:

Head of ravine near point 07.1 x 92.3—
Hill 320 at point 06.2 x 92.2 (incl.)—
High ground at 05.3 x 92.8 (excl.)—
Point in clearing, 04.5 x 92.4.
(See line on map)

THIRD OBJECTIVE:

LES TUILERIES (07.3 x 93.2) (incl.)—
Hill LA FOLLARD (05.1 x 94.5)
(See line on map)

EXPLOITATION LINE:

Point on Hill LES FOURNEAU at 09.1 x 95.2—
TAILLY (excl.)—
NOUART (incl.)—
(See line on map)

(c) PLAN OF ATTACK:

The Division will attack in column of brigades. All phases of the attack will be supported by the heaviest fire of all arms available. All of the objectives will be carried on "D" day. Vigorous exploitation will be pushed forward under artillery protection as soon as the last objective has been taken.

3. (a) The 177th Brigade will make the attack at "H" hour. All elements of the brigade will be at the disposal of the Brigade Commander with the exception of two machine gun companies which are to participate in the preliminary firing and in the support of the advance to the First Objective. The Brigade will be so disposed that in the successive attacks, fresh elements will be presented to each objective. The 177th Brigade must carry the heights of BARRICOURT at all costs and push on to the Exploitation Line.

(b) The 178th Brigade and the Divisional Machine Gun Battalion will constitute the Division Reserve, under the command of the Brigade Commander. Machine guns, stokes mortars, 37 mm. guns, are assigned missions as outlined in sub-paragraphs (c) and (d) below. With the exception of these elements, the brigade will be alerted at "H" hour, at which time it must be assembled in the divisional area North of GESNES with the leading elements just South of the ROMAGNE to SOMMERANCE Road. The Reserves will move under orders of the Division Commander. The 178th Brigade will be prepared to relieve the attacking brigade during the night following the attack, for further advance on the next day.

(c) The Divisional Machine Gun Battalion, all the machine gun companies of the 178th Brigade and two machine gun companies of the 177th Brigade will participate in the preliminary bombardment of two hours and in the support of the infantry advance to the Intermediate and First Objectives, under orders of the Division Machine Gun Officer. The companies of the 177th Brigade will be reformed at "H" plus 2:30 hours and reported to the Commanding Officers respectively of the two reserve battalions of the assaulting brigade at LA DHUY FERME and Point F 5485, respectively. Similarly, the machine gun companies of the 178th Brigade and the Divisional Machine Gun Battalion will be released from their mission at "H" plus 4 hours and reported to the Commanding General, Division Reserves, at points to be designated by him. These eight companies will be used to support by overhead fire, the Infantry on the First Objective and its advance therefrom. The 37 mm. platoons of the 178th Brigade will be under the orders of the Division Machine Gun Officer for the same mission and for the same period and under the same conditions as the machine guns. (See Plan for Using Divisional Machine Guns).

(d) The attack will be supported through its entire length by the Divisional Artillery, consisting of the 57th Field Artillery Brigade, with 1 regiment of French Artillery attached, and the 58th Field Artillery Brigade. The Commanding General, 57th Artillery, will command the Divisional Artillery until the taking of the Third Objective, at which time the command will pass to the Commanding General, 58th Artillery Brigade. Preliminary bombardment of two hours will precede the assault. Each successive attack of the Infantry will be preceded by a rolling barrage, at the following rates:

In the open, 100 meters in 4 minutes.
Up steep slopes, 100 meters in 6 minutes.
In deep woods, 100 meters in 8 minutes.

A heavy smoke barrage of three minutes will be laid down just prior to "H" hour and thereafter 1 smoke shell in 4 will be used in the rolling barrage.
One battery of 75's will be reported at 12 hours "D" minus 1 day, to Commanding General, 177th Brigade, as accompanying guns for his two assault battalions. These guns are entirely under the orders of the Infantry commander and if he so orders, will actually accompanying the front line battalions.

(e) Should the Infantry at any time be unable to keep up with the barrage, it will at once make use of the weapons at hand (rifles, machine guns, 37 M.M.'s, Stokes Mortars) to obtain fire superiority. Overcoming the resistance in this manner, the attack will proceed. At the same time the barrage will be recalled to some well established line to rest until the Infantry can reach it, when the advance will be resumed. The barrage must be entirely under the control of the commanders of the assault battalions. Artillery liaison through artillery officers equipped with proper means of communicating with the batteries must be thoroughly established and maintained throughout the action.

(f) Stokes Mortar Platoons, of the 178th Brigade, will be reported to the Commanding General, Divisional Artillery, on "D" minus 1 day, at 12 hours and serve under his orders until "H" hour. They will then be formed and reported to the Commanding General, Division Reserves, at a point to be designated by him.

(g) Gas and flame troops assigned to the Division will be under the Commanding General, Division Artillery, until "H" hour and then pass under the command of Commanding General, Assaulting Brigade, to join the support battalions at points designated by him. If the Infantry advance is checked, the full-fire power of these gas troops will be developed, using heavy smoke and thermite on the enemy machine gun nests.

(h) Each assaulting and support battalion will have one machine gun company in immediate support. Assault battalions will include the platoons of their machine gun companies in their open formation, so as to realize the full fire effect any time. The companies attached to the support battalions will habitually march in advance of the battalions. They will support the advance of the assault battalions with overhead fire, remaining in fire position during the advance of the Infantry, and advancing when the Infantry is halted. When the support battalion is about to pass through the lines and become an assault battalion, it will absorb its machine gun company in its open formation. Just after this movement, the machine gun company with the relieved assault battalion will support the new advance with overhead fire until the old reserve (now support) machine gun company passes through with its Infantry battalion.

(i) The following time table will be carried out:

LINE	DEPARTURE TIME
Jumping Off Line	"H" hour.
Intermediate Objective	"H" plus 1 hours, 08 minutes.
First Objective	"H" plus 3 hours.
Second Objective	"H" plus 6 hours, 50 minutes.
Third Objective	Vigorous exploitation without waiting for the Divisions on our right or left.

(j) The Infantry attack must be pushed forward with all vigor and the barrage closely followed. In order to accomplish this adequate mopping up details must be provided from the supporting elements to cover known and probable strong points such as LA BERGERIE FERME and the numerous small woods lying in the zone of action.

(k) Upon reaching each of the successive objectives, lines will be promptly thinned out, automatic weapons sited, preparations made for resumption of the forward movement, as well as for resisting counter-attack. Our formation in depth either in motion or halted on an objective affords ample protection against enemy counter-attack, so long as our men hold their ground and develop their full fire action. Troops will dig in for hasty shelter at every halt during the action.

(l) A wire cutting team will be organized in every half platoon of the assaulting battalions to consist of one rifleman, acting as axeman, two riflemen, acting as wire cutters and two automatic riflemen. In each company not in the front line, the automatic rifle teams will be marched in one group under the direct supervision of an officer and only deployed through the company to resist counter-attack or to develop special fire action.

(m) Dense formations will be avoided. Every possible use will be made of machine guns, 37 mm. guns and Stokes mortars to assist the advance. It is essential that fire superiority rather than sheer man power be the driving force of the attack. No effort must be spared to ensure the full vigor and power of the division's driving strength, supported by every available means of delivering fire. Any element able to advance will drive on irrespective of delay of other units.

(n) 314th Engineers will remain under the orders of the Division Engineer in the opening up, and maintenance of routes of communication. One company will be specially detailed to assist the artillery getting out of the Northern part of BOIS de BANTHEVILLE.

(o) For use of the Air Service, see Appendix Paragraph 3 (o).

4\. (a) In addition to his combat equipment, each Infantry soldier will carry three sand bags, two hand grenades, two rifle grenades, and one full clip of automatic rifle ammunition or equivalent number of cartridges, a white cloth to serve as a signal panel.

(b) Reserve rations may be eaten on "D" and "D" plus one days.

(c) Each organization will carry its lister bags and a sufficient number of chlorine capsules to last for two days.

(d) Movement of trains and all other supply and evacuation details will be issued in further instructions. See Plan of Supply and Administration.

5\. (a) Divisional AXIS OF LIAISON—GESNES—BRIGADE P. C. at 05.3 x 84 8—LA TUILERIE FERME—LA DHUY FERME—LA BERGERIE FERME—REMONVILLE—BARRICOURT. Telephonic Axis will follow approximately the line indicated above.

(b) Advance Message Centers will be established as follows:

No. 1—P. C. WINN
No. 2—LA TUILERIE FERME
No. 3—LA DHUY FERME
No. 4—LA BERGERIE FERME
No. 5—REMONVILLE

(c) Brigade and Regimental P. C.'s will be selected beforehand by the respective commanders and report to these Headquarters with the Brigade plan of action. These P. C.'s should be as close to the Divisional Axis of Liaison as practicable.

(d) 177th Brigade will assure combat liaison with the right regiment of the 2nd Division and with the left regiment of the 90th Division, in each case by a detachment of 1 company of infantry and 1 machine gun platoon. On the left this detachment will follow the dividing line between the divisions as far as the First Objective, where it will unite with a similar detachment from the 2nd Division, and under the command of the senior officer present, form a combined liaison detachment for both divisions, following the boundary. Special attention will be paid to Western edge of wood called CAMP D'AVIATION, Eastern edge of ABRE D'REMONVILLE, HILL 269, Western edge of LES BARRICOURT BOIS. The detachment on the right will unite with a similar detachment from the 90th Division and form a combined detachment with the mission of maintaining liaison between the Corps and to protect the flanks of the two divisions. The officer of the 89th Division will command the detachment and will give the necessary instructions as to the time and place of assembly of the combined detachment. Brigade Commander, 177th Brigade, will inform these Headquarters of such dispositions by "D" minus 1 day, at 12 hours.

(e) Time will be synchronized through the Message Center. Special couriers will be sent to Brigade Headquarters. From the Brigade and from each successive P. C. time will be sent down promptly by special runner. Time couriers will leave the Message Center daily at 13 hours and on the night of "D" minus one—D, at midnight.

(f) Hourly reports will continue throughout the division on the hour but no commander will delay the making of an important report in order to conform to this ruling.

(g) Messages from brigades and other troops in action, to the Advance Message Center. All other messages to the Division P. C.

(h) Other liaison details in the Plan of Liaison.

(i) Brigade Commanders of Infantry and Artillery, and the Division Machine Gun Officer, will report to the Division P. C. with the outline of their plans for co-ordination at 13 hours, 29th October, 1918.

WRIGHT,
Commanding.

OFFICIAL:
FRANK WILBUR SMITH,
Major, U. S. A.
Actg. A. C. of S. G-3.

DISTRIBUTION:

No. 1—C.G.	No. 20—314 Engrs.	No. 39—Liaison Officers.
2—C.S.	21—314 F. S. Bn.	
3—G-1.	22—C.O., Hq. Troop.	40—7th Balloon Co.
4—G-2.	23—Hq. Tr. and M.P.	
5—G-3.	24—V Army Corps.	41—104 Aero Squadron.
6—Sig. Officer.	25—32nd Div'n.	
7—M.G. Officer.	26—42nd Div'n.	42—2nd Divn.
8—Engineer.	27—French Mission.	43—1st Army.
9—Engr. Train.	28—314 San. Train.	44)
10—177 Brigade.	29—Div. Inspector.	45)
11—353 Infantry.	30—A. P. M.	46)
12—354 Infantry.	31—90th Div'n.	47)
13—355 Infantry.	32—III Army Corps.	48)—Extras.
14—356 Infantry.	33—War Diary.	49)
15—178 Brigade.	34—File.	50)
16—340 M. G. Bn.	45—57th F.A. Brigade.	51)
17—341 M. G. Bn.	36—58th A.A. Brigade.	52)
18—342 M. G. Bn.	37—Gas Officer.	53)
19—Div. Surgeon.	38—C. O., 314 Amm. Tr.	54)

89th Div., France.
28 Oct., 1918, 23:30 hrs.

Copy No....
SECRET
Field Orders
No........46

(Dun sur MEUSE 1/20.000.

MAPS (BUZANCY
(BUZANCY SPECIAL 1/50,000.

1. In case of withdrawal by the enemy, on the Division front, Brigade Commander of the advance brigade will send out a strong advance guard consisting of one regiment, supported by two machine gun companies, to keep close contact with the enemy.

2. (a) BOUNDARY LINES of 89th DIVISION:

Right Boundary—ANDEVANNE (To the 90th Div.)—
BEAUCLAIR (To the 89th Div.)—
STENAY (To the 90th Div.)

Left Boundary—REMONVILLE—BARRICOURT—NOUART Road (To the 89th Div.) REMONVILLE and BARRICOURT (To the 89th Div.) NOUART (divided)—LE CHAMPY HAUT (To the 2nd Div.)—LE CHAMPY BAS (To the 89th Div.)—LETANNE (To the 2nd Div.)

(b) ROUTE OF ADVANCE.

The main route of advance will be as follows:
Advance Brigade followed by support brigade

REMONVILLE—BARRICOURT—NOUART—
BEAUCLAIR—LANEUVILLE.

3. GENERAL INSTRUCTIONS.

(a) The direction of the enemy withdrawal will necessarily govern the detailed conduct of the pursuit.

(b) The advance of the brigades must be so regulated that the main bodies will not be carried into the zone of effective fire of massed enemy guns, installed in previously prepared positions, before the latter have been uncovered by the advance guard.

(c) The attacking brigade will maintain liaison with the neighboring Divisions by flank guards from which liaison detachments will be sent out.

4. P. C.'s and AXES OF LIAISON.

(a) P. C. (1st Bound)—89th Div. —To NOUART
Advance Brigade—To BARRICOURT.
Support Brigade—To BEAUCLAIR.

(b) AXES OF LIAISON.

89th Div.—GESNES—REMONVILLE—BARRICOURT—NOUART—BEAUFORT.

Advance Brigade—Present P. C.—REMONVILLE—BARRICOURT—NOUART—BEAUCLAIR—LANEUVILLE.

WRIGHT,
Commanding.

OFFICIAL:
FRANK WILBUR SMITH,
Major, U.S.A.,
Actg. A. C. of S., G-3.

DISTRIBUTION:
(Same as Field Orders No. 45.)

HEADQUARTERS
89TH DIVISION
AMERICAN EXPEDITIONARY FORCES.

November 1, 1918.

Copy No....
SECRET
Field Orders
No........47

MAPS (Remonville——Special) 1:20,000
(Buzancy)
(DUN sur MEUSE) 1:20,000

1. (a) Enemy in his defeat is believed to be trying to hold the line South of NOUART-TAILLY. No organized positions are known in this vicinity.

(b) Divisions on our right and left reported to be on the final objective, pushing patrols to the front. Both divisions are to advance to the exploitation line tomorrow. 1st Division in reserve is moving up in the vicinity of Southern part of BOIS de BANTHEVILLE.

2. Division will resume the attack at 5:30 hour tomorrow, 2nd November.

3. (a) 177th Brigade will continue the attack and press on to the exploitation line, which will be organized for defense against counter-attack. Vigorous exploitation will be pushed beyond to develop thoroughly the enemy position.

(b) The defensive position taken will consist of an advance post position to include Cote 288 (308.0 x 279.9), and the commanding bluffs running South Southeast. Position of Resistance to include Hill 295 (306.9—296.01). Both the advance post position line and that of the Position of Resistance will be connected up with similar positions on the right and left. Brigade Commander is charged with this liaison.

(c) The Division Reserves will proceed at 3:30 to points designated in person to the Brigade Commander. Front line elements not to cross the general line North edge ANDEVANNE (305.0 x 293.0) until further orders, and to maintain echelonment in depth. The Commander, Division Reserves, in his subsequent movements of the day will at no time move the 3rd (Reserve) Battalion of his right regiment North of Hill 300—BOIS de ANDEVANNE, unless specifically directed by these Headquarters.

(d) The Divisional Artillery will stand ready to deliver a barrage with one regiment tonight along the road about 400 meters in advance of the right half of the 3rd Objective. The Divisional Artillery will cover probable routes of enemy counter-attack from the Northeast and the NOUART-BARRICOURT valley, calling upon the Corps Artillery for assistance. It will support the advance of the Infantry attack by a barrage, including smoke, advancing at the rate of 100 meters in 4 minutes for the first hour of the operations, and thereafter fire on such sensitive points and on such centers of resistance as may be developed during the course of the action or as may be called for by the Commander of the Attacking Infantry Brigade. Movement forward of one battalion of 75's will commence immediately to the vicinity of REMONVILLE, to be followed by the remainder of the regiment before daylight. As soon as this regiment is adjusted for fire the rear regiment of 75's will be moved by battalions to positions in the North edge of the BOIS de BARRICOURT.

(e) Division Engineers will continue under G-1 in the maintenance of communications.

(f) Division Signal Officer will double his communication lines forward and will carry a telephone axis of liaison as far as one front line battalion.

(g) If during the progress of our advance to the Exploitation Line the enemy launches a counter-attack, the Artillery barrage will be laid down as close to the front line as practicable and the fire will be delivered there. If the situation demands, successive battalions will be moved forward to maintain this line. There will be no withdrawal. After the Exploitation line is reached the development of the defensive position and the Plan of Defense will be along the same lines as in the EUVEZIN sector.

4\. (a) The Infantry Trains will move at 5:30 hour, under the direction of G-1, and rejoin their organizations.

(b) Reserve rations will be eaten 2nd November No other change in administrative details.

5\. (a) Division P. C.—La DHUY Fme.
177th Brigade—REMONVILLE.
178th Brigade (Divisional Reserves)—La DHUY Fme.

(b) Axis of Liaison—La Dhuy Fme.—REMONVILLE—BARRICOURT—TAILLY—BEAUCLAIR.

(c) Until further orders, Commanding General, leading brigade, will at 17:00 hours daily report the correct location of his front line as of 16:00 hours that date. This information must be based on the personal verification of officers.

(d) Hourly reports will continue.

WRIGHT,
Commanding.

OFFICIAL:
FRANK WILBUR SMITH,
Major, U.S.A.,
Actg. A. C. of S., G-3.

DISTRIBUTION:
(Same as Field Order No. 45.)

89th Div., France,
3 November, 1918.

Copy No....
SECRET
Field Orders
No........50

MAPS: BUZANCY SPECIAL 1/50,000
REMONVILLE 1/20,000

1\. (a) The enemy on the left of this Corps is retiring to the north. Information from the Corps Commander indicates probability of enemy withdrawal along our entire front.

(b) 1st American Army is to continue its attack. This Corps is to secure the heights overlooking BEAUCLAIR—Les CHAMPY HAUT—VAUX en DIEULET.

2\. (a) This Division will continue to attack and carry the heights overlooking Les CHAMPY HAUT and BEAUCLAIR and push strong reconnaissance toward STENAY.

(b) The Division Sector is bounded on the right north of the heights by a line running parallel to and about 300 meters east of the main road BEAUCLAIR-LANEUVILLE. It is bounded on the west by the villages of BARRICOURT—NOUART—Les CHAMPY Bs (all inclusive), and a line extending Northeast from Les CHAMPY Bs through the FORET de DIEULET toward INOR.

3\. (a) The Division will continue the attack with the 178th Brigade in advance. The 355th Infantry will attack in the right sub-sector and the 356th Infantry in the left sub-sector. The dividing line between sub-sectors is the main road TAILLY-BEAUCLAIR-BEAUFORT—thence in a direct line to LANEUVILLE. The assaulting lines of each regiment will cross the road leading Southeast from BARRICOURT at 5:30 hours and push forward to the attack, passing through the lines of the 177th Brigade. A distance of 1000 meters will be observed between battalions of attacking regiments and each battalion will be echeloned in depth.

(b) The Commanding General, Divisional Artillery, will detail two accompanying guns for each assaulting battalion and will make the necessary arrangements to insure their joining their battalions before they cross the road indicated in Paragraph 3 (a) at 5:30 hours.

(b) 1. The positions held on the heights will be organized for defense against counter attack. All troops halted during this operation will dig in for protection against shell fire and bombing.

(c) The 124th Field Artillery will clear the North exit of REMONVILLE by 2:00 hours and will proceed to a position in the Northern edge of the BOIS de BARRICOURT. During the attack it will function in close liaison with the Commanding Officer, 355th Infantry Regiment, and will be available to fire upon such special targets as he may request. The 122nd Field Artillery will take position in the Northern edge of the BOIS de BARRICOURT as soon as the Infantry of the 178th Brigade has cleared the road North of REMONVILLE. It will function with relation to the Commanding Officer, 356th Infantry Regiment, in the same manner as the 124th Field Artillery functions with the 355th Infantry.

(d) As soon as the heights have been seized, a battalion of the 355th Infantry and a company of machine guns, to be designated by the Commanding General, 178th Brigade, accompanied by one complete battery of the 124th Field Artillery, will push on as an exploiting column toward STENAY. It will cross the open valley in the vicinity of BEAUCLAIR in suitable formation to avoid losses from artillery fire from East of the MEUSE or elsewhere and will reach a position in the lower end of the FORET de DIEULET from where it will energetically patrol toward STENAY. It will watch for opportunity to fire upon any hostile parties. An exploiting column consisting of a battalion of the 356th Infantry and a machine gun company will be similarly selected and sent out via Les CHAMPY Bs and Southern edge of the BOIS D'BELVEL to establish and maintain touch with exploiting columns from the division on the left which is to be sent in the direction of BEAUMONT.

(e) Combat liaison will be maintained between this division and adjoining divisions as well as between exploiting columns by means of suitable flank guards from which liaison detachments will be sent out.

(f) The 177th Brigade, after having been passed by the 178th Brigade, will camp in convenient places adjacent to their present positions, reporting P. C.'s to these Headquarters.

(g) The 11th Regiment of Field Artillery, the 293rd French Artillery and the available battalions of heavy artillery will be used under direction of the Commanding General, Divisional Artillery, for counter battery work and harassing fire.

4. (a) The Engineers will continue to function under G-1.

(b) Assistant Chief of Staff, G-1, will issue orders regarding administrative details. Distributing point will be established in le FEY BOIS.

(c) The Signal Corps will establish an Advance Message Center at BARRICOURT and TAILLY. Axis of Liaison as previously ordered.

5. Divisional P. C. remains at LA DHUY FERME.

WRIGHT,
Commanding.

OFFICIAL:
ROGER S. FITCH,
Colonel, General Staff,
Actg. A. C. of S., G-3.

DISTRIBUTION:
Same as Field Orders No. 47 (Omit 32nd and 42nd Divisions—Add 1st Division)

89th Division, France,
4 November 1918.
0:40 hours.

Copy No....
SECRET
Field Orders
No........51

MAP: BUZANCY SPECIAL 1/50,000.

1. (a) The enemy is continuing his withdrawal beyond the MEUSE.

(b) Neighboring divisions are continuing in their advance.

2. The 89th Division, in accordance with Corps orders, will advance November 4 and seize the town of LANEUVILLE and the Northern edge of the FORET de DIEULET, push reconnaissance forward to the MEUSE and reconnoiter for river crossings.

3. (a) The 178th Brigade will advance at "H" hour from the line BEAUCLAIR-Le CHAMPY HAUT with one battalion on the right, one in the center and one on the left, echeloned in depth. These battalions will be followed at 1200 yards distance by the remaining battalion similarly echeloned. Full use will be made of accompanying artillery, machine guns, trench mortars and one pounders. Liaison will be established to the right and left. The advance must be vigorously pushed to the final objective, regardless of liaison.

(b) The Artillery will support the attack in accordance with Operations Order dated 24:00 hours, November 3.

(c) Special provision for machine guns for overhead fire will be made by the Division Machine Gun Officer.

(d) The 177th brigade will move forward and occupy by 8:00 hours, the high bluffs at present occupied by the 178th Brigade, where they will camp under shelter, so far as practicable. Two machine gun companies of this brigade will report to the Commanding General, 178th Brigade, at TAILLY at 4:00 hours, November 4.

4. Administrative details will be handled by Assistant Chief of Staff, G-1.

5. Axis of Liaison: BARRICOURT—TAILLY—BEAUCLAIR—LANEUVILLE.

6. P. C. 89th Division remains at BARRICOURT for the present. It will close there at 10:00 hour, 4 November 1918, and will open at TAILLY same date and hour.

WRIGHT,
Commanding.

OFFICIAL:
ROGER S. FITCH,
Colonel, General Staff,
Actg. A. C. of S., G-3.

DISTRIBUTION:
Same as Field Orders No. 50.

89th Division, France,
4 November, 1918,
23:00 hour.

Copy No....
SECRET
Field Orders
No........52

MAP: BUZANCY SPECIAL 1/50,000.

1. (a) Enemy continues his rear guard defense, covering his retreat to the North and Northeast.

(b) 2nd Division on our left is extending its front to include MOUZON, and will seize the bridgehead at BEAUMONT and patrol to the North and East. The 90th Division on our right is to continue its exploitation. The 1st Division continues in support in this Corps.

2. (a) This Division will continue its advance tomorrow, driving the enemy across the MEUSE. This Division will clean all ground of the enemy this side of the MEUSE and will seize and hold all bridges in its front.

(b) The Western boundary of this Division is extended to include the FORET de JAULNAY.

3. (a) The 178th Brigade will continue its advance and carry out the mission of the Division It will prosecute vigorous patrols tonight toward the towns and bridges of POUILLY, INOR, LUZY, CESSE, STENAY. Positions found unoccupied will be held. It will be supported in all its operations by the Divisional Artillery upon the request of the Commanding General, 178th Brigade.

(b) The 177th Brigade will move forward tomorrow its two leading battalions to positions just Southwest of the FORET de DIEULET, with its two reserve battalions in position on the height overlooking BEAUCLAIR. These reserve battalions will continue the organization of the defensive line.

(c) Divisional Artillery will respond to any request of the Commanding General, 178th Brigade, for the support of his operations. Positions will be taken tonight to guarantee the covering of the bridgeheads along the front of this Division.

(d) The Divisional Machine Gun Battalion is placed under the orders of the Commanding General, 178th Brigade. The Divisional Machine Gun Officer will report to the Commanding General, 178th Brigade, to co-ordinate the work of the machine guns.

(e) The regiment of Engineers, less one company, will continue on communications under the direction of G-1. One Company of Engineers will report to the Commanding General, 178th Brigade, to assist in bridge reconnaissance under his orders.

(f) The Commanding General, 178th Brigade, is charged with combat liaison with the divisions on the right and left.

4. (a) Distribution Point —just West of BEAUCLAIR.
(b) Advance M. O. R. S.—TAILLY.
(c) Ammunition Dump —just Southwest of TAILLY.
(d) Brigade and separate organization commanders will report to G-1 by noon, 5 November, list of material captured in the recent operations.

5. (a) P. C. 89th Division—TAILLY.
P. C. 178th Brigade—BEAUCLAIR, after 8:00 hours, 5 November.
P. C. 177th Brigade—NOUART.
Axis of Liaison —TAILLY—BEAUCLAIR—LANEUVILLE—STENAY.

(b) Commanding General, 178th Brigade, will submit his plan of action as soon as practicable to the Division Commander, for approval.

WRIGHT,
Commanding.

OFFICIAL:
ROGER S. FITCH,
Colonel, General Staff,
Actg. A. C of S. G-3.

DISTRIBUTION:
Same as Field Orders No. 51.

89th Division, France.
10 November, 1918,
17:00 hours.

Copy No....
SECRET C O R R E C T E D C O P Y
Field Orders DESTROY ALL PREVIOUS COPIES.
No........58

MAPS: STENAY, MONTMEDY } 1/20,000
MOUZON
SPECIAL 1/50,000

1. (a) Enemy continues general retreat. No change in our immediate front. A foot bridge crossing has been discovered near point 314.9 x 302.5 (STENAY).

(b) 90th Division, pushing North on far side of river, is reaching STENAY.

(c) 2nd Division on our left is to cross tonight.

2. (a) 89th Division will cross the river and maintain contact with the divisions on the right and left.

(b) Boundaries:

Right:	STENAY	(excl.)
	MONTMEDY	(excl.)
	VIRTON	(excl.)
Left:	LETANNE	(excl.)
	AUTREVILLE	(incl.)
	LA FERTE sur CHIERS	(excl.)
	MARGUT	(excl.)
	MARGNY	(excl.)
	GEROUVILLE	(excl.)

(c) Final objective, this operation, the heights Northeast of the river.

3. (a) 178th Brigade will cross near POUILLY, co-ordinating its attack with and maintaining liaison with the 2nd Division. The two battalions between INOR and STENAY will maintain contact with the enemy until relieved by the 177th Brigade.

(b) 177th Brigade will gain combat liaison with the 90th Division, first sending one regiment (less one battalion) via STENAY and one battalion via the the foot bridge VILLEFRANCHE. Brigade will push Northward on the far side of the river, clearing the heights and gaining contact with the 178th Brigade north of INOR. One battalion of infantry will be sent immediately to relieve one battalion, 356th Infantry, and act as escort to Divisional Artillery.

(c) Division Machine Gun Officer will co-ordinate the machine gun support of the attack near POULLY and issue necessary orders for the assignment and return of the various machine gun companies upon the completion of this operation.

(d) Division Engineer, with the entire regiment of Engineers at his disposal will provide crossing for troops operating near POULLY, will install pontoons bridge at most suitable place between INOR and STENAY and will improve any available crossings at STENAY. Troops not used on this work will be continued in the maintenance of roads.

(e) Division Signal Officer will establish and maintain communications with both brigades.

(f) Divisional Artillery will support both operations, co-ordinating to the Corps Artillery the task on the left.

4. Administrative details by G-1.

5. (a) Vth Corps has set the hour for beginning the operation at 18:00 hours, this date.

(b) 177th Brigade will proceed with its mission without delay.

(c) No change in P. C.'s.

(d) The absolute importance of liaison in this operation must be impressed on all commanders.

WRIGHT,
Commanding.

OFFICIAL:

ROGER S. FITCH,
Colonel, General Staff,
Actg. A. C. of S. G-3.

DISTRIBUTION:
Same as Field Orders No. 57.

ADMINISTRATIVE DETAILS
Paragraph 4, Field Order No. 58

(a) (1) Railroad and Refilling Point—No change.
Distributing Point—The Division Quartermaster will load the daily supplies for issue on the 11th at Refilling Point and move them up to BEAUCLAIR, where they will be met by a representative from each Unit and conducted to point on the motor road that the Supply Officers designate, and will be turned over there to the Detachment Supply Officers.

(a) The Division Quartermaster will, as soon as LANEUVILLE is considered safe, establish a rest camp for officers and men in that town in building to be designated by G-1, and will provide dry clothing and arrange with the Division Surgeon for messing and caring for officers and men who have collapsed from exhaustion, or exposure, with a view to returning them to duty in a day or two.

(b) Axial Road — REMONVILLE — BUZANCY — NOUART — BEAUCLAIR — LANEUVILLE — STENAY — MARTINCOURT — INOR — AUTREVILLE and LANEUVILLE — BEAUMONT.

(c) Ammunition, Small Arms:
Advance Dump for Cal. .30 on LANEUVILLE—BEAUMONT road near Point 10.0x 05.1.
BEAUFORT—Cal. .30, Cal. .45, Stokes, 37 m/m and pyrotechnics.
The Ammunition Train, Small Arms, Motor Section, loaded with Cal. .30, will be on BEAUCLAIR—LANEUVILLE road near Point 11.6 x 99.6 at 19:00 hours and will await instructions from G-1, or calls for ammunition from any Munitions Officer.

(d) Ordnance—Distributing Point: BEAUCLAIR.

(e) Sanitary Service—Advance ambulance dressing station will be established at Boche Prison Camp at Point 08.7 x 05.8 and at LANEUVILLE.

(f) The trains will remain in their present location until further orders.
By Direction of Chief of Staff:

W. J. SCOTT,
Lieut. Colonel, General Staff,
A. C. OF S., G-1.

89th Division, France,
11 November, 1918,
21:00 hours.

Copy No....
SECRET
Field Orders
No........59

	STENAY	1/20,000
MAPS:	MONTMEDY	
	MOUZON	
	SPECIAL	1/50,000

1. (a) An armistice with Germany has been signed and all hostilities ceased at 11:00 hours, 11 November, 1918.

(b) The Allied armies will hold themselves in readiness for further advance.

(c) The First American Army, including the V Corps, while holding its present front, will prepare for further advance.

2. The 89th Division will hold its present front, reorganizing in preparation for further advance.

3. (a) The 177th Brigade will occupy the sector STENAY to LUZY (inclusive); one regiment in STENAY and one regiment in support so disposed as to observe the enemy in MARTINCOURT and CERVISY.

(b) The 178th Brigade will hold its present positions.

(c) Divisional Artillery will hold its present positions.

(d) Machine Gun Units will join their proper organization; the Divisional Machine Gun Battalion moving to BEAUFORT.

(e) Engineers will function as directed by G-1.

(f) Troops will be so disposed as to obtain the maximum rest and comfort consistent with necessary arrangements for security and with preparations for further advance.

(g) The lines attained at 11:00 hours, 11 November, 1918, will not be passed by any American troops until further orders. All communication with the enemy is forbidden, pending further instructions. Present arrangements involving cessation of hostilities is an armistice and not a peace, and there must be no relaxation of vigilance. Troops must be prepared at any time for rapid forward movement. Strict discipline must be maintained and troops will be held ready for any eventualities. Brigade commanders will personally inspect all organizations with the foregoing in view.

(h) Troops will be marched in close order in cadence until further notice and strictest march discipline will apply. Every effort will be made to obtain the best possible condition for further advance.

4. (a) Railhead and Refilling Point--No change.
Distributing Points:
For 178th Brigade, 11th, 122nd and 124th F. A—On BEAUMONT-LANEUVILLE road near Point 09.0 x 06.5.
For 177th Brigade—LANEUVILLE.
For 314th Sanitary Train, 314th Engineers, 340th Machine Gun Bn., and 314th Military Police—BEAUCLAIR.
For 314th Field Signal Battalion, 314th Supply Train, 314th Ammunition Train and Headquarters Troop—REMONVILLE.
For Headquarters 58th Field Artillery Brigade—TAILLY.

4. (b) Billeting Areas:
178th Brigade, 11th, 122nd and 124th F. A.—North North of Y 05.0.
177th Brigade—STENAY, LANEUVILLE and CESSE.
340th Machine Gun Battalion—BEAUFORT.
Headquarters Military Police—LANEUVILLE.
314th Ammunition Train—BARRICOURT.
314th Supply Train—REMONVILLE.
314th Sanitary Train—BEAUCLAIR.
314th Engineers, 314th Field Signal Bn. and Headquarters Troop—TAILLY.

5. P. C. 89th Division........TAILLY.
P. C. 177th Brigade........To be selected and reported.
P. C. 178th Brigade........No change.

WRIGHT,
Commanding.

OFFICIAL:
BREHON SOMERVELL,
Lieut. Colonel, Engineers,
A. C. of S. G-3.

DISTRIBUTION:
Same as Field Orders No. 56.

GERMAN OFFICIAL REPORTS OF THE BATTLE OF ST. MIHIEL

Translation of German Documents

(German) Army Headquarters, September 19, 1918.

Army Detachment "C."
Chief of General Staff.
No. 2991. Secret.

Pursuant to verbal order of September 18, 1918.

EVENTS UP TO EVENING OF SEPTEMBER 11

When the first information of an intended hostile attack on the St. Mihiel salient reached the Army Detachment it was holding the 84 km. front of the salient with an average sector of 12 km. for each division in line.

Among the divisions assigned to the salient sector were the 3d Ldw. Division, 1st Austro-Hungarian Division, the completely used-up 192d Division, the 77th Reserve Division, considered unreliable, and the 10th Division which had suffered heavy losses but had been partly filled up again. As reserve behind the Army there was at first only the 31st Division which had just been relieved.

The 123d, 107th and 88th Divisions were hurriedly brought up later.

The Army Detachment, whose front had been weakened by two divisions since the Spring Offensive, had always clearly realized that a great danger existed in holding this dangerous salient with only a slight force. Only a defensive battle called "Michel" was worked out and, in order to prevent deep penetrations in the salient before the evacuation was completed, four assault divisions, two field artillery regiments, ten battalions of heavy artillery and a reinforcement of the air forces were requested (Order Ia No. 1700, secret, July 21, 1918).

When the situation came to a head the Army had issued the following order for the relief of the unreliable 77th Reserve Division:

September (August ?) 31, 1918.

Army Detachment "C."
Ia No. 2592 secret.

To the Army Group of von Gallwitz:

The Army directs that the 77th Reserve Division be relieved as quickly as possible by the 107th Division, which is already moving up. The Division (77th Reserve) is in line in that part of the Army sector especially exposed to hostile attacks, the checking of which is a prerequisite to the execution of the "Michel" Operation without interference.

Since the Division has been in line (7 weeks) a total of 23 Alsace-Lorrainers have deserted. Further desertions must be expected on account of the large number (800) of Alsace-Lorrainers in the Division. At the present time the danger undoubtedly exists that the enemy, reckoning upon the weak and—so far as the Alsace-Lorrainers are concerned—unreliable garrison, will make a surprise attack, which if it succeeds, will entail a very considerable loss in personnel and material for the other divisions in the St. Mihiel salient. It therefore seems imperative to transfer the Division to another part of the front.

(Signed) FUCHS.

With the knowledge that the endangered southern front was too weakly held, the Army had made repeated requests since September 2 for the use of the 31st and 123d Divisions which were being held behind the Army as reserve of the Higher Command. It was the intention of the Army to put in one of these divisions between the 10th and 77th Reserve Divisions in order to reinforce the obviously too-weakly held front at that point and to bring the other division up to the front line. A decision had not yet been made, however, at the time the hostile attack occurred.

On September 2 the representations made on August 27 relative to assigning the sector of the 255th Division to the Army Detachment were renewed and shown to be especially urgent in view of the tense situation. Not until 5:45 a. m. on the day of the battle was approval received, by telephone.

In order to make sure that the divisions being held behind the Army front as reserve of the Higher Command would be engaged at the proper time an order was issued on September 2 that the infantry and accompanying artillery were to be billeted in the southern part of the billeting areas of the divisions. Furthermore, special orders were issued providing for the quickest possible assembling of these divisions at Dampvitoux, St. Julien and Onville and for conducting them into the sectors of the 77th Reserve and 10th Divisions.

By a series of orders beginning August 25, all working forces, minenwerfer companies, pioneer companies, and gas projector companies available and the resting regiment of the 35th Austro-Hungarian Division were assigned to the Gorz Group to complete the construction of the line of artillery protection as quickly as possible, in order that the intended transfer of the main line of resistance to the line of the artillery protection might be accomplished as soon as possible. At the same time other working forces, even sections of the resting battalions, were made available for the rearward positions. On September 9 orders were issued stopping all road and railroad construction and the construction of all dispensable railway track, the curtailment of all ammunition and supply depots and the removal of all ammunition still on the Cotes.

On September 5 the Army sent its entire artillery reserve, in all 9 squadrons and 3 light batteries, into position behind the Gorz Group on a line with Thiaucourt in order to support that flank which was considered to be especially endangered. On September 8, after a considerable number of reinforcement batteries, especially of heavy artillery, had been promised, but before they had arrived, an order was issued (Order No. 2728 secret) for the withdrawal of all unmounted heavy batteries behind the "Michel" position. At the same time it was ordered that the unmounted 5th and 6th guns of the field artillery be taken away from the center divisions which had long marching routes and be assigned to the flank divisions which had the short marching routes.

On September 7 it was tentatively decided, upon recommendation of the Army Group, to shatter the enemy's offensive preparations by an attack with limited objectives upon the southern front. At that time it was ordered that the work of removal be continued on the western front and temporarily stopped (field railroads) only on the southern front. The plan of attack was worked out in a conference with the Army Group at Montmedy on September 9, but was abandoned because a highly important change in the situation had occurred in the meantime—the probability of a simultaneous hostile attack against the western front of Army Detachment "C" had increased materially. It was decided to obtain an order from the Higher Command for the immediate starting of the "Michel" movement (withdrawal to the "Michel" position).

Already on September 10, even before the order was received from the Army Group, the work of removal and destruction was ordered to commence (in a conference of commanding officers), so that this work was in full progress when the order of the Army Group and the decision of the Higher Command arrived. On the same day request was made by telegraph for reinforcements considered necessary. On the evening of September 9 the Gorz Group reported that all preparations had progressed so far that the main line of resistance could be transferred back to the line of artillery protection on the night of September 11-12. Army Headquarters gave its approval and stipulated that the movement, which had been in preparation for weeks, should be completed by 4 a. m., September 12.

Thus on the morning of September 12 the work of removal and destruction was in full progress. Some of the unmounted batteries had already been withdrawn (Mihiel Group) and the others were to be withdrawn that night. The Gorz Group was engaged in moving back its main line of resistance. The available counter-attack divisions were so placed that they could be used either on the western or southern front.

This was the situation when the enemy's attack struck the Army Detachment by surprise on the night of September 11-12.

The Commanding General.
(Signed) FUCHS, Lieutenant General.

(German) Army Headquarters, September 19, 1918.

Army Detachment "C".
Chief of General Staff.
No. 2986. Secret.

Pursuant to verbal order of the Army Group, September 18.

EVENTS OF SEPTEMBER 12

At 2 o'clock on the morning of September 12 very heavy artillery fire commenced along the entire Army front. Although the reserves of the Higher Command had not yet been made available—in spite of several requests—the 31st and 123d Divisions were alerted at 2:30 a. m. and the 88th Division at 2:50 a. m. As it became more and more certain that the expected large scale attack had begun and as the situation, therefore, did not permit waiting for the approval of the Higher Command but demanded an immediate and independent decision, the 31st and 123d Divisions were assembled at Dampvitoux and Onville. The 31st Division was sent forward to Xammes at 6:45 a. m., while the most advanced regiment of the 123d Division, which was already at Onville at 4:15 a. m., was sent to La Grange en Haye Farm at 5:45 a. m.; therefore, before the attack. At 8:15 a. m. the Commanding General gave permission to advance the foremost regiment of the 123d Division to the crossroad 2 kilometers southwest of Preny and to send the rest of the Division forward to La Grange en Haye Farm.

It was also necessary to act independently in the case of the 255th Division which was not assigned to the Army Detachment until 5:40 a. m. on the day of battle. On September 11 this division, in conjunction with the Gorz Group, was made to withdraw its main line of resistance to the Vencheres Position.

The enemy's infantry attacked at 6 a. m. At 4:20 a. m. it was reported to the Army Group, in reply to an inquiry, that the evacuation would not be begun as there were no compelling reasons for such action at that time. The events which took place after the attack had begun, showed, however, that the lightly held southern front was not capable of sustaining the attack of greatly superior forces. The two weak divisions could not make the necessary distribution in depth on their 22 kilometer front and were unable to stop the attack of an enemy from four to five times as strong. The Gorz Group reported at 10:25 a. m. that rearward movements had been observed in Sector H.

In order to restore the situation in the sector of the 77th Reserve Division and to prevent the outflanking of the left wing of the 10th Division one regiment of the divisions in reserve, namely, the 31st and 123d (which were moving forward), was placed at the disposal of these divisions.

Already at 11:15 a. m. it was reported that the enemy had broken through the 77th Reserve Division and appeared to have taken Vieville, that the Gorz Group therefore—inasmuch as it could not establish immediate telephone communication with the Higher Command—had already issued orders on its own responsibility (10:45 and 11 a. m.) that the 31st and 123d Divisions should execute a simultaneous attack against the left flank of the advancing enemy, the former through Thiaucourt, the latter in the direction of Vieville.

Meanwhile the Combres Group in Sectors B and D and the Mihiel Group in Sector F had been attacked and were engaged in heavy fighting.

The report of the Gorz Group at 11:50 a. m. read: "The enemy is southeast of Thiaucourt and at Tautecourt Farm. The 77th Reserve Division appears to be annihilated. No information yet concerning the counter-attack of the 31st and 123d Divisions".

At the time of this report the enemy had, therefore, already advanced to within 1 kilometer of the main line of resistance of the "Michel" position. Furthermore, the left wing of the 10th Division had undoubtedly been outflanked and driven back by the 6 kilometer penetration near Thiaucourt. There was not only the danger of a break-through at the vital point in the "Michel" position, but also a serious threat at the line of retreat of the Mihiel Group which was still in the salient.

The situation required an immediate decision. If the troops in the St. Mihiel sector were to be saved from capture there could no longer be the slightest delay in ordering the withdrawal of the front to the "Michel" position. Army Headquarters therefore issued the following order to the Mihiel Group at noon:

"The withdrawal will begin at once."

At 12:10 p. m. the Combres Group reported that the enemy had taken St. Remy, had penetrated sectors B III and D I and was advancing.

At the same time the Gorz Group reported that deeply echeloned columns were advancing upon Nonsard.

The correctness of the decision which had been made was hereby shown. The 10th Division also was being driven back without having any reserves at its disposal. The entire withdrawal to the "Michel" position was therefore endangered.

As reports up to 1 p. m. showed that Maizerais, Essey, Euvezin and the entire plateau on the right bank of the Meuse were in the enemy's hands, the Combres Group was ordered to make possible the greatly endangered retreat of the Mihiel Group by holding at all costs the line Combres Heights-Herbeuville Heights-line of artillery protection. Beney, too, was taken by the enemy early in the afternoon.

It is due only to the energetic stand of the Combres Group, to the splendid leadership and conduct of the Mihiel Group, and to the timely decision made by the Army Command upon its own responsibility that the Mihiel Group was able to make the 30 kilometer flank march with heavy rear-guard fighting and the loss of only 1,100 men and three guns (with burst in bore) and was able to reach the "Michel" position next morning, after having been joined by the Assault Regiment and the 88th Division. Two flank detachments of the 5th Ldw. Division and the failure of the Americans to recognize their tactically favorable position prevented the latter from bringing catastrophe to Army Detachment "C". At the same time the attacks of the 31st and 123d Infantry Divisions, even though they gained but little ground, prevented the penetration of the "Michel" position northeast of Thiaucourt.

The Commanding General.
(Signed) FUCHS, Lieutenant General.

OPERATIONS REPORT OF THE 12TH RESERVE CORPS (MIHIEL GROUP) TO SEPTEMBER 12, 1918, INCLUSIVE

INTRODUCTION

Since August 27, 1918, indications of an impending hostile offensive had been observed on the front of Army Detachment "C". As a result of the tactical situation it had long been reckoned that the attack would be directed mainly against the Combres and Gorz Groups and would have as an objective the cutting off of the St. Mihiel salient. For such an eventuality preparations had long been made systematically to evacuate the salient and to fight a defensive battle in the Michel I Zone.

At 9 o'clock on the morning of September 8, the Commander of the Army Detachment held a conference with the Commanding Generals at Xonville in which he explained the situation and the problems of the Army Detachment. Accordingly, the evacuation of the salient was only contemplated in the event that the hostile attack, the indications of which were at first only apparent on the southern front of the Army Detachment, should extend from Ailly Woods to the eastern boundary of the Army. Should the attack be made only upon a narrow front, for example, against the Gorz Group alone, the present battle zone was to be held with the forces at the disposal of the Army Detachment.

As a result of the fact that on September 9 reports reached Army Headquarters which strongly indicated a simultaneous attack on the western front of the Army Detachment, it was agreed in a conference of the Army and group commanders on the afternoon of September 10 that all preparations for the systematic evacuation of the salient should begin at once. For the removal of material and supplies within the territory to be evacuated and for the destruction of important works, a period of eight days was determined upon before beginning the movement. The necessary orders were issued on the evening of September 10 to a conference of the chiefs of staff of the Group with the divisional general staff officers and to the commanders of the units immediately subordinate to the Army Group Command.

September 11 passed according to plan without interruptions. Work of removal and destruction was in full progress. This was the situation when the hostile attack was launched by surprise on the night of September 11 to 12.

EVENTS OF SEPTEMBER 12 UP TO 4:45 A. M.

At 2 o'clock on the morning of September 12, the Combres and Gorz Groups were subjected to a violent and heavy artillery fire which extended as harassing fire to the front line trenches of Divisions "E" and "F". The rear areas of Division "E", especially the crossroads, were heavily harassed. The towns of Chaillon, Creue, Heudicourt and the roads from Buxieres to Varneville were bombarded with heavy calibers.

Inasmuch as a hostile attack was expected with certainty the Group, at 2:50 a. m., ordered increased readiness for action for the divisions. This order was carried out by Division "E" at 5:05 a. m. and by Division "F" at 5:16 a. m.

The distribution of forces in the sector of the Group at the beginning of the artillery fire is shown on maps 1 and 2. (Note.)

Note.—These maps were not found with the original document.

After a rather violent gas attack had been made at 3:45 a. m., on the sector E. 1. North, extending as far as the Advance P. C., the entire Group sector became quiet about 4 a. m. The front-line trenches were subjected to searching fire at some points. The fire also became weaker in the sector of the Combres Group. The impression prevailed there that an attack would be made against Sector "B". In the sector of the Combres Group, on the other hand, the fire continued with undiminished violence and fell especially upon the sector of the 77th Reserve Division, the rear areas, Essey, Pannes, Thiaucourt, Jaulny and Bayonville.

The hostile artillery opposite Division "E" fired in general from new positions. In Sector "F", on the other hand, no new batteries were observed in action.

ESTIMATE OF THE SITUATION UP TO 4:50 A. M. BY CORPS HEADQUARTERS

The heavy hostile artillery fire in the neighboring sectors was regarded as preparatory fire of an attack which would be made immediately. The relative quiet in the sector of the Group confirmed the prevailing opinion that the hostile attack would be directed against the flanks of the salient. The main attack was expected against the Gorz Group. If the latter held its position, then the advance battle zone in the sector of the Mihiel Group would have to be held at all costs in order not to permit the enemy without cause to have an easy success. The order issued on the afternoon of September 11 that in each division the resting battalion of the center regimental sector and one company from the resting battalions of the regiments on the flanks were to be withdrawn for the purpose of constructing positions in the Michel I Zone was consequently changed about 4:50 a. m. on September 12, so that only three companies (one company from each battalion) from each division would be withdrawn to the Michel I Zone, and so that the divisions would have sufficient reserves at their disposal for the battle in the salient. Furthermore, the chief general staff officer of each division was instructed first of all to arrange, according to the situation, for the removal of the most important materiel and to take measures to assure the subsequent destruction of water towers, and especially of the water supply constructions, in the event that the evacuation would have to be quickly carried out under pressure of a hostile success.

The 5th Landwehr Division, in addition, received the order at 5:45 a. m. to bring up a field battery at once into one of the reconnoitered crest positions on the Cote near Buxieres, so that with observation in the immediate vicinity of the battery it could flank a hostile attack against the right wing of the Gorz Group.

The Army Commander and the commanders of the neighboring groups were several times advised of the situation.

EVENTS FROM 4:45 A. M. TO 11:15 A. M.

Up to 6 a. m. no increase in hostile fire was noticeable in the group sectors. A moderate fire lay upon the entire sector of the Combres Group, being a little more intense in Sector A I and B in the region of the HUMMERSCHERE. At 6:20 a. m. fire of destruction was requested there. In the Gorz Group the fire continued with undiminished violence.

At 6:25 a. m. it was reported to Corps Headquarters that yellow light signals had been observed in front of the center and the left of the sector of the 10th Infantry Division, and in front of the sector of the 77th Reserve Division. At 6 a. m. the Group observer on the Bocksberg noticed a bright flash in the sector of the Gorz Group resembling a signal given with flame projectors. The infantry attack had apparently begun. Aviators could not make reconnaissances at this time, as stormy weather and squalls, as well as low-hanging clouds, made rising and observation impossible.

While even after 6 a. m. Sector E was generally quiet, hostile artillery fire increased again in the sector of the 5th Ldw. Division, and about 7 a. m. lay upon Sector F I (interspersed with gas), upon Sector F II 2 and Sector F III, especially upon Jaudberg and Apremont Ravine. Le Mont was not so vigorously bombarded. The rear areas were at times under heavy fire, especially the military road and the DOKTORSCHLUCHT.

Between 7 and 8 a. m. the hostile attack was successful against the Jurat Woods and penetrated temporarily into our outpost zone. The situation was re-established by counter-attack. Patrols advancing against F I were driven off.

In order to keep generally informed of the situation with regard to the enemy's fire, the activity of the air forces and the noise of the battle, Corps Headquarters established an observatory with one officer from Corps Headquarters in the Chateau Tower at St. Benoit. This measure proved its worth in the course of the battle.

Towards 8 a. m the fire again decreased noticeably in the sector of the 5th Ldw. Division. In Sector F the enemy continued to fire upon Chaillon and Creue. In the sectors of the Combres and Gorz Groups the artillery fire continued with undiminished violence.

The 192d Division, which had taken over Sector E only a few days before, and the troops of which were consequently not altogether familiar with the terrain, gave orders at 8:12 a. m. for a practice exercise in the occupation of the Schroeter Zone by the resting battalions. The order from Corps Headquarters for the withdrawal of one company from the resting battalions therefore was not carried out.

Telephone connections between the 5th Ldw. Division and the neighboring 10th Infantry Division of the Gorz Group failed. Liaison was reestablished by cavalry patrols and the sending of an intelligence officer to the Headquarters of the 10th Division.

At 8:20 a. m. the Gorz Group reported that the hostile infantry attack had been in progress since 6 a. m. In Sector H the enemy had penetrated the outpost zone; the Bois des Pretres had not yet been attacked. According to the reports on hand at that time the front of attack extended from St. Baussant to one kilometer east of Fey-en-Haye. The artillery fire continued to be very vigorous.

Owing to the fact that in the meantime the weather had so far cleared that aviators and balloons could become active, about 8:35 a. m. the first reports from an infantry aviator of the 37th Reconnaissance Flight and from the 112th Balloon Section came in, reporting only light artillery fire in the Group sector. The aviator had observed infantry columns with wagons near Girovoisin, as well as well-directed friendly artillery fire upon Limey and Seicheprey. The balloon observed three hostile batteries firing from the eastern entrance to Rambucourt and reported that the hostile artillery fire was directed mainly upon the line of artillery protection of the Gorz Group.

At 8:40 a. m. an increase of hostile artillery fire between Montsec and the Moselle was reported. Montsec was suffering a moderate gas bombardment.

At 9:10 a. m. the 5th Ldw. Division reported that the fire had increased upon the front-line trenches and rear areas in Sector F I. A hostile attack was in progress against F II c. The enemy appeared to have entered the village of Apremont. Enemy skirmishers advancing from Besombois Woods against Le Mont were quickly forced to retire by well-directed machine-gun fire.

The Combres Group had sent in no new report up until 9:30 a. m. At 9:37 a. m. the 5th Ldw. Division was able to report that the attack against Apremont had been repulsed. In Sector F I also the enemy artillery fire had again diminished. Quiet reigned in the sector of the 192d Infantry Division.

At 9:45 a. m. the Gorz Group reported, in reply to an inquiry, that the enemy had penetrated the Sonnard Woods at 8:30 a. m. Near Vieville the situation was not clear. Thiaucourt, Pannes and Xammes were under heavy hostile artillery fire.

Towards 10:40 a. m. heavy enemy artillery fire was directed upon Sector E. Deep-flying enemy aviators circled over the position. A hostile attack against Sector F I was broken up by machine-gun fire. The enemy began to confine his efforts to heavy, flat trajectory fire upon the road from St. Benoit to the railway station at Benoit. At 11:15 a. m. the Gorz Group reported that the enemy had advanced to the line just south of Thiaucourt—1½ kilometers north of Vieville—Soulevre Farm. A counter-attack by the 123d and 31st Divisions had been ordered, but at that time had not yet gotten under way.

The situation around Essey and Pannes was not clear.

ESTIMATE OF THE SITUATION BY CORPS HEADQUARTERS AT 11:15 A. M.

The events of the forenoon had shown that the enemy did not intend a serious attack on the front of the Mihiel Group. On the front of the Combres Group also no strong hostile attack had been reported up to this time. On the other hand, the enemy's attack against the Gorz Group had led a deep penetration in the center of the Group sector, which, in case it was not checked and confined to the west, would have very serious consequences for the Mihiel Group still fighting in the salient. At present, to be sure, it was still to be expected that the counter-attack of the 123d and 31st Infantry Divisions would restore the situation in the center of the Gorz Group and prevent a further penetration there by the enemy. It was of vital importance for the Mihiel Group that the 10th Infantry Division hold the heights south of Pannes and northeast of Essey and thereby check the enemy's break-through on the West. Whether the 10th Infantry Division would be able to accomplish this had not been ascertained at this time because the situation near Pannes and Essey was not clear, according to the report of the Gorz Group.

The 5th Ldw. Division therefore, received orders at 10:40 a. m. to send up the resting battalion of the 65th Ldw. Infantry Regiment which was lying southeast of Heudicourt, along with accompanying batteries, into the region Nonsard—Lamarch with orders to assure the left flank of the Group there and, if necessary, attack and occupy Nonsard.

Also along the St. Benoit-Beney road a local protection, at first immediately subordinate to Corps Headquarters, seemed imperative in order to prevent the enemy by increasing his success against the Gorz Group from passing through Thiaucourt or Pannes without hindrance and gaining the possession of the crossroad at St. Benoit, which was vitally important for the Mihiel Group. For this purpose the Group at first had available only three companies of the 5th Ldw. Division which had been sent off in the morning to construct trenches in the Michel Zone I. One of these companies had already reached Dampvitoux. The company was alerted by telephone, sent towards Benoit and its commanding officer ordered to report to Corps Headquarters. The other two companies, as soon as they reached Hassavant Farm and Dampvitoux, were to be ordered by the town majors of these places to proceed immediately to Corps Headquarters.

The Army Commander and the commanders of the neighboring groups were advised of the situation

EVENTS UP TO 11:45 A. M.

The 5th Landwehr Division reported that the enemy had penetrated the outpost zone of Sector F II. Friendly artillery was bombarding with annihilating fire the outpost zone of the sector under attack.

Shortly before 11:45 a. m. the Combres Group reported that the situation on the Combres Heights had not been clear since 11:30 a. m. Heavy fighting was in progress there; it was doubtful whether the Heights were still in our possession. St. Remy had been taken by the enemy. Furthermore, the enemy had reached the large Tranchee and had penetrated to a depth of about 1½ kilometers the sector of the 35th Austro-Hungarian Division.

At 11:45 a. m. the Gorz Group reported that the enemy had apparently broken completely through the 77th Reserve Division. The enemy was also making progress in the sector of the 10th Infantry Division and was now occupying the heights south of Pannes, south of Bouillonville and near Thiaucourt. A regiment of the 31st Division was sent towards Pannes, but it was too early to expect that it had counter-attacked. The right wing of the 10th Division apparently still rested on Montsec.

ESTIMATE OF THE SITUATION BY CORPS HEADQUARRTERS AT 11:45 A. M.

The 192d Infantry Division and the 5th Ldw. Division had up to this time repulsed all of the enemy's efforts and could continue to hold out. However, the progress which the enemy had been making since 11:15 a. m. in the sector of the 10th Infantry Division in conjunction with the enemy's success against the Combres Group continued to bring the danger ever nearer that the troops of the Mihiel Group still remaining in the salient would be cut off.

Therefore the following verbal report was made to the Chief of the Army General Staff about noon:

"The Mihiel Group can hold its position. If it becomes necessary, however, to withdraw to the Michel Zone, the Mihiel Group will require considerable time because the march is a long one. The route of march of the 5th Ldw. Division through St. Benoit is already in danger, inasmuch as only weak forces are available there at the present time to prevent the further progress of the enemy's attack. It is, therefore, possible that the Mihiel Group will be crowded to the north upon the route of march of the 35th Austro-Hungarian Division."

Thereupon Army Headquarters gave orders by telephone that the Loki movement should begin at once and the defense transferred for the present to the Schroeter Zone.

EVENTS UP TO 1:52 P. M.

Between 12:10 and 12:20 p. m. the order from Army Headquarters was transmitted verbally to the 192d Infantry Division and the 5th Ldw. Division. By 1:10 p. m. the instructions which had been delivered verbally had been supplemented by the following order which had been dictated to the orderly officers of the divisions:

GROUP ORDER

1. The Loki movement will begin at once. The defense will be transferred to the Schroeter Zone (right flank of the Group one kilometer east of Deuxnouds, left flank of Group at Champrez Pond).

2. The Schroeter Zone will be held until the receipt of further orders. The forces available for the defense will be grouped accordingly.

Rear guards (infantry with special weapons and single pieces of artillery) will remain in contact with the enemy and will fall back to the Schroeter Zone only when forced to do so by the enemy. In such an event they will do everything possible to impede the enemy without themselves being drawn into a combat whose issue cannot be foreseen.

3. The security garrisons in the Schroeter Zone will establish liaison with the army groups on the flanks and with each other. The fact of the completion of this operation will be telephoned in clear to Corps Headquarters by the divisions.

4. As for the artillery, only those sections or guns required for the support of the most advanced battalions will be left in front of the Schroeter Zone. All the rest of the artillery will be at once withdrawn behind the Schroeter Zone and be placed in position there insofar as required. All apparently dispensible batteries will be brought into a condition of readiness for the withdrawal to the Michel I Zone.

5. All explosions and destructions which have been prepared will be carried out insofar as the short space of time available permits.

Of special importance are all measures which will impede the rapid progress of the enemy. In this category is included, besides the blowing-up of roads, the blowing-up of all water supply constructions.

The Commanding General,
(Signed) LEUTHOLD.

Between 1 and 2 p. m. orders were given by the Group for the necessary regrouping of the subordinate anti-aircraft units and air forces. The Group observatories were to be taken over by the divisions.

Already during the forenoon the Group Signal Officer had made the necessary preparations for the transferring of Corps Headquarters from St. Benoit to Lachaussee. He reported that at 2 p. m. all the necessary communications between the fighting units and Lachaussee would be established.

At 12:30 p. m. about forty deep-flying hostile battle planes made an attack with machine guns and hand grenades upon the chateau garden and crossroad at St. Benoit, but the attack was unsuccessful on account of the wind and rain just at that time.

At 1:05 p. m. the 5th Ldw. Division reported that it had sent the 65th Ldw. Infantry Regiment through Nonsard Woods in the direction of Lamarche. In view of the situation at that moment Corps Headquarters was of the opinion that the battalion should be quickly sent forward to Nonsard by the most direct route in order to protect the open flank at this greatly endangered point in the line. The 5th Ldw. Division was therefore advised accordingly. At the same time it was informed that the three companies of the division which had been designated for trench construction work in the Michel I Zone would be ordered by Corps Headquarters to Sevastopol Farm in order to protect the flank of the division's line of march at that point. The 5th Ldw. Division was again informed of the necessity for strong artillery support of the right wing of the Gorz Group from the slopes of the Cote and of the importance of continuous close liaison with the neighboring divisions.

At 1:15 p. m. the commander of the Gorz Group was advised of the measures which had been taken.

The 5th Ldw. Division reported at 1:20 p. m. that it had sent the Divisional Assault Company to St. Benoit to reinforce the three companies sent to Sevastopol Farm by Corps Headquarters.

In the meantime the commander of the intrenching company of the 5th Ldw. Division which had been stopped at Dampvitoux reported at Corps Headquarters and was given instructions by the chief of staff of the Group. The company itself reached Sevastopol Farm about 2 p. m. At 1:40 p. m. the 5th Ldw. Division reported that the enemy had been again driven out of the outpost zone of Sector F II. and that some prisoners from the 156th Regiment, 39th French Division, had remained in our hands.

The 5th Ldw. Division acting in conjunction with the 192d Division was not to withdraw the front line battalions from the advance position until 8 o'clock in the evening, and was to maintain contact with the enemy by means of officer patrols until the morning of September 13.

The observatory on Le Mont reported two hostile balloons and one battery near Flirey and Xivray.

At 1:52 p. m. the 5th Ldw. Division reported that, according to a report of the Infantry Brigade on the Bocksberg, Pannes and Nonsard had been surrounded and captured by the enemy. Tanks co-operating with infantry were advancing from Nonsard against Heudicourt.

ESTIMATE OF THE SITUATION AT 1:52 P. M. BY CORPS HEADQUARTERS

The loss of Pannes and Nonsard signified that the situation had grown decidedly worse. It showed that the 10th Infantry Division could not with its own means prevent the enemy from breaking through on the west. The order issued by Army Headquarters at noon to hold the Schroeter Zone had become obsolete, because the enemy had already broken through the zone near and east of Nonsard. The regiment of the 31st Infantry Division which had been sent towards Xammes had apparently not yet counter-attacked, and it was also very questionable whether this arrangement would be able to restore the very critical situation of the 10th Infantry Division.

It was imperative for the Mihiel Group to check a further enemy advance in a northerly and northwesterly direction beyond the line Nonsard-Pannes-Bouillonville.

The infantry advancing with tanks from Nonsard in the direction of Heudicourt would, in the opinion of Corps Headquarters, meet with the resting battalion of the 65th Ldw. Infantry Regiment which had been sent in that direction with accompanying artillery. It would probably be sufficient to drive the enemy back to Nonsard. Other forces would have to be sent by the Group to fill up the gaps and assure the flank between Nonsard and Beney.

The 5th Ldw. Division reported that on its own responsibility it had sent the two resting battalions of the 25th and 36th Ldw. Infantry Regiments, which had been originally assigned as the security garrison for the Schroeter Zone, to counter-attack in the region north of Heudicourt, and that these battalions had orders to drive back the enemy beyond the line Pannes-Beney in the direction of Bouillonville and to take over the protection of the left flank of the Division by establishing liaison with the battalion of the 65th Ldw. Regiment at Nonsard, and the companies at Sevastopol Farm.

Corps Headquarters agreed to this arrangement. There were no other forces in sight for the protection of the flanks.

The Army Commander and the commanders of the neighboring Groups were advised of the situation and the measures which had been taken.

EVENTS UP TO 5:30 P. M.

The Gorz Group, in reply to an inquiry, reported at 2:10 p. m. that it had no information to offer concerning the situation around Nonsard and Pannes. Tanks had gained possession of Raulecourt and Rambucourt.

The 192d Division reported at 2:15 p. m. that the enemy had attacked the division. In front of Sector E I North the enemy had been annihilated in the wire entanglements; further south, however, he had succeeded in taking Pioneer Hill and in advancing from there towards the east. Now after all movements had been started division headquarters was about to move to Hassavant Farm.

At 2:30 p. m. the Gorz Group reported that masses of infantry with tanks and cavalry opposite Sector G 1 in the woods south of Montsec were preparing to attack. The artillery fire of the 5th Ldw. Division was immediately directed upon that point.

Shortly after 2:30 p. m. Corps Headquarters transferred its P. C. to Lachaussee. A general staff officer and an orderly officer remained behind in the former Corps Headquarters to temporarily maintain communications. At 2:35 p. m. the Army Commander telephoned an order that no stop was to be made in the Schroeter Zone but that the troops were to be withdrawn without stopping to the Michel I Zone. The reinforced Assault Battalion 14 was brought by rail from Briey to Chambley in the afternoon to take up a position in the Spada sector (192d Division) in the new battle zone; the 88th Division was enroute to relieve the 5th Ldw. Division in the Apremont sector. This order was immediately transmitted to the two divisions.

At 2:50 p. m. the chief general staff officer of the 5th Ldw. Division reached St. Benoit and reported that the resting battalions of the 25th and 36th Ldw. Infantry Regiments had been sent forward for the counter-attack on the line Pannes-Beney. The order to evacuate the salient had been issued to the troops. At 3 p. m. the commander of the Gorz Group reported that the 10th Division had been forced back to the vicinity of Beney and that the garrison of Montsec had just received orders to withdraw. The chief general staff officer of the 5th Ldw. Division who was at St. Benoit declared that this order conformed to the measures taken by the 5th Ldw. Division.

The Combres Group reported at 3 p. m. that the line of artillery protection was for the most part being held. The village of Remy and the western half of Combres had fallen into the enemy's hands.

Shortly after 3 p. m. the commander of the 192d Infantry Division arrived at St. Benoit and reported that the movements which had been ordered were under way. He then left for Lachaussee to make a verbal report to the commanding general.

Towards 3:15 p. m. the 5th Ldw. Division transferred its P. C. to Louiseville Farm and shortly afterwards to Marimbois Farm.

At 3:30 p. m. communications between Lachaussee and the fighting units were brought into use. About 4 p. m. the entire battle staff of Corps Headquarters was reunited in Lachaussee.

Both divisions had issued systematic orders for the withdrawal movements. The division headquarters were on the march to or already arranging their new P. C's.

About 5:30 p. m. the Army Commander reported that the counter-attack of the 31st and 123d Divisions east of Thiaucourt was in progress and gaining ground. No report had as yet been received of the attack being made by the regiments of the 31st Division west of Thiaucourt in the direction of Pannes. The 88th Infantry Division would not be engaged in the Apremont sector but in the Lahayville sector (10th Infantry Division) to take over the right flank of the Gorz Group. The reinforced Assault Battalion 14 was assigned to the Apremont sector (5th Ldw. Division). Army Headquarters could not place any fresh troops at the disposal of the Group for taking over the Spada sector from the 192d Infantry Division.

ESTIMATE OF THE SITUATION AT 5:30 P. M. BY CORPS HEADQUARTERS

Since about 5 p. m. the noise of battle had markedly decreased. It appeared as if, on this day at least, the enemy had been prevented from breaking through between the Mad Brook and the Moselle by the counter-attack of the 31st and 123d Divisions. Only west of Thiaucourt, at the point at which the Mihiel Group was most endangered, did the situation continue to remain unclear. Only the three companies of the 5th Ldw. Division, which Corps Headquarters had sent forward to Sevastopol Farm, were immediately available for safeguarding the important crossroad at St. Benoit. There was no mistaking the danger to the Mihiel Group from a further advance of the enemy from Beney in the direction of St. Benoit.

As telephone communication with the 5th Ldw. Division was temporarily cut, an orderly officer from Corps Headquarters was sent to the 5th Ldw. Division by automobile about 6:10 p. m., with the following order:

> To the 5th Ldw. Division:
>
> 1. The 5th Ldw. division will withdraw to the Apremont sector in the Michel position.
>
> 2. Assault Battalion 14 will be sent to the Division in that sector and placed under its command.
>
> 3. The two battalions east of Heudicourt will cover the retreat of the Division through Benoit and prevent the enemy from advancing beyond Beney.
>
> 4. The 88th Division will occupy the Lahayville sector.
>
> 5. The 192d Division will occupy the Spada sector.
>
> 6. The Michel position, including the outpost zone and outposts, will be occupied and held according to plan.
>
> 7. The change of location of division headquarters will be communicated to the group at once.
>
> 8. One officer will be stationed at Xylanderkreuz to regulate the march through the place.
>
> (Signed) LEUTHOLD.

The 192d Division was advised by telephone of the contents of the Army Order.

EVENTS UP TO 5 A. M., SEPTEMBER 13, 1918

About 6:30 p. m. the commander of Assault Battalion 14, Major von Puttkammer, arrived at Corps Headquarters at Lachaussee and reported that his companies would reach Xonville between 9 and 10 p. m.

The aerial reconnaissance made in the evening brought in no fresh information.

About 2 p. m. the orderly officer who had been sent from Corps Headquarters to the 5th Ldw. Division returned and reported that the 1st Battalion of the 65th Ldw. Regiment of the 5th Ldw. Division was already occupying the left half of the Apremont sector of the Michel I Zone, and that the right half would be taken over by the Assault Battalion. As for artillery, a mixed battalion of field artillery and the 3rd Battery of the 129th Foot Artillery were already in the Michel Zone and ready for action. The enemy had taken Beney and was feeling his way forward with patrols in the Xammes and Dampvitoux Woods. The three companies which had been at Sevastopol Farm were acting as outposts south and east of St. Benoit. Southeast of Marimbois Farm liaison had been established with the unit on the left.

No troops of the 192d Division had reached the Michel I Zone up to 9 p. m. The headquarters of the division was at Jonville.

Hostile artillery fire had completely subsided on the entire front of attack.

At 2:30 a. m. the 192d Division reported that the headquarters and the 3d Battalion of the 183d Regiment had arrived in Jonville. This report was supplemented at 2:50 a. m. by the announcement that the withdrawal of the division along the Roumanian Road was in full progress.

The Assault Battalion reached the 5th Ldw. Division after midnight and was sent into the right half of the divisional sector. Otherwise nothing new had happened there. The enemy had not followed up.

ESTIMATE OF THE SITUATION BY CORPS HEADQUARTERS AT 5 A. M. SEPTEMBER 13

From the reports of the divisions the Corps Commander formed the opinion that the greater part of the troops, who had to execute the difficult and at times apparently very dangerous withdrawal, had reached the Michel I Zone by the morning of September 13. Under the protection of the units which had been the first to arrive and of the Assault Battalion, which units had occupied the Michel I Zone ready for defensive action, the divisions were arranging their elements and organizing the artillery for the defense.

The very great danger which had been continually threatening during the afternoon and evening of September 12, namely, that the enemy would advance from Dampvitoux Woods into the Michel I Zone and break through at that point before forces were available for its defense, was obtained. The enemy had not followed.

After it had been ascertained on the morning of September 13 that the divisions were holding their sectors in the Michel I Zone ready for the defense, as far as the prevailing conditions permitted, and after liaison had been established with the neighboring groups, Corps Headquarters left Lachaussee and moved to Homecourt.

The losses on September 12 amounted to:

5th Ldw. Division:	casualties:	1 officer, 25 men killed 3 officers, 65 men wounded 7 officers, 523 men missing
	materiel:	15 '08 machine guns 36 '08/15 machine guns 13 light minenwerfer 2 guns (on account of burst in bore).
192d Division:	casualties:	21 men killed 71 men wounded 14 officers, 609 men missing
	materiel:	25 '08 machine guns 49 '08/15 machine guns 10 light minenwerfer 2 medium minenwerfer

In spite of the tactically unfavorable situation which compelled the troops of the Mihiel Group in the salient to withdraw to the Michel I Zone in one movement, it was possible during the day of September 12 and the night of September 12-13 to carry out a larger number of the systematically prepared removals and destructions in the area to be evacuated.

According to the reports of the divisions, it was possible to completely destroy the majority of the water supply constructions, such as the water tower on the field railroad near Heudicourt. The water tower near the Bayrisch Zell-Wendelstein station had been previously disconnected by the commander of the railway troops. The Roman Fort was systematically blown up, the majority of the villages and camps were set on fire. Only a small number of the road destructions which had been planned could be carried out (at the most important crossroads), inasmuch as the necessary preparation had not advanced sufficiently in the period preceding the attack. The removal of the civilian inhabitants capable of bearing arms from the villages in the advance battle zone and all inhabitants who had moved into the Michel I Zone from the evacuated area was in general carried according to plan on September 12.

For the Corps Commander.
(Signed) VON HINGST,
Chief of Staff.

DECORATIONS AND CITATIONS

DECORATIONS AND CITATIONS AWARDED TO MEMBERS OF THE
89TH DIVISION
AMERICAN EXPEDITIONARY FORCES

Compiled from announcements in General Orders, 89th Division, records of the Decoration Section, Adjutant General's Office, A. E. F. (corrected to April, 1920), and General Orders of the War Department, Washington, D. C.

Note—Where a higher American decoration was subsequently bestowed for an exploit for which a lower American award had been given originally (as Medal of Honor in place of Distinguished Service Cross (D. S. C.), or D. S. C. in place of Citation), the higher honor takes the place and is in lieu of the lower, which is thereby automatically withdrawn. In such cases, therefore, the earlier and lower award has been omitted on these lists to avoid duplication. This principle does not extend to foreign decorations, many of which were presented as a further tribute to the same exploits or services which were likewise recognized by an appropriate American decoration or citation.

In the case of American honors, dates of the exploits are given, except in a few cases where the information was not available. All exploits dated prior to October 10th, 1918, took place in the St. Mihiel sector. All subsequent to that time occurred in the Meuse-Argonne operation, except those of members of the 164th Field Artillery Brigade, which were all in the St. Mihiel sector.

Second awards of the Croix de Guerre (made to a few members of the Division and authorizing wearing the decoration with a second palm or star) are not shown because complete and accurate information regarding such awards is not available.

The lists include only honors won while serving with organizations of the 89th Division, and do not include those awarded for exploits with other divisions, even though the recipient, either previously or subsequently, belonged to the 89th.

Every effort has been made for accuracy and completeness, but there were discrepancies in spelling, etc., in lists from the several sources, and some awards may have been missed because not credited properly to the Division. Additional awards may be made by the War Department later. It is therefore too much to hope that this record is entirely complete and without error.

AMERICAN MEDAL OF HONOR

The Medal of Honor was awarded to those named below by the President, in the name of Congress, for conspicuous gallantry and intrepidity, above and beyond the call of duty, in action with the enemy. It was given only to officers and soldiers of the American Army, and the standard of conduct required to merit its award during the World War is not exceeded by that for any other decoration in the world. It is doubtful whether it is equalled by any, unless the English Victoria Cross. The cold words of a citation can give little idea of the heroism demanded to earn this honor.

PRIVATE 1/CL. CHARLES D. BARGER, 2205271 COMPANY L, 354TH INFANTRY.

For conspicuous gallantry and intrepidity, above and beyond the call of duty, in action with the enemy, near the Bois de Bantheville, France, 31 October 1918.

Learning that two daylight patrols had been caught out in No Man's Land and were unable to return, Private Barger and another stretcher bearer, upon their own initiative made two trips five hundred yards beyond our lines, under constant machine gun fire and rescued two officers.

Home address: Henry S. McFeron (uncle), Stotts City, Missouri.

PRIVATE DAVID B. BARKELEY, 1488756, COMPANY A, 356TH INFANTRY (DECEASED).

For conspicuous gallantry and intrepidity, above and beyond the call of duty, in action with the enemy, near Pouilly, France, 9 November 1918.

When information was desired as to the enemy's position on the opposite side of the River Meuse, Private Barkeley, with another soldier, volunteered without hesitation and swam the river to reconnoiter the exact location. He succeeded in reaching the opposite bank, despite the evident determination of the enemy to prevent a crossing. Having obtained his information, he again entered the water for his return, but before his goal was reached, he was seized with cramps and drowned.

Next of Kin: Mrs. Antonio Barkeley (mother), 1121 E. Quincy St., San Antonio, Texas.

CAPTAIN MARCELLUS H. CHILES, 356TH INFANTRY (DECEASED).

For conspicuous gallantry and intrepidity, above and beyond the call of duty, in action with the enemy, near Le Champy Bas, France, 3 November 1918.

When his battalion, of which he had just taken command, was halted by machine gun fire from the front and left flank, Captain Chiles picked up the rifle of a dead soldier, and, calling on his men to follow, led the advance across a stream waist deep, in the face of the machine gun fire. Upon reaching the opposite bank, this gallant officer was seriously wounded in the abdomen by a sniper, but before permitting himself to be evacuated he made complete arrangements for turning over his command to the next senior officer, and under the inspiration of his fearless leadership, his battalion reached its objective. Captain Chiles died shortly after reaching the hospital.

Next of Kin: John Horne Chiles (father), 2815 West 37th Ave., Denver, Colorado.

SERGEANT ARTHUR J. FORREST, 2178726, COMPANY D, 354TH INFANTRY.

For conspicuous gallantry and intrepidity above and beyond the call of duty, in action with the enemy, near Remonville, France, 1 November 1918.

When the advance of his company was stopped by bursts of fire from a nest of six enemy machine guns, without being discovered, he worked his way, single-handed, to a point within fifty yards of the machine gun nest. Charging, single-handed, he drove out the enemy in disorder, thereby protecting the advance platoon from annihilating fire, and permitting resumption of the advance by his company.

Next of Kin: William Forrest (father), 112 South Maple St., Hannibal, Missouri.

CORPORAL (THEN PRIVATE) JESSE N. FUNK, 2187583, COMPANY L, 354TH INFANTRY.

For conspicuous gallantry and intrepidity, above and beyond the call of duty, in action with the enemy, near Bois de Bantheville, France, 31 October 1918.

Learning that two daylight patrols had been caught out in No Man's Land and were unable to return, Private Funk and another stretcher bearer, upon their initiative, made two trips five hundred yards beyond our lines, under constant machine gun fire, and rescued two wounded officers.

Next of Kin: Martin Funk (father), Calhan, Colorado.

FIRST LIEUTENANT HAROLD A. FURLONG, 353RD INFANTRY.

For conspicuous gallantry and intrepidity, above and beyond the call of duty, in action with the enemy, near Bantheville, France, 1 November 1918.

Immediately after the opening of the attack in the Bois de Bantheville, when his company was held up by severe machine gun fire from the front, which killed his company commander and several soldiers, Lieutenant Furlong moved out in advance of the line with great courage and coolness, crossing an open space several hundred yards wide. Taking up a position behind the line of machine guns, he closed in on them, one at a time, killing a number of the enemy with his rifle, putting four machine gun nests out of action and driving twenty German prisoners into our lines.

Next of Kin: Arthur D. Furlong (father), 2950 West Grand Boulevard, Detroit, Michigan.

SERGEANT WALDO M. HATLER, 2199881, COMPANY B, 356TH INFANTRY.

For conspicuous gallantry and intrepidity, above and beyond the call of duty, in action with the enemy, near Pouilly, France, 8 November 1918.

When volunteers were called for to secure information as to the enemy's positions on the opposite bank of the Meuse River, Sergeant Hatler was the first to offer his services for this dangerous mission. Swimming across the river, he succeeded in reaching the German lines, after another soldier, who had started with him, had been seized with cramps and drowned in mid-stream. Alone, he carefully and courageously reconnoitered the enemy's positions which were held in force, and again successfully swam the river, bringing back information of great value.

Next of Kin: Troy C. Hatler (father), General Delivery, Neosho, Missouri.

SERGEANT (THEN PRIVATE 1/CL.) HAROLD I. JOHNSTON, 2202872, COMPANY A, 356TH INFANTRY.

For conspicuous gallantry and intrepidity, above and beyond the call of duty, in action with the enemy, near Pouilly, France, 9 November 1918.

When information was desired as to the enemy's position on the opposite side of the River Meuse, Private Johnston, with another soldier, volunteered without hesitation, and swam the river to reconnoiter the exact location of the enemy. He succeeded in reaching the opposite bank, despite the evident determination of the enemy to prevent a crossing. Having obtained his information he again entered the water for his return. This was accomplished after a severe struggle, which so exhausted him that he had to be assisted from the water, after which he rendered his report of the exploit.

Next of Kin: Mrs. Belle Renshaw (mother), 1148 Speer Boulevard, Denver, Colorado.

SECOND LIEUTENANT J. HUNTER WICKERSHAM, 353RD INFANTRY (DECEASED).

For conspicuous gallantry and intrepidity, above and beyond the call of duty, in action with the enemy, near Limey, France, 12 September 1918.

Advancing with his platoon during the St. Mihiel offensive, Lieutenant Wickersham was severely wounded in four places by the bursting of a high explosive shell. Before receiving any aid for himself, he dressed the wounds of his orderly, who was wounded at the same time. He then ordered and accompanied the further advance of his platoon, although weakened by loss of blood. His right hand and arm being disabled by wounds, he continued to fire his revolver with his left hand until, exhausted by loss of blood, he fell and died from his wounds before aid could be administered.

Next of Kin: Mrs. W. E. Damon (mother), 3416 Colfax Ave. B., Denver, Colorado.

AMERICAN DISTINGUISHED SERVICE CROSS

The Distinguished Service Cross was awarded to those named below by the President, or in the name of the President by the Commander in Chief, American Expeditionary Forces in Europe, for extraordinary heroism in action with the enemy.

The honor is confined to those serving in some capacity with the American Army, including members of Allied forces so serving.

NAME, RANK AND ORGANIZATION.	DATE OF EXPLOIT. 1918
1st Sgt. (then Sgt.) Harry J. Adams, 2177024, Co. K, 353rd Inf.	Sept. 12
Capt. Fred C. Albright, M.C. 353rd Inf.	Sept. 13
1st Lieut. John H. Ale, 355th Inf.	Sept. 12
Sgt. Roy C. Anthony, 2178410, Co. B, 354th Inf.	Nov. 1
Capt. Moses D. Atkins, 353rd Inf.	Sept. 12-13
2nd Lieut. Howard A. Bair, 354th Inf. (deceased)	Nov. 2
Cpl. Lloyd Barber, 2175210, Hq. Co., 353rd Inf.	Nov. 2
Pvt. Alex J. Barbier, 1595630, Hq. Co., 356th Inf.	Oct. 22
Cpl. Edward Barry, 2088934, Co. K, 354 Inf. (deceased)	Nov. 1
Capt. Albert F. Baxter, 353rd Inf.	Nov. 1
Sgt. Harry E. Bayly, 2175201, Hq. Co., 353rd Inf. (deceased)	Oct. 22
Cpl. Billie W. Belt, 2195748, Co. B, 314th Supply Train	Oct. ..
Pvt. Roy A. Bess, 2205709, Co. L, 355th Inf.	Nov. 4
2nd Lieut. Albert E. Birch, 342nd M. G. Bn. (deceased)	Nov. 1
Lieut. Col. Geo. W. Blackinton (then Major 353rd Inf.)	Sept. 12-13
Cpl. Tracy S. Blair, 2187066, Co. E, 353rd Inf. (deceased)	Nov. 1-2
Sgt. (then Private) Gus Bordkas, 2334009, Med. Det., 354th Inf.	Nov. 1
Sgt. John Brinda, 2181349, Co. B, 355th Inf.	Sept. 12
Sgt. George L. Busch, 2178732, Co. D, 354th Inf.	Nov. 1
Pvt. Ora Lee Butcher, 2208393, Co. M, 356th Inf.	Sept. 12
Sgt. Claude E. Cavenee, 2178440, Co. B, 354th Inf.	Nov. 1
Capt. (then 1st Lieut.) Arthur S. Champeny, 356th Inf.	Sept. 12
Sgt. (then Pvt. 1/cl.) John W. Childers, 2178442, Co. B, 354th Inf.	Nov. 1
Sgt. (then Cpl.) George Colville, Jr., 2178873, M. G. Co., 354th Inf.	Nov. 1
Pvt. George W. Condit, 2177584, Med. Det., 353rd Inf.	Nov. 2-3
Cpl. Francis L. Daniels, 2176745, Co. H, 353rd Inf.	Nov. 2
1st Lieutenant Thorndike Deland, 340th F. A.	Nov. 4
Cpl. Frank Deskins, 542189, Co. D, 354th Inf.	Nov. 1
1st Sgt. (then Sgt.) Clyde H. Dewalt, 2185154, Co. K, 356th Inf.	Nov. 10-11
Pvt. 1/cl. Edward W. A. Dietz, 2176527, Co. F, 314th Eng.	Nov. 6-7

NAME, RANK AND ORGANIZATION.	DATE OF EXPLOIT. 1918
Pvt. Andrew W. Dilbeck, 3207561, Co. I, 356th Inf.	Nov. 10-11
Sgt. Marquis L. Dillard, 2178369, Co. A, 354th Inf.	Nov. 1
Pvt. Charles Disalvo, 2848232, Co. B, 354th Inf. (deceased)	Nov. 1
Pvt. John J. Dorgan, 2207992, Co. C, 356th Inf.	Sept. 23
Sgt. Otis V. Dozer, 2176368, Co. F, 353rd Inf.	Nov. 2
Pvt. John I. Dugan, 2844913, Co. B, 353rd Inf.	Oct. 23
Cpl. John Duncan, 2178736, Co. D, 354th Inf.	Nov. 1
Pvt. John J. Farrell, 2848308, Co. B, 354th Inf. (deceased)	Nov. 1
2nd Lieut. Frank J. Fisher, 355th Inf. (deceased)	Nov. 3-4
Sgt. Harry E. Flannery, 2192862, Co. D, 341st M. G. Bn.	Nov. 1
Cpl. Alexander Folz, 2194030, Co. B, 354th Inf. (deceased)	Nov. 1
Pvt. 1/cl. Fred M. Forbis, 2845581, Co. D, 354th Inf.	Nov. 1
Pvt. Herman J. Forth, 2180322, Med. Det., 341st M. G. Bn. (deceased)	Nov. 2
Capt. Charles M. Fox, M. C., 353rd Inf.	Oct. 26
Sgt. George W. Gardner, 2176371, Co. F, 353rd Inf.	Nov. 2
Cpl. (then Pvt.) Patrick Garrity, 2087074, Co. C, 354th Inf.	Nov. 1
Pvt. Don Greene, 2213364, Co. H, 353rd Inf.	Nov. 2
Pvt. 1/cl. Charles J. Gude, 2846082, Co. D, 342nd M. G. Bn.	Nov. 3
Sgt. Elmer F. Guthrie, 217635, Co. E, 353rd Inf.	Nov. 1
Cpl. (then Pvt. 1/cl.) Otho M. Hagerman, 2178271, Co. A, 354th Inf.	Nov. 1
Cpl. Joseph C. Hahn, 2178107, M. C. Co., 354th Inf.	Nov. 1
Pvt. 1/cl. Claud P. Hale, 2180240, Med. Det., 354th Inf.	Nov. 1
Pvt. 1/cl. William A. Hall, 2192179, Co. A, 353rd Inf. (deceased)	Sept. 12
1st Lieut. (then 2nd Lieut.) Charles R. Hanger, 356th Inf.	Nov. 10-11
Major Mark Hanna, 356th Inf. (deceased)	Nov. 6-11
Sgt. John A. Hartung, 2178459, Co. B, 354th Inf. (deceased)	Nov. 1
1st Lieut. Eilert G. Heiken, 356th Inf.	Sept. 23 and Nov. 10-11
2nd Lieut. Henry Henderson, 354th Inf.	Nov. 1
Major Henry W. Hobson, 356th Inf.	Sept. 12
2nd Lieut. Frank J. Hoeynck, 314th Eng. (deceased)	Nov. 6-7
Pvt. Earl A. Hoffman, 2180850, Co. C, 341st M. G. Bn.	Oct. 24
Cpl. Alexander Hollingsworth, 2056074, Co. B, 354th Inf.	Nov. 1
Sgt. (then Cpl.) George G. Hollis, 2184500, Co. E, 356th Inf.	Nov. 4
Pvt. 1/cl. Wendell W. Jacobs, 2185701, Co. C, 341st M. G. Bn.	Oct. 30
Sgt. Martin J. Janssen, 2181249, Co. A, 355th Inf.	Sept. 12
Pvt. Alva Kane, 2177538, Med. Det., 353rd Inf.	Oct. 25-27
Sgt. Roy L. Keller, 2178408, Co. B, 354th Inf.	Nov. 1
Sgt. Orlen O. Kelley, 2185003, Co. I, 356th Inf.	Nov. 7, 8, 11
Pvt. John Kelly, 2191080, Co. A, 341st M. G. Bn.	Nov. 2
1st Lieut. Harold W. Kenaston, 356th Inf.	Nov. 4-10
Cpl. Edward M. Kessler, 2176452, Co. F, 353rd Inf. (deceased)	Sept. 12
Pvt. 1/cl. Clifford C. Kidd, 2183276, M. G. Co., 354th Inf.	Nov. 1
Brig. Gen. Charles E. Kilbourne (then Col., Chief of Staff, 89th Div.)	Sept. 12
Pvt. Richard E. King, 2187488, Hq. Co., 340 F. A.	Nov. 4
Pvt. 1/cl. David Kline, 2180319, Med. Det., 341st M. G. Bn.	Nov. 1-2
Pvt. Dwight F. Lamson, 2189236, Co. G, 353rd Inf. (deceased)	Sept. 12
Pvt. Clarence E. Lauber, 3091038, Co. I, 356th Inf. (deceased)	Nov. 10-11
Sgt. (then Cpl.) Charles A. Lemasters, 2193875, Co. C, 314th F. S. Bn.	Nov. 4-11
2nd Lieut. Henri Jean Lescadron, French Liaison Officer, att. 356th Inf.	Sept. 12-14
Pvt. Clarence Loken, 2814509, Co. M, 356th Inf.	Nov. 4
Pvt. 1/cl. Louis H. Loyd, 2189256, Co. F, 356th Inf.	Nov. 4
Sgt. Clayton Malone, 2176872, Co. I, 353rd Inf.	Nov. 1
2nd Lieut. William E. Maloney, 354th Inf.	Nov. 1
Pvt. John R. Manning, 2848637, Co. D, 342nd M. G. Bn.	Nov. 1
Sgt. (then Cpl.) Tharold B. Mansfield, 2193652, Co. C, 314th F. S. Bn.	Nov. 4-11
Cpl. Augustine Martinez, 2846993, Co. I, 356th Inf.	Nov. 10-11
2nd Lieut. Oscar P. May, 356th Inf.	Sept. 12
Cpl. John W. McAfee, 2184365, Co. D, 356th Inf. (deceased)	Nov. 8
Sgt. Roy E. McComb, 2183787, M. G. Co., 356th Inf. (deceased)	Nov. 4
Sgt. Lee B. McDaniel, 2175601, Co. A, 353rd Inf. (deceased)	Oct. 23
Bugler Edward McGee, 2213042, Co. M, 353rd Inf.	Nov. 1-2
Cpl. John W. McKay, 2213386, Co. M, 353rd Inf.	Nov. 1
Capt. (then 1st Lieut.) Herman McNulty, 354th Inf.	Nov. 1
Sgt. (then Cpl.) Herbert H. Miller, 2201262, Co. G, 353rd Inf.	Nov. 2
2nd Lieut. John M. Millis, 354th Inf.	Oct. 30

NAME, RANK AND ORGANIZATION.	DATE OF EXPLOIT. 1918
Sgt. 1/cl. Elgin J. Moore, 2193735, Co. C, 314th F. S. Bn.	Nov. 4-11
Capt. Fred F. Moore, 355th Inf.	Sept. 12
1st Lieut. Francis Morgan, 353rd Inf.	Nov. 1-11
Capt. (then 1st Lieut.) Verne A. Morgan, 355th Inf.	Nov. 4
1st Lieut. John H. Murphy, 356th Inf.	Nov. 10-11
Lieut. Col. (then Major) James L. Peatross, 353rd Inf.	Nov. 2
2nd Lieut. Harry W. Pine, 353rd Inf.	Oct. 4
Cpl. (then Bugler) Chauncey W. Porter, 2202524, Co. B, 355th Inf.	Sept. 12
2nd Lieut Irving Le Nois Ragsdale, 356th Inf. (deceased)	Nov. 4 & 6
Sgt. Earl E. Ramsey, 2176548, Co. G, 353rd Inf.	Nov. 2
1st Lieut. George E. Rand, 353rd Inf.	Nov. 2
Pvt. 1/cl. Cecil E. Reed, 2201115, Co. E, 353rd Inf.	Nov. 2
Sgt. Glenn M. Reed, 2181356, Co. B, 355th Inf. (deceased)	Sept. 13
Col. James H. Reeves, 353rd Inf.	Sept. 12-13
Cook (then Pvt.) Elmer P. Richards, 2847865, Co. D, 354th Inf.	Sept. 18
Pvt. Leo L. Sandman, 2212260, Co. F, 353rd Inf. (deceased)	Nov. 2
Sgt. 1/cl. Roy M. Sauers, 2193727, Co. D, 314th F. S. Bn.	Nov. 4
1st Lieut. James E. Scanlon, 353rd Inf.	Sept. 12
Pvt. Marcelino Serna, 2195593, Co. B, 355th Inf.	Sept. 12
Pvt. Quincy R. Seymour, 2186865, Co. F, 353rd Inf. (deceased)	Nov. 2
1st Lieut. Charles A. Shaw, 353rd Inf. (deceased)	Sept. 12-13
Sgt. Ralph M. Shimeall, 2213015, Co. M, 353rd Inf.	Nov. 1-2
1st Lieut. Leon P. Shinn, 356th Inf.	Sept. 12
Cpl. Edgar Shoultz, 2183705, Co. B, 354th Inf.	Nov. 1
Pvt. Edward Sittler, 2855903, Co. C, 341st M. G. Bn.	Oct. 24
Sgt. John R. Slay, 2179328, Co. G, 354th Inf.	Nov. 2
Lieut. Col. (then Major) Burton A. Smead, Div. Adjutant, 89th Div.	Nov. 1-6
Pvt. Fred S. Smith, 2212976, M. G. Co., 354th Inf. (deceased)	Nov. 1
1st Lieut. Robert O. Smith, Dental Surgeon, 356th Inf.	Nov. 6-11
1st Lieut. Royal H. G. Smith, 353rd Inf.	Nov. 1
Lieut. Col. Brehon B. Somervell, G-1, 89th Div. (then Corps of Engineers, attached to 89th Div.)	Nov. 5-6
Pvt. 1/cl. (then Pvt.) Almon E. Sprague, 2192613, Med. Det., 355th Inf.	Nov. 4
1st Lieut. C. W. Steinhilber, 354th Inf.	Nov. 1-2
Cpl. Thomas Stirling, 2183329, M. G. Co., 354th Inf.	Nov. 1
Cpl. Milton C. Sundin, 2202754, Co. L, 353rd Inf.	Sept. 12-13
Pvt. Joseph A. Szczepanik, Co. M, 353rd Inf.	Sept. 12-13
Bugler Frank F. Tomanek, 2176998, Co. I, 353rd Inf.	Nov. 1
Capt. Francis Trives, French Liaison Officer, att. 164th F. A. Brigade	
Pvt. Benjamin T. Tubbs, 1590382, Co. I, 356th Inf. (deceased)	Nov. 10-11
Pvt. 1/cl. (then Pvt.) Richard Wahler, 2176034, Co. C, 353rd Inf.	Oct. 21
Cpl. Harry M. Ward, 2178243, Co. A, 354th Inf.	Nov. 1
Pvt. 1/cl. (then Pvt.) Edwin Wiese, 2207678, Co. C, 355th Inf.	Sept. 12
Capt. Marshall P. Wilder, 354th Inf.	Sept. 26
Major Thomas F. Wirth, 355th Inf.	Sept. 12
Sgt. Walter S. Witt, 2076194, Co. D, 353rd Inf.	Oct. 22
Pvt. 1/cl. Earl V. Wright, 2185246, Co. K, 356th Inf.	Nov. 10-11
2nd Lieut. Edward M. Young, Inf. Att. Div. Quartermaster, 89th Div. (deceased)	Nov. 8
Sgt. Rudolph A. Zimmerman, 2178114, M. G. Co., 354th Inf.	Nov. 2-3

AMERICAN DISTINGUISHED SERVICE MEDAL

The Distinguished Service Medal was awarded to those named below by the President for exceptionally meritorious service in a duty of great responsibility, in time of war.

NAME, RANK AND ORGANIZATION.

Col. Robert H. Allen, 356th Inf.
Col. Conrad S. Babcock, 354th Inf.
Brig. Gen. Charles E. Kilbourne (then Col., Chief of Staff, 89th Div.).
Col. John C. H. Lee, Chief of Staff, 89th Div.
Brig. Gen. Louis M. Nuttman (then Col., 356th Inf.).
Col. James H. Reeves, 353rd Inf.
Major Gen. Frank L. Winn, 177th Inf. Brig., and later 89th Div.
Major Gen. William M. Wright, 89th Div.

DECORATIONS AWARDED BY OUR ALLIES TO MEMBERS OF THE 89TH DIVISION

FRENCH LEGION OF HONOR

(La Legion D'Honneur)

AWARDED BY THE FRENCH TO OFFICERS ONLY

COMMANDER (COMMANDEUR)

NAME, RANK AND ORGANIZATION.

Major Gen. Frank L. Winn, 89th Div.
Major Gen. William M. Wright, 89th Div.

OFFICER (OFFICIER)

NAME, RANK AND ORGANIZATION.

Brig. Gen. George C. Barnhardt, 178th Inf. Brig.
Col. John C. H. Lee, Chief of Staff 89th Div.

CHEVALIER (CHEVALIER)

NAME, RANK AND ORGANIZATION.

Lieut. Col. George W. Blackinton (then Major 353rd Inf.).
Capt. (then 1st Lieut.) Arthur S. Champeny, 356th Inf.
1st Lieut. Thorndike Deland, 340th F. A.
1st Lieut. Harold A. Furlong, 353rd Inf.
1st Lieut. (then 2nd Lieut.) Charles R. Hanger, 356th Inf.
1st Lieut. Ellert G. Heiken, 356th Inf.
2nd Lieut. Henry Henderson, 354th Inf.
2nd Lieut. William E. Maloney, 354th Inf.
2nd Lieut. Oscar P. May, 356th Inf.
Lieut. Col. (then Major) James L. Peatross, 353rd Inf.
1st Lieut. George E. Rand, 353rd Inf.
Major Thomas F. Wirth, 355th Inf.

FRENCH MILITARY MEDAL

(Medaille Militaire)

AWARDED BY THE FRENCH ONLY TO ENLISTED MEN AND OCCASIONALLY, AS A MARK OF SPECIAL HONOR, TO GENERAL OFFICERS OF GREAT DISTINCTION.

NAME, RANK AND ORGANIZATION.

1st Sgt. (then Sgt.) Harry J. Adams, 2177024, Co. K, 353rd Inf.
Pvt. 1/cl. Chas. D. Barger, 2205271, Co. L, 354th Inf.
Pvt. Fred Berg, Co. L, 354th Inf.
1st Sgt. Clyde H. Dewalt, 2185154, Co. K, 356th Inf.
Sgt. Arthur J. Forrest, 2178726, Co. D, 354th Inf.
Cpl. (then Pvt.) Jesse N. Funk, 2187583, Co. L, 354th Inf.
Pvt. 1/cl. Claud P. Hale, 2180240, Med. Det., 354th Inf.
Sgt. (then Pvt. 1/cl.) Harold I. Johnston, 2202872, Co. A, 356th Inf.
Bugler Edward McGee, 2213042, Co. M, 353rd Inf.
Cpl. John W. McKay, 2213386, Co. M, 353rd Inf.
Cpl. (then Bugler) Chauncey W. Porter, 2202524, Co. B, 355th Inf.
Cook (then Pvt.) Elmer P. Richards, 2847865, Co. D, 354th Inf.
Pvt. Marcelino Serna, 2195593, Co. B, 355th Inf.
Bugler Frank F. Tomanek, 2176998, Co. I, 353rd Inf.
Pvt. 1/cl. (then Pvt.) Edwin Wiese, 2207678, Co. C, 355th Inf.

FRENCH WAR CROSS

(Croix de Guerre)

NAME, RANK AND ORGANIZATION.

1st Sgt. (then Sgt.) Harry J. Adams, 2177024, Co. K, 353rd Inf.
Cpl. Edward H. Alewel, Co. H, 356th Inf.
Sgt. Roy C. Anthony, 2178410, Co. B, 354th Inf.
Col. Conrad S. Babcock, 354th Inf.
Pvt. 1/cl. Charles D. Barger, 2205271, Co. L, 354th Inf.
Brig. Gen. George C. Barnhardt, 178th Inf. Brig.
Capt. Albert F. Baxter, 353rd Inf.
Col. Fred W. Boschen (then Lieut. Col. 353rd Inf.).

NAME, RANK AND ORGANIZATION.

1st Lieut. Paul M. Coleman, 164th F. A. Brig.
Sgt. (then Pvt.) Gus Bordkas, 2834009, Med. Det., 354th Inf.
Sgt. John Brinda, 2181349, Co. B, 355th Inf.
Cpl. Jasper V. Brown, Co. H, 356th Inf.
Lieut. Col. Levi G. Brown, Hq. 89th Div.
Pvt. Ora Lee Butcher, 2208393, Co. M, 356th Inf.
Capt. (then 1st Lieut.) Arthur S. Champeny, 356th Inf.
Sgt. (then Cpl.) George Colville, Jr., 2178873, M. G. Co., 354th Inf.
Cpl. Ray W. Crane, 2178761, Co. D, 354th Inf.
1st Lieut. Thorndike Deland, 340th F. A.
Cpl. Frank Deskins, 542189, Co. D, 354th Inf.
1st Sgt. Clyde H. Dewalt, 2185154, Co. K, 356th Inf.
Pvt. 1/cl. James A. Dickerson, Co. G, 356th Inf.
Lieut. Col. Franz A. Doniat, Hq. 89th Div.
Brig. Gen. Edward T. Donnelly, 164th F. A. Brig.
Pvt. John J. Dorgan, 2207992, Co. C, 356th Inf.
Sgt. Otis V. Dozer, 2170368, Co. F, 353rd Inf.
Pvt. John I. Dugan, 2844913, Co. B, 353rd Inf.
Sgt. Harry E. Flannery, 2192862, Co. D, 341st M. G. Bn.
Sgt. Arthur J. Forrest, 2178726, Co. D, 354th Inf.
Cpl. (then Pvt.) Jesse N. Funk, 2187583, Co. L, 354th Inf.
1st Lieut. Harold A. Furlong, 353rd Inf.
Sgt. George W. Gardner, 2176371, Co. F, 353rd Inf.
Cpl. Patrick Garrity, 2087074, Co. C, 354th Inf.
Pvt. Anton Gordelchuk, Co. E, 354th Inf.
Chaplain Otis E. Gray, 353rd Inf. (later Senior Chaplain, 89th Div.).
Lieut. Paul L. Green, 355th Inf.
Lieut. Chas. Griesha, 356th Inf.
Cpl. (then Pvt. 1/cl.) Otho M. Hagerman, 2178271, Co. A, 254th Inf.
Pvt. 1/cl. Claud P. Hale, 2180240, Med. Det., 354th Inf.
Major W. A. Hale, 340th M. G. Bn.
1st Lieut. (then 2nd Lieut.) Charles R. Hanger, 356th Inf.
Sgt. M. Waldo Hatler, 2199881, Co. B, 356th Inf.
Lieut. Georges W. Hay, Co. D, 355th Inf.
1st Lieut. Ellert G. Heiken, 356th Inf.
2nd Lieut. Henry Henderson, 354th Inf.
Sgt. Orvalle R. Hight, Co. L, 353rd Inf.
Sgt. (then Cpl.) George G. Hollis, 2184500, Co. E., 356th Inf.
1st Lieut. Robert G. Hudson, 354th Inf.
Sgt. Harry C. Hyndman, Co. L, 353rd Inf.
Sgt. Martin J. Janssen, 2181249, Co. A, 355th Inf.
Cpl. John A. Johnson, Co. A, 355th Inf.
Sgt. (then Pvt. 1/cl.) Harold I. Johnston, 2202872, Co. A, 356th Inf.
Lieut. Francis N. Jordan, 356th Inf.
Sgt. Orien O. Kelley, 2185003, Co. I, 356th Inf.
Pvt. John Kelly, 2191080, Co. A, 341st M. G. Bn.
1st Lieut. Harold W. Kenaston, 356th Inf.
Lieut. Col. Edward A. Keyes, 178th Inf. Brig.
Brig. Gen. Charles E. Kilbourne (then Col., Chief of Staff 89th Div.).
Pvt. Richard E. King, 2187488, Hq. Co., 340th F. A.
Col. John C. H. Lee, Chief of Staff, 89th Div.
Capt. John W. Lockwood, Hq. 89th Div. (then 1st Lieut. 177th Inf. Brig.).
2nd Lieut. William E. Maloney, 354th Inf.
Cpl. Augustine Martinez, 2846993, Co. I, 356th Inf.
Major (then Capt.) Clinton J. Masseck, 353rd Inf.
2nd Lieut. Oscar P. May, 356th Inf.
Major Harvey E. McCarthy, M. C., 355th Inf.
Cpl. Hayden McDowell, 2847769, Co. E, 354th Inf.
Bugler Edward McGee, 2213042, Co. M, 353rd Inf.
Cpl. John W. McKay, 2213386, Co. M, 353rd Inf.
Capt. (then 1st Lieut.) Herman McNulty, 354th Inf.
Capt. Fred F. Moore, 355th Inf.
1st Lieut. Francis Morgan, 353rd Inf.
Capt. (then 1st Lieut.) Verne A. Morgan, 355th Inf.
Major John E. Morrison, 354th Inf.
Brig. Gen. Louis M. Nuttman (then Col. 356th Inf.).

NAME, RANK AND ORGANIZATION.
Lieut. Col. F. W. O'Donnell, M. C. Div. Surgeon (then Major Reg. Surgeon 353rd Inf.).
Capt. (then 1st Lieut.) Marion W. Page, M. C. 354th Inf.
Lieut. Col. (then Major) J. L. Peatross, 353rd Inf.
2nd Lieut. Harry W. Pine, 353rd Inf.
Cpl. (then Bugler) Chauncey W. Porter, 2202524, Co. B, 355th Inf.
1st Lieut. George E. Rand, 353rd Inf.
Col. James H. Reeves, 353rd Inf.
Capt. William E. Reid, 355th Inf.
Cpl. Frank R. Rice, Co. L, 353rd Inf.
Cook (then Pvt.) Elmer P. Richards, 2847865, Co. D, 354th Inf.
Cpl. Andrew H. Roach, Co. A, 355th Inf.
Sgt. Walter Rudy, 2184471, Co. E, 356th Inf.
Pvt. Lewis Schumaker, Co. D, 355th Inf.
Pvt. Marcelino Serna, 2195593, Co. B, 355th Inf.
Col. (then Lieut. Col.) John L. Shepard, M. C. Div. Surgeon 89th Div.
Sgt. Ralph M. Shimeall, 2213015, Co. M, 353rd Inf.
1st Lieut. Leon P. Shinn, 356th Inf.
Lieut. Col. Nathan C. Shiverick (then Major 354th Inf.).
Sgt. John R. Slay, 2179328, Co. G, 354th Inf.
1st Sgt. (then Sgt.) Charles P. Smith, Co. H, 356th Inf.
Lieut. Col. Frank Wilbur Smith, G-2, 89th Div. (then Major, Asst. G-3).
Lieut. Col. Rudolph E. Smyser, M. G. Officer, 89th Div.
Cpl. Milton C. Sundin, 2202754, Co. L, 353rd Inf.
Col. James D. Taylor, 355th Inf.
Sgt. Ralph G. Taylor, Co. D, 355th Inf.
Three hundred fifty-third Infantry (Colors decorated).
Bugler Frank F. Tomanek, 2176998, Co. I, 353rd Inf.
Capt. Gregory A. Vigeant, 354th Inf. (att. Hq. 89th Div., Asst. G-3).
Cpl. Harry M. Ward, 2178243, Co. A, 354th Inf.
Major Ernest E. Watson, 341st M. G. Bn.
Col. Warren W. Whitside, C. O. Trains and Military Police 89th Div.
Sgt. Benjamin P. Wicker, Co. H, 356th Inf.
Pvt. 1/cl. (then Pvt.) Edwin Wiese, 2207678, Co. C, 355th Inf.
Capt. Marshall P. Wilder, 354th Inf.
Major Gen. (then Brig. Gen.) Frank L. Winn, 89th Div.
Major Thomas F. Wirth, 355th Inf.
Major (then Capt.) Paul Withington, M. C., 354th Inf.
Sgt. Walter S. Witt, 2076194, Co. D, 353rd Inf.
Capt. Frank M. Wood, 353rd Inf.
Pvt. 1/cl. Earl V. Wright, 2185246, Co. K, 356th Inf.

BRITISH KNIGHT COMMANDER, ORDER OF ST. MICHAEL AND ST. GEORGE.

NAME, RANK AND ORGANIZATION.
Major Gen. William M. Wright, 89th Div.

BELGIAN CHEVALIER OF THE ORDER OF LEOPOLD (CHEVALIER DE L'ORDRE DE LEOPOLD).

NAME, RANK AND ORGANIZATION.
Capt. Moses D. Atkins, 353rd Inf.
Pvt. 1/cl. Sylvester J. Henschel, 2177536, Med. Det., 353rd Inf.
Pvt. 1/cl. Frank L. Hunn, 2176936, Med. Det., 353rd Inf.
Major Milton C. Portmann (then Capt. 353rd Inf.)

ITALIAN WAR CROSS
(Croce di Guerra)

NAME, RANK AND ORGANIZATION.
Pvt. Roy A. Bess, 2205709, Co. L, 355th Inf.
Sgt. (then Pvt. 1/cl.) John W. Childers, 2178442, Co. B, 354th Inf.
Cpl. Francis L. Daniels, 2176745, Co. H, 353rd Inf.
Sgt. Roy L. Keller, 2178408, Co. B, 354th Inf.
Pvt. Clarence Laken, 2814509, Co. M, 356th Inf.
Pvt. 1/cl. Louis H. Loyd, 2189256, Co. F, 356th Inf.
Lieut. Col. (then Major) James L. Peatross, 353rd Inf.

NAME, RANK AND ORGANIZATION.

Pvt. 1/cl. Cecil E. Reed, 2201115, Co. E, 353rd Inf.
Pvt. Marcelino Serna, 2195593, Co. B, 355th Inf.
Cpl. Edgar Shoults, 2183705, Co. B, 354th Inf.
Pvt. 1/cl. (then Pvt.) Richard Wahler, 2176034, Co. C, 353rd Inf.

MONTENEGRIN BRAVERY MEDAL

(Medaille de Bravoure)

NAME, RANK AND ORGANIZATION.

Sgt. Arthur J. Forrest, 2178726, Co. D, 354th Inf.
Cpl. (then Pvt. Jesse N. Funk, 2187583, Co. L, 354th Inf.
Sgt. (then Pvt. 1/cl.) Harold I. Johnston, 2202872, Co. A, 356th Inf.

HONOR CERTIFICATES AND CITATIONS AWARDED TO MEMBERS OF THE 89TH DIVISION BY THE COMMANDER IN CHIEF, AMERICAN EXPEDITIONARY FORCES, AND THE COMMANDING GENERAL, 89TH DIVISION.

KEY TO CITATIONS BELOW.

a—Certificate for distinguished and exceptional gallantry, awarded by the Commander in Chief, American Expeditionary Forces.

b—Certificate for exceptionally meritorious and conspicuous services awarded by the Commander in Chief, American Expeditionary Forces.

c—Citation and commendation by the Commanding General, 89th Division, in Division General Orders, for gallantry.

In numerous cases (a) and (c) are for the same exploit.

See note at head of Decoration Section (page 385) regarding citations omitted here because of subsequent award of higher honors for the same exploits.

CITATION.	NAME, RANK AND ORGANIZATION.	DATE OF EXPLOIT. 1918
a, c	Wagoner (Acting as Ambulance Orderly) Victor W. Allen, 2196822, 355th Ambulance Co.	Sept. 14
a	Col. Conrad S. Babcock, 354th Inf.	Nov. 1-2
a, c	Capt. George R. Baker, M. C., 355th Inf.	Nov. 1
c	2nd Lieut. John Bargfrede (then Sgt., Co. H, 354th Inf.)	
c	Cpl. Henry H. Becher, 2847192, Co. H, 355th Inf.	Nov. 9-10
a	Col. Fred W. Boschen (then Lieut. Col. 353rd Inf.)	Sept. 12
a	1st Lieut. Paul M. Coleman, 164th F. A. Brig.	Nov. 2
c	2nd Lieut. Columbus C. Beverage, 355th Inf.	Nov. 9
c	Cpl. George W. Blankenship, 2184610, Co. F, 356th Inf.	Nov. 10-11
a	Capt. Eugene A. Bond, 353rd Inf.	Nov. 1
c	Cpl. William W. Bonnom, 2193736, Co. C, 314th F. S. Bn.	Nov. 1
a	1st Lieut. Shirley F. Boyce, M. C., 353rd Inf.	Nov. 2
c	Pvt. Roland E. Brail, 2207965, Co. K, 356th Inf.	Oct. 18
c	Pvt. Roma Brannan, 3512706, Co. L, 355th Inf.	Nov. 9-10
c	Sgt. 1/cl. Earl H. Britain, 2173798, Co. C, 314th F. S. Bn.	Nov. 1
c	Pvt. Clifford S. Brown, 2177545, Med. Dept., Co. B, 353rd Inf.	Oct. 1
c	Pvt. Theodore G. Campbell, 2846256, Co. H, 355th Inf.	Nov. 9-10
c	Pvt. James S. Carpenter, 3511269, M. G. Co., 356th Inf.	Oct. 29
a, c	Pvt. Arthur E. Carrell, 2213164, Co. C, 341st M. G. Bn.	Nov. 2
a, c	Capt. Charles A. Case, 314th Eng.	Nov. 11
c	Pvt. 1/cl. Harry Choulett, 2194045, M. G. Co., 356th Inf.	Sept. 12
c	Sgt. Mack Christian, 1560027, Co. F, 355th Inf.	Nov. 9-10
a	1st Lieut. Herbert E. Christiancy, 353rd Inf. (deceased)	Sept. 12
c	Pvt. 1/cl. Archie Comstock, 2211579, M. G. Co., 356th Inf.	Nov. 4
c	Pvt. James R. Cook, 3102697, Co. L, 355th Inf.	Nov. 9-10
a, c	Cpl. Ray W. Crane, 2178761, Co. D, 354th Inf.	Sept. 18
a, c	Capt. (then 1st Lieut.) John L. Crofut, 89th Military Police Co.	Oct. 28
a	Cpl. James E. Cummins, 2187837, Hq. Co., 341st F. A.	Sept. 18
a, c	2nd Lieut. Justin W. Dake, 354th Inf. (deceased)	Nov. 2
a, b	Pvt. Henry W. Damkroger, 2197004, 342nd M. G. Bn.	
c	Capt. John J. Delaney, 353rd Inf.	Nov. 2

CITATION.	NAME, RANK AND ORGANIZATION.	DATE OF EXPLOIT. 1918
a, c	Capt. Frank E. Dennie, 314th Eng.	Nov. 10
c	Pvt. George Desselles, 1610477, Co. H, 355th Inf.	Nov. 9-10
c	Cpl. Ralph T. Dickey, 2847512, Co. B, 340th M. G. Bn.	Nov. 10-11
a	Chaplain Alfred James Dickinson, 356th Inf.	Aug. 28
a, b, c	Sgt. Douglas M. Dimond, 2176708, Co. H, 353rd Inf.	
a	Sgt. Algar H. Dole, 2177229, Co. L, 353rd Inf.	Nov. 2
a, c	Pvt. 1/cl. (then Pvt.) John P. Donovan, 2185351, Co. L, 356th Inf.	Nov. 5
c	Pvt. Julius Dove, 2088958, Co. K, 356th Inf.	Oct. 6
c	Pvt. Archie D. Dunaway, 3703188, Co. F, 356th Inf.	Nov. 10-11
a, c	Pvt. Walter H. Durham, 2186194, Hq. Co., 353rd Inf.	Sept. 21
c	Pvt. Charles W. Earl, 2182829, Hq. Troop, 89th Div.	Sept. 16
a, c	Cpl. Edgar D. Egleston, 2178045, Hq. Co., 356th Inf.	Nov. 10
c	Cpl. William E. Eliason, 2202003, Co. C, 356th Inf.	Sept. 23
c	Pvt. 1/cl. Harry M. Evans, 2185202, Co. K, 356th Inf.	Oct. 6
a, c	Cpl. Lloyd Farber, 2175210, Hq. Co., 353rd Inf.	Nov. 2
c	Sgt. Emery E. Fetters, 2184624, Co. F, 356th Inf. (deceased)	Nov. 4
a, c	2nd Lieut. Edmund Field, 356th Inf.	Nov. 10
c	1st Lieut. Percy G. Forman, Co. F, 314th Eng.	Nov. 5
a, c	1st Lieut. Nathan B. Forrest, S. C., 314th F. S. Bn.	Nov. 1 to 11
b	Cpl. Harry H. Frederick, 2181977, Co. G, 355th Inf.	
c	Sgt. George M. Gable, 2185306, Co. L, 356th Inf.	Sept. 12
c	Pvt. Charles Garrison, 2182675, Hq. Troop, 89th Div.	Oct. 18
c	Pvt. Ernest A. Gill, 2175302, Hq. Co., 353rd Inf.	Nov. 1
c	Pvt. H. F. Goettsch, 2846739, Co. L, 355th Inf.	Nov. 9-10
a, c	Sgt. Harvey E. Gold, 2195721, Co. C, 314th F. S. Bn.	Nov. 10
a	Sgt. Ira L. Graves, 2186062, Co. A, 342nd M. G. Bn.	Nov. 1
a, b	Chaplain Otis E. Gray, Senior Chaplain, 89th Div. (then Chaplain 353rd Inf.)	
a, c	Cpl. Roscoe W. Grisham, 2847946, Co. K, 355th Inf.	Nov. 9-10
c	Pvt. Joseph Gross, 2183313, Co. L, 355th Inf.	Nov. 9-10
a, c	Pvt. 1/cl. (then acting as Ambulance Driver) Charles L. Grout, 2196844, 355th Ambulance Co.	Sept. 14
a	Pvt. 1/cl. Daniel Hammond, 2183346, M. G. Co., 354th Inf.	Nov. 1
c	Mechanic Roy L. Hart, 2176113, Co. D, 353rd Inf.	Oct. 19
a	Sgt. Walter R. Heffron, 2176373, Co. F, 353rd Inf. (deceased)	Sept. 12
a	Pvt. 1/cl. Sylvester J. Henschel, 2177536, Med. Det., 353rd Inf.	Sept. 17
a	Pvt. Oliver W. Holmes, 2847904, Co. G, 353rd Inf. (deceased)	Sept. 12
a	2nd Lieut. Joseph J. Hook, 356th Inf.	Nov. 5
c	Sgt. Charles M. Huber, 2193604, Co. B, 314th F. S. Bn.	Nov. 1-6
c	Pvt. 1/cl. Edward J. Huchins, 2189173, Co. F, 356th Inf.	Nov. 10-11
c	1st Lieut. Robert G. Hudson, 354th Inf.	Oct. 18
a	Pvt. 1/cl. Frank L. Hunn, 2176936, Med. Det., 353rd Inf.	Sept. 17
c	Sgt. Harry C. Hyndman, Co. L, 353rd Inf.	Aug. 30-31
c	Sgt. John D. Irwin, 2197188, Co. M, 356th Inf.	Nov. 7-8-10-11
c	Sgt. Andrew Jarman, 2184518, Co. F, 356th Inf.	Nov. 10-11
c	1st Lieut. Francis N. Jordan, 356th Inf.	Aug. 13-14
c	Cpl. William L. Keith, 2184349, Co. D, 356th Inf.	Oct. 23
c	Cpl. Samuel M. Kinkead, 2185178, Co. K, 356th Inf.	Oct. 6
a, c	Cpl. Frantz Koeppe, 2192946, Co. C, 341st M. G. Bn.	Nov. 2
a, c	Cpl. (then Pvt.) John H. Koontz, 2199362, Co. C, 314th Ammunition Train.	Nov. 7
c	Supply Sgt. Court E. Krumvieda, 2193175, Co. A, 340th M. G. Bn.	Nov. 6
c	Pvt. 1/cl. Martin L. Larson, 2208030, Co. B, 355th Inf.	Oct. 20-21
a	Sgt. Arthur R. Law, 2187823, Hq. Co., 341st F. A.	Sept. 18
c	Cpl. Walter L. Lewis, 2847190, Co. H, 355th Inf.	Nov. 9-10
a, c	Pvt. 1/cl. Aaron Frank Lindsey, 2202484, Co. K, 354th Inf.	Nov. 1
a, c	Pvt. Sigurd Lundstedt, 2185889, Co. B, 342nd M. G. Bn.	Nov. 6
a, c	1st Lieut. Riley W. MacGregor, 356th Inf.	Nov. 10-11
a	Pvt. 1/cl. Joseph J. Maguire, 2182999, M. G. Co., 354th Inf.	Nov. 1
a, c	Pvt. 1/cl. Willard Malloy, 2175107, Hq. Det., 89th Div.	Sept. 12-13
a, c	Pvt. 1/cl. William McAulis, 2177541, Med. Det., 353rd Inf.	Sept. 14
a	Cpl. Hayden McDowell, 2847769, Co. E, 354th Inf.	Sept. 6
c	Pvt. Robert C. McGill, 3511491, Co. H, 355th Inf.	Nov. 9-10
a, c	Cpl. Lawrence C. McKee, 2188281, Battery B, 341st F. A.	Sept. 20-23
c	Wagoner Roscoe C. McTeer, 2196733, 354th Amb. Co., 314th Sanitary Train	Oct. 5-6
a, b	Major Reginald H. Meade, M. C. Reg. Surgeon, 354th Inf.	

CITATION.	NAME, RANK AND ORGANIZATION.	DATE OF EXPLOIT. 1918
c	Cpl. James L. Melton, 2184359, Co. D, 356th Inf	Oct. 23
c	Sgt. Elmer E. Michael, 2185001, Co. I, 356th Inf	Nov. 10-11
a, c	Sgt. Arthur Meyer, 2179718, Co. K, 354th Inf	Nov. 1
a, c	1st Lieut. William T. Milligan, 341st F. A	Nov. 10
c	Pvt. Alfred Moen, 2845097, Co. G, 355th Inf	Nov. 9-10
a	Sgt. David M. Moore, 2176366, Co. F, 353rd Inf. (deceased)	Sept. 12
c	Pvt. Earl P. Morris, 2177620, Hq. Co., 353rd Inf	Nov. 1
a, c	Pvt. 1/cl. James Nathan, 2177518, Med. Det., 353rd Inf	Sept. 14
a, b	Lieut. Col. F. W. O'Donnell, M. C., Div. Surgeon 89th Div. (then Major, Reg. Surgeon, 353rd Inf.)	
c	Sgt. (then Pvt.) Carl R. Olson, 2093687, Co. E, 356th Inf	Nov. 10
a, c	Pvt. Lee H. Ostoff, 2173362, Co. D, 354th Inf	Nov. 1
c	Sgt. (then Cpl.) Gully A. Overton, 2211502, Co. E, 356th Inf	Nov. 10
a, c	Capt. (then 1st Lieut.) Marion W. Page, M. C., 354th Inf	Oct. 31
c	Sgt. Oren C. Page, 2184644, Co. F, 356th Inf. (deceased)	Nov. 10
c	2nd Lieut. Curtis B. Perryman, 356th Inf	Nov. 10-11
c	Wagoner Paul S. Phelps, 2196637, Med. Supply Depot No. 2, 314th Sanitary Train	Sept. 22
a, c	Pvt. Darrelt L. Pigman, 2198969, Hq. Co., 353rd Inf	Sept. 21-22
c	Cpl. Jose A. Pino, 2176322, Co. E, 353rd Inf	Oct. 25
a, c	Major Milton C. Portmann (then Capt.), 353rd Inf	Sept. 12-13
c	Cook (then Pvt.) John Reams, 2192082, Co. K, 356th Inf	Oct. 6
a, c	Pvt. 1/cl. David A. Reavis, 2194343, 89th Div. Military Police Co	Oct. 28
c	Wagoner Howard G. Rounds, 2196629, Med. Supply Depot No. 2, 314th Sanitary Train	Sept. 22
a	Sgt. Walter Rudy, 2184471, Co. E, 356th Inf	Sept. 3
c	Pvt. 1/cl. (then Pvt.) August W. Schmidt, 2213309, Co. M, 356th Inf	Nov. 7
c	1st Sgt. John S. Schoolfield, 2184602, Co. F, 356th Inf	Nov. 10-11
c	Sgt. Oscar E. Schulte, 2180173, Co. M, 354th Inf	Nov. 1
c	Capt. William Schwinn, Co. B, 356th Inf	Oct. 22
c	Cpl. Ernest C. Sexton, 2846226, Co. H, 355th Inf	Nov. 9-10
a	1st Lieut. Carl A. Shadowen, 355th Inf. (deceased)	Nov. 4
c	Pvt. Steve Y. Shears, 2192155, M. G. Co., 356th Inf	Sept. 12
a, b	Col. (then Lt. Col.) John L. Shepard, M. C., Div. Surgeon, 89th Div	
a	Cpl. James E. Shuey, 2185532, Co. M, 356th Inf	Nov. 7
c	Cpl. Roland S. Sloane, 2845062, Co. B, 340th M. G. Bn	Nov. 10-11
a, b	Lt. Col. Frank Wilbur Smith, G-2, 89th Div. (then Major, Asst. G-3)	
a, c	2nd Lieut. Stanley W. Staatz, 356th Inf	Nov. 8
a	Sgt. Henry St. Pierre, 2193191, Co. A, 340th M. G. Bn	Nov. 1
c	Pvt. Onezie Suire, 1610466, Co. H, 355th Inf	Nov. 9-10
c	2nd Lieut. Vernon C. Swihart, 355th Inf	Aug. 27-28
c	Sgt. James A. Taylor, 2184160, Co. C, 356th Inf	Sept. 23
c	Sgt. Carl K. Tebbe, 2184585, Co. F, 356th Inf	Nov. 10-11
c	Pvt. Bernard M. Thompson, 2185646, Sanitary Det., 356th Inf	Sept. 12
c	Three hundred fifty-fourth Infantry (1st Bn.)	Aug. 7-8
c	Three hundred fifty-fifth Infantry (1st Bn.)	Aug. 7-8
c	Pvt. 1/cl. George H. Trible, 2177532, Med. Det., 353rd Inf	Oct. 22
a, c	1st Lieut. James G. Tucker, 353rd Inf	Nov. 1-11
a	1st Lieut. Robert M. Underhill, 353rd Inf	Nov. 2
c	Sgt. (then Cpl.) Walter L. Vercoutere, 2175202, Hq. Co., 353rd Inf	Nov. 1
c	Cpl. William Vodock, 2056199, Co. F, 353rd Inf	Nov. 2
a, b	Major Ernest E. Watson, 341st M. G. Bn	
a, c	Sgt. William K. Wells, 2183472, Hq. Co., 356th Inf	Nov. 10-11
a, c	Sgt. Wesley E. Wendt, 2183429, Hq. Co., 356th Inf	Nov. 10-11
a, c	Cpl. Herschel G. West, 2177358, Co. M, 353rd Inf	Nov. 1
a	Sgt. Seth R. Whitfield, 2185548, Co. M, 356th Inf	Nov. 7
a	Sgt. Henry A. Whitmer, 2177331, Co. L, 353rd Inf	Nov. 2
a, c	Cpl. William B. Whittaker, 1595750, Co. A, 356th Inf	Nov. 3
c	1st Sgt. Grover C. Williams, 2193036, Co. B, 340th M. G. Bn	Nov. 10-11
c	Pvt. William E. Williams, 2203107, Co. A, 314th Eng	Nov. 1
c	Sgt. Edward R. Winebar, 2181941, Co. G, 355th Inf	Nov. 9-10
a	Major (then Capt.) Paul Withington, M. C., 354th Inf	Nov. 3
c	Cpl. Jacob M. Wixson, 2198514, Co. F, 353rd Inf	Nov. 2
a, c	Pvt. 1/cl. Casper G. Wolfskill, 2184538, Hq. Co., 356th Inf	Nov. 10-11
c	Cpl. Clyde S. Worley, 2175262, Hq. Co., 353rd Inf	Nov. 1
c	Pvt. 1/cl. Joseph Zabicki, 2180200, Co. M, 354th Inf	Nov. 1

TABLE OF CASUALTIES, 89TH DIVISION

Line	Organization	Killed Off.	Killed Men	Missing Presumed Dead Off.	Missing Presumed Dead Men	Severely Wounded Off.	Severely Wounded Men	Wounded Degree Undetermined Off.	Wounded Degree Undetermined Men	Gassed Off.	Gassed Men	Slightly Wounded Off.	Slightly Wounded Men	Totals Off.	Totals Men	Totals Off & Men	Line
1	89th Div. Hq. Staff...	1	....	..	....	..	....	..	....	3	....	2	....	6	....	6	1
2	89th Div. Hq. Troop..	..	2	..	....	..	2	..	1	..	6	..	2	..	13	13	2
3	340th M. G. Bn......	..	12	..	....	..	12	..	2	4	47	..	8	4	81	85	3
4	177th Inf. Brig. Hq...	..	1	..	....	..	....	..	....	..	....	..	....	..	1	1	4
5	353rd Inf.	12	349	..	....	15	445	3	100	5	178	12	353	47	1,425	1,472	5
6	354th Inf.	11	334	..	3	12	399	..	47	28	610	4	258	55	1,651	1,706	6
7	341st M. G. Bn.......	1	50	..	....	5	95	..	2	3	87	1	57	10	291	301	7
8	178th Inf Brig. Hq...	..	....	..	....	..	....	..	....	..	....	..	1	..	1	1	8
9	355th Inf.	11	306	1	7	14	378	1	40	14	339	11	287	52	1,357	1,409	9
10	356th Inf.	10	259	..	5	10	278	8	79	9	293	14	200	51	1,114	1,165	10
11	342nd M. G. Bn......	2	37	..	1	1	39	..	8	2	80	1	32	6	197	203	11
12	164th F. A. Brig. Hq..	1	....	..	....	..	....	..	....	..	....	..	....	1	....	1	12
13	340th F. A.	2	11	..	....	1	13	1	28	1	42	..	2	5	96	101	13
14	341st F. A...........	..	4	..	....	..	11	2	....	..	16	1	....	3	31	34	14
15	342nd F. A..........	1	8	..	....	..	13	..	3	3	24	..	15	4	63	67	15
16	314th Tr. Mor. Bat...	..	....	..	....	..	....	..	....	..	....	..	....	..	....	....	16
17	314th Engineers	3	40	..	....	1	71	..	11	..	54	2	49	6	225	231	17
18	314th F. S. Bn.......	1	14	..	....	1	14	..	7	1	34	..	12	3	81	84	18
19	314th Tr. Hq. & M. P.	..	7	..	....	..	7	..	2	..	3	..	3	..	22	22	19
20	314th Eng. Tr.......	..	3	..	....	..	1	..	....	..	....	..	3	..	7	7	20
21	314th Amm. Tr......	..	6	..	....	..	6	..	3	..	17	..	18	..	50	50	21
22	314th Sup. Tr.......	..	4	..	1	..	7	..	5	..	5	..	6	..	28	28	22
23	314th San. Tr........	..	12	..	....	1	19	..	2	1	17	..	7	2	57	59	23
24	314th M. V. S........	..	1	..	....	..	....	..	....	..	....	..	....	..	1	1	24
25	Totals	56	1,460	1	17	61	1,810	15	340	74	1,852	48	1,313	255	6,792	7,047	25
26	Totals, Officers & Men	1,516		18		1,871		355		1,926		1,361		7,047		7,047	26

CASUALTY SECTION

LIST OF CASUALTIES IN THE 89th DIVISION OVERSEAS

Casualties listed are those officially reported to the Division Personnel Adjutant, 89th Division, supplemented by data direct from some organizations of the Division and corrected, since return of the Division from overseas, from records in the War Department, Washington, D. C., as to degree of injury in many cases. Figures on the consolidated table of casualties by organizations were prepared with the same care.

These records are as complete and accurate as facilities permitted; duplications and non-reportable cases (so common when loose and approximate figures are given) have been rigidly excluded.

Nevertheless it must be remembered that variations in spelling and discrepancies in reports from different sources may make it difficult, in a few cases, to place the casualty and detached service of individuals, or failure to report through usual channels may have resulted in the omission of a very few names which might properly appear. Actual casualties of the Division were probably a little larger than here shown.

Ordinarily the date shown is date the man was hit, but sometimes it is the day the casualty was confirmed and reported officially, usually not more than a few days later. In a number of cases when dates were unreported or reports conflicted the day is omitted in these lists.

THE DEAD

OFFICERS

Name, Rank, Company, Regiment	Emergency Address
Aug, Charles H., 2nd Lt., Att. A, 356th Inf	Mrs. Bessie Aug, 89 E. 108th St., New York, N. Y.
Bair, Howard A., 2nd Lt., M, 354th Inf	Mrs. Francis Bair, Ritman, Ohio
Birch, Albert E., 2nd Lt., A, 342nd M. G. Bn	Charles E. Birch, Lawrence, Kansas
Bland, Willian J., Major, 1st Bn., 356th Inf	Mrs. William J. Bland, 3659 Harrison Blvd, Kansas City, Mo.
Boutwell, Lloyd R., 1st Lt., M. C., 314th Eng	Mrs. Lloyd R. Boutwell, 14 Elm Ave., Glendale, Kirkwood, Mo.
Bowles, Martin F., 1st Lt., 355th Inf	Ross Bowles, 5770 Degiverville, St. Louis, Mo.
Burtis, Darrell D., 2nd Lt., F, 354th Inf	Mrs. Darrel D. Burtis, 603 Madison St., Waukegan, Ill.
Campbell, Samuel A., Jr., 1st Lt., K, 355th Inf	Samuel A. Campbell, 1424 Brevok St., Louisville, Ky.
Carr, Roy E., 1st Lt., I, 353rd Inf	Mrs. E. M. Carr, Lockwood, Mo.
Chiles, Marcellus H., Capt., A, 356th Inf	John H. Chiles, 2815 W. 37th Ave., Denver, Colo.
Christiancy, Herbert E., 1st Lt., E, 353rd Inf	J. Christiancy, 605 E. Atlantic, Warren, Ohio
Collins, John F., 1st Lt., H, 354th Inf	Mrs. Jean Dalrymple, 508 W. 108th St., New York, N. Y.
Dake, Justin W., 2nd Lt., Att. G, 354th Inf	Dr. A. J. Dake, Viola, Wis.
Delman, Harry, Chaplain, 354th Inf	Mrs. Harry Delman, New Florence, Mo.
Dixon, W. B., 1st Lt., Hq. 340th F. A.	
Duncker, Charles H., Jr., 1st Lt., A, 340th F. A.	
Evans, Lawrence H., 2nd Lt., A, 314th Eng	D. H. Evans, Gen. Del., Nelplie, Utah
Finlayson, Allan, 2nd Lt., I, 353rd Inf	Pearl Finlayson, 18 Sumner St., Keene, N. H.
Fisher, Frank J., 2nd Lt., B, 355th Inf	Wm. M. Fisher, 2010 N. 5th St., Kansas City, Kan.
Fryer, Clair P., 2nd Lt., B, 342nd M. G. Bn	Emmett Fryer, Plainview, Neb.
Gardner, Robert, 2nd Lt., L, 353rd Inf	Mrs. Mable E. Petts, East Templeton, Mass.
Hanna, Mark, Major, 2nd Bn., 356th Inf	Mrs. Corine E. Hanna, 2514 E. 28th St., Kansas City, Mo.
Harris, Arthur F., 1st Lt., G, 341st M. G. Bn	Mrs. Arthur F. Harris, 2304 Griffith Ave., Louisville, Ky.
Hay, Wendell P., Capt., E, 354th Inf	Mrs. A. J. Gulick, 513 Ryerson Ave., Elgin, Ill.
Hege, Loy A., 2nd Lt., A, 355th Inf	Mrs. Jane L. Hege, 506 Market St., Emporia, Kan.
Hoeynck, Frank J., 2nd Lt., F, 314th Eng	Mrs. Marie L. Lynk, 421 Sherman Ave., Evanston, Ill.
Hughes, Reginald W., Capt., 164th F. A.	Mrs. Clare Wilson Hughes, 1320 N. Delaware St. Indianapolis, Ind.
Jackson, Jared S., 1st Lt., M, 353rd Inf	Mrs. W. A. Jackson, 601 N 2nd St., Atchison, Kan.
Jacobus, Harold F., 1st Lt., E, 342nd F. A.	Phillip Jacobus, Turners Falls, Mass.
Larson, Louis E., 2nd Lt., B, 355th Inf	Chas. A. Larson, R. F. D. 6, Menominee, Wis.
Lewis, Gilbert M., 1st Lt., H, 353rd Inf	J. M. Lewis, Kinsley, Kan.
Lincoln, Atwell T., Capt., Hq. 354th Inf	Anna Lou P. Lincoln, 1508 Washington Ave., St. Louis, Mo.
McGuiggan, Robert F., 1st Lt., D, 354th Inf	E. J. McGuiggan, Winnebago, Minn.
McKinstry, John A., 1st Lt., L, 355th Inf	W. H. McKinstry, Box 221, Canon City, Colo.
Mitchell, Edward A., 1st Lt., M. G. Co., 353rd Inf	
Moore, Jerome E., 1st Lt., I, 356th Inf	George H. Moore, Customs Bldg., St. Louis, Mo.

Name, Rank, Company, Regiment	Emergency Address
Nixon, James G., 1st Lt., K, 353rd Inf	Henry F. Nixon, 1886 E. 97th St., Cleveland, Ohio
Prelwitz, Leo, 2nd Lt., H, 355th Inf	Mrs. Max Prelwitz, 415 Brainard Ave., Grand Rapids, Mich.
Ritchie, Edgar B., 1st Lt., Sup Co., 355th Inf	Mrs. Glen J. Ritchie, 34 Elm St., Ludlow, Ky.
Seith, Alvin N., 1st Lt., M, 353rd Inf	Charles L. Seith, c-o George Worthington Co., Cleveland, Ohio
Schulman, Harry, 1st Lt., Sup. Co., 354th Inf	Samuel Schulman, 22 Baldwin St., Toronto, Canada
Severson, Will C., 2nd Lt., M. G. Co., 356th Inf	Mr. Chas. E. Severson, Jackson, Neb.
Shadowen, Carl, 1st Lt., C, 355th Inf	Mrs. Bell Shadowen, 702 Main St., Ft. Morgan, Colo.
Shaw, Charles A., 1st Lt., E, 353rd Inf	Wm. A. Shaw, Weatherby, Mo.
Smith, Eben L., 1st Lt., 355th Inf	
Spencer, Glen K., 1st Lt., 355th Inf	Samuel T. Spencer, 2011 Glenwood, Pueblo, Colo.
Tait, Lee C., 1st Lt., F, 354th Inf	
Wallin, Victor B., 1st Lt., B, 356th Inf	Mrs. Agnes M. Wallin, c-o August Johnson, Washburn, N. D.
Wear, Arthur Y., Capt., L, 356th Inf	Mrs. James H. Wear, 307 N. 4th St., St. Louis, Mo.
Whitside, Victor M., Major, 354th Inf	Mrs. S. M. Whitside, c-o The Ontario, Washington, D. C.
Wickersham, J. Hunter, 2nd Lt., H, 353rd Inf	Mrs. W. E. Damon, 3416 Colfax B, Denver, Colo.
Willis, Marion L., 1st Lt., F, 356th Inf	Mrs. Ella Willis Smith, Chestnut Apt., Long Beach, Cal.
Wilson, James, 1st Lt., G, 356th Inf	Mrs. James S. Wilson, 205 14th St., West, Prince Albert, Sascatchewan, Canada
Wray, Harry C., 1st Lt., G, 353rd Inf	Mrs. M. B. Oken, 317 3rd Ave., Joliet, Ill.
Young, Edward M., 2nd Lt., Hq. 89th Div.	Wm. W. Young, 139 Ashley St., Hartford, Conn.
Ziesenis, Harry C., 1st Lt., 314th F. S. Bn	Mrs C. H. Ziesenis, 1022 Ala St., Lawrence, Kan.

ENLISTED MEN

Abney, George C., Pvt. 1cl., M, 353rd Inf	George Abney, 203 Killburn Ave., Rockford, Ill.
Achee, Charley, Pvt., B, 355th Inf	Mrs. Louisa Achee, Bellrose, La., c-o Milly Store, Plaquemine, La.
Ackerman, Carl W., Pvt., H, 353rd Inf	Daniel Ackerman, Meriam, Kan.
Ackerman, Harvey P., Pvt., M. G. Co., 356th Inf	Wm. C. Ackerman, Las Cruces, N. M.
Adams, Leslie, Corp., Co. G, 355th Inf	Claude Adams, Superior, Neb.
Adams, Lloyd L., Corp., E, 356th Inf	Mrs. Alice Adams, 3840 E 15th St., Kansas City Mo.
Adolph, Harvey, Corp., E, 353rd Inf	Mrs. Amanda Adolph, Scranton, Kan.
Agar, Tom, Pvt. 1cl., E, 355th Inf	Mrs. Goldie Agar, 1014 Harrison Ave., Kansas City, Mo.
Aheo, Emil, Pvt., B, 353rd Inf	Mrs. T. Recisicky, 1911 S. May St., Chicago, Ill.
Aho, Erick J., Corp., A, 355th Inf	John Aho, Iron Belt, Wis.
Ahrens, William, Corp., I, 354th Inf	Mrs. Louie Kiessling, 2110 Alice Ave., St. Louis, Mo.
Aigner, Egnotz W., Sgt., B, 355th Inf	Mrs. August Aigner, R. F. D. No. 5, Box 46, Phoenix, Ariz.
Alderson, Leonard C., Corp., C, 341st M. G. Bn	Ernest Alderson, Belden, Neb.
Alewel, Edward H., Corp., H, 356th Inf	Mrs. Lena Meyer, 915 Ellis St., St. Louis, Mo.
Alexander, Perry D., Pvt., A, 356th Inf	John S. Alexander, Gen. Del., Rhinehart, La.
Allen, Forrest, Pvt. 1cl., L, 353rd Inf	Mildred Barnes, Earleton, Kans.
Allen, George S., Bugler, E, 340th F. A.	Mrs. Chas. Moun, 330 S. 7th St., West Cedar Rapids, Iowa
Allen, Lance, Corp., B, 355th Inf	
Altenhoff, Paul H., Pvt., E, 356th Inf	Mrs. Frank Altenhoff, 1326 Lincoln Ave., Cincinnati, Ohio
Ament, Jesse R., Pvt., E, 354th Inf	Mrs. Ned Ament, Harrisonville, Mo.
Amsberry, Ora B., Corp., D, 355th Inf	
Anderson, Albert J., Pvt., G, 356th Inf	Andrew Anderson, R. F. D. 2, Osborn, Mo.
Anderson, Andrew M., Pvt., C, 354th Inf	Carl Carlson, 186 Walnut St., Batavia, Ill.
Anderson, Gus A., B, 342nd M. G. Bn	Wm. H. Hempy, 727 Gorden St., St. Joseph, Mo.
Anderson, Harold, Pvt., M, 353rd Inf	Lars Anderson, Box 54, Solway, Minn.
Anderson, John A., Pvt., G, 354th Inf	Mrs. Hilda Anderson, 209 Jefferson St., Geneva, Ill.
Anderson, Moris, Pvt., E, 354th Inf	Herman Lenden, Dear Grove, Ill.
Anderson, Ole F., Pvt. 1cl., B, 342nd M. G. Bn	Frank Anderson, Gen. Del., Platte, South Dakota
Anderson, Ralph P., Pvt. 1cl., F, 353rd Inf	Nels Anderson, Box 42, Scranton, Kan.
Andrews, Ivan Earl, Pvt., A, 353rd Inf	Flora Andrews, Gen. Del., Leon, Kan.
Angell, Henry, Pvt., A, 353rd Inf	Mrs. Teresa Weber, Gen. Del., Breezy Hill, Kan.
Angle, Roscoe L., Pvt., F, 354th Inf	
Armenis, Nick, D, 355th Inf	Kost J. Armenis, Colsmato, Greece
Artz, Henry W., Pvt. 1cl., A, 341st F. A.	Ashton N. Artz, Mina, South Dakota
Augustine, John C., Pvt. C, 341st M. G. Bn	
Aukerman, Wade S., Corp., A, 314th Eng	John W. Aukerman, 917 W. 9th St., Winfield, Kan
Austin, Layton, Pvt., F, 355th Inf	Sis Austin, R. F. D. 2, Harrisburg, Ark
Baatz, Herman T., Pvt. 1cl., G, 355th Inf	
Back, Isaac Looking, Pvt., L, 355th Inf	Geo. L. Back, Little Eagle, S. D.
Backman, Adolph G., Pvt., M. G. Co., 355th Inf	Andrew Backman, R. F. D. 3, Newcastle, Neb.
Badeaux, Michael, Pvt., I, 356th Inf	
Bailey, James O., Pvt., B, 354th Inf	Mrs. Leander S. Hodge, R. F. D. 1, Vichy, Mo.
Baird, Reginald, Pvt., F, 356th Inf	
Baird, Verner A., Pvt. 1cl., M, 355th Inf	Maxwell A. Baird, R. F. D. 2, Brunswick, Neb.
Baker, Harry L., Pvt. 1cl., A, 354th Inf	Mrs. Hazel M. Baker, Duranell, Ill.
Baker, James H., Pvt. 1cl., L, 355th Inf	Floyd Baker, Adams, Neb.
Baker, Lawrence, Pvt., M, 356th Inf	Mrs. Alexander Baker, 315 Church St., Lake Charles, La.
Ball, Charley A., Pvt., C, 354th Inf	Estle Ball, R. F. D. 2, Mountain Grove, Mo.
Ballard, Charles J., Pvt. 1cl., C, 353rd Inf	Mrs. Anna P. Dodge, 720 Hudson St., Burlington, Kan.
Bammann, Fred W., Pvt., E, 354th Inf	Herman Bammann, 428 14th St., Oshkosh, Wis.
Banks, Frank, Pvt., C, 356th Inf	Emma Banks, R. F. D. 1, Springhill, La.
Barkeley, David B., Pvt. 1cl., A, 356th Inf	Mrs. Antonio Barkeley, 909 N. Laredo St., San Antonio, Tex.
Barnby, John T., Pvt., L, 354th Inf	Mrs. Chesman Barnby, 339 S. Colorado Ave., Kansas City, Mo.
Barnes, John E., Pvt., D, 354th Inf	John H. Barnes, R. F. D. 2, Grant City, Mo.
Barnicle, Alias S., Pvt. 1cl., B, 353rd Inf	Mrs. Alice Barnicle, 1018 Pamm Ave. East, New St. Louis, Miss
Barras, Stanley, Pvt., F, 355th Inf	Bernadette Barras, Broussard, La
Barry, Edward, Corp., K, 354th Inf	T. J. Barry, 2335 S. Rideway Ave., Chicago, Ill.
Bartell, Elmer E., Sgt., E, 353rd Inf	Mrs. Lena Bartell, Zeandale, Kan.
Basine, John E., Pvt., E, 353rd Inf	Mrs. Lena Magee, Bradley, Cal.
Bates, Henry J., Pvt., H, 353rd Inf	Thomas H. Dennis, Hayden, Ariz.
Baugh, Cicero T., Pvt., F, Pioneer Det., 314th Eng	Cicero P. Baugh, Ouakman, Ark.
Bayly, Harry E., Sgt., Hq. 353rd Inf	Allen R. Bayly, Tar River, Okla.
Beach, Alfred T., Corp., E, 353rd Inf	Mrs. Mary Beach, Manchester, Kan.
Beaman, Roy, Pvt., E, 353rd Inf	Blanche Beaman, R. F. D. 2, Oakley, Kan.
Bean, Clarence M., Corp., K, 355th Inf	Mrs. Irene Winnek, Lake Mills, Wis.

Name, Rank, Company, Regiment	Emergency Address
Bean, Parley H., Pvt., K, 355th Inf	Lawrence Bean, Oxford, Me.
Bearheart, Henry, Pvt., H, 353rd Inf	Pete Bearheart, Hertel, Wis.
Beattie, John C., Pvt. 1cl., Hq, 354th Inf	Thomas Beattie, 792 S. Sherman St., Denver, Colo.
Beaver, George D., Pvt., B, 356th Inf	William J. Beaver, Gen. Del., Granby, Mo.
Beckett, Frank, Pvt., H, 356th Inf	Mrs. Viva Beckett, R. F. D. 2, Hamburg, Iowa
Beerman, J. H., Pvt. 1cl., L, 354th Inf	Henry Beerman, Concordia, Mo.
Beggs, Chester A., Pvt. 1cl., F, 354th Inf	Mrs. Nellie M. Beggs, 1811 W. Vermijo St., Denver, Colo.
Bell, Fred, Pvt., M. G. Co., 356th Inf	Mrs. Lydia A. Bell, 1208 S. Lamine St., Sedalia, Mo.
Bellizzi, James V., Pvt., Hq. 353rd Inf	212 E. 10th St., Cheyenne, Wyo.
Benardis, George N., Pvt. 1cl., F, 354th Inf	Alexander Papandricos, 1114 S. 8th St., St. Louis, Mo.
Benedetti, Alfredo, Pvt., B, 354th Inf	Carlo Saldi, Box 66, East Belles, Vernon, Pa.
Benham, Thos. E., Pvt. 1cl., I, 355th Inf	
Bennett, Vernon, Pvt., A, 353rd Inf	
Bennett, Owen, Pvt., G, 355th Inf	Mrs. Anna May Bennett, Ellsworth, Neb.
Bennington, Ralph A., Corp., D, 355th Inf	
Benoit, Alcide, Pvt., Hq. 356th Inf	Delfine Benoit. Luke Clores. La., R. F. D. 2, Box 64, Lake Charles, La.
Benson, Arthur W., Pvt., D, 341st M. G. Bn	Oliver A. Benson, R. F. D. 4, Petaluma, Cal.
Benson, Warren E., Pvt., G, 355th Inf	Mrs. Ida Goodwin, Gregory, South Dakota
Berglind, Bror A., Pvt. 1cl., C, 314th F. S. Bn	Miss Selma Romming, Brockings, South, Dakota
Bergner, William C. E., L, 353rd Inf	Paul Bergner, 1017 Michigan Ave., Sheboygan, Wis.
Bergsma, Frank, Pvt., H, 353rd Inf	Anna Bergsma, 1718 N. Campbell Ave., Chicago, Ill.
Berglund, Walter R., Corp., G, 354th Inf	
Berndt, Alvin C., Pvt., G, 353rd Inf	
Berquist, Emil R., Pvt., M, 354th Inf	Mrs. Reckie Berquist, 905 Weeks Ave., Superior, Wis.
Berquist, Arthur C., Corp., M. G. Co., 353rd Inf	Mrs. Arthur Berquist, 1139 Elm St., Kansas City, Mo.
Berry, Harold J., Pvt., K, 354th Inf	Joseph H. Berry, 524 E. Colorado Ave., Colorado Springs, Colo.
Berry, Oscar R., Pvt., Hq. 353rd Inf	Mrs. Ruby E. Berry, 1316 Dear Ave., Parsons, Kan.
Besaw, Charlie A., Pvt., A, 354th Inf	Alvin Besaw, Gen. Del., Cobma, Wis.
Bettenhausen, William, Pvt., G, 314th Amm. Tr	Mrs. Mary Bettenhausen, West Point, Neb.
Betts, Fred L., Pvt., A, 314th Eng	Mrs. Louis Betts, 109½ S. Wheeler Ave., Grand Island, Neb.
Bible, Haskell M., Pvt., E, 356th Inf	
Bies, Bernard M., Bugler, D, 355th Inf	
Bigelow, Dean Walden, Pvt., Hq. 355th Inf	James T. Bigelow, Flandreau, South Dakota
Biggs, Clare W., Pvt. 1cl., 314th Eng. Tr	Ed Biggs, R. F. D. 3, Chickasha, Okla.
Billotts, Leonard W., Pvt., D, 356th Inf	
Binger, Eugene C., Pvt., 1cl., K, 355th Inf	Roy C. Binger, Pulare, South Dakota
Bird, Chester A., Pvt. 1cl., M. G. Co., 353rd Inf	W. S. Bird, Stockton, Kan.
Birmingham, Walter C., Pvt. 1cl., F, 356th Inf	Mrs. Mary Birmingham, Union, Mo.
Bisheau, Oakley, Pvt., D, 355th Inf	George Bisheau, Ringle, Wis.
Bishop, Oscar E., Pvt., A, 342nd M. G. Bn	Fred Bishop, Sedalia, Mo.
Black, Benjamin H., Pvt., M, 353rd Inf	Frank Black, R. F. D. 5, Marion, Kan.
Blair, Robert, Pvt., H, 356th Inf	Charles C. Blair, Fairfield, Ky.
Blair, Tracy S., Pvt., E, 353rd Inf	Mary C. Blair, Cotter, Iowa
Blaisdell, William D., Corp., Hq. 341st F. A.	Mrs. Ora I. Johnson, 820 Frederick St., Oelwein, Iowa
Blakeney, Thomas J., Pvt., E, 356th Inf	Thomas Blakeney, Hope, N. M.
Blanchard, George J., Pvt., A, 342nd M. G. Bn	Fred Blanchard, Woodland Ave., Kansas City, Mo.
Block, Henry J., Pvt., E, 356th Inf	
Block, Joseph H., Pvt., M, 353rd Inf	Albert Carter, Gen. Del., Lyons, Kan.
Bloomquist, Oscar T., Pvt., H, 354th Inf	
Bodmer, Albert E., Pvt., H, 353rd Inf	
Boehmer, Edward W., Pvt., H, 356th Inf	Mrs. Friedereka Boehmer, R. F. D. 2, St. Charles, Mo.
Boehrig, Royal C., Pvt. 1cl., Hq. 356th Inf	
Bohan, John E., Pvt., K, 353rd Inf	Michael Bohan, R. F. D. 5, Box 28, Fond du lac, Wis.
Bolin, Jesse W., Pvt., G, 354th Inf	
Bollinger, August, Pvt., H, 356th Inf	Mrs. Barbara Barbareck, 1411 S. Broadway, St. Louis, Mo.
Bolte, Fred, Pvt., E, 356th Inf	Mrs. Annia Bolte, 2910 Kosseuth St., St. Louis, Mo.
Bond, Herbert L., Pvt. 1cl., G, 355th Inf	Mrs. Sarah O. Bond, Benkelman, Neb.
Bond, John, Pvt. 1cl., F, 354th Inf	Eliza Bond, Route 1, Box 67, Eugene, Mo.
Bookholtz, George M., Pvt. 1cl., C, 354th Inf	Peter Bookholtz, French Village, Mo.
Boone, Jasper A., Corp., F, 356th Inf	
Bossard, Harry Vern, Corp., C, 314th F. S. Bn	L. E. Bossard, Papillion, Neb.
Boswell, Fred A., Pvt., F, 356th Inf	Wentford M. Boswell, R. F. D. 3, Mt. Vernon, Mo.
Bougher, George A., Pvt., A, 353rd Inf	John Bougher, Gen. Del., Independence, Colo.
Bourtzos, Gust G., Pvt., E, 353rd Inf	George Bourtzos, Mantherea, Greece
Bowar, William J., Pvt. 1cl., B, 340th M. G. Bn	Charles Bowar, Faulkton, South Dakota
Bowden, John C., Pvt., K, 356th Inf	Robert Bowden, Gld, La.
Bowe, Paul, Pvt., M. G. Co., 354th Inf	Jacob Bowe, R. F. D. 2, Chiphowa Falls, Wis.
Bower, Elmer M., Pvt., C, 340th F. A.	
Bowman, Arch M., Pvt. 1cl., A, 356th Inf	Mrs. Tenia Bowman, R. F. D. 1, Hamburg, Mo.
Bradburn, Donald, Pvt. 1cl., B, 341st M. G. Bn	W. P. Bradburn, 2336 Octavia St., New Orleans, La.
Bradley, John Pvt. 1cl., E, 341st F. A.	John J. Bradley, Gen. Del., Flat River, Mo.
Bradshaw, Benjamin H., Pvt., H, 354th Inf	Mrs. Sarnh E. Bradshaw, 512 E. College Ave., Fredericktown, Mo.
Branch, Marion A., Pvt. 1cl., I, 353rd Inf	Allen M. Branch, 1021 S. 4th St., Atchison, Kan.
Brandell, Edwin T., Cook, Amb. Co. 355, 314th San. Tr.	Mrs. Hazel Eva Brandell, 4332 Garfield Ave., Kansas City, Mo.
Brandt, Robert H., Corp., F, 355th Inf	Fred Brandt, Creighton, Mo.
Brannan, Roy B., Pvt. 1cl., C, 353rd Inf	Mrs. Lucy O. Tubbs, Kiowa, Kan.
Brannon, Lee, Pvt., F, 356th Inf	Gilbert M. Brannon, Birmingham, Iowa
Branstetter, Reaves, Pvt., A, Inf	Mrs. Francis Keletesen, Gen. Del., Fisher, Ark.
Brassea, Joseph, Pvt., C, 354th Inf	Mr. James Brassea, Gen. Del., Keating, Colo.
Braunguardt, George F. W., Pvt., D, 354th Inf	Mrs. Sophia Braungardt, Old Monroe, Mo.
Brendle, Charles H., Corp., H, 356th Inf	Mrs. Alma Brendle, Gen. Del., McCabe, Mo.
Brewer, John H. L., Pvt., M, 356th Inf	Els. B. Brewer, Gen. Del., Slade, Ky.
Brewer, John L., Pvt., M, 353rd Inf	Mrs. Lula Nelson, Gen. Del., Montrose, Colo.
Brier, Louis, Pvt., H, 355th Inf	Calites Brier, Aoste, Italy
Brock, Clarence J., Corp., L, 354th Inf	Mrs. Clarence J. Brock, 4124 Labadie Ave., St. Louis, Mo.
Broemmer, August R., Pvt. 1cl., A, 356th Inf	Henry H. Taliafevio, 704 Section St., Hannibal, Mo.
Brogden, Joseph D., Corp., E, 353rd Inf	Mary Brogden, 305 Lawrence St., Topeka, Kan.
Brooks, William H., Pvt., A, 342nd M. G. Bn	Armon Brooks, Grandin, Mo.

Name, Rank, Company, Regiment	Emergency Address
Brown, Andrew J., Pvt., 314th San. Tr.	
Brown, Howard E., Corp., B, 355th Inf	Mrs. Pearl W. Brown, 2874 Cable Ave., Lincoln, Neb.
Brown, John, Corp., B, 314th Eng	Mrs. Helen C. Brown, 2773 Creston Ave., Bronx, N. Y.
Brown, Leslie C., Pvt., H, 356th Inf	George L. Brown, Gen. Del., Billings, Mo.
Brown, Ralph Albert, Pvt., Hq. 355th Inf	Charley H. Brown, Crafton, Neb.
Brown, William Joseph, Sgt., F, 354th Inf	Mrs. Mary Brown, 4141A Carter Ave., St. Louis, Mo.
Browning, Stephen C., Pvt., A, 341st M. G. Bn	D. Browning, Gen. Del., New Hampton, Mo.
Bruce, Clarence H., Corp., H, 355th Inf	Helena Mobley, Meeker, Colo.
Bruce, Noah, Pvt. 1cl., C, 353rd Inf	Mrs. Anna Bruce, Gen. Del., Kennett, Mo.
Brullman, Lester B., Bugler, G., 353rd Inf	John W. Brullman, Louisburg, Kan.
Brummer, Harry M., Pvt., G, 354th Inf	Mrs. Antonie Brummer, 7150 Cleveland Ave., Kansas City, Mo.
Brunswick, George W., Pvt., B, 314th Eng	Mary Chapman, R. F. D. 2, Chapman, Kan.
Bruton, Charles, Pvt., C, 356th Inf	Martin L. Bruton, Golden, Mo.
Bruyer, George A., Pvt., C, 342nd M. G. Bn	Mrs. John Bruyer, R. F. D. 2, Burbank, South Dakota
Buberge, Frederick C., Pvt., A, 354th Inf	William Buberge, 1021 Hudson Ave., St. Paul, Minn.
Buckworth, Earl E., Pvt., K, 353rd Inf	Mrs. Minnie Buckworth, Powersville, Mo.
Buehrer, Clayton O., Pvt., L, 356th Inf	Mrs. Emma Zigler, Archbold, Ohio
Buesch, Alfred A., 1st Sgt., H, 356th Inf	Mrs. Mary Buesch, 610 N. Church St., Bellville, Ill.
Burch, Corbett J., Pvt., G, 355th Inf	
Burghardt, Edwin L., Pvt., E, 353rd Inf	Ike Bratsher, R. F. D. 1, Protection, Kan.
Burns, William E., Corp., B, 353rd Inf	Mrs. Lula Burns, R. F. D. 2, Tonganoxie, Kan.
Burt, William R., Pvt. 1cl., G, 353rd Inf	Richard Burt, Cornwall, England
Butler, Homer J., Pvt. 1cl., Med. Det., 354th Inf	W. P. Butler, Midvale, Neb.
Butrick, William E., Pvt., H, 355th Inf	Mrs. Ila Butrick, Presho, S. D.
Buxton, William G., Pvt., B, 356th Inf	Emma L. Buxton, R. F. D. 1, Alba, Mo.
Byars, Charles C., Pvt., F, 354th Inf	Mrs. Nellie Byars, 94 S. 13th St., Kansas City, Mo.
Byers, John C., E, 356th Inf	Mrs. Elizabeth Brehn, R. F. D. 1, Greenville, Ohio
Cabutto, Gaspare P., Pvt., L, 353rd Inf	
Cahoon, Oscar E., Pvt. 1cl., E, 314th M. S. T.	Mrs. Norma Cahoon, Hope Valley, R. I.
Cain, Henry E., Pvt. 1cl., G, 355th Inf	Elizabeth Cain, Anselmo, Neb.
Cain, John, Pvt., E, 355th Inf	J. A. Cain, Leesville, La.
Cain, Joseph, Pvt., M, 355th Inf	Mrs. Mary A. Cain, 509 W. 3rd Ave., Leadville, Colo.
Caldwell, Luther P., Pvt., K, 355th Inf	
Campbell, George W., Corp., E, 354th Inf	Mrs. Hazel Campbell, 1246 S. Vandeventer Ave., St. Louis, Mo.
Campo, Fred, Pvt. 1cl., I, 354th Inf	Mrs. Paul Campo, 513 Cherry St., Kansas City, Mo.
Carlile, Walter W., Pvt., Tr. Co., 314th M. P.	J. Russell Carlile, 1411 N. 15th St., Philadelphia, Pa.
Carlson, Erik M., Pvt. 1cl., B, 341st M. G. Bn	Carl John Carlson, 4224 N. 33rd St., Omaha, Neb.
Carlson, William E., Pvt., M, 354th Inf	Arthur Black, Tampico, Ill.
Carney, Andrew J., Pvt., A, 356th Inf	Thomas J. Carney, Gen. Del., Dover, Tenn.
Carry, Willian E., Pvt., K, 354th Inf	Mrs. Katherine Carry, 4107 Mercier St., Kansas City, Mo.
Carson, George T., Pvt., B, 314th Eng	Mrs. Anna Carson, Peabody, Kan.
Carson, James E., Pvt., G, 356th Inf	Mrs. Frank Carson, Beckmeyer, Ill.
Carter, Leora, Pvt., K, 355th Inf	Sarah Carter, 1310 E. 4th St., Fairbury, Neb.
Carter, Sidney D., Pvt., H, 353rd Inf	Ole McClure, Somerton, Ariz.
Casanover, George Joseph, Pvt., B, 314th M. P.	Mrs. Julia Casanover, 911 8th St., Luxemberg, Mo.
Chamberlain, James W., Corp., M, 353rd Inf	Mrs. Matilda J. Chamberlain, Gen. Del., Parker, Kan.
Chase, John C., Sgt., K, 354th Inf	Mrs. Martha E. Chase, 705 Wilson Ave., Menomonie, Wis.
Chavez, Mauel, Pvt., B, 355th Inf	Ambrocio Chavez, Las Vegas, N. M.
Choltz, Charles J., Pvt., A, 355th Inf	Mrs. Caroline Wehner, 4349 S. Troy St., Chicago, Ill.
Christ, Harry Oliver E., Sgt., E, 356th Inf	Mrs. Ida Christ, 2910 E. 12th St., Kansas City, Mo.
Christenson, Otto H., Pvt., M, 355th Inf	Emil Christenson, Oakland, Neb.
Christopher, Ellis, Pvt., A, 340th M. G. Bn	
Clapper, Carl Joseph, 314th M. V. S.	Calvin Clapper, R. F. D. 3, Neosho, Mo.
Clark, Wray, Corp., F, 353rd Inf	Mrs. Edith E. Clark, R. F. D. 2, Pittsburg, Kan.
Clayton, Charley F., Wag., Sup Co., 355th Inf	Mrs. Alvin McNett, Mayhill, N. M.
Clement, Claud E., Pvt., E, 353rd Inf	Freda Clement, 626 Miami Ave., Kansas City, Kan.
Clemons, David Emery, Pvt., M, 353rd Inf	Mrs. Grace Clemens, R. F. D. 1, Otega, Kan.
Clendening, Foster J., Pvt., B, 353rd Inf	Mrs. Kate Clendening, R. F. D. 2, Fulton, Kan.
Clingan, William E., Pvt., M, 354th Inf	Mrs Sue Clingan, R. F. D. 4, Springfield, Mo.
Clow, Calvin C., Pvt., B, 355th Inf	Mrs. Lydia Clow, Dawson, Tex.
Clown, Moses, Pvt., B, 314th M. P.	Amos Clown, Dupree, South Dakota
Coats, Walter G., Pvt. 1cl., G, 356th Inf	James Coats, Gen. Del., Cabool, Mo.
Cocanougher, Roy, Corp., H, 356th Inf	
Cochran, Thomas M., Bugler, A, 355th Inf	James A. Cochran, Pitman, Ark.
Cody, James, Pvt., F, 340th F. A.	Mrs. Mary Cody, 748 S. Washtenaw Ave., Chicago, Ill.
Coffman, Allen, Pvt., G, 354th Inf	Mrs. Maddie Starky, Peru, Ill.
Coffman, Paul, Pvt., I, 355th Inf	Mrs. Beatrice Coffman, Mason City, Neb.
Cole, McKinley W., Pvt., A, 355th Inf	Herman H. Cole, R. F. D. 2, Adams, Wis.
Collins, Charlie A., Pvt. 1cl., E, 356th Inf	Wm. M. Collins, R. F. D. 1, Kipling, N. C.
Cone, Cornelius B., Corp., K, 355th Inf	Mrs. Mary Cone, 601 Hood St., Waco, Tex.
Cone, William A., Pvt. 1cl., San. Det., 356th Inf	Mary Ella Cone, Ashland, Neb.
Conklin, Walter R., Pvt., A, 354th Inf	Mattie Conklin, R. F. D. 2, Springfield, Mo.
Conrad, Burr M., Pvt., M, 355th Inf	
Conway, William E., Pvt., E, 314th Eng	Mrs. Thomas Conway, 90 Factory Hill, East Braintree, Mass.
Cook, Samuel J., Pvt., H, 354th Inf	Mrs. Anna Cook, R F. D. 3, Loveland, Colo.
Coonrod, John V., Corp., B, 356th Inf	John R. Coonrod, Arcadia, Kan.
Coppus, Jacob J., Pvt., M, 353rd Inf	Jacob Coppus, Box 295, Little Chute, Wis.
Corriston, Frank, Pvt., L, 353rd Inf	
Cosand, Nigel G., Corp., B, 355th Inf	William G. Cosand, Eldorado, Mich.
Court, Louis W., Cook, Sup. Co., 356th Inf	Mrs. Louise Court, 1010 B Ave., Lawton, Okla.
Covey, Gow R., Pvt. 1cl., F, 314th Eng	Mrs Belle Covey, 2405 Virginia Ave., Joplin, Mo.
Cox, Archie, Pvt., G, 356th Inf	N. D. Cox, R. F. D. 3, Troy, Mo.
Cox, Jim, Pvt. 1cl., B, 354th Inf	Jim Tolliver, Versailles, Mo.
Cox, Raymond M., Corp., A, 341st M. G. Bn	Mrs. Mary E. Cox, Missouri Valley, Iowa
Crader, Ray E., Corp., H, 356th Inf	Daniel F. Crader, R. F. D. 1, Buxfordsville, Mo.
Cradic, Charles A., Wag., 314th Eng. Tr	Mrs. Alice Cradic, R. F. D. 1, Piedmont, Mo.
Craig, Samuel Eph, Pvt., C, 354th Inf	Mrs. Bell Craig, 713 Joseph St., Rich Hill, Mo.
Craig, Oscar E., Pvt., I, 353rd Inf	John Craig, 200 E. Park St., Hutchinson, Kan.
Creek, Hosea, Corp., A, 340th F. A.	

Name, Rank, Company, Regiment	Emergency Address
Criscl, Frank, Pvt., A, 314th Sup. Tr.	Miss Sophie Criscl, 303 E. 148th St., New York, N. Y.
Crosley, William G., Pvt., M, 353rd Inf.	Burt Crosley, Gen. Del., Deer Trail, Colo.
Cross, Jesse R., Pvt., E, 356th Inf.	Wm. A. Cross, P. O. Box 282, Estancia, N. M.
Crouch, Joseph H., Pvt., M, 353rd Inf.	James B. Crouch, Gen. Del., Odessa, Mo.
Crowder, Joseph A., Pvt., C, 353rd Inf.	
Crutchfield, Guy B., Corp., H, 356th Inf.	Mrs. Aleena Crutchfield, Gen. Del., Kennett, Mo.
Culp, Herbert R., Pvt., M. G. Co., 356th Inf.	Mr. John Culp, 1401 S. Ransom St., Ft. Scott, Kan.
Cupp, Elijah M., Pvt., D, 355th Inf.	Mrs. Sarah Cupp, R. R. 2, Box 30, Rockhold, Ky.
Curran, Walter C., Pvt., F, 314th Eng.	
Curry, Corlande B., Pvt. 1cl., L, 355th Inf.	Mabel Curry, Mt. Hope, Kan.
Cutts, Raymond B., Corp., H, 354th Inf.	Fred Hines, 503 E. 15th St., Amarillo, Tex.
Czeschin, Benjamin A., Pvt. 1cl., E, 356th Inf.	Mrs. Emma Czeschin, Gen. Del., Chamois, Mo.
Daniels, Jesse A., Pvt., C, 342nd M. G. Bn.	Mrs. Owen Daniels, R. F. D. 2, Box 242, St. Joseph Mo.
Danielson, Axel, Pvt., C, 354th Inf.	
David, Jesse W., Corp., B, 356th Inf.	Caleb C David, Gen. Del., Darlington, Mo.
Davidson, Frank J., Sgt., M. G. Co., 353rd Inf.	Pete Thorsen, Gen. Del., Merriam, Kan.
Davis, Eli, Pvt., I, 353rd Inf.	Tom Miller, Gen. Del., Skull Valley, Ariz.
Davis, John L., Corp., G, 354th Inf.	Griff Davis, Greenlake, Wis.
Davis, Wesley K., Pvt., 355th Inf.	Mrs. Frances Davis, 2505 N. Prairie, St. Louis, Mo.
Davis, William H., Pvt., B, 355th Inf.	William J. Davis, Rushville, Neb.
Davisson, Bernard, Pvt., H, 356th Inf.	Sam B. Davisson, R. F. D. 1, Fristoe, Mo.
Dean, Alvin R., Pvt., H, 356th Inf.	Mrs. Eva Effie Dean, Kennett, Mo.
Dehler, Ernie William, Pvt., E, 356th Inf.	Charles Dehler, R. F. D. 1, Lavalle, Wis.
Dietsch, Louis Frank, Pvt., M. G. Co., 353rd Inf.	Mrs Marie Dietsch, 3710 Lafayette St., Denver, Colo.
Deitz, Herman W., Pvt., A, 341st M. G. Bn.	
Deml, Rudolph, Pvt., F, 355th Inf.	Mrs. Michael Barry, 5128 S. 22nd St., Omaha, Neb.
Dempsey, James A., Pvt., A, 355th Inf.	James W. Dempsey, R. F. D. 4, Lavalle, Wis.
De Wald, Arthur W., Pvt., K, 354th Inf.	Mrs. Jennie Bledsoe, 435 Scott Ave., Kansas City, Mo.
De Witt, Samuel, Pvt., E, 354th Inf.	Mrs. David R. Cane, 3019 Cherry St., Kansas City, Mo.
Dickey, George W., Pvt., I, 356th Inf.	Harry Dickey, 6208 Princeton Ave., Chicago, Ill.
Dickey, James R., Pvt., M, 353rd Inf.	
Dickinson, Harry, Pvt., B, 356th Inf.	Jasper W. Dickinson, Adams, Neb
Dickson, Charles H., Sgt., D, 354th Inf.	
Dier, Walter E., Pvt. 1cl., Hq. 354th Inf.	Mrs. Oena Dier, R. F. D. 3, Sturgeon Bay, Wis
Dietrich, Walter C., Corp., D, 354th Inf.	Mrs. Barbara Dietrich, 4318 Cherokee St., St. Louis, Mo.
Dilbeck, Andrew W., Pvt., I, 356th Inf.	Wm. J. Dilbeck, Grossville, Ala.
Dillon, Cecil E., Pvt. 1cl., Hq. 353rd Inf.	Mrs. Elizabeth Shafer, Gen. Del., Highland, Kan.
Dingfelder, John M., Pvt., G, 354th Inf.	Mrs. Ida Reising, 4255 Oregon Ave., St. Louis, Mo.
Disalvo, Charles, Pvt. 1cl., B, 354th Inf.	Mrs. Rose Disalvo, 3305 Arlington Ave., St. Louis, Mo.
Dittrick, Leo C., Pvt., K, 355th Inf.	Mrs. Mary Dittrick, Stickney, South Dakota
Dixon, Clarence L., Pvt. 1cl., G, 356th Inf.	Ed. Dixon, Gen. Del., Leadwood, Mo.
Dobmeier, Joseph, Pvt., B, 314th Sup. Tr.	Mrs. Augusta Dobmeier, 282 Herman St., Buffalo, N. Y.
Doescher, Edward, Corp., I, 355th Inf.	Henry A. Doescher, Lyons, Neb.
Dokken, George, Pvt., M. G. Co., 355th Inf.	Knutt Dokken, Brookings, South Dakota
Donovan, George W., Pvt., G, 354th Inf.	Mrs. Bell Donovan, Fort Collins, Colo.
Doon, Albert H., Pvt., B, 354th Inf.	
Dopp, Benjamin R., Pvt., K, 355th Inf.	Charles Martin, Mohaska, Kan.
Dotson, Clay, Corp., E, 353rd Inf.	Mrs. Mary Dotson, Gen. Del., Neodesha, Kan.
Downey, Harvey E., Corp., 314th Eng.	Will Downey, Atlanta, Mo.
Drake, Frank G., Corp., A, 353rd Inf.	Frank Drake, 4648 Columbus Ave., South Minneapolis, Minn.
Dubuque, Bertie L., Pvt., San. Det., 356th Inf.	Mrs. Jonnie Dubuque, 1002 Vine St., Lincoln, Neb.
Duffy, Albert J., Pvt., F, 353rd Inf.	Henry Duffey, R. F. D. 4, Wathena, Kan.
Dufrense, Sidney, Pvt., E, 356th Inf.	Albert S. Dufrense, La Place, La.
Dumey, Albert G., Pvt., G, 354th Inf.	Mrs. Hazel Dumey, 1723 Franklin Ave., St. Louis, Mo.
Dunker, Andrew P., Pvt. 1cl., G, 356th Inf.	Matilda Budd, 227 Adelia Ave., Luxemberg, Mo.
Dunker, Arthur E., Pvt., C, 354th Inf.	Wm. Dunker, Box 46, Marengo, Ill.
Dunn, Alvin, Pvt., I, 353rd Inf.	Mrs. R. M. Dunn, Bernard, Mo.
Dunning, Hardman, Corp., G, 356th Inf.	
Duran, Agapito, Pvt., E, 354th Inf.	Juan J. Duran, Ideal, Colo.
Durham, William, Pvt., B, 356th Inf.	Mrs. Tilda Alford, Warren Ky.
Duvall, Claud H., Pvt B, 353rd Inf.	Grant Duvall, Colwich, Kan.
Dyke, Allie B., Pvt. 1cl., L, 354th Inf.	Cad B. Dyke, New Truxton, Mo.
Easley, Green, Pvt., D, 342nd M. G. Bn.	Robert Easley, R. F. D. 2, Eureka Springs, Ark.
Eckhart, John F., Pvt., K, 353rd Inf.	John Eckhart, Norcatur, Kan.
Eocher, Richard, Corp., I, 353rd Inf.	
Eeg, Alfred, Pvt., A, 355th Inf.	Mrs. Oliva Eeg, 1715 S. 10th St., La Crosse, Wis.
Eich, John M., Pvt. 1cl., B, 355th Inf.	Philip J. Eich, Farmer, S. D.
Eichholtz, William H., Corp., E, 354th Inf.	
Elander, Helge, Pvt., M, 355th Inf.	Mrs. Alvaedo Coleman, 1025 Post St., San Francisco, Cal.
Elder, August G., Pvt. 1cl., F, 354th Inf.	Wm. F. Elder, R. F. D. 6, Box 75, Perryville, Mo.
Elwick, Harry H., Pvt., B, 353rd Inf.	
Elliot, Gilbert, G, 353rd Inf.	Mrs. Sarah Elliot, Pooli, Ind.
Elliott, Illiff, Pvt., A, 353rd Inf.	Mrs. Lena M. Elliott, 725 E. 7th Ave., Hutchinson, Kan.
Ellis, Leonidas B., Pvt. 1cl., M. G. Co., 356th Inf.	J. N. Ellis, Box 172, Princeton, Mo.
Ellis, Ralph, Corp., C, 314th F. S. Bn.	Mrs. Sarah B. Ellis, 613 Bloomington St., Iowa City, Iowa, c-o I. B. Ellis, Rocky Ford, Colo.
Ellison, Francis T., Pvt., Hq. 355th Inf.	Mrs. Honour Ellison, Scammon, Kan.
Emerson, Thomas B. C., Pvt., E, 356th Inf.	Thomas A. Emerson, Osceola, Mo.
Engel, Walter E., Pvt., B, 355th Inf.	
Engle, Leonard A., Corp., F, 355th Inf.	
Epperson, Jim W., Pvt., G, 356th Inf.	Mrs. Charley Epperson, Waldron, Ark.
Erdman, August, Pvt., F, 353rd Inf.	
Erickson, Albin, Pvt., F, 353rd Inf.	Daniel Erickson, Gen. Del., Wayne, Kan.
Erickson, Benjamin A., Pvt., I, 354th Inf.	Stanley Erickson, R. F. D. 1, Arkdale, Wis.
Erickson, Charles, Pvt., M, 353rd Inf.	
Erwin, Arthur, Pvt., H, 356th Inf.	
Eshelman, James E., Pvt., F, 354th Inf.	
Estes, Cephas, Pvt. 1cl., F, 354th Inf.	Rachel Hitt, Route 4, Advance, Mo.
Eveland, John W., Pvt., A, 355th Inf.	Mrs. Jennie Eveland, Barneveld, Wis.

Name, Rank, Company, Regiment	Emergency Address
Eylens, Charles, Pvt., E, 354th Inf	Mrs. Jennie Roberts, Silver Plume, Colo.
Fager, Aurie E., Pvt. 1cl., F, 354th Inf	
Falk, Albert F., Pvt. 1cl., F, 356th Inf	
Farrar, Guy S., Corp., M, 356th Inf	Mrs. Kate Farrar, Windsor, Mo.
Farrell, John J., Pvt., B, 354th Inf	Mrs. Frank Delvin, 36 Spring St., Paterson, N. J.
Farrell, Joseph H., Pvt., E, 355th Inf	
Farris, Allen F., Pvt., I, 354th Inf	
Farris, Evan L., Pvt. 1cl., C, 342nd M. G. Bn	James D. Farris, Norwich, Kan.
Fasano, Don A., Pvt. 1cl., D, 356th Inf	Frank Fasano, Gen. Del., Crystal City, Kan.
Faulkner, Virgil, Pvt., E, 354th Inf	Rex M. Faulkner, Rolla, Mo.
Fauth, George J., Pvt., D, 354th Inf	Mrs. Kate Fauth, 4760 Alaska Ave., St. Louis, Mo.
Feck, Ernest, Pvt., F, 353th Inf	Mrs. Augusta Cohn Peck, R. F. D. Box 22, Wausau, Wis.
Fedderson, Carl F., Pvt., B, 356th Inf	Rose Dwelle, Kelleys Island, Ohio
Feely, William James, Pvt., B, 354th Inf	Simon Feely, 3960 Kalamath St., Denver, Colo.
Feldman, Elmer A., Pvt., A, 355th Inf	Edward Feldman, R. F. D. 3, Frendship, Wis.
Feldman, Jacob L., Pvt., K, 354th Inf	Mrs. Pauline Eisen, 2621 Gamble Ave., St. Louis, Mo.
Feniter, John J., Pvt., F, 353rd Inf	Mrs. Mamie Cullen, 4091 5th Ave., Chicago, Ill.
Fenster, Charles, Corp., Hq. 353rd Inf	
Fenton, Daniel C., Pvt., F, 355th Inf	Mrs. Emma Fenton, 306 Broadway, Pueblo, Colo.
Fetters, Emery E., Sgt., F, 356th Inf	Mrs. James K. Fetters, Lees Summit, Mo.
Fidler, Lawrence C., Pvt., E, 356th Inf	Hiram Fidler, R. F. D. 1, Yorkshire, Ohio
Fielder, Joseph G., Pvt., A, 355th Inf	
Finkelstein, Samuel, Pvt., M. G. Co., 353rd Inf	Mrs. Anna Finkelstein, 2930 Sheridan Ave., St. Louis, Mo.
Fiorinzi, Frank, Pvt., A, 353rd Inf	Dominico Fiorinzi, Gen. Del., Gross, Kan.
Fischer, Phillip, Pvt., A, 355th Inf	Math. Fischer, 198 Cove St., Hartford, Wis.
Fish, Charles R., Pvt. 1cl., I, 353rd Inf	Wm. Fish, Skiddy, Kan.
Fitzgerald, George A., Pvt., K, 355th Inf	
Fletcher, James E., Corp., C, 355th Inf	James G. Fletcher, Holcomb, Mo.
Flinn, James W., Corp., F, 354th Inf	Mrs. Mary Flinn, Colvin, Ill.
Flores, George E., Pvt. 1cl., G, 354th Inf	Joshua Flores, Knox City, Mo.
Flores, Dave J., Pvt., E, 356th Inf	Philip Flores, R. F. D. 2, Robeline, La.
Focht, William J., Sgt. 1cl., Med. Det., 353rd Inf	Mrs. Cora E. Focht, 1015 High St., Grinnell, Iowa
Fohman, Walker A., Pvt., B, 354th Inf	
Folda, Albin, Corp., M, 355th Inf	Emil Folda, Clarkson, Neb.
Folz, Alexander, Corp., B, 354th Inf	Mrs. Alexander Folz, 1019 Rural St., Rockford, Ill.
Ford, Alexander L., Pvt., K, 354th Inf	G. E. Ford, 312 Gallais Bldg., Tulsa, Okla.
Ford, Frank M., Pvt., E, 356th Inf	Miss Nettie S. Osborn, 141 Broadway, Cincinnati, Ohio
Forth, Herman J., Pvt., Med. Det., 341st M. G. Bn	Mrs. Dora A. Forth, Wayne City, Ill.
Foster, Harry, Pvt., B, 340th M. G. Bn	Mrs. Willa Foster, Box 176, Elsberry, Mo.
Foster, Horace K., Pvt., C, 356th Inf	
Fox, Chester, Pvt., B, 353rd Inf	
Fraizer, Lloyd M., Pvt. 1cl., Med. Det., 353rd Inf	
Frankowski, Joseph, Pvt., M, 354th Inf	Mary Frankowski, Warsrour, Poland
Frans, Claude L., Corp., K, 356th Inf	Mrs. Martha Frans, Frazer, Mo.
Freeman, Clyde A., Pvt., B, 340th M. G. Bn	Mrs. Clara Stuckey, Cherokee, Okla.
Freimark, Ralph T., Pvt., H, 355th Inf	Ernestine Freimark, St. Lawrence, S. D.
Freitag, Max H., Pvt., F, 354th Inf	Mrs. Emily Freitag, R. F. D. 2, Elkhorn, Wis.
Fry, Lawrence N., Pvt., A, 355th Inf	Mrs. Mary Fry, 805 Johnson Ave., Hickman, Ky.
Fuller, Harry J., Sgt., A, 355th Inf	Willis C. Fuller, 150 Crane St., Schenectady, N. Y.
Fulner, Lewis G., Pvt., E, 356th Inf	John Fulner, R. F. D. 2, Henderson, Ky.
Fulton, Charles G., Pvt., B, 353rd Inf	Mrs. Mary Fulton, Gen. Del., Cuba, Kan.
Fumuso, Marco, Pvt., C, 356th Inf	Mrs. Katrina Bellafire, Cashlvitiano, Trapani, Italy
Gaebler, Frederick, Corp., C, 341st M. G. Bn	
Gaines, Fletcher W., Pvt., G, 356th Inf	John L. Gaines, Bethel, Mo.
Galbraith, John J., Sgt., D, 355th Inf	
Gallegos, Biterba, Pvt., I, 356th Inf	Andrella Gallegos, Central, N. M.
Galligan, Peter F., Corp., B, 356th Inf	Mrs. Maggie Galligan, Aspen, Colo.
Gann, Wyatt, Pvt., L, 355th Inf	Mrs. Anna Gann, Hatfield, Ark.
Gano, Harley Perle, Pvt., Hq. 356th Inf	Mr. George Gano, Gen. Del., Washington, Kan.
Garcia, Antanacio, Pvt., B, 356th Inf	Jesse Garcia, Albuquerque, N. M.
Gandert, Frederick, Pvt., I, 356th Inf	Andrew Gandert, Holeman, N. M.
Gardner, Miles E., Pvt., A, 354th Inf	Gurdon Gardner, Box 184, Wiggins, Colo.
Garrett, Manoll J., Hrsshr., Sup. Co., 355th Inf	Mrs. Pearl L. Keaton, 4146 Zuni St., Denver, Colo.
Garrison, Andrew A., Pvt., D, 354th Inf	Mrs. Samantha Garrison Creede, Colo.
Gartland, Myles P., Corp., E, 354th Inf	Lawrence F. Gartland, Cavalry Cemetery, St. Louis, Mo.
Garvey, William H., Pvt., M, 356th Inf	Mrs. Mary A. Garvey, 675 Adams St., Dorchester, Mass.
Gausden, Frank L., Pvt., B, 314th F. S. Bn	Mrs. Mary Gausden, 879 Rush St., Chicago, Ill.
Gerard, William H., Pvt., C, 354th Inf	Eugene E. Gerard, R. F. D. 3, Bradford, Ill.
Gerhartz, Peter, Pvt., E, 354th Inf	John Gerhartz, R. F. D. 40, Marathon, Wis.
Geroldson, Owen, Pvt., K, 355th Inf	
Gibson, Andrew J., Pvt., B, 355th Inf	Mr. James W. Gibson, Dixon, Ky.
Gilardi, Jaspre, Pvt. 1cl., B, 354th Inf	Andre Santangilo, 621 Townsend St., Chicago, Ill.
Gilbert, Edward E., Pvt., Med. Det., 341st M. G. Bn	John R. Gilbert, Orleans, Cal.
Gill, Frederick J., M. G. Co., 355th Inf	Samuel R. Derry Berry, North Platte, Neb.
Gilmer, John E., Corp., E, 355th Inf	Mrs. Ethel N. Gilmer, 308 D St., Central City, Neb.
Gingrich, Curvin A., Pvt. 1cl., B, 342nd M. G. Bn	Mrs. Maude Gingrich, Gen. Del., Wakonda, S. D.
Gipson, Clyde A., Pvt., C, 355th Inf	Mrs. Dorris L. Gipson, R. F. D. 4, Purdy, Mo.
Godberson, Herman, Pvt. 1cl., B, 341st M. G. Bn	Mrs. Fredericka Godberson, Millard, Neb.
Godfrey James T., Pvt., G, 356th Inf	Mrs. Maggie Werner, Gen. Del., Valley Park, Mo.
Goecks, Arthur W., Pvt., A, 355th Inf	
Goforth, Luther B., Pvt. 1cl., I, 354th Inf	Mrs. Lizzie Conway, Gen. Del., Shawnee, Mo.
Goff, Ira B., Pvt., Hq. 353rd Inf	
Gohl, George B., Pvt., A, 354th Inf	Mrs. Emma L. Gohl, 3921 Highland Ave., Kansas City, Mo.
Gohr, Harry, Pvt., G, 355th Inf	Mr. James Keeler, Fairmont, Neb.
Golden, Victor E., Pvt., M. G. Co., 356th Inf	Mrs. Anna Golden, Byron, Neb.
Goodrich, Roy C., Pvt. 1cl., B, 353rd Inf	James A. Goodrich, Montana, Kan.
Goodman, John W., Corp., B, 341st F. A.	John A. Goodman, 730 E. Cimarron Ave., Colorado Spgs., Colo.
Goodwin, Thomas A., Pvt., L, 355th Inf	Mrs. Josephine Goodwin, Gregory, S. D.
Gordon, Carl E., Pvt. 1cl., B, 341st M. G. Bn	Alexander P. Gordon, 3548A Missouri Ave., St. Louis, Mo.
Gorges, Clarence M., Sgt., B, 341st M. G. Bn	Andrew J. Gorges, R. F. D. 2, Wamego, Kan.

Name, Rank, Company, Regiment	Emergency Address
Gottshall, Ervin O., Pvt. 1cl., C, 314th Eng	Emanuel Gottshall, R. F. D. 1, Treverton, Pa.
Gowen, James, Pvt., C, 355th Inf	William Kinder, R. F. D. 2, Box 176, Caruthersville, Mo.
Grannan, Joseph W., Pvt., F, 353rd Inf	Mrs. Eva Grannan, 7848 S. Morgan St., Chicago, Ill.
Grant, Zachary A., Pvt., K, 353rd Inf	Zachary T. Grant, Burlington, Kan.
Grass, Wilfred W., Pvt., L, 353rd Inf	Mrs. G. L. Vance, R. F. D. 1, Chetopa, Kan.
Graves, William, Pvt. 1cl., A, 355th Inf	Mrs. Augusta Graves, 1448 W. 14th Pl., Chicago, Ill.
Gray, Bertram, Pvt. 1cl., M, 354th Inf	Mrs. Amelia Gray, Miami, Ariz.
Gray, Harry E., Pvt., H, 353rd Inf	Mrs. John Gray, Columbus, Kan.
Gray, James E., Corp., I, 356th Inf	John H. Gray, 108 N. Buchanan St., Maryville, Mo.
Green, Lester B., Pvt., F, 353rd Inf	Mrs. Amelia Green, R. F. D. 4, Paola, Kan.
Green, Lloyd C., Pvt., B, 354th Inf	
Green, Ray R., Pvt., F, 314th Eng	Luther Green, Globe, Ariz.
Greer, Giles R., Corp., H, 356th Inf	
Greiner, Frank, Pvt., B., 355th Inf	Peter J. Greiner, R. F D. 6, Bloomfield, Neb.
Grenda, John, Pvt., L, 354th Inf	Mrs. Peter Grenda, Ironwood, Mich.
Grief, John F., Pvt., B, 314th Eng	
Griesemer, Emanuel, Pvt., K, 353rd Inf	
Griffith Elmer C., Pvt., B, 353rd Inf	John E. Griffith, 621 Menor, Winfield, Kan.
Griffith, Wesley E., Pvt., Hq. 355th Inf	
Grim, Alfred, Wag., Amb. Co., 356th Inf	Mrs. E. E. Grim, 725 Columbia St., Waterloo, Iowa
Grota, Adam E., Pvt., I, 354th Inf	Mrs. Adam Grota, Gen. Del., Berlin, Wis.
Groth, Joseph, Pvt., B, 353rd Inf	John Groth, Sterling, Kan.
Grothe, Martin, Pvt. 1cl., F, 354th Inf	Mrs. Anna Grothe, R. F. D. 1, Box 88, Pine City, Minn.
Grube, Lee A., Corp., C, 353rd Inf	Mrs. Viola Lucas, 425 Neosho, Emporia, Kan.
Gruer, Walter J., Pvt., A, 341st M. G. Bn	Miss Edna Gruer, 3440 Garfield Ave., Kansas City, Mo
Guggisberg, Edward, Corp., D, 353rd Inf	Mrs. Elizabeth Guggisberg, R. F. D. 1, Burns, Kan.
Guilbeau, Romain, Pvt., A, 355th Inf	Mrs. Julia Guilbeau, 813 Dumain St., New Orleans, La.
Gutschenritter, Joseph G., Pvt., A, 355th Inf	Mrs. Jos. Gutschenritter, Hartford, Wis.
Gwinner, Harvey W., Pvt. 1cl., F, 314th Eng	
Hackett, Thomas E., Sgt., Hq. 354th Inf	Samuel F. Hackett, Onick, Mo.
Hackman, Edward E., Sgt., B, 356th Inf	Elizabeth Hackman, 2717 St. Vincent St., St. Louis, Mo.
Hackman, Fritz H., Pvt., D, 354th Inf	Miss Dena Hackman, 822 N. Main St., St. Charles, Mo.
Hadlick, Charles F., Pvt., C, 353rd Inf	Mrs. Emma Hadlick, 706 S. Moore St., Blue Earth, Minn.
Hagerman, Chester R., Pvt., B, 353rd Inf	Mrs. Susie Hagerman, Gen. Del., Medicine Lodge, Kan.
Hake, Antone, Pvt. 1cl., L, 356th Inf	Henry A. Hake, Montrose, Mo.
Hall, Ernest, Corp., M, 354th Inf	A. E. Hall, 411 Dermond, Macon, Mo.
Hall, Marechal E., Pvt. 1cl., C, 354th Inf	Clarence A. Hall, Dudley, Mo.
Hall, Walter, Pvt., E, 314th Eng	Mrs. Emma Nuckols, Dumas, Ark.
Hall, William A., Pvt. 1cl., A, 353rd Inf	William Allen Hall, Sr., 401 E 16th St., Winfield, Kan.
Haller, Richard W., Pvt., I, 356th Inf	
Hallgren, Henry W., Sgt., D, 314th Eng	G. F. Hallgren, Youngsville, Pa.
Halvorson, Carl H., Pvt. 1cl., M, 356th Inf	
Hamil, Lester D., Sgt., B, 353rd Inf	Mrs. J. D. Hamil, Tonganoxie, Kan.
Hamilton, Joseph A., Pvt., Hq. 355th Inf	William Murphy, Belgrade, Neb.
Hamman, Rox, Pvt., 314th F. S. Bn	
Hammond, Claude C., Pvt., L, 355th Inf	Mr. Francis M. Hammond, Estelene, Colo.
Hanlin, Charles H., Mech., D, 353rd Inf	George W. Hanlin, Osawatomie, Kan.
Hanniphan, Raymond W., Pvt., K, 356th Inf	Ed. Gullion, New Madrid, Mo.
Hansen, Arthur, Pvt., M. G. Co., 354th Inf	Robert Hansen, 112 E. Main St., St. Charles, Ill.
Hansen, Arvid L., Corp., M, 353rd Inf	Mr. Swan B. Hansen, McPherson, Kan.
Hansen, Elmer C., Pvt., M, 353rd Inf	Mrs. Cora B. Hansen, 861 15th Ave., E. Moline, Ill.
Hansen, Peter M., Pvt. 1cl., F, 356th Inf	
Harbin, Audley W., Pvt. 1cl., M. G. Co., 354th Inf	Mrs. Emma Jordan, 1419 Tejon St., Colorado Spgs., Colo.
Hardtke, Otto C., Pvt., B, 353rd Inf	Mrs. Otto C. Hardtke, 4921 Kimball Ave., Chicago, Ill.
Hardy, Charles, Pvt., B, 356th Inf	Mrs. Mary Hardy, Washburn, Mo.
Haries, George, Pvt., B, 340th F. A	
Harless, Nain R., Pvt., E, 353rd Inf	Mrs. Mary Cunningham, Lewisburg, W. Va.
Harman, John D., Sgt., C, 341st M. G. Bn	Mrs. Anna Harman, 825 Hutchins Ave., Cincinnati, Ohio
Harmon, Guy B., Sgt., E, 340th F. A	Mrs. Alice Harmon, R. F. D. 1, Higley, Ariz.
Harrington, Parmer, Cook, G, 353rd Inf	Margaret Harrington, Miami, Ariz.
Harris, Homer, Pvt., A, 355th Inf	Mrs. Levada Harris Star Route, Elba, Ala.
Harris, Lucian W., Pvt., B, 356th Inf	Mrs. Florence Harris, Venable, Mo.
Harris, Sparrell, Pvt., A, 356th Inf	Allen Harris, Kearney, Mo.
Hartung, John A., B, 354th Inf	Mrs. Anna E. Hartung, Keokuk, Iowa
Harvey, Charles, Corp., M, 353rd Inf	Mrs. Lillie A. Harvey, Quinter, Kan.
Harvey, Isaac J., Pvt., H, 355th Inf	Mrs. Anna M. Harvey, Wauneta, Neb.
Harvill, William A., C, 354th Inf	Alba M. Harvill, Keltner, Mo.
Hassett, Ellis E., Pvt. 1cl., F, 354th Inf	Mrs. Kate Hassett, 3850 Cote Brilliant Ave., St. Louis, Mo.
Hetlage, Frank, Pvt., B, 356th Inf	Mrs. Louisa Hetlage, 1321 2nd St., St. Louis, Mo.
Haugen, Elvin J., Pvt. 1cl., A, 341st M. G. Bn	Iver S. Haugen, Dufur, Ore.
Haven, Samuel C., Pvt. 1cl., B, 341st F. S. Bn	Miss Jane M. Haven, Ottumwa, Iowa
Hayes, William J., Pvt. 1cl., Hq. 354th Inf	Mrs. Allen Hayes, 1209 N. 17th Ave., St. Louis, Mo.
Haynes, Ezra, Pvt., B, 354th Inf	Robert L. Haynes, Commerce, Ga.
Heald, Arlington A., Pvt. 1cl., G, 353rd Inf	Caleb Healey, Goff, Kan.
Healy, Francis L., Pvt. 1cl., K, 353rd Inf	Margaret Healy, Lincoln, Kan.
Hedrick, Wesley S., Pvt., B, 356th Inf	Lee Hedrick, Marceline, Mo.
Heffron, Walter R., Sgt., F, 353rd Inf	Mrs. William Heffron, Lookeba, Okla.
Heidle, William T., Pvt., C, 353rd Inf	Mrs. Helen Heidle, Junction City, Kan.
Heins, Erwin, Pvt. 1cl., M, 355th Inf	Mrs. Clara Heins, Lyndhurst, Wis.
Heintz, Chas. C., Pvt., D, 342nd F. A	
Heller, Victor, Pvt., B, 341st M. G. Bn	John Heller, 3645 Polk St., S. Omaha, Neb.
Henderson, Oral T., Pvt., G, 353rd Inf	Mrs. Francis Henderson, Cottonwood, Ariz.
Hendrickson, Charles C., Pvt., C, 314th F. S. Bn	Mrs. Rachael Hendrickson, Great Falls, Mont.
Hennessy, Arthur, Pvt., D, 356th Inf	Mrs. Catherine Cronin, 2826 Calumet Ave., Chicago, Ill.
Henning, Joe P., Pvt., B, 355th Inf	
Henrich, Samuel C., Pvt., E, 353rd Inf	Mrs. Lottie McFadden, Natoma, Kan.
Henritz, Alexander P., Pvt., D, 354th Inf	Mrs. Lewellyn E. Henritz, 4014 Troost Ave., Kansas City, Mo.
Henson, Joseph G., Pvt., F, 356th Inf	
Herbold, George C., Pvt., B. 314th F. S. Bn	August Herbold, R. F. D. 4, Thayer, Mo.
Herman, Claude E., Pvt. 1cl., B, 341st M. G. Bn	Susan T. Herman, R. F. D. 28, Topeka, Kan.

Name, Rank, Company, Regiment	Emergency Address
Herman, William C., Corp., C, 355th Inf	Mrs. Caroline Herman, Alliance, Neb.
Herring, Frederick, Pvt., B, 353rd Inf	Mrs. Margaret Herring, Metamora, Ill.
Herzog, William A., Pvt., B, 355th Inf	Mrs. Regian Herzog, 921 Avondale Ave., Springfield, Ohio
Hewitt, Henry L., Corp., I, 353rd Inf	John Hewitt, Mound City, Kan.
Hickerson, Leslie F., Corp., M. G. Co., 354th Inf	Noah Hickerson, Wellsville, Mo.
Hickman, Harry F., Sgt., G, 356th Inf	Orin Hickman, Golden City, Mo.
Hicks, Frank B., Corp., B, 353rd Inf	Charles Hicks, Linwood, Kan.
Higdon, John T., Pvt., H, 354th Inf	Mrs. B. E. Higdon, Brookhaven, Miss.
Higgins, Edward L., Pvt., L, 353rd Inf	William C. Higgins, R. F. D. 2, Stella, Neb.
Higgins, Harold D., Pvt. 1cl., Hq. 354th Inf	George M. Higgins, White, S. D.
Hilburn, Robert F., Corp., L, 355th Inf	James R. Hillburn, 720 3rd St., Douglas, Ariz.
Hiles, Henry G., Pvt., A, 354th Inf	
Hines, Milford, Pvt., E, 356th Inf	Mr. James Hines, Somerset, Ky.
Hinghaus, William J., Wag., Hq. 354th Inf	Mrs. Clara Benz, 2629A Armour Pl., St. Louis, Mo.
Hink, William H., Pvt. 1cl., F, 314th Eng	Mrs. Daisy Hink, 803 N. John St., Joplin, Mo.
Hinkle, Jesse R., Pvt., A, 355th Inf	Mrs. Elizabeth Hinkle, Barron, Wis.
Hinkley, Clarence C., Corp., E, 356th Inf	
Hlava, Ladislaus, Pvt. 1cl., D, 355th Inf	John Hlava, 812 Maple St., Wausau, Wis.
Hobson, James A., Pvt., L, 353rd Inf	Fred Hobson, Bartlett, Kan.
Hodge, Arnold, Pvt., I, 356th Inf	Mary Hodge, Piedmont, Mo.
Hoffman, Ralph, Wag., Amb. Co., 354th Inf	Geo. H. Hoffman, College View, Neb.
Hogan, Thomas J., Pvt. 1cl., I, 353rd Inf	James M. Hogan, Sr., Natoma, Kan.
Hoglund, Leander, Pvt., C, 314th Amm. Tr	Mrs. Agnes Kidwell, Carrizo Springs, Tex.
Hohberg, Albert, Corp., D, 353rd Inf	Mrs. J. C. Weeks, 1614 W 17th St., Topeka, Kan.
Hohensee, Albert C., Pvt. 1cl., A, 355th Inf	Charles Hohensee, R. F. D. 3, Fond du Lac, Wis.
Holmes, Ira G., Pvt., L, 353rd Inf	Mrs. Josephine Holmes, Hartford, Kan.
Holmes, Oliver W., Pvt., G, 353rd Inf	Winfield S. Holmes, Beaver Crossing, Neb.
Holst, Alfred P., Corp., A, 355th Inf	John Holst, Loraine, Wis.
Holtman, George P., Pvt., B, 356th Inf	Peter Holtman, 1703 Washington St., St. Louis, Mo.
Holz, Carl O., Sgt., H, 355th Inf	William Holz, Guide Rock, Neb.
Homer, Henry, Pvt., C, 355th Inf	Thomas Homer, Springfield, Ill.
Hooper, Wilbert G., Pvt., B, 353rd Inf	Mrs. Gladys Hooper, Inavale, Kan.
Hootman, Frank, Pvt. 1cl., C, 356th Inf	Maria Hootman, Mirabile, Mo.
Hopkins, Robert P., Sgt., B, 314th Eng	John Hopkins, 188 Terrace St., Carbondale, Pa.
Houldsworth, Wallace, Corp., D, 354th Inf	James Houldsworth, 2827 (5½) Ave., Rock Island, Ill.
Howard, Amos W., Pvt. 1cl., I, 354th Inf	James G. Howard, Sligo, Colo.
Howard, John M., Pvt., A, 314th Eng	James C. Howard, 253 5th Ave. W., Twin Falls, Idaho
Howe, Francis E., Pvt., L, 355th Inf	Mrs. Gertrude Hannan, Creston, Iowa
Howe, Myrl W., Pvt., F, 314th Eng	O. W. Howe, Elmer, Mo.
Hubbard, Harry H., Wag., Sup. Co., 356th Inf	Miss Nellie Hubbard, Garnett, Kan.
Hubbard, Samuel S., Pvt., E, 353rd Inf	Mrs. Etta Hyes, Atwood, Kan.
Hubbs, Alvis, Corp., E, 356th Inf	
Hudspeth, Onney M., Pvt., B, 353rd Inf	George P. Goodson, Corona, N. Y.
Huey, Howard T., Pvt. 1cl., D, 342nd M. G. Bn	Mrs. Mary Jane Huey, Delmont, S. D.
Hoffman, Harry, Pvt., C, 356th Inf	Mrs. Malissa Petithorn, Sardinia, Ohio
Huffstutler, Virgil, Pvt., E, 356th Inf	Lee Huffstutler, Malden, Mo.
Hughes, Abel J., Corp., B, 355th Inf	
Hull, James A., Pvt., C, 354th Inf	Mrs. Letha Broadbent, R. F. D. 2, Atkinson, Ill.
Humphrey, Glenn, Sgt., C, 356th Inf	Gorsh S. Humphrey, R. F. D. 4, Chillicothe, Mo.
Humphrey, Jake D., Pvt., D, 342nd M. G. Bn	
Hunt, Charles L., Pvt., H, 353rd Inf	John Hunt, Bigelow, Kan.
Hurd, Conrad I., Pvt. 1cl., D, 353rd Inf	Mattie Hurd, Luray, Kan.
Hurlbert, Dexter L., Pvt., C, 353rd Inf	Mrs. Dexter Hurlbert, Waco, Mo.
Hurlburt, Clarence O., Pvt., K, 355th Inf	Ethel Hiedelk, 600 5th St., Fairbury, Neb.
Hurt, Paul G., Pvt., Hq. 355th Inf	James A. Hurt, R. F. D. 5, Kearney, Neb.
Hustedde, Anton, Pvt. 1cl., Hq. Troop	William Hustedde, Campbell, Mo.
Hutchens, Lawrence, Pvt., C, 353rd Inf	Harvey Hutchens, Elk City, Kan.
Hutchinson, Frederick, Corp., E, 353rd Inf	
Hutton, Eugene, Pvt., C, 353rd Inf	Bert Hutton, 305 University St., Wichita, Kan.
Igo, John T., Pvt., I, 354th Inf	Lafayette Igo, Lexington, Mo.
Imhoff, George L., Pvt., C, 355th Inf	Mrs. Rosa Imhoff, 530 Louisa St., New Orleans, La.
Ingerham, Clarence, Pvt. 1cl., I, 353rd Inf	James England, 112 N. Main St., Neosho, Mo.
Isaacson, Clyde, Pvt., L, 353rd Inf	Ben Van Dalson, Fairview, Kan.
Jackson, Wilbur I., Corp., C, 314th F. S. Bn	Mrs. Eva Martha Jackson, 733 Roseville Ave., Salt Lake C., Utah
Jackson, William H., Corp., D, 353rd Inf	Mrs. Emma Jackson, R. F. D. 4, Box 59, Ft. Worth, Tex.
Jacobson, Harley, Pvt. 1cl., L, 353rd Inf	Hans Jacobson, Cadott, Wis.
Jacobson, Leonard, Pvt. 1cl., Amb. Co., 354th Ind	Walter Gemmell, 1836 3rd St., Eureka, Cal.
James, Morris, Corp., L, 353rd Inf	Elmer James, Madison, Kan.
Janzen, Gustave, Pvt., B, 355th Inf	Mrs. Helen Janzen, Hillsboro, Kan.
Jelkin, Wilber, Pvt., L, 355th Inf	Henry Jelkin, Tripp, S. D.
Jennings, Lewis W., Pvt., C, 353rd Inf	Ellis Jennings, Smith Center, Kan.
Jensen, Herman C., Mech., K, 354th Inf	Erik Fester, Lamberton, Minn.
Jensen, Tineus J., Pvt., D, 341st M. G. Bn	Michael Jensen, Karlstad, Minn.
Jenson, Henry C., Pvt. 1cl., B, 353rd Inf	Mrs. Pete Mathison, 302 N. Academy St., Janesville, Wis.
Jessen, Frederick, Pvt. 1cl., B, 355th Inf	Mrs. Anna Jessen, White, S. D.
Johannsen, John H., Corp., A, 355th Inf	John H. Johannsen, R. F. D. 2, Davenport, Iowa
Johns, William K., Pvt., D, 342nd M. G. Bn	Mrs. Elizabeth Johns, Booneville, Mo.
Johnson, Adolph, Pvt., D, 354th Inf	Andrew Johnson, Shiocton, Wis.
Johnson, Andrew J., Pvt., G, 355th Inf	Edward Nelson, Ellis, S. D.
Johnson, Arthur J., Pvt. 1cl., F, 355th Inf	Charles M. Johnson, R. F. D. 1, Box 25, Valparaiso, Neb.
Johnson, Carl, Pvt. 1cl., C, 342nd M. G. Bn	John Granstrom, Halmstead, Halland, Sweden
Johnson, Charles R., Corp., G, 355th Inf	F. C. Johnson, 829 4th St., Superior, Neb.
Johnson, Frederick P., Pvt., C, 355th Inf	William W. Johnson, R. F. D. 1, Summers, Ark.
Johnson, Harold M., Pvt, I, 353rd Inf	Mrs Sarah Johnson, 601 Spruce St., Wamego, Kan.
Johnson, Lawrence D., Pvt. 1cl., A, 355th Inf	
Johnson, Leonard, Corp., A, 353rd Inf	Mrs. Sandra Willies, 104 S 48th St., West Duluth, Minn.
Johnson, Martin, Pvt., 314th F. S. Bn	
Johnson, Oakley V., Pvt., H, 355th Inf	Roy L. Hobson, Grant City, Mo.
Johnson, Oscar, Pvt., B, 354th Inf	Miss Engrid Anderson, Box 44, Odanah, Wis.
Johnson, Otto V, Bugler, K, 355th Inf	John H Johnson, Sutherland, Neb.

Name, Rank, Company, Regiment	Emergency Address
Johnson, William A., Pvt., A, 355th Inf	Mrs. Celia Johnson, Baronett, Wis.
Johnson, William N., Pvt., L, 354th Inf	Christopher T. Johnson, Oregon, Wis
Johnston, Francis M., Corp., G, 356th Inf	Mrs. Retta Johnston, Quitman, Mo.
Jokers, Walter J., Pvt., A, 355th Inf	Mrs. Martha Jokers, R. F. D. 2, Dow, Ill.
Jones, Everett E., Pvt., C, 353rd Inf	Edward G. Jones, Ethel, Mo.
Jones, Earl R., Pvt., E, 355th Inf	
Jones, Floyd E., Pvt., M, 355th Inf	Mrs. Emma Lewis, Madison, Neb.
Jones, Irwin L., Pvt., A, 355th Inf	Theodore Jones, Isabell, Ind.
Jones, Otis L., Corp., E, 354th Inf	Mrs. Ora Burgess, Warrenton, Mo.
Jones, Walter J., Corp., E, 354th Inf	Mrs. Emma Jones, Bonne Terre, Mo.
Joyce, Harry F., Corp., C, 353rd Inf	Mrs. Julia Joyce, 214 Osage St., Leavenworth, Kan.
Kahn, Norman, Corp., G, 353rd Inf	Mrs. Mollie Kahn, Bald Eagle Lake, Minn.
Kail, Robert W., Pvt., A, 355th Inf	Thomas Kail, Highland, Wis.
Kalejak, John, Pvt., C, 314th Sup. Tr	Mrs. Hary Homehoskr, 421 Wasson St., Lackawanna, N. Y.
Kallemeyn, George E., Pvt. 1cl., A, 341st M. G. Bn	N. W. Kallemeyn, 524 E 23rd St., University Place, Neb.
Kalm, Albin L., Pvt., L, 356th Inf	Chas. H. Kalm, R. F. D. 2, White Falls, Mich.
Karastes, George, Pvt., B, 354th Inf	Mrs. Anna Karastes, Hersey, Wis.
Kasha, Henry H., Pvt., G, 353rd Inf	Wesley Kasha, R. F. D. 1, Naika, Kan.
Keane, Harry H., Pvt. 1cl., F, 354th Inf	Mrs. Elizabeth Keane, 4234½ Evans Ave., St. Louis, Mo.
Keck, Harry L., Pvt. 1cl., M, 353rd Inf	
Keeney, Clyde E., Pvt. 1cl., D, 353rd Inf	George Keeney, R. F. D. 3, Onaga, Kan.
Keeney, Fred F., Pvt., H, 356th Inf	Mrs. Lon Anna Keeney, Belton, Mo.
Keif, Charles L., Pvt., A, 355th Inf	
Kelleher, James W., Corp., M, 354th Inf	Mrs. John Harvey, 6500 Bartmer, St. Louis, Mo.
Keller, Ignatz, Pvt., E, 353rd Inf	Alois Keller, Mt. Angel, Ore.
Keller, Martin A., Pvt., I, 353rd Inf	August Keller, R. F. D. 40, Mukwonago, Wis.
Kelley, Joseph, Pvt. 1cl., G, 353rd Inf	Mrs. Leuella Nelson, 302 W. 3rd St., Paola, Kan.
Kelly, Chester T., Pvt. 1cl., C, 314th Amm. Tr	
Kelly, John J., Pvt., F, 356th Inf	Mrs. Mary E. Kelly, 1027 Louise St., New Orleans, La.
Kelsey, Floyd J., Pvt., C, 353rd Inf	Mrs. Olive Kelsey, R. F. D. 1, Tonganoxie, Kan.
Kemp, Floyd W., Pvt., Hq. 353rd Inf	James M. Kemp, 615 Alma St., St. Marys, Kan.
Kendell, George, Corp., E, 354th Inf	Henry W. Kendell, R. F. D. 8, Waukesha, Wis.
Kennedy, Leo Joseph, Pvt., Hq. 354th Inf	Miss Mary Kennedy, 4851 St. Louis Ave., St. Louis, Mo
Kenney, Edward J., Corp., M. G. Co., 356th Inf	Mrs Sarah Kenney, R. F. D. 5, Cameron, Mo.
Kennon, Raymond G., Corp., L, 354th Inf	
Kepple, Clarence G., Mech., A, 356th Inf	Mrs. Alice Kepple, Artesia, N. M.
Kessler, Edward M., Corp., F, 353rd Inf	
Kiefer, William F., Pvt., E, 354th Inf	John R. Kiefer, R. F. D. 1, St. Genevieve, Mo.
Kiely, Patrick, Pvt., L, 353rd Inf	Mrs. Caroline M. Kiely, 4537 Indiana Ave., Chicago, Ill.
Kiely, Thomas J., Pvt., E, 354th Inf	Mrs. Julia Kiely, 3141 Olive St., Kansas City, Mo.
Kierski, Walter, Pvt., B, 353rd Inf	Steve Kierski, 317 E. 119th St., Chicago, Ill.
Kindred, Ernest L., Pvt., B, 342nd M. G. Bn	
King, Clarence, Pvt., M, 353rd Inf	Mrs. Anna King, 15 E. 6th Ave, Emporia, Kan.
King, Howard S., Pvt., H, 353rd Inf	Mrs. Maggie King, 2311 G St., S. Side, Omaha, Neb.,
	c-o W. S. King, Capt. Q. M. C., Quartermaster, Ft. Benj. Harrison, Ind.
Kingery, Lloyd, Pvt., G, 356th Inf	Mrs. Francis E. Kingrey, 4418 Belleview Ave., Kansas City, Mo.
Kingsbury, La Rue S., Pvt. 1cl., C, 353rd Inf	Arthur S. Kingsbury, Smith Centre, Kan.
Kinnier, Thomas S., Corp., H, 355th Inf	James Kinnier, Primrose, Neb.
Kirschbaum, John, Pvt., A, 353rd Inf	Mrs. Kate Kirschbaum, Downs, Kan.
Kitto, Silas, Pvt., G, 354th Inf	Richard Kitto, Runningville, S. D.
Kitto, William, Pvt., L, 355th Inf	Mrs. Mary Kitto, Rockvale, Colo.
Kitzmann, August, Pvt., K, 354th Inf	Peter Kitzmann, Goodrich, Colo.
Klavun, Albert C., Pvt., A, 355th Inf	Mrs. Pauline Klavun, 2633 S. Komensky Ave., Chicago, Ill.
Klegin, Lawrence F., Pvt. 1cl., M. G. Co., 356th Inf	John L. Centlivse, Box 145, Pierce, Neb.
Kleman, Oscar, Pvt. 1cl., K, 353rd Inf	Mrs. Matilda Kleman, Bowler, Wis.
Kline, Roy C., Pvt., B, 355th Inf	Mrs. Ada B. Kline, 704 9th St., Aurora, Neb.
Kline, Wilson R., Corp., K, 353rd Inf	Samuel R. Kline, Box 277, Fleetwood, Pa.
Klonder, Walter, Pvt. 1cl., A, 355th Inf	Frank Klonder, 1622 N. Marshfield Ave., Chicago, Ill.
Klosterman, Elbert, Pvt., I, 356th Inf	
Klumker, George, Bugler, K, 354th Inf	Louis Klumker, Tonopas, Ohio
Knapp, Nicholas A., Pvt. 1cl., C, 353rd Inf	Mrs. G. W. Knapp, R. F. D. 2, Harmon, Ill.
Knobel, Roy D., Pvt., K, 355th Inf	
Knozvich, Fred, Pvt. 1cl., H, 353rd Inf	Nick Lozovich, Globe, Ariz.
Knudson, Elmer A., Wag., Sup. Co., 353rd Inf	Mrs. Mary C. Ahart, 256 W. 2nd St., Salina, Kan.
Knutson, Cournell, Pvt., M, 354th Inf	Ebert Knutson, R. F. D. 3, Blair, Wis.
Knutson, John C., Pvt., K, 355th Inf	Mrs. Martha Stoke, Fertile, Iowa
Koch, Henry J., Pvt. 1cl., L, 355th Inf	Mrs. Anna Koch, 518 S. Boston Ave., Hastings, Neb.
Koch, Otto H., Pvt. 1cl., F, 356th	Mrs. Ida Koch, Sawpington, Mo.
Koeger, Frank O., Sgt., H, 356th Inf	Clifton K. Koeger, 601 Pine St., Nevada, Mo.
Koehl, Edward F., Pvt. 1cl., L, 354th Inf	
Koenecke, Arnold E., Pvt., D, 356th Inf	Herman Koenecke, N. Freedom, Wis.
Koenig, Harold L., Pvt., C, 341st M. G. Bn	Mrs. Ada A. Burns, Wood, S. D.
Kolb, Frederick J., Pvt., I, 353rd Inf	Caroline Kolb, 723 S. 8th St., La Crosse, Wis.
Koller, Mike, Pvt., D, 355th Inf	George Koller, Blenker, Wis.
Kopang, Arthur C., Pvt., K, 353rd Inf	Ole Kopang, 1521 Williamson St., Madison, Wis.
Korff, Carl T., Pvt. 1cl., M, 355th Inf	Henry J. Korff, Hartington, Neb.
Kosakowski, John, Pvt., B, 353rd Inf	Mrs. John B. Kosakowski, 308 Ottawa St., Leavenworth, Kan.
Kosowitz, George, Pvt., I, 354th Inf	Wasili Dudzik, General Russian Counsel, Chicago, Ill.
Krabaum, Victor, Pvt. 1cl., L, 355th Inf	Mrs. Martha Krabaum, Great Bend, Kan.
Kraft, Emil A., Pvt., C, 355th Inf	Adam J. Kraft, 622 S. Church, Bellville, Ill.
Krause, Reginald, Pvt., F, 353rd Inf	Mrs. Hanna Krause, 826 10th St., Milwaukee, Wis
Kray, Frank A., Pvt., B, 354th Inf	Philip Kray, Cold Spring, Minn.
Kregger, William J., Sgt., L, 355th Inf	Mrs. John Kregger, Harvard, Neb.
Krehmeier, John, Pvt. 1cl., L, 355th Inf	Ernest Krehmeier, Monett, Mo.
Kreibaum, George F., Corp., C, 354th Inf	Mrs. Cora Kreibaum, Gerald, Mo.
Kren, Walter R., Pvt., I, 353rd Inf	Joseph Kren, 607 Altman Bldg., Kansas City, Mo.
Krewson, Otto A., Wag., F. H. 353rd, 314th San. Tr	
Kroll, Stanley, Pvt., I, 356th Inf	Mike Kroll, 1028 W. Division St., South Bend, Ind.
Kronlokken, John, Pvt., L, 353rd Inf	Miss Lillian Kronlokken, Renville, Minn.
Kruzinsky, Archie, Corp., A, 355th Inf	

Name, Rank, Company, Regiment	Emergency Address
Kuehn, Edward A., Pvt., B, 354th Inf	John D. Kuehn, Elk River, Minn.
Kuhn, Frank, Pvt., A, 356th Inf	Otto C. F. Kuhn, 2014 Clifton Ave., Chicago, Ill.
Kuykendall, Samuel A., Pvt., A, 356th Inf	
La Fleur, Ebert A., Wag., Hq. 354th Inf	Adeline La Fleur, St. Genevieve, Mo.
La Font, Elmer, Pvt., Hq. 354th Inf	Mrs Emma Gogean, Portageville, Mo.
Lafrenz, Julius H., Corp., K, 355th Inf	Cris. A. Lafrenz, Tekamah, Neb.
Lages, Anthony, Pvt., D, 354th Inf	Peter Lages, Kavno, Staith, Vilkeergas, Pavets, pac Staic, Kupiski Mest, Vestintai, Lazus, Jilvidzai, Russia
Lamb, Ray T., Pvt. 1cl., D, 342nd M. G. Bn	Mrs. Minnie Lamb, Gen. Del., Bloomfield, Neb.
Lambert, Leroy P., Corp., L, 353rd Inf	James A. Lambert, Montana, Kan.
Lamont, Earl A., Pvt., Hq. 355th Inf	Mrs. Minerva H. Lamont, De Smet, S. D.
Lawson, Dwight F., Pvt. G, 353rd Inf	
Lampe, Chris H., Pvt., E, 354th Inf	William Lampe, R. F. D. 1, Collis, Minn.
Landry, Sylvain, Pvt., Hq. 355th Inf	Desire Landry, Belle Rose, La.
Lane, Donald C., Pvt., M, 353rd Inf	Charles Lane, Gen. Del., Quincy, Kan.
Lane, Grover E., Pvt. 1cl., Hq. 354th Inf	
Lang, Accina E., Pvt. 1cl., Hq. 340th F. A	
Langan, Charles P., Corp., B, 356th Inf	
Langdon, Roy V., Pvt., A, 355th Inf	Mrs. Mary Langdon, 245 Northeast Iak St., Resburg, Wis.
Langkamp, Edward I., Pvt., I, 356th Inf	
Lanning, Maurice, Pvt. 1cl., M. G. Co., 354th Inf	Mrs. Florence Lanning, Cozad, Neb.
Lantis, Leo, Corp., F, 353rd Inf	Levi Lantis, R. F. D. 3, Ottawa, Kan.
Larson, Edward H., Sgt., H, 355th Inf	Mrs. H. Larson, Genoa, Neb.
Larson, Rudolph A., Corp., D, 356th Inf	Lars Larson, Highmore, S. D.
Lasher, Arthur E., Pvt., A, 341st M. G. Bn	Thomas J. Lasher, Louisburg, Mo.
Latty, Mernie C., Pvt., B, 354th Inf	Miss Edith Latty, New Bloomfield, Mo.
Lauber, Clarence E., Pvt., I, 356th Inf	Mrs. Elsie Porter, Richmond, Ohio
Laune, Raymond, Corp., M, 354th Inf	Bertha F. Norton, Wendte, S. D.
Lautenslager, Andrew, Corp., A, 355th Inf	Mrs. Mary Avers, 905 4th St., Reading, Ohio
Lawrence, Edward J., Wag., Sup. Co., 354th Inf	
Lawson, George L., Pvt., L, 354th Inf	George Lawson, McGregor, Colo.
Lee, Herbert, Pvt., G, 354th Inf	Mrs. Elen Lee, Depoy, Ky.
Lee, Fred D., Sgt., B, 342nd M. G. Bn	
Lee, Lonnie J., Pvt., D, 341st M. G. Bn	David O. Lee, 1512 Brown Ave., Norfolk, Va.
Lee, Victor C., Sgt., H, 355th Inf	
Leibel, Albert, Pvt., A, 355th Inf	Henry Leibel, Campbellsport, Wis.
Lemanski, Peter, Pvt., C, 353rd Inf	Stani Lamanski, 2822 Edwards St., Pittsburgh, Pa.
Leonard, David F., Pvt., A, 354th Inf	Robert A. Leonard, R. F. D. 1, Rookins, Mo.
Lepore, Louis, Pvt., B, 354th Inf	Dominico Lapore, Provo Ovellins, Prata P. U., Italy
Lesicur, Freamon E., Wag., Sup. Co., 355th Inf	Charles L. Lesieur, R. F. D. 1, Clarkston, Mo.
Lesley, Chester R., Pvt., L, 354th Inf	William McCarthy, 2210 Station St., Indianapolis, Ind.
Lessert, Roy, Pvt. 1cl., G, 355th Inf	
Leul, Ralph C., Sgt., B, 341st M. G. Bn	Joseph Leul, Gen. Del., Comstock, Neb.
Levingston, John, Pvt., A, 354th Inf	John W. Livingston, R. R. 1, Advance, Mo.
Levy, Joseph, Pvt., D, 353rd Inf	Edward Block, 2909 W. Walton St., Chicago, Ill.
Lewelling, Merle T., Corp., E, 356th Inf	Wm. Penn Lewelling, Larned, Kan.
Lewellyn, Vernie D., Pvt., 314th San. Tr	Mrs. Mary McNeff, Lawrence, Kan.
Lewis, Howard M., Pvt., L, 353rd Inf	Mrs. Helen Lewis, 908 Lipan St., Denver, Colo.
Lewis, Taylor E., Sgt., L, 355th Inf	Mrs. Irene Lewis, Superior, Neb.
Libera, George A., Pvt. 1cl., B, 341st M. G. Bn	Mrs. Albert P. Libera, 1176 W. 4th St., Winona, Minn.
Liberatore, Francescho, Pvt., B, 354th Ind	Pasquale Liberatore, Box 14, Belgium, Wis.
Liebman, Joseph, Pvt., G, 354th Inf	Sam Liebman, 2621 E. 34th St., Kansas City, Mo.
Lilly, Clownie W., Pvt., B, 354th Inf	Russell C. Read, Ricksville, Va.
Limback, Gustav G., Pvt., D, 342nd F. A	
Linden, Elmer, Pvt. 1cl., C, 314th F. S. Bn	Klas Linden, 258 Brunson St., Benton Harbor, Mich.
Lindhorst, Henry J., Pvt., B, 353rd Inf	Fred Lindhorst, Vernon, Wis.
Lindner, Henry E., Pvt., A, 342nd M. G. Bn	Mrs. Emile Lindner, 2914 West St., Omaha, Neb.
Lindstrom, Walter R., Pvt., M. G. Co., 353rd Inf	
Linehan, Walter J., Sgt., B, 354th Inf	Mrs. Ida Schroeder, 1037½ W. 2nd St., Davenport, Iowa
Lines, Henry R., Corp., Hq. 341st F. A	Mrs. Henry R. Lines, 416 E Street, Salida, Colo.
Linnell, Paul D., Pvt., M. G. Co., 356th Inf	Mrs. Paul D. Linnell, Junction City, Kan.
Lipsitz, Henry, Pvt., A, 355th Inf	Jacob Lipsitz, R. F. D. 8, Grand Rapids, Mich.
Lisle, Samuel V., Pvt., L, 353rd Inf	Thos. L. Lisle, Bunger, Tex.
Little, John, Pvt. 1cl., B, 342nd M. G. Bn	Mrs. Helen Little, Gen. Del., Winner, S. D.
Litton, Patrick D., Pvt., F, 356th Inf	Mrs. Geo. W. Litton, R. F. D. 1, Potosi, Mo.
Livingston, Glen S., Pvt., C, 356th Inf	Mrs. Susan A. Livingston, Kanapolis, Kan.
Lockman, Henry, Wag., C, 314th Amm. Tr	
Lockwood, Emery C., Pvt., M, 353rd Inf	Frank C. Lockwood, De Quoin, Kan.
Loftus, Michael, Corp., H, 354th Inf	Mrs. Mary Loftus, 4267 Wyoming St., St. Louis, Mo.
Loftus, Patrick J., Pvt. 1cl., E, 314th Amm. Tr	Miss Maiek Loftus, Minneapolis Block, Pueblo, Colo.
London, Marcus L., Pvt., Hq. 353rd Inf	Charley London, R. R. 3, Tarkio, Mo.
Long, William H., Cook, A, 314th Eng	Arthur Long, Routt Co., Dunkley, Colo.
Longenecker, Claude, Pvt. L, 353rd Inf	
Lontkowsky, Frank A., Pvt. 1cl., C, 353rd Inf	Mrs. Kath. Lontkowsky, 1609 N. Grand Ave., Pittsburg, Kan.
Lott, Fred G., Corp., E, 354th Inf	Mrs. Sarah G. Lott, 117 S. Lawn St., Kansas City, Mo.
Love, Cramer C., Pvt., L, 353rd Inf	Mrs. Ophelia Love, Somerton, Ariz.
Lovelady, Grant, Pvt., K, 353rd Inf	Earl Schlect, R. F. D. 2, Belmar, Neb.
Lovell, Norman E., Pvt., D, 341st M. G. Bn	Sylvenus O. Lovell, Springfield, Neb.
Lowder, John C., Pvt. 1cl., E, 354th Inf	Mrs. Tallie Lowder, 3025 E. State St., Kansas City, Mo.
Loy, Willie A., Pvt., F, 355th Inf	Mrs. Geo. Loy, Heiskell, Tenn.
Lucas, Clarence D., Pvt. 1cl., C, 353rd Inf	Frank Lucas, Nashville, Kan.
Lucero, Henry, Pvt., G, 355th Inf	Mrs. Eliza Lucero, Redmesa, Colo.
Lundquist, John A., Corp., B, 342nd M. G. Bn	
Ludwig, Harry L., Corp., I, 354th Inf	Mrs. Anna Ludwig, 3007A Ohio Ave., St. Louis, Mo.
Ludwig, Charles, Corp., M, 354th Inf	
Ludy, Chance, Pvt., C, 356th Inf	Ed. Ludy, Arcanum, Ohio
Lundberg, Hans M., Pvt., C, 354th Inf	Mrs. Marie Lundberg, Dyste, P. O. Box 31, Hartland, Minn.
Lyon, Earl C., Corp., M, 353rd Inf	Mrs. Hattie Lyon, Gen. Del., Lincoln, Kan.
Lyon, Earl Henry, Pvt., M. G. Co., 354th Inf	Mrs. Bessie L. Lyon, 1536 E. 32nd Ave., Denver, Colo.
Lyons, Michael, Pvt., K, 356th Inf	Raymond Lyons, 2147 Osgood St., Chicago, Ill.

Name, Rank, Company, Regiment	Emergency Address
Mabee, Harold H., Sgt., C, 342nd M. G. Bn	Mrs. Rose E. Mabee, Parker, South Dakota
Mack, Joseph A., Pvt., B, 353rd Inf	Mrs. Myrtle Mack, 330 N. James St., Kansas City, Mo.
Mackeprang, Henry, Corp., F, 355th Inf	Carl Mackeprang, Petersdorf Dansehendorf, Germany
Madrid, Agatito, Pvt. 1cl., G, 356th Inf	Ramon Madrid, Arroyo, Seco, N. M.
Madrid, Jose E., Pvt., G, 356th Inf	Tesserita Madrid, Pagosa Junction, Colo.
Maguire, James, Pvt., B, 354th Inf	Mrs. Margaret Maguire, R. F. D. 2, Damey, Wis.
Malliet, Edward J., Pvt., B, 354th Inf	Jule Malliet, Bear Creek, Wis.
Manfre, Charles, Corp., G, 354th Inf	Vincent Manfre, 119 N. Quincy St., Kansas City, Mo.
Mankel, John, Sgt., D, 354th Inf	
Mann, Louis H., Pvt., E, 355th Inf	Mrs. Mary E. Mann, Humboldt, Neb.
Manner, Peter, Pvt., Hq. 356th Inf	
Mannion, Thomas P., Corp., M, 354th Inf	Mary Mannion, 3851 Maffitt St., St. Louis, Mo.
Mantle, Thomas E., Pvt., B, 342nd M. G. Bn	Mrs. Annie Mantle, Lane, Mo.
Marchbank, Charles O., Corp., D, 342nd F. A	Steve Marchbank, Van Buren, Mo.
Marcus, Tom, Cook, A, 314th Eng	George Vellios, 6658 Manchester Ave., St. Louis, Mo.
Margarito, Vrarial, Pvt., F, 356th Inf	
Marshall, Earl C., Pvt., Hq. 353rd Inf	Mrs. Matilda W. Marshall, 117 S. 4th St., Arkansas City, Kan.
Marshall, Frederick A., Corp., E, 354th Inf	Mrs. Edna McIlvain, Smith Center, Kan.
Marshall, Harold D., Pvt., E, 355th Inf	Mrs. Charlotte Marshall, Weeping Water, Neb.
Martin, Alva L., Pvt. 1cl., M. G. Co., 356th Inf	Sherman W. Martin, R. F. D. 1, Middletown, Mo.
Martin, Charles F., Pvt., H, 355th Inf	
Martin, Clyde R., Pvt. 1cl., 356th Inf	Dora Martin, 1507 Irving St., Springfield, Mo.
Martin, Leroy, Sgt., G, 353rd Inf	Mrs. Matilda Martin, Atlanta, Kan.
Martin, William J., Pvt., I, 356th Inf	
Martinez, Alexjandro, Pvt., C, 356th Inf	Mrs. Lusita C. De Martinez, Las Vegas, N. M.
Massengill, Daniel P., Pvt. 1cl., M. G. Co., 356th Inf	Wm. T. Massengill, Edgerton, Neb.
Massey, Charles A., Corp., L, 354th Inf	
Matson, Arvid, Pvt., E, 341st F. A	John Matson, R. F. D. 2, Sebika, Minn.
Matthews, Charles E., Pvt., L, 356th Inf	
Matthews, George, Corp., F, 355th Inf	Mrs. Hattie Matthews, 2345A Ecoff, St. Louis, Mo.
Matthews, James I., Pvt. 1cl., 349th Bakery Co.	James Houston Matthews, Prosser, Wash.
Mattison, William A., Pvt., C, 353rd Inf	Louis Mattison, R. F. D. 2, Box 69, Spring Valley, Mo.
Maupin, Amos, Corp., M. G. Co., 354th Inf	Mrs. Ida Magin, 906 N. Lynor St., Independence, Mo.
McAdams, Wallace J., Corp., L, 356th Inf	Mrs. Sarah B. McAdams, 103 W. Burkhartle St., Moberly, Mo.
McAllister, James L., Bn. Sgt. Maj., Hq. Co., 356th Inf	
McAfee, John W., Corp., D, 356th Inf	James H. McAfee, Gallatin, Mo.
McCabe, Cornelius B., Pvt., C, 354th Inf	Mrs. Mabel F. McCabe, 1208 O Ave., E. Oskaloosa, La.
McCann, Edgar, Bugler, L, 354th Inf	Mrs. Ida McCann, Monroe City, Mo.
McCarren, Andrew J., Pvt., G, 353rd Inf	
McClanahan, Thomas I., Pvt. 1cl., A, 341st M. G. Bn	Alexander McClanahan, R. F. D. 1, Payette, Idaho
McClendon, Madge, Pvt., H, 354th Inf	
McCloskey, Purley E., Corp., A, 353rd Inf	Mrs. Blanch McCloskey, Agra, Kan.
McCloughan, Lester L., Pvt. 1cl., K, 355th Inf	John L. McCloughan, Allerton, Iowa
McComb, Roy E., Sgt., M. G. Co., 356th Inf	Ruth A. McComb, Cameron, Mo.
McCormick, Martin K., Pvt., G, 354th Inf	Mrs. Anna McCormick, Benson, Minn.
McCoy, Albert, Pvt. 1cl., F, 356th Inf	Mrs. Stella Trommele, Box 83, Baxter, Kan.
McCoy, Kenneth L., Pvt., F, 354th Inf	
McCollough, Floyd L., Pvt. 1cl., H, 353rd Inf	Mrs. Floyd McCollough, Cherryvale, Kan.
McCullock, Willis L., Pvt., Hq. 355th Inf	John G. McCullock, Duncan, Ariz.
McCune, Clarence, Pvt., Hq. 340th M. G. Bn	Oscar McCune, R. F. D. 5, Mitchell, South Dakota
McDaniel, Guy F., Pvt., G, 353rd Inf	Mrs. Celia McDaniel, Sabetha, Kan.
McDaniel, Lee B., Sgt., A, 353rd Inf	C. J. Boyd, Columbus, Kan.
McDonald, Carrol A., Pvt. 1cl., K, 355th Inf	Charles J. McDonald, Wall, South Dakota
McDonald, Chester, Pvt. 1cl., Hq. 353rd Inf	Samuel McDonald, Howard, Kan.
McDonald, George R., Corp., H, 354th Inf	
McDonald, Ralph C., Pvt., E, 353rd Inf	Mrs. Minnie McDonald, Logan, Kan.
McElfish, Roy C., Pvt., 314th San. Tr	Cora McElfish, Princeton, Mo.
McElwain, Harley H., Pvt., M, 355th Inf	Wm. H. McElwain, Bailey, Neb.
McEntoffer, Harry M., Pvt., C, 341st M. G. Bn	
McFadden, Odus E., Cook, C, 355th Inf	Grayson E. McFadden, Mesa, Ariz.
McGarry, John J., Pvt. 1cl., B, 356th Inf	Catherine McGarry, Bedison, Mo.
McGowan, Frank T., Pvt., B, 356th Inf	Tom McGowan, 1444 N. 22nd St., St. Louis, Mo.
McGrew, Laverne, Pvt., Hq. 355th Inf	C. E. McGrew, Ord, Neb.
McIntosh, Dan, Pvt., 1cl., M, 355th Inf	
McIntosh, James H., Pvt., L, 355th Inf	Harry H. McIntosh, 509 S. Oak St., Trinidad, Colo.
McIntyre, James E., Pvt., C, 314th F. S. Bn	John McIntyre, R. F. D. 3, Punxsugawnly, Pa.
McKenna, Edward A., Pvt., I, 353rd Inf	Miss Mollie McKenna, 4639 Evans, Chicago, Ill.
McKenna, Hugh A., Pvt., A, 355th Inf	Mrs. Jane McKenna, 705 Oakton St., Evanston, Ill.
McKim, Elza, Corp., B, 340th M. G. Bn	
McKnight, Luther T., Pvt., A, 356th Inf	Johnnie McKnight, Lorenzo, Texas
McLain, John B., Pvt., I, 355th Inf	Harry A. Kessler, Riverton, Neb.
McNabb, Evean G., Pvt., I, 355th Inf	Mrs. W. L. Hudson, R. R. 2, Decatur, Texas
McNeal, Edgar L., Corp., G, 356th Inf	Mrs. Minnie McNeal, Odessa, Mo.
McNeeley, Theodore L., Pvt., L, 353rd Inf	Mrs. Flenora McNeeley, 202 Branner St., Topeka, Kan.
McNulty, Thomas J., Pvt., B, 314th M. S. T	Mrs. Samuel Christie, 795 Glenwood Ave., Detroit, Mich.
McNutt, George, Pvt., C, 356th Inf	Frank McNutt, Palmyra, Neb.
McVey, William C., Corp., G, 354th Inf	Mrs. Emma McVey, 2632A Park Ave., St. Louis, Mo.
McVey, Charles F., Pvt., A, 341st M. G. Bn	
Meador, Ruel, Pvt., B, 356th Inf	
Medigovich, Sam P., Pvt. 1cl., B, 340th F. A	Vasco P. Medigovich, Pertleville, Ariz.
Medlin, John W., Pvt., A, 341st M. G. Bn	Fait Medlin, R. F. D. 1, Marionville, Mo.
Meehan, Lambert C., Pvt., Hq. 354th Inf	Michael J. Meehan, 1268 Goodfellow Ave., St. Louis, Mo.
Melton, Buff E., Corp., A, 355th Inf	Everett Melton, R. F. D. 1, Simpson, Kan.
Mende, Clarence A., Sgt., Hq. 355th Inf	Mrs. Christian Mende, 1940 Garfield St., Lincoln, Neb.
Mendel, Ernest H., Pvt., E, 354th Inf	Peter Mendel, Metz, Mo.
Mendenhall, Elmer, Pvt., B, 342nd M. G. Bn	Willis Mendenhall, Dayton, Idaho
Menzel, Edward, Pvt., B, 354th Inf	Mrs. Bessie Menzel, Box 366, Hopkins, Minn.
Merriam Charles P., Pvt., M. G. Co., 354th Inf	Mrs. Louise I. Merriam, 735 S. Adams St., Pueblo, Colo.
Metcalf, Grant E., Pvt. 1cl., C, 353rd Inf	Mrs. Grace Mathias, Sterling, Ill.
Metzker, William H., Pvt., L, 353rd Inf	Frank L. Metzker, Coldwater, Kan.

Name, Rank, Company, Regiment	Emergency Address
Meyer, Frank W., Pvt., F, 353rd Inf	Bernard Meyer, R. F. D. 1, Belpre, Kan.
Meyer, Henry, Pvt., B, 340th M. G. Bn	Mrs. Fannie Meyer, R. F. D. 2, Castlewood, South Dakota
Meyers, Harry E., Corp., E, 314th Eng	William Meyers, Preston, Neb.
Meyers, Raymond, Pvt., 314th San. Tr.	William Meyers, Route 7, Brookville, Ind.
Michalski, John, Pvt., H, 354th Inf	Mrs. Freda Michalski, 1645 W. 17th St., Chicago, Ill.
Michie, John, Corp., A, 355th Inf	Adam Michie, R F. D. 1, Fort Collins, Colo.
Michelson, Clarence A., Sup. Co., 355th Inf	E Michelson, Blackearth, Wis.
Miers, Clarence F., Pvt., D, 353rd Inf	Roy Walworth, Towanda, Kan.
Mikolajewski, John, Pvt., C, 356th Inf	Mrs. Francisco Mikolajewski, Sumpolno Gub Kaliska, Russia
Milan, James L., Corp., K, 356th Inf	Mrs. Sarah Milan, Lees Summit, Mo.
Milbourne, Charles E., Pvt., B, 354th Inf	Mrs. Alice Milbourne, 221 Colorado Ave., St. Joseph, Mo.
Miller, Charles D., Pvt., D, 353rd Inf	Mrs. John Miller, Ellsworth, Kan.
Miller, Clyde C., Pvt. 1cl., B, 356th Inf	Ida May Drawn, Seneca, Kan.
Miller, Conrad E., Pvt., C, 354th Inf	Ben Miller, R. F. D. 3, Calumet, Okla.
Miller, Daniel W., Pvt., C, 355th Inf	Mrs. Lydia Miller, R. F. D. 1, Swiss, Mo.
Miller, Frank, Pvt, Hq. 355th Inf	
Miller, Felix A., Pvt., C, 341st F. A.	
Miller, Jerald L., Pvt., L, 353rd Inf	Mrs. Minta Mullenueix, 1900 E. 10th St., Wichita, Kan.
Miller, Peter, Pvt., I, 355th Inf	Conrad Miller, R. F. D. 2, Harvard Neb.
Miller, Lloyd C., Corp., D, 342nd M. G. Bn	
Miller, Ernest C., Pvt., A, 356th Inf	
Millet, Charles, Pvt., K, 356th Inf	Marie Millet, Plauquemine, La.
Mills, Elbert F., Pvt., K, 355th Inf	Mrs. Olive D. Mills, Akron, Iowa
Mintert, Frederick W., Pvt. 1cl., Hq. 354th Inf	John Mintert, R. F. D. 1, West Alton, Mo.
Mislivek, Frank, Pvt., E, 355th Inf	Mrs. Anna Mislivek, 1822 O St., Omaha, Neb.
Mitchell, Calvin B., Sgt., Hq. 354th Inf	Mrs. Susan C. Mitchell, 1112 Hodiamont Ave., St. Louis, Mo.
Mitchell, Dorsey E., Corp., D, 354th Inf	
Mitchell, James O., Corp., B, 353rd Inf	Mrs. Jermina Mitchell, 2755 W. Adams St., Chicago, Ill.
Mittlat, William, Pvt., E, 341st F. A.	Mrs. Anna Mittlat, 146 N. 3rd St., Brooklyn, N. Y.
Monk, Martin J., Pvt., A, 353rd Inf	Mrs. Arabella Kreviers, North Kaupkanna, Wis.
Montgomery, Frank, Pvt., K, 354th Inf	Pandy U. Montgomery, Sheldon, Mo.
Montoya, Philip B., Pvt., L, 354th Inf	Mrs. Estefanito B. Montoya, Las Vegas, N. M.
Mooney, Fred W., Pvt., A, 353rd Inf	James D. Mooney, R. F. D. 9, Blue Mound, Kan.
Moore, David M., Sup. Sgt., F, 353rd Inf	Mrs. Ruth Moore, Stromsberg, Neb.
Moore, Ernest L., Pvt., A, 342nd M. G. Bn	
Moore, John A., Pvt. 1cl., H, 354th Inf	
Morgan, Oral M., Pvt., Hq. 354th Inf	Hattie V. Morgan, R. F. D. 28, Urich, Mo.
Morgan, Riley, Pvt., C, 355th Inf	Mrs. Lucinda Morgan, Malden, Mo.
Morgonstern, Sam, Sgt., G, 354th Inf	Jacob Morgonstern, 1426½ N. 18th St., St. Louis, Mo.
Morris, Jacob B., Pvt., D, 355th Inf	Thomas Morris, R. F. D. 1, Walton, Ky.
Morris, John T., Pvt. 1cl., M. G. Co., 356th Inf	John W. Morris, R. F. D. 2, St. Paul, Kan.
Morris, Joseph S., Corp., C, 340th F. A.	
Morrison, Rodney G., Pvt. 1cl., A, 341st M. G. Bn	Mrs. Daisy Morrison, 515 South St., Iola, Kan.
Moyer, Howard W., Pvt. 1cl., B, 342nd M. G. Bn	John T. Moyer, Virginville, Pa.
Muchneck, Abe, Pvt. 1cl., A, 341st M. G. Bn	Asher Muchneck, 1563 St. Clare Ave., E. St. Louis, Mo.
Mueller, Louis E., Pvt., F, 355th Inf	
Mueller, Paul G., Pvt., E, 353rd Inf	Mrs. Emma Achs, 2103A Withnell Ave., St. Louis, Mo.
Muhovich, Pohn, Pvt., Hq. 355th Inf	John Muhovich, Sr., Walsen, Colo.
Munkres, Richard B., Corp., Hq. 356th Inf	Mrs. Anna Munkres, Savanah, Mo.
Munson, Lewis, Pvt., M. G. Co., 353rd Inf	Charles Nelson, Box 58, R. F. D. 1, Spencer, Wis.
Murphy, Joseph M., Corp., G, 353rd Inf	
Murray, Ewell C., Pvt., B, 356th Inf	Geo. Murray, Box 59, Amite, La.
Murry, Henry R., Pvt., C, 355th Inf	Mrs. Henry Murry, Richland, Mo.
Nachtman, Frank, Pvt. 1cl., F, 355th Inf	James Nachtman, Perchville, Neb.
Nagel, Benjamin J., Pvt., B, 342nd M. G. Bn	Joseph Nagel, R. F. D. 1, Stratton, Colo.
Nathan, James, Pvt. 1cl., Med. Det., 353rd Inf	Mrs. Della Nathan, 1094 Union Ave., Memphis, Tenn.
Nelson, Joseph W., Pvt. 1cl., C, 354th Inf	Otto Nelson, R. F. D. 4, Barrington, Ill.
Nester, Albert C., Pvt., F, 355th Inf	Mrs. Hanna Nester, 502 Walnut St., Maryville, Kan.
New, Roy O., Pvt., C, 353rd Inf	Thomas New, R. F. D. 2, Mound City, Kan.
Newberry, Sylvester, Pvt., E, 354th Inf	Geo. H. Newberry, Richland, Mo.
Newman, Elmer L., Corp., K, 355th Inf	Michael J. Newman, New Diggings, Wis.
Newman, Thomas, Pvt., Med. Det., 355th Inf	Wm. Schuessler, Gen. Del., Newkirk, Okla.
Neely, Charles V., Pvt., H. 354th Inf	
Nichols, Earl, Corp., A, 356th Inf	Mrs. Neva F. Nichols, Davenport, Neb.
Niederjohann, Arnold H., C, 356th Inf	Henry Niederjohann, New Melle, Mo.
Niederjohn, Louis M., D, 354th Inf	Henry C. Niederjohn, Waverly, Mo.
Nielson, George C. S., Pvt., M. G. Co., 355th Inf	
Nielson, Lauritz, Pvt., F, 353rd Inf	Anton B. Grobeck, 1708 Van Camp Ave., Omaha, Neb.
Nighbor, Anton L., Pvt., M, 354th Inf	Mrs. Frances Nighbor, 1003 Webster St., Berlin, Wis.
Nilson, Carl, Pvt., K, 356th Inf	August Nilson, Oasio, Wis.
Nissen, Jens A. W., Pvt., B, 355th Inf	
Nixon, Willis G., Pvt. 1cl., I, 353rd Inf	Mrs. Barbara E. Nixon, Medicine Lodge, Kan.
Noll, Merle A., Pvt., H, 356th Inf	Mr. William T. Noll, Lowry City, Mo.
Norris, Claude A., Pvt., M, 353rd Inf	Bert E. Norris, R. F. D. 1, South Haven, Kan.
North, Phillip C., Pvt., L, 356th Inf	Wm. North, 1917 W. 32nd Ave., Denver, Colo.
Nowiekaitys, James J., Pvt., B, 356th Inf	Carl Nowiekaitys, 2931 Milwaukee Ave., Chicago, Ill.
Nuce, Joe A., Pvt., F, 353rd Inf	Mrs. Mary J. Nuce, 406 Vine St., Dodge City Kan.
Nunn, Burrell S., Pvt., B, 356th Inf	Wm. R. Nunn, Buffalo, Mo.
Nunn, Harry W., Pvt., H, 354th Inf	James N. Nunn, Mill Springs, Mo.
Nutter, Lloyd K., Pvt., B, 341st M. G. Bn	Jacob H. Nutter, Nutterville, W. Va.
Nutz, Theodore E., Pvt., C, 353rd Inf	Mrs. Minnie Nutz, 224 Lowman St., Fort Scott, Kan.
Oakes, Arthur A., Pvt., Hq. 354th Inf	Earl E. Oakes, Decorah, Iowa
Oberg, Emil W., Pvt., E, 354th Inf	
O'Connell, Dennis, Pvt., C, 355th Inf	Mrs. Mary O'Connell, 1337 Graham Ave., St. Louis, Mo.
O'Connor, Frank J., Corp., E, 353rd Inf	Mrs. Lillian O'Connor, 2222 W. Monroe St., Chicago, Ill.
O'Farrell, John A., Pvt., E, 356th Inf	
Ohm, Albert, E, 353rd Inf	Mrs. Herman Ohm, R. F. D. 5, Box 53, Albert Lea, Minn.
Ohrn, Nyort L., Pvt., C, 354th Inf	Mrs. Albertine Anderson, 2315 18th St. B, Moline, Ill.
Oliver, John M., Pvt., E, 355th Inf	Steve B. Oliver, R. F. D. 1, Cabot, Ark.
Oliver, Ray M., Pvt., C, 356th Inf	Mrs. Mattie L. Oliver, 3366 Gillham Road, Kansas City, Mo.

Name, Rank, Company, Regiment	Emergency Address
Olmstead, Cortes R., Pvt., I, 353rd Inf	Alden Olmstead, Gen. Del., Great Falls, Mont.
Olsen, Harry T., Pvt. 1cl., C, 354th Inf	Mrs. Bertha Olsen, 1250 Kalamath St., Denver, Colo.
Olsen, Clarence, Pvt., F, 355th Inf	
Olson, Carl K., Pvt., I, 354th Inf	Ole K. Olson, R. F. D. 2, Elbow Lake, Minn.
Olson, Edward, Pvt., D, 353rd Inf	Mrs. Julia Olson, Market St., De Forest, Wis.
Oncale, Bernard F., Pvt., Hq. 355th Inf	Sylvain Oncale, Labadieville, La.
Orcine, Harry, Pvt., K, 354th Inf	Domenick Orcine, 2335 Pine St., Boulder, Colo.
Ordway, Frederick E., Sgt., K, 356th Inf	Helen P. Ordway, Marshall, Mo.
Osness, Henry O., Pvt., G, 355th Inf	Daniel Stolsmark, Pierpont, South Dakota
Ostlund, Andrew J., Pvt., G, 354th Inf	Hilda Gustafsen, 803 Battle Ave., Cleveland, Ohio
Osthoff, Leo H., Pvt., D, 354th Inf	Henry Ostoff, Wellington, Mo.
Ott, Alfred B., Pvt., F, 356th Inf	Mrs. Minnie Biszak, 1135 S. Fairfield Ave., Chicago, Ill.
Owen, Henry Harlan, Pvt., D, 353rd Inf	Mrs. Elizabeth Owen, Fulton, Kan.
Owens, Thomas, Pvt. 1cl., F, 356th Inf	Miss Gavella Owens, 415 Cherokee, Leavenworth, Kan.
Pace, Oren C., Sgt., F, 356th Inf	M. G. Pace, Ashland, Mo.
Padgett, George, Pvt., C, 314th F. S. Bn	Mrs. Ella W. Padgett, 3419 E. Baltimore St., Baltimore, Md.
Painter, Charles E., Pvt., C, 355th Inf	John W. Painter, R. F. D. 1, Hornersville, Mo.
Palka, Whydsaw, Pvt. 1cl., C, 355th Inf	
Palmer, George S., Pvt., K, 355th Inf	Hiram J. Palmer, 716 W. 3rd St., Grand Island, Neb.
Palmer, Harry C., Corp., B, 355th Inf	
Palmer, Leroy G., Cook, B, 341st F. A.	Mrs. Macey Walker, 2614 Race St., Denver, Colo.
Palo, Matt E., Pvt. 1cl. L, 355th Inf	Jacob Palo, Fruitdale, South Dakota
Park, James R., Pvt., B, 356th Inf	
Parker, Arthur R., Pvt., M, 356th Inf	Mrs. Marion C. Cook, Duquoin, Ill.
Parker, John L., Pvt. 1cl., D, 354th Inf	J. M. Parker, Hayden, Mo.
Parker, William P., Pvt., B, 356th Inf	John Parker, Boyce, La.
Parsons, William F., Corp., I, 353rd Inf	Ben Fitzsimmons, Red Rock, Ariz.
Pascoe, Wm. T., Pvt. 1cl., K, 355th Inf	Wm. H. Pascoe, R. F. D. 1, Parker, South Dakota
Passeri, Angelos, Pvt., G, 354th Inf	Lenardo Barnelli, 109 Basdtow St., Waukesha, Wis.
Pate, Aubie U., Pvt., B, 356th Inf	J. S. Pate, Mooringsport, La.
Patrick, Frank J., Hq. 356th Inf	Frank Patrick, Minden Mines, Mo.
Patterson, Duncan J., Pvt., B, 353rd Inf	
Paul, Edward R., Pvt., A, 355th Inf	Mrs. George Hardy, Pearl River, N. Y.
Paul, Fritz R., Chauffeur, Sup. Det., 314th F. C. Bn	Robert Paul, R. F. D. 3, Kimmswick, Mo.
Paustian, Otto H., Pvt., L, 353rd Inf	Henry W. Paustian, 639 Blunt St., Clay Center, Kan.
Payne, Frank F., Cook, F, 354th Inf	
Payne, James L., Pvt., I, 355th Inf	Mrs. Minnie E. Payne, Bridgeport, Neb.
Pearson, Floy, Corp., F, 356th Inf	
Peck, Frederick L., Corp., A, 341st M. G. Bn	Mrs. Mary L. Peck, 17 N. 26th St., Omaha, Neb.
Peck, Ruben L., Pvt., L, Inf	John F. Peck, Belle Foche, South Dakota
Peck, William R., Sgt., C, 354th Inf	Chas. S. Peck, Washburn, Wis.
Pederson, Christopher, Pvt., G, 355th Inf	
Pelleter, Joseph, Pvt., G, 354th Inf	Mrs. Mary D. Pelleter, 1847 Lincoln St., Denver, Colo.
Pender, Joseph L., Pvt., H, 355th Inf	Mrs. Emily Pender, Ainsworth, Neb.
Peninger, Ira A., Pvt., E., 355th Inf	Uriah Peninger, Valpariso, Neb.
Pennock, Joseph, Pvt., M, 354th Inf	Albert Pennock, 610 N. 7th St., Louisiana, Mo.
Perkins, Oscar T., Pvt., M, 353rd Inf	
Perron, Liquori A., B, 353rd Inf	Mrs. Helen Perron, Mendota, Minn.
Perry, Fred L., Pvt., D, 342nd M. G. Bn	Miss Claire Perry, 3096 S. Lincoln St., Denver, Colo.
Peterman, John R., Pvt., H, 354th Inf	Mrs. August Peterman, R. R. 32, Campbellsport, Wis.
Peterson, Nels J., Pvt., M, 353rd Inf	Adolph Anderson, 4009 Wirth St., Omaha, Neb.
Peterson, Ludwig, Pvt., G, 355th Inf	Paul Peterson, Burbank, South Dakota
Peterson, Martin E., Pvt., M, 353rd Inf	
Peterson, Nels, Pvt. 1cl., G, 355th Inf	Nels Hanson, R. F. D. 1, Parker, South Dakota
Pfaff, Jesse L., Pvt., G, 356th Inf	Hubert Pfaff, R. F. D. 1, Willmathseville, Mo.
Phelps, Paul C., Mech., B, 356th Inf	Mary Vance, Peru, Ind.
Phillips, Clyde R., Pvt., A, 356th Inf	Dr. J. L. Philips, Glenmora, La.
Phillips, Walter T., Pvt., I, 355th Inf	George G. Thompson, Freedom, Neb.
Phillips, Cyrus E., Pvt., I, 354th Inf	Pearl C. Phillips, 1658 Jefferson St., Kansas City, Mo.
Phillips, Ray M., Corp., E, 314th Eng	Frank H. Phillips, 3624 Cambridge Ave., Rosedale, Kan.
Piepmeyer, Bernard R., Pvt. 1cl., L, 354th Inf	Mrs. Theresa Piepmeyer, 517 N. Center St., Collinsville, Ill.
Phillips, John, Corp., G, 354th Inf	
Phipps, Clyde R., Pvt. 1cl., K, 356th Inf	
Pierce, Harry A., Pvt., B, 354 Inf	Mrs. Ida Pierce, 510 N. Prospect, Kansas City, Mo.
Pierce, Lester R., Pvt. 1cl., H, 354th Inf	Mrs. Jennie Pierce, 118 S. Whitcomb St., Fort Collins, Colo.
Pike, Raymond A., Pvt. 1cl., L, 355th Inf	Allison E. Pike, Fairfax, South Dakota
Pilarski, Stanley J., Pvt., E, 314th Eng	Miss Francis Pilarski, 638 5th Ave., Milwaukee, Wis.
Piper, Ralph A., Pvt. 1cl., B, 355th Inf	Lucian Piper, Woodlake, Neb.
Pippert, Herman W., Pvt., M, 353rd Inf	Mrs. Ella Pippert, 30 S. Galapago St., Denver, Colo.
Plamenaz, Pvt. 1cl., L, 353rd Inf	Charley Wiles, Bisbee, Ariz.
Plov, John, Pvt., A, 353rd Inf	John Plov, Lubay, Russia
Poels, Anton, Pvt., Amb. Co., 314th San. Tr	Peter Venbommel, David City, Neb.
Pollock, William H., Pvt. 1cl., E, 354th Inf	John Pollock, R. F. D. 4, S. Lancaster, Wis.
Polst, Curt J., Pvt., Hq. 356th Inf	Mrs. Helen Polst, 4264 Kossuth Ave., St. Louis, Mo.
Poole, Sam C., Pvt. 1cl., A, 354th Inf	John W. Poole, Downing, Mo.
Porchella, Augusta, Pvt., A, 355th Inf	Joseph Porchella, 1433 Wentworth Ave., Chicago, Ill.
Porter, Carl E., Sgt., D, 354th Inf	
Post, Gustave E., Pvt. 1cl., Hq. 355th Inf	Sifred Post, Marquette, Neb.
Poths, Harry, Pvt., G, 354th Inf	
Potter, Oscar G., Pvt. 1cl., B, 342nd M. G. Bn	Oscar Potter, Chamberlain, South Dakota
Powell, Charles O., Pvt., E, 355th Inf	Mrs. Bridget Powell, Neligh, Neb.
Prosser, John H., Pvt., Sup. Co., 353rd Inf	Mrs. Martha O'Connell, Glidden, Wis.
Proud, Earl, Sgt., D. M. G. Bn	Mrs. Chas E. Smith, 1600 49th Ave. North, Minneapolis, Minn.
Pryor, Preston P., Pvt., Hq. 354th Inf	James C. Pryor, R. F. D. 1, Saxton, Mo.
Pugh, William W., Pvt., E, 354th Inf	Mrs. Mary E Pugh, Acorn, Mo.
Pupka, Joseph A., Pvt., D, 354th Inf	Mrs. Eva Bergielle, 2852 W. 39th St., Chicago, Ill.
Racobs, Dan B., Corp., H, 355th Inf	Wm. W. Racobs, Smithland, Iowa
Radant, Oscar A., Pvt. 1cl., M., 355th Inf	A. Radant, Madison, Neb.
Rader, Valentine S., Corp., K, 353rd Inf	Jackson L. Rader, Howard, Kan.
Raduechel, Walter, Pvt. 1cl., A, 355th Inf	

Name, Rank, Company, Regiment	Emergency Address
Raible, Joseph R., Corp., L, 353rd Inf	Minnie Raible, Overbrook, Kan.
Ramsey, Earl E., Sgt., G, 353rd Inf	Tillman H. Ramsey, Cedarvale, Kan.
Ramsey, James W., Pvt., L, 354th Inf	Mrs. Fannie Ramsey, Western Grove, Ark.
Rasmussen, John, Cook, E, 340th F. A.	Knud Rasmussen, Skrillinge, Middlefardt, Denmark
Ratliff, Denver T., Pvt., I, 356th Inf	Mrs. Nora N. Ratliff, 111 Switzer St., Greenville, Ohio
Rauls, William F., Pvt., E, 354th Inf	Mrs. Josephine Rauls, Hornersville, Mo.
Rauscher, Richard, Pvt., B, 355th Inf	
Raymond, Jesse C., Sgt., E, 353rd Inf	Mrs. Martha Raymond, Hillsboro, Kan.
Reagan, Daniel D., Sgt., M. G. Co., 354th Inf	Mrs. Bridget Reagan, 5743 Cote Brilliant Ave., St. Louis, Mo.
Redd, Charles E., Pvt., Hq. 353rd Inf	Mrs. Mamie Redd, Norton, Kan.
Redmon, Eddie, Pvt., K, 356th Inf	Maggie Redmon, R. F. D. 4, Marshall, Ill.
Reed, Glen M., Sgt., B, 355th Inf	Milton H. Reed, Aux Vasse, Mo.
Reed, Roy C., Sgt., I, 355th Inf	
Reeves, Jesse C., Pvt., C, 353rd Inf	Mrs. Martha Reeves, Medicine Lodge, Kan.
Reis, Eugene John, Pvt. 1cl., M. G. Co., 354th Inf	Martin Reis, 7600 Michigan Ave., St. Louis, Mo.
Reithel, Henry C., Corp., M. G. Co., 356th Inf	Mrs. Clara Reithel, 3944 N. 19th St., St. Louis, Mo.
Remick, Earl F., Pvt. 1cl., B, 353rd Inf	Fred E. Remick, R. F. D. 3, Osborne, Kan.
Remley, George A., Pvt., D, 342nd F. A.	Michael S. Remley, R. F. D. 5, Benton, Pa.
Rendle, Herman J., Mech., M, 356th Inf	Mrs. Rose Jordan, Wagner Place, Jefferson City, Mo.
Reuter, Bernard S., Sgt., E, 354th Inf	Otto H. Reuter, 4229 Lexington Ave., St. Louis, Mo.
Reyelts, Charles P., Pvt. 1cl., D, 353rd Inf	Betty Young, 7435 Champlain St., Chicago, Ill.
Reynolds, Daniel, Pvt., D, 342nd F. A.	Mrs. Rose Reynolds, 2450 2nd Ave., New York, N. Y.
Rhoades, Roy Glen, Corp., C, 354th Inf	George Rhoades, Rose Hill, Kan.
Rhodes, Roscoe B., Sgt., A, 342nd M. G. Bn	Mrs. Rhodes, Ansley, Neb.
Rice, Otis W., Pvt., K, 353rd Inf	Ed. Rice, 216 E. 2nd St., Hutchinson, Kan.
Ridge, Edward L., Pvt. 1cl., K, 353rd Inf	Howard T. Ridge, 432 S. Chicago St., Los Angeles, Cal.
Ridgeway, John C., Mech., M, 356th Inf	John W. Ridgeway, R. F. D. 2, Columbia, Mo.
Riemenapp, Albert, Pvt., G, 353rd Inf	Anton Riemenapp, R. F. D. 5, Potosi, Wis.
Riley, Joseph, Pvt., M, 354th Inf	Mrs. Mollie Oliver, 4930 Chouteau Ave., St. Louis, Mo.
Riley, William S., Pvt. 1cl., M, 353rd Inf	Wilford H. Riley, Fort Morgan, Colo.
Rish, Joseph C., Pvt., H, 355th Inf	Norma A. Rish, Winton, Neb.
Rizzuto, Francisco, Pvt. 1cl., K, 354th Inf	Teresa Rizzuto, Mongone Cosanza, Italy
Roach, John D., Corp., A, 356th Inf	John Roach, R. F. D. 7, St. Joseph, Mo.
Roberson, Charley D., Corp., B, 354th Inf	J. T. Roberson, Haleyville, Ala.
Robbins, George A., Pvt., G, 354th Inf	
Roderick, Thaddeus, 2nd Lt., M. G. Co., 354th Inf	Mrs. Thaddeus D. Roderick, Strong, Me.
Rogers, Clarence Otho, Corp., A, 314th Eng	Floyd Wood, Protem, Mo.
Rogers, Frank, Pvt., F, 356th Inf	
Rolan, John B., Pvt., D, 354th Inf	Oolie Rolan, Portageville, Mo.
Roland, Annie L., Pvt., C, 356th Inf	Thomas Roland, Conway, Mo.
Romack, Francis R., Corp., G, 353rd Inf	Miss Lucy Romack, Katy, Texas
Romick, James E., Pvt., F, 353rd Inf	James E. Romick, Mescotah, Kan.
Rooney, John P., Pvt., C, 341st M. G. Bn	
Rosaker, Chris C., Pvt., A, 341st M. G. Bn	Henry F. Rosaker, 300 S. 12th St., Norfolk, Neb.
Rosencrantz, Geo. C., Corp., H, 355th Inf	Jacob Rosencrantz, St. Edwards, Neb.
Rosenthal, Joseph J., Pvt., A, 342nd M. G. Bn	
Rosentretter, Wm. R., Pvt., A, 355th Inf	Mrs. Anna Rosenstretter, 3446 Evergreen Ave., Chicago, Ill.
Rostretter, Frank L., Pvt. 1cl., M, 353rd Inf	Victor A. Shintaffer, Gen. Del., Fairview, Kan.
Roszkoski, John, Pvt. 1cl., A, 356th Inf	Frank Roszkoski, 808 Jamison St., Flint, Mich.
Roth, Albert V., Pvt. I, 355th Inf	Mrs. Eva I. Roth, Goehner, Neb.
Roth, Herman, Corp., B, 341st M. G. Bn	Mrs. Herman Roth, 2109 Wirth St., Omaha, Neb.
Rouner, Glen L., Pvt., I, 353rd Inf	Geo. W. Rouner, Luray, Kan.
Rouse, Clare, Pvt., D, 355th Inf	Wm. A. Rouse, Glenmore, Wis.
Rouse, Thomas J., Pvt., A, 340th M. G. Bn	P. A. Rouse, Monroe City, Mo.
Rowe, Edward, Corp., F, 353rd Inf	W. M. Rowe, R. F. D. 4, Scranton, Kan.
Rowland, Roy, Pvt., E, 356th Inf	Caleb Rowland, Excelsior Springs, Mo.
Royster, George R., Sgt., H, 354th Inf	Elizabeth Royster, c-o Nell Shay, East DuBuque, Ill.
Runnestrand, Alfred T., Pvt., M, 356th Inf	Knudt E. Runnestrand, Ettrich, Wis.
Rush, Ralph G., Pvt. 1cl., K, 353rd Inf	John R. Rush, Eugene, Mo.
Russell, Samuel D., Pvt., B, 314th M. P	Mrs. Samuel Russell, Merriam, Kan.
Ryan, Clifford T., Pvt., E, 356th Inf	
Ryan, John, Pvt., Hq. 353rd Inf	Mrs. Anna Ryan, 1750 Fletcher St., Chicago, Ill.
Ryan, William C., Pvt., E, 356th Inf	Mandy Ryan, Doniphan, Mo.
Sabatier, Charles A., Pvt., B, 355th Inf	Eliza Sabatier, Marvell, Ohio
Salazar, Manuel, Pvt., I, 356th Inf	Juan Salazar, Rosa, N. M.
Sanchez, Solomon, Pvt., M. G. Co., 353rd Inf	Mrs. Felicita C Sanchez, 337 Garcia St., Raton, N. M.
Sanders, Arthur Frederick, Corp., E, 356th Inf	John Thomas Sanders, R. F. D. 6, St. Joseph, Mo.
Sandman, Leo L., Pvt., F, 353rd Inf	Miss Minnie Sandman, Gen. Del., Barrington, Ill.
Sanstrom, Carl E., Pvt., D, 353rd Inf	Mrs. Tekla Wickstrom, 7353 Eberhart Ave., Chicago, Ill.
Sanjyk, Peter, Pvt., B, 356th Inf	Miss Walyi Sanjyk, 649 Michigan St., Grand Rapids, Mich.
Saunders, Gladwyn M., Pvt. 1cl., L, 356th Inf	Frank Saunders, Ada, Kan.
Schaeffer, Edward Pvt., B, 354th Inf	Mrs. Anna Schaeffer, 1429 Paradise Alley, Milwaukee, Wis.
Schalk, Arthur E., Pvt., F, 314th Amm. Tr	
Schapendonk, John, Pvt., B, 356th Inf	
Scharer, Walter J., Pvt., E, 314th Sup. Tr	Mrs. John Scharer, 1608 Cherry St., Toledo, Ohio
Scharf, Albert, Pvt. 1cl., B, 355th Inf	Peter Scharf, 7232 82nd St., Portland, Ore.
Schaunaman, Otto F., Pvt., D, 341st M. G. Bn	Henry Schaunaman, Sisseton, South Dakota
Schavone, Tony, Pvt., A, 353rd Inf	Frank Schavone, Gen. Del., Conversano, Barra, Italy
Schellinger, William A., Pvt., I, 355th Inf	Wm. Schellinger, R. F. D. 3, Nebraska City, Neb.
Schildbach, William F. H., Pvt., I, 354th Inf	William Schildbach, 822 7th Ave., Peoria, Ill.
Schiller, John S., Pvt., K, 355th Inf	Mrs. Margaret Schiller, 63 Block H, Pueblo, Colo.
Schinck, Frank J., Pvt., M, 355th Inf	Jacob Schinck, Tilden, Neb.
Schimmin, Thomas A., Pvt., H, 353rd Inf	Mrs. Anna Kneen, Andres Isle of Man, England
Schlender, Ferdinand W., Pvt., K, 355th Inf	Christ Schlender, Herman, Mo.
Schlesner, Herbert W., Pvt., B, 354th Inf	Herman Schlesner, R. F. D. 1, Johnson Creek, Wis.
Schlight, Carl E., Pvt., G, 354th Inf	Mrs. Agusta Schlicht, 1714 S. 9th St., La Crosse, Wis.
Schlott, Aloysious A., Pvt., H, 354th Inf	
Schmer, Conrad, Pvt., B, 355th Inf	John Schmer, 900 L St., Lincoln, Neb.
Schneikart, Rudolph, Pvt., M, 353rd Inf	George Schneikart, 81 N. Mill St., Kansas City, Kan.
Schnabel, John J., Pvt., F, 355th Inf	

Name, Rank, Company, Regiment	Emergency Address
Scholz, Arthur E., Pvt., Hq. 354th Inf	Mrs. Emma Scholz, 288 Wise St., Oshkosh, Wis.
Schooling, Clarence Pvt. 1cl., H, 354th Inf	Mrs. Sallie Schooling, Box 45, Clark, Mo.
Schroeder, Ernest E., Pvt., E, 353rd Inf	Gus D. Schroeder, 300 E. 10th St., Newton, Kan.
Schultz, Ben, Pvt., 314th San. Tr.	
Schultz, Fred J., Pvt., H, 353rd Inf	Bertha Schultz, 514 Chatfield St., Winona, Minn.
Schumacher, John M., Pvt. 1cl., E, 341st F. A.	John W. Schumacher, 82 Dwight St., Ansonia, Conn.
Schwandt, Carl F., Pvt., A, 353rd Inf	August Schwandt, 516 Dakota St., Leavenworth, Kan.
Schwiekert, William P., Pvt., Sup. Co., 356th Inf	
Schwerdtmann, Walter C., Pvt. 1cl., C, 354th Inf	Mrs. Sophie Schwerdtmann, 4214 Conn. St., St. Louis, Mo.
Scott, Clarence, Pvt., F, 354th Inf	Enoch H. Scott, Dulany, Ky.
Sellards, Wayne, Pvt., F, 314th Eng	Att. Sellards, E. Lynn, W. Va.
Semenske, Edward, Pvt., A, 355th Inf	
Severin, Alvin, Pvt., Hq. 353rd Inf	Andrew Severin, 529 N. Nevada St., Colorado Springs, Colo.
Sexton, Ernest C., Corp., H, 355th Inf	
Shafer, Francis W., Wag., Sup. Co., 353rd Inf	Mrs. Opal Shafer, 330 W. 2nd St., Cherryvale, Kan.
Sheffer, Perry, Pvt. 1cl., M, 354th Inf	Elizabeth McClendon, R. F. D. 9, Brownington, Mo.
Shale, Arthur E., Wag., A, 340th M. G. Bn	Mrs. Frances Shale, 415 5th St. S. E., Watertown, S. Dak.
Shannon, Edward, Sgt., M. G. Co., 353rd Inf	William Shannon, Mapleton, Kan.
Sharp, Frank W., Corp., B, 353rd Inf	William Sharp, Sterling, Kan.
Shaw, George M., Pvt., A, 354th Inf	Mrs. Hattie M. Shaw, 1524 Lister Ave., Kansas City, Mo.
Shea, Michael, Pvt. 1cl., B, 341st M. G. Bn	Mrs. Mary Shea, 2723 Francis St., St. Joseph, Mo.
Shea, William, Pvt., L, 356th Inf	
Sheehan, John P., Pvt., F, 314th Eng	
Sheets, Wiley, Pvt., M. G. Co., 355th Inf	Mrs. Wiley Sheets, Durango, Colo.
Shelton, Joe, Pvt., B, 354th Inf	Mrs. Ida Shelton, Pleasant Hill, Mo.
Shemoski, John, Pvt., Hq. 355th Inf	John Vandewege, R. F. D. 1, Panama, Neb.
Shepard, Frank M., Pvt. 1cl., Hq. 355th Inf	
Shephard, Albert E., Pvt., K, 354th Inf	Thomas Shephard, Golding, Colo.
Sherman, Arthur O., Pvt., A, 341st M. G. Bn	
Sherold, Ralph E., Pvt. 1cl., K, 354th Inf	Mrs. Caroline Schuster, 206 S. 33rd St., Billings, Mont.
Sherrill, Thomas H., Pvt., F, 353rd Inf	Millia H. Sherrill, Alta Vista, Va.
Shields, James R., Pvt., F, 355th Inf	Mrs. Myrtle Shields, 718 E. High St., Colorado Springs, Colo.
Shields, Newell C., Corp., M. G. Co., 354th Inf	Mrs. Venora Shields, 232 W. 4th St., Loveland, Colo.
Shields, Thomas O., Corp., H, 355th Inf	W. B. Shields, Uplands, Neb.
Shiffler, George L., Pvt. 1cl., E, 354th Inf	Mrs. Ada Shiffler, Chilton, Mo.
Shroyer, Ernest W., Pvt., G, 354th Inf	Henry Shroyer, R. F. D. 3, Mountain Home, Ark.
Shultz, Claire W., Pvt. 1cl., D, 341st M. G. Bn	Mrs. Rachel Shultz, O'Neil, Neb.
Sibbel, Henry, Pvt., A, 354th Inf	Mrs. Anna Sibbel, Butte, Neb.
Siebenthaler, Geo. H., Pvt., L, 353rd Inf	Gottfried P. Siebenthaler, Merriam, Kan.
Siebrecht, Max J., Corp., B, 353rd Inf	
Sigurd, Anton A., Pvt., C, 354th Inf	Mrs. Anna Sigurd, 528 Allen St., Belvidere, Ill.
Silcott, Harry M., Pvt., E, 314th Eng	Chas. W. Scott, Nelsonville, Mo.
Silk, Elmer, Pvt., C, 356th Inf	Sophia Raines, 2902 Washington Ave., St. Louis, Mo.
Simmons, Frank L., Pvt., F, 353rd Inf	Mrs. Mattie Bogue, 1718 Haskell Ave., Kansas City, Kan.
Sipes, Walker O. H., Pvt., F, 353rd Inf	
Sitterman, Frank J., Pvt. 1cl., C, 354th Inf	John Sitterman, Leslie, Mo.
Skaggs, Herschel, Pvt., Hq. 177th Brig	Clint H. Skaggs, Sharon, Kan.
Skala, George W., Sgt., C, 341st M. G. Bn	James Skala, 1450 E. 16th St., Des Moines, Iowa
Slaughter, John H., Pvt., I, 353rd Inf	Mrs. Mollie Owens, Springville, Ariz.
Sletten, Anthony M., Pvt. 1cl., K, 355th Inf	
Slezak, Edward, Pvt., B, 355th Inf	
Slomski, Martin, Pvt., Hq. 353rd Inf	August Slomski, Gen. Del., Tonganoxie, Kan.
Smart, William M., Pvt. 1cl., D, 353rd Inf	Ralph B. Smart, R. F. D. 2, Mulvane, Kan.
Smiejkowski, Frank S., Sgt., L, 353rd Inf	
Smith, Donald F., Sgt., G, 354th Inf	Mrs. Wm. E. Smith, Odessa, Mo.
Smith, Eben L., 1st Lt., K, 355th Inf	
Smith, Elbert L., Sgt., H, 354th Inf	Mrs. Ida Smith, 4119 W. Kossuth St., St. Louis, Mo.
Smith, Elmer W., Pvt., K, 355th Inf	Mrs. Viola Smith, 1618 S. Jefferson St., St. Louis, Mo.
Smith, Ernest A., Pvt., B, 354th Inf	Mrs. Elijah W. Smith, Galena, Mo.
Smith, Frank E., Pvt., B, 314th Eng	Robert Murphy, Casper, Wyo.
Smith, Fred S., M. G. Co., 354th Inf	Mrs. Jessie Smith, 46 S. Lincoln St., Denver, Colo.
Smith, Grant C., Pvt., I, 354th Inf	Newell R. Smith, Vernon, Kan.
Smith, Henry A., Pvt., K, 354th Inf	Wm. Smith, 5631 S. Green St., Chicago, Ill.
Smith, Jacob L., Bugler, G, 353rd Inf	Valentine A. Smith, Cawker City, Kan.
Smith, Lehi, L., Pvt., I, 353rd Inf	Mrs. Drucilla M. Smith, Box 314, Malad City, Idaho
Smith, Lester W., Pvt., H, 354th Inf	
Smith, Neal, Pvt. 1cl., M, 354th Inf	Chas. Smith, Unionville, Mo.
Smith, Pearl G., Pvt. 1cl., D, 356th Inf	Wm. F. Smith, Queen City, Mo.
Smith, Samuel A., Pvt., E, 354th Inf	Miss Hazel Norton, 1909 S. 17th St., St. Joseph, Mo.
Smith, Walter P., Pvt., C, 355th Inf	Walter D. Smith, R. F. D. 2, Kennett, Mo.
Snyder, Harry N., Pvt., F, 353rd Inf	James G. Snyder, R. F. D. 1, Memphis, Mo.
Solomon, Frank, Pvt., M, 353rd Inf	Philip Solomon, R. F. D. 1, Hiawatha, Kan.
Solomon, Guy F., Pvt. 1cl., C, 355th Inf	Mrs. Eva Solomon, Huntsville, Mo.
Sondker, Edward H., Pvt., E, 355th Inf	Henry F. Sondker, Holton Kan.
Sorg, William, Pvt., I, 355th Inf	Mrs. Louisa Sorg, Arthur, Neb.
Southerland, Samuel, Pvt., F, 355th Inf	Margaret Southerland, Moreland, Ky.
Spadafore, Nicola, Pvt., D, 342nd F. A.	James Spadafore, 115 Cherry St., New York, N. Y.
Sparling, Clare F., Corp., E, 353rd Inf	Mrs. Ida Sparling, Oneida, Kan.
Spayer, Edward S., Pvt., K, 353rd Inf	
Spellman, John A., Pvt., C, 354th Inf	Mrs. John Spellman, 4143 Sarpy Ave., St. Louis, Mo.
Spencer, Monroe J., Sgt., C, 354th Inf	Hiram Spencer, Shelbyville, Mo.
Sperling, Henry, Pvt., 1cl., D, 342nd F. A	
Sperr, Joe R., Sgt., I, 353rd Inf	
Spicer, Harris T., Pvt. 1cl., C, 356th Inf	Samuel E. Spicer, 311 Kansas Ave., Atchison, Kan.
Spidell, George F., Pvt., M, 354th Inf	Mrs. Florence Spidell, 717 25th St., Denver, Colo.
Spivey, Ocie C., Pvt., B, 342nd M. G. Bn	Kenie T. Spivey, R. F. D. 1, Windsor, Va.
Sponhauer, Harry F., Pvt., H, 353rd Inf	Mrs. Melvina Sponhauer, R. F. D. 6, Cherryvale, Kan.
Sprague, James M., Pvt., D, 353rd Inf	Mrs. Mary Sprague, Lena, Ill.
Sprenger, Henry J., Corp., H, 355th Inf	Joe Sprenger, Linn, Mo.
Springer Simon D., Corp., I, 356th Inf	

Name, Rank, Company, Regiment	Emergency Address
Spyrczak, Adam, Pvt., E, 314th Eng	Felix Rucara, 1406 Chene St., Detroit, Mich.
Squibb, Reginald G., Corp., M, 354th Inf	Frederic Squibb, 4040 Broadway, Chicago, Ill.
Staas, Charles S., Pvt., A, 356th Inf	Wm. H. Staas, R. R. 1, Wishart, Mo.
Staley, David R., Corp., K, 354th Inf	Miss Bertha Pearson, 3131 Main St., Kansas City, Mo.
Stamm, Boyd, Pvt., F, 353rd Inf	Mary Miller, Severance, Kan.
Stanbarger, Orval E., Corp., C, 355th Inf	Mrs. Ella Stanbarger, Gen. Del., McCook, Neb.
Starks, William H., Pvt., M. G. Co., 356th Inf	Mrs. Mary Starks, 625 W. Allen St., Clinton, Mo.
Stavrianos, Stamatis N., Pvt., Hq. 354th Inf	Nick Savakis, 3332 La Clede Ave., St. Louis, Mo.
Steeby, Carl H., Corp., D, 356th Inf	
Steele, Aubrey T., Wag., Sup Co., 354th Inf	
Steffen, John O., Pvt., G, 354th Inf	
Steidley, Robert B., Pvt., H, 355th Inf	Joseph V. Steidley, Adams, Neb.
Steinbeck, Russell, Pvt., M, 354th Inf	James F. Steinbeck, Lake City, Colo.
Stenger, Arthur J., Pvt., C, 356th Inf	Kit Stenger, Council Grove, Kan.
Stephens, Lawrence J., Pvt., Hq. 354th Inf	Mrs. Clara Stephens, 3262 Walter Ave., Maplewood, Mo.
Stephens, Oscar W., Pvt., A, 355th Inf	Jim Allen, R. F. D. 1, Lufkin, Texas
Sternberger, Ferdinand, Pvt., L, 356th Inf	
Stevenson, Wilbur A., Pvt. 1cl., B, 353rd Inf	
Steward, Herbert S., Pvt. 1cl., I, 353rd Inf	
Stewart, Ray E., Pvt., C, 342nd M. G. Bn	
Stinson, Harold -M., Pvt., E, 353rd Inf	
Stockwell, Christopher, Pvt. 1cl., C, 356th Inf	Wm. M. Stockwell, Stafford, Kan.
Stockwell, Lynn J., Pvt., H, 355th Inf	James Stockwell, Butte, Neb.
Stoenner, Albert J., Pvt., C, 354th Inf	Mrs. Louise Stoenner, 511 Colorado Ave., Kansas City, Mo.
Stone, Lynn, Pvt., C, 355th Inf	John L. Stone, Columbia Crossroads, Bradford Co., Pa.
Story, George, Pvt., I, 356th Inf	Matt Story, Craig, Mo.
Straker, Charles E., Pvt., 314th Eng. Tr.	Burgess E. Straker, 308 W. Maryland Ave., Evansville, Tenn.
Strand, Martin H., Pvt., Hq. 355th Inf	Henry M. Strand, Newman Grove, Neb.
Stroemer, Otto R., Pvt., D, 355th Inf	Gustave Stroemer, 2249 S. Polin St., Chicago, Ill.
Stroh, Henry, Corp., B, 341st M. G. Bn	
Strommer, Melvin, Pvt., Tr. Co., 314th M. P.	Lawrence Strommer, Gen. Del., St James, Minn.
Stuart, Jackson, Pvt., E, 356th Inf	William F. Stuart, Bismarck, Mo.
Sturn, Jacob E., Pvt. 1cl., M, 353rd Inf	
Suding, Joseph A., Pvt., K, 354th Inf	Anna Suding, P. O. Box 184, Clayton, Wis.
Sullivan, John L., Pvt. 1cl., M, 355th Inf	
Swan, William H., Mech., D, 353rd Inf	
Swanson, Herman P., Pvt., H, 354th Inf	Emil Swanson, R. R. 4, Box 59, Geneseo, Ill.
Swart, Irvin M., Pvt., M. G. Co., 353rd Inf	Lola Swart, Gen. Del., Newberg, Ore.
Swiderski, Victor, Corp., C, 353rd Inf	Mrs. Emilia Swiderski, R. F. D. 2. Leavenworth, Kan.
Szylobrit, Alex S., Pvt., M. G. Co., 353rd Inf	Louie Szylorbrit, 1807 Hamilton St., Manitowoc, Wis.
Taake, Elmer W., Pvt., Hq. 356th Inf	Henry Taake, Baden Sta., St. Louis, Mo.
Tafoya, Juan B., E, 353rd Inf	Jose Tafoya, Truchas, N. M.
Take-The-Shield, Joseph, Pvt., B, 314th M. P.	Joseph Take-The-Shield, Sr., Wakpala, South Dakota
Tate, Bertie, Pvt., C, 356th Inf	Etsie W. Tate, Hodgenville, Ky.
Tatum, Bee, Corp., B, 354th Inf	Mrs. Mary Tatum, Deventer, Mo.
Tatum, Oscar W., Corp., B, 354th Inf	Mrs. Mona Laws, Fuget, Mo.
Taylor, Arthur C., Pvt., 1cl., B, 341st M. G. Bn	
Taylor, Arthur C., Pvt. 1cl., B, 341st M. G. Bn	Mrs. Elizazbeth Taylor, 1414 S. St., Lincoln, Neb.
Taylor, George D., Pvt., L, 355th Inf	
Taylor, Thomas W., Pvt., F, 314th Eng	George Taylor, Rowe, S. D.
Teachenor, Iven B., Pvt. 1cl., Amb. Co., 355th Inf	Mrs. Monroe Teachenor, Shelbina, Mo.
Teal, Fred, Pvt., Hq. Troop, 89th Div	Mrs. M. A. Teal, R. F. D. 3, Lake City, S. C.
Teigeler, Henry, Jr., Sgt., A, 355th Inf	Henry Teigeler, Sr., 1808 N. Broad St., Freemont, Neb.
Tennis, Fred N., Pvt., H, 354th Inf	Mrs. Edna S. Tennis, 1101 W. 11th St., Pueblo, Colo.
Thelen, Alfred A., Corp., F, 354th Inf	
Theobold, Jacob K., Pvt., I, 353rd Inf	
Thieme, Eitel F., Corp., M. G. Co., 353rd Inf	August Thieme, Goff, Kan.
Thomas, Frank G., Pvt., C, 314th Eng	
Thompson, Fred A., Pvt., A, 341st M. G. Bn	A. H. Thompson, 432 Ain Broke Ave., Wilmerding, Pa.
Thompson, Geo. Daniel, Pvt. 1cl., C, 354th Inf	Geo. Thompson, 249 Grant St., Oshkosh, Wis.
Thompson, George W., Pvt., L, 353rd Inf	Elizabeth Thompson, R. F. D. 1, Liberal, Kan.
Thompson, James F., Pvt., I, 354th Inf	Alexander Thompson, Belle, Mo.
Thompson, John I., Pvt., Hq. 353rd Inf	Janie Thompson, Englewood, Kan.
Thompson, Olaf, Pvt., M, 356th Inf	Ole Thompson, Gen. Del., Black River Falls, Wis.
Thompson, Otto, Pvt. 1cl., C, 354th Inf	Mrs. Nancy Thompson, 117 N. 12th St., Lexington, Mo
Thoms, Charles H. L., Pvt., A, 355th Inf	Mrs. Esther Thoms, 3918 Arsenal St., St. Louis, Mo.
Thoms, Johnny R., Pvt., 314th San. Tr.	Claris Thoms, Albion, Neb.
Tice, Ellwood P., Pvt., F, 314th Eng	Mrs. Louise A. Tice, Box 10, Westville, Gloucester, N. J.
Tillman, Dennie F., Pvt., E, 356th Inf	Mrs. Hester Frazier, 709 N. 2nd St., Phoenix, Ariz.
Tilton, Shirley, Pvt., D, 355th Inf	Mrs. Eliza Tilton, 409 N. 4th St., Oregon, Ill.
Timlin, Eugene C., Corp., D, 355th Inf	James Holloren, Bear Creek, Wis.
Tindall, Marvin, Pvt., Med. Det., 353rd Inf	J. M. Tindall, Ballinger, Texas
Titolski, Joe, Pvt., B, 353rd Inf	
Tofoya, Silas, Pvt., B, 353rd Inf	
Todd, John I., Pvt., Med. Det., 355th Inf	
Tohtieff, Solamagary Dozi, Pvt. 1cl., F, 356th Inf	Kisiko Tohtieff, 121 Wyoming St., Butte, Mont.
Tornow, Martin F., Pvt., H, 353rd Inf	Charles Tornow, R. F. D. 3, Box 74, Walnut, Kan.
Tosch, John A., Pvt., A, 355th Inf	John Tosch, R. F. D. 31, Vesper, Wis.
Tousch, Frank, Corp., Hq. 355th Inf	
Tracy, Victor A., Pvt. 1cl., G, 355th Inf	John Tracy, Elk Creek, Neb.
Tracy, Victor Andrew, Pvt. 1cl., G, 355th Inf	
Trapp, Peter C., Corp., M, 353rd Inf	Mrs. Mary Trapp, Gen. Del., Herington, Kan.
Traube, James S., Sgt., H, 356th Inf	Mrs. Estella Traube, Pleasant Hill, Mo.
Trautman, Emanuel, Pvt., Tr. B. 314th M. P	Conrad Trautman, Artas, South Dakota
Trobough, Henry Clinton, Pvt. 1cl., M. G. Co., 355th Inf	Mrs. Anna Trobough, Fairfield, Neb.
Trout, Orvie C., Pvt., H, 355th Inf	Ida F. Trout, Fleming, Colo.
Troyer, Jesse F., Pvt., G, 354th Inf	
Trujillo, Jose E., Pvt. 1cl., Hq. 341st F. A.	Juanita Trujillo, Box 73, Durango, Colo.
Tubbs, Benjamin T., Pvt., I, 356th Inf	Homer H. Tubbs, Farmersville, La.
Tucker, Ellis A., Sgt., H, 355th Inf	A. E. Tucker, Crofton, Neb.

Name, Rank, Company, Regiment	Emergency Address
Tucker, Fred L., Pvt. 1cl., D, 353rd Inf	Jesse Tucker, Englewood, Kan.
Tucker, Richard, Pvt., D, 356th Inf	Mrs. Sadie Tucker, 1410 Dillon St., St. Louis, Mo.
Tunks, Rolla N., Pvt., D, 356th Inf	Mark Tunks, R. F. D. 2, Maysville, Mo.
Turek, Mike, Pvt. 1cl., B, 342nd M. G. Bn	
Turnbull, August, Sgt., A, 355th Inf	Thomas G. Turnbull, Burchard, Neb.
Turner, James C., Pvt., F, 354th Inf	Mrs. James V. Turner, 898 Main St., Oshkosh, Wis.
Turner, Lawrence W., Corp., B, 353rd Inf	Plinn S. Turner, c-o A. A. Minert, Newton, Kan.
Turner, William, Pvt. 1cl., K, 354th Inf	Mrs. Jennie Lathayn, 509 N. Liberty, Webb City, Mo.
Tuttle, Lewis F., Pvt., H, 353rd Inf	James E. Tuttle, Anthony, Kan.
Underwood, Clinton H., Pvt. 1cl., A, 354th Inf	Elihue C. Underwood, 4212 Locust St., Kansas City, Mo.
Valero, Procopio, Pvt., I, 356th Inf	Gavrielta Valero, Las Vegas, N. M.
Van Dyke, John G., Pvt., C, 314th Eng	Mrs. Dena Van Dyke, R. R. 2, Prairie View, Kan.
Van Noffert, Norris, Pvt., G, 354th Inf	Mrs. Rachel Rinaldi, 2558 Superior St., Chicago, Ill.
Vass, John, Wag., Amb. Co., 354th Inf	John Vass, Laramie, Wyo.
Vaughan, Leon B., Pvt., H, 356th Inf	Mrs. Mary G. Vaughan, Raton, N. M.
Verch, Carl, Pvt., K, 354th Inf	Herman Verch, Billings, Mont.
Verhoeff, Leonard C., Corp., M, 353rd Inf	Mrs. Nellie Verhoeff, Gen. Del., Grinnel, Kan.
Verhuest, Cornelius R., Pvt., L, 353rd Inf	
Vetter, Albert, Pvt., B, 354th Inf	
Vickroy, Lawrence P., Pvt., M, 353rd Inf	Mrs. Elsie Stunbaugh, R. F. D. 1, Box 162, Aurora, Ill.
Vilott, Fletcher, Pvt., G, 355th Inf	Mrs. Lute Vilott, Mankato, Kan.
Vis, Leonard, Pvt., C, 341st M. G. Bn	Marinis Vis, Whitelake, South Dakota
Vogel, Charles A., Pvt., H, 354th Inf	Charles Vogel, Nottingham St., St. Louis, Mo.
Vogel, John A., Pvt. 1cl., C, 354th Inf	Mrs. Julia Vogel, 3219 N. Newstead Ave., St. Louis, Mo.
Voris, Frank Landes, Pvt., Hq. 354th Inf	J. M. Voris, Halfway, Mo.
Voss, Remmer, Pvt., B, 355th Inf	
Wagner, Harold R., Pvt., L, 353rd Inf	Mrs. Jennie E. Wagner, Fruita, Mesa Co., Colo.
Wakeman, Arthur H., Corp., K, 353rd Inf	Delinda Wakeman, Wathena, Kan.
Walker, John A., Pvt., D, 353rd Inf	Joe Kazmierzah, 738 7th Ave., Milwaukee, Wis.
Walker, William H., Corp., Hq. 355 Inf	Mrs. M. L. Keefer, 1819 L St., Havelock, Neb.
Wallace, W. N., Pvt., K, 354th Inf	Mrs. Mary Sailer, 2839 Arlington Ave., St. Louis, Mo.
Wallwork, Geo. H., Pvt. 1cl., M. G. Co., 354th Inf	
Wambean, Floyd, Pvt., 356th Amb. Co	Mrs. Flora Wambeau, Wahoo, Neb.
Ware, Hugh H., Corp., B, 353rd Inf	Mrs. John E. Ware, Chickasha, Okla.
Ware, James C., Pvt., G, 354th Inf	James C. Ware, 1007 W. Ontario St., Centerville, Iowa
Warren, Clarence I., Pvt. 1cl., M, 355th Inf	Mrs. Eva Shreffer, Fairfield, Neb.
Warren, Thomas E., Pvt., C, 342nd M. G. Bn	Mrs. Alice Warren, 1357 Newton St., Denver, Colo.
Washakas, Felix J., Pvt., E, 354th Inf	Mrs. Mary Washakas, 3218 Lime St., Chicago, Ill.
Wassinger, George, Pvt., M, 354th Inf	Mrs. Lizzie Wassinger, Byers, Colo
Wasson, Joseph H., Pvt., A, 354th Inf	Mrs. Ella Thomas, 108 County Road, Monett, Mo.
Watkins, Dass S., Wag., D, 314th Eng	Monroe Watkins, Neosho, Wis.
Watson, Walter W., Pvt. 1cl., K, 353rd Inf	Mrs. Harriet Watson, Platteville, Wis.
Weaver, Herman, Pvt., E, 353rd Inf	Mrs. Grace Weaver, Eldorado, Kan.
Weaver, Taylor B., Pvt., E, 353rd Inf	Mrs. Lula Weaver, Brinkley, Ark.
Weber, Jacob J., Pvt., G, 355th Inf	John Weber, Freeman, South Dakota
Wedlake, John C., Pvt., H, 354th Inf	William Wedlake, Beverly, Neb.
Wehry, William A., Pvt., A, 353rd Inf	Andrew P. Wehry, Gen. Del., Peabody, Kan.
Weigel, Nick A., Pvt., L, 354th Inf	August Weigel, Marshfield, Wis.
Weinberg, Louis B., Corp., K, 353rd Inf	Otto Weinberg, Troy, Kan.
Weinheimer, Adolph, Pvt., B, 355th Inf	Wm. Weinheimer, R. F. D. 4, Greenville, Ill.
Wellnitz, Frank, Corp., C, 353rd Inf	Albert Wellnitz, Emporia, Kan.
Wells, Lawrence G., Corp., D, 356th Inf	Inez Conrad, 3509 St. Louis Ave., St. Louis, Mo.
Wells, Curt, Sgt., H, 354th Inf	Mrs. Curt Wells, 216 N. 16th St., Green Castle, Mo.
Wendorf, Emil A., Pvt., I, 353rd Inf	Herman Wendorf, 1456 7th St., Milwaukee, Wis.
Wengert, Bernie, Pvt., Hq. 354th Inf	Charley Wengert, R. F. D. 1, St. Marys, Mo.
West, James W., 1st Sgt., H, 353rd Inf	Mrs. Anna L. West, Gen. Del., Kansas City, Mo.
West, Owlen J., Pvt. 1cl., H, 353rd Inf	Laura B. West, Mildred, Kan.
Westhoff, Peter A., Pvt. 1cl., B, 314th Eng	Elizabeth Westhoff, R. F. D. 2, O'Fallon, Mo.
Westling, John R., Corp., G, 353rd Inf	Mrs. Ruben Westling 1637 Filmore St., Topeka, Kan.
Westrun, William G., Pvt., B, 340th M. G. Bn	Mrs. Martha Cotton, Bruce, South Dakota
Wetzel, William W., Pvt., 314th San. Tr	Mrs. Helen Payne, Drake Apts. 33, Omaha, Neb.
Weyerts, Tony, Pvt., K, 355th Inf	
Wharton, Hugh C., Pvt., F, 356th Inf	Mrs. Wharton, 1104 Scott Ave., Wichita Falls, Tex.
Wheeler, Clarence W., Pvt., A, 353rd Inf	Mrs. Mary E. Colentine, Joplin, Mo.
White, Benjamin R., Pvt., A, 354th Inf	Mrs. Anna R. White, c-o Kendall Hotel, Lindell St., St. Louis, Mo.
White, Jack A., Pvt. 1cl., C, 354th Inf	Mrs. Julia White, 225 W. 18th St., Kansas City, Mo.
White, Harry A., Pvt., I, 355th Inf	Mrs. Margaret A. White, Delta, Colo.
White, Travis B., Pvt., G, 354th Inf	Wm. P. White, R. F. D. 1, Kenefic, Okla.
Whitford, William, Pvt., L, 355th Inf	Mrs. Clara Whitford, Box 81, Davis, Okla.
Whiting, Clark, Sgt., H, 356th Inf	Ira Whiting, Dighton, Kan.
Whittle, John Q., Corp., F, 354th Inf	Patrick W. Whittle, 4525 St. Louis Ave., St. Louis, Mo.
Whitworth, James L., Corp., C, 354th Inf	Jas. L. Whitworth, Catawissa, Mo.
Wideman, Alfred C., Pvt., D, 356th Inf	Andrew Weideman, Crystal City, Mo.
Widlansky, George G., Pvt., H, 354th Inf	Herman Widlansky, 1405 Wabash Ave., Kansas City, Mo.
Wiegert, Arthur G., Pvt., B, 341st M. G. Bn	Wm. Wedlake, Beverly, Neb.
Wiensch, Joseph, Pvt., I, 354th Inf	Mrs. Gertrude Wiensch, R. F. D. 1, Cornell, Wis.
Wiley, William G., Pvt., G, 355th Inf	Mrs. Agnes A. Wiley Shongaboo, Ia.
Wilcox, Fred, Pvt., D, 355th Inf	Fred Wilcox, Sr., Milletteville, S. C.
Willcut, Kibble B., Pvt., D, 356th Inf	Mrs. Catherine Willcut, Poplar Bluff, Mo.
Willhoit, Van O., Pvt., H, 356th Inf	M. Willhoit, Knowles, N. M.
Williams, Arthur A., Pvt., M, 354th Inf	Mrs. Fannie Williams, 6085 Minerva Ave., St. Louis, Mo.
Williams, David R., Sgt., C, 353rd Inf	Mrs. Matilda A. Williams, R. F. D. 3, Tonganoxie, Kan.
Williams, Grover C., Sgt., B, 340th M. G. Bn	Mrs. E. T. Forrester, Havana, Ark.
Williams, Robert L., Pvt. 1cl., G, 355th Inf	Louis O. Williams, 805 W. 16th St., University Place, Neb.
Williams, Sam J., Pvt., A, 355th Inf	Mrs. Sallie Williams, Macon, Miss.
Willison, Warren H., Sgt., Hq. 354th Inf	Charles E. Williams, 612 Callahan St., Muskogee, Okla.
Willmore, Ralph, Pvt., I, 354th Inf	Mrs. Dorothea Willmore, 1430A Temple Place, St. Louis, Mo.
Willoughby, James W., Pvt. 1cl., A, 356th Inf	Mrs. E. Willoughby, Strafford, Mo.
Wills, Robert L., Corp., D, 353rd Inf	W. T. Wills, Butte, Neb.
Wilmore, William W., Corp., C, 354th Inf	William Wilmore, 38th and Wadsworth Sts., Denver, Colo.

Name, Rank, Company, Regiment	Emergency Address
Wilson, Glen R., Corp., E, 353rd Inf	Threaa Marie Wilson, Box 192, Oberlin, Kan.
Wilson, Harold E., Pvt., E, 355th Inf	Thos. P. Wilson, Clifton, Ariz.
Wilson, Irving F., Pvt., M, 353rd Inf	Mrs. Clara S. Wilson, 822 9th St., Oshkosh, Wis.
Wilson, Ross, Pvt., A, 355th Inf	Mrs. Matilda Wilson, S. Mansfield, La.
Wilt, Mark L., Pvt., G, 354th Inf	Wilson R. Wilt, 508 Reynolds, Goshen, Ind.
Wimmer, Lawrence M., Sgt., D, 353rd Inf	Mrs. Wetha Wimmer, 623 N. Sherman St., Liberal, Kan.
Winemiller, Marion, Pvt., C, 356th Inf	John Winemiller, Hollywood, Mo.
Wingerter, Henry J., Pvt., E, 356th Inf	Leo Wingerter, Gen. Del., Biehle, Mo.
Witkowski, Frank S., Pvt., A, 355th Inf	Mrs. Mary Witkowski, 5514 S. Lincoln St., Chicago, Ill.
Witt, George J., Pvt., D, 353rd Inf	Mrs. Josephine Witt, R. R. 1, Milladore, Wis.
Witters, Joseph J., Pvt. 1cl., I, 355th Inf	Mrs. Joseph Witters, Kolin, Mont.
Wittrock, William Fred, M. G. Co., 354th Inf	John Wittrock, R. R. 13, Kendrick, Colo.
Wojnowski, Vincent I., Pvt., E, 354th Inf	Ignatz Wojnowski, 1010 12th Ave., Milwaukee, Wis.
Wolf, Ervin G., Pvt., E, 354th Inf	Mrs. Martha Wolf, 807 Harrison St., Topeka, Kan.
Wolf, Henry L., Pvt., L, 355th Inf	Henry Wolf, Ramona, South Dakota
Wolf, Jacob H., Corp., F, 354th Inf	Mrs. Mary C. Wolf, 1414 E. Prairie Ave., St. Louis, Mo.
Wolf, John, Pvt. 1cl., E, 354th Inf	Jacob Wolf, 1845 S. 10th St., St. Louis, Mo.
Wolfe, Lawrence, Corp., A, 355th Inf	Mrs. Florence Wolfe, 3003 Elim Ave., Zion City, Ill.
Wolff, Adolph, Pvt., A, 340th M. G. Bn	Mathias J. Wolff, Java, South Dakota
Wombles, Ora, Pvt., D, 354th Inf	Lucy Wombles, Leaton, Mo.
Wood, Claude C., Pvt. 1cl., C, 356th Inf	Bessie Wood, King City, Mo.
Wood, Everett D., Pvt. 1cl., C, 356th Inf	William H. Wood, R. F. D. 2, Baldwin, Ky.
Wood, Jasper M., Pvt., B, 353rd Inf	William Wood, R. R. 1, Hiattville, Kan.
Woodward, Burley, Pvt. 1cl., C, 342nd M. G. Bn	Mrs. Emil Woodward, 3760 Broadway Ave., Kansas City, Mo.
Wright, Arthur A., Pvt. 1cl., D, 340th F. A.	
Wright, Friend E., Jr., Pvt., 341st M. G. Bn	Homer Wright, R. F. D. 2, Longmont, Colo
Wright, Roy E., Mess Sgt., G, 353rd Inf	Mrs. Allie Wright, 1108 Greeley Ave., Kansas City, Kan.
Wright, William E., Pvt. 1cl., H, 353rd Inf	Miss Bessie Matoon, 321 Seneca St., Leavenworth, Kan.
Wroflewski, Joseph A., Pvt., C, 353rd Inf	Mrs. Frances Wroflewski, 247 Burnham St., Milwaukee, Wis.
Wunsch, Charles H., Pvt., C, 355th Inf	Mrs. Anna Wunch, 2721 Missouri Ave., St. Louis, Mo.
Wymore, Verne, Pvt., B, 353rd Inf	Betta Wymore, 936 Spalding, Wichita, Kan.
Wysowatcky, John, Pvt., G, 354th Inf	Mrs. Mary Wysowatcky, 4663 Penn Ave., Denver, Colo.
Yates, Homer M., Pvt., M. G. Co., 355th Inf	Mrs. Effie J. Yates, Whitman, Neb.
Yerko, John, Pvt., E, 314th Eng	Mrs. Mary Yerko, Drifton, Pa.
Yocam, Fred V., Pvt., M, 356th Inf	Mrs. Olive Yocam, 408 Prairie Ave., Joplin, Mo.
Yocum, John, Pvt., B, 355th Inf	E. E. Yocum, Ohio City, Ohio
Yore, Louis A., Pvt. 1cl., H, 353rd Inf	Mrs. Katherine Bradley, 2827 W. Quincy St. Chicago, Ill.
Yund, Harry R., Pvt., H, 355th Inf	James H. Yund, Grand Island, Neb.
Young, Roscoe D., Corp., D, 356th Inf	Roy O. Young, R. F. D. 1, Forest Green, Mo.
Young, Robert, Pvt., B, 353rd Inf	Simon W. Young, Rodley, Colo.
Youngerman, George, Pvt., E, 354th Inf	Mrs. Mary Youngerman, 4346 Hologan Ave., St. Louis, Mo.
Yousits, Charles E., Pvt., F, 355th Inf	
Zabroki, Stanley B., Pvt., K, 353rd Inf	Stanley B. Daniels, 262 Duluth Ave., St. Paul, Minn.
Zachrison, Raleigh, Pvt., D, 314th Eng	Mrs. Hanna Zachrison, Arvada, Colo.
Zadig, Charles, Pvt., A, 355th Inf	Joseph Zadig, 651 Center St., Chicago, Ill
Zeller, Michael, Pvt. 1cl., C, 342nd M. G. Bn	Mrs. Mary Zeller, 3734 Tennessee Ave., St. Louis, Mo.
Zenk, Leo L., Pvt., M, 353rd Inf	Miss Clara Zenk, 473 Washington St., Winona, Minn
Zink, Louis F., Pvt., G, 354th Inf	Mrs. Elizabeth Zink, 2514 S. 3rd St., St. Louis, Mo.
Zukaitis, Charles, Pvt., C, 353rd Inf	Mrs. John Karalus, 3088 Wallace St., Chicago, Ill.
Zwickey, Harry J., Sgt., A, 355th Inf	Mrs. Daisy D Zwickey, 915 E. 10th St., Freemont, Neb.

OFFICERS AND MEN MISSING IN ACTION

(Presumed Dead)

Name, Rank and Organization	Emergency Address
Yarbrough, Walter S., 1st Lt., Co. F, 355th Inf	W. S. Yarbrough, Nashville, Tenn.
Alendale, Ole, Pvt., Co. H, 355th Inf	Knut Alendale, Viborg, S. D.
Christian, Mack, Sgt., Co. F, 355th Inf	A. C. Christian, Rarden, Ohio
Coll, John B., Pvt., Co. H, 356th Inf	
Glad, Frank E., Pvt., Co. E, 356th Inf	
Heath, Carl, Corp., Co. G, 355th Inf	John Heath, Wallace, Neb.
Howard, Claud C., Pvt., M. G. Co., 356th Inf	Guy Howard, Deming, N. M.
Kramer, Emil, Pvt., Prov. 314th M. S. T.	
Lee, Victor C., Sgt., Co. H, 355th Inf	Pearl Newman, 539 W. 9th St., Freeman, Neb.
Limle, David Gus, Pvt., Co. I, 356th Inf	Mrs. Violet Limle, 818 Capital Ave., Omaha, Neb.
Loucher, Jacob, Pvt., Co. B, 355th Inf	
McPherson, Charles, Pvt., Co. D, 355th Inf	George McPherson, Polo, Ill.
Montoya, Arturo, Pvt., Co. G, 356th Inf	Jose Montoya, Roy, N. M.
Potts, Leland E., Pvt., Co. I, 354th Inf	
Roberts, John W., Pvt., Co. K, 355th Inf	John Roberts, Riverside, Neb.
Smith, Thomas R., Pvt., Co. D, 342nd M. G. Bn	Mrs. Nellie Johnston, 300 2nd St., Petaluma, Cal.
Warmowski, Alexander, Pvt., Co. B, 354th Inf	Mrs. August Warmowski, 2237 Ward St., Chicago, Ill.
Willichowski, Joseph W., Co. L, 354th Inf	Valentine Willichowski, Marathon, Wis.

SEVERELY WOUNDED

OFFICERS SEVERELY WOUNDED

Name, Rank, Organization	Date, 1918
Ale, John H., 1st Lt., 355th Inf	9-12
Allen, Jacob W., 1st Lt., 355th Inf	10-21
Baker, George R., Capt., M. C., M. D., 355th Inf	10-22
Barney, Carey W., 1st Lt., 354th Inf	9-13
Barney, Carey W., 1st Lt., M. G. Co., 354th Inf	11- 2
Barr, Jesse W., 1st Lt., 353rd Inf	11- 3
Bates, Vernon E., 1st Lt., 354th Inf	11- 2
Brock, Raymond O., 2nd Lt., 356th Inf	10-21
Broyles, Watkins A., 2nd Lt., 355th Inf	11- 7
Byrum, Paul, Capt., 341st M. G. Bn	11- 1
Clancy, Richard E., 1st Lt., M. G. Co., 354th Inf	9-19
Clark, Gideon T., 2nd Lt., 353rd Inf	9-12
Cline, Earl M., Capt., 355th Inf	9-12
Cushing, John B., 1st Lt., 353rd Inf	10- 8
Darst, James E., 2nd Lt., 341st M. G. Bn	11- 1
Doherty, Joseph T., 2nd Lt., 356th Inf	11- 5
Dolan, William H., 1st Lt., 353rd Inf	10-24
Driscoll, Michael A., 2nd Lt., M. G. Co., 356th Inf	11- 4
Ensign, Chester O., 1st Lt., 353rd Inf	10-22
Fickett, Fred W., 1st Lt., M. G. Co., 354th Inf	11- 9

Name, Rank, Organization	Date, 1918
Garin, Rene G., 2nd Lt., M. G. Co., 353rd Inf	9-12
Gaston, Alpheus D., 1st Lt., Hq. 314th F. S. Bn	10-15
Gilbert, Frank, 1st Lt., 356th Inf	11- 6
Goff, William, Capt., M. C., M. D., 354th Inf	10-22
Hagenbuch, Charles C., 1st Lt., 340th F. A	10-17
Hayden, Richard, 2nd Lt., 354th Inf	11- 1
Heiken, Ellert G., 1st Lt., 356th Inf	11-11
Heim, Russell R., Capt., M. C., M. D., 356th Inf	10-22
Herrick, Myron C., 2nd Lt., 355th Inf	10-22
Herrington, Cass M., 1st Lt., 355th Inf	10-21
La Rue, Benn V. M., Capt., 355th Inf	11- 9
Little, James B., 1st Lt., 355th Inf	9-13
Luchtenberg, Carl O., 2nd Lt., 355th Inf	11- 1
McCollum, John, 1st Lt., Hq. 353rd Inf	10-30
McNulty, Herman, 1st Lt., 354th Inf	11- 1
Metzger, Leon D., 2nd Lt., 353rd Inf	10-30
Millis, John M., 2nd Lt., 354th Inf	10-30
Morrison, Lewis Richard, 2nd Lt., 353rd Inf	9-12
Mundell, Walter M., Capt., M. C., 314th San. Tr	11- 2
Nanninga, Simon P., 2nd Lt., 341st M. G. Bn	10-30
Platt, William P., Capt., 353rd Inf	10-26
Portmann, Milton C., Capt., 353rd Inf	10-21
Reese, Tom M., Capt., 353rd Inf	10-26
Rice, Walter L., 2nd Lt., 342nd M. G. Bn	11- 3
Rowell, Ernest G., 1st Lt., 354th Inf	10-31
Rush, Roy L., 1st Lt., Hq., 355th Inf	10-21
Sample, John G., Capt., 356th Inf	10- 3
Scheibla, Harry D., 341st M. G. Bn	11- 1
Shea, Patrick E., 2nd Lt., 355th Inf	10-22
Shriver, Ray O., 1st Lt., 314th Eng	11- 1
Smith, Frank, Capt., 356th Inf	11- 9
Smith, Royal H. G., 2nd Lt., 353rd Inf	9-18
Smith, Sam, 1st Lt., 355th Inf	10-22
Staatz, Stanley W., 2nd Lt., 356th Inf	11-11
Steinhilber, C. W., 1st Lt., 354th Inf	11- 2
Strain, Frank E., 1st Lt., 356th Inf	10- 6
Strauss, Leonard A., 2nd Lt., 353rd Inf	10-28
Tait, Lee C., 1st Lt., 354th Inf	11- 3
Thompson, Paul E., 2nd Lt., 341st M. G. Bn	11- 3
Torrey, William B., Capt., 355th Inf	11- 4
Webster, Thomas M., 1st Lt., 353rd Inf	10-24

ENLISTED MEN SEVERELY WOUNDED

Name, Rank, Company, Regiment	Date 1918
Aarons, A. Doyle, Pvt., A, 340th M. G. Bn	11-11
Aaronson, Brother A, Pvt., B, 353rd Inf	10-22
Aasen, Torvald, Pvt., B, 355th Inf	10-20
Abbit, Elmer R., Pvt., A, 314th Eng	10-26
Abraham, Walter E., Pvt. 1cl., G, 355th Inf	11- 5
Adams, Frank, Pvt., H, 354th Inf	11-11
Adkins, George L., Pvt., C, 355th Inf	11- 4
Adkins, Joseph, Pvt., A, 356th Inf	10-21
Agnew, Henry, Pvt., B, 353rd Inf	11- 1
Aguirre, Alberto, Pvt. 1cl., B, 355th Inf	11- 4
Akers, Carmel J., Pvt., L, 354th Inf	11- 1
Albers, August, Wag., Hq. 342nd M. G. Bn	10- 2
Albrecht, Fred J., Corp., I, 354th Inf	11- 1
Aleksiebes, Toni, Pvt., F, 353rd Inf	11- 3
Allen, Clyde V., Corp., B, 353rd Inf	10-25
Allen, Horace E, Pvt., E, 356th Inf	11- 6
Alley, Vern, Pvt., H, 356th Inf	9-13
Almond, Claud L, Pvt., E, 354th Inf	9-16
Alper, Israel, Pvt., D, 355th Inf	11- 4
Altberg, John V., Pvt., B, 341st M. G. Bn	10- 5
Alton, Wm. J., Mech., H, 356th Inf	9-12
Alavarez, Santiago, Pvt., H, 356th Inf	11-11
Amen, George L., Pvt., C, 354th Inf	11- 1
Ames, James A., Pvt., E, 353rd Inf	11- 1
Andersen, Hans E., Corp., C, 354th Inf	11- 1
Anderson, Carl C., Pvt., F, 353rd Inf	11- 4
Anderson, Carl R., Pvt. 1cl., B, 354th Inf	11- 1
Anderson, George E., Pvt., F, 314th Eng	11- 1
Anderson, Gunder, Pvt., B, 355th Inf	9-14
Anderson, James, Pvt. 1cl., B, 355th Inf	11- 5
Anderson, Thomas P., Pvt., E, 356th Inf	11- 7
Andrew, Henry, Pvt., H, 356th Inf	11- 3
Andrews, Albert R., Pvt., B, 342nd M. G. Bn	10- 1
Anekos, Joseph, Pvt., M, 353rd Inf	9-13
Anstine, Leslie C., Corp., L, 355th Inf	9-12
Anthony, Commodor, Pvt., F, 356th Inf	11- 5
Anthony, Walter J., Pvt., L, 355th Inf	11- 4
Apel, Nicholas, Pvt., F, 354th Inf	11- 3
Applebee, Clyde M., Pvt., A, 341st M. G. Bn	9-27
Applegit, Gilbert J., Pvt., I, 355th Inf	10- 2
Argentino, Gasperi, Pvt., K, 354th Inf	11- 1
Armstrong, Charles W., Pvt., D, 354th Inf	11- 1
Arnold, Clarence B., Pvt., F, 314th Eng	11- 8
Arnold, Isaac, Pvt., Sup. Co., 353rd Inf	11- 5
Arthur, Earl, Pvt., A, 353rd Inf	10- 2
Arvanitopeulos, Vissilious, Pvt., M, 354th Inf	10- 6
Ashbury, George T., Wag., Amb Co. 314th San. Tr	11- 1
Ashley, Harry T., Bugler, M. G. Co., 356th Inf	10-22
Ashley, Roscoe, Corp., E, 340th F. A	9-19
Aubrey, Clem, Pvt., B, 355th Inf	11- 5
Ausemus, Elmer R., Corp., F, 353rd Inf	11- 2
Austin, George, Pvt., D, 353rd Inf	9-12
Austin, George W., Pvt. 1cl., B, 342nd M. G. Bn	10- 5
Axotis, Alex A., Pvt., D, 354th Inf	9-26
Baber, Walter E, Pvt. 1cl., K, 354th Inf	11- 1
Bagby, Marion B., Pvt., B, 341st M. G. Bn	10-22
Bailey, Septimus, Pvt., D, 341st M. G. Bn	9-13
Baker, Everett E., Corp., D, 354th Inf	11- 1
Baker, Robert C., Pvt., Med. Det., 356th Inf	9-23
Bailey, Wm. G. H., Pvt., M, 353rd Inf	9-30
Balinsky, Wm., Pvt., B, 354th Inf	11- 1
Balk, Lawrence M., Pvt., G, 354th Inf	10-22
Ballard, Elva, Sgt., G, 355th Inf	9-16
Ballard, Frank, Pvt., A, 356th Inf	10-21
Baltremas, Charles, Pvt., C, 354th Inf	10-28
Banta, Edgar W., Pvt., E, 354th Inf	11- 6
Barbier, Alex J., Pvt., Hq. 356th Inf	10-22
Barbo, Geo. W., Cook, M, 354th Inf	11- 2
Barger, Elmer V., Cook, B, 355th Inf	10-20
Barkley, Wm. M., Sgt., A, 353rd Inf	11- 3
Barlage, John H., Corp., C, 354th Inf	10-28
Barnes, Frank, Pvt. 1cl., K, 355th Inf	9-14
Barnett, Edgar B., Pvt., Hq. 356th Inf	10-27
Barnett, Ralph G., Corp., K, 355th Inf	9-12
Barrick, Sam, Pvt., D, 355th Inf	11- 4
Barsl, John G., Pvt., C, 341st M. G. Bn	11- 1
Bartlett, Archer L., Pvt., D, 356th Inf	9-12
Bartlett, Russel, Pvt., A, 355th Inf	9-22
Bartley, Wm., Pvt., D, 355th Inf	10- 5
Barton, Harold, Pvt. 1cl., C, 355th Inf	9-13
Bates, Chester I., Pvt., A, 353rd Inf	10-26
Batt, Conrad, Corp., B, 341st M. G. Bn	9-13
Baustain, Bryan W., Pvt., Hq. 353rd Inf	10- 7
Baxendale, Gilbert E., Corp., D, 353rd Inf	10-23
Baxter, Fred M., Corp., L, 353rd Inf	10-22
Baxter, Ronald C., Pvt., L, 353rd Inf	10-28
Bay, Dervin A., Pvt., K, 355th Inf	9-14
Bayer, John, Pvt., D, 356th Inf	9-23
Bayerlein, Gregor, Pvt., I, 353rd Inf	10-30
Beach, Earl G., Sgt., A, 355th Inf	9-13
Beahm, Sherman E., Pvt., F, 355th Inf	9-12
Beamer, Clinton R., Cook, E, 353rd Inf	11- 5
Bearly, Samuel D., Pvt., D, 353rd Inf	10-30
Beasley, Edmond A., Corp., K, 353rd Inf	9-12
Beck, Henry, Corp., I, 354th Inf	11- 3
Becker, Fred, Pvt., L, 353rd Inf	11- 6
Becker, Paul T., Corp., H, 355th Inf	10-21
Beeson, Jesse K., Pvt., B, 314th Eng	9-24
Behrendt, Albert G., Saddler, Sup Co., 356th Inf	10-28
Beimford, Robert E., Pvt., K, 354th Inf	11- 2
Beine, Wesley A., Pvt., Med. Det., 353rd Inf	10-22
Belau, Louie W., Pvt. 1cl., M. G. Co., 355th Inf	9-19
Bell, David T., Pvt. 1cl., C, 353rd Inf	10-22
Bell, Wm. J., Pvt., M, 354th Inf	11- 1
Bell, Wm. M., Pvt., G, 354th Inf	10-22
Bell, Wm. R., Pvt., C, 354th Inf	11- 1
Bender, Wm., Pvt., G, 354th Inf	9-14
Bennett, Glenn E., Corp., F, 353rd Inf	11- 2
Bennett, Norman, Pvt. 1cl., H, 353rd Inf	9-14
Bennett, Rollie G., Pvt., E, 356th Inf	10- 6
Bennett, Roy E., Pvt., M. G. Co., 353rd Inf	11- 5
Benson, Ben, Pvt., M, 353rd Inf	10-30
Benson, Robert F., Pvt., D, 355th Inf	11- 4
Benyas, David, Pvt., E, 354th Inf	9-15
Bergemann, Walter B., Pvt., F, 355th Inf	10-21
Bergin, Louis D., Pvt. 1cl., A, 353rd Inf	10-20
Bergkamp, Fred E., Pvt., 314th San. Tr	11- 1
Berglund, Walter R., Corp., G, 354th Inf	10-27
Bergman, Henry M., Pvt., F, 354th Inf	10-21
Bergstraesser, Otto A., Pvt., D, 341st M. G. Bn	9-12
Bernoll, Albert, Pvt., F, 355th Inf	11- 6
Berquist, Allen A., Pvt., Hq. 353rd Inf	11- 1
Berry, Harold J., Pvt., K, 354th Inf	11- 1
Berryman, Lloyd M., Sgt., I, 355th Inf	9-14
Best, Edward T., Corp., H, 355th Inf	11- 5
Best, Orville W., Corp., E, 354th Inf	11- 8
Beverlin, Wm. A., Pvt., C, 353rd Inf	10-26
Bianchi, Ambrogio, Pvt., B, 341st M. G. Bn	10-26

Name, Rank, Company, Regiment	Date 1918
Bibb, Charles D., Pvt., B, 354th Inf	11- 1
Bicha, Joseph C., Pvt., D, 353rd Inf	10-21
Billesbach, Joseph, Pvt., G, 355th Inf	10-22
Bird, Harless P., Pvt., G, 354th Inf	10-22
Bischoff, Eugene A., Pvt., 354th Amb. Co.	10-22
Bishop, Lewis C., Pvt. 1cl., Med. Det., 356th Inf	10-21
Bishop, Raymond P., Pvt., L, 353rd Inf	11- 1
Black, Melvin C., Pvt. 1cl., B, 314th F. S. Bn	11- 5
Blackburn, Emil, Pvt., H, 353rd Inf	11- 5
Blackburn, Silas M., Pvt. 1cl., Sup. Co., 354th Inf	11- 1
Blair, Glenn D., Pvt. 1cl., 341st M. G. Bn	10-25
Blair, Wm. J., Pvt., K, 355th Inf	11- 4
Blakeley, Fred O., Pvt., I, 353rd Inf	11-11
Blakeman, Otto C., Corp., D, 355th Inf	11- 5
Blanton, George G., Sgt., A, 353rd Inf	10-23
Blob, Joseph A., Pvt., H, 353rd Inf	11- 1
Blincoe, Claud F., Pvt., A, 353rd Inf	10-25
Blom, Gustave R., L, 353rd Inf	11- 3
Blume, Herman F., Pvt., B, 353rd Inf	9-14
Bodenstein, Martin J., Pvt., G, 356th Inf	11- 5
Bodine, Harold C., Pvt., M, 353rd Inf	11- 8
Bocsek, John S., Pvt., M. G. Co., 355th Inf	11- 1
Boise, Paul E., Pvt., A, 354th Inf	9-22
Boley, Wm. J., Pvt., H, 355th Inf	9-17
Bollin, Frank M., Pvt. 1cl., K, 356th Inf	10- 3
Bolzenthal, Arthur, Pvt., H, 353rd Inf	11- 3
Bomsta, Max P., Pvt., F, 354th Inf	10-25
Bennett, Aubry, Pvt. 1cl., K, 355th Inf	11- 5
Bonnom, Wm. W., Corp., C, 314th F. S. Bn	11- 1
Boone, Richard B., Pvt., A, 342nd M. G. Bn	11- 1
Booth, Charles E., Corp., E, 355th Inf	11- 8
Borowiak, Walter, Pvt., D, 353rd Inf	10-24
Bose, Roy E., Pvt., D, 356th Inf	10-28
Bosseck, Lorane, Pvt., M, 353rd Inf	9-30
Boston, Wm. E., Pvt., F, 354th Inf	10-21
Boswell, John E., Pvt. 1cl., B, 341st M. G. Bn	11- 7
Botts, Oscar P., Corp., C, 356th Inf	9-29
Bouchon, Louis V., Pvt., B, 356th Inf	11- 4
Boudar, Emil, Pvt., E, 355th Inf	10-21
Bouray, Thomas F., Pvt., I, 353rd Inf	11- 3
Boutelle, Vernon W., Pvt., M. G. Co., 355th Inf	9-15
Bowman, Joseph E., Pvt., C, 355th Inf	11- 5
Bowman, Rudolph M., Pvt. 1cl., Hq. Troop, 89th Div.	11- 5
Bowman, Samuel D., Pvt., F, 355th Inf	10-21
Bowman, Walter E., Corp., K, 355th Inf	9-14
Bowyer, Harry J., Pvt. 1cl, C, 314th Eng	9-25
Box, Claude, Pvt., D, 355th Inf	11- 6
Boxleitner, John H., Corp., E, 353rd Inf	11- 1
Boyce, Ernest R., Pvt., M. G. Co., 353rd Inf	9-28
Boyd, Clay C., Pvt., L, 355th Inf	11- 5
Boyd, Earl L., Pvt., K, 355th Inf	9-13
Boyd, Harold, Pvt., E, 356th Inf	10- 6
Boyd, Ralph, Mech., C, 356th Inf	11- 3
Bradish, Joseph M., Pvt. 1cl., D, 340th F. A.	9-25
Bradley, Wm. D., Pvt., C, 355th Inf	11- 5
Brand, Wm. C., Pvt. 1cl., E, 354th Inf	9-14
Breakfield, Wm. J., Pvt., M, 355th Inf	11- 4
Breitweg, William J., Pvt., A, 353rd Inf	10-21
Brenaman, Roland C., Pvt. A, 353rd Inf	11- 3
Brennels, Carl E., Corp., L, 353rd Inf	11- 3
Bressman, Henry, Sgt., B, 341st M. G. Bn	9-18
Bricker, Elijah E., Pvt. 1cl., M. G. Co., 353rd Inf	10-30
Bridge, Burton R., Pvt., M, 356th Inf	11- 1
Briefer, Sherman A., Pvt., F, 355th Inf	10-22
Brigham, Paul L., Pvt., M. G. Co., 354th Inf	11- 3
Bright, Herbert M., Pvt., C, 356th Inf	10-22
Brinkley, Lee B., Pvt., B, 342nd F. A.	10- 7
Brinner, Willie B., Pvt., A, 356th Inf	11- 4
Brissolara, Rocco A., Pvt., M, 354th Inf	10-25
Brock, Fred, Corp., M. G. Co., 356th Inf	10-22
Brockman, John H., Sgt., L, 356th Inf	9-14
Brownfield, Gilbert, Pvt., Hq. 356th Inf	11- 3
Brommer, Charles T., Pvt. 1cl., Hq. 356th Inf	11- 6
Bron, Richard H., Pvt., B, 353rd Inf	9-18
Brocker, Marvin G., Pvt., Hq. 356th Inf	10-27
Brooks, Harry C., Pvt., H, 354th Inf	9-26
Brooks, Jesse J., Corp., M. G. Co., 354th Inf	10-21
Brooks, Leslie E., Pvt. 1cl., Hq. 342nd F. A.	9-29
Brosnan, Jeremiah C., 1st Sgt., F, 314th Eng	11- 1
Brough, Johnnie, Pvt., 314th San. Tr	10-21
Brown, Charles, Pvt., F, 353rd Inf	11- 1
Brown, Charles B., Pvt. 1cl., B, 341st M. G. Bn	10-25
Brown, Eddie M., Pvt., C, 314th F. S. Bn	11- 8
Brown, Edward A., Wag., Sup. Co., 353rd Inf	9-22
Brown, Otis T., Pvt. 1cl., Hq. 356th Inf	10- 2
Brown, Ray, Pvt., B, 341st M. G. Bn	11- 1
Brown, Wm. H., Pvt., H, 354th Inf	11- 2
Browning, Floyd C., Pvt. 1cl., D, 341st M. G. Bn	9-30
Browning, Floyd C., Pvt. 1cl., 341st M. G. Bn	11- 1

Name, Rank, Company, Regiment	Date 1918
Bruce, Harold, Sgt., C, 355th Inf	11- 5
Bruton, Grover C., Pvt. F, 353rd Inf	11- 3
Budd, Charlie E., Pvt., G, 356th Inf	9-15
Buddon, Charles E., Pvt., F, 353rd Inf	9-12
Bumgarner, Harry, Pvt., L, 353rd Inf	11- 1
Bunney, Ernest C., Wag., 314th Eng. Tr	9-25
Burgardt, Joseph, Pvt., A, 353rd Inf	10-21
Burgin, Ramus, Pvt., E, 356th Inf	10- 6
Burkholder, Wm. M., Corp., Hq. 353rd Inf	10-21
Burnham, Maxie H., Pvt., E, 356th Inf	10- 7
Burns, Raymond H., Sgt., Hq. 355th Inf	11-11
Burnside, Edgar, Pvt., H, 355th Inf	10-21
Burow, John C., Pvt., A, 341st M. G. Bn	10-22
Burr, Frederick N., Pvt. 1cl., M. G. Co., 355th Inf	11- 4
Bursvold, Louis L., Pvt. 1cl., B, 340th M. G. Bn	9-12
Burton, Willard J., Pvt. 1cl., K, 355th Inf	11- 4
Busby, John, Pvt., B, 354th Inf	11- 1
Bushman, Fred E., Pvt., K, 355th Inf	9-13
Buskirk, John R., 1st Sgt., L, 353rd Inf	11- 1
Bushwell, John M., Pvt., G, 356th Inf	9-13
Butcher, Ora L., Pvt., M, 356th Inf	11-11
Bute, Joy E., Corp., L, 355th Inf	11- 7
Butler, Elias H., Corp., E, 355th Inf	10-22
Butler, Fred N., Pvt., E, 353rd Inf	10-31
Butzlaff, Otto, Pvt., B, 353rd Inf	10-22
Bylo, Henry J., Pvt., I, 354th Inf	9-28
Byxbe, Jasper C., Pvt., E, 354th Inf	11- 3
Cabanne, Jean S., Sgt., E, 354th Inf	10-21
Cahill, Wm. P., Pvt., Hq. 355th Inf	10-21
Cain, Turner, Corp., Sup. Co., 353rd Inf	11- 5
Caldwell, Harry A., Pvt., C, 355th Inf	9-12
Callahan, Alfred M., Pvt. 1cl., A, 354th Inf	11- 1
Callaway, John E., Pvt., G, 355th Inf	11- 5
Camden, Otto O., Sgt., H, 355th Inf	11- 3
Campbell, Chester W., Pvt., F, 314th Eng	9-18
Campbell, Elmer, Pvt. 1cl., D, 314th Eng	10-29
Campbell, Jesse T., Pvt., M, 354th Inf	11 1
Campbell, John H., Pvt., C, 356th Inf	11- 5
Campbell, William, Pvt. 1cl., I, 354th Inf	9-20
Campion, Edmund, Pvt. 1cl., I, 354th Inf	11- 3
Canady, Courtland, Pvt., E, 356th Inf	11- 8
Cancrenne, Lynn, Pvt., F, 355th Inf	10-22
Cannady, Wm. R., Pvt., G, 355th Inf	10-22
Carberry, Isaac B., Pvt., M. G. Co., 354th Inf	11- 3
Card, Chas M., Corp., M. G. Co., 356th Inf	10-31
Card, Roy A., Pvt. 1cl., Med. Det., 354th Inf	9-26
Cardinelli, Domenick, Pvt., F, 354th Inf	10-25
Cardwell, Fred, Pvt., K, 356th Inf	10- 6
Carl, Gilbert E., Pvt., B, 314th M. P.	10-22
Carlson, Carl, Pvt. 1cl., L, 353rd Inf	11- 1
Carlson, Gust, Pvt., E, 355th Inf	10-22
Carpenter, Glen E., Pvt. 1cl., B, 341st M. G.	9-14
Carpenter, Willis R., Corp., A, 353rd Inf	10-25
Carpenter, Wm. R., Pvt., Sup. 353rd Inf	11- 5
Carr, Robert E., Pvt., A, 314th M. P.	10-27
Carroll, James E., Corp., A, 354th Inf	11- 1
Carson, Carl B., Pvt., M. G. Co., 355th Inf	9-18
Casanova, Geo. A., Pvt. 1cl., B, 355th Inf	11- 5
Casel, Casim H., Pvt., H, 356th Inf	11- 2
Cashatt, Robert G., Pvt., E, 356th Inf	10- 6
Catt, Marion E., Corp., L, 353rd Inf	11- 4
Cecil, Albert L., Corp., F, 355th Inf	9-12
Centlivre, Henry, Pvt., F, 353rd Inf	9-29
Chadwick, Clyde B., Pvt. 1cl., H, 354th Inf	11- 2
Chaffin, Ira W., Pvt. 1cl., F, 355th Inf	11-11
Chalmers, Robert R. 1cl., Hq. 353rd Inf	10-23
Chaney, Thomas A., Pvt., F, 314th Eng	9-26
Chapman, Roy M., Pvt. 1cl., E, 314th Eng	9-15
Cheek, Frank G., Corp., C, 356th Inf	11- 4
Cherry, Wm. U., Pvt., D, 353rd Inf	10-23
Cheyka, Frank J., Pvt. B, 354th Inf	11- 1
Childs, Alonzo C., Sgt., I, 353rd Inf	11- 1
Chinn, John H., Pvt., C, 341st M. G. Co	10-25
Choate, Claude, Pvt. 1cl., Hq. 354th Inf	11- 2
Choulette, Harry, Pvt. 1cl., M. G. Co., 356th Inf	10-22
Christensen, Christian H., Pvt., B, 356th Inf	9-16
Christian, Harold M., Corp., F, 353rd Inf	11- 2
Christian, Wm. L., Pvt., A, 355th Inf	11- 5
Christiansen, Carl A., Pvt. 1cl., F, 355th Inf	10-22
Christine, Nigal L., Pvt. 1cl., E, 353rd Inf	9-19
Church, George J., Sgt., M, 364th Inf	9-30
Chrzanoske, Peter, Pvt., L, 353rd Inf	11- 3
Cizek, Edward, Corp., F, 314th Eng	10-22
Clark, Harlan O., Corp., C, 342nd M. G. Co	9-29
Clark, Nicholas W., Corp., L, 353rd Inf	9-13
Clark, Roy L., Pvt. 1cl., C, 355th Inf	11- 5
Clark, Warren, Pvt. M. G. Co., 355th Inf	11- 1
Clatterbuck, Guy W., Pvt. 1cl., D, 354th Inf	11- 3
Clauser, Charles, Pvt., A, 354th Inf	11- 8

Name, Rank, Company, Regiment	Date 1918
Cleffman, Vernie R., Pvt., C., 355th Inf	11- 5
Clifton, Carl, Pvt., L, 354th Inf	10-23
Cline, Charles L., Cook, B, 355th Inf	9-16
Clouett, Patrick, Sgt., C, 353rd Inf	9-25
Coats, Charles E., Pvt., Hq. 353rd Inf	10-21
Cockran, James H., Pvt., G, 354th Inf	10-30
Coder, Frederick C., Pvt. 1cl., E, 353rd Inf	11- 1
Coe, Elmon F., Pvt., M. G. Co., 355th Inf	11- 1
Coen, John P., Corp., C, 354th Inf	11- 5
Coffman, Charles W., Pvt., B, 356th Inf	10-31
Coffman, Thomas E., Pvt., G, 353rd Inf	9-19
Cohn, Samuel, Pvt. 1cl., A, 356th Inf	9-23
Coleman, Thomas H., Pvt., I, 356th Inf	10- 6
Coleman, Wm. A., Pvt., E, 353rd Inf	11- 1
Colleto, Sulley, Pvt., M. G. Co., 354th Inf	11- 3
Collins, Elzey F., Corp., A, 341st M. G. Bn	10-22
Collobert, Louis, Pvt., I, 354th Inf	10-21
Colwell, Frank W., Mech., I, 355th Inf	9-22
Compton, Oscar F., Pvt., M. G. Co., 356th Inf	9-21
Conn, Arthur G., Pvt., L, 354th Inf	11- 1
Connor, Wm., Pvt., C, 356th Inf	11-11
Conrad, Paul E., Pvt., L, 353rd Inf	11- 1
Conway, Edward F., Pvt., M. G. Co., 353rd Inf	11- 1
Cook, Arthur E., Sgt., Hq. 353rd Inf	10-23
Cook, James H., Pvt. 1cl., K, 354th Inf	11- 2
Cook, Joseph M., Pvt., C, 356th Inf	11- 3
Cook, Milo J., Pvt., M, 353rd Inf	10-22
Cookson, John H., Pvt., C, 314th F. S. Bn	9-26
Corbin, Rollie S., Pvt., Med. Det., 356th Inf	10-22
Cordova, Joseph B., Corp., H, 355th Inf	11-10
Corliss, George A., Pvt. 1cl., B, 355th Inf	9-19
Corneilius, Henry C., Pvt. 1cl., K, 353rd Inf	10- 3
Cornell, Wesley P., Corp., B, 314th F. S. Bn	11- 9
Corrough, Fay M., Pvt. 1cl., B, 356th Inf	10-21
Costello, John H., Pvt., H, 356th Inf	11- 5
Costo, Tony, Pvt., A, 356th Inf	11- 6
Cottin, Leland F., Pvt., C, 354th Inf	11- 5
Coughlin, Michael, Pvt., F, 354th Inf	10-22
Coulson, Emmett, Pvt., G, 353rd Inf	9-12
Courtney, Lester F., Pvt., C, 356th Inf	11- 3
Courtney, Roy B., Mech., C, 354th Inf	11- 1
Covington, Josie A., Pvt., C, 355th Inf	11- 5
Cox, Gideon L., Pvt. 1cl., K, 354th Inf	11- 3
Cox, Robert E., Pvt., E, 356th Inf	11- 6
Cowalski, Clarence G., Pvt., F, 355th Inf	10-29
Craig, Charles T., Pvt., E, 354th Inf	11- 2
Craig, George, Pvt., H, 354th Inf	10-23
Crain, Guthrie C., Sgt., M, 356th Inf	9-12
Craine, John N., Pvt., F, 353rd Inf	11- 2
Craman, Ray, Pvt., Med. Det., 356th Inf	11- 1
Crebo, William R., Corp., Hq. 353rd Inf	10- 4
Creighton, James H., Pvt., I, 355th Inf	11- 8
Cresswell, Clarence S., Pvt., B, 356th Inf	11- 4
Cripe, Cecil L., Pvt., 355th Amb. Co	9-26
Cubbiery, Robert A., Pvt. 1cl., B, 354th Inf	11- 5
Cucchiara, Tony, Pvt., M, 353rd Inf	9-12
Cuddy, Peter J., Corp., F, 354th Inf	11- 3
Culbertson, Gary M., Corp., L, 353rd Inf	11- 3
Cullum, James L., Pvt., H, 355th Inf	9-25
Cummings, Cecil F., Pvt. 1cl., A, 356th Inf	11- 3
Cunha, Manuel, Pvt., B, 353rd Inf	10-26
Cunningham, Rex K., Corp., D, 355th Inf	11- 5
Cunningham, Vernon, Pvt., G, 356th Inf	10-22
Cunningham, Wayne J., Pvt. 1cl., K, 355th Inf	9-12
Cunningham, Wayne J., Pvt. 1cl., K, 355th Inf	11- 5
Curran, John B., Pvt. 1cl., A, 341st M. G. Bn	9-20
Curran, Mike F., Pvt., D, 353rd Inf	9-12
Curry, Samuel W., Corp., C, 355th Inf	10- 2
Curtis, Francis W., Pvt., B, 353rd Inf	10- 1
Curtis, Richard O., Pvt., E, 355th Inf	10-22
Curtner, Joseph C., Pvt., E, 356th Inf	10- 6
Czaplicki, Stefen, Pvt., B, 354th Inf	11- 1
Czarescki, John M., Pvt., E, 353rd Inf	11- 1
Czenkunsch, Arthur H., Pvt. 1cl., A, 341st M. G. Bn.	9-24
Dahl, Clyde E., Pvt. 1cl., B, 355th Inf	11- 4
Daley, Ira L., Pvt., A, 353rd Inf	10-23
Dalwitz, August, Sgt., I, 354th Inf	11- 2
Dame, John T., Pvt. 1cl., F, 354th Inf	10-21
Daniel, Joseph, Pvt., B, 314th Sup Tr	11- 1
Danselmo, Dominick, Pvt., M, 355th Inf	11- 5
Davenport, Norman, Pvt., C, 353rd Inf	10-22
David, Francis M., Corp., B, 356th Inf	9-20
Davidson, States, Pvt., H, 356th Inf	11- 4
Davis, Bert A., Mech., C, 353rd Inf	10-22
Davis, Carl E., Pvt., F, 314th Eng	11- 1
Davis, Claude H., Pvt., M. G. Co., 356th Inf	11- 5
Davis, Fred, Pvt., F, 353rd Inf	11- 8
Davis, Joseph, Pvt. 1cl., B, 341st M. G. Bn	10-23
Davis, Leo M., Pvt., Hq. 356th Inf	10- 6
Davis, Neil E., Pvt., K, 355th Inf	9-14
Day, William F., Pvt., H, 354th Inf	11-11
Dean, William E., Pvt., C, 355th Inf	11- 4
Deatherage, Paul H., Pvt., B, 342nd M. G. Bn	10- 5
De Baca, Damiano C., Pvt., E, 356th Inf	11- 5
De Bouny, Thomas A, Pvt., B, 354th Inf	11- 1
Deer, James O., Pvt., B, 314th Eng	9-21
Defreez, Albert C., Corp., G, 353rd Inf	9-12
Degenhardt, Jacob, Pvt., L, 353rd Inf	11- 4
De Groft, Charles F., Pvt., L, 355th Inf	9-13
Deiters, Benjamin, Jr., Pvt., G, 356th Inf	11- 5
De Jaeger, Manchar, Pvt., D, 353rd Inf	11-11
De Jong, William, Pvt., H, 355th Inf	10-21
Delzite, Edward, Corp., K, 353rd Inf	10-26
Denness, Elmer, Sgt., E, 314th Eng	10-26
Dennis, Joseph, Pvt., A, 355th Inf	11- 5
Dennis, Ralph D., Pvt., E, 355th Inf	10-22
Dennison, Atley, Pvt., A, 355th Inf	11- 5
Denst, Ferdinand J., Pvt., C, 354th Inf	10-28
Deskins, Frank, Pvt., D, 354th Inf	11- 1
Devine, Nancy L., Pvt. 1cl., D, 356th Inf	9-19
Dickerson, James A., Pvt., G, 356th Inf	11- 7
Dickinson, Richard, Pvt., A, 314th Sup. Tr	11- 4
Diediker, Elmer J., Corp., F, 353rd Inf	11- 1
Dietzschold, Reinhold E., Corp., E, 353rd Inf	9-23
Dillon, Clarence, Corp., G, 355th Inf	10-22
Dix, Walter G., Pvt., G, 356th Inf	11- 2
Dloogoff, Morris M., Pvt. 1cl., I, 354th Inf	9-26
Dobbins, Dan, Pvt., H, 356th Inf	11- 7
Doby, William J., Corp., A, 342nd M. G. Bn	11- 1
Dodderidge, Kenneth C., Pvt. 1cl., D, 341st M. G Bn.	9-24
Dodson, Melvin, Pvt., M, 355th Inf	10-21
Doll, John J., Pvt., D, 356th Inf	11- 3
Donbarger, Arthur, Pvt., I, 353rd Inf	9-12
Doner, Forrest E., Pvt. 1cl., H, 355th Inf	11-10
Donovan, Cyril, Pvt. 1cl., E, 354th Inf	9-25
Donze, Henry, Wag., Sup. Co., 354th Inf	9-14
Dopman, Charles, Pvt., E, 314th Eng	11- 1
Dorgan, John J., Pvt., C, 355th Inf	9-23
Douglass, Harry, Pvt., K, 356th Inf	11- 6
Douthitt, Levi A., Pvt., F, 354th Inf	11- 2
Dowdell, John, Pvt., F, 355th Inf	10-22
Downard, Murry, Pvt., M, 356th Inf	9-28
Downs, Oscar B., Pvt., F, 353rd Inf	11- 5
Dragoun, John, Pvt., C, 341st M. G. Bn	11- 4
Drennon, William R., Pvt., L, 355th Inf	9-13
Dubois, Stephen M., Pvt. 1cl., K, 353rd Inf	10-21
Duckett, Herman, Pvt., I, 353rd Inf	11- 1
Dugger, Bert L., Pvt. 1cl., G, 353rd Inf	9-12
Dull, Charles F., Pvt., Med. Det., 354th Inf	10-24
Dunaway, Alva R., Sgt. 1cl., C, 314th Eng	10-30
Dunbar, Otto C., Pvt. 1cl., 353rd Amb. Co	10-28
Duncan, John C., Corp., D, 354th Inf	11- 1
Dunn, John, Sgt., G, 354th Inf	11- 2
Dunn, John B., Pvt., I, 355th Inf	11- 6
Dunn, Robert, Pvt., F, 355th Inf	10-22
Durham, Walter H., Pvt., Hq. 353rd Inf	10-23
Duscynski, Arthur S., Pvt., E, 355th Inf	10-22
Dutcher, Henry H., Pvt., G, 354th Inf	11- 3
Dutcher, James A., Pvt., K, 354th Inf	10-22
Dye, William W., Pvt., B, 354th Inf	11- 5
Eaton, Wright E., Pvt., F, 354th Inf	10-22
Ebert, George C., Pvt., C, 355th Inf	11- 4
Eberts, Bert, Pvt., Hq. 353rd Inf	10-30
Eckstein, Henry E., Corp., G, 356th Inf	11- 5
Edelbrook, John, Corp., A, 353rd Inf	9-14
Edgren, Victor A., Pvt., F, 355th Inf	10-22
Edwards, Clarence M., Pvt., Hq. 314th Eng	10-25
Edwards, George, Pvt., A, 355th Inf	11-11
Ehert, John, Pvt., B, 353th Inf	11- 5
Ehrike, Frederick R., Corp., E, 355th Inf	10-21
Eicksteadt, George F., Pvt., C, 354th Inf	10-28
Elam, Milo V., Pvt., H, 353rd Inf	9-13
Elder, Glen W., Corp., H, 353rd Inf	9-14
Elder, John C., Pvt., E, 355th Inf	11- 8
Eller, James W., Pvt., L, 353rd Inf	11- 1
Eller, Luther J., Sgt., G, 356th Inf	11- 5
Elliott, Chester A., Sgt., H, 354th Inf	9-26
Elliott, Ray C., Pvt. 1cl., K, 355th Inf	11- 5
Elmer, Albert B., Pvt., D, 341st M. G. Bn	9-29
Elmore, Barna O., Pvt., E, 356th Inf	10- 6
Elvin, Alfred T., Pvt., F, 353rd Inf	11- 1
Emmons, Ross S., Pvt. 1cl., Amb. Co., 353rd Inf	9-23
Engberd, David E., Corp., K, 353rd Inf	9-18
Engelbrecht, Henry, Pvt., B, 353rd Inf	10-27
Englehorn, Phillip J., Pvt., I, 353rd Inf	10-31
Ennen, Henry H., Pvt. 1cl., G, 355th Inf	10-30
Enoch, Howard, Pvt., L, 356th Inf	11-11
Erickson, Charles, Pvt., M, 353rd Inf	10-23

Name, Rank, Company, Regiment	Date 1918
Erickson, C. W., Pvt., G, 356th Inf	11- 5
Ermel, Edward J., Corp., C, 314th F. S. Bn	11- 1
Ertl, Roland C., Pvt., L, 354th Inf	9-28
Eshelman, Tom D., Pvt. 1cl., D, 356th Inf	10-22
Estabrook, Ralph C., Pvt., L, 353rd Inf	11- 1
Estabrooks, Carloso M., Pvt., M, 354th Inf	11- 4
Etter, John, Master Eng., Jr., Hq. 314th Eng	10-26
Euell, Ira L., Pvt., M. G. Co., 356th Inf	10-21
Evans, Roy C., Pvt., M. G. Co., 354th Inf	11- 1
Everett, Terance, Pvt., M, 356th Inf	9-12
Eysell, Erick E., Pvt., M. G. Co., 354th Inf	11- 3
Fagan, Joseph J., Pvt., K, 353rd Inf	11- 1
Fagerli, Ole, Pvt., M, 355th Inf	11- 5
Fahnstrom, Elmer F., Corp., F, 353rd Inf	11- 3
Fallon, Frank W., Pvt., E, 356th Inf	10- 6
Farrel, Ellick, Pvt., C, 354th Inf	11- 3
Faulkner, Frederick J., Pvt., H, 356th Inf	11- 7
Fedde, Reimer F., Pvt. 1cl., H, 355th Inf	9-14
Felbish, Max, Pvt. 1cl., A, 314th Eng	10-26
Felber, Henry G., Sgt., C, 341st M. G. Bn	10-24
Felice, Michel, Pvt., F, 355th Inf	10-21
Fidler, John F., Pvt., Hq. 353rd Inf	9-25
Fiebig, Harry G, Pvt., F, 314th Eng	9-18
Fiedler, Vincent, Pvt., Hq. 354th Inf	10-21
Fields, Ambrose R., Pvt., C, 354th Inf	10-29
Finch, James R., Pvt., D, 355th Inf	10- 8
Fine, Royal A., Pvt. 1cl., Amb. Co., 354th Inf	11- 6
Fingerson, John M., Corp., A, 355th Inf	9-13
Firgens, Edward, Pvt., A, 353rd Inf	10-23
Fisher, Calvin, Pvt., E, 356th Inf	10- 6
Fisher, Charles, Pvt., A, 353rd Inf	10-21
Fisher, Lonnie, Pvt., A, 342nd F. A.	
Fisher, Roy T., Pvt., C, 342nd M. G. Bn	9-30
Fitzpatrick, Vincent J., Pvt., Amb. Co., 354th Inf	11- 8
Fitzwater, Alfred M., Pvt., B, 341st M. G. Bn	10-23
Flack, Harold B., Pvt., M. G. Co., 355th Inf	9-26
Flannery, Harry E., Sgt., D, 341st M. G. Bn	11- 1
Flinn, Roy H., Corp., F, 354th Inf	10-25
Flom, Oscar, Pvt. 1cl., K, 354th Inf	11- 2
Flood, Joe, Pvt., G, 353rd Inf	10-22
Flynn, George W., Pvt., A, 355th Inf	11- 5
Flynn, Patrick, Pvt., D, 354th Inf	9-14
Fogarty, Richard A., Pvt., B, 354th Inf	11- 1
Forbis, Fred M., Pvt., D, 354th Inf	11- 1
Ford, Robert E., Pvt., C, 341st M. G. Bn	10-26
Forslund, Carl G., Pvt., F, 353rd Inf	9-29
Foster, Herbert, Pvt., M. G. Co., 353rd Inf	11- 8
Foster, William F., Sgt., H, 353rd Inf	10-23
Fox, Guy, Pvt., F, 314th Eng	9-25
Fox, Homer J., Pvt., A, 342nd F. A.	10- 7
Franxmann, Bernard J., Pvt., K, 355th Inf	11- 5
Fraser, Daniel W., Sgt., D, 341st M. G. Bn	11- 1
Fratto, Carmeno, Pvt., B, 353rd Inf	10-22
Freeman, Earl A., Pvt. 1cl., H, 353rd Inf	9-12
Freeman, Joseph A., Pvt., F, 354th Inf	9-24
Freeman, Zanoani B., Sgt., Med. Det., 355th Inf	11- 4
Frehse, William F., Pvt., E, 355th Inf	10-21
Freise, William, Pvt., A, 314th Eng	9-12
French, William, Pvt., E, 356th Inf	10- 6
Frost, Roy N., Pvt., E, 353rd Inf	10-22
Fry, Benjamin H., Pvt., F, 353rd Inf	11- 2
Fry, Samuel M., Pvt., C, 356th Inf	11- 5
Fry, Sylvester, Pvt. 1cl., A, 353rd Inf	11- 2
Frye, Chesley F., Pvt. 1cl., B, 354th Inf	11- 1
Fulton, William C., Corp., B, 340th F. A.	10- 1
Fuschino, Pasquale, Pvt., B, 354th Inf	11- 1
Fussell, Fred M., Pvt. 1cl., C, 355th Inf	11- 5
Futter, Frank R., Pvt., Prov. Co., 314th Sup. Tr	11- 1
Gabe, Ambrose, Pvt., B, 314th M. P.	11- 1
Galk, Walter F., Pvt. 1cl., F, 354th Inf	10-22
Gann, Harrison, Pvt., D, 356th Inf	9-23
Gannon, John F., Pvt. 1cl., M, 355th Inf	9-14
Garba, Gustave A., Pvt. 1cl., A, 355th Inf	11- 5
Garcia, Pedro, Pvt., D, 356th Inf	11-11
Garcia, Onecimo, Pvt., H, 355th Inf	9-12
Garcia, Pablo S., Pvt., E, 356th Inf	11- 5
Gardner, Clare L., Pvt., E, 314th Sup. Tr	11- 3
Garton, Percy F., Pvt., H, 355th Inf	11- 8
Gasbler, Frederick, Corp., C, 341st M. G. Bn	10-31
Gates, Inness H., Pvt. 1cl., Hq. 354th Inf	10-23
Gaulrapp, George B., Pvt., I, 354th Inf	11- 2
Geanakoplos, James, Pvt., F, 354th Inf	11- 3
Gearhart, Earl E., Pvt., A, 353rd Inf	10-21
Geest, Roy R., Pvt., E, 356th Inf	11- 6
Gehrke, Julius D., Pvt., G, 354th Inf	10-22
George, Albert H., Pvt., I, 354th Inf	10-31
Geracimos, Gust N., Pvt. 1cl., M. G. Co., 356th Inf	10-21
Gerety, Paul P., Cook, G, 353rd Inf	11- 5
German, Edward F., Corp., K, 356th Inf	11- 4
Gezecki, Frank, Pvt., K, 353rd Inf	11- 1
Gifford, Bernard P., Pvt. 1cl., A, 356th Inf	11- 3
Gilbert, Ed. L., Pvt., H, 356th Inf	10- 7
Gilbert, Roy, Pvt., H, 353rd Inf	11- 3
Gillenberg, Robert, Pvt., H, 356th Inf	11-10
Gilles, John, Pvt., L, 353rd Inf	10-22
Gilroy, Julius J., Pvt., 314 San. Tr	11- 1
Ginakis, William G., Pvt., M, 355th Inf	9-13
Giorgos, Louis, Pvt., M, 354th Inf	11- 3
Glass, Wilber H., Pvt., I, 353rd Inf	11- 7
Glenn, Clifford N., Pvt. 1cl., I, 355th Inf	11- 5
Glofka, Walcon, Pvt., M, 356th Inf	9-13
Godair, Willard, Corp., H, 354th Inf	11- 1
Godlesky, Konstanty, Pvt., F, 353rd Inf	11- 1
Godsman, Sidney P., Pvt. 1cl., D, 354th Inf	11- 1
Goetz, Oscar F., Pvt., F, 355th Inf	10-22
Goldblum, William, Pvt., G, 354th Inf	11- 2
Golden, John W., Pvt. 1cl., E, 354th Inf	10-22
Golden, Louis, Pvt., L, 354th Inf	10-29
Golembski, Stanley, Pvt., E, 356th Inf	9-13
Gonzales, Carlos, Pvt., C, 355th Inf	11- 5
Gonzales, Jose C., Pvt., K, 354th Inf	9-23
Gonzales, Tobias, Pvt., B, 355th Inf	11- 5
Gooden, Judd D., Mess. Sgt., E, 353rd Inf	11- 5
Goodenow, John H., Pvt., E, 355th Inf	9-16
Goodsell, James H., Pvt., E, 353rd Inf	10-30
Gordon, Charles A., Pvt., F, 354th Inf	10-21
Gordon, James J., Pvt., F, 353rd Inf	11- 3
Grabowski, Walter R., Pvt., E, 354th Inf	10-21
Graichen, Theodore M., Pvt., B, 354th Inf	11- 1
Grandpre, Eddie, Pvt., D, 342nd M. G. Bn	11- 1
Graverbolt, Hans C. J., Pvt., M, 355th Inf	9-14
Graves, Fred W., Pvt. 1cl., M, 355th Inf	9-12
Gravesen, Peter, Pvt., K, 353rd Inf	10-23
Gray, Eddie F., Sgt., A, 356th Inf	10-21
Gray, John, Pvt., B, 340th F. A.	10- 6
Green, Allis E., Pvt., E, 354th Inf	10-30
Green, Alois F., Pvt., A, 355th Inf	11- 5
Gregg, Elbert B., Pvt., K, 353rd Inf	11- 1
Gregory, Fred E., Pvt. 1cl., H, 355th Inf	11- 6
Gregory, Perry F., Pvt., E, 354th Inf	11- 4
Grenfell, Thomas A., Pvt., K, 356th Inf	11- 2
Gribben, Christopher S., Bugler, M. G. Co., 353rd Inf	9-12
Griesbaum, Edward L., Pvt. 1cl., D, 354th Inf	9-23
Griffin, Hiram C., Pvt., I, 353rd Inf	11- 3
Grimm, Ralph O., Pvt., I, 355th Inf	11- 4
Grimmer, Clifford R., Sgt., M, 353rd Inf	9-30
Gross, Edward C., Pvt. 1cl., M. G. Co., 356th Inf	11- 4
Gross, Walter E., Pvt., G, 354th Inf	11- 1
Grove, John L., Pvt. 1cl., 355th Inf	11- 5
Groves, Frank Benj. F., Pvt., D, 355th Inf	11- 5
Groves, William P. A., Pvt., B, 356th Inf	11- 4
Grubb, James L., Pvt., H, 354th Inf	11- 1
Grundeman, William O., Pvt., B, 353rd Inf	10-21
Guenther, Otto H., Pvt., Amb. Co., 355th Inf	9-28
Guerin, Victor A., Pvt., F, 355th Inf	10-22
Guitar, James H., Sgt., E, 354th Inf	10-22
Gulliford, John H., Pvt., F, 314th Eng	11- 1
Gunter, James, Pvt. 1cl., A, 356th Inf	9-23
Gustafson, Lloyd S., Corp., F, 353rd Inf	11- 3
Guthrie, Wiley C., Pvt., C, 314th F. S. Bn	9-23
Gutierez, Guadalupe J., Pvt. 1cl., E, 314th Eng	9-12
Haap, William J., Corp., F, 354th Inf	11- 1
Haas, Edward C., Pvt., E, 354th Inf	11- 3
Haberman, Chris, Sgt., M, 355th Inf	10-21
Haffner, Rollie J., Pvt., D, 341st M. G. Bn	11- 3
Hagan, Harold J., Pvt., Med. Det., 354th Inf	10- 1
Hagelin, Paul A., Corp., C, 341st M. G. Bn	10-31
Hagman, Charles A., Pvt. 1cl., D, 342nd M. G. Bn	9-25
Hagstrand, John A., Pvt., Sup. Co., 353rd Inf	11-10
Hall, Albert, Pvt., I, 353rd Inf	11- 3
Hall, William, Pvt., D, 355th Inf	10-21
Hallock, Philip, Pvt., Hq. 354th Inf	11- 2
Halloren, Francis A., Corp., B, 355th Inf	9-12
Halverson, Gilbert, Pvt., D, 341st M. G. Bn	11- 2
Hamilton, Floyd W., Pvt., F, 354th Inf	11- 3
Hamilton, John A., Pvt., B, 355th Inf	11- 5
Hamilton, Porter A., Sgt., F, 356th Inf	10- 6
Hamlin, John, Pvt., A, 356th Inf	9-14
Hammond, John I., Sgt., D, 353rd Inf	9-12
Hammond, Louis A., Pvt. 1cl., F, 354th Inf	9-30
Hancock, James, Pvt., C, 355th Inf	11- 5
Handlan, William A., Pvt., H, 354th Inf	11-11
Haney, James W., Corp., B, 342nd M. G. Bn	11- 1
Hanners, Landy F., Corp., C, 341st M. G. Bn	10-25
Hansen, Adolph, Pvt., B, 353rd Inf	10-23
Hansen, Edward C., Pvt., D, 355th Inf	11- 8
Hansen, James G., Pvt., E, 355th Inf	11- 4
Hansen, Jens P., Sgt., F, 353rd Inf	9-18

Name, Rank, Company, Regiment	Date 1918
Hansen, John W., Corp., B, 341st M. G. Bn.	10-22
Hansen, Martin, Pvt., G, 354th Inf	11- 3
Hansen, Phillip L. P., Pvt., H, 353rd Inf	9-12
Hanson, Walter, Pvt. 1cl., B, 340th M. G. Bn.	11- 1
Hantzon, Petros, Pvt., I, 354th Inf	11- 3
Happel, Roy E., Corp., I, 353rd Inf	11- 1
Harbaugh, Malcolm E., Pvt., F, 353rd Inf	11- 3
Hariman, John J., Pvt. 1cl., A, 355th Inf	11- 5
Hardin, David W., Pvt., A, 356th Inf	10-22
Hargis, Walter J., Pvt., E, 353rd Inf	11- 1
Harmon, Charles L., Pvt., H, 354th Inf	11-11
Harmon, Millard, Pvt., E, 356th Inf	10- 6
Harper, Henry C., Pvt., I, 356th Inf	9-13
Harper, Henry C., Pvt., I, 356th Inf	11-11
Harris, Charles, Pvt., E, 356th Inf	10- 6
Harris, Clovis, Pvt., C, 354th Inf	11-11
Harris, Lloyd E., Pvt., B, 355th Inf	11- 5
Harris, Richard L., Sgt., F, 355th Inf	10-22
Harris, Walter K., Pvt., F, 355th Inf	10-22
Harris, William, Pvt. 1cl., M. G. Co., 356th Inf	11- 5
Harrison, Richard T., Pvt., B, 354th Inf	9-14
Harsh, James A., Pvt., I, 353rd Inf	11- 7
Hart, Wilbur J., Corp., H, 353rd Inf	11- 3
Hartley, Howard B., Pvt. 1cl., M. G. Co., 353rd Inf	9-21
Hartley, Paul T., Pvt. 1cl., C, 314th F. S. Bn.	10-31
Hartshorn, Clyde C., Pvt., D, 353rd Inf	10-31
Harvey, John J., Pvt., C, 353rd Inf	11- 1
Haselwood, Leroy, Pvt., F, 353rd Inf	9-12
Hauber, Anthony W., Pvt., A, 353rd Inf	10-23
Havener, Herbert L., Pvt., E, 356th Inf	11- 3
Havens, Ernest L., Pvt., Hq. 354th Inf	9-26
Hawkins, Albert, Corp., H, 354th Inf	11-11
Hawkins, Clay H., Pvt., H, 353rd Inf	10-30
Haworth, Burton J., Pvt., A, 353rd Inf	10-22
Hays, Guerney V., Sgt., F, 355th Inf	10-22
Hazeltine, Warren J., Pvt., M. O. Co., 354th Inf	11- 1
Hazlip, Claud, Pvt., E, 353rd Inf	11- 1
Head, Thomas, Pvt., D, 355th Inf	11- 6
Healy, John L., Pvt., I, 356th Inf	11-11
Heath, Robert M., Cook, F, 340th F. A.	9-29
Heathman, Marcus J., Sgt., L, 354th Inf	11- 3
Hedlund, Hilding A., Corp., A, 355th Inf	11- 5
Heier, George, Pvt., M. G. Co., 354th Inf	11- 1
Heiser, John W., Jr., Pvt. 1cl., F, 354th Inf	10-21
Heim, Aloysius, Pvt., G, 353rd Inf	9-23
Heim, Phil. F., Pvt., Sup. Co., 356th Inf	11- 5
Heintz, Charles E., Pvt., D, 342nd F. A.	9-21
Helding, Albert, Pvt., E, 354th Inf	10-21
Helgeson, Peter C., Pvt., B, 354th Inf	11- 2
Helsing, Hjalmer B., Pvt., A, 341st M. G. Bn.	11- 4
Henderson, Oral T., Pvt., G, 353rd Inf	11- 1
Hendricks, Frank I., Pvt., E, 353rd Inf	11- 1
Hendricks, Jyloe C., Corp., H, 355th Inf	11- 6
Hendricks, Richard L., Pvt., A, 355th Inf	11- 1
Hendricks, Pink, Pvt., Sup. Co. 355th Inf	10- 4
Hendrickson, Frank L., Pvt., M, 356th Inf	9-12
Henke, Joseph J., Corp., I, 354th Inf	10-20
Hennessy, Benjamin O., Pvt., A, 356th Inf	10-21
Herberger, Fred L., Pvt., L, 354th Inf	11- 1
Herbert, John E., Pvt., F, 354th Inf	10-21
Hering, Raymond, Pvt., G, 355th Inf	10-21
Herman, Charles J., Pvt., A, 356th Inf	10-21
Herwig, Phillip, Pvt., B, 355th Inf	11- 5
Hiatt, Elmer E., Sgt., C, 355th Inf	11- 4
Hibbart, Frederick A., Pvt., M. G. Co., 356th Inf	9-13
Hierenymus, John O., Pvt. 1cl., H, 354th Inf	10-25
Higgins, George H., Sgt., I, 355th Inf	9-14
Higgins, Henry E., Pvt., A, 353rd Inf	10-21
Hight, Orvalle R., Sgt., L, 353rd Inf	11- 3
Hild, Emil J., Sgt., M. G. Co., 355th Inf	11- 1
Hildebrand, Archie, Pvt. 1cl., B, 342nd M. G. Bn.	11- 1
Hildebrandt, Erich F., Pvt., H, 354th Inf	10-25
Hiles, Mason J., Pvt., D, 342nd M. G. Bn.	11- 5
Hill, Benjamin, Pvt., E, 356th Inf	10- 6
Hill, John J., Pvt., B, 353rd Inf	10-21
Hill, Thomas, Pvt., F, 355th Inf	10-21
Hill, Walter O., Pvt., B, 356th Inf	9-21
Hill, William D., Pvt., H, 354th Inf	11- 1
Hilton, Frank G., Pvt. 1cl., L, 354th Inf	10-21
Hoagland, Clinton T., Sgt., E, 355th Inf	10-21
Hock, James E., Corp., K, 356th Inf	10- 6
Hoffman, Earl A., Pvt., C, 341st M. G. Bn.	10-25
Hogans, Mack, Pvt., G, 355th Inf	10-26
Holden, Frank E., Cook, A, 314th Eng	9-12
Holder, William C., Pvt., E, 354th Inf	9-24
Holdren, Benjamin F., Pvt., I, 353rd Inf	11- 3
Holland, Earl, Pvt., G, 353rd Inf	11- 1
Holley, George B., Pvt., K, 314th Amm. Tr.	10- 6
Hollingsworth, Alexander, Corp., B, 354th Inf	11- 1
Hollis, Ward, Sgt., L, 354th Inf	11- 1
Holman, Earl E., Pvt., H, 353rd Inf	11- 5
Holmberg, Fred L., Mech., C, 355th Inf	11- 4
Holmes, William, Pvt., Hq. 356th Inf	11- 1
Holscher, Gust. A., Pvt., K, 355th Inf	9-23
Holt, William R., Pvt. 1cl., M, 353rd Inf	10- 3
Holtz, George W., Pvt., F, 353rd Inf	9-23
Hood, Oscar W., Pvt. 1cl., G, 355th Inf	11- 5
Hooper, Harry, Sgt., K, 356th Inf	11-11
Hoover, William H., Pvt., C, 355th Inf	9-13
Hopkins, Alexander, Pvt., L, 353rd Inf	9-24
Hopkins, James A., Pvt., A, 355th Inf	11- 5
Hopkins, Marion L., Pvt., H, 354th Inf	11-11
Hoskins, Charles W., Pvt., Hq. 356th Inf	9-12
Houg, Phillip M., Pvt. 1cl., D, 355th Inf	9-13
Houghton, Hugh J., Pvt. 1cl., M. G. Co., 356th Inf	10-30
Houk, John, Corp., B, 354th Inf	11- 1
Howard, Robert, Sgt., H, 354th Inf	11- 3
Howisey, George H., Sgt., A, 341st M. G. Bn.	11- 3
Hoxeny, Charles J., Pvt., B, 340th M. G. Bn.	11- 8
Hoyle, Charles R., Pvt., B, 341st M. G. Bn.	10-24
Hreljoc, Luke F., Bugler, G, 354th Inf	9-14
Huber, Edward E., Pvt., M. G. Co., 356th Inf	10-22
Huddleston, Lue A., Pvt., O, 355th Inf	10- 4
Hudspeth, Silas C., Pvt., I, 355th Inf	10- 2
Huebner, Hugo, Pvt., D, 353rd Inf	10-31
Huffman, Wilbur D., Pvt., F, 356th Inf	10-21
Huitt, John G., Pvt., D, 342nd F. A.	9-21
Hullihan, John L., Pvt., K, 356th Inf	9-14
Hundley, Jacob, Pvt., C, 356th Inf	11- 3
Hunt, Harrison, Pvt., B, 314th Eng	9-15
Hunt, Samuel L., Pvt., C, 353rd Inf	10-24
Hunting, King L., Pvt., E, 314th Eng	10-26
Hurlburd, Ernest W., Pvt., D, 342nd M. G. Bn.	11- 8
Hurley, George J., Pvt., A, 354th Inf	9-28
Hurst, Joe E., Pvt., I, 354th Inf	9-23
Hurwitz, Simon W., Corp., D, 353rd Inf	10-25
Huse, George G., Pvt. 1cl., K, 356th Inf	11- 2
Hyde, Harry, Pvt., L, 353rd Inf	11- 3
Hynek, Jerry, Pvt., F, 353rd Inf	9-29
Hynes, Albert D., Pvt., F, 355th Inf	11-21
Hynes, Frederick, Pvt., A, 355th Inf	10-31
Hyser, Charles T., Pvt. 1cl., H, 355th Inf	11- 6
Ingraham, William, Pvt. 1cl., G, 353rd Inf	11- 3
Irving, John F., Pvt., F, 354th Inf	11- 2
Jackson, Bronce, Sgt., E, 353rd Inf	11- 1
Jackson, Charles L., Sgt., H, 354th Inf	9-28
Jackson, Clark L., Pvt., G, 355th Inf	9-13
Jackson, John E., Corp., I, 353rd Inf	11- 1
Jackson, John V., Pvt. 1cl., A, 356th Inf	9-16
Jackson, Orral O., Corp., D, 342nd M. G. Bn.	11- 5
Jacobs, Edward E., Corp., G, 354th Inf	11- 1
Jacobs, Everett J., Wag., Sup. Co., 355th Inf	11- 5
Jacobs, George, Pvt., E, 353rd Inf	11- 5
Jacobs, Henry J., Pvt. 1cl., Hq. 354th Inf	11- 1
Jacobs, Wendell W., Pvt. 1cl., C, 341st M. G. Bn.	10-31
Jacobson, Nels, Pvt., F, 355th Inf	10-22
Jacoby, Clifford, Pvt., A, 353rd Inf	10-23
Jacques, Charles S., Pvt., A, 341st M. G. Bn.	10-21
Jacques, Joseph H., Pvt., L, 354th Inf	10-21
Jagodzinski, Vincent J., Pvt., F, 354th Inf	11- 3
James, Glen O., Sgt., C, 341st M. G. Bn.	9-18
James, Russel F., Pvt., M. G. Co., 356th Inf	9-21
James, Walter L., Pvt., B, 354th Inf	9-26
Janitell, Joseph, Pvt., M, 353rd Inf	11- 1
Janke, Leonard, Pvt., K, 355th Inf	9-15
Jarboe, Robert L., Corp., C, 354th Inf	11- 1
Jefferies, Benjamin H., Mech., L, 353rd Inf	9-24
Jennings, George W., Pvt., A, 356th Inf	10-21
Jennings, Harry C., Pvt. 1cl., F, 355th Inf	10-21
Jensen, Reuben, Pvt., H, 355th Inf	11- 8
Jensen, Soren C., Pvt., B, 355th Inf	11- 5
Jewett, Homer R., Pvt., Hq. 353rd Inf	10-23
Johansen, Oscar, Mech., C, 356th Inf	9-14
Johansson, Johannes P., Pvt. 1cl., M. D., 354th Inf	11- 1
Johnson, Arthur, Pvt., C, 354th Inf	10-28
Johnson, Arthur R., Pvt., H, 354th Inf	10-23
Johnson, Bennie E., Pvt., M. G. Co., 355th Inf	11- 2
Johnson, Carl E., Corp., F, 355th Inf	11- 3
Johnson, Charles H., Pvt., D, 353rd Inf	11- 1
Johnson, Dock V., Pvt., C, 355th Inf	11- 5
Johnson, Eddie, Pvt., G, 355th Inf	10-22
Johnson, Edwin E., Pvt., B, 353rd Inf	10-22
Johnson, Gottfred, Pvt., H, 354th Inf	10-23
Johnson, Gus., Pvt. 1cl., E, 314th Eng	9-12
Johnson, James M., Pvt., F, 355th Inf	10- 5
Johnson, John A., Pvt., C, 354th Inf	10-28
Johnson, Lovel F., Pvt., E, 354th Inf	9-30
Johnson, Paul, Pvt., A, 355th Inf	11- 5

Name, Rank, Company, Regiment	Date 1918
Johnson, Thura K., Pvt., L, 353rd Inf	10-22
Johnson, Walter B., Pvt. 1cl., E, 353rd Inf	11- 1
Jokich, Arthur, Pvt., G, 355th Inf	10-21
Jones, Clifton V., Pvt. 1cl., F, 355th Inf	10-22
Jones, George W., Pvt., B, 341st M. G. Bn	10-22
Jones, Glenn L., Corp., M, 355th Inf	9-12
Jones, Ross, Pvt. 1cl., Hq. 354th Inf	9-17
Jones, Walter W., Corp., B, 353rd Inf	9-12
Jones, William W., Pvt. 1cl., F, 356th Inf	11- 4
Jonkel, Frank F., Pvt. 1cl., E, 354th Inf	11- 2
Judkins, Leo R., Pvt., E, 353rd Inf	11- 1
Junkman, David W., Pvt. 1cl., K, 355th Inf	9-12
Justice, Lawrence, Pvt., D, 355th Inf	11- 5
Kaddatz, Fred W., Pvt., B, 354th Inf	11- 1
Kain, Edwardo G., Pvt., C, 356th Inf	11- 3
Kaiser, Oliver P., Pvt., E, 354th Inf	11- 3
Kalina, Frank, Pvt., F, 355th Inf	10-21
Kampen, Thomas, Pvt., B, 353rd Inf	11- 1
Kane, George E., Pvt., C, 353rd Inf	10-21
Karman, Ignatius, Pvt., D, 353rd Inf	11- 1
Karouzos, George K., Pvt., D, 356th Inf	9-23
Karr, John H., Pvt., B, 356th Inf	11- 4
Kasel, Aloysius O., Pvt., B, 342nd M. G. Bn	10- 5
Kasten, Arthur C., Pvt., H, 353rd Inf	11- 3
Kastrup, Henry, Pvt., B, 356th Inf	11- 4
Katzberg, Fred W., Pvt., K, 355th Inf	9-23
Kaufmann, Martin, Pvt., Sup Co., 353rd Inf	11- 8
Keals, James, Pvt., M, 353rd Inf	11- 1
Keddy, Clyde A., Pvt. 1cl., F, 355th Inf	10-21
Keel, George B., Corp., E, 354th Inf	10-28
Keith, Samuel G., Pvt., G, 356th Inf	9-13
Keithley, John, Pvt. 1cl., C, 356th Inf	11- 8
Keller, Harry, Pvt., M. G. Co., 356th Inf	9-13
Keller, Robert E., Pvt., 356th Inf	9-15
Kelly, Howard, Pvt. 1cl., I, 356th Inf	9-13
Kelso, Stephen E., Pvt., E, 356th Inf	10- 8
Keltner, Jeff, Pvt., D, 356th Inf	11- 5
Kendle, Ralph S., Pvt. 1cl., A, 356th Inf	9-12
Kennedy, Lester L., Sgt., G, 353rd Inf	9-24
Kerler, Charles, Pvt., I, 354th Inf	11- 2
Kerlin, Richard, Pvt., G, 354th Inf	11- 3
Kersten, Otto F., Pvt., K, 356th Inf	11-11
Kessler, Joseph G., Pvt., B, 353rd Inf	10-22
Kester, Jay P., Pvt., H, 356th Inf	11- 5
Ketheart, Oral W., Pvt. 1cl., M, 353rd Inf	9-30
Key, Claude, Pvt., E, 356th Inf	10-22
Keyahian, Kay, Pvt., M, 354th Inf	10-21
Kice, Orville A., Pvt. 1cl., E, 353rd Inf	9-20
Kimble, Belar, Pvt., F, 354th Inf	10-21
Kimberg, John, Pvt., C, 356th Inf	9-28
Kindsfather, Jacob, Pvt. 1cl., A, 353rd Inf	10-23
King, Jack, Pvt., G, 355th Inf	10-22
King, Harley, Pvt., M, 353rd Inf	10-23
Kinkade, Walter E., Pvt. 1cl., A, 341st M. G. Bn	10-22
Kinkead, George G., Pvt., A, 353rd Inf	10-24
Kirkakos, Xenophone, Pvt., M, 353rd Inf	11- 1
Kirkbride, Emmons W., Pvt., L, 353rd Inf	11-11
Kirkpatrick, Dean F., Corp., G, 353rd Inf	11- 2
Kirkpatrick, Noah R., Pvt., Hq. 354th Inf	11- 2
Kistler, Walter R., Pvt., D, 353rd Inf	10-21
Kjelland, Ole, Pvt. 1cl., A, 340th M. G. Bn	10-28
Klastow, Stanley, Pvt., D, 354th Inf	11- 1
Klatt, Fred L., Pvt. 1cl., A, 342nd M. G. Bn	11- 3
Klein, Joseph P., Corp., E, 354th Inf	11- 2
Kleinschmidt, Lester G., Corp., Hq. 354th Inf	11- 1
Klever, Charles E., Pvt., F, 354th Inf	11- 1
Kline, Harry R. Pvt., K, 353rd Inf	9-12
Klinkenberg, Edward G., Corp., C, 353rd Inf	10-22
Klix, Otto A., Pvt., A, 354th Inf	11- 2
Knapp, Adam J., Corp., C, 356th Inf	9-13
Knapp, Gus. L., Pvt., K, 355th Inf	11- 4
Knapp, Henry P., Pvt., L 353rd Inf	10-22
Knierim, George, Pvt., M, 354th Inf	11- 2
Knox, Archie, Pvt., C, 353rd Inf	10-22
Knox, Robert, Pvt., M, 353rd Inf	9-18
Knox, Frank J., Pvt., G, 354th Inf	9-25
Kobelt William, Pvt. 1cl., M, 354th Inf	9-15
Koehler, Bernard G., Pvt., B, 342nd M. G. Bn	8-16
Koenig, Adolph, Pvt., K, 355th Inf	9-14
Koepsel, Herman, Pvt., B, 353rd Inf	10-23
Kohring, Ben, Pvt., G, 354th Inf	10-27
Koken, Ralph R., Sgt., G, 355th Inf	10-21
Kokenos, Harry, Pvt. 1cl., B, 353rd Inf	10-22
Konetchy, Leo F., Pvt., D, 354th Inf	11- 1
Kosky, Frank, Pvt., H, 353rd Inf	11- 1
Kotrba, Charles, Pvt., A, 353rd Inf	10-23
Koranda Stephen, Corp., M, 355th Inf	11- 4
Kraatz, Randolph P., Sgt., C, 341st M. G. Bn	10-25
Krahenbuhl, Fritz, Corp., G, 356th Inf	10-21
Kramer, Harry, Pvt., A, 353rd Inf	9-22
Krapelin, Herman, Pvt., B, 354th Inf	11- 1
Kraus, William J., Pvt., G, 356th Inf	11- 9
Krieger, Martin A., Pvt., C, 354th Inf	10-28
Kreuger, Leonard A., Pvt., C, 353rd Inf	10-31
Kreuger, Rudolph A., Pvt., D, 356th Inf	9-13
Kubal, George N., Pvt., B, 354th Inf	11- 1
Kucewski John, Pvt., Hq. 353rd Inf	10-26
Kueck, Edwin F., Cook, M. G. Co., 355th Inf	9-26
Kuehnl Joseph, Pvt., M, 354th Inf	11- 1
Kuhn, Henry M., Pvt. 1cl., L, 354th Inf	11- 1
Kuklock, Peter, Pvt., B, 354th Inf	11- 1
Kuss, Frank W., Pvt., L, 353rd Inf	11- 1
Kuss, John M., Corp., Hq. 314th Eng	10-25
Labatus, Louis, Pvt., D, 355th Inf	11- 5
LaFore, J. S., Pvt., E, 354th Inf	11- 2
LaFrance, Frank, Pvt., M, 356th Inf	11-11
Lager, Gust. R., Pvt., G, 353rd Inf	11- 1
Lamb, Fred R., Pvt., A, 341st M. G. Bn	9-20
Lamb, Paul E., Pvt. 1cl., B, 342nd M. G. Bn	10- 4
Lane, Edward E., Pvt., B, 341st M. G. Bn	10-22
Lang, Herbert A., Pvt., M. G. Co., 354th Inf	10-31
Lang, Oscar T., Pvt., E, 354th Inf	11- 2
Lanham, Roy U., Pvt. 1cl., A, 314th Eng	10-26
LaPalme, Arthur, Pvt., Hq. 353rd Inf	10-23
Lappin, George A., Pvt. 1cl., F, 354th Inf	10-21
Larson, Charles W., Pvt., E, 353rd Inf	11- 1
Larson, Ivar J., Pvt., M, 354th Inf	10-25
LaRue, Charles L., Pvt., F, 314th Eng	9-18
Laschinger, Fred, Pvt., F, 353rd Inf	11- 3
Lash, Raymond J., Pvt., B, 356th Inf	9-23
Latall, Theodore F., Pvt., A, 354th Inf	11- 1
Latiner, Ralph V., Pvt., C, 356th Inf	11-11
Lauber, Emil, Pvt., L, 353rd Inf	11- 6
Lauer, Herman F., Pvt., L, 353rd Inf	11- 3
Lautenslauger, John H., Pvt., Hq. 340th F. A	9-29
Law, Clarence G., Pvt., Hq. 353rd Inf	9-19
Lawrence, Joseph, Pvt., 355th Amb. Co	9-26
Lawson, William J. S., Pvt., K, 355th Inf	11-10
Lay, Arthur M., Pvt., A, 342nd M. G. Bn	10-28
Laycock, Simon, Pvt., K, 355th Inf	9-15
Leavens, Elmer, Corp., A, 355th Inf	11- 4
Ledbetter, William B., Pvt. 1cl., G, 353rd Inf	9-26
Lee, Conrad, Pvt., B, 354th Inf	11- 1
Lee, Herman, Pvt., L, 355th Inf	9-14
Lee, Joseph M., Pvt., D, 341st M. G. Bn	11- 1
Leeder, William M., Pvt., E, 355th Inf	10-21
Leeper, Elias W., Pvt., A, 341st M. G. Bn	9-11
Leeper, Silas F., Pvt. 1cl., E, 354th Inf	11- 2
LeGrand, Lopis W., Pvt., M, 353rd Inf	11- 1
Lehrman, Charles H., Corp., D, 342nd F. A	10- 7
Leiferman, Mike Pvt., F, 355th Inf	10-22
Leighty, Frank M., Pvt. 1cl., B, 342nd M. G. Bn	11- 1
Leiker, Jacob F., Pvt., K, 353rd Inf	11- 5
Leikon, Peter C., Pvt., K, 353rd Inf	10-31
Leitner, John F., Pvt., E, 356th Inf	10- 6
Lemmons, James A., Pvt., H, 354th Inf	9-16
Lendorf, August H., Corp., I, 354th Inf	11- 3
Lentz, Herman, Mech., F, 355th Inf	10-22
Leonard, Otto F., Pvt., M. G. Co., 356th Inf	9-23
Leul, Foster A., Pvt., C, 355th Inf	11- 1
Lewin, Sam., Pvt., K, 354th Inf	11- 1
Levine, Simon, Pvt., E, 356th Inf	11- 2
Levitt, Benjamin, Pvt., A, 354th Inf	11- 2
Lewis, Weldon C., Pvt., C, 356th Inf	10-21
Lightbody, John M., Corp., H, 353rd Inf	11- 1
Likins, Millard B., Pvt., H, 354th Inf	10-28
Lindon, Harrison, Pvt., K, 356th Inf	10- 6
Lindsay, David, Pvt. 1cl., Hq. 356th Inf	10- 6
Litterest, Clarence F., Pvt., C, 354th Inf	11- 3
Little, Crow Isaac, Pvt., G, 355th Inf	10-21
Lloyd, Stanley W., Sgt., B, 353rd Inf	10- 2
Lobban, James L., Corp., M. G. Co., 355th Inf	11- 4
Lobel, Joseph, Pvt., C, 314th Amm. Tr	10-25
Locke, Leslie C., Pvt., M. G. Co., 353rd Inf	10-31
Leddick, Leon W., Pvt., L, 353rd Inf	10-22
Logan, Franklin W., Wag., Sup. Co., 353rd Inf	9-22
Lopez, Amarante, Pvt., L, 354th Inf	11- 1
Lopez, Jose B., Pvt., B, 353rd Inf	10-22
Lorig, Julius E., Pvt., K, 353rd Inf	10-26
Louk, Palmer, Pvt., B, 356th Inf	10-25
Lovitt, Paul, Pvt., F, 355th Inf	10-21
Lloyd, John L., Pvt., D, 354th Inf	11- 1
Luder, Jacob, Corp., Hq. 353rd Inf	11- 5
Ludwig, John W., Pvt. 1cl., A, 341st M. G. Bn	11- 1
Lukovich, John, Pvt., L, 353rd Inf	11- 1
Lundberry, Clyde H., Pvt., M, 355th Inf	10- 1
Lundstad, John, Pvt., B, 354th Inf	11- 1
Lutz, Charles H., Corp., F, 354th Inf	10-22

Name, Rank, Company, Regiment	Date 1918
Lynch, Sam. L., Pvt., Med. Det., 354th Inf	10-31
Lynes, Sherman F., Pvt., K, 354th Inf	11- 1
Lyons, Richard C., Pvt., E, 355th Inf	10-21
Madden, Harvey L., Pvt., I, 356th Inf	10- 6
Mader, Willie L., Pvt. 1cl., I, 353rd Inf	9-25
Madsen, Carl A., Pvt., E, 355th Inf	11- 9
Magelky, Peter M., Pvt., D, 341st M. G. Bn	11- 1
Maggard, Pearl M., Pvt., M, 354th Inf	11- 1
Mahan, Dan., Pvt. 1cl., M. G. Co., 355th Inf	11- 5
Mahane, Henry, Pvt., A, 355th Inf	11- 4
Maher, Michael A., Pvt., Sup. Co., 353rd Inf	10- 5
Mahutga, Mathew, Pvt., E, 353rd Inf	11- 3
Makamul, Joseph, Pvt., C, 354th Inf	11- 1
Malm, Emil, Pvt. 1cl., C, 355th Inf	9-17
Maloney, Leonard, Pvt., A, 355th Inf	11- 5
Mangoficio, Paul, Pvt., Amb. Co., 356th Inf	11- 4
Manson, Burton P., Pvt. 1cl., E, 314th Sup. Tr	11- 8
Manzanares, Manuel, Pvt., C, 356th Inf	9-17
Marek, Jerry, Corp., C, 341st M. G. Bn	11- 3
Marko, Charles, Pvt., D, 354th Inf	10- 3
Marks, Edward H., Pvt., L, 353rd Inf	11- 3
Marks, Mathew, Pvt., E, 353rd Inf	10-18
Marr, William H., Pvt., E, 353rd Inf	10-22
Marshall, Claude S., Pvt. 1cl., B, 341st M. G. Bn	10-24
Marsteller, Luther S., Pvt. 1cl., K, 355th Inf	9-14
Martens, Herman R., Pvt. 1cl., M, 356th Inf	11-11
Martin, John C., Pvt., M. G. Co., 354th Inf	11- 3
Martinez, Rafael A., Pvt., H, 353rd Inf	11- 1
Martinson, Gilbert, Corp., F, 355th Inf	10-22
Matson, Chris, Pvt. 1cl., M, 355th Inf	11- 5
Masterson, Edward J., Pvt. 1cl., Ord., 353rd Inf	9-26
Mastio, Robert G., Pvt., K, 356th Inf	10- 5
Mattley, Ray D., Pvt., F, 353rd Inf	9-29
Mattox, Marion R., Pvt. 1cl., A, 356th Inf	9-23
Maucini, Joseph J., Pvt. 1cl., B, 340th M. G. Bn	9-13
Maupin, Louis M., Pvt., M. G. Co., 356th Inf	9-23
Mayer, Charles H., Pvt., M. G. Co., 356th Inf	9-27
McBride, Charles A., Corp., D, 353rd Inf	10-25
McCaffery, Leo J., Pvt., L, 354th Inf	11- 1
McCallister, Jack C., Pvt., B, 342nd M. G. Bn	10- 4
McCann, Pleas, Sgt., L, 354th Inf	11- 1
McCargo, George, Pvt., C, 314th F. S. Bn	10-27
McCarthy, John C., Pvt. 1cl., C, 341st M. G. Bn	9-13
McCartney, Charles E., Pvt. 1cl., K, 354th Inf	10-22
McClain, Walter A., Pvt., K, 353rd Inf	11- 1
McClintock, John W., Pvt. 1cl., C, 356th Inf	11- 3
McCormack, Joseph J., Pvt. 1cl., C, 314th Sup. Tr	11- 4
McCready, Charles E., Sgt., E, 356th Inf	10- 6
McDaniel, Sylvester E., Pvt., I, 353rd Inf	11- 1
McDaniels, Frank L., Sgt., D, 342nd M. G. Bn	11-10
McDermott, Patrick F., Pvt., I, 354th Inf	11- 3
McDonald, David G., Pvt., M. G. Co., 354th Inf	11- 2
McElveney, John, Corp., C, 341st M. G. Bn	10-25
McGee, Otis E., Pvt., F, 356th Inf	11- 3
McGhee, Terry W., Pvt., D, 356th Inf	9-18
McGrath, Patrick, Pvt., M, 354th Inf	11- 2
McHalffey, Natha C., Pvt. 1cl., K, 355th Inf	11- 4
McHeney, Edward C., Pvt., G, 356th Inf	11- 5
McKane, Charles A., Pvt., D, 314th Sup. Tr	11- 3
McLaughlin, James A., Pvt., M, 353rd Inf	11- 1
McMahan, William E., Pvt., G, 355th Inf	10-21
McManemin, Robert A., Pvt., E, 314th Eng	11- 1
McManus, Thomas J., Pvt. 1cl., M. G. Co., 356th Inf	9-13
McMullen, Barnett, Pvt. 1cl., L, 354th Inf	9-27
McNaughton, Roy, Corp., G, 356th Inf	11- 5
McNeilly, Chester F., Pvt., B, 314th M. P	10- 5
McPherson, John J., Corp., D, 355th Inf	11- 4
McQuaid, Charles R., Pvt. 1cl., M. G. Co., 356th Inf	11- 3
McRae, Simon B., Pvt., D, 355th Inf	11- 4
McRoberts, George, Pvt. 1cl., I, 353rd Inf	11- 1
McVay, John J., Pvt., 314th San. Tr	11- 5
McVeigh, James, Pvt., M. G. Co., 355th Inf	9-20
Mead, William P., Pvt. 1cl., H, 355th Inf	10-21
Meador, Clarence, Sgt., I, 353rd Inf	11- 1
Meastes, Eugenio, Pvt., D, 356th Inf	9-13
Meder, George, Pvt. 1cl., L, 353rd Inf	10-22
Medina, Alejandro, Pvt., B, 355th Inf	10-20
Mehrle, Arthur J., Mech., A, 356th Inf	9-21
Melton, Clifford, Pvt., C, 356th Inf	10-23
Melvin, Claude T., Pvt. 1cl., M. G. Co., 354th Inf	11- 1
Menkeschi, Marion, Pvt., C, 353rd Inf	10-21
Merrell, Robert L., Corp., B, 354th Inf	11- 1
Meusborn, Walter, Pvt. 1cl., C, 341st M. G. Bn	10-25
Mevius, Arthur, Pvt., A, 356th Inf	10-21
Meyer, Arthur, Sgt., K, 354th Inf	11- 2
Meyer, Warren F., Pvt., H, 355th Inf	11- 4
Meyers, Alvin J., Pvt., H, 355th Inf	11- 8
Meyn, Gust. C., Pvt., G, 354th Inf	10-21
Middleton, Carr, Pvt., G, 356th Inf	11- 5
Miles, Harry B., Pvt., H, 353rd Inf	11- 3
Milbelic, Frank, Pvt., L, 354th Inf	11- 2
Miller, Charles A., Pvt., D, 353rd Inf	9-26
Miller, Claude L., Pvt., C, 341st M. G. Bn	10-25
Miller, Frank J., Pvt., H, 353rd Inf	10-30
Miller, Fred H., Pvt., Hq. 353rd Inf	10-26
Miller, James F., Pvt., B, 341st M. G. Bn	10-24
Miller, Joe B., Corp., C, 342nd M. G. Bn	9-29
Mills, Floyd, Pvt., Sup. Co., 354th Inf	11- 3
Mincher, James L., Corp., B, 314th Eng	10-26
Mirasky, Frank J., Sgt., A, 341st M. G. Bn	10-22
Mitchell, Arden H., Sgt., M, 353rd Inf	9-16
Mitchell, John A., Pvt., G, 353rd Inf	9-18
Mitchell, Roscoe W., Pvt., B, 341st M. G. Bn	10-22
Moarhaus, Clarence, Pvt., M, 356th Inf	9-20
Mobley, John E., Pvt., A, 356th Inf	10-21
Moehlmann, Ernest, Pvt., G, 353rd Inf	11- 2
Moerschel, Andrew J., Pvt., E, 356th Inf	11-11
Moffit, Frank, Pvt., A, 341st M. G. Bn	11- 1
Molenda, Peter, Pvt., A, 353rd Inf	10-23
Moley, Battista, Pvt., D, 354th Inf	9-24
Mondragono, Pedro A., Pvt., D, 314th Eng	10-29
Montagne, Rang E., Corp., C, 342nd M. G. Bn	11- 3
Moore, Jasper B., Pvt. 1cl., D, 355th Inf	11- 7
Moore, Lester G., Corp., M. G. Co., 354th Inf	9-15
Moore, Walter R., Jr., Pvt. 1cl., B, 314th Eng	9-24
Moraville, Isadore Augustus, Pvt. 1cl., G, 355th Inf	10-22
Morlan, Oscar M., Pvt., Hq. 354th Inf	11- 9
Morris, Burrin L., Pvt., H, 354th Inf	10- 7
Morris, Meridith, Pvt., E, 356th Inf	10- 6
Morrison, Andrew W., Pvt., H, 353rd Inf	11- 2
Morton, Linus C., Cook, F, 314th Eng	9-23
Metz, Edward L., Pvt., A, 341st M. G. Bn	9-14
Mueller, Alred H. E., Pvt., D, 356th Inf	9-23
Muller, James T., Pvt., F, 355th Inf	10-21
Mundale, Harold O., Pvt., K, 353rd Inf	10-26
Munday, William L., Pvt. 1cl., L, 354th Inf	9-26
Munsch, Edwin S., Sgt., L, 354th Inf	11- 1
Munson, John B., Pvt., E, 354th Inf	10-22
Murphy, Claud, Pvt., C, 355th Inf	10- 2
Murphy, John T., Pvt., C, 354th Inf	9-16
Murphy, Peter Paul, Pvt., C, 354th Inf	9-29
Murphy, Stephen, Pvt., K, 354th Inf	11- 2
Murray, John J., Sgt. 1cl., A, 314th Eng	9-26
Myhre, Nordahl, Pvt., G, 354th Inf	10-21
Nation, Walter R., Pvt., G, 353rd Inf	9-24
Naunez, Encarnacion, Pvt., A, 353rd Inf	10-22
Navarra, Jim, Pvt., D, 341st M. G. Bn	9-14
Neely, Eunus R., Pvt. 1cl., M. G. Co., 354th Inf	10-22
Neff, Oliver R., Pvt., M, 353rd Inf	11- 1
Negro, Angelo, Pvt. 1cl., C, 341st M. G. Bn	10-23
Neill, Alton H., Pvt., M, 353rd Inf	11- 1
Nelson, Alfred, Pvt. 1cl., C, 341st M. G. Bn	10-31
Nelson, Charles, Pvt., M, 355th Inf	11- 5
Nelson, Charles E., Pvt., M, 354th Inf	11- 2
Nelson, Gustave A., Pvt., F, 353rd Inf	11- 3
Nelson, Harry, Pvt., E, 353rd Inf	10-22
Nelson, Raymond E., Pvt., D, 356th Inf	11-11
Nelson, Richard J., Pvt., F, 353rd Inf	11- 3
Neshiem, Brynjulf, Pvt., M. G. Co., 355th Inf	11- 1
Nevin, William F., Pvt., B, 314th Eng	9-25
Newman, Walter D., Pvt., L, 355th Inf	9-13
Newport, James J., Pvt. 1cl., A, 341st M. G. Bn	11- 3
Newton, Arthur T., Pvt., C, 356th Inf	10-23
Nichols, Denver, Pvt., C, 355th Inf	11- 5
Nicholson, William H., Corp., E, 354th Inf	11- 2
Nielsen, William N., Mech., B, 341st M. G. Bn	10-24
Nieuwenhuis, William, Pvt., B, 340th M. G. Bn	9-12
Nieweg, Fritz J., Pvt., L, 354th Inf	10-29
Norby, Oscar M., Pvt. 1cl., H, 353rd Inf	10- 1
Nord, Henry E., Pvt., C, 354th Inf	10-28
Nordstrom, Fred E., Pvt., G, 355th Inf	10-22
Northey, Neil W., Sgt., C, 314th F. S. Bn	10- 2
Norton, Edward J., Corp., E, 354th Inf	10-21
Noyok, Alexander, Pvt., L, 353rd Inf	11- 1
Nulick, Joseph, Pvt., D, 314th Eng	10-29
Nyberg, Harold G., Pvt., D, 356th Inf	11- 4
Nydam, Ed., Pvt. 1cl., D, 342nd M. G. Bn	11- 4
O'Brien, John J., Corp., C, 354th Inf	11- 5
O'Brien, Joseph J., Corp., E, 314th Eng	10-26
O'Brien, Michael F., Sgt., L, 354th Inf	11- 2
O'Connor, James J., Pvt. 1cl., M. G. Co., 355th Inf	9-13
Odle, Silas A., Pvt., G, 356th Inf	11- 7
Olguin, Jaun H., Pvt., A, 356th Inf	9-21
Olinger, Elmer M., Sgt., K, 355th Inf	9-23
Olinger, William H., Pvt., H, 354th Inf	11- 1
Oliver, Stonewall J., Wag., Sup. Co., 353rd Inf	9-22
Olliges, Henry H., Pvt., K, 354th Inf	11- 1
Olney, Earl E., Pvt., L, 354th Inf	11- 1

Name, Rank, Company, Regiment	Date 1918
Olsen, George A., Pvt. 1cl., C, 341st M. G. Bn.	10-25
Olson, Joel, Pvt., B, 354th Inf	11- 1
Olson, Henry A., Pvt. 1cl., D, 342nd M. G. Bn.	9-24
Olson, Olaf N., Pvt., F, 353rd Inf	11- 3
O'Neill, John R., Pvt., C, 355th Inf	11- 4
Olesewicz, Necystau, Pvt., E, 353th Inf	10-18
O'Rourke, John T., Pvt., G, 354th Inf	9-23
Orr, John C., Pvt. 1cl., L, 353rd Inf	9-12
Orr, Miledge O., Pvt., C, 342nd F. A	10- 5
Orris, William, Pvt., L, 353rd Inf	9-25
Orvold, Clarence, Pvt., C, 353rd Inf	10-22
Osgood, George L., Pvt., C, 356th Inf	9-23
Oswalt, Lee S., Pvt. 1cl., Hq. 354th Inf	9-29
Otero, Benedicto, Corp., C, 314th F. S. Bn	10-27
Otten, Otto, Pvt., Sup. Co., 355th Inf	10-31
Otto, Oscar A., Pvt., B, 354th Inf	11- 1
Ouimet, Frank, Pvt., L, 353rd Inf	9-28
Owens, Owen J., Pvt., A, 314th Eng	9-12
Padilla, Teodocio, Pvt., F, 341st F. A	9-28
Palmore, Clarence C., Pvt., Med. Det., 354th Inf	10-31
Papagianopolus, Gust., Pvt. 1cl., K, 355th Inf	9-14
Papathemetrious, Paleologos, Pvt., E, 354th Inf	11- 3
Park, Edward S., Mech., B, 354th Inf	11- 1
Parker, Oliver E., Pvt., B, 340th M. G. Bn	11-11
Parmenter, Clifford A., Pvt. 1cl., M⁹ G. Co., 353rd Inf.	11- 1
Parrish, Earl C., Pvt., K, 354th Inf	11- 1
Parsons, Joseph, Pvt., D, 353rd Inf	10-23
Patterson, Harry, Pvt. 1cl., D, 314th Eng	11- 2
Pawlowski, Wladislaw S., Pvt., Hq. 314th Eng	9-25
Pazeer, Charles, Pvt., F, 354th Inf	9-15
Pederson, Obel C., Pvt., A, 355th Inf	11- 4
Peltz, Sam, Pvt., E, 355th Inf	11- 2
Penas, Joe, Pvt. 1cl., B, 314th Amm. Tr	9-19
Pendegrass, Roy E., Pvt., A, 353rd Inf	10-28
Pepowski, Charles F., Pvt., C, 354th Inf	10-28
Perkins, Charles L., Corp., B, 355th Inf	11- 5
Perkins, Lester, Pvt., M, 354th Inf	11- 1
Persow, Meyer J., Pvt., E, 354th Inf	10-23
Peters, William A., Pvt., Hq. 342nd F. A	9-29
Petersen, Emil L., Pvt. 1cl., E, 355th Inf	10-22
Peterson, Carl, Pvt., D, 314th Eng	11- 1
Peterson, Clyde F., Cook, A, 354th Inf	9-20
Peterson, Clarence E., Sgt., A, 356th Inf	10-21
Peterson, Emil G., Pvt., B, 353rd Inf	10-22
Peterson, Emil E., Pvt., D, 353rd Inf	9-26
Peterson, Fred H., Pvt., E, 354th Inf	11- 1
Peterson, Lawrence, Pvt., D, 353rd Inf	10-26
Peterson, Timothy E., Pvt. 1cl., F, 314th Eng	9-24
Pettit, John W., Pvt., I, 353rd Inf	10-26
Petty, Earl H., Pvt., E, 355th Inf	10-22
Phillips, Clyde B., Pvt. 1cl., M, 356th Inf	9-24
Phillipson, Victor R., Sgt., C, 355th Inf	9-13
Pickard, Harry S., Sgt., C, 341st M. G. Bn	10-25
Pierce, Howard G., Pvt. 1cl., K, 355th Inf	9-13
Pierce, Joseph S., Sgt., E, 354th Inf	10-21
Piercy, Anthony K., Sgt., C, 341st M. G. Bn	10-26
Pietz, Emil, Pvt., Hq. 353rd Inf	10-30
Pirtle, Andrew C., Corp., F, 354th Inf	10-22
Pitre, Moise, Pvt., K, 356th Inf	11-11
Pitchford, William T., Pvt., H, 353rd Inf	11- 3
Pitts, Garfield, Pvt., D, 355th Inf	11- 5
Pitts, Griffie, Pvt., D, 356th Inf	10-22
Pittsenbarger, William R., Pvt. 1cl., E, 356th Inf	11- 4
Plats, Norton S., Pvt., G, 353rd Inf	11- 5
Plotts, Oliver J., Pvt., C, 353rd Inf	10-22
Pohl, Herman L., Pvt., H, 354th Inf	10-23
Pollex, Otto A., Pvt., M, 354th Inf	11- 1
Poole, Bruce B., Pvt., A, 354th Inf	10-28
Pooley, Fay Arville, Pvt., G, 355th Inf	10-22
Popham, Raymond W., Pvt., Hq. 314th Eng	10-25
Potter, Harvey B., Pvt., K, 355th Inf	11- 5
Poulsen, Hans C., Pvt. 1cl., K, 355th Inf	9-13
Powell, Melvin D., Pvt., B, 340th M. G. Bn	11- 1
Powell, Robert C., Pvt., D, 356th Inf	11- 5
Preslar, Finas Elsia, Corp., I, 354th Inf	11- 3
Pressmann, Charles, Pvt., E, 353rd Inf	9-12
Prews, Martin J., Pvt., K, 354th Inf	11- 2
Price, Anton, Pvt., E, 355th Inf	10-22
Prichard, Elijah, Pvt., D, 356th Inf	11- 1
Prior, Joseph Henry, Pvt. 1cl., M. G. Co., 354th Inf	10-24
Pritchett, Charles B., Pvt., M, 356th Inf	9-12
Prockish, Edward, Pvt. 1cl., G, 353rd Inf	9-24
Proffitt, Murrell C., Pvt., L, 353rd Inf	9-25
Protocolla, Carmelo, Pvt., B, 355th Inf	11- 5
Puehbauer, Arthur, Pvt. 1cl., F, 314th Eng	11- 9
Pues, Joseph P., Pvt., M, 356th Inf	11-11
Pulse, Harold L., Corp., I, 355th Inf	11- 5
Pund, John F., Sgt., Hq. 354th Inf	11- 2
Queener, David H., Pvt., B, 354th Inf	9-13

Name, Rank, Company, Regiment	Date 1918
Quigley, Leonard, Corp., H, 355th Inf	10-21
Quirk, Nikel F., Pvt., M, 354th Inf	10-22
Ramm, Fred, Pvt., F, 356th Inf	11- 5
Rader, Leslie, Pvt., I, 354th Inf	11- 1
Ramsey, Ethrian, Corp., G, 356th Inf	11- 5
Randolph, Jefferson C., Pvt., C, 353rd Inf	10-22
Random, Gilman, Pvt., E, 354th Inf	11- 2
Rankin, John B., Pvt., E, 355th Inf	11- 1
Rapp, Frank E., Corp., B, 354th Inf	11- 1
Rasa, Otto F., Pvt., M, 354th Inf	11- 1
Rasberry, Charles C., Pvt., E, 356th Inf	11- 5
Rasmussen, Christian, Bugler, K, 353rd Inf	11- 1
Rasmussen, Hans, Pvt., B, 355th Inf	10-20
Ratskopf, Roy Pvt., H, 355th Inf	10- 1
Rauch, Rudolph, Corp., A, 355th Inf	11- 5
Ray, Elmer, Pvt., C, 356th Inf	10-23
Rayburn, Leonard, Pvt., B, 342nd M. G. Bn	11- 1
Rea, Harry, Pvt., D, 353rd Inf	10-20
Reano, Joseph C., Pvt. H, 355th Inf	11- 5
Rebmann, Emil H., Pvt. 1cl., C, 314th F. S. Bn	10-30
Reed, Elmer, Pvt., A, 353rd Inf	10-24
Reed, Frank, Pvt., Sup. Co., 356th Inf	11- 8
Reesch, Peter J., Pvt., M, 353rd Inf	11- 2
Reezor, Ed. H. Pvt., D, 355th Inf	11- 5
Regan, Joseph E., Pvt., E, 354th Inf	11- 3
Reggini, Bert, Pvt., A, 356th Inf	11- 4
Rehu, Swan J, Pvt., D, 353rd Inf	10-22
Reid, William H., Pvt., A, 356th Inf	10-27
Reiger, Frederick E., Pvt. M, 353rd Inf	10-30
Reimers, Charley Fred, Pvt., L, 355th Inf	9-25
Reisacker, Joseph H., Pvt., C, 356th Inf	11-11
Reisbig, John, Pvt., C, 355th Inf	11- 5
Reisher, Robert B., Sgt., F, 355th Inf	10-21
Remington, Phillip Judson Pvt., I, 354th Inf	9-24
Remley, Allie A., Cook, L, 354th Inf	10-29
Rempel, John J., Pvt., G, 354th Inf	10-21
Remus, Herman L., Corp., A, 355th Inf	10- 3
Reumschussel, Charles, Pvt., B, 314th Eng	11- 2
Reynolds, Albert W., Bugler, H, 353rd Inf	9-18
Rhodes, James L., Pvt., F, 355th Inf	10-22
Rice, Oren B., Corp., G, 356th Inf	11- 6
Richards, Earl B., Pvt., H, 355th Inf	10-22
Richardson, Leander A., Corp., B, 356th Inf	10-24
Richardson, William L., Corp., A, 354th Inf	11- 2
Ridgeway, George H., Pvt., B, 341st M. G. Bn	10-24
Rieger, Otto A., Pvt., C, 314th F. S Bn	10-21
Rigney, William W., Pvt., Hq. Troop, 89th Div	9-26
Risch, Leo F., Pvt., B, 314th Eng	11- 9
Risk, Jarad, Pvt., B, 314th M. P	10-28
Ristau, Arthur O., Pvt., E, 353rd Inf	10-22
Ritzo, Tony J., Pvt. 1cl., E, 355th Inf	10-21
Roach, Paul A., Pvt. 1cl., A, 342nd M. G. Bn	11- 1
Roach, William, Pvt., I, 356th Inf	11- 4
Robben, William B., Pvt. 1cl., K, 354th Inf	11- 1
Roberts, Otis E., Pvt., C, 356th Inf	11- 3
Robertson, Robert S., Sgt., K, 355th Inf	11- 4
Robinson, James F., Pvt., I, 356th Inf	10- 5
Robinson, John L., Pvt., H, 353rd Inf	9-14
Robinson, Leo M., Corp., D, 354th Inf	11- 1
Robinson, Louis F., Corp., G, 354th Inf	11- 2
Robinson, Orville, Pvt. 1cl., B, 354th Inf	11- 1
Rodenberry, Ernest, Pvt. 1cl., E, 356th Inf	11-11
Rodrigo, Adolph B., Pvt., D, 356th Inf	9-13
Roe, Willie, Pvt., B, 356th Inf	10-21
Roehl, Mathias, Corp., I, 353rd Inf	11- 1
Roels, Leo August, Corp., B, 355th Inf	11- 5
Roethel, William H., Pvt. 1cl., H, 354th Inf	11-11
Rogers, Arthur I., Pvt., B, 353rd Inf	10-22
Rogers, James G, Pvt. 1cl., K, 356th Inf	9-13
Rohacek, Harry L., Sgt., F, 314th Eng	11- 9
Rohr, Harry, Cook, D, 341st M. G. Bn	9-12
Rowland, Cladene E., Pvt., B, 314th Eng	9-25
Rollman, Leades C., Pvt., B, 354th Inf	9-23
Romero, Claud, Pvt., G, 355th Inf	10-21
Romero, Cresinino, Pvt., B, 353rd Inf	10-26
Rooney, Edward C., Pvt., D, 355th Inf	11- 9
Rooney, Henry M., Pvt., I, 355th Inf	9-14
Rooney, William J., Corp., F, 353rd Inf	11- 3
Rorer, Harry Wade, Pvt., A, 341st M. G. Bn	11- 3
Roten, Ben, Pvt, C, 341st M. G. Bn	9-12
Rothwell, Roscoe L., Pvt. 1cl., F. H., 353rd Inf	10-30
Roudebush, Lester G., Pvt., K, 355th Inf	9-23
Rouillard, Eugene, Bugler, H, 355th Inf	10-21
Roush, Earl W., Corp, A, 354th Inf	11- 1
Rozwadowski, Leon, Corp., H, 354th Inf	11- 1
Rubach, Paul F., Pvt., A, 353rd Inf	10-24
Rubino, Joe, Pvt., M, 353rd Inf	11- 1
Rude, Floy A., Sgt., I, 356th Inf	9-13
Rudolph, William, Pvt., E, 355th Inf	10- 7

Name, Rank, Company, Regiment	Date 1918
Rudy, Walter, Sgt., E, 356th Inf	11-11
Ruh, Lawrence Fred, Corp., C, 353rd Inf	10-25
Rupp, Henry J., Pvt., D, 356th Inf	9-23
Rush, Alva J., Pvt., M. G. Co., 356th Inf	9-13
Russell, Albert T., Pvt., D, 354th Inf	9-13
Russell, Arthur L., Pvt., F, 353rd Inf	11- 1
Russell, Frank, Pvt., C, 341st M. G. Bn	9-18
Rutstein, William B., Pvt., C, 356th Inf	11- 3
Rybicki, Joseph B., Pvt., D, 356th Inf	11- 3
Sager, Louie, Pvt., B, 342nd F. A	10- 7
Sallee, Harry J., Pvt., C, 355th Inf	10- 4
Salley, Roy G., Sgt., K, 356th Inf	10-30
Salomon, Solly, Pvt., A, 353rd Inf	9-22
Salsbury, Vern L., Pvt. 1cl., A, 353rd Inf	10-21
Saltzman, Edwin N., Pvt., D, 353rd Inf	10-24
Salvatori, Victor, Pvt., L, 354th Inf	10-20
Sampson, Thomas W., Pvt., B, 354th Inf	11- 2
Sanderson, Lawrence H., Pvt., G, 354th Inf	11- 3
Sandfort, Henry J., Pvt. 1cl., B, 314th Eng	9-25
Santo, William T., Pvt. 1cl., L, 353rd Inf	9-29
Sartori, Joseph, Pvt., E, 354th Inf	10-28
Sasnett, William T., Pvt. 1cl., L, 353rd Inf	10-22
Sather, John A., Pvt., B, 341st M. G. Bn	10-30
Saukles, James, Pvt., B, 353rd Inf	11- 2
Savedra, Andres, Pvt., B, 353rd Inf	9-12
Savlers, Harold D., Pvt., I, 353rd Inf	11- 3
Scanlon, James, Pvt., E, 354th Inf	11- 1
Scarpinate, Joseph, Pvt., C, 353rd Inf	10-31
Schaaf, Jordon W., Pvt., E, 354th Inf	11- 3
Schade, Ernest C., Corp., E, 354th Inf	10-28
Schalkopf, William John, Sgt., Hq. 355th Inf	9-12
Schamel, George C., Farrier, Amb. Co., 356th Inf	11- 1
Schatz, Julius L. A., Mech., M, 356th Inf	9-12
Scheetz, John L., Wag., Sup. Co., 354th Inf	11- 1
Schlerloh, John Henry, Pvt., B, 354th Inf	11- 1
Schinp, Frank H., 1st Sgt., I, 354th Inf	11- 1
Schirr, Theodore A., Pvt., D, 354th Inf	9-16
Schmale, Henry W., Pvt., I, 356th Inf	9-14
Schmid, Albert H., Pvt., F, 354th Inf	11- 3
Schmid, Karl O., Pvt. 1cl., B, 314th Eng	9-12
Schmidt, Benjamin C., Pvt., H, 355th Inf	9-16
Schmidt, Herbert, Pvt., B, 355th Inf	11- 5
Schmit, Felix, Pvt., E, 340th F. A	9-28
Schmitt, Albert, Pvt. 1cl., I, 354th Inf	9-27
Schmitz, William A., Pvt., B, 341st M. G. Bn	9-22
Schmode, Julius C., Pvt. 1cl., F, 355th Inf	10-22
Schneider, Edwin P., Pvt. 1cl., H, 354th Inf	11- 1
Schoenfeld, Joseph, Pvt. 1cl., E, 355th Inf	10-22
Scholle, Oscar H., Pvt. 1cl., Hq. 354th Inf	10-22
Scholten, James E., Pvt., D, 342nd M. G. Bn	11- 4
Schooley, Frank L., Pvt., D, 353rd Inf	10-26
Schooler, Harry N., Pvt. 1cl., L, 355th Inf	10- 2
Schowalter, Marcus M., Sup. Sgt., G, 353rd Inf	11- 5
Schramm, Alvin W., Sgt., F., 355th Inf	10-22
Schreckengast, Ray, Pvt. 1cl., G, 355th Inf	10-22
Schreier, Benhard, Pvt., C, 353rd Inf	10-24
Schreier, Oscar P., Sgt., H, 355th Inf	9-12
Schroder, Gus., Pvt., B, 314th Eng	10-30
Schroder, Henry W., Corp., M, 353rd Inf	11- 1
Schulte, Oscar E., Sgt., M, 354th Inf	11- 2
Schultz, Elmer, Pvt., F, 355th Inf	10-22
Schultz, Henry N., Pvt., E, 354th Inf	10-21
Schwab, Edward, Pvt., E, 354th Inf	10-21
Schwartz, Charles H., Pvt., B, 341st M. G. Bn	10-22
Schwem, Albert H., Pvt., G, 355th Inf	10-22
Schwemmer, David, Pvt., M, 353rd Inf	11- 1
Scofield, Virgil A., Pvt. 1cl., A, 340th F. A	10- 2
Scott, Andrew J., Corp., B, 356th Inf	11- 4
Scott, Jeff D., Pvt., H, 356th Inf	11- 5
Scott, John, Pvt., C, 353rd Inf	9-15
Scott, Louis R., Corp., Hq. 353rd Inf	10-26
Scott, Rado, Pvt., M, 354th Inf	9-26
Scott, William H., Pvt., M. G. Co., 355th Inf	11- 1
Sebastian, Lester L., Pvt., E, 356th Inf	10- 3
Sebastian, Nicholas C., Pvt., C, 356th Inf	10-21
Sedlacek, Charles J., Pvt., M. G. Co., 356th Inf	10-21
Seegrist, Robert R., Pvt., L, 355th Inf	11- 5
Seeman, Carl, Pvt., A, 355th Inf	11- 5
Seems, Bundy, Pvt., G, 355th Inf	10-21
Self, James F., Pvt., A, 354th Inf	11- 2
Sessions, Edward L., Pvt., I, 353rd Inf	11- 1
Seyler, Jacob, Pvt., M, 354th Inf	11- 1
Shafer, Harry, Pvt., E, 354th Inf	9-26
Shafman, John M., Pvt., H, 354th Inf	11- 1
Shakelford, Ollon, Pvt., A, 356th Inf	11- 6
Shannon, Harmon W., Pvt., M, 356th Inf	9-12
Shannon, Patrick F., Pvt., 314th San. Tr	11- 8
Sharp, Elmer, Pvt., A, 354th Inf	11- 1
Shaw, Leslie A., Corp., A, 342nd M. G. Bn	11- 1

Name, Rank, Company, Regiment	Date 1918
Shearin, Wm. J., Corp., M, 354th Inf	9-23
Shears, Stevey, Pvt., M. G. Co., 356th Inf	9-12
Sherwood, Orval C., Corp., M. G. Co., 356th Inf	11- 5
Shields, Edward J., Pvt., F, 353rd Inf	11- 3
Shock, Fred J., Pvt., L, 355th Inf	11- 5
Shoemaker, William E., Pvt., F, 354th Inf	11- 3
Shroyer, Willis, Pvt., M, 354th Inf	11- 1
Shuck, Edgar N., Pvt., C, 341st M. G. Bn	10-25
Shwartz, Harry, Corp., B, 353rd Inf	10-22
Sidler, Carl E., Pvt., B, 356th Inf	11- 4
Siebert, Lampher W., Pvt., I, 354th Inf	11- 1
Siegel, Fred C., Pvt., A, 355th Inf	11- 5
Sielmantkowski, Stanley, Pvt., G, 356th Inf	10-22
Silbaugh, Alvie Herbert, Pvt., B, 341st M. G. Bn	10-23
Simmons, Charley B., Pvt. 1cl., M, 353rd Inf	9-18
Simonson, Simon, Pvt., A, 356th Inf	9-18
Sisneros, Jacob, Pvt., B, 356th Inf	11- 4
Sites, George W., Pvt. 1cl., C, 356th Inf	11-11
Sittler, Edward, Pvt., C, 341st M. G. Bn	10-25
Skaggs, Harry D., Sgt., B, 353rd Inf	9-11
Skaggs, Harry D., Sgt., B, 353rd Inf	10-25
Skarson, Severt, Pvt., A, 356th Inf	11- 2
Skillington, Herbert E., Sgt., Hq. 354th Inf	11- 1
Slay, John R., Pvt., G, 354th Inf	11- 2
Sloane, Roland Snyder, Corp., B, 340th M. G. Bn	11-11
Small, Joe, Pvt., C, 353rd Inf	9-23
Smarinsky, Herman G., Pvt., M, 354th Inf	11- 2
Smiley, Chester A., Pvt., Med. Det., 356th Inf	9-21
Smith, Albert M., Pvt., E, 353rd Inf	11- 1
Smith, Benjamin F., Pvt., B, 314th Eng	9-12
Smith, Carl, Pvt., G, 356th Inf	11- 6
Smith, Cecil F., Pvt., B, 353rd Inf	11- 9
Smith, Charley B., Pvt., M. G. Co., 353rd Inf	11- 4
Smith, Clayton L., Pvt. 1cl., A, 356th Inf	10-21
Smith, Clifford H., Pvt., B, 355th Inf	11- 5
Smith, Frank G., Pvt., M, 353rd Inf	11- 3
Smith, Frank J., Pvt., I, 353rd Inf	9-24
Smith, Guy E., Corp., Hq. 342nd F. A	9-29
Smith, Joseph C., Pvt., H, 353rd Inf	11- 3
Smith, Logan S., Pvt., B, 353rd Inf	10-24
Smith, Mack R., Pvt., C, 353rd Inf	10-22
Smith, Magnus K., Sgt., E, 341st M. G. Bn	10-22
Smith, Robert S., Pvt., K, 355th Inf	9-14
Smith, Roscoe R., Corp., D, 353rd Inf	10-26
Smith, Ruick E., Pvt., E, 353rd Inf	9-19
Smith, Seth A., Pvt., B, 355th Inf	11- 8
Smyth, Joseph H., Pvt., A, 354th Inf	11-10
Snider, Charles A., Pvt., A, 353rd Inf	9-14
Snodgrass, Alex J., Corp., H, 354th Inf	10-23
Snow, Virgil H., Pvt., C, 354th Inf	9-13
Snowbarger, Junior E., Pvt., D, 356th Inf	9-18
Snyder, George D., Pvt., F, 353rd Inf	11- 3
Snyder, James A., Pvt., I, 354th Inf	11- 3
Snyder, Walter A., Pvt., H, 354th Inf	11- 2
Southern, Christopher, Pvt., C, 353rd Inf	10-21
Spargur, James R., Bugler, E, 354th Inf	9-30
Sparks, Francis F., Pvt., 314th San. Tr	11- 5
Specter, Harry, Pvt., I, 355th Inf	9-14
Sperry, Charles C., Corp., B, 341st M. G. Bn	11- 8
Spicer, James L., Bugler, A, 356th Inf	11- 3
Spitzenberg, Harry L., Pvt., Hq. 354th Inf	9-26
Stables, William S., Pvt., D, 342nd M. G. Bn	11- 1
Stambaugh, Herbert E., Pvt., F, 355th Inf	9-16
Stangel, George W., 1st Sgt., K, 355th Inf	9-14
Stanley, Allen G., Pvt., B, 356th Inf	11- 8
Stanley, Ray A., Pvt., F, 314th Eng	11- 8
Stapp, Boyd, Pvt. 1cl., E, 314th Eng	9-15
Stark, Robert K., Sgt., K, 353rd Inf	10-26
Starr, Lue E., Pvt. 1cl., K, 355th Inf	11- 5
Steinbach, Benjamin, Pvt., K, 353rd Inf	11- 1
Steiner, Percy R., Corp., I, 354th Inf	11- 8
Steinford, Herman, Pvt. 1cl., K, 353rd Inf	9-16
Steinmetz, Richard A., Corp., E, 354th Inf	10-22
Steinreide, Edward B., Pvt., C, 341st M. G. Bn	10-31
Stejspal, John F., D, 342nd F. A	
Stelsel, Gerrit, Pvt., D, 353rd Inf	9-23
Stenderup, Mads, Pvt., 342nd M. G. Bn	11- 1
Stephens, Charles F., Pvt., H, 353rd Inf	9-20
Sterry, Frank R., Pvt., B, 353rd Inf	9-13
Stevens, Clyde W., Sgt., C, 353rd Inf	10-22
Stevens, George W., Pvt., M. G. Co., 356th Inf	11- 5
Stevens, Roy Edwin, Pvt., M. G. Co., 356th Inf	9-15
Stevenson, William M., Pvt., K, 355th Inf	9-12
Steward, Roy W., Pvt., C, 356th Inf	9-23
Stock, Carl J., Pvt. 1cl., E, 340th F. A	9-27
Stock, Glenn, Pvt., H, 353rd Inf	11- 3
Stock, Louie, Pvt., E, 314th Eng	9-26
Stolte, Emil L., Corp., A, 353rd Inf	10-21
Stonis, Harry T., Pvt., C, 353rd Inf	10-21

Name, Rank, Company, Regiment	Date 1918
Straube, Herbert August, Pvt., L, 356th Inf	11-11
Strautmann, Anthony A., Pvt., Hq. 355th Inf	9-22
Street, Clarence W., Pvt., C, 342nd M. G. Bn	11- 6
Strohm, Peary C., Corp., F, 356th Inf	10-30
Stromstead, Andrew, Pvt., E, 354th Inf	10-22
Stumme, August F., Mech., Hq. 341st F. A	9-19
Sturman, Harold A., Pvt., A, 355th Inf	9-14
Suages, Walte, Pvt., K, 355th Inf	11- 4
Sullivan, Edward, Pvt., I, 353rd Inf	11- 1
Summers, Aaron C., Pvt., H, 353rd Inf	9-12
Summers, Arthur, Pvt., A, 355th Inf	11- 5
Sumner, Oscar C, Pvt., D, 356th Inf	9-24
Sumrall, Louis V., Pvt., A, 355th Inf	11- 4
Sunderman, John V., Pvt., B, 314th Eng	9-25
Sundsrud, Ole John, Pvt., B, 314th M. P	11- 1
Sutherland, Henry E., Pvt., E, 354th Inf	11- 2
Sutton, Harry J., Pvt., D, 353rd Inf	10-22
Svec, Charles, Pvt., D, 356th Inf	9-23
Swain, Alexander A., Pvt., I, 353rd Inf	11- 1
Swanson, Per E., Pvt., M. G. Co., 353rd Inf	9-28
Swanson, Sterling M., Corp., F, 355th Inf	10-21
Sweeney, Eugene P., Pvt. 1cl., M, 353rd Inf	9-16
Sweet, Peter T., Pvt., E, 356th Inf	10- 6
Swenson, John V., Pvt., E, 355th Inf	10-22
Swanson, Oscar F., Pvt., F, 353rd Inf	11- 2
Szezepanik, Joseph A., Pvt., M, 353rd Inf	9-13
Tacha, Frank W., Sup. Sgt., Sup Co., 353rd Inf	11- 8
Talberg, Roy L., Pvt., K, 353rd Inf	11- 2
Tamietti, Felix, Pvt. 1cl., K, 354th Inf	11-11
Tanner, Ralph A., Pvt., K, 354th Inf	11- 1
Tappan, Charles F., Pvt., I, 353rd Inf	10-30
Tate, George B., Pvt., B, 356th Inf	10-22
Taylor, Donald C., Pvt. 1cl., M. G. Co., 355th Inf	11- 1
Taylor, Floyd F., Pvt., F, 355th Inf	10-21
Taylor, Henry L., Pvt., K, 355th Inf	10- 5
Taylor, Louis, Sgt., L, 353rd Inf	9-14
Teare, Daniel, Corp., I, 353rd Inf	11- 1
Teckemeier, Edward A., Pvt. 1cl., H, 354th Inf	11-11
Tehee, Henry, Pvt., E, 355th Inf	10-22
Thater, Paul Sgt., M, 354th Inf	9-26
Thierolf, Phillip, Pvt. 1cl., B, 355th Inf	11- 4
Thomas, Franklin L., Pvt., K, 354th Inf	10-22
Thomas, Herbert O., Pvt. 1cl., L, 353rd Inf	9-18
Thomas, Melvin D., Pvt. 1cl., C, 341st M. G. Bn	10-25
Thomas, Ralph D., Sgt., F, 314th Eng	11- 1
Thomas, Rudolph E., Pvt. 1cl., D, 355th Inf	11- 5
Thompson, Alfred, Pvt., D, 353rd Inf	10-24
Thompson, James W., Pvt., M. G. Co., 353rd Inf	11- 4
Thompson, Jay W., Pvt., C, 353rd Inf	10-21
Thompson, Morris T., Pvt., Hq. 353rd Inf	10-23
Thompson, Pozey H., Pvt., D, 356th Inf	9-13
Thompson, Richmond S., Pvt., D, 355th Inf	11- 5
Thompson, Tom S., Pvt., C, 341st M. G. Bn	11- 5
Thornberg, Arthur A., Corp., C, 355th Inf	11- 5
Thornburg, Charles Scott, Pvt., B, 354th Inf	9-22
Thornhill, Elmer, D, 342nd F. A	
Thornton, Clarence, Pvt., M, 354th Inf	11- 1
Thunee, Mathias, Pvt., I, 353rd Inf	11- 7
Thurman, Pirk P., Pvt., 314th San. Tr	11- 4
Tienken, Heinie L., Bugler, A, 355th Inf	9-25
Timmerberg, Charles John, Pvt., L, 356th Inf	9-30
Tindall, Elmer J., Pvt., D, 355th Inf	11- 5
Toal, Peter M., Pvt., C, 354th Inf	10-27
Todd, George B. Pvt. 1cl., E, 314th M. S. Tr	11- 1
Tolley, James H., Pvt., A, 342nd M. G. Bn	10-26
Tomaszlwski, Vincent J., Corp., G, 354th Inf	10-23
Tomes, Alois F., Corp., Hq. 355th Inf	11- 1
Torkelson, Clarence, Pvt., E, 353rd Inf	11- 1
Torres, Felimon, Pvt., B, 355th Inf	10-20
Torres, John D., Pvt., H, 356th Inf	11- 5
Torson, Gilbert C. Pvt., C, 353rd Inf	10-26
Totta, Peter, Pvt., H, 354th Inf	10-23
Touzinski, Joseph W., Bugler, I, 354th Inf	11- 3
Tovatt, Vernon Joseph, Pvt., D, 342nd M. G. Bn	11- 4
Townsend, Harve, Pvt., D, 341st M. G. Bn	11- 1
Trail, James E., Pvt. 1cl., F, 314th Eng	11- 5
Trample, Emil A., Corp., C, 355th Inf	11- 4
Tramulto, Jerry, Pvt., M, 354th Inf	11- 1
Treon, Charley, Pvt., F, 314th Eng	11- 1
Tricarico, Ernest, Pvt., Hq. 354th Inf	9-13
Trice, Louis, Pvt., E, 354th Inf	10-28
Trimble, Troy L., Pvt., F, 353rd Inf	9-29
Trout, Orvie C., Pvt., H, 355th Inf	9-13
Troxell, Robert H., Pvt., 314th San Tr	10-22
Thrower, Louis V. Pvt. 1cl., D, 356th Inf	9-18
Trujillo, Canuto, Pvt., B, 355th Inf	9-12
Truppa, Edward, Pvt., B, 355th Inf	10-20
Tubbs, Severt D., Pvt., B, 353rd Inf	10-24
Tucker, Patrick J., Pvt., F, 314th Eng	10-29
Tuma, Frank A., Pvt., E, 355th Inf	10-21
Turner, Charles H., Corp., H, 354th Inf	10-25
Turner, Paul C., Corp., B, 354th Inf	11- 1
Turner, Paul E., Pvt., B, 356th Inf	10-21
Tvedt, Carl W., Pvt., 355th Inf	10-22
Tyner, Albert F., Pvt. 1cl., C, 314th Eng	9-13
Udaekes, Stanley, Pvt., H, 354th Inf	10-25
Uhelsky, George J., Pvt., D, 354th Inf	11- 1
Ulrich, Frank E., Pvt., D, 355th Inf	9-13
Ullrich, John, Corp., H, 353rd Inf	11- 3
Ulibarri, Juan A., Pvt., B, 355th Inf	11- 5
Umholtz, Corlett, Pvt., B, 353rd Inf	9-21
Underwood, Pled, Pvt., F, 355th Inf	11-11
Uphoff, Carl J., Bugler, M, 355th Inf	11- 5
Upton, Odes K., Pvt., C, 340th F. A	10- 7
Urieste, Alige, Pvt., M, 355th Inf	11- 5
Urrea, Augustine, Pvt., E, 355th Inf	10-22
Urrutia, Jose, Pvt., I, 353rd Inf	10-30
Valenzuela, Jose, Pvt., L, 353rd Inf	11- 3
Van Fleet, Charles H., Pvt., Hq. 355th Inf	11- 6
Van Gorder, Clifford R., Pvt., Med. Det., 314th Eng	10-27
Van Hoosen, Wilber R., Pvt., M, 355th Inf	11- 4
Vander, Milton B., Pvt., I, 353rd Inf	11- 1
Van Lant, Guy, Pvt., E, 353rd Inf	11- 1
Van Liew, Charles L., Bugler, M, 353rd Inf	9-30
Van Loenen, John H., Sgt., B, 353rd Inf	9-15
Van Vuren, Ray, Pvt., F, 356th Inf	11- 5
Vaughn, John E., Pvt., B, 314th M. P	10- 5
Vaught, Grover C., Pvt., F, 314th Eng	11- 9
Vermerien, Joseph H., Pvt., B, 342nd M. G. Co	10-27
Vessells, Frank H., Pvt., C, 342nd M. G. Co	11- 4
Vickery, Benjamin F., Pvt. 1cl., F, 355th Inf	10-21
Villers, Heber, Pvt., K, 356th Inf	11- 2
Virginia, Paul, Pvt., B, 353rd Inf	10-26
Vizinat, Rene, Pvt., C, 356th Inf	11- 3
Vogt, Harry J., Pvt., M, 354th Inf	11- 1
Vollpe, Tony, Pvt., E, 314th Eng	10-30
Voss, Herman C., Pvt., A, 356th Inf	11- 9
Waddell, Wm. D., Pvt. 1cl., Med. Det., 341st M. G. Bn	9-12
Wagner, Fred W., Pvt., D, 355th Inf	10- 5
Wagner, William R., Pvt., E, 353rd Inf	11- 1
Waits, Lathen, Pvt., L, 356th Inf	10- 6
Walden, William G., Pvt., F, 353rd Inf	11- 1
Waldhauser, Henry G., Pvt., F, 364th Inf	9-24
Waldron, Thomas L., Cook, K, 354th Inf	11- 3
Wales, Barger R., Pvt., Hq. 354th Inf	11- 1
Walker, Gay, Pvt. 1cl., L, 353rd Inf	9-14
Walker, Jacob V., Sgt., F, 356th Inf	11- 6
Walker, Orva M., Pvt., M. G. Co., 354th Inf	10-21
Walker, Ronald W., Pvt. 1cl., M. G. Co., 354th Inf	9-14
Wall, Samuel J., Pvt., B, 354th Inf	11- 1
Wall, William R., Pvt. 1cl., G, 355th Inf	10-22
Walls, Harlan, Pvt., B, 356th Inf	10-21
Walsh, Walter T., Pvt. 1cl., B, 341st M. G. Bn	9-14
Walter, John E., Pvt. 1cl., Hq. 341st F. A	9-19
Wamego, Harry, Pvt., D, 353rd Inf	9-15
Wampler, Javen, Pvt., I, 354th Inf	11- 2
Wampler, William H., Pvt., E, 354th Inf	10-23
Ward, Lee F., Pvt., K, 353rd Inf	11- 3
Ward, Leo S., Corp., Hq. 353rd Inf	11- 1
Warren, Clarence A., Pvt., Hq. 356th Inf	11-11
Washatko, John, Pvt., C, 353rd Inf	10-21
Wastrack, Henry A., Pvt., H, 354th Inf	11- 1
Watson, Harry D., Pvt., G, 354th Inf	10-23
Weaver, James M., Pvt., E, 353rd Inf	11- 1
Weaver, Turner C., Pvt., I, 355th Inf	9-14
Wedlaka, John C., Pvt., H, 354th Inf	11- 2
Wegman, Herbert F., Pvt. 1cl., M, 354th Inf	9-14
Weigel, John A., Pvt., K, 354th Inf	11- 1
Weigner, Floyd H., Pvt., E, 314th Eng	9-23
Weiland, Frank, Pvt., G, 355th Inf	9-25
Weisner, Leo L., Pvt., G, 353rd Inf	11- 1
Weiss, Arnold H., Pvt., D, 353rd Inf	9-23
Welborn, LeRoy A., Pvt., Hq. 356th Inf	9-22
Welch, Raymond R., Corp., C, 314th F. S. Bn	11- 5
Welch, Thomas E., Bugler, M. G. Co., 353rd Inf	9-27
Wells, James A., Pvt., F, 340th F. A	9-24
Wenger, Jacob, Pvt., E, 353rd Inf	11- 1
Werly, August H., Corp., B, 353rd Inf	10-20
Wermuth, Elmer W., Pvt., B, 341st M. G. Bn	10-23
Wesley, Silas, Pvt., F, 355th Inf	10-21
Wesolowski, Alexander, Pvt., B, 353rd Inf	10-22
Wessel, Edwin L., Corp., M, 354th Inf	11- 1
Wesselman, Hubert J., Pvt., L, 354th Inf	11- 1
West, Sie A., Pvt., E, 355th Inf	10-22
Westerberg, Martin L., Pvt., B, 354th Inf	11- 1
Westerbuhr, Focke E., Corp., K, 355th Inf	11- 5
Westfall, Leonard LeRoy, Pvt., A, 341st M. G. Bn	11- 3
Wheeler, Charles S., Pvt., B, 340th M. G. Bn	11- 1

Name, Rank, Company, Regiment	Date 1918
Wheeler, Harold S., Pvt., D, 341st M. G. Bn	11- 1
Wheeler, John H., Pvt., A, 314th Eng	9-12
Wherrett, Ortley N., Sgt., Hq. 341st F. A	9-19
White, John E., Sgt., C, 354th Inf	11- 5
White, Cecil D., Pvt., M. G. Co., 356th Inf	10-21
White, Joseph H., Pvt., B, 354th Inf	11- 1
Whitish, Edward, Pvt., D, 353rd Inf	10-25
Whitlaw, Walter, Pvt., K, 353rd Inf	10-26
Whitmer, Elmer, Pvt., K, 353rd Inf	9-12
Whittaker, Maurice, Pvt., M. G. Co., 356th Inf	9-22
Wiese, Edwin, Pvt. 1cl., C, 355th Inf	11- 5
Wiesner, Frank, Pvt., C, 353rd Inf	10-22
Wilbers, Emil H., Pvt., K, 354th Inf	11- 2
Wilcox, Allie LeRoy, Pvt. 1cl., A, 353rd Inf	9-22
Wilde, Thomas H., Pvt., G, 314th Amm. Tr	11- 6
Wilkerson, Roy, Pvt., B, 340th F. A	10- 6
Wilkinson, Herbert L., Sgt., B, 356th Inf	9-23
Willis, Willie R., Pvt., I, 355th Inf	11- 8
Williams, Claud A., Pvt. 1cl., E, 354th Inf	10-21
Williams, Daniel D., Pvt., G, 356th Inf	10-30
Williams, Edson G., Pvt., K, 353rd Inf	10-28
Williams, Enos, Pvt., A, 431st M. G. Bn	11- 2
Williams, Porter A., Pvt., F, 355th Inf	10-21
Williams, S. C., Pvt., G, 356th Inf	10-30
Williamson, Earl H., Pvt. 1cl., M. G. Co., 356th Inf	10-21
Willis, Arch A., Pvt., M, 353rd Inf	9-20
Wilshire, Noble A., Pvt., M, 353rd Inf	11- 3
Wilson, Everett, Pvt., I, 354th Inf	11- 3
Wilson, Oscar W., Pvt. 1cl., F, 340th F. A	10-14
Wilson, Ralph W., Corp., L, 355th Inf	9-13
Wilson, Repps H., Sgt., I, 356th Inf	10- 6
Wilson, Theodore, Pvt., B, 314th Eng	9-24
Wing, Marion W., Pvt. 1cl., B, 356th Inf	9-23
Wingate, Charles R., Pvt., L, 353rd Inf	11- 1
Wiskirchen, Henry C., Corp., G, 314th Amm. Tr	10-31
Wittig, Edward E., Pvt. 1cl., B, 355th Inf	9-13
Wixson, Jacob M., Pvt., F, 353rd Inf	11- 3
Wolfe, Nicholas H., Pvt. 1cl., D, 356th Inf	9-14
Wolff, Henry J., Pvt., C, 354th Inf	11- 2
Wolford, Ernest H., Pvt. 1cl., M, 355th Inf	11- 5

Name, Rank, Company, Regiment	Date 1918
Wolsfeld, Henry, Pvt., B, 353rd Inf	10-22
Wood, Charles A., Wagoner, Hq. 353rd Inf	11- 1
Wood, John E., Mus., B, 353rd Inf	9-13
Wood, Oscar, Wagoner, F, 314th Eng	11- 1
Woods, Irving, Pvt., H, 354th Inf	10-24
Woods, Richard, Pvt., Hq. 353rd Inf	10-23
Woods, Roy E., Pvt., G, 354th Inf	9-30
Woods, William C., Pvt., F, 353rd Inf	11- 2
Woods, William J., Pvt., B, 355th Inf	11- 4
Worl, Harry L., Pvt., L, 355th Inf	11- 5
Wright, Emmett F., Pvt. 1cl., B, 341st M. G. Bn	10-23
Wright, James, Pvt., Hq. 356th Inf	11- 9
Wright, James B., Pvt., H, 353rd Inf	11- 3
Wright, Martin, Pvt., A, 353rd Inf	10-29
Wright, Robert L., Pvt., I, 356th Inf	11- 3
Wright, William W., Pvt., H, 354th Inf	10-24
Wuenscher, Nicolaus G., Pvt., B, 355th Inf	11- 5
Wyatt, Edmond, Pvt., E, 314th Amm. Tr	10- 6
Wyre, Burney H., Corp., L, 353rd Inf	11- 3
Yager, .Willard, Pvt., I, 354th Inf	11- 3
Yakaitis, John, Pvt., I, 353rd Inf	11- 1
Yarnall, Raymond W., Pvt. 1cl., G, 353rd Inf	9-24
Yates, David C., Jr., Pvt. 1cl., 356th Inf	10-27
Yerchus, Joseph F., Pvt. 1cl., D, 355th Inf	11- 2
Yocom, Glenn F., Pvt., C, 353rd Inf	10-26
Young, Anton L., Pvt., B, 356th Inf	9-23
Young, Carl C., Pvt., E, 355th Inf	11- 5
Young, George G., Corp., A, 340th M. G. Bn	11- 9
Young, Morrill A., Pvt., A, 353rd Inf	10-23
Young, Quay, Corp., G, 354th Inf	11- 8
Youngman, Elmer J., Corp., D, 355th Inf	11- 4
Yust, John, Pvt., Hq. 354th Inf	10-21
Zabicki, Joseph, Pvt. 1cl., M, 354th Inf	10-27
Zapolski, Jake, Pvt. 1cl., K, 354th Inf	10-22
Zies, Ray M., Pvt., M, 353rd Inf	11- 1
Zacharias, Charles, Pvt., E, 354th Inf	11- 2
Zarzano, Antonio, Pvt., C., 354th Inf	9-26
Zimmerman, Raymond L., Sgt., K, 353rd Inf	11- 1
Zivielle, Anthony, Pvt., B, 341st M. G. Bn	11- 3
Zullo, Joseph A., Pvt., E, 354th Inf	11- 4

WOUNDED — DEGREE UNDETERMINED

OFFICERS WOUNDED, DEGREE UNDETERMINED

Name, Rank, Organization	Date 1918
Athins, Moses D., Capt., 353rd Inf	9-12
Bach, Joseph P., 2nd Lt., 356th Inf	9-21
Coffman, Frank, 2nd Lt., 356th Inf	11-11
Gardner, Ward A., 2nd Lt., 353rd Inf	9- 9
Griesa, Chas. H., 1st Lt., 356th Inf	9-17
Hazlett, John C., Capt., 353rd Inf	9-18
Irwin, W J., 1st Lt., 340th F. A	10-18
Kemp, Philip C., 1st Lt., Hq. 341st F. A	9-19

Name, Rank, Company, Organization	Date 1918
Lake, Chas. E., 1st Lt., 356th Inf	
Lamy, Joseph E., 1st Lt., 356th Inf	11- 9
Perryman, Curtis B., 2nd Lt., 356th Inf	11-11
Poteet, Charles A., 2nd Lt., 355th Inf	11- 9
Robinson, Dewey, 2nd Lt., 356th Inf	11-11
Shafroth, Morrison, Capt., Hq. 341st F. A	10-23
Stout, Francis R., 2nd Lt., 356th Inf	11- 3

ENLISTED MEN WOUNDED, DEGREE UNDETERMINED

Name, Rank, Company, Organization	Date 1918
Aasen, Sam, Corp., B, 355th Inf	10-22
Adams, Robert H., Pvt., H, 353rd Inf	11-10
Adlum, Wilford M., Corp., G, 356th Inf	11-11
Allen, Clyde V., Corp., B, 353rd Inf	10-27
Anderson, Ernest, Pvt., M, 356th Inf	8- 2
Anderson, Frank G., Pvt., F, 356th Inf	11-11
Atzenbeck, Joe J., Pvt., B, 355th Inf	9-23
Ayres, Francis, Cook, 314th F. S. Bn	...
Baker, John H., Pvt., G, 354th Inf	10-26
Barnesberger, John G., Sgt., A, 340th F. A	10-17
Beachtel, Harry L., Pvt., H, 354th Inf	10-27
Beeber, John A., Cook, F, 353rd Inf	9-19
Belford, Lloyd O., Pvt., G, 354th Inf	10-23
Benadik, Paul, Pvt., Med. Det., 355th Inf	9-15
Bendon, Leo, Sgt., F, 353rd Inf	9-19
Berquist, Andrew G., Pvt., G, 353rd Inf	11- 6
Berry, Benj. L., Pvt 1cl., 314th F. S. Bn	...
Bleener, William, Wag., 314th Eng	11-11
Binkley, Ralph J., Pvt., 1cl., C, 340th F. A	9-21
Bishop, Ralph C., Pvt., F, 353rd Inf	9-19
Blaha, Charles, Pvt. 1cl., A, 355th Inf	11-10
Bogard, William, Pvt., L, 353rd Inf	9-18
Bonar, Lester M., Pvt., F, 353rd Inf	11-10
Boroughs, Ruble, Corp., D, 353rd Inf	10-27
Bowen, Iris A., Pvt., A, 353rd Inf	10-29
Bowman, Samuel E., Pvt., A, 353rd Inf	10-21
Bradford, Albert L., Pvt., A, 356th Inf	10-29
Branaman, William, Pvt., L, 353rd Inf	9-19
Brancato, Mattis, Pvt., Hq. 353rd Inf	9-16
Brandt, Robert J., Pvt., L, 356th Inf	9-16
Brant, P. B., Pvt., E, 342nd F. A	

Name, Rank, Company, Organization	Date 1918
Bratton, Paul B., Pvt., A, 353rd Inf	9-19
Brennan, Joseph P., Pvt., E, 354th Inf	10-28
Brickner, Carl B., Pvt., F, 354th Inf	11-11
Broaddus, James W., Pvt. 1cl., A, 353rd Inf	10-29
Bryant, William M., Pvt., A, 353rd Inf	10-26
Budde, George, Pvt., K, 356th Inf	9-14
Bugenhagen, Otto C., Pvt., C, 314th Sup. Tr	
Burleson, Charles W., Pvt., Hq. 354th Inf	9-14
Burlew, Ernest M., Pvt., C, 356th Inf	11-11
Burt, James F., Pvt., F, 356th Inf	11-11
Burt, Joseph S., Pvt., K, 353rd Inf	8-25
Burton, Bert, Pvt., K, 353rd Inf	11-10
Buth, John O., Pvt., M, 353rd Inf	11-10
Cahill, Edward, Pvt., I, 355th Inf	9-18
Carlson, Albert B., Pvt. 1cl., K, 355th Inf	11-11
Carpenter, Elvaro M., Pvt. 1cl., Med. Det., 355th Inf.	9-17
Carver, Jack, Corp., A, 354th Inf	9- 2
Cederholm, Francis C., Corp., M, 355th Inf	11-10
Chalice, William G., Pvt., F, 314th Eng	9-17
Chase, Frank W., Pvt. 1cl., F, 356th Inf	11-11
Chorum, Marvin, Pvt., A, 342nd M. G. Bn	11-11
Christine, Nigal L., Pvt. 1cl., E, 353rd Inf	9-19
Christofilopulos, George, Pvt., I, 354th Inf	8-25
Cohan, Louis Edwin, Corp., B, 355th Inf	11-11
Coleman, Seymour D., Pvt., F, 353rd Inf	11-10
Conley, Francis C., Pvt., G, 356th Inf	9-17
Conley, James E., Corp., H, 354th Inf	9-14
Conwell, Bernard, Pvt., B, 356th Inf	9-16
Coonts, Harry L., Pvt., F, 356th Inf	11-11
Cope, Clinton C., Corp., E, 353rd Inf	9-19
Cox, Floyd E., Sgt. 1cl., Med. Det., 340th F. A	9-26

Name, Rank, Company, Organization	Date 1918
Crader, Roy N., Pvt., H, 356th Inf	11-11
Cross, Roy L., Sgt., E, 314th Sup. Tr	
Cucchiara, Tony, Pvt., M, 353rd Inf	9-20
Daniel, Frederick C., Pvt., I, 355th Inf	9- 9
Davis, Charles, Sgt., H, 353rd Inf	9- 9
DeBoer, Fred C., Pvt., A, 353rd Inf	10-25
Dickson, John H., Pvt., F, 354th Inf	9-10
Dobberstein, Henry F., Pvt., K, 353rd Inf	11-10
Dosher, Sam R., Mech., 340th F. A.	9-26
Drennon, Earl W., Pvt., M, 353rd Inf	10-27
Duran, Manuel, Pvt., A, 342nd M. G. Bn	11-11
Durazo, Esimiro, Pvt., G, 353rd Inf	11- 6
DuShane, James H., Pvt., B, 353rd Inf	10-27
Echterling, Eugene J., Pvt., G, 356th Inf	11-11
Eliason, Wm. E., Corp., C, 356th Inf	9-23
English, Frank E., Wag., Sup. Co., 356th Inf	8-15
Ennis, Everett, Pvt., A, 314th Eng	9-23
Ernest, Kenneth C., Pvt., D, 355th Inf	11- 8
Fanti, Basilie, Pvt. 1cl., H, 355th Inf	10-31
Ferguson, Richard V., Pvt., E, 353rd Inf	9-19
Ferris, Harold B., Pvt., Hq. 353rd Inf	10-21
Fisher, Ed. Albert, Pvt. 1cl., E, 356th Inf	10- 7
Foltz, Floyd C., Pvt., A, 356th Inf	9-23
Foster, Wm. E., Pvt., I, 355th Inf	9- 9
Francis, Allen C., Pvt. 1cl., B, 340th F. A.	10-17
Fuller, Guy H., Corp., D, 342nd M. G. Bn	8-16
Gale, John H., Pvt. 1cl., C, 314th F. S. Bn	10-29
Gannon, Edwin F., Pvt., G, 356th Inf	11- 6
Garcia, John O., Corp., D, 353rd Inf	10-27
Gates, Ruphus C., Corp., G, 355th Inf	9-17
Gee, Alfred A., Sgt., H, 355th Inf	11- 6
Geller, Jack, Corp., A, 356th Inf	11- 8
Gilles, John, Pvt., L, 353rd Inf	10-24
Gillham, Roger R., Pvt., Hq. 353rd Inf	9-23
Gnade, Chris, Corp., D, 354th Inf	11- 5
Gomez, Francisco, Pvt., G, 356th Inf	11- 6
Goodbar, Earl G., Corp., Hq. 340th F. A.	11- 8
Goodbrod, Walter E., Corp., H, 355th Inf	10-27
Goodenough, Ernest, Pvt. 1cl., H, 356th Inf	9-17
Goodier, Henry A., Corp., B, 356th Inf	11- 7
Graham, Ed., Pvt., B, 356th Inf	11-11
Graves, Ira L., Sgt., A, 342nd M. G. Bn	11- 1
Gray, Edward J., Cook, G, 353rd Inf	11-10
Gray, John, Pvt., B, 340th F. A.	10- 6
Green, Fred, Pvt., E, 354th Inf	9-10
Green, George B., Corp., B, 340th F. A.	9-25
Green, Roy V., Pvt. 1cl., C, 353rd Inf	9-19
Gullet, Richard E., Sgt., C, 354th Inf	11-11
Habermann, Louis, Pvt., H, 354th Inf	11- 3
Hackman, Leland, Pvt., B, 356th Inf	11- 9
Halbert, John L., Pvt. 1cl., E, 354th Inf	9-17
Hale, Jack C., Pvt. 1cl., B, 353rd Inf	9-16
Hall, Everett L., Corp., B, 353rd Inf	10-25
Holloran, Hubert V., Pvt. 1cl., B, 353rd Inf	9-21
Halter, Ernest G., Pvt. 1cl., B, 355th Inf	9-23
Hancock, Joseph H., Pvt., G, 353rd Inf	9-19
Hansen, Charles E., Pvt., C, 340th F. A.	9-22
Hansen, Columbus C., Pvt., I, 353rd Inf	11- 6
Hansford, Jim, Pvt., G, 353rd Inf	9-24
Havins, Earl F., Pvt. 1cl., 89th M. P.	11- 7
Hawke, Henry A., Pvt., D, 340th F. A.	10-14
Hendren, Cylde N., Pvt., C, 353rd Inf	10-27
Henson, Arthur, Pvt., L, 354th Inf	11-10
Higgins, James E., Cook, B, 353rd Inf	10-27
Hinkhouse, Roy, Pvt. 1cl., H, 353rd Inf	9-19
Holbrook, Harry S., Pvt., 356th Amb. Co	10-30
Hoppe, Henry Alvin, Pvt. 1cl., F, 356th Inf	11- 6
Hosking, Fred C., Mech., C, 340th F. A.	9-24
Hummel, Louis C., Pvt., B, 355th Inf	9-22
Humphries, Douglas A., Pvt. 1cl., D, 340th F. A.	9-24
Hurst, William A., Corp., A, 356th Inf	11- 8
Jagels, Edw. G., Corp., C, 314th Sup. Tr	
Jameson, Rudolph, Pvt., H, 353rd Inf	9-19
Johnson, Martin H., Pvt., F, 353rd Inf	9-19
Johnson, Roy, Pvt. 1cl., F, 355th Inf	9-23
Johnson, Walter, Pvt., C, 353rd Inf	9-18
Johnston, Jamie N., Corp., F, 354th Inf	9-16
Joslin, Oscar D., Pvt. 1cl., Med. Det., 355th Inf	9-17
Juers, Edward H., Pvt., L, 353rd Inf	10-27
Kalbfell, Arthur F. D., Pvt. 1cl., C, 355th Inf	11-11
Karalis, Nicholas Sam., Pvt., B, 355th Inf	11-11
Kelley, Lee D., Pvt., L, 353rd Inf	10-24
Kinder, Roy A., Pvt., I, 354th Inf	11-11
King, Ardalla, Sgt., F, 353rd Inf	9-19
King, Charles S., Pvt., Hq. 353rd Inf	10-28
Kinney, Wm. W., Corp., D, 356th Inf	10-5
Kirby, Alva, Pvt., B, 356th Inf	11- 9
Kochleos, Nick, Pvt., H, 353rd Inf	9-19
Kolshorn, Wm., Pvt., G, 353rd Inf	10-22
Koronkiewicz, Alexander, Pvt., C, 356th Inf	11- 8
Krause, Herman, Pvt., Med. Det., 342nd M. G. Bn	11- 1
Kreider, Herbert W., Pvt., G, 356th Inf	11- 9
Kreitz, Wm. E., Pvt. 1cl., K, 355th Inf	9-28
Krizinger, Adolph, Pvt., H, 355th Inf	9-17
Kuhn, Raymond A., Pvt., B, 356th Inf	11- 9
Lamb, Harry D., Pvt., C, 356th Inf	11-10
Landa, Louis, Pvt., I, 353rd Inf	10-29
Larkin, John L., Pvt., E, 353rd Inf	9-18
Laws, Wm. L., Pvt., C, 355th Inf	11- 4
Lentz, Gust T., Pvt E, 353rd Inf	9-19
Lewis, Ben S., Corp., C, 353rd Inf	10-27
Lichtenberger, Warren H., Pvt., B, 353rd Inf	10-27
Lievense, Simon, Corp., 89th M. P.	11-11
Lindsey, Jesse J., Pvt., C, 314th Amm. Tr	10-26
Lingwood, Iver T., Corp., C, 355th Inf	11- 3
Linnerts, Arthur S., Pvt., C, 354th Inf	9- 2
Loftus, Wm. M. C., Pvt. 1cl., C, 353rd Inf	10- 5
Longueppe, Ernest T., Pvt., Hq. 356th Inf	11- 6
Loyd, Charles L., Corp., B, 314th Eng	10- 6
Lucero, Conrade, Pvt., Hq. 356th Inf	11- 6
Lucey, James F., Pvt., C, 314th Amm. Tr	10 30
Lynn, Harold F., Mech., A, 340th F. A.	10-17
March, James, Pvt., F, 353rd Inf	9-28
Mare, Maopin, Pvt., C, 356th Inf	9-23
Marianna, John L., Pvt., H, 356th Inf	11-11
Maritz, Alvin, Pvt., C, 355th Inf	11- 4
Markovetz, Martin S., Corp., Bat. F, 340th F. A	10- 9
Marks, Charles, Pvt., D, 354th Inf	10- 3
Martin, Paul V., Pvt., C, 356th Inf	9-19
Martinez, Jose, Pvt., Bat. A, 340th F. A.	10-20
Mata, Felipe, Pvt., H, 356th Inf	8 14
Maurer, John W., Corp. B, 340th M. G. Bn	11- 5
Maupin, Carey J., Sgt., E, 342nd F. A.	
McBeath, Robert W., Pvt., Hq. 356th Inf	11-11
McBroom, Clarence B., Pvt., G, 353rd Inf	11- 5
McCarty, Charles A., Pvt., B, 356th Inf	9-21
McConnell, Harry, Pvt., D, 353rd Inf	9-20
McCrachen, Elmer C., Corp., F, 314th Eng	10-31
McCullough, Charles L., Sgt., Bat. C., 340th F. A.	9-19
McDonald, Joe, Pvt., Hq. 356th Inf	11- 7
McDonald, Louis C., Corp., Hq. 356th Inf	9-12
McDowell, Hayden, Corp., E, 354th Inf	9- 7
McKimens, Wilder D., Sgt., H, 353rd Inf	9-23
McKinnon, Charlie, Pvt., B, 314th Eng	10-31
McMahan, William E., Pvt., G, 355th Eng	10-25
McMahon, Bert J., Pvt., E, 314th Eng	10-30
Medius, Arthur, Pvt., A, 356th Inf	10-24
Mendenhall, Earl, Pvt., C, 354th Inf	9- 5
Miner, John, Pvt., C, 355th Inf	11- 3
Mork, Melvin, Cook, H, 353rd Inf	11- 4
Morlan, Oscar M., Pvt., Hq. 354th Inf	11- 9
Mudd, Frank G., Corp., M, 354th Inf	11- 5
Mueller, Bernardt C., Pvt. 1cl., Hq 356th Inf	11- 6
Muninger, Fred E., Pvt., I, 353rd Inf	9-20
Murray, Patrick J., Pvt., E, 354th Inf	9-10
Murrell, Leonard W., Pvt. 1cl., M, 354th Inf	9-18
Nadin, John, Pvt. 1cl., A, 355th Inf	11- 5
Nalle, Louis B., Pvt., B, 356th Inf	11- 9
Nelson, George C., Pvt. 1cl., H, 353rd Inf	8-14
Nichols, Garry F., Pvt., K, 356th Inf	8-22
Nichols, Luther P., Pvt., D, 314th Eng	10-30
Nichols, William B., Pvt. 1cl., L, 356th Inf	9-16
Niehous, John H., Pvt., Hq. Tr., 89th Div	8-10
Noonan, Eugene A., Corp., A, 356th Inf	11- 8
Noonan, John F., Pvt., C, 356th Inf	11- 9
Nordell, John A., Pvt., E, 353rd Inf	11-10
Northrup, Charles R., Pvt., H, 354th Inf	9-18
Ogle, Mitchell E., Pvt. 1cl., K, 356th Inf	8-26
O'Gorman, Clarence W., Pvt. 1cl., L, 356th Inf	10-27
Ohnesorgen, William, Pvt., H, 356th Inf	11-11
Ostasiewski, Frank, Pvt., B, 353rd Inf	10-22
Pardue, Charles L., Pvt. 1cl., I, 355th Inf	8-15
Paulson, John, Pvt. 1cl., K, 356th Inf	9-16
Penfield, William A., Pvt., F, 340th F. A.	10-23
Peterson, Carl R., Pvt., H, 354th Inf	11- 5
Peterson, Harry B., Pvt., M, 354th Inf	11- 5
Phegley, James W., Pvt., Hq. 356th Inf	10-25
Pindell, Isaac L., Pvt. 1cl., K, 355th Inf	9-17
Pinder, Robert L., Pvt. 1cl., E, 314th Eng	10 30
Poecinnos, George, Pvt., L, 356th Inf	11-11
Poffenburger, Donald C., Pvt., B, 353rd Inf	10-27
Pokojski, Anthony E., Pvt. 1cl., C, 356th Inf	11- 8
Polkki, Emil, Pvt., I, 353rd Inf	10-29
Post, Simon O., Pvt., G, 354th Inf	10-28
Price, Eugene W., Pvt., C, 356th Inf	11- 8
Priem, Ralph E., Pvt., L, 353rd Inf	10-28
Proffitt, Murrell C., Pvt., L, 353rd Inf	9-25
Pullins, Luther L., Pvt. 1cl., A, 341st M. G. Bn	9-19

Name. Rank, Company, Organization	Date 1918
Ralston, Walter L., Sgt., A, 353rd Inf	9- 4
Ramsbottom, James H., Corp., C, 356th Inf	11- 8
Ravey, Herman A., Pvt., B, 353rd Inf	10-27
Reasoner, Henry C., Pvt. 1cl., M. G. Co. 356	11- 6
Reed, William D., Pvt. 1cl., Bat. D, 340th F. A.	9-19
Ribas, Juan, Pvt., M, 353rd Inf	8-24
Robinson, Edward G., Hq. Co., 340th F. A	10- 1
Roff, Louis J., Pvt., E, 314th Eng	11- 3
Ruble, Claude, Bugler, F, 353rd Inf	10-12
Ruppert, Otto, Pvt., Sup., 354th Inf	9- 7
Russel, John P., Pvt., A, 353rd Inf	10-25
Ryason, Charles E., Pvt., H, 356th Inf	8-13
Sampal, George C., Pvt., B, 340th M. G. Bn	7-23
Sanders, John E., Pvt. 1cl., K, 356th Inf	9-17
Sauer, James, Pvt., F, 353rd Inf	10-26
Schalla, Otto M., Pvt., D, 355th Inf	9-17
Schlau, Alexander H., Pvt., G, 354th Inf	9-14
Schloe, Otto H., Pvt. 1cl., D, 341st M. G. Bn	10-19
Schmidt, George, Pvt., K, 353rd Inf	9-20
Schmidt, Harry J., Corp., B, 353rd Inf	9-19
Schneider, Clarence R., Pvt., C, 356th Inf	9-17
Schofield, Virgil A., Pvt. 1cl., A, 340th F. A	10-11
Schofield, Wm. C., Pvt. 1cl., M, 353rd Inf	9-18
Schultz, Leo A., Pvt., B, 353rd Inf	10-27
Scordos, Gabriel, Pvt., B, 342nd M. G. Bn	11-11
Scott, Chester A., Pvt. 1cl., A, 358th Inf	9-19
Sealey, Morris E., Corp., B, 356th Inf	11- 9
Seal, Otto G., Corp., 314th F. S. Bn	
Sebeck, Charles J., Corp., B, 358th Inf	11- 9
Seitner, Antonius G. H. W., Sgt., D, 355th Inf	9-17
Serna, Marcelino, Pvt., F, 355th Inf	11-11
Sherman, Orrin W., Pvt. 1cl., K, 356th Inf	11- 8
Shockey, Fred D., Corp., A, 314th Sup. Tr	
Shoup, Robert A., Pvt., E, 354th Inf	9-30
Silvermintz, Maurice, Pvt., I, 354th Inf	10- 3
Skaarer, Herbert P., Pvt., G, 354th Inf	10-23
Smart, Robert L., Corp., M. G. Co., 356th Inf	11- 6
Smith, Frank A., Pvt., L, 353rd Inf	10-27
Smith, Louis W., Pvt. 1cl., E, 354th Inf	10-28
Spires, Joseph, Mess Sgt., B, 314th Amm. Tr	
Sprekelmeyer, Harry G., Pvt. 1cl., K, 356th Inf	9-19
Steele, Joseph L., Pvt. 1cl., C, 314th F. S. Bn	10-29
Stegle, Charles W., Sgt., B, 353rd Inf	9-30
Steinke, Henry G., Pvt., H, 354th Inf	11- 5
Stephens, Ralph, Corp., Bat. D, 340th F. A	9-19
Stewart, David J., Cook, Sup. Co., 340th F. A	9-28
Stilley, Leon L., Pvt., G, 356th Inf	11-11
Stuppy, Meinrad A., Pvt. 1cl., Hq. 356th Inf	11- 3
Styginski, A., Pvt., B, 353rd Inf	10- 2
Summers, William A., Corp., L, 356th Inf	9-16
Swift, Robert D., Pvt., Med. Det., 355th Inf	9-17
Taylor, James H., Wag., Sup., 340th F. A	10-14
Tenquist, Clarence G., Pvt., A, 353rd Inf	10-25
Ternes, John B., Pvt., I, 355th Inf	9-17
Thatcher, Dolan, Pvt., Amb. Co., 355th Inf	11-10
Thompson, Emil A., Pvt., K, 355th Inf	9-17
Thrash, Preston M., Pvt., A, 356th Inf	11- 8
Tinkelemberg, Jacob, Pvt., F, 355th Inf	11-10
Tipton, Floyd L., Pvt., L, 354th Inf	10-24
Titus, Andrew, Pvt., Prov., 314th Sup. Tr	
Toups, Edgar J., Pvt., B, 356th Inf	11- 9
Tracy Asa R., Pvt. 1cl., 314th F. S. Bn	
Trokey Frank, Pvt., M, 354th Inf	9-14
Truelove, Chester, Pvt. 1cl., D, 342nd M. G. Bn	11- 5
Tucker, Fred, Sgt., B, 356th Inf	11- 9
Turner, Charles L., Pvt., M, 354th Inf	9-19
Upton, Odes K., Pvt. 1cl., C, 340th F. A	10- 6
Urich, Gordon C., Pvt., D, 356th Inf	9-18
Van De Wall, Luther B., Pvt., Hq. 353rd Inf	10-30
Van Dusen, Roland G., Pvt. 1cl., A, 353rd Inf	9-24
Van Haren, Arthur, Pvt. 1cl., M, 353rd Inf	9-20
Vanvalkenburg, Ernest, Corp., B, 353rd Inf	10-27
Waetzig, William, Pvt., B, 353rd Inf	10-26
Wahls, William, Pvt., B, 353rd Inf	10-28
Walker, Emil, Pvt. 1cl., 314th F. S. Bn	
Walker, Patrick J., Pvt., E, 314th Eng	11- 8
Wallace, Harry H., Pvt., S. C. U. No. 5, 89th Div	10- 5
Weant, Samuel A., Pvt., K, 356th Inf	9-16
Weaver, George S., Pvt. 1cl., K, 356th Inf	9-18
Webster, William J., Sgt., Bat. F, 340th F. A	9-26
Webster, Howard P., Pvt., C, 340th F. A	10-21
Welland, John P., Pvt., D, 355th Inf	9- 2
Weller, Nicholas P., Pvt., C, 353rd Inf	10-27
Wesselman, Hubert J., Pvt., L, 354th Inf	11- 5
White, Guy B., Pvt. 1cl., B, 353rd Inf	9-19
White, Maney D., Pvt., B, 353rd Inf	10-27
White, Paul, Pvt., C, 353rd Inf	10-27
Wickert, Arthur O., Pvt. 1cl., C, 354th Inf	9- 5
Wilkerson, Roy P., Pvt., B, 340th F. A	10- 6
Wilson, Glen E., Pvt., C, 356th Inf	11- 3
Wilson, Oscar W., Pvt. 1cl., F, 340th F. A	10- 3
Wolf, Harry, Pvt., C, 354th Inf	9- 5
Wolz, Gussie, Pvt., K, 355th Inf	9-17
Worth, Lee, Pvt., E, 342nd F. A	
Wright, Wellington P., Pvt., M, 354th Inf	9-14
Yates, Clyde, Pvt., I, 354th Inf	9- 3
Young, Bernard L., Sgt., I, 353rd Inf	9-20
Young, Ralph A., Pvt. 1cl., A, 342nd M. G. Bn	11-11
Zerkel, Carl O., Corp., H, 354th Inf	11-11
Zimmerman, Harry L., Corp., B, 353rd Inf	10-27
Zweifel, Edward, Pvt., B, 353rd Inf	10-27

GASSED

GASSED OFFICERS

Name, Rank, Organization	Date, 1918
Arnold, Emmett L., 1st Lt., 356th Inf	10- 7
Barr, Chas. F., 1st Lt., M. C., 354th Inf	8-10
Beck, Henry A., 1st Lt., M. C., 355th Inf	8-10
Becker, Seth A., 2nd Lt., 354th Inf	9-25
Boschen, Fred W., Lt. Col., 353rd Inf	10-22
Bottomley, Myrl E., 2nd Lt., 355th Inf	8- 8
Boyle, Ernest E., 1st Lt., 354th Inf	8-10
Brown, Levi G., Lt. Col., F. A., Hq. 89th Div	8- 9
Caldwell, Leslie O., 1st Lt., 355th Inf	11- 5
Calhoun, Allen P., 2nd Lt., 356th Inf	10- 7
Chase, Erskine H., 1st Lt., 353rd Inf	10-25
Churchill, Gerald E., 2nd Lt., 354th Inf	8-10
Clemente, Humbert J., 1st Lt., 354th Inf	10-27
Cook, Lewis H., 2nd Lt., 354th Inf	10-27
Cox, Harvey B., 1st Lt., 354th Inf	8- 7
Dake, Justin W., 2nd Lt., 354th Inf	9-26
Davis, Vernon W., 1st Lt., D. C., M. C., 356th Inf	11-10
Dearing, Harry L., 2nd Lt., 355th Inf	11- 5
Deland, Thorndike, 1st Lt., 340th F. A	10- 5
Earl, John J., 2nd Lt., 354th Inf	8-10
Edmonds, Leslie E., Capt., 341st M. G. Bn	10-22
Eldridge, Harold C., 2nd Lt., 355th Inf	8- 9
Ellison, William F., 2nd Lt., 356th Inf	10- 7
Engle, Stanley L., 1st Lt., 354th Inf	10-27
Ernsberger, Dale D., Capt., 356th Inf	10- 7
Farrell, Henry C., 1st Lt., 340th M. G. Bn	10- 5
Ferguson, Albert E., 2nd Lt., 342nd F. A	10-14
Floete, Franklin G., Capt., 342nd F. A	
Fox, Chas. M., 1st Lt., M. C., M. D., 353rd Inf	10-29
Gartner, William, Capt., M. C. M. D., 354th Inf	10-28
Gomez, Louis G., 1st Lt., 314th F. S. Bn	8-10
Green, Charles O., 2nd Lt., 342nd F. A	
Griffith, Grove B., 1st Lt., 355th Inf	11- 1
Hale, William A., Major, 340th M. G. Bn	10- 5
Hanna, Myron, 1st Lt., 314th San. Tr	10-27
Hansen, Arthur J., Chaplain, Hq. 89th Div	11-11
Hastings, Harllah E., 1st Lt., 341st M. G. Bn	10- 2
Hay, George W., 1st Lt., 355th Inf	8- 9
Holcombe, William S., 1st Lt., 354th Inf	8-11
Johnson, William G., 1st Lt., 354th Inf	10- 5
Keller, Dallas C., 1st Lt., 342nd M. G. Bn	10- 5
Kelly, James A., 2nd Lt., 355th Inf	8- 9
Kellogg, Hugh B., 1st Lt., 353rd Inf	10-23
Kelly, Farmer, Capt., 354th Inf	8-10
La Driere, Raymond E., 1st Lt., 354th Inf	8-10
McLaughlin, Richard M., 1st Lt., 355th Inf	8- 9
Maclear, Arthur A., 1st Lt., 355th Inf	8- 9
Maloney, William E., 2nd Lt., 354th Inf	8-10
Meade, Reginald H., Major, M. C., 354th Inf	9-27
Miekle, Chas. H., Major, M. C., Hq. 340th M. G. Bn	10- 5
Moreland, Julius C., 2nd Lt., 356th Inf	10- 7
Morrow, Walter J., 2nd Lt., 355th Inf	11- 5
Muchmore, Clyde E., 2nd Lt., 340th M. G. Bn	10- 5
Murdock, Clarence T., 2nd Lt., Hq. 354th Inf	9-26
Newcomber, Lloyd A., 1st Lt., 354th Inf	10-25
Odom, Paul W., 2nd Lt., 341st M. G. Bn	8-15
Page, Lloyd, Capt., 356th Inf	9-21
Passmore, Claude A., 1st Lt., Hq. 354th Inf	10-28
Pelstrup, Edward C., 1st Lt., Hq. 354th Inf	8-10
Reif, Carl T., 2nd Lt., 354th Inf	8-10
Rhodes, George E., 1st Lt., 354th Inf	8-10
Rice, Harry D., 2nd Lt., 356th Inf	8-10
Salmon, Ivan R., 2nd Lt., 355th Inf	11- 5
Scherf, Louis M., Capt., 355th Inf	8-10

Name, Rank, Organization	Date, 1918
Schrof, William H., 2nd Lt., 354th Inf	10-24
Schuh, Harold, 2nd Lt., 355th Inf	8- 9
Shiverick, Nathan C., Major, Hq. 354th Inf	8-10
Stivers, Howard B., Major, Hq. 354th Inf	9-28
Toney, Lee E., Capt., M. C., M. D, 356th Inf	10- 9
Topping, Chas R., 2nd Lt., 354th Inf	8-10
Vigeant, Gregory, Capt., 354th Inf., Hq. 89th Div	8- 9
Whitt, Ollie B., 2nd Lt., 342nd M. G. Bn	10- 5
Woods, Judson E., 1st Lt., Chaplain, 354th Inf	8-10
Zipoy, Frank J., 1st Lt., 353rd Inf	10-23

GASSED ENLISTED MEN

Name, Rank, Company, Regiment	Date, 1918
Abbott, Charles W., Pvt., A, 354th Inf	8-10
Abbott, Oscar L., Pvt. 1cl., E, 354th Inf	8-10
Abraham, Walter E., Pvt. 1cl., M. G. Co., 355th Inf	11- 2
Abrams, Harry M., Pvt., B, 355th Inf	8-15
Abrams, Joseph, Pvt., 354th Inf	10-27
Ackerman, Carl P., Pvt. 1cl., H, 353rd Inf	10- 2
Adair, Ora, Corp., G, 354th Inf	9-26
Adams, Charles L., Pvt., M, 355th Inf	10- 6
Adams, Daniel R., Pvt., F, 354th Inf	10-28
Adams, Ernest W., Pvt., A, 354th Inf	8-10
Adams, James, Mech., F, 340th F. A	10-24
Addington, Hadwen A., Pvt., L, 355th Inf	11- 5
Adkins, George M., Corp., B, 353rd Inf	10- 7
Aodlph, Ervin E., Pvt. 1cl., E, 356th Inf	10- 7
Agnitch, John P., Pvt. 1cl., F, 355th Inf	11- 2
Ahlstrom, Albin, Pvt., L, 355th Inf	11- 5
Akers, Albert L., Pvt., A, 340th M. G. Bn	11- 3
Akert, Paul, Pvt., B, 342nd Inf	10- 5
Alexander, Audie J., Pvt., E, 356th Inf	10- 6
Alley, James F., Pvt., L, 353rd Inf	10-27
Altenburg, George, Pvt., B, 354th Inf	10- 5
Altenhoff, Julius J., Pvt., E, 356th Inf	10- 7
Alvig, Melvin L., Pvt., G, 354th Inf	10-30
Ames, Norman, Corp., D, 355th Inf	8- 9
Anderson, Albert, Pvt., L, 355th Inf	11- 5
Anderson, Andrew J., Wag., Sup. Co., 355th Inf	10- 2
Anderson, Arthur, Pvt., Hq., 355th Inf	8-10
Anderson, Clyde, Sgt., Hq., 355th Inf	8- 8
Anderson, Gus A., Pvt., B, 342nd M. G. Bn	10- 5
Anderson, Hilmer T., Pvt. 1cl., Med Det., 355th Inf	8- 9
Anderson, James F., Pvt., H, 354th Inf	10- 5
Anderson, Judd W., Corp., M. G. Co., 353rd Inf	11- 5
Anderson, Max, Corp., F, 340th F. A	10-24
Andrews, Hall Paul, Pvt., I, 356th Inf	10- 7
Anzalone, Antonino, Pvt., D, 341st M. G. Bn	9-30
Apodaca, Jose S., Pvt., F, 354th Inf	10-27
Archuleta, Jose B., Pvt., I, 356th Inf	11- 2
Ardin, Artellus, Pvt., E, 356th Inf	10- 7
Argus, George L., Pvt., F, 354th Inf	9-26
Armstrong, Frank T., Pvt., B, 354th Inf	10- 5
Armstrong, William G., Sup. Sgt., D, 355th Inf	8- 9
Arndt, Henry, Pvt., A, 355th Inf	8- 9
Artrip, Fullen H., Corp., Hq. 354th Inf	9-26
Ash, Fred A., Pvt. 1cl., A, 340th M. G. Bn	10-26
Ashercraft, Allie, Pvt., I, 356th Inf	10- 6
Ashinhurst, Guy C., Pvt., L, 353rd Inf	10- 3
Atchley, Perry D., Pvt. 1cl., D, 355th Inf	8- 9
Atterbury, William J., Pvt. 1cl., L, 356th Inf	10- 7
Atwell, Millard, Pvt., F, 314th Eng	9-29
Atwood, Paul, Pvt., D, 355th Inf	8- 9
Aumuchon, Charlie E., Pvt., B, 342nd M. G. Bn	10- 5
Auflick, Thomas J. R., Pvt., C, 354th Inf	8-10
Austin, George W., Pvt., B, 342nd M. G. Bn	10- 5
Ayres, Thomas J., Pvt., A, 340th M. G. Bn	10-27
Ayres, Carl W., Pvt. 1cl., Med. Det., 314th Eng	10- 5
Babe, William M., Corp., D, 355th Inf	8- 9
Backer, William E., Mess Sgt., B, 354th Inf	10- 5
Backus, Benjamin L., Pvt., L, 355th Inf	11- 5
Bagnek, Victor J., Corp., D, 355th Inf	8- 9
Baker, Edward R., Pvt., I, 356th Inf	10- 6
Baker, Luther C., Pvt., F, 354th Inf	10-27
Baker, Stephen S., Corp., C, 314th F. S. Bn	8- 9
Baladam, Benjamin, Pvt., H, 354th Inf	10-28
Balducci, Attilio, Pvt., G, 354th Inf	10-28
Baldwin, Louis E., Pvt. 1cl., Hq., 354th Inf	8-10
Balkin, Edward, Pvt., D, 355th Inf	8- 9
Balton, William, Pvt., G, 354th Inf	8-10
Baltzell, Edward L., Sgt., Hq. 355th Inf	8- 9
Bangert, George, Pvt., G, 354th Inf	9-26
Bankstrom, Ernest, Pvt., E, 356th Inf	10- 7
Bardell, Arthur W., Corp., L, 355th Inf	11- 5
Barlen, Douglas, Pvt., F, 314th Eng	9-26
Barry, David J., Wag., Sup. Co., 355th Inf	10- 3
Barry, John R., Pvt., C, 354th Inf	8-10
Bartlett, Lehman A., Pvt., I, 356th Inf	10- 7
Bassman, Arthur A., Sgt., D, 314th Eng	10- 7
Baumann, Fred, Pvt., F, 354th Inf	10-27
Baxter, Glenn B., Pvt. 1cl., B, 314th F. S. Bn	10- 5
Bayless, George H., Pvt., Hq. 355th Inf	10- 4
Beach, Earl G., Sgt., A, 355th Inf	8- 9
Beach, Perly I., 1st Sgt., A, 355th Inf	8- 9
Beals, Alonso R., Pvt., Hq., 354th Inf	10-29
Bean, James V., Pvt., F, 354th Inf	10-27
Beardsley, Clifford L., Corp., C, 341st M. G. Bn	10- 1
Beaty, Thomas E., Sgt. 1cl., C, 314th F. S. Bn	9-26
Beaver, Doss H., Pvt. 1cl., M. G. Co., 354th Inf	10-27
Bebermiss, Walter, Pvt., A, 342nd M. G. Bn	10-27
Beck, Claus A., Pvt., L, 353rd Inf	10-27
Becker, Geo. W., Corp., E, 342nd F. A	
Beeding, Arthur D., Corp., Hq. 354th Inf	8-10
Beegle, Frederick C., Pvt., F, 354th Inf	10-28
Beeler, Vernon C., Pvt., Hq. 353rd Inf	9-27
Behling, Arthur, Pvt., E, 314th Eng	9-18
Behnke, Joseph, Pvt., F, 353rd Inf	11- 1
Behrens, Fred H., Pvt., M. G. Co., 355th Inf	11- 9
Beirne, Charles V., Pvt., I, 356th Inf	10- 7
Belcher, Guy T., Pvt., H, 353rd Inf	10- 2
Belford, Philip H., Pvt., B, 353rd Inf	10- 6
Bellman, Harry, Pvt. D, 354th Inf	8-10
Bellomo, Paul O, Pvt., D, 355th Inf	8- 9
Belman, Charles E., Corp., M, 355th Inf	10- 5
Benard, William A., Pvt., A, 342nd M. G. Bn	10-26
Bendel, Walter E., Pvt. 1cl., F, 354th Inf	11- 3
Benefiel, Noble W., Pvt., D, 341st M. G. Bn	8-10
Benoit, Edward, Pvt., I, 356th Inf	10- 7
Benson, Lawrence E., Pvt. 1cl., A, 355th Inf	8- 9
Berg, Otto, Pvt., F, 314th Eng	9-30
Bergeron, Antone J., Pvt. 1cl., F, 354th Inf	10-27
Bergjans, Harry, Pvt., H, 354th Inf	11- 1
Bergman, William R., Pvt., B, 354th Inf	8-10
Berkel, John W., Pvt., E, 356th Inf	10- 7
Berta, Jerry, Pvt., F, 354th Inf	10-28
Bevinetto, Francesco, Pvt., G, 354th Inf	10-28
Billac, James B., Pvt., E, 356th Inf	10- 7
Billings, Harry C., Pvt., A, 342nd M. G. Bn	8- 9
Billyeu, Roy M., Pvt., M. G. Co., 355th Inf	11- 9
Bingham, Harry H., Pvt., Hq. 353rd Inf	10- 6
Bird, Everett E., Corp., I, 356th Inf	10- 6
Bird, William, Pvt., F, 354th Inf	10-29
Black, Elzy, Pvt., I, 356th Inf	10- 7
Blades, Oscar M., Pvt., B, 354th Inf	10- 5
Blakley, Elbert R., Pvt. 1cl., I, 356th Inf	10- 7
Blanchard, Albert, Pvt., I, 356th Inf	10- 7
Blanchard, Chester R., Pvt., M. G. Co., 354th Inf	10-28
Blankenship, William J., Pvt., I, 356th Inf	10- 7
Blasko, Joseph F., Pvt., G, 354th Inf	11- 1
Bloodworth, John W., Pvt., I, 356th Inf	10- 7
Blum, Walter E., Sgt., L, 355th Inf	11- 5
Blunt, Clark, Pvt., I, 356th Inf	10- 6
Bocher, Jim E., Pvt. 1cl., E, 356th Inf	10- 7
Bock, Arthur P., Corp., A, 355th Inf	10- 5
Bock, Gerhard, Pvt., G, 354th Inf	10-29
Bock, Harry A., Pvt., E, 314th Eng	10-29
Boehlein, Paul, Pvt., D, 354th Inf	8-10
Boente, Frank J., Pvt., D, 341st M. G. Bn	9-28
Bolan, Walter C., Corp., A, 355th Inf	8- 9
Boland, Hylary J., Pvt., A, 342nd M. G. Bn	10-29
Bolander, Andrew J., Pvt., 314th San. Tr	10-28
Bond, Edward F., Pvt., M. G. Co., 355th Inf	11- 3
Bond, William A., Pvt., M. G. Co., 354th Inf	10-28
Bookout, Henry C., Pvt. 1cl., F, 354th Inf	10-27
Boone, William M., Pvt. 1cl., D, 355th Inf	8-13
Borland, Charles M., Pvt., M. G. Co., 354th Inf	10-21
Borman, John, Pvt., L, 355th Inf	11-10
Borst, Jay H., Pvt., G, 354th Inf	10-28
Bosch, Walter C., Corp., G, 354th Inf	10-29
Bosley, Harold S., Pvt., B, 353rd Inf	10- 6
Bosley, Henry D., Pvt., B, 353rd Inf	10- 6
Boston, Robert L., Sgt., F, 314th Eng	9-29
Boultas, Benjamin H., Pvt., D, 354th Inf	8-10
Bounds, Frank J., Sgt., F, 354th Inf	10-28
Bounds, Walter A., Pvt., I, 356th Inf	10- 7
Bourne, Harvey E., Corp., L, 355th Inf	11- 5
Bowen, James G., Pvt., A, 342nd M. G. Bn	8- 9
Boy, John J., Sgt., A, 341st F. A	
Boyd, Harold, Pvt., E, 356th Inf	10- 6
Boyer, Albert R., Pvt., F, 354th Inf	10-27
Brabham, Clarence F., Pvt. 1cl., C, 355th Inf	11-13
Brace, Sylvanus, Pvt., M. G. Co., 354th Inf	11- 6

Name, Rank, Company, Regiment	Date, 1918
Bradeen, James W., Pvt., A, 355th Inf	8- 9
Bradford, Hudson, Sgt., D, 353rd Inf	9-26
Bradford, Ovid G., Pvt., I, 356th Inf	10- 7
Bradley, Stephen A., 1st Sgt., L, 355th Inf	11- 6
Bradshaw, Larry T., Sgt., G, 354th Inf	9-25
Brake, Cecil W., Pvt. 1cl., M. G. Co., 354th Inf	11- 6
Branch, Emmet M., Pvt., G, 354th Inf	9-25
Brandenberg, Frank H., Pvt., G, 354th Inf	10-28
Braham, Percy, Pvt. 1cl., B, 354th Inf	9-23
Braunstein, Phillip J., Sgt., A, 341st F. A	10- 4
Bray, Aubrey O., Pvt., Hq. 340th F. A	10- 4
Brazeal, Thomas, Pvt. 1cl., M. G. Co., 354th Inf	10-28
Breaux, Beauregard, Pvt., K, 356th Inf	10- 9
Breeding, Pearl, Corp., E, 314th Amm. Tr	
Breig, Henry J., Sgt. D, 354th Inf	8-10
Breitenstein, Walter W., Corp., A, 354th Inf	8-10
Brewer, Amos, Pvt., M. G. Co., 354th Inf	10-27
Bright, Lenna E., Pvt., A, 354th Inf	8- 7
Briner, Ravid, Corp., E, 354th Inf	10-28
Bristow James M., Pvt., D, 341st M. G. Bn	9- 3
Brittain, Earl M., Corp., B, 356th Inf	10-21
Brock, Perry L., Pvt., I, 356th Inf	10- 7
Broschears, Isaac, Pvt., M. G. Co., 356th Inf	10- 9
Brouder, Joseph F., Pvt., Hq. 355th Inf	8- 9
Brown, Dement, Corp., L, 355th Inf	11- 5
Brown, Edwin, Pvt. 1cl., A, 355th Inf	8- 9
Brown, Elbert R., Corp., I, 356th Inf	10- 7
Brown, John A., Pvt. 1cl., F, 314th Eng	9- 9
Brown, LeRoy S., Pvt., D, 355th Inf	8-24
Brown, Linn T., Pvt., D, 355th Inf	8- 9
Brown, Thomas H., Pvt. 1cl., M. G. Co., 354th Inf	10-28
Brown, William E., Pvt., C, 354th Inf	8-19
Browning, Floyd C., Pvt. 1cl., D, 341st M. G. Bn	9-30
Bruz, Zedenek L., Corp., A, 355th Inf	8- 9
Brubaker, Estelle R., Pvt., E, 314th Sup. Tr	11- 8
Brule, Sidney J., Corp., C, 341st F. A	
Brummall, Clarence E., Corp., I, 356th Inf	10- 7
Brundige, Clarence E., Pvt., A, 340th M. G. Bn	11- 1
Brunner, David, Pvt., B, 341st M. G. Bn	10-22
Bryan, Paul F., Sup. Sgt., A, 355th Inf	8- 9
Bucciarelli, Carmine, Pvt., F, 354th Inf	10-28
Buchanan, Silas A., Pvt., E, 355th Inf	10- 7
Buchanan, Simon, Pvt., G, 354th Inf	9-25
Buchold, Albert H., Corp., C, 355th Inf	8- 9
Buderman, George A., Pvt., F, 354th Inf	10-28
Buller, Harry, Pvt., E, 356th Inf	10- 6
Bunn, Harry R., Pvt., M. G. Co., 354th Inf	10-28
Burdi, Domineo, Pvt., F, 354th Inf	11- 3
Burke, John, Pvt., E, 356th Inf	10- 6
Burkert, Franklin P., Pvt., C, 314th F. S. Bn	10-30
Burlin, Charles G., Pvt., A, 354th Inf	8-11
Burlison, Roy D., Pvt., Hq. 354th Inf	10-27
Burnett, Lewis C., Pvt., C, 314th F. S. Bn	10- 6
Burnham, Andrew C., Sgt., B, 354th Inf	8-10
Burnham, Mamie H., Pvt., 356th Inf	10- 7
Burns, Robert H., Pvt., C, 341st F. A	
Burrow, William C., Pvt., I, 356th Inf	10- 7
Burtch, Marion W., Pvt. 1cl., M. G. Co., 356th Inf	10-21
Busby, Jehu, Pvt., B, 354th Inf	10- 1
Buteff, Vladimir T., Pvt., D, 354th Inf	8-10
Butler, Harry, Pvt., G, 354th Inf	10-29
Button, Joseph M., Pvt, 1cl., Hq. 355th Inf	10- 6
Butzlaff, Gustav, Pvt., G, 354th Inf	10-31
Buxton, Oliver, Pvt., A, 342nd M. G. Bn	8- 8
Byrd, Ellis E., Pvt., I, 356th Inf	10- 7
Byrum, Dow L., Corp., L, 353rd Inf	10- 8
Cahill, Thomas J., Pvt., B, 354th Inf	8- 7
Cain, Lewis J., Corp., G, 354th Inf	9-25
Caldwell, John D., Pvt., G, 354th Inf	9-25
Caldwell, Jos. C., Sgt., E, 342nd F. A	
Caldwell, Raleigh L., Corp., B, 356th Inf	9-21
Calhoun, Robert, Pvt., B, 354th Inf	10- 6
Callender, Arthur R., Sgt., B, 314th F. S. Bn	10- 5
Calvert, Kenneth, Pvt., G, 354th Inf	9-25
Campbell, Andrew A., Pvt., D, 314th Eng	9-28
Campbell, Charles, Pvt., E, 354th Inf	10- 2
Campbell, George D., Pvt., B, 340th M. G. Bn	10-27
Campbell, Wesley W., Pvt., C, 354th Inf	8-10
Campbell, Winfield P., Pvt., I, 353rd Inf	10-27
Cannon, Cecil W., Sup. Sgt., D, 354th Inf	8-10
Cannon, Elmer M., Pvt., F, 354th Inf	10-27
Cannon, Houston B., Pvt., Med. Det., 354th Inf	10-28
Cantaño, Dominick, Pvt., D, 354th Inf	8-10
Cantu, Manuel B., Pvt., Med. Det., 355th Inf	11- 5
Caputo, Louis, Pvt., B, 354th Inf	10- 6
Carlesimo, Pasquale, Pvt., D, 314th Eng	8-23
Carley, Dennis J., Pvt., G, 354th Inf	10-28
Carlson, Charles A., Sgt., F, 354th Inf	10-27
Carlson, Edwin J., Pvt., C, 354th Inf	8-10
Carlson, Otto E., Pvt., F, 354th Inf	10-28
Carpenter, James E., Pvt., I, 356th Inf	10- 7
Carrell, Arthur E., Pvt., C, 341st M. G. Bn	9-26
Carrano, Tony C., Pvt., D, 355th Inf	8- 9
Carriger, Thomas D., Pvt., M, 355th Inf	11- 8
Carter, Charles T., Pvt., I, 356th Inf	10- 6
Carter, Marvin, Pvt., Hq. 354th Inf	8-10
Carter, Verdie E., Pvt., F, 354th Inf	10-28
Casey, Ernest R., Sup. Sgt., B, 355th Inf	8- 9
Casey, LeRoy, Wag., Sup. Co., 353rd Inf	10- 3
Casey, William E., Pvt., F, 354th Inf	10-28
Caster, James W., Pvt. 1cl., B, 353rd Inf	10- 6
Cave, Jess, Pvt. 1cl., E, 356th Inf	10- 7
Cavenaugh, Thomas P., Sgt., F, 354th Inf	10-28
Cavenee, Claude E., Sgt., E, 354th Inf	9-27
Cavett, Yale H., Sgt., A, 355th Inf	8- 9
Cawyer, Abe, Pvt., I, 356th Inf	10- 7
Cervantes, Jose, Pvt., I, 356th Inf	10- 7
Chadwick, Charles J., Corp., A, 342nd M. G. Bn	8- 9
Champion, Lewis, Pvt., B, 354th Inf	8-10
Chapman, Roy, Pvt., A, 354th Inf	8-10
Chappell, Henry H., Corp., H, 354th Inf	10-28
Charles, Ray A., Pvt., I, 353rd Inf	10-27
Chavez, Edurado, Pvt., B, 355th Inf	10-12
Cherry, Calvin, Sgt., E, 356th Inf	11-11
Childers, Leonard, Pvt., B, 354th Inf	10- 5
Chleboun, Laddie, Pvt., D, 355th Inf	8- 9
Christensen, Alfred H., Sgt., A, 341st F. A	
Christensen, Harry M., Corp., C, 354th Inf	8-10
Christian, Jack C., Pvt., F, 340th F. A	10-23
Christian, Joe W., Pvt., F, 354th Inf	10-27
Christopherson, John H., Sgt., D, 355th Inf	8- 9
Chuman, Oran F., Pvt., E, 342nd F. A	
Church, Claud H., Pvt. 1cl., Med. Det., 354th Inf	9-27
Claar, Frank O., Pvt., D, 355th Inf	8- 9
Clark, George, Pvt., I, 356th Inf	10- 7
Clark, John, Sgt., B, 353rd Inf	10- 6
Clark, John F., Pvt., Hq. 354th Inf	10-27
Clark, Josh B., Pvt., M, 354th Inf	9-27
Clark, Warren, Pvt., M. G. Co., 355th Inf	11- 2
Clatterbuck, Paul W., Pvt. 1cl., B, 354th Inf	8-10
Clary, Ray C., Corp., B, 353rd Inf	10- 6
Clinton, Allen R., Sgt., C, 314th F. S. Bn	8-10
Clover, Willie A., Pvt., A, 354th Inf	8-10
Cody, Richard A., Pvt., F, 354th Inf	8-10
Cohen, Frank, Pvt., E, 342nd F. A	
Cohen, Joseph, Pvt., B, 354th Inf	9-11
Cohn, Arthur, Pvt., L, 356th Inf	10- 5
Colt, Harry C., Pvt. 1cl., A, 354th Inf	8-11
Colburn, Clarence L., Sgt., A, 355th Inf	8- 9
Cole, Frank H., Pvt., Hq. 355th Inf	8- 9
Cole, Frank L., Pvt., K, 353rd Inf	8-30
Coleman, Otis T., Bn. Sgt. Maj., Hq. 354th Inf	8-10
Coligan, Mike, Pvt., E, 314th Eng	10-27
Collins, George, Pvt., L, 355th Inf	11- 8
Collins, James F., Pvt., B, 354th Inf	10- 5
Collins, Joseph W., Pvt., E, 340th F. A	10-24
Comboy, Raymond P., Pvt. 1cl., B, 341st M. G. Bn	10-22
Combs, John A., Pvt., A, 354th Inf	10- 5
Comella, Matthew V., Pvt., I, 353rd Inf	11- 1
Connell, John, Pvt., B, 354th Inf	10- 5
Conner, James W., Pvt. 1cl., C, 355th Inf	8- 9
Connor, Joe, Pvt., B, 354th Inf	8-10
Conyers, Hal, Sgt., B, 340th M. G. Bn	10- 5
Cook, Earl, Pvt. 1cl., Hq. 354th Inf	8-10
Coons, Harrison F., Pvt., F, 354th Inf	10-28
Cooper, Ed., Pvt., E, 342nd F. A	
Cooper, Hallie B., Pvt., E, 314th Eng	9-18
Cooper, Oliver B., Pvt., D, 341st M. G. Bn	9-29
Copas, Roy W., Pvt., C, 355th Inf	8- 9
Cope, Wallace C., Pvt., Med. Det., 355th Inf	8- 9
Copestake, Spencer, Pvt. 1cl., M. G. Co., 355th Inf	11- 4
Corbus, Victor H., Pvt., I, 356th Inf	11- 2
Cordes, John H., Pvt., B, 340th M. G. Bn	10- 7
Coring, John L., Pvt., A, 342nd M. G. Bn	11-13
Cortese, Sam, Pvt., D, 355th Inf	8- 9
Costanzo, James, Pvt., C, 341st M. G. Bn	9-27
Coulomb, George A., Pvt., E, 356th Inf	10- 7
Courtney, Michael F., Pvt. 1cl., D, 355th Inf	8- 9
Cox, Joseph N., Pvt., F, 354th Inf	10-30
Crader, E. L., Sgt., E, 342nd F. A	
Craig, Hugh L., Pvt. 1cl., F, 354th Inf	8-10
Crain, Buddie, Pvt., E, 356th Inf	10- 7
Crame, Clarence, Pvt., E, 354th Inf	10-29
Cramer, Harry H., Pvt., M. G. Co., 354th Inf	10-28
Creager, Robert J., Pvt., M. G. Co., 356th Inf	10-29
Cribbs, Paul C., Corp., C, 314th F. S. Bn	8-16
Crites, Harrison, Pvt., I, 356th Inf	10- 7
Crockett, Clyde F., Pvt., H, 353rd Inf	10- 3

Name, Rank, Company, Regiment	Date, 1918
Cromwell, Chester A., Sgt., L, 356th Inf	10- 6
Crossland, William R., Pvt., C, 314th F. S. Bn	10-27
Crouch, Harrison, Pvt., G, 354th Inf	9-25
Crowe, Louis A., Pvt., F, 354th Inf	10-27
Crowl, Frank A., Pvt., E, 353rd Inf	11- 1
Crowley, Francis D , Pvt., G, 354th Inf	9-25
Crum, Robert, Pvt., B, 355th Inf	10- 9
Crump, Nichols J., Pvt. 1cl., E, 340th F. A	10-24
Cullim, Ernie B., Pvt., M, 354th Inf	9-28
Cummins, Thomas, Pvt., Hq. 354th Inf	8-10
Crueton, Daniel W., Sgt., I, 356th Inf	10- 7
Curtis, Walter E., Corp., I, 356th Inf	10- 7
Curzon, George H., Pvt., M. G. Co., 354th Inf	10-28
Dahmer, Martin V., Pvt., B, 341st M. G. Bn	10-22
Dally, Glenn L., Pvt., Hq. 355th Inf	8-10
Dale, Jarvis G., Pvt., I, 356th Inf	10- 7
Dame, George W., Sgt., B, 353rd Inf	10- 7
Damm, Chris H., Corp., D, 355th Inf	8- 9
Damoude, Phillip C., Pvt., A, 355th Inf	8- 9
Davenport, Jay E., Pvt. 1cl., F, 314th Eng	9-19
David, Francis M., Corp., B, 356th Inf	9-21
Davis, Fred J., Pvt., I, 356th Inf	10- 7
Davis, Larkin E., Corp., D, 353rd Inf	11- 5
Davis, Perry L., Corp., B, 353rd Inf	10- 6
Davis, Sidney E., Pvt. 1cl., F, 354th Inf	10-27
Davis, William A., Pvt., B, 354th Inf	10- 5
Daxey, Fred A., Pvt. 1cl., I, 356th Inf	10- 6
Dean, William E., Pvt., C, 355th Inf	8- 9
Dearmin, Mark T., Pvt., B, 354th Inf	8-10
Deatherage, Paul H., Pvt., B, 342nd M. G. Bn	10- 5
Deavenport, James M , Pvt., I, 356th Inf	10- 6
DeBell, Michael, Pvt., M, 353rd Inf	10- 4
DeBlaere, Archie, Mech., E, 354th Inf	10-30
Decker, Wilbur A., Pvt., I, 356th Inf	10- 7
Dees, Roszel P., Pvt., B, 355th Inf	9- 7
Delorum, Clarence H., Pvt., G, 354th Inf	9-26
Dembowski, Thomas A., Pvt., L, 355th Inf	11- 5
Dempsey, Harry F., Corp., D, 355th Inf	8- 9
Dennis, Roy C., Pvt. 1cl., D, 355th Inf	8- 9
Denson, Nelson M., Pvt., A, 341st M. G. Bn	10-29
Depew, Andy, Pvt., B, 353rd Inf	10- 6
DeRoos, John, Pvt., B, 353rd Inf	10- 6
Desperida, Joseph, Pvt., D, 355th Inf	8- 9
Desvaux, Victor A., Corp., A, 354th Inf	8-10
Detschel, Edward J., Pvt., G, 354th Inf	9-26
DeVane, John T., Pvt. 1cl., A, 355th Inf	8- 9
Devlin, Ralph E., Pvt., F, 314th Eng	9-29
DeWitt, Roy Torrence, Pvt., I, 356th Inf	10- 7
Dexter, John J., Pvt., G, 354th Inf	9-26
Dichtenmiller, George E., Sgt., Hq. 340th F. A	10- 4
Dick, Charles W., Pvt. 1cl., C, 355th Inf	8-10
Dickenson, Ira L., Pvt., A, 355th Inf	8-17
Dickerson, Albert, Pvt., I, 356th Inf	10- 7
Dickinson, Clarence D., Pvt 1cl., B, 354th Inf	10- 6
Dickson, James H., Pvt., I, 356th Inf	10- 6
Diehl, Newlee, Pvt. 1cl., H, 354th Inf	10-29
Diel, Raymond F., Pvt., I, 356th Inf	10- 7
Diorio, Lawrence, Pvt., E, 356th Inf	10- 6
Dipella, Tony, Pvt., F, 314th Eng	9-29
Divan, Fay, Cook, C, 355th Inf	10- 5
Dixon, Joseph, Pvt., C, 354th Inf	8-10
Dobbins, Jefferson, Pvt., E, 356th Inf	10-27
Dodge, Allie, Pvt., M. G. Co., 355th Inf	11- 1
Dodge, Benton J. O., Corp., A, 340th M. G. Bn	10-27
Dodge, Herbert G., Corp., A, 355th Inf	8- 9
Dodson, Richard H., Pvt., B, 354th Inf	10- 5
Dohrman, George C., Pvt. 1cl., D, 341st M. G. Bn	10- 4
Dolan, Aloysius D., Sgt., G, 354th Inf	9-26
Doles, Eaph R., E, 342nd F A	
Donath, Herman, Pvt , F, 314th Eng	9-29
Donlan, Daniel W., Pvt., D, 355th Inf	8- 9
Dorris, Francis L., Pvt., B, 354th Inf	8-10
Dorris, Winfred E., Corp., F, 340th F. A	10-24
Dorsey, Chester W., Pvt. 1cl., Hq. 355th Inf	10- 4
Dorsey, Daniel B., Pvt., I, 356th Inf	10- 7
Dorsey, Harvey E., Pvt., C, 354th Inf	8-10
Dougherty, Chester A., Pvt., Med. Det., 354th Inf	11- 2
Dougherty, Joseph A., Pvt., G, 354th Inf	9-25
Douglass, Roscoe A., Pvt., B, 354th Inf	10- 5
Downey, Hugh R., Mess Sgt., D, 355th Inf	8- 9
Downey, John, Pvt., M. G. Co., 354th Inf	10-27
Doyle, Ralph J., Pvt., Med. Det , 355th Inf	8- 9
Drake, James I , Pvt. 1cl., Hq. 353rd Inf	10-27
Drake, Theodore, Pvt., B, 342nd M. G. Bn	10-28
Drevson, George P., Pvt., Hq. Troop, 89th Div	8- 7
Drew, Joe, Pvt., B, 354th Inf	10- 5
Dreyer, George M., Sgt., F, 354th Inf	8-10
Driver, Moses, Pvt. 1cl., B, 341st M. G. Bn	10-22
Drury, Joseph, Pvt., E, 356th Inf	10- 7
Dugelman, Emil, Pvt., F, 354th Inf	10-30

Name, Rank, Company, Regiment	Date, 1918
Dillallo, Paul, Pvt., B, 354th Inf	8-10
Dummit, Iliff L., Pvt. 1cl., C, 355th Inf	8- 9
Duncan, Benjamin, Pvt., D, 354th Inf	8-10
Duncan, Earl I., Pvt., A, 355th Inf	8- 9
Duncan, Harry J., Pvt. 1cl., F, 354th Inf	10-27
Dunham, George M., Corp., I, 356th Inf	10- 6
Durant, Roscoe C., Pvt., D, 341st M. G. Bn	10- 3
Durham, Arley, Pvt., D, 353rd Inf	10-28
Duvall, Frank U., Pvt., E, 356th Inf	10- 7
Duvall, Jacob L., Corp., B, 354th Inf	8-10
Dye, William W., Sgt. B, 354th Inf	10- 6
Dye, Willie, Pvt. 1cl., E, 356th Inf	10- 7
Eads, George, Pvt., I, 356th Inf	10- 7
Eales, Feran K., Pvt., Med. Det., 355th Inf	11- 5
Earll, William H., Pvt. 1cl., B, 353rd Inf	10- 6
Easton, Walter, Pvt. 1cl., A, 356th Inf	10-28
Ebert, Charles, Sgt., B, 353rd Inf	10- 6
Ebert, William, Corp., B, 353rd Inf	10- 6
Eckert, Alexander, Corp., I, 353rd Inf	10-27
Edge, Lee R., Pvt., B, 354th Inf	10- 5
Edler, Tony W., Corp., M. G. Co., 354th Inf	10-27
Edmondson, Chester M., Sgt., D, 353rd Inf	9-26
Eierman, Walter W., Pvt., L, 355th Inf	11- 5
Eiseman, Eugene F., Pvt., H, 354th Inf	8-10
Eitel, William H., Pvt., F, 354th Inf	10-28
Elam, Louis, Pvt., I, 356th Inf	10- 6
Elfrink, Fredrick W., Pvt., E, 342nd F. A	
Elkins, Charles H., Pvt. 1cl., Med. Det., 354th Inf	8-10
Ellington, Nathan C., Pvt., I, 356th Inf	10- 7
Ellis, Adrien, Pvt., Hq. 355th Inf	10- 9
Ellis, Charles F., Corp., C, 341st F. A	
Ellis, William A., Pvt., C, 314th F. S. Bn	8-10
Ellmers, Crisse H., Pvt., Med. Det., 355th Inf	8-17
Elmer, Alfred P., Pvt., D, 341st M. G. Bn	9-29
Emmons, Tipton E., Pvt., Hq. 355th Inf	8- 9
Endsley, James R., Pvt., Med. Det., 342nd M. G. Bn	11-11
Engle, Amos H., Pvt., K, 353rd Inf	11- 8
Engler, Bernard C., Sgt., D, 355th Inf	8- 9
Engstrom, George, Pvt., Hq. 355th Inf	8- 9
Enright, Edward P., Cook, I, 356th Inf	10- 7
Ensinger, Eugene E., Pvt., H, 354th Inf	10-28
Epperson, Ernest, Pvt., I, 356th Inf	10- 7
Erb, Harry G., Pvt., Sales Comm., Unit No. 5	10- 5
Erickson, Albert, Pvt., E, 314th Eng	9-18
Erickson, George H., Sgt., C, 355th Inf	8-10
Erickson, Oscar R., Corp., A, 355th Inf	8- 9
Erlinger, Herbert C., Pvt., B, 354th Inf	8-10
Erman, Walker L., Pvt., H, 354th Inf	10-28
Erwin, Harry, 89th M. P. Co	10- 7
Espinosa, Joseph R., Corp., A, 340th M. G. Bn	10-27
Estabrooks, Leslie, Pvt., B, 354th Inf	10- 5
Estes, Kirk, Pvt., E, 353rd Inf	10- 3
Estes, Raymond O., Pvt., D, 340th F. A	9-19
Evans, Everett S., Corp., G, 354th Inf	9-29
Evans, Joseph W., Corp., D, 354th Inf	8-10
Everson, Alfred, Pvt., G, 355th Inf	8-10
Everson, Emmett J., Corp., F, 354th Inf	10-27
Evjen, Henry, Pvt., F, 353rd Inf	11- 1
Ewert, Edward W., Pvt., A, 355th Inf	8- 9
Faber, Frank, Pvt., Amb. Co., 356th Inf	10-28
Fahrenbach, Harold O., Pvt., A, 355th Inf	8- 9
Fall, Arley W., Pvt. 1cl., M. G. Co., 356th Inf	11-11
Fairchild, John H., Pvt. 1cl., Med. Det., 354th Inf	8-10
Farley, Charles F., Corp., I, 356th Inf	10- 7
Farmer, Hubert T., Sgt., M. G. Co., 354th Inf	10-27
Farmer, LeRoy, Sgt., D, 355th Inf	8- 9
Farrar, Lawrence E., Pvt. 1cl., F, 340th F. A	10-24
Farrow, Milford A., Pvt., I, 356th Inf	10- 7
Faxon, Frank, Pvt. 1cl., A, 355th Inf	8- 9
Fayman, Adolph J., Pvt. 1cl., A, 355th Inf	8- 9
Fecht, Harry E., Pvt., I, 356th Inf	10- 7
Feigum, Martin A., Pvt., B, 314th Amm. Tr	9-19
Feldman, Carl, Saddler, Hq. Troop, 89th Div	8- 9
Fellnagel, Robert R., Pvt., D, 355th Inf	8- 9
Ferguson, Roy E, Sgt., G, 354th Inf	9-26
Ferrell, Andrew T., Pvt., B, 354th Inf	8-10
Fillipelli, Fillippo, Pvt., B, 314th Amm. Tr	9- 9
Filson, Bertie, Corp , D, 355th Inf	8- 9
Fine, Leon, Pvt., 356th Amb. Co	10-28
Fink, Milton G., Corp., I, 356th Inf	10- 7
Fink, Richard, Pvt., D, 355th Inf	8-15
Finkelstein, Ike, Pvt., F, 314th Eng	9-30
Finks, Raymond T., Pvt. 1cl., 89th Div. Mail Det	10- 5
Finley, James A., Pvt., D, 354th Inf	8-10
Fisher, James F., Pvt. 1cl., C, 355th Inf	8- 9
Fissell, Cyrus, Pvt., C, 355th Inf	8- 9
Fitch, Elba M., Sgt., E, 356th Inf	10- 6
Fitch, Melvin A., Pvt. 1cl., D, 355th Inf	8- 9
Fitzgerald, Frank W., Sgt., F, 354th Inf	10-28

Name, Rank, Company, Regiment	Date, 1918
Fitzgerald, Joseph W., Pvt., A, 340th M. G. Bn.	11-11
Fix, Alfred W., Pvt., I, 356th Inf.	10- 7
Flenner, William C , Pvt , I, 356th Inf.	10- 7
Fletcher, Cecil O., Corp., F, 354th Inf.	10-27
Fletemeyer, Florance A., Pvt., M. G. Co., 354th Inf.	10-27
Flewelling, Golden W., Pvt. 1cl., C, 341st M. G. Bn.	9-26
Flinn, Roy R., Corp., F, 354th Inf.	10-27
Flohrs, Claud H., Pvt., B, 353rd Inf.	10- 6
Flood, Benjamin H., Pvt., I, 356th Inf.	10- 7
Flottman, Fritz R., Pvt. 1cl., Hq. 353rd Inf.	10- 6
Floyd, James, Pvt., Hq. 354th Inf.	9-26
Flynn, Roy R., Corp., F, 354th Inf.	10-28
Foley, Thomas A., Pvt., H, 354th Inf.	10-29
Ford, Arnold B., Pvt., H, 354th Inf.	10-28
Ford, Arthur D., Pvt., I, 356th Inf.	10- 7
Ford, Emmet J., Pvt. 1cl., D, 355th Inf.	8- 9
Ford, Joseph F., Pvt., Hq. 354th Inf.	10- 5
Foreman, Frank W., Pvt., A, 354th Inf.	8- 9
Forgeron, Louis A., Pvt. 1cl., B, 354th Inf.	10- 5
Foster, Elmer W., Pvt. 1cl., B, 342nd M. G. Bn.	10- 5
Foutes, Reuben N., Pvt., D, 354th Inf.	8-10
Fox, Ray P., Pvt., A, 354th Inf.	8- 9
Foy, Edward J., Pvt., Mail Det., 89th Div.	8- 9
Framaschi, Vincenzo, Pvt., B, 314th Amm. Tr.	9- 9
Frank, Hubert D., Pvt., G, 354th Inf.	10-29
Frank, Miles E, Pvt. 1cl., D, 353rd Inf.	9-27
Franken, Edward H., Pvt., E, 356th Inf.	10- 7
Franklin, Adolph J., Corp., G, 354th Inf.	10- 7
Frechette, Arthur S., Pvt., A, 355th Inf.	8- 9
Freelin, Fred J., Pvt. 1cl., B, 341st M. G. Bn.	10-24
Freeman, Clarence, Pvt., E, 356th Inf.	10- 7
Freeman, Paul, Pvt. 1cl., B, 354th Inf.	8-10
Freiberg, Alvin A., Corp., H, 354th Inf.	10-28
French, Earl D., Pvt., A, 354th Inf.	8-10
French, Norman C., Corp., B, 353rd Inf.	10- 6
Fresquez, Pedro, Pvt., I, 356th Inf.	10- 6
Freymiller, Richard F., Pvt., F, 340th F. A.	10-24
Friar, Charles C., Pvt., 1cl., F, 355th Inf.	10-22
Fringer, Karl P., Pvt. 1cl., D, 353rd Inf.	9-26
Frisk, Noling, Pvt., I, 356th Inf.	10- 7
Fritch, George, Pvt., H, 353rd Inf.	10- 2
Froelich, William, Pvt. 1cl., D, 355th Inf.	8- 9
Frost, George, Corp., D, 355th Inf.	8- 9
Fuchsgruber, Raymond M. Pvt., E, 354th Inf.	10- 5
Funk, Harold D. Pvt. 1cl., A, 342nd M G. Bn	10-27
Fuqua, James G, Pvt., Sales Com. Unit No. 5	10- 5
Fuse, Giovanni, Pvt. 1cl , B, 354th Inf.	10- 5
Gable, George M., 1st Sgt., L, 356th Inf.	10- 7
Gaede, Jacob E., Pvt., B, 341st M. G. Bn.	10-24
Gaffney, Charles J., Pvt. 1cl., H, 354th Inf.	8-10
Gafford, Harry D., Mech., C, 355th Inf.	8- 9
Gaines, Fred I., Pvt., E, 356th Inf.	10- 7
Gallegos, Edwardo, Pvt., I, 356th Inf.	10- 7
Gallegos, Fidel, Pvt., I, 356th Inf.	10- 7
Gallitz, Theodore, Pvt., G, 354th Inf.	10-29
Galloway, Loran D., Cook, D, 355th Inf.	8- 9
Gammorata, Rosario, Pvt., Amb. Co., 356th Inf.	10-28
Gardner, Arthur J., Pvt. 1cl., Med. Det., 356th Inf.	10- 7
Gardner, Austin S., Pvt., C, 354th Inf.	9- 6
Garlett, Jacob L., Pvt 1cl., B, 354th Inf.	10- 5
Garst, Fred L., Pvt., D, 355th Inf.	8- 9
Gates, William G., Sgt., D, 355th Inf.	8- 9
Gaughan, Leonard, Pvt., B, 340th M. G. Bn.	10-27
Gautt, Charles F., Pvt., E, 340th F. A.	10-24
Gelwix, Joe M., Pvt., D, 341st M. G. Bn.	9- 3
Gelwix, Joe M., Pvt., D, 341st M. G. Bn.	9-29
Genrich, Gustave F., Pvt., Med. Det., 355th Inf.	8- 9
Gentry, Elmer, Pvt., E, 356th Inf.	10- 7
Gentry, William, Pvt., E, 356th Inf.	10- 7
Geritis, Themistocles, Pvt., Amb. Co., 356th Inf.	10-27
Germer, Richard E., Pvt., G, 354th Inf.	10-29
Gerrard, James T., Pvt., G, 354th Inf.	8-28
Gervais, Thomas, Pvt., B, 354th Inf.	10- 5
Giardano, Fillipo, Pvt., F, 354th Inf.	10-27
Gibbons, John J., Pvt., F, 355th Inf.	11- 5
Gibson, Rozier, Corp., I, 356th Inf.	10- 7
Gill, Thomas W., Corp., F, 354th Inf.	10-27
Gilmore, Benjamin H., Corp , D, 353rd Inf.	9-27
Gish, Gilbert M., Pvt., C, 355th Inf.	8- 9
Glantz, Gustaf A., Pvt. 1cl., B, 354th Inf.	8-10
Glauert, William F., Bugler, F, 354th Inf.	10-28
Glynn, Tommy, Pvt. 1cl., Med. Det., 353rd Inf.	11- 1
Gobrke, Gustave A., Pvt., G, 354th Inf.	10-27
Goldberg, Peter, Pvt., F, 354th Inf.	10-27
Goldburg, Alfred, Pvt., E, 354th Inf.	9-26
Goldman, Otto, Pvt., F, 354th Inf.	10-27
Goldsmith, Floyd E., Cook, D, 354th Inf.	10- 5
Goldstein, Joseph, Pvt. 1cl., A, 355th Inf.	8-17
Goldstein, Sylvester, Pvt. 1cl., F, 354th Inf.	10-28
Goldstein, William, Pvt., D, 355th Inf.	8- 9
Gomez, Joseph M., Pvt. 1cl., Amb. Co., 356th Inf.	10-28
Goodfellow, Frank R., Sgt., A, 340th M. G. Bn.	10-27
Goodrich, Alpheus, Pvt. 1cl., I, 356th Inf.	10- 7
Goodstein, Harry, Pvt., 1cl., F, 354th Inf.	10-27
Goodwin, Mike H., Pvt , E, 354th Inf.	10- 7
Gothe, Wm., Pvt., E, 314th Amm. Tr.	
Gott, Robert N., Pvt., A, 354th Inf.	8-10
Gough, Joseph P., Pvt. 1cl., B, 354th Inf.	8-10
Gowen, George O., Pvt., A, 341st M. G. Bn.	8- 9
Grandstaff, Mell B., Pvt., I, 356th Inf.	10- 6
Granby, Joseph, Pvt., 356th Amb. Co.	10-28
Grannemann, Harry L. C., Pvt. 1cl., B, 354th Inf.	8-10
Granthan, Charles J., Pvt., Hq. 355th Inf.	8-20
Gray, James F., Sgt., E, 314th Eng.	9-18
Gray, James W., Corp., L, 356th Inf.	10- 7
Green, Norbert, Corp., M. G. Co., 354th Inf.	10-24
Green, Raymond J., Pvt. 1cl., D, 355th Inf.	8- 9
Green, Roy M., Pvt., F, 340th F. A.	10-26
Greene, Charles C., Pvt., C, 353rd Inf.	10- 2
Greene, Max, Pvt., C, 314th F. A. Bn.	10-27
Greene, Ralph E., Sgt., H, 356th Inf.	10-12
Greer, Oren J., Pvt., B, 353rd Inf.	10-20
Gregg, Alvin A., Pvt. 1cl., L, 353rd Inf.	10- 3
Gregg, Earl W., Pvt., F, 314th Eng.	9-29
Gregory, Benjamin M., Pvt., H, 354th Inf.	9-10
Gregory, Harry E., Pvt., Hq. 355th Inf.	8-15
Greis, William J., Pvt., C, 354th Inf.	9- 6
Griepp, Rudolph G., Pvt. 1cl., A, 355th Inf.	8- 9
Griffin, Guy G., Corp., D, 314th Amm. Tr.	
Griffith, Leslie G., 1st Sgt., A, 341st M. G. Bn.	10- 3
Griffith, Walter R., Pvt , B, 354th Inf.	8-10
Grimes, Leroy J., Pvt. 1cl., C, 314th F. S. Bn.	10-26
Grinstead, Louis R., Pvt., A, 354th Inf.	8-10
Grint, Harold A., Mess Sgt., D, 355th Inf.	8- 9
Gritton, Henry, Pvt., B, 354th Inf.	10- 5
Gritzner, Frederick, Pvt., A, 355th Inf.	8- 9
Groiton, Walter J., Pvt., C, 341st M. G. Bn.	10- 1
Grosh, George A., Pvt., Hq. 355th Inf.	10- 6
Gross, Casper P., Corp., F, 354th Inf.	10-28
Gross, John A., Corp., B, 314th Eng.	10-29
Grove, Frank B , Pvt., D, 355th Inf.	8- 9
Gruar, Oran J., Pvt., B, 353rd Inf.	10- 6
Gruber, William L., Corp., L, 356th Inf.	10- 7
Gruendeman, Henry A., Pvt., D, 354th Inf.	8-10
Gunther, Herman F., Pvt. 1cl., D, 355th Inf.	8- 9
Guerrero, Martin, Pvt., B, 314th Amm. Tr.	9- 9
Guey, John, Pvt., B, 353rd Inf.	10- 6
Gushi, Sam, Pvt., D, 355th Inf.	8- 9
Haase, Louis J., Pvt., D, 355th Inf.	8- 9
Hader, Leslie W., Pvt., I, 356th Inf.	10- 7
Haffner, Rollie J., Pvt., D, 341st M. G. Bn.	9-29
Hagen, Roy, Pvt., F, 340th F. A.	10-24
Hagen, Thomas E., Sgt., C, 353rd Inf.	10-22
Hahn, Charles, Pvt., E, 342nd F. A.	
Hafls, Charles E., Pvt., I, 356th Inf.	10- 6
Halbeisen, John F , Pvt., A, 341st M. G. Bn.	10- 3
Hale, Tom J., Pvt., E, 356th Inf.	10- 7
Hall, Alfred M., Pvt., Hq. 354th Inf.	8-10
Hall, James F., Pvt., B, 353rd Inf.	10-26
Halley, Homer H., Pvt., K, 356th Inf.	10- 5
Hamer, Maurice A., Pvt. 1cl., F, 354th Inf.	10-28
Hamilton, Arthur, Pvt., Hq. 356th Inf.	10- 9
Hamilton, George R., Pvt., B, 354th Inf.	8-10
Hamilton, George R., Pvt., B, 354th Inf.	9-29
Hamilton, Walter, Pvt. 1cl., Med. Det., 354th Inf.	9-27
Hampton, Lee J., Pvt., M, 355th Inf.	10- 7
Haney, Leslie B., Pvt., I, 356th Inf.	10- 7
Hankins, Charley, Pvt., C, 354th Inf.	8-10
Hanks, Grover, Pvt. 1cl., G, 356th Inf.	10- 6
Hanna, Clyde W., E, 314th Amm. Tr.	
Hannah, Ernest E., Sgt., C, 314th F. S. Bn.	8- 9
Hannem, Alfred, Pvt., A, 355th Inf.	8- 9
Hanno, William, Pvt., H, 354th Inf.	10-30
Hannom, James, Pvt., A, 355th Inf.	9-27
Hansen, Ernest W., Pvt., H, 354th Inf.	10-29
Hanson, Edmund, Wag., Sup. Co., 355th Inf.	11- 8
Hanson, Edwin T., Pvt. L, 355th Inf.	11- 8
Hanson, Hans, Pvt., C, 341st F. A.	
Hanson, James A., Pvt., D, 355th Inf.	8-15
Happy, William E., Corp., M, 354th Inf.	10- 1
Hardesty, Roy, Corp., E, 314th Eng.	10-29
Hardin, Benjamin A., Pvt., D, 354th Inf.	8-10
Hardwick, Ned, Pvt., E, 354th Inf.	10- 6
Hare, Calvin H., Pvt., I, 356th Inf.	10- 6

Name, Rank, Company, Regiment	Date, 1918
Hargate, Hubbard C., Pvt., G, 354th Inf	9-25
Hargis, Elmer W., Pvt., A, 89th M. P. Co	10- 5
Harmon, Millard, Pvt., E, 356th Inf	10- 6
Harpster, Percy, Corp., C, 314th F. S. Bn	10-27
Harrington, Charles L., Corp., B, 342nd M. G. Bn	10- 5
Harsen, Henry F., Pvt., M. G. Co., 354th Inf	11- 3
Hart, Andy, Pvt., Amb. Co., 356th Inf	10- 2
Hart, Carl E., Pvt., M. G. Co., 354th Inf	10-27
Hart, Henry, Pvt., E, 342nd F. A	
Harter, Fred L., Pvt., Hq. 353rd Inf	10- 6
Hartman, Edward, Jr., Sgt., Sales Com. Unit No. 5	10- 5
Hartman, Edward C., Pvt., G, 354th Inf	11- 9
Harvey, Lester G., Corp., E, 340th F. A	10-29
Harvey, Frank, Pvt., D, 314th Eng	8-22
Harvey, Samuel M., Pvt., I, 356th Inf	10- 7
Harvey, Wallace A., Pvt. 1cl., D, 341st M. G. Bn	9- 7
Hauge, Carl, Pvt. 1cl., D, 355th Inf	8- 9
Haugen, John O., Pvt., L, 355th Inf	11- 6
Hauser, Arthur S., Pvt., Med. Det., 356th Inf	9-13
Havens, Ernest L., Pvt., Hq. 354th Inf	9-26
Hawalleck, Edward R., Pvt., A, 355th Inf	8- 9
Hawe, William A., Pvt., F, 354th Inf	10-27
Hawkins, Eugene, Pvt., B, 355th Inf	11- 5
Hawkins, Jesse B., Pvt., I, 356th Inf	10- 7
Haylor, Frank A., Pvt. 1cl., B, 353rd Inf	10- 6
Haynes, David B., Pvt., H, 353rd Inf	10- 2
Haynes, Roscoe A., Pvt., Med. Det., 354th Inf	10-28
Hays, Jesse L., Pvt., C, 341st F. A	
Healy, Vincent J., Pvt., D, 355th Inf	10- 6
Heath, Almon T., Pvt., M. G. Co., 354th Inf	10-27
Heatherington, Ilo M., Pvt., Sup. Co., 353rd Inf	8-31
Heaton, William B., Pvt., A, 354th Inf	9-28
Heidbreder, Elmer L., Pvt. 1cl., I, 356th Inf	10- 7
Heienefeld, LeRoy F., Pvt., D, 355th Inf	8- 9
Heimburger, William F., Pvt., C, 341st M. G. Bn	10- 2
Heleker, Ralph P., Corp., B, 341st M. G. Bn	10-21
Heltemes, Harry S., Corp., G, 354th Inf	9-29
Helton, John W., Pvt., I, 356th Inf	10- 7
Hembree, Otto C., Pvt., F, 314th Eng	9-29
Hendricks, John, Pvt., I, 355th Inf	10- 6
Henke, Reinbold, Pvt., D, 355th Inf	6- 9
Henkins, Sherman, Pvt., Hq. 356th Inf	9-22
Henning, Charles E., Pvt., H, 356th Inf	10- 7
Henning, Gustave, Pvt. 1cl., D, 355th Inf	8- 9
Henry, Eugene, Pvt., I, 356th Inf	10- 6
Henry, Jacob O., Pvt., I, 356th Inf	10- 8
Herbison, John, Pvt., F, 354th Inf	10-27
Herring, George E., Pvt., L, 356th Inf	10- 7
Herron, John B., Pvt., I, 356th Inf	10- 7
Hesket, Noble W., Pvt., I, 353rd Inf	10-28
Hesse, Stephen W., Corp., I, 356th Inf	11- 1
Hesse, William, Pvt., Amb. Co., 355th Inf	10-22
Hetmanek, August R., Pvt., Hq. 355th Inf	8-16
Herisen, Louis S., Pvt., B, 353rd Inf	10- 7
Hibbard, Donald, Sgt., B, 340th M. G. Bn	10- 6
Hickman, Carl S., Sgt., A, 340th M. G. Bn	10-27
Hickcox, Clarke, Pvt. 1cl., E, 340th F. A	10-24
Hicks, John N., Corp., E, 353rd Inf	11-11
Higgins, Daniel, Pvt., F, 354th Inf	10-27
Higgins, Thomas E., Pvt., G, 354th Inf	10-27
Higley, Delbert N., Pvt., A, 355th Inf	8- 9
Hild, Emil J., Sgt., M. G. Co., 355th Inf	11- 2
Hildebrand, Archie, Pvt. 1cl., B, 342nd M. G. Bn	10- 5
Hill, Arnold, Pvt. 1cl., I, 356th Inf	10- 7
Hill, Henry H., Corp., E, 354th Inf	10- 5
Hill, Howard, Pvt. 1cl., B, 314th F. S	11- 9
Hill, John A., Pvt., I, 356th Inf	10- 6
Hillker, Charles E., Sgt., Hq. 355th Inf	8- 9
Hinkle, Warren H., Corp., L, 355th Inf	11- 6
Hinton, Robbie C., Pvt., E, 314th Eng	9-18
Hoag, Charles M., Cook, Hq. 340th M. G. Bn	10- 5
Hoch, Charles J., Pvt., B, 354th Inf	10- 5
Hockberger, Fred J., Corp., L, 356th Inf	10- 7
Hodges, James A., Reg. Sgt. Maj., Hq. 355th Inf	8- 9
Hodges, Stephen E., Pvt. 1cl., L, 353rd Inf	8-24
Hodgson, Owen E., Sgt., B, 353rd Inf	10-25
Hodson, Albert N., Corp., I, 356th Inf	10- 7
Hoenshel, Frank L., Pvt., C, 355th Inf	8-14
Hoffer, Martin, Sgt., B, 342nd M. G. Bn	10- 5
Hogue, Archie H., Pvt., A, 354th Inf	8-11
Holford, Frank D., Pvt., F, 354th Inf	10-27
Holm, Oscar A., Pvt., G, 354th Inf	10-28
Holmes, Edward, Pvt., E, 356th Inf	10- 6
Holston, Julius, Pvt., G, 354th Inf	10-24
Holyfield, John G., Pvt., I, 356th Inf	10- 7
Holzer, Fritz C., Pvt., D, 355th Inf	8- 9
Hook, Thomas W., Mess Sgt., I, 356th Inf	10- 7
Hooper, Austin M., Pvt., E, 340th F. A	10-24
Hoover, Robert P., Pvt., B, 342nd F. A	
Hopkins, Charles W., Pvt. 1cl., I, 356th Inf	10- 7
Hopper, Joseph H., Pvt. 1cl., I, 356th Inf	10- 7
Hopper, Lawrence, Pvt., E, 342nd F. A	
Hornstein, Charles L., Pvt. G, 354th Inf	10- 5
Horton, Fred H., Pvt., F, 354th Inf	10-27
Houghton, Chas E., Pvt. 1cl., E, 314th Amm Tr	
Houlihan, John P., Pvt. 1cl., I, 356th Inf	10- 7
Houser, Dennis M., Sgt., B, 353rd Inf	10- 2
Howard, Roy, Pvt., Med. Det., 354th Inf	9-26
Howard, Walker E., Pvt., I, 356th Inf	10- 7
Howe, Franklin, Pvt., Hq. 354th Inf	8-10
Howell, Charles A., Pvt., D, 354th Inf	8-10
Howell, Floyd R., Sgt., Hq. 354th Inf	6-26
Hubbard, John G., Sgt., G, 354th Inf	9-27
Huber, William C., Pvt. 1cl., B, 342nd M. G. Bn	10- 5
Huebschman, Alvin G., Pvt., D, 354th Inf	8-10
Huffman, Henry M., Pvt., B, 354th Inf	10- 5
Hufstedler, G. C., Pvt., E, 342nd F. A	
Huggins, D. H., Pvt., I, 356th Inf	10- 7
Hughes, Harry B., Pvt., C, 354th Inf	8-10
Hughes, Norman, Pvt., E, 354th Inf	10- 7
Hugunin, Ray, Pvt., Hq. 353rd Inf	10- 7
Hulce, Albert E., Pvt. 1cl., B, 342nd M. G. Bn	10- 5
Hull, Victor L., Wag., Sup. Co., 355th Inf	10- 2
Humfeld, Lawrence H., Pvt. 1cl., I, 356th Inf	10- 7
Hunt, James H., Pvt., I, 356th Inf	10- 7
Hunt, Michael P., Pvt., B, 355th Inf	8- 9
Hunter, Darwin, Sgt., E, 342nd F. A	
Huntling, Harry C., Pvt., Amb. Co., 356th Inf	11- 2
Hurley, Joseph H., Pvt., D, 355th Inf	8- 9
Hurley, Matthew M., Pvt., Med. Det., 354th Inf	10-28
Hyde, Adriant, Pvt., L, 353rd Inf	10- 4
Hyland, Clyde F., Corp., C, 341st M. G. Bn	9-26
Hyland, Clyde F., Corp., C, 341st Bn	10-31
Ikenberry, Charles W., Pvt., Med. Det., 354th Inf	8-10
Illig, Herman F., Pvt., B, 354th Inf	10- 5
Inman, Roy W., Pvt., B, 354th Inf	8-10
Irvin, William J., Pvt., K, 355th Inf	10- 3
Irving, Richard F., Pvt., B, 354th Inf	10- 6
Isaak, Albert, Pvt., A, 340th M. G. Bn	11- 5
Isenberg, George H., Corp., I, 356th Inf	10- 5
Isgrig, Earl W., Sgt., C, 314th Sup. Tr	
Isitt, Douglas C., Div. Maj., Hq. 340th F. A	10- 7
Iten, Charley, Pvt., F, 354th Inf	10-27
Jackson, Paul S., Corp., D, 355th Inf	8- 9
Jacobs, William S., Pvt., A, 341st M. G. Bn	10- 3
Jacox, Charles F., 1st Sgt., D, 355th Inf	8- 9
Jaggers, Ray F., Pvt., H, 353rd Inf	10- 2
Jahnke, Edward E., Pvt., E, 356th Inf	10- 7
James, Clyde W., Pvt. 1cl., C, 314th F. S. Bn	8-16
James, Loyd R., Pvt., Med. Det., 353rd Inf	11- 2
Jansen, Frank W., Pvt. 1cl., G, 354th Inf	9-26
Jacquez, Genovero, Pvt., M, 356th Inf	11- 1
Jarrell, Elbert F., Pvt., D, 354th Inf	10- 8
Jarvis, Charlie E., Pvt., F, 354th Inf	10-27
Jeffers, Walter R., Pvt., C, 353rd Inf	11- 3
Jensen, Max, Mech., Hq. 355th Inf	8- 9
Jensen, Nels P., Corp., H, 356th Inf	11- 6
Jensen, Nick, Pvt. 1cl., B, 341st M. G. Bn	10-24
Jenson, Axel, Pvt. 1cl., B, 340th M. G. Bn	10-28
Jeske, William F., Pvt., D, 355th Inf	8- 9
Jewett, Marion L., Pvt. 1cl., I, 356th Inf	10- 7
Johnson, Andrew J., Pvt., C, 353rd Inf	10-25
Johnson, Arthur E., Pvt., E, 354th Inf	8-10
Johnson, Ben W., Pvt., E, 354th Inf	11- 5
Johnson, Bennie E., Pvt., M. G. Co., 355th Inf	11- 2
Johnson, Charles R., Pvt., M. G. Co., 354th Inf	10-27
Johnson, Clarence E., Corp., I, 356th Inf	10- 7
Johnson, Earl D., Pvt., H, 354th Inf	10-30
Johnson, Elmer, Pvt., A, 355th Inf	8- 9
Johnson, James, Pvt., B, 353rd Inf	10- 6
Johnson, Joseph W., Pvt., H, 354th Inf	10-25
Johnson, Lee B., Corp., I, 356th Inf	10- 7
Johnson, Lloyd H., Sgt., I, 356th Inf	10- 7
Johnson, Olee, Pvt. 1cl., E, 340th F. A	10-24
Johnson, Oscar W., Pvt., A, 355th Inf	8- 9
Johnson, Rollie C., Pvt., A, 355th Inf	8- 9
Johnson, Victor N., Pvt., H, 354th Inf	10-28
Joint, Leslie G., Corp., B, 353rd Inf	10- 6
Jolly, Theodore, Pvt., D, 355th Inf	8- 9
Jones, Avery R., Pvt., A, 355th Inf	8- 9
Jones, Ben T., Corp., G, 354th Inf	9-25
Jones, Clifton V., Pvt. 1cl., F, 355th Inf	10-28

Name, Rank, Company, Regiment	Date, 1918
Jones, Eldrige, Pvt., F, 356th Inf	11- 5
Jones, George E., Cook, D, 354th Inf	8-10
Jones, George W., Corp., C, 354th Inf	8-10
Jones, George W., Pvt., B, 341st M. G. Bn	8-10
Jones, Joseph G., Pvt. 1cl., B, 342nd M. G. Bn	10- 5
Jones, William F., Pvt., G, 354th Inf	9-30
Jones, William K., Pvt., C, 314th F. S. Bn	8-10
Jordon, William M., Pvt., A, 314th Eng	11- 3
Journey, James R., Pvt., A, 354th Inf	10- 5
Joyce, Alonzo, Pvt., K, 353rd Inf	11- 1
Juan, Joseph, Pvt., L, 355th Inf	11- 5
Juergensmeyer, Alvin H., Pvt., Med. Det., 354th Inf	10- 5
Kaempf, Walter R., Pvt., C, 355th Inf	8- 9
Kalambokis, Nicholas, Pvt., D, 314th Eng	8-22
Kalenbach, Leonard E., Pvt., D, 354th Inf	8-10
Kane, Alva, Pvt., Med. Det., 353rd Inf	10-29
Kane, Raymond J., Sgt., F, 355th Inf	10-22
Kaplan, Louis, Pvt., G, 354th Inf	10-29
Karafios, George, Pvt. 1cl., F, 340th F. A.	10-24
Karl, Robert, Pvt., I, 356th Inf	10- 6
Kasel, Aloysius, Pvt., B, 342nd M. G. Bn	10- 5
Kasitz, Frank, Pvt. 1cl., A, 342nd M. G. Bn	8- 9
Kays, Dorris T., Pvt. 1cl., B, 342nd M. G. Bn	10- 5
Keating, Thomas F., Pvt., M. G. Co., 354th Inf	10-29
Keegan, Emmett, Pvt., I, 356th Inf	10- 7
Keeton, William, Cook, D, 354th Inf	8-10
Keller, Roy L., Sgt., B, 354th Inf	8-10
Kelley, Frank, Pvt., I, 356th Inf	10- 6
Kellogg, Martin, Pvt., A, 340th M. G. Bn	10-27
Kelly, John R., Pvt., D, 355th Inf	8- 9
Kelly, William A., Pvt., C, 341st M. G. Bn	10- 1
Kempf, John, Pvt., I, 356th Inf	10- 7
Kendal, Walter E., Pvt. 1cl., B, 353rd Inf	10- 7
Kendall, William W., Pvt. 1cl., B, 340th M. G. Bn	10-28
Kendrick, David, Pvt., E, 356th Inf	10- 7
Kennedy, Ambrose, Pvt., F, 355th Inf	10- 6
Kennedy, Benjamin E. B., Pvt., Hq. 355th Inf	8- 9
Kennedy, Luther C., Pvt., E, 354th Inf	10-27
Kennedy, Preston V., Pvt., F, 340th F. A.	10-24
Kent, Lee Curtiss, Pvt., G, 354th Inf	10-26
Kerkman, William F., Pvt., B, 341st M. G. Bn	10-28
Kerr, Francis P., Mech., F, 355th Inf	10-22
Keslin, Albert, Pvt., G, 354th Inf	10-28
Key, Frank, Corp., F, 354th Inf	10-28
Kimbrell, Roy, Pvt., A, 341st M. G. Bn	9- 4
Kimmel, Clarence F., Sgt., E, 354th Inf	10-28
Kimber, Robert F., Pvt., K, 356th Inf	10- 6
King, John R., 1st Sgt., B, 342nd M. G. Bn	10- 5
King, Rufus, Wag., Sup. Co., 354th Inf	8-10
King, William J., Pvt., B, 354th Inf	8-10
King, William O., Corp., I, 356th Inf	10- 7
Kinneth, Clarence, Pvt., E, 356th Inf	10- 7
Kinnison, Frank A., Corp., H, 355th Inf	8- 9
Kintner, Lawrence, Mech., I, 356th Inf	10- 7
Kirk, Eugene J., Pvt., G, 354th Inf	9-26
Kirk, Frank G., Pvt., C, 314th Eng	10- 1
Kittleson, Clarence G., Pvt., E, 354th Inf	10- 6
Klassen, Jacob, Pvt., Att. 314th San. Tr.	10-27
Klaumann, Lawrence, Pvt., E, 356th Inf	10- 6
Klein, Jay, Pvt., I, 356th Inf	10- 7
Klentz, Louis, Pvt. 1cl., F, 354th Inf	10-28
Kline, Hammond F., Pvt., D, 355th Inf	8- 9
Klopp, Edward F., Pvt., D, 355th Inf	8- 9
Knabe, Henry H, Pvt., I, 356th Inf	10- 6
Knappe, Joseph, Pvt., M, 353rd Inf	10- 3
Knasiak, Peter M., Corp., F, 354th Inf	10-27
Kneist, Edward, Pvt., B, 341st M. G. Bn	9-13
Knight, Freeman D., Pvt. 1cl., D, 355th Inf	8- 9
Knisley, Byron T., Corp., Hq. 354th Inf	9-26
Knoles, Carl, Pvt., A, 354th Inf	8-11
Knott, James B., Pvt., I, 356th Inf	10- 7
Knowlton, Arthur D., Pvt., G, 354th Inf	1-25
Knox, Frank J., Pvt., G, 354th Inf	9-25
Knox, William H., Mech., A, 340th F. A.	10- 5
Knussman, Fred, Pvt., F, 354th Inf	10-23
Koarik, Charles, Pvt. 1cl., F, 340th F. A.	10-24
Koenigs, William A., Mech., F, 354th Inf	10-27
Koerner, Elmer E., Corp., D, 355th Inf	8- 9
Kohring, Ben, Pvt., G, 354th Inf	10-27
Kopp, Alfred, Pvt., D, 355th Inf	8- 9
Kopp, Walter C., Corp., L, 353rd Inf	10- 3
Koronsos, John, Pvt. 1cl., H, 354th Inf	10-28
Kortner, Chris. H., Pvt. 1cl., H, 353rd Inf	10- 2
Koth, Frank, Corp., G, 354th Inf	10-28
Kradle, John W., Pvt. 1cl., D, 355th Inf	8- 9
Kratz, Roy G., Sgt., C, 341st M. G. Bn	11- 5
Kraus, John G., Corp., F, 354th Inf	10-27
Kreft, Frank E., Pvt. 1cl., D, 354th Inf	8-11
Kretschmer, Frank J., Sgt., C, 341st M. G. Bn	9-26
Krieger, Henry, Pvt., B, 342nd M. G. Bn	10- 5
Kriley, Paul L., Pvt., A, 354th Inf	8-10
Kroll, Stanley, Pvt., I, 356th Inf	10- 7
Krommnacker, Edward E., Pvt., G, 354th Inf	10-28
Krueger, August E., Pvt., E., 354th Inf	10-31
Krug, George A., Pvt., Hq. 353rd Inf	10- 6
Kuchner, Arthur O., Sgt. 1cl., C, 314th F. S. Bn	8-10
Kulik, Joseph, Pvt., M. G. Co, 354th Inf	10-28
Kunzman, Charles, Corp., F, 354th Inf	10-27
Kwiatkowski, Thomas, Pvt., I, 356th Inf	10- 6
LaChasse, Ralph F., Pvt. 1cl., Hq. 354th Inf	10-22
Lacy, Albert C., Pvt., E, 356th Inf	10- 7
Lade, Walter A., Pvt. 1cl., A, 355th Inf	8- 9
Lafemina, Ralph, Pvt. 1cl., D, 355th Inf	8- 9
Lake, Wilmer B., Sgt., I, 356th Inf	10- 6
Lakonde, John S., Pvt., I, 356th Inf	10- 7
Lamb, Paul E., Pvt. 1cl., B, 342nd M. G. Bn	10- 5
Lambert, Charles W., Pvt., E, 354th Inf	10-28
Lambert, Fred A., Pvt. 1cl., F, 353rd Inf	11- 5
Lambert, LeRoy G., Pvt., Hq. 355th Inf	8- 9
Lambrigger, Frank, Pvt. 1cl., B, 353rd Inf	10- 6
Lamon, Cecil G., Corp., C, 314th F. S. Bn	9-26
Lamparter, Frederick C., Mech., I, 356th Inf	10- 7
Landis, Edwin C., Pvt., A, 355th Inf	8- 9
Lane, Alvin, Pvt., E, 355th Inf	10- 7
Lanford, Walter C., Pvt., A, 340th M. G. Bn	10-28
Lang, Edwin J., Pvt., D, 355th Inf	8- 9
Lanning, Edward H., Pvt. 1cl., M. G. Co., 354th Inf	10-27
Lantz, Henry J., Pvt., Hq. 353rd Inf	10- 6
Larsen, Chris, Pvt., H, 353rd Inf	10- 2
Larson, William, Pvt. 1cl., B, 342nd M. G. Bn	10- 5
Lasch, Dilmus L., Pvt., H, 354th Inf	10-21
Laughlin, Robert W., Pvt., A, 355th Inf	8- 9
Laum, Ralph J., Pvt. 1cl., B, 341st M. G. Bn	9- 29
Lauterer, Henry, Pvt., D, 355th Inf	8- 9
Lawson, John B., Corp., B, 354th Inf	10- 6
Lawson, Roy, Corp., L, 356th Inf	10- 7
Lay, DeWitt T., Ord. Sgt., Ord. Det., 354th Inf	9-26
Lea, Fred E., Pvt., Hq. 355th Inf	8- 9
Leavitt, Bernard, Pvt., I, 356th Inf	10- 6
Leavitt, John, Pvt., D, 353rd Inf	10-24
Leavitt, Porter, Pvt., M. G. Co., 354th Bn	10-27
Lebarton, Maurice, Pvt., B, 342nd M. G. Bn	10- 5
Lee, Chester L., Pvt., G, 353rd Inf	10-28
Lefarth, John H., Pvt. 1cl., Hq. 354th Inf	9-28
Lefevre, Raymond C., Wag., Hq. Det., 340th M.G. Bn	10- 5
Legg, Charles O., Pvt., B, 341st M. G. Bn	10-24
Leinhaupel, George J., Pvt., B, 340th M. G. Bn	10- 5
Leitner, John F., Pvt., E, 356th Inf	10- 6
Lemen, James O., Pvt., F, 353rd Inf	10- 3
Lemmerman, Henry, Pvt., A, 355th Inf	8- 9
Lepper, Harry, Pvt., D, 355th Inf	8- 9
Lesley, James L., Pvt., L, 356th Inf	10- 7
LeVora, John J., Pvt., G, 354th Inf	10-28
Lewallen, Jesse A., Pvt., B, 354th Inf	10- 5
Lewis, Arthur E., Mech., L, 353rd Inf	10-29
Lewis, Logan, Pvt., I, 356th Inf	10- 7
Lewis, Onis, Pvt., H, 356th Inf	10- 7
Lewis, Ralph, Pvt., D, 355th Inf	8- 9
L'Hommadieu, Ira L., Pvt., 314th San. Tr.	10-27
Lichterman, Leon LeRoy, Pvt., C, 354th Inf	9- 6
Lien, Earl H., Sgt., B, 340th M. G. Bn	10- 5
Lierman, August J., Pvt., M, 356th Inf	10- 5
Lindeman, Lawrence, Pvt., M. G. Co., 354th Inf	10-27
Lindon, Harrison, Pvt., K, 356th Inf	10- 6
Lindstrom, George H., Pvt. 1cl., B, 353rd Inf	10- 6
Lingenfelter, William H., Pvt., H, 354th Inf	8-11
Lipta, Stephen, Pvt. 1cl., C, 355th Inf	8- 9
Little, George W., Pvt., E, 356th Inf	10- 7
Little, John, Pvt., E, 342nd F. A.	
Little, Phillip, Mech., E, 356th Inf	10- 7
Littrell, Manley F., Pvt., Hq. 354th Inf	8-10
Livesey, Robert E., Corp., C, 314th Fld. Sig. Bn	9-29
Lloyd, Stanley W., Sgt., B, 353rd Inf	10- 2
Lobban, James L., Sgt., M. G. Co., 355th Inf	11- 2
Lochner, Ellsworth, Pvt. 1cl., H, 354th Inf	10-28
Lockman, Wilbur F., Pvt., F, 354th Inf	10-27
Lodwick, Paul M., Sgt., M. G. Co., 354th Inf	10-27
Loehde, Christian C., Pvt. 1cl., D, 354th Inf	9-26
Logan, Chester E., Corp., I, 356th Inf	10- 7
Logan, James A., Pvt., E, 356th Inf	10- 6
Londo, Louis, Pvt., G, 353rd Inf	10-26
Long, Alex. L., Pvt. C, 355th Inf	8- 9
Long, Hardy B., Pvt. 1cl., E, 340th F. A.	10-24
Long, William J., Corp., D, 355th Inf	8- 9
Longhauser, John, Corp., H, 355th Inf	10-29
Longinette, Edward, Corp., F, 354th Inf	10-28
Lopes, Tiburcio, Pvt., M, 353rd Inf	11- 6

Name, Rank, Company, Regiment	Date, 1918
Lord, Robert W., Pvt. 1cl., H, 354th Inf	9-30
Losey, James H., Pvt. 1cl., B, 342nd M. G. Bn	10- 5
Lou on, Jerrel A., Mech., L, 353th Inf	11- 5
Loutsch, Henry, Pvt., A, 355th Inf	8- 9
Love, James W., Pvt. 1cl., B, 342nd M. G. Bn	10- 5
Loveland, Fred M., Pvt., G, 354th Inf	9-25
Loving, Th.odore E., Pvt., C, 314th Amm. Tr	9-19
Lowe, Lloyd L., Pvt., C, 354th Inf	8-10
Lowe, Robert E., Pvt., I, 356th Inf	10- 7
Lowrance, William E., Sgt., H, 354th Inf	8-10
Lowry, Robert, Pvt., E, 340th F. A	10-24
Loyd, Charles L., Corp., B, 314th Eng	10- 6
Luepke, Alfred H., Pvt. 1cl., A, 355th Inf	8- 9
Luff, Robert J., Pvt. 1cl., M. G. Co., 354th Inf	10-31
Lujan, Benisislac, Pvt., I, 356th Inf	11- 2
Lukasaritz, Felix, Pvt., D, 355th Inf	8- 9
Luker, Charles W., Sgt., G, 354th Inf	9-25
Luna, Leopoldo, Pvt., I, 356th Inf	10- 6
Lun.quist, Ralph E., Pvt., E, 354th Inf	10-28
Lun:quist, Rudolph N., Pvt., F, 340th F. A	10-24
Luster, Edward, Pvt., E, 356th Inf	10- 8
Lybarder, Thomas F., Pvt., G, 354th Inf	8-10
Ly :on, Martin J., Pvt., M. G. Co., 354th Inf	10-28
Lyle, Si n.y B., Pvt., E, 353rd Inf	11- 3
Lynch, John J., Pvt., A, 355th Inf	8- 9
McAdams, Edward T., Pvt., B, 354th Inf	10- 5
McBride, Pliny G., Pvt., B, 354th Inf	10- 5
McCallister, Jack C., Pvt., B, 342nd M. G. Bn	10- 5
McCampbell, Willis R., Wag., Sup. Co., 355th Inf	8- 9
McCarrick, John P., Pvt. 1cl., M. G. Co., 354th Inf	10-28
McCarthy, Michael S., Sgt., A, 353rd Inf	11- 5
McClain, Ralph A., Pvt. 1cl., B, 356th Inf	9-21
McCoy, Charles G., Sgt., K, 353rd Inf	10- 3
McCoy, John S., Sgt., E, 340th F. A	10-24
McCulloch, George S., Corp., H, 354th Inf	10-28
McCullough, Joseph I., Pvt., M. G. Co., 354th Inf	11- 6
McCune, Leonidas H., Pvt., B, 342nd M. G. Bn	10- 5
McDaniels, Joseph C., Sgt., B, 340th M. G. Bn	10-27
McDonald, Bill, Pvt., I, 356th Inf	10- 6
McDonough, John M., Pvt., I, 354th Inf	9-26
McEwen, Fenton E., Corp., D, 355th Inf	8- 9
McFarland, Ben H., Mech., Hq. 340th F. A	11- 8
McFate, Claude C., Pvt., M. G. Co., 354th Inf	11- 1
McGee, Keith E., Sgt., A, 356th Inf	8- 9
McGinley, Benjamin, Pvt., B, 353rd Inf	10- 2
McGuffin, Robert A., Pvt., F, 314th Eng	9-30
McGuire, Everett D., Corp., C, 314th F. S. Bn	8-10
McGuire, Patrick H., Pvt. 1cl., D, 355th Inf	8- 9
McInerny, Joseph, Pvt., B, 342nd M. G. Bn	10- 5
McKane, John, Corp., Hq. 340th F. A	10- 7
McKeen, John L., Corp., E, 354th Inf	10- 5
McKenney, Griff R., 1st Sgt., M. G. Co., 354th Inf	10-27
McKenzie, Dwight C., Pvt., B, 342nd M. G. Bn	10-21
McKinley, William D., Pvt., A, 354th Inf	9-20
McKinney, Harry, Sgt., I, 354th Inf	8-10
McKinnon, Guy E., Pvt., I, 356th Inf	10- 7
McKinstry, Robert E., Pvt., B, 354th Inf	8-10
McLain, Henry C., Pvt., H, 354th Inf	10-28
McLaughlin, John A., Pvt., M. G. Co., 354th Inf	10-27
McMillan, James, Pvt., I, 356th Inf	10- 7
McNichols, John, Pvt., F, 354th Inf	10-27
Machecek, Anthony F., Pvt., C, 354th Inf	8-10
Magruder, Cecil T., Pvt., D, 354th Inf	8-11
Maher, Michael A., Pvt. 1cl., Sup. Co., 353rd Inf	10- 5
Maher, William P., Pvt., D, 354th Inf	8-10
Mai, Fred, Pvt., A, 355th Inf	8- 9
Malecek, Joseph M., Pvt., C, 354th Inf	8-10
Maloney, Thomas H., Corp., H, 354th Inf	10-27
Maltese, Dominick, Pvt., F., 314th Eng	9-29
Mangimelli, Carmelo, Pvt. 1cl., C, 341st M. G. Bn	9-26
Mannebach, Richard W., Sgt., E, 354th Inf	9-26
Manning, Alvin A, Pvt. 1cl., B, 342nd M. G. Bn	10- 5
Manning, Bernard, Pvt., H, 354th Inf	10-31
Mansfield, Tharold B., Sgt., C, 314th F. S. Bn	9-16
Markland, David L., Pvt., H, 354th Inf	10-28
Marler, James, Pvt., A, 356th Inf	10-27
Martl, Robert C., Pvt., G, 354th Inf	10-29
Martl, Robert G., Pvt. 1cl., B, 340th M. G. Bn	10-11
Martin, Elmer B., Pvt., Med. Det., 354th Inf	9-27
Martin, George L., Pvt., Hq. 355th Inf	8- 9
Martin, Wesley D., Pvt., B, 354th Inf	10- 5
Martin, William J., Pvt., A, 354th Inf	8-10
Martinez, Augustin, Corp., I, 356th Inf	11- 2
Martinez, Prudencio, Pvt., I, 356th Inf	10- 7
Masowski, Joe, Pvt., G, 354th Inf	10-28
Massey, Daniel C., Pvt., F, 354th Inf	9-29
Math r, Frank, Cook, C, 355th Inf	10- 5
Mathewson, David A., Pvt., B, 341st M. G. Bn	10-22
Matteson, Charles J., Pvt. 1cl., A, 355th Inf	8- 9
Mauch, Aloys B., Sgt., E, 340th F. A	10-24

Name, Rank, Company, Regiment	Date, 1913
Mauel, Harry H., Pvt., E, 354th Inf	10-27
May, Ardo, Pvt. 1cl., B, 341st M. G. Bn	10-22
May, Delbert E., Pvt., E, 354th Inf	10- 6
Mead, Frank, Pvt., I, 356th Inf	10- 7
Medlin, Verdie C., Pvt., Hq. 354th Inf	10- 7
Meek, James E., Pvt. 1cl., B, 356th Inf	10-20
Meer, Frank H., Pvt., D, 354th Inf	10- 5
Meisky, Floyd C., Pvt., D, 342nd M. G. Bn	11- 6
Menken, George H., Pvt., B, 340th M. G. Bn	10-27
Mercer, Ellis W., Pvt. 1cl., E, 354th Inf	10- 6
Mestre, Guy, Pvt., 314th San. Tr	10-25
Metcalf, Phillip I., Pvt., E, 354th Inf	10-29
Metzinger, Charles F., Pvt. 1cl., F, 314th Eng	9-29
Meyer, Charles W., Pvt. 1cl., F, 355th Inf	10-22
Meyer, Joseph J., Pvt. 1cl., G, 354th Inf	9-26
Meyer, William, Pvt., B, 354th Inf	8-10
Micheels, Walter E., Corp., A, 355th Inf	8- 9
Mihm, William A., Corp., F, 354th Inf	10-28
Milan, William G., Pvt., D, 355th Inf	8- 9
Miles, Floyd A., Corp., F, 354th Inf	10-25
Miller, Andrew M., Pvt., B, 340th M. G. Bn	10-27
Miller, Charles A., Pvt., D, 353rd Inf	9-26
Miller, Clarence M., Sgt., B, 342nd M. G. Bn	10- 5
Miller, Clayton L., Pvt., L, 353rd Inf	10- 3
Miller, Emil H., Pvt. 1cl., Hq. 354th Inf	9-28
Miller, Emil H., Pvt. 1cl., Hq. 353rd Inf	10-30
Miller, Ernest, Pvt., A, 340th M. G. Bn	10-27
Miller, George F., Pvt., D, 355th Inf	8- 9
Miller, Gilbert L., Pvt. Hq. 353rd Inf	10- 6
Miller, Henry C., Pvt., A, 354th Inf	8-10
Miller, Irie Lee, Pvt., B, 341st M. G. Bn	10-21
Miller, Jack, Pvt., C, 314th F. S. Bn	10- 2
Miller, John L., Pvt., A, 354th Inf	10- 5
Miller, Lester, Pvt. 1cl., D, 314th Eng	8-18
Miller, Oliver, Pvt., B, 354th Inf	10- 5
Miller, Otto W., Pvt., I, 353rd Inf	10-28
Miller, Ray V., Pvt. 1cl., E, 314th Eng	10-27
Miller, Thomas, Pvt., L, 353rd Inf	10-24
Miller, Virgil, Pvt., D., 354th Inf	10-31
Million, Britton A., Corp., B, 354th Inf	10- 5
Minmutis, John, Pvt., 314th San. Tr	10-27
Misch, Leo, Pvt., D, 355th Inf	8- 9
Miskinas, John, Pvt., F, 354th Inf	10-28
Mitchell, Roscoe W., Pvt., B, 341st M. G. Bn	10-28
Mitchell, Walter H., Pvt., A, 354th Inf	8-11
Mizer, Herb, Pvt., G, 356th Inf	10- 5
Moberg, Clarence, Pvt., A, 353rd Inf	10-27
Moe, Joseph A. T., Pvt., B, 340th M. G. Bn	10-27
Monohan, William B., Corp., E, 314th Eng	10-27
Montgomery, Thomas O., Pvt., C, 341st M. G. Bn	10-27
Monti, Leo J., Pvt., F, 354th Inf	10-27
Moody, Frank H, Pvt. 1cl., B, 353rd Inf	10-25
Moore, Charles F., Corp., M. G. Co., 356th Inf	11-10
Moore, Ernest E., Pvt., A, 342nd M. G. Bn	10-28
Moore, Jasper B, Pvt. 1cl., D, 355th Inf	8- 9
Moore, Paul A, Pvt., I, 356th Inf	10- 6
Morehead, Eugene P., Corp., E, 314th Eng	9-26
Mores, George, Pvt., B, 354th Inf	8-10
Morgan, John E., Pvt., I, 356th Inf	10- 6
Morgan, Jules, Pvt., I, 356th Inf	10- 7
Morris, John S., Pvt. 1cl., E, 354th Inf	10-28
Morris, Ray, Pvt. 1cl., E, 356th Inf	10- 7
Morrow, Aleck, Pvt., D, 353rd Inf	9-26
Morts, Luther E., Cook, B, 354th Inf	10- 6
Moseley, Jack S., Corp., B, 354th Inf	8-10
Moseman, Walter A., Pvt. 1cl., A, 341st M. G. Bn	10- 3
Mosher, Harry C., Pvt. 1cl., D, 355th Inf	8- 9
Mott, Joseph E., Pvt., D, 355th Inf	8- 9
Mozeko, John, Sgt., C, 354th Inf	8-10
Mrstik, John, Pvt., C, 341st M. G. Bn	10- 1
Mrzila, Joseph, Pvt., F, 354th Inf	10-29
Mueller, Frederick C., Pvt. 1cl., E, 356th Inf	10- 6
Mueller, Harry A., Sgt., F, 354th Inf	10-28
Muesbeck, Ralph K., Pvt., I, 356th Inf	11- 2
Mulligan, James J., Pvt. 1cl., I, 356th Inf	10- 7
Mulvehill, Emmett P., Pvt., E, 356th Inf	10- 7
Mulvogue, Lewis W., Pvt. Hq. 354th Inf	9-27
Mumford, Joseph R., Pvt. 1cl., E, 314th Eng	11- 6
Munsch, Russell F., Corp., E, 354th Inf	10-28
Munson, Albin S., Pvt. 1cl., F, 340th F. A	10-24
Munson, John B., Pvt., E, 354th Inf	11- 3
Murphey, Van Horn, Pvt. 1cl., B, 342nd M. G. Bn	10- 5
Murray, Mark R., Sgt., D, 355th Inf	8- 9
Musselman, Lester G., Pvt., Hq. 355th Inf	8-10
Mutz, Albert L., Pvt. 1cl., B, 340th M. G. Bn	10- 9
Myers, Dale H., Pvt., H, 354th Inf	10-28
Myers, George C., Pvt., I, 356th Inf	10- 6
Myers, James M., Sgt., D, 355th Inf	8- 9
Myers, Wayne, Pvt., A, 354th Inf	8-10
Nabors, Henry O., Pvt., E, 356th Inf	10- 7

Name, Rank, Company, Regiment	Date, 1918
Nadin, John, Pvt. 1cl., A, 355th Inf	8- 9
Nalty, John F., Pvt., H, 354th Inf	10-28
Nance, Sylvester, Pvt., E, 356th Inf	10- 7
Narbutt, Charles J., Pvt., B, 354th Inf	10- 5
Nasse, Fred, Corp., Hq. 354th Inf	8-10
Neece, John E., Pvt., I, 356th Inf	10- 6
Neely, Clark, Sgt., B, 354th Inf	10- 6
Nehl, Alexander N., Pvt. 1cl., D, 341st M. G. Bn	11- 3
Nelson, Alfred G., Pvt., B, 354th Inf	10- 6
Nelson, Everett L., Bugler, B, 342nd M. G. Bn	10- 5
Nelson, Harry L., Pvt., Amb. Co., 356th Inf	11- 2
Nelson, John L., Pvt. 1cl., B, 342nd M. G. Bn	10- 5
Nelson, Paul I., Pvt., D, 341st M. G. Bn	9-29
Nelson, William, Pvt., B, 340th M. G. Bn	10- 6
Nesmith, Henry W., Pvt., I, 353rd Inf	10- 3
Neville, Darius B, Corp., I, 356th Inf	10- 7
Nicholson, X. L., Pvt., C, 314th F. S. Bn	8- 6
Nickerson, Arthur W., Corp., M. G. Co., 354th Inf	10-27
Nider, Leslie D., Sgt., D, 355th Inf	8- 9
Niehaus, Paul H., Pvt., M. G. Co., 354th Inf	11- 3
Nielsen, Anton M., Mech., B, 341st M. G Bn	10-28
Nielson, Axle W., Pvt., D, 355th Inf	8- 9
Niewald, George W., Pvt., H, 354th Inf	8-11
Nigro, Jim, Pvt., B, 342nd M. G. Bn	10- 5
Nizzlo, Batiste, Pvt., F, 314th Eng	9-29
Nolan, John L., Corp., L, 353rd Inf	10-22
Nolte, Albert W., Pvt., A, 355th Inf	8- 9
Nordgren, Edward W., Pvt. 1cl., A, 355th Inf	8- 9
Northey, Ernest G., Pvt., F, 314th Eng	9-29
Norton, Evan E, Cook, D, 354th Inf	8-10
Notari, Anthony T., Pvt. 1cl., D, 355th Inf	8-15
Nowotny, Edward, Pvt. 1cl., B, 342nd M. G. Bn	10- 5
Nyffeler, William, Pvt., A, 355th Inf	8- 9
Oballe, Max, Pvt., F, 354th Inf	10-27
Oberlin, Edward, Pvt., D, 354th Inf	8-10
Oberreitber, Edward C., Pvt., D, 354th Inf	8-10
O'Brien, Joseph A., Pvt., B, 342nd M. G. Bn	10- 5
O'Connell, John J., Pvt., G, 354th Inf	10-28
O'Donnell, James A., Pvt. 1cl., D, 353rd Inf	9-26
Ofiel, Charles G., Pvt. 1cl., F, 340th F. A	10-24
Ogden, Harry, Pvt., A, 342nd M. G. Bn	10- 5
Olander, Gilbert G., Pvt., D, 355th Inf	8- 9
Oldham, Henry J., Pvt., F, 340th F. A	10-24
O'Leary, Charles, Pvt., B, 354th Inf	8-10
Oliphant, Charles W., Sgt., L, 353rd Inf	10- 3
Olson, Carl R., Sgt., E, 356th Inf	10- 7
Olson, Ibert, Pvt., F, 340th F. A	10-24
Olson, James J., Pvt., D, 341st M. G. Bn	9-29
Olson, William A., Pvt., G, 354th Inf	10-30
O'Neil, William P., Pvt., F, 314th Eng	9-30
O'Reilly, John J., Sgt., B, 342nd M. G. Bn	10- 5
Orick, Erick E., Pvt. 1cl., G, 354th Inf	9-26
O'Shaughnessy, John P., Pvt., D, 355th Inf	8- 9
Osipochack, Jack, Pvt., F, 354th Inf	10-27
Otting, Julius G., Pvt., E, 354th Inf	10- 6
Ouimet, Frank F., Pvt., L, 353rd Inf	9-28
Oulton, Martin J., Pvt., E, 356th Inf	10- 7
Overton, Monroe, Pvt., I, 356th Inf	10- 7
Owen, Earl, Sgt. 1cl., Med. Det., 340th M. G. Bn	10-10
Owen, Guy W., Pvt. 1cl., G, 354th Inf	9-26
Padillo, Tiodoro, Pvt., I, 356th Inf	10- 7
Pafford, Maurice W., Pvt. 1cl., Med. Det., 356th Inf.	10- 7
Page, John C., Pvt., D, 314th Eng	8-22
Pahlmann, Clifford M., Pvt., Hq. 354th Inf	10-28
Pallozolo, Leo, Corp., G, 354th Inf	9-25
Panchot, John, Pvt., M. G. Co., 354th Inf	10-28
Pankowsky, Joseph R., Pvt. 1cl., C, 341st M. G. Bn	10- 2
Parshall, Delbert A., Pvt., B, 342nd M. G. Bn	10- 5
Parsons, Davis E., Pvt. 1cl., C, 353rd Inf	9-21
Paschall, Fred B., Pvt., L, 354th Inf	9-28
Patterson, Paul R., Pvt., E, 354th Inf	10- 6
Patterson, Walter A., Pvt., B, 354th Inf	8-10
Patton, Guy, Pvt., M. G. Co., 354th Inf	10-28
Paulson, David M., Corp., B, 342nd M. G. Bn	10- 5
Payne, Alonzo, Pvt., A, 355th Inf	8- 9
Peak, Edgar W., Corp., 89th Div. Mail Det	10- 5
Pearson, Columbus C., Mess Sgt., D, 354th Inf	8-10
Peel, Chas., Pvt., E, 342nd F. A	
Penas, Joe, Pvt. 1cl., B, 314th Amm. Tr	9- 9
Penman, Donald, Pvt., Med. Det., 354th Inf	9-26
Penman, Frank A., Pvt. 1cl., E, 314th Eng	9-18
Penney, William E., Pvt., Hq. 354th Inf	10-27
Pennington, William R., Pvt., A, 354th Inf	8-10
Peoples, Arthur H., Pvt., B, 342nd M. G. Bn	10- 5
Perdun, Melvin L., Pvt., E, 354th Inf	10-28
Perkins, George H., Pvt., D, 355th Inf	8- 9
Perrault, Roy A., Bugler, E, 356th Inf	10- 7
Perry, Taylor L., Pvt., E, 340th F. A	10-24
Peterka, Edward E., Pvt., H, 353rd Inf	10- 2
Peters, Martin P., Sgt., L, 355th Inf	11- 6
Peters, William, Corp., B, 354th Inf	10- 5
Peterson, Frank R., Wag., C, 314th Amm. Tr	10-27
Peterson, Magnus, Pvt., D, 341st M. G. Bn	9-29
Peterson, Ole, Pvt., L, 355th Inf	9-19
Peterson, Oluf, Pvt., B, 340th M. G. Bn	10-27
Peterson, Raymond L., Sgt., L, 355th Inf	11- 6
Petoros, Angelos, Pvt., G, 354th Inf	11- 8
Petritis, Anton, Pvt., L, 353rd Inf	10-27
Pettis, John F., Pvt., A, 355th Inf	8- 9
Petty, James A., Pvt., E, 354th Inf	10-29
Pfuhl, Walter H., Pvt., Hq. 354th Inf	8-10
Phebus, Roy G., Pvt. 1cl., B, 340th M. G. Bn	10- 6
Phelps, Isaac, Pvt., I, 356th Inf	10- 7
Phelps, Lester A., Pvt., I, 356th Inf	10- 7
Phillips, Charles M., Pvt., G, 354th Inf	9-29
Philpot, DeWight H., Pvt. 1cl., C, 341st M. G. Bn	9-26
Pian, William, Pvt., Med. Det., 354th Inf	9-26
Pieper, Edward, Pvt. 1cl., A, 355th Inf	8- 9
Pierce, Henry H., Pvt., B, 354th Inf	8-10
Pierce, Rollie T., Pvt 1cl., B, 341st M. G. Bn	10-24
Pinchatorie, Frank J., Pvt., C, 314th Amm. Tr	11- 2
Pinkston, Geo. C., Pvt., E, 314th Sup. Tr	
Piper, Arthur R., Corp., D, 314th Eng	8-22
Piskos, Frank G., Pvt., E, 354th Inf	10- 5
Podojil, Joseph F., Wag., C, 314th Amm. Tr	11- 1
Pollock, Clifford L., Mech., D, 355th Inf	8- 9
Pollock, Clifford L., Mech., D, 355th Inf	11- 5
Pomeranke, Frank L., Pvt., D, 354th Inf	8-10
Pope, Aaron J., Pvt., E, 356th Inf	10- 7
Pope, Vilas E., Sgt., L, 356th Inf	10- 7
Porter, William H., Pvt., E, 356th Inf	10- 7
Poudevigne, Albert M., Pvt., B, 354th Inf	8-10
Povenmire, Harvey E., Pvt., I, 356th Inf	10- 7
Powell, Frank E., Pvt., F, 355th Inf	10-22
Powell, Frank P., Sgt., D, 355th Inf	8- 9
Powers, William J., Pvt., C, 354th Inf	8-10
Pratt, Jesse L., Pvt., E, 354th Inf	10-28
Price, Asa D., Corp., D, 353rd Inf	9-26
Priest, Louie C., Corp., D, 353rd Inf	9-26
Przybyl, Joseph A., Pvt., F, 354th Inf	10-28
Psalidas, Anzel A., Pvt., E, 354th Inf	10- 6
Pyeatt, Irvan, Pvt., E, 354th Inf	10-28
Pyle, John M., Pvt., B, 354th Inf	10- 5
Quick, Joseph W., Corp., H, 356th Inf	9-19
Quigley, Carl R., Pvt., E, 354th Inf	9-26
Quintana, Delfido, Pvt., I, 356th Inf	10- 7
Quintana, Isaac, Pvt., I, 356th Inf	10- 7
Quarles, James W., Pvt., I, 356th Inf	10- 3
Radaker, Harry E., Sgt., B, 314th F. S. Bn	10- 6
Rades, Herman C., Pvt., L, 354th Inf	11- 6
Radziswski, Adam C., Pvt., I, 356th Inf	10- 7
Ragland, George R., Corp., B, 354th Inf	8-10
Railton, George C., Pvt., D, 354th Inf	8-11
Rainwater, Thomas, Pvt., I, 356th Inf	10- 7
Ralfston, Nelson G., Pvt., B, 342nd M. G. Bn	10- 5
Rampy, Clyde H., Pvt 1cl., Hq. 354th Inf	10-27
Ramsey, Grover C., Pvt., Field Hosp., 354th Inf	10-11
Randolph, John G., Pvt., I, 356th Inf	10- 7
Rankin, Thomas A., Pvt., L, 356th Inf	10- 5
Raper, Jack L., Sgt., Med. Det., 354th Inf	8-10
Raper, Simon, Pvt., E, 354th Inf	10- 5
Rathstone, Irwin D., Pvt. 1cl., B, 340th M. G. Bn	10-27
Rauch, Paul O., Pvt., 314th San. Tr	10-27
Raumschuh, Joseph, Pvt. 1cl., E, 354th Inf	11- 3
Rausch, Anton F., Pvt., E, 354th Inf	11- 5
Rauscher, Arthur F., Pvt. 1cl., D, 341st M. G. Bn	10- 4
Rayburn, Chas. W, Sgt., F, 342nd F. A	
Reacke, Alfred, Pvt., I, 356th Inf	10- 7
Realph, Harvey W., Sgt., Hq. 355th Inf	8- 9
Rebenesborn, William H., Pvt., B, 340th M. G. Bn	10- 5
Reed, Clyde V., Corp., E, 342nd F. A	
Reed, Rufus R., Pvt., E, 342nd F. A	
Reed, Tyler, Pvt., I, 356th Inf	10- 7
Reese, Oscar N., Pvt., E, 356th Inf	10- 7
Reikat, Eitel E., Pvt. 1cl., C, 355th Inf	8- 9
Reilly, Eugene J., Bn. Sgt. Maj., 354th Inf	10-27
Reinhard, Virgil, Pvt. 1cl., Hq. 354th Inf	9-26
Renfro, Benjamin H., Corp., E, 354th Inf	10- 5
Renner, George H., Pvt., L, 356th Inf	10- 7
Renner, Henry, Pvt., Hq. 354th Inf	10-29
Replinger, Wilbur R., Corp., E, 354th Inf	10- 6
Reshefsky, Reubin, Pvt., A, 355th Inf	8- 9
Remiker, Frank W., Corp., G, 354th Inf	10-28
Revard, Nicholas N., Pvt. 1cl., Hq. 356th Inf	10- 5
Reynolds, Elwood Ellis, Mech., L, 355th Inf	11- 5
Rhea, Harry R., Pvt., I, 356th Inf	10- 6
Rhodes, Howard, Pvt., L, 353rd Inf	10-28
Ribera, Nasario, Pvt., I, 356th Inf	10- 6

Name, Rank, Company, Regiment	Date, 1918
Rice, James V., Pvt. 1cl., K, 355th Inf	10- 8
Rich, Delbert, Pvt., C, 355th Inf	8- 9
Richards, Claude G., Corp., I, 356th Inf	10- 7
Richards, Ernest W., Pvt., H, 354th Inf	8-10
Richards, Stanley B., Pvt. 1cl., D, 341st M. G. Bn.	9-28
Richard, William F., Pvt. 1cl., E, 354th Inf	10- 6
Richter, William A., Pvt., E, 354th Inf	10-29
Ricketts, Clinton, Pvt., E, 314th Amm. Tr	
Rickmann, Albert P., Pvt., E, 354th Inf	10-29
Riddle, Charles H., 89th M. P. Co	10- 6
Riley, Martin A., Pvt., 314th San. Tr	10-27
Rine, Halsey A., Pvt., I, 353rd Inf	10-31
Rinker, Grover C., Corp., H, 356th Inf	11- 5
Roberson, Roscoe C., Pvt. E, 356th Inf	10- 7
Roberts, Albert Leo, Pvt., C, 355th Inf	9-19
Roberts, Benjamin H., A, 342nd M. G. Bn	8- 9
Roberts, Frank W., Sgt., A, 342nd M. G. Bn	8-9
Roberts, James C., Pvt., D, 314th Eng	8-22
Roberts, Paul O., Corp., I, 356th Inf	10- 7
Roberts, Russell C., Pvt., A, 355th Inf	8-11
Robertson, Robert, Pvt., G, 354th Inf	9-29
Robertson, Tracy R., Pvt., B, 342nd M. G. Bn	10- 5
Roderick, Roy F., Corp., A, 355th Inf	8- 9
Rodgers, Lawrence, Cook, C, 355th Inf	10- 5
Roeder, George C., Cook, D, 355th Inf	8- 9
Roese, Truman, Pvt., M, 353rd Inf	10-26
Rogers, Henry, Pvt., E, 354th Inf	10-27
Rogge, George J., Pvt. 1cl., B, 342nd M. G. Bn	10- 5
Rooney, Edward C., Pvt., D, 355th Inf	8-15
Rosa, Frank, Pvt., E, 356th Inf	10- 7
Rosenberg, Lewis, Pvt., D, 355th Inf	8- 9
Rosenbloom, Joe, Pvt., B, 354th Inf	8-10
Rosentreter, Meyer, Corp., F, 314th Eng	9-29
Rosewall, Thomas L., Pvt., B, 354th Inf	8-10
Ross, Howard E., Corp., F, 354th Inf	10-28
Rosson, William H., Corp., I, 356th Inf	10- 7
Rothove, John C., Pvt. 1cl., C, 355th Inf	10- 5
Rothrock, Fred, Pvt., A, 355th Inf	8- 9
Rothrock, Samuel H., Pvt., E, 354th Inf	10-28
Rowland, Robt. M., Pvt., E, 354th Inf	10- 6
Royer, Clinton S., Pvt. 1cl., Med. Det. 355th Inf.	8- 9
Rudd, Frank F., Sgt., B, 354th Inf	10- 5
Ruf, Frank B., Corp., F, 354th Inf	10-28
Rummel, Chester A., Corp., C, 314th F. S. Bn	8-10
Runyon, William L., Corp., L, 356th Inf	10- 7
Russell, Clifford S., Pvt., K, 353rd Inf	9-18
Ryan, Edward J., Pvt., C, 314th F. S. Bn	8-11
Ryan, Leonard P., Pvt., E, 342nd F. A	
Sallila, John, Pvt. 1cl., A, 342nd M. G. Bn	8- 9
Salvo, Nick, Pvt., E, 355th Inf	11- 2
Salyers, Otho, Pvt., H, 354th Inf	8-15
Sandberg, Henry T., Pvt. 1cl., F, 340th F. A	10-24
Sanders, Edward H., Pvt., I, 356th Inf	10- 7
Sanford, Thomas W., Pvt. 1cl., M. G. Co., 354th Inf.	10-28
Saterfield, William E., 1st Sgt., H, 354th Inf	10-28
Saubert, Charles A., Sgt., F, 354th Inf	10-27
Saunders, Charley J., Corp., Hq. 354th Inf	8-10
Saunders, Joseph P., Pvt. 1cl., M. G., 356th Inf	11- 1
Sauter, Richard D., Pvt., A, 355th Inf	8- 9
Saylors, Ulysses L., Pvt., I, 356th Inf	10- 7
Schaffrus, Otto R., Corp., G, 354th Inf	10-29
Schalk, John J., Sgt., B, 340th M. G. Bn	10- 7
Schalla, Otto M., Pvt., D, 355th Inf	8- 9
Schallman, Sydney M., Pvt., D, 355th Inf	8- 9
Scheib, Howard J., Pvt., Med. Det., 354th Inf	8-10
Scherrel, Raymond P., Pvt., F, 354th Inf	10-27
Scheumeman, Frank A., Corp., A, 355th Inf	8- 9
Schewe, Fred W., Pvt., D, 355th Inf	8- 9
Schick, Miles, Pvt., M, 353rd Inf	10-26
Schilpp, Albert C., Pvt. 1cl., A, 342nd M. G. Bn	8- 9
Schilling, Carl, Pvt., F, 354th Inf	10-28
Schindler, Fred W., Pvt., Hq 355th Inf	8- 9
Schloe, Hugh C., Corp., C, 341st M. G. Bn	9-26
Schmedake, Henry A., Pvt., G, 354th Inf	10-29
Schmedinghoff, Francis B., Pvt., A, 353rd Inf	10-26
Schmidt, George H., Sgt., C, 341st M. G. Bn	10- 2
Schmidt, Hurbert, Sgt., B, 342nd M. G. Bn	10- 5
Schmidt, William, Corp., G, 354th Inf	9-25
Schmitt, Frank, Pvt., F, 353rd Inf	11- 1
Schmitzehe, William, Corp., F, 314th Eng	9- 8
Schneider, Erwin L., Pvt., F, 354th Inf	10-28
Schneider, Roy S., Corp., C, 353rd Inf	10-22
Schoenberg, William, Pvt., Hq. 355th Inf	10- 9
Schoenfeld, Joseph, Corp., F, 355th Inf	10-22
Schoenfeld, Joseph J., Pvt. 1cl., F, 355th Inf	10-22
Schoepp, Charles G., Pvt. 1cl., C, 314th F. S. Bn	11- 5
Schollmeyer, George M., Pvt., E, 354th Inf	10- 5
Scholten, John H., Pvt. 1cl., D, 355th Inf	8- 9
Schoppenhorst, Clarence H., Pvt., A, 354th Inf	8-10

Name, Rank, Company, Regiment	Date, 1918
Schrader, Nelson L., Pvt., G, 354th Inf	10-27
Schreiber, Carl W., Pvt., H, 354th Inf	9-26
Schricker, Luther Paul, Pvt., A, 342nd M. G. Bn.	8- 9
Schroeder, Charles F., Pvt. 1cl., K, 355th Inf	10- 8
Schroeder, John G, Pvt. 1cl., H, 354th Inf	10-29
Schroder, Joseph, Pvt., I, 353rd Inf	10-28
Schuerman, Adam E., Pvt., E, 353rd Inf	11- 6
Schultz, William C., Pvt., A, 355th Inf	8- 9
Schulz, Peter F., Pvt., M. G. Co., 354th Inf	10-27
Schumacher, Jacob Emil, Corp., E, 356th Inf	10- 6
Schumacker, Louis H., Pvt. 1cl., D, 355th Inf	8-15
Schumaker, Theodore A., Sgt., E, 354th Inf	11- 4
Schurmann, Theobald H., Sgt., A, 355th Inf	8- 9
Schussler, George H., Pvt. 1cl., E, 354th Inf	10-28
Schwab, William L., Pvt., F, 355th Inf	10-22
Schwahn, Stanley E., Pvt. 1cl., H, 353rd Inf	10- 2
Schwartzlow, Oscar W., Pvt. 1cl., A, 354th Inf	8-10
Scott, Carl C., Pvt., Hq. 340th M. G. Bn	10- 5
Scott, William, Pvt. 1cl., B, 355th Inf	10- 6
Scott, William H., Pvt., M. G. Co., 355th Inf	11- 2
Seabaugh, Tivus J., Corp., E, 356th Inf	10- 6
Seagraves, Logan B., Pvt., Med. Det., 355th Inf	10-21
Seal, Pleas A., Pvt., D, 353rd Inf	9-26
Secrest, Richard, Pvt., D, 353rd Inf	8-10
Sedillo, Solomon, Pvt., I, 356th Inf	10- 7
Seitel, Lloyd H., Pvt. 1cl., B, 342nd M. G. Bn	10- 5
Seema, Antonio A., Pvt., I, 353rd Inf	11-11
Schackelford, Frank H., Corp., I, 356th Inf	10- 7
Shafer, Harry, Pvt., E, 354th Inf	9-26
Schanafelt, John K., Pvt., M. G. Co., 354th Inf	10-28
Sharp, Wilbur T., Sgt., F, 354th Inf	8-10
Sharrott, Arthur, Corp., F, 340th F. A	10-23
Shebilsky, George J., Pvt. 1cl., D, 341st M. G. Bn.	9-30
Sheehy, Frank C., Pvt., F, 354th Inf	10-27
Shepherd, Frank H., Pvt. 1cl., Hq. 354th Inf	9-27
Schoemaker, Harold E., Pvt. 1cl., C, 314th F. S.	9-26
Shoop, Albert L., Corp., D, 353rd Inf	9-26
Shouse, Walter P., Pvt., Hq. 354th Inf	10-27
Sidenstricker, Aaron M., Pvt., B, 314th Eng	10-27
Seifert, Harry, Corp., G, 354th Inf	9-29
Simmering, Wm. F., Pvt. 1cl., E, 356th Inf	11-11
Simmons, Frank, Pvt., E, 354th Inf	10-27
Simonson, Aage A., Corp., D, 355th Inf	8- 9
Simpich, Philip R., Pvt., A, 354th Inf	8-10
Simpson, Aaron L., Pvt., B, 354th Inf	8-10
Siorfanes, George A., Pvt. 1cl., E, 354th Inf	10- 6
Siver, Wm. M., Pvt., F, 355th Inf	9-19
Skaggs, Harry D., Sgt., B, 353rd Inf	10- 6
Skelley, George A., Pvt., Hq. 353rd Inf	10-27
Skibmore, Edward, Pvt., B, 355th Inf	8- 9
Slack, Henry D., Pvt. 1cl., E, 340th F. A	10-24
Slaminski, Mike, Pvt., A, 355th Inf	8- 9
Sloane, Roland S., Corp., B, 340th M. G. Bn	10- 5
Smiley, Chester A., Pvt., Med. Det., 356th Inf	9-21
Smith, Albert, Pvt. 1cl., L, 353rd Inf	10-22
Smith, Charles E., Pvt. 1cl., A, 355th Inf	8- 9
Smith, Edwin R., Pvt., A, 340th M. G. Bn	10-28
Smith, Henry L., Pvt., B, 340th M. G. Bn	10-29
Smith, James Marion, Sup. Sgt., Hq. 355th Inf	8- 9
Smith, John, Pvt., F, 354th Inf	8-10
Smith, Miles, Pvt., L, 355th Inf	11- 8
Smith, Omer J., 1st Sgt., E, 354th Inf	10-30
Smith, Sanford A., Corp., B, 353rd Inf	10- 6
Smith, Virgil B., Pvt., H, 356th Inf	10- 7
Smithson, John R., Sgt., M. G. Co., 354th Inf	10-27
Snethen, Theora, Pvt. 1cl., B, 356th Inf	9-21
Snodgrass, Francis M., Corp., C, 341st M. G. Bn	9-26
Snyder, Edgar U., Sgt., D., 353rd Inf	9-27
Soda, Alexander M., Pvt., M. G. Co., 354th Inf	10-27
Soley, Stanley G., Pvt., H, 354th Inf	10-23
Songer, Harry O., Pvt. 1cl., D., 353rd Inf	9-26
Sorenson, Harold J., Pvt., F, 354th Inf	10-27
Spahn, Fred, Pvt., Med. Det., 353rd Inf	10-28
Sparks, Sydney, Pvt. 1cl., H, 356th Inf	11-11
Sparr, Herman A., Pvt., E, 355th Inf	10-18
Speaker, Neal F., Sgt., I, 356th Inf	10- 7
Spencer, Albert C, Pvt. 1cl., 354th Inf	10-28
Spenrath, Eric, Pvt., I, 356th Inf	10- 7
Stitler, Carroll, Pvt., E, 314th Eng	9-18
Spitzenberg, Harry L., Reg. Sgt. Maj., Hq. 354th Inf.	9-26
Spooner, Walter E, Sgt., D, 355th Inf	8- 9
Spotts, James L., Wag., Sup. Co., 353rd Inf	9-25
Spring, Ray, Pvt., B, 342nd M. G. Bn	10- 5
Staley, Ellis, Pvt., A, 342nd M. G. Bn	8- 9
Stapleton, Dell L., Pvt., D, 353rd Inf	9-26
Stapp, Billie, Corp., C, 341st M. G. Bn	10-27
Stasevicsh, Alexander, Pvt., C, 314 Amm. Tr	9-19
Stech, Mike, Pvt. 1cl., F, 354th Inf	10-27
Steel, Robert H., Pvt. 1cl., A, 354th Inf	8-10

Name, Rank, Company, Regiment	Date 1918
Stehlin, Robert L., Pvt., F, 354th Inf	10-28
Steiner, Emil J., Pvt., D, 355th Inf	8-15
Steinkiste, Medard, Pvt., E, 356th Inf	10- 6
Steinman, Bernard, Pvt., B, 354th Inf	10- 5
Stephens, Albett B., Pvt., Hq. 354th Inf	9-28
Stephens, Benjamin F., Pvt., 314th San. Tr	10-27
Stephens, Elias O., Pvt., E, 314th Eng	9-18
Stephens, Harold I., Pvt. 1cl., B, 342nd M. G. Bn	10- 5
Stephens, James L., Sgt., K, 355th Inf	11- 6
Stephens, Joseph J., Pvt., Mech., A, 355th Inf	8- 9
Stephensen, Duke, Pvt., F, 354th Inf	10-27
Stephenson, Ellis F., Pvt. 1cl., Hq. 354th Inf	9-26
Stevens, Clyde W., Sgt., C, 353rd Inf	10-22
Stevens, Monte G., Pvt., L, 356th Inf	10- 9
Stewart, Ralph T., Pvt., Med. Det., 354th Inf	8-10
Stiefel, Roy L., Pvt., I, 356th Inf	10- 7
Stiff, Andrew, Pvt., B, 353rd Inf	10- 3
Stinnett, Macy, Pvt. 1cl., E, 356th Inf	10- 6
Stitt, David D., Pvt., D, 353rd Inf	9-26
Stockinger, George J, Pvt., D, 355th Inf	8- 9
Stoecklein, Alexander C., Pvt., I, 353rd Inf	10-30
Stout, Cecil J., Pvt., B, 353rd Inf	10- 2
Stout, Grover C., Pvt., B, 353rd Inf	10- 6
Straub, John J., Pvt., D, 353rd Inf	9-26
Streck, George A., Pvt., Med. Det., 355th Inf	8- 9
Streeby, Robert E., Pvt., C, 354th Inf	8-10
Stricklett, Gail E., Pvt. 1cl., C, 341st M. G. Bn	10- 5
Strowig, Homer F., Corp., L, 353rd Inf	10- 3
Struttman, Alvin F., Mech., M. G. Co., 354th Inf	10-27
Stude, Walter C., Pvt. 1cl., D, 341st M. G. Bn	9-28
Stufflebean, Elmer L., Pvt., Hq. 354th Inf	10-27
Stull, Kenneth L., Sgt., I, 356th Inf	10- 7
Sullivan, Edward R., Pvt., Hq. 340th F. A	10- 4
Sullivan, Frank J., Pvt. 1cl., C, 341st M. G. Bn	10- 2
Sullivan, Howard S., Sgt., F, 354th Inf	10-28
Sullivan, James, Pvt., D, 355th Inf	8- 9
Sullivan, Thomas J., Pvt., Hq. 354th Inf	9-26
Sullivan, Thomas P., Pvt., B, 342nd M. G. Bn	10-21
Summers, Francis, Pvt., C, 354th Inf	8-10
Summers, Jesse E., Corp., K, 355th Inf	11- 6
Sumrow, Robert C., Pvt. 1cl., G, 354th Inf	9-26
Sundeen, Paul E., Pvt., F, 354th Inf	10-28
Sundholm, Carl G., Pvt., G, 354th Inf	10-30
Sundeen, Paul E., Pvt., F, 354th Inf	10-29
Swanson, David L., Corp., C, 314th Sup. Tr	11- 2
Swanson, Harold V., Sgt., A, 341st M. G. Bn	10- 3
Swarts, LeRoy W., Pvt., C, 354th Inf	9-27
Swearingen, Silas H., Corp., E, 354th Inf	10-28
Sweet, William H., Pvt., D, 341st M. G. Bn	9-28
Sweetin, Claude E., Sgt., G, 354th Inf	10-30
Swift, Dean, Pvt., M. G., 355th Inf	11- 4
Swinchowski, Anthony, Pvt., G, 354th Inf	9-28
Swinney, Richard D., Sgt., E, 356th Inf	10- 7
Sylvis, James E., Sgt., K, 355th Inf	11- 6
Szadezumas, Ignatz, Pvt., G, 353rd Inf	11- 3
Talamonti, Angelo, Pvt., Med. Det., 354th Inf	10-27
Tanberg, Henry J., Pvt., G, 354th Inf	10-28
Tarquiny, Tony, Pvt. 1cl., F, 354th Inf	10-27
Tate, Claud E., Pvt. 1cl., A, 342nd M. G. Bn	8- 9
Taylor, Everett S., Pvt., A, 355th Inf	8-10
Taylor, Houston, Pvt., A, 342nd M. G. Bn	10-28
Taylor, James, Pvt., A, 342nd M. G. Bn	8- 9
Taylor, Maurice H., Pvt. 1cl., A, 342nd M. G. Bn	8- 9
Templeton, Robert B., Corp., C, 314th F. S. Bn	8-10
Tenorio, Esmel, Corp., I, 356th Inf	10- 7
Teorroasvez, Walter, Pvt., B, 356th Inf	9-21
Teschner, William C., Pvt., I, 353rd Inf	10-27
Teutsch, Roy P., Pvt. 1cl., F, 314th Eng	9-30
Thatcher, Jonas W., Pvt., I, 356th Inf	10- 7
Thoeni, Christian, Pvt. 1cl., E, 354th Inf	10- 6
Thomas, Edward, Pvt., D, 354th Inf	8-10
Thomas, John, Wag., Hq. 341st M. G. Bn	11- 9
Thomas, Joseph, Pvt., A, 355th Inf	8- 9
Thomas, Robert J., Sgt., Med. Det., 354th Inf	10-28
Thompson, Alexander J., Jr., Sgt., E, 340th F. A	10-24
Thompson, Axel, Pvt., B, 340th M. G. Bn	10-10
Thompson, Donnell C., Pvt. 1cl., E, 354 Inf	10- 5
Thompson, John L., Pvt. 1cl., E, 354th Inf	10- 5
Thompson, James W., Jr., Reg. Sup. Sgt., Sup. Co., 355th Inf	8- 9
Thornton, Verne L., Pvt., I, 353rd Inf	10-28
Thornton, Walter W., Cook, D, 355th Inf	8- 9
Thrams, Leonard L., Pvt., C, 341st M. G. Bn	10- 1
Thurston, Charles A., Pvt., L, 356th Inf	10- 7
Tietgen, Emil, Pvt., D, 341st M. G. Bn	9-29
Till, Henry F., Wag., Sup. Co., 355th Inf	10- 2
Tilzey, Howard M., Corp., B, 353rd Inf	10- 6
Titsworth, Claud C., Corp., B, 341st M. G. Bn	10-24
Tokespeta, Mack, Pvt., D, 354th Inf	8-10
Toston, Wm. E., Pvt., D, 314th Sup. Tr	
Trahan, Philip, Pvt., I, 356th Inf	10- 7
Tribant, Louis C., Mess. Sgt., Hq. 354th Inf	10- 4
Triplett, Heber, Pvt., I, 356th Inf	10- 7
Triscari, Sebastino, Pvt., I, 356th Inf	10- 2
Trook, Nicholas J., Pvt., E, 355th Inf	10- 2
Troute, Ovid E., Corp., B, 353rd Inf	10-25
Truby, Edwin L., Pvt., A, 342nd M. G. Bn	8- 9
Trujillo, Anastacio, Pvt., B, 356th Inf	9-21
Tubbs, Vernon O., Sgt., D, 355th Inf	8- 9
Tuhill, Patrick H., Pvt. 1cl., B, 341st M. G. Bn	10-22
Turck, Harry, Sgt., F, 354th Inf	10-21
Turnquist, Alfred, Pvt. 1cl., B, 353rd Inf	10- 6
Tweed, John H., Pvt., L, 353rd Inf	11- 1
Twents, John W., Sgt., Med. Det., 353rd Inf	10-27
Underhill, Ira W., Corp., B, 354th Inf	10- 5
Underwood, John M., Corp., I, 356th Inf	10- 6
Upton, Wm. J., Pvt., E, 342nd F. A	
Urzi, Sebastiano, Pvt., D, 314th Eng	9-28
Valle, Andrew R., Corp., F, 354th Inf	10-27
Vandenbrouche, Kamiel, Pvt., D, 341st M. G. Bn	8-31
Vandergrift, Hubert G., Pvt., G, 354th Inf	10-27
Vandewalker, William F., Pvt., C, 341st M. G. Bn	10- 1
Vanhoosen, John L., Pvt., B, 341st M. G. Bn	10-22
Vanlanker, Achiel, Pvt., A, 354th Inf	8-10
Vanscoy, Warren G., Pvt., I, 356th Inf	10- 6
Vaughan, Charles A., Cook, B, 354th Inf	10- 5
Veale, Claud W., Pvt., E, 342nd F. A	
Veillon, Juste, Pvt., I, 356th Inf	10- 7
Vermoilen, Joseph H, Pvt., B, 342nd M. G. Bn	10-27
Vetter, Albert, Pvt., B, 354th Inf	10- 5
Vicknir, Vieves, Pvt., I, 356th Inf	10- 9
Vincent, Frank, Pvt. 1cl., Hq. 355th Inf	8- 9
Vinckel, Nicholas, Pvt. 1cl., M. G. Co., 355th Inf	11- 3
Vipond, Roger W., Pvt., Hq. 354th Inf	8-10
Vitts, Walley, Mech., I, 356th Inf	10- 7
Vives, Vickmair, Pvt., I, 356th Inf	10- 7
Vlean, Andrew J. B., Pvt. 1cl., A, 355th Inf	8- 9
Vogelsang, Joseph G., Pvt., B, 355th Inf	8- 9
Vollbracht, Aaron F., Pvt. 1cl., A, 342nd Inf	8- 9
Vollus, Julius E., Pvt., H, 354th Inf	8-10
Vondracek, Joseph A., Pvt. 1cl., B, 342nd M. G. Bn	10- 5
Voss, Christopher F., Pvt., H, 353rd Inf	10- 2
Voss, William, Pvt., E, 356th Inf	10- 7
Wachsmuth, Edward C., Corp., G, 354th Inf	10-27
Waddell, Ray C., Pvt., F, 354th Inf	10-27
Wade, Fred E., Pvt., I, 353rd Inf	11- 3
Wagner, Everett J., Corp., F, 354th Inf	10-27
Wagner, Nicholas J., Sgt., D, 341st M. G. Bn	9-28
Wagoner, Charles W., Pvt., Sales Com. U. No. 5	10- 5
Walch, Henry A., Sgt., Hq. 340th M. G. Bn	10- 5
Walbourne, Jess R., Pvt., B, 354th Inf	8-10
Walker, Charles W., Pvt., B, 354th Inf	8-10
Walker, Charles W., Corp., K, 353rd Inf	11- 3
Walker, Irl J., Sup. Sgt., A, 355th Inf	8- 9
Walker, Roy, Pvt., B, 354th Inf	8-19
Wall, Jesse H., Pvt., E, 354th Inf	10- 5
Walls, Jerry J., Pvt., D, 355th Inf	8- 9
Wallace, Roy, Pvt. 1cl., F, 340th F. A	10-24
Walleski, George, Pvt., B, 341st M. G. Bn	10-24
Walls, Clares M., Corp., B, 353rd Inf	10- 7
Walsh, James E., Pvt., F, 354th Inf	10-28
Walsh, John J., Pvt., L, 353rd Inf	10- 4
Walters, Orville J., Corp., D, 355th Inf	8- 9
Ward, Samuel B., Pvt., L, 355th Inf	11- 5
Warner, Charles I., Pvt., A, 342nd M. G. Bn	8- 9
Warner, Henry A., Pvt., D, 353rd Inf	11- 3
Warner, Pearl A., Stable Sgt., M. G. Co., 356th Inf	11- 9
Warren, Clarence D., Pvt. 1cl., B, 314th F. S. Bn	10- 5
Warrender, Orville L., Corp., A, 355th Inf	8- 9
Washburn, Orval R., Sgt., E, 314th Eng	9-26
Waters, Arthur B., Pvt., A, 353rd Inf	11- 5
Waters, John M., Sgt., C, 354th Inf	8-10
Watkins, Ernest E., Corp., C, 341st M. G. Bn	10- 1
Watkins, Harrison, Pvt., K, 353rd Inf	10- 1
Watson, James E., Pvt., Hq. Troop, 89th Div	9-25
Watson, James M., Pvt. 1cl., I, 353rd Inf	10-27
Wattenbarger, Raymond, Pvt., Hq. 354th Inf	8-10
Wayenberg, John; Pvt. 1cl., B, 340th M. G. Bn	10- 5
Weaver, George S., Pvt. 1cl., K, 356th Inf	10- 6
Weaver, James F., Pvt., E, 354th Inf	10- 6
Weber, Frank G., Pvt., E, 354th Inf	10-28
Weikal, Ralph E., Pvt. 1cl., Hq. 353rd Inf	10- 6
Weirich, Hugh, Pvt., A, 342nd M. G. Bn	8- 9
Welch, Lloyd, Sgt., B, 353rd Inf	10- 6
Wenan, Herman, Pvt., D, 355th Inf	8- 9
Wells, William L., Pvt., E, 354th Inf	10- 5
Welter, Fred J., Pvt. 1cl., B, 342nd M. G. Bn	10- 5
Werner, Arthur E., Pvt. 1cl., B, 342nd M. G. Bn	10- 5

Name, Rank, Company, R-giment	Date 1918
Wcsselschmeidt, Henry W., Pvt., C, 354th Inf	8-10
Westberg, Edward, Pvt., B, 353rd Inf	10- 6
Westbrook, Earl R., Pvt. 1cl., C, 341st M. G. Bn	10- 1
Westbrook, Fred E., 1st Sgt., I, 356th Inf	10- 7
Westfall, Walter E., Corp., Hq. 353rd Inf	10- 6
Westlake, Earl V., Corp., Hq. 354th Inf	8-10
Wharton, Lee R., Pvt., H, 356th Inf	10- 7
Whipple, Joe, Corp., F, 340th F. A	10-24
White, Edward R., Sgt., Hq. 354th Inf	8-10
White, James A., Pvt., C, 314th F. S. Bn	10-27
Whitesell, John W., Pvt., D, 354th Inf	10- 6
Whitney, Fred, Pvt., M. G. Co., 355th Inf	11- 2
Whitsett, Gilbert C., Sgt., C, 314th F. S. Bn	10-27
Whorton, Andy, Pvt., L, 355th Inf	11- 5
Widell, Bert L., Pvt. 1cl., D, 341st M. G. Bn	9-29
Wieland, William C., Bug., B, 342nd M. G. Bn	10- 5
Wiesel, Fred W., Wag., Sup. Co., 355th Inf	10- 6
Wieesler, Joseph B., Pvt., B, 355th Inf	8-10
Wiesner, Albert C., Pvt., I, 356th Inf	10- 7
Wiggert, William, Pvt., I, 356th Inf	10- 7
Wilcott, James E., Pvt. 1cl., D, 355th Inf	8- 9
Wilcox, Franklin P., Sgt., E, 353rd Inf	11- 2
Wilde, George, Bug., F, 354th Inf	10-27
Wilde, Henry, Pvt., E, 342nd F. A	
Wilhelms, Henry M., Pvt., C, 354th Inf	8-10
Wilkinson, Odie J., Corp., A, 354th Inf	8-10
Willer, William, Mech., F, 354th Inf	10-28
Williams, John B., Pvt., Sup. Co., 356th Inf	10- 9
Williams, Lewis J., Pvt. 1cl., H, 354th Inf	10-30
Williams, Marvin E., Corp., A, 354th Inf	8-10
Williams, Raymond T., Pvt. 1cl., M. G., 354th Inf	10-27
Williams, William A., Corp., E, 314th Eng	10-27
Williamson, Ingwald, Pvt., G, 354th Inf	10-28
Willis, Eugene E., Pvt., B, 342nd M. G. Bn	10- 5
Wills, Walter J., Pvt., C, 314th F. S. Bn	10- 2
Wilson, Dallas W., Sgt., A, 354th Inf	8-10
Wilson, Eugene T., Pvt., A, 355th Inf	8- 9
Wilson, Harry C., Corp., I, 356th Inf	10- 6
Wilson, Roy E., Pvt. 1cl., L, 353rd Inf	10-28
Wilson, Ward J., Pvt., B, 355th Inf	8-28
Wines, Harry R., Pvt., M. G. Co., 355th Inf	11- 2
Winton, Percy W., Pvt., I, 356th Inf	10- 7
Wiscow, Henry W., Pvt., G, 354th Inf	10-29
Wise, Conrad T. J., Pvt., D, 355th Inf	8- 9
Wiss, Bernard J., Pvt., Med. Det., 354th Inf	8-10
Witte, Otto J., Pvt., G, 354th Inf	9-25
Wittig, Robert, Pvt. 1cl., H, 354th Inf	10-25

Name, Rank, Company, R.giment	Date 1918
Wobst, Albert C, Pvt., B, 353rd Inf	10- 6
Woebe, Ray W., Wag., Sup. Co., 355th Inf	8- 9
Woerner, Fred W., Pvt., A, 355th Inf	8- 9
Wolff, Theodore O., Pvt., A, 355th Inf	8- 9
Wonderly, Charles H., Pvt. 1cl., D, 355th Inf	8- 9
Woodard, Austin C., Corp., D, 354th Inf	8-11
Woodruff, Thomas E., Pvt. 1cl., C, 341st M. G. Bn	10- 2
Woods, Charles B., Pvt., G, 354th Inf	9-25
Woods, Joe T., Pvt., E, 354th Inf	10-28
Woodson, Everett L., Sgt., B, 354th Inf	10- 5
Woodson, Lloyd H., Sgt., B, 354th Inf	8-10
Woodward, Walter S., Corp., C, 341st M. G. Bn	10- 1
Worth, Charley W., Pvt., A, 340th M. G. Bn	10- 8
Wright, John W., Pvt. 1cl., Hq. 354th Inf	9-26
Wright, Zemar, Pvt. 1cl., D, 355th Inf	8-15
Wurdack, Edward F., Corp., Hq. 354th Inf	8-10
Wurster, Claude L., Pvt., D, 353rd Inf	10-31
Wurtenberger, Frank A., Pvt., E, 354th Inf	10- 6
Yancey, David F., Cook, B, 354th Inf	10- 5
Yancey, Gustaf A., Pvt., B, 354th Inf	8-10
Yancey, Lyman K., Pvt. 1cl., B, 354th Inf	8-10
Yates, Robert L., Pvt., A, 354th Inf	8-10
Yearwood, Henry F., Corp., B, 354th Inf	10- 5
Yocom, Glenn F., Pvt., C, 353rd Inf	10-26
Yoder, Benjamin, Pvt., Hq. 355th Inf	10- 4
Yordt, William, Corp., I, 356th Inf	11- 1
Yost, Harold, Corp., A, 355th Inf	8- 9
Young, Dale A., Pvt., M. G. Co., 354th Inf	10-22
Young, Dale G., Pvt., M. G. Co., 354th Inf	10-28
Young, David, Pvt., E, 354th Inf	8-10
Young, Desray, Pvt., B, 340th M. G. Bn	10-27
Young, Edward A., Pvt., G, 354th Inf	9-25
Young, Louis E., Corp. D, 340th F. A	9-19
Young, Ora G., Pvt., D, 353rd Inf	9-26
Yowell, Charles B., Sgt., G, 354th Inf	10-29
Zadnichek, Edward, Pvt., H, 354th Inf	10-31
Zamora, Christobal, Pvt., B, 354th Inf	10- 5
Zamfes, Harry S., Pvt., G, 355th Inf	8-18
Zarek, Edward E., Corp., F, 354th Inf	10-28
Zeuschel, William B., Pvt., D, 354th Inf	8-10
Zielhke, Peter J., Pvt., A, 354th Inf	8-10
Zinser, Mike, Pvt., A, 355th Inf	8- 9
Zudoni, Mons, Corp., E, 314th Amm. Tr	
Zuhlke, Elmer A., Pvt., A, 341st F. A	
Zurlo, Raffael P., Jr., Pvt., Sales Com. U, No. 5	10- 5
Zutz, Carl E., Pvt., Hq. 355th Inf	8-10

SLIGHTLY WOUNDED

OFFICERS SLIGHTLY WOUNDED

Name, Rank, Organization	Date 1918
Breen, Frederick, 2nd Lt., 353rd Inf	10- 2
Brown, Sanford Perry, Capt., 342nd M. G. Bn	9-17
Carpenter, Lewis G., Capt., F. A., Hq. 89th Div	11-11
Christoph, Charles De Guire, 1st Lt., 353rd Inf	11- 4
Davis, James Edgar, 1st Lt., 356th Inf	11-14
Dykes, John H., Capt., 356th Inf	9-23
Ellis, Ward, Capt., 353rd Inf	9-12
Evans, John E., 2nd Lt., 355th Inf	10-21
Galvin, Francis L., 2nd Lt., 354th Inf	11- 6
Gramley, William, Capt., M. C., Med. Det., 356th Inf.	11- 7
Ham, Victor H., 2nd Lt., 355th Inf	9-16
Hanna, Mark, Capt., 356th Inf	9-23
Hansen, Amos M., 1st Lt., 356th Inf	10-28
Hansen, John C., Capt., 356th Inf	9-13
Heiken, Ellert G., 1st Lt., 356th Inf	9-23
Hobson, Henry W., Major, 356th Inf	9-12
Kelly, James A., 2nd Lt., 355th Inf	11- 7
Kelly, Francis M., Capt., 355th Inf	9-12
Little, James B., 1st Lt., 353th Inf	9-13
McCoy, William Stewart, 1st Lt., 355th Inf	9-17
McDonough, Gilbert, 1st Lt., 355th Inf	9-17
Macatee, Edward V., 2nd Lt., 356th Inf	9-12
Macdonald, Allan C., 2nd Lt., 353rd Inf	11- 1
Marks, Edward A., Jr., 2nd Lt., Hq. 354th Inf	10- 7

Name, Rank, Organization	Date 1918
Millard, Leslie J., 2nd Lt., 353rd Inf	10-21
Miller, Ben W., 1st Lt., 353rd Inf	10-25
Miller, David B., 1st Lt., 353rd Inf	9-18
Moore, Fred F., Capt., 355th Inf	9-17
Moore, William V., 2nd Lt., 341st M. G. Bn	11- 3
Murphy, John H., 1st Lt., 356th Inf	11-11
Nelson, Norman O., Capt., M. C., San. Det., 356th Inf.	10- 4
Newman, John, Capt., 353rd Inf	9-30
Oakes, Harold S., 1st Lt., Hq. 341st F. A	9-21
Ohlandt, Beverly C., 2nd Lt., 353rd Inf	10-31
Peatross, James L., Major, 353rd Inf	
Portmann, Milton C., Capt., 353rd Inf	9-12
Potter, Wilson, Major, Ord., Hq. 89th Div	11-11
Rose, Maurice, 1st Lt., 353rd Inf	9-16
Sallee, Julius O., Capt., 314th Eng	11- 9
Shinn, Leon P., 1st Lt., 356th Inf	9-14
Sutton, Wade H., 2nd Lt., 356th Inf	11-11
Throckmorton, Burton H., 2nd Lt., 356th Inf	11-15
Traynor, Mack Vincent, 1st Lt., 355th Inf	11- 8
Webster, Harold Melvin, 1st Lt., 356th Inf	9-13
Wheatley, Edwin T., 1st Lt., 354th Inf	10-27
Wilkinson, E. R., 2nd Lt., 314th Eng	11- 9
Woods, Peter D., 1st Lt., 354th Inf	11- 2
Yohe, David A., 2nd Lt., 355th Inf	11- 7

ENLISTED MEN SLIGHTLY WOUNDED

Name, Rank, Company, Organization	Date 1918
Abbot, Lloyd E., Pvt., Hq. 314th Sup. Tr	11- 1
Abdo, William G., Pvt., K, 353rd Inf	10-30
Accorsi, Joseph, Pvt., E, 353rd Inf	11- 1
Adair, Lewis O., Pvt., B, 342nd M. G. Bn	11- 1
Adams, Henry F., Pvt., F, 314th Eng	10-30
Adams, Lewis E., Pvt., F, 314th Eng	10-20
Adee, James F., Mech., G, 353rd Inf	9-18
Adkins, Ballard, Pvt., A, 355th Inf	11- 5

Name, Rank, Company, Organization	Date 1918
Aeby, John A., Pvt., K, 353rd Inf	9-13
Aitken, Edmund J., Pvt. 1cl., L, 355th Inf	9-14
Akkerman, Dick, Pvt., K, 355th Inf	10- 7
Alberter, Frank F., Pvt. 1cl., L, 354th Inf	9-13
Albertson, Clarence A., Pvt., I, 353rd Inf	11- 6
Allard, Louis, Pvt. 1cl., H, 354th Inf	11-11
Allen, Fred F., Pvt., D, 314th Eng	12-24
Allen, Thurman R., Pvt., Hq. 353rd Inf	10-20

Name, Rank, Company, Organization	Date 1918
Alleshouse, Arthur A., Corp., D, 314th Eng	9- 5
Allie, Albert, Pvt., 314th Eng. Tr	11-11
Alton, Clarence, Pvt., M, 356th Inf	10- 2
Amos, Ray A., Pvt. 1cl., M, 353rd Inf	9-24
Amundsen, Harry, Pvt., Hq. 356th Inf	10-22
Anderson, Alfred, Pvt. 1cl., D, 356th Inf	9-17
Anderson, Alfred J., Pvt. 1cl., B, 355th Inf	9-19
Anderson, Arthur H., Pvt., B, 340th M. G. Bn	9-12
Anderson, Ben L., Corp., G, 354th Inf	11- 1
Anderson, Elmore T., Pvt., I, 355th Inf	9-16
Anderson, Ernest, Pvt., I, 354th Inf	11- 5
Anderson, Herman, Pvt. 1cl., B, 354th Inf	9-15
Anderson, James A., Pvt., B, 356th Inf	10-28
Anderson, John A., Pvt. 1cl., F, 354th Inf	9-23
Anderson, Judson B., Pvt., C, 354th Inf	11- 1
Anderson, Martin N., Pvt., I, 353rd Inf	11- 3
Anderson, Ray B., Pvt., B, 353rd Inf	10- 2
Anderson, Roy V., Pvt. 1cl., D, 355th Inf	9-12
Andrezejewski, Leo, Pvt. 1cl., 314th Eng	9-18
Anthony, Roy C., Sgt., B, 354th Inf	11- 1
Appelgate, Charlie, Pvt., G, 355th Inf	11- 4
Archer, Sherman, Pvt., F, 314th Eng	9-18
Archuleta, Mercelino, Pvt., B, 355th Inf	11-11
Armijo, Manuel, Sgt., M, 354th Inf	11- 2
Armstrong, David D, Pvt., C, 314th Eng	10-28
Armstrong, Frank T., Pvt., B, 354th Inf	9-20
Arndt, George N., Corp., K, 356th Inf	9-14
Arnold, Fred K., Pvt., F, 354th Inf	9- 9
Arnold, Joe Christ Henry, Pvt., Hq 355th Inf	9-13
Arnoldy, Mike Edward, Pvt. 1cl., G, 355th Inf	9-28
Arvine, John C., Corp., Hq. 314th F. S. Bn	10-25
Asbeck, Dick Richard, Pvt., B, 354th Inf	9-14
Aubuchon, Charlie E., Pvt., B, 342nd M. G. Bn	11- 5
Aukschum, Otto, Pvt., M, 355th Inf	11-22
Austin, Willie M., Pvt., C, 355th Inf	11- 7
Bach, Herman J., Pvt., B, 342nd M. G. Bn	9-14
Bachman, Ray A., Pvt. 1cl., L, 353rd Inf	9-15
Bachman, Julius H., Pvt. 1cl., D, 341st M. G. Bn	11- 1
Bade, George H., Sgt., C, 354th Inf	11- 8
Badsky, Frank, Pvt., E, 353rd Inf	11- 4
Bailey, Frank E., Corp., B, 353rd Inf	10- 2
Bailey, John D., Pvt., I, 356th Inf	10- 2
Baillie, Effel, Pvt., C, 355th Inf	11- 8
Baird, Harry W., Pvt. 1cl., D, 353rd Inf	9-15
Baker, George W., Sgt., E, 353rd Inf	9-16
Baker, Glen A., Pvt., I, 355th Inf	8-20
Baker, Merrill, Pvt., 314th San. Tr	10-28
Baldwin, John Benjamin, Pvt. 1cl., C, 354th Inf	11-11
Balistreri, Joseph, Pvt., I, 354th Inf	11-11
Barnes, Carol H., Corp., H, 355th Inf	9-17
Barnes, John J., Pvt., L, 356th Inf	9-12
Barry, Lawrence O., Pvt. 1cl., L, 354th Inf	11- 8
Barschak, Thomas E., Pvt. 1cl., C, 353rd Inf	9- 2
Barth, Paul A., Pvt., H, 356th Inf	9-14
Bartlett, Archer L., Pvt., D, 356th Inf	9-13
Bartley, Devaun, Pvt., D, 355th Inf	11- 4
Bauer, Henry F., Pvt., D, 353rd Inf	11- 9
Bauer, John Wenzel, Pvt., I, 354th Inf	9-19
Bareles, Nick, Pvt., D, 356th Inf	9-13
Bean, Thomas R., Pvt. 1cl., A, 356th Inf	10-23
Beck, William I., Pvt., C, 355th Inf	11-11
Beckman, Henry George, Sgt. 1cl., 314th F. S. Bn	9-18
Beighlie, Harry I., Pvt. 1cl., F, 355th Inf	10- 2
Belmford, Robert E., Pvt., K, 354th Inf	9-22
Belau, Louie W., Pvt. 1cl., M. G. Co., 355th Inf	11-24
Belk, Albert, Jr., Pvt., K, 354th Inf	11- 1
Bell, Frank L., Pvt., M. G. Co., 354th Inf	11- 1
Bender, Walter, Pvt., F, 354th Inf	8-11
Benfield, Early G., Corp., K, 354th Inf	8-24
Bennett, Charles W., Pvt., G, 354th Inf	9-23
Bennett, Edward, Pvt. 1cl., A 355th Inf	9-13
Bennett, Thomas Ransom, Pvt., L, 355th Inf	9-12
Benson, Earl, Corp., K, 353rd Inf	11- 5
Benson, Harry W., Sgt., H, 355th Inf	9-23
Benson, Leon C., Pvt., H, 355th Inf	9-16
Bentley, Alfred T., Pvt., E, 356th Inf	10-14
Benyas, David, Pvt., E, 354th Inf	11-14
Bersin, Peter, Pvt., B, 355th Inf	11- 6
Berthold, William F., Pvt. 1cl., G, 354th Inf	9-14
Bess, Roy Alvin, Pvt., L, 355th Inf	11- 6
Besselman, John M., Pvt., F, 355th Inf	10- 7
Bettgar, John, Pvt., G, 355th Inf	9-17
Bezona, Roy E., Pvt., H, 356th Inf	11-11
Bickmeyer, John H., Cook, A, 354th Inf	9-22
Billings, Dean R., Corp., L, 353rd Inf	9- 2
Billups, Robert F., Pvt., M. G. Co., 354th Inf	11- 2
Bilyeu, John H., Pvt., Hq. 356th Inf	11-11
Birdsong, Lee E., Pvt. 1cl., D, 356th Inf	9-18
Biros, George A., Pvt., C, 353rd Inf	10-27
Bishop, John M., Pvt., L, 353rd Inf	10-22
Bitz, Walter Jacob, Pvt., A, 353rd Inf	9- 9
Bivins, Francis Abraham, Pvt., A, 353rd Inf	9-14
Blaha, Charles, Cook, H, 353rd Inf	11- 5
Blair, Paul Frank, Pvt. 1cl., Hq. 355th Inf	11-11
Blake, Andrew, Pvt., F, 353rd Inf	11- 3
Blake, Carroll G., Pvt., A, 353rd Inf	9-24
Blakey, Angus G., 1st Sgt., B, 354th Inf	9-15
Blalack, James A., Pvt., C, 355th Inf	10-23
Block, Henry J., Pvt. 1cl., K, 355th Inf	9-16
Blum, Walter E., Sgt., L, 355th Inf	9-14
Blumenstein, Oscar F., Pvt., H, 353rd Inf	11- 3
Blumenthal, Arnold, Corp., F, 353rd Inf	10-30
Boatman, Willis G., Corp., H, 354th Inf	11-11
Bock, Robert, Pvt., F, 353rd Inf	11- 3
Bogard, William, Pvt., L, 353rd Inf	9-18
Bohan, James, Pvt., H, 355th Inf	11- 6
Bohning, Paul, Sgt., B, 341st M. G. Bn	9-13
Boleschka, George, Pvt. 1cl., K, 355th Inf	9-13
Bolin, John W., Pvt., G, 353rd Inf	9-12
Bond, George F., Pvt., F, 355th Inf	11- 5
Borden, Oliver V., 1st Sgt., M. G. Co., 355th Inf	9- 9
Borman, John, Pvt., L, 355th Inf	9-14
Botts, James A., Corp., G, 353rd Inf	11-11
Bourgeois, Ovide, Pvt., D, 355th Inf	11- 4
Bouton, Leslie Melvin, Pvt., L, 355th Inf	9-15
Bovee, Chester J., Pvt. 1cl., E, 314th Amm. Tr	10- 6
Bowans, Arthur L., Pvt., F, 353rd Inf	9-12
Bowers, Floyd, Corp., E, 353rd Inf	9-12
Bowman, Jesse Coleman, Pvt., Hq. 356th Inf	10-29
Boxberger, William John, Pvt., L, 355th Inf	9-14
Boyce, Roy J., Corp. Ord., 314th Amm T	
Boyd, Robert E., Bn. Sgt. Maj., Hq. 353rd Inf	11- 1
Boyle, Patrick J., Pvt., H, 353rd Inf	9-23
Bradshaw, Ellis E., Corp., E, 353rd Inf	9-12
Brady, Frank, Sgt., B, 342nd M. G. Bn	10-26
Braeger, Walter W., Pvt., E, 353rd Inf	10- 2
Bragg, Clarence E., Pvt., A, 341st M. G. Bn	9-13
Brandenburg, Frederick, Pvt. 1cl., I, 358th Inf	11- 5
Brandhorst, Frank F., Pvt. 1cl., I, 354th Inf	9-26
Brandt, George, Pvt., M, 354th Inf	11- 1
Brattin, Olon B., Pvt., B, 356th Inf	10-21
Brauch, Henry J., Pvt. 1cl., E, 354th Inf	9-19
Breaux, Beauregard, Pvt., K, 356th Inf	11- 5
Breen, August Lawrence, Pvt., G, 356th Inf	10-21
Breitbarth, Charles Paul, Pvt. 1cl., E, 314th Eng	9-18
Bressman, Henry, Sgt., B, 341st M. G. Bn	9-18
Bridgford, John F., Sgt., D, 353rd Inf	9-15
Briscoe, Earl E., Sgt., F, 354th Inf	10-21
Broadway, Ralph, Pvt., I, 354th Inf	8-29
Broderick, Bert J., Corp., B, 353rd Inf	9- 9
Brooks, Clarence F., Pvt., F, 354th Inf	10-22
Brown, Carl E., Pvt., C, 314th F. S. Bn	11- 8
Brown, John Davis, Corp., A, 341st M. G. Bn	9-14
Brown, Osborne L., Corp., B, 353rd Inf	11- 6
Brown, Stanley, Pvt. 1cl., E, 356th Inf	11-11
Bruns, Phillip J., Corp., I, 353rd Inf	11- 1
Bruton, Grover C., Pvt., F, 353rd Inf	8-31
Buecclarelli, Carmine, Pvt., F, 354th Inf	9-20
Buchold, Albert H., Corp., C, 355th Inf	11- 5
Buck, George C., Pvt. 1cl., C, 341st M. G. Bn	11- 7
Bucksath, Christopher W. H., Pvt., E, 354th Inf	10-29
Buenting, John E., Pvt., M. G. Co., 356th Inf	9-13
Burkett, Paul J., Pvt., Hq. 353rd Inf	10-30
Burklin, William H., Mech., F, 354th Inf	11- 2
Burlison, Roy Dalton, Pvt., Hq. 354th Inf	9-15
Burrichter, Frank A., Sgt., K, 354th Inf	9-26
Burton, George B., Pvt., H, 355th Inf	11-11
Butler, Lowell R., Corp., L, 354th Inf	10-29
Cahill, Edwin, Pvt., D, 354th Inf	9-22
Cain, Harry V., Pvt. 1cl., I, 356th Inf	9-19
Cain, James G., Pvt. 1cl., K, 356th Inf	11-11
Caldwell, Earl W., Sgt., F, 354th Inf	9-26
Campbell, Harry C., Corp., M, 353rd Inf	9-18
Campbell, Harry M., Pvt., K, 353rd Inf	11- 1
Campbell, Harry T., Pvt., C, 341st M. G. Bn	9-15
Candravia, Ralph, Pvt., B, 353rd Inf	10-22
Carey, Morris W., Pvt., A, 314th Eng	11- 9
Carlson, Frank A., Sgt., G, 353rd Inf	9-12
Cartohers, Glen H., Corp., B, 355th Inf	10-20
Carr, Reuben, Pvt. 1cl., G, 355th Inf	11- 5
Carr, John B., Bugler, I, 353rd Inf	11- 1
Cash, Wirt, Sgt., K, 354th Inf	11- 2
Castor, Cleo D., Pvt. 1cl., C, 356th Inf	11-11
Castro, Joe M., Pvt., A, 353rd Inf	10-24
Cato, James T., Pvt., A, 355th Inf	11- 6
Catterlin, Ben Harrison, Pvt. 1cl., C, 354th Inf	11- 1
Cattin, Marcel E., Pvt., L, 353rd Inf	9-12
Cermak, Joe, Pvt., K, 355th Inf	9-15

Name, Rank, Company, Organization	Date 1918
Chambers, Frank A., Pvt., H, 353rd Inf	9-18
Chapman, Louis A., Pvt., M, 354th Inf	9-14
Chapman, Roy Manson, Pvt. 1cl., E, 314th Eng	9-12
Chauvin, Ilson C., Pvt. 1cl., A, 355th Inf	12-15
Chauvin, Joseph V., Pvt., E, 356th Inf	10- 7
Chrismar, John, Pvt., K, 353rd Inf	9-18
Chittenden, Joel B., Pvt., F, 353rd Inf	11- 5
Choulett, Harry, Pvt. 1cl., M. G. Co., 356th Inf	9-13
Christie, John G., Corp., F, 354th Inf	10-23
Cissell, William W., Pvt., B, 355th Inf	11- 3
Clark, Ernest A., Pvt., C, 355th Inf	11- 5
Clark, Harry A., Pvt., H, 353rd Inf	9-18
Clark, Milburn D., Pvt. 1cl., 314th Amm. Tr	9-24
Clarkson, Walter E., Pvt., F, 354th Inf	11- 3
Clary, William L., Pvt., L, 353rd Inf	10-24
Claymore, John M., Pvt., K, 355th Inf	9-13
Cleary, Leo A., Pvt. 1cl., I, 353rd Inf	9-14
Clement, Albert H., Pvt., D, 355th Inf	11- 5
Cleveland, Grover Francis, Pvt., Hq. 355th Inf	10-21
Clogston, Jeffrey B., Pvt. 1cl., Amb. Co., 353rd Inf	10-27
Clough, Fay J., Sgt., I, 355th Inf	9-15
Coder, Frederick G., Pvt. 1cl., E, 353rd Inf	9-19
Coffman, Thomas E., Pvt., G, 353rd Inf	9-18
Cogdal, Paul R., Pvt., F, 356th Inf	10-30
Cohen, Samuel, Pvt. 1cl., D, 355th Inf	8-20
Coleman, Floyd W., Pvt., A, 342nd M. G. Bn	9-19
Collins, Steven, Corp., G, 353rd Inf	10-26
Comella, Matthew V., Pvt., I, 353rd Inf	9-12
Comman, David H., Corp., K, 354th Inf	11- 1
Conner, Carl A, D, 342d F. A	
Conner, James W., Pvt., I, 353rd Inf	10-28
Connors, Benjamin, Pvt., E, 354th Inf	9-20
Conrad, Carl T., Pvt., F, Hq. 353rd Inf	10-30
Cook, Cromer W., Pvt., Hq. 353rd Inf	11- 1
Cook, Everett T., Pvt., C, 355th Inf	10- 6
Cook, Henry L., Pvt. 1cl., M. G. Co., 356th Inf	10-30
Coots, Willie A., Pvt., Med. Det., 355th Inf	10-26
Copeland, Arthur, Pvt. 1cl., Hq. 354th Inf	11- 2
Copeland, John M., Pvt., C, 356th Inf	9-14
Corey, Samuel R., Mech., B, 353rd Inf	9- 2
Corneilison, Roscoe S., Pvt. 1cl., Hq. Det., 314th Eng	9-25
Cornell, Ralph W., Pvt., A, 354th Inf	11- 1
Cotter, Charles F., Pvt., A, 314th Eng	11- 4
Cottier, Eddie, Pvt., I, 353rd Inf	10-23
Coughlin, Leo J., Corp., D, 341st M. G. Bn	11- 1
Coursey, Henry, Pvt., A, 342nd F. A	
Cox, Charles E., Pvt. 1cl., C, 355th Inf	11- 5
Coxon, Wayne, Sgt., A, 356th Inf	11-11
Craig, John R., Pvt. 1cl., A, 342nd F. A	
Cram, Alfred P., Pvt., C, 342nd M. G. Bn	9-19
Cranefield, Benjamin Franklin, Pvt., Hq. 355th Inf	11- 2
Creal, Russell J., Cook, E, 356th Inf	11-11
Crews, Wm. E., D, 342nd F. A	
Crigger, Clifford, Pvt., E, 356th Inf	10- 7
Crosno, Sherman A., Pvt., C, 356th Inf	11- 3
Crumbs, Oliver, Pvt., D, 355th Inf	10- 6
Cruzan, Jacob L., Pvt. 1cl., M. G. Co., 355th Inf	9-26
Culbertson, Cary H., Corp., L, 353rd Inf	11- 3
Cummings, James H., Sgt., G, 353rd Inf	11- 1
Cunningham, Louis R., Pvt. 1cl., 355th Amb. Co	8- 9
Curran, Mike F., Pvt., D, 353rd Inf	9-18
Curry, John David, Pvt., Hq. 178th Inf. Brig	11- 9
Curtis, Francis W., Pvt., B, 353rd Inf	10- 2
Curtis, George F., Pvt., I, 353rd Inf	9-13
Curtiss, Lyle L., Corp., A, 355th Inf	9-16
Czermiak, Max Frank, Pvt. 1cl., L, 356th Inf	9-12
Dahlin, Rolland E., Corp., E, 314th Sup. Tr	8-23
Dale, George B., Pvt., C, 341st M. G. Bn	9-27
Daniels, Francis L., Corp., H, 353rd Inf	9-13
Dannerik, John M., Sgt., K, 353rd Inf	10-30
Darring, Ralph H., Pvt., C, 342nd M. G. Bn	11- 6
Daum, Henry Wm., Pvt. 1cl., M. G. Co., 353rd Inf	9-19
Davidson, John, Pvt., M. G. Co., 353rd Inf	10-29
Davis, Deb, Pvt., M, 356th Inf	10-24
Davis, Louis E., Pvt., I, 353rd Inf	11- 1
Davis, Thorpe, Corp., H, 353rd Inf	9-12
Dawson, Ernest L., Pvt., C, 355th Inf	11- 4
Day, Arthur L., Pvt., C, 353rd Inf	8-10
Day, Howard E., Sgt., A, 355th Inf	11- 5
Decker, James M., Pvt., M, 355th Inf	9-15
De Feo, Michael S., Pvt., I, 354th Inf	9-20
Deitz, Herman, Pvt., A, 341st M. G. Bn	11- 2
Delgado, Jose Ignacio, Pvt. 1cl., A, 314th Eng	9-13
Delker, Henry W., Corp., K, 353rd Inf	11- 1
Demnio, Dominico, Pvt., G, 354th Inf	11-15
Demonbrum, Roy, Pvt., L, 354th Inf	10-31
Dempsey, John F., Pvt., L, 353rd Inf	9-15
Demski, Frank H., Pvt., B, 353rd Inf	10-22
Dopperschmidt, Seraphine, Corp., M, 353rd Inf	10-22

Name, Rank, Company, Organization	Date 1918
Devine, Nancy L., Corp., D, 356th Inf	9-13
Dewey, Walter, Corp., C, 314th Amm. Tr	11- 9
Didway, Vile, Pvt., I, 355th Inf	11- 6
Diediker, Elmer J., Corp., F, 353rd Inf	9-12
Dietz, Edward W. A., Pvt. 1cl., F, 314th Eng	11- 9
Dill, Frank, Pvt., E, 354th Inf	11-10
Dillon, Francis Marion, Sgt., Hq. 356th Inf	11- 8
Dimond, Roy G., Pvt., K, 355th Inf	9-15
Dixon, Charles H., Corp., K, 355th Inf	9-13
Dobson, Otto S., Pvt., Hq. 355th Inf	11- 5
Dodge, Bayard A., Corp., E, 355th Inf	10-21
Donnelly, William, Pvt., C, 314th M. P	11- 8
Dorn, Chester C., Pvt., K, 354th Inf	10- 3
Dortland, Herbert, Pvt., G, 353rd Inf	9-12
Douds, Edwin E., Sgt., E, 356th Inf	11-11
Dowdy, James L., Mech., L, 354th Inf	9-24
Dozer, Otis V., Sgt., F, 353rd Inf	11- 3
Dreckshage, Roy E., Sgt., I, 354th Inf	10-28
Driver, Moses, Pvt. 1cl., B, 341st M. G. Bn	11- 7
Duda, Michael, Pvt., G, 354th Inf	11- 2
Dugan, John L., Pvt., B, 353rd Inf	10-24
Dugan, Thomas L., Pvt., D, 314th Eng	10- 4
Dugger, Bert L., Pvt. 1cl., G, 353rd Inf	9-13
Dunavent, Virgil, Pvt., A, 355th Inf	10- 4
Duncan, Clifford, Pvt., C, 342nd M. G. Bn	11- 5
Duncan, William Henry, Pvt., B, 354th Inf	11- 1
Dupaquier, Maynier, Pvt., L, 355th Inf	11- 5
Duplen, Joseph, Pvt., E, 353rd Inf	9-29
Duren, George, Pvt., M. G. Co., 358th Inf	10-26
Durst, Alfred Jacob, Pvt., L, 354th Inf	9-25
Dusheko, Peter William, Pvt., C, 354th Inf	11- 1
Duss, Leonard A., Pvt., L, 353rd Inf	11- 3
Duvic, Joseph Ewing, Corp., L, 355th Inf	9-13
Dvorak, Fred Albert, Pvt., G, 354th Inf	11- 2
Dybvig, Helmer A., Pvt., M. G. Co., 355th Inf	11- 9
Echols, Olin, Pvt., Hq. 355th Inf	11- 6
Eck, Ray B., Sgt., D, 353rd Inf	10- 8
Eckerd, Thomas H., Pvt. 1cl., A, 342nd M. G. Bn	10- 5
Edmisten, Jesse N., Corp., D, 355th Inf	9-13
Edmonds, William L., Pvt., A, 355th Inf	11- 5
Eichelberg, Fred John, Pvt., F, 356th Inf	9-21
Eimers, Henry, Pvt. 1cl., B, 342nd M. G. Bn	11-11
Eipperle, Arthur G., Pvt. 1cl., C, 341st M. G. Bn	10-25
Eisenstein, Jacob, Corp., M, 354th Inf	9-15
Ellis, Monroe, Pvt. 1cl., A, 314th Amm. Tr	10-12
Ellwanger, Carl S., Pvt., B, 353rd Inf	10-22
Elmer, Lee, Pvt. 1cl., F, 355th Inf	9-10
Elwood, Ben Oliver, Pvt. 1cl., K, 356th Inf	9-14
Emrick, Alva E., Pvt., K, 355th Inf	9-12
Engberg, David E., Corp., K, 353rd Inf	9-18
Ennis, James O., Pvt., D, 341st M. G. Bn	10- 2
Erhard, Clymer O., Pvt. 1cl., K, 355th Inf	9-14
Erickson, Matt, Pvt., I, 353rd Inf	11- 3
Erle, Francis A., Pvt. 1cl., M. G. Co., 353rd Inf	10-29
Ervin, Jesse J., Pvt., D, 356th Inf	9-12
Eskildson, Sigurd E., Pvt., C, 341st M. G. Bn	10-25
Essary, Sherman E., Pvt., B, 354th Inf	10- 5
Estill, Coy F., Pvt., A, 356th Inf	10-25
Evans, George C., Pvt. 1cl., K, 355th Inf	11- 4
Exline, Riley R., Pvt., B, 353rd Inf	9-13
Eymann, Will K., Pvt., H, 355th Inf	11-11
Farbelow, August H., Pvt., E, 354th Inf	11- 3
Faris, Claude C., Corp., A, 356th Inf	10-25
Farmer, Samuel D., 1st Sgt., G, 353rd Inf	9-12
Farrington, John E., Corp., K, 354th Inf	11- 2
Faulconer, Charles C., Corp., M, 353rd Inf	9-30
Fauth, Charles M., Corp., G, 354th Inf	11- 2
Featherston, William, Pvt., G, 356th Inf	10- 5
Feeley, Walter L., Pvt., F, 353rd Inf	11- 1
Feeney, Harold Patrick, Pvt., Hq. 356th Inf	11- 5
Feeney, Joseph M., Pvt., B, 353rd Inf	9-13
Fegley, William J., Corp., K, 355th Inf	9-14
Fehrman, Ervin J., Pvt. 1cl., E, 353rd Inf	11- 8
Fellows, George, Pvt. 1cl., K, 355th Inf	9-13
Ferguson, Frank, Pvt., K, 353rd Inf	10-22
Ferguson, Robert T., Pvt. 1cl., B, 353rd Inf	9-12
Fett, Harry G., Pvt. 1cl., H, 354th Inf	11- 2
Fickes, Orvin Emmett, Pvt. 1cl., Hq. 355th Inf	11- 4
Fields, Hiram, Pvt., E, 314th Eng	11- 4
Fink, Ray O., Corp., G, 342nd M. G. Bn	9-12
Finley, Tillman R., Pvt., E, 354th Inf	11- 2
Finnigan, James Francis, Pvt. 1cl., G, 355th Inf	9-13
Fishbach, William J., Cook, C, 354th Inf	10-28
Fisher, Harry E., Pvt., Hq. 353rd Inf	9-13
Fisher, James, Sgt., E, 355th Inf	9-14
Fisher, John L., Corp., K, 353rd Inf	9-12
Fite, Clyde L., Pvt., G, 355th Inf	11- 6
Fitzpatrick, James Timothy, Corp., B, 341st M. G. Bn	9-14
Fleming, Robert W., Pvt., L, 353rd Inf	9-14

Name, Rank, Company, Organization	Date 1918
Flohr, William J., Pvt. 1cl., H, 354th Inf	9-11
Flood, Olof, Pvt., M, 356th Inf	9-15
Fly, William F., Pvt. 1cl, C, 355th Inf	9-13
Flynn, Cornelius T., Corp., B, 354th Inf	9-15
Follis, Earl C., Sgt., A, 341st M. G. Bn	9-15
Follis, Robert H., Pvt., A, 355th Inf	9-15
Foote, Lawrence, Corp., A, 353rd Inf	10-28
Ford, Walter W., Pvt., B, 354th Inf	11- 1
Foss, Lewis H., Pvt., H, 356th Inf	11-11
Foster, Herbert, Pvt., M. G. Co., 353rd Inf	9-16
Foust, Walter Bee, Cook, Hq. 355th Inf	11- 8
Fowler, Fred L., Pvt., C, 342nd M. G. Bn	9-15
Fox, Edgar C., Pvt., H, 356th Inf	9-21
Frechette, Arthur S., Pvt., A, 355th Inf	11- 5
Freeman, Earl A., Pvt. 1cl., H, 353rd Inf	9-14
Fretwell, Hurley B., Pvt. 1cl., K, 354th Inf	10-24
Fritsch, Raymond J., Pvt., H, 353rd Inf	9-18
Fugate, Bud, Pvt., E, 356th Inf	11-11
Fuller, John, Pvt., C, 354th Inf	10-23
Funk, Jesse N., Pvt., L, 354th Inf	10-31
Funk, Ralph E., Bugler, K, 353rd Inf	11- 2
Gallegos, Benjamin, Pvt., H, 353rd Inf	9-18
Galloway, Howard E., Pvt., F, 353rd Inf	9-13
Gammons, Hull A., Pvt., G, 356th Inf	11- 6
Gann, Adam S., Sgt., A, 342nd M. G. Bn	11- 1
Garduino, Manuel F., Pvt., B, 355th Inf	9-12
Garnier, Alfred, Pvt., B, 353rd Inf	10-28
Gartzke, Milo A., Pvt., Hq. 353rd Inf	11- 1
Garrett, Nora R., Corp., H, 354th Inf	9-20
Garrison, Charles, Pvt., Hq. Troops, 89th Div	10-19
Garrison, Russell L., Sgt., M, 356th Inf	9-17
Gates, Claude, Pvt., B, 355th Inf	11- 4
Gedroics, Mikalaj, Pvt., B, 355th Inf	11- 3
Gehrke, Ferdinand W., Pvt., B, 353rd Inf	10-22
Gerety, Nicholas C., Corp., I, 353rd Inf	9-16
German, Edward F., Corp., K, 355th Inf	9-12
Gervais, Alphonse, Pvt., L, 353rd Inf	10-22
Geyer, William S., Pvt., G, 353rd Inf	11- 5
Gibson, Thomas A., Pvt., Hq. Det., 314th Eng	10-25
Gilbert, Robert L., Pvt., C, 356th Inf	9-16
Gilham, Charles B., Sgt., H, 353rd Inf	11- 1
Gill, Lew W., Corp., H, 353rd Inf	9-14
Gill, William, Pvt. 1cl., F, 355th Inf	8-17
Gillen, Harry E., Sgt., M. G. Co., 353rd Inf	9-18
Ginakis, William George, Pvt., M, 355th Inf	9-15
Gipson, Henry W., Pvt., A, 340th F. A	10- 4
Glasgow, Lloyd M., Pvt. 1cl., K, 353rd Inf	9-18
Glenn, Thomas J., Pvt., L, 355th Inf	11- 5
Gmiech, Albert G., Pvt., H, 353rd Inf	10-25
Godbey, Lyle B., Sgt., M. G. Co., 354th Inf	10-22
Godlewski, Vincent, Pvt., C, 356th Inf	11-11
Goforth, Albert J., Pvt., K, 355th Inf	11-10
Goldsbury, Leslie Louis, Pvt. 1cl., D, 342nd M. G. Bn.	11- 9
Gompf, Albert H., Pvt., E, 314th Eng	9-19
Gonzales, Clotario, Pvt., E, 356th Inf	11-11
Goodman, Alma D., Pvt. 1cl., F, 355th Inf	10-22
Goodrich, Orrie Lester, Pvt., G, 355th Inf	9-12
Gorda, Charles, Pvt. 1cl., D, 354th Inf	11- 1
Gordelchuk, Anton, Pvt., E, 354th Inf	10-25
Gorcham, Charles R., Pvt., M, 355th Inf	10- 1
Gorman, Leland, Pvt., C, 341st M. G. Bn	10-26
Goshen, Edward E., Pvt. 1cl., H, 354th Inf	11- 1
Goss, Corbett, Pvt., C, 354th Inf	9-13
Gossitt, Marion B., Pvt., F, 354th Inf	11- 2
Gould, George E., Pvt. 1cl., B, 342nd M. G. Bn	11-11
Gowan, George O., Pvt., A, 341st M. G. Bn	9-15
Gowdy, Jackson C., Sgt., B, 355th Inf	9-15
Grabowski, Gustav, Pvt., Hq. 356th Inf	11- 1
Graham, Charles, Pvt., H, 355th Inf	10-21
Graham, John J., Pvt., B, 353rd Inf	9-18
Grant, Vern J., Pvt., H, 354th Inf	11-11
Graves, Ansel Edward, Pvt. 1cl., L, 355th Inf	9-18
Greeley, Josh B., Pvt., A, 340th F. A	10- 4
Green, Christopher B., Pvt., B, 342nd M. G. Bn	11- 1
Green, Harry D., Corp., M, 355th Inf	11- 5
Green, James R., Pvt., D, 341st Inf	10-29
Green, Wallace C., Pvt., D, 355th Inf	11- 5
Greenberg, Isadore, Pvt., M, 356th Inf	11-11
Greenstreet, Archie M., Pvt., B, 353rd Inf	10-24
Greenwood, Edward F., Pvt., D, 314th Eng	8-13
Grefarud, Carl O., Pvt., E, 353rd Inf	11- 1
Gregory, Harry Edgar, Pvt., Hq. 355th Inf	9-15
Gribbin, Christopher S., Bugler, M. G. Co., 353rd Inf.	9-18
Grieser, Frank, Pvt., I, 355th Inf	9-12
Griffiths, Claud A., Pvt., A, 355th Inf	11- 5
Grindemann, Herbert A. R., Pvt. 1cl., D, 355th Inf.	11- 5
Grisham, Herbert A., Pvt., M. G. Co., 354th Inf	9- 8
Groff, Jacob R., Pvt., H, 355th Inf	9-18
Groh, Arthur, Pvt., I, 354th Inf	9- 6
Grosh, George A., Pvt., Hq. 355th Inf	9-17
Gruendeman, Henry A., Pvt., D, 354th Inf	11- 1
Gryniewicz, Ludwig, Pvt., G, 354th Inf	10-25
Gust, Urban J., Wag., A, 314th Eng	9-17
Hageleen, Aaron W., Sgt., M. G. Co., 355th Inf	9- 8
Hagmann, John T., 1st Sgt., E, 314th Amm. Tr	10- 6
Hahn, Fred C., Pvt., C, 314th San. Tr	11- 5
Haley, Louis, Pvt., L, 356th Inf	9-13
Hall, McClure Elliott, Pvt. 1cl., I, 354th Inf	9-28
Hall, Ward Avery, Pvt., B, 355th Inf	11- 6
Halloran, Francis Arthur, Corp., B, 355th Inf	9-12
Halter, Albert, Pvt., 1cl., D, 354th Inf	9-24
Halter, Ernest George, Pvt., B, 355th Inf	9-15
Hamernik, Frank, Pvt., M. D., 353rd Inf	9-12
Hamilton, Howard J., Pvt. 1cl., H, 355th Inf	9-12
Hamlett, Arthur, Pvt., F, 314th Eng	9-17
Hamm, Chester C., Pvt., F, 353rd Inf	11- 1
Hammerbacker, Walter, Corp., Hq. 354th Inf	9-14
Hammerlun, Wm. H., Pvt. 1cl., C, 341st M. G. Bn.	11- 1
Hancock, Joel H., Pvt., C, 356th Inf	9-12
Hanline, Alva C., Pvt., E, 356th Inf	9-13
Harkins, John F., Pvt., H, 353rd Inf	9-16
Harkness, John W., Pvt., B, 354th Inf	11- 2
Harman, Amaziah Z., Pvt., B, 341st M. G. Bn	10-28
Harp, Virgil F., Pvt., A, 354th Inf	9- 2
Harrell, Alfred H., Pvt., D, 342nd M. G. Bn	9-15
Harris, Andrew, Pvt., D, 341st M. G. Bn	11- 1
Harrison, William N., Pvt., A, 341st M. G. Bn	11- 1
Hartigan, Vincent E., Corp., L, 354th Inf	11- 1
Harvey, Nathaniel L., Pvt., H, 355th Inf	11-10
Harvey, William A., Pvt. 1cl., G, 353rd Inf	9-18
Haselwood, Leroy, Pvt., F, 353rd Inf	9-18
Hasenpflug, Paul, Pvt., A, 355th Inf	9-16
Haslouer, Joe A., Corp., H, 353rd Inf	9-12
Haugen, John C., Pvt., L, 355th Inf	9-14
Hauptli, Walter J., Pvt., E, 353rd Inf	9-12
Hause, Joseph A., Sgt., C, 356th Inf	11- 3
Hawk, Jesse J., Pvt., A, 340th M. G. Bn	9-15
Hayes, Harold P., Corp., Hq. 353rd Inf	9-22
Hayes, John, Cook, I, 356th Inf	11-11
Hayes, Stanley M., Pvt. 1cl., M. G. Co., 354th Inf.	9-15
Haynes, Pearl J., Pvt., G, 354th Inf	9- 8
Hays, Elijah H., Pvt., G, 353rd Inf	9-23
Hays, William, Corp., A, 356th Inf	9-21
Heckeler, Edward K., Pvt., A, 341st M. G. Bn	10-22
Hedegaard, William, Pvt 1cl., K, 353rd Inf	9-18
Hefner, Harry O., Pvt., A, 354th Inf	9-20
Hellner, Carl P., Sgt., C, 355th Inf	9-13
Hellyer, William, Pvt. 1cl., A, 356th Inf	8- 8
Helweg, Hugo W., Pvt., K, 353rd Inf	11- 1
Henderson, John, Pvt., I, 355th Inf	11- 8
Henderson, Vern L., Pvt., F, 356th Inf	11- 5
Hendrix, Alva B., Pvt., D, 341st M. G. Bn	9-10
Hendrix, George A., Corp., F, 354th Inf	10-21
Henke, Arthur, Pvt., L, 353rd Inf	10-22
Henkel, Harvey W., Pvt., L, 353rd Inf	10-29
Henley, Fielding B., Corp., A, 354th Inf	11- 2
Hennessy, Joseph B., 1st Sgt., D, 342nd M. G. Bn	9-15
Henry, George H., Pvt., C, 353rd Inf	10-22
Henson, Aaron C., Pvt., C, 355th Inf	9-13
Heusler, George J., Pvt., G, 355th Inf	11- 5
Herrera, Nemesio, Pvt., M. G. Co., 356th Inf	11- 8
Herrera, Osbaldo G., Pvt., M. D., 314th Amm. Tr	11- 9
Herring, Raymond A., Pvt., G., 355th Inf	10-25
Hershey, Earl P., Pvt., A, 356th Inf	10-28
Heynes, George Orin, Pvt., D, 342nd M. G. Bn	10- 6
Hill, Joseph B., Pvt., B, 353rd Inf	10-28
Hill, Rolland R., Pvt. 1cl., B, 341st M. G. Bn	10-24
Hillery, William, Pvt., L, 354th Inf	10-31
Hites, Raymond J., Corp., G, 354th Inf	10-21
Hobbs, Tonnie, Pvt., F, 353rd Inf	11- 5
Hoffmann, Charles, Pvt., L, 354th Inf	11- 1
Hoke, George, Pvt., D, 341st M. G. Bn	9-11
Holding, Edwin, Pvt., Hq. 353rd Inf	11- 5
Holland, Frank B., Pvt., B, 355th Inf	9-30
Holland, Frank D., Wag., Sup. Co., 355th Inf	9-29
Holy, Frank, Pvt., D, 342nd M. G. Bn	9-15
Holser, Fritz C., Pvt., D, 355th Inf	11- 5
Hood, Lincoln, Pvt., E, 353rd Inf	9-12
Hoopingarner, Zeno Herman, Wag., 314th Eng. Tr	9-20
Hopkins, Joseph J., Pvt. 1cl., H, 353rd Inf	9-12
Hoppe, Norbert M., Pvt., D, 354th Inf	10-20
Hopper, Carrol W., Pvt., K, 356th Inf	10- 6
Houltberg, Arthur T., Pvt., H, 353rd Inf	8-17
Howard, Irwin D., Pvt., K, 353rd Inf	11- 1
Howarth, George W., Pvt. 1cl., E, 356th Inf	11- 6
Huddleston, Merril D., Pvt., L, 353rd Inf	9- 4
Huebner, Arthur Christ., Pvt., Sup. Co., 356th Inf	11- 4
Huebner, William J., Corp., E, 355th Inf	9-14

Name, Rank, Company, Organization	Date 1918
Huff, Amos E., Pvt., F, 314th Eng	11- 1
Huffman, Wilber L., Wag., Sup. Co., 355th Inf	10-28
Hughart, Charles H., Pvt. 1cl., A, 354th Inf	11- 6
Hugh.s, Charles G., Pvt., I, 354th Inf	8-24
Hughes, James Henry, Pvt., E, 314th Eng	10-27
Hundley, Raymond, Sgt., F, 353rd Inf	9-18
Hunt, Harry D., Pvt., C, 356th Inf	11- 8
Hutson, Ross E., Pvt. 1cl., F, 354th Inf	9-11
Hyland, John M., Pvt., B, 342nd M. G. Bn	11- 5
Hynek, Prokop J., Pvt. 1cl., C, 341st M. G. Bn	10-25
Hyronimus, Heiko, Pvt., G, 355th Inf	10-22
Imler, Chester M., Pvt., G, 356th Inf	11- 7
Irmisik, August, Sgt., M, 354th Inf	9-14
Jach, Lacy Benton, Pvt., Hq. 354th Inf	9-14
Jack, Roy Kenneth, Pvt., C, 353rd Inf	10- 2
Jackson, Thomas K., Corp., K, 355th Inf	9-13
Jackson, Willie Lee, Pvt., I, 356th Inf	9-16
Jacobie, Lee M., Pvt., L, 353rd Inf	11- 3
Jacobs, Joseph A., Pvt., A, 354th Inf	11-26
Jacobson, Leslie E., Pvt., D, 354th Inf	9-20
Jacques, Lancelot B., Pvt., F, 353rd Inf	9-12
Jabubiak, Frank M., Pvt. 1cl., K, 355th Inf	9-14
Jamison, William Edgar, Pvt. 1cl., A, 353rd Inf	9-13
Jarrett, Lyon, Pvt., C, 354th Inf	9-27
Jereczek, Frank A., Pvt., K, 356th Inf	9-15
Jeffery, Sylvester, Pvt. 1cl., Hq. 355th Inf	9- 6
Jelinek, Rudolph J., Musc. 3cl., Hq. 355th Inf	10-25
Jenkins, Lester R., Pvt. 1cl., A, 356th Inf	9-26
Jenner, William B., Pvt. 1cl., D, 356th Inf	9-13
Jensen, Jens B., Pvt. 1cl., C, 341st M. G. Bn	11-11
Jepson, Chris, Pvt., M, 355th Inf	11- 5
Johnson, Albert, Pvt., B, 356th Inf	9-25
Johnson, Albert R., Corp., F, 353rd Inf	11-11
Johnson, Erford O., Pvt. 1cl., A, 341st M. G. Bn	9- 4
Johnson, Eskil E., Pvt., B, 353rd Inf	10-24
Johnson, Fred Eugene, Pvt. 1cl., F, 355th Inf	9-10
Johnson, Harold, Pvt., K, 353rd Inf	11- 1
Johnson, Nelson R., Pvt., K, 353rd Inf	11- 1
Johnson, Oscar T., Pvt. 1cl., A, 355th Inf	11- 5
Johnson, Randall A., Pvt. 1cl., L, 353rd Inf	8-28
Johnston, Henry E., Corp., M, 356th Inf	9-12
Jones, Hobart, Pvt., M. G Co., 356th Inf	8-27
Jones, James A., Pvt., G, 356th Inf	11- 5
Jones, Kelly C., Pvt., K, 354th Inf	10-22
Jordan, Arthur, Pvt., D, 355th Inf	11- 9
Jorgenson, Aage W., Pvt. 1cl., Hq. 356th Inf	9-13
Kain, Ray, Pvt., F, 356th Inf	11-11
Kamman, Wilton C., Pvt., C, 356th Inf	11-11
Kamradt, Walter L., Corp., D, 355th Inf	11- 5
Kamrath, William A., Corp., K, 354th Inf	10-28
Kane, Charles F., Pvt., D, 355th Inf	9-12
Kane, Hubert E., Pvt., M. G Co., 353rd Inf	9-12
Kane, Raymond J., Sgt., F, 355th Inf	9-16
Kanstrup, Peter, Pvt., F, 355th Inf	9-14
Kapfer, Charley D., Corp., A, 354th Inf	9-20
Karnes, Anthony E., Pvt. 1cl., M. G. Co., 353rd Inf	10-28
Karr, Floyd, Corp., A, 356th Inf	9-21
Kasner, Emil B., Pvt., C, 341st M. G. Bn	9-12
Kaune, William J., Pvt., E, 354th Inf	9-13
Kavanaugh, Herman Loyal, Corp., B, 341st M. G. Bn	11- 8
Keating, Michael W., Pvt., I, 354th Inf	11- 2
Keen, Allen T., Pvt., B, 356th Inf	9-12
Keith, William L., Corp., D, 356th Inf	10-24
Keller, John Grover, Pvt., K, 356th Inf	10-29
Kelly, Frederick, Pvt., A, 342nd F. A.	
Kelly, Patrick, Wag., D, 354th Inf	11-10
Kemblowski, John, Pvt., D, 356th Inf	9-13
Kemp, Charles O., Pvt., H, 353rd Inf	9-12
Kemp, Vincent K., Sgt., K, 314th Eng	10-27
Kennedy, Guy Houston, Pvt., M, 353rd Inf	11- 7
Kennedy, John Edward, Pvt., M. G. Co., 354th Inf	10-24
Kenning, Emell, Pvt. 1cl., Amb. Co., 354th Inf	11- 6
Kersey, Roy D., Pvt., G, 353rd Inf	9-26
Kershaw, Marsden, Pvt., E, 356th Inf	9-13
Kersting, George E., Sgt., E, 354th Inf	11- 2
Ketchem, Carl, Sgt., C, 356th Inf	9-16
Ketchum, Clinton Orval, Pvt., K, 356th Inf	10-30
Kettner, Arthur L., Pvt., H, 353rd Inf	9-12
Keulkes, George, Sgt., G, 354th Inf	9-20
Kice, Orville A., Pvt. 1cl., E, 353rd Inf	9-12
Kimbrough, Harry, Pvt., K, 356th Inf	9-12
Kimsey, John C., Cook, H, 353rd Inf	10-19
King, Elmer, Pvt., M, 353rd Inf	11- 1
King, Rufus, Pvt. 1cl., D, 341st M. G. Bn	11- 1
Kirk, Arthur, Sgt., A, 355th Inf	9-16
Kirkbridge, Emmons W., Pvt., L, 353rd Inf	9- 3
Kirkwood, Lester J., Pvt., B, 353rd Inf	10-26
Klabunde, Paul A., Pvt., D, 353rd Inf	9-27
Klenk, Frank R., Pvt. 1cl., M, 353rd Inf	11-11

Name, Rank, Company, Organization	Date 1918
Kleyboecker, Herbert G., Pvt., L, 354th Inf	10-29
Klein, John A., Corp., E, 356th Inf	9-13
Kilkunos, George, Pvt., F, 354th Inf	9-15
Kling, Fred, Pvt., G, 353rd Inf	9-19
Kloekser, Charles A., Sgt., Hq. 354th Inf	11-11
Knapp, Edward J., Pvt. 1cl., F, 356th Inf	11- 6
Knofler, James G., Pvt., M. G. Co., 356th Inf	9-12
Knopfel, William, Pvt., L, 356th Inf	11-11
Knowles, Clyde C., Sgt., D, 353rd Inf	9-11
Knox, James E., Sgt., F, 353rd Inf	9-12
Knox, James E, Sgt., F, 353rd Inf	11- 1
Knox, Robert, Pvt., M, 353rd Inf	9-17
Koeppel, August, Pvt. 1cl., F, 356th Inf	11- 6
Kohl, Phillip Andrew, Pvt., G, 354th Inf	9-15
Kohlman, Leo B., Pvt., B, 353rd Inf	10-22
Kohnen, Edward H., Pvt. 1cl., M, 354th Inf	11- 1
Kokenos, Harry, Pvt. 1cl., B, 353rd Inf	9-14
Kolatz, Michael, Pvt., G, 356th Inf	11- 6
Kountz, Erwin O., Pvt., Hq. 356th Inf	9-13
Krezcl, Bladau, Pvt., B, 355th Inf	11- 5
Kraettly, Benjamin H., Pvt. 1cl., K, 354th Inf	11- 2
Krellis, Tom T., Pvt., D, 356th Inf	10-22
Kreuter, Earl L., Corp., M, 356th Inf	11- 3
Krieser, George E., Pvt., G, 353rd Inf	9-24
Kritsellis, Nicolas G., Pvt., Sup. Co., 356th Inf	11- 9
Kritzer, Joseph William, Pvt., L, 355th Inf	9-18
Krueger, Walter H., Pvt. 1cl., K, 356th Inf	11-11
Kuhnert, Paul J., Pvt., G, 354th Inf	9-14
Kuhl, William Fred, Pvt., M, 354th Inf	11- 2
Kuhn, George A., Pvt., B, 356th Inf	11- 4
Kuhn, James R., Pvt., F, 355th Inf	9-14
Kuligowski, John, Corp., B, 354th Inf	11- 4
Kunstman, William A., Pvt., E, 353rd Inf	9-13
Kurtz, Charles F., Pvt., C, 341st M. G. Bn	10-25
Kivernes, Olger Arthur, Pvt., G, 355th Inf	9-17
Lamar, Lon, Cook, H, 356th Inf	11- 7
Lambert, Dallas, Pvt., K, 355th Inf	11- 5
LaMere, Lester, Pvt. 1cl., M, 356th Inf	9-13
Lamm, Charles L., Sgt., K, 353rd Inf	8-30
Lamond, James, Pvt., C, 353rd Inf	10-24
Lampe, Joseph G., Pvt., A, 355th Inf	11- 5
Lamprecht, Walter A., Pvt., G, 353rd Inf	8-15
Lanahan, George M., Corp., F. H., 355th Inf	10-31
Lancaster, Emmett W., Pvt., F, 356th Inf	11-11
Land, Ralph W., Pvt. 1cl., I, 354th Inf	11- 5
Langan, George E., Pvt., H, 354th Inf	11-11
Lanoue, Eugene H., Pvt., E, 353rd Inf	9-14
Lapka, Jacob, Pvt., K, 356th Inf	11-11
Larew, Otto Estel, Pvt. 1cl., M. D., 353rd Inf	10-28
LaRose, Theodore, Pvt., B, 314th Amm. Tr	
Larsen, Hans L., Pvt., B, 353rd Inf	11-25
Larsen, Hans A., Pvt., C, 353rd Inf	10-22
Larsen, Lars A., Wag., G, 314th Amm. Tr	9-28
Larson, Emil L., Sup. Sgt., K, 353rd Inf	9-19
Larson, John E., Pvt., I, 353rd Inf	9-20
Larson, Ole E., Mech., D, 356th Inf	11- 7
Larson, Oscar M., Pvt. 1cl., D, 341st M. G. Bn	9- 8
Larson, Walter W., Pvt. 1cl., L, 356th Inf	11-11
Laskaris, Nicholas, Pvt., D, 341st Eng	8-22
Lauer, Joseph Allen, Corp., F, 356th Inf	11- 6
Law, Clarence G., Pvt., Hq. 353rd Inf	9-18
Law, Ernest F., Pvt., E, 354th Inf	10-20
Lawrence, James R., Pvt., A, 355th Inf	10-21
Lawson, Ernest L., Pvt., F, 356th Inf	11-11
Lawson, Rufus H., Pvt. 1cl., H, 356th Inf	11-11
Lay, Arthur M., Pvt., A, 342nd M. G. Bn	10-28
Lee, Wilfred C., 1st Sgt., G, 356th Inf	9-12
Leeper, George W., Mech., A, 356th Inf	9-13
Leeper, Harry, Pvt., B, 355th Inf	11- 4
Leiker, Jacob F., Pvt. 1cl., K, 353rd Inf	9-13
Lemon, Walter D., Pvt., B, 353rd Inf	10-26
Lemons, Henry D., Pvt. 1cl., A, 356th Inf	11-11
Lencioni, Louis J., Pvt., D, 314th Eng	9- 5
Lenhard, Harry W., Pvt., C, 341st M. G. Bn	10-25
Lentner, Adolph F., Pvt. 1cl., E, 353rd Inf	9-18
Leopold, John F., Pvt., C, 353rd Inf	9-27
Lewis, Ernest C., Bugler, D, 356th Inf	9-13
Lewis, Florus V., Pvt., F, 356th Inf	11-11
Lewis, Thomas, Pvt., F, 314th Eng	10- 1
Liebman, Sam, Pvt., E, 354th Inf	11- 2
Liftchild, George E., Pvt., Sup. Co., 354th Inf	11- 2
Light, Wm., Pvt., E, 342nd F. A.	
Lincoln, Samuel R., Pvt., Hq. 356th Inf	9-13
Lindsey, Aaron F., Pvt. 1cl., K, 354th Inf	11- 2
Lindsey, Paul J., Pvt. 1cl., F, 353rd Inf	10-26
Lindsey, Sherman A., Pvt., K, 356th Inf	9-14
Lindstrom, Leon H., Sgt., B, 354th Inf	11- 1
Lloyd, Vaughn B., Bugler, F, 353rd Inf	9-12
Lockard, Carl A., Corp., D, 353rd Inf	9-12

Name, Rank, Company, Organization	Date 1918
Lockas, Harry C., Pvt., G, 353rd Inf	9-26
Lokofski, Michal, Pvt., G, 353rd Inf	9-12
Long, Harvey Joyce, Pvt., M. G. Co., 354th Inf	10-27
Lonog, Charles C., Corp., I, 356th Inf	9-16
Lopp, John R., Pvt. 1cl., L, 354th Inf	10-28
Loutsch, Henry, Pvt., K, 355th Inf	11- 5
Lovato, Eusebio H., Pvt., E, 356th Inf	11-11
Loveless, Arlington Hights, Pvt., M. G. Co., 355th Inf	11- 1
Lovett, Ernest B., Pvt., B, 355th Inf	11- 4
Lukasik, Frank, Pvt., Hq. 355th Inf	11-11
Luking, William, Pvt., B, 356th Inf	10-22
Lund, Earl A., Pvt. 1cl., G, 353rd Inf	11- 5
Lundahl, Gunnard, Pvt., L, 356th Inf	11-11
Lusk, Earl R., Pvt. 1cl., C, 353rd Inf	9-12
Lusnie, Joseph, Pvt., M, 354th Inf	11- 2
Luttmann, Hugo W., Pvt., C, 342nd M. G. Bn	11- 5
Lynch, Jesse Clifford, Pvt., L, 356th Inf	9-12
Lyons, Archie O., Corp., L, 353rd Inf	8-30
Lyons, William M., Pvt., G, 353rd Inf	9-12
Madden, Paul, Corp., M. G. Co., 353rd Inf	9-25
Madrid, Juan E., Pvt., D, 356th Inf	10-25
Maestas, Juan I., Pvt. 1cl., H, 356th Inf	11-11
Makemson, Emil A., Pvt., H, 354th Inf	11-11
Malcom, Robert, Pvt., A, 342nd M. G. Bn	10-26
Malinowich, Maurice B., Pvt., H, 354th Inf	11- 5
Mall, Anthony, Sgt., I, 353rd Inf	11- 1
Mallory, William A., Pvt., A, 353rd Inf	9-14
Malm, Emil, Pvt. 1cl., C, 355th Inf	9-13
Malone, Floyd, Pvt. 1cl., K, 355th Inf	10-28
Maloney, Gus T., Corp., H, 353rd Inf	9-18
Manject, William, Pvt. 1cl., D, 353rd Inf	9- 7
Manne, Tony, Pvt., H, 353rd Inf	9-12
Manning, Robert E., Pvt. 1cl., B, 355th Inf	11- 5
Manning, Thomas M., Pvt., F. H. 354, 314th San. Tr.	10-30
Manning, William J., Pvt., H, 354th Inf	10-28
Mansholt, Charles, Pvt., D, 355th Inf	11- 5
Mantzeoros, Sotereos, Pvt., I, 356th Inf	11-11
Mareus, Luther C., Pvt. 1cl., C, 355th Inf	9-15
Marks, Matthew, Pvt., E, 353rd Inf	10-18
Marks, William F., Pvt., E, 314th Eng	11- 2
Mart, Charles C., Pvt., I, 355th Inf	9-12
Martello, Joseph J., Pvt. 1cl., A, 314th Eng	10-26
Martilla, Abram, Pvt., F, 355th Inf	10-29
Martin, Harry C., Pvt., H, 353rd Inf	9-14
Martin, Mark S., Pvt., K, 355th Inf	9-16
Martin, Patrick, Pvt., B, 342nd F. A	....
Martin, Weldon S., Corp., C, 354th Inf	10-28
Martinez, Fidel F., Pvt. 1cl., M. G. Co., 353rd Inf	10-22
Martinez, Jose M., Pvt., I, 355th Inf	9-16
Mason, Charlie, Corp., K, 355th Inf	9-13
Massey, Elijah F., Corp., D, 356th Inf	9-13
Matlick, Scott, Pvt., E, 354th Inf	11- 3
Matson, Andrew O., Pvt., K, 353rd Inf	11- 2
Matthews, John F., Pvt., H, 355th Inf	11-10
Maurer, Elmer J., Pvt., Hq. 353rd Inf	9-13
Maurer, Frank J., Pvt., B, 354th Inf	11- 1
Maxwell, Charley T., Pvt., L, 353rd Inf	11- 1
May, Guy C., Pvt., H, 353rd Inf	9-18
McAllister, Luther, Pvt., H, 353rd Inf	11- 5
McCallum, John A., Pvt., D, 355th Inf	11- 9
McCarl, Roy, Pvt., M, 355th Inf	9-14
McCarthy, John C., Pvt. 1cl., C, 341st M. G. Bn	9-12
McCartney, Walter H., Pvt., B, 314th Sup. Tr	11- 2
McCashland, Ivan L., Sgt., M, 355th Inf	9-12
McCoy, John F., Pvt., E, 355th Inf	10-22
McCoy, Ralph S., Corp., F, 356th Inf	11-11
McCrumb, George E., Wag., Sup. Co., 355th Inf	9-16
McCullah, Ira F., Wag., A, 340th M. G. Bn	9-16
McDonald, Edward P., Sgt., C, 341st M. G. Bn	9-12
McDonald, Steve, Pvt., Sup. Co., 354th Inf	11- 1
McDonald, Thomas, Pvt., M. G. Co., 354th Inf	10-24
McGarvey, John H., Corp., E, 356th Inf	11-11
McGee, Harry T., Pvt., B, 314th F. S. Bn	10- 1
McGill, Robert C., Pvt., A, 355th Inf	11-11
McHenry, Foster B., 1st Sgt., M, 356th Inf	9-13
McIntosh, Howard H., Pvt. 1cl., M, 355th Inf	10-21
McKay, Willis, Pvt., K, 353rd Inf	9-12
McKee, Robert J., Pvt., D, 355th Inf	9-13
McKinney, Joe V., D, 342nd F. A	
McKinney, Riley E., Pvt., L, 353rd Inf	9-14
McLaughin, Charles W., Cook, E, 356th Inf	11-11
McLaughlin, Fred A., Pvt., D, 353rd Inf	9-13
McLean, James B., Corp., H, 353rd Inf	9-12
McPhee, Charles A., Sgt., C, 314th F. S. Bn	10-25
McPherson, George D., Pvt. 1cl., F, 354th Inf	10-21
McQuistan, Edward W., Corp., F, 355th Inf	8-15
McTernan, John S., Pvt. 1cl., L, 355th Inf	9-12
Meador, Ernest H., Pvt., H, 354th Inf	11- 1
Medina, Nicolas, Corp., M, 356th Inf	9-13
Meier, Carl J., Pvt., C, 314th Amm. Tr	10-26
Meimer, Edward J., Pvt. 1cl., B, 355th Inf	9-15
Melonas, John, Pvt., H, 353rd Inf	11- 1
Merritt, Glenn G., Pvt., E, 353rd Inf	11- 1
Meyer, August, Corp., C, 355th Inf	11- 5
Meyer, Mike W., Pvt., Hq. 353rd Inf	10-26
Meyer, Paul E., Pvt. 1cl., E, 354th Inf	11- 2
Meyers, Henry C., Pvt., Hq. 354th Inf	11-11
Meyers, John, Pvt., B, 355th Inf	10-20
Meyers, Peter J., Pvt. 1cl., E, 353rd Inf	11- 1
Miche, Edgar L., Pvt., L, 354th Inf	11- 1
Mikolajczak, John, Pvt., C, 356th Inf	10-28
Milenbach, Maurice, Pvt., F, 353rd Inf	11- 3
Miles, Gilbert H., Pvt., H, 353rd Inf	9-18
Miles, Gilbert H., Pvt., H, 353rd Inf	11- 3
Miles, Loyd D., Pvt., F, 314th M. S. Tr	11- 5
Miller, Alvin H., Pvt., F, 353rd Inf	11- 3
Millr, Frank, Wagoner, B, 314th Amm. Tr	...
Miller, George, Pvt., A, 340th M. G. Bn	11- 5
Miller, Jarvis C., Pvt. 1cl., G, 356th Inf	11-11
Miller, Joe A., Pvt., M. G. Co., 353rd Inf	9-16
Miller, Lamoine C. F., Pvt., F, 354th Inf	10-23
Miller, Otto E., Pvt., L, 354th Inf	10-23
Mills, Lewis R., Pvt. 1cl., B, 354th Inf	11- 1
Minnick, Herbert L., Pvt., A, 341st M. G. Bn	11- 1
Minnis, Joseph, Corp., E, 342nd F. A	
Minogue, Eugene V., Pvt. 1cl., D, 355th Inf	11- 5
Mishlove, Henry, Pvt., G, 354th Inf	11- 2
Mitchell, James R., Pvt., Hq. 354th Inf	11- 3
Mitchell, John A., Pvt., G, 353rd Inf	9-12
Mitchell, John A., Pvt., G, 353rd Inf	11- 3
Mitchell, Lawrence D., Pvt., D, 355th Inf	11- 5
Montagne, Rene E., Corp., C, 342nd M. G. Bn	9-29
Montoya, Estoban, Pvt., F, 355th Inf	10-22
Moody, William H., Pvt., A, 353rd Inf	10-22
Moorberg, Paul G., Corp., H, 355th Inf	9-15
Moore, Clinton A., Bugler, B, 354th Inf	10- 1
Moore, Jonathan B., Pvt. 1cl., K, 353rd Inf	11- 1
Moore, Leslie C., Pvt., L, 355th Inf	9-20
Moore, Nelson G., Pvt., A, 356th Inf	10-23
Moreland, Arthur E., Pvt. 1cl., D, 354th Inf	11- 1
Morris, Ross E., Sgt., M. G. Co., 355th Inf	11- 3
Morrison, Charles S., Corp., L, 354th Inf	10-31
Morrison, Ralph E., Pvt., Hq. 355th Inf	10-21
Mortenson, Martin A., Pvt., L, 354th Inf	11- 1
Mortensen, Weaver J., Pvt. 1cl., Hq. 355th Inf	9-15
Morton, Robert L., Corp., Hq. 355th Inf	9-23
Mueth, Joseph J., Pvt., C, 355th Inf	11-11
Muhlenfeld, William, Pvt. 1cl., L, 354th Inf	10-21
Mullarkey, William, Corp., C, 314th Eng	10-25
Mullen, Charles R., Pvt. 1cl., B, 355th Inf	9-12
Mullett, George, Pvt. 1cl., C, 314th F. S. Bn	10-29
Munson, DeForrest, Pvt. 1cl., H, 355th Inf	9-13
Murphy, Daniel C., Pvt., D, 355th Inf	9-12
Murphy, James, Pvt. 1cl., H, 354th Inf	11-11
Murphy, John, Pvt., G, 354th Inf	9-15
Murphy, John F., Pvt., H, 354th Inf	11-11
Murray, Harrison A., Pvt., G, 354th Inf	9-14
Mutchie, Lawrence L., Corp., H, 354th Inf	10-25
Naccarato, John, Pvt., I, 355th Inf	9-16
Nass, Julius H., Pvt., C, 353rd Inf	11- 1
Navarra, Jim, Pvt., D, 341st M. G. Bn	9-12
Navarra, Jim, Pvt., D, 341st M. G. Bn	10-28
Nelsen, Otto F., Corp., D, 356th Inf	9-23
Nelson, Alfred, Corp., A, 341st M. G. Bn	9-13
Nelson, Alfred, Pvt. 1cl., C, 341st M. G. Bn	9-14
Nelson, Carl E., Pvt. 1cl., F, 314th Eng	9-24
Nelson, Casper L., Pvt., D, 350th Inf	11-11
Nelson, Ernest W., Pvt. 1cl., H, 353rd Inf	9-16
Nelson, Frank J., Pvt., H, 355th Inf	11- 1
Nelson, John S., Pvt., M, 356th Inf	9-12
Nelson, Martin, Corp., M, 353rd Inf	11- 3
Nester, William J., Cook, G, 353rd Inf	11- 6
Nettles, Sam, Pvt., D, 356th Inf	11- 7
Newman, Grover C., Pvt., M. G. Co., 354th Inf	10-27
Newman, Jesse, Corp., A, 314th Eng	9-12
Newport, James J., Pvt. 1cl., A, 341st M. G. Bn	9-29
Newport, Mark J., Pvt., H, 356th Inf	9-16
Newton, James E., Pvt., E, 355th Inf	11-10
Nicodemus, George, Corp., H, 354th Inf	11-11
Niehaus, Herman J., Sgt., E, 354th Inf	11- 2
Noack, Paul E., Sgt., A, 341st M. G. Bn	11- 1
Norman, William S., Wag., Sup. Co., 355th Inf	9-16
Novak, Jos. J., Corp., Hq. 342nd F. A	
Oellien, William H., Pvt. 1cl., D, 354th Inf	11- 1
Oertwich, Otto A., Pvt., H, 355th Inf	11- 8
Ohlemier, Bert H., Pvt., D, 353rd Inf	9- 7
Olesewicz, Mecyslaw, Pvt., E, 353rd Inf	10-19
Olsen, Alfred, Pvt., G, 355th Inf	9-17

Name, Rank, Company, Organization	Date 1918
Olson, Sigvold, Pvt. 1cl., M, 355th Inf	11-11
Olszewski, Vincent, Pvt., A, 314th M. S. Tr	10-29
Orndorff, Stanton, Pvt. 1cl., C, 341st M. G. Bn	11- 6
Osborn, Willie J., Pvt., G, 356th Inf	10- 5
O'Shaughnessy, John, Pvt., H, 355th Inf	10-28
Ost, Howard C., Sgt., L, 354th Inf	9-26
Oulcelt, Harry C., Pvt., C, 354th Inf	11-11
Overgaard, Oscar, Corp., B, 342nd M. G. Bn	11- 1
Owen, Allen H., Pvt. 1cl., C, 314th F. S. Bn	10-27
Owen, Ray A., Pvt. 1cl., B, 353rd Inf	11- 3
Owens, Carl L., Pvt., E, 354th Inf	10-21
Padilla, Tiodoro, Pvt., I, 356th Inf	11- 3
Paleska, Louis W., Pvt., B, 353rd Inf	10-27
Palm, Gustaf A., Pvt. 1cl., M, 356th Inf	9-12
Parker, Jim, Pvt., A, 314th Eng	10-26
Patton, John E., Pvt., E, 355th Inf	11- 9
Paul, Claude W., Pvt., Hq. 354th Inf	9-15
Paulk, Albert W., Pvt., B, 353rd Inf	9-13
Paulsen, Christian M., Pvt., K, 354th Inf	11-11
Pâwlowski, Wladislaw, Pvt., Hq. Det., 314th Eng	9-25
Payne, Ernest H., Pvt., E, 354th Inf	9-20
Peet, Groucher, Corp., B, 353rd Inf	10-20
Peltier, Cyril M., Pvt., H, 353rd Inf	9-24
Penny, Orsmus N., Jr., Pvt., A, 356th Inf	10- 9
Perrett, Emilie, Pvt., H, 353rd Inf	9-18
Peters, Clifford C., Pvt. 1cl., D, 353rd Inf	10-29
Peters, John L., Pvt., C, 356th Inf	9-20
Peterson, Andrew, Pvt., E, 356th Inf	9-13
Peterson, Paul, Corp., C, 353rd Inf	9- 7
Peterson, Walter A., Pvt., Hq. 354th Inf	10-28
Petot, Alves, Wag., Sup. Co., 354th Inf	11- 2
Pettit, Amel L., Pvt., I, 356th Inf	11- 2
Peyton, Thomas, Pvt., L, 355th Inf	9-14
Phillips, Clark C., Sgt., D, 353rd Inf	9-15
Phillips, Frank L., Pvt. 1cl., L, 353rd Inf	9- 2
Phillipson, Victor R., Sgt., C, 355th Inf	11- 8
Piano, Anthony, Pvt., 89th M. P.	10-20
Pickinpaugh, Edward W., Cook, E, 353rd Inf	11- 5
Pieczynski, Frank, Pvt., D, 355th Inf	11-10
Pierce, Edward W., Corp., F, 353rd Inf	9-22
Pierce, Frederick B., Pvt., B, 354th Inf	11- 1
Pine, Walter L., Pvt., F, 353rd Inf	11- 1
Pitonyak, John A., Pvt., A, 355th Inf	11- 4
Pittman, Alva E., Pvt. 1cl., C, 314th San. Tr	10- 2
Plagens, Otto, Pvt., M, 353rd Inf	11- 1
Plimmer, Harry L., Pvt., K, 356th Inf	10- 7
Ploetz, Rudolph R., Pvt., D, 353rd Inf	10-29
Plotkin, Isadore, Pvt., M, 353rd Inf	9-30
Pohlman, Fred H., Pvt., Med. Det., 314th M. G. Bn.	9-10
Polcelli, Felice, Pvt., C, 314th Amm. Tr	
Pollack, Jake, Pvt. 1cl., E, 314th Eng	9-20
Pollara, Frank, Pvt., A, 314th Eng	9-18
Polston, Frank M., Pvt., K, 356th Inf	11-11
Popple, Geo. E., Pvt., B, 354th Inf	11- 1
Poezinas, George, Pvt., L, 356th Inf	11-11
Potter, Edward C., Pvt. 1cl., C, 341st M. G. Bn	10-25
Powers, Garman M., Pvt., G, 354th Inf	9-11
Powers, Thimothy J., Pvt., H, 354th Inf	10-25
Price, Leslie A., Pvt., I, 353rd Inf	9-12
Primm, Shelby, Pvt., D, 355th Inf	10-21
Proffer, Henry O., Pvt. 1cl., 314th F. S. Bn	11-11
Pucilla, Gennaro, Pvt. 1cl., D, 314th M. S. Tr	10-29
Pulver, Fred, Pvt., I, 353rd Inf	11- 7
Pulver, James F., Pvt., B, 353rd Inf	10-24
Quaid, Wm. J., Pvt., K, 356th Inf	9-24
Quammen, John, Pvt., F, 353rd Inf	9-18
Quammen, John, Pvt., F, 353rd Inf	11- 3
Rafferty, Peter J., Pvt., B, 354th Inf	10- 1
Raisig, Geo. A., Pvt., D, 353rd Inf	9-25
Rankin, Bert L., Pvt., E, 353rd Inf	10-19
Rasmussen, Gottfred A., Pvt., M. G. Co., 353rd Inf.	10-31
Rasmussen, Rockwell, Pvt., L, 353rd Inf	11- 8
Rasque, Edward E., Pvt., M. G. Co., 353rd Inf	10-30
Rathkey, Fred L., Wag., 314th Eng. Tr	11-13
Razor, James, Corp., B, 342nd F. A	
Redlin, Alvin W., Pvt., B, 353rd Inf	10-26
Redwine, Owen P., Pvt., D, 355th Inf	11- 9
Reed, Harold J., Pvt. 1cl., C, 354th Inf	9-20
Reed, Silas A., Pvt., A, 340th M. G. Bn	11- 1
Reefe, John J., Pvt., M, 355th Inf	9-16
Reiman, Ernest A., Sgt., H, 353rd Inf	9-12
Reis, Joseph G., Cook, E, 356th Inf	11-11
Reisbick, John R., Pvt., E, 355th Inf	11- 2
Reisher, Robert B., Sgt., F, 355th Inf	9-17
Remer, Edwin G., Pvt., M. G. Co., 356th Inf	9-22
Remington, Phillip J., Pvt., I, 354th Inf	9-24
Rengstorff, James E., Pvt., D, 356th Inf	9-18
Reuter, Edmond A., Pvt., E, 356th Inf	10-26
Rice, Frank R., Corp., L, 353rd Inf	9-13
Richards, Elmer P., Pvt., D, 354th Inf	9-23
Richardson, Levi T., Sgt., I, 356th Inf	9-13
Richardson, Wm. A., Pvt., I, 356th Inf	8-28
Richel, Edward L., Pvt., B, 354th Inf	11- 1
Ridder, Fred, Pvt., E, 354th Inf	9-14
Ridgeway, Floyd L., Pvt., B, 314th Eng	9-12
Riebock, Lewis W., Pvt., B, 353rd Inf	10-24
Ries, Fred E., Pvt., C, 353rd Inf	10-26
Riley, Charley, Pvt., A, 356th Inf	10-29
Riley, Joseph A., Pvt. 1cl., B, 354th Inf	10- 6
Riley, Martin A., Pvt., 314th San. Tr	10-27
Riley, Wm., Pvt., I, 354th Inf	9-20
Rink, Wm., Pvt., M, 355th Inf	11- 5
Risley, Wm. H., Sgt., F, 353rd Inf	9-18
Rivera, Jose M., Pvt., B, 355th Inf	11- 5
Robbins, Jay L., Pvt. 1cl., C, 314th Eng	9-13
Robbins, Mearle E., Pvt., H, 353rd Inf	9-12
Roberts, Harry E., Sgt., B, 355th Inf	9-13
Robertson, Guy S., Pvt. 1cl., K, 356th Inf	11- 5
Robertson, James, Pvt., C, 354th Inf	8-31
Robinson, Earle T., Corp., H, 356th Inf	11-11
Robinson, James H., Corp., K, 355th Inf	11- 5
Robinson, John M., Pvt., C, 356th Inf	11- 2
Robinson, Melvin, Pvt., B, 314th Eng	10-27
Robitsch, Jacob, Pvt., I, 354th Inf	8-24
Roemer, Lem, Pvt., B, 353rd Inf	10-24
Roemer, Wm. H., Corp., C, 354th Inf	9-24
Rogers, Wilber A., Sgt., E, 355th Inf	11- 8
Rohacek, Harry L., Sgt., F, 314th Eng	11- 7
Romero, Nicanor C., Pvt., I, 356th Inf	9-16
Romme, Peter J., Pvt., L, 353rd Inf	10-22
Rose, Edward, Pvt., E, 356th Inf	11-11
Ross, Amos A., Mech., K, 355th Inf	9-15
Roth, Arthur W., Pvt. 1cl., C, 341st M. G. Bn	10-25
Royal, Thomas V., Sgt., G, 354th Inf	10-24
Ruediger, Emil, Corp., E, 354th Inf	9-15
Rulle, Frank G., Pvt., A, 356th Inf	9-16
Rumsey, Geo. L., Pvt., F, 355th Inf	11- 9
Rupp, John, Pvt., G, 314th Amm. Tr	11- 8
Ruppert, Joseph G., Pvt., I, 355th Inf	9-12
Russell, Guy, Pvt., A, 356th Inf	10- 7
Russell, Herbert D., Pvt., D, 354th Inf	10- 2
Ruzicka, Edward E., Pvt., Hq. 355th Inf	11-10
Ryder, John S., Pvt., A, 340th M. G. Bn	10-30
Ryslavy, Wm., Pvt. 1cl., C, 341st M. G. Bn	10-26
St. Clair, Raymond C., Pvt. 1cl., K, 354th Inf	11- 2
Sacca, Joseph, Pvt., B, 341st M. G. Bn	10-22
Safley, Arthur E., Cook, B, 314th F. S. Bn	10-29
Salas, Filiberto, Pvt., K, 355th Inf	9-14
Salbic, Erick J., Pvt., K, 353rd Inf	10-30
Salzman, Harry C., Corp., E, 354th Inf	11- 2
Sandow, Julius C., Pvt., M. G. Co., 353rd Inf	10-25
Sandwith, Alfred E., Pvt., D, 353rd Inf	9- 8
Sargent, Donald M., Pvt., E, 353rd Inf	9-18
Saulles, James, Pvt., E, 353rd Inf	11- 1
Sauser, Edward M., Pvt., G, 355th Inf	10-22
Savchik, Harry, Pvt., C, 356th Inf	10-29
Sawyer, Owen William, Pvt., A, 314th Eng	9-19
Scavotto, Leo, Pvt., K, 355th Inf	9-13
Schaeffer, Argyle A., Pvt. 1cl., F, 354th Inf	10-21
Schalla, Otto M., Pvt., D, 355th Inf	10-20
Scheetz, Aloysious Bernard, Pvt., E, 314th Eng	10-27
Schindler, Fred W., Pvt., Hq. 355th Inf	11- 4
Schlutsmeier, Emil J., Pvt. 1cl., B, 314th M. S. T.	11- 6
Schmidt, Bernard, Pvt., B, 342nd F. A	
Schmidt, Emil H., Pvt., B, 353rd Inf	10-22
Schneider, Wm. A., Sgt., A, 354th Inf	9-14
Schofield, Ralph P., Corp., B, 354th Inf	11- 5
Schrimph, Frank, Pvt., E, 353rd Inf	9-12
Schrodt, Elmer E., Corp., I, 354th Inf	9-23
Schroen, Carl R., Pvt., A, M. G. Co., 356th Inf	9- 4
Schuessler, Walter P., Pvt., M, 355th Inf	11- 5
Schulte, Reuben, Pvt., B, 355th Inf	9-15
Schultz, John, Pvt., F, 354th Inf	11- 1
Schwab, Edward, Pvt., E, 354th Inf	9-20
Schwartz, Edwin, A, Pvt., E, 354th Inf	10-21
Schwartz, Fred, Pvt., A, 353rd Inf	10-26
Schwenn, John, Corp., F, 354th Inf	11- 3
Scoppenhorst, Frank R., Mech., I, 354th Inf	11- 1
Scott, Fred, Pvt., K, 353rd Inf	10-30
Scott, Ross, Sgt., L, 356th Inf	9-26
Scott, William Anthony, Pvt., E, 355th Inf	9-12
Scroggin, Ray Oliver, Pvt., Hq. 355th Inf	10- 9
Searer, Ned. C., Pvt. 1cl., I, 354th Inf	11- 1
Seeley, Walter C., Pvt. 1cl., Med. Det., 89th Div	9-13
Seganti, Anthony, Pvt. 1cl., C, 354th Inf	9-15
Segur, Albert L., Pvt., H, 354th Inf	10-21
Sellers, Austin W., Pvt., E, 355th Inf	9-13
Senter, Ray, Pvt., E, 353rd Inf	11- 5

Name, Rank, Company, Organization	Date 1918
Settles, William H., Amb. Co., 356th Inf	11- 7
Severson, Selmer T., Pvt., M, 356th Inf	9-12
Seward, James W., Pvt., L, 353rd Inf	9-14
Seymour, Ronold, Pvt., D, 341st M. G. Bn	11-11
Shannon, Earl L., Pvt., H, 355th Inf	9-16
Sharp, Sephus S., Pvt., H, 354th Inf	9-14
Sheanhan, Albert, Pvt., M, 353rd Inf	9-18
Sheddan, Mack F., Corp., H, 353rd Inf	9-18
Sherman, Robert, Pvt., A, 354th Inf	9-24
Shinkle, Charles, Pvt. 1cl., C, 355th Inf	11- 4
Showalter, John F., Wag., Sup. Co., 355th Inf	11- 9
Simmer, Cecil A., Pvt., B, 314th Sup. Tr	10-28
Siorfanes, George A., Corp., E, 354th Inf	9-20
Sirclum, Edward, Corp., B, 314th Eng	9-14
Shejel, Marvin O., Pvt., D, 342nd F. A	
Skoog, John, Pvt., L, 354th Inf	11- 3
Slaathaug, Hans I., Pvt., Hq. 355th Inf	9-15
Slattery, Thomas, Pvt., F, 353rd Inf	11- 5
Smalley, Elmer E., Pvt., D, 354th Inf	10-21
Smith, Anton B., Pvt., Sup. Co., 354th Inf	11- 2
Smith, Clifford, Pvt., E, 354th Inf	11- 2
Smith, George C., Pvt., E, 353rd Inf	10-26
Smith, Henry Irva, Pvt., Hq. 356th Inf	11- 1
Smith, James C., Pvt., 89th Div., M. P	11- 8
Smith, LeRoy B., Corp., I, 355th Inf	11- 8
Smith, Luther L., Bugler, H, 353rd Inf	9-12
Smith, Moses C., Amb. Co., 356th Inf	11- 4
Smith, Riley I., Pvt., D, 353rd Inf	9-28
Smith, Reuben A., Pvt., E, 354th Inf	10-21
Smull, Charles W., Pvt., M. G. Co., 353rd Inf	11- 1
Snodgras, Harry J., Pvt. 1cl., I, 356th Inf	9-16
Sollman, Oscar H., Bugler, C, 342nd M. G. Bn	9-12
Solvie, Erick J., Pvt., K, 353rd Inf	10-23
Sommers, Arthur C., Wagoner, A, 314th Amm. Tr	
Sowers, Earl H., Pvt., C, 353rd Inf	10-26
Sowienski, Alexander, Pvt., C, 353rd Inf	10-22
Sparks, Clyde A., Pvt., M. G. Co., 356th Inf	9-23
Sparks, Warren A., Pvt. 1cl., M, 356th Inf	11-11
Sprecher, Irwin D., Corp., C, 314th F. S. Bn	9-26
Springfield, George L., Pvt., H, 355th Inf	11-11
Staarmann, Herman E., Pvt., F, 355th Inf	10-29
Stahl, Dwight M., Pvt., H, 354th Inf	11- 1
Staton, Edward, Pvt. 1cl., E, 353rd Inf	9-18
Stedman, Charles C., Sgt., H, 354th Inf	11-11
Stein, Edward, Pvt., G, 356th Inf	11- 5
Stein, Leon E., Pvt., B, 354th Inf	11- 1
Stein, Lester F., 1st Sgt., M, 353rd Inf	9-30
Steiner, Emery F., Pvt. 1cl., C, 356th Inf	11- 4
Steinkirchner, William H., Pvt., L, 353rd Inf	9-12
Stenzinger, Ernest H., Pvt. 1cl., E, 354th Inf	9-14
Stephenson, George E., Pvt., I, 355th Inf	11- 5
Stertz, Peter, Pvt., G, 355th Inf	11- 5
Stewardson, James B., Pvt., D, 353rd Inf	10-22
Stiegelmeier, Dave, Pvt. 1cl., A, 340th M. G. Bn	10-26
Stiehl, Herman H., Pvt., K, 353rd Inf	9-12
Stivers, Milo C., Corp., H, 353rd Inf	9-19
Stoble, George B., Pvt., C, 354th Inf	11- 1
Stoker, Frank, Pvt., E, 353rd Inf	9-17
Stommer, Elmer N., Pvt. 1cl., L, 355th Inf	9-14
Stone, Howard L., Pvt. 1cl., H, 355th Inf	9-16
Stone, Walker P., Corp., H, 356th Inf	9-18
Storm, Charley, Pvt., G, 353rd Inf	10-19
Strawn, Cecil G., Pvt., Hq. 355th Inf	9-23
Strayhorn, Louis R., Pvt., L, 354th Inf	9-15
Streete, Joseph E., Pvt., F, 355th Inf	10-22
Strom, Clarence B., Pvt., D, 354th Inf	11- 1
Stromberg, Carl O., Corp., K, 353rd Inf	11- 3
Stuckmeyer, John, Pvt., M, 353rd Inf	11- 1
Stull, James L., Sgt., M. G. Co., 356th Inf	9-12
Sullivan, Walker, Sgt., G, 355th Inf	11- 2
Sundin, Milton C., Corp., L, 353rd Inf	9- 2
Sutherlin, Ambirs E., Pvt. 1cl., C, 356th Inf	11- 9
Sutton, William A., Corp., B, 342nd M. G. Bn	9-15
Swan, John, Wag., Sup. 354th Inf	9-25
Swanson, Hal E., Corp., H, 356th Inf	10-31
Swenson, Charley, Pvt. 1cl., L, 355th Inf	11-11
Swigart, Oscar A., Sgt., Sup. 356th Inf	10-17
Swoboda, William H., Pvt., C, 354th Inf	11- 1
Swoger, Melvin E., Pvt., E, 314th Amm. Tr	
Swogger, Leo C., Pvt., L, 353rd Inf	9-18
Szymkiewicz, Martin, Pvt., B, 355th Inf	11- 5
Tabke, Walter C., Pvt. 1cl., Hq. 355th Inf	9-12
Taglier, Henry C., Pvt. 1cl., M, 355th Inf	10- 4
Taylor, Charles E., Pvt., E, 353rd Inf	9-18
Taylor, Frank B, Pvt. 1cl., C, 342nd M. G. Bn	9-29
Taylor, Fred H., Pvt., Sup. Co., 353rd Inf	11- 1
Taylor, Paul Evan, Corp., B, 353rd Inf	10- 2
Tefft, Ralph E., Pvt., E, 353rd Inf	11- 1
Teply, Benjamin J., Mech., M, 353rd Inf	9-15
Terry, Oscar B., Wag., Sup. Co., 353rd Inf	10-20
Thieman, Emil A., Pvt., Med. Det., 342nd F. A	
Thiess, Gottfried, Pvt., B, 342nd F. A	
Thomas, Charles, Pvt., K, 355th Inf	10- 6
Thompson, Albert Perry, Pvt., B, 341st M. G. Bn	9-12
Thompson, Alfred I., Pvt., G, 354th Inf	11- 1
Thompson, Andrew J., Pvt. 1cl., F, 356th Inf	11- 5
Thompson, Frank A., Pvt., K, 353rd Inf	9-12
Thompson, Nelson W., Corp., C, 356th Inf	9-16
Thoren, Arnold Victor, Corp., L, 355th Inf	9-12
Thorn, Howard Harry, Pvt., A, 353rd Inf	9-15
Thrower, Louis V., Corp., D, 356th Inf	9-14
Thurmon, Roland R., Sgt., H, 354th Inf	11- 3
Timlin, John F., Corp., E, 356th Inf	10-25
Tincher, Robert S., Pvt., A, 354th Inf	9- 2
Tindsley, William A. M., Pvt., C, 341st M. G. Bn	10-25
Todd, Bruce H., Mech., F, 353rd Inf	9-13
Tofall, Henry J., Pvt. 1cl., Hq. 354th Inf	11- 2
Tomkin, William T., Pvt., M, 355th Inf	9-15
Tours, Thomas Nash, Pvt. 1cl., L, 355th Inf	9-13
Toulme, Alcide J., Pvt., M, 355th Inf	11- 1
Tracy, Albert, Pvt., A, 353rd Inf	11- 3
Travis, John M., Pvt., F, 353rd Inf	9-12
Trucksess, Martin, Pvt., C, 342nd M. G. Bn	9-30
Trudell, James A., Mech., D, 355th Inf	9-11
Tucker, Harry, Pvt., F, 314th Eng	11- 8
Turner, Arthur O., Pvt., D, 355th Inf	11- 5
Ude, George Edgar, Pvt. 1cl., L, 355th Inf	9-12
Ulm, Roy E. W., Corp., B, 355th Inf	9-15
Ulrich, Albert, Pvt., D, 355th Inf	11-10
Underhill, Sylvester M., Sgt., Hq. 353rd Inf	10- 2
Unland, William Joseph, Mech., I, 354th Inf	8-24
Urner, Joseph E., Pvt. Hq. 354th Inf	11- 1
Valadez, Noberto, Pvt., L, 353rd Inf	10-23
Van Buren, Roy F., 1st Sgt., F, 354th Inf	9-24
Vancil, Charley W., Pvt., C, 341st M. G. Bn	10-25
Van Cleave, Thomas W., Pvt., G, 356th Inf	9-18
Van Nordheim, Frank, Pvt. 1cl., K, 355th Inf	9-13
Van Nostrand, Louis C., Corp., K, 355th Inf	9-15
Vaught, Grover C., Pvt., F, 314th Eng	11- 8
Van Vuren, Ray, Pvt., F, 356th Inf	9-16
Van Vuren, Ray, Pvt., F, 356th Inf	11- 5
Van Zandt, Amos, Pvt., B, 340th M. G. Bn	9-12
Veitch, Harry G., Corp., E, 354th Inf	9-28
Vermillion, Robert M., Pvt., F, 353rd Inf	9-12
Vernon, Charles E., Sgt., K, 355th Inf	10-24
Vest, Jake, Pvt., G, 356th Inf	11- 2
Vickery, John E., 1st Sgt., F, 354th Inf	11- 3
Vierling, Frank, Wag., A, 314th Eng	9-12
Vincent, Herbert, Pvt., Hq. 356th Inf	10-29
Voelkel, John W., Pvt., A, 355th Inf	11- 5
Voigt, Raymond B., Pvt., D, 353rd Inf	10-31
Waddell, Wm. D., Pvt. 1cl., M. D., 341st M. G. Bn	9-14
Wagner, Charles H., Pvt., M, 353rd Inf	11- 1
Wait, Pvt., M, 355th Inf	11- 9
Walts, Perry D., Pvt., I, 355th Inf	9-15
Walche, Frank, Pvt., L, 353rd Inf	9-13
Walker, Henry M., 1st Sgt., A, 314th Amm. Tr	
Walker, Jesse L., Pvt. 1cl., F, 355th Inf	9-14
Walker, Jesse L., Pvt. 1cl., F, 355th Inf	10-22
Walker, Joseph L., Pvt., Med. Det., 353rd Inf	10-29
Walkup, Miller H., Pvt., C, 341st M. G. Bn	10-31
Wallace, William S., Pvt., D, 355th Inf	9-30
Walsh, Edward, Jr., Pvt., L, 354th Inf	10-30
Walsh, John J., Corp., C, 353rd Inf	10-26
Ware, Guy F., Sgt., A, 314th Eng	9-13
Warfel, John Emanuel, Pvt. 1cl., K, 356th Inf	11- 2
Warren, John H., Pvt., C, 355th Inf	10-20
Waskow, Henry, Pvt., L, 354th Inf	10-31
Watry, Louis T., 1st Sgt., F, 314th Eng	11- 2
Watson, Reed LaFollette, Pvt. 1cl., M, 355th Inf	9-13
Watters, Charles F., Pvt., D, 356th Inf	11- 5
Weigand, Alex H., Pvt., K, 353rd Inf	11- 1
Weiss, Arnold H., Pvt., D, 353rd Inf	9-12
Welcome, Fred J., Pvt., M, 353rd Inf	11- 1
Wells, William L., Pvt., E, 354th Inf	11- 1
Wesley, Silas, Pvt., F, 355th Inf	10-21
Wessling, Erwin R., Pvt., D, 354th Inf	11- 8
West, Herschel Glen, Corp., M, 353rd Inf	10- 3
Westfall, Gus, Pvt., M. G. Co., 354th Inf	10-28
Wetterer, William C., Sgt., B, 314th Amm. Tr	9-20
Wheeler, William E., Pvt., F, 355th Inf	9-26
Whitacre, Joseph A., Pvt., E, 353rd Inf	9-12
White, Clarence D., Corp., A, 341st M. G. Bn	9-19
White, Gene, Pvt. 1cl., H, 354th Inf	11- 2
White, Herbert H., Pvt., B, 354th Inf	11-11
Whitney, Oliver, Pvt., K, 353rd Inf	11- 1
Whittlock, Archie E., Pvt., C, 342nd M. G. Bn	9-29
Wickstrom, Carl A., Pvt., B, 355th Inf	11- 5

Name, Rank, Company, Organization	Date 1918
Wiley, Charles H., Corp., D, 353rd Inf	9-18
Wilkerson, Mosby, Pvt., E, 355th Inf	11- 9
Wilkerson, Ray W., Sgt., G, 356th Inf	8-14
Wilkofsky, Max, Pvt., D, 355th Inf	9-15
Williams, Chester H., Pvt., I, 355th Inf	11- 5
Williams, Wayne W., Sgt., D, 355th Inf	9-13
Willis, Floyd M., Pvt., Med. Det., 353rd Inf	11- 5
Willis, Sydney, Pvt., D, 356th Inf	9-18
Willman, Albert A., Pvt., G, 353rd Inf	10-27
Wilson, Archie, Pvt. 1cl., C, 342nd M. G. Bn	11- 5
Wilson, James H., Pvt., F, 353rd Inf	9-18
Wilson, John H., Pvt., C, 314th F. S. Bn	9-17
Wilson, Kemper S., Pvt., H, 354th Inf	10-30
Wilson, Levi V., Corp., H, 353rd Inf	9-14
Wilson, Ord, Corp., B, 314th F. S. Bn	10-24
Wingbermuehle, George J., Pvt., D, 341st M. G. Bn	11- 3
Winslow, Orette B., Pvt., D, 353rd Inf	10-25
Wintle, Harry, Pvt., F, 353rd Inf	9-12
Wise, James L., Pvt., C, 353rd Inf	10-22
Wiss, Euphratis Edward, Pvt., L, 356th Inf	9-12
Withey, Hubert D., Pvt., I, 355th Inf	11- 5
Witt, Frank, Pvt., L, 354th Inf	11- 1
Woerner, Conrad, Mech., I, 355th Inf	9-15
Wofford, Arthur, Pvt., M, 356th Inf	9-13
Wolf, Joe N., Pvt., I, 353rd Inf	9-18
Wolfe, Clell O., Sgt., D, 356th Inf	9-18
Wolfe, Philip A., Pvt., B, 354th Inf	11- 1

Name, Rank, Company, Organization	Date 1918
Woodford, Mark M., Pvt., F, 353rd Inf	9-18
Woodhull, Charles E., Pvt., M. G. Co., 353rd Inf	10-29
Woodman, Bruce S., Pvt. 1cl., Hq. 353rd Inf	10-21
Worthington, Robert S., Pvt., H, 353rd Inf	9-23
Wright, Charles W., Pvt., F, 353rd Inf	8-16
Wright, Perry H., Pvt., C, 354th Inf	10-28
Wright, Victor Paul, Pvt. 1cl., G, 355th Inf	9-30
Wyatt, Edmond, Wag., E, 314th Amm. Tr	10- 6
Yaple, Albert E., Corp., Hq. 356th Inf	10-21
Yates, Claude Charles, Pvt., L, 356th Inf	9-12
Yelm, George Edward, Corp., K, 355th Inf	9-13
Yoritimo, Sexiro, Pvt. Hq. 355th Inf	9-14
York, Richard Bland, Pvt., M, 354th Inf	10-21
York, William R., Pvt., K, 353rd Inf	9-18
Young, Benjamin H., Pvt., F, 355th Inf	11- 5
Youngblood, Agnew R., Pvt D, 314th Eng	8-29
Youngmark, Oscar E., Pvt., M, 355th Inf	11- 5
Yung, Randall, Pvt. 1cl., M, 355th Inf	9-16
Zabrowski, Frank P., Pvt., Hq. 314th San. Tr	10-30
Zahler, Edward, Mech., L, 355th Inf	9-16
Zamora, Catarino, Pvt., B, 353rd Inf	9-15
Zander, Edward, Pvt., K, 353rd Inf	11- 1
Zullo, Joseph A., Corp., E, 354th Inf	11- 2
Zane, Roscoe H., Pvt. 1cl., E, 353rd Inf	9-18
Ziemann, August H., Pvt. 1cl., I, 354th Inf	9-18
Ziercher, William F., Corp., D, 356th Inf	10-28
Zimmerman, Rudolph A., Sgt., M. G. Co., 354th Inf	11- 1
Zimpfer, Charles J., Sgt., F, 354th Inf	11- 2

Field Hospital of the 314th Sanitary Train, 89th Division, in Bernecourt, St. Mihiel Sector, September 24th, 1918. S. C. 25281.

SIGNAL CORPS PHOTOGRAPHS

All Signal Corps photographs throughout this book may be identified by the official Signal Corps (S. C.) numbers included in the captions.

Persons desiring prints from these negatives (which will usually be somewhat larger and sharper than the printed half-tones) may obtain them at 15c each from the Photographic Section, Signal Corps, Washington, D. C., describing the pictures wanted by their official numbers given here, as S. C. 71144, etc.

SPECIAL PICTURE SECTION.

Review of the 89th Division by General Pershing at Trier, Germany, April 23, 1919. Men to be decorated massed and advancing for presentation of the honors, followed by colors of the organizations of the Division to which General Pershing affixed ribbons for combat service as a part of the same ceremony.

German civil population, Saarburg, Germany, watching American troops of the Army of Occupation marching into the town, which became headquarters of the 355th Infantry, 89th Division. S. C. 42168.

View of the burning American ammunition dump, north of Royaumeix and Menil la Tour, St. Mihiel Sector, from Royaumeix, on August 31st, 1918. Trees at the extreme left border the road from Menil la Tour to Bernecourt. S. C. 38548.

Vertical aeroplane photograph of Limey, St. Mihiel Sector, taken October 30th, 1918. At this time roads were repaired, but the trenches and shell-wrecked buildings appear as they did while occupied by troops of the 89th Division prior to the St. Mihiel Offensive.

Euvezin, which was taken by the 89th Division during the St. Mihiel Offensive. The chateau (to right, with shell hole in roof) was headquarters of the 89th Division from September 14th to September 26th, 1918. Then headquarters moved to the partly wrecked buildings at the extreme left of the picture, where the hill lent some protection from German shelling, which was carried on spasmodically during the entire period of occupancy. Photographed September 26th, 1918. S. C. 25289.

"Opening the tail" of a 155 G. P. F. near Flirey on September 13th, 1918, during the St. Mihiel Offensive. These guns are "Corps Artillery," are usually placed well behind the front lines, and have an accurate range of 16 kilometers. G. P. F. stands for "Grande Puissance Filloux" (great power Filloux), Filloux being the name of the French manufacturer of these powerful pieces of artillery. S. C. 25248.

Ivoiry, between Montfaucon and Epinonville, was headquarters of the 314th Supply Train and elements of the 314th Sanitary Train for a time during the Meuse-Argonne Offensive. It was also location of the Division Quartermaster Dump. Montfaucon can be seen in distance on the hill at the left. Pup tents and wagons under cover of trees and camouflaged in foreground. Soldier cemetery in front of church. The 37th Division advanced over this ground on September 27th, 1918. S. C. 26215

Gesnes, Headquarters of the 89th Division during the Meuse-Argonne offensive, as it appeared October 30, 1918. Trucks covered with camouflage in foreground. Wagons under cover of trees at right. The town was more battered by shell fire than this picture suggests, most of the destruction not being visible from the point where it was taken. S. C. 35532

Street in Romagne, October 29th, 1918, while the town was occupied by the 89th Division. The town was under constant shellfire until the advance, November 1st. Church steeple shown in distance was hit, burned and fell shortly after this picture was taken. S. C. 30018.

Troops of the 89th Division dodging German shell fire by keeping in the lee of buildings as they advanced through Bayonville on November 2nd, 1918, during the Meuse-Argonne Offensive. S. C. 31487.

Looking northeast over Tailly on November 12, 1918. Behind the town, on hill to right, Bois de Tailly. On hill to left, Bois de Nouart. In the distance is Beauclair; behind it the Foret de Dieulet, and in the far distance the hills beyond the Meuse. S. C. 34977.

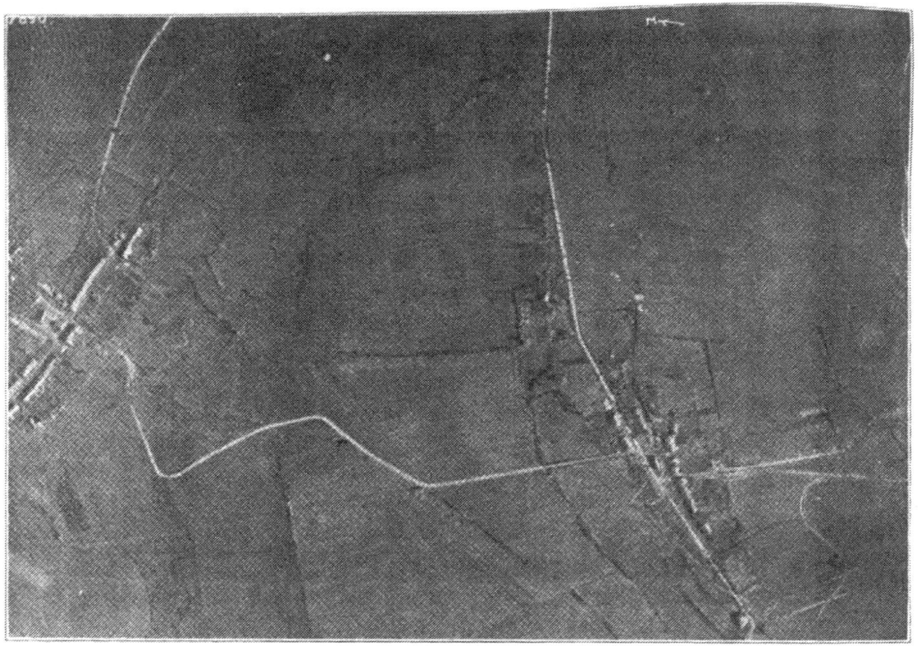

Beaufort (left) and Beauclair (right). Meuse-Argonne Offensive, photographed from the air October 30th, 1918

The 354th Infantry, 89th Division, in the barracks yard at Trier, Germany, in the spring of 1919. Trier was Advanced G. H. Q. and was garrisoned by the 354th Infantry.

Aeroplane view of the men and colors massed for presentation of decorations at the review of the 89th Division by General Pershing near Trier, Germany, April 23rd, 1919. Only a very small portion (part of one infantry regiment and machine gun units) of the troops participating in the ceremony can be seen.

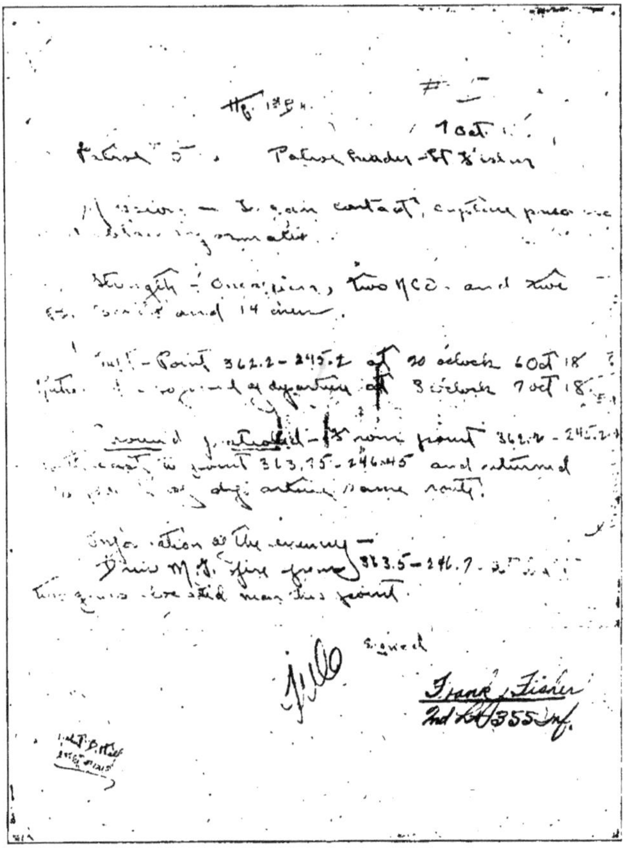

Hq. [illegible]

1 Oct. [illegible]

Patrol [illegible] Patrol leader — Lt Fisher

Mission — to gain contact, capture prisoners [illegible] information.

Strength — One officer, two NCO. and [illegible] and 14 men.

[illegible] — Point 362.2 - 245.2 at 10 o'clock 6 Oct 18
[illegible] departure at 3 o'clock 7 Oct 18

Ground patrolled — from point 362.2 - 245.2 [illegible] to point 363.75 - 246.45 and returned [illegible]

Information of the enemy —
[illegible] M.G. fire from 363.5 - 246.7 [illegible]

Signed
Frank J. Fisher
2nd Lt 355 Inf.

Photographic reproduction of typical patrol report. This report was made by Lieutenant Frank J. Fisher, 355th Infantry, patrol leader, covering reconnaissance just before the Division was relieved in the St. Mihiel Sector. The officer was killed in the Meuse-Argonne Offensive a few weeks later.

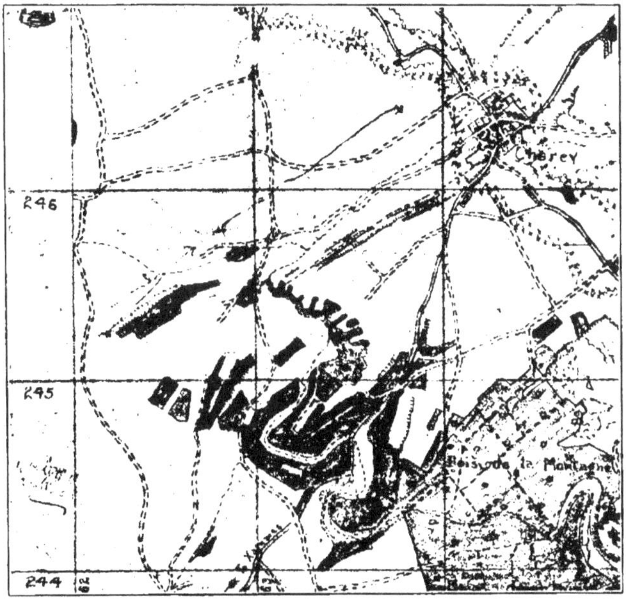

Photograph of sketch map accompanying patrol report of Lieutenant Frank J. Fisher, 355th Infantry, reproduced herewith.

Barbed wire entanglements in the St. Mihiel Sector. Contrary to popular impressions at home and the practice of training days, wire at the front was not stretched neatly between vertical posts, but was a tangled mass such as is here shown.

Building dugout under ruined house in Rambucourt, St. Mihiel Sector. S. C. 14941.

Dugout under observation post, Lironville, St. Mihiel Sector.

Railhead and quartermaster depot, Menil la Tour, St. Mihiel Sector, where supplies were received on standard gauge railroad and stored by the Division Quartermaster. From here they were distributed by truck or on the narrow gauge railroad (also called "soisante," "60-centimeter" and "Decauville") to troops of the Division in the line in the Lucey Sector. S. C. 14276.

Traffic jam on September 13th, 1918, during the St. Mihiel Offensive. Congestion of traffic like this existed on all roads back of the front. The large trucks (camions) are French. The light trucks and water carts are American. S. C. 22441.

Flirey, as seen through a shell hole in a wall, after the St. Mihiel Offensive. The flag of a dressing station at the left. Quartermaster and engineer dump across the road. S. C. 25162.

Crater in the American ammunition dump north of Royaumiex and Menil la Tour (St. Mihiel Sector) after it was blown up August 30, 1918. The man climbing out gives some idea of the size of the hole. S. C. 22168.

Camouflaged German 77-mm. gun captured in position, concealed in wrecked house on road to Thiaucourt. St. Mihiel Offensive. S. C. 27110.

Regimental P. C. of the 354th Infantry at Xammes, St. Mihiel Sector, upon which a direct hit was made by a German "210," killing Chaplain Delman.

Headquarters of 314th Sanitary Train, 89th Division, September 20th, 1918, at Bouillonville, St. Mihiel Sector, in a dugout which had been a German officers' club. The Germans had fitted the place out with beamed ceilings, electric lights, tapestries and musical instruments, to all of which the Americans fell heir when they moved in with field desk, typewriter and files. S. C. 25265.

314th Engineers, 89th Division, making barbed-wire entanglements at Bouillonville, September 30th, 1918. This was after the St. Mihiel Offensive, and when completed the entanglements were placed in front of the new trenches further north. S. C. 25264.

Street scene, looking south, in Xammes, St. Mihiel Sector, taken after the armistice, showing effect of German artillery fire. Roadway repaired to carry traffic.

Captured German stone and concrete dugouts at St. Baussant, St. Mihiel Sector, used as headquarters, 314th Ammunition Train, 89th Division, October 17, 1918. S. C. 27105.

The 354th Infantry, 89th Division, in the barracks yard at Trier, Germany, in the spring of 1919. Trier was Advanced G. H. Q. and was garrisoned by the 354th Infantry.

Aeroplane view of the men and colors massed for presentation of decorations at the review of the 89th Division by General Pershing near Trier, Germany, April 23rd, 1919. Only a very small portion (part of one infantry regiment and machine gun units) of the troops participating in the ceremony can be seen.

Church in Romagne just hit by German shell and burning, October 29th, 1918, during the Meuse-Argonne Offensive. The steeple and roof burned and fell shortly after the picture was taken. The town was under constant shell fire until the advance, November 1st. Some of the shell holes shown were made about two weeks earlier by American artillery, but the two men huddled in the doorway suggest the direction from which present shelling comes. S. C. 30019.

Interior of ruined church at Romagne, after the Meuse-Argonne Offensive. S. C. 34647.

Third Battalion, 354th Infantry, 89th Division, crossing the line from Belgium into Luxembourg, December 1st, 1918. S. C. 40648.

Rations and forage (piles of bread, cases of corned willie and bales of hay) at railhead of the 89th Division, Clerges, November 4, 1918, during the Meuse-Argonne Offensive. S. C. 35010.

German dugouts used by 314th Sanitary Train as dressing station, Epinonville, Meuse-Argonne Offensive, October 18, 1918. Roof of 89th Division P. C. in background. S. C. 26687.

354th Ambulance Company, 314th Sanitary Train, 89th Division, bringing wounded (most of them from the 355th Infantry) back to first-aid station in Tailly, Meuse-Argonne Offensive, November 4th, 1918. S. C. 31479.

Trucks of the 314th Supply Train in Beaufort on November 13th, 1918. The town was captured by the 355th Infantry, 89th Division, during the Meuse-Argonne Offensive, on November 4th. A brigade headquarters and quartermaster dump were established there a day or two later, and maintained in spite of the fact that the place was a frequent target for German shells, which caused numerous casualties. S. C. 34939.

Company A, 314th Engineers, 89th Division, starting to build a new bridge across the canal at Stenay on November 11th, 1918. The retreating Germans had blown up the bridge and lock gates. S. C. 34934.

A thorough job of demolition. Ruins of the railway station at Stenay on November 15, 1918. The town is seen across the Meuse in the left background. S. C. 34962.

Infantry of the 89th Division passing in review before General Pershing at Trier, Germany, April 23, 1919.

Chateau de Verdier, Stenay, Nov. 14th, 1918. For many months this was the home of the German Crown Prince, who lived here during the memorable attack on Verdun in 1916. Stenay was seized by the 89th Division on November 11th, 1918, just before the armistice went into effect, and this chateau was successively used as headquarters by Colonel James H. Reeves, commanding the 177th Infantry Brigade, and Major General Frank L. Winn, commanding the 89th Division. Officers shown, from left to right, are Major General H. T. Allen, Colonel James H. Reeves, Colonel J. J. Kingman and Lieutenant Colonel (then Major) George H. English, Jr. S. C. 34967.

The victorious 89th Division Football Team.
Left to right, lower row: Clark, end; Thompson, tackle; Withington, guard; Garside, guard; Lewis, center; Schweiger, tackle; Laslett, end.
Upper row: Lindsey, halfback; Nelson, fullback; Gerhardt, quarterback; Clark, halfback
Absent: Higgins, end; Flannigan, guard; Padfield, fullback; Fletcher, end.

Porta Nigra, Trier, Germany. An ancient town gate, with towers for defense, built by the Romans in the 4th century. S. C. 42621.

Entrance to P. C. Davis (341st Field Artillery) at Beney, St. Mihiel Sector.

General Pershing inspecting troops of the 89th Division
at the review near Trier, April 23rd, 1919.

The flooded Meuse between Laneuville and Stenay on November 11th, 1918. The retreating Germans had blown up bridges and thrown wagons and all sorts of material into the river to back up the water and impede pursuit. S. C. 24982.

Entraining at Trier in May, 1919, for return to the United States. The packs are big, but a fair part of their contents consists of souvenirs.

COMMANDING OFFICERS

COMMANDING OFFICERS OF UNITS OF THE 89TH DIVISION DURING SERVICE OVERSEAS
(Artillery From Arrival in Division Sector, September, 1918.)

89TH DIVISION

Brigadier General Frank L. Winn....June 23, 1918—September 7, 1918
Major General William M. Wright....September 7, 1918—November 12, 1918
Major General Frank L. Winn....November 12, 1918— Return to U. S.

HEADQUARTERS TROOP

Captain Tom A. Velie....June 23, 1918—November 10, 1918
Captain Thomas J. Reid, Jr....November 10, 1918—January 13, 1919
Captain Fenton S. Jacobs....January 13, 1919—April 2, 1919
1st Lieutenant Harry D. Rice....April 2, 1919—April 7, 1919
Captain Fenton S. Jacobs....April 7, 1919—May 3, 1919
1st Lieutenant Harry D. Rice....May 3, 1919—Return to U. S.

340TH MACHINE GUN BATTALION

Lieutenant Colonel Rudolph E. Smyser....June 23, 1918—September 26, 1918
Major William A. Hale....September 26, 1918—October 4, 1918
Captain Harry A. Miller....October 4, 1918—November 23, 1918
Major William A. Hale....November 23, 1918—February 3, 1919
Captain Harry A. Miller....February 3, 1919—February 17, 1919
Captain David P. Janes....February 17, 1919—March 13, 1919
Major William A. Hale....March 13, 1919—April 27, 1919
Captain Harry A. Miller....April 27, 1919—April 30, 1919
Major William A. Hale....April 30, 1919—Return to U. S.

177TH INFANTRY BRIGADE

Colonel James H. Reeves....June 23, 1918—July 13, 1918
Colonel George H. McMaster....July 13, 1918—July 20, 1918
Colonel Americus Mitchell....July 20, 1918—July 31, 1918
Colonel James H. Reeves....July 31, 1918—September 7, 1918
Brigadier General Frank L. Winn....September 7, 1918—November 12, 1918
Colonel James H. Reeves....November 12, 1918—November 17, 1918
Brigadier General Herman Hall....November 17, 1918—February 18, 1919
Colonel Conrad S. Babcock....February 18, 1919—February 24, 1919
Colonel James H. Reeves....February 24, 1919—March 30, 1919
Brigadier General Herman Hall....March 30, 1919—Return to U. S.

353RD INFANTRY

Colonel James H. Reeves....June 23, 1918—July 31, 1918
Lieutenant Frank B. Hawkins....July 31, 1918—August 17, 1918
Colonel Conrad S. Babcock....August 17, 1918—September, 7, 1918
Colonel James H. Reeves....September 7, 1918—November 12, 1918
Major George W. Blackinton....November 12, 1918—November 17, 1918
Colonel James H. Reeves....November 17, 1918—January 8, 1919
Lieutenant Colonel Daniel W. Spurlock....January 8, 1919—January 13, 1919
Colonel James H. Reeves....January 13, 1919—Return to U. S.

354TH INFANTRY

Colonel Americus Mitchell....June 23, 1918—September 7, 1918
Colonel Conrad S. Babcock....September 7, 1918—November 20, 1918
Lieutenant Colonel Joseph H. Barnard....November 20, 1918—December 10, 1918
Colonel Conrad S. Babcock....December 10, 1918—Return to U. S.

341ST MACHINE GUN BATTALION

Major Edward A. Keyes....June 23, 1918—July 2, 1918
Captain John Dross....July 2, 1918—July 12, 1918
Lieutenant Colonel Rudolph E. Smyser....July 12, 1918—July 19, 1918
Major Ernest E. Watson....July 19, 1918—March 3, 1919
Major William Aird....March 3, 1919—April 21, 1919
Major Ernest E. Watson....April 21, 1919—Return to U. S.

178TH INFANTRY BRIGADE

Brigadier General Thomas G. Hanson	June 23, 1918—November, 9, 1918
Brigadier General Herman Hall	November 9, 1918—November 16, 1918
Brigadier General George C. Barnhardt	November 16, 1918—Return to U. S.

355TH INFANTRY

Colonel William G. Sills	June 23, 1918—July 15, 1918
Lieutenant Colonel Ralph McCoy	July 15, 1918—July 20, 1918
Colonel George H. McMaster	July 20, 1918—August 16, 1918
Colonel James D. Taylor	August 16, 1918—October 20, 1918
Lieutenant Colonel T. P. Bernard	October 20, 1918—November 16, 1918
Colonel William A. Cavenaugh	November 16, 1918—January 11, 1919
Lieutenant Colonel Levi G. Brown	January 11, 1919—January 14, 1919
Colonel William A. Cavenaugh	January 14, 1919—March 20, 1919
Lieutenant Colonel Levi G. Brown	March 20, 1919—Return to U. S.

356TH INFANTRY

Colonel Louis M. Nuttman	June 23, 1918—September 20, 1918
Lieutenant Colonel Edward A. Keyes	September 20, 1918—October 8, 1918
Colonel Alonzo Gray	October 8, 1918—October 20, 1918
Colonel Robert H. Allen	October 20, 1918—Return to U. S.

342ND MACHINE GUN BATTALION

Major T. P. Bernard	June 23, 1918—July 13, 1918
Captain John B. Donovan	July 13, 1918—July 22, 1918
Lieutenant Colonel Rudolph E. Smyser	July 22, 1918—July 31, 1918
Major T. P. Bernard	July 31, 1918—August 10, 1918
Captain Sandford Sellers, Jr.	August 10, 1918—August 15, 1918
Captain A. L. Ford	August 15, 1918—August 21, 1918
Major David H. Scott	August 21, 1918—September 16, 1918
Captain A. L. Ford	September 3, 1918—September 16, 1918
Lieutenant Colonel David H. Scott	September 16, 1918—October 9, 1918
Major Harry N. Burkhalter	October 9, 1918—December 25, 1918
Captain A. L. Ford	December 25, 1918—January 2, 1919
Captain William Laidlaw	January 2, 1919—January 14, 1919
Captain A. L. Ford	January 14, 1919—February 3, 1919
Major Harry N. Burkhalter	February 3, 1919—February 11, 1919
Captain A. L. Ford	February 11, 1919—February 16, 1919
Major Horace C. Bates	February 16, 1919—Return to U. S.

164TH FIELD ARTILLERY BRIGADE

Brigadier General Edward T. Donnelly	September 16, 1918—January 9, 1919
Colonel Ernest S. Wheeler	January 9, 1919—January 15, 1919
Brigadier General Edward T. Donnelly	January 15, 1919—Return to U. S.

340TH FIELD ARTILLERY

Colonel Ernest S. Wheeler	September 16, 1918—January 9, 1919
Major Leland A. Wind	January 9, 1919—January 15, 1919
Colonel Ernest S. Wheeler	January 15, 1919—February 16, 1919
Major Leland A. Wind	February 16, 1919—March 29, 1919
Lieutenant Colonel Joseph C. King	March 29, 1919—April 18, 1919
Colonel Ernest S. Wheeler	April 18, 1919—Return to U. S.

341ST FIELD ARTILLERY

Colonel Robert Davis	September 16, 1918—March 28, 1919
Captain Harry A. Randel	March 28, 1919—April 11, 1919
Colonel Robert Davis	April 11, 1919—Return to U. S.

342ND FIELD ARTILLERY

Colonel Earl Biscoe	September 16, 1918—February 11, 1919
Lieutenant Colonel William W. Overton	February 11, 1919—February 25, 1919
Colonel Earl Biscoe	February 25, 1919—April 13, 1919
Lieutenant Colonel Joseph C. King	April 13, 1919—Return to U. S.

314TH TRENCH MORTAR BATTERY

Captain J. L. Milburn	September 16, 1918—Return to U. S.

314TH FIELD SIGNAL BATTALION

Major David Reeves	June 23, 1918—July 13, 1918
Captain John R. Ruddick	July 13, 1918—July 31, 1918
Major David Reeves	July 31, 1918—September 24, 1918
Captain John R. Ruddick	September 24, 1918—October 17, 1918
Major H. E. Strider	October 17, 1918—Return to U. S.

314TH ENGINEERS

Colonel Robert P. Johnston	June 23, 1918—November 13, 1918
Lieutenant Colonel Brehon B. Somervell	November 13, 1918—November 26, 1918
Lieutenant Colonel O. M. Leland	November 26, 1918—January 7, 1919
Colonel D. D. Pullen	January 7, 1919—Return to U. S.

314TH TRAIN HEADQUARTERS AND MILITARY POLICE

Colonel George H. McMaster	June 23, 1918—July 18, 1918
Colonel Warren W. Whitside	July 18, 1918—March 28, 1919
Major Ancil Davis	March 28, 1919—April 15, 1919
Colonel Warren W. Whitside	April 15, 1919—Return to U. S.

89TH MILITARY POLICE CO.

Major Robert K. Schutt	September 7, 1918—November 15, 1918
Captain Roy R. Coyne	November 15, 1918—March 16, 1919
Captain John L. Crofut	March 16, 1919—Return to U. S.

314TH SANITARY TRAIN

Lieutenant Colonel Bruce F. Ffoulkes	June 23, 1918—October 29, 1918
Major Frederick C. Huff	October 29, 1918—December 5, 1918
Lieutenant Colonel F. W. O'Donnell	December 5, 1918—February 9, 1919
Major Frederick C. Huff	February 9, 1919—February 25, 1919
Lieutenant Colonel F. W. O'Donnell	February 25, 1919—Return to U. S.

314TH SUPPLY TRAIN

Major Walter C. Cole	June 23, 1918—March 31, 1919
Captain Frank C. Wilkins	March 31, 1919—April 26, 1919
Major Walter C. Cole	April 26, 1919—Return to U. S.

314TH AMMUNITION TRAIN

Colonel James D. Tilford	September 16, 1918—February 18, 1919
Major Ancil G. Davis	February 18, 1919—March 28, 1919
Major James R. Lysaght	March 28, 1919—April 15, 1919
Major Ancil G. Davis	April 15, 1919—April 27, 1919
Major James R. Lysaght	April 27, 1919—Return to U. S.

314TH ENGINEER TRAIN

1st Lieutenant William D. Stuart	June 23, 1918—July 17, 1918
1st Lieutenant Lawrence D. Pike	July 17, 1918—October 16, 1918
1st Lieutenant Halley M. Fishwood	October 16, 1918—April 2, 1919
1st Lieutenant Harvey D. Miller	April 2, 1919—April 15, 1919
1st Lieutenant Halley M. Fishwood	April 15, 1919—Return to U. S.

AMERICA IN EUROPE

A PAPER PUBLISHED IN THE INTEREST OF GOOD FELLOWSHIP AMONG ALL NATIONS.

MONDAY, JULY 29, 1918

NEWS FROM AMERICA.

Men and Money in the War.

[illegible]

Mayor Thompson's Speech in the Chicago Colosseum.

[illegible]

Peace: "The road to me is near enough, but

TIMELY THOUGHTS OF THE FOURTH OF JULY

A few extracts from GEORGE WASHINGTON'S celebrated "Farewell-Address"

[illegible]

WAR NEWS.

[illegible]

Heavy American losses in the recent battles.

[illegible]

Photographic reproduction of first page of a German propaganda newspaper, the sort sent over the lines to American troops. This paper was found in the St. Mihiel Sector on the morning of August 21st, 1918, in Trench de Seres at point 65.1-34.1.

OFFICERS' ROSTER

OFFICERS SERVING OVERSEAS WITH 89th DIVISION

Rank given, with few exceptions, is the highest attained while assigned to the Division. Branch of service in which commissioned is shown by assignment except where otherwise marked. Organization designated is the one in which the officer served the longest time or with which he was most closely identified.* A few names appear of officers assigned to the Division but who did not serve with it.

Name, Rank and *Organization

Abbott, Harry C., 1st Lt., 353rd Inf.
Abeel, Alan C., 2nd Lt., 355th Inf.
Abel, Oscar B., Capt., 355th Inf.
Adams, Clarence, Capt., S. C., Hq. 89th Div.
Adams, Franklin A., 2nd Lt., Inf., Hq. 89th Div.
Adams, Lawrence B., 2nd Lt., V. C., 340th F. A.
Adams, Samuel, Capt., M. C., 314th Eng.
Addison, D. E., 2nd Lt., Q. M. C., Bathing and Clothing Unit No. 326.
Adler, Herbert G., 2nd Lt., F. A., Hq. 89th Div.
Aird, William A., Major, Inf., 341st M. G. Bn.
Albert, Fred Craig, Capt., 314th Eng.
Albright, Fred C., Capt., M. C., 353rd Inf.
Ale, John H., 1st Lt., 355th Inf.
Alexander, Arthur P., 1st Lt., D. C., 353rd Inf.
Alexander, Joseph E., 2nd Lt., Inf., 314th Sup. Tr.
Allen, Darius, 1st Lt., 355th Inf.
Allen, E. L., 2nd Lt., Inf., 341st M. G. Bn.
Allen, George A., 2nd Lt., 340th F. A.
Allen, Gerard, 1st Lt., 341st F. A.
Allen, Jacob W., 1st Lt., 355th Inf.
Allen, Robert H., Col., 356th Inf.
Allen, Robert J., 2nd Lt., 341st F. A.
Allen, William B., Capt., 354th Inf.
Allis, Leland C., 1st Lt., 354th Inf.
Allmond, Angus R., 2nd Lt., 341st F. A.
Allport, Harold E., 1st Lt., 356 Inf.
Alps, Bayard G., 1st Lt., 356th Inf.
Amerime, Ivan R., 2nd Lt., 354th Inf.
Amermann, Ralph K., 1st Lt., 342nd F. A.
Amet, Herbert P., 1st Lt., 314th Eng.
Ammons, Olly C., 1st Lt., D. C., 314th Tr. Hq. and M. P.
Anderson, Adolph A., 1st Lt., D. C., 341st F. A.
Anderson, Carl M., 2nd Lt., 355th Inf.
Anderson, Hanson H., 1st Lt., 342nd F. A.
Anderson, James W., 2nd Lt., 356th Inf.
Anderson, Oswald K., 1st Lt., Inf., 342nd M. G. Bn.
Androp, Serge, Capt., M. C. 342nd F. A.
App, Leo B., 2nd Lt., 353rd Inf.
Armstrong, George L., Capt., 354th Inf.
Arnold, Emmet L., 1st Lt., 356th Inf.
Arnold, Frank P., 1st Lt., 314th Eng.
Artz, George E., 1st Lt., M. C. 314th San. Tr.
Ashmore, C. M., Chaplain, 353rd Inf.
Atkins, Moses D., Capt., 353rd Inf.
Auchard, Virgil M., 2nd Lt., 355th Inf.
Aug, Charles H., 2nd Lt., 356th Inf.
Avery, Charles D., 2nd Lt., Inf., Hq. 89th Div.
Avery, Floyd B., 1st Lt., 314th Eng.
Avery, W. F., 1st Lt., D. C., 354th Inf.
Axon, Elmer R., Capt., 314th Eng.

Babcock, Conrad S., Col., Cav., 354th Inf.
Bach, Joseph P., 2nd Lt., 356th Inf.
Backman, S. G., Capt., 314th Eng.
Backstrom, A. G., 2nd Lt., 340th F. A.
Bailey, George R., 2nd Lt., 353rd Inf.
Bailey, Morton S., 1st Lt., 353rd Inf.
Bailey, Virgil S., 2nd Lt., Inf., 342nd M. G. Bn.
Bair, Howard A., 2nd Lt., 354th Inf.
Baker, Ernest, 2nd Lt., Inf., Hq. 89th Div.
Baker, George D., Capt., Inf., 342nd M. G. Bn.
Baker, George R., Capt., M. C., 355th Inf.
Baker, Tracy, Capt., Inf., 341st M. G. Bn.
Baker, Wilfred W., 1st Lt., 314th Eng.
Baldwin, Arthur D., Capt., Hq. 164th F. A. Brig.
Baldwin, Benjamin B., 2nd Lt., 355th Inf.
Ball, E. C., 1st Lt., 353rd Inf.
Ballard, Chester N., 2nd Lt., 341st F. A.
Balliett, Kenneth E., 2nd Lt., 356th Inf.
Ballinger, Robert, 1st Lt., D. C., 314th Eng.
Ballweg, Raymond A., 1st Lt., 353rd Inf.
Banks, Frank E., 2nd Lt., 341st F. A.
Baonel, Henry H., 2nd Lt., 353rd Inf.
Barbour, Ira J., Capt., 355th Inf.

Name, Rank and *Organization

Barger, Harold B., 1st Lt., 340th F. A.
Bargfrede, John, 2nd Lt., 354th Inf.
Barkmann, H. A., Capt., D. C., 340th M. G. Bn.
Barnard, Joseph H., Lt. Col., 354th Inf.
Barnett, Allen, Capt., 353rd Inf.
Barnett, Raymond G., 1st Lt., Inf., Hq. 177th Inf. Brig.
Barnett, William H., 1st Lt., M. T. C., Hq. 89th Div.
Barney, Carey W., 1st Lt., 354th Inf.
Barney, James W., Capt., Inf. Hq. 89th Div.
Barnhardt, Geo. C., Brig. Gen., Hq. 178th Inf. Brig.
Barone, Richard F., 2nd Lt., 342nd F. A.
Barr, Charles F., 1st Lt., D. C., 354th Inf.
Barr, Harry E., 1st Lt., 340th F. A.
Barr, Jesse W., 1st Lt., 353rd Inf.
Barrett, Edward J., 2nd Lt., 355th Inf.
Barron, Stephen F., Chaplain, Hq. 89th Div.
Bartlett, Charles W., Major, Q. M. C., Hq. 89th Div.
Bartlett, G. D., 1st Lt., 340th F. A.
Bartlett, John D., Major, M. C., 314th San. Tr.
Barton, James F., Capt., Inf, 342nd M. G. Bn.
Bartsch, Fred S., 2nd Lt., 356th Inf.
Baskett, Lindsay Webster, Major, M. C., 356th Inf.
Basye, Edmund H., 1st Lt., 355th Inf.
Bates, Horace C., Major, Inf, 342nd M. G. Bn.
Bates, Vernon E., 1st Lt., 354th Inf.
Bauer, Raymond G., 2nd Lt., 314th Eng.
Baxter, A. F., Capt., 353rd Inf.
Bayless, Walter J., 1st Lt, 341st F. A.
Bayley, Earnest R., 1st Lt., 354th Inf.
Beach, Alfred H., Major, F. A., Hq. 89th Div.
Beale, Raymond H., 2nd Lt., M. P. C., Hq. 89th Div.
Beaman, Walter L., Capt., 353rd Inf.
Beardslee, Claude G., 2nd Lt., 340th F. A.
Beaver, Thurman R., Capt. M. C., 314 San. Tr.
Beck, Henry A., 1st Lt., M. C., 355th Inf.
Becker, Seth A., 2nd Lt., 354th Inf.
Behrend, Jerome V., 1st Lt., 356th Inf.
Behrman, Roland A., Capt., M. C., 314 San. Tr.
Belot, Monte L., Capt., M. C., 314 San. Tr.
Benedict, B. W., 1st Lt., Inf., Hq. 89th Div.
Bennett, John D., 1st Lt., 353rd Inf.
Bennett, Louis E., Col., C. A. C., 342nd F. A.
Benning, Lloyd H., 1st Lt., 353rd Inf.
Bente, Oscar F., 1st Lt., Inf., Hq. 89th Div.
Bentley Bruce M., 1st Lt., Inf., 340th M. G. Bn.
Berg, Harold, 1st Lt., Inf., 341st M. G. Bn.
Bergfield, Geo. A., 2nd Lt., 354th Inf.
Bernard, Thomas P., Lt. Col., 355th Inf.
Bernet, Milton E., 1st Lt., Q. M. C., 314 Sup. Tr.
Beukema, Herman, Major, F. A., Hq. 164th F. A. Brig.
Beverage, Columbus A., 2nd Lt., 355th Inf.
Biezis, Stephen, 1st Lt., M. C., 354th Inf.
Biggs, Clyde H., Capt., 353rd Inf.
Birch, Albert E., 2nd Lt., Inf., 342nd M. G. Bn.
Bird, Owen I., 1st Lt., D. C., 354th Inf.
Biscoe, Earl, Col., C. A. C., 342nd F. A.
Bishop, George M., 1st Lt., Eng., Hq. 89th Div.
Bissell, Harry B., Major, 353rd Inf
Black, Gurdon G., Major, 314th Eng.
Blackinton, George W., Lt. Col., 353rd Inf.
Blair, Bard B., 2nd Lt., 342nd F. A.
Blair, Glen F., 1st Lt, Inf., 341st M. G. Bn.
Blair, L. L., 1st Lt., M. C., 314th San. Tr.
Blair, Leon M., 2nd Lt., 353rd Inf.
Bland, William J., Major, 356th Inf.
Blattner, Carl H., 1st Lt, Q. M. C., Bakery Co. 349.
Blelock, William W., 2nd Lt., 342nd F. A.
Block, Gary E, Capt., 314th Eng.
Block, Oscar E., Capt., M. C., 356th Inf.
Bodie, Davis P., 2nd Lt., 353rd Inf.
Boesch, Clarence E., Major, Eng., Hq. 89th Div.
Boldon, Harry, 2nd Lt, 356th Inf.
Bolton, Louis E., 1st Lt., 356th Inf.
Bond, Eugene A., Capt., 353rd Inf.
Bondi, Anthony, 1st Lt., M. C., 314th San. Tr.

Name, Rank and *Organization

Borst, Ralph P., 2nd Lt., 356th Inf.
Bosch, Nick, Jr., 2nd Lt., 353rd Inf.
Boschen, Fred W., Lt. Col., 353rd Inf.
Bosley, Carl E., Capt., M. C., 356th Inf.
Bottomley, Myrl E., 2nd Lt., 355th Inf.
Bottorff, Guy W., 1st Lt., Inf., 314th Sup. Tr.
Bourck, William, 2nd Lt., Inf., 314th Amm. Tr.
Boutwell, Lloyd R., 1st Lt., M. C., 314th Eng.
Bowen, Ivan, Capt., F. A., 314th Amm. Tr.
Bower, Albert G., 1st Lt., M. C., 353rd Inf.
Bowie, Louis L., Capt., M C., 314 San. Tr.
Bowland, Ray E., Capt., 353rd Inf.
Bowler, John F., 2nd Lt., 353rd Inf.
Bowles, Martin F., 1st Lt., 355th Inf.
Bowman, Matt C., 2nd Lt., 341st F. A.
Bowser, Charles K., 1st Lt., 355th Inf.
Boyce, Shirley R., Capt., M. C., 353rd Inf.
Boyd, A. S., Major, 353rd Inf.
Boyle, Ernest E., 1st Lt., 354th Inf.
Boyle, Peter, 1st Lt., 354th Inf.
Braden, Clyde O., 2nd Lt., 341st F. A.
Bradfield, Lloyd, 1st Lt., 355th Inf.
Bradley, Edward C., 1st Lt., Inf., 342nd M. G. Bn.
Brannigan, Frank, Capt., Inf., 314th Amm. Tr.
Bratcher, Claude, 2nd Lt., 354th Inf.
Braucher, Hawley H., 1st Lt., 342nd M. G. Bn.
Breen, Frederick, 1st Lt., 353rd Inf.
Brennan, Alfred F., 1st Lt., 342nd F. A.
Briber, Frank E., 2nd Lt., 314th Eng.
Bridges, Thomas S., Major, 354th Inf.
Brinkley, Charles A., Capt., Q. M. C., 314th San. Tr.
Brinkman, Walter N., 2nd Lt., 356th Inf.
Brock, Raymond O., 2nd Lt., 356th Inf.
Brockmeyer, Edwin J., 2nd Lt., 314th Eng.
Brockway, Fred, 2nd Lt., 355th Inf.
Brod, Benjamin, 1st Lt., M. C., 314th San. Tr.
Brodie, Francis R., 1st Lt., 341st F. A.
Bromfield, Donald C., 1st Lt., 355th Inf.
Bronston, Jason L., 1st Lt., 353rd Inf.
Brookshire, Willie S., 2nd Lt., 354th Inf.
Brouse, Don, 2nd Lt., 356th Inf.
Brown, Eugene H., 1st Lt., M. C., 314th San. Tr.
Brown, George P., 1st Lt., 354th Inf.
Brown, Herbert A., Capt., 353rd Inf.
Brown, J. Angus, Capt., 355th Inf.
Brown, Joseph E., Major, A. G. D., Hq. 89th Div.
Brown, Levi G., Lt. Col., F. A., Hq. 89th Div.
Brown, Russell V., 2nd Lt., Q. M. C., Sales Commissary Unit No. 5.
Brown, Sanford P., Capt., Inf., 342 M. G. Bn.
Browne, Harold F., 1st Lt., 353rd Inf.
Broyles, Watkins A., 2nd Lt., 355th Inf.
Brugger, A. E., 1st Lt., 314th Eng.
Brunckhorst, Frank O., Capt., M. C., 354th Inf.
Brunzell, Otto L., Col., 342nd F. A.
Brush, Percy P., 2nd Lt., 342nd F. A.
Bryan, Henry C., 1st Lt., 314th Amm. Tr.
Bryant, Kuebel A., 1st Lt., M. C., 314th San. Tr.
Bryson, Harold L., Major, 342nd F. A.
Buckbee, E. J., Major, Q M. C., Hq. 89th Div.
Buleo, Leo F., 2nd Lt., 355th Inf.
Bulkley, Ralph G., 1st Lt., F. A., Hq. 164th F. A. Brig.
Bump, Floyd S., 2nd Lt., F. A., 314th Tr. Mortar Bty.
Bunger F. S., 2nd Lt., 340th F. A.
Bunker Sydney, Capt., M. C., 314th San. Tr.
Bunts, Alexander T., 2nd Lt., 341st F. A.
Burgener, Charles E., 1st Lt., 341st F. A.
Burgess, Herbert R., Capt., 356th Inf.
Burke, John J., 2nd Lt., 354th Inf.
Burkhalter, Harry N., Major, Inf., 342nd M. G. Bn.
Burks, Amos L., Capt., 354th Inf.
Burns, David S., 2nd Lt., 356th Inf.
Burns, Harry J., Capt., M. C., 314th San. Tr.
Burns, William, 1st Lt., 342nd F. A.
Burruss, David N., 1st Lt., 341st F. A.
Burstien, Louis L., 1st Lt., M. C., 355th Inf.
Burtis, Darrel D., 2nd Lt., 354th Inf.
Burton, Charles M., Capt., Q. M. C, Hq. 89th Div.
Busch, Claus M., 2nd Lt., 353rd Inf.
Bush, Martin M., 1st Lt., 354th Inf.
Butler, Charles E., 1st Lt., 353rd Inf.
Butler, F. W., Major, 354th Inf.
Byerley, Cecil B, 2nd Lt., 356th Inf.
Byrd, John H., Capt., 314th Eng.
Byrne, Gerald D., Major, D. C., Hq. 89th Div.
Byrnes, James, Capt., 342nd F. A.
Byrum, Paul R., Capt., Inf., 341st M. G. Bn.

Name, Rank and *Organization

Caffey, Hugh W., 2nd Lt., 340th F. A.
Cagle, A. F., Chaplain, 355th Inf.
Cain, John M., Capt., 342nd F. A.
Cain, Louis A., 1st Lt., 355th Inf.
Caldwell, Leslie O., 1st Lt., 355th Inf.
Caldwell, Will P., 2nd Lt., 341st F. A.
Calhoun, Allen P., 2nd Lt., 356th Inf.
Calver, Homer N., 1st Lt., San. Corps., 314 San. Tr.
Campbell, Raymond, 2nd Lt., 340th F. A.
Campbell, Samuel A., 1st Lt., 355th Inf.
Campbell, Thomas R., Major, 355th Inf.
Cannon, Peter L., 2nd Lt., 353rd Inf.
Cansler, Edwin T., Capt., Inf., Hq. 89th Div.
Carey, Frank L., 2nd Lt., 342nd F. A.
Carey, Marc R., 1st Lt., D. C., 314th San. Tr.
Carlson, George N., Capt., 356th Inf.
Carlson, Harry, Capt., 356th Inf.
Carlton, Berne S., 2nd Lt., 356th Inf.
Carpenter, Lewis G., Capt., F. A., Hq. 89th Div.
Carpenter, Wm. S., Chaplain, Hq. 89th Div.
Carr, Roy E., 1st Lt., 353rd Inf.
Carr, Walter A., Major, M. C., 314th San. Tr.
Carson, Frank P., Capt., 356th Inf.
Carter, A. H., 1st Lt., M. C., 314th San. Tr.
Carter, Charles B., Capt., Ord. Corps, 314th Mobile Ord. Repair Shop.
Carwile, Walker P., 2nd Lt., Inf., 341st M. G. Bn.
Cary, Logan W., 2nd Lt., 355th Inf.
Case, Charles A., Capt., 314th Eng.
Case, Maurice A., 1st Lt., D. C., 341st M. G. Bn.
Casey, James B., 2nd Lt., 354th Inf.
Casey, Thomas W., 1st Lt., 341st F. A.
Cassidy, Thomas J., Major, D. C., 314th Eng.
Cassin, Frank J., 2nd Lt., 314th Eng.
Catterlin, Oscar, 1st Lt., 355th Inf.
Cavanaugh, Jesse, 2nd Lt., 353rd Inf.
Cavaness, Ernest W., Capt., M. C., 314th San. Tr.
Cavenaugh, Wm. A., Col., 355th Inf.
Chaffee, Glenn R., 1st Lt., D. C., 314th San. Tr.
Chalmers, Clifford, 1st Lt., 353rd Inf.
Chamberlain, Guy R., 2nd Lt., 355th Inf.
Champeny, Arthur S., Capt., 356th Inf.
Chandler, Kent, Capt., Inf., 341st M. G. Bn.
Chanler, Winthrop, Capt., Inf., Hq. 89th Div.
Chapman Charles, 1st Lt. Inf., Hq. 89th Div.
Chase, Albert G., Capt., 354th Inf.
Chase, Edward, Capt., 354th Inf.
Chase, Erskine H., 1st Lt., 353rd Inf.
Cheney, Morris S., 1st Lt., 340th F. A.
Chiera, H. J., Chaplain, 355th Inf.
Chiles, Marcellus H., Capt., 356th Inf.
Chittenden, R. M., 2nd Lt., 340th F. A.
Chittenden, Rollin d'E., 1st Lt., 341st F. A.
Chittick, M. B., Capt., Eng., Hq 89th Div.
Chouteau, Auguste, 2nd Lt., Q. M. C., 314th Sup. Tr.
Christiancy, Herbert E., 1st Lt., 353rd Inf.
Christmann, H. A., 1st Lt., 340th F. A.
Christoph, Charles D., 1st Lt., 353rd Inf.
Chubb, Robert W., Capt., 342nd F. A.
Churchill, Gerald E., 2nd Lt., 354th Inf.
Claiborne, Leonard J., 2nd Lt., 340th F. A.
Clancy, J. L., 1st Lt., M. C., 314th Amm. Tr.
Clancy, Richard E., 1st Lt., 354th Inf.
Clark, Charles B., Col., G. S., Hq. 89th Div.
Clark, George, 1st Lt., 342nd F. A.
Clark, Gideon T., 2nd Lt., 353rd Inf.
Clark, Howard, 2nd Lt., Eng., Hq. 89th Div.
Clark, James A., 2nd Lt., 342nd F. A.
Clark, Robert W., Lt. Col., F. A., Hq. 89th Div.
Clark, W. K., 1st Lt., 340th F. A.
Clarke, Robert C., 1st Lt., 354th Inf.
Clarkson, Freeman, Capt., 314th Eng.
Clausing, Roth, 2nd Lt., 341st F. A.
Clement, William B., Capt., 354th Inf.
Clemente, Humbert J., 1st Lt., 354th Inf.
Cline, Earl M., Capt., 355th Inf.
Cline, Neal F., 2nd Lt., 354th Inf.
Cloud, Paul W., 2nd Lt., 314th F. S. Bn.
Clough, William P., 1st Lt., M. C., 314th San. Tr.
Coats, Ralph B., 2nd Lt., Inf., 340th M. G. Bn.
Coatsworth, William M., Capt., 356th Inf.
Cochran, F. M., Lt. Col., 356th Inf.
Cochrane, Walter C., 1st Lt., 356th Inf.
Coffman, Frank, 2nd Lt., 356th Inf.
Colburn, Daniel N., 1st Lt., D. C., 353rd Inf.
Cole, Charles C., 1st Lt., 356th Inf.
Cole, Walter C., Major, Q. M. C., 314th Sup. Tr.
Coleman, James C., 1st Lt., 314th F. S. Bn.
Coleman, Paul M., 1st Lt., F. A., Hq. 164th F. A. Brig.

Name, Rank and *Organization
Collins, John F., 1st Lt., 354th Inf.
Combs, C. J., Major, M. C., 340th F. A.
Comstock, Arthur T., 2nd Lt., 342nd F. A.
Condie, Walter D., 1st Lt., 342nd F. A.
Conklin, Deane L., 2nd Lt., 355th Inf.
Connally, Horace P., 2nd Lt., 314th F. S. Bn.
Connell, Carleton A., 1st Lt., Ord. Corps, 314th Mobile Ord. Repair Shop.
Connors, Edward M., 1st Lt., 353rd Inf.
Conover, George R., 1st Lt., Ord. Corps, 314th Mobile Repair Shop.
Converse, Charles W., 1st Lt., V. C., 342nd F A.
Cook, Chauncey W., Capt., Hq. 89th Div.
Cook, Lewis H., 2nd Lt., 354th Inf.
Cook, Paul B., Major, M. C., 314th San. Tr.
Coolidge, Walter L., Capt., M. C., 353rd Inf.
Cooper, Joseph A., Chaplain, Hq. 89th Div.
Cooper, Wm. S., 2nd Lt., 353rd Inf.
Corboy, William J., Chaplain, 314th Amm. Tr.
Cordis, Samuel L., 2nd Lt., 340th F. A.
Corell, Fred A., 2nd Lt., 355th Inf.
Cornell, T. E., 2nd Lt., 342nd F. A.
Corvese, Anthony, 1st Lt., M. C., 314th San. Tr.
Costella, James L., Lt. Col., Q. M. C., Hq. 89th Div.
Cotton, Herbert M., 2nd Lt., Inf., 342nd M. G. Bn.
Cottrell, Joseph F., Lt. Col., 342nd F. A.
Couchman, Floyd H., 1st Lt., 353rd Inf.
Cousins, Dennis E., 2nd Lt., 314th F. S. Bn.
Covington, John W., 1st Lt., 353rd Inf.
Cowan, Vern L., 1st Lt., D. C., 314th San. Tr.
Cox, Harvey B., 1st Lt., 354th Inf.
Coy, Burgis G., Major, 314th Eng.
Coyne, Roy R., Capt., Inf., 89th M. P. Co.
Coyner, Howard D., 2nd Lt., 340th F. A.
Craig, M. L. Weems, 1st Lt., Inf., Hq. 89th Div.
Crandall, Herbert R., 2nd Lt., 355th Inf.
Crane, R. W., 1st Lt., 340th F. A.
Crans, Roy E., 1st Lt., 314th Eng.
Cravens, Charles R., 1st Lt., 354th Inf.
Crawford, Abbott L., 2nd Lt., 355th Inf.
Crawford, Benjamin H., Capt., D. C., 353rd Inf.
Crawford, Earl R., 2nd Lt., 314th Amm. Tr.
Crawford, Geo. E., 2nd Lt., 354th Inf.
Crawford, Robert Leighton 3rd, Capt., F. A. Hq. 164th F. A. Brig.
Creaghe, St. George S., 1st Lt., 356th Inf.
Crews, Thomas B., Jr., Capt., 342nd F. A.
Crites, Clarence D., 1st Lt., Inf., 314th Amm. Tr.
Crockett, Dura P., Capt., Inf., Hq. 89th Div.
Crockett, James C., Capt., 356th Inf.
Crofton, Geo. H., 1st Lt., M. C., 355th Inf.
Crofut, Henry, Capt., Cav., 314th Tr. Hq. and M. P.
Crofut, John L., Capt., Inf., 89th M. P. Co.
Cronkite, Francisco M., 1st Lt., 354th Inf.
Cross, Walter S., Chaplain, 314th Tr. Hq. and M. P.
Crossland, Clarence, 2nd Lt., 354th Inf.
Crothers, George M., 1st Lt., 356th Inf.
Cruise, John D., 2nd Lt., 341st F. A.
Crump, Clay K., Capt., 353rd Inf.
Cruse, Charles G., 1st Lt., Inf., 341st M. G. Bn.
Crystal, T. L., Lt. Col., 354th Inf.
Cubbison, Paul K., Capt., 354th Inf.
Cullen, Lawrence K., 1st Lt., 356th Inf.
Cuming, Ulmont O., 2nd Lt., 340th F. A.
Cummins, J. T., 1st Lt., 314th Eng.
Curfman, Lawrence E., Lt. Col., 314th Eng.
Curlee, Francis M., Capt., 340th F. A.
Currey, Bradley, Capt., 353rd Inf.
Curry, Walter, 1st Lt., 354th Inf.
Curtis, Raleigh T., 2nd Lt., Inf., Hq. 89th Div.
Cushing, John B., 1st Lt., 353rd Inf.

Dauge, Howard D., 2nd Lt., Inf., 314th Sup. Tr.
Dahmke, Frederick, Major, 353rd Inf.
Dake, Justin W., 2nd Lt., 354th Inf.
Daly, J. B., 2nd Lt., 342nd F. A.
Danforth, George L., Capt., 341st F. A.
Darley, Christian P. J., Chaplain, 355th Inf.
Darrin, H. M., 1st Lt., Inf., Hq. 89th Div.
Darst, James E., 2nd Lt., Inf., 341st M. G. Bn.
Davidson, Hartley G., 2nd Lt., F. A., 314th Amm. Tr.
Davidson, John H., 2nd Lt., 355th Inf.
Davis, Ancil G., Major, Inf., 314th Amm. Tr.
Davis, Charles O., 1st Lt., 353rd Inf.
Davis, Dean W., 1st Lt., 354th Inf.
Davis, George A., Major, Inf., Hq. 89th Div.
Davis, George F., Capt., M. C., 314th San. Tr.
Davis, Henry, Lt. Col., J. A. G. D., Hq. 89th Div.
Davis, Howard P., 2nd Lt., M. P. C., 89th M. P. Co.
Davis, James E., 1st Lt., 356th Inf.

Name, Rank and *Organization
Davis, John E.; 2nd Lt., 353rd Inf.
Davis, Manton, Capt., 354th Inf.
Davis, Manvel H., 1st Lt., Hq. 177th Inf. Brig.
Davis, P. R., 1st Lt., M. C., 355th Inf.
Davis, Robert, Col., 341st F. A.
Davis, Robert F., 1st Lt., Inf., Hq. 89th Div.
Davis, Vernon W., 1st Lt., D. C., 356th Inf.
Davis, William M., 1st Lt., 341st F. A.
Dearing, Harry L., 2nd Lt., 355th Inf.
Deem, Frederick S., 1st Lt., M. C., 314th San. Tr.
Dehmel, Richard W. A., Capt., M. C., 356th Inf.
Deiman, Harry, Chaplain, 354th Inf.
Deland, Thorndike, 1st Lt., 340th F. A.
Delaney, G. A., 1st Lt., 340th F. A.
Delaney, John J., Capt., 353rd Inf.
Dennie, Frank E., Capt., 314th Eng.
Dennis, Orville L., 1st Lt., 355th Inf.
Deuchar, Chas. D., 2nd Lt., Cav., 341st M. G. Bn.
Dickey, Burton F., Capt., Inf., 314th Sup. Tr.
Dickey, C. H., Chaplain, 341st M. G. Bn.
Dickinson, Alfred J., Chaplain, 356th Inf.
Dickson, Clarence C., 1st Lt., Inf., 341st M. G. Bn.
Dienst, Charles F., Capt., 353rd Inf.
Dierking, Irwin S., 1st Lt., 355th Inf.
Dillard, Fielding, 2nd Lt., 353rd Inf.
Dillard, Miles H., 1st Lt., 356th Inf.
Dinsmore, Arthur M., 2nd Lt., 354th Inf.
Dobson, Gilbert C., Capt., 314th Eng.
Dodd, Charles G., Capt., 353rd Inf.
Dodge, S. P., Capt., 340th F. A.
Doherty, Joseph T., 2nd Lt., 356th Inf.
Doherty, William T., 1st Lt., M. C., 355th Inf.
Dolan, William H., 1st Lt., 353rd Inf.
Donahue, J. D., 2nd Lt., 342nd M. G Bn.
Doneghy, John T., Jr., 1st Lt., 342nd F. A.
Doniat, F. A., Lt. Col., G. S., Hq. 89th Div.
Donnelly, Edward T., Brig. Gen., Hq. 164th F. A. Brig.
Donohoe, Wm. T., 2nd Lt., 356th Inf.
Donovan, John B., Capt., Inf., 342nd M. G. Bn.
Dooling, Henry C., 1st Lt., M. C., 314th San. Tr.
Dorety, Philip J., 1st Lt., M. C., 314th San. Tr.
Dorfmeier, Virgil Z., 1st Lt., 353rd Inf.
Dorn, Ralph W., Capt., 355th Inf.
Dorris, Charles L., 1st Lt., 355th Inf.
Dost, Paul F., 2nd Lt., 356th Inf.
Dougherty, James R., 2nd Lt., 355th Inf.
Dougherty, Lew W., Capt., D. C., 341st F. A.
Douglas, James M., 1st Lt., 342nd F. A.
Downey, Thomas, 2nd Lt., 355th Inf.
Downey, Wm. J., 2nd Lt., 353rd Inf.
Downing, Roy H., Capt., 340th F. A.
Drake, A. N., 1st Lt., 355th Inf.
Draper, George, Major, M. C., 355th Inf.
Draper, Henry E., 2nd Lt., 353rd Inf.
Dreher, Henry S., Capt., M. C., 314th San. Tr.
Driscoll, Cornelius J., 2nd Lt., 353rd Inf.
Driscoll, Michael A., 2nd Lt., 356th Inf.
Drollinger, Clyde F., 1st Lt., 342nd F. A.
Dross, John, Capt., 314th Tr. Hq. and M. P.
Drybread, Joseph W., 1st Lt., F. A., 314th Amm. Tr.
Dudley, Edward C., 1st Lt., 356th Inf.
Dugan, Patrick C., 2nd Lt., 355th Inf.
Dumont, Fernald G., Capt., 355th Inf.
Duncan, Edgar C., Major, M. C., 314th San. Tr.
Duncker, C. H., Capt., 340th F. A.
Dunn, Charles H. E., 1st Lt., 353rd Inf.
Durham, A. Z., 1st Lt., D. C., 314th Eng.
Durham, Louis A., 1st Lt., 355th Inf.
Durnell, Aubert, Capt., M. C., 355th Inf.
Duvall, Thomas W., 2nd Lt., 342nd M. G. Bn.
Dye, J. T. Jr., 2nd Lt., Inf., 314th Amm. Tr.
Dykes, John H., Capt., 356th Inf.

Eades, Carl G., Capt., 353rd Inf.
Earl, John J., 2nd Lt., 354th Inf.
Early, Bynum T., Major, Q. M. C., Hq. 89th Div.
Eaton, Gilbert M., 2nd Lt., Inf., 341st M. G. Bn.
Ebersole, Benjamin S., Capt., 342nd F. A.
Edmonds, Leslie E., Capt., Inf., 341st M. G. Bn.
Edmondson, Wm. O., 1st Lt., Inf., 342nd M. G. Bn.
Edwards, Will E., 1st Lt., Inf., 342nd M. G. Bn.
Egbert, P. S., 1st Lt., C. W. S., Hq. 89th Div.
Egen, Lothar F., Capt., M. C., 314th San. Tr.
Egloff, G. E., Capt., M. C., 342nd F. A.
Eigonauer, John E., 2nd Lt., 354th Inf.
Eikenbary, Charles F., Capt., M. C., 314th San. Tr.
Eiskant, Anthony J., 1st Lt., M. T. C., M. S. T. U. No. 390.
Eldridge, Charles D., Chaplain, 341st F. A.

Name, Rank and *Organization

Eldridge, Harold C., 1st Lt., 355th Inf.
Elliott, Clarence E., Capt., 342nd F. A.
Elliott, G. S., 2nd Lt., Inf., Hq. 178th Inf. Brig.
Ellis, Herbert A., 2nd Lt., 314th Eng.
Ellis, Ward, Capt., 353rd Inf.
Ellison, William F., 2nd Lt., 356th Inf.
Elmiger, Hans, Major, 340th F. A.
Elmore, Derrill G., 2nd Lt., 355th Inf.
Elsaesser, Otto H., 1st Lt., 356th Inf.
Elston, Allen V., 1st Lt., 314th Eng.
Embury, Aymar, Capt., Eng., Hq. 89th Div.
Engel, Carl A., 2nd Lt., Inf., Hq. 89th Div.
Engelhard, George, Capt., 341st F. A.
Engle, Stanley L., 1st Lt., 354th Inf.
English, George H., Jr., Lt. Col., Inf., Hq. 177th Inf. Brig.
Ensign, Chester O., 1st Lt., 353rd Inf.
Erickson, John E., 1st Lt., 341st F. A.
Ernsberger, Dale D., Capt., 356th Inf.
Ervin, Edwin A., 1st Lt., 355th Inf.
Erwin, John M., 1st Lt., Inf., Hq. 178th Inf. Brig.
Esmiol, Morris A., Capt., 340th F. A.
Etling, Walter P., 2nd Lt., 355th Inf.
Evans, F. E., 1st Lt., 340th F. A.
Evans, John E., 2nd Lt., 355th Inf.
Evans, Lawrence H., 1st Lt., 314th Eng.
Evans, Roy E., Capt., M. C., 314th San. Tr.
Evans, Walter O., 2nd Lt., Q. M. C., Hq. 89th Div.
Everett, Harry, Capt., D. C., 342nd F. A.
Everly, R. G., 2nd Lt., 356th Inf.
Eves, Herbert, 2nd Lt., 314th Eng.
Ewers, Clyde, 1st Lt., 354th Inf.

Fahley, Anton N., Capt., 354th Inf.
Fairless, John K., Capt., 340th F. A.
Fales, John C., 1st Lt., 314th Eng.
Fancher, Harvey A., Major, 341st F. A.
Fann, John J., 2nd Lt., 356th Inf.
Farbar, Ralph M., 1st Lt., 356th Inf.
Farmer, Ellery W., Lt. Col., I. G. D., Hq. 89th Div.
Farrar, James M., Jr., 2nd Lt., 354th Inf.
Farrar, Russel Johnson, 2nd Lt., 314th Eng.
Farrell, Guy C., 2nd Lt., 314th F. S. Bn.
Farrell, Henry C., 1st Lt., 340th M. G. Bn.
Farris, Carl H., Capt., 353rd Inf.
Farrish, George C., 2nd Lt., 356th Inf.
Fasig, Howard W., 2nd Lt., 341st F. A.
Fast, John O., 1st Lt., 342nd F. A.
Faus, Raymond G., 2nd Lt., 341st F. A.
Fehrenbaker, Carlin E., 2nd Lt., 341st F. A.
Felton, Hilbert O., 2nd Lt., 355th Inf.
Fenn, Gustave C., 2nd Lt., 355th Inf.
Fenton, Joseph H., 1st Lt., 355th Inf.
Ferguson, Allan P., 2nd Lt., 353rd Inf.
Ferguson, Albert E., 2nd Lt., 342nd F. A.
Ffoulkes, Bruce, Lt. Col., M. C., 314th San. Tr.
Fickett, Fred W., Capt., 354th Inf.
Fickle, Melvin E., 2nd Lt., 314th Eng.
Field, Edmond, 2nd Lt., 356th Inf.
Finger, Ted J., 1st Lt., 355th Inf.
Finkbiner, D. E., Capt., 342nd F. A.
Finlayson, Allen, 2nd Lt., 353rd Inf.
Fischer, Joseph W., 2nd Lt., 341st F. A.
Fisher, Frank J., 2nd Lt., 355th Inf.
Fisher, Hart Ellis, Capt., M. C., 356th Inf.
Fisher, Neville C., Capt., 355th Inf.
Fisher, S. L., Major, M. C., 354th Inf.
Fishwood, Halley M., 1st Lt., 314th Eng. Tr.
Fitch, Roger S., Col., G. S., Hq. 89th Div.
Fitzgerald, James A., 1st Lt., 341st F. A.
Fitzpatrick, Francis X., 2nd Lt., 342nd F. A.
Fletcher, Claude C., Capt., 354th Inf.
Floete, Franklin G., Capt., 342nd F. A.
Flora, Loren, 2nd Lt., V. C., 314th Tr. Hq. and M. P.
Flynn, William H., 2nd Lt., 314th F. S. Bn.
Font, Anthony, 1st Lt., M. C., 356th Inf.
Ford, Alexander L., Capt., Inf., 342nd M. G. Bn.
Ford, Walter A., Capt., M. C., 354th Inf.
Forman, Percy G., 1st Lt., 314th Eng.
Forrest, Nathan B., 1st Lt., 314th F. S. Bn.
Forsythe, Samuel, Capt., M. C., 354th Inf.
Foster, Bryant E., 1st Lt., 314th Amm. Tr.
Fournet, William J., 2nd Lt., 314th Eng.
Fowler, B. C., Capt., 355th Inf.
Fox, Alphonsus C., 1st Lt., 314th F. S. Bn.
Fox, Charles M., Capt., M. C., 353rd Inf.
Fox, Earl F., 2nd Lt., 354th Inf.
Fox, Jesse W., 2nd Lt., 342nd F. A.
Fox, Sylvester D., 1st Lt., M. C., 314th San. Tr.
Fraine, J. R., 1st Lt., Inf., 354th Inf

Name, Rank and *Organization

Franklin, Clyde R., 2nd Lt., Inf., 341st M. G. Bn.
Franklin, John F., Lt. Col., F. A., Hq. 89th Div.
Freeberg, Solomon, 1st Lt., 355th Inf.
Freeman, James E., 1st Lt., 355th Inf.
Freeman, John G., Capt., 314th Eng.
Frick, George F., 2nd Lt., 314th Eng.
Fryer, Clarie P., 2nd Lt., Inf., 342nd M. G. Bn.
Fulkerson, Walter S., Capt., Inf., 314th Sup. Tr.
Fullerton, Kenneth M., 2nd Lt., 341st F. A.
Fulton, Russell P., 2nd Lt., 354th Inf.
Furbur, Wallace R., 2nd Lt., 356th Inf.
Furlong, Harold A., 1st Lt., 353rd Inf.
Fuson, Charles M., Capt., M. C., 342nd F. A.

Gaffner, Karl A., 1st Lt., 356th Inf.
Gagnon, Arthur T. P., Chaplain, 314th Amm. Tr.
Gallagher, Edward F., 1st Lt., 356th Inf.
Gallenkamp, Charles O., 1st Lt., 353rd Inf.
Galvin, Francis L., 2nd Lt., 354th Inf.
Gammage, A. E., Capt., M. C., 353rd Inf.
Ganter, Maxwell, Chaplain, 356th Inf.
Gardner, Robert, 2nd Lt., 353rd Inf.
Gardner, Roy E., 2nd Lt., 314th Eng.
Gardnet, Ward A., 1st Lt., 353rd Inf.
Garin, Rene G., 2nd Lt., 353rd Inf.
Garside, B. C., 1st Lt., 340th F. A.
Gartner, William, Capt., M. C., 354th Inf.
Gaskill, John, 2nd Lt., 355th Inf.
Gassaway, Floyd E., Capt., 354th Inf.
Gaston, Alpheus D., 1st Lt., 314th F. S. Bn.
Gatchell, Theodore A., 2nd Lt., 341st F. A.
Gaydash, John A., 2nd Lt., 356th Inf.
Gaylord, Paul L., 1st Lt., 355th Inf.
Gentry, Roy I., Capt., 342nd F. A.
George, Harvey L., 2nd Lt., 354th Inf.
George, John C., Capt., M. C., 314th San. Tr.
Gerhardt, Charles H., Capt., Cav., Hq. 89th Div.
Gerteisen, John, Jr., 1st Lt., 353rd Inf.
Getelson, Joseph, Capt., M. C., 341st M. G. Bn.
Getsinger, J. W., Capt., 340th F. A.
Gibson, Chas. E., Capt., Q. M. C., Hq. 89th Div.
Gilbert, Frank, 1st Lt., 356th Inf.
Gilbert, Syl C., 2nd Lt., 356th Inf.
Gill, Denson D., Capt., M. C., 314th San. Tr.
Gillette, Frank O., 1st Lt., 355th Inf.
Ginsberg, William, Capt., M. C., 314th San. Tr.
Glaeser, Hugo W., 2nd Lt., 353rd Inf.
Glenn, Edgar M., 2nd Lt., 353rd Inf.
Glinski, Chester S., 2nd Lt., 355th Inf.
Glover, Rodney C., 1st Lt., 353rd Inf.
Goebel, William R., 1st Lt., 353rd Inf.
Goff, William, Capt., M. C., 354th Inf.
Golberg, A., 2nd Lt., 342nd F. A.
Goldsberry, Carl, 2nd Lt., 355th Inf.
Gomez, Louis G., 1st Lt., S. C., 354th Inf.
Good, Gilbert, Capt., 356th Inf.
Goodman, John B., Major, G. S., Hq. 89th Div.
Goodwin, F. E., Capt., 340th F. A.
Goodwin, Walton, Jr., Lt. Col., 355th Inf.
Gore, Robert J., 2nd Lt., Inf., 340th M. G. Bn.
Goss, Henry A., 1st Lt., 356th Inf.
Gottenborg, Archie C., 1st Lt., D. C., 341st F. A.
Gottschalk, Telesphor G., Lt. Col., 341st F. A.
Goujot, J. E., Lt. Col., 356th Inf.
Gould, Robin, Chaplain, 354th Inf.
Gowenlock, Thomas R., Capt., Inf., Hq. 89th Div.
Gramley, William, Capt., M. C., 356th Inf.
Gray, Alonzo, Col., Cav., 356th Inf.
Gray, Moses, Capt., 355th Inf.
Gray, Otis E., Chaplain, 353rd Inf.
Greable, Robert W., Capt., 341st F. A.
Greeley, A. W., Jr., Major, 314th F. S. Bn.
Green, Charles O., 2nd Lt., 342nd F. A.
Green, Estill I., Capt., Inf., Hq. 177th Inf. Brig.
Green, John O., 2nd Lt., 353rd Inf.
Greenman, E. N., 1st Lt., M. C., 314th San. Tr.
Greenwood, Albert E., 2nd Lt., 353rd Inf.
Greever, Paul R., 1st Lt., F. A., 314th Tr. Mtr. Bat.
Greiss, Charles H., 1st Lt., 356th Inf.
Grider, Neal, 1st Lt., 356th Inf.
Griffith, Groves B., 1st Lt., 355th Inf.
Griffith, Shannon A., Chaplain, 341st F. A.
Grinde, J. C., Capt., 354th Inf.
Griswold, H. C., 1st Lt., 354th Inf.
Grossman, Wm. F., Capt., 354th Inf.
Guilliano, Vincent, 2nd Lt., Q. M. C., Hq. 89th Div.
Gunby, Fred W., 2nd Lt., 353rd Inf.
Gunn, Charles H., Capt., 356th Inf.
Guy, Walter P., Capt., M. C., 314th San. Tr.

Name, Rank and *Organization

Hackman, Logan F., 1st Lt., Inf., 314th Sup. Tr.
Hackett, Wayne H., Capt., 355th Inf.
Hadley, Howard, 2nd Lt., 340th F. A.
Hagenbuch, C. O., 1st Lt., 340th F. A.
Hager, Frank J., Capt., M. C., 314th San. Tr.
Haigh, James A., 1st Lt., 314th M. P.
Halbert, William C., 2nd Lt., 314th Eng.
Hale, William A., Major, 340th M. G. Bn.
Hall, Herman, Brig. Gen., Hq. 177th Inf. Brig.
Hall, John F., Chaplain, 314th F. S. Bn.
Hall, Robert B., 2nd Lt., 355th Inf.
Hall, William F., 2nd Lt., 356th Inf.
Hall, William L., Capt., M. C., 314th San. Tr.
Ham, Victor H., 2nd Lt., 355th Inf.
Hammer, John E., Capt., M. C., 314th San. Tr.
Hancock, Albert B., 1st Lt., Inf., 342nd M. G. Bn.
Handlan, Edward R., Major, 342nd F. A.
Hanger, Charles R., 1st Lt., 356th Inf.
Hanks, Charles, 2nd Lt., 356th Inf.
Hanna, Henry P., 1st Lt., M. C., 314th Eng.
Hanna, Mark, Major, 356th Inf.
Hanna, Myron, 1st Lt., M. C., 314th San. Tr.
Hannigan, John J., 1st Lt., 314th F. S. Bn.
Hannigan, John Joseph, Capt., 353rd Inf.
Hannon, Edmund D., 2nd Lt., Inf., 341st M. G. Bn.
Hansen, Amos M., 1st Lt., 356th Inf.
Hansen, Arthur J., Chaplain, 314th San. Tr.
Hansen, Clarence J., 2nd Lt., 342nd F. A.
Hansen, John C., Capt., 356th Inf.
Hanson, Clinton E., 2nd Lt., 354th Inf.
Hanson, Harry W., Capt., 354th Inf.
Hanson, Thomas G., Brig. Gen., Hq. 178th Inf. Brig.
Harbison, McClarty, 1st Lt., Inf., 342nd M. G. Bn.
Hardy, Aldo E., 2nd Lt., V. C., 340th F. A.
Haring, Graham B., 2nd Lt., 353rd Inf.
Harkins, Leon R., 2nd Lt., V. C., 340th F. A.
Harlow, Alonzo W., Capt., 354th Inf.
Harney, Louis G., Major, M. C., Hq. 89th Div.
Harrel, George B., 2nd Lt., 356th Inf.
Harris, Arthur F., 1st Lt., Inf. 341st M. G. Bn.
Harris, James A., 1st Lt., 354th Inf.
Harris, John W., Major, 356th Inf.
Harris, John W., Jr., 2nd Lt., 353rd Inf.
Harris, Martin H., 1st Lt., 314th Eng.
Harris, Urban B., Capt., M. C., 314th San. Tr.
Harrison, Harry C., 1st Lt., 353rd Inf.
Hartig, Carl, 2nd Lt., 356th Inf.
Harting, Walter C., Capt., 314th Eng.
Harvey, Fred E., Major, M. C., 314th San. Tr.
Harvill, Halbert, 2nd Lt., 356th Inf.
Harwood, Ralph W., 2nd Lt., 353rd Inf.
Hastings, Havilah E., 1st Lt., Inf, 341st M. G. Bn.
Hastings, Roy, 1st Lt., 342nd F. A.
Hausmann, John E., Capt., Q. M. C., Hq. 89th Div.
Haverick, Harley D., 2nd Lt., 355th Inf.
Hawkins, Frank B., Col., 353rd Inf.
Hay, Donald D., Lt. Col., I. G. D., Hq. 89th Div.
Hay, George W., 1st Lt., 355th Inf.
Hay, Wendell P., Capt., 354th Inf.
Hayden, Herbert B., Lt. Col., 341st F. A.
Hayden, Richard V., 2nd Lt., 354th Inf.
Hayes, Ernest T., 1st Lt., Inf., 342nd M. G. Bn.
Hayes, Francis E. A., 2nd Lt., 356th Inf.
Hayes, William H., 1st Lt., 353rd Inf.
Hazard, Leland W., Major, A. G. D., Hq. 89th Div.
Hazlett, John C., Capt., 353rd Inf.
Heacock, Alvin E., 2nd Lt., 340th M. G. Bn.
Headley, Joseph B., Capt., F. A., 314th Amm. Tr.
Heagerty, William B., Major, M. C., 314th San. Tr.
Heath, Warren E., Capt., 340th F. A.
Hebblethwaite, Mark P., 2nd Lt., 356th Inf.
Hege, Loy A., 2nd Lt., 355th Inf.
Heibner, Eugene A., 1st Lt., M. C., 314th Eng.
Heidenheim, Arthur I., 2nd Lt., 342nd F. A.
Heiken, Eilert G., 1st Lt., 356th Inf.
Heim, Russel Rule, Capt., M. C., 356th Inf.
Heindsmann, Theodore E., 2nd Lt., Inf., 342nd M. G. Bn.
Helm, Meredeth E., Capt., D. C., 355th Inf.
Hemen, Edwin S., 2nd Lt., 354th Inf.
Henderson, George V., 1st Lt., 354th Inf.
Henderson, Henry, 2nd Lt., 354th Inf.
Hendricks, Earl L., Capt., M. C., 355th Inf.
Hennessy, C. A., 2nd Lt., 355th Inf.
Hennigan, James D., 1st Lt., F. A., 314th Amm. Tr.
Hensley, John J., 2nd Lt., 353rd Inf.
Henson, Lynn H., 2nd Lt., 314th F. S. Bn.
Herres, M. M., 1st Lt., 342nd F. A.
Herrick, Myron C., 2nd Lt., 355th Inf.
Herrington, Cass M., 1st Lt., 355th Inf.

Name, Rank and *Organization

Herring, Edgar T., 1st Lt., 340th F. A.
Heutel, Emil, 1st Lt., 356th Inf.
Hewitt, James S., 1st Lt., 353rd Inf.
Hexter, Percy K., Capt., M. T. C., Hq. 89th Div.
Hickey, T. F., 1st Lt., Cav., 341st M. G. Bn.
Higbee, H. G., Capt., 356th Inf.
Higgins, Robert A., 1st Lt., 355th Inf.
Hildebrand, John A., 1st Lt., 342nd F. A.
Hill, James W., 2nd Lt., 342nd F. A.
Hill, Nathaniel P., 1st Lt., 356th Inf.
Hilldring, John H., 1st Lt., 355th Inf.
Hinemon, John H., Jr., Lt. Col., S. C., Hq. 89th Div.
Hissem, Ralph W., Major, M. C., 314th San. Tr.
Hitchcock, William B., Capt., 354th Inf.
Hitz, Leonard J., Capt., D. C., 314th Amm. Tr.
Hobson, Henry W., Major, 356th Inf.
Hockaday, J. B., 1st Lt., 354th Inf.
Hodges, C. M., Capt., Inf., Hq. 89th Div.
Hodges, Walter A., Capt., M. C., 314th San. Tr.
Hoeynck, Frank J., 2nd Lt., 314th Eng.
Hofacre, Michael H., 1st Lt., 355th Inf.
Hogan, Raymond P., Capt., 341st F. A.
Holcombe, Wm. S., 1st Lt., 354th Inf.
Holland, Henry, Capt., San C., 314th San. Tr.
Hollensteiner, Arno. J., 2nd Lt., 314th Amm. Tr.
Hollingsworth, Thomas E., Jr., 2nd Lt., 341st F. A.
Holman, Harry A., Capt., 341st F. A.
Holmes, Carl N., 1st Lt., Inf. 341st M. G. Bn.
Holt, Henry, 2nd Lt., 314th F. S. Bn.
Hook, Ingraham D., Capt., 356th Inf.
Hook, Joseph J., 1st Lt., 356th Inf.
Hope, Percival G., 2nd Lt., 356th Inf.
Hopkins, Elliott B., Major, 342nd F. A.
Hopkins, Horace H., Capt., 355th Inf.
Horner, James L., 2nd Lt., 355th Inf.
Houghkirk, William E., 2nd Lt., 353rd Inf.
Hout, Earl L., Capt., 354th Inf.
Hovey, Howard W., 2nd Lt., 341st F. A.
Howard, Wm. L., 2nd Lt., 356th Inf.
Howbert, VanDyne, 1st Lt., 314th Eng.
Howe, Clifton C., 1st Lt., 356th Inf.
Howe, Wm. M., 1st Lt., 314th Eng.
Howell, John S., Capt., 354th Inf.
Hoy, George W. R., 1st Lt., 355th Inf.
Hubbard, Clifford W., 2nd Lt., 355th Inf.
Hudson, John W., 2nd Lt., F. A., 314th Amm. Tr.
Hudson, Robert G., 1st Lt., 354th Inf.
Hudson, W. A., 2nd Lt., 314th Eng.
Huff, Frederick C., Major, M. C., 314th San. Tr.
Hughes, Dan H., Capt., 355th Inf.
Hughes, Delmar R., Capt., 342nd F. A.
Hughes, Percy M., Jr., 1st Lt., 356th Inf.
Hughes, Reginald W., Capt., F. A., Hq. 164th F. A. Brig.
Hulen, Ruby M., 1st Lt., 353rd Inf.
Hull, J. D., 2nd Lt., 314th Eng.
Humphrey, James V., 2nd Lt., 353rd Inf.
Hunt, Marion L., Capt., F. A., 314th Amm. Tr.
Hunt, Paul C., Major, A. G. D., Hq. 178th Inf. Brig.
Hunter, Vernon D., Capt., 353rd Inf.
Hurst, Frank A., Major, M. C., 314th San. Tr.
Husted, Elbert E., Capt., 353rd Inf.
Huston, Gary, 1st Lt., Inf., 341st M. G. Bn.
Hutchinson, Grover E., 1st Lt., Inf., 340th M. G. Bn.
Hutchinson, Walter C., 2nd Lt., 355th Inf.
Hutton, John H., 1st Lt., 342nd F. A.
Hyde, E. A., 1st Lt., 340th F. A.
Hymes, John E., Major, D. C., Hq. 89th Div.
Hyssong, Clyde L., 1st Lt., 355th Inf.

Ingram, Charles H., Capt., 356th Inf.
Ireland, Rutherford, Capt., 354th Inf.
Irones, Rutherford B., Capt., M. C., 314th San. Tr.
Irwin, Wendell W. J., 1st Lt., 340th F. A.

Jaccard, Eugene G., Capt., Inf., 314th Amm. Tr.
Jackson, Benjamin R., 1st Lt., 354th Inf.
Jackson, George M., 1st Lt., Inf., 341st M. G. Bn.
Jackson, Jared F., 1st Lt. 353rd Inf.
Jackson, Rufus, Capt., M. C., 314th San. Tr.
Jacobs, Fenton S., Capt., Cav., Hq. Troop, 89th Div.
Jacobson, Andrew S., 2nd Lt., Inf, 314th Amm. Tr.
Jacobus, Harold F., 1st Lt., 342nd F. A.
Jamison Allen R., Capt., 356th Inf
Janes, David P., Capt. Inf., 340th M. G. Bn.
Janney, J. G., Capt., M. C., 342nd F. A.
Jansing, Joseph H., Capt., M. C., 340th F. A.
Jenkins, Charles E., Capt., M. C., 314th San. Tr.
Jenkins, George W., Capt., 354th Inf.
Jennings, Henry C., 1st Lt., 355th Inf.

Name, Rank and *Organization

Johnson, A. B., 2nd Lt., 314th Eng.
Johnson, Andrew M., 2nd Lt., 314th Eng.
Johnson, Arthur E., 1st Lt., 355th Inf.
Johnson, Czar C., Lt. Col., M. C., 342nd F. A.
Johnson, Earnest B., 2nd Lt., 356th Inf.
Johnson, Harry L., 2nd Lt., 355th Inf.
Johnson, Henry D., 1st Lt., 342nd F. A.
Johnson, James F., Major, 355th Inf.
Johnson, John D., 1st Lt., 356th Inf.
Johnson, Keen, 1st Lt., 354th Inf.
Johnson, La Roy G., 1st Lt., 354th Inf.
Johnson, Orlando, 2nd Lt., 356th Inf.
Johnson, Paul A., 2nd Lt., 342nd F. A.
Johnson, Ronald E., 2nd Lt., 356th Inf.
Johnson, Roy F., 1st Lt., 314th Amm. Tr.
Johnson, Sebastian K., 2nd Lt., 353rd Inf.
Johnson, W. F., 1st Lt., 342nd F. A.
Johnson, Will M., 1st Lt., Inf., 341st M. G. Bn.
Johnson, William G., 1st Lt., 354th Inf.
Johnston, Frank E., 2nd Lt., Inf., Hq. 89th Div.
Johnston, Robert P., Col., 314th Eng.
Jones, Clifford C., 1st Lt., 353rd Inf.
Jones, Cloyse J., 2nd Lt., 342nd F. A.
Jones, Erwin M., Capt., 341st F. A.
Jones, Morton T., Major, 354th Inf
Jones, Robert T., Capt., M. C., 314th San. Tr.
Jones, Thomas, Jr., Capt., Inf., 314th Amm. Tr.
Jordan, Francis N., 1st Lt., 356th Inf.
Joseph, Wm. A., Capt., M. C., 314th San. Tr.
Jumer, John A., 1st Lt., D. C., 340th M. G. Bn.

Kaiser, Eugene, 1st Lt., Q. M. C., Hq. 89th Div.
Kalina, Karl, 1st Lt., 342nd F. A.
Kaniewski, Walter L., 2nd Lt., 354th Inf.
Kapka, Horace L., 1st Lt., 355th Inf.
Kapper, Willard B., 2nd Lt., Inf., 341st M. G. Bn.
Karkow, Waldemar, 2nd Lt., 314th Eng.
Kassler, George W., 2nd Lt., 341st F. A.
Kavanaugh, Josiah B., Capt., 341st M. G. Bn.
Keel, James F., 2nd Lt., 314th Sup. Tr.
Keene, Robin C., Capt., 356th Inf.
Keezer, Dexter M., 1st Lt., Inf., 340th M. G. Bn.
Keim, Thurman E., Capt., 353rd Inf.
Keith, Richard H., 1st Lt., 341st F. A.
Keller, Dallas G., 1st Lt., Inf., 342nd M. G. Bn.
Kelley, James, 2nd Lt., 355th Inf.
Kellogg, George M., Capt., Q. M. C., Hq. 89th Div.
Kellogg, Gladstone B., 2nd Lt., 354 Inf.
Kellogg, Hugh B., Capt., 353rd Inf.
Kellogg, James G., 1st Lt., 341st F. A.
Kelly, Farmer, Capt., 354th Inf.
Kelly, Francis M., Capt., 355th Inf.
Kelsey, Carleton G., Capt., M. C., 341st F. A.
Kemp, Philip C., 1st Lt., 341st F. A.
Kenaston, Harold W., 1st Lt., 356th Inf.
Kendall, A., Major, 356th Inf.
Kennedy, Allen J., 1st Lt., 355th Inf.
Kennedy, John W., 1st Lt., 356th Inf.
Kent, Wallace C., Capt., M. C., 314th Tr. Hq. and M. P.
Kenter, Frank H., 2nd Lt., 341st F. A.
Kersting, Ferdinand, 2nd Lt., 314th F. S. Bn.
Keyes, Edward A., Lt. Col., Inf., Hq. 178th Inf. Brig.
Kilbourne, Charles E., Brig. Gen., Hq. 89th Div.
Kilgore, Leonard L., 2nd Lt., 355th Inf.
Kimball, Russell H., 2nd Lt., 341st F. A.
King, Joseph C., Lt. Col., 342nd F. A.
Kingston, Harry L., 1st Lt., Hq. 89th Div.
Kinnaman, Clarence H., 1st Lt., M. C., 314th San. Tr.
Kinnamon, Perry P., 2nd Lt., 340th F. A.
Kinne, Birge W., 2nd Lt., 340th F. A.
Kinsman, Hugh J., 2nd Lt., 341st F. A.
Kirn, G. W., 2nd Lt., 340th F. A.
Kirn, R. W., 1st Lt., C. W. S., Hq. 89th Div.
Kistler, Erle O., Major, 355th Inf.
Kleckner, Joseph B., Capt., 355th Inf.
Knapp, Robert W., 2nd Lt., 342nd F. A
Koch, Milton H., 2nd Lt., 314th Eng.
Koefoot, Theodore H., Capt., M. C., 314th F. S. Bn.
Koentz, Christian H., Capt., M. C., 314th San. Tr.
Kohler, Frank E., Jr., 1st Lt., 353rd Inf
Koontz, Ezra W., Capt., Inf., 314th Amm. Tr.
Kouri, Martin F., 1st Lt., M. C., 314th San. Tr.
Krasa, John M., Capt., M. C., 314th San. Tr.
Kretchmer, Fred R., 1st Lt., Inf., 341st M. G. Bn.
Kring, Jesse B., 2nd Lt., 342nd F. A.
Kulp, Mark R., 1st Lt., 314th Eng.

Name, Rank and *Organization

LaBuhn, Edmond C., 2nd Lt., 355th Inf.
Lacey, Clifton P., 1st Lt., 355th Inf
La Driere, Raymond E., Capt., 354th Inf.
Laidlaw, William, Capt., 342nd M. G. Bn.
Laing, George S., 1st Lt., 340th F. A.
Lake, John P., 1st Lt., 356th Inf.
Lally, John J., Capt., D. C., 314th Eng.
Lamm, Donald S., Capt., 340th F. A.
Lamphere, Leo., 2nd Lt., 354th Inf.
Lamy, Joseph E., 1st Lt., 356th Inf.
Lanagan, Frederic R., Capt., 341st F. A.
Lancaster, A. A., Chaplain, 342nd M. G. Bn.
Landfield, Joseph N., 2nd Lt., A. G. D., 356th Inf.
Lane, Olgar R., 1st Lt., 341st F. A.
Langlard, Henri, 1st Lt., C. of I., Hq. 89th Div.
Larkin, John H., Capt., 341st F. A.
Larson, Louie E., 2nd Lt., 355th Inf.
La Rue, Benn V. M., Capt., 355th Inf.
Law, Charles E., 2nd Lt., 355th Inf.
Leach, James A., 1st Lt., 355th Inf.
Leatherman, George A., 2nd Lt., 341st F. A.
LeBow, I. V., 2nd Lt., 340th F. A.
Lecher, Neal D., 2nd Lt., 342nd F. A.
Ledford, Robert C., 1st Lt., Inf., 314th Sup. Tr.
Lee, John C. H., Col., G. S., Hq. 89th Div.
Lee, William J., 2nd Lt., 353rd Inf.
Leedy, Harold G., 2nd Lt., 353rd Inf.
Lefler, Jay C., Capt., 314th Eng.
Lehman, Dorrance R., Major, 356th Inf.
Lehmann, John S., Capt., 342nd F. A.
Lehnhard, Carl J., Capt., 340th F. A.
Leigh, Francis, Capt., 353rd Inf.
Leipold, Karl R., 1st Lt., 314th F. S. Bn.
Leland, O. M., Lt. Col., 314th Eng.
Leonard, Leverett T., 2nd Lt., 342nd F. A.
Leonard, Ward H., Capt., M. C., 314th San. Tr.
Leslie, Herbert H., 2nd Lt., 356th Inf.
Lever, Charles M., Chaplain, 353rd Inf.
Levinson, Adrian M., Capt., 342nd F. A.
Lewis, Gilbert M., 1st Lt., 353rd Inf.
Lewis, H. R., 2nd Lt., Q. M. C., Clothing and Bathing Unit No. 326.
Lewis, John C., 2nd Lt., 353rd Inf.
Lewis, Leroy B., 1st Lt., 354th Inf.
Lewis, Monroe C., 1st Lt., 342nd F. A.
Lewis, Stanley W., 1st Lt., F. A., 314th Amm. Tr.
L'Homadieu, Leonard, 2nd Lt., 355th Inf.
Likely, Charles W., Capt., V. C., 314th Mobile Vet. Sect.
Lillard, Ross N., Capt., Inf., Hq. 89th Div.
Lincoln, Atwell T., Capt., 354th Inf.
Lindsay, Courteney T., 1st Lt., Q. M. C., Salvage Squad No. 1.
Lindsay, Edwin I., Capt., Inf., 342nd M. G. Bn.
Lindsey, Adrian H., 1st Lt., 342nd F. A.
Linley, Louis D., 2nd Lt., 354th Inf.
Listoe, Alexander F., Major, M. C., 340th M. G. Bn.
Little, James B., 1st Lt., 355th Inf.
Lockhart, Lee McD., 2nd Lt., 342nd F. A.
Lockwood, John W., Capt., Inf., Hq. 177th Inf. Brig.
Logan, F. F., Capt., D. C., 340th F. A.
Loney, Ellis, 2nd Lt., 340th F. A
Long, Forrest E., 1st Lt., 342nd M. G. Bn.
Long, George W., 2nd Lt., 355th Inf.
Long, Joseph F., Capt., M. C., 314th Amm. Tr.
Long, Norman B., 2nd Lt., 356th Inf.
Long, Orval O., 1st Lt., V. C., 314th Amm. Tr.
Long, Stewart L., Chaplain, 355th Inf.
Long, Wm. H., Capt., M. C., 314th San. Tr.
Loomis, John F., Capt., C. A. C., 314th Amm. Tr
Louden, Chester C., 2nd Lt., 355th In.
Loughridge, Paul, Major, 355th Inf.
Lucas, Lawrence W., 1st Lt., 354th Inf.
Luchtenberg, Carl O., 2nd Lt., 353rd Inf.
Luddy, Leo A., 2nd Lt., 353rd Inf.
Lukins, Raymond A., Capt., Inf., 341st M. G. Bn.
Lupton, Edwin H., 2nd Lt., 342nd F. A.
Lyon, Ralph P., 2nd Lt., Bak'y Co. No. 349.
Lynch, David M., 2nd Lt., 353rd Inf.
Lysaght, James R., Major, 314th Amm. Tr.

Macatee, Edward V., 1st Lt., 356th Inf.
Macauley, Kenneth, 2nd Lt., 356th Inf.
MacDonald, Allan C., 2nd Lt., 353rd Inf.
MacGregor, Riley W., 1st Lt., 356th Inf.
MacKenzie, I. D., 2nd Lt., Inf., 340th M. G. Bn.
Maclean, J. M., 1st Lt., 342nd F. A.
Maclear, Arthur A., 1st Lt., 355th Inf.
Madden, John C., 1st Lt., 355th Inf.
Mahoney, Daniel J., 1st Lt., 354th Inf.

Name, Rank and *Organization

Malm, Frank O., 2nd Lt., 342nd F. A.
Maloney, Willard F., 2nd Lt., Cav., Hq. 89th Div.
Maloney, Wm. E., 2nd Lt., 354th Inf.
Manderson, Raymond G., 2nd Lt., 341st F. A.
Mandigo, Clark R., Capt., 314th Eng.
Mangiere, Joseph M., 2nd Lt., 342nd F. A.
Mann, Robert H., 2nd Lt., Inf., 342nd M. G. Bn.
Mannebach, John J., 2nd Lt., Inf., 341st M. G. Bn.
Manning, Frank B., Capt., 314th Amm. Tr.
Markgraf, Carl A., 2nd Lt., 314th Eng.
Marks, Edward A., Jr., 2nd Lt., 354th Inf.
Martin, Albert, Capt., M. C., 314th San. Tr.
Martin, John J., 2nd Lt., V. C., 341st F. A.
Martin, Mark H., 2nd Lt., Q. M. C., Sales Comm. Unit No. 5.
Martin, Paul A., 2nd Lt., 354th Inf.
Mason, Charles D., Capt., M. C., 314th San. Tr
Mason, Fred T., Capt., Ord. Corps, 314th Amm. Tr.
Mason, J. B., Capt., M. C., 314th San. Tr.
Mason, Ralph C., 2nd Lt., T. C., 314th Sup. Tr.
Masseck, Clinton J., Major, 353rd Inf.
Matheson, Norman, 2nd Lt., Inf., 342nd M. G. Bn
Matthews, Stanley, 1st Lt., 340th F. A.
Maule, George J., 2nd Lt., 355th Inf.
Maupin, Curtman, 1st Lt., 356th Inf.
Mans, J. P., 1st Lt., M. C., 314th San. Tr.
Maw, Herbert B., Chaplain, 342nd F. A.
Maxwell, Albert C., Capt., D. C., 356th Inf.
Maxwell, Raymond W., Capt., 340th F. A.
May, Oscar P., 2nd Lt., 356th Inf.
Mayo, James B., 2nd Lt., Q. M. C., Bak'y Co. No. 349.
McBride, John S., Capt., 355th Inf.
McCabe, Frank M., Capt., 314th F. S. Bn.
McCabe, Fordyce H., Major, M. C., 314th San. Tr.
McCaleb, Charles G., 2nd Lt., 342nd F. A.
McCalla, Lee A., Major, 342nd F. A.
McCandliss, Edgar S., Capt., 314th Eng.
McCarthy, Harvey E., Major, M. C., 355th Inf.
McCaskey, F. H., Capt., M. C., 341st F. A.
McCave, Mark L., 2nd Lt., 353rd Inf.
McClanahan, Ross, 2nd Lt., Inf., 314th M. P.
McClellan, George B., 2nd Lt., 341st F. A.
McClellan, George R., 1st Lt., 355th Inf.
McClure, R. G., 2nd Lt., 314th Eng.
McClure, Thomas M., 2nd Lt., 342nd M. G. Bn
McCollum, John, 1st Lt., 353rd Inf.
McCormack, Alphonsus L., 2nd Lt., 355th Inf.
McCormack, John, 1st Lt., 355th Inf.
McCoy, Ralph, Lt. Col., 354th Inf.
McCoy, William S., 1st Lt., 355th Inf.
McCurdy, Joseph E., Capt., 356th Inf.
McDonnall, Zara H., 2nd Lt., V. C., 355th Inf.
McDonnough, Gilbert, 1st Lt., 355th Inf.
McElroy, Hubert E., 2nd Lt., 355th Inf.
McElroy, Leo O., 2nd Lt., 353rd Inf.
McGee, Ralph, Capt., Inf., 314th Sup. Tr.
McGinnis, Clive Sidney, Major, M. C., 356th Inf.
McGivney, Eugene J., 2nd Lt., 354th Inf.
McGlammery, John W., 2nd Lt., 354th Inf.
McGrann, Owen L., 1st Lt., Inf., 341st M. G. Bn.
McGrath, John E., 2nd Lt., 356th Inf.
McGrath, John F., 1st Lt., 354th Inf.
McGuffey, Erle M., 1st Lt., 314th Sup. Tr.
McGuiggan, Robert F., 1st Lt., 354th Inf.
McGuire, Herbert, Capt., 354th Inf.
McGurn, Peter F., 2nd Lt., 356th Inf.
McIlwain, James C., 1st Lt., M. C., 314th Sup. Tr.
McInnes, R. G., 1st Lt., Q. M. C., Hq. 89th Div.
McIntyre, Charles E., 2nd Lt., 340th F. A.
McIntyre, Charles J., Capt., 356th Inf.
McKinley, Floyd C., 1st Lt., 356th Inf.
McKinney, George E., 1st Lt., Inf., 314th Sup. Tr.
McKinstry, John A., 1st Lt., 355th Inf.
McKnight, Arthur W., 1st Lt., 355th Inf.
McLaughlin, Fred, Major, Inf., 340th M. G. Bn.
McLaughlin, Richard M., 1st Lt., 355th Inf.
McLean, Robert E. H., Capt., F. A., 314th Amm. Tr.
McLeod, Duncan C., 2nd Lt., Q. M. C., Salvage Squad No. 1.
McLeod, France C., 2nd Lt., 340th F. A.
McMahon, Donald, 2nd Lt., Inf., 341st M. G. Bn.
McMaster, George H., Col., Inf., 314th Tr. Hq. and M. P.
McMenamy, John M., 1st Lt., 314th Amm. Tr.
McNally, Carlton F., 1st Lt., Inf., 340th M. G. Bn.
McNally, Martin V., 2nd Lt., 353rd Inf.
McNaughton, Guy P., 1st Lt., M. C., 356th Inf.
McNeill, Augustine P. F., Chaplain, 354th Inf.
McNulty, Herman L., Capt., 354th Inf.

Name, Rank and *Organization

McPheeters, Samuel B., Capt., F. A., 314th Amm. Tr.
McReaken, Chalmer, 1st Lt., 356th Inf.
McWhorter, Wm. P., 2nd Lt., Inf., 341st M. G. Bn.
Meade, Reginald H., Major, M. C., 354th Inf.
Means, Louis M., 2nd Lt., 356th Inf.
Meany, Francis P., 1st Lt., D. C., 353rd Inf.
Meister, Elmer, 2nd Lt., 354th Inf.
Mellier, Mabry, Capt., Inf., 341st M. G. Bn.
Melville, Max D., 1st Lt., 355th Inf.
Melvin, Robert L., 1st Lt., 353rd Inf.
Menefee, Thomas K., 1st Lt., 356th Inf.
Meserole, George V., 1st Lt., 353rd Inf.
Metheny, Earl, 1st Lt., M. C., 314th San. Tr.
Metzger, Leon D., 1st Lt., 353rd Inf.
Mewhinney, Edwin F., 2nd Lt., 340th F. A.
Mewhirter, Sydney, 1st Lt., 314th Eng.
Mielke, Charles H., Major, M. C., 340th M. G. Bn.
Milburn, John L., Capt., 314th Tr. Mortar Bat.
Milgram, Abraham, 1st Lt., 355th Inf.
Millard, Leslie J., 2nd Lt., 353rd Inf.
Miller, Ben W., 1st Lt., 353rd Inf.
Miller, Benjamin W., 1st Lt., 342nd F. A.
Miller, Bryan R., 2nd Lt., 356th Inf.
Miller, Charles Y., 2nd Lt., 355th Inf.
Miller, David B., 1st Lt., 353rd Inf.
Miller, George A., Capt., 314th Amm. Tr.
Miller, George C., Capt., M. C., 354th Inf.
Miller, George G., Major, V. C., Hq. 89th Div.
Miller, George W., 2nd Lt., V. C., 314th Tr. Hq. and M. P.
Miller, Harry A., Capt., F. A., 340th M. G. Bn.
Miller, Harvey D., 1st Lt., 314th Eng.
Miller, John, 2nd Lt. 356th Inf.
Miller, Myron C., 1st Lt., 354th Inf.
Miller, Richard J., Capt., M. C., 314th San. Tr.
Miller, Stuart N., 2nd Lt., 314th Eng.
Milligan, William T., 1st Lt., 341st F. A.
Milliken, Carl S., 1st Lt., 355th Inf.
Millis, John M., 2nd Lt. 354th Inf.
Milne, Robert B., 2nd Lt., Inf., 341st M. G. Bn.
Mitchell, Americus, Col., 354th Inf.
Mitchell, Edward A., 1st Lt., 353rd Inf.
Modisette, Demott, 1st Lt., 341st F. A.
Moffit, James T., Capt., D. C., 356th Inf.
Moll, Frank H., 2nd Lt., 354th Inf.
Molony, L. A., Capt., M. C., 341st F. A.
Montee, Jesse A., 2nd Lt., 356th Inf.
Montgomery, Plummer H., 1st Lt., Inf., Hq. 177th Inf. Brig.
Montgomery, Ray C., Capt., 340th F. A.
Montgomery, Wm. P., Capt., Inf., Hq. 89th Div.
Moody, Samuel S., Capt., M. C., 314th San. Tr.
Moora, John C., Capt., 355th Inf.
Moore, Frank M., Capt., Inf., 341st M. G. Bn.
Moore, Fred F., Capt., 355th Inf.
Moore, Jerome E., 1st Lt., 356th Inf.
Moore, M. S., Capt., 356th Inf.
Moore, Pierce J., 2nd Lt., 355th Inf.
Moore, Robert L., 2nd Lt., 353rd Inf.
Moore, Washington N., Capt., 355th Inf.
Moore, William B., 2nd Lt., Inf., 341st M. G. Bn.
Mooring, Scott W., Major, M. C., 314th San. Tr.
Moreland, Julius C., 2nd Lt., 356th Inf.
Morgan, David A., 1st Lt., M. C., 314th San. Tr.
Morgan, Francis M., 1st Lt., 353rd Inf.
Morgan, Verne A., Capt., 355th Inf.
Morrill, Wilbur H., Capt., D. C., 356th Inf.
Morrison, Fred L., Capt., 355th Inf.
Morrison, John E., Major, 354th Inf.
Morrison, Lewis R., 2nd Lt., 353rd Inf.
Morrison, Mark B., 1st Lt., 356th Inf.
Morrow, Walter J., 2nd Lt., 355th Inf.
Morse, Frank L., Lt. Col., M. C., Hq. 89th Div.
Morse, Robert DeVere, 2nd Lt., 356th Inf.
Morse, Taylor, 2nd Lt., 355th Inf.
Mosher, Elbert F., 2nd Lt., 353rd Inf.
Moss, William C., Capt., M. C., 314th San. Tr.
Moth, Michael V., Capt., M. C., 355th Inf.
Moulton, Ellis V., M. C., 314th Amm. Tr.
Moynahan, Harold J., 2nd Lt., 354th Inf.
Muchmore, Clyde E., 1st Lt., 340th M. G. Bn.
Mulheron, Thomas M., 1st Lt., Inf., 314th Sup. Tr.
Muller, Herbert, 1st Lt., 354th Inf.
Mulvill, Dennis F., Capt., 314th Eng.
Munck, Harold F., Capt., 354th Inf.
Mundell, Walter M., Capt., M. C., 314th San. Tr.
Murdock, Clarence T., 2nd Lt., 354th Inf.
Murphy, Earle N., 1st Lt., F. A., 314th Amm. Tr.
Murphy, Jerome A., 1st Lt., M. C., 354th Inf.

Name, Rank and *Organization

Murphy, John H., 1st Lt., 356th Inf.
Murray, Everett B., Capt., 314th Eng.
Murray, Ralph E., 1st Lt., 356th Inf.
Myer, Erskine R., 1st Lt., 356th Inf.
Mylon, Wm., 2nd Lt., 341st M. G. Bn.

Nagle, William J., 2nd Lt., 354th Inf.
Nance, Kidd F., Chaplain, 340th M. G. Bn.
Nanninga, Simon P., 2nd Lt., Inf., 341st M. G. Bn.
Nash, George E., 2nd Lt., 353rd Inf.
Nash, J. G. C., 2nd Lt., 340th F. A.
Natanson, David M., 1st Lt., M. C., 356th Inf.
Neale, William G., 1st Lt., D. C., 342nd F. A.
Neel, Percy C., 1st Lt., 314th Eng.
Neff, James F., Capt., 356th Inf.
Nelson, Norman Oscar, Capt., M. C., 356th Inf.
Nelson, Oscar C., 2nd Lt., Inf., Hq., 89th Div.
Neville, Maurice P., 2nd Lt., 354th Inf.
Newbold, Douglas T., 2nd Lt., 341st F. A.
Newcomb, Harry V., 1st Lt. 314th Eng.
Newcomer, Loyd H., 1st Lt., 354th Inf.
Newman, John, Capt., 358rd Inf.
Nigg, Milton W., 2nd Lt., 342nd F. A.
Nixon, James O., 1st Lt., 353rd Inf.
Norman, William G., 1st Lt., M. C., 341st F. A.
Noyles, George S., Jr., 2nd Lt., 353rd Inf.
Nugent, George A., Brig. Gen., 342nd F. A.
Nuttman, Louis M., Brig. Gen., 356th Inf.
Nyberg, Milton O., Capt., M. C., 314th San. Tr.

Oakes, Harold S., 1st Lt., 341st F. A.
O'Brien, Francis M., 2nd Lt., 356th Inf.
Ocker, Erwin L., 1st Lt., 354th Inf.
Odom, Paul W., 2nd Lt., Inf., 341st M. G. Bn.
O'Donnell, F. W., Lt. Col., M. C., 314th San. Tr.
O'Fallon, John J., Jr., Capt., 342nd F. A.
Ogilbee, Donald W., 2nd Lt., F. A., 314th Amm. Tr.
O'Hara, Benjamin H., Capt., 342nd F. A.
Ohlandt, Beverly C., 2nd Lt., 353rd Inf.
Ohler, W. R., Capt., M. C., 314th San. Tr.
Ojers, Roy H., Capt., 314th F. S. Bn.
O'Kane, Lawrence, 1st Lt., Inf., Hq. 178th Inf Brig.
Olson, Hjalmar A., 2nd Lt., Inf., 342nd M. G. Bn.
O'Neill, J. L., Chaplain, 355th Inf.
Orr, Albert S., 2nd Lt., 340th F. A.
Orr, Caleb W., Capt., 314th Sup. Tr.
Osborne, Francis W., 1st Lt., 341st F. A.
Oster, L. A., 1st Lt., M. C., 356th Inf.
O'Toole, E. L., Chaplain, 340th F. A.
O'Toole, John A., 2nd Lt., 354th Inf.
Overton, William W., Lt. Col., 342nd F. A.

Packer, Gouveneur V., Lt. Col., J. A. G. D., Hq. 89th Div.
Padfield, Grover, 1st Lt., 340th F. A.
Page, A. C., Major, 356th Inf.
Page, Cecil H., 1st Lt., 356th Inf.
Page, Lloyd P., Capt., 356th Inf.
Page, Marion W., Capt., M. C., 354th Inf.
Paine, W. D., Capt., Ord. Corps, 342nd F. A.
Palmer, D. B., Major, V. C., Hq. 89th Div.
Palmer, Horace R., 2nd Lt., F. A., Hq. 164th F. A. Brig.
Palmer, John R., 1st Lt., 314th F. S. Bn.
Palmer, Walter C., Major, 355th Inf.
Pardey, Herbert C., 2nd Lt., Inf., 342nd M. G. Bn.
Parish, John C., 1st Lt., 355th Inf.
Parker, Van. H., Capt., 341st F. A.
Parsons, Douglas E., 2nd Lt., F. A., 314th Tr. Mortar Bat.
Paschal, Boykin, 2nd Lt., 353rd Inf.
Passmore, Claude A., 1st Lt., 354th Inf.
Pastorius, Washington, Capt., 340th F. A.
Patten, Ivan M., 2nd Lt., 341st F. A.
Patton, Farish, 2nd Lt., Cav., Hq. 89th Div.
Patton, Joseph L., 1st Lt., Inf., 314th M. P.
Paul, Herbert W., 1st Lt., 354th Inf.
Pearce, R. B., Capt., 314th Eng.
Pears, Thomas T., 2nd Lt., 342nd F. A.
Peatross, James L., Lt. Col., 353rd Inf.
Peck, Roland C., 2nd Lt., 355th Inf.
Pederson, Hans C., Capt., M. C. 355th Inf.
Pegues, Henry S., 1st Lt., 353rd Inf.
Peistrup, Edward C., 1st Lt., 354th Inf.
Pemberton, M. O., Capt., M. C., 340th F. A.
Pendelton, Charles P., 2nd Lt., A. G. D., Hq. 89th Div.
Pepperdine, Fred F., Capt., 314th F. S. Bn.
Perkins, Alvin S., Lt. Col., 340th F. A.
Perkins, James R. O., 2nd Lt., 340th F. A.

Name, Rank and *Organization

Perry, H. C., 2nd Lt., 356th Inf.
Perryman, Curtis B., 2nd Lt., 356th Inf.
Perten, Ernest, 2nd Lt., 354th Inf.
Pettus, John H., 2nd Lt., Hq. 164th F. A. Brig.
Petzing, Edwin R., 1st Lt., 314th F. S. Bn.
Phillips, Maurice, 2nd Lt., 341st F. A.
Phillips, Nilus P., 2nd Lt., 355th Inf.
Phillips, Rose M., 2nd Lt., V. C., Hq. 177th Inf. Brig.
Phillips, Walter E., 1st Lt., 353rd Inf.
Piatt, William P., Capt., 353rd Inf.
Piersall, Claude, Capt., 314th San. Tr.
Pierson, William M., 1st Lt., Inf., 314th Sup. Tr.
Pike, Lawrence D., 1st Lt., 314th Eng. Tr.
Pine, Harry W., 2nd Lt., 353rd Inf.
Pinkerton, Hugh M., Major, 354th Inf.
Pinkerton, William P., Capt., 354th Inf.
Pitcher, Fred, 1st Lt., 355th Inf.
Plummer, Howard E., 2nd Lt., Q. M. C., Clothing Squad No. 6.
Poague, William T., Capt., 340th F. A.
Pollock, Woolsey McA., 2nd Lt., 355th Inf.
Pommerane, Milton C., 2nd Lt., 353rd Inf.
Poore, C. W., 1st Lt., Inf., 341st M. G. Bn.
Porter, Aubrey A., 2nd Lt., 314th F. S. Bn.
Porter, George F., Capt., M. C., 314th San. Tr.
Portmann, Milton C., Major, 353rd Inf.
Postin, William R., Capt., 353rd Inf.
Poteet, Charles A., 2nd Lt., 355th Inf.
Potter, Lyman J., 1st Lt., 314th F. S. Bn.
Potter, Wilson, Lt. Col., Ord. Corps., Hq. 89th Div.
Powell, William H., 1st Lt., 342nd F. A.
Powers, Edmond, 2nd Lt., 341st F. A.
Powers, H. M., 2nd Lt., Inf., 340th M. G. Bn.
Pratt, B. L., Capt., 340th F. A.
Pratt, Harold S., 1st Lt., 314th F. S. Bn.
Prelwitz, Leo., 2nd Lt., 355th Inf.
Pressly, Thomas A., Capt., M. C., 355th Inf.
Pritchard, Allen E., 1st Lt., 356th Inf.
Prosser, Francis H., Capt., D. C., 314th F. S. Bn.
Puffer, Ray K., Capt., 356th Inf.
Pugh, James W., Capt., 341st F. A.
Pullen, D. D., Col., T. C., 314th Eng.
Pusch, Herbert V., Capt., Inf., 314th Sup. Tr.
Putman, Robert B., Capt., 342nd F. A.

Quinn, James M., 2nd Lt., 354th Inf.

Rader, Ralph D., Major, 314th Eng.
Ragsdale, Clarence E., 1st Lt., Inf., 340th M. G. Bn.
Ragsdale, Irving, 2nd Lt., 356th Inf.
Rand, George E., 1st Lt., 353rd Inf.
Randall, A. B., 1st Lt., 314th Eng.
Randel, Harry E., Capt., 341st F. A.
Randolph, Lewis, 2nd Lt., 354th Inf.
Rasmussen, Alvin M., 2nd Lt., 354th Inf.
Rastall, Charles W., Capt., Q. M. C., Hq. 89th Div.
Rawlings, John W., 1st Lt., 341st F. A.
Ray, Grover W., 2nd Lt., 353rd Inf.
Ray, James R., 2nd Lt., 356th Inf.
Raymond, Arthur W., 1st Lt., 342nd F. A.
Reagan, Frank L., Capt., Inf., 314th Amm. Tr.
Reardon, Wm. C., 2nd Lt., Inf., 341st M. G. Bn.
Reece, Henry E., Capt., M. C., 314th San. Tr.
Reed, William M., 2nd Lt., 342nd F. A.
Reed, Willis C., 1st Lt., D. C., 353rd Inf.
Reeder, Clarence O., 2nd Lt., 341st F. A.
Reese, Tom M., Capt., 353rd Inf.
Reeves, David, Major, 314th F. S. Bn.
Reeves, Henry E., 2nd Lt., 354th Inf.
Reeves, James H., Col., 353rd Inf.
Reid, Leslie, 1st Lt., 354th Inf.
Reid, Thomas J., Jr., Capt., 354th Inf.
Reid, William E., Capt., 355th Inf.
Reif, Carl F., 2nd Lt., 354th Inf.
Reiter, William, 1st Lt., 340th F. A.
Reser, Ernest F., Capt., F. A., Hq. 89th Div.
Ressel, Oscar, 1st Lt., 354th Inf.
Reynolds, Charnell A., Capt., 354th Inf.
Reynolds, Karl W., 2nd Lt., 341st F. A.
Rhoads, Geo. W., 2nd Lt., Inf., 341st M. G. Bn.
Rhodes, George E., 1st Lt., 354th Inf.
Rhodes, John F., Capt., 356th Inf.
Rice, Harry D., 1st Lt., Hq. Troop, 89th Div.
Rice, Leonard M., 1st Lt., 353rd Inf.
Rice, Walter L., 2nd Lt., 342nd M. G. Bn.
Rich, Kenneth F., Capt., 353rd Inf.
Richards, John S., 1st Lt., 355th Inf.
Richardson, John E., 1st Lt., 355th Inf.
Rieman, Gilbert, 1st Lt., Hq. 177th Inf. Brig.

Name, Rank and *Organization

Rifenbary, Reinhold F., 1st Lt., Inf., 342nd M. G. Bn.
Riggs, William A., 2nd Lt., 356th Inf.
Rimmele, Carl L., 1st Lt., 314th Eng.
Rinehart, B. T., Capt., Inf., Hq. 177th Inf. Brig.
Ritchie, Edgar B., 1st Lt., 355th Inf.
Ritter, Murl E., 1st Lt., 354th Inf.
Roberts, Clair C., 2nd Lt., 353rd Inf.
Roberts, Harold M., 1st Lt., 356th Inf.
Robertson, Harold H., 2nd Lt., 353rd Inf.
Robinson, Dewey, 2nd Lt., 356th Inf.
Robinson, William G., 1st Lt., Inf., Hq. 89th Div.
Roderick, Thaddeus, 2nd Lt., 354th Inf.
Rodgers, Grover, 1st Lt., M. T. C., M. S. T. U. 397.
Rogers, Earl L., 1st Lt., Inf., 341st M. G. Bn.
Rogers, Edmund, Capt., 355th Inf.
Rogers, Harry L., 1st Lt., M. C., 355th Inf.
Rolinson, Caleb W., 2nd Lt., 354th Inf.
Root, Frank P., Capt., 354th Inf.
Rose, Maurice, 1st Lt., 353rd Inf.
Rosenthal. S. E., 1st Lt., M. C., 356th Inf.
Roska, Herbert C., 2nd Lt., 353rd Inf.
Row, George W., 1st Lt., F. A., Hq. 89th Div.
Rowan, Hugh W., Capt., C. W. S., Hq. 89th Div.
Rowan, Joel W., 2nd Lt., 314th F. S. Bn.
Rowell, Ernest G., 1st Lt., 354th Inf.
Royer, Karl, 2nd Lt., 356th Inf.
Royse, Frank E., Major, Inf., Hq. 178th Inf. Brig.
Ruddick, John R., Capt., 314th F. S. Bn.
Rudisill, Theodore F., Chaplain, 314th Eng.
Ruff, Harry, 2nd Lt., 355th Inf.
Runkle, Daniel, Capt., F. A., Hq. 89th Div.
Runyan, John F., 1st Lt., 314th M. P.
Rush, Roy L., 1st Lt., 355th Inf.
Rush, Weaver A., Capt., M. C., 353rd Inf.
Russell, Barney, 1st Lt., D. C., 355th Inf.
Russell, Clarence E., Major, 314th Eng.
Russell, George S., Capt., 314th Eng.
Russell, Robert C., 2nd Lt., 314th Eng.
Rutherford, Ray C., Major, 341st F. A.
Ryan, Edward F., Chaplain, Hq. 89th Div.
Rymer, Donald H., 2nd Lt., 342nd F. A.

Sabin, Henry P., Major, 355th Inf.
Sallee, Julius C., Capt., 314th Eng.
Salmon, Ivan R., 2nd Lt., 355th Inf.
Salzberg, Ben A., 1st Lt., M. C., 314th San. Tr.
Sample, John G., Capt., 356th Inf.
Sampson, James O., 1st Lt., F. A., 314th Amm. Tr.
Samuelson, Samuel B., 2nd Lt., 356th Inf.
Sanborn, Fred W., 1st Lt., 354th Inf.
Sanders, Newton A., 1st Lt., 353rd Inf.
Sanderson, Samuel B., 2nd Lt., 356th Inf.
Sandhouse, Raymond M., 2nd Lt., 355th Inf.
Sandusky, Richard M., 2nd Lt., 354th Inf.
Sanford, Loren A., 1st Lt., 356th Inf.
Sarver, Albert F., 1st Lt., M. C., 355th Inf.
Sauter, Joseph I., 2nd Lt., 354th Inf.
Savage, Howard M., 1st Lt., V. C., Hq. 178th Inf. Brig.
Sawyer, Charles, Major, Inf., Hq. 178th Inf. Brig.
Scanian, Henry, 2nd Lt., 342nd F. A.
Scanlon, James E., 1st Lt., 353rd Inf.
Scheibla, Harry D., 1st Lt., Inf., 341st M. G. Bn.
Schell, Carl E., 1st Lt., 356th Inf.
Scherf, Louis N., Capt., 355th Inf.
Schlegel, Walter L., Capt., Inf., 342nd M. G. Bn.
Schlemmer, Ferdinand L., 1st Lt., 356th Inf.
Schlink, Henry A., Capt., M. C., 353rd Inf.
Schmidt, George W., 1st Lt., 356th Inf.
Schmitt, William A., Capt., 354th Inf.
Schnell, Benjamin C., Major, M. C., Hq. 89th Div.
Schofield, William M., 1st Lt., 342nd F. A.
Scholes, George P., Capt., 356th Inf.
Schrof, Wm. H., 2nd Lt., 356th Inf.
Schuck, Harold T., 1st Lt., 355th Inf.
Schuh, Harold, 2nd Lt., 355th Inf.
Schulman, Harry, 1st Lt., 354th Inf.
Schultz, Elmer H., 2nd Lt., 354th Inf.
Schultz, Robert L., 1st Lt., 341st F. A.
Schutt, Robert K., Major, Inf., 314th M. P.
Schweiger, Carl A., 1st Lt., 341st F. A.
Schwinn, William H., Capt., 356th Inf.
Scoggin, Clyde, 1st Lt., D. C., 314th Sup. Tr.
Scoggin, G. W., 2nd Lt., 340th F. A.
Scott, Albert, 2nd Lt., 355th Inf.
Scott, David H., Lt. Col., Inf., 342nd M. G. Bn.
Scott, George C., 2nd Lt., 354th Inf.
Scott, Harry P., 2nd Lt., 341st F. A.
Scott, Hugh, 2nd Lt., 340th F. A.
Scott, LeRoy E., 2nd Lt., 314th F. S. Bn.

Name, Rank and *Organization

Scott, Walter J., Lt. Col., G. S., Hq. 89th Div.
Sear, Jesse L., 1st Lt., M. C., 314th San. Tr.
Searle, Jack, 1st Lt., 354th Inf.
Seddon, Bruce, 2nd Lt., C. W. S., Hq. 89th Div.
Seggel, Louis W., 2nd Lt., 354th Inf.
Seiler, Vincent H., 2nd Lt., 353rd Inf.
Seith, Alvin N., 1st Lt., 353rd Inf.
Sellers, Sanford, Jr., Capt., Inf., 342nd M. G. Bn.
Senecal, James N., 2nd Lt., 341st F. A.
Settle, Wilford L., 1st Lt., 354th Inf.
Severson, Will C., 2nd Lt., 356th Inf.
Seymour, Pliny B., 2nd Lt., Hq. 89th Div.
Shade, Grant K., 2nd Lt., 353rd Inf.
Shadowen, Carl, 1st Lt., 355th Inf.
Shafroth, Morrison, Capt., 341st F. A.
Shanks, Angus, 2nd Lt., Inf., 342nd M. G. Bn.
Shanor, Paul G., 1st Lt., 314th Eng.
Shaw, Charles A., 1st Lt., 353rd Inf.
Shea, Patrick F., 2nd Lt., 355th Inf.
Shelly, I. N., Capt., M. C., 314th San. Tr.
Shepard, John L., Lt. Col., M. C., Hq. 89th Div.
Shepard, Morton B., 1st Lt., 353rd Inf.
Shifrin, Hymen, 1st Lt., 314th Eng.
Shimman, Wm. M., Capt., 314th F. S. Bn.
Shinn, Leon P., 1st Lt., 356th Inf.
Shiverick, Nathan C., Major, 341st M. G. Bn.
Shriver, Fred M., 2nd Lt., 353rd Inf.
Shriver, Ray O., 1st Lt., 314th Eng.
Showalter, Freeman B., 2nd Lt., 355th Inf.
Shy, Joseph J., 2nd Lt., 354th Inf.
Sichterman, Arie J., Capt., 353rd Inf.
Silberman, Horace L., 2nd Lt., 355th Inf.
Sills, William G., Col., 355th Inf.
Silverman, Mose, 2nd Lt. 356th Inf.
Simon, Robert E., 1st Lt., 355th Inf.
Simpson, Joseph H., 1st Lt., 355th Inf.
Simpson, Lester I., Capt., M. C., 314th San. Tr.
Sinclair, Leo H., 1st Lt., F. A., 314th Tr. Mortar Bat.
Sinke, James, Capt., 354th Inf.
Skeele, Edward E., Jr., 2nd Lt., 356th Inf.
Slaughter, Samuel B., 1st Lt., 354th Inf.
Slothower, Lewis C., 2nd Lt., 355th Inf.
Small, W. L., Capt., 340th F. A.
Smallwood, Charles S., Major, Inf., 314th M. P.
Smalzried, H. L., 1st Lt., Inf., 341st M. G. Bn.
Smead, Burton A., Lt. Col., Inf., Hq. 89th Div.
Smiley, Arthur C., Capt., M. C., 342nd F. A.
Smiley, Earl J., 2nd Lt., 355th Inf.
Smith, Andrew L., 2nd Lt., Inf., 341st M. G. Bn.
Smith, A. M., Chaplain, 314th Tr. Hq. and M. P.
Smith, Charles B., 2nd Lt., 353rd Inf.
Smith, C. H., 1st Lt., 340th F. A.
Smith, Clifton T., Major, 353rd Inf.
Smith, Eben L., 1st Lt., 355th Inf.
Smith, Emery T., Col., 342nd F. A.
Smith, Francis T., 2nd Lt., 353rd Inf.
Smith, Frank, Capt., 356th Inf.
Smith, Frank A., 1st Lt., 353rd Inf.
Smith, Frank Wilbur, Lt. Col., G. S., Hq. 89th Div.
Smith, Harry A., 2nd Lt., Inf., 341st M. G. Bn.
Smith, Henry, 1st Lt., M. C., 354th Inf.
Smith, Henry W., 2nd Lt., Q. M. C., 314th San. Tr.
Smith, Heyl B., 1st Lt., D. C., 314th San. Tr.
Smith, Herbert A., Capt., 354th Inf.
Smith, Leland A., 2nd Lt., 340th F. A.
Smith, Raymond, 1st Lt., 353rd Inf.
Smith, Robert O., Capt., D. C., 356th Inf.
Smith, Royal H. G., 1st Lt., 353rd Inf.
Smith, Sam, 1st Lt., 355th Inf.
Smyser, Rudolph E., Lt. Col., Hq. 89th Div.
Snellgrove, Neal F., 2nd Lt., T. C., 314th Sup. Tr.
Snider, Randolph, Capt., M. C., 356th Inf.
Solomon, Clair, 2nd Lt., 342nd M. G. Bn.
Somervell, Brehon Burke, Lt. Col, G. S., Hq. 89th Div.
Sommer, Lyman H., 2nd Lt., 353rd Inf.
Sorensen, Arthur A., 2nd Lt., Inf., Hq. 89th Div.
Sorose, Bernard, 1st Lt., M. C., 356th Inf.
Spalding, Merrill E., Lt. Col., G. S., Hq. 89th Div.
Spear, Albion W., 2nd Lt., 314th F. S. Bn.
Spear, Robert, 2nd Lt., 354th Inf.
Speer, James P., 2nd Lt., 354th Inf.
Spencer, Glen K., 1st Lt., 355th Inf.
Sperry, Langley, 2nd Lt., 353rd Inf.
Sprague, Gale A., 2nd Lt., 314th Eng.
Spurlock, Daniel W., Lt. Col., 353rd Inf.
Spurr, John P., Col., C. A. C., 342nd F. A.
Staatz, Stanley W., 2nd Lt., 356th Inf.
Stahl, Milton R., 2nd Lt., 340th F. A.
Stalvey, Wm. E., 2nd Lt., 89th M. P. Co.

Name, Rank and *Organization

Stamm, Eugene, Capt., D. C., 354th Inf.
Stanley, Eugene B., 1st Lt., 353rd Inf.
Stapelton, George A., 2nd Lt., 355th Inf.
Stark, William J., Capt., D. C., 314th San. Tr.
Starkey, John R., Lt. Col., 340th F. A.
Steel, James A., 2nd Lt., 314th Eng.
Steiner, Alexander, Capt., 354th Inf.
Steinhilber, C. W., 1st Lt., 354th Inf.
Steiwer, Karl, Capt., F. A., 314th Amm. Tr.
Stenjem, E. M., 2nd Lt., 356th Inf.
Sterner, Howard, 1st Lt., 355th Inf.
Stewart, Duncan M., Major, 356th Inf.
Stewart, Emerson E., 2nd Lt., Inf., 342nd M. G. Bn.
Stewart, Harold A., 1st Lt., Inf., 340th M. G. Bn.
Stewart, Thomas G., Capt., 342nd F. A.
Stiles, Wm. B., 2nd Lt., 356th Inf.
Stites, Luke S., 1st Lt., 314th Eng.
Stivers, Howard B., Major, 354th Inf.
Stoll, Roland A., 1st Lt., Inf., Hq. 89th Div.
Stone, Harry R., Capt., M. C., 356th Inf.
Stoner, Oscar C., 1st Lt., 340th F. A.
Stott, Charles, 2nd Lt., 314th F. S. Bn.
Stout, Francis R., 2nd Lt., 356th Inf.
Stout, J. W., 1st Lt., 340th F. A.
Strain, Frank E., 1st Lt., 356th Inf.
Strauss, Leonard A., 2nd Lt., 353rd Inf.
Strider, H. E., Major, 314th F. S. Bn.
Stringfellow, Walton B., 1st Lt., F. A., 314th Amm. Tr.
Stuart, Wm. D., Jr., Capt., 314th Eng. Tr.
Sturges, Gould A., Jr., Capt., 340th F. A.
Sturman, Walter I., 2nd Lt., 340th M. G. Bn.
Summers, Paul A., 1st Lt., 354th Inf.
Sutphen, Joseph W., Major, Inf., Hq. 89th Div.
Sutton, Daniel F., 1st Lt., 353rd Inf.
Sutton, George S., 1st Lt., 342nd F. A.
Sutton, Wade H., 2nd Lt., 356th Inf.
Swaim, John E., Capt., 356th Inf.
Swatts, Henry, 2nd Lt., 356th Inf.
Swift, John P., Major, 341st F. A.
Swihart, Vernon C., 2nd Lt., 355th Inf.
Sykes, Herbert B., 1st Lt., 355th Inf.
Symes, John F., Major, 355th Inf.

Tabbert, Theodore, 1st Lt., 341st F. A.
Taggart, M. H., Lt. Col., I. G. D., Hq. 89th Div.
Tait, Lee C., 1st Lt., 354th Inf.
Talbot, George K., 1st Lt., 354th Inf.
Tanner, Roscoe W., Capt., 341st F. A.
Taylor, James D., Col., 355th Inf.
Taylor, Thomas J., 2nd Lt., 355th Inf.
Tayntor, Clark O., 1st Lt., Inf., Hq. 89th Div.
Temple, William O., 1st Lt., 353rd Inf.
Tenison, Alonzo M., 2nd Lt., 342nd F. A.
Tenney, H. H., 2nd Lt., 354th Inf.
Terrell, Horace P., 2nd Lt., 355th Inf.
Terry, M. L., 2nd Lt., 340th F. A.
Thalman, R. P., 1st Lt., Ord. Corps. 342nd F. A.
Thielicke, Charles G., 2nd Lt., 314th Eng.
Thien, Leo H., 1st Lt., 314th Eng.
Thomas, Abraham L., Capt., 356th Inf.
Thomas, John R., 2nd Lt., 354th Inf.
Thomas, Ralph R., 1st Lt., A. G. D., Hq. 89th Div.
Thompson, Paul E., 2nd Lt., Inf., 341st M. G. Bn.
Thomson, Wm. R., Capt., M. C., 353rd Inf.
Throckmorton, Burton H., 2nd Lt., 356th Inf.
Throckmorton, Robert J., Capt., F. A., 314th Amm. Tr.
Thurlow, Ralph M., Capt., M. C., 314th San. Tr.
Tilford, J. D., Col., Inf., 314th Amm. Tr.
Tinker, John W., Major, 356th Inf.
Tipton, Campbell G., 1st Lt., D. C., 355th Inf.
Tipton, J. Holt., 1st Lt., 354th Inf.
Tischbein, Louis, 2nd Lt., 353rd Inf.
Todd, Frank G., Capt., 354th Inf.
Tompkins, Howard R. K., Capt., F. A., 314th Amm. Tr.
Toney, Lee E., Capt., M. C., 314th San. Tr.
Topham, Joseph L., Lt. Col., Hq. 89th Div.
Topping, Charles R., 2nd Lt., 354th Inf.
Torrey, William B., Capt., Inf., 355th Inf.
Towle, Thorborn E., Capt., Inf., 314th M. P.
Trainer, Leo E., 2nd Lt., 354th Inf.
Traynor, Mack V., 1st Lt., 355th Inf.
Triplett, Orle F., 1st Lt., 354th Inf.
Trompeter, Oscar H., 1st Lt., 354th Inf.
Trowbridge, Irvin, 2nd Lt., 356th Inf.
Truemper, Louis G., 1st Lt., Inf., 341st M. G. Bn.
Tubbs, Lon F., 2nd Lt., 353rd Inf.
Tucker, James G., Capt., 353rd Inf.

Name, Rank and *Organization

Tucker, James R., 2nd Lt., 353rd Inf.
Tunell, Garfield F., 1st Lt., 355th Inf.
Turner, Courtney S., Capt., 353rd Inf.
Turner, Floyd C., 1st Lt., M. C., 314th San. Tr.
Turner, Grover C., Capt., 314th Sup. Tr.
Turner, John R., 1st Lt., M. C., 355th Inf.
Tuttle, Ovid S., Capt., D. C., 314th San. Tr.

Uhl, Leland M., Capt., 342nd F. A.
Undem, Louis, 2nd Lt., 356th Inf.
Underhill, Robert M., 1st Lt., 353rd Inf.
Unrath, Frederick, 2nd Lt., 353rd Inf.
Upp, John W., 1st Lt., Q. M. C., 314th Sup. Tr.
Urban, Carl G., 1st Lt., 353rd Inf.

Vandegrift, John L., Capt., 341st F. A.
Van Der Vort, C. O., Capt., 314th F. S. Bn.
Van Frank, H., 2nd Lt., 353rd Inf.
Van Kirk, John A., 1st Lt., M. C., 342nd M. G. Bn.
Van Krug, K. L., Chaplain, 356th Inf.
Van Meter, Glen E., 2nd Lt., 354th Inf.
Van Osdel, Paul, 1st Lt., 356th Inf.
Van Wye, Thomas A., 2nd Lt., 340th F. A.
Varner, Harry H., Capt., M. C., 353rd Inf.
Velie, Tom A., Capt., F. A., Hq. Troop, 89th Div.
Vigeant, Gregory, Capt., Inf., Hq. 89th Div.
Vogel, John C., 2nd Lt., 354th Inf.
Vollmer, Albert M., 1st Lt., 354th Inf.
Voorhees, Claude H., 2nd Lt., Inf., 341st M. G. Bn.
Voorhis, Charles D., 2nd Lt., 354th Inf.

Wadell, Frank R., Capt., 340th F. A.
Waddell, St. John, Jr., 1st Lt., C. A. C., 314th Trench Mortar Bat.
Wait, Lloyd, 1st Lt., 342nd F. A.
Walden, Ewell K., 2nd Lt., Inf., 341st M. G. Bn.
Waldo, Elmer E., 1st Lt., M. C., 355th Inf.
Waldo, Hubert D., 1st Lt., Inf., 342nd M. G. Bn.
Walker, James M., 2nd Lt., 355th Inf.
Walker, Merle R., Capt., 341st F. A.
Walkey, Daniel W., Capt., 356th Inf.
Walking, Lynd A., 2nd Lt., 340th F. A.
Wallace, Edgar D., 2nd Lt., 353rd Inf.
Wallace, George C., 1st Lt., 356th Inf.
Waller, Archibald S., 2nd Lt., 354th Inf.
Wallick, Guy P., Capt., 341st F. A.
Wallin, Victor B., 1st Lt., 356th Inf.
Walsh, John K., 2nd Lt., 340th F. A.
Walter, Martin L., 2nd Lt., V. C., 340th F. A.
Wanter, Walter, 2nd Lt., 356th Inf.
Wanzer, Howard S., 2nd Lt., 341st F. A.
Ward, D. A., 1st Lt., 340th F. A.
Ward, Paul C., 1st Lt., 355th Inf.
Wardell, Henry, Capt., 355th Inf.
Watkins, Boaz B., 1st Lt., Inf., 340th M. G. Bn.
Watkins, Ferre C., 1st Lt., 356th Inf.
Watkins, Miles A., Major, M. C., 340th M. G. Bn.
Watson, Albert J., Major, 342nd F. A.
Watson, Ernest E., Major, 341st M. G. Bn.
Watson, Willie C., 2nd Lt., 353rd Inf.
Weager, Warren C., 1st Lt., 356th Inf.
Wear, Arthur Y., Capt., 356th Inf.
Weatherwax, Lester F., 2nd Lt., 341st F. A.
Weaver, Homer J., Capt., 355th Inf.
Weaver, Ralph M., 1st Lt., 341st F. A.
Webb, Elbert L., Capt., 356th Inf.
Webber, Harry, 2nd Lt., 340th M. G. Bn.
Webster, Grant M., 2nd Lt., A. G. D., Hq. 89th Div.
Webster, Harold M., 1st Lt., 355th Inf.
Webster, James L., 2nd Lt., 355th Inf.
Webster, Milon M., 2nd Lt., 354th Inf.
Webster, Thomas M., 1st Lt., 353rd Inf.
Weeks, Leon W., Capt., 354th Inf.
Weer, Percy H., 2nd Lt., 340th F. A.
Weis, Herman W., Capt., 342nd F. A.
Weissenborn, Walter, 2nd Lt., 342nd F. A.
Welles, T. L., Jr., 2nd Lt., 314th Eng.
Wellington, Marcellus B., Capt., 353rd Inf.
Wells, Lloyd P., 1st Lt., 314th Amm. Tr.
Welsh, Frank B., Capt., 356th Inf.
Welsh, W. P., 1st Lt., Hq. 89th Div.
Wentworth, A. J., Capt., M. C., 354th Inf.
Wentworth, Edward N., Capt., F. A., Hq. 164th F. A. Brig.
Werts, Joseph R., 1st Lt., 354th Inf.
West, Robert R., Capt., C. W. S., Hq. 89th Div.
West, W. B., 2nd Lt., 356th Inf.
Westfall, Geo. A., 1st Lt., M. C., 340th F. A.
Whalen, William F., 1st Lt., 355th Inf.
Wheatley, Edwin T., 1st Lt., 354th Inf.

Name, Rank and *Organization

Wheaton, H. M., 1st Lt., 340th F. A.
Wheeler, Ernest S., Col., 340th F. A.
Whitall, Lawrence W., 2nd Lt., 342nd F. A.
White, Arthur E., 2nd Lt., 356th Inf.
White, Roscoe A., 2nd Lt., Inf., 342nd M. G. Bn.
White, Theodore, Capt., 314th Amm. Tr.
Whitside, Victor M., Major, Cav., 354th Inf.
Whitside, Warren W., Col., F. A., 314th Tr. Hq. and M. P.
Whitt, Ollie B., 2nd Lt., 342nd M. G. Bn.
Whitten, Frederick E., 1st Lt., 356th Inf.
Wickersham, J. Hunter, 2nd Lt., 353rd Inf.
Wiedeman, Geo. J., Jr., 2nd Lt., 356th Inf.
Wilder, Marshall P., Capt., 354th Inf.
Wilder, Throop M., Major, A. G. D., Hq. 89th Div.
Wilkins, Frank C., Capt., Inf., 314th Sup. Tr.
Wilkins, Herbert J. Jr., 1st Lt., Inf., Hq. 178th Inf. Brig.
Wilkinson, E. P., 2nd Lt., 314th Eng.
Williams, Clarence J., 2nd Lt., F. A., 314th Amm. Tr.
Williams, Frederick J., Major, 342nd F. A.
Williams, George H., Jr., 2nd Lt., 356th Inf.
Williams, Harry V., 1st Lt., 355th Inf.
Williams, Paul R., Capt., M. C., 314th San. Tr.
Williamson, Llewellyn P., Col., M. C., Hq. 89th Div.
Willis, Marion L., 1st Lt., 356th Inf.
Wilson, Frank B., 2nd Lt., 355th Inf.
Wilson, George B., 1st Lt., 314th F. S. Bn.
Wilson, Harry W., Major, D. C., 354th Inf.
Wilson, Henry W., Capt., 353rd Inf.
Wilson, James, Jr., 1st Lt., 356th Inf.
Wilson, John, Capt., M. C., 314th San. Tr.
Wilson, Roy G., 2nd Lt., 353rd Inf.
Wilson, Roy H., Major, 341st F. A.
Wilson, Scott, 1st Lt., 356th Inf.
Wilson, Thomas E., 2nd Lt., 353rd Inf.
Winans, David E., 2nd Lt., 355th Inf.
Winchester, Theo. D., 1st Lt., 354th Inf.
Wind, Leland A., Major, 340th F. A.
Winfrey, Geo. W., 2nd Lt., 354th Inf.
Wing, Harold E., 1st Lt., 314th Eng.
Wing, R. H., 2nd Lt., 355th Inf.
Winn, Frank L., Major-General, Hq. 89th Div.
Winter, James, 2nd Lt., Inf., 314th Amm. Tr.
Winters, Mathew, Capt., 356th Inf.

Name, Rank and *Organization

Wirth, Thomas F., Major, 355th Inf.
Withington, L., 1st Lt., C. W. S., Hq. 89th Div.
Withington, Paul, Major, M. C., 354th Inf.
Withington, Winthrop, Lt. Col., G. S., Hq. 89th Div.
Wolff, Herman C., Capt., 354th Inf.
Wolle, Francis, Capt., 356th Inf.
Wolverton, Vance, 1st Lt., F. A., Hq. Troop, 89th Div.
Wood, Dan P., 2nd Lt., 340th F. A.
Wood, Frank M., Capt., 353rd Inf.
Wood, George W., Major, 353rd Inf.
Wood, Harry B., 1st Lt., Inf., 342nd M. G. Bn.
Wood, James W., 2nd Lt., 355th Inf.
Wood, Jefferson K., 2nd Lt., 353rd Inf.
Wood, John W., 2nd Lt., F. A., Hq. Troop, 89th Div.
Woods, Judson E., Chaplain, 354th Inf.
Woods, Peter D., 1st Lt., 354th Inf.
Woodward, Jesse A., 2nd Lt., 314th Eng.
Woodzelle, Guy W., 2nd Lt., 354th Inf.
Wray, Harry C., 1st Lt., 353rd Inf.
Wright, Charles A., Capt., 355th Inf.
Wright, Eugene P., Major, M. C., 314th Amm. Tr.
Wright, Stanley, 1st Lt., 314th Eng.
Wright, Wm. M., Major-General, Hq. 89th Div.
Wyatt, Benjamin F., 1st Lt., 342nd M. G. Bn.
Wyatt, Grant, Jr., 2nd Lt., 341st F. A.
Wynn, G. E., 2nd Lt., Inf., 341st M. G. Bn.
Wyon, W. B., 1st Lt., Inf., 342nd M. G. Bn.

Yaeger, Norbert F., 2nd Lt., 354th Inf.
Yager, George F., 2nd Lt., V. C., 341st F. A.
Yarbrough, Walter S., 1st Lt., 355th Inf.
Yates, Oscar W., 2nd Lt., 353rd Inf.
Yohe, David A., 2nd Lt., 355th Inf.
Yontz, Edward, 2nd Lt., 354th Inf.
York, William B., 1st Lt., M. C., 353rd Inf.
Young, Edward J., 2nd Lt., 353rd Inf.
Young, Edward M., 2nd Lt., Inf., Hq. 89th Div.
Young, Roy M., 2nd Lt., 356th Inf.
Younglove, Frank J., Capt., V. C., Hq. 89th Div.

Zane, Clarence J., 2nd Lt., 354th Inf.
Zergiebel, Charles, 2nd Lt., 355th Inf.
Ziesenis, Harry, 1st Lt., 314th F. S. Bn.
Zinser, Alvah L., 2nd Lt., 356th Inf.
Zipoy, Frank J., 1st Lt., 353rd Inf.

COMMENDATIONS

The list of commendations printed below might be extended almost indefinitely by the inclusion of those from higher headquarters for specific organizations and individuals within the Division, and those so general in character as to be applicable to many units in the A. E. F. With propriety it might include the congratulatory messages sent out at large by higher commanders, by the President, the Secretary of War and various of our allies upon the successful conclusion of engagements in which the Division participated. Space forbids, and the record is limited to a partial list of orders, letters and telegrams referring specifically to the 89th and, except for certain orders, exclusively to it.

They cover the period from the very first night of original entry into the line until return to the United States, and may be considered as typifying the character of service of the 89th Division and the regard with which it was universally held.

HEADQUARTERS 89TH DIVISION
FRANCE

September 27, 1918.
HP

General Orders
No. 75

1. Report of the Battalion Commander, 1st Battalion, 354th Infantry, and of the Inspectors of the VIIIe French Army, recently submitted to the Division Commander, invite attention to the courage and fortitude of the personnel of the 1st Battalion, 354th Infantry, and the 1st Battalion, 355th Infantry, on the night of August 7-8, during the gas attack by the Germans on the center regimental zones of the Lucey Sector.

This attack was made during the period of the relief of the 82nd Division by the 89th Division. In most instances it was the first night the troops had been in the line; in practically every instance it was the first time the personnel had been under fire.

The orders in force at the time required troops of the advanced post position to hold that position to the death unless withdrawal was ordered by the Army Commander. This order was faithfully carried out in spite of the intensity of the attack and the helplessness of the troops to retaliate. It was an example of courage and steadfastness deserving the highest praise, and the spirit of the troops was further indicated by the fact that they requested to remain in the line and finish their tour of duty when relief was proposed.

The Division Commander commends the officers and men of these battalions.

This order will be read at the first assembly of each organization after its receipt.

By command of Major General Wright:

C. E. KILBOURNE,
Colonel, General Staff,
Chief of Staff.

OFFICIAL:
BURTON A. SMEAD,
Major of Infantry,
Acting Adjutant.

H.Q. August 16th, 1918.

32nd FRENCH ARMY CORPS
Staff
Third Office
No. 4131/3

General Order
No. 141.

(Translation)

The General Commanding the 32nd Army Corps highly congratulates the patrol of the 356th I. R. U. S. which, on August 14th, having encountered an enemy detachment, succeeded capturing 4 prisoners.

For a long time, in that difficult sector where both adversaries have been using best artifice, we had not taken any prisoners to identify the troops in front of us.

This action shows the care taken by the 89th D. I. U. S. in the preparation of night raids. It also shows the Go and the Dash of the soldiers of this fine Division.

The General Commanding the 32nd A. C.
(Signed) PASSAGA.

To the 89th Division.

32nd FRENCH ARMY CORPS
Headquarters
Third Bureau

General Order
No. 142.

August 20, 1918.

(Translation)

The command of the sector of Lucey will be taken over today (August 20), at 3:00 P. M., by General Dickman, Commanding the 4th Army Corps, United States Army, the Headquarters of which will be at Toul.

Upon relinquishing the command of this sector, the General Commanding the 32nd Corps of the French Army, wishes to congratulate the 89th Division, U. S. A., upon its discipline, its spirit and its determination, all of which surely guarantee laurels soon to be gained by this fine division, under the distinguished command of its chief, General Winn.

GENERAL PASSAGA,
Commanding the 32nd Army Corps,
(Signed) Passaga.

To the 89th Division.

HEADQUARTERS FOURTH ARMY CORPS
American Expeditionary Forces

September 13, 1918.

CORRECTED COPY
General Order
No. 6

1. The Fourth Corps* has defeated the enemy and driven him back on the whole Corps front. All objectives were reached before the time prescribed in orders, a large number of prisoners and a considerable amount of booty captured. The rapid advance of the Corps, in conjunction with the action of the other elements of the First Army, rendered the ST. MIHIEL salient untenable to the enemy, who has retreated.

2. The greatest obstacle to the advance was thought to be the enemy wire, which presented a problem that caused anxiety to all concerned. The Corps Commander desires to express in particular his admiration of the skill shown by the small groups in the advance battalions and their commanders in crossing the hostile wire, and in general to express his appreciation of the high spirit and daring shown by the troops, and the rapidity and efficiency with which the operation was conducted.

By command of Major General Dickman:

STUART HEINTZELMAN,
Chief of Staff.

Official:
PHILIP L. SCHUYLER,
Adjutant.

*Consisted of 1st, 42nd and 89th Divisions, with 3rd Division in reserve.

HEADQUARTERS 32ND DIVISION
American Expeditionary Forces
France

October, 1918.

From: Commanding General, 32nd Division.
To: Commanding General, 89th Division.
Subject: Relief of 32nd Division by 89th Division.

The Brigade and Regimental Commanders of the 32nd Division have reported on the conduct of the troops of the 89th Division in making the relief of that division October 19-20. Each and every report indicates most excellent discipline in the organizations of the 89th Division. The Brigade and Regimental Commanders had previously, by reconnaissance and the collection of information, informed themselves as to the location of our elements, and when it came to make the relief hardly any guides from the 32nd were necessary. This was most fortunate, as you are aware that our troops were very much worn out by the long fighting they had in this sector. It, therefore, gives me unusual pleasure to express to you the great satisfaction that my division felt and we are all hoping that the two divisions may serve close together in the future.

(Signed) W. G. HAAN,
Major General, U. S. A.

HEADQUARTERS FIRST ARMY
AMERICAN EXPEDITIONARY FORCES
FRANCE
OFFICE OF THE CHIEF OF STAFF

October, 26, 1918

From: Chief of Staff.
To: Commanding General, 5th Corps, American E. F.
Subject: Commendation on recent success of 89th Division.

The Army Commander directs that you convey to the Commanding General, officers and men of the 89th Division, his appreciation of their persistent and successful efforts in clearing the Bois de Bantheville of the enemy.

(Signed) H. A. DRUM,
Chief of Staff.

ebh. Hq. V Corps, Received 27 Oct., 1918.

HEADQUARTERS FIFTH ARMY CORPS
American Expeditionary Forces

France, 28 October, 1918.

From: Chief of Staff, V Army Corps.
To: Commanding General, 89th Division, U. S.
Subject: Commendation on recent success of 89th Division.

In transmitting the inclosed letter* to you, your officers and men, the Corps Commander desires me to add his commendation to that of the Army Commander, and to congratulate you on the morale and spirit of your Division as shown by its recent work.

(Signed) W. B. BURTT,
Chief of Staff.

I Incl.

*Letter from Chief of Staff, First Army, printed above.

WHAT THE GERMANS SAID
Extract from Order of 88th Division (German)

October 30, 1918

* * * * * * * * * * * * *

(Translation)

5. In the last days considerable losses have been caused by enemy artillery fire. These are only to be prevented when the troops dig themselves in well. Moving about in prominent places is without object, as the American Artillery places all landmarks and woods under fire.

I expect that the commanders personally see to it that the troops dig in and build shelters. Wood may be obtained in the Pioneer Park at MONTIGNY.

6. In the preceding night an American patrol hailed the 170th J. D. in German. This use of our tongue with the intention of deceiving our outpost has often been observed lately. The command has therefore ordered the use of a pass word. Pass word for tonight "Dansig." Pass word from November 2nd, noon, "Feuerschein." Pass word from November 5th, noon, "Fischotter."

7. The division is again opposite the 89th American Division as in the St. Mihiel region. This division is, as at that time, still known as a good American shock division which undertakes many strong patrol movements. In the present sector the 89th Division is probably in line with three regiments in the front line, the fourth regiment in reserve. The Division is at full strength, its combat strength is high; namely, 5 officers and 250 non-coms. and men per company. From the words of prisoners brought in in the last few days the Division has been placed in the present sector for an advance. From various maps and other notes it attempts to take as its objective the line from BUZANCY heights southwest of STENAY.

The capture of new prisoners for the further clearing of the situation is urgently commanded.

* * * * * * * * * * * * *

---

(100)

MESSAGE CENTER

2 November 18
01:35 Hour FJL

TELEGRAM (Received by telephone).

To C. G. 89th Divn.

Army commander desires to record and express to you his appreciation for the work done this day. He desires you to convey his appreciation to Virginia* and Peggy*. Please have this information transmitted to all organizations as far as practicable this night.

‡DRUMM

ACTION COPY C. of S.
G-3
File
Adjt.
P. C. Irwin
L. F.
Mc. L. F. 100
G-1
G-2

*89th and 2nd Divisions.
‡Chief of Staff, 1st American Army.

HEADQUARTERS FIFTH ARMY CORPS
American Expeditionary Forces

France, 2d November, 1918.

From: Commanding General, V Army Corps.
To: Commanding General, 89th Division.
Subject: Commendation.

In addition to my telephone message, I desire to convey to you and to the officers and soldiers of the 89th Division my profound appreciation and great admiration for the splendid manner in which the Division accomplished the mission allotted to it in the advance of the Fifth Corps on November first.

With a dash, courage, and speed that is worthy of the best traditions of our service, the 89th Division quickly overran the enemy's strong organization, followed its barrage, and planted itself on all objectives in accordance with the schedule previously arranged. It has captured many prisoners, guns and spoils of war, showing that the enemy was afforded no opportunity to escape.

The Division has more than justified the high confidence of the Commander in Chief when he selected it to form the advance in the great operations that have begun.

It is a high honor to command such troops, and I beg that you will convey to your officers and soldiers the assurances of my abiding wishes for their continued success in the campaigns that lie before it.

(Signed) C. P. SUMMERALL,
Major General, Commanding.

HEADQUARTERS EIGHTY-NINTH DIVISION
FRANCE

General Orders
No. 86.

12 November, 1918.

In leaving the 89th Division to assume command of the First Corps, I want to thank the officers and men for their splendid support and loyal service throughout the recent operations.

You have won a reputation which my praise cannot increase. I am proud to have been your commander.

W. M. WRIGHT,
Major General, U. S. A., Commanding

HEADQUARTERS SECOND DIVISION (REGULAR)
AMERICAN EXPEDITIONARY FORCES

France, November 13, 1918.

ORDER.

In the crossing of the MEUSE on the night of November 10th, * Companies "G" and "H," 9th Infantry, assisted the 2nd Engineers in throwing the bridges across the river. The 8th and 23rd Machine Gun Companies (Marine) accompanied the 1st and 2nd Battalion of the 5th Marines in their crossing; the 2nd Battalion, 356th Infantry (89th Division), and Company "C" of the 342nd Machine Gun Battalion (89th Division) crossed immediately after the above mentioned organizations; and, at dawn, the 1st Battalion of the 9th Infantry, accompanied by Company "D" of the 5th Machine Gun Battalion, moved forward to the east bank in support of the advanced force.

The names of the officers and men of these organizations belong on the roll of heroic men who did heroic deeds in the last battle of the war.

JOHN A. LEJEUNE,
Major General, U. S M. C., Commanding.

*At Letanne.

HEADQUARTERS FIFTH ARMY CORPS
American Expeditionary Forces

CORRECTED COPY

France, November 20, 1918.

General Order
No. 26

I. The following citations are announced:

The 1st, 2nd, and 89th Divisions, V Corps, American E. F., for their part in the memorable attack launched by the 1st American Army on November 1st. Throughout this operation all officers and men, by their high courage, devotion to duty, and disregard for the innumerable hardships encountered, made for themselves a place in the history of our country.

* * * * * * * * * *

The 89th Division, American E. F. (Maj. Gen. William M. Wright, Commanding), preceding the attack of November 1st, cleaned up the difficult and strongly held BOIS de BANTHEVILLE and attacked on November 1st. It broke through the enemy's lines, advanced strongly day and night, defeating the enemy and his reserves in its front, and drove him across the Meuse. Under heavy fire and against stubborn resistance, it constructed bridges and established itself on the heights. The cessation of hostilities found this Division holding strong positions across the Meuse and ready for a continuation of the advance.

* * * * * * * * * *

C. P. SUMMERALL,
Major General, Commanding.

OFFICIAL:
HARRY C. KAEFRING,
Adjutant General.

MEMORANDUM
No. 10.

28TH DIVISION
American Expeditionary Forces

8 November, 1918.

1. The Division Commander, with a feeling of sincere pride, publishes below a letter of commendation from the Commanding General, Second Army. It is indeed a pleasure to realize that our recent activities have been appreciated, and that the efforts of all who have taken part in this work have brought additional credit to the Division.

The 164th F. A. Brigade, now attached as Divisional Artillery, has done much towards the success of these operations.

HEADQUARTERS SECOND ARMY
American Expeditionary Forces

France, 5 November, 1918.

From: Commanding General, Second Army.
To: Commanding General, 28th Division, American E. F. (Through Commanding General, IV Corps).
Subject: Recent Activity of 28th Division.

1. I desire to inform you of my gratification at the vigorous and successful activities of your division since its entry into line on the front of the Second Army. The recent patrols and raids have resulted in making No Man's Land our land and in lowering the morale of the hostile units on your front, as well as in inflicting losses on them, and capturing a considerable number of prisoners. Such conduct exemplifies the American spirit and cannot fail to create a feeling of confidence on the part of our troops and of corresponding depression on the part of the enemy. The 28th Division has shown its ability to execute promptly the tasks which have been given to it to perform, and its officers and men have exhibited an efficiency and dash which are highly commendable.

R. L. BULLARD,
Lieutenant General, U. S. A.

W. H. HAY,
Major General, Commanding.

HEADQUARTERS 28TH DIVISION
American Expeditionary Forces
France

MEMORANDUM. November, 1918.

For Commanding General, 164th Field Artillery Brigade.

The Division Commander desires me to express to the officers and enlisted men of your command his appreciation of the excellent work which they have done during the time that the 28th Division has been in this sector.

Our infantry states that the barrage work of your brigade is uniformly good, and the proof that your artillery work is good is that it has the confidence of the infantry of the 28th Division.

The work of Captain Wentworth, your Operations Officer, and the uniform desire to assist the infantry manifested by yourself and by all of your staff are especially appreciated.

By Command of Major General Hay:

(Signed) W. C. SWEENEY,
Chief of Staff.

G. H. Q.
AMERICAN EXPEDITIONARY FORCES

France, December 26, 1918.

GENERAL ORDERS
No. 238.

It is with soldierly pride that I record in General Orders a tribute to the taking of the St. Mihiel Salient by the First Army.

On September 12, 1918, you delivered the first concerted offensive operation of the American Expeditionary Forces upon difficult terrain against this redoubtable position, immovably held four years, which crumpled before your ably executed advance. Within twenty-four hours of the commencement of the attack, the salient had ceased to exist and you were threatening Metz.

Your divisions, which had never been tried in the exacting conditions of major offensive operations, worthily emulated those of more arduous experience and earned their right to participate in the more difficult task to come.

Not only did you straighten a dangerous salient, capture 16,000 prisoners, and 443 guns, and liberate 240 square miles of French territory, but you demonstrated the fitness for battle of a unified American Army.

We appreciate the loyal training and effort of the First Army. In the name of our country, I offer our hearty and unmeasured thanks to these splendid Americans of the 1st, 4th and 5th Corps, and of the 1st, 2nd, 4th, 5th, 26th, 42nd, 82nd, 89th and 90th Divisions, which were engaged, and of the 3rd, 35th, 78th, 80th and 91st Divisions, which were in reserve.

JOHN J. PERSHING,
General, Commander-in-Chief.

G. H. Q.
AMERICAN EXPEDITIONARY FORCES

France, December 19, 1918.

GENERAL ORDERS
No. 232.

It is with a sense of gratitude for its splendid accomplishment, which will live through all history, that I record in General Orders a tribute to the victory of the First Army in the Meuse-Argonne battle.

Tested and strengthened by the reduction of the St. Mihiel salient, for more than six weeks you battered against the pivot of the enemy line on the western front. It was a position of imposing natural strength, stretching on both sides of the Meuse River from the bitterly contested hills of Verdun to the almost impenetrable forest of the Argonne; a position, moreover, fortified by four years of labor designed to render it impregnable; a position held with the fullest resources of the enemy. That position you broke utterly, and thereby hastened the collapse of the enemy's military power.

Soldiers of all of the divisions engaged under the First, Third and Fifth American Corps and the Second Colonial and Seventeenth French Corps—the 1st, 2nd, 3rd, 4th, 5th, 26th, 28th, 29th, 32nd, 33rd, 35th, 37th, 42nd, 77th, 78th, 79th, 80th, 81st, 82nd, 89th, 90th and 91st American Divisions—you will be long remembered for the stubborn persistence of your progress, your storming of obstinately defended machine gun nests, your penetration, yard by yard, of woods and ravines, your heroic resistance in the face of counter-attacks supported by powerful artillery fire. For more than a month, from the initial attack of September 26th, you fought your way slowly through the Argonne, through the woods and over the hills west of the Meuse; you slowly enlarged your hold on the Rotesde-Meuse to the east, and then, on the 1st of November, your attack forced the enemy into flight. Pressing his retreat, you cleared the entire left bank of the Meuse south of Sedan, and then stormed the heights on the right bank and drove him into the plain beyond.

The achievement of the First Army, which is scarcely to be equaled in American history, must remain a source of proud satisfaction to the troops who participated in the last campaign of the war. The American people will remember it as the realization of the hitherto potential strength of the American contribution toward the cause to which they had sworn allegiance. There can be no greater reward for a soldier or for a soldier's memory.

JOHN J. PERSHING,
General, Commander-in-Chief,
American Expeditionary Forces.

---

1 May, 1919. ADC-lad.

From: Chief of Staff, Third Army, American E. F.
To: Commanding General 89th Division, A. E. F. (Thru Commanding General, 7th Corps).
Subject: Condition of Transportation of 89th Division.

1. The Army Commander directs me to inform you that he is well pleased with the condition and appearance of the transportation (animals, vehicles and harness) of the 89th Division, which is being turned in to the Army Depot at Sinzig.

2. The excellent care of these animals and this property reflects credit upon the Train Commander, the officer in charge of the convoy, and all other officers and men on duty therewith, and the Army Commander desires to compliment you and them upon the showing they have made.

(Signed) MALIN CRAIG,
Chief of Staff.

1st Ind.
Hq. VII Army Corps, A. E. F., A.P.O. 792, 5/5/19. To C. G., 89th Division, A. E. F.

ADVANCE EMBARKATION SECTION, S. O. S.
PERSONNEL DEPARTMENT

May 1, 1919.

From: Captain L. E. Van Vleck, Personnel Adjutant, A. E. F., S. O. S.
To: Commanding General, 89th Division.
Subject: Report of Inspection of Records.

1. Having completed the inspections of the 89th Division in connection with the preparation of the Division for return to the United States, desire to report that the records and paper work have been found in a most gratifying condition, there being absolutely no criticisms to make. This shows the most careful and painstaking supervision and work on the part of the officers responsible.

(Signed) LYLE E. VAN VLECK,
Captain, Infantry,
Personnel Adjutant,
Adv. Emb. Sec., S. O. S.

HEADQUARTERS 89TH DIVISION
American Expeditionary Forces

General Orders
No. 44.
6 May, 1919. HP.

1. The movement home begins today. The Division Commander cannot let the occasion pass without expressing to officers and men his congratulations and gratitude. The Division is to be congratulated upon the accomplishment of its final mission of duty in occupied Germany, in a manner that has won the commendation of military superiors, increased the regard of our associate divisions and gained the respect of the inhabitants. It is with a heart full of gratitude that record is made of the whole-souled, intelligent and successful response the Division has made to every demand. The best tradition of the American Army for fair dealing in a foreign land have been maintained.

2. In training, in civil affairs, in the care of animals and transportation, in entertainments, in schools and in all routine duty, the Division has not only done its part well, but in many ways its record has been distinguished; in conduct and clean living it has been exemplary; in athletics it has won the football championship of the A. E. F. and excelled in other sports. The spirit and discipline of the Division have been remarkable, and for this the intelligence, sound common sense and superior character of the personnel as a whole are in large measure responsible.

3. The game has been played to the full, and in Germany to the last. This was strikingly exemplified in the splendid appearance of the men, the excellent condition of equipment and transportation, and the efficient team-work of the entire force on the occasion of the Review by the Commander-in-Chief at Treves Aviation Field, April 23, 1919. The record during the trying times of the Armistice is one comparable in every respect to that fighting record which, for the time the Division was in the line, is unexcelled in the A. E. F. It is confidently expected that it will be the determination of officers and men alike to see that the standards of the Division are preserved so long as a single member remains in the service.

4. This opportunity is taken to express appreciation of the services of the Staff Officers of the Division. Zealous, loyal and able, they have done their part toward maintaining the fighting efficiency that stamps the character of the Division.

5. The Commander-in-Chief has sent a letter* which all will read with pride and satisfaction, and which is published as the final message, most highly valued by the officers and men, who have made the Division worthy of the praise and assured of the friendship of General Pershing.

(Signed) FRANK L. WINN,
Major General, U. S. A., Commanding.

*Printed below.

AMERICAN EXPEDITIONARY FORCES
OFFICE OF THE COMMANDER-IN-CHIEF
FRANCE

Major General Frank L. Winn,
Commanding 89th Division, American E. F.

April 27, 1919.

My dear General Winn:

It was very pleasing to me to note the fine appearance of your Division at the inspection and review held on April 23rd at the Aviation Field near Treves. The high morale of all ranks was very evident, and was what I had expected to find in a division with such a splendid fighting record as the 89th.

After its arrival in France in early June, for two months it trained near Reynel. It then joined the 1st American Army in the Toul sector, where on September 12th it took part in the St. Mihiel offensive, capturing the strong position of Bois de Mort Mare and by the 13th advancing 18 kilometers. It then consolidated its position and after relieving the 42nd and 78th Divisions was itself relieved on October 7th. On October 19th it entered the Meuse-Argonne offensive as part of the 5th Corps, taking the Bois de Bantheville the next day. On November 1st it surged forward with the 1st Army, and from that time until November 11th it was advancing constantly. Breaking through the enemy's line, it pushed on day and night to a depth of 30 kilometers, defeating the enemy and the reserves on its front and driving him across the Meuse. Under heavy fire bridges were constructed and by the signing of the Armistice it was established on the heights east of the river. In the short space of this letter it is impossible to mention the names of the places which will live in the history of the Division on account of the gallant deeds done. Barricourt Woods, Remonville, Tailly, Nouart, Barricourt, Bois des Dames, Beauclair, Pouilly, the brilliant crossing of the River Meuse, and Autreville are but a few of them.

Please extend my congratulations to the officers and men of your Division on their appearance at inspection as well as their splendid record in France. They may well return home proud of themselves, safe in the assurance of the admiration and respect of their comrades in the American Expeditionary Forces.

Respectfully yours,

(Signed) JOHN J. PERSHING.

Coblenz, Germany, 8 May, 1919.

From: Chief of Staff, Third Army.
To: Commanding General, 89th Division.
Subject: Appreciation of services of the Division.

The Army Commander desires to express to you, and through you to the officers and men of your command, his appreciation of the service rendered to the Nation by the "Middle West Division."

Seasoned by your occupation of the defensive sector of Toul, you engaged the enemy in the St. Mihiel Offensive with a dash and a determination worthy of the best traditions of the American Army. During the Meuse-Argonne Operation, where you served under the Army Commander as the Commanding General of the First Army, you won new laurels. Since joining the Army of German Occupation the conduct of your officers and men has been above criticism: their morale, military appearance and high state of training have impressed all who have come in contact with them.

The fine record made by the Division while in the American Expeditionary Forces reflects credit on its home training and the worth of the citizens of those States from which its personnel was drawn.

By command of Lieutenant General LIGGETT:

(Signed) MALIN CRAIG,
Chief of Staff.

MESSAGE CENTER
Telegram

S-303 — 12 May, 1919.
18 ZAB 85 OB — 19:27 hrs. lf.
From: Hdqrs., Third Army 12.
To: Commanding General, 89th Div.

C. A. 51 Army Commander directs me to express appreciation for work your division in administration civil affairs and for excellent report submitted.

Hunt, Col., Charge Civil Affairs.

FRENCH REPUBLIC
(Translation)

THE PRESIDENT OF THE COUNCIL*
DEPARTMENT OF WAR

Paris, May 12, 1919.

To the General Commanding the 89th American Division.
My dear General:

I cannot but call to mind, before your Division leaves French soil, the record of the glorious part it has played in the war for liberty and civilization.

When, on the 12th of September, it was called on to attack at St. Mihiel, it reached by the end of the first day the objectives which had been assigned it for the first two days: three thousand prisoners, twelve cannon, and sixty machine guns were its trophies.

The following month, in the Verdun sector, its attack in the Bois de Bantheville showed that it had lost none of its offensive spirit. In the month of November it was keen in the pursuit of the enemy, and on that account it won the glory of entering the town of Stenay.

I beg you to express to your soldiers the gratitude of the Government of the Republic. France will never forget the generous aid which they have given her. In the same thought of remembrance I join the living and the dead, and I wish all those who are going to return to their country good fortune and a happy life.

For and by order of the President of the Council.

The General charged with the Franco-American Affairs of War.

(Signed) TARDIEU.

*M. Clemenceau,
Le President du Conseil,
Ministre de la Guerre.

SIGNAL CORPS, U. S. ARMY
TELEGRAM

Treves, May 14, 1919.

Received at
14 BR W N 71 OB

Commanding General, 89th Division, Brest:

A. E. S. 366. Following telegram to Commanding General, S. O. S., repeated for your information: "Twenty-third and last train 89th Division left for Brest at twelve hours two minutes this date. Medical examination, records, condition of equipment and property, discipline and condition of billets highly satisfactory, and reflects great credit upon the Division."

*CONRAD,
10:26 A.

*Chief, Advance Embarkation Service.

MISCELLANEOUS

RATINGS SHOWN ON DIVISION INSIGNIA

(See Page 309)

At the close of each training period, while the Division was in the Army of Occupation, the regiments in each brigade, battalions in each regiment and companies in each battalion were given, by their respective commanders, a relative rating. The Division commander determined the relative rating of the brigades and of divisional troops.

(A) The members of each company or battery rated as No. 1 in its battalion were authorized to wear a white patch or inlay in the lower forward space of the division shoulder insignia.

(B) The members of the battalion rated as No. 1 in each regiment, or among divisional troops, were authorized to wear a white inlay in the upper forward space of the division insignia.

(C) The members of the regiment rated highest in its brigade were authorized to wear a white inlay in the upper rear space of the division shoulder insignia.

(D) The members of that brigade declared by the Division commander as having the greatest degree of excellence were authorized to wear a white inlay in the lower rear space of the division shoulder insignia.

Thus every member of a highest rated organization was enabled to wear a striking evidence of that fact, and relative excellence was indicated by the number of white inlays. Hence, a member of that company rated highest in the winning battalion of the winning regiment of the winning brigade would have four white inlays, entirely surrounding the "W" of the shoulder insignia, for the "shell" (S) or middle section of the "W" was already filled with an inlay of appropriate color for his branch of the service, blue for infantry, red for artillery, etc.

These white inlays were worn until a new rating at the end of the next training period brought changes in standing. The competitive instinct was stimulated and results were considered very beneficial, although for practical reasons ratings were not always made as between infantry and artillery brigades and the divisional troops.

The following illustrates these markings:

White inlay, (A) Best company or battery in the battalion.
White inlay, (B) Best battalion in the regiment.
White inlay, (C) Best regiment in the brigade.
White inlay, (D) Best brigade in the division.
Colored inlay, (S) "Shell" colored according to branch of the service.

MUSKETRY COMPETITION—APRIL, 1919

(See Page 309)

1. The silver trophy offered by the Division commander to the company having, in record practice, the smallest number of poor shots, was won by Company B, 353rd Infantry, 1st Lieutenant Morton B. Shepard, Commanding.

2. The silver trophy offered by the Division commander to the platoon chosen to represent the Division in the A. E. F. Musketry Match (held at LeMans, France, in May) was won by the First Platoon, Company H, 356th Infantry, 2nd Lieutenant Edward V. Macatee, Commanding. In this competition, held April 17th, one platoon from each infantry regiment participated. The results were:

1st—Platoon from 356th Infantry (noted above).
2nd—Platoon from 353rd Infantry.
3rd—Platoon from 355th Infantry.
4th—Platoon from 354th Infantry.

On account of the early return of the Division to the United States, the winning platoon was unable to participate in the A.E.F. contest at LeMans.

3. The silver trophy offered by the Division commander to the enlisted man making the highest total score in record practice, qualification course, was won by Private Oscar J. Peterson, Headquarters Company, 356th Infantry.

4. The machine gun competition, held April 19th, to select a machine gun platoon to represent the Division in the A.E.F. contests at LeMans was won by the First Platoon, Company B, 340th Machine Gun Battalion, 1st Lieutenant Grover Hutchinson, Commanding. In this competition one platoon from each infantry brigade and one from the 340th Machine Gun Battalion participated. The results were:

1st—Platoon from 340th Machine Gun Battalion (noted above)
2nd—Platoon from 341st Machine Gun Battalion.
3rd—Platoon from 342nd Machine Gun Battalion.

On account of the early return of the Division to the United States, the winning platoon was unable to participate in the A.E.F. contests at LeMans.

MAP READING

For the reader who has had no experience with French military maps a word concerning the method of reading map coördinates will be necessary. Maps based on the coördinate system had been made for almost all of France prior to 1914. It will be noticed that each one of these maps, no matter what its scale may be, is divided into equal squares by a number of vertical and horizontal lines. These lines are known as coördinates, and they are exactly one kilometer apart on the map. The origin point or zero for both coördinates is an arbitrarily selected point in the ocean west of France. It will also be noticed that the coördinates are numbered serially from the left to the right and from the bottom to the top of the map. Thus in the map of the

St. Mihiel attack, the coördinates from left to right are numbered from 355 to 367, and are known as the X coördinates, and the coördinates from bottom to top from 228 to 251 are known as the Y coördinates. In order to find the coördinate reading of any point on the map it is only necessary to determine which of the coördinate lines it lies between. The town of Xammes, for instance, falls between lines 362 and 363, measuring horizontally, and between lines 243 and 244, measuring vertically. Upon estimating the fractions beyond the lower coördinates 362 and 243, and designating them by decimals, the coördinates of the town are found to be 362.4 by 243.3. For convenience, however, the first figures of each coördinate are omitted, since it may be seen at a glance that they are the same for every point on the map. The coördinates of Xammes then become 62.4 by 43.3.

Further simplicity in designation was sometimes attained by expressing both coördinates in one series of four figures, the first two figures used being those just before and after the decimal point in the X coördinate and the last two being the corresponding figures of the Y coördinate. These were often placed on airplane photographs to indicate corresponding points on the maps. An example may be seen on the composite air photograph of the terrain of the St. Mihiel battle, shown in this book. The figures 3356 shown at the edge of the Bois d'Euvezin, above and to the left of Robert Menil Farm, will be found, by reference to the map to indicate 363.3x235.6.

The kilometer squares permitted another simple form of designation by the use of two figures only, which was frequently used, especially when it was unnecessary to locate the point or small area referred to with the precision possible by use of decimals above described. The first figure used in this method was the one before the decimal point in the X coördinate and the second the figure before the decimal point in the Y coördinate, the two together being the number of the kilometer square. Thus Xammes is located in the center of square 23 and the Robert Menil Farm is in square 35. On some maps these figures were shown in the corner of each kilometer square, but since coördinates were always shown on the maps, the system could be used even though squares were not individually marked.

A few remarks about the French maps of the trenches may also prove of interest. These were made for the most part from airplane photographs. On coördinate maps of scale 1/5,000, 1/10,000, and 1/20,000 like those described above there was overprinted all available information of Allied and enemy works, including trenches, wire, dugouts, emplacements, railroads, etc. The Allied works were printed in red. Maps showing them were sparingly distributed and closely guarded. On the maps commonly distributed to troops the works of the Germans were printed in blue, and Allied works were not shown, except by a single red line indicating the front line. These maps, known as the "plans directeurs," had been made for the territory from twenty to forty kilometers on both sides of the lines before the United States entered the war. They were supplied to American troops, and were the real maps by which all fighting was done. These maps also show the elevations and depressions in the ground by a system of lines called contours, each of which is traced on the map following the line of a specified level above the sea. The contour lines are shown at a specified distance in elevation, as for example, each 10 meters of elevation will be indicated by a contour line. It is thus evident that where the ground is steep the contour lines will come close together, while level ground will show the contours widely separated. It it thus possible for one skilled in map reading to obtain a perfect idea of the ground, and by the use of the coördinates to describe points upon it with the utmost precision.

89TH DIVISION

LOCATION OF DIVISION HEADQUARTERS

Arrived:	
LE HAVRE, France	June 21, 1918.
REYNAL, Haute-Marne, France	June 22, 1918, to 12 hours August 5, 1918.
LAGNEY, Meurthe et Moselle, France	12 hours August 5, 1918, to 8 hours August 10, 1918.
LUCEY, Meurthe et Moselle, France	8 hours August 10, 1918, to 12 hours September 10, 1918.
Dugout R. R. of NOVIANT Meurthe et Moselle, France	12 hours September 10, 1918, to 10 hours September 12, 1918.
FLIREY, Meurthe et Moselle, France	10 hours September 12, 1918, to 10 hours September 14, 1918.
EUVEZIN, Meurthe et Moselle, France	10 hours September 14, 1918, to 23 hours October 7, 1918.
COMMERCY, Meurthe et Moselle, France	23 hours October 7, 1918, to 18 hours October 9, 1918.
RECICOURT, Meuse, France	18 hours October 9, 1918, to 9 hours October 13, 1918
BOIS de MONTFAUCON, Meuse, France (Point 105-752, Map VERDUN A. 1/20,000)	9 hours October 13, 1918, to 12 hours October 14, 1918.
EPINONVILLE, Meuse, France	12 hours October 14, 1918 to 13:30 hours October 24, 1918.
GESNES, Meuse, France	13:30 hours October 24, 1918, to 14 hours November 1, 1918.
LA DHUY FERME, Meuse, France	14 hours November 1, 1918, to 9 hours November 3, 1918.
REMONVILLE, Meuse, France	9 hours November 3, 1918, to 13:30 hours November 3, 1918.
BARRICOURT, Meuse, France	13:30 hours November 3, 1918, to 10 hours November 4, 1918.
TAILLY, Meuse, France	10 hours November 4, 1918, to 15 hours November 21, 1918.
STENAY, Meuse, France	15 hours November 21, 1918, to 15 hours November 25, 1918.
DAMPICOURT, Belgium	15 hours November 25, 1918, to 15 hours November 30, 1918.
ST. LEGER, Belgium	15 hours November 30, 1918, to 15 hours December 3, 1918.
MERSCH, Luxembourg	15 hours December 3, 1918, to 8 hours December 4, 1918.
ECHTERNACH, Luxembourg	8 hours December 4, 1918, to 15 hours December 7, 1918.
KYLLBURG, Germany	15 hours December 7 1918, to 12 hours May 13, 1919.
Sailed from:	
BREST, France	May 19, 1919.

TOTAL NUMBER OF PRISONERS CAPTURED

	Officers	Men
ST. MIHIEL DRIVE	78	2,209
MEUSE-ARGONNE OFFENSIVE	114	2,660
TOTAL	192	4,869
GRAND TOTAL		5,061

PARTIAL LIST OF MATERIAL CAPTURED IN EACH OPERATION

ST. MIHIEL DRIVE: 72 cannon, 10 minenwerfers, 95 machine guns, 1,000 rifles.
MEUSE-ARGONNE OFFENSIVE: 42 pieces light artillery, 12 pieces heavy artillery, 1 anti-aircraft gun, 15 minenwerfers, 7 one-pounders, 360 machine guns, 400 rifles.
In addition vast quantities of ammunition, equipment and supplies of all kinds were captured in both offenses.

TOTAL DEPTH OF ADVANCE IN EACH OFFENSIVE	Average Depth	Extreme Depth
ST. MIHIEL DRIVE, 12-13 September, 1918	12 km.	18 km.
MEUSE-ARGONNE OFFENSIVE, 1-11 November, 1918	24 km.	30 km.
TOTALS	36 km.	48 km.

A. E. F. BATTLE DEATHS BY BRANCH OF THE SERVICE

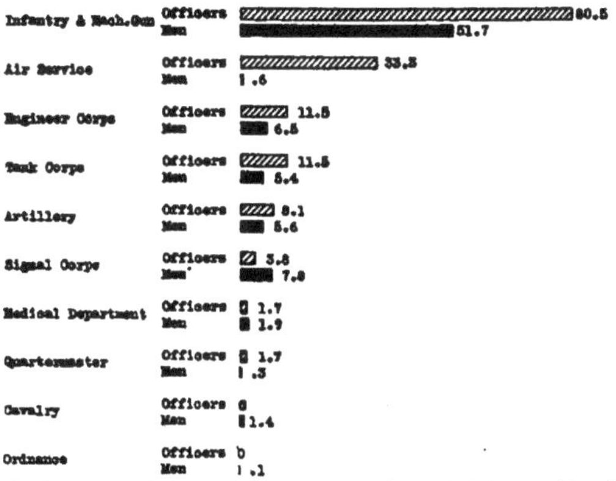

Battle deaths among each thousand officers and men who reached France. From "The War with Germany, a Statistical Summary" (Ayres) 2nd Edition, an official compilation prepared by the Statistics Branch of the General Staff, War Department, Washington, D. C.

RELIGIOUS CENSUS OF THE 89th DIVISION

January 22, 1919

Church members	13,818
No Church preference	5,320

Denominations

Catholic	3,691
Methodist	2,973
Baptist	1,698
Presbyterian	1,336
Lutheran	1,318
Christian	1,071
Protestant (unclassified)	718
Episcopalian	352
Congregational	252
Hebrew	187
Mormon	77
Christian Science	75
United Brethren	71
Evangelist	70
Greek Orthodox	28
Reformed	18
Adventist	14
Quaker	12
Dunkard	10
Unitarian	8
Holiness	11
Church of God	6
Salvation Army	6
Free Methodist	6
Spiritualist	7
Free Thinker	5
Church of Christ	5
Miscellaneous	26

TYPICAL DAILY REGIMENTAL REPORT

354TH INFANTRY
INTELLIGENCE AND OPERATION REPORT
12.00 Sept. 6th to 12:00 Sept. 7/1918.

I. ORDER OF BATTLE—A prisoner captured during an enemy raid of this morning. Name: Reinhold Fietze; 294; Kamin, Flatow. W. P. R. 93; R. J. R. 257; K. N. 1249; E. B. R. J. R. 65, supplies the following information regarding enemy:

"Each battalion holds a front of 1,100 meters; light machine guns 6 to each company are placed along the front; heavy machine guns further back; one company to each two battalions of infantry. Their supplies come through Thiaucourt along the Thiaucourt-Regnieville road and then into the woods. Machines are used for the greater part of the trip and then carried over good paths to final disposition. They intend to hold the line in front of Thiaucourt as a main or last line of resistance, but have one line just back of the woods and another between that and Thiaucourt. The openings in the woods along the roads to Essey and Euvezin are protected by machine gun emplacements, some near the front and then back to the rear edge of the woods. There are also battery emplacements back of the Mort Mare and Bois Rendu, but prisoner could not state where or what kind of guns were used. There still some French inhabitants in Thiaucourt, but most of population has moved out. German snipers and light machine guns occupy their front line trench. The raiding party of which he was a member consisted of 60 men, 1 officer and 1 unterofficer. He knew of a similar raiding party going out towards Limey. The mission of the raid was to capture prisoners. Their party came over the top and through the wire, having to cut only when they came into the very edge of our trenches. This prisoner had all his marks of identification on his person, which shows some disorganization on their side. He stated that they would probably let this raid settle for awhile and then come over on another raiding party. He further stated that the Germans expected an attack by the American forces at any time, and all men in their ranks feared the American soldier."

II. GENERAL IMPRESSION OF THE DAY—Continued enemy artillery activity.

III. ACTIVITY OF INFANTRY—

(a) American—Successfully repulsed enemy raiding of 60 men.

(b) German—Enemy raiding party of 60 men attacked the 4th platoon of our left center company near point 61.6-32.3 during their artillery bombardment. Private Hayden McDowell, upon hearing a noise in wire challenged and fired his rifle; also threw a grenade. Four Germans came over the top of trench in front of him. He got the first German with his bayonet; the other Germans hit him on the head with rifle and pulled him out of trench. He was successful in fighting his way free with trench knife which the enemy had not taken away from him. Captain W. P. Hay of Company "E" was killed by grenade; at the same time Private Gordechak was wounded. One German prisoner was taken by Company "E;" also two prisoners were taken by Company "F." One of the enemy killed and a number wounded.

IV. ACTIVITY OF ARTILLERY—

(a) Allied—Intermittent firing during the day; active reply to enemy bombardment of this A. M.

(b) German—Enemy unusually quiet during the day until the hour of the raid; during that time and 6:30 the enemy heavily shelled the area among our battalion headquarters, located near bridge of railroad, from hour 6.10 to 6.27. Sixteen shells fell in rear of this area in Bois de la Hazelle. These shells were fired from the direction of Mort Mare.

V. AERONAUTICS—

(a) American—Usual aerial activities. At hour 8.30 two enemy planes circled over our right sector, signalled and then returned to their lines. At hour 8.40 two enemy planes circled over the area of our battalion headquarters and returned upon being fired upon. Two enemy planes flying over our front lines at hour 18.10. Two enemy planes circled over our enter sector were fired upon by machine gun. At hour 18.25 two planes flying low in a southwesterly direction. At hour 20.30 two planes flying close together back and forth over our lines. At 6.32 enemy plane circled over the area shelled by their artillery.

ENEMY OBSERVATION BALLOONS

	Up	Down
Grange	18.55	19.14
Beney	18.55	19.14
Hattonchatel	19.07	19.15
Beney		19.25
Jaulny	5.32	
Billy	5.34	

VI. MOVEMENTS—

(a) Visibility—Poor.
(b) American (Troop Movement)—N. T. R.
(c) French—N. T. R.
(d) German—N. T. R.

1. Trains—N. T. R.
2. Decauville—N. T. R.
3. Motor Trucks and Wagons—N. T. R.
4. Men—N. T. R.

VII. WORK—

(a) American—Old dugouts repaired, shelters repaired, drains put in trenches, and general policing of trenches.

(b) German—Two of the enemy were observed at point 61.82-33.87, which has been a center of their activities in the past. The enemy were not visible at any other point of their line.

VIII. LOSSES—

Hay, Wendell P., Captain, killed by grenade in enemy raid of this morning.
McDowell, 2847769, Hayden, Private 1-cl., wounded during enemy raid.
Gordeichak, Private, wounded during this encounter.
Ruppert, 2201265, Otto, Private, Supply Co., gun shot wound, accidental.

IX. MISCELLANEOUS—

At hours 20.13, 20.20, 20.21, 20.25, 21.25, white flares from the enemy right sector; 21.30, red rocket from opposite our right; 21.55, 21.56, white flares opposite our right. Hours 22.02, 22.04, white flares opposite our left. At hour 24.40, flare and smoke from locomotive plainly seen in a direction opposite our left sector, smoke rolling from the locomotive as though laboring under heavy load. The noise of this train was heard between hours 1.25 and 2.35.

JOHN F. McGRATH,
1st Lt., Inf., N. A., R. I. O.

Approved:

AMERICUS MITCHELL,
Colonel, 354th Infantry, Commanding.

NOTE—Full report covering details, also statements of two other prisoners will follow. This information delayed account interruption of field telephone communication.

TYPICAL DAILY DIVISION G-2 REPORT

NOT TO BE TAKEN INTO
FRONT LINE TRENCHES.

89TH DIVISION HEADQUARTERS
Second Section, G. S.
No 19—FEH

SUMMARY OF INTELLIGENCE—AUGUST 27-28, 1918

ORDER OF BATTLE

Three prisoners, one sergeant and two corporals, were captured last night southeast of RICHECOURT at about 11 p. m. by a patrol of the 355th Infantry. The order of battle was confirmed in that the 47th Infantry occupies the center formerly held by the 477th Infantry, and that the relief took place about seven days ago. They confirmed the fact that the center is occupied by one regiment of infantry with two battalions side by side, each battalion with two companies in the front line and two companies in support. The third battalion is in reserve. Statements as to the size of the companies varied from 80 men to 200 men in a company. Each company is equipped with six machine guns. Prisoners stated that two or three of the enemy patrol were wounded.

ACTIVITY OF THE ENEMY

(a) Infantry—One of our patrols, consisting of one officer and nineteen men encountered an enemy patrol southeast of RICHECOURT, gained contact with the enemy and captured three prisoners. Enemy patrol seen crossing No Man's Land at vicinity 62.5-33.72. Our patrol lay in ambush, but enemy patrol did not return by same route. 7.50 machine gun fire from BOIS de MORT MARE. From 0.10 to 1.00 bursts of machine gun fire from vicinity ANSONCOURT Farm. 22.10 to 22.15 six bursts machine gun fire from SONNARD Woods. 22.10 several bursts machine gun fire from RICHECOURT. 8.00 fifty shots from machine gun from BURLY Woods. 23.25 six rounds of machine gun fire from vicinity GERECHAMP Woods. 4.07 to 4.45 intermittent machine gun fire from GERECHAMP Woods. 5.48 two bursts of machine gun fire from GERECHAMP Woods. 10.45 six rifle shots from direction ANSONCOURT Farm. 11.30 several enemy rifle shots struck wire at 64.6-32.1 and 64.7-32.2. From 6.30 to 3.00 rifle shots fired from PONCE Woods at approximately three-minute intervals. German sentry heard to challenge and fire two shots at 51.8-31.3. Several rifle shots heard XIVRAY-MARVOISIN, 23.20, and again at 2.01 to 2.25.

(b) Artillery—

Time	37	77	105	155	Point of Contact	Origin
7:15			10		Limey	Bois du Four
7:47	5				Lironville	" " "
7:55- 8:10	10	2			Limey	" " "
8:14		4			65.3-22.8	" " "
8:38		1			64.1-33.1	Bois de Mort Mare
8:45	1				64 2-33.2	Promenade des Moines
9:10- 9:25	20				Limey	Bois la Haie l'Eveque
9:21-10:57			32		"	Bois du Four
9:41-10:12		10			65.3-33.4	" " "
10:48	9				Limey	Ansoncourt Farm
11:50-12:03			36		64.0-33.1	Bois du Four
11:58-12:54			104		64.1-33.1	" " "
12:06-12:20		10				Bois de Mort Mare
12:51			27		63.8-33.3	Bois du Four
12:58		8			63.0-32.1	Bois la Haie l'Eveque
13:25			7		64.1-33.1	Promenade des Moines
15:35	15				64.1-33.1	Bois du Four
14:17-15:20			50		63.8-33.6	" " "
14:30	10				64.9-31.4	" " "
14:50		12			64.1-33.3	Bois de Mort Mare
15:05			3		64.9-31.4	" " " "
15:25		10			64.1-33.3	Bois du Four

Time	37	77	105	155	Point of Contact	Origin
16:00-17:20		21			66.0-32.7	Bois de Mort Mare
16:03	12				64.3-34.1	Promenade des Moines
16:05		4			64.1-33.3	Bois du Four
17:05			11		64.9-31.4	" " "
17:55			12		64.9-31.4	Bois de Mort Mare
19:50		2			Limey	Bois du Four
17:18- 7:22		2			Beaumont	Burly Woods
13:30-14:30		7			Hazelle Woods	Sonnard Woods
14:45-16:37		34			60.0-29.2	Unknown
16:50-18:45		184 (77's and 105's)			Jury Woods	Sonnard Woods
18:45		6			" "	Quart Reserve
17:02		1			E. of Rambucourt	Burly Woods

Total shells reported in sector.. 692

AERONAUTICS

(a) Balloons—

Location	Ascended	Descended
Beney	6:42	6:55
"	16:34	18:14
"	18:17	20:08
Hattonchatel	13:26	13:37
"	17:55	19:43
Jaulnay	16:17	
Laginau	18:05	19:41
Vigneulles	18:10	18:28
Thiaucourt	19:07	19:50

On 26th, August, 1918, Beney moved from old position in BOIS DE BENEY to vicinity around NONSARD (closer). Beney rose at this position (NONSARD) at 13:27 p. m. today and soon went down. Beney rose in another position near PANNES just before firing on rest camp in BOIS REHANNE, and in the BOIS du ROYAUMEIX. Just before this firing, WOEL maneuvered from in rear (far back) up to vicinity of Beney's old position, in line with BENEY, perhaps moved up four or five kilometers. Hattonchatel maneuvered to the right about two kilometers from old position. All balloons, especially these three, were much closer to the lines than ordinarily. This approach closer to the lines and bunching of enemy balloons may be an effort to locate guns in BOIS REHANNE by intersection. At 10:10 A. M. enemy plane shot down our balloon southeast of RAULECOURT at 25.0-52.0. At about 11:30 A. M. enemy plane shot down our balloon southwest of Ansauville at 25.0-60.0, and also one east of Division area, the exact location of which is unknown.

(b) Aeroplanes—10:35 enemy plane flying northwest over our line. 18:10 enemy plane appeared over BOIS de MORT MARE, disappeared over BOIS du FOUR. 18:40 enemy planes patrolling behind their lines from west to east. At 18:52 enemy planes attempted to cross Allied line at XIVRAY-MARVOISIN, driven back by anti-aircraft guns.

MOVEMENTS

Visibility—Fair.

Eleven Germans seen standing and sitting on parapet of trench at 63.8-35.4, apparently doing nothing but standing around.

Trains—At 5:46 train VIGNEULLES to BENEY. 5:48 train ESSEY to BENEY. At 6:15 train switching at BENEY. At 6:17 train going south through BENEY station. At 6:30 train going through BENEY station northwest. At 6:31 train went through ESSEY station southwest. At 14:05 train going from BENEY to PANNES. At 16:48 train disappeared in woods at 58.8-43.5. At 19:13 engine and two cars BENEY to VIGNEULLES. At 19:32 train from VIGNEULLES to BENEY. At 19:32 train from BENEY to VIGNEULLES. Usual amount of activity consisting of trucks, automobiles, wagons and pedestrians back area, except unusual activity reported on HATTONCHATEL road.

MISCELLANEOUS

Enemy outpost reported at 51.7-30.4 to 52.1-30.4 which has twice fired on our forces. no time given. Usual flares, rockets and lights. At 21.30 enemy used a flash light on BERNECOURT Road. At 22:30 flash of light behind hill 365 repeated frequently. Smoke seen rising at following points:

At 18:55 and again at 19:12 trench at 64.4-35.5.
At 11:45 at 48.2-36.2.
At 18:00 cloud af smoke at HEUDICOURT.
At 14:56 at point 59.8-37.7

GENERAL IMPRESSION OF THE DAY

Somewhat above normal in activity artillery and movements in back area.

ESTIMATE OF THE ENEMY'S INTENTIONS

N. T. R.

J. B. GOODMAN, JR.,
Major of Infantry, N. G.,
A. C. of S., G-2.

AMERICAN COMMUNIQUE, AUGUST 27TH. 9 P. M.

Aside from renewed local combats along the VESLE between RAZOCHES and FISMES there is nothing to report.

FRENCH COMMUNIQUE, AUGUST 28TH

The French have forced the Germans to precipitate their retreat across the AVRE. On a front of about 20 kilometers, breaking all resistance, they have realized an advance of over four kilometers on certain points. They hold the line immediately west of OULCHY, VERPILLIERS. They have occupied HALLU, FRONSART, CREMERY, CRUMY, ROYE, HANCOURT and CRAPEAUMESNIL. They captured prisoners. The battle goes on quite lively between the OISE and the AISNE.

BRITISH COMMUNIQUE, AUGUST 28TH. 15 h. 30.

BAPAUME, CROISILLES and many villages fell in the hands of the British. More than 21,000 prisoners in five days. A new army commanded by General Home entered in action, giving a rather sad surprise to the Huns.

TYPICAL DAILY DIVISION G-3 REPORT

SECRET OPERATION
REPORT NO. 44

HEADQUARTERS 89TH DIVISION
G-3 Section

23rd September, 1918.

OPERATION REPORT
From Noon, September 22nd, to Noon, September 23rd, 1918

1. HOSTILE SITUATION AT BEGINNING OF DAY.
No change.

2. INFORMATION RECEIVED OF ENEMY DURING DAY.
Prisoners captured in raid September 22nd-23rd confirm enemy order of battle.

3. HOSTILE MOVEMENTS, CHANGES AND CONDUCT DURING DAY.
Infantry—Usual machine gun and rifle fire. Enemy activity confined to observation and defensive tactics.
Artillery—XAMMES and BENEY heavily shelled intermittently. BOUILLONVILLE shelled between 20.00 and 21.00 hour. Between 14.30 and 15.00 hour 5 shells, calibre unknown, fell in EUVEZIN.
Aeronautics—Weather unfavorable for too extensive activity. Five enemy balloons reported up.
Movements—Usual traffic in back area. Large amount of movement behind enemy line with apparently no attempt at concealment. Considerable movement of men on CHAREY-DOMMARTIN Road.

4. MAPS ILLUSTRATING ABOVE.
None required.

5. OWN SITUATION AT BEGINNING OF DAY.
No change.

6. OWN CHANGES, MOVEMENTS AND ACTION DURING DAY.
Infantry—
353rd Inf. Necessary protective screens thrown out.
354th Inf. Patrol of 2 officers, 5 N. C. O.'s and 33 men left point 62.1x45.15 at 22.30 hr. Mission—To reconnoiter woods at 63x45.55, drive enemy out of same and gain contact with his line to rear of woods.
Ground Patrolled—Proceeded N. E. to point 63.05x45.7. Encountered no enemy up to cross roads 63.1x45.8, but just E. of this point light M. G. opened fire on patrol. When patrol replied enemy retired. Enemy trenches located in general direction 63.1x46.05 to 63.8x45.3 with no wire. Patrol returned by same route to point of departure at 2.30 hour.
355th Inf. In reserve training in accordance with instructions from 89th Division Headquarters.
356th Inf. Preceded by artillery barrage a raid was made at 4.00 hour by 2 companies, with mopping up parties on each flank on Dommartin Woods. Mission—to drive enemy out of woods, capture prisoners and secure identification.
Ground raided—The raid extended in a northeasterly direction covering the area 60.6x45.8; 61.55x46.9; 62.15x46.4, and 61.25x45.3.
The enemy put down an artillery barrage, and a heavy cross fire of machine guns from MARIMBOIS FARM-The DOMMARTIN WOODS and northwest thereof. The raiding party advanced through this fire and took the objective. The woods were cleared out and a number of the enemy killed and wounded. Four prisoners belonging to 2nd Co., 352nd Regiment, 88th Division, were captured. Seven of our men were killed, and approximately 33 wounded. All of our troops returned, bringing the dead and wounded with them.

Artillery—
Effective barrage preceding raid by 356th Infantry. Increased harassing fire. No. of rounds fired, 17,095.

Aeronautics—
Active at intervals owing to bad weather. No Allied balloons reported up.

Movements—
Internal movements without event.

Work—

Engineers working on positions of resistance	760
Infantrymen working on positions of resistance	490
Engineers working on Division P. C.	200
Engineers working on roads and miscellaneous	140
Total	1,590

7. INFORMATION ON NEIGHBORING UNITS.
   Divisions on our right and left report a quiet day.

8. ORDERS RECEIVED.

From	Class	No.	Date of Issued	Date of Rec'd	Summary
4th A. C.	G-3 Memo	118	22	22	
4th A. C.	G-3 Memo	119	22	22	

9. ACTION DURING DAY AND ORDERS RECEIVED AND ISSUED.
   The following orders were received from 177th Brig. F. O. 8, September 22nd; from 178th Brig. F. O. No. 8 September 22nd. The following orders were issued by 89th Division: F. O. 23, September 21st, and F. O. 24, September 22nd.

10. RESULTS OF ACTION—OWN AND ENEMY.
    Casualties—
    353rd Inf.—2 E. M. wounded, artillery fire.
    356th Inf.—7 E. M. killed (approximately); 33 E. M. wounded (approximately).

11. MAPS ILLUSTRATING ABOVE.
    None required.

12. ESTIMATE OF SITUATION.
    No change.

13. PLANS FOR FUTURE.
    In accordance with instructions from 4th Army Corps.

14. MORALE—Good; SUPPLIES—Normal; WEATHER—Unsettled; VISIBILITY—Fair.
    By direction of Chief of Staff.

JOHN C. H. LEE,
Colonel, General Staff,
Asst. Chief of Staff, G-3.

(Per) F. W. SMITH,
Major, U. S. A.
Asst., G-3.

THE LAST STATION LIST IN GERMANY

G-3 OFFICE, 89TH DIVISION, AMERICAN E. F., GERMANY, 3 MAY, 1919
STATION LIST NO. 20, 10:00 hours, 3 May, 1919

ORGANIZATION	COMMANDER	LOCATION OF P. C.
89TH DIVISION HEADQUARTERS	Major General Winn	KYLLBURG
Headquarters Troop	Captain Jacobs	"
177TH INFANTRY BRIG. HDQRS.	Brigadier General Hall	PRUM
353rd Infantry Hq., Hq. and Sup. Cos.	Colonel Reeves	"
Machine Gun Co.	Lieutenant Lee	WEINSHEIM
1st Bn. (less Cos. A and B)	Major Dahmke	PRUM
Cos. A and B	Captain Rich	NIEDERPRUM
2nd Bn. (less Cos. E and H)	Major Bissell	WAXWEILER
Co. E	Lieutenant Morgan	PRONSFELD
Co. H	Captain Atkins	LUNEBACH
3rd Bn.	Major Masseck	NEUERBURG
354th Infantry Hq., Hq., Sup. and M. G. Cos.	Colonel Babcock	TRIER
	Lieutenant Colonel Crystal	
1st Bn.	Major Page	"
2nd Bn.	Captain W. P. Pinkerton	"
3rd Bn.	Major H. M. Pinkerton	"
341st Machine Gun Bn.	Major Watson	RUWER PAULIN
178TH INFANTRY BRIG. HDQRS.	Brigadier General Barnhardt	PALLIEN
355th Infantry Hq., Hq., Sup. and M. G. Cos.	Lieutenant Colonel Brown	SAARBURG
1st Bn.	Major Wirth	"
2nd Bn. (less Co. G)	Captain Abel	BEURIG
Co. G	Captain Barbour	CURTWEILER
3rd Bn.	Lieutenant Colonel Goodwin	SAARBURG
356th Infantry Hq. and Sup. Co.	Colonel Allen	QUINT
Hq. and M. G. Cos.	Captain Walkey	EHRANG
1st Bn.	Major Tinker	SCHWEICH
2nd Bn.	Major Harris	EHRANG
3rd Bn. (less Co. L)	Major Lehman	SCHWEICH
Co. L	Lieutenant Shinn	ISSEL
342nd Machine Gun Bn. (less Co. D)	Major Bates	PFALZEL
Co. D	Captain Ford	BIEWER
164TH F. A. BRIG. HDQRS.	Brigadier General Donnelly	BITBURG
340th F. A. Reg. Hq., Hq. and Sup. Cos.	Colonel Wheeler	SCHONECKEN
1st Bn. (less Bat. C)	Major Elmiger	MURLENBACH
Battery C	Lieutenant Barr	BIRRESBORN
2nd Bn. (less Bat. F)	Major Wind	SCHONECKEN
Battery F	Lieutenant Matthews	ROMMERSHEIM
341st F. A. Reg. Hq., Hq. and Sup. Co.	Colonel Davis	SPEICHER
1st Bn. (less Bats. A and B)	Captain Vandegrift	DUDELDORF
Battery A	Captain Tanner	METTERICH
Battery B	Lieutenant Wallick	ORDORF
2nd Bn.	Major Fancher	SPEICHER
342nd F. A. Reg. Hq. and Hq. Co.	Lieutenant Colonel King	NIEDERWEISS
Supply Co.	Captain Elliott	ALSDORF
1st Bn.	Major Watson	IRREL
2nd Bn.	Captain O'Hara	WOLSFELD
3rd Bn.	Major Handlan	HOLSTHUM

314th Ammunition Train Hq.	Major Lysaght	BITBURG
Motor Bn. Hq. and Co. D	Captain Hunt	BADEM
Co. A	Lieutenant Bryan	MOTSCH
Co. B	Captain Manning	GINDORF
Co. C	Captain McLean	ROHL
Horsed Bn. (less Cos. F and G)	Captain White	ZEMMER
Co. F	Lieutenant Brannigan	SCHLEIDWEILER
Co. G	Lieutenant Young	ORENHOFEN
314th Engineers Reg. Hq.	Colonel Pullen	CONZ
Hq. Detachment	Lieutenant Kulp	CONEN
Supply Office	Captain Block	BITBURG
1st Bn.	Major Coy	CONZ
2nd Bn. (less Co. F)	Major Black	KARTHAUS
Co. F	Captain Sallee	WASSERLIESCH
314th Engineer Train	Lieutenant Fishwood	CONEN
340th Machine Gun Bn.	Major Hale	ERDORF
314th Field Signal Bn.	Major Strider	RITTERSDORF
Hdqrs. 314th Trains	Colonel Whitside	KYLLBURG
314th Motor Supply Train (less Co. F and Det. Co. B)	Major Cole	BITBURG
Co. F	Captain Pusch	TREVES
Detachment Co B.		PRUM
314th Sanitary Train	Lieutenant Colonel O'Donnell	BOLLENDORF
Supply Office	Captain Brinkley	BITBURG
Hq. Ambulance Section	Major Duncan	BOLLENDORF
353rd Ambulance Co.	Captain W. C. Hodges	OBERWEISS
354th " "	Captain Jenkins	ERNZEN
355th " "	Captain Jones	FUSCHWEILER
356th " "	Captain Smiley	METTENDORF
Hq. Field Hospitals	Major Huff	BOLLENDORF
353rd Field Hospital	Major Harvey	BITBURG
354th " "	Major McCabe	BOLLENDORF
355th " "	Major Haegerty	BITBURG
356th " "	Major Carr	BOLLENDORF
89th Military Police Co.	Captain Crofut	KYLLBURG
Division Quartermaster	Lieutenant Colonel Costella	BITBURG
Division Ordnance Hq.	Lieutenant Colonel Potter	KYLLBURG
Division Munitions Hq.	Major Lysaght	BITBURG
Division Motor Transport Hq.	Major Cole	"
Division Veterinary Hq.	Major Palmer	KYLLBURG
314th Mobile Veterinary Unit	Captain Likely	KIRSCH
Division Remount Hq.	Captain Kellogg	BITBURG
A. P. O. 761	Lieutenant Davis	TRIER
French Mission	Lieutenant Braun	KYLLBURG

ATTACHED UNITS:

349th Bakery Co.	Lieutenant Blattner	BITBURG
349th Bakery Co. Det.	Lieutenant Lyons	PRUM
56th Pioneer Inf. 1st Bn.	Major Fogg	BITBURG
Det. Co. B	Lieutenant Thivent	"
Det. Co. B	Lieutenant Towle	PRUM

WELFARE WORKERS

It was intended to include in the appendix a roster of the welfare workers who served with the 89th Division. Requests for their names were sent to the national headquarters of the several welfare organizations and to individual representatives.

In some cases partial lists were returned. In others it was frankly admitted that their records did not show divisional assignments. Even where names were furnished, a casual inspection showed so many obvious errors and omissions that publication of the names given would be an inaccurate and doubtful compliment to those included, and a regrettable (though unintentional) slight to those others who served as faithfully and well but whose names were not reported.

Since all could not be included, it would seem invidious to list any.

Yet simple justice and a keen realization of their contribution to the comfort, the contentment, the morale, the health and general well being of the men of the Division demand some expression of grateful appreciation for their tireless devotion, their loyal and efficient service

Inadequate though this tribute is to the earnest workers, men and women, of the American Red Cross, the Y. M. C. A., the Knights of Columbus, and the Salvation Army, there is no lack of gratitude in the hearts of the men in the Division they served.

CPSIA information can be obtained
at www.ICGtesting.com
Printed in the USA
BVHW032202101222
653949BV00012B/500

9 781015 52686